PLATINUM EDITION

USING
WINDOWS® 95

PLATINUM EDITION

USING
WINDOWS® 95

Written by Ron Person with

Michael Desmond • John Gordon • Gerald Honeycutt
David Johnson • Brady Merkel • Ken Poore • Bob Voss • Craig Zacker

Platinum Edition Using Windows 95

Library of Congress Catalog No.: 96-67567

ISBN: 0-7897-0797-7

98 97   6 5

Interpretation of the printing code: the rightmost double-digit number is the year of the book's printing; the rightmost single-digit number, the number of the book's printing. For example, a printing code of 96-1 shows that the first printing of the book occurred in 1996.

All terms mentioned in this book that are known to be trademarks or service marks have been appropriately capitalized. Que cannot attest to the accuracy of this information. Use of a term in this book should not be regarded as affecting the validity of any trademark or service mark.

Screen reproductions in this book were created using Collage Plus from Inner Media, Inc., Hollis, NH.

Credits

PRESIDENT
Roland Elgey

VICE PRESIDENT AND PUBLISHER
Marie Butler-Knight

PUBLISHING DIRECTOR
Brad R. Koch

EDITORIAL SERVICES DIRECTOR
Elizabeth Keaffaber

MANAGING EDITOR
Michael Cunningham

DIRECTOR OF MARKETING
Lynn E. Zingraf

SENIOR SERIES EDITOR
Chris Nelson

ACQUISITIONS MANAGER
Elizabeth A. South

ACQUISITIONS EDITOR
Thomas E. Barich

PRODUCT DIRECTORS
Lorna Gentry
Kevin Kloss
Joyce Nielsen
Jim Boyce
Lisa Wagner

TECHNICAL EDITORS
Robert Bogue
James Johnston
Karl Kemerait
Gary King
Bob Reselmen

PRODUCTION EDITORS
Thomas F. Hayes
Julie A. McNamee

EDITORS
Charlie Bowles
Lori A. Lyons
Theresa Mathias
Susan Ross Moore
Rebecca Mounts
Lynn Northrup
Christy Prakel
Linda Seifert

TECHNICAL SPECIALIST
Nadeem Muhammed

ACQUISITIONS COORDINATOR
Tracy Williams

OPERATIONS COORDINATOR
Patty Brooks

EDITORIAL ASSISTANT
Carmen Krikorian

BOOK DESIGNERS
Ruth Harvey
Kim Scott

COVER DESIGNER
Jay Corpus

PRODUCTION TEAM
Marcia Brizendine, Brian Buschkill, Jason
Carr, Jenny Earhart, Bryan Flores,
DiMonique Ford, Trey Frank, Amy Gornik,
Jason Hand, Sonja Hart, Damon Jordan, Dan
Julian, Daryl Kessler, Betty Kish, Glenn
Larsen, Stephanie Layton, Michelle Lee, Bob
LaRoche, Tony McDonald, Kaylene Riemen,
Laura Robbins, Bobbi Satterfield,
Julie Quinn, Kelly Warner, Todd Wente

INDEXER
Craig Small

Composed in *Century Old Style* and *Franklin Gothic* by Que Corporation.

About the Authors

Ron Person has written more than 18 books for Que Corporation, including *Special Edition Using Excel for Windows 95*, *Web Publishing with Word for Windows*, and *Special Edition Using Windows 3.11*. He is the lead author of *Special Edition Using Windows 95*. He has an M.S. in physics from Ohio State University and an M.B.A. from Hardin-Simmons University. Ron was one of Microsoft's original 12 Consulting Partners and is a Microsoft Solutions Partner.

Michael Desmond is executive editor of *Multimedia World* magazine, a 200,000 circulation national monthly publication serving the needs of multimedia computing enthusiasts. Previously an editor with *PC World,* Michael is also vice-president of the Computer Press Association. He has an M.S. in journalism from Northwestern University's Medill School of Journalism, and a B.A. in Soviet Studies from Middlebury College in Vermont. A native of Cleveland, Ohio, Michael is an inveterate Cleveland Indians fan, but finds time to write articles for publications like *Working Woman* and *Video* magazine. You can reach Michael via the *Multimedia World* web site at **http://www.mmworld.com**.

John R. Gordon is a senior marketing consultant with Intergraph Corporation in Huntsville, Alabama. He has held many positions in his nine years with Intergraph, most recently as the Intergraph Forum Manager for The Microsoft Network. He also contributes to the strategic planning effort for Corporate Internet, Intranet, World Wide Web, and Electronic Commerce issues. John devoted five years with the Mapping Sciences Division producing and marketing MGE PC-1, an entry-level GIS (Geographic Information System) application for the desktop, as well as several years in Intergraph's Federal Systems Division designing and marketing mapping solutions to the federal government.

John resides in Huntsville with his wife Diane, and three-year-old son Jimmy. He can be reached on The Microsoft Network at **jrgordon@msn.com** or on CompuServe at **70524,2420** when he's not engaged in cordial debate with his neighbor Eddie over whether the Apple II or TRS-80 was the first "real" PC available. It's a friendly debate, actually, although its been raging for some ten years now.

John dedicates this work to all his family, especially his parents, sisters, wife and son, all whom he loves very much.

Jerry Honeycutt is a business oriented, technical manager with broad experience in software development. He has served companies such as The Travelers, IBM, Nielsen North America, and most recently Information Retrieval Methods as Director of Windows Application Development. Jerry has participated in the industry since before the days of Microsoft Windows 1.0, and believes that everyone must eventually learn to use the Internet to stay in touch with the world.

Jerry wrote *Using Microsoft Plus!* and was a contributing author on *Special Edition Using Windows 95*, for Que. He also has been printed in *Computer Language Magazine* and is a regular speaker at the Windows World and Comdex trade shows on topics related to software development and corporate solutions for Windows 95.

Jerry graduated from the University of Texas at Dallas in 1992 with a B.S. degree in Computer Science. He currently lives in the Dallas suburb of Frisco, Texas, with Becky, two Westies, Corky and Turbo, and two cats, Scratches and Chew-Chew. Please feel free to contact Jerry on the Internet at **jerry@honeycutt.com**, on CompuServe at **76477,2751**, or on The Microsoft Network at **Honeycutt**.

Dave Johnson is a freelance writer and president of HLA Consulting, a computer training firm serving the Colorado front range. He has written *The Desktop Studio* and contributed to such magazines as *Computer Shopper* and *Digital Video*. Dave can be reached at **djohns@rmii.com**.

Brady P. Merkel is a senior software consultant and technical Webmaster for Intergraph Corporation in Huntsville, Alabama. He has co-authored popular internet books such as *Web Publishing with Word for Windows* and *Building Internet Applications with Visual C++*. One of his ongoing projects includes the development of Intergraph Online, Intergraph Corporation's World Wide Web server at **http://www.intergraph.com**. Brady can be reached by e-mail at **bpmerkel@ingr.com.**

Kenneth W. Poore is a marketing consultant for the Technical Information Management and Delivery division of Intergraph Corporation in Huntsville, Alabama. He currently develops strategic product plans, but has written technology white papers, conducted customer training, and worked in presales and marketing roles over the past 10 years. Ken lives with his wife Molly in Harvest, Alabama, and can be reached at **kwpoore@ingr.com**.

Robert Voss, Ph.D., deserves special thanks for his help in bringing this book together. Beyond applying his writing and training skills to the original writing, Bob made a significant contribution to this book and many of Que's best-selling books, including *Special Edition Using Word Version 6 for Windows*. Bob is a senior trainer in Microsoft Excel and Word for Windows for Ron Person & Co.

Craig Zacker got his first experience with computers in high school on a minicomputer "with less memory than I now have in my wristwatch." His first networking responsibility was a NetWare 2.15 server and six 286 workstations, which eventually evolved into NetWare 4 and more than 100 WAN connections to remote offices.

He's done PC and network support on-site, in the field, and over the phone for more than five years, and now works for a large manufacturer of networking software on the East coast as a technical editor and online services engineer.

We'd Like to Hear from You!

As part of our continuing effort to produce books of the highest possible quality, Que would like to hear your comments. To stay competitive, we *really* want you, as a computer book reader and user, to let us know what you like or dislike most about this book or other Que products.

You can mail comments, ideas, or suggestions for improving future editions to the address below, or send us a fax at (317) 581-4663. For the online inclined, Macmillan Computer Publishing has a forum on CompuServe (type **GO QUEBOOKS** at any prompt) through which our staff and authors are available for questions and comments. The address of our Internet site is **http://www.mcp.com** (World Wide Web).

In addition to exploring our forum, please feel free to contact me personally to discuss your opinions of this book: I'm **74201,1064** on CompuServe, and I'm **kkloss@que.mcp.com** on the Internet.

Thanks in advance—your comments will help us to continue publishing the best books available on computer topics in today's market.

Kevin Kloss
Product Director
Que Corporation
201 W. 103rd Street
Indianapolis, Indiana 46290
USA

N O T E Although we cannot provide general technical support, we're happy to help you resolve problems you encounter related to our books, disks, or other products. If you need such assistance, please contact our Tech Support department at 800-545-5914 ext. 3833.

To order other Que or Macmillan Computer Publishing books or products, please call our Customer Service department at 800-835-3202 ext. 666. ■

Contents at a Glance

Table of Contents

III | Configuring and Optimizing Windows 95

V | Working with Applications

16 Installing, Running, and Uninstalling Windows Applications   471

Introduction

Windows 3.0 and 3.1 forever altered the face of PC computing. At one time regarded as a plaything, Windows became the standard for hardware and software compatibility. Now with Windows 95, Microsoft has added a new look to computers, and the look and feel of graphical PC computing has taken another major turn.

Microsoft has devoted years of extensive research to making Windows 95 easier to learn and use than its predecessors. New users will be able to start programs, create documents, and become productive much more quickly with Windows 95.

That's where *Platinum Edition Using Windows 95* steps in to help. This book is the single source you need to quickly get up to speed and greatly enhance your productivity with Windows 95. ■

How to Use this Book

This book was designed and written from the ground up with two important purposes:

■ First, *Platinum Edition Using Windows 95* makes it easy for you to find any task you need to accomplish and see how to do it most effectively.

■ Second, this book covers Windows 95 in a depth and breadth that you won't find anywhere else. It has been expanded beyond the best-selling *Special Edition Using Windows 95* to include almost 200 additional pages of in-depth technical detail, tips, techniques, and troubleshooting solutions. It also includes two CD-ROMs of 32-bit software.

With those goals in mind, how do you use this book?

If you have used Windows 3.1, you may just want to skim through the first few chapters of this book to see what changes there are in Windows 95. After all, you may have read magazine articles and heard from colleagues about all of the new features. The first two chapters help you get a grip on what changes to expect. After that, keep *Platinum Edition Using Windows 95* handy by your computer as a reference.

Platinum Edition Using Windows 95 was written for the experienced Windows computer user. You may be experienced with Windows 3.x, or you have already started working with Windows 95. Either way, you will find comprehensive coverage on Windows 95 features. Throughout the book there are techniques for customizing Windows 95 to work the way you need Windows to work.

How this Book is Organized

Platinum Edition Using Windows 95 is a comprehensive book on Windows 95. The book is divided into 10 parts, 43 chapters, and four appendixes to help you quickly find the coverage you need. The parts begin with the most common and basic topics and move forward into more specialized or advanced subjects. The rest of this section describes the contents more specifically, chapter by chapter.

Part I: Getting Started

Chapter 1, "What's New in Windows 95," shows you an overview of the new features in Windows 95. After reading this chapter, you should be aware of why you moved or need to begin the move from Windows 3.1 to Windows 95.

Chapter 2, "Understanding Windows 95," presents the big picture of Windows 95. If you're new to Windows 95, you'll want to get a feel for the important concepts. This chapter points out the important user interface differences from Windows 3.x.

Part II: Navigating Windows 95

Chapter 3, "Windows Navigation Basics," gives you an explanation of the parts of the Windows screen, and how to start Windows and applications.

Chapter 4, "Managing Files," is devoted to showing you how to use Windows Explorer and folder windows to work with and manage the files on your computer. You also learn how to carry out many file management tasks using My Computer. The chapter includes many tips and Registry modifications that enhance Explorer.

Part III: Configuring and Optimizing Windows 95

Chapter 5, "Adding New Hardware to Windows 95." The objective of Plug and Play is to make new device installation a "hands-off" process. Thus, much of this chapter is devoted to explaining what happens "behind-the-scenes" to make Plug and Play work. This chapter also describes how to install the many older "legacy" devices that do not take advantage of Plug and Play. When hardware doesn't install correctly, we've included descriptions on how to use the Device Manager to troubleshoot and resolve the problem.

Chapter 6, "Configuring Windows 95 for Notebook Users," describes how to take advantage of Windows 95 support for PC Cards (formerly called PMCIA adapter cards), advanced power management, docking stations, file synchronization with My Briefcase, and all the other new features useful to laptop users. We've included in-depth installation and use instructions for Windows 95's new infrared communication. This software upgrade is available free in Service Pack 1.

Chapter 7, "Controlling Printers," explains how to use Windows 95 printing. It also introduces each of the new printing features, describes the options, and explains how to create a quality print job. You are guided through installing new printers.

Chapter 8, "Working with Fonts," explains fonts and how Windows 95 uses them. It also shows you how to install and manage fonts in Windows 95.

Chapter 9, "Installing and Configuring Modems," explains how Windows' communications system works for you, how to install your Plug and Play modem or legacy modem, how to configure your modem after it's installed, and what TAPI means and does.

Chapter 10, "Configuring and Using CD-ROM Drives," shows how to install drivers for Plug and Play and legacy CD-ROM drives, how to use CD-ROM applications, and how to optimize your CD-ROM to get the best performance possible.

Chapter 11, "Configuring and Using Sound Boards," shows how to install drivers for Plug and Play and legacy sound cards. You see how to use Windows accessories for recording, playing, and editing sound files, and how to play audio CDs on your computer.

Chapter 12, "Optimizing Video Performance," describes video enhancements in Windows 95. You see the procedure for installing video drivers, adding to your video capabilities with QuickTime for Windows, and how to play videos with Media Player.

Part IV: Customizing Windows 95

Chapter 13, "Customizing with Property Sheets," shows you how to customize Windows 95 to fit the way you work. You learn to customize the taskbar, the Start menu, the Program menu, the desktop pattern or graphic, as well as all the colors used by Windows elements. This chapter includes many secret techniques such as adding custom commands to the Send To menu and how to modify the Registry to add your own custom commands to the context (right-click) menus.

Chapter 14, "Introduction to REGEDIT," describes the Registry, the database of settings used by Windows, applications, and customer preferences. When you learn how to use REGEDIT to make changes, many new opportunities for customizing Windows are available to you.

Chapter 15, "Customizing with REGEDIT," illustrates how you can use REGEDIT to customize Windows 95.

Part V: Working with Applications

Chapter 16, "Installing, Running, and Uninstalling Windows Applications," shows you how to install Windows applications (both Windows 95 and older applications are covered), how to run applications, and how to remove applications, including coverage of uninstalling software with Windows 95's new Remove feature. Tips and techniques show you how to uninstall older applications and how to improve your productivity with application tips such as Shortcuts and Scraps on the desktop.

Chapter 17, "Installing, Running, and Uninstalling DOS Applications," shows you how to use DOS programs in Windows. This version of Windows makes more memory available to DOS applications and runs DOS games faster and better than previous versions.

Chapter 18, "Using Windows 95's Accessories." Although many small accessory programs come with Windows 95, two of the most frequently used are WordPad and Paint. This chapter gives you some bare-bones instructions on using them and tips on how they can be used with your larger applications.

Part VI: Sharing Data Effectively

Chapter 19, "Simple Ways of Sharing Data Between Applications." Generally, all Windows applications provide some means for sharing data with another application. This chapter shows you the most basic and commonly used of these means, including cutting, copying, and pasting within and between documents in Windows and DOS applications, as well as how to link data from one document to another.

Chapter 20, "Creating Compound Documents with OLE," shows how to create and modify documents based on the concept of *compound documents*—documents you create by using multiple types of data. You see how to build documents that incorporate different types of data, such as text from a word processor, a spreadsheet, and graphics. You also learn how to use this data within a single application without having to switch between applications to edit the different data types.

Chapter 21, "Introduction to Visual Basic for Applications," introduces you to Microsoft's new Visual Basic for Applications programming language that will be shared by Microsoft applications. VBA enables programmers to learn one language that has core statements and concepts shared by multiple applications. It makes integrating applications much easier. Applications in Office 95 that include or can be controlled by VBA include Excel, Access, PowerPoint, and Project. Word continues to use WordBASIC, but it can be integrated with other applications in the suite through VBA.

Part VII: Managing Disk Drives and Backups

Chapter 22, "Working with Disks and Disk Drives," shows you how to work with and maintain your floppy and hard disks. Windows 95 comes with a tool to help you check for and repair some kinds of damage. You can monitor the performance of your system using the System Monitor. You can improve the performance of your hard disks by using Disk Defragmenter and enable your system to act as if it has more memory (RAM) than is actually installed by using *virtual memory*. This chapter covers all these topics and more. To increase the effective size of your hard disk, you can use DriveSpace or DriveSpace 3 (available with Plus!) to compress your hard disk, giving it two to three times more storage.

Chapter 23, "Backing Up and Protecting Your Data," explains how to copy one or more files from your hard disk to another location (usually a floppy disk, a tape drive, or another computer on your network), restore your backed up files to any location you choose (including their original locations), and compare files on your backup disks with the original files to ensure their validity.

Part VIII: Networking with Windows 95

Chapter 24, "Installing Windows 95 as a Network Client," familiarizes you with the various options you have available in Windows 95 to quickly get connected in a networked environment, and then steps you through the process.

Chapter 25, "Connecting to a NetWare Network," takes a more in-depth look at effectively using Windows 95 as a Network Client to the most popular corporate network, Novell's NetWare. This chapter details the differences between Microsoft's and Novell's 32-bit Network Clients for NetWare as well as the 16-bit real mode clients.

Chapter 26, "Accessing Client/Server Network Services," is designed to present the client/server networking tools and concepts that are part of the Windows 95 operating system, not only to complete the immediate task at hand, but also as a way of gaining additional insight into how your company network is laid out, and what other resources are available to you. You learn to map network drives, change passwords, browse the "Network Neighborhood," and access network printers.

Chapter 27, "Installing Windows 95 Peer-to-Peer Networking," shows you how to set up your own workgroup network, as well as integrate it with a "Server" based network like Windows NT or NetWare for a client/server environment. It explains the different types of sharing and security available, as well as administration.

Chapter 28, "Accessing Windows 95 Workstation Resources," covers the actual mechanics of sharing workstation resources, and in the process, examines the user policies and limitations that should be adopted in order to create a smoothly functioning, productive environment. You learn how to share CD-ROMs and Fax-modems, install and use remote network access (RAS) and even how to create a workgroup over the Internet.

Chapter 29, "Windows 95 Network Administration." The Windows 95 operating system includes an assortment of tools and utilities that integrate many day-to-day network administration tasks into the user interface. This chapter concentrates on tools intended for the workgroup administrator, which will be used on a daily basis.

Chapter 30, "Customizing Windows 95 Network Installations," discusses issues that are primarily of concern to the corporate network administrator who is responsible for engineering a large scale migration to the Windows 95 operating system. Things like installing Windows 95 from a network server, using installation scripts, creating user profiles and system policies, and detailing the use of the system administration utilities found on the CD like POLEDIT.EXE are also covered.

Part IX: Using the Internet and Online Services

Chapter 31, "Using the Universal Inbox," shows how to use the Universal Inbox, a central communications client that organizes "received" electronic mail and faxes in one convenient location. You learn how to use Exchange as your universal inbox and how to compose, store, organize, and send messages via e-mail and fax.

Chapter 32, "Using Fax, Address Book, and Phone Dialer." Windows 95 includes fax services that integrate with the Universal Inbox to give you an easy way to send faxes from within documents. You can use the built-in address book to make it easy to send e-mail and fax messages through the Universal Inbox.

Chapter 33, "Getting Connected to the Internet," introduces you to the Internet and World Wide Web, two of the fastest growing and most talked about topics in computing. You learn what TCP/IP is, how to choose an Internet service provider, and how to connect to the Internet with Windows 95's built-in connectivity tools.

Chapter 34, "Using Internet Explorer and the World Wide Web," covers what to do once you get connected to the Internet. You see how to use Microsoft's Internet Explorer 2.0— an impressive Web browser. You can use IE 2.0 to browse through the World Wide Web, download files via FTP, log in to remote computers with Telnet, and create and receive e-mail. This chapter even describes how to create Web pages with Microsoft's Internet Assistant.

Chapter 35, "Using The Microsoft Network," describes how to get started using The Microsoft Network (MSN). MSN is fully integrated into Windows and offers you online access to the world by giving you access to a variety of people and resources. With MSN, you can exchange electronic mail (e-mail) with other people, exchange ideas on bulletin boards, participate in live discussions in chat rooms, access the resources of the Internet, and more.

Chapter 36, "Using HyperTerminal," discusses using HyperTerminal, the Windows accessory that enables you to connect your computer to another PC or online service. HyperTerminal is a full-featured communications tool that greatly simplifies getting online. With HyperTerminal, you can connect to a friend's computer, a university network, an Internet service provider, or an online service like CompuServe. In this chapter, you learn how to use HyperTerminal for some common tasks, such as creating a connection or downloading a file. You also learn how to configure HyperTerminal and customize your connections.

Part X: Exploring Multimedia in Windows 95

Chapter 37, "Working with Multimedia," explains the foundation of Windows 95's multimedia capabilities and outlines material to be covered in depth in later chapters. It includes a description of the hardware necessary to take advantage of multimedia. An overview of the Multimedia Properties sheet found in the Windows 95 Control Panel acts as an introduction to more specific tips and concepts discussed later.

Chapter 38, "Working with Graphics," is a guide to getting the most out of Windows 95's enhanced graphics capabilities, including a primer on changing settings such as color depth, refresh rates, and resolution. It includes an in-depth description of the critical DirectDraw technology and new driver system. There is a discussion of Windows 95's 3-D graphics capabilities and the software and hardware necessary to work with them.

Chapter 39, "Working with Video and Animation," describes how to get the most out of video playback in Windows 95, including a primer on the DirectVideo technology. It features a description of compression schemes and formats, including an in-depth exploration of MPEG video.

Chapter 40, "Working with Audio," discusses the specifics of wave audio and MIDI sound, explaining where each should be used. The chapter introduces the DirectSound technology as a core Windows 95 component, and discusses 3-D audio capabilities.

Chapter 41, "Playing with Windows 95: The Games," reveals Windows 95 as a game platform. The chapter introduces DirectPlay and DirectInput technologies, and provides a game-centric discussion of previously explained Direct X components. It includes a guide to setting up joysticks, multiplayer gaming, and other devices. It also includes tips and tricks for optimizing DOS games.

Part XI: Appendixes

Appendix A, "Installing Windows 95," presents the steps for preparing your computer for Windows 95 and then for installing Windows 95. Standard and custom installation options are discussed, including a multiple-boot configuration. The appendix also explains how to remove Windows 95 from your system.

Appendix B, "Using Microsoft Plus!," presents how to install MS Plus!, the add-on software that gives you additional Windows 95 features such as Internet services, desktop customizing "themes," and more effective disk compression software.

Appendix C, "Additional Help and Resources," tells you where to find what wouldn't fit between our covers. This appendix lists the telephone and fax support numbers for Microsoft and third-party suppliers. You'll also learn how to use the Internet, The Microsoft Network, CompuServe, and TechNet CDs to get the same databases of support information available to Microsoft's telephone support staff and consultants.

Appendix D, "File Listing of the Windows 95 CD," contains a list of all files that come with the Windows 95 CD.

Appendix E, "What's on the CDs," describes the software and utilities you find on the CDs that accompany this book.

Special Features in the Book

Que has over a decade of experience writing and developing the most successful computer books available. With that experience, we've learned what special features help readers the most. Look for these special features throughout the book to enhance your learning experience.

Chapter roadmaps

On the first page of each chapter, you'll find a list of topics to be covered in the chapter. This list serves as a roadmap to the chapter so you can tell at a glance what is covered. It also provides a useful outline of the key topics you'll be reading about.

Notes

Notes present interesting or useful information that isn't necessarily essential to the discussion. This secondary track of information enhances your understanding of Windows, but you can safely skip notes and not be in danger of missing crucial information. Notes look like this:

N O T E Ctrl+Esc is a shortcut key combination used to access the Start menu. Throughout this book, when you see a key+key combination, that signifies a shortcut to accessing an application or opening a menu.

Tips

Tips present advice on quick or often overlooked procedures. These include shortcuts that save you time. A tip looks like this:

 Nearly every item in Windows 95 contains a property sheet you can customize. Right-click an item and choose Properties to see its property sheet.

Cautions

Cautions serve to warn you about potential problems that a procedure may cause, unexpected results, and mistakes to avoid.

CAUTION

If you have a similar printer that could use the same drivers, do not remove the software. Deleting the associated software might remove that driver from use by other printers.

Troubleshooting

No matter how carefully you follow the steps in the book, you eventually come across something that just doesn't work the way you think it should. Troubleshooting sections anticipate these common errors or hidden pitfalls and present solutions. A troubleshooting section looks like this:

TROUBLESHOOTING

I've always been able to set the number of copies I print from the control panel of my printer. When I print in Windows 95, however, I always get one copy no matter how I set the printer. In Windows 95, the settings in your programs for the number of copies to be printed overrides the setting on your printer. To print multiple copies, change the setting in the program you are printing from.

Internet references

Throughout this book you will find Internet references that point you to World Wide Web addresses or online addresses where you can find additional information about topics. Internet references look like this:

ON THE WEB

You can learn about the Registry's organization on the Internet, too. *PC Magazine* has a three part description of the Registry on the Web that you can read by pointing your Web browser to:

www.zdnet.com/~pcmag/issues/1418/pcm00083.htm

www.zdnet.com/~pcmag/issues/1419/pcm00116.htm

www.zdnet.com/~pcmag/issues/1422/pcm00140.htm

Cross References

Throughout the book, you see references to other sections and pages in the book, like the one that follows this paragraph. These cross references point you to related topics and discussions in other parts of the book.

▶ **See** "Improved Performance and Reliability," **p. 20**

In addition to these special features, there are several conventions used in this book to make it easier to read and understand.

Underlined Hot Keys, or Mnemonics

Hot keys in this book appear underlined, like they appear on-screen. In Windows, many menus, commands, buttons, and other options have these hot keys. To use a hot-key shortcut, press Alt and the key for the underlined character. For instance, to choose the Properties button, press Alt and then R.

Shortcut Key Combinations

In this book, shortcut key combinations are joined with plus signs (+). For example, Ctrl+V means hold down the Ctrl key while you press the V key.

Menu Commands

Instructions for choosing menu commands have this form:

> Choose File, New.

This example means open the File menu and select New, which in this case opens a new file. Instructions involving the new Windows 95 Start menu are an exception. When you are to choose something through this menu, the form is

> Open the Start menu and choose Programs, Accessories, WordPad.

In this case, you open the WordPad word processing accessory. Notice that in the Start menu you simply drag the mouse pointer and point at the option or command you want to choose (even through a whole series of submenus); you don't need to click anything.

This book also has the following typeface enhancements to indicate special text, as shown in the following table.

Typeface	Description
Italic	Italics are used to indicate terms and variables in commands or addresses.
Boldface	Bold is used to indicate text you type, Internet addresses, and other locators in the online world.
Computer type	This command is used for on-screen messages and commands (such as DOS copy or UNIX commands).
MYFILE.DOC	File names are set in all caps to distinguish them from regular text, as in MYFILE.DOC.

Getting Started

What's New in Windows 95

by Ron Person

Windows 95 changes the way you work with computers. Microsoft's new operating system is more than just a better interface or an easier way of working with the computer—it incorporates more features, better performance, and greater compatibility than any previous operating system. This chapter gives you an overview of the new features in Windows 95 and teaches you ways to take advantage of the system's vast new capabilities.

Windows 95 is an improvement over Windows 3.1 and Windows for Workgroups 3.11. Both of these programs, although significantly easier to use than DOS, needed enhancements to accommodate both first-time users and experienced "power" users.

Windows 95 compatibility with DOS and previous Windows programs and data

DOS applications can now load their own drivers and have more memory available than under Windows 3.x.

Changes to the Windows graphical interface that make Windows much easier for first time users

New features like the Start button, the taskbar, and shortcut icons contribute to an interface that is more customizable.

Windows 95 uses property sheets to display and change information about screen elements, programs, and documents

A right-click on objects on the screen such as files, icons, or the background displays a property sheet.

Shortcut icons point to programs or documents to make programs easier to start and manage

Shortcuts are one of the most powerful features for users of Windows 95. Shortcuts are icons that point to a file, folder, or resource. Double-click the shortcut and you run, load, or display the resource.

As an experienced computer user you may need to support or train novices. If you work with people who used Windows 3.x in the past, you need to know some of the areas where people had difficulty:

- Overlapping windows caused confusion due to visual clutter. Windows that filled the screen hid other programs that were open.
- Windows seemed to disappear when minimized.
- The hierarchical display of directory structures in the File Manager was intimidating and not intuitive to non-technical users.
- The File Manager and Program Manager shared some functionality, such as starting applications, but they used different metaphors and appearance.
- Switching between running applications and knowing which applications were running was not obvious. Many users started multiple instances of the same application, thereby using up system resources and increasing the potential for an application failure.
- Double-clicking and many keystrokes, such as Alt+Tab, while important, were not obvious.
- File names were limited to eight characters with a three-letter extension.

Windows 95 was created to make work easier for novice and beginning computer users. Yet at the same time it contains many extensions and features that add value for advanced or power users. Some of the areas where power users faced problems with previous versions of Windows were:

- Resources and utilities needed for customizing and fine-tuning were scattered all over the Windows system in different groups, such as Control Panel, Print Manager, Setup, File Manager, and Program Manager.
- Information such as IRQ and I/O address settings were difficult to find.
- Many graphical elements could not be customized.
- Networking with non-Microsoft networks required a lot of study, work, and work-arounds.
- Hardware was difficult to install and could easily cause conflicts with existing hardware. The conflicts were difficult to resolve.

This chapter introduces:

- Windows 95 compatibility with DOS and previous Windows programs and data
- Windows 95's improved performance in many areas, including file handling, memory management, and application speed

- A graphical interface using the Start menu, taskbar, and desktop that make Windows much easier for first-time users

- Property sheets about items in Windows 95 that show you information about the item and enable you to customize the item

- Program startup and file management can be handled from within the same My Computer windows

- Shortcut icons that start programs and documents and give you quick access to frequently used folders

- Long names for files and folders that make file management easier than previously

- Networking and communication that is much easier to install. Networking works with adapters and protocols from more vendors than before

- Easier hardware installation where Windows 95 recognizes the hardware and installs the appropriate drivers and settings automatically

- Features for road warriors who travel with a portable computer ■

N O T E If you are an experienced Windows 3.x user, you will want to go to Chapter 2, "Understanding Windows 95," for a quick understanding of the basic concepts in Windows 95. ■

Keeping Your Copy of Windows 95 Up to Date

Windows 95 was released August 24, 1995. Rather than coming out with a Windows 96 version, Microsoft has committed to keeping Windows 95 up-to-date with new and improved features through the continuous release of additional features and software patches. These upgrades are free and will be released as Service Packs approximately every quarter. At the time this book was printed, the first release—Service Pack 1—was just released for the first quarter 1996.

 T I P This copy of *Platinum Edition Using Windows 95* describes the procedures and tips you need to work with the features and upgrades available in Service Pack 1.

To order a copy of the Microsoft Windows 95 Service Pack 1, call 800-360-7561 and request the Windows 95 Service Pack. There is a shipping and handling charge of $14.95. Service Pack 1 also can be downloaded from the Internet, The Microsoft Network, and CompuServe.

ON THE WEB

You can get a free upgrade by downloading portions or all of the Service Pack from Microsoft's site on the World Wide Web. To find the Service Pack on the World Wide Web, use the URL:

http://www.microsoft.com/windows/software/updates.htm

Compatibility with Windows 3.1 and DOS Programs

With more than 60 million people using Windows 3.1, Microsoft had to include a high degree of compatibility in Windows 95 so that data and applications from previous versions of Windows would still work. Windows 95 also handles DOS programs better than previous versions of Windows. DOS programs can now run in a window that includes a toolbar for commonly used features.

File Manager and Program Manager are Available

A company with thousands or tens of thousands of Windows users may not want to think about having to train them on how to use Windows 95. One way to make this transition and upgrade smoother is to continue to use the File Manager and Program Manager that are familiar to users of previous versions of Windows. Over time, you can help your users migrate to the File Manager and Program Manager replacement—either My Desktop or Windows Explorer.

Windows 3.1 and DOS Data Files are Compatible

The effective use of data seems to be what differentiates winners from losers in the information age. With that in mind, files created in Windows 95 are compatible with files from earlier versions of DOS and Windows.

▶ **See** "Working with Long File Names," **p. 134**

Windows 95 is capable of handling file names up to 255 characters long. (The entire pathname can be up to 260 characters.) The long file names can include spaces. For example, what was BUDGET96.DOC can now be TRAVEL BUDGET FOR 1996.DOC. When you move a file with a long name to a system that uses the older eight-character name with a three-letter extension, the older system sees only an abbreviated version of the long name.

> **CAUTION**
>
> Don't use file utility software designed for DOS and older versions of Windows in Windows 95 or on files from Windows 95. Windows 95 stores name and file tracking information in different locations. Although this makes no difference to applications, some file-manipulation utilities can scramble this data. The types of utilities to beware of do such things as recover lost files.

Compatible Drivers

Device drivers act as translators between hardware and software. They make sure the two work together efficiently. Windows 95 comes with 32-bit device drivers for major hardware such as disk drives, display adapters, and CD-ROM drives. This means that when you install Windows 95, it will install new device drivers that give you the hardware's advanced features as well as any speed that comes from a 32-bit driver. Unfortunately, there are thousands of different hardware devices. This makes it almost impossible for Microsoft to ensure that every device driver has been included in the set that initially installs with Windows. Because of that, if Windows 95 cannot find a new device driver during installation, it continues to use any 16-bit device driver that you have already installed from a previous version of Windows or from MS-DOS.

 To see the device drivers you have and information about them, open the Start menu and choose Settings, Control Panel. Double-click the System icon and select the Device Manager tab. Double-click any device to see its Properties sheet.

If you want to ensure you have the latest device driver, contact the manufacturer of your hardware device. Microsoft has made device drivers much easier to create for Windows 95, and your hardware manufacturer should have a new version available.

▶ **See** "Reviewing Your Computer's System Information," **p. 413**

Installing Windows 95 is Easy

You don't have to be a hardware guru to install Windows 95. In previous versions of Windows you were often forced into making choices about hardware configurations. It was up to you to select the appropriate options and settings so that hardware and software were compatible. Windows 95 takes care of many of those decisions and options for you. Hardware is also being redesigned to work with Windows 95. The new Plug-and-Play devices work with Windows 95 to automate installation and configuration. If you have hardware, such as modems that aren't Plug and Play, Windows 95 prompts you for the information necessary for setup.

▶ **See** "Installing Plug and Play Hardware," **p. 158**
▶ **See** "Installing a Plug and Play Modem," **p. 284**
▶ **See** "Using Windows 95 Setup," **p. 1187**

Improved Performance and Reliability

One of the design goals for Windows 95 was that its speed should be the same or better than Windows 3.11. Although Microsoft has lower minimum recommended hardware configuration, you should be able to run many applications with a 486 33MHz with 8M of RAM. If you want to run multiple applications at adequate performance or want to run a larger program such as Access, then you will usually need 16M or more of RAM.

As you add more memory, you find that Windows performance improves proportionally. You should see a significant performance improvement for new 32-bit applications designed for Windows 95, too. Microsoft Excel for Windows 95 and Microsoft Word for Windows 95 are up to 50 percent faster in many of their operations.

Even 16-bit applications will have improved performance in Windows 95 in areas that involve the 32-bit system such as printing and file handling. That Windows terror, the *out of memory* error, is less likely to occur. Although Windows 95 still uses a 64K heap to store systems information for 16-bit applications, a lot of the information that was stored in this area by older versions of Windows is now stored elsewhere. As a result, there is less chance of your application failing.

Windows 95 uses a new 32-bit VCACHE, which replaces the older SmartDrive that ran under DOS and previous versions of Windows. VCACHE uses more intelligent caching algorithms to improve the apparent speed of your hard drive as well as your CD-ROM and 32-bit network redirectors. Unlike SmartDrive, VCACHE dynamically allocates itself. Based on the amount of free system memory, VCACHE allocates or reallocates memory used by the cache.

▶ **See** "Improving Performance with Disk Defragmenter," **p. 646**

An Easier but More Powerful Interface

To most personal computer users, the interface they see on-screen *is* the computer. Because of that, the world of DOS computers was too difficult for many people. There was a lot of learning involved just to get started with simple tasks. And there was no way to learn as you worked. You had to devote part of your time to learning DOS and the applications and use the remaining time to try and get productive work done. The advent of

Windows improved this quite a bit. With a few hours of instruction on Windows, you could learn on your own by exploring. The work-to-learning ratio improved significantly.

Research by Microsoft found that Windows was still difficult to learn for many people and some people were still too timid to explore and learn on their own. For that reason they had two primary design goals for Windows 95:

- To make windows more accessible to novice users so that they can quickly get what they need.
- To make windows more customizable and productive for advanced users by including accessible shortcuts and power techniques.

Windows 95 does a good job on both of these goals. Tests in Microsoft's usability laboratory show that inexperienced computer users are able to find and start applications significantly faster with Windows 95 than with previous versions of Windows.

 T I P Without an overview of Windows 95, your previous experience with Windows may get in the way of how easy it is to use Windows 95.

Experienced and novice computer users will want to review the basics of Windows 95 in order to get a good idea as to how much easier Windows 95 is to operate than previous operating systems. The Windows 95 desktop interface is shown in figure 1.1.

FIG. 1.1
When Windows 95 first loads, your desktop will look similar to this. Depending on the type of setup you used, you may have additional icons, or some of these icons may not be present.

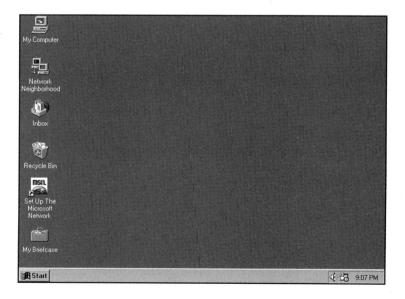

The Start Button Makes Starting Applications Easier

The Start button is one of the most important changes to Windows 95. It makes Windows 95 more accessible. By clicking the Start button, you open the Start menu, which is your avenue to Windows 95.

The Start button makes Windows easier to use for beginners, and it's an excellent improvement for power users. When you click the Start button, or press Ctrl+Esc, you see a menu that includes not only applications, but also lists of frequently used documents, customizable settings, and frequently used features such as Find, Help, and Run (see fig. 1.2).

N O T E Ctrl+Esc is a shortcut key combination used to access the Start menu. Throughout this book, a key+key combination signifies a shortcut to accessing an application or opening a menu. ▪

FIG. 1.2
Tests show that Windows 95 is easier to use for beginners and more customizable for experts.

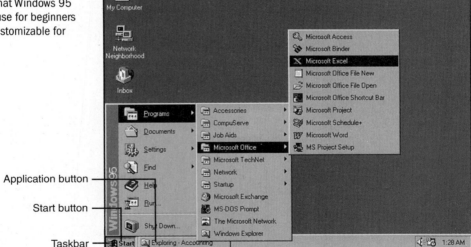

The Taskbar Makes it Easy to Switch Between Applications

In previous versions of Windows, switching between applications was difficult. Microsoft estimates that nearly 70 percent of users didn't know they could press Alt+Tab to switch between applications (the Alt+Tab combination still works in Windows 95). With the new taskbar, all the applications that are running appear as buttons on the taskbar (refer to fig. 1.2). Clicking a button opens that running application into its own window.

▶ **See** "Customizing the Taskbar," **p. 366**

Right Mouse Button Information

Windows 95 has many customizable features, and the key to unlocking them is clicking the right mouse button. Nearly every item you see on the Windows 95 screen contains a shortcut menu. To see that shortcut menu, right-click the item. For example, if you want to customize the taskbar, put the tip of the mouse pointer on a gray area of the taskbar and click the right mouse button, then choose Properties. The Taskbar Properties sheet displays (see fig. 1.3). In it, you can change how the taskbar appears and what it contains.

FIG. 1.3

Clicking the right mouse button on the taskbar brings up the Taskbar Properties sheet.

N O T E Properties dialog boxes in Windows 95 are referred to as *sheets*. When you click a tab within the sheets, the open dialog boxes are referred to as *pages*. Figure 1.3 displays the Start Menu Programs page of the Taskbar Properties sheet. ▪

My Computer for Easy Understanding of What's in Your Computer

Hierarchical displays of directories and files confused many new computer users. Microsoft developed My Computer and Network Neighborhood to resolve that problem. Double-click the My Computer icon to see a window that displays the resources available on your computer (see fig. 1.4). Doing the same on the Network Neighborhood icon displays all the resources available on any network to which you are connected. The Network Neighborhood icon does not appear unless Windows has been installed for a network.

T I P If you find it confusing to have too many windows open, you can specify that all the views of My Computer or Network Neighborhood appear in the same window.

FIG. 1.4
Use the My Computer window to access the drives on your computer. Double-clicking a drive displays the folders and files within that drive.

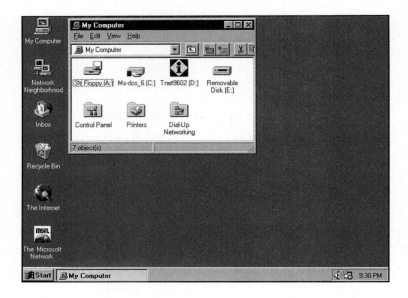

Notice in the My Computer window that the drives and resources available within your computer are displayed. In the example in figure 1.4, the computer has an A, C, D, and E drive. My Computer always displays a Control Panel icon, and in this case a Printers, and Dial-Up Networking icon.

N O T E The name of the C drive in this example depends on the hard drive having a volume name prior to Windows 95 installation. Most My Computer windows just show a (C:) drive. ■

Folders Make File Management More Intuitive

The metaphor of folders and documents in Windows 95 makes file management easier to understand. Double-clicking the My Computer icon on the desktop displays the My Computer window shown in figure 1.4. This window shows the drives on your computer and other peripherals. You can get to files and directories by double-clicking any of the drives.

Double-clicking on the MS-DOS 6 (C:) icon that represents a hard drive in the computer opens the window C:\. Within this window, double-clicking on the My Documents folder opens the window titled C:\My Documents. (Depending on preference settings, another window may open.) This window contains document icons. Notice that each icon represents a type of file.

▶ **See** "Using My Computer to Manage Files," **p. 117**

TIP You can perform work on documents by dragging their icon into other folders, onto the desktop (the background), or dropping them onto other icons that represent resources such as printers or applications. Use a right mouse click on a document icon to see frequently used tasks that control documents or to see the properties of the document.

In figure 1.5, the My Computer icon has been opened to show selected contents of the computer. Double-clicking the My Computer icon opened the My Computer window. Double-clicking the C: drive icon opened the window titled MS-DOS_6 (C:). Finally, double-clicking the My Documents folder opened a My Documents window.

Each of these windows shows a different view of the computer resources available to you. As the windows open, they layer over the previous window.

FIG. 1.5
Double-clicking items in My Computer windows either opens the item to show its contents or opens the document or program.

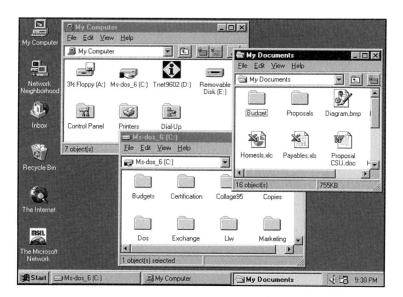

Windows Explorer for Powerful File Management

Expert users may find My Computer and Network Neighborhood limiting when they need to do a lot of file management and examine different types of computer resources. Windows provides Explorer (see fig. 1.6) for more advanced users. It uses a single window composed of two panes. The left side shows a hierarchical structure of all the computer resources from hard drives and CD-ROMs to control panels and printers. Once you understand how to use Explorer, you will be able to do more than you could with the old File Manager. For example, you can drag files and folders from the right panel in Explorer to a subfolder at any level in the right panel. You also can right-click files to display a shortcut menu that enables you to view the file, print, create a shortcut, and see the file's properties. To open Windows Explorer, right-click the Start button, then choose Explore.

▶ **See** "Using Explorer to View Files and Folders," **p. 96**

FIG. 1.6
Explorer is a powerful file management tool.

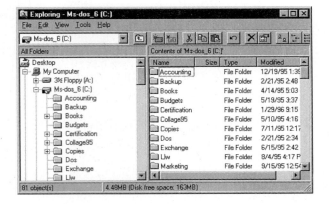

Displaying Properties of Programs, Documents, and Resources

Almost everything in Windows can be customized. If you can't customize it, you can at least see what its current settings or properties are. To change or view properties of an object such as the desktop background, the taskbar, the Recycle Bin, a file, a folder, and so on, click the right mouse button on the item. When a shortcut menu displays, choose Properties. A properties sheet displays. Figure 1.7 shows the property sheet for the desktop. It appears when you right-click the desktop and choose Properties. Selecting different tabs in the sheet enables you to change the colors, background, and screen savers in Windows.

Shortcuts Add Power

Shortcuts are a powerful way of customizing your desktop. You can use a shortcut to start applications, load a document, act as a drop-box into a folder located elsewhere, and so on. You can even put a printer shortcut on your desktop. Dragging a file onto a printer shortcut will then print the file. You can put shortcuts anywhere on the desktop or in any folder.

▶ **See** "Using Shortcuts and Icons on the Desktop," **p. 82**

FIG. 1.7
Right-click almost any item and choose Properties to display a sheet like this Display Properties sheet.

Quick View Displays File Previews

Quick View enables you to see a preview of a file without starting the application that created the file and opening the file. It's a handy browser that can save you time. Quick View works with the files from most major applications. Figure 1.8 shows a Quick View of an Excel sheet. To see a Quick View, right-click a file's icon, then choose Quick View.

▶ **See** "Previewing a Document with Quick View," **p. 112**

FIG. 1.8
Use Quick View to preview a file without opening it.

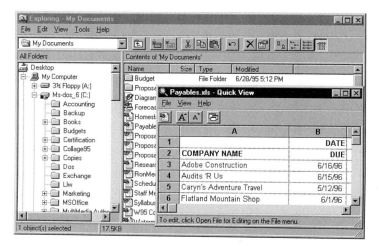

Long File Names Make File Names Easier to Read

One of the most aggravating things faced by everyone who used DOS or previous versions of Windows was the 8.3 file naming restriction. File names were a maximum of eight characters, and file extensions were a maximum of three characters. This limit lead to very inventive, but pretty undecipherable, file names. In Windows 95, you can use file names that are up to 255 characters long—they can even include space characters. When a file with a long name is brought back to an 8.3 file system, the long file name is truncated so that files are still compatible.

▶ **See** "Working with Long File Names," **p. 134**

Agents Automatically Backup or Improve Disk Performance

Agents are software monitors that run programs at a time you schedule. They enable you to set times for utilities or programs to run automatically. Agents are installed from Microsoft Plus!. They are discussed more fully in Chapter 22, "Working with Disks and Drives," and in Chapter 23, "Backing Up and Protecting Your Data." For example, you can specify that backups be made every afternoon at 6 p.m. or that the disk defragmenter should run every Friday after work.

Help is Easy to Use

Help has been simplified, while at the same time it contains more information. Help now enables you to type in phrases and get back a list of related items. Help also includes graphical displays that are designed to help you understand the big picture of how a function or feature works.

More Useful Accessories

Windows includes accessories that are helpful in routine work and performing more challenging tasks, such as file and disk management. The simple word processor, WordPad, is more than adequate for most school work or personal letter writing. And it uses a file format that is compatible with Word for Windows, the powerful and most widely sold word processor. Windows also includes accessories such as a new paint program, calculator, and clock.

A valuable set of disk management accessories comes with Windows. These accessories improve the performance, integrity, and safety of data on your hard drives. DriveSpace compresses data on your disk so that you can fit almost twice as much data on a drive. DriveSpace 3, available on the Plus! disk, can compress drives on Pentium computers to fit almost three times as much data. The ScanDisk utility checks your hard disk for errors.

Disk Defragmenter collects file segments that are stored all over the disk and relocates them so that files are stored in contiguous segments. As a result, your disk runs faster and wastes less storage space. Finally, Windows 95 includes Backup. You can use the Backup utility to make magnetic tape or disk backups of all or parts of your hard disk.

Windows 95 has been improved for use with multimedia equipment. It includes the CD Player that enables you to play music CDs on computers equipped with a CD-ROM and sound board. The new AutoStart feature makes installing CDs automatic. Windows 95 detects when a new CD is put in the drive, searches for the installation files, and either runs the program from the CD or asks you whether you want to install it on your disk drive.

Improved Printing

Windows 95's printing speed is something everyone will appreciate. Windows now uses a 32-bit print subsystem that enables you to print in the background without causing the application you are using to show significant delays. The apparent print time has been improved because it takes less time for Windows to return to your control after you give a print command.

If you need high-quality print output, you will be able to take advantage of Windows' support for PostScript Level II printers as well as better color matching between the display and output devices.

Mobile computer users will be able to take advantage of *deferred printing*. This enables people with laptop computers to print even though their laptop is not in a docking station. Printed files are stored on hard disk until the computer is connected to a printer or docking station that has a printer. At that time, Windows prompts the user whether the deferred print jobs should be printed.

Windows 95 also supports more than 800 printer models. With newer models that support the Plug and Play standard, installation is simple. Network administrators will enjoy the automatic printer driver installation from Windows 95, Windows NT, or Novell NetWare servers.

MS-DOS Applications Run Better

The new Windows 95 protected-mode drivers enable MS-DOS virtual machines to have more than 600K free conventional memory. Real-mode drivers can still be used if a protected mode driver is not available. Failure in any virtual machine does not affect the MS-DOS applications running in other virtual machines.

Drivers can be loaded separately for each MS-DOS virtual machine. In addition, you can specify batch files that run prior to the execution of an MS-DOS program.

▶ **See** "Configuring Your MS-DOS Application," **p. 519**

Networking and Communication in Windows 95

Windows 95 is designed to meet the requirements of a corporate networking environment. It also is easier to use for people on a network and for mobile computer users who connect to a network.

Windows uses a high-performance 32-bit network architecture that includes 32-bit versions of network client software, file and print sharing software, network protocols, and network card drivers. Windows 95 is a fast 32-bit client for NetWare and Windows NT Server networks. It supports NDIS 2.x, 3.x, and ODI drivers. Protocols supported are 32-bit NetBEUI, IPX/SPX, and TCP/IP.

▶ **See** "Introducing the Windows 95 Client for NetWare Networks," **p. 718**

Windows 95 users can now log on and have their system settings follow them to the new workstation.

System administration is easier. Administrators can use the Policy Editor to control which operations are available to specific users. The Policy Editor also can be used to control desktop appearance.

Windows 95 computers are easier to manage with the system Registry. The Registry is a database containing information about a computer, hardware, software, user preferences, and privileges. The Registry can be controlled through SNMP, DMI, and Remote Procedure Call.

You can build your own network using the integrated peer-to-peer networking capability of Windows. Windows 95 is capable of supporting up to ten 32-bit, Protected-mode network clients. With today's heterogeneous networking environments, it's important that Windows be able to run as a client for many different networks. Windows runs client support for Windows NT Server, NetWare, Banyan, DEC PathWorks, and Sun NFS.

Windows 95 includes HyperTerminal, an improved 32-bit version of the basic communications program Terminal that came with previous versions of Windows.

▶ **See** "Using the Peer Advantage," **p. 778**
▶ **See** "Installing the Windows 95 Client for NetWare Networks," **p. 719**

Internet and Microsoft Network Connection

Besides supporting corporate networking, Windows 95 has access to The Microsoft Network and the Internet. Windows includes TCP/IP support, Windows Socket services, and widely used protocols such as PPP and SLIP, so you can connect to the Internet through your corporate network or directly via your own modem or ISDN connection.

The Internet Explorer enables you to browse the World Wide Web through your own Internet provider or by using The Microsoft Network as an Internet service provider.

The Microsoft Network is a collection of databases, services, software libraries, and forums. Although MSN has many informative areas on topics ranging from gourmet cooking to flying, it's extremely valuable as a reservoir of technical knowledge on Windows 95 and all Microsoft products. It gives you access to the Knowledge Base, the same database used by Microsoft's telephone support people.

Better Features for the Road Warrior

Windows 95 addresses many of the difficulties inherent with mobile computing such as operating with portable and laptop configurations, temporarily connecting to networks, printing while disconnected from a printer, quickly installing PC Cards, synchronizing files between laptop and desktop computers, monitoring battery life, and more.

With Windows 95, mobile computer users can easily switch between different named setup configurations. If the mobile computer uses a docking station, the software transition can be completely automatic. Putting the laptop in the docking station causes the laptop to reboot in the correct configuration and connect to the appropriate network, printers, and so on.

The use of PCMCIA cards also has been improved (in Windows 95, however, PCMCIA cards are now referred to as PC Cards). You can install newer PC Cards while the computer is on. Windows 95 recognizes the new card through Plug and Play, immediately installs the correct drivers, and then makes its features available.

One of the advances that Windows 95 includes is the Briefcase, a feature used to store files shared between desktop and mobile computers. The Briefcase automatically updates files between the systems and asks you to judge files that may be in conflict.

▶ **See** "Synchronizing Files with the Briefcase," **p. 140**

Any mobile computer user will tell you how important power management is. You can't have a battery go dead at the wrong time. In laptop computers that support the new Power Management APIs, Windows can monitor system power, reduce power loss, and warn you when power gets low.

With deferred printing, you can print the documents you want. Windows 95 spools them to disk for storage if you aren't connected to a printer. As soon as you connect your laptop to a printer, it will begin printing.

The new Infrared communication support became available in Microsoft's first free upgrade, Service Pack 1. Infrared communication uses infrared light between hardware devices in the same manner as a serial or parallel cable. No more will you have to crawl around on the floor and switch cables when you want to do something as easy as print in a temporary office.

Easier Hardware Installation and Maintenance

One of the most aggravating situations you can face with a computer is installing a sound board, disk drive, or network adapter card that you are unfamiliar with. In fact, many hardware devices used with computers require some arcane knowledge and a few tricks that aren't in the book before they finally work. Plug and Play is designed to do away with the trickery and make the hardware side of computers as easy as installing refrigerators and toasters.

The Plug and Play specification is an industry-wide specification designed to make adding hardware easy. Plug and Play enables you to install or connect Plug-and-Play-compatible devices and let Windows figure out the technical details such as IRQs, I/O addresses, DMA channels, and memory addresses. Where there is conflict, Windows resolves the problem rather than you having to spend hours trying different settings.

The information about all installed hardware and software is stored in the Registry, a database of system information. Plug and Play even makes it easier to install hardware that does not meet Plug and Play specifications, so-called *legacy hardware*. Windows detects that the legacy hardware may cause a conflict with current system settings and then gives you information from the Registry that makes it easier for you to decide how to install the hardware. You don't have to keep notecards containing all the settings from previous hardware you installed, nor do you have to pull out hardware manuals that you have probably misplaced.

▶ **See** "Installing Legacy (non-PnP) Hardware," **p. 165**
▶ **See** "Installing Plug and Play Hardware," **p. 158**

Plug and Play's ease of use is apparent with, for example, the use of Plug and Play printers or PC Cards. With a Plug and Play printer, as soon as you connect the printer, your computer recognizes the new printer, installs a new device driver for it, and sets up your printer configuration to print with that printer. With PC Cards used in portable computers, you can slide in a modem card and immediately send a message. Plug and Play configures the modem card for you.

Troubleshooting conflicts between hardware devices is significantly easier with the Device Manager. The Device Manager enables you to select a hardware device and see what driver it uses, and whether it is operating correctly. The Device Manager also shows the system resources assigned to a device such as the IRQ settings and Input/Output range.

▶ **See** "Troubleshooting Hardware Installation," **p. 177**

Improved Multimedia and Games

Windows 95 has improved multimedia capability. Windows includes Video for Windows so that you don't have to install video drivers. It also includes drivers for the most commonly used CD-ROM drives and sound cards. And to make it easy for anyone at home to use games or edutainment software, Windows automatically installs and runs newer CD-ROMs when you put them in the computer. Its improvements aren't limited to multimedia however, Windows now includes WinG, a programming interface used by game programmers, so they can write faster games that run on Windows.

Collect Mail and Faxes with the New Universal Inbox

Windows 95 includes a new system of collecting e-mail, the Universal Inbox. The Universal Inbox is the client for Microsoft Exchange. The Universal Inbox retrieves messages from Microsoft Mail, Faxes, Internet mail, The Microsoft Network, CompuServe Mail, and other services. You'll learn how to install new mail services so you can use the Universal Inbox with non-Microsoft mail systems.

▶ **See** "The Universal Inbox," **p. 875**

In addition to acting as a universal inbox, you can use Microsoft Exchange to send mail through different transmission methods. If one transmission method will not work when you attempt to send an e-mail or fax, then it automatically tries another method. It even includes Microsoft Fax software so you can send and receive faxes as well as create your own fax cover sheets.

Remote Network Access

Windows 95 supports a much more robust remote-access environment than Windows for Workgroups did. Windows 95 dial-up networking has been tested with Windows NT Server, Netware servers running NetWare Connect, Siva NetModem, and LANRover. Protocols include Windows 3.1 RAS, PPP, and NetWare Connect. The Dial-up Wizard helps you connect to remote networks so it looks like Windows 95 has a physical network connection. ●

CHAPTER 2

Understanding Windows 95

by Ron Person

This chapter gives you "the big picture" to help you understand Windows 95. As an experienced Windows user, you'll want to know what is different and what is the same in this new version of Windows compared to previous versions. And if you are a power user or consultant, you'll want a quick introduction to ways you can customize and troubleshoot Windows 95. ■

What are the most important elements in a Windows 95 screen?

Learn the different parts of a Windows 95 screen.

How are programs started and documents loaded?

Intermediate and expert users can customize Windows 95 to start programs on startup, from desktop icons, or directly from files.

How to customize Windows 95

Learn how to customize Windows 95 by changing property sheets.

Who should use My Computer and who should use Windows Explorer for their file management needs?

Shows advantages to using both single pane windows and double pane windows to manage files.

T I P People who have used previous versions of Windows should read this chapter so that they can quickly grasp what has changed. Experienced Windows 95 users can probably skip this chapter.

Understanding the Most Important Screen Elements in Windows 95

The appearance of the Windows 95 screen, shown in figure 2.1, is completely different from previous versions of Windows. The backdrop of the screen, called the *desktop,* holds icons that represent programs or documents, a taskbar containing a Start button and application buttons, and windows that contain programs. If your Windows 95 machine has been used previously and customized, it may appear slightly different from the figure.

FIG. 2.1
The Windows 95 screen is designed to be easier to use for first-time users, yet more powerful and customizable for power users.

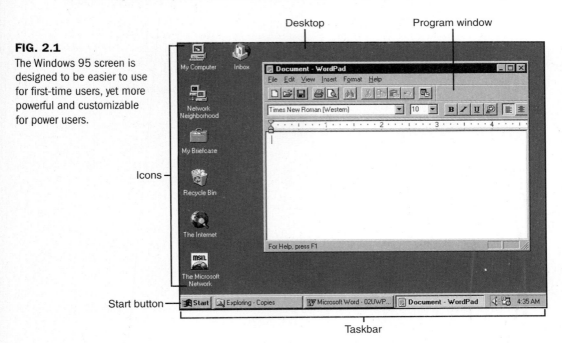

If you are familiar with previous versions of Windows, important changes to notice are:

- Icons on the desktop represent programs, documents, or shortcuts. *Shortcuts* are pointers or links to a program or document.

- You use the Start button and taskbar shown at the bottom of figure 2.1 to start and switch between programs.

■ Running programs appear in three ways—as a button on the taskbar, in a window on the screen, or filling the entire screen. You can always tell which programs are running because all running programs appear on the taskbar.

■ Much more of Windows can be customized than in previous Windows versions. Customize by clicking an item with the right mouse button, clicking Properties, and then changing options on the Properties sheet for the item.

■ The Program Manager is gone. In its place are icons that appear on the desktop and a taskbar with a Start button shown at the bottom of figure 2.1.

■ You can drag icons on the desktop to any location and they will stay there. You can even place folders on the desktop. (*Folders* is the new name for directories.)

■ *Shortcut* icons on the desktop act as pointers to programs or documents that you don't want to put directly on the desktop. Shortcuts display a small curved arrow at their lower-left corner. Double-clicking a shortcut icon opens the document or program. Deleting a shortcut icon does not delete the file to which it points.

> **See** "Learning the Parts of the Windows Display," **p. 64**

> **See** "Opening Programs and Documents from Explorer or My Computer," **p. 78**

> **See** "Customizing the Mouse," **p. 402**

> **See** "Making Windows Accessible for the Hearing, Sight, and Movement Impaired," **p. 405**

> **See** " Using the Power of Shortcuts and Desktop Icons," **p. 71**

Starting Programs and Documents

Depending on your experience level and the task, you can start programs or documents in different ways. Some of the ways in which you can start programs and documents are:

■ *Start button.* Click the Start button to see the Start menu. Click the Programs item to see programs you can start. Click the Documents item to see a list of the most recently used documents you can reopen.

■ *Shortcuts.* Double-clicking icons that appear on the desktop or in folders starts programs or documents.

■ *Files.* Double-clicking program files or documents that appear in the Windows Explorer or in folder windows starts programs and opens documents.

Starting from the Start Button

The Start button is a significant enhancement to Windows. Clicking the Start button displays a menu like the one directly above the Start button in figure 2.2. As you move the pointer over an item on the menu, a submenu appears. When you see the program or document you want to open, click it.

FIG. 2.2
Click the Start
button to display the
Start menu and your
computer's
programs and
documents.

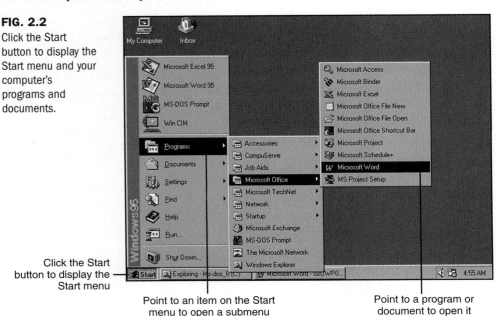

Click the Start
button to display the
Start menu

Point to an item on the Start
menu to open a submenu

Point to a program or
document to open it

When compared with previous versions of Windows, some important changes have been made to the process of starting and shutting down programs:

- Click the Start button to see menu items that display your programs and most frequently used documents. Click the item you want to open.

- Start a recently used document by clicking Start and pointing to the Documents menu item and then clicking the document. The program opens automatically.

- Find documents or programs by clicking Start and pointing to the Find button and clicking Files or Folders. Enter information about the document or program file you want to find.

- Get Help or demonstrations by clicking Start and the Help button.

- Your existing Group windows from the Program Manager in previous versions of Windows now appear as submenus off the Programs item of the Start menu.

- Go directly to the Control Panel or printer settings from the Settings item on the Start menu.

- Shut down Windows by clicking the Start button and then clicking Shut Down.

As an experienced Windows user you will learn that you can quickly customize Windows 95 to make it fit your operating style. Some easy ways to customize are:

- Make frequently used programs more accessible on the Start menu by dragging their file icon from Explorer or My Computer and dropping it on the Start button.

- Access programs faster on the Start menu by adding your own submenus that contain programs, documents, or shortcuts. You also can reposition items on a submenu.

- Change the properties of shortcuts that point to programs so that the program opens as a button on the taskbar, as a window, or maximized to fill the screen.

   ▶ **See** "Customizing the Start Menu," **p. 369**

   ▶ **See** "Starting Windows after Technical Problems Occur," **p. 54**

   ▶ **See** "Customizing the Taskbar," **p. 366**

Part
I

Ch
2

Starting from Shortcuts

Shortcuts are icons that point to files or folders (see fig. 2.3). In that respect they are similar to the icons found in Program Manager; however, shortcut icons can be nested inside folders or shortcuts to folders.

When you double-click a program or document shortcut, it starts the program or opens the document. Double-clicking a shortcut to a folder opens that folder into a *folder window.* You can create shortcuts to folders on your desktop so that when you drag a file onto the folder shortcut, the file is stored in the folder.

Shortcuts make it easy to start programs, move files into frequently used folders, or organize programs and documents on a desktop. Some of the things you can do with shortcuts are:

- You can create a shortcut for any program, document, or folder by dragging the file or folder from the Explorer or My Computer with the right mouse button and dropping it on the desktop.

- You can create shortcuts that automatically run procedures or programs. For example, in Word or Excel you can create a shortcut to a document or spreadsheet that contains a macro that runs when opened. Another example is the Windows 95 Backup program. It enables you to create shortcuts that automatically back up selected files.

- Customize shortcuts by right-clicking the Shortcut icon, clicking Properties and then clicking the Shortcut tab in the shortcut's Properties sheet. You can add shortcut keys, change the file to which the shortcut points, specify how a program runs, and change the icon.

▶ **See** "Using Shortcut Icons on the Desktop," **p. 73**

▶ **See** "Editing a Shortcut Name and Deleting Shortcuts," **p. 74**

FIG. 2.3
Double-click a shortcut icon to open the program or document.

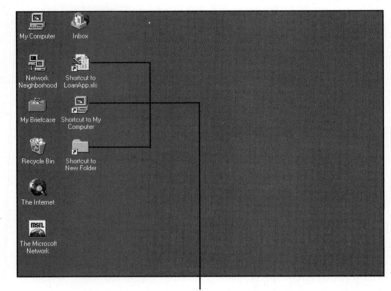

Shortcut icons have small curved arrows at their lower-left corners

Starting from My Computer or Explorer

My Computer and Explorer are windows used to manage the program and document files on your computer. Figures 2.4 and 2.5 show the My Computer and Explorer windows. You can manage files as well as start programs or load documents into programs from My Computer or Explorer. Here are some important issues to keep in mind when you work with My Computer or Explorer:

FIG. 2.4
You can manage program and document files with the My Computer window.

FIG. 2.5
The Explorer window allows you to do the same thing.

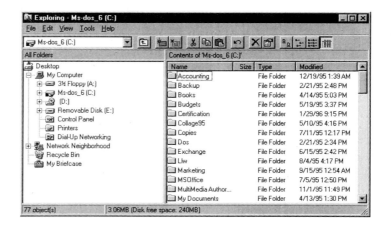

- Start programs and open documents by double-clicking the file. It's the same in Windows 3.x File Manager, Explorer, or a folder window from My Computer.

- You can register a file type with an application so that double-clicking a file of that type opens a specific application and loads the file. Most file types are automatically registered, but you can manually register a file or change a file type's registration by choosing View, Options, selecting the File Types tab, and then either adding a new type or editing an existing type.

- In Windows 3.x File Manager or Program Manager you can only open one file at a time. In Windows Explorer you can open multiple files at a time. Open multiple files at the same time from My Computer or Explorer by selecting the files with Shift+Click or Ctrl+Click, and then right-click one of the selected files. From the shortcut menu, click Open.

▶ **See** "Using My Computer to Start Programs and Open Documents," **p. 79**

▶ **See** "Using Explorer to View Files and Folders," **p. 96**

▶ **See** "Managing Your Files and Folders," **p. 101**

▶ **See** "Registering File Types Causing Documents to Open Applications," **p. 147**

▶ **See** "Customizing the Shortcut (Right-Click) Menu," **p. 375**

Customizing Windows 95

Property sheets are an important part of Windows 95. Nearly every item you see on-screen has a property sheet that contains the item's characteristics. You can change some of these characteristics. To display a properties sheet, click an item with the right mouse button and then click Properties from the shortcut menu. Figure 2.6 shows the Taskbar Properties sheet.

FIG. 2.6
Use properties sheets to get information about an item and change how the item behaves.

Windows 95 customization offers some significant improvements over previous versions of Windows:

■ In Windows 3.x you had to go through the Control Panel to customize most things. Many Windows features weren't customizable. In Windows 95 click the right mouse buttons on items you see and choose Properties to learn what you can customize.

■ In Windows 3.x changing hardware configurations to match temporary conditions, such as working on a laptop on the road or at your desk, required reinstalling drivers each time you changed. In Windows 95 you can predefine hardware configurations. At startup you can choose the configuration you need. For example, choosing a laptop configuration could change your settings to use the battery monitor, the internal hard disk, and PC Card modem. Choosing a desktop configuration when your laptop is connected to its docking station could enable a high-resolution monitor, an extra hard drive, a network adapter, and so forth.

■ In Windows 3.x it was difficult to have a user's customized settings follow them to different stations on the network. In Windows 95 it takes selecting a single check box for custom settings to follow a user. Each user's custom settings are associated with their log-on ID.

▶ **See** "Customizing the Desktop Colors and Background," **p. 382**

▶ **See** "Working with Desktop Themes," **p. 388**

▶ **See** "Reviewing Your Computer's System Information," **p. 413**

▶ **See** "Changing Custom Settings for Each User," **p. 412**

How to Manage Files

Windows 95 has two different approaches to managing files. You may want to train the new or inexperienced user (or people familiar with Macintosh) to use My Computer. It uses a folder metaphor, where files appear as program or document icons (see fig. 2.7). (Your folders may appear different from these figures if your Windows 95 has had settings changed.) These icons can be moved or copied between folder icons. If you're on a network, examine Network Neighborhood. It shows network files in the same way.

Anyone familiar with previous versions of Windows will want to use the more powerful Explorer (see fig. 2.8). (Your folders may appear different from these figures if your Windows 95 has had settings changed.) The Explorer displays folders and files using two panes in a window. The left pane shows the hierarchical relationship between folders (which folder is inside another). The right pane displays the contents of the folder that has been selected in the left pane.

FIG. 2.7
My Computer displays the contents of your computer in windows that contain folders and program/document icons.

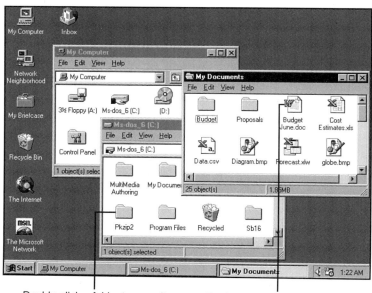

Double-click a folder to open it   Double-click an icon to open it

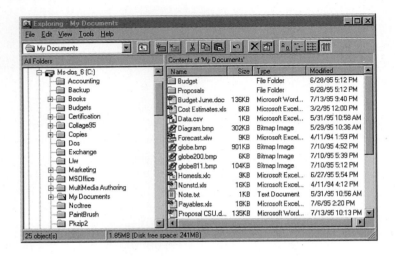

FIG. 2.8
The hierarchical relationship of folders shows in the left pane of the Explorer window.

Important differences between the File Manager in previous versions of Windows and My Computer or Explorer are:

- It's more efficient to do file management tasks in Windows 95 because commands are more readily available than in Windows 3.x. Right-click files in My Computer or Explorer to see the numerous shortcut commands for copying, deleting, printing, and so on.

- At first, you may get frustrated using Explorer because, unlike Windows 3.x File Manager, it doesn't employ multiple windows that display separate drives or folders. You can actually do more in the Explorer than you did in File Manager, but you will need to check the tips in Chapter 4, "Managing Files," to learn how to employ the power built into Explorer.

- There are more ways to view files in Windows 95 than in Windows 3.x. You can change the displays in either My Computer or Explorer to show lists of names with details, and small or large icons.

- In Windows 95 system resources such as the Control Panel, hardware devices, and printers are more accessible and grouped better than in Windows 3.x. My Computer and Explorer also give you access to computer resources such as the Control Panel, Printers, Internet URLs, hardware device settings, and more. Double-click these resources or folders to access the file, folder, or resource.

  ▶ **See** "Using Explorer with Shared Resources on a Network," **p. 148**
  ▶ **See** "Monitoring Your System," **p. 653**

▶ **See** "Using My Computer to Manage Files," **p. 117**

▶ **See** "Managing Your Files and Folders," **p. 101**

▶ **See** "Working with Long File Names," **p. 134**

▶ **See** "Improving Performance with Disk Defragmenter," **p. 646**

Part

I

Ch

2

P A R T

II

Navigating Windows 95

Windows Navigation Basics

by Ron Person

What you learn in this and the next chapter will help you operate Windows and any Windows application. This chapter describes the parts of the Windows screen, how to start Windows and applications, and reveals numerous productivity tips.

This chapter also briefly introduces Windows Explorer (which Chapter 4, "Managing Files," covers in more detail). ■

Techniques for starting and quitting Windows

You are given explanations of the multiple choices for starting and shutting down Windows 95.

How to troubleshoot problems that occur when starting Windows or programs

Use guidelines for finding causes and executing remedies.

The terms for and parts of Windows and Windows applications

Learn the jargon and terminology, and understand what they mean.

How to run programs automatically at startup

If you launch the same program every time you start your day, why not let Windows 95 launch it for you?

How to start programs with different Windows properties

Learn to configure your system's environment so programs with special requirements get exactly what they need to run productively.

How to create shortcuts for starting programs and opening documents

Learn how to skip the menu system by getting where you want to go directly from the desktop.

Starting and Quitting Windows

If you have not yet installed Windows, turn to Appendix A, "Installing Windows 95," to learn how. After you install Windows, you can start Windows simply by turning on your computer. In most cases, computers start directly into Windows 95. If your computer requires a real-mode (16-bit) driver, you might see a DOS-like text screen as the drivers load. (Windows 95 has many new drivers, but real-mode drivers might be required for hardware that does not have a Windows 95 32-bit driver. These real-mode drivers are the ones used by Windows 3.x or DOS.) Also, if your Windows has multiple configurations installed, as a laptop or desktop version for example, then a text screen will display asking you to choose between the configurations. After you make your choice, Windows starts.

 T I P   For a faster startup, press the Esc key during startup of Windows 95 to bypass the Windows 95 logo. To permanently bypass the logo, use Notepad or WordPad to edit the MSDOS.SYS file. Add LOGO=0 to the Options section. To see the logo on startup, just change the 0 to 1.

When Windows starts, it displays a dialog box that contains your name and a space for you to enter your password. Windows uses the name and the password from the login dialog box for several purposes:

■ Windows uses the name to match it against a User Profile so that when users log in, the system displays the desktop and the software settings they configured.

■ If the computer is connected to a network, Windows logs you into the network using the name as the network username and the password to enforce network security. (If the computer is connected to a Microsoft Network, an additional field will be displayed in the dialog box for the Domain.)

N O T E   If you are not using the login dialog box to enter a network password or to load custom settings, then you might as well avoid seeing it each time you start Windows. To prevent the login dialog box from appearing, follow this procedure:

1. Right-click Network Neighborhood, then click Properties.

2. Click the Configuration tab, then choose Windows Logon from the Primary Network Logon pull-down list. Click OK.

3. Click No when Windows prompts to restart the computer.

4. Open the Start menu and choose Settings, Control Panel to open the Control Panel.

5. Double-click the Passwords icon.

6. Choose the Change Passwords tab, then click the Change <u>W</u>indows Password button. Click OK, then enter a blank password. ▨

After login is complete, the Windows 95 desktop is displayed, with the My Computer, Recycle Bin, and Network Neighborhood icons. You might also see the My Briefcase icon and shortcut icons created by prior users. The *taskbar* usually appears at the bottom of the screen.

N O T E The taskbar might appear in another location if you are not the only user of the machine, as it can be placed at any edge of the screen, or not at all, except for a very thin line. This means the "Auto hide" feature was enabled, and moving your mouse to that line will "roll out" the taskbar. ▨

 T I P When you initially run Windows, it displays a Welcome to Windows 95 sheet. People usually check this sheet off so it doesn't appear at each startup. If you ever want to rerun the Welcome sheet, click Start, <u>R</u>un, type Welcome in the edit box, and click OK.

If you share a computer with others, you must restart to use your customized features. Windows 95 saves desktop and network settings by name (in profile files with the extension PWL). Shut down with the <u>C</u>lose All Programs and Log On as a Different User? option (see fig. 3.1).

FIG. 3.1
Windows enables you to shut down the computer, restart the computer, restart the computer in MS-DOS mode, or close all applications and log on with another user ID.

 T I P If there are multiple desktop profiles on your Windows 95 system (either because there are multiple users or because you've created different desktops for different configurations), sometimes you can't tell which desktop you're using currently. To know who and where you are at all times, create a folder for the desktop for every profile. Name the folder to indicate the login name—for example, "This is Mary's Desktop." If you do this for each configuration, a glance at this empty folder's title will let you know which desktop you are currently working on. If you want, you can place a text file in the folder that enumerates the settings for this desktop profile.

Running Applications at Startup

You can customize programs to start automatically when Windows starts. You can even specify whether the program starts in a minimized, maximized, or normal window.

Running Programs or Documents on Startup   To specify the programs or documents you want to run at startup, you add them to the Windows\Start Menu\Programs\Startup folder. When documents are in the Startup folder, Windows starts the document's program, then loads the document

 TIP Create shortcuts to frequently used folders, then drag the shortcuts into the Startup folder if you want the folders to open when Windows starts. Set the shortcut's properties so the folder opens minimized to keep the desktop uncluttered.

To specify programs or documents that you want Windows to run at startup, follow these steps:

1. Right-click in a gray area of the taskbar, then click Properties.
2. Select the Start Menu Programs tab (see fig. 3.2).

FIG. 3.2
Use the Start Menu
Programs page to specify
programs to run at startup.

3. Choose Add, then click Browse.
4. Select the program you want to add to the Startup folder, then click Open (or double-click on the program).
5. Click Next.
6. Select the Startup folder, then click Next.

7. Accept the default title for the program or type a new title in the Select a Name for the Shortcut text box. The name you enter appears in the Startup menu.

8. Click Finish.

9. Repeat steps 3 through 8 to add more programs to the Startup folder, or choose OK if you are finished adding programs.

N O T E If you frequently change the programs or documents that you want to run on startup, make the Startup folder accessible as a shortcut on the desktop so you can drag shortcuts to program or document files. Don't drag the actual program or document file to the Startup folder because you might delete the actual file during later changes to the Startup folder. Creating shortcuts is described in "Using Shortcut Icons on the Desktop" later in this chapter.

 T I P To bypass the Startup group during Windows startup—preventing the objects in the Startup group from opening—hold down the Shift key while Windows is starting (after you enter your logon user name and password). Release the Shift key after the desktop appears.

To remove a program or document from the Startup folder, follow these steps:

1. Choose Remove on the Start Menu Programs page.

2. Double-click the Startup folder.

3. Select the program you want to remove and choose Remove.

4. Choose Close.

Controlling the Window in which Startup Programs Appear   After specifying that a program run at startup, you must choose to have the program run maximized, in a normal window, or as a button on the taskbar (minimized).

To control how a program appears on startup, follow these steps:

1. Add the program to the Startup folder, as described in the preceding section "Running Programs and Documents on Startup." (If you manually drag a file into the Startup folder, use a right-drag and create a shortcut rather than leaving the actual file in the Startup folder.)

2. Open the Startup folder in either My Computer or Explorer. The Startup folder is located as a subfolder in Windows\Start Menu\Programs\Startup.

3. Right-click the program object, then choose Properties.

4. Select the Shortcut tab.

Part
II

Ch
3

5. Select one of the three options, Normal Window, Minimized, or Maximized, from the Run drop-down list (see fig. 3.3).

FIG. 3.3
Use the Shortcut Properties page to configure how Word for Windows will run on startup.

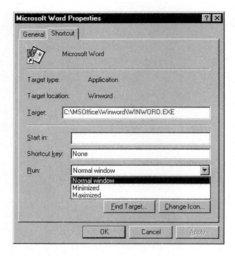

6. Choose OK.

TROUBLESHOOTING

After putting some applications in the Startup folder so they would run on startup, Windows fails to start correctly. Check to see if the applications in the Startup folder are causing the problem by holding down the Shift key as Windows starts. This prevents applications in Startup from starting. If Windows starts correctly, then a problem exists with one of the applications. Remove all the applications from the folder, then put each back, one at a time, until you find the offending application.

▶ **See** "Using Windows Explorer to View Files and Folders," **p. 96**

Starting Windows After Technical Problems Occur

If you have trouble starting Windows, there are a number of paths you can take, both to continue working with your system and to troubleshoot the problem so it doesn't recur.

Using the Startup Disk   During the installation of Windows 95, there was an opportunity to create a Startup Disk. If you didn't take advantage of the opportunity, you should have created a Startup Disk once you'd configured your system. Then, if you have trouble starting Windows, you can use the startup disk to start your computer. For example, if you inadvertently delete a file that Windows needs for startup, you must start Windows with the startup disk in your disk drive and then remedy the problem so you can start Windows normally.

CAUTION

If you didn't create the startup disk during installation or have misplaced the disk, you can create one after Windows is installed. Make sure to do so now, before you need the disk.

To create a startup disk, follow these steps:

1. Open the Start menu and choose Settings, Control Panel.
2. Double-click the Add/Remove Programs button.
3. Click the Startup Disk tab (see fig. 3.4).

FIG. 3.4
Use the Startup Disk Properties Page to create a startup disk or to update an existing startup disk after you've made changes to your system.

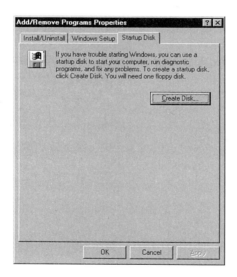

4. Insert a disk in drive A. The contents of this disk will be deleted.
5. Choose Create Disk and follow the instructions as they appear on-screen.

   To create the startup disk, you must have your original Windows program disks (or CD-ROM) because the Startup Disk boot files are copied from the source disks to be sure of their integrity.
6. Click OK.

Keep your startup disk safe and keep a copy of it accessible.

To use the startup disk, insert it in the disk drive and reboot the computer. Read the next section, "Starting Windows in an Alternate Startup Mode," for instructions on diagnosing and correcting problems.

TIP Label the Startup Disk and write-protect it to make sure it's going to be there when you need it and to prevent anyone from using it. Make two copies of your startup disk—one for your office and one for the vault.

Starting Windows in an Alternate Startup Mode   If the computer has difficulty starting, you will want to start Windows in one of its diagnostic modes. In most troubleshooting situations, you will want to start in *safe mode.* In safe mode, Windows uses basic default settings that restart Windows with minimal functionality. For example, if you install the wrong driver for a new monitor, you might not be able to see the Windows display when you restart Windows. In this case, restarting Windows in safe mode enables you to see the display so you can use the Control Panel or the Device Manager to correct problems.

The default safe mode settings use a generic VGA monitor driver, the standard Microsoft mouse driver, and the minimum device drivers necessary to start Windows. When you start Windows with the default settings, you cannot access CD-ROM drives, printers, modems, or other external hardware devices. One of the safe modes allows networking.

To start Windows in a different mode, follow these steps:

1. Turn on the computer.
2. As soon as you see the message `Starting Windows` on your monitor, press F8 to display the Windows 95 Startup Menu. This menu displays choices for different starting modes.

CAUTION
You need fast reflexes to boot into safe mode. If you press F8 before the "Starting Windows" message appears, it won't work because the keypress won't be noticed by Windows. If you wait longer than a second or so after the message appears, it's too late, so you'll have to shut the computer off and try again, and perhaps again and again until you get it timed properly. Incidentally, if you have dual boot choices you have to select Windows 95 before all of this occurs.

The Microsoft Windows 95 Startup Menu offers choices that reflect the configuration of your system. You may see some or all of the following choices:

1. Normal
2. Logged (\BOOTLOG.TXT)

3. Safe mode

4. Safe mode with network support

5. Step-by-step confirmation

6. Command prompt only

7. Safe mode command prompt only

8. Previous version of MS-DOS

9. Type the selection number for the mode in which you want to start, then press Enter.

To skip the Windows 95 Startup Menu and start directly in a mode, start your computer and press one of the key combinations in the following table when the message Starting Windows appears.

Operating Mode	Key Combination	Actions
Windows 95 in safe mode without networking	F5	Loads HIMEM.SYS and IFSHLP.SYS, loads DoubleSpace or DriveSpace if present, then runs Windows 95 WIN.COM. Starts in safe mode.
Windows 95 in safe mode with minimum network functions	F6	Loads HIMEM.SYS and IFSHLP.SYS. Processes the Registry, loads COMMAND.COM, loads DoubleSpace or DriveSpace if present, runs Windows 95 WIN.COM, loads network drivers and runs NETSTART.BAT.
DOS 7.0 without disk compression	Ctrl+F5	Loads COMMAND.COM.
DOS 7.0 with disk compression	Shift+F5	Loads COMMAND.COM and loads DoubleSpace or DriveSpace if present.

TIP Windows 95 automatically starts in safe mode if you restart Windows 95 after it has failed to start successfully.

A message informs you that Windows is running in safe mode and that some of your devices might not be available. The words `Safe mode` appear at each corner of the screen.

Understanding How Windows Achieves Safe Mode   Windows boots to safe mode using settings that enable most computers to run their basic system. The following steps describe what Windows does as it boots in safe mode:

1. Bypasses the Registry, AUTOEXEC.BAT, and CONFIG.SYS files.
2. Loads HIMEM.SYS without processing command line switches.
3. Loads IFSHLP.SYS.
4. Loads path information from the MSDOS.SYS file.
5. If Windows 95 files are available, then Windows executes from the command

   ```
   Win /D:m
   ```

   to boot into safe mode.

   If Windows 95 files are unavailable, then COMMAND.COM executes leaving the system in DOS mode.
6. If Windows booted correctly, then it looks for the Windows\SYSTEM.CB file. The SYSTEM.CB file loads virtual device drivers. If it cannot be found, a clean copy of SYSTEM.CB is created, which loads the following virtual device drivers:

   ```
   mouse=*vmouse
   device=*configmg
   device=*vwin32
   device=*vfbackup
   device=*vshare
   device=*vcomm
   device=*ifsmgr
   device=*ios
   device=*vfat
   device=*vcache
   device=*vcond
   device=*int13
   device=*vxdldr
   device=*vdef
   device=*dynapage
   device=*reboot
   ```

```
device=*vsd
device=*parity
device=*biosxlat
device=*vmcpd
device=*vkd
device=*vdd
device=*ebios
device=*vtdapi
device=*vmpoll
woafont=dosapp.fon
```

7. The SYSTEM.CB file is discarded and WIN.COM loads Windows. Windows 95 then uses the original Registry settings, SYSTEM.INI and WIN.INI files. This process effectively disables all the protected mode devices.

8. Finally Windows 95 resizes the desktop to 640×480 resolution.

Troubleshooting in Safe Mode

Running in safe mode enables you to check and change device drivers that might be causing a problem or failing to work. For example, if you selected an incorrect video device driver, Windows 95 might fail on restart and leave you in safe mode.

If you suspect an incorrect video driver, follow these steps:

1. Right-click the desktop and choose Properties.

2. Select the Settings tab.

3. Click Change Display Type to display the Change Display Type dialog box in which you can check or change the Monitor or Adapter type. Click the appropriate Change button to select a different monitor or adapter using the Select Device dialog box.

4. Select Show All Devices from the Manufacturers list, then choose the right device from the Models list. If you're having serious problems or aren't sure about your hardware, choose the Standard device from each list (which will work with almost any hardware).

5. If you're changing a device, you need the original Windows 95 disks (or CD-ROM) or a disk from the hardware manufacturer in order to transfer the correct drivers. The drivers for the Standard devices are installed as part of your Windows 95 system.

Part

II

Ch

3

If you suspect other hardware problems, refer to Chapter 5, "Adding New Hardware to Windows," for information on hardware troubleshooting.

Using a BOOTLOG.TXT to Troubleshoot Failures

Test for failure in loading device drivers by following the procedure mentioned in the earlier section "Starting Windows in an Alternate Startup Mode" and then selecting 2. Logged (\BOOTLOG.TXT). This will attempt to start a normal load of Windows 95. During the loading of Windows, each action is recorded in the file BOOTLOG.TXT. This file is in the root directory of the boot disk.

If Windows fails to load, restart in Windows safe mode or DOS mode and read BOOTLOG.TXT by typing the command type **bootlog.txt|more** at a command prompt. This is a hidden file so you will not see it in a directory listing, but you can type it out.

BOOTLOG.TXT lists successful and failed actions as it loads devices. For example, you may see the following lines among the many lines in the file:

    Loading Device = C:\WINDOWS\HIMEM.SYS
    LoadSuccess = C:\WINDOWS\HIMEM.SYS
    Loading Vxd = VCOMM
    LoadSuccess = VCOMM
    Loading Vxd = msmouse.vxd
    LoadSuccess = msmouse.vxd
    SYSCRITINIT = VCACHE
    SYSCRITINITSUCCESS = VCACHE
    DEVICEINIT = PAGEFILE
    DEVICEINITSUCCESS = PAGEFILE
    Dynamic load device netbeui.vxd
    Dynamic init device NETBUI
    Dynamic load success netbeui.vxd
    Dynamic init success NETBUI

If a process failed, the word FAILED appears instead of SUCCESS. That means you either have a missing or bad driver, or for some reason Windows 95 can't load it.

Incidentally, in the above list, *vxd* means virtual device drivers and the references to NETBUI indicate network protocols that have to be loaded if the configuration included the installation of them.

Using Step-by-Step Mode to Interactively Test Startup

Interactively test each action in the boot process by following the procedure mentioned earlier in "Starting Windows in an Alternate Startup Mode" and then selecting 4. Step-by-Step Confirmation. Each action will be displayed on-screen. You must type a **Y** (Yes) or **N** (No) for each action. You can boot Windows 95 but bypass suspect drivers by responding with **N**.

Frequently Used Troubleshooting Techniques

Windows 95 is far more stable than previous versions of Windows. However, if you face startup problems, the following sections describe some of the more frequently used troubleshooting tips.

Missing Files Message on Startup   If during startup you receive the error message Bad or missing *filename* and the file is a SYS file, then check the spelling and path names in CONFIG.SYS and check the existence of the file. Any device drivers that refer to the drive containing Windows should be moved to the beginning of CONFIG.SYS so files on the drive can be accessed.

If a system file is corrupt or missing, Windows might not run or operate. In that case, you will probably have to run the Windows 95 Setup and choose the option to reinstall in order to replace missing files.

Lost or Failed System Registry Files   Windows 95 stores user customization information as well as system and application information in Registry files that are required for operation. These files, SYSTEM.DAT and USER.DAT, are described in detail in Chapters 14 and 15. If the files are corrupt or lost, Windows 95 will attempt to recover on its own.

TIP   Read Chapter 14, "Introduction to REGEDIT," to learn how to back up your SYSTEM.DAT and USER.DAT before ever making changes to the Registry files.

Windows 95 makes backup copies of SYSTEM.DAT and USER.DAT, which are stored with the extension DA0. If SYSTEM.DAT fails, Windows uses the backup SYSTEM.DA0. If Windows starts and displays the Registry Problem dialog box, then click the Restore From Backup and Restart button to restore both Registry files from their DA0 backups. If both SYSTEM.DAT and SYSTEM.DA0 files are missing, the Registry will not be restored. In that case, you need to copy backup copies of SYSTEM.DAT and USER.DAT back to the Windows folder. If you do not have backup copies, reinstall Windows.

Suspected Hardware Problem   If Windows cannot recognize certain installed devices, it will cause problems. Restart Windows in safe mode if it is not running, and make safety copies of your CONFIG.SYS and the device driver files referenced by CONFIG.SYS. These files may be useful for restoring your system to its previous configuration.

Use the Device Manager, as described in Chapter 5, "Adding New Hardware to Windows 95," to see if the device has conflicts. If the device has memory, IRQ, or SCSI port conflicts, try changing these values so they don't conflict with other devices. If you cannot resolve conflicts, use the Device Manager to remove the device, then reinstall the device using the Add New Hardware program found in the Control Panel. Chapter 5 discusses the Add New Hardware program.

Checking the Failure of Compression, Partitioning, and Hard Disk Operation   Some computers are configured to use compression software, or have a partitioned hard drive (especially if the partitioning was for multiple operating systems), or use special drivers for the hard disk in order to access all the available space on a large disk (for instance, drivers for large IDE drives in computers that don't have enhanced IDE controllers). These schemes can complicate attempts to remedy boot problems.

Real-mode drivers may have been required for the correct operation of some software programs, such as compression and partition utilities, as well as the operation of hardware such as hard disk drives. To check if a real-mode driver is required and if it is loaded during Windows 95 startup, go into an alternate startup mode by pressing F8 during startup and choose Step-by-Step Confirmation. Press Y to confirm each device driver as it loads. Watch for drivers that fail to load. When this occurs, check for missing files. If all drivers load, then compare the list of loaded device drivers to the device drivers that you think might be needed by your system.

Troubleshooting a Failure to Boot into MS-DOS   You will have trouble if you attempt to dual-boot into MS-DOS if the MS-DOS files are missing or are a version earlier than 5.0. The message `Previous MS-DOS files not found` will appear. If you need to start your computer using an earlier version of MS-DOS, use a startup disk. When using an earlier version, drivers such as DBLSPACE.SYS might not be available.

Incorrect Application Starts on Startup   First open the Windows\Start Menu\Programs\Startup folder and see if the shortcuts there are the same as the programs you want to start. Delete shortcuts for programs you do not want to start.

Programs that start when Windows starts but do not appear in the Startup folder might be incorrect entries in the Registry. To check that the Registry points to the Startup folder as the folder containing the startup files, open the Start menu and choose Run, type **Regedit**, and choose OK. Choose Edit, Find and search for the Key "Shell Folders." You want to find the following key,

```
HKey_Current_User\Software\Microsoft\Windows\CurrentVersion\Explorer\
Shell Folders
```

In the right pane, the Startup value should be *Windows*\Start Menu\Program\Startup. *Windows* is the drive and folder of the Windows 95 files. If the Startup folder is incorrect, double-click Startup and edit the Startup folder path in the Value Data edit box.

Restarting and Reinstalling from Your Startup Disk

If Windows 95 fails to boot and you can't get alternative boot modes such as fail safe to run, then you might need to start using the startup disk you made. After booting from the startup disk, you will be in DOS mode. You can copy important files or reinstall Windows 95 from this mode. If you did not make a startup disk, you might be able to use one from another Windows 95 computer to access your system.

If you need to access a CD-ROM drive or a drive with compression installed, you will need to create an AUTOEXEC.BAT and CONFIG.SYS file on your startup disk that loads the appropriate drivers in real mode. Don't forget that any driver or file loaded by either AUTOEXEC.BAT or CONFIG.SYS has to exist on the disk.

To start your computer using the startup disk, turn off your system, insert the startup disk, and turn your system back on. Your computer will start in DOS mode.

N O T E If the boot from Drive A process doesn't work and your computer goes directly to Drive C to boot, you'll have to check your system setup and make sure it's configured for a drive boot sequence of A, C. Getting into the CMOS setup varies depending upon the manufacturer of your BIOS.

Before reinstalling Windows 95, create backup copies of the SYSTEM.DAT and USER.DAT files. After reinstalling, you can restore these files to regain system changes and user customization. SYSTEM.DAT and USER.DAT are hidden system files. To copy them, follow these steps:

1. At the DOS prompt, type **CD C:\WINDOWS** to change to the Windows folder. The files are in this directory, but are hidden.

2. Remove the system and hidden attributes for these two files by entering the command

   ATTRIB -h -s -r SYSTEM.DAT

   Repeat this command for USER.DAT.

3. Use the COPY command to copy these files to disk.

After reinstalling Windows, make backup copies of the default SYSTEM.DAT and USER.DAT files created by the reinstalled Windows. If you continue to have a problem, then copy your original two files back to the Windows folder. Restore their Hidden,

System, and Read Only attributes by opening Explorer, right-clicking the file name, choosing Properties, and checking these attributes.

Learning the Parts of the Windows Display

Figure 3.5 shows a Windows desktop that contains multiple applications, each in its own window. The figure identifies the parts of a typical Windows screen.

FIG. 3.5
The Windows desktop can contain multiple icons and program windows.

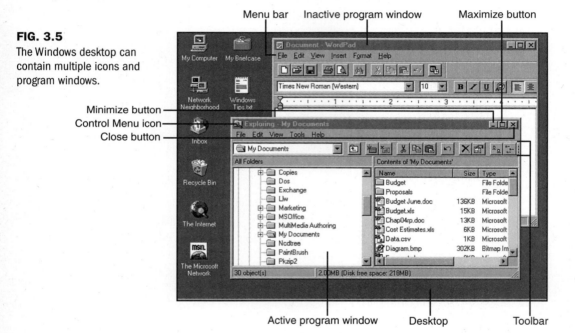

Menu bar   Inactive program window   Maximize button

Minimize button
Control Menu icon
Close button

Active program window   Desktop   Toolbar

The Start button provides one of the easiest ways to start programs or to open documents you have recently used. (The Start button and taskbar might appear along different edges of the screen if a previous user has moved them.) Click the Start button to open the Start menu or press Ctrl+Esc.

The taskbar displays all programs currently running. You can switch between different programs by clicking the mouse pointer on the program's button in the taskbar. Press Alt+Tab to select programs by keyboard.

The right side of the taskbar shows the time by default (you can eliminate it by deselecting it in the Taskbar settings) and there may be other icons placed there by software. For example, your sound card installation may put a permanent icon on the right side of the taskbar in order to let you change speaker volume. On a portable computer there is usually a power management icon. You can usually right-click these icons to display a dialog box that includes an option to remove them from the taskbar.

TROUBLESHOOTING

Pressing Alt+Tab just seems to alternate between two applications. Hold down the Alt key as you press Tab and you will see a bar displaying icons of all the running applications. As you continue to hold down the Alt key, each press of the Tab key selects the next application icon on the bar. When the application you want is selected, release both the Alt and the Tab keys.

To reduce the clutter of a filled desktop, you can minimize windows so they appear as buttons on the taskbar. Even if you don't see an application on your screen, an application is still running if the taskbar displays its button.

▶ **See** "Customizing the Taskbar," **p. 366**

▶ **See** "Moving the Taskbar," **p. 366**

Part II

Ch

3

Using the Start Menu

The Start menu, which you access from the Start button on the taskbar, is the starting place for many of the tasks you will accomplish in Windows. You can open the Start menu at any time, from within any program, with one mouse click. From the Start menu, you can open your programs, customize the look and feel of Windows, find files and folders, get Help, and shut down your computer (see fig. 3.6). While providing all the power of immediate access, the Start menu also is integral to the clean look of the Windows desktop, enabling you to minimize the clutter on your desktop.

Use the Start menu when you need to open a program or access other features of Windows. You can open the Start menu at any time, even when you are working in another application like Excel, as shown in figure 3.7. This is much simpler than in earlier versions of Windows, where you had to switch back to Program Manager to open other programs.

When you install Windows software (or when the Windows 95 installation program finds existing software), the installation program usually places a shortcut for each program on a submenu that appears off of the Start menu. You can open the program simply by selecting it from a menu (see fig. 3.8).

FIG. 3.6

The Start menu is just a mouse click away and gives you instant access to all your programs and many other Windows features.

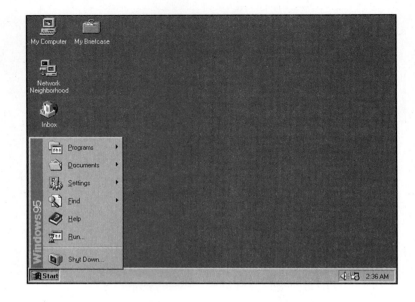

FIG. 3.7

You can open the Start menu without having to leave the program in which you are working. Here the Start menu appears at the bottom of the Excel program.

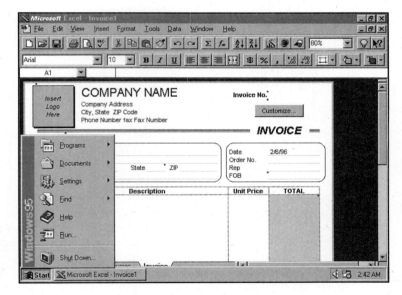

FIG. 3.8
You can select the program you want to start from one of the menus that cascades from the Start menu. Here the user is selecting to start WordPad.

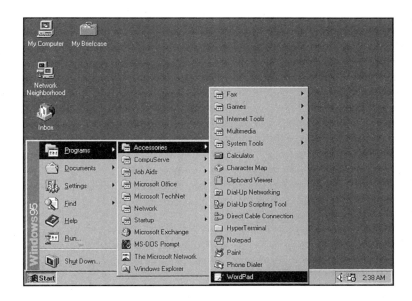

NOTE If you are upgrading from an older version of Windows to Windows 95, the Group windows that appeared in the Program Manager will become submenus that appear off Programs in the Start menu. ▓

▶ **See** "Customizing the Start Menu," **p. 369**

TROUBLESHOOTING

The windows of some programs written for older versions of Windows cover the taskbar; it is difficult to switch between applications or click the Start button. To simultaneously display the taskbar and open the Start menu, even when the taskbar is hidden, press Ctrl+Esc.

Starting a Program from the Start Menu

To start a program from the Start menu, use the mouse to select the program from a menu and then click (see fig. 3.9). It's that easy. To find the program you want, you might have to move through a series of submenus. You also can use the keyboard, although Windows is definitely designed to work most efficiently with a mouse.

FIG. 3.9
Open the submenu that contains the program you want to start and then click the program.

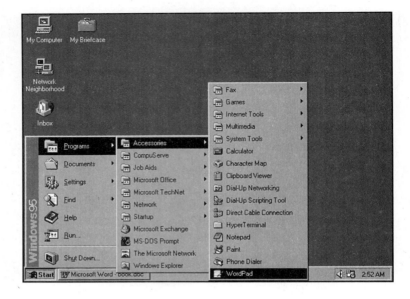

N O T E   If you have customized the taskbar, you might not see the taskbar and Start button on screen. If the Auto Hide feature is enabled, the taskbar resizes itself to a thin line at the edge of the screen. It may be difficult to locate this line if the taskbar has been moved to a screen edge other than its default position at the bottom of the screen. To display the taskbar and Start button, move the pointer to the edge of the screen where it is stored. Or, press Ctrl+Esc to display the taskbar and open the Start menu. (Press Esc to close the Start menu and keep the taskbar displayed.) ▪

If you are using a keyboard and do not have a mouse available, open the Start menu by pressing Ctrl+Esc, and then use arrow keys to move up and down the menu. Press Enter to select the currently highlighted menu or program.

When you open a program, a button for the program appears in the taskbar. These buttons tell you what programs are open and they enable you to move quickly from one open program to another. You learn more about switching between programs later in this chapter in "Using the Taskbar to Switch Between Programs."

N O T E   Usually, you should find the program you want to open in one of the Start menu's submenus. When you install Windows, the installation program looks for all your applications and puts each in one of the menus. If, however, you can't find your program in the Start menus, you can add a program or folder to the Start menu by following the procedures described in Chapter 5. ▪

TIP Make the Start menu open faster or slower by modifying the Registry. Make it open faster if you want quicker access to submenus. If submenus popping up as you move the pointer bothers you, then delay submenu display so submenus only display when you click their name. Before you modify the Registry, read Chapter 15 to learn how to back up Registry files before proceeding. Search through the Registry for

    H_KEY_CURRENT_USER\Control Panel\Desktop

Right-click Desktop and choose New, String Value. In the selected area in the right panel, type **MenuShowDelay**, then press Enter. Double-click MenuShowDelay and enter a small value in the range of 1 to 10 (with 1 being the fastest display of the Start menu). If you don't like submenus to display as you move the pointer over the Start menu, enter a large number—up to 65,534. Using 65,534 delays by approximately 65 seconds. When you do want a submenu to display, click the submenu name. The change takes affect the next time you start Windows.

▶ **See** "Using the Taskbar to Switch Between Applications," **p. 71**
▶ **See** "Customizing the Start Menu," **p. 369**

Starting a Document from the Start Menu

After you click the Start button, you will notice a Documents command in the Start menu. When you choose this command, the Documents submenu appears with a listing of the files you have worked on recently (see fig. 3.10). Notice that only 32-bit Windows 95 programs display their documents on the most recently used list. Older 16-bit programs do not display documents in the list.

NOTE The reason older programs don't display documents is that it's the software placing documents on the list, not the operating system. The software application takes advantage of the operating system's features by calling on Windows to display the name of the document.

To open a document in this list, simply click it. Windows then automatically starts the associated application, if it is not already running, and opens the document.

After a while, the listing in the Documents menu can become quite long and contain documents you no longer are working with. To clear the list, open the Start menu and choose Settings, Taskbar. Select the Start Menu Programs tab on the Taskbar Properties sheet and choose the Clear button (see fig. 3.11). Click OK to close the Taskbar Properties sheet.

FIG. 3.10
The Start menu maintains a list of the documents you have worked with most recently so you can quickly reopen your most recently used documents

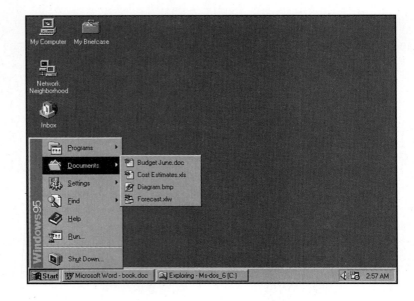

FIG. 3.11
Click Clear on the Start Menu Programs page to clear out your document list so you don't have to wade through a long list of documents.

 TIP If you often want to pare down your most frequently used documents list, create a shortcut on your desktop that points to the Windows\Recent folder. Double-clicking this folder will show you shortcuts to all the documents on the most recently used list. You can selectively delete documents you want off the list.

Using the Taskbar to Switch Between Programs

The taskbar is one of the most important and innovative features in Windows 95, making everything a lot easier than it was in previous versions of Windows. Beyond ease of use, there's plenty of power and enhanced productivity levels available in the taskbar once you become more experienced and begin to customize it.

 If you can't see the full name of a program and document on a crowded taskbar, just pause the mouse pointer over the taskbar button and the full name will show in a pop-up label.

If you work with a lot of open applications, your screen can become cluttered with many open windows. Rather than clutter the screen with several open windows, you can reduce the applications you're not using currently to buttons on the taskbar. As more buttons appear on the taskbar, the other buttons shrink to make room. To activate an application, you simply click its button on the taskbar. Figure 3.12 shows a taskbar with several buttons. To close an application from the taskbar, just right-click and choose <u>C</u>lose.

Part
II

Ch
3

 When the taskbar gets crowded, it's usually easier to make it larger so you can see everything (rather than letting the buttons get so small you're not sure what they represent). You can drag the edge of the taskbar to resize it just as you can drag a window. Once it's larger, the buttons expand so you can read them.

FIG. 3.12
Use the taskbar to temporarily store applications while you're not using them.

To reduce an application to a button on the taskbar, click the Minimize button. To reactivate an application, click its button in the taskbar.

Using the Power of Shortcuts and Desktop Icons

Shortcuts are one of Windows 95's most powerful new features. You see shortcuts as icons with a small curved arrow at the icon's lower-left corner. They are actually pointers to a program, document, disk, folder, or other object such as a printer.

The flexibility of working with shortcuts is more amazing the more you work with them. Some of the things you can do with shortcuts are:

- Start programs, open documents, or open folders
- Drag and drop documents onto printer or fax shortcuts
- Double-click shortcuts to Backup or Defragmenting tools to run them with settings you specify
- Open documents directly to a specific location
- Run DOS batch files that run DOS or Windows applications
- Display a file in different folders or drives without creating multiple copies of the file
- Link to World Wide Web URLs or pages in the Microsoft Network
- Send shortcuts to other Windows users as embedded objects within a document

---

Registry Close-up

If you don't need (or want) to see those little curved arrows on shortcuts to remind you that a shortcut is a pointer, you can eliminate them:

1. Choose Run from the Start menu and enter REGEDIT in the Open text box. Choose OK.
2. In the Registry Editor window, click the plus sign next to the HKEY_CLASSES_ROOT folder.
3. Find the folder named lnkfile and select it to display its contents in the right pane.
4. In the right pane, right-click the IsShortcut item and choose Rename.
5. When the name is highlighted, use your arrow keys to move to the beginning of the name. Insert a letter (any letter) at the beginning of the name (for example, if you use an x the name will be xIsShortcut). Press Enter or click anywhere outside the name to complete the process.
6. Repeat the process in the folder named piffile (which eliminates the arrow in DOS shortcuts, including the shortcut to the MS-DOS prompt that is a must for every desktop).

Be aware that this action will give you no visual distinction between a shortcut and a program.

Creating Shortcuts to Programs or Documents

To create a shortcut on your desktop for a program or document, follow these steps:

1. Using Explorer or My Computer, locate the program for which you want to create a shortcut. Position Explorer or My Computer window so you can see a portion of the desktop.

    See Chapter 5, "Managing Files," to learn how to use Explorer and My Computer for browsing files and folders.

2. Right-drag the file onto the desktop, then release the right mouse button.

3. Choose Create Shortcut(s) Here to create the shortcut.

If the document to which you created a shortcut is associated (or registered) with a program, you can start the program and open the document by double-clicking its shortcut.

Create a shortcut on the desktop to a program or document without opening Explorer or My Computer by right-clicking the desktop. Choose New, Shortcut to open a shortcut wizard. In the Wizard's first dialog box, choose Browse and select the program or document file to which you want a shortcut. Choose Next and edit the label for the shortcut. Finally, choose Finish.

N O T E   If you're creating a shortcut for a program file, you don't have to right-drag the file object from Explorer or My Computer and then choose to place the shortcut from the right-drag menu. Windows 95 is smart enough to know that you're not moving an executable, you're making a shortcut. A simple left drag will accomplish the feat for program files.

The left-drag technique does not work for batch files. If you want to create a shortcut for an executable with a BAT extension, you must use the right-drag method. ▨

TROUBLESHOOTING

Double-clicking a shortcut icon no longer opens the document or program. What might have happened is that the file to which the shortcut pointed was moved or deleted. To correct this problem, you can either delete and then recreate the shortcut, or you can correct its Properties sheet. To delete the shortcut icon, right-click the icon, then choose Delete. Choose Yes when asked to confirm the deletion. Recreate the shortcut with the methods described in this section. To fix a shortcut to a file that has moved, right-click the icon, then choose Properties. Click the Shortcut tab. Check the file and path name in the Target box. They might be wrong. To find the file, click the Find Target button. This opens a window in My Computer to the file if it is found. If it cannot be found, you can search in My Computer for the correct file and path name.

▶ **See** "Registering FileTypes Causing Documents to Open Applications," **p. 147**

Using Shortcut Icons on the Desktop

To start a program, you simply double-click its shortcut. If you don't like using menus to start your programs, you might prefer using shortcuts. A drawback to this method, however, is that to access the shortcut icons, your desktop must be visible. If a program is maximized, you cannot see the shortcuts. See "Accessing the Desktop" later in this chapter.

To open a document, double-click its shortcut. If the document's program is running, it will activate and open the document. If the program is not running, the program will start, then open the document. A document must be associated with a program for this to occur automatically. Normally, file associating or registration occurs during program installation.

Creating Shortcuts to Frequently Used Folders

Use shortcuts to folders as time savers. A shortcut to a folder into which you frequently move files can save you time moving files. A shortcut folder on the desktop also can help organize your desktop. Within the desktop shortcut folder, you can drag and drop the program and document shortcut icons you use. When you want to use one of these stored shortcuts, just double-click the folder shortcut.

If you frequently move files from Explorer into a specific folder, make a shortcut to that folder on the desktop. Now you can drag files from Explorer and drop them onto the folder shortcut. The shortcut acts like a tunnel, guiding the files into the real folder.

To make a shortcut that points to a folder using Explorer or My Computer, follow these steps:

1. Open Explorer or My Computer to display the folder from which you want to create a shortcut.

2. Right-drag the folder from either the right or left pane onto the desktop.

3. Choose Create Shortcut(s) Here.

TROUBLESHOOTING

After creating a shortcut to a folder, the folder doesn't appear to exist in Explorer or My Computer, but it does exist on the desktop. What has happened is that, in the process of right-dragging the folder onto the desktop, you accidentally chose the Move Here command instead of Create Shortcut(s) Here. Your folder still exists, but it is now located in the Windows\Desktop folder. To move it back to its original location, open Explorer and left-drag the folder from the Windows\Desktop folder back to the location where you want it.

Editing a Shortcut Name and Deleting Shortcuts

If you want to modify the name that appears under the icon, click once on the name to select it. Then click the text and pause the mouse pointer. The pointer changes to an

I-beam. You can press Delete to delete the name or click the I-beam where you want the insertion point. After you edit the name, press Enter or click a blank spot on the desktop.

To delete a shortcut, highlight it and press the Delete key (or right-click the shortcut and choose <u>D</u>elete). Choose <u>Y</u>es when the confirmation dialog box appears.

 TIP You can arrange icons on the desktop by right-clicking the desktop, then choosing the Arrange Icons command. You are given alternative ways of arranging them.

CAUTION

Be careful when deleting shortcuts from the desktop. When you delete a shortcut for a file, you delete only the shortcut, not the file. However, when you delete an icon that represents a file, you delete the file. Icons that appear with a small arrow at a lower corner are shortcuts. They can safely be deleted. Shortcuts that are deleted are sent to the Recycle Bin so you can retrieve them if you've deleted something by mistake.

Part
II

Ch
3

Setting the Properties for a Shortcut Icon

You can change how a shortcut icon acts and how it appears by opening its Properties sheet and changing its properties. On the Properties sheet, you can find information such as when a shortcut was created. You also can make a variety of changes, such as the following:

- Change the file that the shortcut opens.
- Make an application start in a folder you specify.
- Add a shortcut key that activates the shortcut.
- Indicate whether you want the document or application to run minimized, maximized, or in a window.
- Change the icon used for a shortcut.

To display the Properties sheet and set the properties for a shortcut icon, follow these steps:

1. Right-click the shortcut icon.
2. Click P<u>r</u>operties to display the General page of the Shortcut Properties sheet (see fig. 3.13).

FIG. 3.13

The General page shows you file information about the shortcut icon.

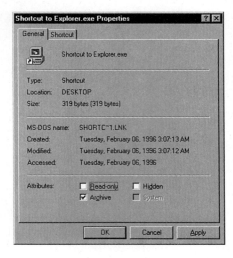

On the General page, you can read where the LNK file for the shortcut is stored, as well as when it was created, modified, and last used. You also can change its file attributes.

3. Click the Shortcut tab to see the Shortcut page (see fig. 3.14).

FIG. 3.14

The Shortcut page enables you to specify the file, startup folder, shortcut key, and icon used by a shortcut.

At the top of the page, you can read the type of shortcut it is and the folder in which it is located. In the figure, the shortcut is to Explorer application in the Windows folder.

4. If you want a different file to start from the shortcut, type the folder and file name in the Target text box.

   If you are unsure of the location, click Find Target to open the My Computer window in which you can look for the file and folder you want. After you find the folder and file, close the My Computer windows and type the name in the Target text box.

5. To specify a folder that contains the file or files necessary for operation, enter the drive and folders in the Start In text box.

6. To specify a shortcut key that will activate this shortcut icon, type the key you want as the shortcut key in the Shortcut Key text box. The key must be a letter or a number. You cannot use Esc, Enter, Tab, the space bar, Print Screen, or Backspace. To clear the Shortcut Key text box, select the text box and press the space bar.

   To use this shortcut key, you press Ctrl+Alt and the key you indicated. Shortcut keys you enter take precedence over other access keys in Windows.

 TIP You can press a shortcut's key combination to run the shortcut's program or document even when another program is active.

7. To specify the type of window in which the application or document will run, choose Normal Window, Minimized, or Maximized from the Run drop-down list.

8. To change the icon displayed for the shortcut, click Change Icon to display the Change Icon dialog box (see fig. 3.15).

   The Change Icon dialog box displays a list of icons stored in files with the extensions EXE, DLL, and ICO.

FIG. 3.15
You can select the icon you want for your shortcut.

9. Select the icon you want and choose OK.

10. Click the OK button to make your changes and close the Shortcut Properties sheet. Click Apply to make your changes and keep the Shortcut Properties sheet open for more changes.

Part
II

Ch
3

N O T E When selecting icons for a shortcut, you don't have to restrict yourself to the icons in the file the shortcut points to. You can select an icon from any other DLL, EXE, or ICO file. To see other icon files in the Change Icon dialog box, click the Browse button. ▨

 T I P You can find icons in the Windows 95 file Windows\Subsystem\SHELL32.DLL. There are additional files hidden in the same folder in the files PIFMGR.DLL and COOL.DLL. If you still have access to Windows 3.x files, you can use Windows\PROGMAN.EXE and Windows\MORICONS.DLL.

Opening Programs and Documents from Explorer or My Computer

Windows Explorer is an application that comes with Windows 95. Explorer is similar to the earlier Windows versions' File Manager, but is much more powerful. You can use Explorer to view the files and folders on your computer; move, copy, rename, and delete files and folders; and perform other file-management tasks. You also can start programs and open documents from Explorer. My Computer is similar to Explorer. The main difference between them is that, unlike the Explorer window, the My Computer window does not enable you to view the overall structure of or relationships among all your computer's resources. Typically, when you use My Computer, you view the contents of one folder at a time.

Starting Programs and Documents from their Files

N O T E Although My Computer and Explorer are more flexible, you might prefer to make the transition slowly and take your time learning the new features of Windows 95. If you prefer to use File Manager and Program Manager from Windows 3.x, you can easily do so. Windows 95 equivalent files, WINFILE.EXE and PROGMAN.EXE, are located in the Windows folder. You can add these programs to your Start menu, create shortcut icons for the desktop, or run them when Windows starts. ▨

Windows 3.1 used one program, the File Manager, to manage files and another, the Program Manager, to start programs or documents. In Windows 95 there is no distinction between file management and starting programs or opening documents.

There are two different views you can take of your files. The simplest view is that from a folder window, a window opened from My Computer. The second view is a hierarchical view of the folders as seen from the Windows Explorer.

Using Explorer to Start Programs and Open Documents

You can use Explorer to find any file on your computer. After you find the file, you also can use Explorer to start the program or open the document. If the file is a program file, you can start the program by double-clicking the file in Explorer. If the file is a document, you can start its associated application and open the document simultaneously. If the application is already running, Windows opens the document in that application.

Figure 3.16 shows the Explorer window displaying files in Detail view. Look at the Type column in the right pane of Explorer to see the file type.

FIG. 3.16
Explorer window displays all
of your computer's resources,
including folders and files.

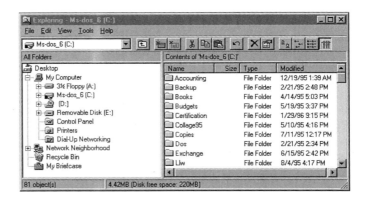

Part
II

Ch
3

TROUBLESHOOTING

Double-clicking a file in Explorer doesn't immediately open the file. The Open With dialog box displays asking which program should be used to open the file. Windows does not recognize the application used to open the document you double-clicked. Windows displays the Open With dialog box so you can select the application to open. Windows records this application so it can open the same application the next time you double-click this type of document.

Many users prefer to organize their documents in the Explorer folders, which are named by category. Rather than work in a program such as Word to open files, they leave Explorer open. When they want to open a document, they open the appropriate folder in Explorer and double-click the document's file.

Using My Computer to Start Programs and Open Documents

The first time you start Windows, you see an icon called My Computer on your desktop. If you double-click this icon, the My Computer window appears (see fig. 3.17). You can use My Computer to view your computer's resources, including folders and files. Figure 3.18 shows a window of folders that displays after double-clicking the C: drive icon.

FIG. 3.17
The My Computer window is an all-encompassing view of the folders and objects in your computer.

FIG. 3.18
Double-click a folder to display its contents.

After you open a window for a folder so you can view its contents, you can start a program or open a document by double-clicking its file. New users and Macintosh users find this window simpler and less confusing than the Explorer window shown in figure 3.16.

Working from Your Desktop

The desktop is a convenient location for storing frequently used folders and shortcuts. Some computer users do the majority of their work directly from the desktop and rarely use the Start menu or Explorer.

 Reduce the chance of deleting important files and folders by putting only shortcuts to files and folders on your desktop. If you put the actual files and folders directly on the desktop, you could delete them when they are selected by pressing the Delete key.

Create custom desktops for each person who uses Windows. A custom desktop can include desktop preferences, customized Start menus, and distinct shortcut icons. Use the Password program found in the Control Panel as described in Chapter 13, "Customizing with Property Sheets," to enable custom desktops.

Making a Desktop Folder to Hold Other Shortcuts

Keeping folders on the desktop is an efficient way of storing shortcuts so your desktop doesn't become cluttered. To clear your desk of icons, just drag and drop shortcut icons into the folder. When you want to use one of the shortcut icons, double-click the folder and, when the folder opens, double-click the program or document icon.

A folder on the desktop does not have to point to a folder you have created in Explorer. To create a folder directly on your desktop, right-click the desktop, then choose New, Folder. A folder appears on the desktop with its name selected so you can type a new name.

Folders on the desktop are actually folders that are in the Windows\Desktop folder. You can see these folders and manipulate them like any other folder by opening Explorer or My Computer and displaying the Windows\Desktop folder.

Accessing the Desktop

It can be difficult to get to the desktop when it is covered with open program windows. Some users go through long, difficult processes to make their desktops accessible. Some magazines have listed complex methods that modify the Registry so the desktop appears on the Start menu. Or you can go through a laborious method of creating shortcuts that duplicate everything on the desktop and placing them on the Start menu. There are some very easy solutions to making the desktop accessible.

Creating a Shortcut to the Desktop   To customize your system so items on the desktop are available in the taskbar, follow these steps:

1. Double-click My Computer.
2. If the toolbar is not visible, choose View, Toolbar.
3. Pull down the Different Folder list from the toolbar, scroll to the top, and choose Desktop. This displays the full contents of the desktop in the folder window.
4. Choose View, Arrange Icons, Auto Arrange to arrange icons in this folder, which is now a miniature desktop.
5. Choose View, Toolbar to remove the toolbar from the folder. The folder should now look like figure 3.19.

FIG. 3.19
Create a Desktop folder and
keep it on your taskbar for
quick access to the desktop.

6.   Leave the folder open on the desktop or minimize it to the taskbar.

The desktop folder you just created shows everything the desktop would. If you are using a mouse, drag to the screen edge where the taskbar is and click the Desktop button to display it. If you are using a keyboard, press Alt+Tab until the Desktop folder is selected. Leave the Desktop folder on the taskbar when you shut down Windows and it will be there when you restart.

To put the desktop on the Start menu, drag the folder you just created to the Start button. This will place the Desktop on the top of the Start menu.

If you use the Microsoft Natural keyboard, notice that it has a Windows key—the keycap looks like the Windows logo. To minimize all program windows so the desktop is accessible, press Windows+M. This gives you quick desktop access. To restore minimized programs to their windows, press Shift+Windows+M.

If you have many windows open, you can minimize them by right-clicking the taskbar and choosing Minimize All Windows. To restore the minimized windows, right-click the taskbar and choose Undo Minimize All.

Using Shortcuts and Icons on the Desktop

The previous sections in this chapter, "Creating Shortcut Icons on the Desktop to Start Programs or Open Documents," and "Making a Desktop Folder To Hold Other Short-cuts," describe how to create shortcut icons on your desktop that point to programs, documents, and folders. To activate or modify those shortcuts, you must select them.

If you want to select an icon, just click it. To select it and display the shortcut menu, right-click the icon. Double-clicking a program icon opens the program. Double-clicking a document opens the document's program if necessary and loads the document. When you double-click a folder icon, the folder opens with its last used settings.

Select multiple adjacent icons on the desktop by clicking the first icon, holding down the Shift key, and clicking the last icon in the adjacent group.

Select multiple non-adjacent icons on the desktop by clicking the first icon, then holding the Ctrl key as you click additional icons. To remove icons from a selected group, hold the Ctrl key as you click an icon that is currently selected.

Select multiple icons on a desktop to delete, copy, or move them at the same time. Figure 3.20 shows a rectangular group of icons selected by dragging the mouse. To select a group of icons that are in a rectangular area of the desktop, click at one corner of a rectangle that would enclose the icons, then drag to the opposite corner of the rectangle. An enclosing rectangle appears as you drag. When you release the mouse button, all icons in the rectangle are selected. Add or remove icons from the selection by clicking icons while holding the Ctrl key.

Deselect all icons on the rectangle by clicking the desktop.

FIG. 3.20
Drag across multiple icons to select them.

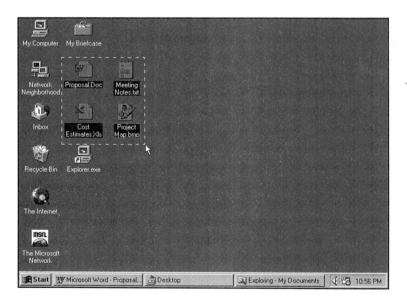

Arranging Icons on Your Desktop

After you create folders on your desktop in which to store shortcuts and icons, you will want to arrange the icons on your desktop. To arrange icons (except for the system icons like My Computer and Network Neighborhood), right-click the desktop, then click one of the following commands in the shortcut menu:

Part
II

Ch
3

Command	Action
Arrange Icons	
by Name	Arrange icons in alphabetical order except for system icons
by Type	Arrange icons grouped by type except for system icons
by Size	Arrange icons by file size except for system icons
by Date	Arrange icons by creation date
Auto Arrange	Command toggles on or off. When the command is on icons snap back to fill the left side of the desktop and align on the invisible grid
Line Up Icons	Align icons on an invisible grid in their current order

You might work better if you arrange icons on your desktop so they are grouped in different areas. To group icons anywhere on-screen, make sure the Arrange Icons, Auto Arrange command is turned off. When it is turned off, you can drag desktop icons into any position. Figure 3.21 shows icons arranged in groups.

 TIP After arranging icons on your desktop, you can get them to align—but not move significantly out of your arrangement—by right-clicking the desktop, and choosing Line Up Icons.

FIG. 3.21
Turn off Auto Arrange so you can drag icons into groups.

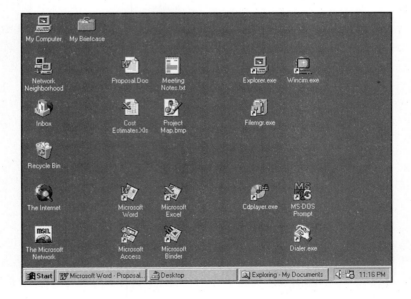

Change the vertical and horizontal spacing of the grid on which icons position themselves by right-clicking the desktop, choosing Properties, and selecting the Appearance tab.

Working on Your Desktop with the Keyboard

If your mouse fails at an important time or you're trapped in a cramped airline seat, you know how important it is to know a few important Windows keystroke commands. One set of important keystroke commands are the ones used to work on the desktop.

To activate or select icons on the desktop by keyboard, follow these steps:

1. Minimize or move program windows so you can see the desktop icons you want to work with. Press Alt+Spacebar to activate the program's control menu so you can minimize or move the application.

2. Press Ctrl+Esc or the Windows button to activate the shortcut menu, then press Esc to remove the menu and select the Start button.

   At this point, each press of the Tab key will cycle the focus from the Start button, to the taskbar, and to the desktop.

3. Press Tab to activate the taskbar. (Move between task buttons with the arrow keys.)

4. Press Tab again to activate the desktop. Use the keystrokes in the following table to select or activate desktop icons.

Action	Do this
Select an icon	Press arrow keys
Select adjacent icons	Press Shift+arrow key
Select non-adjacent icons	Select first icon, then press Ctrl+arrow to next icon to select, then press Ctrl+Spacebar to select it
Activate an icon	Select the icon, press Enter
Delete an icon	Select the icon, press Delete

 If you work long hours at the keyboard, seriously consider buying a Microsoft Natural Keyboard or other ergonomic keyboard that places keys at a less stressful angle. Use a wrist rest to keep your wrists straight. I can attest to the fact that tendonitis and carpal tunnel syndrome can seriously affect your quality of life—not just your career. Take care of the problem before you even notice the symptoms.

If you use the Microsoft Natural keyboard with Windows 95, you can use a number of shortcut keys that are faster than using the mouse. The Windows key referenced in the table is the key on the Microsoft Natural keyboard that has the Windows logo.

Action	Keystroke
Display the Run dialog box	Windows+R
Minimize all windows	Windows+M
Undo minimize windows	Shift+Windows+M
Help	Windows+F1
Display the Windows Explorer	Windows+E
Display Find:Computer	Ctrl+Windows+F
Cycle through taskbar buttons	Windows+Tab
Display System Properties sheet	Windows+Break

Learning about Drag and Drop

The term *drag and drop* exactly describes what you do with the mouse to an object. You click an object, such as a folder, and then hold down the mouse button as you drag the object to a new location. You drop the object by releasing the mouse button. You can drag and drop with either the left or right mouse button. If you drag and drop with the right mouse button, a context sensitive menu appears when you release the button.

Full functionality of drag and drop is only available for applications that are OLE 2-compliant. For drag-and-drop methods to work, each Windows object has to know how to behave when dropped on other Windows objects. For example, if in Explorer you drag the icon of a file and drop it on the icon for a program, the program starts and loads that file.

Figure 3.22 illustrates how you can use drag and drop to make frequently used folders more accessible. Instead of having to find the folder each time in Explorer, you can put a shortcut icon on the desktop that enables you to open the folder directly. To create a shortcut icon with drag and drop, follow these steps:

1. Double-click the My Computer icon to open its window. Make sure that the window does not fill the screen.

2. Double-click the local drive icon for your computer.

3. With the right mouse button, drag the folder out of the window and release the folder over the desktop.

   In figure 3.22, the user has dragged the Budgets folder to the desktop.

FIG. 3.22

The user has dragged the reverse-colored Budgets folder (by holding down the right mouse button) and dropped the folder to the desktop. When you release the mouse button, a context sensitive shortcut menu appears.

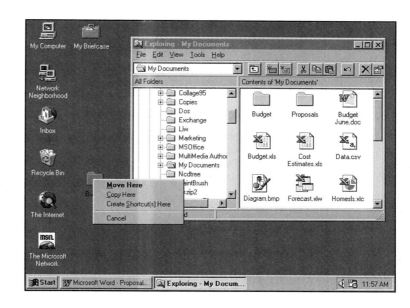

Part II Ch 3

4. When you release the right mouse button, a menu appears over the folder on the desktop as shown in figure 3.22.

5. Choose the Create Shortcut(s) Here command.

 You can tell at a glance that an icon is a shortcut by the small arrow at the lower-left corner.

The Shortcut to Budgets icon, shown in figure 3.23, remains on the desktop even after you close the My Computer windows. You can open the folder at any time by double-clicking the shortcut icon.

CAUTION

When dragging and dropping a file or folder, make sure that you use the right mouse button and choose Create Shortcut(s) Here from the shortcut menu. This creates a shortcut icon while leaving the original file or folder in its original location. If you delete the shortcut icon, the original file or folder remains intact. If you delete an original icon (which you create by dragging with the left mouse button) from your desktop, Windows deletes the original file or folder along with the icon. If the file is important, this causes a disaster and a lot of intra-office panic.

FIG. 3.23
Choosing the Create
Shortcut(s) Here command
produces on the desktop a
shortcut icon that you can
click to start the application.

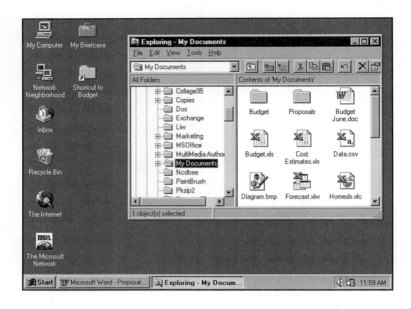

NOTE All of Windows 95's drag-and-drop features are available only with Windows applications that are compatible with OLE. ■

There are many ways that you can use the drag-and-drop method to save time. You can move and copy files and folders, which makes reorganizing the contents on your computer easy. You can drag a shortcut for your printer onto your desktop, drag documents from My Computer or Explorer, and then drop them onto the printer icon, which prints the documents. With applications compatible with the OLE 2 specifications, you can even drag and drop objects from one application to another. For example, you can drag a table from a spreadsheet into a word processing document.

Throughout this book, you accomplish your computer tasks by using drag-and-drop methods. Always look for ways to use these methods for saving time and trouble.

▶ **See** "Drag-and-Drop Printing from the Desktop," **p. 251**
▶ **See** "Using Drag and Drop to Embed Information," **p. 582**
▶ **See** "Backing Up with a Simple Drag and Drop," **p. 675**

Changing Settings and Properties with the Right Mouse Button

One important Windows concept is that most *objects* that you see on-screen have *properties* related to them. Objects that display a properties sheet are such items as desktop icons, shortcuts, files, the desktop, and the taskbar. Properties displayed in the properties sheet can include such characteristics as an object's appearance and behavior.

You can change some properties, but others are *read only*—you can view them, but you cannot change them.

You can experiment to find the properties of objects on the desktop, in Explorer, in My Computer, and in most Windows 95 applications. To see an object's properties, point to the object and click the right mouse button (that is, you *right-click* the object). A Properties sheet displays, or a context menu displays a Properties command. For example, you can place the pointer's tip on most objects, such as the desktop or a file, and then click the right mouse button. From the context menu that appears, select the Properties command.

N O T E Don't be afraid to experiment when you look for properties. To discover how you can customize Windows, right-click on files, taskbars, and so on. If you do not want to change the object's properties, press the Esc key or click the Cancel button in the Properties sheet that appears. ■

To see the properties that you can change on the desktop, right-click on the desktop and then choose the Properties command. The Display Properties sheet shown in figure 3.24 appears. In this dialog box, you can change the display's background, color, and screen saver, and display adapter settings. To learn how to change these settings, see Chapter 13, "Customizing with Property Sheets." Click the Cancel button to remove the dialog box without making changes.

FIG. 3.24
Right-click the desktop and then choose Properties to see the desktop properties. The Screen Saver page, shown here, enables you to choose a screen saver.

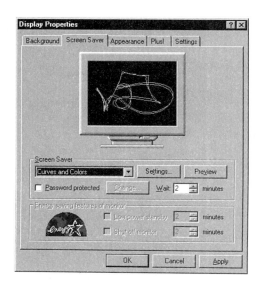

Using the Send To Command for Frequent Operations

Microsoft included the Send To command on many shortcut menus; it is a real time-saver and is one of the most powerful, customizable features in Windows 95. Figure 3.25 shows the Send To command after right-clicking a file. The Send To command appears when you right-click files in Explorer, in folder windows, or on the desktop.

FIG. 3.25

Use Send To as a shortcut for dragging an object to a target.

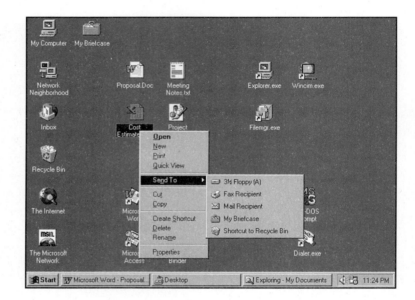

At first, the Send To command appears to be a simple little device to make it easy to send documents to a printer, fax, e-mail, Briefcase, or disk. That in itself is very useful, but Send To can do a lot more.

T I P For information on how to use Send To with a specific application, such as a fax or e-mail program, look in the chapter that describes that application.

When you learn how to customize Send To, you can add items to the Send To menu to give it greater functionality. Chapter 13 describes how to customize Send To by adding programs, disk drives, and folders to it. Some of the custom things you can have Send To do are:

- Send documents to the same printer using different printer setups
- Send documents to local or network folders or disks

- Move a file or folder to the desktop
- Send documents to applications that start with unique parameters

To perform an operation on a document with Send To, display the document icon or shortcut you want to work on. The document might be on the desktop, in a folder window, or in Explorer. Right-click the document icon, then choose Se<u>n</u>d To. A submenu appears giving you locations where you can send the document. The default locations on Send To for Windows with a full install are:

Floppy (A:)

FAX Recipient

Mail Recipient

My Briefcase

Shortcut to Recycle Bin

▶ **See** "Customizing the Send To Menu," **p. 373**

Part

II

Ch

3

Arranging Windows from the Taskbar

There are times when you want to quickly arrange a few applications on your desktop so that you can compare documents, drag and drop between documents, and so forth. Manually moving and resizing each Window is a tedious job, so Windows 95 has a few shortcuts that can make this type of work easier.

 T I P When the taskbar has a lot of application buttons, the titles may be too truncated to read. Pause the pointer over a button to see a pop-up title.

First, you can make your desktop easier to work on by minimizing all applications so they appear as buttons on the taskbar. To do this quickly, right-click on an area between buttons on the taskbar. When the shortcut menu appears, click on <u>M</u>inimize All Windows. To restore minimized applications, right-click in a clear area of the taskbar and choose <u>U</u>ndo Minimize All. If you have the Microsoft Natural Keyboard, minimize applications by pressing Windows+M. Restore minimized applications by pressing Shift+Windows+M.

N O T E The Minimize All Windows command does not work on applications that are currently displaying a dialog box. ▨

If you want to compare documents in two or three applications, minimize all applications except the two or three you want to work with and then right-click on a gray area of the taskbar. When the shortcut menu appears, click either Tile <u>H</u>orizontally or Tile <u>V</u>ertically. Your applications will appear in adjacent windows that fill the screen as shown in figure 3.26.

FIG. 3.26
Tiling application windows horizontally or vertically makes it easy to compare documents or to drag and drop contents.

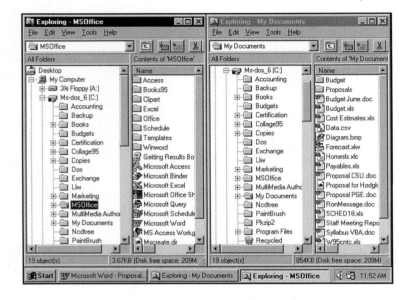

FIG. 3.27
Cascading application windows overlays them so that you can see each title bar. It is then easy to move among windows by clicking the title bars.

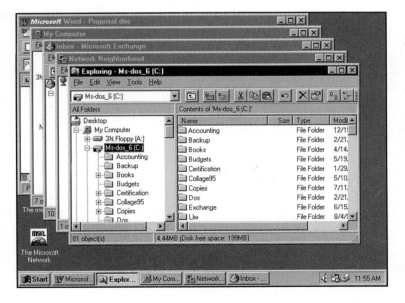

If you want to be able to quickly see all the application title bars so that you can click title bars to switch between many application windows, right-click in the gray area of the taskbar. When the shortcut menu appears, click on Cascade. The windows will arrange as shown in figure 3.27.

Managing Windows after an Application Failure

In Windows 3.0, if an application quit working, the user had two options: prayer and prayer. A hung program meant lost data. Windows 3.1 improved on this by allowing *local reboot*, the capability to trap errant application behavior, thus protecting other applications and data. Under Windows 3.1's local reboot, pressing Ctrl+Alt+Delete didn't restart your computer; it closed the misbehaving application and was supposed to leave Windows and other applications running correctly.

Local reboot had two main problems:

- People didn't always know which application was misbehaving, so pressing Ctrl+Alt+Delete often closed the wrong application.

- Windows 3.1 didn't always respond quickly to the Ctrl+Alt+Delete command. Users would continue to press Ctlr+Alt+Delete until the computer restarted. (A single Ctrl+Alt+Delete would bring up a blue screen warning that a second Ctrl+Alt+Delete would reset the system.)

Windows 95 significantly improves on how failed or misbehaving applications are handled. Windows 95 continuously polls the applications to see if they are running and responding. When an application fails to respond, Windows 95 displays the Not Responding dialog box. In this dialog box, you can click the End Task button to close the application. You lose all changes to data in the application since the last time you saved. Click Cancel to return to the application.

If the application misuses memory or has a fatal error that causes the application to crash, other applications in Windows usually will not be involved. When an application fails to respond—for example, clicks or keystrokes get no response—press Ctrl+Alt+Delete to display the Close Program dialog box.

The application that has trouble will show the phrase [Not responding]. To continue working in Windows on your other applications, you must shut down this application. Select the application and click End Task. If you click Shut Down or press Ctrl+Alt+Delete again, all applications and Windows 95 will shut down. ●

Part

II

Ch

3

CHAPTER 4

Managing Files

by Ron Person

To gain the most from Windows 95, it is essential that you learn how to efficiently work with and manage files.

The first part of this chapter explains how to use Windows Explorer to work with and manage the files on your computer. You also learn how to carry out many file-management tasks using My Computer. The later part of the book describes how you can customize Explorer, synchronize files between different computers, and associate new document files with an application. ■

Use Explorer and My Computer to manage files and folders

This chapter contains many tips and some undocumented tricks that will improve your productivity.

Manage the Recycle Bin so you can undelete files

Learn how to restore deleted files or permanently delete files.

View and change file attributes

Using Explorer, change hidden, system, read-only file attributes. It's also easy to specify that Explorer or My Computer hide files that are not EXE or documents.

Learn to synchronize files between laptop and desktop computers

The Briefcase enables you to synchronize files between two computers. This is very useful when you need to take work off your desktop with a laptop. When you return, the Briefcase updates files between the desktop and laptop.

How to use Explorer on a network

The majority of personal computers today are linked together by networks. Explorer and My Computer show you what resources are shared across the network.

Understanding Files and Folders

If you are familiar with the MS-DOS/Windows system for organizing files, a folder is analogous to a directory, and a folder within a folder is analogous to a subdirectory of a directory. If you like to think hierarchically, you can continue to visualize the organization of your files in exactly the same way as you did with DOS and earlier versions of Windows. The only difference is that instead of directories and subdirectories, you have folders and folders within folders. And, as you see in the next section, you can view the hierarchical arrangement of your folders using Explorer.

 If you misplace a file, use the Find command (Start, Find, Files or Folders) to search for the file by name, type, date saved, or content.

This capability to have folders within folders enables you to refine your filing system, categorizing your files in a way that makes it easy for you to locate a file even if you haven't used it for a long time. If you prefer to use the folder metaphor, you will want to use folder windows created from My Desktop.

 Folder windows created from My Desktop are actually single-pane Explorer windows—the right pane that contains a hierarchical structure is not shown in folder windows. Many of the tips and techniques described in the Explorer section of this book work in folder windows.

Using Explorer to View Files and Folders

Windows 95 comes with a new tool, *Windows Explorer,* that you can use to see how the files and folders on your computer are organized. With Explorer, you can view the hierarchical arrangement of the folders on your computer, and you can look into each folder to see what files are stored there. You also can use Explorer to reorganize and manage your files and folders. You can create new folders; move and copy files from one folder to another, to a floppy disk, or to another computer (if you are on a network); rename and delete files and folders; and perform other file-management tasks.

 The File Manager used in Windows 3.x is still available in Windows 95. Open the file WINFILE.EXE located in the Windows folder to see the new File Manager. Be careful—File Manager does not support long file names. If you use it, you will lose long file names you have created with Windows 95 applications or Explorer. Once you learn a few of the Explorer tips described in this chapter, you'll see that Explorer is more powerful.

N O T E If you are interested in another file manager that is similar to Windows Explorer but has additional features, take a look at Norton Navigator for Windows 95. Although it has a more complex interface and is slower than Explorer, some features are addictive. For example, I use Explorer in daily file management, but I use Norton Navigator to manage sets of compressed ZIP files. Its capability to view, add, and remove files from within a compressed ZIP file is a real timesaver. Never use Norton Navigator for Windows 3.x in Windows 95; it will corrupt files.

For more information on Norton Navigator contact Symantec at:

Symantec
175 West Broadway
Eugene, OR 97401

Phone: 800-441-7234
CompuServe: **GO SYMANTEC**
World Wide Web: **www.symantec.com**
FTP: **ftp.symantec.com**

To open Explorer, right-click Start, then choose <u>E</u>xplore. Explorer also can be found in <u>P</u>rograms in the Start menu or by right-clicking My Computer. Figure 4.1 shows Explorer with the left pane showing system resources and the right pane showing the folders in the local C: drive.

Part
II

Ch
4

FIG. 4.1
Use Explorer to view the files and folders on your computer. This view shows Explorer with large icons and a toolbar.

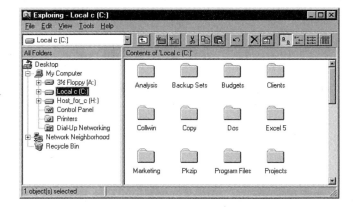

 T I P You'll use Explorer frequently to work with your files and folders. If you need to open Explorer to display frequently used folders, create Explorer shortcuts. Make these shortcuts quickly accessible by adding them to the Start menu.

▶ **See** "Starting Explorer at Specific Directories or Files," **p. 128**

▶ **See** "Customizing the Start Menu," **p. 369**

Viewing Your Computer's Resources

The Explorer window is divided into two panes (refer to fig. 4.1). Move between different panes in Explorer by pressing the Tab key. The left pane displays a hierarchical view of the organization of the folders on your computer. At the top of the hierarchy is the Desktop icon. This represents all the hard disks and resources available to your computer. Just beneath desktop is My Computer, represented by an icon of a computer. Under My Computer are listed all the resources on your computer. These resources include floppy drives (represented by a floppy drive icon) and local hard drives (represented by a hard drive icon). Three special folders—the Fonts, Control Panel, and Printers folders—are used for managing the fonts and printers on your computer and for customizing your computer's settings.

Two other folders that are branches off the Desktop icon are *Network Neighborhood* and the *Recycle Bin.* Network Neighborhood appears on your desktop if you installed a network adapter. Open this folder to browse the computers in your workgroup or on your entire network. The Recycle Bin temporarily holds files when you delete them from a folder, so you have the opportunity to recover them if you change your mind.

Depending on the resources on your computer, you may see other folders displayed under My Computer. If you have a CD-ROM drive or a removable media drive installed on your computer, for example, you will see their icons under My Computer. You may also see an icon for the *Briefcase* folder. The Briefcase is a special folder used for working on the same files at two locations and keeping them synchronized.

Just beneath the menu bar is the toolbar. If the toolbar is not displayed, choose View, Toolbar to see it. You can use the drop-down list at the left end of the toolbar to open the main folders in the Desktop and My Computer folders. This drop-down list shows all the drives on your computer, including network drives. If you scroll through the list, you'll also find your Control Panel, Briefcase (if installed), printers, Network Neighborhood, and Recycle Bin at the bottom of the list. This list also displays the folder hierarchy of the currently open folder, as shown in figure 4.2. You can, for example, quickly select the Recycle Bin folder without having to scroll to the bottom of the list in the left pane of Explorer. To select from the list, click the down arrow next to the text box and click the folder you want to open.

▶ **See** "Managing Print Jobs," **p. 246**
▶ **See** "Deleting Files and Folders," **p. 107**
▶ **See** "Synchronizing Files with the Briefcase," **p. 140**

FIG. 4.2

The folders in the hierarchy above the current folder (Apps) are shown in addition to the list of drives and other main resources. The rest of the folder hierarchy is collapsed for quick access.

Browsing the Contents of a Folder

The right pane of the Explorer window displays the contents of whatever folder is selected in the left pane. If you select the Local C: drive under My Computer, for example, you see a list of all the resources on your computer, including the floppy and hard drives (see fig. 4.3). To display the contents of your hard disk, click its icon in the left pane. To see the contents of a folder, select the folder on the left and its contents are listed on the right. You can select a folder by clicking it with the mouse or by using the up- and down-arrow keys on the keyboard.

 TIP You can open a specific folder without wading through the Explorer hierarchy by selecting Tools, Go To. Enter the path of the folder you want to open and then click OK.

You can expand and collapse the hierarchical view to display more or less detail. If a plus sign (+) appears next to an icon in the left pane of Explorer, additional folders are within this folder. To display these folders, click the plus sign (or double-click the folder). All the folders within this folder are displayed. Some of these folders, in turn, may have folders within them, which you can view using the same procedure. To hide the folders within a folder, click the minus sign (–) next to the folder, or double-click the folder. By collapsing and expanding the display of folders, you can view as much or as little detail as you want. Figure 4.3 shows an expanded view of the Local C: drive folder, which is collapsed in figure 4.1. Notice that some of the folders on the C drive have plus signs next to them, indicating that they contain additional folders.

FIG. 4.3
An expanded view of the Local C: drive in the My Computer folder, showing its folders.

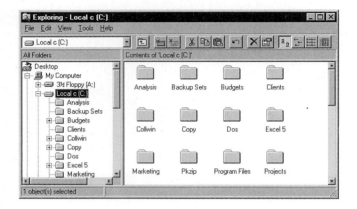

Understanding the File Icons in Windows

Windows uses various icons to represent folders and different types of files. In figure 4.4, folders within the Windows folder are represented with a folder icon. You can quickly display the contents of a folder within a folder by double-clicking its icon in the right pane of Explorer. The easiest way to redisplay the original folder is to click the Up One Level button on the toolbar. The Up One Level button is a picture of a folder with an up arrow in it. You also can redisplay the contents of the original folder by clicking its icon in the left pane of the window.

FIG. 4.4
Folder icons in the right pane of Explorer represent folders within the folder selected in the left pane.

N O T E Icons that have a small curved arrow in the lower left corner are shortcut icons. They are pointers to the actual file and folders that may be located in another folder. ■

In addition to folders, many types of files can appear in the list of contents. Each type is represented by its own icon. Calendar files, for example, are represented by a calendar icon, and Help files have their own special icon. These icons are helpful for visually associating a file with its program. You can, for example, readily distinguish a file created in the Calendar program from a file created in Paint (see fig. 4.5). You can open a file in its program by double-clicking the file's icon in Explorer.

FIG. 4.5
Different icons are used to represent different file types.

Text file

Calculator program

CD Player program

Bitmap file

 TIP Unlike in the Windows 3.1 File Manager, you don't need to refresh Explorer to see changes to the disk contents that were made from the DOS prompt.

You may need to update the display of files and folders in the right pane of Explorer. If you are viewing the contents of a floppy disk, for example, and you switch disks, you won't see the contents of the new disk unless you *refresh* the window. To refresh the window, click the icon for the folder you want to refresh, in this case the icon for the floppy drive, in the left pane of the Explorer. You also can refresh by choosing View, Refresh or by pressing the F5 key.

Managing Your Files and Folders

Explorer is an essential tool for managing the files and folders on your computer. You can use Explorer to create new folders, move folders from one location to another, copy and move files from one folder to another, and even move files from one disk drive to another. You also can use Explorer to delete and rename files and folders.

Selecting Files and Folders

To select a file or folder, click it. If another file in the right pane of Windows Explorer is already selected, then you can use the up- and down-arrow keys on the keyboard. The selected file is highlighted.

To select multiple files at once, click the first file; and then hold down the Ctrl key and click on each additional file you want to select. To deselect a file, continue holding down the Ctrl key and click a second time on the file. To quickly select a group of contiguous files, select the first file in the group, hold down the Shift key, and select the last file in the group. All the files between the first and last file will also be selected.

If files are in one of the icon views, then you can select a group of contiguous files by dragging a box around the group of files with the mouse.

If your files are arranged free form, you may find it convenient to select groups of files by dragging a rectangle around them using the pointer. Figure 4.6 shows how you can click and drag a rectangle around multiple icons. All the icons within the rectangle will be selected. Once they are selected, you can deselect or select additional files by holding down Ctrl and clicking on icons.

FIG. 4.6

Drag a rectangle around the group of file icons you want to select.

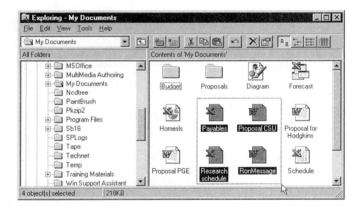

You also can select multiple files with the keyboard. To select multiple adjacent files, select the first file by tabbing into the right pane, then press and hold down the Shift key while moving to the last file by pressing the arrow key. To select nonadjacent files, select the first file, hold down the Ctrl key, use the arrow keys to move to the next file to be selected, and press the space bar. While you continue to hold down the Ctrl key, move to each file you want to select and press the space bar. To deselect a file and retain the other selections, hold down the Ctrl key, use the arrow key to move to the file, and press the space bar.

To select all the files and folders displayed in the right pane, choose Edit, Select All (or press Ctrl+A). If you want to select all but a few of the files and folders in the right pane, select the files and folders you don't want to select; then choose Edit, Invert Selection.

To cancel the selections you have made, simply select another file or folder, using either the mouse or the keyboard.

Renaming Files

Renaming individual files is much easier in Windows 95 than in Windows 3.x. To rename a file, click the file name, pause, then click the file name again. The name will be selected and the pointer changes to an I-beam to indicate you can edit the text underneath. Click the pointer in the name where you want the insertion point and rename the file. To undo your edits, press Esc. To accept your edits, press Enter or click another file.

Renaming Multiple Files

Unlike MS-DOS or Windows 3.x, Explorer has no facility for renaming multiple file names with a single command. However, you can preserve long file names while renaming multiple files by going to a DOS window and using the RENAME command to rename multiple files. You can even rename long file names.

> **CAUTION**
>
> Using the Windows 3.x or Windows 95 File Manager to rename one or more files converts the long file names for those files into their 8.3 equivalents.

Part
II

Ch
4

To rename long file names in multiple files using MS-DOS, follow this procedure:

1. Click Start, Programs, MS-DOS Prompt to open an MS-DOS window.
2. At the DOS prompt, type **CD** *pathname* to switch to the directory containing the files you want to rename.
3. Type **RENAME** *originalname.ext newname.ext*. If originalname or newname are long file names or include spaces, then enclose the name and extension in quotes. Press Enter.

When you use the DIR command to see the file names in a DOS window, remember that file names using 8.3 format will be on the left and long file names will be on the right of the listing.

The following list of file names will be used as examples:

Jun Forcast 01.xls
Jul Forcast 12.xls
Aug Forcast 05.xls
Sep Forcast 07.xls

To correct the spelling of "forcast," use the ? wildcard to match against any single letter in that character position. Use the MS-DOS command line,

```
rename "??? forcast ??.xls" "??? forecast??.xls"
```

This renames the files to:

Aug forecast05.xls
Sep forecast09.xls
Jul forecast12.xls
Jun forecast01.xls

Match against any number of characters by using the * wildcard, even within the quotes needed for long file names. For example, the MS-DOS command line,

```
rename "??? Forcast???.*" "??? Forcast.xls"
```

renames the original collection of files to

Jun Forcast.xls
Jul Forcast.xls
Sep Forcast.xls
Aug Forcast.xls

Creating New Folders

You can use Windows Explorer to create new folders.

TIP Create a new folder by right-clicking in the blank area of the right pane in Explorer. Choose New, Folder. Type a name for the folder and press Enter. In Windows 95 applications that use the common Save As dialog box, you can create new folders using this same process before you save a file.

To create a new folder, follow these steps:

1. Select the subfolder in the left pane of Explorer in which you want to create a new subfolder.
2. Choose File, New, Folder.

   A new folder appears in the right pane of Explorer, ready for you to type in a name.
3. Type a name for the folder and press Enter.

Folders can use long names just like files. Folder names can be up to 255 characters and can include spaces. Folder names can't use these characters:

\ ? : " < > |

Moving and Copying Files and Folders

Moving and copying files and folders is an essential file-management task. Using Explorer and the mouse, you can quickly move and copy files and folders without ever touching the keyboard.

You can use two approaches for moving and copying files and folders. You can either use the Cut or Copy commands or use the mouse to drag and drop the files.

To move or copy files using the menu, follow these steps:

1. Select the files or folders you want to move in the right pane of Explorer.

2. Perform one of the following actions:

   - To cut the file so it can be moved

     Choose Edit, Cut; or

     right-click, choose Cut; or

     press Ctrl+X; or

     click the Cut button on the toolbar

   - To copy the file so a duplicate can be made

     Choose Edit, Copy; or

     right-click, then choose Copy; or

     press Ctrl+C; or

     click the Copy button on the toolbar

3. In either pane of Explorer, select the folder in which you want to paste the cut or copied file, then follow one of these methods:

   - To paste the file

     Choose Edit, Paste; or

     right-click, then choose Paste; or

     press Ctrl+V; or

     click the Paste button on the toolbar

To move or copy files using the drag-and-drop method, follow these steps:

1. Select the files or folders you want to move in the right pane of Explorer.

2. If the folder to which you want to move the selected items is not visible in the left pane of Explorer, use the scroll bar to scroll it into view. If you need to display a subfolder, click the + sign next to the folder containing the subfolder.

Part
II

Ch
4

3. To move the selected items, drag the selected items to the new folder in the left pane of Explorer.

   or

   To copy the selected items, hold down the Ctrl key and drag the selected items to the new folder in the left pane of Explorer.

   A plus sign (+) appears beneath the mouse pointer when you hold down the Ctrl key, indicating that you are copying the files.

   Make sure that the correct folder is highlighted before you release the mouse button.

 Drag selected items to the destination folder with the right mouse button. When the shortcut menu appears, click Move Here to move items or Copy Here to copy items to the new location.

If you attempt to drag and drop a program file to a new folder, Windows creates a shortcut for that program in the new location. This is to prevent you from inadvertently moving a program file from its original folder. When you attempt to drag a program file, an arrow appears beneath the mouse pointer, indicating that you are about to create a shortcut for that program.

 To quickly move selected items to a floppy disk, click the selected items with the right mouse button. Click Send To and then click the disk drive to which you want to send the selected files. Add other drives or folders to the Send To menu through customization.

N O T E   If you routinely copy or move files to particular folders or a disk drive, you can create a shortcut for the folder or drive on your desktop. Then you can quickly drag and drop files onto the shortcut icon instead of having to scroll to the folder or drive in Explorer. To create a shortcut for a folder (or drive), select the folder (or drive) in Explorer, drag it with the right mouse button onto your desktop, and release the mouse button. Choose the Create Shortcut(s) Here command. You can now drag and drop files onto this shortcut icon to copy or move files to this folder (or drive). ▪

▶ **See** "Using the Power of Shortcuts and Desktop Icons," **p. 71**
▶ **See** "Customizing the Send To Menu," **p. 373**

Copying Disks

At times, you may want to make an exact copy of an entire floppy disk. This is easy to do in either Explorer or My Computer.

You can copy from one floppy disk to another using the same drive, but both disks must have the same storage capacity. The disk you copy onto will be erased in the process.

To copy a disk, follow these steps:

1. Insert the floppy disk you want to copy.

2. Right-click the disk in My Computer or in the left pane of the Explorer window.

3. Choose Copy Disk from the shortcut menu. This opens the Copy Disk dialog box shown in figure 4.7.

FIG. 4.7
The Copy Disk dialog box shows the selected drives for the copy operation.

If you have only one drive of this size, that drive will be highlighted for both the Copy From and Copy To areas of the dialog box. If you have another drive of this same size, it will be listed, as well, and you can select it to copy from drive to drive.

4. Choose Start.

5. If you are using the same drive for the master and the copy, you will be prompted to switch floppy disks when necessary.

6. When the disk is duplicated, you can copy another disk by choosing Start, or choose Close if you are done.

Copying disks is much faster in Windows 95 than in prior versions of Windows. This is due to the addition of a high-speed floppy driver. If you frequently copy disks, you will notice the improvement in speed.

Deleting Files and Folders

Windows now has a folder called the Recycle Bin, where deleted files are temporarily stored. The Recycle Bin empties on a rolling basis with the oldest files in the Recycle Bin actually being removed to make room for more recently deleted files. You can restore files from the Recycle Bin if you change your mind or accidentally delete a file.

▶ **See** "Formatting Disks," **p. 612**

 TIP If you realize right away that you have accidentally deleted a file or folder, choose Edit, Undo Delete to restore the files. Press F5 to refresh the file listing and see the restored file or folder.

Part

II

Ch

4

To delete a file or folder, follow these steps:

1. Select the file or folder you want to delete.

   You can select multiple files or folders using the techniques described in "Selecting Files and Folders," earlier in this chapter.

2. Click the selection with the right mouse button and click Delete.

   or

   Choose File, Delete (or press the Delete key or click the Delete button on the toolbar).

   or

   Drag and drop the file onto the Recycle Bin icon on the desktop.

> **TIP** To change whether a confirmation is required to delete a file, right-click the Recycle Bin, choose Properties, and select Display Delete Confirmation Dialog.

3. Click Yes when the Confirm File Delete dialog box appears (see fig. 4.8), or click No if you want to cancel the file deletion.

   If you are deleting multiple files, Explorer displays the Confirm Multiple File Delete dialog box.

FIG. 4.8
The Confirm File Delete dialog box gives you a chance to check your decision before deleting a file.

CAUTION

If you delete a folder, you also delete all the files and folders contained in that folder. The Confirm Folder Delete dialog box reminds you of this. Be aware of what you are doing before you delete a folder.

You also should be careful not to accidentally delete a program file. If you attempt to delete a program file, the Confirm File Delete message box warns you that you are about to delete a program. Click No if you don't mean to delete the program, but other selected files will be deleted. Click Cancel to stop all deletions.

▶ **See** "Viewing and Changing the Properties of a File or Folder," **p. 114**

CAUTION

Files deleted from the MS-DOS prompt, or from a disk or network drive, are not saved to the Recycle Bin. If you delete them, they are gone. You can use utilities such as Norton Utilities for Windows 95 from Symantec to give a broader range of undelete capabilities.

 T I P Permanently delete files without sending them to the Recycle Bin by holding down the Shift key as you delete them.

When deleting some files, you may see a message warning you that the file is a system, hidden, or read-only file. System files are files needed by Windows 95 to operate correctly and should not be deleted. Hidden and read-only files may be needed for certain programs to work correctly, or they may just be files that you have protected with these attributes to prevent accidental deletion. Before deleting any of these file types, you should be certain that your system does not need them to operate correctly.

Restoring Deleted Files

You can open the Recycle Bin folder just as you do any other folder and select a file and restore it to its original location. You also can move or copy files from the Recycle Bin to a new location, in the same way you learned how to move and copy files from other folders.

To restore a deleted file or folder, follow these steps:

 1. Double-click the Recycle Bin icon on the desktop to open the Recycle Bin window, as shown in figure 4.9.

FIG. 4.9
Select files to restore in the Recycle Bin.

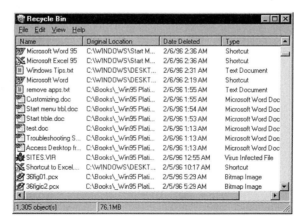

Part
II
Ch
4

2. Select the file or files you want to restore.

   You can use the techniques described in the earlier section, "Selecting Files and Folders," to select multiple files.

3. Click the selected files with the right mouse button and click R̲estore, or choose F̲ile, R̲estore.

   The files are restored in the folders from which they were deleted. If the folder a file was originally in has been deleted, the folder also is restored.

   ▶ **See** "Moving and Copying Files and Folders," **p. 105**

You also can restore a file to a different folder than the one from which it was deleted. Open the Recycle Bin folder in Explorer, select the files you want to restore, and use one of the techniques discussed earlier in this chapter to move the file where you want it.

Emptying the Recycle Bin   Periodically, you may want to empty the Recycle Bin to free up space on your hard disk. To empty the Recycle Bin, follow one of these procedures:

- If the Recycle Bin is already open, choose F̲ile, Empty Recycle B̲in.
- Click the Recycle Bin icon on the desktop with the right mouse button and click Empty Recycle B̲in.

Once you have emptied the Recycle Bin, you can no longer recover the deleted files and folders that were stored there.

You also can delete selected files from the Recycle Bin. To delete selected files from the Recycle Bin, follow these steps:

1. Open the Recycle Bin and select the files you want to delete.

2. Click the selected files with the right mouse button and click D̲elete.

3. Choose Y̲es to confirm the deletion.

> **CAUTION**
>
> The Recycle Bin can be a lifesaver if you accidentally delete a critical file. But don't forget to delete confidential files from the Recycle Bin so that others can't retrieve them.

Changing the Size of the Recycle Bin   You might prefer having more free disk space rather than storing a large history of deleted files. If so, you can change the amount of disk space used for the Recycle Bin.

To change the size of the Recycle Bin, follow these steps:

1. Right-click the Recycle Bin icon on the desktop or in Explorer and click P̲roperties.

The Recycle Bin Properties sheet appears, as shown in figure 4.10.

FIG. 4.10
Change the size of the
Recycle Bin on the Recycle
Bin Properties sheet.

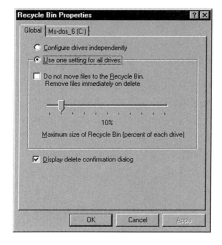

2. Select the Configure Drives Independently option if you want to change the Recycle Bin size separately for each drive.

   or

   Select the Use One Setting for All Drives option if you want to use the same size Recycle Bin for all drives.

3. Drag the slider to change the maximum size of the Recycle Bin, as a percentage of the total disk size.

4. Click OK.

Deleting Without Using the Recycle Bin   If you don't want to use up disk space storing deleted files, you can tell Windows to purge all files when they are deleted instead of storing them in the Recycle Bin. To purge all files when deleted, follow these steps:

1. Right-click the Recycle Bin icon on the desktop or in Explorer and click Properties.

2. Select the Purge Files Immediately on Delete option.

3. Click OK.

When you select this option and delete a file, the Confirm File Delete dialog box warns you that the file will not be moved to the Recycle Bin.

N O T E   You can turn off the confirmation message for the Recycle Bin by deselecting the Display Delete Confirmation Dialog check box on the Recycle Bin Properties sheet. ▨

Part

II

Ch

4

Previewing a Document with Quick View

As you manage the files on your computer, you may want to look at the contents of a file before you make decisions about opening, moving, copying, deleting, and backing up the file. It can be very tedious and time-consuming to open each file in the program that created the file. Windows has a tool called *Quick View* for previewing many types of files without having to open the original program. You can access Quick View from Explorer or from any folder window.

N O T E A worthwhile product to add to your toolkit is Quick View Plus from the people who wrote Quick View for Microsoft. Quick View Plus extends the Quick View that comes with Windows. It works with over 200 file formats from Windows, DOS, and Macintosh applications. It works with Microsoft Exchange so you can view e-mail and their attachments no matter what their source. It replaces the Quick View command on the Context menu so it's easy to access. Quick View Plus sets its viewing screen side-by-side with Explorer so the two act almost like one program. Quick View Plus also enables you to find documents, print, and copy. And Quick View Plus is inexpensive. For more information or trialware software contact:

Inso Corporation
401 North Wabash, Suite 600
Chicago, IL 60611
Phone: (312) 329-0700
Web: **http://www.inso.com**

To preview a file using Quick View, follow these steps:

T I P Preview documents by right-clicking the file and choosing Quick View.

1. Select the file you want to preview.
2. Choose File, Quick View. The Quick View item does not appear on the menu if the file type you select does not have a viewer installed.

   or

   Right-click the selected file and click Quick View.

   or

   Drag the file into an existing Quick View window.

   The Quick View window opens, displaying the contents of the file, as shown in figure 4.11.

You can scroll through the document using the scroll bars or keyboard. If you decide you want to edit the file, choose File, Open File for Editing (or click the Open File for Editing button at the left end of the toolbar).

FIG. 4.11

Quickly preview the contents of many types of files using Quick View.

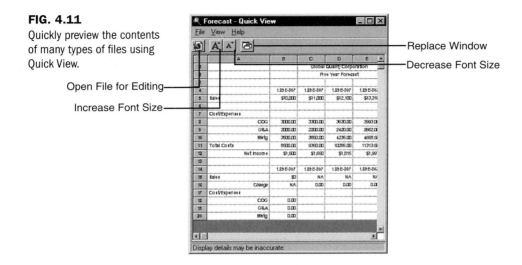

Replace Window

Decrease Font Size

Open File for Editing

Increase Font Size

TIP If you want to compare the contents of two files, you should have a new window opened for each file.

Part
II

Ch
4

By default, Quick View opens a new window for each file. If this default has been changed, or you need to change it back, choose View and look at the menu. If a check mark appears next to Replace Window in Quick View, choose that option to deselect it and have a new window opened for each file. If you want the contents of the current Quick View window to be replaced when you select a new file for previewing, choose View, Replace Window to select this option. You can use the Replace Window button on the toolbar to activate and deactivate this option.

When you first open Quick View, you see a portion of the page of your document. To view whole pages, choose View, Page View. A check mark appears next to the command when it is activated. When you are in page view, you can click the arrows in the upper-right corner of the page to scroll through the document. To return to viewing portions of a page, choose the command again.

When you are in page view, you can rotate the display to preview the file in landscape orientation by choosing View, Landscape. Choose the command again to return to portrait orientation.

You also can change the font and font size used in the display by choosing View, Font and selecting a new font or size. To quickly increase or decrease the font size, click the Increase Font Size or Decrease Font Size tools on the toolbar. When you change the font and font size, it affects only the display in Quick View and does not alter the original file. It's handy to be able to increase the font size if you can't easily read the contents of the file, especially when you are in Page view.

To exit Quick View, choose File, Exit, or double-click the Quick View icon at the left end of the title bar.

Viewing and Changing the Properties of a File or Folder

In Windows, it is easy to check the properties of a selected file or folder. You can find out the type of a file; the location and size of the selected item; the MS-DOS name; and when the file or folder was created, last modified, and last accessed. Each file and folder on a disk also has a set of *attributes,* or descriptive characteristics. Attributes describe whether the file has been backed up, is a Windows system file, is hidden from normal viewing, or can be read but not written over. With Windows Explorer, you can display these attributes and change them.

To display the properties of a particular file or folder, follow these steps:

1. In Explorer (or any folder), select the file or folder whose properties you want to check.

2. Right-click and choose Properties, or choose File, Properties. Windows opens a Properties sheet (see fig. 4.12).

3. View the file or folder's properties.

4. If you want, change the attributes for the file or folder, as described in the following table:

Attribute	Description
Read Only	Sets the R or Read-Only attribute, which prevents a file or folder from being changed or erased. Set this attribute for a file or folder when you want to prevent someone from accidentally changing a master template or erasing a file that is critical to system operation.
Archive	Sets the A or Archive attribute. Marks with an A any file that has changed since being backed up using certain backup programs, including Backup, which comes with Windows. If no A appears, the file has not changed since you backed it up.
Hidden	Sets the H or Hidden attribute, which prevents files from displaying in Explorer and My Computer.
System	Sets the S or System attribute, which prevents files from displaying. System files are files that your computer requires to operate. Deleting a system file could prevent your computer from working. Folders cannot have the System attribute set.

5. Click OK.

CAUTION

Read-only files can still be deleted from within Explorer. You will see one additional warning dialog box prompting you if you attempt to delete a read-only file. So, setting this attribute does not entirely protect a read-only file from deletion.

FIG. 4.12
You can check the properties of a file or folder on its Properties sheet.

If you want to reduce the odds of accidentally changing or erasing a file, set the attributes to Read-Only and Hidden or System. But remember that Read-Only and System files require only one additional confirmation to delete. So be careful when confirming the messages that prompts you to delete files.

N O T E To display files with the Hidden or System attribute, choose View, Options. Click the View tab and select the Show All Files option. Now hidden and system files are displayed in the list of files. You can carry out these steps in either Explorer or My Computer. ▪

Opening a Document from Explorer

You can open documents directly from Explorer. In fact, if you like to think in terms of opening documents rather than opening programs and then opening documents, you can use Explorer as your primary interface with your computer, doing all your viewing, opening, and printing of files from Explorer.

To open a document from Explorer, the file type for that document must be registered with a program in order for Windows to know what application to use to open and print the document. Windows automatically registers file types when you install an application.

Part
II

Ch
4

To open a document in Explorer, double-click the file icon in Explorer or in a folder window. Explorer starts the program for the file and opens the file. If the program is already running and it works with a multidocument interface, then the document loads into the program.

▶ **See** "Registering File Types Causing Documents to Open Applications," **p. 147**

Opening an Unrecognized File Type   If Windows does not recognize the file type of the file you double-click, it displays the Open With dialog box shown in figure 4.13. This dialog box enables you to tell Windows which application should be used to open the file. Choose the program you want to open the file from the <u>C</u>hoose the Program list. If you want the program to always be used to open a file of this type, make sure the Always <u>U</u>se This Program To Open This File check box is selected.

 TIP   You may want to open a file with a program different from the program it has an association with. To do that, hold the Shift key as you right-click the file. Choose Op<u>e</u>n With, and then choose the program with which you want to open the file.

FIG. 4.13
Double-clicking a file that is not recognized produces the Open With dialog box so you can tell Windows which program to use to open the file.

Printing Files

You can send files directly to the printer from Explorer. When you print with Explorer, you send the file to the default printer. To change the default printer, use Control Panel.

To print a file with Explorer, the file must be registered with a program. To print a file using Explorer, follow these steps:

1. Open the folder that contains the file or files you want to print.

2. Select the file or files you want to print.

3. Choose File, Print.

or

If you have created a shortcut for your printer on your desktop, drag and drop the selected file or files onto the Printer icon on the desktop.

 TIP Quickly print files by right-clicking the file, choosing Send To, and then selecting the printer. To add a printer to the Send To menu, right-drag a printer icon from the Printer folder in My Computer into the Windows\SendTo folder. Choose Create Shortcut(s) Here.

▶ **See** " Drag-and-Drop Printing from the Desktop," **p. 251**

▶ **See** "Registering a New File Type," **p. 375**

Using My Computer to Manage Files

New users of Windows may prefer to use My Computer to work with their files. My Computer is a folder on your desktop containing all the resources on your computer. When you first open My Computer, by double-clicking its icon on the desktop, the My Computer window displays an icon representing each of the resources on your computer, as shown in figure 4.14. Notice that the folder window opened from My Computer is the same as the right pane from the Explorer window.

FIG. 4.14
The My Computer window is another way to view the files and folders on your computer.

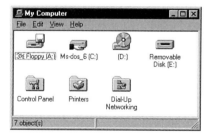

To look at the contents of a resource, double-click the appropriate folder. To view the folders on your hard drive, for example, double-click the hard disk icon. A new window opens, displaying the folders on your hard drive (see fig. 4.15). You can continue browsing through the folders on your computer by double-clicking any folder whose contents you want to view.

As you open up new windows in My Computer to view the contents of the different folders, you won't really have a sense of the organization of the folders the way you do in Explorer. In Explorer, you always have a map of the organization of your folders in the left pane. With My Computer, it is more difficult to visualize the hierarchical structure of your

Part
II

Ch
4

folders. If you don't think hierarchically, this may be a relief, as you may prefer to simply think of folders inside other folders that you open up one by one. You can move back through a series of opened folders by clicking the Up One Level button in the toolbar. This is a handy way to retrace your steps.

FIG. 4.15
You can browse through the folders in My Computer by double-clicking the folders whose contents you want to see.

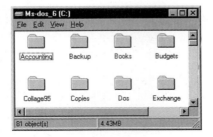

 Move up one level in a folder window by pressing the Backspace key.

If you find it annoying to end up with layer upon layer of folder windows as you open the folders on your computer, you can choose to have the contents of a newly opened folder replace the current contents of the My Computer window, instead of opening a new window. Choose View, Options and select the Browse Folders by Using a Single Window option. Now when you open a new folder, the folder's contents replace the contents of the current window. You can still use the Up One Level button to move back through a series of folders that you opened.

If Windows currently uses a single window to display the contents of folders you open, but you want a new window to open when you open a folder, then hold down the Ctrl key as you double-click a folder. Conversely, if Windows is currently opening a new window when you open a folder but you want to use a single window and replace its contents with the contents of the new folder, hold down the Ctrl key as you double-click a folder.

 If you have opened a trail of new single pane folder windows, you can close them all by holding the Shift key as you click the Close button (X) at the top-right corner of the window.

 If you prefer to run your programs from a folder rather than from the Start, Programs menu, here's a shortcut for making a program folder. Double-click the file PROGRAMS.GRP in the Windows folder. This opens a folder window showing a folder for each submenu off the Start, Programs submenu. Minimize this folder so its always accessible on your taskbar.

You can perform virtually all the file management tasks in My Computer that you learned to carry out in Explorer. To manage your files in My Computer, use the same techniques described throughout this chapter. You can use either the menus or the mouse to open, move, copy, rename, delete, and preview your files. You can drag and drop files from one folder window to another. And all the shortcuts accessible with the right mouse button in Explorer also can be used in My Computer. The display options described for customizing Explorer work exactly the same way in My Computer, as well.

As you work with Windows, you can decide whether you prefer to use Explorer or My Computer to manage your files. You may find a combination of the two approaches works best for you. Because the commands are identical in both, you can move back and forth between the two with ease. Whichever approach you take, you will undoubtedly come to appreciate how easy it is to manage your files in Windows.

Finding Files

Part II
Ch 4

If you are familiar with the Search command from the Windows 3.1 File Manager, you should be impressed by the new features added for finding files in Windows 95.

The Find tool enables you to look for a specific file or group of related files by name and location. When searching by name, it's no longer necessary to use "wild cards" to specify your search, although you can still use them to fine-tune a search. In addition to this improvement, you can search by date modified, file type, and size. The most powerful new feature allows you to search by the text contained in the file or files. If you ever need to look for a file and you can remember a key word or phrase in it, but don't know the name of the file, this will be a real timesaver.

To find a file or group of related files, follow these steps:

1. Open the Start menu, choose Find, and then choose Files or Folders.

   or

   In Explorer, choose Tools, Find, Files or Folders or right-click in the left pane and choose Find, Files or Folders.

   The Find dialog box appears (see fig. 4.16).

2. Type an entry in the Named text box.

   If you know the name of the file, type it in the text box. If you don't know the complete name of the file, just type whatever portion of file name you do know. Windows 95 will find all files that have these characters anywhere in the name.

FIG. 4.16

Specify information about files you are searching for in the Find dialog box.

You also can use wild cards to look for all files of a particular type. (You can also use the Type criteria discussed in step 6 to limit files by type.) The following are some examples of how to use wild cards to look for groups of related files:

Entry	What It Finds
*.xls	Files with XLS extension (Excel worksheet files)
d*.xls	Excel worksheet files with file names beginning with the letter d (for example, DRAFT1.XLS)
report??.txt	TXT files beginning with file names starting with *report*, followed by two more characters (for example, REPORT23.TXT)

To reuse the same search criteria as one used previously, click the arrow at the end of the Named text box and select the name search criteria you want to use from the list.

3. Specify where Find should look for the file in the Look In text box.

   You can type a pathname in the text box, select from the entries in the drop-down list, or click the Browse button to select the location to which you want to restrict the search.

   Select the Include Subfolders option if you want to include the subfolders of whatever folders you selected in the search.

T I P To search an entire drive, select the drive letter from the drop-down list and select Include Subfolders.

4. To limit the search to files created or modified within a specific time period, click the Date Modified tab (see fig. 4.17).

   You can restrict the search to files created or modified between two specified dates, or you can search for files created or modified during a specified number of months or days prior to the current date.

FIG. 4.17
You can narrow your search to a specified time period using options on the Date Modified page.

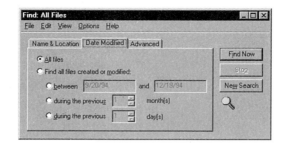

5. Click the Advanced tab to refine your search even more (see fig. 4.18).

FIG. 4.18
Restrict your file search to files containing specific text or files of a specific size on the Advanced page of the Find dialog box.

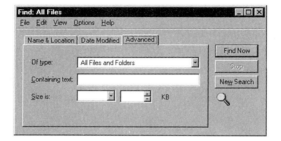

Part
II

Ch
4

6. Select a file type from the Of Type drop-down list to restrict the search to a specific type of file. The types listed here are the registered file types discussed in "Registering Files to Automatically Open an Application" later in this chapter. These include document types created by application programs, as well as various types of files needed by Windows such as icons, control panels, and fonts.

7. Enter a text string in the Containing Text text box to search for files containing a specific string of text. If you enter several words separated by spaces, Windows treats the entry as a phrase and finds only documents containing those words in that order.

8. Specify the size of the file in the Size Is box. You can specify that the file be exactly a particular file size, or at least or at most a specified size. Select from the drop-down list to select which of these options to use; and then specify a size in the Size Is box.

9. When you have finished setting up your search parameters, click the Find Now button.

The Find dialog box expands at the bottom to show the results of the search (see fig. 4.19). If your search parameters were very specific, the search may take a few moments, especially if you told Find to look for files with a specific text string. All files matching the search specifications are listed, along with their location, size, and file type.

FIG. 4.19
The results of a search are listed at the bottom of the Find dialog box.

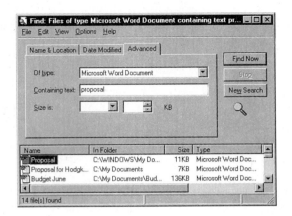

Use Find to do large-scale or disk-wide file deletions. You can use a search parameter that searches for a specific file type, such as *.XLS, or search for all old files, those files prior to a specific date. When the files display in the bottom of the Find window, use Quick View or view the file's properties to decide which files you want to delete.

At this point, you can perform all the same operations on any of the found files that you can on a file in Explorer. To work with a file in the Find dialog box, select the file and choose the File menu, or click the file with the right mouse button to open the shortcut menu. You can open, print, preview, move, copy, delete, rename, or view the properties of the file. You also can drag and drop the file to any folder in Explorer. This is handy if the file you located is in the wrong folder, and you want to quickly move it to the correct folder. The Edit menu contains commands for cutting and copying files, and for all the files, or all but the selected files.

Searching Through Compressed ZIP Files

Find will search for file names within files compressed with PKZIP or a PKZIP-compatible compression program. This can be very useful if you archive files in ZIP format and later need to find a specific file that is within a ZIP file.

The reason Find can do this is that the file names within a ZIP file are not compressed. The file names are stored in the ZIP file as text. You can use Find to search through the contents of the ZIP files for specific names.

To search for a file name within a ZIP file, follow these steps:

1. Click Start, Find, Files or Folders.
2. Choose the Options menu and make sure that Case Sensitive is not selected.

3. Select the Name & Location tab. Specify the drive to search and select the Include Subfolders check box. Type ***.ZIP** in the Named edit box.

4. Select the Advanced tab. Type the file name in the Containing Text edit box. Wild cards will not work.

5. Click the Find Now button.

When Find displays a list of ZIP files containing the file name, you can use Quick View Plus to view all the files in the ZIP file. Utilities such as Norton Navigator can selectively unzip a single file from the ZIP file you found.

▶ **See** "Previewing a Document with Quick View," **p. 112**

Saving the Search Criteria

You can save the search criteria as well as the results in an icon on your desktop. You also can save just the search criteria without saving the results. If you want to save the results with the search criteria, choose Options, Save Results so that Save Results is selected and shows a check mark. To save the criteria and the results if you specified that, choose File, Save Search. The saved criteria, and the results if you specified them, will appear on your desktop as a document icon. You can label the icon by changing its name.

To open the Find dialog box using the saved criteria and result, double-click the icon. The Find dialog box will show the criteria and results as they were when saved. To redo the search, click Find Now.

The View menu has the same commands as Explorer for selecting how you want the files to be displayed in the results pane and for sorting the list of files.

The Options menu has two commands for fine-tuning your search. Choose the Case Sensitive command if you want Find to distinguish between upper- and lowercase characters in any text you specified in the Containing Text text box.

If you want to set up a new search, click New Search to clear the criteria for the current search. Now you can enter the criteria for the new search.

▶ **See** "Changing How Folders and Files Display," **p. 124**

Customizing Explorer's Appearance

Windows offers many options for changing how the Explorer window looks. You can change how folders and files are listed; hide or display the toolbar and status bar; sort the folder and file icons by name, type, size, or date; hide the display of certain types of files; and make other changes to the Explorer window. Any changes you make remain in effect until you make new changes, even if you close and reopen Explorer.

Part
II

Ch
4

N O T E If you're used to opening multiple Windows in File Manager, take note of the fact that you can't do that in the Explorer. For most work, you don't need to open multiple windows in Explorer because you can drag from any file or folder in the right pane into any drive or folder in the left pane. You can display drives or folders in the left pane by clicking on their + sign without disturbing the contents of the right pane. Should you ever need to have multiple windows in Explorer, just open additional copies of Explorer. You can then copy or move files between them.

▶ **See** "Opening Side-by-Side Folder Windows from a Desktop Shortcut," **p. 131** ∎

 T I P Most of the settings and preferences you choose for viewing a folder remain with that folder. The next time you open that folder, it will have the same settings.

Changing the Width of Panes

Use the mouse to change the size of the left and right panes of Explorer. To change the width of the two panes of the Explorer window, move the mouse pointer over the bar dividing the two panes (the mouse pointer changes to a double-headed arrow), hold down the left mouse button, and drag the bar left or right to adjust the size of the two panes to your liking. However, you can't hide one pane or the other completely as you could in Windows 3.1 File Manager.

Changing the Status Bar

The status bar at the bottom of the Explorer window provides information on the item you select. If you select a folder, for example, you see information on the number of items in the folder and the total amount of disk space used by the folder. You can hide the status bar if you don't use it to make more room for displaying files and folders. To hide the status bar, choose View, Status Bar. Choosing this command again displays the status bar.

Customizing the Toolbar

The tools on the toolbar are shortcuts for commands you otherwise access with menu commands. These tools are discussed in the appropriate sections in this chapter. If you don't use the toolbar, you can hide it by choosing View, Toolbar. To display the toolbar, choose the command again.

Changing How Folders and Files Display

When you first start using Explorer, notice that folders and files are represented by large icons in the right pane of the window, as shown earlier in figures 4.4 and 4.5. You also can display files and folders as small icons, as a list, or with file details.

To change the way folders and files are displayed, follow these steps:

1. Open the View menu.

2. Choose one of the following commands:

Command	Result
Large Icons	Large icons
Small Icons	Small icons arranged in multiple columns
List	Small icons in a single list
Details	Size, type, and date modified

The currently selected option appears in the View menu with a dot beside it. Figure 4.20 shows files displayed using small icons.

If the toolbar is displayed, you also can click one of the four tools at the right end of the toolbar to change how items are displayed.

FIG. 4.20

You can view more files and folders in Explorer when you use small icons.

 TIP To automatically adjust column widths in the Detail view of Explorer to show the full content width, double-click the line between the column heads.

When you select the Details option, information on the size, type, and date the folder or file was last modified appears in columns next to the item in the list, as shown in figure 4.21. You can change the width of these columns by moving the mouse pointer over the line that divides the buttons at the top of each column (the mouse pointer changes to a double-headed arrow), holding down the left mouse button, and dragging the line to change the width.

FIG. 4.21

To see information on the folders and files in the Explorer window, choose the Details view. Resize columns by dragging the line between header titles.

Arranging File and Folder Icons

If you select either the Large Icons or Small Icons option for displaying your files and folders, you can choose to let Windows automatically arrange the icons, or you can move the icons around to locate them wherever you want. To arrange the icons automatically, choose View, Arrange Icons. If a check mark appears next to the Auto Arrange command in the submenu, the command is already selected. If not, select Auto Arrange. The icons are now automatically arranged in a grid. If you want to arrange icons at any location in the right pane, deselect Auto Arrange. Some people prefer to have their files and folders arranged in an order of priority, frequency of use, or some other creative arrangement. Figure 4.22 shows files grouped by usage. Some are forecasting files and other are budgetary files.

FIG. 4.22

When Auto Arrange is off you can arrange icons in any way you want.

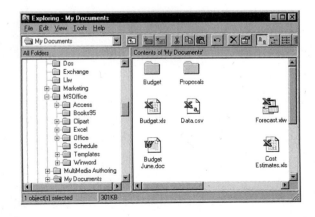

If the Auto Arrange command is not enabled, you can quickly arrange your icons in a grid by choosing View, Line Up Icons.

Sorting Files and Folders

You can sort the files and folders in the right pane of Explorer by name, type, size, and date. To sort the items in the Explorer display, follow these steps:

1. Choose View, Arrange Icons.

2. Select one of the four options from the submenu.

Command	Result
By Name	Sorts folders and then files by their name
By Type	Sorts folders and then files by the type column (this may not be the same as file extension)
By Size	Sorts folders and then files by their size
By Date	Sorts folders and then files by their date

If you selected the Details option for displaying your folders and files, you can quickly sort the list of items by name, size, type, and date modified by clicking the button at the top of the column you want to sort by. Click Size, for example, to sort the list of items by size.

TIP When you see a list in Windows 95 and the list headings appear to be buttons, try clicking them to sort the information according to the column on which you click. Each click toggles between ascending or descending order.

Displaying or Hiding Different File Types

You can change several other options in the View Options dialog box. To change these options, follow these steps:

1. Choose View, Options to display the Options dialog box (see fig. 4.23).

2. Select Show All Files to list all file types in the Explorer window.

   or

   Select Hide Files of These Types to hide the display of several types of system files.

   Hiding these files, which you normally don't have to deal with, shortens the list of items displayed for some folders, and also prevents you and other users from accidentally deleting or moving crucial system files.

FIG. 4.23
You can change several options on the View page of the Options dialog box.

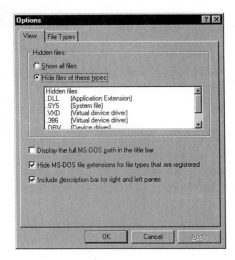

3. Select the Display the Full MS-DOS Path in the Title Bar option if you want to see the full DOS path for the folder selected in the left pane.

4. Select the Hide MS-DOS File Extensions for File Types that Are Registered option if you don't want the extensions for files associated with a particular program to be displayed.

   (In Windows, a file's icon indicates what program it is associated with, if any; so you may have no reason to see file extensions.)

5. Select the Include Description Bar for Right and Left Panes option to display a descriptive bar at the top of the right and left panes of the Explorer window. The Description Bar shows you such information as the drive letter and pathname for the current view.

6. Click OK when you have finished making the selections you want.

Starting Explorer at Specific Directories or Files

One of Explorer's potentially annoying features is that when it opens it displays the directory or resource of the object from which it was opened. For example, if you right-click Start and choose Explore, Explorer opens displaying the contents of the Start menu folder. If you right-click the My Computer icon on the desktop and choose Explore, then Explorer opens displaying the contents of My Computer. While this design is understandable, many of us expect or would like Explorer to open in a folder we designate or in the last folder in which it was used. Use the following tips and you'll be able to create shortcuts that open Explorer the way you want.

Opening Explorer at Specific Folders or Files

Opening Explorer from a command line enables you to use switches that control how Explorer opens. The command line can be entered in the _T_arget box of a shortcut's Property sheet, entered from an MS-DOS prompt, or typed within an MS-DOS batch file. Understanding how these switches work enables you to open Explorer in the following ways:

- In a single pane, Open view, or with the double pane in the Explorer view.
- With full access to all folders or restricted to a _root_ folder or UNC.
- With a folder open and no file selected or with a specific file selected.

N O T E   Be sure that you type a comma between each switch. Long file names or UNC names entered in the Target line of a shortcut's property sheet do not need to be enclosed in quotes.

The syntax for using switches with Explorer is

```
Explorer/n, /e,/root,<object>,/select,<sub object>
```

These switches do the following:

Switch	Description
/n	Opens a new window even when a window is already open in the same folder.
/e	Without /e Explorer opens in the single pane Open view seen from My Computer. With /e Explorer opens with two panes.
/root,<object>	Specifies the highest level folder shown in Explorer, and then opens in this folder. Explorer is restricted to the root folder and its subfolders. Use a local path or UNC name. If no root is specified the Desktop is used.
/select,<sub object>	The object specified by <sub object> is selected when Explorer opens. The object can be a file, folder, or resource. Specify the path or UNC unless it is specified by /root.

Opening Explorer and Restricting It to a Folder   A lot of file management time is spent scrolling up and down through the left pane of Explorer looking for the same two or three frequently used folders. With the following trick you can create shortcuts that open Explorer to the specific folder you want. Two or three of these shortcuts on your desktop or Start menu will save a lot of time.

The _root_ switch opens Explorer to the folder or UNC path that you specify, but it also restricts the user to that root and all the subfolders underneath it.

Part

II

Ch

4

Follow these steps to create a shortcut that opens in the folder you want:

1. Create a desktop shortcut to EXPLORER.EXE in the Windows folder.

2. Right-click the shortcut icon and choose Properties.

3. Select the Shortcut tab.

4. Modify the Target line to read:

   ```
   C:\WINDOWS\EXPLORER.EXE /e,/root,C:\my documents
   ```

   This opens Explorer in the double pane window like the one shown in figure 4.24. Notice that the /root switch forces Explorer to display only the My Documents folder and its subfolders. Use the following command line to open a single pane folder window.

   ```
   C:\WINDOWS\EXPLORER.EXE /root,C:\my documents
   ```

FIG. 4.24
Open Explorer in a double-pane view with unlimited scope or restricted to a folder as shown here.

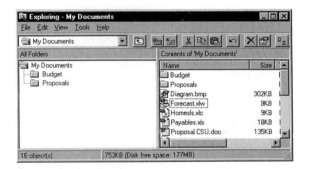

5. Change the icon by clicking the Change Icon button if you want, then click OK.

6. Relabel the shortcut icon to indicate the view that it opens.

When you want to open Explorer to the folder designated by the root switch, just double-click the shortcut. To copy a file or folder into that folder, just drag and drop the file or folder onto the shortcut.

Opening the Explorer and Selecting a File   To open an Explorer window and display a specific file, create a shortcut icon as described in the previous section. Open the shortcut's Property sheet and select its Shortcut tab.

In the Target line enter, a line similar to:

```
C:\WINDOWS\EXPLORER.EXE /select,C:\my documents\schedule.xls
```

If you have restricted Explorer to a root folder with a dual pane view, then your command line might look something like this:

```
C:\WINDOWS\EXPLORER.EXE /e,/root,C:\my documents,/select,schedule.xls
```

The resulting windows look like figure 4.25.

FIG. 4.25
Explorer windows can be restricted to a folder and have a specific file or folder selected when they open.

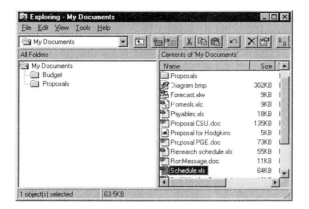

Customizing Explorer for Side-by-Side Views or Program Groups

While Explorer is very powerful, there are a few things about the old File Manager and Program Manager that some people still miss. One of the nice features of the Windows 3.x File Manager was its capability to display side-by-side windows. This enabled you to quickly drag and drop files between widely separated folders. Although you can drag and drop between folders in Explorer, it's sometimes more awkward to do so. The following section shows you how to use Explorer switches and a batch file to create a shortcut that opens side-by-side Explorer windows.

Some people prefer the Windows 3.x Program Manager as a way of viewing programs and documents they want to start. If you prefer to see your programs and documents grouped on the desktop, you will want to see how easy it is to create a programs group that duplicates everything in the Programs submenu of your Start menu.

▶ **See** "Creating Windows 3.1-Like Program Groups," **p. 133**

Opening Side-by-Side Folder Windows from a Desktop Shortcut

The following procedure creates an MS-DOS batch file that opens two folder windows and positions them side-by-side, as shown in figure 4.26. A shortcut to the batch file enables you to rerun it whenever you need it. To use this batch file, you won't need to minimize the other programs that are running.

FIG. 4.26

Run side-by-side folder windows from a batch file whenever you want.

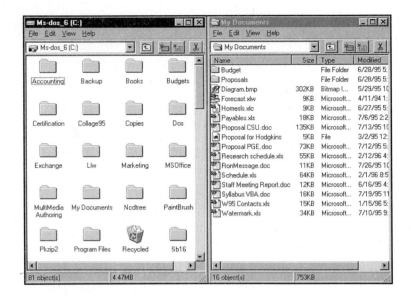

To create the side-by-side folder batch file, follow these steps:

1. Double-click My Computer to open a single pane window. Choose <u>V</u>iew, <u>O</u>ptions and then select Browse Folders by Using a Si<u>ng</u>le Window and choose OK.

2. Create an MS-DOS batch file by clicking Start, Accessories, Notepad and entering two Explorer command lines that open folder windows into the drives or folders you want. If you want the windows to open side-by-side, the initial folder for each window must be different. If the folders are the same, they will open on top of each other. Save this batch file with the extension BAT.

   For example, to open two folder windows with one showing c:\ and the other showing c:\MSOffice you would use:

   ```
   Explorer C:\
   Explorer /n,C:\MSOFFICE
   ```

   In this example, the first line opens a folder window at the C: drive. The second line opens a new folder window at C:\MSOffice.

3. After you have saved the batch file, you can create a shortcut directly from the batch file by right-clicking the batch file and choosing P<u>r</u>operties. Select the Program tab and change the name at the top of the sheet. This name is a descriptive name to help you. It does not appear as the file name. Select Minimize from the <u>R</u>un drop-down list. Select the Close on E<u>x</u>it check box. These actions prevent the batch file window from displaying. Choose OK.

Windows automatically creates a shortcut because you modified the batch file's properties. The shortcut is stored in the same folder as the original batch file.

4. Drag the shortcut onto the desktop if you want it available from the desktop or add it to the Start menu.

5. Close or minimize all programs and run the batch shortcut by double-clicking it.

6. When the two folder windows appear, click the window you want on the left, then right-click the taskbar in a clear area and choose Tile Vertically. Set any viewing options for the windows, such as column widths, then close each window. If these windows display different folders the next time they are opened, they will open in the same position and with the same viewing options.

To run your batch file, double-click the shortcut you created. If you opened both windows into the same folder, the windows will open using the position and viewing options of the last window you closed in step 6.

▶ **See** "Customizing the Start Menu," **p. 369**

Creating Windows 3.1-Like Program Groups

Part
II

Ch

4

Some people who used Windows 3.1 really liked the way the Program Manager visually grouped their programs and documents. If you prefer this method of starting and visualizing your programs and documents, then follow these steps to quickly create a folder window displaying groups of programs and document files that are in your Start menu. Figure 4.27 shows the window that duplicates the contents of the Programs menu.

FIG. 4.27
Put the contents of your Start, Programs menu in a window with a single click.

To create a window duplicating the contents of the Programs submenu of the Start button, double-click the PROGRAM.GRP file in the Windows folder. A Group Conversion window displays while the group file converts into a folder window. When it's done you see a single pane window displaying the contents of the Start, Program menu. Adding or removing programs or documents to the Start, Program menu automatically updates the contents of the window.

Working with Long File Names

Windows 95 gives you the capability to type file and folder names up to 255 characters long and include spaces. This makes understanding file and folder names much easier than older versions of Windows or DOS.

CAUTION

Although a file name can be up to 255 characters long, you shouldn't make them longer than 50 to 75 characters because the full path name cannot be more than 260 characters. From a usability standpoint, file names that are too long are difficult to type and difficult to read in a list.

TIP You can display or hide the three-character file extension by choosing View, Options, and then clicking the View tab and deselecting the option Hide MS-DOS File Extensions for File Types that Are Registered.

Both of these improvements do not restrict your ability to use Windows files with older Windows or DOS systems that do not use long file names. An abbreviated version of the long file names enables files to be backward compatible.

Renaming Files and Folders

As part of your efforts to keep the files and folders on your computer organized, you may want to rename a file or folder. This is easy to do in Explorer.

TIP If you're using a keyboard, you can rename a file or folder by selecting it and then either choosing File, Rename, or pressing F2.

To edit or rename a file or folder, follow these steps:

1. Click the file or folder name to select it.
2. Pause the pointer over the text in the name until the pointer changes to an I-beam and click where you want the insertion point in the text.

CAUTION

If you accidentally double-click the file name, the program for that file opens and loads the file. To return to naming the file, close the program and click once on the file name.

3. Edit using normal Windows editing methods. Press Enter to complete your edit.

If you change your mind while typing in a new name, just press the Escape key to return to the original name. If you have already pressed Enter and the file has been renamed, click the Undo button in the toolbar, choose <u>E</u>dit, <u>U</u>ndo, or press Ctrl+Z.

> **CAUTION**
>
> If you change the three-letter DOS file extension for a name, you will see a Rename alert box with this message: `If you change a file name extension, the file may become unusable. Are you sure you want to change it?` This box warns you that by changing the extension you will not be able to double-click the file and open its program. You can still open the file from within the application by choosing <u>F</u>ile, <u>O</u>pen.

Using Long File Names with Older Windows and DOS Systems

Folders and files with long names can be used on older Windows and DOS systems. The *FAT (File Allocation Table)*, an area on the disk that stores file information, has been especially modified to store both old-style 8.3 file names as well as long file names.

> **CAUTION**
>
> Beware of using MS-DOS based or previous Windows versions of hard disk utilities, file management software, or file utilities with Windows 95. In most cases, long file names will be destroyed and you may lose data.
>
> Some programs that will cause problems with Windows 95 are the Windows 3.x versions of:
>
> Norton Utilities™ by Symantec
> PC Tools™ by Central Point Software, Inc.
> Microsoft Defragmenter for MS-DOS versions 6.0, 6.2, 6.21, or 6.22
> Stacker 4.0 by STAC Electronics
>
> These companies have released or are releasing Windows 95-compatible upgrades for their utilities. Check with these companies for the correct version to use with Windows 95.
>
> If you must run an old backup or disk-management utility with Windows 95, use the LFNBK utility to remove long file names from the disk. After using the old utility you can restore long file names. LFNBK is described in the troubleshooting section at the end of Chapter 23, "Backing Up and Protecting Your Data."

> **CAUTION**
>
> Long file names cannot use the following characters:
>
> / \ : * ? " < > |

Part

II

Ch

4

When you use a long file name, Windows automatically creates a file name fitting the 8.3 convention. This 8.3 file name is saved in its normal location in the FAT so that older Windows and DOS systems can still use the 8.3 file name.

You can see the MS-DOS file name that will be used for a file by right-clicking the file name, choosing Properties, and selecting the General tab. Figure 4.28 shows the File Properties sheet. The long file name is shown at the top of the box, and the MS-DOS name appears near the middle.

FIG. 4.28

Find out about a file by right-clicking its name and then choosing Properties.

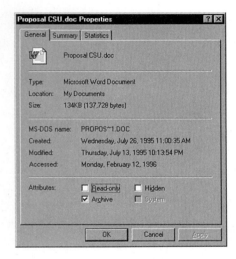

The rules used to convert long file names to 8.3 file names are as follows:

1. Remove the special characters: \ ; * ? " < > | <space> and any period except the right-most period.

2. Create the first portion of the name by taking the first six characters in the long file name and adding a *numeric tail* by adding a tilde (~) followed by the number 1. If a file in the same directory already uses that number, increase the number to 2. Continue trying numbers through 9. If that does not yield a unique name, take the first five characters and create a unique numeric tail using numbers from 10 to 99.

3. Create the file extension by taking the first three characters after the last period. If the long file name does not have a period, then there won't be a file extension.

Administering Long File Names in a Mixed-Name Environment

If you are working in an environment that uses Windows 95 as well as computers that still use the 8.3 naming convention, there are a number of things you can do to lessen the confusion caused by mixed names:

- Familiarize yourself with the LFNBK utility and use it with any pre-Windows 95 disk or file utilities that you use on Windows 95 files. Upgrade to Windows 95 utilities as soon as possible.

  ▶ **See** "Troubleshooting Tools," **p. 257**

- Users should check the resultant 8.3 file name if they have any doubt about the resolution of a long file name down to an 8.3 file name. See the MS-DOS file name by opening a file's Property sheet and checking the MS-DOS name on the General page.

- Modify your Windows 95 computers so they truncate long file names at the first eight characters rather than truncating at six letters and adding the ~# numeric tail. Many users prefer this modification because it enables you to use the first eight characters of a long file name as part of the MS-DOS file name. To learn how to modify the Registry so the numeric tail is not used on MS-DOS file names, see "Modifying the Registry to Truncate Long File Names," later in this chapter.

- Create a naming convention for files and train your users on using it and understanding its importance.

If you decide to create naming conventions for your users, here are some possible conventions:

- Make the first six characters of long file names significant and unique. In this way each file's 8.3 file name will be readable and unique. In the following tables you can see the difference between how long file names convert.

Part
II

Ch
4

Non-Unique Leading Six Characters	
Long File Name	**8.3 Equivalent**
Sales Report Jan.Xls	SALESR~1.XLS
Sales Report Feb.Xls	SALESR~2.XLS
Sales Report Mar.Xls	SALESR~3.XLS

Unique Leading Six Characters	
Long File Name	**8.3 Equivalent**
Jan Sales Report.Xls	JANSAL~1.XLS
Feb Sales Report.Xls	FEBSAL~1.XLS
Mar Sales Report.Xls	MARSAL~1.XLS

■ Create the long file name and the 8.3 name within the same name. Start long file names with the first six characters (eight if you modify the Registry) of the MS-DOS file name, then add a long file name, and then end with a period and the three-letter extension. Use underscore (_) characters to fill unused spaces in the first eight characters. This method makes it easy to read the 8.3 name, yet you can still do complex searches with Find on text in the long file. See the examples in the following tables.

Unmodified Registry Using Numeric Tails	
Long File Name	**8.3 Equivalent**
JanSale_.Sales Report	JANSAL~1.XLS January 1996.Xls
BdgTA___.Budget, Dept	BDGTA~1.XLS A Final version.Xls

Modified Registry Without Numeric Tails	
Long File Name	**8.3 Equivalent**
JanSaleRp.Sales Report	JANSALRP.XLS January 1996.Xls A Final version.Xls

Modifying the Registry to Remove Numeric Tails from File Names

Many people find it difficult to read and remember the MS-DOS file names that have *numeric tails*. The numeric tail is the tilde (~) and number at the end of an MS-DOS file name, for example, SALESR~1.XLS. Windows 95 adds a numeric tail when it creates an 8.3 file name from a long file name. These tails are designed to make sure that long file names can be converted to unique 8.3 names.

With a simple modification to the Registry, you can get rid of the Windows habit of adding numeric tails. The lack of a numeric tail not only makes file names easier to read, it also gives your file name space for two more characters.

To modify the Registry so Windows does not use numeric tails,

1. Click Start, Run and type **Regedit**, then choose OK to open the Registry Editor.

2. Expand the HKEY_LOCAL_MACHINE branch by clicking the + sign to its left.

3. Expand all branches in the following path,
   HKEY_LOCAL_MACHINE\System\CurrentControlSet\Control\FileSystem

4. Select FileSystem in the left pane.

5. Choose Edit, New, Binary Value, then type **NameNumericTail** and press Enter. Your entry, NameNumericTail, appears in the name column.

6. Double-click NameNumericTail. In the Edit Binary Value dialog box that appears, type a 0 and choose OK. The value 00 should appear in the value column to the right of NameNumericTail.

7. Close the Registry Editor.

The next time you start Windows, MS-DOS file names will be created by truncating long file names to the first eight valid characters. Numeric tails will only be used if there is another file with the same name in the same folder.

Working with Long File Names in MS-DOS

If you use a DOS command from the command prompt, such as dir to list a directory containing files with long names, you see the normal file information as well as the long file names. The long file name is displayed in the far right column when using the DOS dir command.

When working from the MS-DOS command line in Windows 95, you can use either the 8.3 or the long file name assigned to each file. Use long file names in MS-DOS command lines as you would 8.3 names. If the name includes spaces, then put quotes around the entire path.

From the MS-DOS prompt the default command line character limit is 127 characters. Command lines cannot be longer than 127 characters. To enable longer command lines, add the following line to CONFIG.SYS:

```
shell=c:\windows\command.com /u:255
```

If your computer already has the SHELL command in the CONFIG.SYS file, change the /u switch to a value of 255.

Part
II

Ch
4

If your computer does not have a CONFIG.SYS file in the root, create one by opening Notepad, typing the line as shown, then saving the text file to your boot disk root folder with the name CONFIG.SYS.

The command line will now be limited to 255 characters. This limit includes the MS-DOS command, switches, spaces, quotes, and long file name. You will be able to use 255 character command lines in all MS-DOS virtual machines running in Windows 95. Making this change will not enable MS-DOS on non-Windows 95 computers to use long file names.

Synchronizing Files with Briefcase

With the proliferation of home computers, laptop computers, and networks, you may often find yourself working on the same file on different computers. The inherent difficulty in working with the same file at more than one location is keeping the files synchronized—that is, making sure that the latest version of the file is at both locations. This used to be a daunting and dangerous task. It is not too difficult to accidentally copy the older version of a file on top of the newer version, rather than the other way around. A new feature in Windows, *Briefcase*, makes the task of synchronizing files in different locations much easier.

N O T E   If you frequently transfer files between computers, must maintain synchronized files, or want to control one computer from another, consider using LapLink for Windows 95. It's features are more robust, it updates files faster, and it operates over more communication media than Briefcase. ▨

Briefcase is really a folder with some special features. When you want to work on files at a different location—for example, on your laptop while you are away from your office—you first copy the files from your desktop computer into Briefcase. You then transfer Briefcase to your laptop and work on the files in Briefcase. When you return to the office, you transfer Briefcase back to your desktop and issue a command that automatically updates any files on your desktop that were modified while they were in Briefcase. The files on your desktop are then synchronized with the files in Briefcase.

The Briefcase procedure works whether you transfer Briefcase using a floppy disk, keep Briefcase on one of two computers that are physically connected, or use Briefcase to synchronize files across a network.

▶ **See** "Maintaining Laptop and Desktop Files with Briefcase," **p. 221**

Installing Briefcase

Unless you chose the Portable option when you were setting up Windows, or specified the installation of Briefcase in a custom installation, you will not have the Briefcase feature. One way to check to see if you do have the Briefcase feature installed is to look for a Briefcase icon on your desktop. However, the Briefcase icon may have been moved or deleted, so a second way to check is to right-click in a folder or on the desktop. Choose New and if the Briefcase appears as an item, choose Briefcase. If a new Briefcase appears, then the Briefcase feature is installed.

> **CAUTION**
>
> If Briefcase is already installed, then Briefcase will not appear in the Accessories portion of the Components list in Add/Remove Programs as described in step 4 of the following instructions. Briefcase will only appear if it has not been previously installed. Once Briefcase is installed, it cannot be uninstalled with Add/Remove Programs. This is to prevent the accidental loss of data from a Briefcase.

Part
II

Ch
4

To install Briefcase, follow these steps:

1. Open the Start menu; then choose Settings and Control Panel.
2. Double-click the Add/Remove Programs icon.
3. Click the Windows Setup tab.
4. Select Accessories in the Components list and then click Details.
5. Select Briefcase in the Components list and then click OK.

N O T E   Briefcase will only be listed in these options if it isn't installed. Unlike the other accessories, which are listed here regardless of whether they are currently installed, Briefcase disappears from the list once you install it. If you delete Briefcase, it will not appear in the list and you won't be able to reinstall it without rerunning the Windows setup.

6. Click OK again and insert the Windows disk specified in the Insert Disk message box that appears. Click OK.
7. Click OK to close the dialog box.

Creating a New Briefcase on the Desktop

If your PC does not already include a Briefcase on your desktop, you can easily create a new Briefcase. To create a Briefcase, follow these steps:

1. Decide where you want the Briefcase to be created (on the desktop, in a floppy disk folder, in a folder on the hard disk, and so on).

2. Right-click in the location in which you want the Briefcase created. If you want the Briefcase created on the desktop, for example, right-click the desktop.

3. From the pop-up menu, choose New, Briefcase. Windows 95 will create a Briefcase and add an icon for it in the location you have selected.

4. If you want to rename the Briefcase, click the Briefcase icon to select it, then click the Briefcase's description. Type a new description and press Enter.

As previously explained, you can create as many Briefcases as you like. By default, Windows 95 creates a Briefcase called My Briefcase on your desktop. You can rename the default Briefcase to suit your preferences.

Synchronizing Files with a Laptop or Another Computer on a Network

You can use Briefcase to keep files synchronized between a laptop and a desktop computer. This is useful because you may update files on the laptop while it is disconnected from the desktop. Upon reconnecting the two computers, you can ask Windows to synchronize the files between the two computers—comparing and updating files between the two computers. The most up-to-date file replaces the unchanged file. If files on both computers have been changed, then you will be asked to choose which file should replace the other.

> **CAUTION**
>
> Be sure that the times and dates are correctly set on any computer on which you use synchronization. Incorrect dates or times could cause the wrong file to be overwritten.

Keeping synchronized files between your laptop and desktop computers is most convenient if they can be physically connected by a cable or network. Physically linking two computers is a much faster way to transfer files than by using a floppy disk. Using Briefcase helps you keep the files you are using on both computers synchronized. You can work on either the file on the original computer or the file in Briefcase, and use the Update command to keep the files synchronized.

TIP The recommended approach is to put Briefcase on the computer you use less often.

You may have two computers on which you need to keep synchronized files, but you don't have the computers connected. You can still keep files synchronized by putting Briefcase on a floppy disk and using the disk to move Briefcase between computers. You can use this method to synchronize files between your work computer and your home computer or between your desktop and laptop computers. Although it's not as fast as synchronizing files between two connected computers, it works well if you are not working with a large number of files and don't have the means to physically connect the computers.

To synchronize files on two computers that are connected by cable or network or that use a floppy disk to transfer the Briefcase, follow these steps:

▶ **See** "Moving and Copying Files and Folders," **p. 105**

1. Copy the files and folders you want to use on both computers into Briefcase.

   The simplest way to copy the files to Briefcase is to drag and drop them on the My Briefcase icon on the desktop.

 T I P The fastest way to move the Briefcase is to right-click the My Briefcase icon, click <u>S</u>end To, and then click the floppy drive you want to move Briefcase to.

▶ **See** "Sharing Local Resources via Parallel or Serial Connection," **p. 196**

2. Move Briefcase to the computer on which you will be working with the Briefcase files. If your computer is not connected to the other computer, move Briefcase to a floppy disk.

   Once you move Briefcase, it will not be located on the original desktop. It can only be at one place at a time.

   The idea is to move, not copy, Briefcase onto the other computer, so that it exists in only one location. An easy way to move Briefcase is to select the My Briefcase icon with the mouse, drag it to the new location with the right mouse button, and choose <u>M</u>ove Here from the shortcut menu that appears.

3. If you are using a floppy disk, transfer the floppy disk to the other computer you want to work on.

4. Open and edit the files in Briefcase, as you normally would.

   If Briefcase is on a floppy disk and the other computer you are working on has Windows installed on it, you can transfer the files to the hard disk on that computer to speed up editing. Drag the files to the hard disk; and after you have edited them, drag the files back to Briefcase.

   If you are working on computers that are physically connected, open and edit the files from Briefcase. You can work on the files on your portable or laptop even when the portable is not connected to the desktop.

Part
II

Ch
4

CAUTION

If the other computer you are working on does not have Windows, you shouldn't transfer files to the hard disk. Open and edit them in the Briefcase on the floppy disk. Otherwise, you'll defeat the purpose of using Briefcase for keeping the files synchronized.

5. Once you are finished editing the files and you need to synchronize the files between the two computers, reconnect the computers if a cable or network connects them.

   If Briefcase was on a floppy disk, you can open Briefcase from the floppy disk or move Briefcase back to the desktop of the original computer. Then open Briefcase.

   Double-click the My Briefcase icon to open it (see fig. 4.29).

FIG. 4.29

Use Briefcase to keep files in different locations synchronized.

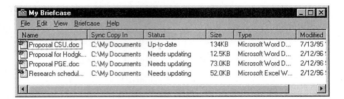

N O T E By default, My Briefcase displays files in the Details view. This view is much like the Details view in Explorer with two additional columns. The Sync Copy In column lists the location of the original file. The Status column indicates whether the file is up-to-date, or whether it's older or newer than the original. Like the other columns in the Detail view of a folder, you can sort the list by clicking the column headings.

6. Choose Briefcase, Update All.

   or

   Select only those files you want to update and choose Briefcase, Update Selection.

   The Update My Briefcase dialog box appears, as shown in figure 4.30.

7. Check the proposed update action for each file as it is synchronized with its corresponding file on the other computer.

   The default update action is to replace the older version of the file with the newer version. If you want to change the update action for a file, right-click the file name and change the action using the pop-up menu that appears (see fig. 4.31).

8. Click the Update button to update the files. (The computers must be connected for you to update the files.)

FIG. 4.30
All files that need to be updated are listed in the Update My Briefcase dialog box.

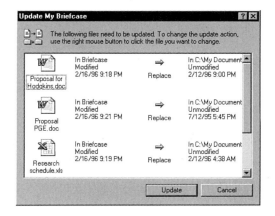

FIG. 4.31
Change the update action that will be applied to a file by right-clicking it and selecting the desired action.

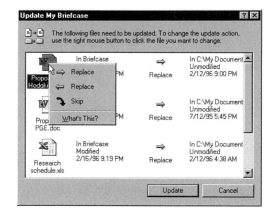

Part
II

Ch
4

Checking the Status of Briefcase Files

You can check the update status of the files in Briefcase at any time. To check the status of a file or folder in Briefcase, open My Briefcase by double-clicking it. Examine the Status column in the window.

If you have the Briefcase files displayed in a view other than Details, you won't see this Status column. To check the status, you can choose View, Details to switch to Details view. Or you can select the file to check and choose File, Properties; then click the Update Status tab (see fig. 4.32). The middle portion of the Update Status page shows the status of the file in the Briefcase on the left and that of the original file on the right. If the files are the same, Up to Date is indicated in the center. If the files are not the same, Replace is shown in the center along with an arrow. The arrow points to the file that is out-of-date and should be replaced.

FIG. 4.32
In this figure, the copy of Proposal PGE.Doc in C:\My Documents is newer than the copy in Briefcase, so Windows indicates that the copy in Briefcase should be replaced.

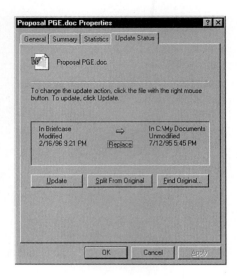

From within this Properties sheet, you can update the file (as described in the preceding section) by choosing Update. You also can prevent a file from being updated (which is discussed in the next section) by choosing Split From Original.

You can choose Find Original to open the folder with the original file, without having to work your way through the hierarchy of folders in Explorer or My Computer.

TROUBLESHOOTING

I modified the original of a file in My Briefcase, but the status still shows Up to Date. If you have Briefcase or the folder with the original open, the status may not be updated immediately. Choose View, Refresh both in My Briefcase and in the folder containing the original file. This ensures that the status indicates any recent changes.

Preventing a File from Synchronizing

You may want to break the connection between a file in Briefcase and its original file, so that when you issue the Update command, the two copies of the file are not synchronized. You may want to do this to preserve the original file or if the portable file is now a file that has changed into a document unrelated to the original.

To split a file from its original, follow these steps:

1. Open Briefcase and select the file you want to split.

2. Choose Briefcase, Split From Original.

   Notice that the file is now referred to as an orphan in the Status field of the Briefcase window.

You also can split a file by clicking the Split From Original button on the Update Status page of the Properties sheet.

Registering File Types Causing Documents to Open Applications

When you register a file type with Windows, you tell Windows that the file type has a certain MS-DOS extension and that a particular program should be used to open the file. The most useful reason for registering a file type is that you can then double-click any file of that type, and the file will be opened using the program you have instructed Windows to use.

 TIP If you want to open a file with a program other than the program it's associated with, hold down the Shift key and right-click the file. The context menu displays an Open With command. Choose this command to see a list of programs you can use to open the file.

N O T E If you learn how to create and edit your own file types, you can customize the context menu that appears when you right-click a file. ■

▶ **See** "Customizing the Shortcut (Right Click) Menu," **p. 375**

If you double-click a file and the file opens in a program, then the file is registered with that program. If Windows does not have a program associated with the file you double-clicked, the Open With dialog box shown in figure 4.33 opens.

To register the file type with a program, follow these steps:

1. Type a description of the file type in the Description edit box. The description displays under the Type column in Explorer for all files with this extension.

2. Scroll through the Choose the Program list to the program you want to open the file in and click the program. If the program is not shown in the list, click the Other button and select the program's EXE file from an Open dialog box.

Part
II

Ch
4

3. If you want to open other files of this type with the same program, check the Always Use This Program To Open This File check box.

4. Choose OK.

FIG. 4.33
Double-clicking an unassociated file type displays the Open With dialog box which prompts you for the program to run.

TROUBLESHOOTING

After double-clicking a file, it opens in a program other than the program I expected it to open in. You need to change the program this file type is registered with. To do this, open the Options dialog box from Explorer, select the File Type sheet, and edit the association for that file type. This process is described in the section, "Editing an Existing File Type," in Chapter 13.

Using Explorer with Shared Resources on a Network

If you are using Windows on a network, you can share resources with other users in your workgroup and use resources that other users have designated as shared. You can open the files in any folder that has been designated as shared by another user, and you can share any of your folders so that the files in that folder can be used by other users. You can use Explorer to designate resources on your computer as shared and to browse the shared resources in your workgroup or on your entire network.

▶ **See** "User-Level versus Share-Level Security," **p. 789**
▶ **See** "Sharing Network Drives," **p. 750**

Browsing Shared Folders

You browse a shared folder using Explorer in the same way you browse a folder on your computer.

To browse a shared folder, follow these steps:

1. Under Network Neighborhood in the left pane of Explorer, find the computer on your network where the folder you want to browse is located.

   If a plus sign appears next to the name of the computer, click the plus sign to display the shared resources on that computer (see fig. 4.34).

   Shared resources can include folders, entire drives, CD-ROM drives, and printers.

FIG. 4.34
View the shared resources on another user's computer in Explorer.

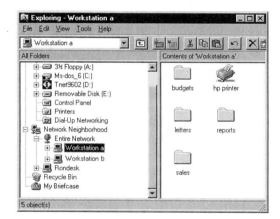

2. Select the shared folder to display its contents in the right pane of Explorer, as shown in figure 4.35.

FIG. 4.35
View the contents of a shared folder by selecting it in Explorer.

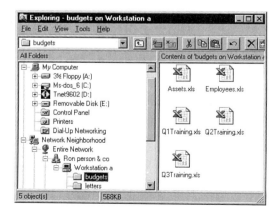

3. To open a shared file from Explorer, double-click the file name in the right pane.

   ▶ **See** "Sharing Network Drives" **p. 750**

Sharing Resources on Your Computer

You can designate any folder on your computer as shared. When you share a folder, you can assign a *share name* and *password* to that folder. You also can specify what type of access users have to the shared folder. Once you have shared a folder, other users have access to the files in that folder. The computers that have the folders you want to share must be on and logged into the network.

To share a folder, follow these steps:

1. In Explorer, select the folder you want to share.

2. Right-click the folder, and then click Sharing to display the Sharing page on the Properties sheet.

3. Select the Shared As option, as shown in figure 4.36.

FIG. 4.36
Designate a folder as shared on the Sharing page of the Properties sheet.

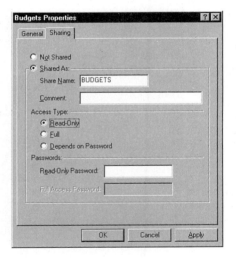

4. You can accept the default share name for the folder or type a new name in the Share Name text box.

5. Enter a comment in the Comment text box, if you want.

   The comment appears in the Details view of your computer when other users select it in Explorer or Network Neighborhood. Comments can help users locate shared information.

6. Select one of the Access Type options to specify the access for the shared resource.

You can grant users two levels of access to a shared folder. If you want users to be able to only read files and run programs in a folder, select the Read-Only option. If you want users to be able to read, modify, rename, move, delete, or create files and run your programs, select the Full option. If you want the level of access to depend on which password the user enters, select the Depends on Password option.

If you want to limit access to the files in the shared folder to certain users, assign a password to the folder and give the password to only those users. If you select the Depends on Password option, you need to enter two passwords—one for users who have read-only access to your files and one for users with full access. If you want all users to have access to your files, don't assign a password.

7. Click OK.

You can share an entire disk drive by selecting the drive and following the preceding steps.

You can quickly tell if you have designated a folder as shared by looking for a hand beneath its folder icon in Explorer or Network Neighborhood, as shown in figure 4.37.

FIG. 4.37

Shared folders are indicated by a hand beneath their folder icons in the Explorer.

shared folders ——

To change the properties of a shared folder, right-click the folder and change the share name, comment, access privileges, or password for the shared folder.

CAUTION

If the Sharing tab is not visible when you open the Properties sheet, you must enable file and printer sharing services.

▶ **See** "File and Printer Sharing for NetWare Networks," **p. 726**

▶ **See** "Sharing Network Drives," **p. 750**

▶ **See** "Mapping Network Drives," **p. 754**

▶ **See** "Creating Workgroups," **p. 786**

Part
II

Ch
4

Stop Sharing a Folder

To stop sharing a folder, follow these steps:

1. Select the folder you want to stop sharing.
2. Right-click the folder, and then click Sharing.
3. Select the Not Shared option and click OK.

Mapping a Network Drive

Windows has greatly simplified working with networks by listing all shared resources in Explorer and Network Neighborhood. You no longer have to map a drive to the shared folder. However, if you prefer to map a drive to a shared resource on another computer, you can still do it. The mapped drive appears under My Computer, just like any other drive. This makes it easy for you to access files on another computer, while making it obvious that the files are in a drive on the network.

To map a drive to a shared folder, follow these steps:

1. Select the shared folder you want to map in Explorer or Network Neighborhood.
2. Right-click the folder, and then click Map Network Drive. The Map Network Drive dialog box appears, as shown in figure 4.38.

FIG. 4.38
You can map a shared folder to a drive letter in the Map Network Drive dialog box.

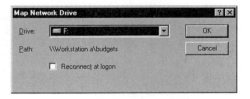

3. By default, Windows assigns the next available drive letter on your computer to the folder you select to map. To assign a different letter, click the drop-down arrow and select a letter from the list.
4. If you want to automatically reconnect to this shared folder at log on, select the Reconnect at Startup option.
5. Click OK.

To remove the mapping for a shared folder, click the Disconnect Network Drive button in Explorer or Network Neighborhood, select the network drive you want to disconnect, and click OK. Or select the drive in the left pane of Explorer, click the right mouse button, and then click Disconnect.

Finding a Computer on Your Network

If you know its name, you can quickly find a computer on your network by using the Find Computer command. To find a computer on your network, follow these steps:

1. Open the Start menu; then choose <u>F</u>ind, <u>C</u>omputer.

   or

   In Explorer, choose <u>T</u>ools, <u>F</u>ind, <u>C</u>omputer.

2. Enter the name of the computer you want to find in the <u>N</u>amed text box of the Find: Computer dialog box, as shown in figure 4.39.

FIG. 4.39
Find a computer on your network using Find, Computer.

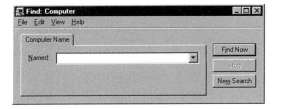

3. Click the F<u>i</u>nd Now button.

   The dialog box expands, listing the location of the specified computer if it is found on the network, as shown in figure 4.40.

FIG. 4.40
The location of the found computer is listed at the bottom of the Find: Computer dialog box.

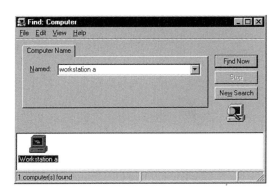

4. To open a browse window displaying the shared files and folders on the found computer, double-click the name of the computer at the bottom of the dialog box, or right-click the name and click <u>O</u>pen.

   ▶ **See** "Creating Workgroups," **p. 786**

Using Network Neighborhood to View Network Resources

When you install Windows and you are connected to a network, you see an icon for Network Neighborhood on your desktop. Open Network Neighborhood by double-clicking its icon on the desktop. The Network Neighborhood appears, as shown in figure 4.41.

FIG. 4.41

The Network Neighborhood window displays all the resources on your network.

To view the shared resources on a particular computer on your network, double-click the icon for the computer to open a new window. You can continue this process to open shared folders and view the contents. Many options discussed in the sections on using Explorer earlier in this chapter are also available in Network Neighborhood. You can, for example, change the way files are displayed; add or remove the toolbar; and move, copy, and delete files.

N O T E If you have file sharing enabled for your computer, it will appear in Network Neighborhood. However, you can't access your own computer from within Network Neighborhood. Use Explorer or My Computer to access your computer. ■

By default, each time you open a folder, a new window appears. This can result in a desktop full of windows and lots of confusion. If you prefer to have a single window open for browsing files, with the contents of that window changing as you open new folders, choose View, Options, click the Folder tab, select the Browse Folders by Using a Single Window option, and then click OK.

 When browsing folders using a separate window for each folder, you can hold the Ctrl key while double-clicking the subfolder and prevent a new window from opening. The original window becomes the subfolder. This can help to minimize desktop clutter.

Whether you use Explorer or Network Neighborhood to work with the files on your network depends on your style of working. Try them both and see which works best for you. ●

Configuring and Optimizing Windows 95

CHAPTER 5

Adding New Hardware to Windows 95

by Michael Desmond

Windows 95 brings a host of important capabilities to the desktop PC, but none more so than Plug and Play (PnP). Anyone who has stayed up all night or stayed in all weekend trying to get a new sound card to work will tell you that. PCs are built specifically for flexibility and upgrades, yet installing an adapter card can be a grueling exercise in futility.

Microsoft recruited the participation of companies like Intel, Compaq, Phoenix Technologies, and others to develop an industry standard for managing PC hardware and peripherals. Windows 95 Plug and Play enables PCs, peripherals, and the Windows 95 operating system to communicate with each other, allowing for automatic configuration of hardware.

Plug and Play can take the complexity out of hardware installations, but there is a catch—for Plug and Play to work to its full potential, the PC's motherboard, add-in cards, and operating system must all be Plug and Play compliant. But even if your hardware is not PnP-compliant, Windows 95 is able to make educated guesses about your PC's configuration to ease installations.

Installing Plug and Play hardware

Learn how to take full advantage of Windows 95's revolutionary Plug and Play technology.

Installing legacy (non-PnP) hardware

This guide to working with older hardware helps you avoid troublesome conflicts during installation.

Troubleshooting hardware installation

When things go wrong, this section helps you get out of trouble and back to work.

TROUBLESHOOTING

When I use the Add New Hardware Wizard, it fails to detect a device upgrade for an unsupported device. What am I doing wrong? If you have upgraded a sound card or other device that uses Windows 3.1 drivers, the new sound card may not be detected by the Add New Hardware Wizard. This occurs because Windows 95 is still seeing the reference to the older card's 16-bit drivers in the SYSTEM.INI file. To resolve the problem, you must go into SYSTEM.INI with a text editor such as NOTEPAD.EXE, and remove the lines referring to the 16-bit drivers. Run the Add New Hardware Wizard, and the new sound card or other device should be set up correctly.

This problem occurs because Windows 95 still looks into DOS/Windows 3.x configuration files to maintain compatibility with 16-bit applications. During setup, Windows 95 looks to CONFIG.SYS, AUTOEXEC.BAT, and SYSTEM.INI files to check for legacy drivers.

This chapter helps you understand how Plug and Play works—and more importantly, what to do when it doesn't. You learn how to use the Add New Hardware wizard and other tools to work with peripherals that are not Plug and Play compliant. You also learn how to handle conflicts. ■

Installing Plug and Play Hardware

Plug and Play can make adding peripherals easy for users of all levels of expertise. With the proper hardware, installing peripherals can be as simple as plugging in an add-in card and starting up the PC. This section guides you through the steps involved in setting up a Plug and Play device. You also learn how Plug and Play technology works.

How Windows 95 Plug and Play Works

Because it addresses so many components in the PC, Plug and Play is a complex technology. Plug and Play enables all parts of the PC to communicate with each other, from the low-level BIOS to the various add-in cards. When Windows 95 starts, the operating system and PC go through a series of steps to establish configurations, arbitrate conflicts, and record changes.

The Components of Plug and Play   To understand how Plug and Play works, you have to know what elements are involved. Four major technologies work together under Plug and Play:

- *System BIOS (basic input/output system).* The system BIOS is the low-level code that boots your system, detects the hard disk, and manages basic operations. Plug and

Play systems employ a specially-tuned BIOS that has the intelligence to detect hardware and manage configuration changes.

N O T E Under the Plug and Play specification, PnP BIOSes are identified as Plug and Play BIOS version 1.0a or later. To find out what BIOS version you have, look for the BIOS information on your monitor at the beginning of the boot up process. ▓

■ *Operating system.* The operating system interacts with the BIOS and hardware, playing a critical role in Plug and Play. Windows 95 is the first Plug and Play operating system, but Microsoft intends to bring the technology to Windows NT in the future.

■ *Hardware peripherals.* To be Plug and Play compliant, adapter cards and other hardware must include circuitry that stores configuration data and allows interaction with other PnP components. PCI add-in cards, by definition, are PnP-compliant, while ISA and EISA cards must be specifically designed for PnP. External peripherals like modems or printers can be PnP as well.

■ *Device drivers.* Drivers let your peripherals talk to Windows 95. Under Windows 95's Plug and Play, hardware must employ 32-bit *virtual device drivers* (called VxDs), as opposed to the 16-bit, real-mode drivers used under DOS/Windows 3.x.

N O T E The 32-bit VxDs for most devices are supplied by the hardware vendors. If the appropriate driver is not available on the Windows 95 CD-ROM or disks, contact your peripheral manufacturer to get the latest PnP-compliant drivers. ▓

Walking Through the PnP Process Each time you boot up the system a series of steps occurs that launches the Plug and Play process. All the hardware on the system is checked at boot time, so if new hardware has been installed, it will be detected and the appropriate steps taken by the PnP system.

The following list details the steps that Windows 95 goes through during system startup:

1. The system BIOS identifies the devices on the motherboard (including the type of bus), as well as external devices such as disk drives, keyboard, video display, and other adapter cards that are required for the boot process.

2. The system BIOS determines the resource (IRQ, DMA, I/O, and memory address) requirements of each boot device. The BIOS also determines which devices are legacy devices with fixed resource requirements, and which are PnP devices with flexible resource requirements. Notice that some devices don't require all four resource types.

N O T E   Microsoft uses the term *legacy device* to refer to older hardware peripherals that do not comply with the Plug and Play specification. As a general rule, any ISA card bought before 1995 is probably a legacy device. ▪

3. Windows 95 allocates the resources remaining after allowing for legacy resource assignments to each PnP device. If many legacy and PnP devices are in use, Windows 95 may require many iterations of the allocation process to eliminate all resource conflicts by changing the resource assignments of the PnP devices.

4. Windows 95 creates a final system configuration and stores the resource allocation data for this configuration in the registration database (the Registry).

5. Windows 95 searches the \Windows\System folder to find the required driver for the device. If the device driver is missing, a dialog box appears asking you to insert into drive A the manufacturer's floppy disk containing the driver software. Windows 95 loads the driver into memory and then completes its startup operations.

Notice that Windows 95 makes educated guesses about the identity and resource requirements of legacy devices. Windows 95 includes a large database of resource settings for legacy devices, allowing it to detect and configure itself to a variety of existing hardware. However, this detection is not perfect, and it forces dynamic PnP peripherals to be configured around the static settings of legacy hardware.

Understanding Plug and Play Hardware

Of course, Windows 95 Plug and Play works best on systems properly equipped to support it. This section helps you to determine if your existing PC is Plug and Play ready; and if not, what you can do to upgrade it. This section also can help you to determine whether a new system you plan to buy is PnP-compliant.

Determining Whether Your PC Supports Plug and Play   So is your PC Plug and Play? To make that claim, a system must have a BIOS that conforms to Plug and Play version 1.0a or later. Vendors generally began building Plug and Play into motherboards at the beginning of 1995, so older PCs probably won't support direct PnP features.

N O T E   Even if your BIOS is PnP-compliant, you won't have a true Plug and Play system until all the peripherals in your system are PnP, too. Remember, legacy devices force Windows 95 to make educated guesses about their requirements and their resources can't be dynamically allocated. ▪

How can you find out if your Windows 95 system is PnP-ready? Go to Windows 95's System Properties sheet and do the following:

1. Click the Device Manager tab of the System Properties sheet to display devices by type. (Click the View Devices by Type option button if necessary.)

2. Double-click the System Devices icon in the device list to expand the System Devices list.

3. If your PC supports Plug and Play, you see a Plug and Play BIOS entry (see fig. 5.1). The I/O Read Data Port for ISA Plug and Play Enumerator item appears regardless of whether your PC is Plug and Play.

FIG. 5.1
The System Properties sheet lets you explore Windows 95's hardware settings.

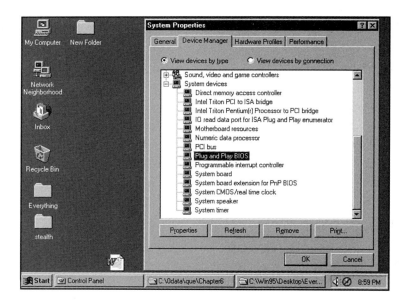

4. Double-click the Plug and Play BIOS icon to open the Properties sheet for the Plug and Play BIOS (see fig. 5.2).

5. Click the Driver tab to display the device driver (BIOS.VXD) that Windows 95 uses to connect to the PnP feature of your system BIOS (see fig. 5.3).

6. To leave the sheet, click OK, and then click OK on the System Properties sheet.

What does a Plug and Play BIOS do exactly? As the cornerstone of PnP functionality, the BIOS adds three major enhancements to conventional PC BIOS:

- *Resource management* handles the basic system resources—direct memory acces (DMA), interrupt requests (IRQs), input/output (I/0), and shared memory address ranges. Resource managment allows various devices to access limited system resources without causing conflicts. The Plug and Play BIOS resource manager configures boot devices on the motherboard and any PnP devices in the system.

FIG. 5.2
Check the System Devices list to determine whether your PC has Plug and Play BIOS.

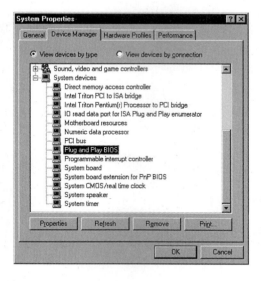

FIG. 5.3
Click the Driver tab to check the properties of Windows 95's Plug and Play BIOS device driver.

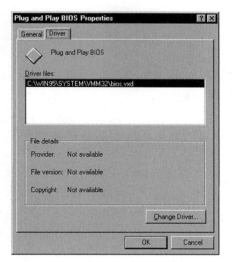

■ *Runtime management* of configuration is new to PCs. PnP BIOS includes the capability to reconfigure devices after the operating system loads. This feature is particularly important for notebook PCs that have PCMCIA (also known as the PC Card) devices that you can change at will. Previously, the operating system considered all devices detected by the BIOS to be static, which required restarting the system anytime a PC Card or other device was swapped out.

■ *Event management* detects when devices have been removed or added to the system while the computer is running. PnP BIOS 1.0a provides event management, such as detecting when your notebook PC is connected to a docking adapter. (Note that installing or removing desktop add-in cards while the PC is running is not a safe practice). Event management relies on runtime management to reconfigure the system.

CAUTION

Some brands of computers whose motherboards were produced in 1994 display messages during the boot process, indicating that the motherboard supports Plug and Play. Many of these motherboards, however, have early versions of the PnP BIOS that do not conform to the 1.0a specification. Even if your computer displays a PnP message during the boot process, check Device Manager for the Plug and Play BIOS entry to verify that you have PnP BIOS 1.0a.

Upgrading to Plug and Play   If you have an older 486 or Pentium PC, you may not be able to take advantage of Plug and Play. The problem is that the BIOS in these systems was written before there was a PnP standard to support. Still, you may be able to upgrade your PC to support PnP, so that future installations of PnP-compliant hardware go more smoothly.

Generally, there are three options for upgrading an older PC to a Plug and Play BIOS:

■ *Flash the BIOS*. This is an option for those systems with a Flash BIOS, a nonvolatile memory chip (NVRAM) that retains BIOS instructions when the power is turned off. Updating a Flash BIOS is as easy as running an upgrade utility from a floppy disk. The utility writes a newer BIOS to the NVRAM chip, effectively turning your PC into a PnP system. Contact your system vendor for an updated Flash BIOS.

■ *Replace the BIOS chip*. If your system is two years old or more, you probably don't have a Flash BIOS. But you may be able to replace the BIOS chip, which is often seated into a socket on the motherboard. You'll need to call your PC or motherboard vendor about a PnP BIOS upgrade kit, which lets you pull the existing BIOS chip(s) and plug in the replacement(s).

■ *Replace the motherboard*. This is the most radical (and expensive) approach, but it's the only solution if the BIOS chip is soldered directly onto the motherboard and is not Flash-upgradable. You need to make sure the new motherboard fits in your system's chassis, and accepts your existing add-in cards, memory, and processor.

N O T E   While a motherboard upgrade can update older BIOSes to Plug and Play, it may make more sense to wait and purchase a new system. A new PC comes with updated peripherals such as a larger hard drive and faster graphics board, which improve overall system performance. ■

Part
III

Ch
5

Purchasing a Plug and Play System   Owners of older PCs may have to do a little investigating to determine if their systems support Plug and Play, but new systems should be PnP-compliant right out of the box. Now that Microsoft has committed to bringing PnP to its other Windows operating system—Windows NT—the presence of PnP on Intel-compatible PCs becomes even more important.

Making sure you have a PnP-ready PC is not difficult. Generally, any machine that displays the "Designed for Windows 95" logo is PnP-compliant. Lacking that logo, look for the following:

- *Plug and Play BIOS 1.0a or later*. Also make sure that the system uses a Flash BIOS, because future updates to the PnP specification or other system architectures may require a BIOS upgrade.

- *PCI bus expansion slots*. Unlike ISA peripherals, all PCI cards are PnP-compliant. Even in non-PnP systems, PCI cards arbitrate configuration among themselves, and offer the further convenience of being software configurable. Also, the VESA Local Bus (VLB) standard is on the wane as Pentium systems replace 486s, which makes VLB peripherals harder to find.

You should also check if the ISA peripherals installed in the PC, such as sound boards or modems, are PnP-compliant. Remember, the presence of non-PnP, or legacy hardware in your system makes the task of hardware configuration more difficult and prone to failure. You should also check on the CD-ROM and fixed disks to ensure that they are also designed for the specification.

TROUBLESHOOTING

Why does my PCI graphics card show an IRQ conflict in the System Properties sheet? Under Plug and Play, PCI cards can share IRQs; however, Windows 95 does not support PCI cards that try to share IRQs with non-PCI devices. While Windows 95 display drivers do not require IRQ resources, PCI graphics cards request an IRQ in order to maintain full compatibility. As a result, all PCI graphics cards attempt to assign an IRQ. You must use Device Manager to assign a new IRQ setting to the device that is conflicting with the PCI graphics card.

Why does Device Manager show a resource conflict with a PCI-to-ISA bridge? There is no conflict here. If your Plug and Play BIOS reports both a PCI and an ISA bus, the Device Manager may report a conflict with that component. Users see an exclamation point in a yellow circle next to the PCI-to-ISA bridge entry in Device Manager. However, the PCI and ISA buses both work normally. There is no actual conflict. If you wish, you can contact your hardware vendor to see if an updated Plug and Play BIOS is available that will only report a PCI bus.

Installing Plug and Play Hardware

If you've been through a few nightmarish upgrades, you'll find installing a PnP adapter card into a PnP-compliant PC to be a refreshing experience. To install both a new card and its 32-bit VxD driver, do the following:

1. Turn off power to the PC.

2. Open the case and install the adapter card, following the instructions provided with the card.

3. Close the case and power up your PC.

4. Insert the driver software floppy disk in your A or B drive, if requested, and follow the steps for installing the driver software.

5. Restart Windows 95, if requested.

It's that easy. If the driver for your card is included with Windows 95, you may not need the card's floppy disk; Windows 95 automatically sets up the driver for your device. (Note that in this case, you may need to put the Windows 95 CD-ROM or requested floppy disk into the appropriate drive so the bundled VxD can be loaded.)

 TIP Windows 95 and your hardware may both provide a 32-bit VxD for your device. Compare the dates of the driver files using Explorer, and install the more recent file.

The same basic procedure applies for PnP-compatible external devices, such as printers, scanners, or external modems. If your PC has PnP-compliant serial and parallel ports, you will follow a procedure similar to the one in the preceding list. When you add or change a peripheral device, you don't need to open the PC, and in some cases (modems, for example), a new driver is not required.

▶ **See** "Using Your Laptop with a Docking System," **p. 192**

Part

III

Ch

5

Installing Legacy (non-PnP) Hardware

As a Plug and Play operating system, Windows 95 may eventually make even complex upgrades a simple manner of plugging in a card and booting to a new configuration. But the existence of millions of add-in cards and external peripherals with no PnP support means that that day is still sometime in the future. Understanding this, Microsoft has gone to great effort to ensure that non-PnP peripherals are adequately supported under the new regime.

The effort seems to have paid off. While installing legacy devices can still be tricky, the experience is simpler and less-hazardous than under 16-bit Windows 3.x. This section shows you how to install legacy devices.

How Windows 95 Operates with Legacy Hardware

Windows 95 cannot fully automate the configuration of legacy devices; however, it does interact with non-PnP devices to ease the process. Detection routines, for example, allow Windows 95 to recognize popular add-in cards such as Creative Labs Soundblaster boards, even though they lack PnP capability. The System Properties sheet, meanwhile, provides a one-stop shop for determining hardware conflicts, editing resource setting values, and optimizing performance. Finally, Windows 95's automated handling of PnP devices makes managing the remaining legacy hardware that much easier.

Almost all PC adapter cards require at least one interrupt request (IRQ) level and a set of I/O base memory addresses for communication with your PC's processor. Some cards require one or more DMA (Direct Memory Access) channels for high-speed communication with your PC's RAM. IRQ's, I/O memory, and DMA channels collectively are called *device resources*.

Legacy adapter cards use the following two methods for setting device resource values:

- *Mechanical jumpers* that create a short circuit between two pins of a multipin header. Jumpers are commonly used to designate resource values for sound cards, and they must be set to match the resource settings of Windows 95. If jumper settings do not match those set in Windows 95, the device will not operate.

- *Nonvolatile memory (NVM)* for storing resource assignments. Nonvolatile memory—such as electrically erasable, programmable read-only memory (EEPROM)—retains data when you turn off your PC's power. Network adapter cards and sound cards commonly use NVM. Usually, you must run a setup program for the card to match the board settings to those of the operating system.

N O T E   PCI adapter cards do not have jumpers or nonvolatile memory to designate resource values. Instead, the system BIOS and Windows 95 automatically allocate resources needed by PCI adapter cards during the boot process.

The following sections describe how Windows 95 deals with a variety of legacy adapter cards. Later chapters of this book describe in detail the installation process for specific device types, such as modems, CD-ROM drives, and sound cards.

▶ **See** "Installing a Plug and Play Modem," **p. 284**

▶ **See** "Installing Plug and Play CD-ROM Drives," **p. 319**

▶ **See** "Installing Legacy CD-ROM Drives," **p. 320**

Legacy Device Detection during Windows 95 Setup

When you run Windows 95's Setup program, Windows 95 attempts to detect all the hardware devices in your PC, including legacy devices such as ISA sound cards and network adapters. It then installs 32-bit protected mode drivers for peripherals for which updated drivers are available. However, Windows 95 often keeps references to real-mode (16-bit) device drivers in the CONFIG.SYS and AUTOEXEC.BAT files, which are used when the system runs DOS software in DOS-only mode.

If Windows can't identify the legacy device, you need to install the device manually. This procedure is described in "Installing Legacy Cards After Setting Up Drivers," later in this chapter.

Setting Resource Values for Legacy Adapter Cards

You must enter the IRQ, I/O base address, and DMA channel of a new adapter card to values that do not conflict with the resource values that are already assigned to system devices, PCI slots, or other legacy adapter cards. One of the problems with the basic design of IBM-compatible PCs is that only 16 interrupts are available, and the majority of these interrupts are likely to be in use. Therefore, your choice of IRQs is limited.

N O T E The word "base" in *I/O base address* refers to the location at which the block of I/O addresses for the adapter card begins. The actual number of address bytes occupied by the I/O system of the adapter card varies with the type of card. I/O addresses are separated by 16 bytes, and most adapter cards require fewer than 16 bytes of I/O address space. ■

Table 5.1 lists the PC's IRQs and most common use of each interrupt level.

Table 5.1 Interrupt Assignments and Options for ISA Cards Installed in 80 × 86-Based PCs

IRQ	Function	Most Common Use
0	Internal timer	Dedicated; not accessible
1	Keyboard	Dedicated; not accessible
2	Tied to IRQ9	Dedicated; see IRQ9

continues

Part
III

Ch

5

Table 5.1 Continued

IRQ	Function	Most Common Use
3	Second serial port	COM2 and COM4; usually assigned to a modem
4	First serial port	COM1 and COM3; usually for a serial mouse
5	Second parallel printer	Often used for bus mouse, network, and scanner cards
6	Floppy disk drives	Dedicated; do not use
7	First parallel printer	Used by some scanner cards; otherwise available
8	Time-of-day clock	Dedicated; not accessible
9	IRQ2 on 80 × 86 computers	IRQ2 is rerouted to IRQ9; often shown as IRQ2/9
10	Unassigned	Good choice for sound card, if offered
11	Unassigned	Not a common option; use if 12 is assigned
12	Usually unassigned	Sometimes dedicated to an IBM-style mouse port
13	80 × 87 coprocessor	Dedicated; do not use even if an 80×87 is installed
14	Fixed-disk drive	Dedicated; do not use
15	Usually unassigned	Used for secondary disk controller, if installed

Assigning IRQs is a real shell game, with many legacy devices being limited to just two or three specific IRQ numbers. In addition, many ISA boards won't support high IRQ numbers (any setting above IRQ9), which further limits your options.

 TIP When you install a new legacy device, you should assign it the highest IRQ number that it will support, leaving the lower IRQs for cards that don't support interrupts above IRQ9 or IRQ10. The Soundblaster 16 audio adapter card, for example, supports only IRQ2/9, IRQ5 (default), IRQ7, and IRQ10.

Virtually all PCs come with two serial port devices (COM1 and COM2) and one parallel port (LPT1) device. COM1 is usually occupied by the serial mouse, unless your PC has a separate IBM PS/2-compatible mouse port that requires an assignable interrupt. The default interrupt for the Soundblaster and most MPC-compatible audio adapter cards is IRQ5, the same setting preferred by many network adapters. Although IRQ7 is assigned to the second parallel printer (LPT2), few users have two printers, and printers seldom require an interrupt—so IRQ7 is a good candidate when space gets tight.

T I P   If you can't get sound on a networked PC, it may be that the network and sound cards are conflicting. IRQ5 is the preferred setting for both network adapters and sound cards, which makes this problem very common.

N O T E   Most legacy PC adapter cards use jumpers to set resource values. Cards that store resource settings in nonvolatile RAM require that you run their setup applications to set IRQ, I/O base address, and DMA channel (if applicable). If the setup program unavoidably installs real-mode drivers for the device, don't forget to disable the real-mode drivers by adding temporary REM prefixes before restarting Windows 95. See "Changing Resource Settings," later in this chapter. ▨

Installing Adapter Cards with Automatic Detection

The easiest way to install a new legacy card in a Windows 95 system is to use the Add New Hardware Wizard's automatic detection feature to identify your added card. The wizard is also capable of determining if you have removed a card. Auto-detection is best suited for PCs that have few or no specialty adapter cards, such as sound and video capture cards.

The following steps describe the automatic-detection process in installing a Creative Labs Sound Blaster AWE 32 card:

1. Set nonconflicting resource values for your new adapter card, using jumpers or the card's setup program.

2. Shut down Windows 95, and turn off the power on your PC.

3. Install the new adapter card in an empty ISA slot, and make any required external connections, such as audio inputs and speaker outputs for sound cards.

4. Turn the PC power on, and restart Windows 95.

5. Launch Control Panel, and double-click the Add New Hardware icon to start the Add New Hardware Wizard (see fig. 5.4).

6. Click Next. The Add New Hardware Wizard dialog box appears. You can choose manual or automatic hardware detection and installation. Accept the default Yes (Recommended) option (see fig. 5.5).

7. Click Next to display the wizard's boilerplate (see fig. 5.6).

8. Click Next to start the detection process (see fig. 5.7).

   After a few minutes of intense disk activity, often interspersed with periods of seeming inactivity, the wizard advises you that detection is complete (see fig. 5.8).

Part

III

Ch

5

FIG. 5.4

The Add New Hardware Wizard provides a step-by-step guide to installing new devices into your PC.

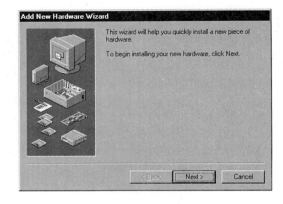

FIG. 5.5

The Add New Hardware routine lets you choose between automatic or manual hardware detection. Be warned that automatic selection can take a while, particularly on slower machines.

FIG. 5.6

The wizard warns you that detecting installed hardware is not without its perils.

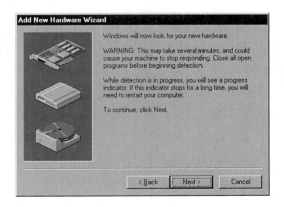

FIG. 5.7
The wizard detection-progress dialog box tells you when detection is complete.

FIG. 5.8
The wizard has finally finished the detection process.

Part
III

Ch
5

9. Click <u>D</u>etails to display what the wizard detected. Figure 5.9 shows that the Sound Blaster AWE-32 was detected.

   If the wizard does not detect your newly installed card, you must install the card manually. Click Cancel to terminate the automatic detection process.

10. Click Finish to install the required drivers from the Windows 95 CD-ROM or floppy disks. The message box shown in figure 5.10 indicates the expec'   ^dium, in this case, the Windows 95 CD-ROM.

11. Insert the Windows 95 CD-ROM into the drive, and click OK '

12. If Windows 95 can't find the required device driver file in th
    will be prompted to browse for the necessary files.

13. When driver installation is complete, a message box adv'
    settings have changed and asks whether you want to r
    Restart Now so that your driver change takes effect.

FIG. 5.9
The wizard detected the new
Sound Blaster AWE 32
sound card.

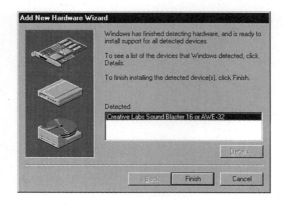

FIG. 5.10
If the driver software isn't
available on your hard drive,
Windows 95 prompts you to
install the media that
contains the drivers.

Installing Legacy Cards After Setting Up Drivers

The alternative to automatic device detection is to install the new adapter card *after* you install its driver software. The advantage to this method is that you can determine in advance resource settings that don't conflict with existing devices.

The following steps describe the process of reinstalling the drivers for the Sound Blaster 32-AWE card:

1. Launch the Add New Hardware Wizard from Control Panel, and click Next in the opening dialog box to display the Add New Hardware Wizard dialog box. Here you choose between manual and automatic hardware detection and installation (refer to fig. 5.5).

2. Choose the No option to select manual installation; then click Next to display the wizard's Hardware Types dialog box (see fig. 5.11).

3. Select the card type in the Hardware Types list; then click Next to display the Manufacturers and Models dialog box (see fig. 5.12).

4. Make the appropriate selections in the Manufacturers and Models list boxes; then click Next to display the default settings for the new device.

FIG. 5.11

The Add New Hardware Wizard's Hardware Types dialog box lists a variety of adapter card categories.

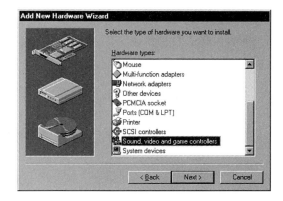

FIG. 5.12

The Wizard dialog box lists manufacturers and models of devices for whose drivers are included with Windows 95.

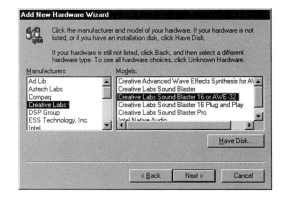

N O T E If you don't see the manufacturer or model in the list boxes, you need a floppy disk or CD-ROM that contains Windows 95 drivers for your device (Windows 3.1 or later drivers won't work). If you have the required Windows 95 drivers, click Have Disk to install the drivers from floppy disk or CD-ROM. If you don't have Windows 95 drivers, click Cancel to terminate the installation. ▨

5. Windows 95 can't determine what resource value settings you made for your new or replacement adapter card, so the default settings for the device appear in the wizard's Resource Settings dialog box (see fig. 5.13). You should write down or print these default settings.

FIG. 5.13

Default values for the Sound Blaster AWE-32 card appear when you open the Resource Setting dialog box.

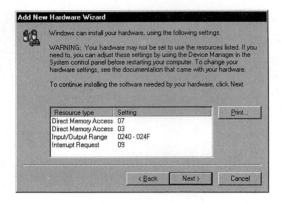

6. Click Next to display the System Settings Change message box (see fig. 5.14).

   If the default settings in the preceding step correspond to the resource settings of your card, click Yes to shut down Windows 95. If you haven't installed the card (which is the normal situation for manual device detection), turn off the power to your PC, install the card, turn the power back on, and restart Windows 95 with the new card activated.

   If any of the resource values in the preceding step are incorrect, or you receive a "resource conflict" message, click No in the System Settings Change message box so that you can alter the resource values as necessary.

FIG. 5.14

The System Settings Change message box gives you the option to restart Windows 95.

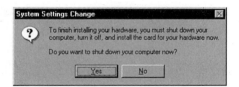

7. Open Control Panel's System Properties sheet, click the Device Manager tab, and expand the entries for the type of device that you're installing. Exclamation points superimposed on the device's icon(s) indicate that the device is not yet fully installed or has been removed from your PC.

8. If you're replacing a card, entries for both cards appear in the Device Manager list. To remove the old entry, select the entry and click Remove. A message box requests that you confirm the removal process (see fig. 5.15).

9. Double-click the entry for the new adapter card to display the Properties sheet for the device.

FIG. 5.15
Windows 95 asks for
confirmation before you
remove a device from the
Device Manager.

10. In the Resource Settings list box, select the resource whose value you want to change; then click the Change Settings button to display the Edit Interrupt Request dialog box for the resource.

11. Use the spin buttons of the Value text box to select the value that corresponds to the preset value for your adapter card. If a conflict with the existing card occurs, the card that has the conflicting value is identified in the Conflict Information text box (see fig. 5.16).

FIG. 5.16
Change the IRQ setting for
the new adapter card to
avoid a conflict.

12. Change the Value setting to a value that displays No Devices are Conflicting in the Conflict Information box; then make the corresponding change in the card, using the jumpers or nonvolatile RAM. (Turn off power to your PC before making jumper changes.) Figure 5.17 shows an I/O base address setting changed to remove a conflict at Input/Output Range 0260-026F.

13. After making all the changes necessary to remove resource conflicts, click OK to close the resource's Edit Input/Output Range dialog box, and then click OK to close the Properties page for the specific device.

14. Click OK to close the System Properties sheet.

15. Shut down and restart Windows 95 so that your new settings take effect.

FIG. 5.17
Change the I/O base address (Input/Output Range) to a nonconflicting value.

The process of manually installing a legacy device, described in the preceding steps, appears to be complex, but it is a much more foolproof method than the one used by Windows 3.x. For example, the ability to detect potential resource conflicts before the new setting is locked in helps eliminate many problems associated with installing new devices under Windows 3.x.

N O T E Windows 95 includes drivers for an extraordinary number of popular devices but not for low-volume products, such as digital video capture and MPEG-1 playback cards. Most manufacturers of specialty legacy devices should provide 32-bit protected-mode drivers for Windows 95. You can find updated Windows 95 drivers on manufacturer's forums on CompuServe, America Online, and The Microsoft Network, as well as on World Wide Web sites. ■

Removing Unneeded Drivers for Legacy Devices

If you remove a legacy device from your PC and don't intend to reinstall it, it's good Windows 95 housekeeping to remove the driver for the device from the Device Manager list. Follow these steps to remove the Device Manager entry for permanently removed adapter cards:

1. Double-click Control Panel's System icon to open the System Properties sheet.
2. Click the Device Manager tab and double-click the icon for the hardware type of the device removed to display the list of installed devices. An exclamation point super-imposed on a device icon indicates a removed or inoperable device.
3. Click the list item to select the device you want to remove and then click Remove.

4. Confirm that you want to remove the device by clicking OK in the Confirm Device Removal message box.

If you have more than one hardware configuration, a modified version of the Confirm Device Removal message box appears. Make sure the Remove from All Configurations option button is selected; then click OK to remove the device and close the message box.

Troubleshooting Hardware Installation

Windows 95 is clearly superior to Windows 3.x when it comes to installing and managing hardware, but it is not perfect. The peaceful coexistence that Windows 95 tries to foster between PnP and legacy devices can break down into bitter conflict, particularly when new legacy hardware is being installed. But Windows 95 does provide a wealth of tools for managing these conflicts when they occur. This section helps you troubleshoot hardware installation problems under Windows 95, with tips for using the Device Manager and other tools.

Understanding the Device Manager

The Device Manager displays all the system components in hierarchical format, allowing you to dig down to individual devices and sub-systems. In essence, the Device Manager is the user interface for the Windows 95 Registry. But unlike working in the Registry, the Device Manager is designed to avoid the kind of catastrophic crashes that making changes in the Registry can cause.

The Device Manager gives you quick access to hardware configurations for virtually all the devices in your PC. To open the Device Manager, double-click the System icon in Control Panel and click on the Device Manager tab. You will see a list of items, some with a plus (+) sign to the left. This plus sign indicates that more detailed device information is available. Selecting the plus sign expands the display to show any listings below that item.

The Device Manager displays hardware information from two separate perspectives, by device type and by device connection. By default, Device Manager opens with the View Devices by Type radio button selected (see fig. 5.18). In this mode, similar devices are grouped under a single item, such as the entry under Ports (COM & LPT). Clicking the View Devices by Connection radio button shows the same information, but now most of the devices appear under the Plug and Play BIOS item (see fig. 5.19).

FIG. 5.18
The Device Manager provides two views of the devices installed in the PC.

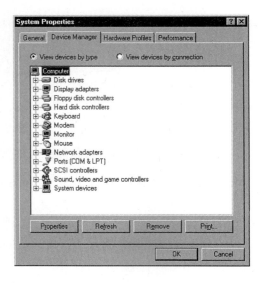

FIG. 5.19
The second radio button lets you view components by their physical connections in the system.

To access the configuration for a sound card, do the following:

1. Go to the Device Manager page of the System Properties sheet.
2. Click the plus (+) sign found next to the Sound, Video, and Game Controllers item.
3. Click the specific sound hardware item that appears on the sheet.
4. Click the Properties button to display the tabbed properties sheet for the sound hardware device.

Changing Resource Settings

After you are at the General page of a device's properties sheet, you can access the IRQ, I/O address, and DMA resource settings by clicking on the Resources tab. Here you see the resources that are currently assigned to that device. Any conflicts are indicated with an asterisk next to the resource having a problem.

To change the resource settings for a device, do the following:

1. In the Resource settings box, click on the resource item you want to view or edit.
2. Uncheck the Use Automatic Settings check box (see fig. 5.20).

FIG. 5.20

Before you can make changes to device settings, you must disable the Use Automatic Settings item.

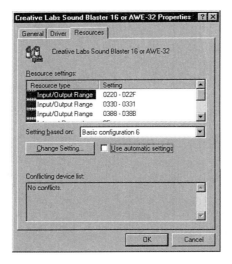

3. Click the enabled Change Setting button.
4. In the Resource Edit dialog box, click on the spinner buttons to switch among system resources.

N O T E Device Manager shows all the resources, indicating those that are already in use by another peripheral. Be sure you don't create a conflict by assigning a resource to a device that is already being used by another device. ▪

You can get an effective roster of system settings by double-clicking on the Computer icon at the top of the Device Manager tree. Doing so brings up the Computer Properties sheet, which features two tabs—View Resources and Reserve Resources (see fig. 5.21).

Part
III

Ch
5

TROUBLESHOOTING

Why do I get a "resource conflict" message when I install a Plug and Play adapter card?
Most PC adapter cards require at least one I/O base address and one or more interrupts.
("Setting Resource Values for Legacy Adapter Cards" describes I/O base addresses and
interrupts.) Most adapter cards support only a few of the available I/O base addresses and
interrupts. If you already have several legacy adapter cards in your PC, you may have a situation
where the I/O base addresses or, more likely, the interrupts supported by the new card are
occupied by existing legacy cards. In this case, you need to change the settings of one or more
of your legacy cards to free the required resource(s) for use by your new card.

The worst-case condition occurs in PCI bus PCs where all of the available interrupts are assigned
before you install the new card. (In many PCI-bus PCs, PCI slots consume one interrupt each,
whether the slot is in use.) The only solution in this instance is to free an interrupt by reconfiguring
your PC's system BIOS to reassign an interrupt from an unused PCI slot. Obviously, this action will
disable that slot, rendering it useless. If your system BIOS does not permit reconfiguration, you
must remove an existing adapter card to free an interrupt.

FIG. 5.21
The Computer Properties
sheet provides a bird's eye
view of your system resource
status.

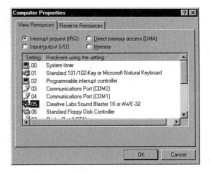

The View Resources tab displays these four radio buttons that cause the page to display
the status of key system resources:

- Interrupt Request (IRQs)
- Input/Output (I/O)
- Direct Memory Address (DMA)
- Memory

Clicking the radio button brings up a scroll down list of occupied settings, and the device
which is using it.

N O T E The View Resources page of the Computer Properties sheet is an excellent place to get an overview of your system's resource status. ▨

The Reserve Resources page lets you view any resources that have been excluded from use by hardware devices (see fig. 5.22). You also can use this page to reserve resources. For example, follow these steps to reserve IRQ12 (some older BIOSes won't recognize an IRQ12 device unless it is a PS/2 mouse):

FIG. 5.22
The Reserve Resources page lets you set aside key resource settings to avoid conflicts.

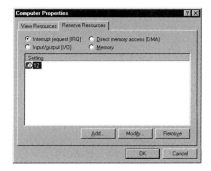

 TROUBLESHOOTING

Why does my system hang during shutdown? This problem can occur when a system BIOS expects a PS/2-style mouse port to occupy IRQ12, but a software-configured PnP adapter occupies it instead. You need to change the software-configurable device in Device Manager to another IRQ number. You might also consider reserving IRQ12 in Device Manager, so Plug and Play does not later assign a device to that resource. Also consider getting a BIOS upgrade that allows you to make full use of IRQ12.

Part
III

Ch
5

1. Click the Reserve Resources tab.
2. Click the Interrupt Request (IRQ) radio button.
3. Click Add to bring up the Edit Resource Setting dialog box (see fig. 5.23).

FIG. 5.23
Set the resource to reserve in the Edit Resource Setting dialog box.

4. Use the spinner controls to select the IRQ you want to change.

5. Click OK to change the settings.

6. If a device is currently logged into the IRQ being reserved, the Resource Conflict Warning dialog box will apprise you of the possible problem and ask for confirmation (see fig. 5.24).

FIG. 5.24

If Windows 95 detects a device already using the resource being reserved, it will warn you and ask for confirmation.

Checking for Resource Conflicts with the Device Manager

The Device Manager is an excellent tool for resolving hardware resource conflicts, allowing you to see if any devices are experiencing a conflict. Device Manager displays an exclamation point or a strikethrough symbol through the icon of any item with a conflict, allowing you to quickly zero in on problems. The symbols indicate different situations:

- *Exclamation point inside a yellow circle.* Indicates a device that is experiencing a direct conflict with another device.

- *Red X symbol.* Indicates a device that is disabled, either due to a conflict or by user selection.

Hardware Problems with the Registry Editor

If you have a problem that changing resources won't solve, the card supplier's product-support staff will need additional information about your system. The primary source of system information in Windows 95 is the Registry. All device information that appears in the Device Manager is obtained from entries in the Registry.

> **CAUTION**
>
> Viruses can cause Windows 95 to report hardware conflicts. You should sweep your system for viruses regularly, and particularly when you encounter unexpected problems.

N O T E   You should be able to manage most hardware problems without resorting to editing
the Registry. Windows 95's Device Manager provides tools for managing hardware
conflicts.

To examine the Registry, you need to set up and use the Registry Editor (REGEDIT.EXE)
application. REGEDIT is not a Start menu choice because Microsoft did not intend all
users to access its settings directly. Entering incorrect settings into REGEDIT can cause
the system to fail to boot up.

1. Open the Start menu, and choose Run.

2. Type **regedit** to open the Registry Editor.

3. Choose Find, Edit to open the Find dialog box.

4. In the Find What text box, type the keyword for the card in question; then click the
   Find Next button to locate the first instance of the keyword.

   The support person usually gives you the keyword on which to search. The phrase
   sound blaster, for example, finds all references to Sound Blaster hardware in the
   Registry.

5. The first or second instance of the keyword is likely to display the Plug and Play
   device assignment data for the card. Press F3 to find the successive instances of the
   keyword.

   Figure 5.25 shows the PnP device data for the Sound Blaster 16 card.

6. Pressing F3 should turn up additional instances of Registry entries for the device in
   question. Figure 5.26 shows the Registry entry that defines the driver for the Line
   Input device of the Sound Blaster 16, SB16SND.DRV.

Part
III

Ch
5

FIG. 5.25
The Windows 95 Registry
Editor displays Plug and Play
device assignment values for
a Sound Blaster 16 card.

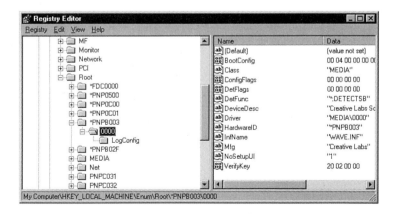

FIG. 5.26
Continued searching in
RegEdit displays the settings
of the driver for the Line
Input device of the Sound
Blaster 16 card.

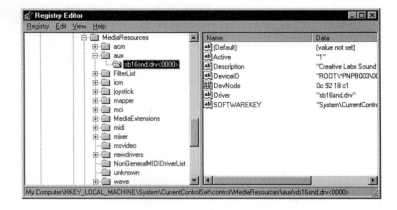

CAUTION

Using the Windows 95 Registry can be dangerous. If you enter an improper value, it can disable key system components, and even prevent your system from rebooting altogether.

Unfortunately, it is not possible to cover all the various things that can go wrong during hardware installation under Windows 95. Many problems are the result of interactions between specific types of hardware. If you discover a problem with hardware you are installing, you should seek guidance from the vendor, since they should know about potential driver updates and other fixes that can help resolve the problem.

TROUBLESHOOTING

I can't get my second IDE drive to appear in My Computer or Explorer. Most PCs with recent system BIOS automatically detect an additional drive connected to the primary IDE controller as a primary slave drive. If you have an older BIOS, you need to use the PC's BIOS setup application to specify the type of drive installed (number of cylinders, number of heads, landing zone, and other drive parameters). If you connect a third drive to a PC with a recent BIOS, you need to enable the secondary IDE controller in the BIOS setup program so BIOS can recognize the drive. IDE CD-ROM drives connected to sound cards usually can be installed as secondary, tertiary, or quaternary IDE drives. Use the default (secondary) setting for an IDE CD-ROM if you don't have a secondary IDE controller in your PC; if your PC has a secondary IDE controller, use the tertiary I/O base address and interrupt for the CD-ROM.

CHAPTER 6

Configuring Windows 95 for Notebook Users

by Jim Boyce and Doug Kilarski with Ron Person

Many business professionals want to be able to take their office with them. Portable technology and Windows 95 make a hard-to-beat combination. Portable computers enable you to work nearly anywhere, and Windows 95's features for portable computing—which include 32-bit support for PC Card (PCMCIA) devices, file synchronization, Dial-Up Networking, remote mail, and more—make Windows 95 a perfect operating system for your portable computer. Not only does Windows 95 make it easy for you to take your work with you, but features such as Dial-Up Networking and remote mail enable you to keep in touch with coworkers and access disk and printer resources in your main office from anywhere in the world.

Laptop computers and changing hardware configurations

Learn how laptops can now automatically reconfigure themselves when inserted in docking stations.

Direct Cable Connection and infrared communication

Moving files between notebook computers and other computers is now easier.

Use Dial-Up Networking to connect your laptop to a network

Laptops become even more flexible when you access corporate data while in the field or at home.

Synchronize files between laptop and desktop with the Briefcase

Taking files off your desktop or network presents a problem when you return files that have been changed. This brief section outlines the advantages to using the Briefcase.

Windows 95 responds to the demands of mobile users. PC Card, Plug and Play, disk compression, power management, and support for port replicators and docking stations all complement portable computer hardware. Windows 95 architectural enhancements conserve battery power and manage configuration changes, which helps extend the life of older portables. Dial-Up Networking enables you to access your office file server(s) using your modem and send and receive e-mail to coworkers. Windows 95 keeps users organized as well. Using an advanced file synchronization system called Briefcase and a deferred printing option, roaming users remain "in-sync" with their desktop environments (and vice versa). ■

Using PC Card Devices

Many notebook computers contain one or two special bus slots called *PC Card slots* (formerly called PCMCIA slots) that accommodate credit card-sized adapters for various functions. Although initially only flash memory cards were available in PCMCIA format, today many types of devices—including modems, hard disks, network cards, sound cards, and other devices—are available in PC Card/PCMCIA format. In addition, PC Card docking stations enable you to use PC Card devices in desktop computers, making it possible, for example, to use the same PC Card modem in a notebook and a desktop computer.

N O T E There are three official types of PC Card slots, referred to as Type I, Type II, and Type III. The specification for a fourth type of slot—Type IV—is being finalized by the PCMCIA organization (Personal Computer Memory Card International Association). One of the primary differences between the types of PC Card slots is that each higher-numbered slot accommodates a thicker PC Card than the previous slot. PC Card hard disks, for example, generally require a Type III slot, but modems can be installed in a Type I or Type II slot. Most of today's newer notebook computers can accommodate one Type III device, or two Type II devices (or any combination of two Type I and Type II devices). ■

The primary advantage of PC Card devices for portable computer users is that these devices make it possible to expand the capabilities of portable computers in the same way you can expand desktop systems, enabling you to add optional hardware to the portable computer. Windows 95 improves on the PCMCIA support in DOS and Windows 3.x by providing 32-bit device drivers to support the PC Card controllers in most computers. This makes it possible for Windows 95 to support a wide variety of PC Card devices without requiring 16-bit, real-mode drivers that slow down the system and use conventional memory.

Another improvement for PC Card devices in Windows 95 is expanded support for *hot swapping,* which is the ability to remove and insert PC Card devices in the computer without powering down the computer. If you need to temporarily remove your hard disk card to use a modem, for example, you first use the PC Card object in the Control Panel to turn off the hard disk card (see fig. 6.1). Then, you remove the hard disk card from its slot and insert the modem. Windows 95 disables the hard disk driver(s) temporarily and enables the modem drivers.

▶ **See** "Installing Plug and Play Hardware," **p. 158**

FIG. 6.1
Use the PC Card (PCMCIA) Properties sheet to enable and disable PCMCIA devices.

Installing PC Card Support

Each computer with PC Card slots or a PC Card docking station includes a PC Card controller that enables the CPU to communicate with the PC Card bus. This controller requires a set of drivers that enable the operating system (in this case, Windows 95) to communicate using the PC Card bus. In addition, each PC Card device requires a device-specific driver that enables the device to function and communicate with the operating system. If you are using a PC Card network card, for example, Windows 95 requires a set of drivers for the PC Card slot itself and a separate driver for the network card.

When you install Windows 95, Setup automatically detects your computer's PC Card controller and installs support for it. Setup does not, however, enable the 32-bit PC Card controller drivers. Setup takes this approach because some portable computers require that you continue to use 16-bit drivers (which come with the portable computer) to control the PC Card slots.

Part
III

Ch

6

N O T E   Windows 95 supports 32-bit drivers for systems based on either an Intel PCIC-compatible PC Card controller or Databook PC Card controller. ▩

In addition to enabling 32-bit PC Card support (if your computer supports it), you must install the drivers for the PC Card devices you'll be using. In many cases, Windows 95 can install these devices automatically using Plug and Play, even on systems without a Plug and Play BIOS. To install a PC Card modem, for example, simply insert the modem in its slot. Windows 95 detects the new device and starts the Add New Modem Wizard to install the modem driver.

Enabling 32-Bit PC Card Support   After you install Windows 95, you must use the PC Card object in the Control Panel to enable 32-bit support for your PC Card controller. Enabling 32-bit support provides better overall system performance and more effective memory use. In addition, enabling 32-bit PC Card support is required to support Plug and Play installation of PC Card devices and hot-swapping.

N O T E   When Windows 95 enables 32-bit PC Card support, your existing 16-bit real-mode PC Card drivers are disabled. If you are installing Windows 95 from a network server, you must have local access to the Windows 95 source (cabinet) files. Therefore, you must have a set of Windows 95 floppy disks or have a CD-ROM connected to your portable PC to enable Windows 95 to read the 32-bit driver files for the PC Card controller. Optionally, you can copy the Windows 95 cabinet files from the network server to your portable computer's hard disk prior to enabling 32-bit support. ▩

To enable 32-bit PC Card support for your computer, follow these steps:

1. Verify that you have local access to the Windows 95 cabinet files, as explained in the previous note.
2. Open the Start menu and choose Settings, Control Panel.
3. Double-click the PC Card (PCMCIA) program icon. The first time you open this object, the PC Card (PCMCIA) Wizard appears (see fig. 6.2).
4. Choose No and then Next to inform the Wizard that you are not setting up Windows 95 from a network server.
5. If the PC Card Wizard detects existing real-mode PC Card drivers, it displays the dialog box shown in figure 6.3, enabling you to view the drivers and control the way the Wizard handles the existing drivers. If you want the Wizard to automatically remove the drivers, choose the No option button and then choose Next. If you want to view and verify the deletion of the existing real-mode PC Card drivers, choose Yes and then choose Next.

FIG. 6.2

The opening dialog box of the PC Card (PCMCIA) Wizard checks to see whether you are using a PC Card to install new PC Card drivers.

FIG. 6.3

To verify your drivers, choose Yes.

6. If you select Yes, the Wizard displays a set of dialog boxes that show the device entries in CONFIG.SYS, AUTOEXEC.BAT, and SYSTEM.INI that it will delete (see fig. 6.4). If you do not want the Wizard to delete a specific driver from one of these files, deselect the line in the appropriate dialog box, and then choose Next.

7. After the PC Card Wizard removes the real-mode drivers (if any) as directed by you, it displays a final dialog box that prompts you to choose Finish to complete the PC Card setup process and enable 32-bit PC Card support. Choose the Finish button to complete the process. Windows 95 shuts down your computer so the change takes effect.

Installing PC Card Devices After you enable 32-bit PC Card support, Windows 95 can typically install PC Card devices automatically. If you insert a network card in the computer, for example, Windows 95 detects the new card and automatically installs the necessary drivers for the card. If, for some reason, Windows 95 does not automatically recognize your PC Card device, you must manually install support for it.

Part
III

Ch
6

FIG. 6.4

The PC Card (PCMCIA) Wizard enables you to verify real-mode driver deletion.

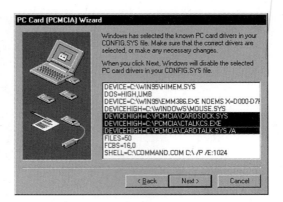

To manually install a PC Card device other than a modem or network adapter, use the following procedure:

1. Insert the new PC Card device in the appropriate slot. (Check the PC Card device's manual to determine if the device must be installed in a specific slot.)

N O T E   If you are installing a PC Card network adapter, use the Network object in the Control Panel to install it. If you are installing a PC Card modem, use the Modems object in the Control Panel. ■

2. Open the Control Panel and double-click the Add New Hardware program icon to start the Add New Hardware Wizard. Then choose Next.

3. Choose Yes and then Next to enable the Wizard to automatically detect your new PC Card device.

4. If the Wizard is unable to detect the new device, the Wizard displays a hardware selection dialog box similar to the one shown in figure 6.5. Choose the type of device you are installing and then choose Next.

FIG. 6.5

Choose the type of device you are installing and then choose Next.

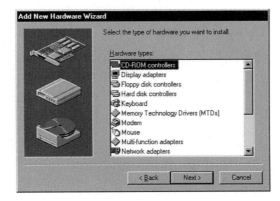

5. From the <u>M</u>anufacturers list, choose the manufacturer of the device you are installing. Then from the Mo<u>d</u>els list, choose the device model. If your manufacturer or model is not listed and you have a driver disk for the device, choose <u>H</u>ave Disk and then follow the prompts to direct the Wizard to the directory on the floppy disk where the necessary files are located.

6. After you have selected the correct manufacturer and model, choose OK to complete the setup process.

   ▶ **See** "Installing a Plug and Play Modem," **p. 284**

   ▶ **See** "Installing a Network Adapter," **p. 691**

Hot-Swapping PC Cards

Windows 95 enables you to remove a PC Card device and replace it with another without powering down the system. This capability enables you to quickly swap PC Card devices. Before you remove a device, however, you should first shut it down. To do so, choose the PC Card object in the Control Panel. Windows 95 displays a PC Card (PCMCIA) Properties sheet similar to the one shown in figure 6.6, which displays information about the computer's PC Card slots and any currently inserted devices.

FIG. 6.6
You can view information about slots and installed devices in the PC Card Properties sheet.

To remove a PC Card device from the system, first select the device from the list on the Socket Status tab and then choose <u>S</u>top. Windows 95 shuts down the device and temporarily disables its drivers (the socket is listed as empty). You then can remove the PC Card device.

Insert the new device in the proper slot. If you have previously installed support for the device, Windows 95 detects the device and automatically enables its drivers. If you have not used the device in the computer previously, Windows 95 detects the new hardware and automatically installs support for the device.

TROUBLESHOOTING

The System Agent reports the ScanDisk error message, Check was stopped because of an error, but the ScanDisk log file does not show an error. This occurs if you created a ScanDisk with a PC Card or docking station disk drive and later removed that drive. To resolve that problem, delete the existing ScanDisk task and schedule separate new ScanDisk tasks for permanent and removable drives.

Using Your Laptop with a Docking System

With Windows 95, *hot-docking support* integrates hardware and software for quick and easy docking between a laptop computer and its desktop docking station. Docking and undocking can occur when the power is on or off. Windows 95 automatically detects any configuration changes and manages any conflicts or file disruptions. It also loads and unloads hardware drivers as required. To undock your computer when Windows 95 is running, open the Start menu and choose Eject PC. Windows 95 reconfigures the system automatically for the undocked configuration and then prompts you to remove the computer from the docking station.

> **CAUTION**
>
> Not all docking stations support hot-docking with a laptop. Even if your laptop supports PC Cards and Plug and Play, check the laptop and docking station manuals before inserting a laptop into a docking station with the power on.

Creating and Modifying Hardware Profiles

Windows 95 enables you to create multiple hardware profiles to accommodate different hardware configurations, such as when your computer is docked and when it is undocked. Windows 95 automatically creates two hardware profiles for your computer—one for the docked configuration and one for the undocked configuration. Windows 95 detects which profile is required at startup and automatically uses the correct one.

N O T E   If your portable computer contains a Plug and Play BIOS, Windows 95 does not have to use multiple hardware profiles to accommodate hot docking. Instead, the Plug and Play BIOS can detect which devices are available and Windows 95 can configure the system accordingly. ■

If you want to change an existing profile or create a new one, you can do so through the Control Panel. Use the following procedure to create a new hardware profile:

1. Open the Start menu and choose Settings, Control Panel.
2. Double-click the System program icon to display the System Properties sheet.
3. Click the Hardware Profiles tab to display the Hardware Profiles page (see fig. 6.7).

FIG. 6.7
The Hardware Profiles tab enables you to modify and create hardware profiles.

4. Select the hardware profile you want to use as a basis for the new profile, and then choose Copy. Windows 95 displays a Copy Profile dialog box, in which you specify the name for the new hardware profile (see fig. 6.8).

FIG. 6.8
Specify a name for the hardware profile.

Part
III

Ch
6

5. Enter a name for the new profile and choose OK. The new hardware profile appears in the Hardware Profiles list.

In some cases, you might want to modify a hardware profile. If Windows 95 is unable to properly detect the hardware in a particular configuration, for example, you can modify the profile to add and remove hardware from the profile.

N O T E   Windows 95 is unable to link hardware profiles to user profiles. This means you cannot create sets of hardware profiles that automatically load according to the logon
name. ■

To modify a hardware profile, use the following procedure:

1. Open the Control Panel and double-click the System program icon, then click the
    Device Manager tab to display the Device Manager property sheet (see fig. 6.9).

FIG. 6.9

Use the Device Manager
page to modify a hardware
profile.

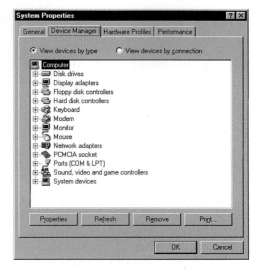

2. Select the hardware device that you want to add or remove from a particular profile,
    and then choose Properties to display the General tab of its Properties sheet (see
    fig. 6.10).

3. At the bottom of the device's General tab is a Device Usage list that defines which
    profiles use the device. Place a check in the check box beside a hardware profile to
    enable the device for that profile. Clear the check box to disable the device for that
    profile.

4. Choose OK to apply the changes.

When you start the system, Windows 95 detects the hardware configuration you are using
and automatically applies the appropriate hardware profile. If the hardware profiles are so
similar that Windows 95 cannot determine which profile should be used, Windows 95
displays a menu containing a list of the available profiles and prompts you to select the
profile to be used.

FIG. 6.10
Use the Device Usage list to
add and remove hardware
from a profile.

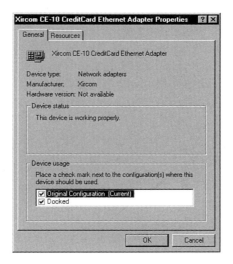

Working with Different Configurations   Most hardware settings in Windows 95 are
stored relative to the current hardware profile. Changes that you make to a device's
settings are applied to the current profile, but not to other hardware profiles. Therefore,
you can maintain different settings for the same device in two or more hardware profiles.
For example, you might use a display resolution of 640×480 in one profile (for your
portable's LCD display), but use 800×600 in a different profile (for an external monitor).

To configure unique settings for a device, first start Windows 95 using the hardware profile in which you want the changes to be made. If you want to use a high-resolution mode
with an external monitor, for example, select the hardware profile you normally use with
the external monitor (or create a profile for use with the external monitor as explained in
the previous section). After you've started Windows 95 with the appropriate hardware
profile, change the settings for the device. The changes are applied to the current hardware profile and do not affect other profiles you have created.

TROUBLESHOOTING

My LCD monitor is not working properly. Windows 95 might not have chosen the correct
display type when it built the initial configuration. Check the monitor type in the hardware profile
that's used when you're working with the internal display. To set the monitor type, right-click the
desktop and choose Properties. Click the Settings tab. Choose Change Display Type to open the
Change Display Type dialog box. Choose the Change button to display the Select Device dialog
box. Choose the Show All Devices button, choose Standard Monitor Types from the Manufacturers
list, and then choose the appropriate Laptop Display Panel selection from the Models list.

Part
III

Ch
6

Using Deferred Printing

When your portable computer is not docked, you probably have no access to a printer. Windows 95 addresses that problem through *deferred printing*. When you print a document, Windows 95 places it in the printer's queue, where it remains even when you turn off your computer.

When you dock your computer, Windows 95 senses that the printer is available and begins spooling the document to the printer. Deferred printing is handled automatically by Windows 95.

▶ **See** "Controlling Printing," **p. 247**

Sharing Local Resources via Parallel or Serial Connection

A growing number of portable users also have a desktop system. They regularly transfer files between systems by using either a floppy disk and/or a direct parallel or serial cable, and a third-party application to handle the transfer. Windows 95 includes a feature called Direct Cable Connection that integrates the same capability in Windows 95—essentially, you can use a serial or parallel cable to network together your portable and desktop computers, creating a small peer-to-peer network. If you update Windows 95 to include IrDA compatibility, you also can use Direct Cable Connect with infrared communication. The two computers can then access each other's files and other resources (such as a fax modem) as if they were joined by a traditional network interface.

 If you frequently move files between your laptop and desktop computer, you need to be familiar with the Briefcase described later in this chapter. For a more capable and faster method of transferring and updating files, use LapLink for Windows 95. There is a note about LapLink for Windows 95 in the section, "Maintaining Laptop and Desktop Files with Briefcase," later in this chapter.

In a direct cable connection, one computer acts as the host (server) and the other computer acts as a guest (client). The host computer also can act as a gateway, enabling the client to access the network to which the host is connected. The host can serve as a gateway for NetBEUI and/or IPX/SPX protocols, but cannot serve as a gateway for TCP/IP.

▶ **See** "Using Infrared to Communicate with Devices," **p. 210**

Setting Up Direct Cable Connection

If you select the Portable option when you install Windows 95, Setup installs Direct Cable Connection on your computer. If you use a different option or deselected the Direct Cable Connection option during Setup, you must install it. To add Direct Cable Connection, use the following procedure:

1. Open the Start menu and choose Settings, Control Panel.

2. Double-click the Add/Remove Programs program icon.

3. Click the Windows Setup tab to display the Windows Setup page.

4. Select Communications from the Components list, and then choose Details.

5. Select the Direct Cable Connection check box, and then choose OK.

6. Choose OK again to cause Windows 95 to add Direct Cable Connection to your computer.

N O T E If Direct Cable Connection is already checked in the Components list, the software is already installed on your computer.

After installing the Direct Cable Connection software, you must connect the two computers with an appropriate cable. You can use either a parallel or null-modem serial cable to connect your two computers. The types of cables you can use for the connection are described in the following list:

- Standard or Basic 4-bit cable, and LapLink and InterLink cables made prior to 1992.

- Extended Capabilities Port (ECP) cable. To use this type of cable, your parallel port must be configured as an ECP port in your system BIOS. This cable allows faster data transfer than a standard cable

- Universal Cable Module (UCM) cable, which supports connecting different types of parallel ports. You can use a UCM cable to connect two ECP ports for fastest performance.

Configuring your parallel ports as ECP ports provides the best performance; but to use ECP, your computer's ports must be ECP-capable, and the ports must be configured as ECP ports in the system BIOS. Older computers do not contain ECP-capable parallel ports.

The final step in setting up the Direct Cable Connection is to ensure that both the guest and host computers are using the same network protocol. You can use the NetBEUI, IPX/SPX, or TCP/IP protocols. In addition, you must use an appropriate network client, such as Client for NetWare Networks or Client for Microsoft Networks. The host computer must be running either the File and Printer Sharing for Microsoft Networks service or the File and Printer Sharing for NetWare Networks service.

Part
III

Ch
6

Setting Up the Host

In a Direct Cable Connection between two computers, one computer acts as the host and the other computer acts as the guest. The first step in enabling the connection is to configure the host. To do so, use the following procedure:

1. Open the Start menu and choose Programs, Accessories, Direct Cable Connection. Windows 95 displays the dialog box shown in figure 6.11.

FIG. 6.11

Choose whether your computer will act as host or guest.

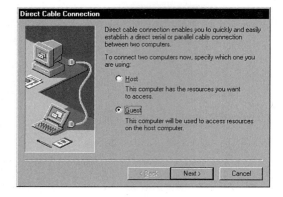

2. Select the Host option button and then choose Next. Windows 95 displays the dialog box shown in figure 6.12.

FIG. 6.12

Select the port to be used by the connection.

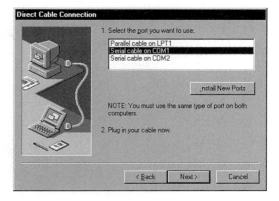

3. Choose the port you want to use on the host for the connection. You can choose one of the host's parallel or serial ports. After selecting the port, choose Next.

4. Specify whether you want to use password protection to prevent unauthorized access to the host. To use password protection, enable the Use Password Protection

check box, then choose Set Password. In the dialog box that appears, enter the password that must be provided by the guest computer to access the host. Choose Finish to complete the host setup.

Setting Up the Guest

After configuring the host, you're ready to configure the guest computer. To do so, use the following procedure:

1. On the guest computer, open the Start menu and choose Programs, Accessories, Direct Computer Connection.
2. From the Direct Cable Connection dialog box, choose Guest and then Next.
3. Choose the port on the guest computer through which the connection will be made, then choose Next.
4. Choose Finish to complete the setup.

Before you begin sharing files using the Direct Cable Connection, you must share a folder in which the files will be transferred.

▶ **See** "Sharing Network Drives," **p. 750**

Using the Direct Cable Connection

When you want to begin using your mini-network connection, you need to start the Direct Cable Connection software on both the host and the guest computers. On the host, open the Start menu and choose Programs, Accessories, Direct Cable Connection. Windows 95 displays a dialog box similar to the one shown in figure 6.13.

FIG. 6.13

Choose Listen to set up the host for the connection.

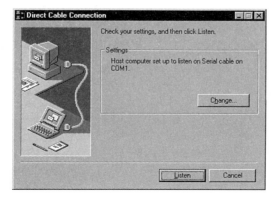

Part
III

Ch
6

If the settings you specified previously are correct, choose Listen to place the host computer in listen mode to listen for a connection by the guest. If you need to change the password or port settings, choose Change.

After placing the host computer in listen mode, start the Direct Cable Connection software on the guest computer. Open the Start menu and choose Programs, Accessories, Direct Cable Connection. Windows 95 displays a dialog box similar to the one shown in figure 6.13, except that the Listen button is replaced by a Connect button. Choose Connect to connect to the host and begin using the connection.

▶ **See** "Using Explorer with Shared Resources on a Network," **p. 148**
▶ **See** "Installing Peer-to-Peer Services," **p. 781**

Using Power Management

Most portable computers (and an increasing number of desktop computers) support some form of power management that allows the computer's devices to be shut down to conserve power while the computer remains on. Power management, for example, can power down the hard disk when the disk is not being used, conserving battery power. When the system is idle, power management can shut down the display and even the CPU to further conserve power. Windows 95 integrates power management into the operating system and adds features to the interface that enable you to easily take advantage of power management.

TIP In order for your computer to use power management, the computer's BIOS must include support for power management, and power management must be enabled in the computer's BIOS.

If your portable computer supports power management and power management software (such as MS-DOS's POWER.EXE) is enabled when you install Windows 95, Setup adds support for power management automatically. If power management software was not enabled during Setup, you must enable power management yourself through the Control Panel. The following steps explain how to enable power management:

1. Open the Start menu and choose Settings, Control Panel.
2. Double-click the System program icon.
3. Click the Device Manager tab and then double-click the System devices item to expand the System devices tree.
4. Select the Advanced Power Management support item and then choose Properties.
5. Click the Settings tab to display the Settings tab shown in figure 6.14.

FIG. 6.14
Use the Settings page to
control power management.

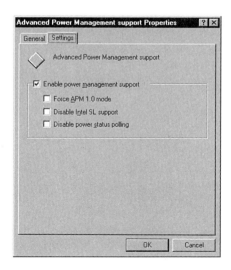

6. Select the Enable Power Management Support check box and then choose OK.

7. Choose OK to close the System Properties sheet. Windows 95 prompts you to restart the computer for the change to take effect.

The other options on the Settings page control the way power management works. These options are explained in the following list:

- *Force APM 1.0 Mode.* Enable this option if your computer's power management features do not work properly. This option causes Windows 95 to use an APM 1.1 BIOS in 1.0 mode, which overcomes problems with some portable computers.

- *Disable Intel SL Support.* If your computer uses the SL chipset and stops responding at startup, enable this option.

- *Disable Power Status Polling.* Enable this option if your computer shuts down unexpectedly while you are using it. This option prevents Windows 95 from calling the APM BIOS to check battery status, consequently also disabling the battery meter in the tray.

Part
III

Ch
6

Setting Power Management Options

The Power object in the Control Panel enables you to specify options that control power management features. Double-clicking the Power program icon in the Control Panel displays the Power Properties sheet shown in figure 6.15. The large SL button appears on the Power Properties sheet if your computer uses an SL processor.

FIG. 6.15
Use the Power page to set
power management options.

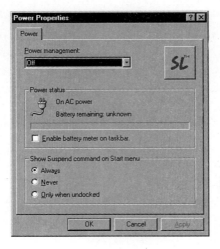

The Power Management list enables you to specify the level of power management your
system uses. The options you can select are explained in the following list:

- *Standard.* Choose this setting to use only the power management features supported by your computer's BIOS. Additional features, such as battery status monitoring, are not enabled when you choose this feature.

- *Advanced.* Choose this setting to use full power management support, including features provided by Windows 95 in addition to those provided by your computer's BIOS. These include battery status monitoring and power status display on the tray.

- *Off.* Choose this setting to turn off power management.

Additional options on the Power property page control whether or not the Suspend command is displayed in the Start menu. Choose Always if you want the Suspend command always displayed in the Start menu. Choose Never if you do not want it to appear in the Start menu, even when the system is undocked. Choose Only when Undocked if you want the Suspend command to appear in the Start menu only when the computer is not connected to a docking station.

 When you want to place the computer in suspend mode, open the Start menu and choose
Suspend. Windows 95 will immediately place the computer in suspend mode. If you have files
open across the network, you should first save or close the files before placing the computer in
suspend mode to avoid losing data.

The Power property page also displays information about battery status and enables you to turn on or off the power status indicator on the tray. To view the amount of power remaining in your battery, rest the cursor on the power indicator in the taskbar for a second and Windows 95 will display a ToolTip that lists how much battery power remains. Or, double-click the power indicator to display a Battery Meter dialog box similar to the one shown in figure 6.16.

FIG. 6.16
The Battery Meter dialog box shows how much power remains in the battery.

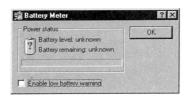

N O T E As you can see in figure 6.16, Windows 95 cannot always detect the amount of power remaining in the battery. This is often due to the way in which the batteries used in portable computers drain their charges. The voltage remains fairly steady through the battery's cycle, then begins to drop rapidly as the battery nears the end of its useful charge. ■

Setting SL Options

If your computer uses an Intel SL processor such as the 486SL, you can use SL-specific options to control additional power-management features. As described earlier in this chapter, an SL button appears on the Power property page on systems containing an SL processor. Choosing the SL button displays the SL Enhanced Options dialog box shown in figure 6.17.

FIG. 6.17
The SL Enhanced Options dialog box controls SL-specific power options.

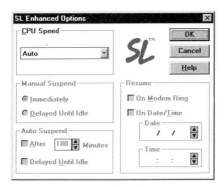

Part
III

Ch
6

TROUBLESHOOTING

The Windows 95 marketing literature describes more power management features than are available on my laptop computer. Older computers do not have BIOS that are compatible with APM. Some newer computers have known incompatibilities with the APM 1.1 specifications. Consequently, some or all of Windows 95's Advanced Power Management features might not be available.

The following list explains the groups in the SL Enhanced Options dialog box:

- *CPU Speed.* This drop-down list enables you to control how the CPU is managed. Choose Auto to cause the CPU to run at full speed but power down whenever possible to conserve power. Choose 10 percent, 25 percent, or 50 percent to run the CPU at a specific reduced speed. Choose 100 percent to run the CPU at full speed and prevent the CPU from powering down.

- *Manual Suspend.* The two settings in this group control the way the system powers down when you press the Suspend button, close the display (on a notebook computer), or choose Suspend in the Start menu. Choose Immediately in the Manual Suspend group to cause the computer to suspend immediately when you press the computer's Suspend button or close the display. Windows will suspend all applications even if they are currently processing. Choose the Delayed Until Idle option to cause Windows to wait for all applications to finish processing before it powers down the computer. Some applications appear to Windows to be processing when they actually are just waiting for input, so the system might not enter suspend mode if such an application is running and the Delayed Until Idle option is selected.

- *Auto Suspend.* This option controls how the system powers down automatically after a specified period of time with no keyboard or mouse activity. The After option lets you specify an amount of time after which the system powers down automatically. The Delayed Until Idle option causes the system to power down automatically only if there are no active applications. These settings don't affect the screen, hard disk, or other devices individually. Instead, they control shutdown of the entire system, including the CPU.

- *Resume.* These settings control how the system resumes after it has been suspended. The On Modem Ring option, if enabled, causes the system to resume if a call comes in to a line that is connected to the computer's modem. The On Date/Time option enables you to specify a specific date and time at which the system will resume.

Using Dial-Up Networking

Windows 95 expands and improves on the remote access client in Windows for Workgroups, integrating remote access almost seamlessly within the Windows 95 interface. With the remote access features in Windows 95—collectively called Dial-Up Networking—you can connect to a remote computer to access its files and printer(s). If the remote computer is connected to a network and you have the necessary access rights on the remote LAN, dialing into the server is just like connecting locally to the network. You can use the shared resources of any computer on the network, send and receive e-mail, print, and perform essentially any task remotely that you can perform with a workstation connected directly to the network.

N O T E   A Windows NT server can act as a TCP/IP gateway, routing TCP/IP traffic for your dial-in computer. If your office network is connected to the Internet, for example, you can dial into a server to gain access to the Internet from home. To use this capability, you must install the TCP/IP network protocol and bind it to the dial-up adapter. The Windows NT server's Remote Access Server service must also be configured to allow TCP/IP dial-in and route TCP/IP traffic. ■

If you did not install Dial-Up Networking when you installed Windows 95, you must do so with the following procedure:

1. Open the Start menu and choose Settings, Control Panel, and then click the Add/ Remove Programs icon. Choose the Windows Setup tab to display the Windows Setup dialog box.
2. Double-click the Communications item to display the Communications dialog box.
3. Select the Dial-Up Networking check box, then choose OK. Choose OK again, and Windows 95 installs Dial-Up Networking on your computer.

Before you can begin using Dial-Up Networking, you must install the dial-up adapter and network protocol required by the remote server. The following section explains how to set up Dial-Up Networking.

Part
III

Ch
6

Setting Up Dial-Up Networking

Setting up Dial-Up Networking requires four steps: installing the dial-up adapter, installing the network protocol(s) used by the remote server, installing a network client, and installing an appropriate file and printer sharing service.

The dial-up adapter is a special driver supplied with Windows 95 that acts as a virtual network adapter, performing much the same function that a typical hardware network adapter performs. Instead of handling network traffic across a network cable, the dial-up adapter handles network traffic through your computer's modem.

To install the dial-up adapter, follow these steps:

1. Open the Control Panel and double-click the Network program icon.

2. Click Add in the Configuration tab of the Network property sheet.

3. Choose Adapter from the Select Network Component Type dialog box, and then choose Add. Windows 95 displays the Select Network Adapters dialog box shown in figure 6.18.

FIG. 6.18

You must install the dial-up adapter before you can use Dial-Up Networking.

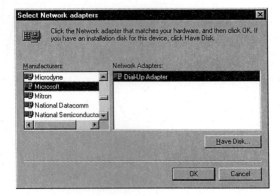

4. From the Manufacturers list, choose Microsoft.

5. From the Network Adapters list, choose Dial-Up Adapter, then choose OK. Windows 95 will add the dial-up adapter to your system.

After you install the dial-up adapter, you must install at least one network protocol to be used for the dial-up connection. The protocol you select depends on the protocol used by the remote server. On Microsoft-based networks, the protocol typically used is NetBEUI, although Microsoft is moving rapidly toward TCP/IP. On NetWare-based networks, the protocol typically used is IPX/SPX. If you are connecting to a remote network that uses TCP/IP, you should install the TCP/IP protocol.

To install a protocol and bind it to the dial-up adapter, use the following procedure:

1. Open the Control Panel and double-click the Network program icon.

2. From the Configuration tab of the Network sheet, choose the Add button.

3. Choose Protocol from the Select Network Component Type dialog box, then choose Add.

4. From the Manufacturers list, choose Microsoft.

5. From the Network Protocols list, choose the appropriate network protocol, then choose OK.

In addition to a network protocol, you also might need to install a network client. The network client enables your computer to access files and printers on the remote server and network. If you are connecting to a Microsoft network-based computer, you should install the Client for Microsoft Networks client. If you are connecting to a NetWare system, you should install the Client for NetWare Networks client.

 TIP If you are using TCP/IP to gain access to the Internet through a dial-up server, and you do not want to have access to the remote server's files or shared resources on the LAN to which the server is connected, you do not need to install a network client.

To install a network client and bind it to the dial-up adapter, use the following procedure:

1. Open the Control Panel, double-click the Network icon, then choose Add from the Configuration page.

2. From the Select Network Component Type dialog box, choose Client, then choose Add.

3. From the Manufacturer's list, choose Microsoft, choose the appropriate client from the Network Clients list, then choose OK.

4. In the Configuration tab of the Network sheet, select Dial-Up Adapter from the list of installed network components, then choose Properties. This displays the Dial-Up Adapter Properties sheet.

5. Click the Bindings tab to display the Bindings tab shown in figure 6.19.

FIG. 6.19
Use the Bindings tab to bind a network protocol to the dial-up adapter.

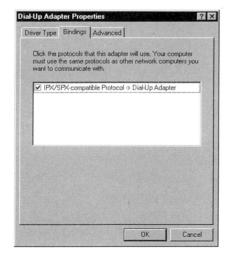

Part
III

Ch
6

6. In the Bindings tab, select the network protocols you want to use with the dial-up adapter, then choose OK. Choose OK again to close the Network dialog box.

Your computer is now configured to act as a Dial-Up Networking client. Making a connection is explained in the following section.

> **N O T E** If you have not already installed your modem, do so before continuing. Your modem must be installed in order to use Dial-Up Networking. ■

▶ **See** "Understanding the Windows 95 Communications System," **p. 284**

Creating a Connection

To create a new Dial-Up Networking connection, first open My Computer, then choose the Dial-Up Networking folder. The Dial-Up Networking folder contains an object named Make New Connection that starts a wizard to help you create Dial-Up Networking connections. The following steps help you start the Wizard and create a Dial-Up Networking connection:

1. Open the Dial-Up Networking folder and double-click the Make New Connection object. Windows 95 displays the Make New Connection Wizard shown in figure 6.20.

FIG. 6.20
The Make New Connection Wizard helps you create Dial-Up Networking connections.

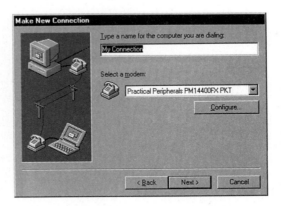

2. By default, the wizard names the connection "My Connection." Highlight the name and enter a name that describes the remote system to which you are connecting. This is the name that will appear under the connection's icon in the Dial-Up Networking folder.

3. Use the Select a Modem drop-down list to choose the modem you want to use for the Dial-Up Networking connection, and then choose Next. The dialog box changes, as shown in figure 6.21.

FIG. 6.21
Specify the phone number for the remote connection.

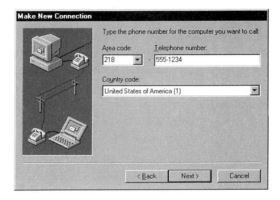

4. Enter the area code and telephone number in the appropriate text boxes.
5. Use the Country Code drop-down list to choose the country in which the remote system is located, and then choose Next.
6. Choose Finish to create the connection and add its icon to the Dial-Up Networking folder.

Connecting to a Remote System

Connecting to a remote system through a Dial-Up Networking connection is simple. Open the Dial-Up Networking folder, and then double-click the icon of the server to which you want to connect. Windows 95 displays a dialog box for the Dial-Up Networking connection similar to the one shown in figure 6.22.

FIG. 6.22
You can verify and change settings prior to making the connection.

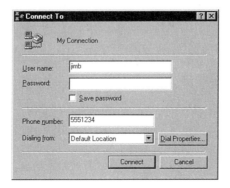

In the Uuser Name and Password text boxes, enter the account name and password required by the remote server. If you want Windows 95 to save the password so you don't have to enter it each time you use the Dial-Up Networking connection, select the Save password check box.

Next, verify that the phone number and dialing location specified in the connection are correct, then choose Connect. Dial-Up Networking dials the remote server and attempts to connect and log on using the name and password you have provided. After the connection is established, you can begin using the shared resources of the remote server and the shared resources of other computers on the remote network as if your computer were connected locally to the network.

▶ **See** "Using Network Neighborhood to View Network Resources," **p. 154**

Using Infrared to Communicate with Devices

One of the nuisances you face when moving around with laptop computers is the extra burden of carrying cables, network adapters, and PC Cards. In a temporary office, you have to get out cables, pull out printers, crawl around on the floor routing cables, and install drivers before you can finally print. Then you leave a few hours later.

Most of these nuisances go away if you use a laptop computer with IrDA in an office with IrDA-compatible equipment. IrDA is an abbreviation for the Infrared Developers Association—an industry association that has agreed on communication standards between infrared devices. The IrDA standard ensures that devices from different hardware and software manufacturers will work together.

Infrared communication enables you to communicate between hardware devices without a cable of any type. Instead, a beam of infrared light substitutes for a serial cable that carries data.

CAUTION
Always remove any previously installed infrared drivers before upgrading or changing to a new driver. You will need to do this if you upgrade to a newer infrared driver or if you change IR adapters in your computer.

Installing IrDA Support

Before you go to the effort of downloading the IrDA software upgrade, make sure your computer will support it. After you examine the Device Manager for IrDA software and the IRQ it uses, follow the steps listed in the section "Installing the Infrared Monitor Software" to install the Infrared Monitor.

Checking for IrDA Hardware and its IRQ   Before upgrading your Windows 95 software, check your computer manufacturer's manuals to make sure your computer is IrDA-compliant. If you are unsure, look on the back of your laptop for a small blackish-maroon window approximately 1/2" by 1". This is the infrared window. It may be next to a wave or signal icon.

Check in System Properties for IrDA-compliant hardware by opening the Start menu and choosing Settings, Control Panel. Double-click the System program. Select the Device Manager tab, then select the View Devices by Type option. Click the Ports (COM & LPT) icon in the hierarchy. Check if there is a Generic IRDA Compatible Device item. This listing will be there if there is an IrDA device built-in to your computer.

With Generic IRDA Compatible Device selected, click the Properties button. Select the General tab from the Generic IRDA Compatible Device Properties sheet. Look at the Device Status check box for the message This device is working properly. If you see a message indicating a problem with your IRDA device, check the hardware manuals from your computer's manufacturer for support.

While the Properties sheet is still displayed, select the Resources tab to check which Interrupt Request (IRQ) the IRDA device uses. Write down the IRQ listed under Resource Settings. COM2 and COM4 correspond to IRQ 3 and are usually assigned to a modem. COM1 and COM3 correspond to IRQ 4 and are usually assigned to a serial mouse.

Installing the Infrared Monitor Software   Infrared communication capability was not in the original release of Windows 95. It was added with Service Pack 1 during the first quarter of 1996. For a small shipping and handling fee, you can have Service Pack 1 shipped to you by calling Microsoft at (800) 426-9400.

Part
III

Ch
6

ON THE WEB

http://www.microsoft.com/windows/software.htm   You can download components of Service Pack 1 for free by visiting this Microsoft software upgrade Web site.

When you are at Microsoft's software upgrade page, select the hyperlink for Service Pack 1, then download the file W95IR.EXE into its own folder. This self-extracting file, approximately 300K in size, contains the IrDA installation software.

To install the IrDA upgrade you received from Microsoft, make sure you have uninstalled any previous IrDA drivers, then follow these steps:

1. Double-click the W95IR.EXE file to expand the files it contains.

2. Double-click RELNOTES.DOC to open it in WordPad. Read the release notes for information that may apply to your computer. Close the release notes when you are done.

3. Double-click the SETUP.EXE file that came from the W95IR.EXE file. Messages will flash while a setup database is built and when Windows detects your infrared hardware. The first Add Infrared Device Wizard appears as shown in figure 6.23. Click Next.

FIG. 6.23

The Add Infrared Device Wizard installs the software for infrared communication.

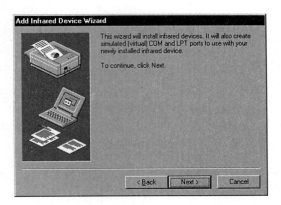

4. Select the manufacturer and model of your IrDA hardware from the lists in the second wizard, as shown in figure 6.24. If your computer has a built-in IrDA port, choose (Standard Infrared Devices) from the Manufacturers list, then click Next.

5. Select the COM port that the IrDA device uses. It may be automatically detected, as shown in figure 6.25. If not, select a COM port using the IRQ information you saw in the Device Manager, then click Next.

6. Change the simulated Infrared Serial (COM) port or Infrared Printer (LPT) port if you do not want to use these simulated ports. Figure 6.26 shows the simulated infrared port sheet. Select whether you want to use the default simulated ports or enter new simulated ports, then click Next.

7. Click Finish to complete the installation.

FIG. 6.24

If your IrDA device is built-in to your computer, choose *(Standard Infrared Devices)*.

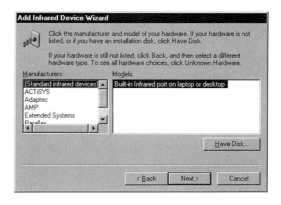

FIG. 6.25

Select the COM port used by your IrDA device.

FIG. 6.26

Change the simulated infrared serial and printer ports or accept the defaults.

Part

III

Ch

6

TIP If you are unsure which COM port to use during installation, take a guess at one that appears unused. If your IrDA communication does not work, uninstall it, then reinstall it using the other COM port.

Starting and Controlling Infrared Communications Support

The Windows 95 Infrared Monitor program must be running if you want your computer to check its surroundings for other IrDA devices, such as printers and network connections. While it is running, the Infrared Monitor sends out an infrared beam and checks for responses every few seconds. If the Monitor gets a response from another IrDA device, it keeps a log that the device is available, and indicates whether a driver for that device is loaded.

The Monitor also tracks which devices are currently communicating with your computer and the quality of that communication. You can see the quality level and communication status by opening the Infrared Monitor whenever it is working. Figure 6.27 shows communication in progress with a Hewlett-Packard (HP) printer. Use the Monitor to change the communication rate and enable or disable communication with devices in range.

FIG. 6.27
This Status tab shows that data is being sent to an HP 5P printer and that the communication rate is good at 115.2 Kbps.

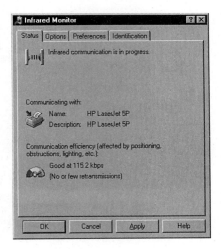

Starting the Infrared Monitor and Turning On Communication   To start the Infrared Monitor, open the Start menu and choose Settings, Control Panel. When the Control Panel appears, double-click the Infrared program. The Infrared Monitor sheet will display.

If you selected the Display the Infrared Icon in The Taskbar option from the Preferences tab of the Monitor, an Infrared icon will appear at the right side of the taskbar. Double-click this icon to display the Infrared Monitor sheet.

When the Infrared Monitor is running, you can turn communication on and off with a right mouse click. To turn on infrared communication, right-click the Infrared icon on the taskbar, then check the Enable Infrared Communication On check box. Turn off infrared communication by clearing the Enable Infrared Communication On check box.

T I P The Search For and Provide Status For Devices in Range option and the Enable Software Install For Plug and Play Devices in Range option are turned off when infrared communication is turned off.

 Changing the Infrared Monitor Settings   To change the Infrared Monitor settings, display the Infrared Monitor by double-clicking the Infrared icon on the taskbar, or by double-clicking the Infrared program in the Control Panel.

Figure 6.28 shows the Status tab when no devices are detected; figure 6.29 shows the Status tab when an IrDA-compatible printer is within range.

FIG. 6.28

The Status tab shows if devices are in range and the quality of their communication.

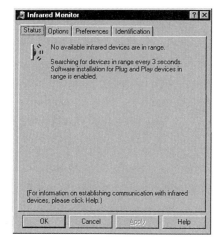

FIG. 6.29

The Status tab shows an IrDA-compatible printer is in range.

Part

III

Ch

6

Figure 6.30 shows the Options tab. The following table describes its options.

FIG. 6.30
The Options tab enables or disables infrared communication.

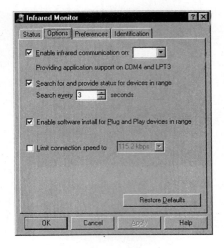

Option	Description
Enable Infrared Communications On	Enables infrared communication when selected and specifies which physical port is being used. You can choose between the physical COM ports you have available.
Search For and Provide Status For Devices In Range	This must be selected if you want devices to detect each other.
Search Every *x* Seconds	Specifies how frequently devices search for each other.
Enable Software Install for Plug and Play Devices In Range	When selected, Plug and Play devices will automatically install their drivers when the computer is within range. If the driver is already installed, it is not reinstalled. You will probably want to leave this unselected most of the time.
Limit Connection Speed To	The Infrared Monitor attempts to transmit at the highest possible speed, but this may cause lower effective transmission rates if a large number of retries are required. In some cases, a lower speed may improve the effective transmission rate.

Figure 6.31 shows the options available on Preferences tab. The following table describes those options.

FIG. 6.31
The Preferences tab specifies personal options about how the Infrared Monitor appears.

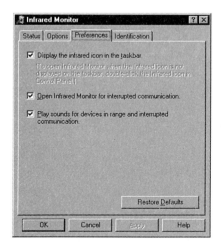

Option	Description
Display the Infrared Icon in the Taskbar	Select this check box to display a small Infrared icon in the taskbar. Right-click the icon for controls, or double-click it to display the Infrared Monitor.
Open Infrared Monitor for Interrupted Communication	When selected, a warning message displays when infrared communication is interrupted. The message box closes when communication resumes.
Play Sounds for Devices In Range and Interrupted Communication	When selected, a sound plays when communication is interrupted. If you have a sound card, you can customize these sounds by double-clicking the Sounds program in the Control Panel and selecting the sounds to play for infrared events.

Figure 6.32 shows the options available on Identification tab. The following table describes these options.

Part
III

Ch
6

FIG. 6.32
Use the Identification tab to specify a network name and description for your computer.

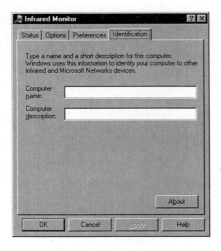

Option	Description
Computer Name	Specify the name you want for your computer to be identified by on the network.
Computer Description	Specify the description for your computer to help in identifying it on a network.

Finding and Monitoring the Status of Infrared Devices

For infrared devices to communicate, they must be turned on and oriented so they send infrared light to each other. The infrared windows on the devices must be facing each other within an approximate 30-degree cone. They should be from six inches to nine feet apart. Most devices are designed for a range of three to nine feet.

To check the status of communication between two devices, open the Infrared Monitor by double-clicking the Infrared icon on the taskbar, or by double-clicking Infrared in the Control Panel. Select the Options tab. Select the Enable Infrared Communication On check box, select the Search For and Provide Status For Devices In Range check box, and then click Apply.

If the transmission quality is poor, lower the transmission speed by selecting a smaller number from the Limit Connection Speed To: list. Normally, infrared communication occurs at the highest possible speed. In cases of a poor link, a lower transmission rate may actually improve throughput by decreasing retries.

Installing Software for Your Infrared Device

Some Plug and Play IrDA devices will install the appropriate driver on your computer when your computer comes within range. Figure 6.33 shows the dialog box that displays when an IrDA computer comes within range of a Hewlett-Packard 5P printer.

FIG. 6.33
Windows indicates when it is within range of a device for which it does not have a driver.

To install software for an infrared device, follow these steps:

1. Right-click the Infrared icon on the taskbar.
2. Select the Enable Plug and Play check box.

You also can display the Infrared Monitor sheet and check the Enable Software Install For Plug And Play Devices In Range check box. If you want to prevent unwanted drivers from being installed on your computer, leave this check box clear.

If the IrDA device is not Plug and Play-compliant, you'll need to install the driver for that IrDA device. This driver should be on a disk that came with the device.

If the IrDA device is not Plug and Play-compliant, click Start, Settings, Control Panel; then double-click the Add New Hardware program. Keep the infrared windows of the devices in range and run the Add New Hardware Wizard, or manually install the drivers using manual selections from the Add New Hardware Wizard.

▶ **See** "Installing Legacy (non-PnP) Hardware," **p. 165**

Part
III
Ch
6

Using Infrared for Direct Cable Connection

You can use infrared to transfer files with Direct Cable Connection. The infrared communication acts the same as communication via a serial or parallel cable. Make sure that infrared is enabled in both devices, then turn on Direct Cable Connection by opening the Start menu and choosing Programs, Accessories, Direct Cable Connection. Follow the Direct Cable Connection procedures described earlier in this chapter.

Printing with an Infrared Printer

Printing to an infrared printer is the same as printing to any other printer. However, you do need to make sure that the infrared windows on the devices are within an angle of 30 degrees and within six inches to nine feet of the printer.

If you have not assigned the printer to an infrared port, follow these steps:

1. Open the Start menu and choose Settings, Printers.
2. Right-click the Printers icon and choose the Properties sheet.
3. Select the Details tab.
4. Select Infrared from the Print to the Following Port list.

Removing Infrared Support

You must remove infrared support from your computer before upgrading to new or different infrared support. You may need to upgrade if you change the infrared adapter in your computer, or if you upgrade from Infrared Support for Windows v1.0 that was released in Service Pack 1 during the first quarter of 1996.

To remove infrared support, follow these steps:

1. Open the Start menu and choose Settings, Control Panel; then double-click the Add/Remove Programs program.
2. Select the Install/Uninstall tab.
3. Select Infrared Support for Windows 95 Version 1.0 from the list.
4. Click the Add/Remove button.

Troubleshooting when Infrared Communication Fails

If you are having trouble with infrared communication and you know the Infrared Monitor is on and the communication is enabled, follow this checklist to search for possible problems:

- Make sure all non-IrDA communication has stopped. Non-IrDA communication prevents IrDA communication.
- Both devices should be IrDA-compliant.
- Check that infrared is on and enabled in both IrDA devices.
- The search option must be turned on by selecting the Search For and Provide Status For Devices in Range check box on the Options tab of the Infrared Monitor.

- Check that the search interval is long enough so the devices can detect each other. Set the Search Every *x* Seconds box for approximately three seconds on the Options tab. The Search For and Provide Status For Devices in Range check box must be selected.

- Check that the devices are between six inches and nine feet apart and their infrared windows are pointing at each other and within a 30-degree cone. Check that the infrared windows are clean.

- Make sure sunlight is not shining on either infrared window.

Maintaining Laptop and Desktop Files with Briefcase

Many users of portable computers also use a desktop system and often need to juggle files between the two systems. You might, for example, have a set of reports you are preparing with your desktop system and you need to move those files to your portable computer to work on them while you are out of town. Windows 95 includes a feature called Briefcase that simplifies the task of synchronizing the files on your desktop and portable computers, helping you keep track of which copy of the file(s) is most current.

N O T E If you need to do a lot of file transfer and synchronizing between computers, you should examine LapLink for Windows 95. It is far more robust and faster than Briefcase. By using a Windows Explorer-like interface, it can access and transfer files, remotely run applications, and read and send e-mail in a single communication session. An amazing feature is its capability to update files to a common file when both files have changed. In addition to cable and network connection, it supports infrared (IrDA), TCP/IP, and the Internet. Both 16-bit and 32-bit Windows 95 compatible products ship in the same package. For more information about LapLink for Windows 95 contact:

Traveling Software
18702 North Creek Parkway
Bothell, WA 98011
(206) 483-8088
http://www.travsoft.com

Part
III

Ch
6

The following is a simplified example of how you might use the Briefcase:

- You create a Briefcase (which appears as a typical folder) on your portable computer.

- You copy one or more files to the Briefcase using a Direct Cable Connection to your desktop computer or through your docking station's network connection.

- You work on the documents contained in the Briefcase while you are away from the office, modifying and updating the files.

- While you are away from the office, a coworker modifies one of the files on your desktop system that you copied to your Briefcase.

- When you return to the office, you reconnect your portable to your desktop computer, then open the Briefcase on your portable.

- You use the Briefcase to update the files. The Briefcase informs you which files have been modified, and enables you to easily copy the files from the Briefcase to their original locations on the desktop computer. The Briefcase also informs you that a file on your desktop computer (the file modified by your coworker), has changed, and gives you the option of updating your copy in the Briefcase. When both the Briefcase and original files have changed, the Briefcase warns you so you can check the files for their changes.

The Briefcase also can detect when the original and Briefcase copies of a file have been changed. The Briefcase then prompts you to specify which copy of the file should be retained. The Briefcase also supports *reconciliation* of the two copies of the file. If the document's source application supports reconciliation, the Briefcase uses OLE to communicate with the source application and merge the two files, retaining the changes made in each copy of the file.

N O T E   Because the Briefcase is a new feature, few applications currently support reconciliation. The number of applications that support it should grow as developers take advantage of this feature.

You are not limited to creating a Briefcase on your portable computer. In fact, you can create a Briefcase on a floppy disk or your desktop computer. You might find a Briefcase useful for synchronizing files on which multiple users on the network collaborate. And, you are not limited to creating a single Briefcase—you can create as many as you like. For example, you might create a separate Briefcase for each project on which you are currently working.

N O T E   Placing a Briefcase on a floppy disk is useful if you do not have the necessary cable to connect your desktop and portable computers using Direct Cable Connection, or your docking station is not connected to the network. Simply create the Briefcase, then move it to a floppy disk. Drag files from your desktop computer to the Briefcase, then move the Briefcase disk to your portable computer and begin working on the files.

▶ **See** "Synchronizing Files with the Briefcase," **p. 140**

LCD Screen Mouse Trails

Pointing device features are also enhanced with the mobile user in mind. Switching between integrated pointing devices—track ball or clip-on mouse—to a desktop mouse (Plug and Play–compatible) is now automatically detected and enabled by Windows 95. Installing a serial, Plug-and-Play mouse amounts to plugging it in, and the system enables its use.

Windows 95 has a few special features that make it easier to see the cursor on a passive-matrix LCD panel, which many portable computers use for their displays (active-matrix panels have much better image quality, and consequently it is much easier to see the cursor on an active matrix LCD). The following sections explain these features.

Using Mouse Trails

When you move the cursor on a passive LCD display, the display typically cannot update fast enough to adequately display the pointer as it moves across the display. This makes it difficult to see the cursor. To alleviate this problem, you can turn on *mouse trails*. This feature creates a set of "ghost" pointers that trail the pointer as it moves across the display to make it much easier to locate the cursor.

To enable mouse trails, open the Start menu and choose Settings, Control Panel. From the Control Panel, select the Mouse icon, and then click the Motion tab to display the Motion property page.

Select the Show Pointer Trails check box to enable mouse trails. Use the accompanying slider control to specify the length of the mouse trail; then choose OK to apply the changes.

Using Large Pointers

In addition to using mouse trails, you also might want to increase the size of pointer you use on your portable computer to make it easier to see. Windows 95 enables you to create pointer schemes much like you create desktop color schemes, saving the pointer schemes by name. Windows 95 includes a small selection of predefined schemes, two of which use large pointers that are much easier to see on a passive LCD panel than the standard Windows 95 mouse pointers.

N O T E If you did not install the optional pointers when you installed Windows 95, you must install them before you can use the large pointer schemes. To do so, open the Control Panel, then double-click the Add/Remove Programs icon. Double-click Accessories, then scroll through the Accessories list to find the Mouse Pointers item. Place a check beside Mouse Pointers, choose OK, then choose OK again to add the pointers to your system. ▪

To use a large-pointer scheme, open the Control Panel and double-click the Mouse icon, then choose the Pointers tab to display the Pointers property page. From the <u>S</u>chemes drop-down list, choose either the Windows Standard (Large) or Windows Standard (Extra Large) scheme, then choose OK. Windows 95 immediately begins using the new pointers.

 To add a new scheme, customize as many pointers as you want; then click Sa<u>v</u>e As on the Pointers property page to identify the new scheme.

In addition to using a predefined scheme, you can create your own custom schemes. Display the Pointers property page as described earlier, then select the pointer you want to change. Choose <u>B</u>rowse, and Windows 95 displays a dialog box from which you can select a pointer file. When you select a pointer file, a sample of the pointer appears in the Preview box. When you have selected the pointer you want to use, choose <u>O</u>pen to select the pointer and return to the Pointers page. Choose Sa<u>v</u>e As to specify a name for your new pointer scheme. ●

CHAPTER 7

Controlling Printers

by William S. Holderby with Bob Voss

Microsoft has packed a great deal of experience into the features of the Windows 95 printing system. To appreciate this system, take a brief look at the new feature changes Microsoft has made to enable faster printing while producing a higher quality output. Although some changes, at first glance, appear to be ho-hum, don't be fooled. Windows 95's new print model is both faster than its predecessors and designed with the user in mind.

This chapter discusses each of the new printing features and how they work in concert to produce a quality print job:

- *Rapid return from printing* is enabled by the 32-bit printer drivers, preemptive spooler, and enhanced meta file spooling.

- *Deferred printing* enables you to configure your computer to conveniently print to a file when you are on the road or away from your printer. After you reattach the printer, simply release the print files to the appropriate printer.

- *Bi-directional printer communications* sends print files to your printer and listens for a response. Windows can quickly identify a printer that cannot accept a print file.

How to install and delete printers

You learn how to install a new printer using the Add Printer Wizard or Plug and Play, and how to delete a printer already installed on your system.

How to configure your printers

Use the properties sheet to customize the settings for your printer, including the printer port configuration, sharing capabilities, paper handling, and graphics settings.

How to print from Windows applications and to manage print jobs

Find out how to start a print job from a Windows application and to manage print jobs using the Print Manager.

How to print from MS-DOS applications

Learn about the changes in how Windows 95 handles printing from MS-DOS applications.

How to use the special printing features for laptop and docking station users

Set up a hardware profile that allows you to manage print jobs when you are not connected to your printer.

- *Plug and Play* supports the addition of new printers by quickly identifying the brand and model of a printer and assisting you in configuring the appropriate drivers for that printer.

- *Extended capability port support* enables Windows 95 to use the latest in high speed parallel port technology to connect your printer. ■

Installing and Deleting Printers

The printer installation process depends largely on the make and model of your printer. The following sections describe how to fully install a printer—with an emphasis on the specific areas in which you can expect to find printer differences. The following sections use the HP LaserJet IIIP printer configured with 5M of internal RAM and an HP PostScript cartridge as an example.

Installing a New Printer

Before you install a printer, you should follow these preliminary steps:

- Determine your printer's make and model (for example, Hewlett-Packard IIIP).

- Refer to the printer manual, or print a test page using the printer's test feature, to find the amount of RAM contained in your printer (for example, 2M).

- Identify the type of communications interface required to connect your printer to the computer (for example, serial, parallel, or a special interface).

- Identify any special features or functions supported by your printer, such as PostScript compatibility. Some printers are multimode and may require installation as two separate printers (such as the HP LaserJet IV with PostScript option).

- Find the location of a suitable port on your computer to connect your printer. The selected port must correspond to the same port type as required by your printer (that is, serial to serial, parallel to parallel).

This information is required by the Windows Add Printer Wizard later in the installation process.

Installing a Printer with the Add Printer Wizard   The Windows 95 print architecture corporates a printer installation wizard to step you through the labor-intensive chore of alling a printer.

se the Add Printer Wizard, follow these steps:

Open the Start menu and choose Settings, Printers. If the control panel is open, ouble-click the Printer folder. The Printers window appears, showing each installed printer as an icon (see fig. 7.1). Don't worry if you have no installed printers yet: the window also includes the Add New Printer icon. The program associated with the Add New Printer icon is the Add Printer Wizard.

FIG. 7.1

Start a printer installation by opening the Printer folder.

2. Double-click the Add New Printer icon to start the Add Printer Wizard. Windows displays the initial wizard screen.

3. Choose <u>N</u>ext. Windows displays the Add Printer wizard screen shown in figure 7.2.

FIG. 7.2

The Add Printer Wizard steps you through the printer installation procedure by first asking whether you are installing a local or network printer.

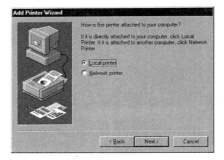

4. Choose the <u>L</u>ocal Printer option to install a printer attached directly to your computer. Choose <u>N</u>ext. The screen shown in figure 7.3 appears.

FIG. 7.3

Select the make and model of the printer you are installing from the lists provided.

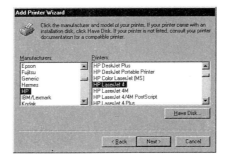

Part

III

Ch

7

5. Locate the make and model of your printer by scrolling through the wizard's screen lists (Windows 95 has drivers that support more than 300 printers). Select the appropriate options, then choose Next to display the screen shown in figure 7.4.

    If you're adding a printer after initial installation, you need the Windows 95 installation disks or CD. Windows will ask for these if it does not have an existing driver available. You also can use a manufacturer's disk to install custom printer drivers.

    If you are installing a new driver for an existing printer, click <u>H</u>ave Disk and locate the new driver in the Install From Disk dialog box. Choose OK.

T I P Many laser printers are Hewlett-Packard compatible and many dot-matrix printers are Epson compatible. If you can't get a driver or the generic driver doesn't work well, try one of the commonly emulated printers.

Scroll the screen on the far left to select your printer's manufacturer. Then select the appropriate printer model. If your printer isn't on the list, you can install your printer by choosing either the generic printer or the Have <u>D</u>isk button. If your printer came with its own software driver, insert the disk from your printer manufacturer and choose Have <u>D</u>isk to complete the requirements of this screen.

N O T E If your printer is not listed, you should contact your printer manufacturer for an updated driver. Choose a generic printer until you get an updated driver version. ▨

FIG. 7.4
Select the printer port to which you want to attach the printer.

6. Provide the printer port information. The wizard screen shown in figure 7.4 displays ports based on the survey Windows did of your computer hardware. You may have several COM and LPT ports. Refer to the list of information you compiled before you started the installation and choose the port to which you want to attach the printer. The port selected in figure 7.4 is LPT1, a very typical selection.

7. Choose <u>C</u>onfigure Port. The wizard displays the Configure Port window (see fig. 7.5). The window contains a check box that enables Windows 95 to spool your MS-DOS print jobs. This is the only configuration in the Add Printer Wizard for the LPT1 port. This check box should always be selected to enable MS-DOS printing,

unless your MS-DOS applications prove to be incompatible with Windows 95 printing. Select the Check Port State before Printing check box if you want Windows 95 to determine whether the printer port is available prior to starting the print job.

FIG. 7.5

Configure your parallel printer port to enable MS-DOS applications to use the same driver.

8. After you configure the port, choose OK and Next to open the dialog box shown in figure 7.6. Use this dialog box to name the new printer and define it as your default printer, if desired. In the Printer Name field, type the name of the printer. The name can be up to 128 characters long and can contain spaces and nonalphanumeric symbols. The printer's name should include location or ownership.

FIG. 7.6

The printer name and default status are specified using this wizard screen.

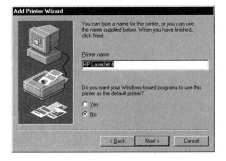

N O T E If you have access to two printers of the same type, add unique identifiers to their names, such as "HP LaserJet Series II Room 5, Building 10" and "HP LaserJet Series II Room 25, Building 15."

9. Choose Yes to set this printer as the system default. By setting this printer as your default, you instruct all applications to use this printer, unless you tell the application to use a different printer. (You can set the default to any other installed printer at any time.) Click Next to continue. The final wizard screen appears (see fig. 7.7).

10. Specify whether you want to print a test page. Printing a test page tests the overall operation of the printer based on the settings you just entered. Choose Yes and click Finish to print the test page.

Part

III

Ch

7

FIG. 7.7
Printing a test page is the final step in configuring and testing your printer installation.

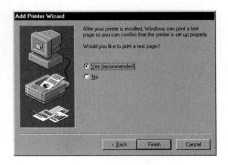

N O T E   The test page contains information specific to your printer, its configuration, and the drivers Windows uses to interface with it. After this page is printed, save it for future reference. If others use your computer, you might have to return to a known installation configuration someday.

You also can get information on your printer using the MSINFO32.EXE utility located in the \Program Files\Common Files\Microsoft Shared\MSInfo folder. Run this utility and click Printing in the left pane of the Microsoft System Information window to view information on all installed printers. ▥

▶ **See** "Using the Add New Printer Wizard," **p. 766**

Installing a Plug and Play Printer   Plug and Play printers interact with Windows to automatically configure printers by using a dialog transparent to the user. Many printer manufacturers have cooperated with Microsoft to not only make configuration easier, but to automatically update the software when you make changes to the printer hardware configuration.

If your printer is Plug and Play compatible, see Chapter 5, "Adding New Hardware to Windows 95," for an explanation of how Plug and Play devices are installed.

Renaming an Existing Printer

You can quickly rename printers named during installation using the Printers folder. The Printers folder displays all installed printers; their individual names are located immediately below the printer's icon (refer to fig. 7.1).

To rename a printer after it is installed, follow these steps:

1. Open the Printers folder by opening the Start menu and choosing Settings, Printers. If the Control Panel is open, double-click the Printers folder.

2. Select the desired printer and choose File, Rename. Or, click the printer name, wait a second, and click a second time.

   Windows creates a text box around the printer name and highlights that name.

3. Change the name by typing a new name or editing portions of the existing name.

4. When finished, press Enter. The new printer name is used throughout the Windows operating system.

   ▶ **See** "Right Mouse Button Information," **p. 23**

Deleting an Existing Printer

You can delete an installed printer from the Printers folder, which displays all installed printers as icons. To delete a printer from the Printers folder, follow these steps:

1. Select the printer you want to delete and press the Delete key.

   Windows opens a dialog box and asks whether you're sure that you want to delete the printer.

2. Choose OK; the printer is now deleted. Windows then asks whether it can remove the associated software from your hard disk.

> **CAUTION**
>
> If you have a similar printer that could use the same drivers, do not remove the software. Deleting the associated software might remove that driver from use by other printers.

3. Choose OK to remove the deleted printer's software driver.

The printer and its driver are now removed. Windows signifies this event by removing that printer icon from the Printers folder.

N O T E If you plan to reattach this printer in the future, do not remove the software drivers. This can save you time when reattaching the printer. ▪

N O T E If a new driver becomes available for your printer, you can update your existing driver using the Add Printer Wizard. A new driver can add new capabilities, correct bugs, or increase the performance of your printer. In step 5 of the steps in "Installing a Printer with the Add Printer Wizard," choose <u>H</u>ave Disk to specify the location of the new driver, and then continue as if adding a new printer.

One source for new drivers is the printer manufacturer. Most manufacturers have a private BBS or a site on CompuServe or the Internet where you can download updated drivers. Check your printer manual for online addresses. You also can find updated drivers in the Windows 95 Driver Library (W95DL), which is available at several online locations:

CompuServe: **GO MSL**

Microsoft Download Service (MSDL): (206) 936-6735

Part
III

Ch

7

Internet (anonymous FTP): **ftp.microsoft.com** (SOFTLIB/MSLFILES directory)

The Microsoft Network: Go To Other Location MSSL, then double-click Microsoft Windows Software Library and then Microsoft Windows 95 Software Library

World Wide Web: **http://www.microsoft.com/windows/software** ■

Configuring Your Printer

By now, you have installed one or more printers for use by Windows 95 applications. Both Windows and MS-DOS applications can use these resources without further effort. The initial installation of the printer created a default configuration. You might want to make changes to that configuration. Because few default configurations satisfy all printing requirements, you might want to change the printer's configuration frequently.

 T I P   If you change printer settings frequently, you can install duplicate printers and configure each printer with its own set of properties. This eliminates repeated property changes.

N O T E   Windows 3.1 provided a setting to change the priority of background printing. This feature does not appear in Windows 95. However, the print spooler in Windows 95, which uses 32-bit device drivers and DLLs, handles background printing much more smoothly than Windows 3.1 did, obviating the need to optimize the background printing settings. ■

Options for Your Printer

Printer properties are preset during installation of the printer. The preset values for the many variables might not meet your current printing needs. You might also have to make changes to meet special printing needs or to solve any performance problems that arise.

Like many other printing issues discussed in this chapter, the exact options available depend on the capabilities of your printer. The following discussion focuses on the basic procedures; you must adapt these to fit your specific printer.

To change printer options, open the Printer Properties sheet (see fig. 7.8). Use one of these two methods:

■ If the Print Manager for the printer whose options you want to change is open, choose Printer, Properties.

■ Open the Printer control panel and select the printer whose options you want to change. Choose File, Properties or right-click the printer icon and choose Properties from the shortcut menu.

This sheet has several tabbed pages. The settings on each page depend on the manufacturer, printer model, and printer options.

FIG. 7.8

Use the General page of the Printer Properties sheet to get and specify basic information about the printer.

The Printer Properties sheet typically contains the following information. (The details of these tabs will change with different printers.)

- *General page.* Enables you to identify your printer, print a test page, and choose a separator page to separate print jobs of different users. Each page includes a user name and job-specific information such as date, time, and file name.

- *Details page.* Contains controls to attach or change ports, add or delete ports, change time-out periods, and specify how Windows will process print files. Use the Details page to configure enhanced meta file printing and the spooler.

- *Sharing page.* Enables a printer to be shared with other workstations attached to your computer over a network.

- *Paper page.* Provides several controls that set the printer's default paper handling, orientation, and number of pages to be printed.

- *Graphics page.* Sets the resolution, halftone capabilities, scaling, and other options that define how the printer treats graphic files.

- *Fonts page.* Enables you to adjust how fonts are treated by Windows for this printer. Configurable fonts include printer, cartridge, and software fonts.

 Be certain to accurately configure the available printer memory. An incorrect value in this variable can change the speed of your printouts or cause your printer to time out or fail during printing sessions.

Part

III

Ch

7

■ *Device Options page.* Configures the options associated with the printer's hardware, such as the printer memory capacity settings, page protection, and other device-specific options. The number and type of controls are specific to the printer's make, model, and hardware.

TROUBLESHOOTING

I've always been able to set the number of copies I print from the control panel of my printer. When I print in Windows 95, however, I always get one copy no matter how I set the printer. In Windows 95, the settings in your programs for the number of copies to be printed overrides the setting on your printer. To print multiple copies, change the setting in the program you are printing from.

I'd like to be able to print multiple copies from WordPad but this option is not available. WordPad and Paint do not support printing multiple copies, so if your printer does not support printing multiple copies, this option will not be available.

When I try to print a page I receive the message, `Not enough memory to render page.` If your printer has bi-directional communication with your computer, there may be a problem with the amount of memory the printer driver detected. To have Windows 95 recheck the printer for memory, follow these steps:

1. With the printer online, open the Start menu and choose Settings, Printers.
2. Right-click the icon for the printer you want to check and choose Properties.
3. Select the Device Options tab and choose the Restore Defaults button.
4. Click OK.

Printing with Color

Microsoft uses licensed Image Color Matching (ICM) technology from Kodak to create an image environment that treats color consistently from the screen to the printed page. The Windows ICM goal is to be able to repeatedly and consistently reproduce color-matched images from source to destination.

ICM provides more consistent, repeatable quality among various brands of printers and scanners and provides a higher quality color rendering (the term *color* includes grayscale rendering). To fully benefit from ICM technology, choose a color printer that is compliant with Kodak's ICM specifications.

Setting Color Printing Properties   Figure 7.9 shows the Graphics page of the Printer Properties sheet for a color printer. The controls on this page allow you to configure your printer to produce the best color possible.

FIG. 7.9

The Graphics page of the Printer Properties sheet for a color printer lets you adjust color and output quality.

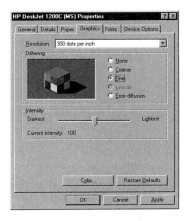

- *Resolution.* This drop-down list box specifies the number of dots per inch (dpi) that the printer can produce. The higher the dpi, the clearer the graphics.

- *Dithering.* This error-correcting tool used by Windows 95 more accurately represents an object's color and grayscale.

- *Intensity.* This brightness control lightens or darkens a printout to more accurately reflect its screen appearance and to compensate for deficiencies in toner or paper quality.

To access the color settings for a color printer, click the Color button. Use the Graphics—Color dialog box to set ICM compliance alternatives (see fig. 7.10).

FIG. 7.10

Display this box by choosing the Color button on the Graphics page.

Use the color settings to adjust the level of compliance of your printer with the ICM standards. The dialog box is also useful for trial-and-error adjustment of color printer output quality. Following is a list of the settings:

- *Color Control.* A macro command that enables you to direct the printer to print only black and white or to specify whether you want ICM technology.

- *Color Rendering Intent.* Provides the best ICM settings for three of the major uses of color printing: presentations, photographs, and true color screen display printing. Select the choice that works best for your purpose.

Part

III

Ch

7

Using the 32-bit Subsystem

Naturally, a 32-bit application is faster than its 16-bit equivalent. However, in Windows 95, 32-bit performance means more than speed; it also means safety. 32-bit applications run in their own address space so a failure in one application doesn't propagate to others. Because printing is a resource-dependent function, 32-bit performance results in better use of your resources. It permits Windows 95 designers to provide a more robust, feature-rich user interface.

When using the 32-bit printing subsystem, you will find the following differences in Windows 95 versus Windows 3.1 performance:

- *Return from Printing*. When an application prints, it shares memory and resources with the print system. In the Windows 32-bit architecture, 32-bit applications do not share the same memory—each has its own virtual memory resources. Virtual memory, combined with the faster performance of 32-bit drivers, results in the printing subsystem quickly releasing resources. 32-bit printer drivers share existing resources more equitably, resulting in smoother background printing.

- *System Stalls*. Because the printing subsystem runs in its own 32-bit virtual processor, a printing failure no longer locks out other applications. Another benefit from this design is that Windows can clean up resources after a print failure.

- *Printing Independence*. 32-bit virtual drivers enable Windows to support each printer with an individual, dedicated Print Manager. Multiple Print Managers result in the independent configuration of each printer and maximize the use of all printers without the need for frequent reconfiguration.

To verify that all Windows 95 printing components are 32-bit, perform the following checks:

- Using the Port Configuration dialog box, verify that all port drivers are VXD files. The VXD extension designates a virtual device driver.

- Using the Print Manager Properties sheet, print a test page from the General page. The test page displays the name and version of the current printer driver. Verify that the version of the driver is the latest available for Windows 95. As a general rule, this driver should also have a VXD (virtual device driver) extension. If your drivers are not VXD, check with your printer manufacturer to obtain the latest releases of these drivers. Then perform the Add a Printer installation procedure using the new drivers.

▶ **See** "Improved Performance and Reliability," **p. 20**

Using Enhanced Meta File Spooling (EMF)

The new enhanced meta file (EMF) feature appears to fall in the "so-what" category—or does it? Historically, PostScript printing has employed meta files to produce excellent hard copy results. A printer meta file contains specific printer instructions to produce a hard copy printout. Many printer manufacturers use proprietary meta file formats, such as PostScript, to produce their best results. Now meta files can be created in the operating system and be standardized for most printers.

The EMF Process   An application submits a print stream to Windows. If the printer is configured to support enhanced meta files, the print stream is converted into a series of high-level printer instructions.

The process of changing a print stream to a meta file converts each page into a series of printer-recognizable macro instructions. Printing EMF files transfers much of the processing overhead from the computer to the printer. Windows uses its 32-bit graphics device interface (GDI) and its device independent bitmap (DIB) engine to create the image to print.

Print Spooling   Print spooling creates a temporary disk file that stores print files— Windows only stores these files until it has finished printing. The spooler is an integral part of the Windows 32-bit print architecture. The spooler itself is a 32-bit virtual device driver.

An application sends a print stream to Windows for printing. The printer driver reviews the printer configuration and verifies that the spooler is required. The spooler creates a memory-mapped file on the system's hard disk to store the application's print stream. Although this process takes time, it uses fewer system resources for a shorter period of time than does sending the print stream directly to the printer.

Using the spooler enables Windows to smooth out background printing and return resources to the application more quickly.

Configuration of the EMF Print Spooler   The enhanced meta file (EMF) print spooler is responsible for converting your documents into a printable format prior to sending them to the printer. The spooler is important because it affects both printing speed and how quickly Windows returns control to you after printing.

N O T E   You cannot configure PostScript printers using the EMF print spooler. PostScript is itself a substitute for EMF, and Windows will only configure RAW for PostScript printers. ▨

Part

III

Ch

7

To use the spooler, follow these steps:

1. From a desktop shortcut printer icon or the Start menu, choose Settings and start the Print Manager. Select a non-PostScript printer.

2. Choose Printer, Properties.

3. Select Spool Settings. Windows displays the Spool Settings dialog box (see fig. 7.11).

   The Spool Settings dialog box has four basic controls: spooler printing, bypassing the spooler, spooler formats, and printer communications.

FIG. 7.11

The Spool Settings dialog box provides controls to modify the operation of the Windows printer spooler.

4. Select the Spool Print Jobs So Program Finishes Printing Faster option. Selecting this option enables the spooler.

   Alternatively, select Print Directly to Printer; this option disables the spooler.

5. If you selected the Spool Print Jobs So Program Finishes Printing Faster option, you can then choose when you want Windows to start printing during the spooling process. Printing after the last page is spooled provides the smoothest background printing, even though you wait longer for the printout.

6. Specify EMF in the Spool Data Format drop-down list box (the RAW option saves the print stream to a spooler, but does not convert the print stream to EMF format). Select RAW when printing to a PostScript printer or to a printer with a proprietary meta file print driver. The EMF setting should produce superior results on most printers. However, if your printing slows down or produces poor-quality graphics, try the RAW setting for possible improvement.

7. Select the Enable Bi-Directional Support option or the Disable Bi-Directional Support option to specify whether Windows can communicate in both directions with the attached printer. If a printer cannot support any level of bi-directional communications or is not attached, the correct choice is Disable Bi-Directional Support. In all other cases, the appropriate choice is Enable Bi-Directional Support, which allows the Print Manager to monitor the printer status during the printing process.

N O T E   To take advantage of bi-directional printer communication, you must have a bi-directional printer using an IEEE 1284-compliant printer cable, your printer port must be configured to PS/2 mode (versus AT-compatible mode), and your Windows 95 printer driver must support bi-directional communication. ▨

TROUBLESHOOTING

I shut down Windows 95 while I was printing a document and didn't get a warning message telling me the job was canceled. If you are using the RAW spool data format and you shut down before the print job has finished spooling, the job may be canceled without warning. Use the EMF spooling format to receive a warning message when you close Windows 95 before a print job has finished spooling.

Configuring the Printer Port

In addition to configuring settings that affect the printer itself, you can make a few configuration changes to the port to which the printer is attached. These options vary depending on which port you use to print. The most common printing port is an LPT port, usually LPT1 (or LPT2, if you have a second LPT port). You might have to change the printer port if you attach a printer to a serial port or add a printer switch.

Follow these steps to change the configuration options for port LPT1:

1. Open the Start menu and choose Settings, Control Panel.
2. Double-click the System icon.
3. Windows displays the System Properties sheet; choose the Device Manager tab to configure printer ports (see fig. 7.12).

FIG. 7.12
The Device Manager page of the System Properties sheet identifies the port, its present state of operation, and the hardware configuration being used.

Part

III

Ch

7

4. Double-click the Printer Ports icon to show the attached ports. Choose the printer port whose configuration you want to change, such as LPT1 or COM1. For this example, choose LPT1. If your printer is attached to another parallel port or a COM (serial) port, choose that port instead.

5. Click Properties. The Printer Port Properties sheet shown in figure 7.13 appears. Note that Printer Port Properties are divided among three tabs: General, Driver, and Resources.

FIG. 7.13

The General page of the Printer Port Properties sheet provides current status and information about the port's hardware.

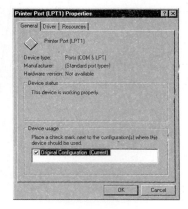

6. Choose the Driver tab.

7. Verify that the driver file selected on the Driver page is the most current printer driver available (see fig. 7.14). Note that the VXD extension signifies a 32-bit virtual driver that can be expected to provide the best performance. If you have a driver with a DRV extension, you are not using a 32-bit driver. Check with your printer manufacturer for the latest version.

FIG. 7.14

The Driver page of the Printer Port Properties sheet provides the name and version of the currently installed port driver.

8. To install a different driver, click Change Driver. Windows displays the Select Device dialog box shown in figure 7.15. Use this dialog box to load a new driver from a vendor-supplied disk or to choose a previously installed driver. If you have a vendor-supplied disk that contains the new port driver, choose Have Disk.

FIG. 7.15
Select a new or existing printer port driver.

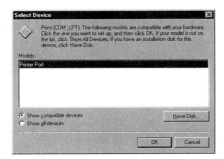

9. Windows displays an instruction window that directs you to insert the manufacturer's disk in drive A. The window also allows you to browse and select a driver from another location. Windows requests a vendor disk. Insert the appropriate disk and click OK. Otherwise, click Cancel to stop the installation process. Windows installs the vendor software and links it to the selected printer port.

The Resources page contains detailed information about the printer port's addresses and any configuration conflicts. Reviewing this information to verify that Windows has properly installed the driver. In the background, Windows cross-checked the ports configuration with the system startup settings. Windows can and does spot configuration problems, but doesn't necessarily notify the user that there's a problem. The resources contain the Input/Output Range of addresses. The addresses of the LPT1 port are shown under the Setting column. If a device uses an interrupt, that interrupt is also shown. If Windows spots a problem, it will designate that a conflict exists and list the information in this window. You can then choose alternative configurations to test other configurations.

To configure the printer port, click the Resources tab. The critical information is the Conflicting Device List (see fig. 7.16). This list contains all items that conflict with your printer port. When installing new hardware, always verify that its address and interrupts do not conflict with existing hardware properties.

You should normally choose Use Automatic Settings. If you have any conflict problems, the Settings Based On list box shown in figure 7.16 provides several optional configurations that Windows can use to configure the printer port.

Part

III

Ch

7

FIG. 7.16

The Resources page of the Printer Port Properties sheet displays detailed hardware information vital to port operation and the diagnosis of communications problems.

To use this control, first deselect the Use Automatic Settings check box. You then can use the Settings Based On option to select from a list of Windows configurations. Each configuration shows the port configured to different devices and interrupts. As each configuration is considered, problems associated with the new configuration are shown in the Conflicting Device List information box at the bottom of the page.

N O T E Carefully review the hardware properties for all devices to identify potential conflicts. Windows cannot discover and display all problems in normal operation. Use the Device Manager to check for conflicting devices; doing so can prevent problems later. ■

Most printer installations do not require changes to the printer port settings. However, unusual address conflicts from older equipment or Enhanced Capability Ports (ECP) technology provide more configuration options. The number of possible decisions and potential conflicts between pieces of hardware increase as the number of options increase. Select OK to complete the port configuration.

Printing from Applications

When you print from an application under Windows 95, you use the same commands and techniques available under previous versions of Windows; however, there have been changes. You find that application printing now takes less time, the operating system releases your resources quicker, and the color/gray scale found in the printer output is substantially more consistent and accurate. However, many details of the printing architecture are transparent to application users.

Basic Windows 95 Printing Procedures

Depending on the application from which you are printing, you may have some slightly different printing options. In this section, we look at the printing options available to all applications written for the Windows 95 operating system. The two most common Windows 95 applications are WordPad and Paint, included with Windows 95. The options you see in these applications are the same as the options in many Windows 95 applications.

To print from an application, follow these steps:

1. Load the file to be printed.

2. Initiate the printing command. In most Windows applications, do this by choosing File, Print. Figure 7.17 shows a typical Print dialog box. The controls in this dialog box let you specify the portion of the file to be printed and the printer designated to complete the job.

FIG. 7.17
A typical application's Print dialog box lets you send a print job to a specific printer.

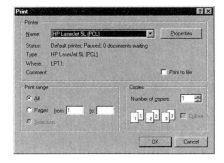

3. Select the desired printer from the Name list box.

4. Specify the number of copies you want to print in the Number of Copies text box.

5. Define the print range in the Print Range area. By default, most applications choose All as the print range.

 TIP The sheets-of-paper icon next to the collate option show whether the print job will be collated.

6. If you are printing more than one copy of the document, you can have the copies collated (each copy of the multipage document is printed completely before the next copy of the document). To collate copies, select the Collate check box. If you don't select this option, all the copies of each page are printed together. The Collate option is not available in all applications.

7. To output the printer information to a print file, select the Print to File check box. Print files were used in earlier versions of Windows to store print jobs, but Windows

95 uses Deferred Printing to create its own spooled print file, eliminating the need to check this box. Print files also are used for transferring printouts between computers with dissimilar applications.

8. To initiate the links between your application and the Windows print drivers, click OK. Your application should now begin printing the specified document.

   If you change your mind and don't want to print, click Cancel to return to the document without making any changes or starting the print job.

This basic printing procedure applies to most applications, even if their Print dialog boxes are slightly different than the one shown previously in figure 7.17. Some applications have additional options, as discussed in the next two sections.

N O T E   If you plan to print to a file frequently, set up a bogus printer. For example, set up a second PostScript printer to create EPS files. Use the Options, Printer Setup command (or the Printers application in Control Panel) to install a new printer; accept the current driver if you already have a PostScript printer installed or add the PostScript driver if you don't have one installed. Follow the preceding steps to direct this printer's output to an EPS file. When you're ready to print from the application, choose File, Print Setup to select the bogus printer and print.

▶ **See** "The Print Manager," **p. 246**

▶ **See** "Working Offline," **p. 249**

▶ **See** "Previewing and Printing Paint Files," **p. 549**

Applications with Special Print Options

Some applications take the basic printing features in Windows 95 and add a few features of their own. This section looks at some of the additional features you may find in other programs, with Word 95 as an example. Although these features vary from application to application, this section should give you an idea of what to look for.

Figure 7.18 shows the Word 95 Print dialog box.

FIG. 7.18
The Print dialog box in Word 95 includes several enhancements not found in the standard Windows 95 Print dialog box.

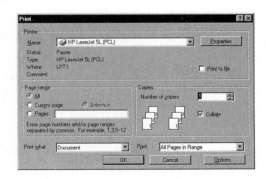

Here is a quick summary of some of the additional (and different) options provided by this application compared to the standard Windows 95 printing options:

- *The Current Page option in the Page Range section.* When this option is selected, Word prints the page in which the insertion point is currently located.

- *An enhanced Pages option.* This enhanced option allows you to specify a page range in the variable box located to the right of the Pages label. The range can be individual pages separated by a comma, a page range separated by a hyphen, or both.

- *The Print What drop-down list.* In Word, you can select to print the document itself or other information such as summary information, annotations, and styles.

- *The Print option.* From this drop-down list, you select to print odd, even, or all pages in the range.

- *The Options button.* When you click this button, Word displays the Options dialog box, opened to the Print tab. Use this dialog box to set printing options specific to Word.

N O T E For a more complete discussion of Word's printing features, see Que's *Special Edition Using Word for Windows 95*. ▓

Keep in mind that the options described here are not the same in all applications.

Windows 3.1 Applications with Special Print Options

The other common type of Print dialog box you may encounter is from a Windows 3.1 application that has a customized dialog box, such as the one for Word 6 shown in figure 7.19.

FIG. 7.19
The Word 6 Print dialog box is still styled like a Windows 3.1 Print dialog box.

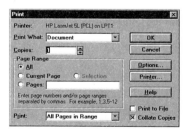

Most options in this dialog box are the same as those shown previously in figures 7.17 and 7.18. However, there are some differences:

- There is no status entry or comment field that describes the printer's current activity.

■ You select a different printer by clicking the Printer button and selecting from a dialog box instead of choosing a printer from a drop-down list.

■ There is no Properties button.

As with the other printing options discussed in this chapter, the options displayed in the Print dialog box vary from application to application.

▶ **See** "Options for Your Printer," **p. 232**

Managing Print Jobs

Like Windows 3.1, Windows 95 offers the option of printing directly to the configured port or using its 32-bit Print Manager. For most applications, the Print Manager provides facilities to better manage the printing of documents.

The Print Manager

To start the Print Manager, open the Start menu and choose Settings; then choose Printers and double-click the icon for the printer you want to manage in the Printer control panel (see fig. 7.20).

FIG. 7.20
The Printers control panel has icons for each of your installed printers as well as the icon to add a new printer.

 To create a desktop shortcut for your printer, see "Creating a Desktop Printer Icon," later in this chapter.

Unlike Windows 3.1, Windows 95 uses a separate Print Manager for each printer. Therefore, make certain that you choose the correct Print Manager to view the status of your print jobs.

The Print Manager shown in figure 7.21 displays the current printer status for each print job.

FIG. 7.21
Each printer has its own Print Manager; make sure that you select from the Printer control panel the correct printer for the print jobs you want to check.

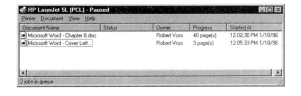

The printer status includes the following information:

- The *Document Name section* shows the name of each application that has submitted a print job as well as the name of each document job in the print queue.

- The *Status column* describes the current condition of each print job, such as paused or spooling.

- The *Owner column* gives the user's name associated with each document. A print job on your printer may belong to someone else when you share your printer.

- The *Progress column* shows the relative progress of each job in the print queue. The progress of each job monitors the printing of each document and provides information concerning the number of pages printed and the number of pages left to print.

 TIP By default, print jobs are listed in the order they entered the queue. You can sort them according to name, status, owner, progress, or start time by clicking the appropriate column heading.

- The *Started At column* provides the time and date when each job entered the queue. This is important for those users with deferred print jobs.

  ▶ **See** "Using Network Printers," **p. 766**

Controlling Printing

The Print Manager coordinates and schedules the printing of files received from your applications. These applications may be Windows-based or MS-DOS based.

The Print Manager pull-down menus provide you with the following capabilities, all of which are described in the next several sections:

- Pause printing
- Purge printing
- Work offline
- Set printer as default
- Change a printer's properties

Part

III

Ch

7

- Pause a selected document's printing
- Cancel a selected document's printing
- View the status bar
- Access Windows Help

N O T E If you are using a network printer, you can cancel only your own print jobs. You cannot pause the printing, even of your own documents. Canceling someone else's print jobs or pausing printing requires network supervisor rights. ■

▶ **See** "Using Network Printers," **p. 766**

Pausing Printing   Pausing a printer temporarily stops print jobs from being sent to a printer. Once a paused printer is restarted, all pending print jobs are started and sequentially sent to the printer. This feature is useful when changing toner or performing printer maintenance.

To pause printing, choose Printer, Pause Printing. The Print jobs are paused and the Print Manager's title bar displays Paused.

To restart printing, choose Printer, Pause Printing again, which is now prefaced by a check mark. The Pause Printing check mark disappears and printing resumes.

T I P You can exit Print Manager without purging print jobs, unlike in Windows 3.1. All print jobs in progress will continue printing. Paused print jobs will remain in the print queue and can be resumed by reopening Print Manager and releasing them. In fact, you can shut down Windows 95 when a print job has been paused and it will not be lost from the print queue. When you restart Windows, a message box appears informing you that your printer has print jobs pending and a flashing "Printers Folder" button appears in the taskbar. To resume printing, choose Yes, to pause printing choose No, and to cancel the print job(s), choose Cancel.

Purging Print Jobs   The Purge Print Jobs command permanently removes all queued print jobs. Choose Printer, Purge Print Jobs. The documents listed by the Print Manager disappear.

TROUBLESHOOTING

The printer has started my print job and the Purge Print Jobs command won't stop it. Purging print jobs stops Windows 95 from sending print jobs to the printer. However, it does not purge the print jobs currently being processed by the printer. You may have to reset the printer to terminate unwanted printing.

Working Offline   Windows 95 enables you to initiate a print job without being physically attached to a printer. This feature is known as Deferred Printing, or Working Offline. Deferred Printing is available for network printers and laptop computers. Deferred Printing tracks deferred print jobs and releases them under configuration control when the computer is connected to the printer locally or networked, or attached through a docking station.

 T I P   The Work Offline command is only available for laptop computers and network printers. Use the Pause Printing command to delay printing on a computer that uses a local printer. See "Pausing Printing" earlier in this chapter for more information on that option.

N O T E   The spooler must be turned on for you to use Deferred Printing.

To configure a printer to work offline, choose Printer, Work Offline. A check mark appears in front of the Work Offline command. The Printer is now configured to work offline and defer printouts. The Print Manager changes its title to read User Intervention Required. This information is then placed in the status line of each print job being sent to this printer. The Print Manager defers printouts until you change the status of the Work Offline flag.

To change the status of the Work Offline flag, choose Work Offline for a second time. The check mark disappears and the deferred printouts are sent to the printer.

The taskbar normally displays a printer when a document is being printed. If deferred documents are pending, the icon changes to include a question mark circled in red.

To print documents that have been deferred, follow these steps:

1. Physically connect the target printer to the system by putting the laptop in the docking station or connecting to the network printer.

2. From the Print Manager window, choose Printer, Work Offline to remove its check mark.

   If you have multiple printers configured, be sure to select the correct printer before releasing the print jobs.

3. Verify that printing begins immediately to the target printer and that the deferred print jobs are no longer displayed by the Print Manager.

   ▶ **See** "Using Your Laptop with a Docking System," **p. 192**
   ▶ **See** "Configuration of the EMF Print Spooler," **p. 237**
   ▶ **See** "Using Network Printers," **p. 766**

Setting a Default Printer   If you have more than one printer available (either locally or on a network), you can choose a default printer. All applications use the default printer, unless you choose another from within the application.

To set a printer as the default, start that printer's Print Manager and then choose Printer, Set as Default. A check mark appears next to the Set as Default command on the pull-down menu, signifying that this printer is now the Windows default printer.

To remove the printer as the system default, select the Set as Default option again to reset the flag. Alternatively, from the Print Manager of another printer, select the Printer, Set as Default command. Windows allows only one default printer.

Pausing a Document   You may pause a document to stop the Print Manager from sending it to the printer. Pausing suspends processing of the print job, but it does not stop the document from being spooled. The Print Manager displays a list of documents being printed; any paused print jobs are labeled Paused.

To pause documents, choose them from the list of documents in the print queue, then choose Document, Pause. The selected documents now display a Paused status.

To release a paused document, repeat the preceding steps. The paused status toggles off, and the selected documents no longer display a Paused status.

Canceling a Document from Printing   You also can permanently remove selected documents from the list of documents being printed. To cancel documents, choose one or more documents from the documents in the print queue; then choose Document, Cancel.

> **CAUTION**
> When you cancel a document, Windows immediately removes that document from the print queue. You do not receive a confirmation prompt. You might try Pause first and make certain you want this document's printout terminated.

Turning the Status Bar Off and On   The status bar lists the status of the print queue and contains the number of print jobs remaining to be printed. To turn off the display of the status bar, choose View, Status Bar. Repeat this action to turn the status bar display back on. The Status Bar option is a standard Windows toggle control: if the option is not preceded by a check mark, the status bar is not visible.

 Closing Print Manager   To close the Print Manager, choose Printer, Close; or click the Close button.

 Closing the Print Manager in Windows 95 does not purge the associated print jobs (unlike Windows 3.1). Printing continues based on the Print Manager's settings.

To rearrange the print queue, select a document, drag it to the correct queue position, and drop it. Dragging and dropping a document in the print queue works only with documents that are not currently being printed.

Drag-and-Drop Printing from the Desktop

A new feature of the Windows 95 operating system is the ability to print a document without first initiating the associated application or the File Manager. Using desktop icons, you can quickly launch print jobs from the desktop.

In earlier versions of Windows, printing used a four-step operation: open an application, load a file, initiate printing, and finally shut down the application after printing. Windows 95 uses a two-step printing procedure that is quick and convenient. However, before you can print from the desktop, you must take certain steps to set up your system.

Creating a Desktop Printer Icon

Before you can drag and drop documents to desktop icons, you must first create the icons. Although some icons are automatically created during Windows setup, printer icons are not.

To create a shortcut icon for a printer, follow these steps:

1. Open the Start menu, choose Settings, Printers. You also can open the Printers folder by double-clicking the Printers icon in the Control Panel window. The Printer's folder is now open.

2. Select the desired printer, drag it onto the desktop, and release it.

3. Windows displays a question window that asks permission to create a shortcut (see fig. 7.22). Answer Yes; the shortcut icon is created. If you answer No, the icon disappears from the desktop.

FIG. 7.22
A Windows question window asks your permission to create a shortcut.

Part
III

Ch
7

After you have created the shortcut to the printer, you can modify it by creating a shortcut key or changing the icon. Modifying shortcuts is discussed in Chapter 3, "Windows Navigation Basics."

▶ **See** "Editing a Shortcut Name and Deleting Shortcuts," **p. 74**

▶ **See** "Using Shortcut and Icons on the Desktop," **p. 82**

▶ **See** "Using the Power of Shortcuts and Desktop Icons," **p. 71**

Print from the Desktop

After you create a shortcut icon on the desktop for your printer, you can print any document from the desktop. To print from the desktop, simply open a folder that contains a printable document and select that document. Drag the document's icon to a printer desktop icon and drop the file there.

Make sure the document is associated with an application and the application is available to Windows, or your printing will be terminated.

Another way to quickly print a file is to add a shortcut for your printer to the SendTo folder (which is in the Windows folder). You can then right-click a file in Explorer or a folder window, choose Send To and choose the printer from the Send To list. If you have multiple printers or multiple configurations for the same printer, add shortcuts for each one to the Send To folder.

Windows starts the associated application configured to handle that file type. Windows executes that application's print command. Once the printing has been committed to the background print spooler, Windows releases the associated application, closes it, and background prints the spooled files.

TROUBLESHOOTING

I still use File Manager in Windows 95 because I prefer it over Explorer. However, when I try to print a file from File Manager by dragging the file icon to the printer icon on my desktop, I get an error message informing me that an illegal operation has been performed and that I should save my work and restart the computer. Drag-and-drop printing is not supported by File Manager when running in Windows 95. Use Explorer or a folder window if you want to print using drag and drop.

▶ **See** "Selecting Files and Folders," **p. 101**

▶ **See** "Using My Computer to Manage Files," **p. 117**

▶ **See** "Adding Items to the Send To Menu," **p. 373**

Desktop Printing of Multiple Documents

Using Windows, you can print several files at once by dragging them to the shortcut icon on the desktop. Follow these steps to print several files at once:

T I P You can select and print multiple documents created using different applications.

1. Select several documents to print.

2. Drag the selected documents to the desktop printer icon.

3. Drop the documents on the icon.

4. The message window shown in figure 7.23 appears. Click Yes to print. Click No only if you want to stop all documents from printing.

FIG. 7.23
This message window asks permission to print the multiple documents.

Windows starts each of the applications associated with the selected documents and begins printing.

N O T E Before trying to print multiple documents, check whether your system has the resources (memory and disk space) to support the number of applications Windows has to open to print the files.

Printing from MS-DOS Applications

Windows provides support for printing from MS-DOS applications in much the same way it does for printing from Windows applications. Although EMF support for MS-DOS applications is not supported, the print stream is spooled using the RAW setting for the print spooler. The result is a faster return to MS-DOS applications and the ability to mix Windows and MS-DOS print streams (avoiding contention problems that occurred under Windows 3.1).

The major change Windows 95 brings to MS-DOS applications is direct access to the Windows print spooler. MS-DOS applications no longer compete for a share of the printer; you can actually use the Print Manager to queue your MS-DOS printouts with those of Windows applications.

When you print from an MS-DOS application in the Windows environment, the DOS application spools print jobs to the 32-bit print spooler, which takes the output destined for the printer port and spools it before printing. Windows automatically installs the print spooler for MS-DOS applications; the spooler is transparent to users. Although your MS-DOS

Part
III

Ch
7

printouts automatically use the 32-bit spooler, they cannot be processed into Enhanced Metafiles.

Printing from a Docking Station

Every time you start Windows, it performs an inventory check of all attached hardware. Windows also provides a choice of configurations during startup (that is, it lists the configurations it recognizes). You must choose one of the selections from this list.

You can configure Windows to work offline when the computer is undocked and online when the computer is docked. You can set the system configurations for the printer port to be configured only when the laptop is attached to the docking station. You also can configure the port to be automatically unavailable when the system is being used as a laptop.

▶ **See** "Using Your Laptop with a Docking System," **p. 192**

Configuring a Hardware Profile

A hardware profile specifies whether Windows will use a specific peripheral. Hardware profiles provide a tool that you can use to specify the hardware configurations to operate your system. Hardware configurations are created and changed through the Control Panel's System icon.

Because the printer is not a system resource, it isn't part of the hardware configuration. However, the printer is attached to the system through the LPT1 port. This port *is* a system resource and can be configured to be available when the computer is in a docking station. The port also can be configured as unavailable when the system is used as a laptop.

Use the following steps to create the hardware profile:

1. Open the Start menu; choose Settings, Control Panel.

2. Double-click the System icon. The System Properties sheet appears.

3. Choose the Hardware Profiles tab. This page contains a text window with a single item: Dock 1. When Windows is first installed at a docking station, it creates the Dock 1 setting in the text window.

4. Select the Dock 1 setting and click Copy.

N O T E Windows automatically detects most docking stations and creates a Dock 1 profile. Even if you initially install Windows on a laptop, Windows checks the system components each time it starts and creates profiles automatically when it finds changes. ▪

5. Change the name of the newly created configuration from Dock 1 to **Lap Top** or some other name that indicates that the lap top isn't in its docking station. Click OK.

6. Choose the Device Manager tab from the System Properties sheet.

7. Select the port (COM or LPT) from the Device Manager page.

8. Choose the printer's port (LPT1)and choose Properties.

   The Printer Port (LPT1) Properties sheet that appears contains a Device Usage block with a hardware configuration window (see fig. 7.24). The Device Usage block now contains two hardware configurations: the initial Dock 1 and the new Lap Top. The two items are check box controls. A check in the Dock 1 box directs Windows to include port LPT1 in its hardware configuration whenever a docking station has been detected.

FIG. 7.24

The Printer Port Properties sheet shows which hardware profile is currently config-ured.

9. Check the Dock 1 box. Leave the Lap Top box unchecked.

10. Reboot your Windows system. During initial boot-up, Windows asks for a configuration. Choose Lap Top.

To verify that you have configured the hardware profile correctly, do not change the hardware and follow these steps:

1. Open the Start menu; choose Settings, Control Panel.

2. Double-click Device Manager.

3. Select the port (COM or LPT) from the Device Manager page.

4. Note that the printer port is now offline, signified by a red X through the port's icon. Printing now results in a diagnostic message that the printer is not attached. The Print Manager deletes all print files. Therefore, you must set the printer to Work Offline so the system will save all print files.

Part

III

Ch

7

Repeat the process first by rebooting Windows, this time selecting the Dock 1 configuration setting. The printer port returns. The saved print files can then be released for printing.

Common Printer Problems

The most useful tool in identifying and correcting printer problems is a thorough knowledge of your printer's installation and properties. During installation, test your printer and the wide range of properties available to better identify a starting point for dissecting most problems.

Windows provides fundamental troubleshooting aid with Bi-Directional Printer Communication. If a printer can talk to its drivers, many potential causes for problems can be routinely identified.

Advance preparation is always an excellent safeguard against any computer problem. The following checklists can be useful when you are diagnosing a local printer problem.

Before the Problem: Initial Preparation

Following initial installation of the printer, perform these steps:

1. Make a test-page printout and save the resulting printout for future use. The test page can contain important configuration information including the current printer driver, memory size, and port information. On PostScript printers, it will contain version level and settings.

2. If your printer can perform a self test, make a printer self-test printout. For most printers, this test page contains the printer's internal configuration. This information may contain the number of pages printed, memory size, a list of configured options, and internal software revision level. Save the printout for future use. This information may be useful in describing your printer to its manufacturer at a later date, for upgrading or troubleshooting.

3. Note the proper configuration of your printer's indicators: the Ready or Online light and the display status.

4. Make a record of your printer's internal menu settings for paper size, orientation, interface, and so on.

5. Record the installation results and the information from the Printer Properties screens.

▶ **See** "Options for Your Printer," **p. 232**

Diagnosing the Problem: A Checklist

For a local printer, perform the following steps to start diagnosing a problem:

1. Verify that all cabling is free of nicks, tears, or separations.
2. Verify that all cabling is fully inserted and locked at both the computer and the printer ends.
3. Verify that the printer is online and that all proper indicators are lit (for example, that the Online or Ready indicators are lit).
4. Verify that the printer is properly loaded with paper and that there are no existing paper jams.
5. Verify that the printer has toner (laser), ink (inkjet), or a good ribbon (dot-matrix).
6. Verify that cabinet doors and interlocks are closed and locked.
7. Verify that the printer's display, if available, shows a normal status.
8. Verify that the Windows printer driver can communicate with the printer using the Printer Properties sheets. You should be able to print a test page to verify communication. If you cannot print a test page, Windows generates a diagnostic message providing you with a starting point to diagnose the problem.
9. Verify that the Windows Printer Properties sheets display the same information that was contained in the Properties sheets when you installed the printer.
10. Attempt to print to the errant printer using another application and a different type of print file (for example, print a text file or a graphics file).

Troubleshooting Tools

If the basic troubleshooting steps listed in the preceding section fail, Windows comes with three important tools you can use to further investigate printer problems. The first tool is Windows 95's new Help file. Initiate the Help file from the Print Manager's Help menu. Then select the Troubleshooting icon.

The Troubleshooter steps you through several of the most probable causes of printing problems (see fig. 7.25). Primarily, this tool verifies that the printer can communicate with the computer. If basic communication is lost, none of the software tools can provide any real assistance. You must resort to hardware exchange until you resolve which component or components are defective. However, with the exception of toner and paper problems, most printing problems are not hardware failures; the problems are primarily software settings or corrupted printer drivers.

Part
III

Ch
7

FIG. 7.25

The Windows Print Trouble-shooter assists you in isolating problems using logical fault-isolation techniques.

The Windows 95 Print Manager provides a diagnostic tool that can aid you during the process of equipment interchange. The diagnostic screen shown in figure 7.26 is usually the first indication you receive that a printer fault has occurred. The information on this screen varies (Windows provides as much detail as possible about the problem). The increased amount of information is a result of the Bi-Directional Communications between the computer and the printer. For those printers without bi-directional capability, you will receive a standard `Unable to print` diagnostic.

FIG. 7.26

The Print Manager diagnostic reports problems as they are found and continues until either the problem is fixed or the print job is canceled.

If you click the diagnostic's Retry button, Windows continues to monitor the printer's status at approximately five-second intervals. If you click the Cancel button, the diagnostic discontinues and the Print Manager pauses the print file.

The third troubleshooting tool is the Enhanced Print Troubleshooter, shown in figure 7.27. This software application steps you through your problem by asking you questions concerning the problem. As you answer each question, you are provided with a range of possible alternatives to help you narrow in on the potential source of the problem. Clicking the hot buttons next to the most accurate answer brings up another screen with additional insight and questions. This tool is a Windows 95 executable file named EPTS.EXE, which is located in the \Other\Misc\Epts folder on the Windows 95 CD-ROM. Copy all the files in this folder to the \Windows\System folder on your hard disk and run the program by double-clicking EPTS.EXE in Explorer or a folder window. You also can type **epts.exe** in the Start Run dialog box.

FIG. 7.27

The Enhanced Print Troubleshooter steps you through a printer problem using questions in plain English.

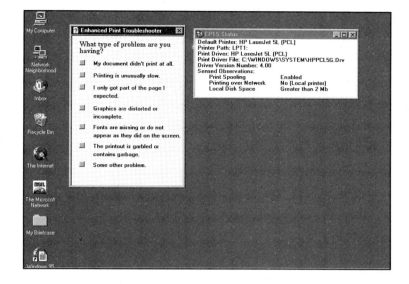

TROUBLESHOOTING

My first print job of a Windows 95 session always seems to take longer than subsequent print jobs. The print spooler must be started the first time you print a file. Depending on your system configuration, this can take several seconds—adding to the time it takes to print your first file. After the print spooler is started, subsequent print jobs take less time.

Part
III

Ch
7

CHAPTER 8

Working with Fonts

by William S. Holderby

The term *font* refers to one complete set of characters in a given typeface design, such as Arial, `Courier`, or Bookman. A *typeface* (the word is frequently used interchangeably with the word "font") is a group of characters that are considered a set, with a name (frequently derived from the designer's name). Each font has a distinctive look, and there is sometimes an obvious personality trait for the font that makes it unsuitable body text, or for small print.

Fonts have specifications, which include font size (such as 12-point and 14-point) and font style (such as **bold,** *italic,* and SMALL CAPS). Font styles are sometimes referred to as *attributes.*

Font technology is the term for the way fonts are created, stored and used, and the technology has improved a great deal over the years. More font types are available than ever before, and working with fonts has never been easier.

Changing fonts in Windows 95 is straightforward and almost effortless, whether you want to resize, change the spacing, or change the orientation (rotation).

Using fonts in Windows 95

Learn how to choose fonts for your screen display and your printed documents. Get to know the terminology for font technology.

Working with TrueType and other fonts

Understand the font files, and the way Windows 95 uses them. Learn about TrueType and other font technologies.

Installing and deleting fonts

Learn how to install new fonts. Recognize font files and what's safe to move around or delete.

Installing printer fonts

Learn how to install proprietary fonts from your printer manufacturer. Understand the choices you can make when you use printer fonts instead of Windows 95 fonts.

This chapter shows you how to use the standard font offerings available with Windows 95. Although Windows comes equipped with several font technologies, the Windows preference is the TrueType font technology. Microsoft's TrueType technology provides standard fonts that do not change appearance from the on-screen display to the printed page. Although TrueType fonts were available in previous versions of Windows, Windows 95 includes new architectural features (such as the 32-bit Rasterizer discussed later in this chapter) that make the process of displaying fonts faster in Windows 95. ■

▶ **See** "Using TrueType Fonts," **p. 271**

Understanding Fonts

Font technology may seem complex and confusing because of the large number of fonts in use, the somewhat obscure constraints, and the advantages touted by various vendors. Windows 95 and your applications eliminate much of this confusion by providing standard font choices and enabling you to customize their selection. Windows 95 supports numerous font technologies from many vendors. New fonts are available from Adobe, Bitstream, and other software suppliers.

To review fonts, you should first understand a few terms:

- *Font family* is a set of fonts in several sizes (heights) and weights (widths or thicknesses) that share the same typeface design.

- *Font size* is the definition of how large, or tall, a font character is when it is printed. Sizes are normally described in points. Each point is approximately 1/72 of an inch, so if you see printed characters an inch high, you're seeing 72 point type.

N O T E   When fonts are measured in points, the points are a measurement of height. Windows 95 uses points for sizing all the fonts provided through the operating system.

If, however, you choose a printer's built-in font you may be confused a bit by the sizing scheme. Before using Windows 95 you may have seen the size measure of CPI, especially using the font named Courier, which is built into all printers (and may be the only built-in font available for some dot-matrix printers).

CPI measures characters per inch, which is a width measurement indicating how many characters can fit in one inch. To give you a frame of reference, the standard 12 cpi you may have been used to is actually about 10 points in height. ■

■ *Font style* indicates whether characters are displayed as bold, normal, italic, or bold italic.

■ *Font effects* define things that are added to characters. These effects can include color, special instructions (such as an underline or strikethrough), and in some cases, gradient grayscale fill for outlined fonts.

■ *Serif fonts* have projections called serifs (usually short lines) that are appended to the edges of characters. The `Courier` font is an example of a serif font. Sans-serif fonts, such as Helvetica, do not have these projections.

 TIP The presence of serifs is important to you as a design issue because the serifs add a decorative "complication" to characters. This means that if you're creating a document with sections of very small characters (for instance, less than 7 or 8 points), you'll want to use a sans serif font to make it easier to read. Also, many designers feel that sans serif is the appropriate font type for headlines.

■ *Font spacing* refers to the amount of space (in width) a character uses on the screen or printed page. Fixed-spaced fonts (called monospace fonts) use identical widths for each character and there is the same amount of space between each character. This means a slim character such as an i takes the same amount of width as a broad character such as an m. Courier is a fixed-spaced font. Proportional-spaced fonts, such as Arial, occupy an amount of space that is proportional to the character's width. The inter-character space varies based on the width of the individual characters. This means an i takes up half the space of an o and a third the space of a w.

■ Kerning is a process by which characters in a proportional font are moved to fit better with the adjacent character(s). For instance, a capital W followed by a lowercase o can be kerned to bring the o closer to the W because there's room under the right-hand sweep of the top of the W.

32-Bit TrueType Font Rasterizer

Microsoft has included a new *rasterizer* in Windows 95 that improves the time it takes to create TrueType fonts. A rasterizer prepares a TrueType font for display or printing from a file that contains a mathematical model of the font's characters. The Microsoft 32-bit TrueType Font Rasterizer was developed as part of Windows' new 32-bit printing architecture. You can make a scalable font such as TrueType larger or smaller without losing its distinctive shape and appearance; as a result, the appearance of a character shown in

6 point is identical to the same font character in 18 point. The Rasterizer creates special parameters to use in displaying font characters of different sizes, orientations, and effects (such as Arial 12 bold italic).

In Windows 95, a single file—the TTF file—replaces the two sets of files used in previous Windows versions. In earlier font technology, there was an FOT file for each font, that kept track of the location of the TTF file. The Windows 95 TTF file contains all the information needed to create fonts of different sizes and complexity.

TIP If you upgraded to Windows 95 from Windows 3.x, you can remove all the files with an extension of FOT. This will give you a little bit of additional disk space (the files aren't very large but if you have a lot of fonts, there could be quite a few of them). The FOT files are in the Windows\System subdirectory.

TROUBLESHOOTING

I receive the following error message when I start Windows 95: `True Type Rasterizer Is Not Enabled.` If you upgraded to Windows 95 from Windows 3.1 or Windows for Workgroups 3.1, and you had disabled TrueType fonts, you get this message. To enable TrueType fonts and avoid this message, delete the `TTEnable=` line in your WIN.INI file or change its value to 1.

This same condition results in the following error message when you try to send a fax with Microsoft Fax: `Insufficient Memory to perform operation in Cover Page Editor.`

Registry-Based Font Support

Windows 3.1 identified and loaded fonts using INI files. Windows 3.1 dutifully loaded each font during startup. The time Windows 3.1 took to start increased as it loaded more and more fonts into the system. In addition, the number of fonts available was restricted under Windows 3.1.

Windows 95 attaches fonts through the Registry and therefore can access fonts quickly. The Registry not only saves time but also provides better management and enables access to many more fonts. Windows uses the Registry rather than the INI files to configure software options for Windows access. The Registry provides a systematic structure and interface that is available to all software regardless of manufacturer. If you upgrade to Windows 95 from Windows 3.1 or Windows for Workgroups 3.1, the font listings in the WIN.INI file are moved to the Registry. An exception is that information for PostScript fonts remains in the WIN.INI file.

Changing to Registry-based fonts provides the following benefits:

- You can use all the fonts installed on your system because there is no limit to the number of fonts the Registry can handle.

- Registry-based fonts create an environment where more than one person can use your PC hardware. Each user can individually configure a unique environment that can include individual font selection.

- Improved font handling through the universal Registry enables an efficient standard access for both Windows and applications.

N O T E The maximum number of TrueType fonts you can install in Windows 95 is approximately 1,000, depending on the length of the font names and file names. All font files are registered under a single key in the Registry, and the maximum size for a Registry key is 64K. This size limitation determines the maximum number of fonts you can install.

Windows 3.1 used initialization files to identify which font files were available for use. Most 16-bit Windows applications use the WIN.INI file to identify which fonts are installed. Under Windows 95, 32-bit applications use the system Registry to access installed fonts. Windows 95 still maintains the WIN.INI file to stay compatible with 16-bit applications.

Required Fonts for Windows

The number of fonts that Windows 95 requires is defined by the applications that you plan to run under the operating system. If you are primarily interested in word processing, then 10 to 12 scalable fonts are more than adequate. A page of text may require only one or two fonts for emphasis. If you plan to use CAD (computer-aided design), desktop publishing, or imaging applications, consult these packages for their special requirements. Because fonts provide an additional dimension you can use to create special effects or distinguish a particular area of a document, CAD or desktop publishing documents may require a large number of fonts.

The following list describes the standard Windows fonts that are shipped with the operating system:

- *System fonts* are used by Windows to draw menus and controls and to create specialized control text. System fonts are proportional fonts that Windows can size and manipulate quickly. Therefore, Windows uses these fonts to save time when it creates your screen environment.

- *Fixed-width fonts* are included with Windows 95 to maintain compatibility with earlier versions of Windows 2.0 and 3.0.

- *OEM fonts* are provided to support older installed products. The term *OEM* refers to Original Equipment Manufacturers. This font family includes a character set designed to be compatible with older equipment and software applications.

Fonts You Should Keep

Although Windows 95 does not slow down when loaded with additional fonts, the extra fonts do take up valuable disk real estate. Carefully weigh the value of all fonts before you load them on your system. Microsoft has optimized the font-handling drivers for TrueType fonts, but you can use other fonts as well. The decision about which fonts to keep depends on which applications you use.

The only way to make this determination is to experiment by adding, changing, displaying, printing, and eventually deleting unneeded fonts. Experiment with all the fonts on both the display and printed page before you make this decision.

> **CAUTION**
>
> Don't delete a font just because you don't recognize the name as one you use in your documents. Some fonts cannot be deleted, they are the system fonts that Windows 95 uses for dialog boxes and other features. The \Windows\Fonts folder houses VGAOEM.FON, VGASYS.FON, and 8514OEM.FON, which you cannot delete. The file named SSERIFE.FON holds the system MS Sans Serif font, which is used on the desktop (although you can change the fonts you use on the desktop if you wish).

N O T E   Experimenting with other font families from various manufacturers provides you with a wide range of optional selections. You can add other font families, such as those from Adobe, to Windows. However, Adobe fonts require more Windows resources because they require the Adobe Type Manager to be running. You may want to look for TrueType fonts that serve your needs if your applications or typesetting service don't specifically require ATM. Adobe fonts and the ATM are discussed in the following section. ■

Reviewing Font Types

Some fonts are designed to be compatible with special printing devices. These fonts use mathematical outline descriptions to create their character set. You can scale and rotate the resulting characters. However, fonts designed for special printers are often difficult to display. To solve this problem, Adobe has created the Adobe Type Manager (ATM), a Windows application that converts Adobe PostScript printer fonts into displayable characters for use by Windows 95 applications.

N O T E Many printer vendors have designed custom software drivers to support their printers. Your printer manufacturer may have special Windows 95 handler software.

These output devices involve different font-handling technology and drivers:

- PostScript printers use PostScript meta file printing that is similar to, but not compatible with, Windows Enhanced Meta Files (EMF).

- Dot-matrix printers range from older, very simple models to newer Near Letter Quality (NLQ) printers. Many of the older dot-matrix printers do not support downloading of soft fonts, and some of the newer printers may provide better results using proprietary drivers.

- Hewlett-Packard PCL printers use various levels of HP's Printer Control Language (PCL). For example, the Laserjet II supports level 4 and the Laserjet III supports level 5 PCL. Both Windows and HP provide up-to-date drivers that provide the best font settings.

- Plotters primarily use vector fonts as plotter software converts plotter outputs into a series of straight lines.

- Specialized OEM printers may use proprietary fonts to create unique symbols or increase the speed of graphic character creation. Most of the specialized printers provide optimum performance when they are interfaced with their manufacturer's proprietary drivers.

N O T E If your printer came with special drivers, check with the manufacturer for the latest Windows 95 driver.

By default, Windows provides support for three font technologies:

- *Raster fonts.* Bit-mapped for fast display, these fonts are created in specific sizes and rotation angles.

- *Vector fonts.* These fonts are created from mathematical line models, with each character consisting of a series of lines (vectors). Vector fonts are ar plotter technology. Pen plotters are used extensively in CAD to crea

- *TrueType fonts.* These scalable, rotatable fonts are created from ma models. TrueType fonts are a compromise between displayable an

The following sections discuss these and other font technologies.

▶ **See** "Using Enhanced Meta File Spooling (EMF)," **p. 237**

Raster Fonts

Raster fonts, sometimes called *bit-mapped fonts*, describe a font set that was designed primarily for the raster display. You cannot scale raster fonts in odd multiples or rotate them effectively. Raster fonts consist of arrays of dots and are stored in bit-map files with the extension FON. Raster fonts need separate files for each point size, resolution, and display device. Therefore, each raster font file has a letter designating its targeted device:

D = printer

E = VGA display

F = 8514 display

The Courier raster font has three files associated with it: COURD.FON for the printer font, COURE.FON for the VGA font, and COURF.FON for the fonts optimized for the 8514 display. Each raster file is optimized for its intended display device and contains attribute-specific information:

- Font type
- Font character set
- Font sizes
- Font optimized resolution

Although you can scale bit-mapped fonts in a limited sense, scaling is accomplished by adding more dots to each dot in the bit map as you enlarge the font. By their nature, bit maps that are expanded too far become more and more ragged looking. To increase size with a raster font, ideally you should use a font set for that point size. The advantages of raster fonts are that they display quickly and reduce the Windows screen refresh time, and each raster font set is optimized for its size. The Windows 95 Rasterizer uses a technique called *anti-aliasing* to smooth display mode curves and reduce the jagged effects of the font enlargement.

Raster fonts are printable only if the chosen font set is compatible with your printer's horizontal and vertical resolution.

N O T E Not all printers can print raster fonts acceptably. Before you combine any font type with your printer, first test the compatibility. You can test the appearance of printed fonts by creating a page of text using that font type and then printing that page. Another way to test printed fonts is to print the font family from the Control Panel's Font folder, shown later in this chapter. ▨

Five raster fonts are supplied with Windows 95: MS Serif, MS Sans Serif, Courier, System, and Terminal. Several other vendors supply additional font sizes.

Vector Fonts

Vector fonts are derived from lines or vectors that describe each character's shape. The characters are stored as a set of points and interconnecting lines that Windows 95 can use to scale the font to any required size. As with the raster fonts, vector fonts are stored in FON files.

To handle vector fonts, Windows 95 rasterizes the various characters by using function calls to the Graphics Device Interface (GDI). The number of calls required for each font increases the display time required to create the characters and to refresh the display. The fonts are useful for CAD, desktop publishing, and plotting because they are readily extensible. Large vector font sizes maintain the same aspect ratio as smaller sizes. Windows 95 supplies three vector fonts: ROMAN, SCRIPT, and MODERN. Additional fonts are available from several sources including CAD and desktop publishing software vendors.

TrueType Fonts

TrueType fonts use s*calable* font technology. Scalable fonts have many advantages over raster fonts and have greatly simplified the use and management of fonts. Scalable fonts are stored in files that contain both the outline information and the ratios necessary to scale the font. Windows uses this information to render the fonts, that is, to produce the dots needed to display and print the font.

Windows 95 supplies many TrueType fonts including Arial (ARIAL.TTF), New Courier (COUR.TTF), Times New Roman (TIMES.TTF), and Swiss (TT0007M_.TTF). Now that TrueType fonts are included with Windows, scalable fonts are available to all users at no extra cost. A market still exists for Adobe PostScript Type 1 fonts, because these fonts are the standard in the typesetting world. For most users, however, TrueType fonts are more than sufficient.

TROUBLESHOOTING

I have Adobe Type Manager (ATM) PostScript Type 1 fonts installed on my computer, but they are not listed in the Fonts folder. When you install fonts using ATM, these fonts are not added to either the [FONTS] section in the WIN.INI file or to the Registry. Because the Fonts folder displays only those fonts listed in the WIN.INI file or the Registry, you don't see your ATM PostScript fonts. Use the ATM application in the Control Panel to manage your ATM fonts.

I installed Adobe Type Manager on my Windows 95 system. When I tried to open the ATM tool in the Control Panel, I received the following message: `Invalid Fonts Directory`. ATM does not work properly if you install it in the Windows\Fonts folder because this folder is a system folder. To correct the problem, delete the ATM fonts in the Windows\Fonts folder and delete the ATM.INI file in the Windows folder. Reinstall ATM, making sure not to install it in the Windows\Fonts folder. Another solution is to move the ATM fonts from the Windows\Fonts folder to another folder and edit the path listed in the ATM.INI file to point to the new folder.

▶ **See** "Using TrueType Fonts," **p. 271**

Other Fonts

In addition to raster, vector, and TrueType fonts, other fonts exist that perform specialized services. Your printer may have an entire set of fonts or may be capable of being configured with font sets through the use of font cartridges or additional cards. The following list describes additional Windows fonts:

- *System fonts.* The system font files included with Windows 95 are 8514SYS.FON and VGASYS.FON.

- *OEM fonts.* The OEM font files included with Windows 95 are 8514OEM.FON and VGAOEM.FON.

- *Fixed fonts.* The fixed-font files included with Windows 95 are 8514FIX.FON and VGASYS.FON.

- *MS-DOS legacy fonts.* Windows 95 includes several MS-DOS compatible font files for DOS applications to use while running in the Windows 95 environment. These files provide backward compatibility to the real-mode DOS environment. Files included are CGA40WOA.FON, CGA80WOA.FON, DOSAPP.FON, EGA40WOA.FON, and EGA80WOA.FON. Although these fonts are primarily used for application display, the DOSAPP.FON is a good choice for printing.

■ *Printer soft fonts.* Depending on your printing hardware, you may download soft fonts to your printer. Downloading fonts reduces the time taken by the printer to process printouts. You download soft fonts one time to speed up subsequent print jobs.

Using TrueType Fonts

Because TrueType fonts are an integral part of Windows 95, many font styles come bundled with the operating system, as described earlier. TrueType scalable fonts offer several advantages over previous font technologies:

■ A single font file can print and display the font over a wide range of point sizes. Raster files require many font files to cover the same range of sizes.

■ The same font file can render both screen display and printer output. Raster fonts require a screen font and printer font file for each font set.

■ The technology for scalable fonts has standardized the production of fonts, bringing the cost of font production way down.

■ You can use the same font with any printer that has a Windows printer driver. Individual printer manufacturers don't need to worry about creating fonts for their printers.

■ By using the same font file to render both the screen and printer fonts, the match between what you see on your screen and the printer output is very close.

TrueType fonts have certain limitations, however. The anti-aliasing technology described earlier in this chapter needs a 256-color mode or higher, requiring more complex and higher priced hardware. For specific printing applications and CAD applications, PostScript fonts repeatedly provide better printing results. In addition, not every printer is compatible with TrueType fonts, causing some printers to treat TrueType fonts as graphics and thus reducing printer speed.

Through the use of icons in the Fonts folder, Windows enables you to easily identify your TrueType fonts.

If you work with many MS-DOS applications, note that TrueType and other fonts are also distinguishable by their file extensions. TrueType fonts have the TTF extension; other font types have the FON extension.

Adding or Removing TrueType Fonts

You add or delete TrueType fonts the same way you add or delete other font types. To add or remove TrueType fonts, use the procedures described later in this chapter for adding a font or deleting a font, selecting only fonts with TTF file extensions.

TROUBLESHOOTING

When I removed a TrueType font, the font file was deleted from my hard disk. In Windows 3.1, I had the option of removing a font without deleting its file from the hard disk. Can I do this in Windows 95? The only way to keep a TrueType font file on your hard disk when you remove the font using the Font manager is to keep a copy of the file in a folder other than the Windows\Fonts folder. Before removing any TrueType font files, use Explorer to make copies into another folder you create for this purpose. Now you can remove the files using the Font manager. You can reinstall these fonts from the folder you created at any time. Be sure you select the Copy Fonts to Fonts Folder option in the Add Fonts dialog box so copies of the reinstalled fonts are made in the Fonts folder.

When I try to use the TrueType Font Assistant that comes with Microsoft TrueType Font Pack II, I don't see the fonts on my system. Font information is stored in the Registry in Windows 95. Because the Font Assistant uses information stored in the WIN.INI file, you cannot use it to manage fonts in Windows 95. To manage your fonts in Windows 95, use the Fonts folder in the Control Panel.

I received the following error message when I tried to install some new TrueType fonts: `Unable to install the <fontname> font. The font file may be damaged.` If the TrueType font file is indeed damaged, you must replace the file. You also get this message if you exceed the maximum number of fonts you can install in Windows 95. In this case, you must remove at least one TrueType font installed on your system.

When I removed a desktop theme that came with Microsoft Plus!, I lost one of the fonts I had installed on my system. When you remove a desktop theme, any font files associated with the theme are also removed. You can use the application originally used to install the font to reinstall it. To avoid the same problem in the future, rename the font in the Windows\Fonts folder before you remove the desktop theme. Then remove the theme and rename the font back to its original name.

Using Windows 3.1 TrueType Fonts

In Windows 3.1, each TrueType font was maintained by two files, TTF and FOT. Windows 95 eliminates the need for an FOT by implementing faster font creation. You can add your existing TrueType fonts to Windows 95 by specifying the TTF file when adding a font. Windows does not ask for a separate FOT file and accepts Windows 3.1 TrueType fonts as well as fonts created from most existing applications.

Using Only TrueType Fonts

When you're working on a document in an application and you want to change fonts, it can be annoying to have to scroll through a lot of font names you're never going to use. However, deleting fonts is not a good idea because there may be some special document that needs exactly the font you deleted. One of the ways to resolve this dilemma is to restrict the display of fonts to TrueType fonts. This should give you all the flexibility and choices you need for your application tasks.

The decision to use TrueType fonts almost exclusively makes sense because the capacity inherent in these fonts is robust enough to meet all your needs.

For one thing, you can send a document created with the built-in TrueType fonts to anyone else who has these fonts and it will look exactly the way you designed it when they view or print it on their own machines.

All TrueType fonts, those that come with Windows 95 and those you purchase and install, provide the capability to replicate what you see on your screen (as long as your printer can either print graphics or accept downloaded fonts). All TrueType fonts are scalable, so you can get exactly the size you need for any given project.

If you want to use only TrueType fonts in your applications, follow this procedure:

1. Choose the Fonts folder from the Control Panel. Windows displays the Fonts folder containing a list of the registered fonts.
2. Choose View, Options.
3. Choose the TrueType tab in the Options dialog box.
4. Check the box that reads Show Only TrueType Fonts in the Programs on My Computer. Now only TrueType fonts are shown as available to applications.

Using Other Font Configurations

Each printer in your Windows 95 system is configurable through its Printer Properties pages. The printer property options vary from printer to printer. Many printers support downloaded soft fonts. And many of these printers support TrueType fonts as downloaded soft fonts or support printing them as graphics. You can set these options on the appropriate Printer Properties Fonts page, but you should understand the ramifications of any changes you make.

Downloading TrueType fonts as soft fonts stores the fonts in your printer. If your printer has adequate memory to store fonts, downloading speeds up the printing operation. If the printer is unable to store these fonts, you usually receive a `memory overflow` error on the printer following the download. Printing TrueType fonts as graphics increases your printing time, but on some printers it substantially improves the look and quality of the printed font.

PostScript printers provide an option to substitute PostScript fonts for TrueType fonts by use of a Font Substitution Table. The Printer Properties Fonts page for those printers enables you to change which fonts are substituted by changing the table.

▶ **See** "Displaying Properties of Programs, Documents, and Resources," **p. 26**

Smoothing Fonts with Microsoft Plus!

If you have installed Microsoft Plus! on your system, a font-smoothing feature uses anti-aliasing to smooth out the jagged edges of large fonts displayed on-screen. To use font smoothing, you must have a 486 or Pentium processor, and a video card and monitor that support either 16-bit high color or 32-bit true color.

To turn on font smoothing, follow these steps:

1. Right-click the desktop and choose Properties.
2. Click the Plus! tab and select the Smooth Edges of Screen Fonts option.
3. Choose OK.

Installing and Deleting Fonts

During the Windows installation process, Windows loads its standard suite of font files onto the system disk. Windows and your applications use these files as default fonts. And, to satisfy your creative instincts, you can install additional fonts that change the look of your system or that may be useful in certain applications (especially word processing, desktop publishing, and CAD).

> **CAUTION**
>
> Be careful to hold font change auditions before you delete fonts. You may not like the substitute fonts you choose or that are provided by Windows after a deletion. Change the fonts, and, if you like the changes, delete the fonts you've replaced.
>
> Then, just to be sure, make certain you have a backup copy of all fonts you delete, in case you want to put them back in the future.

Installing New Fonts

Windows enables you to install new fonts quickly, using the Control Panel. You may install fonts from the Windows disks or from vendor supplied disks. This procedure installs new fonts into the Windows Registry for use by Windows and applications:

1. Open the Start menu and choose Settings; then choose Control Panel. Double-click the Fonts folder in the Control Panel.

2. Windows displays the Fonts window that contains a list of all the fonts currently registered by the system (see fig. 8.1).

FIG. 8.1

The Fonts window shows which fonts are loaded in Windows 95.

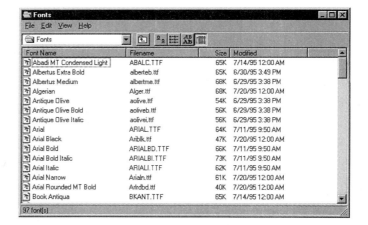

You can display the list as individual icons with the name of each font below the icons. Or you can display a detailed list that contains the name of the font, the name and extension of the font file, the size of the file, and the date of its creation.

3. To change the look of this list, choose View and then choose Large Icons, List, or Details. Refer to figure 8.1 for an example of Details view.

N O T E On occasion, you may want to look at the list of font types displayed without their many variations (like Bold). You may choose this option in conjunction with other View menu selections by choosing View, Hide Variations (Bold, Italic, etc.). ▪

4. Choose File, Install New Font. Windows displays the Add Fonts dialog box, shown in figure 8.2.

FIG. 8.2

The Add Fonts dialog box provides the controls needed to add a new font to Windows 95.

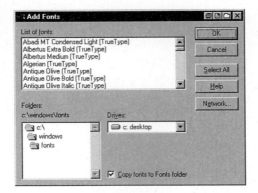

5. Using the Drives and Folders controls, choose the location of the font you want to install. This location may be a directory on the hard drive or a manufacturer's floppy disk.

6. Windows displays a roster in the List of Fonts window. Select the font or fonts to add.

   If these fonts are in a location other than the Windows font directory, you may have the files automatically copied to this directory by checking the Copy Fonts to Fonts Folder box at the bottom of the Add Fonts dialog box.

7. Choose OK to add the selected font(s). Windows installs the new fonts and enters them in its Registry.

N O T E You can install fonts by dragging and dropping them from a disk into the Fonts folder, using Explorer. However, this procedure doesn't always register the font correctly. After you install a font this way, print a test copy to verify installation. ▪

Deleting Fonts from the Hard Disk

Windows enables you to quickly delete installed fonts from the Control Panel. The following procedure deletes unwanted fonts and removes them from the Windows Registry:

1. Open the Start menu and choose Settings; then choose Control Panel. Double-click the Fonts folder in the Control Panel. In the Fonts window, Windows displays the fonts currently registered by the system (refer to fig. 8.1).

2. Highlight the font or fonts to delete.

3. Choose File, Delete.

 T I P If you mistakenly delete fonts, you may recover them from the Recycle Bin.

4. Windows displays a warning asking if you really want to delete these fonts. Choose Yes. Windows shows the font going to the Recycle Bin as it removes the deleted fonts from the Registry.

 T I P For faster deletion, you can delete fonts by dragging and dropping them from the Fonts folder into the Recycle Bin, using Explorer.

▶ **See** "Restoring Deleted Files," **p. 109**

Managing Fonts in Windows 95

In Windows 95, fonts are a managed resource. Applications can quickly access fonts through standardized registration, making your fonts quickly available for viewing, printing, comparing, sorting, adding, and deleting.

Previewing and Printing Font Samples

Windows provides quick access for previewing or printing a font sample before you commit it to a document. To preview and/or print a font sample, follow these steps:

1. In the Control Panel, double-click the Fonts folder. Windows displays the Fonts window containing the list of registered fonts.

2. Select the font you want to view and choose File, Open; or double-click the font to view it. Windows displays the font in various sizes (see fig. 8.3).

3. To print the sample page, choose Print.

4. When you are finished previewing and printing the font, choose Done.

FIG. 8.3
This sample of a font type shows sizes and font detail information.

Showing Font Properties

Fonts, like most other Windows objects, have properties. The properties include version information that may be important for purposes of upgrading your fonts. Although at present you have no way of changing these font properties, you can view the information contained in these screens through the following procedure.

To view font properties, double-click the Fonts folder in the Control Panel. From the list of registered fonts, select the font you want to view, then choose File, Properties. Windows displays a Properties sheet like the one shown in figure 8.4. The Properties sheet contains version and management information for each font type registered by Windows.

FIG. 8.4

A Properties sheet for the Arial TrueType font provides file and configuration information.

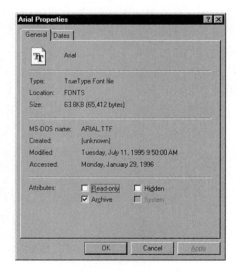

Viewing Fonts by Similarity

You distinguish fonts by their differences, but you also can group them by similar features. Grouping fonts by similarity may be important when you show subtly different text in a document or when your printed document doesn't match the display. Substituting a similar font may correct this problem.

Sometimes Windows has insufficient Panose information to make a comparison to group fonts by similarity. *Panose* refers to a Windows internal description that assigns each font a Panose ID number. Windows uses several internal descriptions to categorize fonts. The Panose information is used to register a font class and is a means to compare similar font features.

You can group similar fonts by following this procedure:

1. Double-click the Fonts folder in the Control Panel. Windows displays the Fonts window containing the list of registered fonts.

2. To change the way the fonts are displayed, choose View, Details, List, or Large Icons.

3. To see which fonts are similar to a specific font, choose View, List Files by Similarity. Windows redisplays the Font list as shown in figure 8.5.

4. Click the List Fonts by Similarity To drop-down list arrow and select a font from the list to use as a master against which you test other fonts for similarity.

   The list now shows all fonts with an assessment of their similarity to the master font. Fonts are shown as being very similar, fairly similar, not similar, or insufficient Panose information available.

   In the case shown in figure 8.5, the Arial font is the master font. Univers is listed as being fairly similar to Arial. Compare the similarity between Univers and the Arial font.

 T I P You can test the similarity of other fonts by choosing the List Fonts by Similarity To drop-down list and selecting another font type.

FIG. 8.5
This list shows how closely other font types match the Arial font.

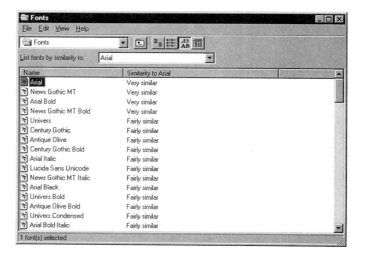

Installing Printer Fonts

Printer fonts reside in the printer as a cartridge or within the printer's memory. You can install printer fonts through Windows or through installation applications that usually accompany your printer. Follow these steps to install printer fonts using Windows:

1. Open the Start menu and choose Settings, then choose Printers.

2. Right-click the appropriate printer icon and choose Properties.

3. Choose the Fonts tab on the Properties sheet. See the Printer Properties Fonts page shown in figure 8.6. Note that each printer type is supported by a different set of Properties pages, which depend on the make, model, and hardware configuration of the printer.

FIG. 8.6

A typical Printer Properties Fonts page displays the available font options for the printer so you can select the ones you've installed, as well as choices for installing and using software fonts.

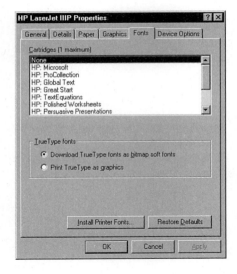

4. Choose Install Printer Fonts. A dialog box similar to the one in figure 8.7 appears. The printer fonts installer for your printer may look different from the one shown in the figure, but all installers perform similar functions.

N O T E   You cannot use the HP Font Installer shown in figure 8.7 to download TrueType fonts to HP printers. PCL printers can download only PCL-compatible fonts. Be certain that your printer and the fonts you specify for download are compatible. Refer to the installer's Help file for more information on compatible fonts. ■

FIG. 8.7
The HP Font Installer dialog
box is designed to let you
install or remove HP
Compatible fonts.

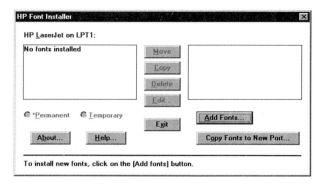

5. In the list on the right side of the Font Installer dialog box, select the fonts to install.

6. Choose Copy to move the selected fonts to the left window.

7. Choose Add Fonts to register the printer's fonts. A dialog box then asks for the location of the fonts.

8. Identify where the font files are located. If you want, use the Browse button to find the disk location of the fonts. Click OK to install the selected fonts.

Most Printer Properties Fonts pages include a set of radio button controls on the Font Installer dialog box that enables you to select whether to temporarily or permanently download a font.

To print faster, download frequently used fonts as permanent. However, permanently downloaded fonts limit the amount of printer memory available for printing. To stay within normal printer memory limits, keep the number of fonts you specify as permanent to three of four.

Downloading fonts as temporary does not store the font in the printer's memory until you need it. Windows 95 loads the font in the printer before you print the document and removes the font after the printing is complete. Using temporarily downloaded fonts increases printing time, but it also increases the amount of available printer memory and reduces print overrun errors. Downloading fonts as temporary is the default setting and works well with most applications. ●

CHAPTER 9

Installing and Configuring Modems

by Gordon Meltzer with Brady P. Merkel

Windows 95 incorporates a rich, reliable, full-featured communications subsystem capable of operating today's fastest modems. Better, Windows 95 is an extensible system that works well with tomorrow's communications devices, such as ISDN adapters, parallel-port modems, and cable modems. These forthcoming devices work at speeds beyond even the fastest of today's modems. Windows 95 can handle all these devices, and more, at the same time. ■

How the Windows communications system works for you.

The TAPI features of Windows 95 allow you to focus on your work and not worry about the details of modem communication.

How to install your Plug and Play modem or legacy modem.

Use Plug and Play for quick and easy installation of your PC Card modem, or use the auto-detect feature to install a legacy modem.

About the Universal Standard Modem Driver and other drivers.

Windows 95 supports all Hayes-compatible modems through a single modem driver. If you have a Hayes-compatible modem, you can use it with Windows 95 without additional software.

How to configure your modem after it is installed.

Choose the right port, speed, error control, compression, and flow control for your modem.

How to dial and work with your modem.

Configure your dialing preferences and test your modem with Phone Dialer.

Understanding the Windows 95 Communications System

The sophisticated Plug and Play communications subsystem in Windows 95 is designed to automatically recognize, install, and configure modems when they are installed. Even if you have a standard modem that does not support Plug and Play, Windows provides a wizard to help you install and configure the modem.

Windows 95 can use your modem to communicate more reliably and with better data throughput than ever before. The three reasons for this are:

- New 32-bit TAPI (Telephony Applications Programming Interface) communications system for 32-bit applications
- Support for the new 16550A-compatible UART (Universal Asynchronous Receiver Transmitter) chips found in new modems and modern serial ports
- Improved 16-bit communications driver for older 16-bit programs

Windows uses these features to give you more control over your communications with your modem, and to make your modem do a better job for you.

▶ **See** "Sharing a Modem Between Applications," **p. 304**

Installing a Plug and Play Modem

Like other devices that support this new technology, Plug and Play modems communicate with Windows to cooperate in setting themselves up. Internal modems always contain the serial communications port and modulator/demodulator/dialer on the same card, so Windows can configure them to work together at the same time.

Many Plug and Play modems are located on *PC Cards* (formerly known as PCMCIA cards). These cards support full Plug and Play functionality, including hot swapping.

N O T E   *Hot swapping* lets PC Cards be removed or inserted while the system is running. The system loads and unloads any required software automatically on the fly. ■

Some Plug and Play modems may be on ISA cards; these do not benefit from hot swapping, because the ISA bus was originally designed for fixed components inside the computer that are not removed during operation.

TIP Make sure any internal ISA card modem you buy includes a modern type of UART (Universal Asynchronous Receiver/Transmitter) chip with at least the capabilities of the 16550A. All PC Card modems already do.

N O T E Internal modems consist of three main functional sections. The Serial Communications Port handles communications with your computer. The Modulator/Demodulator handles communications over the phone lines with another modem. The Dialer handles communications with the telephone network and connects your call.

External modems do not contain the Serial Communications Port; they attach to one that is built in to your computer.

Plug and Play modems add another section which identifies the modem's capabilities and resource needs to Windows 95 setup.

During Windows setup, information is exchanged between your modem and the system. This is what happens, automatically, when Windows comes to the part of setup in which your modem will be configured:

1. Windows searches through all the system's input-output (I/O) ports and finds the Plug and Play modem.

2. The system assigns the card an identification number, which Windows stores in the Registry.

3. Windows requests the modem speeds and specifications. The modem gives the information to Windows setup.

4. Setup then assigns a communications-port number (COM1, COM2, and so on) and resources to be used by the port. These resources are an interrupt and an I/O address. If the Plug and Play modem is on a PC Card, Windows also assigns a memory address to the modem.

   ▶ **See** "Installing Plug and Play Hardware," **p. 158**
   ▶ **See** "Understanding Plug and Play Hardware," **p. 160**
   ▶ **See** "Port Settings," **p. 301**
   ▶ **See** "Understanding Windows 95 Setup Requirements," **p. 1180**
   ▶ **See** "How Windows 95 Setup Works," **p. 1186**

Part

III

Ch

9

Plug and Play In Action

If a Plug and Play modem is installed in your computer before you install Windows, the modem setup occurs automatically and transparently. This section examines what happens if you have a PC Card modem installed in PC Card slot 1 when you install Windows 95.

First, Windows configures the PC Card slots. The PC Card Wizard appears during installation (see fig. 9.1).

CAUTION

Notice in figure 9.1, the Wizard warns you that it is about to disable all PC Cards while it works. If you are installing Windows from a CD-ROM connected through a PC Card, Setup will fail. For a workaround, use floppy disks for this portion of Setup.

FIG. 9.1
The PC Card Wizard begins installing your PC Card modem.

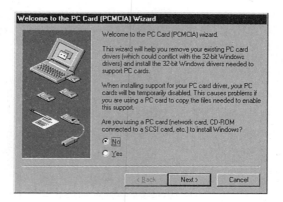

Next, Windows suggests removing the old DOS-based 16-bit Card and Socket Services drivers from the CONFIG.SYS, AUTOEXEC.BAT, and SYSTEM.INI files. To review the changes before proceeding, choose Yes and then click Next.

Figure 9.2 shows the real-mode, 16-bit drivers in CONFIG.SYS. They are the last five lines in the file. For best results, you should permit the Wizard to comment out the old drivers. Click Next to accept the changes. After the Wizard processes CONFIG.SYS, it processes the AUTOEXEC.BAT and SYSTEM.INI files in the same way.

When the Wizard finishes setting up the PC Card slots, it installs the 32-bit protected mode Card and Socket Services driver software. These drivers control all the Plug and Play features.

FIG. 9.2
Real mode drivers in
CONFIG.SYS that will be
commented out by
Windows 95.

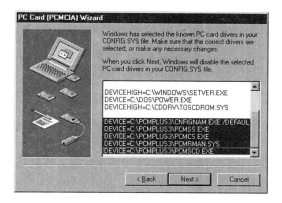

After the drivers are installed, you need to restart Windows to activate the new drivers. Click Finish in the Wizard dialog box, close any other applications that are running, and click Yes when you are ready to shut down.

Windows loads with the 32-bit drivers enabled for the first time. Now it can configure the modem in your PC Card slot. Using the new, protected-mode 32-bit Card and Socket Services, Windows can install any modem in your PC Card slot. In figure 9.3, Windows detected a new modem and installed the software drivers for it automatically.

FIG. 9.3
Windows Setup finds
your modem.

Your Plug and Play modem is now installed. Next, the modem must be configured to allow all Windows' advanced features to operate.

▶ **See** "Advanced Settings," **p. 298**

Plug and Play—How it Works

The Windows user interface for the installation of the Plug and Play modem is the Setup Wizard. The wizard does all the setup work, and a lot happens behind the scenes.

What has actually happened during the Plug and Play modem installation is this:

1. Windows asks the modem to identify itself, the modem responds, and Windows installs the software to run the modem. Then, the wizard tells you its job is complete and your modem is installed.

2. Windows installs the Unimodem driver for any modems that support AT (Attention) commands. Most modems do. Windows then looks in its database of INF files. If information is found on the specific modem, it installs the modem mini-driver.

N O T E Windows assigns the IBM-compatible standard communications port names to ports and modems. The names are assigned in order, using the standard resources:

Port Name	I/O Port Resource
Com1	3F8
Com2	2F8
Com3	3E8
Com4	2E8

CAUTION

If Windows finds a modem configured to a base address that is not listed in the previous table, it assigns COM5 to that modem. Programs designed for Windows 3.1 or DOS may not be able to work with a modem on this port. The workaround is to change the non-standard address in the Device Manager, found in the System Control Panel.

TROUBLESHOOTING

I can't get the modem to install. First, check the Device Manager to see whether the hardware communications port exists and is working properly. If the port does not exist in Device Manager's list of ports, follow the steps in "Installing a Legacy Modem," in the next section to install the communications port. A legacy modem is a modem that does not incorporate the Plug and Play standards. Turn your external modem off and then on again. If you are using an internal modem, shut down Windows, power down the computer, and try again.

▶ **See** "Understanding the Device Manager," **p. 177**
▶ **See** "Customizing Hardware Support," **p. 1205**

Installing a Legacy Modem

A legacy modem can't tell Windows about its capabilities, or its resource requirements. Legacy modems can be either internal or external modems, but are not Plug and Play devices.

Windows considers the serial port to be a separate device from the modem, even if you have an internal modem, in which both the modem and the serial port are on the same card. Windows configures these devices separately.

If you are trying to install an internal modem, Windows may act differently with different modems. You may be able to install the serial port at the same time you install the modem. If Windows cannot detect and initialize the serial port, you can use the Add New Hardware option in the Control Panel to set up the port.

Part

III

Ch

9

In Windows 95, you can install a legacy modem in any of the following ways:

- Use the Add New Hardware Wizard.
- Double-click the Modem icon in the Control Panel.
- Start a 32-bit program that uses a modem. If no modem is installed, Windows suggests you install one.

The following procedure uses the Add New Hardware Wizard to install the modem. Follow these steps:

1. Open the Start menu and choose Settings, Control Panel.
2. Double-click the Add New Hardware icon. The first Add New Hardware Wizard window appears.
3. Click Next.
4. You should allow Windows to try to find your modem by itself, so choose Yes when the wizard asks if you want Windows to detect it automatically. You will see a progress report during the detection process.

   If Windows can, it sets up the serial port and the modem at the same time. Windows may not find the modem when it finds the port. In that case, run the Add New Hardware Wizard again.

   The report from the Add New Hardware Wizard shown in figure 9.4, shows that Windows has found a new Communications Port. This report is correct and represents new hardware, COM3, added at I/O address 03E8-03EF.
5. Click Finish.
6. When prompted, restart the computer.

After Windows restarts, look in the Device Manager. In the Ports section, you see that a new Communications Port—COM3—has been added (see fig. 9.5).

FIG. 9.4

This report from the Add New Hardware Wizard shows two new devices detected.

FIG. 9.5

The new Communications Port and its resources.

N O T E Often, Windows won't find the port and the modem on the same pass through the installation process. Don't be concerned; just follow the next set of steps. ■

In this common example, Windows could not detect and install the port and modem in one step. Therefore, you need to visit the Control Panel again. Now that COM3 is working properly, Windows should be able to detect and install the modem connected to that port.

1. Double-click the Modems icon in the Control Panel. When the Install New Modem Wizard starts, choose Other.

2. In the next dialog box, the wizard asks for another chance to detect the modem. Click Next, and allow the wizard to detect which modem you have. Figure 9.6 shows the window that appears just before automatic modem detection.

FIG. 9.6

The Modem Installation Wizard set to auto-detect your modem.

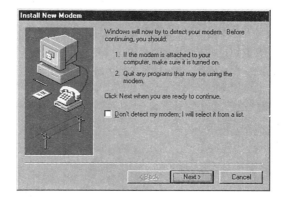

3. Windows reports that it found the modem attached to COM3, as shown in figure 9.7. If the detected modem does not match the type that is installed, click Change and select your modem from the ensuing list.

4. Click Next to finish the modem installation and close the dialog box.

FIG. 9.7

The Modem Wizard has detected the new modem.

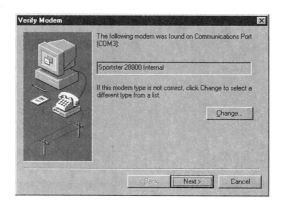

N O T E Windows chooses slow port speeds by default. If you have a fast computer, change the port speeds in the Modems Properties Control Panel to the modem's maximum port speed. The port speed is the speed of communication between the computer and the modem, which usually needs to be faster than the modem-to-modem speed. As a simple rule, set the port speed to four times the modem-to-modem speed (with V.34 28.8Kbps modems, 115,200bps is correct). Setting the port speed to four times the modem speed will keep the modem's input buffer full and allow compression to raise throughput beyond the modem's maximum speed on the phone line. ▨

TROUBLESHOOTING

When I use the modem, another program—or the entire system—locks up or crashes. This problem usually results from an interrupt conflict. Two devices may be trying to use the same interrupt. If you have a serial mouse on COM1, which uses Interrupt 4, and you set up a modem on COM3, which also uses Interrupt 4, a conflict exists.

Use Device Manager to look for a modem or mouse icon that has a yellow exclamation point. Double-click the icon and choose Resources. If a conflict is listed, Windows offers to start the Hardware Conflict Troubleshooter. This program can help you resolve interrupt conflicts by reassigning resources such as interrupts.

See Chapter 5 for more information concerning the Device Manager and troubleshooting hardware conflicts.

▶ **See** "Installing Legacy (non-PnP) Hardware," **p. 165**
▶ **See** "Advanced Installation Techniques," **p. 1203**

Understanding the Unimodem Driver

Most of the modems on the market use a variation of the AT command set, which Dennis Hayes developed for the original Smartmodem in 1980. Because the vast majority of modems are Hayes-compatible, Microsoft created a universal modem driver—the Unimodem driver.

Table 9.1 shows the basic AT commands used by the Unimodem driver.

Table 9.1   Basic Modem Commands for the Unimodem Driver

AT Command	Function
AT	Attention
ATZ	Reset modem
	Dial modem
	Identify modem
	Hang up modem
	Go off hook in Originate mode

em driver is talking to the modem, the basic AT commands provide ity for the driver to interrogate the modem, find its manufacturer and model number, and try to find a match in the Windows modem database. If a match is found, the driver tells Windows to install the mini-driver that matches the modem. This mini-driver works with the modem to enable advanced features such as data compression and error correction. These features are likely to be implemented differently by each manufacturer.

Even without a mini-driver, the Unimodem driver can make a partially Hayes-compatible modem dial, connect, and disconnect. Modems that are running without a mini-driver are shown in the Control Panel as Standard modems.

Using Drivers Provided by Modem Manufacturers

You may encounter a modem that comes with a Windows 95 driver disk. This disk indicates that Windows 95 has no appropriate mini-driver, or the modem has features that are not supported by the Unimodem driver.

ON THE WEB

You can find a list of modem manufacturers on the YAHOO search engine

http://www.yahoo.com/Business_and_Economy/Companies/Computers/Peripherals /Modems/

To install the modem with its own driver software, follow these steps:

1. Double-click the Modem icon in Control Panel.
2. Choose Add.
3. Choose Do Not Detect My Modem; I Will Select It From a List.
4. Now choose Have Disk.
5. Insert the manufacturer's driver disk into the proper disk drive when prompted, and then choose OK.
6. Choose the driver for your modem model from the list that appears if more than one driver appears.
7. Choose Finish.

Your modem's drivers are installed in Windows, and the modem's special features are enabled.

Configuring Your Modem

Now that your modem is installed, configure Windows to work cooperatively with it. For communication programs to operate your modem with the greatest possible intelligence, configure Windows with the following information:

- Your location
- Your area code
- Access number(s) needed to get an outside line
- Type of dialing used at this location (tone or pulse)

This information, however, is not enough to make your modem operate at peak efficiency and at maximum data-transfer rates. Configure Windows with other information about your modem, including the following:

- Maximum port speed (computer to modem)
- Default data-formatting properties
- How to handle "no dial tone" situations
- How long the modem should try to connect before stopping
- When to disconnect an idle modem connection
- Whether to use error-control and compression for robust and fast communication
- What kind of flow control to use with your modem
- How to handle low-speed connections
- How to record a log file of the modem's interaction with the system, for use in troubleshooting
- How to manually send extra AT commands to the modem during initialization

General Properties

Use the Modems Control Panel to select the modem you are working with, and then choose Properties. The Modem Properties sheet appears. The General properties page, as shown in figure 9.8, contains settings that can make your modem work better when the ___er values are selected.

The Port identification shows the communications port to which Windows ___d the modem. If the modem is an internal Plug and Play type, in which Windows ___figure the serial port, you may have a choice in setting which communications ___se with the modem. If other communications ports are used, or if the modem ___configured by Windows (you must use jumpers to set its port and address), you ___ble to change the communications port assigned to this modem.

FIG. 9.8

The General page of a modem's Properties sheet displays basic information about your modem.

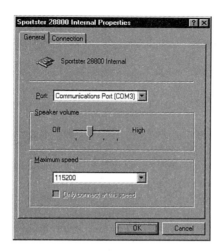

Speaker Volume　The Speaker Volume control is a handy way to tell 32-bit Windows 95 communication programs how loud to set the volume of the modem's speaker.

The volume-control slider works with modems that have physical speakers and with modems (such as PC Cards) that rely on the computer's speaker for their sound. If the volume control is grayed out, the modem has no speaker and no way of using the speaker in the computer. (Many ISDN Terminal Adapters have the Speaker Volume grayed out.)

N O T E　16-bit Windows and DOS communication programs ignore the Speaker Volume setting; instead, they set the modem speaker volume themselves. These older programs set the volume themselves because when they were written, the operating system had no way to keep track of your preferences. ■

Maximum Speed　The Maximum Speed parameter is extremely important. This setting has nothing to do with the speed at which your modem connects to another modem; it represents the speed at which your *computer* connects to your modem.

Why is this important? Any modem that operates at 9600 bits per second or faster typically supports data compression. The International Telecommunications Union (ITU), the professional society that sets world-wide communications standards, has established four data-compression standards. Your modem may support one or all of these standards.

The V.42bis data compression standard offers up to 4X compression. If your modem provides V.42bis, configure the port speed to four times that of your maximum modem speed. To use V.42bis compression, you must enable V.42 error-control.

Table 9.2 shows the standards, the modem speed associated with each standard, and the port speed that you should use with your modem. These general guidelines work for almost all modems.

N O T E   The "bis" suffix to an ITU standard means that it is a revision to another standard. The "bis" term derives from the French word for "two." The V.32 ITU standard defines the 9,600bps modulation rate, while V.32bis revises V.32 to allow up to 14,400bps. V.42 is an error-control standard, and V.42bis is the accompanying compression standard. V.34 defines the 28,800bps modulation standard. Soon there will be a V.34bis which should offer speeds up to 33,600bps. Coupled with V.42/V.42bis, you should see effective throughput nearing 134,400bps. ■

T I P   Do not confuse the term *baud* with the data rate of modem communications. Baud refers to the number of analog signals per second, which cannot exceed 2400 using current phone line equipment. To achieve high rates of data throughput, modem manufacturers squeeze multiple bits into each signal, and rate their modems in bits per second (bps).

Table 9.2   Modem Port Speed Settings

Modem Speed	ITU Standard	Port Speed (bps)
9600	V.32	38,400
14400	V.32bis	57,600
19200	V.32ter	76,800
28800	V.34	115,200

N O T E   You may not be able to set the port speed as high as 115,200bps on older, slower computers. These computers may not have the right type of serial-port hardware, which is based on the type 16550A UART chip. In such a case, use 57,600bps or 19,200bps. See "Port Settings," later in this chapter for more details about the 16550A UART. ■

ON THE WEB

Frequently Asked Questions about modems

http://www.cis.ohio-state.edu/hypertext/faq/usenet/modems/top.html

When modems connect, they negotiate the fastest and most reliable connection. Use compression to raise the effective throughput of the connection. Compression works only if the port speed is fast enough to feed the data to the modem as quickly as the modem needs it. If a 14,400bps V.32bis/V.42bis modem compresses data into a fourth of the space the data takes up on disk, the port must feed data to the modem at least four times as fast as the 14,400bps connect speed. Setting the port to 57,600bps allows for the high speed data feed to the modem.

▶ **See** "Advanced Settings," **p. 298**

Only Connect at this Speed   Select this box if you don't want your modem to adjust its speed to match the speed of the modem on the other end. Checking this box allows only high speed connections between two modems that are each capable of high speeds.

Sometimes bad conditions on the telephone line can make two high speed modems connect at low speeds. Checking this box prevents the low speed connection from taking place. In that case, you have to keep trying the call, until the modems connect at their full-rated speed.

TROUBLESHOOTING

My communication application seems to be running excessively slow. Is there something I can do to improve the performance? Slow communications can be the result of many factors, but one often overlooked is that your modem speed may be too high. Fast data rates can cause overrun errors. If Windows cannot process data as fast as it arrives, the receiving modem has to tell the sending modem to resend the prior data. If overruns occur frequently, the problem worsens. To remedy the situation, experiment with lower speed settings. Alternatively, upgrade your serial port to a 16550A UART chip.

▶ **See** "Port Settings," **p. 301**

Connection Properties

To define the default modem settings used for new connections, click the Connection tab of the Modems Control Panel properties sheet, as shown in figure 9.9.

FIG. 9.9
Use the Connection page to set your default modem connection settings.

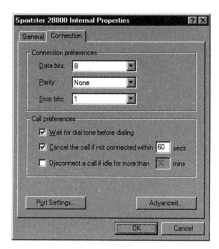

Connection Preferences   The default settings—8 bits, no parity, and 1 stop bit—work for most online services, BBSes, remote-access and remote-control programs, data-transfer services, dial-up networking, and so on. Change these settings only if the resource you are dialing requires different values.

Wait for Dial Tone Before Calling   When this option is enabled, Windows cancels the connection if no dial tone is present when the modem tries to dial. Under normal circumstances, this option should be checked; however, uncheck it if you have any of the following situations:

- You have to dial the phone manually for your modem.
- You are using a phone system with a dial tone that your modem fails to detect.
- You want to speed up the dialing process by a few milliseconds, such that the modem does not wait for a dial tone before dialing.

Cancel the Call if Not Connected Within X Seconds   If the modem you are calling does not answer within 60 seconds, a problem may exist. When you choose this option, you are notified if your call did not connect, so you can check to see whether you have the right phone number. If 60 seconds is not long enough, type a longer duration in the text box.

Disconnect a Call if Idle for More Than X Minutes   This option can save you money if you use commercial online services regularly. If you get interrupted or called away from your computer, Windows disconnects from the service so you won't continue to accumulate expensive online charges.

Advanced Settings

At the bottom of the Connection page is the Advanced button. When you click this button, you see the dialog box shown in figure 9.10.

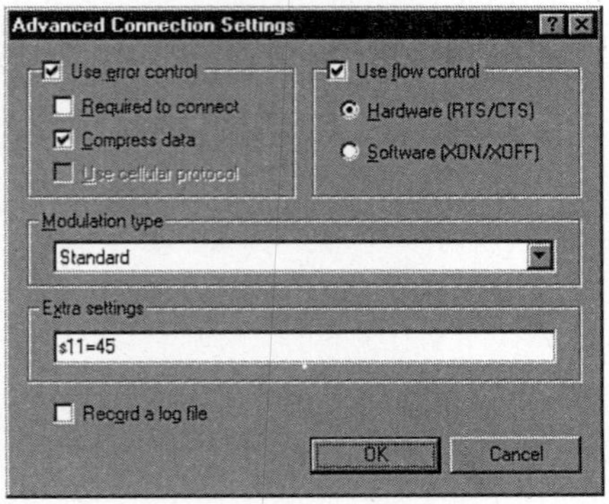

FIG. 9.10
Use the Advanced Connection Settings dialog box to configure modem error control, flow control, modulation, log files, and additional settings.

Your choices in the Advanced Connection Settings dialog box will determine if your modem will work as fast, and as reliably, as its manufacturer intended it to.

Error Control   For modems with data speeds of 9,600bps or faster, Windows turns on the Use Error Control option automatically. When using error control, such as V.42 or MNP 4, the receiving modem verifies data when it arrives. If a bad data transmission is detected, the receiving modem requests the data again.

When modems connect, they negotiate the highest level of error control and compression. If you don't want error control or compression, simply uncheck the Use Error Control check box. To insist that connections use error control, check the Required to Connect check box.

Check the Use Cellular Protocol check box if you use a cellular modem. The cellular error control protocol offers more robust connections for mobile communications moving between cells.

If your modem supports compression, such as the V.42bis or MNP 5 compression standards, choose the Compress Data option. MNP 5 offers 2X compression. MNP 5 doesn't sense when it is sending previously compressed data, such as a ZIP or GIF file, and results in slower effective throughput. Better, V.42bis offers 4X compression and senses when data has already been compressed. Refer to your modem manual to see what level of compression your modem supports.

TIP   If you connect to the Internet via a SLIP (Serial Line Internet Protocol), CSLIP (Compressed-SLIP), or PPP (Point-to-Point Protocol) connection, you should still enable modem compression. CSLIP and PPP compress only the TCP header and do not compress the data. Enabling modem compression can still improve the effective throughput of Internet dial-up connections.

Flow Control   Use flow control to throttle data between your computer and the modem. If data buffers on either side become full, the receiving side will notify the sender to hold off for a moment. If you do not use flow control, data collisions occur resulting in garbled or illegible information.

Check the Use Flow Control check box and choose Hardware if you are using an internal or PC Card modem. You should also choose Hardware when using an external modem rated at 9,600bps or faster, but be sure you are using a hardware-handshaking cable that includes the necessary lines for the Request To Send/Clear To Send (RTS/C?) shake. If you don't choose Hardware, high port speeds can cause data overru and result in excessively slow throughput.

Choose <u>S</u>oftware if you cannot use <u>H</u>ardware flow control. Software flow control (also referred to as XON/XOFF flow control) uses byte sequences in the data of the connection, and can cause problems when transmitting binary files.

Modulation Type   The <u>M</u>odulation Type setting controls how your modem handles connections at 300bps and 1,200bps. Sometimes, your modem may fall back to the slow setting if phone lines are noisy. If your modem tries to connect at 300bps or 1,200bps, you have to decide whether to use U.S. or European standards. <u>B</u>ell works with American modems, and CCITT V.21 works with modems in the rest of the world. If you want to connect to a CCITT V.21 or V.22 modem, make sure your modem can use these standards.

NOTE   U.S. and European modems used different standards until 9,600bps modems became popular. At that time, American manufacturers adopted the standards set by the CCITT (in English, the International Telegraph & Telephone Consultative Committee) and its successor, the ITU (International Telecommunications Union). Now modems all over the world can communicate at 9,600bps and faster. ▪

Extra Settings   If you need to send the modem an AT command that Windows does not include in the modem initialization procedure, type the command in the E<u>x</u>tra Settings box. The AT prefix is not required.

Windows hides extra settings away in this obscure location because Windows architects believe the operating system should handle all details of communicating with the modem. The user should be deterred from sending raw AT commands. Because each brand of modem implements the AT command set differently, an AT command that works on one 28,800bps modem may not work the same on any other brand of modem.

However, if you are certain about your modem's implementation of the AT command set, use the E<u>x</u>tra Settings text box to send additional commands at modem initialization time, right before the modem dials. For example, if you want to speed up the pulse dialing for a modem, enter **S11=55** in the E<u>x</u>tra Settings text box.

Using Log Files   If you repeatedly have trouble making a connection, tell Windows to keep a record of the commands it sends to the modem and the replies from the modem so you can use that record to troubleshoot the problem. You can look for responses from the modem that contain the word ERROR and see what commands caused the errors. To activate this feature, select the Rec<u>o</u>rd a Log File check box.

NOTE   The log file is stored in the Windows directory as MODEMLOG.TXT. You can use Notepad or WordPad to examine the log file. ▪

When you are done making your choices in the Advanced Connection Settings dialog box, click OK. This returns you to the Modem Properties sheet.

Port Settings

At the bottom of the Connection page in the Modem Control Panel is the Port Settings button. When you click this button, you see the dialog box shown in figure 9.11.

FIG. 9.11
Use the Port Settings dialog box to configure the UART settings.

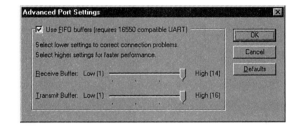

> **NOTE** You can use the Modem Diagnostics tool to determine the type of UART your serial ports use. To use the Modem Diagnostics tool, start the Modems Control Panel. When the Modem Properties sheet appears, click the Diagnostics tab. Select your serial port and choose More Info. The UART for the serial port is shown in the Port Information box. ▪

If you are using either a PC Card modem, an internal modem equipped with a 16550A compatible UART, or an external modem connected to a serial port using a 16550A compatible UART, select the Use FIFO Buffers check box. FIFO (First-In, First-Out) buffers give Windows more time to respond to interrupts, and greatly reduces the chance that data is lost, or overrun errors occur.

You can set the buffer sizes (in bytes,) that the UART uses when communicating to the modem and Windows. Set the Transmit Buffer to the highest level to permit your communication programs to send the modem as much data as available. This reduces the total number of send requests, and can improve the performance of your system when using the modem.

For the Receive Buffer, select the highest value if you have a fast CPU that can respond and process frequent bursts of data. This reduces the total number of Windows interrupts, and can improve the performance of your system when using the modem. If your CPU cannot process bursts of data fast enough, and data overruns occur, reduce the Receive Buffer setting. This offers more reliable communications at the cost of reduced system performance.

Working with Your Modem

Windows 95 uses a technology called the *Telephony Applications Programming Interface* (TAPI) to provide a common and efficient layer between communication programs and the modem. Communication programs written specifically for Windows 95 talk to the TAPI layer, which then issues the appropriate commands to the modem. The benefits of TAPI allow you to:

- Customize your calling locations
- Dial using a calling card
- Share a modem with several applications at the same time
- Share a fax modem with other users over a network

N O T E TAPI features only work with new, 32-bit communications programs that are written to support Windows 95. ■

Customizing Your Calling Locations

A modem used at home usually dials differently from a modem in a hotel room or at the office. In addition to the phone number of the computer you want to dial with the modem, you also have area codes and outside-line codes to deal with, and you might be using a calling card to pay for the calls. Windows 95 collects this information from you as Dialing Properties. Use Dialing Properties to:

- Create and choose from a list of dialing locations, which is especially useful for mobile users
- Define when your modem needs to dial an access code to get an outside line
- Make a calling card call with your modem
- Disable call waiting, so your modem calls will not be interrupted by incoming calls
- Tell your modem whether it can use touch-tone dialing on your phone line, or if the modem must use rotary style pulse dialing

To define dialing properties, click the Dialing Properties button on the General sheet in the Modem Control Panel.

Figure 9.12 shows the Dialing Properties sheet. If you are using your modem at home, where you do not need to dial a code for an outside line but do have the call-waiting feature, your settings may look like the ones shown in figure 9.12.

FIG. 9.12
Set your location information in the Dialing Properties sheet.

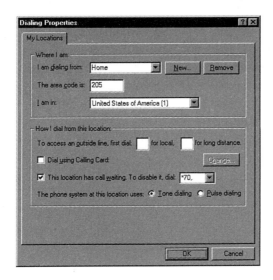

Suppose, however, that you are working in a hotel room in Washington, D.C.; that you need to dial 9 to get an outside line; and that you want to charge the call to a calling card. Type a **9** into the First Dial text box, then check the Dial Using Calling Card box, define the calling card type and account number in the Change Calling Card dialog box. Your settings would look like those shown in figure 9.13.

FIG. 9.13
You can define a calling card to be used for outgoing modem calls.

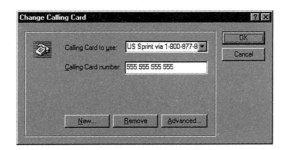

In the Dialing Properties sheet, Windows has created your first Location for you, based on information you gave Setup during Windows installation. Windows has named this the Default Location.

Create additional locations by choosing New on the Dialing Properties sheet. Then, name the location, and fill out the other settings, such as the country and area code. If you no longer need a Dialing Property location, choose the location and click Remove.

Sharing a Modem Between Applications

Suppose that at 3 o'clock in the afternoon, Microsoft Fax is waiting for an incoming fax to arrive. At the same time, the CompuServe Mail driver in Microsoft Exchange is scheduled to check CompuServe to see whether any new mail has arrived. Without missing a beat, TAPI allows the mail driver to use the modem; once the mail driver is finished, TAPI hands modem control back to Microsoft Fax.

If your modem is waiting for a fax under control of the program Microsoft Fax, and you need to use it to call CompuServe with your Windows 3.1 version of WinCIM, which is not TAPI-aware, you must first turn off Microsoft Fax.

In the same way, if your modem is waiting for a fax under control of your legacy Windows 3.1 version of Delrina Winfax Pro, you must turn Winfax off before you can use the modem with any other program

For the TAPI features to work, all the applications in the mix must be TAPI-aware, 32-bit, and written specifically to support Windows 95.

When you use a communications program that is TAPI-aware and Windows 95-aware, you can specify your location before dialing. Examples of programs that take advantage of TAPI locations are Windows HyperTerminal, Windows Phone Dialer, The Microsoft Network online service, Dial-Up Networking, Microsoft Exchange, and any of Exchange's MAPI modules, such as CompuServe Mail.

To learn more about Microsoft Exchange, and MAPI modules that use modems, see Chapter 31, "Using the Universal Inbox."

Sharing a Fax Modem Over a Network

Any user on a Windows 95 network can send faxes via another network user's fax modem. The user who has the fax modem enables the modem as a shared device.

N O T E Windows 95 does not include a way to share data modems over a network. However, there are third-party programs that provide this capability. ■

▶ **See** "Installing and Configuring Microsoft Fax," **p. 914**

Getting Your Modem to Dial

After you define your modem settings, you need to test the modem to verify that it dials properly. Phone Dialer, an accessory that comes with Windows 95, is a good program to perform the test. Run Phone Dialer by opening the Start menu, and choosing Programs, Accessories, Phone Dialer. Figure 9.14 shows the main Phone Dialer dialog box.

FIG. 9.14
Use Phone Dialer to test dial your modem.

When you tell Phone Dialer to dial the number shown in the Number to Dial box, it knows how to handle the area code. Because you defined your location in Dialing Properties, Phone Dialer knows if you are dialing a number in the same area code as your computer; in that case, it leaves off the area code and dials the call as a local call, as shown in figure 9.15. Phone Dialer also knows whether to dial 1 before the number, based on what you define as your dialing properties. When you must dial 1 and the area code for long distance calls in your same area code, select the Dial as a Long Distance Call check box in the Dialing Properties sheet.

FIG. 9.15
When calling in the same area code, Windows dials only seven digits.

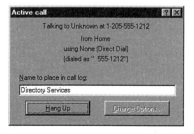

TROUBLESHOOTING

The modem won't dial. In the Modems Control Panel, check to see whether the modem displayed matches your model. If not, choose Add New Modem to install your modem. If any modems that are not in your system appear in the Control Panel, delete their entries.

In the System Control Panel, choose Device Manager. Choose Modems, select your modem, double-click to display the Properties sheet, and click the General tab. The page shown in figure 9.16 indicates that the device is used in the current configuration and that it is working properly

continued

FIG. 9.16
Use Device Manager to see
if your modem is working
properly.

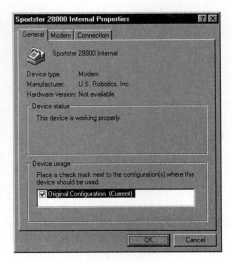

Make sure that the communications port is set correctly. Click the Modem tab, shown in figure 9.17, and check the port name and port speed.

Make sure the port name matches the port that your application wants to use. If the port is set to COM2, for example, make sure your application is trying to use the modem on COM2.

You also can try lowering the port speed. Perhaps your serial port hardware does not support the selected speed. Try a range of speeds between the data speed of your modem and the maximum speed. Use the highest setting that works reliably.

If these suggestions do not work, use Windows' built-in diagnostic tool that tests the communication from your computer to the modem. To use the Modem Diagnostic tool, start the Modem Control Panel. When the Modem Properties sheet appears, click the Diagnostics tab.

Select your modem and choose More Info. Windows issues a series of interrogatory commands to the modem and notes the responses. Figure 9.18 shows sample results. Use the results to verify that the modem is responding to Windows commands. Also, some modems respond with their model number. Cross-check this with your modem settings. Refer to your modem reference manual for the meaning of the responses.

FIG. 9.17
Check the communications
Port and Maximum Speed if
your modem is not working
properly.

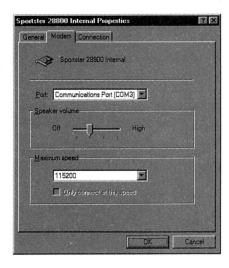

FIG. 9.18
Use Modem Diagnostics to
show modem responses
to basic information
commands.

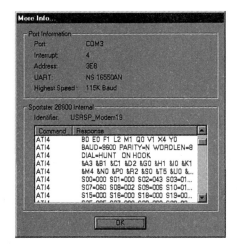

My modem connects, but it does not stay connected. If your phone line has call waiting, incoming calls may be throwing you offline. Use Dialing Properties to disable call waiting. You reach the Dialing Properties sheet by choosing Dialing Properties from the Modem Control Panel.

If that doesn't work, flow control may be set incorrectly. For 9,600bps and faster modems, make sure flow control is set to Hardware.

 To get to the flow control setting, use the Control Panel, double-click the Modem icon, and then choose Properties. Click the Connection tab, and then choose Advanced.

Also, confirm that the cables are good by swapping them with cables that you know to be good—serial cables for external modems as well as your regular phone cables.

continues

continued

My Windows 95 communications programs work fine, but I can't access the modem with a DOS or old Windows communications program. You ran into the TAPI gotcha. TAPI only works if all the communications programs you will be using are TAPI-aware, 32-bit, Windows 95 programs. If Microsoft Fax is waiting for an incoming fax or Dial-Up Networking is waiting for an incoming call, DOS and old Windows programs cannot access the modem; this capability is reserved for TAPI-enabled Windows 95 applications.

My Windows 95 application keeps dialing the wrong number. Check to see whether the Dialing Location properties are set correctly. To do this, use the Control Panel and double-click the Modem icon. Then click Dialing Properties.

Make sure the entry in I Am Dialing From matches your location, and the area code and country shown match where you are as well. If they don't, Windows 95 programs will be dialing phone numbers incorrectly.

Errors occur in file transfers with DOS and old Windows programs. How do I track them down and fix them? If you are using DOS and Windows 3.1 communications programs, you have probably upgraded from Windows 3.1 to Windows 95. There are settings in the old Windows 3.1 SYSTEM.INI file that can cause problems in your new installation of Windows 95.

To correct these problems, some manual editing of SYSTEM.INI may be necessary. You can use NOTEPAD.EXE to perform these tasks.

In the [boot] section of your SYSTEM.INI file, make sure COMM.DRV=COMM.DRV. If it doesn't, edit it so it says **COMM.DRV=COMM.DRV**. This ensures that Windows 95 is using its own communications driver for older, 16-bit programs.

In the [386Enh] section, make sure a line exists that says DEVICE=*VCD. If you don't see DEVICE=*VCD, type it on a line by itself anywhere in the [386Enh] section. Use NOTEPAD.EXE to do this.

Next, set the FIFO buffer to 512 bytes. Determine the communications port you are using with these DOS and old Windows programs. If the port is COM2, for example, add the line **COM2BUFFER=512** in the [386Enh] section of your SYSTEM.INI file. Use the same syntax for other ports. You can add COM2BUFFER=512 on a line by itself, anywhere in the [386Enh] section of SYSTEM.INI. You can use NOTEPAD.EXE to do this.

▶ **See** "Working with Phone Dialer," **p. 934**

CHAPTER 10

Configuring and Using CD-ROM Drives

by Dave Johnson

The CD-ROM has become nearly as essential to computing as the floppy drive; more so, in fact, when you consider that e-mail has effectively replaced floppies around the office and software is increasingly shipped on CD rather than disk, making the CD-ROM a more common sight than the floppy disk for many people. Most new computers, in fact, ship with a CD-ROM drive already installed. Demand for CD-ROM software titles has mushroomed, and vendors are rushing to satisfy the demand.

Most multimedia applications rely on such a quantity of sounds, videos, and images that would not be possible without this ubiquitous little silver disc. A multimedia encyclopedia like Encarta, for instance, consumes about 600M—the equivalent of 500 floppy disks! Also, software vendors ship software on CD for economic reasons: a single CD-ROM is significantly less expensive to press—less than a dollar—than a handful of floppy disks.

Optimize your CD-ROM drive in Windows 95

Squeeze the most performance out of your CD-ROM with the tips in this section.

Use your CD-ROM drive with Windows and other applications

Look here for all the details on using AutoPlay, installing software from the CD and sharing a CD-ROM across a network.

Install a CD-ROM drive

Windows 95 makes the task easier than it used to be, but installing a CD-ROM drive is still anything but child's play.

Increasingly, popular software packages—such as Microsoft Office—ship on CD as well. Installing an application as large as Office is much quicker from CD-ROM: swapping disks can take more than 90 minutes, whereas a CD-ROM installation is done in about 15 minutes. ■

Optimizing CD-ROM Drives in Windows 95

Windows 95 incorporates a new file system specifically designed and optimized for CD-ROM drives. CDFS (CD File System) is a 32-bit, protected-mode file system that provides the following benefits:

- Replaces MSCDEX with a driver that occupies no conventional memory.
- Improves performance of your applications by providing 32-bit, protected-mode caching, and is more efficient than SmartDrive. Your multimedia applications run more smoothly.
- Requires no configuration. CDFS is a dynamic cache.

 TIP Check the contents of your AUTOEXEC.BAT and CONFIG.SYS files—if they only load your CD-ROM and SmartDrive, you don't need your start-up files anymore! Check for MSCDEX.EXE in the AUTOEXEC.BAT and a complementary CD-ROM driver line in the CONFIG.SYS. CDFS can supplant both of these lines.

The CD-ROM cache is separate from your disk cache because it is specifically optimized for use with a CD-ROM drive. Windows normally caches the CD-ROM to memory. However, when Windows needs more memory for your applications, it transfers the cache to the hard drive instead of simply flushing it. The next time Windows needs that particular data, it reads it from the hard drive instead of the CD-ROM. This significantly improves performance, as reading data from the hard drive is as much as ten times faster than reading data from the CD-ROM.

To optimize your CD-ROM do the following:

1. Right-click My Computer and select Properties.
2. Click the Performance page of the System Properties sheet, click File System, and select the CD-ROM tab. The CD-ROM tab appears as shown in figure 10.1.

FIG. 10.1
Your hard disk and
CD-ROM use
separate caches.
They both can be
adjusted in the File
System Properties
sheet.

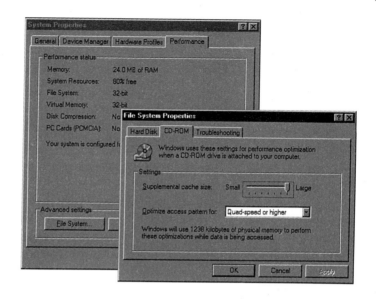

Part
III

Ch
10

3. Drag the Supplemental cache size slider to the setting indicated in table 10.1.

TIP If you need to conserve RAM, keep in mind that a large CD-ROM cache offers a comparatively little performance boost over a small or moderately-sized cache.

Table 10.1 Cache Sizes Based on System RAM

	Up to 8M	8M to 12M	12M or more
Single Speed	64K	576K	1088K
Double Speed	114K	626K	1138K
Triple Speed	164K	676K	1188K
Quad Speed	214K	726K	1238K

4. Select the type of CD-ROM in the Optimize Access Pattern For list, and then click OK.

ON THE WEB

The Internet continues to be a dynamic source of information. For more information about CD-ROMs, try one of these sites

- **ftp://ftp.cdrom.com/pub/cdrom/faq/faq1**   A Frequently Asked Question list from the alt.cdrom newsgroup.

continues

continued

- **gopher://news.wu-wien.ac.at:7119/1comp.publish.cdrom.hardware**   An archive of the comp.publish.cdrom.hardware newsgroup.
- **http://www.cs.yorku.ca/People/frank/**   A home page packed with comparisons of and specifications for many CD-ROM drives.

Using Your CD-ROM Drive

Using your CD-ROM drive in Windows is not much different than using any other drive. Figure 10.2 shows the D: drive icon in My Computer as a CD-ROM. You can access it in My Computer or Explorer just like the other drives in your computer—double-click the icon to open its folder or right-click to display its context menu.

FIG. 10.2
Double-clicking the CD-ROM icon displays a "legacy" disc's contents; if it is an AutoPlay disc, double-clicking runs the main program. Right-clicking the icon provides a menu which includes options like Open, Properties, Share, and Eject.

▶ **See** "Windows Navigation Basics," **p. 49**
▶ **See** "Adding New Hardware to Windows 95," **p. 157**

TROUBLESHOOTING

I have a CD-ROM installed in my machine, but it doesn't show up in My Computer or Explorer. If you are using an external CD-ROM drive, make sure it is turned on.

Windows may not detect your CD-ROM drive when you install Windows for the first time. In this case, use the Add New Hardware Wizard to allow Windows to automatically detect your CD-ROM as described in "Installing Legacy CD-ROM Drives" later in this chapter. If your CD-ROM drive still does not show up in My Computer, right-click My Computer and select Properties. Click the

Device Manager page, select your CD-ROM, and click Properties. A description of the problem and a possible solution is displayed in the Device Status area. If your CD-ROM does not appear in the Device Manager, consult the manual that came with your CD-ROM for more troubleshooting information, or contact the vendor.

I can use my CD-ROM in Windows and in a DOS window, but if I restart Windows in DOS mode, my CD isn't available. The protected-mode driver that Windows uses to control your CD-ROM doesn't function if you boot directly into DOS. You'll need to load a real-mode driver in the AUTOEXEC.BAT and CONFIG.SYS for those special DOS occasions. If you purchased a computer with Windows 95 preinstalled, it is entirely possible that the CD-ROM drive came without such DOS drivers. If that's the case, contact your vendor for the disk containing a compatible CD-ROM driver.

You also may be able to adjust your DOS settings so that the offending program runs without having to reboot to a DOS session. Select MS-DOS Prompt from the Start Menu, and right-click in the title bar when it appears. Select Properties. On the Program page, select the Advanced button and check the button labeled "Prevent MS-DOS based programs from detecting Windows." This won't work for all programs, but it should keep you out of DOS sessions most of the time.

Playing a CD-ROM Automatically

Windows automatically detects when you insert a CD-ROM. As a result, it displays the label of the CD-ROM next to the drive letter in My Computer. When you remove the CD-ROM, it clears the label.

▶ **See** "Installing, Running, and Uninstalling Windows Applications," **p. 471**

Some CD-ROMs for Windows 95 are set up to automatically run when they are inserted into the CD-ROM drive. If Windows detects an *AutoPlay* CD-ROM, it runs the appropriate program on the disc. The Windows 95 CD-ROM is a good example. After you have installed Windows 95, reinsert the CD-ROM in the drive. Almost immediately, a window opens, which gives you the opportunity to add or remove Windows components or play with the multimedia samples on the disc (see fig. 10.3).

N O T E   Of course, only newer CD-ROM discs utilize AutoPlay. There are utilities available from online services which enhance non-AutoPlay "legacy" discs.

AutoPlay Extender (a component of Microsoft's free PowerToys accessories), runs a user-specified shortcut whenever a new disc is inserted. A similar program, FlexiCD (also from the PowerToys collection), adds a convenient icon to the system tray for controlling music CDs. ■

ON THE WEB

These tools are available from Microsoft's World Wide Web site,
http://www.microsoft.com.

FIG. 10.3
This window opens
when you insert the
Windows 95 CD-
ROM. You don't have
to search for
SETUP.EXE.

In the future, software vendors will no doubt use AutoPlay as a marketing tool. AutoPlay
certainly simplifies software installation and saves valuable time.

TIP
You may not always want a program to start when the disc is inserted. To disable AutoPlay, hold
down the Shift key while inserting a CD-ROM in the drive.

It is possible to "permanently" disable the AutoPlay feature of audio CDs as well. Open any file
folder and select View and Options. Look at the File Types page and Edit the AudioCD entry. The
Actions list should include an entry called Play (see fig. 10.4). Select the button marked Set
Default. To re-enable AutoPlay audio CDs, select Set Default again to change the word Play back
to bold.

FIG. 10.4
Audio CDs are a
registered file type,
just like DOC or
BMP files. You can
even specify a
different CD player
for your CDs by
selecting Edit in the
Edit File Type
requester.

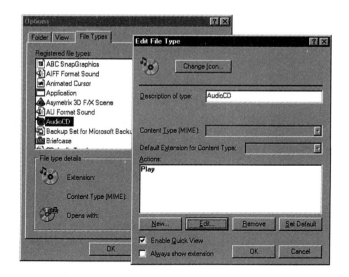

TROUBLESHOOTING

Audio CDs don't automatically play when I insert them. When I go to the Edit File Type page in a folder's View Options, there is no Action listed for AudioCDs. You haven't installed Windows 95's CD Player. Install the CD Player from the Multimedia component section in the Control Panel's Add/Remove Programs.

Windows doesn't automatically recognize a CD-ROM when I insert it. I have to refresh My Computer or Explorer to see the CD-ROM's contents. Auto Insert notification is buried in an unexpected location. Right-click My Computer, select Properties, and select your CD-ROM drive under the CD-ROM heading in the device list. Click the Properties button, and select the Settings page of the property sheet. Make sure the Auto Insert Notification option is checked.

Sharing Your CD-ROM Drive on a Peer-to-Peer Network

If other users on your peer-to-peer network don't have a CD-ROM drive, you may want to share yours. Sharing your CD-ROM drive is similar to sharing any other drive on your computer. However, there are two considerations when sharing a CD-ROM drive:

- If a user *maps* to your shared CD-ROM drive and no disc is in it, he will receive a message that says X:\ is not available when he tries to open it.

- You are sharing a drive, not a particular CD-ROM title. Therefore, if you share the drive with the Windows 95 CD-ROM in it, and then change the disc, you will be sharing the new disc.

 TIP With Windows 95 file sharing for Novell Networks, you can share a CD-ROM drive with other Novell clients, even though Novell is a client/server network.

▶ **See** "Sharing Workstation Drives," **p. 802**

Installing a Software Application from a CD-ROM Drive

Installing software from a CD-ROM drive is similar to installing from floppy disk. For non-AutoPlay discs, there are three methods to install software:

- Double-click the Add/Remove Programs icon in the Control Panel and click the Install button on top of the page where it says, To install a program from a floppy disk or CD-ROM drive.

- Double-click the CD-ROM icon and then double-click either SETUP.EXE or INSTALL.EXE in the Explorer window.

- Open the Start menu and choose Run and type either SETUP.EXE or INSTALL.EXE, as appropriate.

In addition to these methods, many new CD-ROMs are AutoPlay-enabled. In this case, simply insert the CD-ROM in the drive and follow the instructions.

▶ **See** "Installing, Running, and Uninstalling Windows Applications," **p. 471**

 TROUBLESHOOTING

When I try to install a program from a CD-ROM using the Control Panel, I get the message Windows was unable to locate the installation program. Your CD-ROM did not have a SETUP.EXE or INSTALL.EXE file in its root directory. This probably means that the program is intended to be run directly from the disc; simply double-click the application's icon.

If that doesn't work, check the documentation for the correct installation program name, or click Browse to search the CD-ROM for setup program names such as WINSTALL.EXE.

I successfully installed a program from a CD-ROM on my hard drive. When I run the program now, I get an error that says `File not found`**. Or, if I try to use Help, the Help window pops up and displays an error that says** `Help file not found`**.** First, make sure that you have inserted the proper CD-ROM in the drive.

If the error message persists, check to see if the CD-ROM is still assigned to the same drive letter as when you installed the program (adding a hard disk, for instance, can change the CD-ROM's drive letter). If the drive has moved, you need to tell Windows where to find the program. Many CD-ROM programs place an INI file in the Windows directory, which you simply need to edit with the proper drive letter. As an example, Maris's RedShift 2.0 REDSHIFT.INI file looks like this:

```
[RedShift 2.0]
CDDrive=D
[Preferences]
PlanetsQuality=3
WhenFound=3
StartUpLocation=3,15300,3015
```

Change the CDDrive= line and restart the program. As a last resort, if you cannot find the appropriate INI file, simply reinstall the offending program.

Complete Installation   Many applications perform a complete installation: All of the files required to run the program are copied to the hard drive. This is typical of applications that don't require a large amount of space, but are distributed on CD-ROM for convenience.

Partial Installation   Most applications enable you to do a partial installation (see fig. 10.5). In this case, only core components are copied to the hard drive. While a partial installation doesn't sacrifice a significant amount of hard-drive space to store the application, you must always return the CD-ROM to the drive to run the application. It may also run more slowly than if you install the program to your hard drive.

 Often, the speed gain from a complete installation is surprisingly small because the core program is copied to the hard disk in either case. If choosing between a 50M loss to your hard disk or a minor speed advantage, consider the partial installation—particularly if you plan to use the program infrequently.

FIG. 10.5
Selecting partial installation installs only the program files, leaving the data files on the CD-ROM. In the case of Asymetrix 3D F/X, you can install as little as 12M or as much as 37M to your hard disk.

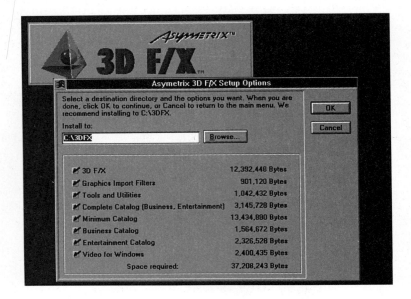

Running Applications from the CD-ROM Drive

A limited number of applications can be run directly from the CD-ROM drive. Few programs work this way because there is a noticeable speed penalty when *all* of the program files must be read from the relatively slow CD-ROM. Commonly, data browsers (like clip art collection programs) and digital magazines are the sort of software which run exclusively from the CD without depositing any data on your hard disk. The HoverHavoc game on your Windows 95 CD-ROM is another example of an application you can run directly from disc.

 If the CD-ROM contains a SETUP.EXE file in the root directory, you probably can't run the application from the CD.

Although most programs generally can't be run directly from the CD-ROM, some discs are compilations of files not meant to be kept on the hard disk:

- *Data Files.* Data such as clip art, bitmaps and 3-D objects occupy a prohibitive quantity of space on your hard drive. You can use these files directly from the CD-ROM or copy them as needed to your hard drive.

  ▶ **See** "Managing Files," **p. 95**
  ▶ **See** "Adding or Removing TrueType Fonts," **p. 272**

▶ **See** "Working with Multimedia," **p. 1083**

■ *Fonts.* Some discs contain collections of fonts that you install via the Control Panel. You cannot use fonts directly from the CD, but you can install them to your hard disk as needed.

■ *Multimedia.* Some CD-ROMs are packed with sounds and videos you can preview directly from the CD-ROM. These are useful for inclusion in presentation programs like PowerPoint. Some discs even embed audio CD tracks along with the data.

> **CAUTION**
>
> Never attempt to play a CD-ROM in an audio CD player, even if it includes audio tracks. The nonaudio data stored on the disc can destroy a set of speakers faster than you can say *Abbey Road*.

■ *Audio CD.* Playing your favorite music from the computer can pick up the pace while you are working—especially if you work in a room without a sound system.

▶ **See** "Using CD Player," **p. 339**

 ON THE WEB

Let your CD-ROM drive help you get up to speed in Windows 95. Internet sites which offer inexpensive discs packed with Windows utilities, games, and drivers include

● http://www.morse.net/w95comp.html

● http://www.cdrom.com/

Installing Plug and Play CD-ROM Drives

In Chapter 5, "Adding New Hardware to Windows 95," you learned how to install Plug and Play devices. Installing a Plug and Play CD-ROM is similar to installing other Plug and Play devices.

Windows takes care of CD-ROM drive installation details that previously drove ordinary people to the brink of insanity: It identifies the hardware and resource requirements, creates the configuration, programs the device, loads the 32-bit device drivers, and notifies the system of the change. The newly installed CD-ROM appears in My Computer the next time you boot Windows.

▶ **See** "Installing Legacy (non-PnP) Hardware," **p. 165**

Part III
Ch 10

Installing Legacy CD-ROM Drives

Installing legacy CD-ROM drives is not as easy as installing Plug-and-Play drives. However, Windows' Add New Hardware Wizard greatly simplifies the task. This wizard looks for clues in your computer that tell it what hardware is installed. Some clues include the following:

- Signatures or strings in ROM
- I/O ports at specific addresses that would indicate a particular class of hardware
- Plug-and-Play devices that report their own ID
- Drivers loaded in memory before you run Setup
- Telltale `device=` lines in the CONFIG.SYS that indicate specific device drivers

N O T E The CD-ROM drive defaults to the next sequential drive letter following your installed hard drives. To specify a particular letter after installation, right-click My Computer and select Properties. Select the Device Manager page and display CD-ROM drive's properties. Select the Settings page and choose the desired drive letter from the list (see fig. 10.6). ■

FIG. 10.6
Setting the designation of your CD-ROM couldn't be easier—just select a letter from the Property sheet in the Device Manager.

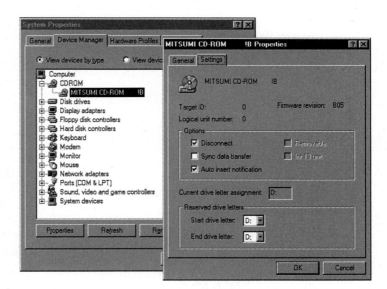

Windows-Supported CD-ROM Types

Windows supports three types of CD-ROM drives—SCSI, IDE, and proprietary CD-ROM drives. The following list describes these drive types:

- *SCSI.* A Small Computer System Interface adapter lets you daisy-chain as many as seven peripherals such as scanners, hard-drives, and CD-ROMs together. SCSI drives—particularly Fast SCSI and Wide SCSI—are faster than IDE hard drives.

- *IDE.* An Interface Device Electronics adapter provides an inexpensive interface for floppy disks, hard drives, and CD-ROMs.

- *Proprietary.* Some manufacturers, such as Sony and Mitsumi, sell CD-ROMs that require a proprietary adapter. These drives require a unique adapter or a sound card that supports the drive's interface. Some sound cards include several interfaces, increasing the odds that your proprietary CD-ROM will fit one of them.

N O T E If you haven't purchased your CD-ROM yet, look for a Plug and Play model. Even if your computer doesn't have a Plug and Play BIOS, Windows can still take advantage of many Plug and Play features. Also, you can transplant the device to a Plug and Play computer later.

If you are running out of open slots and want to purchase a sound card as well, consider a combination sound/CD-ROM adapter card—or purchase a CD-ROM which can plug into your motherboard's IDE port. ■

> **CAUTION**
>
> When buying a Plug and Play adapter, be wary of packaging that says "Plug and Play Ready." Verify that it is truly a Plug and Play device before you purchase it. In many cases, your best gauge is whether the box carries a Windows 95 logo.

ON THE WEB

You also can get a list of Microsoft-approved products from their World Wide Web site at **http://www.microsoft.com**.

Installing the CD-ROM on an Existing Adapter

If you install your CD-ROM drive to an existing adapter that Windows already recognizes, you do not need to do anything else. Simply connect the drive and cables as described in your manufacturer's documentation. Your CD-ROM drive appears in your device list the next time you boot Windows.

CAUTION

If you daisy-chain a CD-ROM drive to an existing SCSI adapter, take care to properly configure the SCSI ID number and terminator pack for proper operation. The last peripheral in the chain must be "terminated" with a resistor pack, which you can probably just move from the previous end of the line—such as your hard disk—to the CD-ROM. As for the SCSI ID, you can use a utility which came with the SCSI card to figure out which ones are in use, or simply experiment.

Remember that Plug and Play doesn't sort out SCSI numbering or termination for you.

Installing a Legacy CD-ROM and Adapter

By installing the driver for your new CD-ROM adapter before actually installing the hardware, you can let Windows suggest a configuration that does not conflict with existing devices in your computer. Therefore, make sure that your have not installed your adapter in your computer before following these steps.

N O T E   If you are installing one of the popular combination sound/CD-ROM adapters, install the sound card device drivers as described in Chapter 11, " Configuring and Using Sound Boards," before continuing installation as described in this chapter. ■

T I P   If you are absolutely sure that your CD-ROM adapter will not conflict with existing devices in your computer, go ahead and install the adapter and allow Windows to automatically detect it.

1. Open the Control Panel and double-click the Add New Hardware icon. The Add New Hardware Wizard opens.

2. Click Next. The wizard allows you to choose between automatically detecting new hardware and manually installing new hardware. Select No and click Next.

3. Choose your adapter—SCSI or CD-ROM Adapter—from the dialog box shown in figure 10.7.

FIG. 10.7

Select either CD-ROM controllers or SCSI controllers from the list, depending on which type of adapter you are installing.

4. Select a manufacturer from the <u>M</u>anufacturers list and a specific model from the Mo<u>d</u>els list (see fig. 10.8). Make sure that your selection matches your adapter. Click Next. The wizard displays information about the recommended settings for this device.

FIG. 10.8

Select a manufacturer and model. If your exact adapter doesn't appear in these lists, you'll need a disk from the manufacturer—this is one occasion that "close enough" doesn't apply.

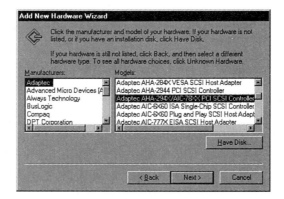

5. Click <u>P</u>rint to output the recommended settings to the printer or write them down on paper. You'll use these settings to configure your hardware before installing it in your computer.

6. Click Next; then click Finish, and Windows installs the necessary drivers on your computer.

7. After Windows has installed the drivers, shut down Windows and turn off your computer.

8. Configure and install the CD-ROM adapter and drive using the instructions provided by the manufacturer and the settings recommended by Windows. For additional information on setting an adapter's I/O address, IRQ line, and DMA address, see Chapter 5, "Adding New Hardware to Windows 95."

The CD-ROM adapter is installed, but you still have to ensure that the CD's sound can get to the computer's speakers. If you are attaching the CD-ROM sound output to a separate sound card, things can get dicey.

Unfortunately, it often seems as if no two CD audio connectors are the same, and unless you get a system preconfigured at the point of sale or purchase a multimedia "kit," it's just dumb luck if your CD-ROM happens to plug directly into your existing sound card.

All CD-ROM audio cables have four wires—a signal and ground for each channel. Knowing that, you can easily create your own cable, assuming you have the actual plug for each end of the connection.

If you're not handy with a soldering iron, an easier solution is to search out a custom cable designed for your specific hardware combination. Many companies, such as Cables to Go (800-225-8646) and AMC (800-882-0587) sell them.

▶ **See** "Setting Resource Values for Legacy Adapter Cards," **p. 167**
▶ **See** "Using CD Player," **p. 339**

TROUBLESHOOTING

I successfully installed my CD-ROM (I can see the files on the CD-ROM using Explorer), but it won't play audio CDs. First, check the volume by clicking the Volume icon in the system tray. Then, run Media Player, select Device, and make sure that there is a menu entry that says CD Audio. If not, install the MCI CD Audio driver as shown in Chapter 37, "Working with Multimedia."

Test the CD-ROM by plugging a pair of headphones into the external audio jack of the CD-ROM. If you hear music using the external audio jack but not through your sound card, your CD-ROM is not properly connected to the sound card; check the connectors both at the sound card and CD-ROM.

I tried to connect my CD-ROM to the sound card but the cable doesn't fit both cards. You'll need a new cable that can connect your CD-ROM drive to your sound card, as previously discussed. Contact the manufacturer or a specialty cable company.

My computer dies during setup after installing my new CD-ROM adapter. Restart your computer. Run Setup again and it will ask you if you want to use Safe Recovery to continue the installation. Choose Safe Recovery and click Next. Continue using the steps described previously in this section. Setup will skip the portions of the hardware detection that caused the failure.

I installed Windows 95 and my computer can no longer find the CD-ROM. Your CD-ROM is probably trying to use incompatible real-mode drivers in the AUTOEXEC.BAT. Run the Control Panel's Add New Hardware to install new 32-bit drivers for your CD-ROM.

Configuring and Using Sound Boards

by Dave Johnson

So many systems now come with a sound card pre-installed that it almost seems like a standard feature. But beware—sound boards are an afterthought in the world of the PC, and they can be frustrating enough to prove it.

There is a bright side, however. Multimedia-ready computers, equipped with a sound card, speakers, and a CD-ROM drive, are capable of playing and recording high quality sounds. Sound cards are essential for video, games, and reference programs. ■

Installing and configuring sound boards

Look here for the procedures and pitfalls for installing sound hardware.

An overview of the sound capabilities in Windows 95

A guide to WAVs, CODECs, and MIDI files.

Using Windows 95 sound accessories

Make the most of your sound card with the software built into Windows 95.

Resolving problems with sound

These troubleshooting tips will help your system sound the way it should.

Using the PC speaker

Someday you might need it—here's how to install the PC speaker driver using Windows 95.

Configuring Sound Boards

Unfortunately, sound cards are just about the trickiest peripherals to install in a PC. Any number of things can lead to sound features not working properly. This section describes how proper configuration can help you avoid sound problems.

Choosing a Sound Board

Sound card technology and features have been changing rapidly. Some of the most important qualities to watch for include the following:

- *8-bit vs. 16-bit.* This refers to the "width" of the sound—more data points in each sample mean greater sonic detail. In fact, 16-bit is fairly close to the threshold for human perception of sound, so it's unlikely the industry will move past 16-bit cards any time soon.

- *8-bit vs. 16-bit DMA.* A 16-bit DMA significantly reduces the overhead on the CPU itself while processing sound, using as little as 8 percent of the CPU's time.

> **CAUTION**
>
> Many 16-bit sound cards feature only an 8-bit DMA, and product packages rarely clarify this specification. If in doubt, call the vendor.

- *Wavetable lookup vs. FM synthesis.* Because MIDI only tells you how to play a note and doesn't contain the actual sound data, the sound card must have some way to generate the necessary tones. *FM synthesis* mimics real sounds by generating artificial tones with an FM-synthesis chip. *Wavetable lookup,* on the other hand, stores actual samples of musical instruments in ROM. Consequently, wavetable cards can sound significantly more realistic.

- *Digital Signal Processing (DSP).* DSP chips can be used as multi-purpose processors for performing all sorts of signal processing tasks on-board the card, freeing the CPU for more pressing matters. DSP-populated cards, for instance, can serve as combination sound and modem boards.

NOTE Wavetable sound cards are typically only as good as the amount of ROM reserved for storing samples. Specifically, more memory typically means higher quality samples and a greater variety of instruments. Most boards feature between 1 and 4M of ROM.

Some cards—like the Sound Blaster AWE32—swap samples as needed from your hard disk to a special cache of RAM located on the sound card. This allows the card to play high-quality wavetable sounds without forcing the card to have egregiously large amounts of memory. ■

ON THE WEB

One of the best ways to stay on top of current drivers and even shop for Windows 95-compatible sound boards is via the Internet. Here's a list of some sites to investigate:

http://creative.creaf.com/www/sound.html   One-stop shopping for Creative Labs.

http://www.mediavis.com/support/win95faq.htm   What works and what doesn't in Windows 95? This page for MediaVision keeps you up-to-date.

http://www.reveal.com   Learn about Reveal's sound cards and pick up a Windows 95 driver to boot.

http://www.teleport.com/~crystal   CrystaLake shows their wares on this page.

Sound Blaster and Windows   Creative Labs' Sound Blaster family of add-on audio boards deserves mention because it has become something of a pseudo-standard among multimedia PCs. Most, though not all sound cards, advertise Sound Blaster compatibility, principally to support DOS applications which can't hook into the Windows' standard sound driver.

Most DOS programs don't care which sound card you have as long as it emulates a standard. You can typically configure it for Sound Blaster digital audio and General MIDI or MPU-401 for MIDI. Check your sound card manual to be sure.

Part
III

Ch
11

Windows Sound System   Another emulation mode which has become moderately popular is the Windows Sound System (WSS), first marketed by Microsoft as a sound card with voice recognition software. While Microsoft's WSS sound card has had a limited impact in the market, it is increasingly common to see vendors emulate the card. Most cards today support either Sound Blaster or Windows Sound System.

Adding a Sound Board

One notorious problem with installing sound cards in the past was figuring out which IRQs and DMAs were in use before installing a card—there was no simple way to do that in older versions of Windows. Windows 95 provides an easier method, however.

To see exactly which resources are available before attempting an installation, follow these steps:

1. Right-click My Computer.
2. Select Properties, and then click the Device Manager tab.
3. Double-click the Computer icon at the top of the list. You'll see a useful li such resources as IRQs, DMAs, and memory addresses in use.
4. Click OK twice to exit the Properties sheet.

CAUTION

From My Computer's Properties sheet, resources may be viewed, not changed, using the Computer icon. To change resources, click the Device Manager tab, select the hardware in question, and view its Properties. Select the Resources tab. Deselect Use Automatic Settings and change the resource as desired.

You should not manually change the settings provided by Windows unless directed by a technical support advisor. Selecting the wrong IRQ can cripple the mouse, for instance, and force you to repair the problem using nothing but keyboard shortcuts. Always write down the original settings before changing them.

Sound problems are often the result of an improperly installed sound card suffering from resource conflicts. The next section discusses the installation of a sound board using Windows 95's Add New Hardware Wizard, which reduces the possibility of conflicts.

TROUBLESHOOTING

I get no sound at all, or when I do it's distorted. Common settings problems, such as an IRQ conflict or a wrong DMA channel selection, can result in no sound at all. A wrong DMA driver setting may also result in distorted WAV file playback. Legacy devices most commonly cause these sorts of problems, and the only solution is to experiment with different jumper settings on the sound card until the sound functions normally.

To define the hardware settings, particularly on older sound cards, you often need to configure groups of pins, called *jumpers*, on the audio board. Jumper configurations vary depending on the board being installed. As a result, a careful reading of the documentation accompanying your new board is a must.

Thankfully, Windows 95 now simplifies the installation of sound cards by recommending a hardware configuration for you via the Add New Hardware Wizard.

N O T E You might want to hold the sound card's own installation program "in reserve," and attempt to install the card with the installation software if the wizard runs into problems identifying the correct configuration for your sound board. ■

CAUTION

With some sound boards, installation problems may occur if you try to install enhanced utilities that come with the board after you use Windows 95's Add New Hardware Wizard. This is because older sound cards rarely offer an option to install the utilities separately from the drivers, and may write older drivers to your hard drive. Contact the manufacturer to see if this will be a problem with your system.

N O T E Some cards come with CD controllers built-in. When this happens, you need to install the card in Windows 95 and then configure the CD portion at the same time you install the sound card.

If the card contains multiple CD-ROM interfaces, you may need to run a utility provided with the card in order to prepare the card. This allows Windows to recognize the proper interface. ■

If you are installing a Plug and Play sound card, install the hardware using the manufacturer's instructions, and then power up your computer. Windows should recognize the device and install its device drivers.

▶ **See** "Installing Legacy CD-ROM Drives," **p. 320**

To install a legacy device, see Chapter 5, "Adding New Hardware to Windows 95." In brief, the sound card can be installed this way:

1. Don't install the card itself until the Add New Hardware Wizard has recommended specific resource settings.

2. Select Add New Hardware from the Control Panel. Then, select Sound, Video and Game Controllers from the manual installation list (see fig. 11.1).

Part
III

Ch
11

FIG. 11.1
Select Sound, Video and Game Controllers from the wizard's Hardware Type list.

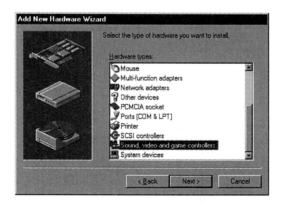

3. When the wizard displays the recommended hardware settings for your sound card, write them down and configure your card to match those settings. Shut down the computer and install the card (see fig. 11.2).

FIG. 11.2

The Add New Hardware Wizard recommends settings for your sound card based on information stored in the Registry.

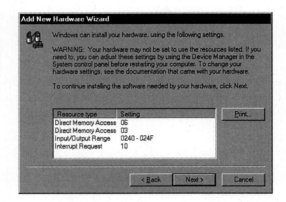

N O T E   You also can install the sound card prior to running the Add New Hardware Wizard, and then choose Yes to the question, "Do you want Windows to search for your new hardware?" However, this method is less reliable when installing legacy devices. ■

Adding or Changing Hardware Drivers

Any time you add a component or peripheral to your PC, you need to make sure a software driver is also installed. The driver acts as a liaison between the computer operating system and the device, so they can communicate. You may need to change drivers if an updated one becomes available. With Windows 95, you can easily add or change hardware device drivers using Device Manager. Follow these steps to update a sound card driver:

1. Right-click My Computer and select Properties.

2. Select the Device Manager tab (see fig. 11.3).

3. Double-click Sound, Video and Game Controllers.

4. Double-click your sound card.

5. In the Properties sheet, click the Driver tab (see fig. 11.4).

FIG. 11.3

Device Manager enables you to change driver settings.

FIG. 11.4

The Driver page for your sound card (in this case, Sound Blaster AWE32) enables you to change drivers.

6. Click Change Driver. The Select Device dialog box appears. A list details the models compatible with your hardware. Depending on your hardware, you may have only one or many choices. If the hardware you want to set up is not on the list, select the Show All Devices option. The list changes to show all devices (use this category with caution, as it includes drivers that are, by definition, incompatible with your hardware).

7. Click the device you want to set up, and then OK.

8. Continue clicking OK until you exit the System Properties sheet.

Setting Up a MIDI Instrument

One benefit of some sound boards is the ability to plug a MIDI instrument into a MIDI port to record and play back music. Here is how to set up a MIDI instrument:

1. Plug the instrument into the sound card's MIDI port.

2. Open the Start menu and choose Settings, Control Panel.

3. Double-click the Multimedia icon.

4. In the Multimedia Properties sheet, click the MIDI tab (see fig. 11.5).

FIG. 11.5
Assign an external MIDI instrument to your sound card using the Multimedia Properties sheet.

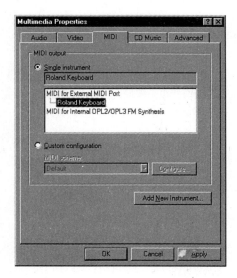

5. Click Add New Instrument.

6. Follow the instructions on-screen to install the instrument.

7. Choose Single Instrument on the MIDI page.

8. Select the instrument you just installed and click OK.

TROUBLESHOOTING

My MIDI instrument doesn't seem to be "talking" to the computer. Often, MIDI instruments can operate in multiple settings, such as "multitimbral" and "performance" modes. Check your instrument's manual to see which modes accept MIDI commands.

Moving a MIDI Instrument to Another Sound Board

You can move MIDI instruments between sound boards using these steps:

1. Open the Start menu and choose Settings, Control Panel.

2. Double-click the Multimedia icon.

3. On the Multimedia Properties sheet, click the Advanced tab.

4. Click the plus sign next to MIDI Devices and Instruments. A sub-list of devices appears.

5. From the resulting list, click the plus sign next to the sound board your MIDI instrument was connected to (see fig. 11.6).

FIG. 11.6
Clicking the plus sign next to your sound device expands the list to show your MIDI instrument.

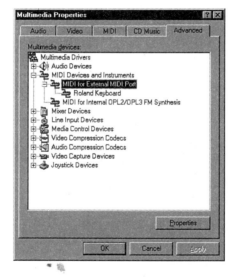

6. Click the instrument you want to move, and then click Properties.

7. Click the Detail tab.

8. Select the name of the sound board you want to connect the instrument to from the MIDI Port list.

9. Connect your MIDI instrument into the new sound board you just specified using the appropriate port, by following the instructions that came with your sound board.

MIDI and WAV Sound Files

Windows is designed to play two types of audio formats in addition to CD audio:

- *Digital* (or *Waveform*) audio, called *WAV* files

■ *Musical Instrument Digital Interface*, or *MIDI*

Windows 95 includes built-in support for both MIDI and WAV audio. However, you'll need a sound card to appreciate these formats.

WAV files constitute a digital copy of the actual sound, and consequently consume a great deal of disk space. Several variables contribute to file size, such as the number of bits per sample, sample frequency, and stereo or mono recording.

MIDI, on the other hand, isn't a digital clone of the original sound. MIDI keeps only a record of *how* the sound is played, much as how a vector drawing doesn't store every pixel to be drawn. The MIDI file consults these "instructions" when you want to play the sound back and relies on hardware to shape the actual tones. MIDI, consequently, is significantly more vulnerable to sound card quality than are WAV files.

N O T E   MPU-401 is a MIDI interface which many sound cards claim to have and most DOS games look for to produce high quality sound. Not all sound boards provide the MPU-401 in hardware, though, and instead try to emulate it in software. That can be a problem with some DOS programs that disable TSRs before the program begins. Result: no music. ■

MIDI works well in multimedia presentations, where small files are preferable and it's important to be able to synchronize music with the display.

N O T E   Many new PCs are billed as multimedia-ready with built-in CD-ROM and sound board capabilities, but these PCs rarely contain high-end sound cards with wavetable synthesis. Be sure to ask which sound card is included in the system, and, if necessary, swap it out for one that meets your needs. ■

Audio Codecs

Capturing sound to your hard drive takes a great deal of disk space. Therefore, Windows 95 offers a collection of sound compression technologies, called *codecs*. Codecs compress audio as it is recorded, and decompress it on-the-fly as it is played back. You can see the codecs installed by Windows by double-clicking Multimedia in the Control Panel. Select the Advanced page and double-click Audio Compression Codecs (see fig. 11.7). Table 11.1 shows how well each codec compressed the same 3.5 second file (most codecs are configurable—the highest quality was selected for comparison):

Table 11.1 Comparison of Audio Codecs

File Format	Attributes	Sound Quality	File Size
PCM	44,100 Hz 16-bit Stereo	Excellent— use for "lossless" masters	602K
ADPCM	44,100 4-bit Stereo	Good general purpose codec	150K
CCIT	44,100 Hz 8-bit Stereo	Good general purpose codec	300K
GSM	44,100 Hz Mono	Good, somewhat noisy	30K
TrueSpeech	8000 Hz 1-bit Mono	Appropriate for voice recordings only	3.7K

FIG. 11.7
Windows 95 installs a variety
of audio codecs in the
Multimedia Properties sheet.

ON THE WEB

Want to learn more about computers and music? Here are a few Internet locations with something to offer in that area:

http://ac.dal.ca/~dong/music.htm   An online music lesson, this site talks about file formats, audio players, and has lots of music-related links.

http://www.teleport.com/~crystal/   There's an info-packed MIDI tutorial here on CrystaLake's home page.

Can't get enough of the technical details? These sites can tell you more than you want to know regarding audio formats on a variety of computing platforms:

ftp://ftp.eecs.umich.edu/pub/nextmusic/FAQ. AudioFormats.part1

ftp://ftp.eecs.umich.edu/pub/nextmusic/FAQ.AudioFormats.part2

▶ **See** "Using Sound Recorder," **p. 341**

Windows 95 Sound Accessories

Windows 95 has some useful accessories for recording and playing sounds, either from audio CDs or recorded files.

CD Player enables you to play audio CDs from your CD drive while you are working in another application. CD Player offers many of the controls found in standalone audio CD players and operates much the same way. In addition, CD Player enables you to edit your play list for each CD, and the program remembers that list each time the disc is inserted.

Sound Recorder is a very rudimentary digital recording system. It enables you to make small recorded files that you can edit and mix into other sound files or insert in documents like Web pages and multimedia presentations.

ON THE WEB

When you need more features than Sound Recorder provides, commercial programs abound. Shareware and freeware programs are available as well, and they often match the features found in more expensive products. Investigate these programs online, from sources such as CompuServe and Cnet Central Online (**http://www.cnet.com**):

>   Cool Edit

>   Gold Wave

>   Wham

Using CD Player

CD Player enables you to play audio CDs in the background while you are working in another application (see fig. 11.8). To access CD Player, open the Start menu. Then choose Programs, Accessories, Multimedia, CD Player.

FIG. 11.8
The CD Player allows you to play audio CDs and edit play lists like a "real" CD player.

Menu bar

Standard CD player controls

Time indicator

Artist name

CD title

Current track

Status bar

CD Player includes a number of advanced functions that you access from the menu bar, such as Random Order, Continuous Play, and the ability to edit your play list.

Using the View and Options Menus   The View menu offers three sets of options. The first set of options enables you to customize the general CD Player screen:

- Toolbar enables seven toolbar icons which control such functions as time display (time elapsed and time remaining) and play mode (random or continuous).

- Disc/Track Info enables the CD disc and track information at the bottom of the general CD Player screen.

- Status Bar enables the status bar at the bottom of the window.

The second set of options on the View menu enables you to change the time displayed in the time indicator window, and is self-explanatory.

The final item on the View menu is the Volume Control, which enables you to set levels for volume, wave, and MIDI (see fig. 11.9).

 The Volume Control can be added to the system tray for easy access. Double-click Multimedia in the Control Panel and select the Audio tab. Select the Show Volume Control on the Taskbar check box.

The Options menu lets you choose between play modes like random and continuous play. Intro play is like the scan mode on some systems; it plays just the first few seconds of a song and then moves to the next song.

FIG. 11.9

The Volume Control option in the View menu lets you set CD audio, WAV, and MIDI volumes, plus speaker balance as well.

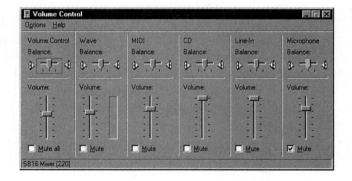

 T I P You can adjust the length of the Intro Play sample by choosing Options, Preferences. Ten seconds is the default.

Editing a Play List A play list is a queue of songs that you want to play. With CD Player, you can specify the tracks you want played from a CD and the order in which they should play.

You can change the play list by first choosing Edit Play List from the Disc menu in CD Player. The CD Player's Disc Settings dialog box appears (see fig. 11.10).

FIG. 11.10

You can customize each CD's play list by moving Available Tracks to the Play List column.

The left window shows the desired Play List, and the right window lists all Available Tracks on the audio CD. To remove a track from the Play List, highlight it and choose Remove. To add a track to the Play List from the Available Tracks list, highlight it and click Add.

Using Sound Recorder

The Sound Recorder provides an introduction to the world of digital recording. Use Sound Recorder to record and edit small sound files.

This section provides an overview of the basic features of Sound Recorder. You access Sound Recorder in much the same way you access CD Player:

1. Open the Start menu and choose Programs, Accessories, Multimedia.
2. Choose Sound Recorder to open the Sound Recorder dialog box (see fig. 11.11).

> **CAUTION**
>
> Most sound cards have both line and microphone inputs, and attaching a powered microphone—like the one which comes with the Windows Sound System—to the wrong input can damage your speakers. Microphone inputs are amplified because they expect a much lower signal than line inputs, so test your connection at a low volume to be sure you won't overdrive the system.

FIG. 11.11
Sound Recorder enables you to record sounds for future playback.

Visual wave display
Length
Menu bar
Progress bar
Position
Control buttons

The Sound Recorder display shows several important bits of information:

- *Position*. Your current location in a sound file, akin to a cursor in a Word document.
- *Length*. Total size of the file, in seconds.
- *Visual Wave display*. A graphic representation of the sound sample. More sophisticated sound editors allow you to edit start and end points in this display and show "clipping limits," where the sound will distort from over-amplification.

The File menu contains two particularly useful options. Revert enables you to undo a deleted section of a sound file, and Properties enables you to change the size and quality of a recorded sound (see fig. 11.12).

 Sound Recorder initially captures all sounds in PCM format. To shrink the file size, you must apply a Codec from the Properties sheet.

FIG. 11.12
The Properties option from the File menu enables you to change the quality of the recording by changing the format.

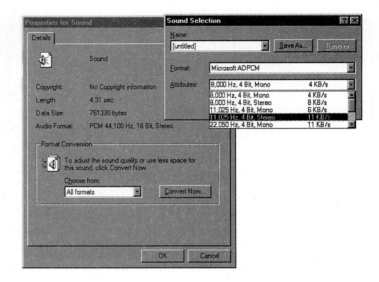

 T I P The Revert command works only if you have *not* saved the sound file.

The Edit menu offers a variety of options, some of which may sound familiar but actually accomplish tasks not normally associated with those commands:

- *Copy.* Copies a sound to the clipboard.
- *Paste Insert.* Inserts a sound into a document.
- *Paste Mix.* Inserts a mixed sound file.
- *Insert File.* Enables you to insert a file into another file at the point where you position the slider.
- *Mix with File.* Enables you to mix another file with the file playing at the point where you position the slider.
- *Delete Before Current Position.* Deletes everything before a specified point, once you have moved the slider to the point in the sound file where you want to cut.
- *Delete After Current Position.* Deletes everything after a specified point, once you have moved the slider to the point in the sound file where you want to cut.
- *Audio Properties.* Opens the Audio Properties sheet, from which you can change various properties for both recording and playback, such as volume (see fig. 11.13).

FIG. 11.13

Change recording and playback specifications, such as volume level and desired sound device (if you have more than one) using the Audio Properties option.

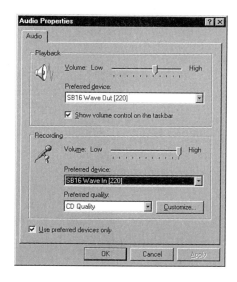

The Effects menu offers options that allow for effects to be added to the sound file:

- *Increase Volume [by 25%]*. Increases the volume of a sound file.
- *Decrease Volume*. Decreases the volume of a sound file.
- *Increase speed [by 100%]*. Increases the speed of a sound file.
- *Decrease Speed*. Decreases the speed of a sound file.
- *Add Echo*. Adds an echo effect to a sound file.
- *Reverse*. Plays a sound file in reverse.

T I P You cannot change the speed of a sound or add an echo if the sound file has been compressed.

▶ **See** "Compressing a Hard Disk," **p. 626**

N O T E Increasing the volume of a sample also amplifies the noise. For best results, optimize your hardware so ramping the volume isn't necessary in "post production."

Some ways to ensure optimal sound quality include:

- Ensuring that the microphone is attached to the appropriate input.
- Adjusting the volume slider on your sound card, if there is one.
- Positioning the microphone away from sources of background hum.

Part

III

Ch

11

Problems with Sound

Many problems can occur when you are trying to get sound capabilities working on a PC because of the complexity of the operation between the system and the components. Windows 95's Plug and Play and easy-to-use Device Manager registry help keep track of available IRQs and I/O addresses, but things can still go wrong.

TROUBLESHOOTING

I hear a hissing sound during playback of sound files. If you hear a hissing sound during the playback of a sound file, the file may be recording in 8 bits and playing back in 16 bits.

Converting the sound file into a different codec will often solve this problem.

When I play video and sound files together, they appear out of step with each other. You may have a computer that isn't fast enough to keep up with the data. You may improve performance by adding RAM, but only if you have 8M or less. Expanding beyond 16M offers few benefits.

If your system has an older, slower processor and a relatively slow hard drive, you can solve this problem by upgrading your PC.

I've installed my sound card, but instead of audio through the speakers, sound is coming from the PC speaker. Believe it or not, the speakers are simply inserted in the wrong plug on the sound card. Some sound cards can sense the presence of speakers, and in their absence, route audio to the PC speaker.

Should hardware conflicts occur, Windows 95 includes a troubleshooting guide to help you solve them. From the Start menu, select Help. Click the Contents tab, and then double-click Troubleshooting. Finally, select "If you have a hardware conflict." The Hardware Conflict Troubleshooter will take you through an investigative process that should resolve most hardware conflicts, or at least identify the conflict (see fig. 11.14).

FIG. 11.14
The Troubleshooting Wizard steps you through hardware conflicts, and points out solutions you might not otherwise be aware of.

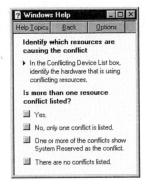

Using the PC Speaker

In rare cases, you may need to resort to enabling the PC speaker. Clearly, *any* sound card is preferable to using the tiny speaker built into your PC, but there are occasions when you may need to—if your sound card fails, for instance. In addition, PC speaker sound may be valuable in offices where installing sound cards would be a prohibitive expense.

Installing the PC Speaker The driver for the PC speaker isn't included with the Windows 95 installation. You'll need to download it from an online service. It can, for instance, be found in the Microsoft Connection on CompuServe as SPEAK.EXE. To install the file after you have downloaded it, follow these steps:

1. Copy SPEAK.EXE to an empty directory and run the program to extract the files.
2. Install the driver by choosing Add/Remove Hardware in the Control Panel. Select No when Windows asks to search automatically. Then, select Sound, Video and Game Controllers.
3. Select the directory which contains the SPEAK program using Have Disk, and follow the remaining instructions.

N O T E The SPEAK driver for the PC speaker only plays WAV files; it will not play MIDI files because it cannot perform FM synthesis or wavetable lookup to reproduce MIDI instruments.

Part III
Ch 11

CAUTION
If your mouse freezes during audio playback while using the speaker driver, your computer hasn't crashed. By default, this driver disables PC interrupts (IRQ) for higher quality sound.

To assure mouse control, double-click the Multimedia icon in the Control Panel. Select the Advanced tab and click Audio for Sound Driver for PC Speaker. Select Properties, then Settings, and check the button marked Enable Interrupts during Playback.

CHAPTER 12

Optimizing Video Performance

by Dave Johnson

Until 1992, Windows PCs more closely resembled high-tech typewriters than the multimedia jack-of-all-trades they represent today. In fact, until PCs could actually *do* multimedia, most people regarded the very idea of multimedia as a gimmick.

A few years can make quite a difference. Today, video technology hasn't quite matured, but it has certainly reached a level of sophistication allowing everyone from educators to salesmen to see why it's important. Video's time has come in part due to faster processors, the proliferation of CD-ROMs, and improved video playback software, such as Microsoft's Video for Windows and Apple's QuickTime. And MPEG-1, though only an interim technology, vividly demonstrates that full screen video is a key part of our computing future.

Microsoft introduced Windows 95 by calling it an immediate multimedia upgrade. And while Windows 95 doesn't yet have all the multimedia goodies that Microsoft initially promised, it does contain substantial improvements from the ground up. Features such as

Video enhancements in Windows 95

Find out about a host of improvements Windows 95 has added to the video display engine.

Video compression and decompression drivers available for Windows 95

Look here to learn about compression/decompression schemes that Windows 95 uses to display video.

Using full-motion video in Windows 95

A balanced system is essential for Windows 95 to effectively play videos. These tips help you optimize your system for video playback.

Optimizing Windows 95 for broadcast-quality video

Capturing broadcast-quality video isn't rocket science, but it's close. This section describes the hardware you need to make it work.

Playing video in Windows 95.

Learn how to use Windows' video playback software.

the *CDFS* (CD File System) and *DCI* (Display Control Interface) have removed the soft-ware bottlenecks that Windows 3.1 presented getting data from disc to screen. ▪

▶ **See** "Configuring and Using CD-ROM Drives," **p. 309**

Video for Windows 95

Windows 95 incorporates significant enhancements in the video for Windows architec-ture. Video sets up easier now and performs significantly better. In short, Windows 95 has made multimedia accessible to virtually every desktop.

▶ **See** "Configuring and Using Sound Boards," **p. 327**

▶ **See** "Working with Video and Animation," **p. 1119**

Easy Video Setup

The Video for Windows architecture is built into Windows. Windows automatically in-stalls and configures the components necessary to use video when you first set up Win-dows, removing much of the anguish that accompanied multimedia in the past. This means that users are more likely to tap into the power of video, and you can distribute multimedia files such as AVI to any Windows 95 user without worrying about whether they have Video for Windows installed.

Default Video Devices   Figure 12.1 shows the multimedia devices installed on a typical Windows computer. Though several of these devices, like QuickTime, have been added by other programs, Windows installs support for video compression, video capture, and specialized tools like laser disc players. To see the list of devices installed on your computer, double-click the Multimedia icon in the Control Panel and select the Advanced tab of the property sheet.

▶ **See** "Exploring the Multimedia Properties Sheet," **p. 1092**

Plug and Play Devices   Plug and Play and the Add New Hardware Wizard are Windows 95 features that enable users to easily install new video hardware. Unlike in the past, you can now literally insert a Plug and Play video device into your computer, turn it on, and Windows recognizes it.

The Add New Hardware Wizard also simplifies the task of setting up legacy devices by automatically detecting the hardware and configuring the drivers. Windows comes with drivers for most of the popular video devices available on the market today.

▶ **See** "Adding New Hardware to Windows 95," **p. 157**

FIG. 12.1
View your multimedia devices through the Multimedia icon of the Control Panel.

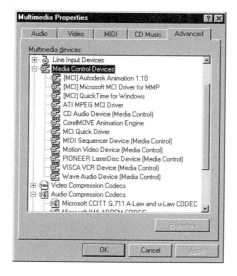

Improved Video Performance

An uncompressed 60-second video that is 320×240 pixels and 15 frames per second requires more than 200M of video data—that's 3M per second! Even when compressed, the sheer amount of data moving through the system can overwhelm your hardware, leading to jerky video.

The performance improvements incorporated into Windows 95 directly address this shortcoming. It's now possible to play high-quality videos in a larger window, potentially up to 640×480 pixels with the right hardware. Windows 95 has these performance enhancements:

- *DCI.* The Display Control Interface (DCI) greatly improves the rate at which video memory is updated. DCI enables video software to interact more directly with the hardware.

- *CDFS.* The CD File System (CDFS) improves throughput from the CD-ROM by providing an optimized, 32-bit protected-mode file system. Because Windows reads data from the drive more efficiently, videos are smoother.

- *Multitasking.* Windows preemptive multitasking minimizes "stutters" during video playback caused by background tasks stealing too much processor time.

More Exciting Video

Very few multimedia games were ever published for Windows 3.1 and with good reason: performance was too slow for graphically intense games such as *Doom*. Many games

Part
III

Ch
12

relied on painting directly to the video device and using device-dependent features—functions which could only be done in DOS.

Windows 95 provides such significant performance improvements that game developers can finally take a serious look at Windows. WinG provides for virtually direct access to the display device while retaining complete compatibility with Windows. Games like *Doom* have been ported to Windows using WinG and perform nearly as well as in DOS.

▶ **See** "Playing with Windows 95: The Games," **p. 1159**

DCI Standard in Windows 95

Display Control Interface (DCI) is the result of a joint effort between Microsoft and Intel to produce a display driver interface that enables fast, direct access to the video frame buffer in Windows. Also, DCI enables games and video to take advantage of special hardware support in video devices that improves the performance and quality of video. For example, a video player can take advantage of color-space conversion that enables color conversion to RGB (Red Green Blue) to occur in hardware rather than software. Although DCI enables direct access to the frame buffer, like WinG, it too retains complete compatibility with Windows GDI.

DCI is available for all display devices in Windows. DCI improves access to SVGA display devices and newer devices that include hardware support for stretching, double buffering, and more. Some of the possible hardware-specific features are described here:

- *Stretching*. Stretching enables the hardware to change the size of the image instead of having the software do it. Therefore, the software sends the same number of pixels as before, but the hardware stretches the image to the requested size.

- *Color-space conversion*. Colors are stored in a video using YUV—a representation of color based on how people perceive colors. Before the image can move to the display device, it must be converted to RGB values. Hardware conversion saves a lot of time—potentially as much as 30 percent—by freeing the software from this task.

- *Double-buffering*. Double-buffering is an animation technique that draws the "next" screen in memory while displaying the current one. Because the new screen can be copied very quickly to the display buffer, video playback appears much smoother.

- *Chroma key*. Chroma key enables two streams of video to merge. A particular color in one of the streams is designated a "matte" and made transparent, so video behind it shows through. This process is similar to the "blue screens" that weather forecasters and special effects artists rely on.

- *Asynchronous drawing*. In conjunction with double-buffering, asynchronous drawing provides for faster screen painting outside the display buffer.

Applications using Windows 95 notice performance improvements. On a 486 DX/2 66 with local bus video, DCI provides reasonable 640 × 480 video at 15 frames per second. This is full-screen, but visibly jerky, video.

On the same computer, DCI also provides smooth video in a 320 × 240 pixel (quarter-screen) window at 30 frames per second. This playback is much better, but unfortunately, there are few videos recorded at 30 frames per second. Figure 12.2 shows a quarter-screen video playing.

FIG. 12.2
Videos can be viewed from the Preview page of the .AVI icon's properties sheet.

N O T E DCI has no effect on hardware video co-processors such as MPEG. MPEG video processors don't use software to draw pixels on-screen and therefore receive little or no benefit from DCI. ▪

▶ **See** "Capturing Video," **p. 1135**

Part
III

Ch
12

Codec Implementation in Windows 95

It's not surprising why consumers were initially so blasé about Video for Windows. Television—the contemporary standard for audio-video—produces a fuzzy analog display that roughly equates to 640 × 480 pixels drenched in about four million glorious colors. Video for Windows, by comparison, provided a 160 × 120 pixel window with just 256 grainy colors.

For Video for Windows to duplicate the television's level of realism with the much sharper computer display, however, images need to go right to the threshold of human color perception—about 16 million colors. At TV resolution, that translates into 27M of data per second without audio, well in excess of anything you'd find in any mail order catalog then or now.

In an effort to make computer-based video achievable, you need to make the picture smaller—much smaller. A 320 × 240 pixel video playing at 15 frames per second requires the file system to deliver just 3M of data each second. Unfortunately, even that small fraction of the earlier data rate isn't remotely possible even with today's quad-speed CD-ROMs. Thus, *codecs* have evolved over the last few years to handle *co*mpression and *de*compression of video. Video for Windows isn't itself a codec. It is a shell that supports a variety of compression schemes. Windows 95 includes support for four video codecs, and third-party vendors can add their own codecs as needed. Figure 12.3 shows the codecs installed in a typical computer. Only videos which use a codec listed in this property sheet can be viewed on this computer. The miro driver near the bottom of the list supports a hardware-based codec from a video capture card. A few years ago, PCs weren't fast enough to decompress video in real-time via software, so all codecs were based in hardware. Today, only high performance codecs like this miro driver still need to be based in silicon.

FIG. 12.3
View the video codecs on the Advanced page of the Multimedia Properties sheet.

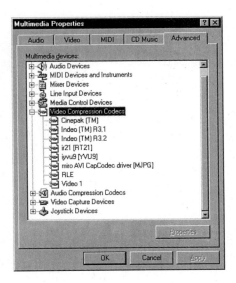

The following list describes the video codecs in Windows 95:

- *Cinepak.* Cinepak is licensed from SuperMac. It provides good quality video playback at 15 frames per second or better and 320 × 240 pixels. Cinepak is used for both Windows and Macintosh, making it a natural choice for "multiplatform" applications.

- *Indeo*. Indeo was developed by Intel. It, too, provides good quality video playback at 15 frames per second or better and 320 × 240 pixels. Indeo is another common codec used primarily on Windows.

- *Video 1*. Video 1 has low overhead and is a good, average quality codec. This codec was developed by Microsoft.

- *RLE*. RLE stands for *run length encoding*. RLE cannot handle rapidly changing frames. Instead, it is often used to compress bitmaps.

 T I P If you want the codecs to install automatically when installing Windows 95, don't select the "Compact" installation option.

N O T E MPEG (Motion Pictures Experts Group) is a codec, not currently supplied by Windows, that provides high-quality 640 × 480 video at 30 frames per second. Approximately 75 minutes of VHS-quality video can be compressed and stored on a single CD-ROM. A full-length feature film can be distributed on two CD-ROMs.

Because MPEG is so computationally intensive, software-based playback schemes are usually inadequate—MPEG plays back best with hardware support. Many new video cards include MPEG hardware, alleviating the need for separate MPEG cards.

▶ **See** "Working with Video and Animation," **p. 1119**

To see which codec a particular video uses, right-click the AVI file and click the Details tab of the Property sheet. Figure 12.4 shows the property sheet for GOODTIME.AVI as found on the Windows 95 CD-ROM.

 T I P The AVI file's property sheet holds a lot of information. Most importantly, it reveals the data rate required for playback.

Part

III

Ch

12

Apple's QuickTime for Windows

QuickTime is the standard video player for Macintosh computers. More and more, though, QuickTime is becoming the video player of choice within Windows because of its superior performance, "VR" mode (which allows the user to wander around very large, panoramic scenes), and its capability to play MIDI tracks from within a video.

Another advantage, at least from the developer's point of view, is that QuickTime is available for both Windows and Macintosh. That means that developers need only create videos once for dual release, saving time and money.

Apple has made QuickTime 2.0 for Windows available for download from CompuServe. To download, **GO QTIME**. Select Download QuickTime 2.0 for Windows from the list and follow the instructions.

ON THE WEB

QuickTime 2.0 for Windows is also available on other online services, such as America Online, or directly from Apple at

http://quicktime.apple.com/

N O T E   QuickTime 2.0 for Windows is not a Windows 95 application. Therefore, if you select its property sheet (right-click a QuickTime file and choose Properties) it will not display the same information as a Video for Windows file. ■

FIG. 12.4
The details of GOODTIME.AVI on your Windows 95 CD-ROM. Notice the transfer rate of 197 KB/s—most computers will have trouble with videos which need much more than about 600 KB/s.

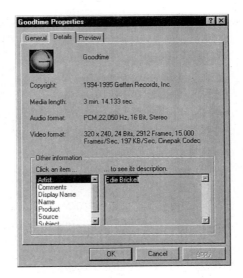

Windows System Requirements for Full-Motion Video

If you expect to achieve satisfying video performance with your PC, you have to start with a solid foundation. No amount of system tweaking, for instance, will overcome a single speed CD-ROM drive. To bring some order to the chaos of defining adequate systems for multimedia performance, the Multimedia PC Marketing Council in 1991 established the Multimedia PC (MPC) specifications. The MPC specs were designed to aid computer buyers in the selection of a balanced system that was capable of delivering the multimedia goods. Today, those initial MPC standards are woefully inadequate. Revised MPC Level 2 and recently released MPC Level 3 standards are a good guide to selecting a system—but are still somewhat conservative. Table 12.1 outlines the current MPC specifications, as well as our recommended system capabilities.

Table 12.1   Multimedia PC System Specifications

	MPC 2	MPC 3	Recommended
RAM	8M	8M	16M
CPU Speed	25 MHz 486SX	75 MHz Pentium	90 MHz Pentium
Hard Disk size	160M	540M	1G
CD-ROM	Double speed, 400 ms seek time, multi-session, 64K buffer	Quad-speed, 250 ms seek time, multi-session, "Red Book"	Quad-speed, 250 ms seek time, multi-session, "Red Book"
Sound	16-bit digital, 8 note synthesizer, MIDI, ADPCM compression compatible	16-bit digital, wavetable synthesis capable of 6 voices plus 2 percussion tracks	16-bit wavetable synthesis
Video	640 × 480 pixels, 65,536 colors	30 frames per second video at 352 × 240 pixels, MPEG 1 hardware support	1024 × 768 pixels, 65,536 colors, MPEG 1 hardware support

Playing full-motion video is just about the most taxing activity your computer performs. If the data cannot get from the CD-ROM to the video display in a continuous, uninterrupted stream, the images will pause, skip, and lurch. There are numerous places for this data to get bogged down. The drive's file system may not be able to transfer data quickly enough. The video data must go through computationally exhausting decompression, and the bus must pump megabytes of data to the video device every second to play smoothly. If any one of these components isn't up to the job, your video experience will be disappointing.

If your CPU is any variety of Pentium, it isn't likely to be a significant bottleneck. Instead, the two primary places to point your finger are the CD-ROM and the video device. If you are creating broadcast or near-broadcast quality video by capturing video to a hard disk for later output to tape, the hard disk also can be—and probably is—the car wreck

Part

III

Ch

12

slowing down the video traffic. The following list shows the bottom line for achieving high-quality 320×240 pixel video at 30 frames per second:

- As already discussed, a balanced system is essential. Just like a good home audio system in which each of the components must be equally matched, the same is true here. Remember, a subwoofer provides little benefit to a set of $50 speakers, and likewise, even a PentiumPro processor is worthless without a fast video device.

- Make sure your computer can display at least a 1024×768 screen with 16-bit color (65,536 colors). Unless you really need 24-bit color (16.7 million colors), however, the higher color count slows down your system for negligible gain in quality. Eight-bit (256 colors) video, on the other hand, just doesn't have enough colors to make a realistic-looking image. Most new computers have display adapters, such as Matrox Millenium, ATI Mach 64, or the Diamond Stealth, which support at least 16-bit color.

- A local bus video device is essential for the multimedia experience, preferably with DCI support for improved performance. Local bus video devices are up to 10 times faster than some ISA devices. In addition, an adapter that provides a DCI driver offers substantial improvements by supporting color conversion and other DCI functionality. VESA local bus is quickly becoming an historical curiosity; PCI systems are the logical choice throughout the foreseeable future.

  ▶ **See** "Configuring and Using CD-ROM Drives," **p. 309**

  ▶ **See** "Optimizing Windows for Broadcast Quality Full-Motion Video," **p. 358**

ON THE WEB

Shopping for a video card? The Internet is a good place to look. Visit some of these sites for specifications, current drivers, and information about the company:

http://www.semiconductors.philips.com/paradise/

The place to go for the newest information on Paradise video cards.

http://www.atitech.ca/

ATI maintains an excellent page for their line of video products.

http://www.diamondmm.com/products/

One stop shopping for Diamond video.

You also might want to check out these locations for more information and other links:

http://www.whidbey.net/~mdixon/win4000c.htm

comp.sys.ibm.pc.hardware.video

misc.forsale.computers.pc-specific.cards.video

■ Make sure you purchase a CD-ROM drive with a transfer rate of at least 300K per second (double speed). This rate is required to play 320 × 240 pixel video at 15 frames per second with reasonable quality. As video quality rises, so do file sizes and transfer rates, so you may want to consider a quad-speed CD-ROM drive. In fact, the price difference between a double- and quad-speed drive has dropped to the point that it makes little sense not to purchase the faster drive. Owners of 6- and 8-speed drives, on the other hand, will not realize many practical benefits from that extra speed for quite some time—because videos are intended for playback at a specific speed, so extra-fast CD-ROM drives have no effect on presentation quality.

■ Use at least 16-bit audio. Modern sound cards should include wavetable synthesis as well. Before purchasing a sound card for your computer, play samples of WAV (Waveform-audio) and MIDI (Musical Instrument Digital Interface) formats on the demo units at the store. Only the ear can tell.

▶ **See** "Configuring and Using Sound Boards," **p. 327**

N O T E Spend your upgrade money wisely. Search out tools which measure not just your system's overall performance, but also how each of your main components—video, drives, and CPU—stack up. *Windows Magazine's* WinTune 2.0, available from online services such as CompuServe, is a good example of such a program. ■

TROUBLESHOOTING

Videos don't play smoothly even though I have a fairly fast system. What's wrong? Videos don't play well over a network, so run them directly from your local computer. In addition, your CD-ROM drive might be using real-mode drivers. In the Control Panel, open System Properties by double-clicking the System icon. Select the Performance tab and note the description next to "File System."

You can get the best performance from the drive by installing a new 32-bit driver—contact the drive's manufacturer. If that isn't possible, you can improve performance by running SmartDrive (found in the Windows directory) in your AUTOEXEC.BAT, which supports CD-ROM caching. If you cannot find SmartDrive on your hard drive, copy it directly from the Windows 95 CD (it is found in the Win95 directory), don't try to use an older version from Windows 3.1.

Optimizing Windows for Broadcast Quality Full-Motion Video

It is only recently that Windows-based PCs have been capable of "desktop video"—that is, capturing, editing, and outputting broadcast quality video back to tape. This is a demanding chore, and many aspects of the PC are taxed to their limit. And though choppy video is an annoyance while watching an Encarta clip, it is embarrassing and potentially expensive for the same thing to occur during the playback of a corporate training film or flying logo sequence. Besides the tips provided here, this kind of video absolutely demands a fast hard drive. Though there are some fast IDE hard drives, you'll probably need to invest in a SCSI adapter, both to ensure reliable video playback and to gain the elbow room offered by many-gigabyte drives. In addition to SCSI's higher data rates, many SCSI drives are designed specifically for video. The following is a partial list of hard drives that are robust enough for capturing full-motion video.

IDE Drives

Seagate SG1080A (1G)

SCSI Drives

Micropolis 4211AV (2G)

Micropolis 1991AV (9G)

Quantum Grand Prix XP34280 (4G)

Seagate ST15150N-W (4G)

TROUBLESHOOTING

Even though I have a fast hard drive, captured video sometimes stutters during playback.
This is because a typical hard drive's head pauses frequently to perform thermal calibrations as it travels across the platter. The pauses are too short to affect ordinary data, but it can play havoc with video capture and playback. You can avoid this problem by capturing to a hard drive specifically rated for audio-video, such as the Micropolis AV or Seagate Barracuda series.

N O T E   AV-optimized drives aren't always easy to spot. Clues are rotational speed (7200 RPM) and a very fast interface (usually either Fast- or Wide-SCSI 2). Some manufacturers, like Micropolis and Fujitsu, label their drives with the AV suffix. If in doubt, call the vendor and ask. ∎

In addition to hard disk performance, the sound card you use to capture audio for your video can have a serious impact on the quality of your presentation. Specifically, not all

16-bit cards are equal. Some use an 8-bit DMA, which can eat as much as 18 percent of your CPU's time recording audio data. That's a serious slice of processor power that isn't available to capture video. Be sure the sound card you purchase uses true 16-bit DMA, which reduces the processor load to a more reasonable eight percent.

N O T E If you have a fairly robust system and have access to video capture equipment, you might be interested in video teleconferencing. Prices are slowly dropping and this is becoming a more mainstream way to conduct tele-business. ▓

ON THE WEB

http://fiddle.ee.vt.edu/succeed/videoconf.html

Finally, try these housekeeping tips to "tweak" your system's video capture capabilities:

- ▓ If you have more than one hard drive, use the fastest one to capture video. Use a speed test utility like WinTune 2.0 or a program that comes with your video card to test each drive.

- ▓ Video should be recorded in a nearly continuous stream—defragment your hard disk before each capture session.

- ▓ If you have a hard disk utility that lets you place files in a specific order on your disk, place program files on the inside of the platter and video on the outside, where access times are shorter.

- ▓ Use the highest quality input available—an S-Video cable is always preferable to a composite input.

  ▶ **See** "Adding New Hardware to Windows 95," **p. 157**

Part

III

Ch

12

TROUBLESHOOTING

I've installed a new video card and the display acts erratically or the mouse behaves oddly.
You need an updated driver from the vendor, usually available from their World Wide Web page or BBS. You don't need to reinstall your old video card in the meantime, though. Virtually any card should work with the basic VGA driver, so right-click anywhere on the Windows desktop. Select Properties from the menu, then select the Settings page (see fig. 12.5). Click Change Display Type and Change the Adapter Type. Click the Show all Devices radio button and pick the [Standard Display Types] on the left side of the screen. Then choose the Standard VGA display and click OK. You can use this setting until you get a reliable driver.

FIG. 12.5

It really is worthwhile to get the latest drivers, even if you're not having trouble. The new driver for the ATI Mach 64 video card (below) offers more speed and many features lacking in the original version (at right).

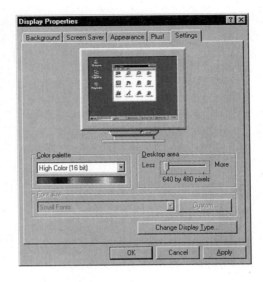

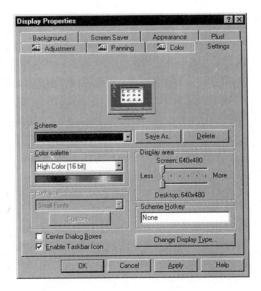

Using Windows Media Player

Media Player is a Windows accessory that allows you to play multimedia files. It supports Video for Windows (AVI), sound (WAV), MIDI (MID), and CD audio. However, The primary use of Media Player is to play videos. This section shows you how to play videos, insert portions of a video in your document, and configure Media Player.

Playing Videos in Media Player

Using Media Player to play a video is simple: Double-click an AVI file in the Explorer. Media Player loads the AVI file and immediately starts playing it. Alternatively, you can load Media Player first (see fig. 12.6) and use the instructions that follow to play a video.

1. Select Device, 1 Video for Windows.

2. Select an AVI file in the Open dialog box and click Open.

3. Click the Play button in Media Player.

When a video is playing, the Play button changes to a Pause button. You can stop the video by clicking the Stop button or pause the video by clicking the Pause button.

FIG. 12.6
Click the Play button to play your video. The Play button changes to a Pause button while the video is playing.

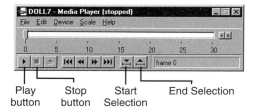

Play button   Stop button   Start Selection   End Selection

 TIP You can call up the Media Player controls while watching a video by double-clicking the movie's title bar.

You also can put a portion of a video in your documents. Then, you can play the video by double-clicking it. To copy a portion of a video to your document, do the following:

1. Position the trackbar thumb on the starting frame of the portion you want to copy.

2. Click the Start Selection button.

3. Position the trackbar thumb on the last frame of the portion you want to copy.

4. Click the End Selection button.

5. Select Edit, Copy Object to copy that portion of the video to the Clipboard.

6. Open the document and paste the video clip by choosing Edit, Paste.

If you want to deselect the clip, select Edit, Selection from Media Player's menu, select None, and click OK.

Video Options in Video for Windows

You can change many aspects of how Media Player plays a video. For example, you can have Media Player use time or frames to display its progress by choosing Scale, Time or Scale, Frames, respectively.

Part
III

Ch
12

To choose whether Media Player plays a video full screen or a window, choose <u>D</u>evice, Properties. Then select <u>W</u>indow or <u>F</u>ull Screen in the Video Properties sheet.

> **TIP** You can vary the size of a video in four increments by selecting Ctrl+1 (normal) through Ctrl+4 (full-screen), while the movie's window is selected.

Use the following instructions to set additional options for Media Player:

1. From the Media Player menu, choose <u>E</u>dit, <u>O</u>ptions.
2. Select <u>A</u>uto Rewind if you want the video clip to automatically rewind after it has finished playing.
3. Select Auto <u>R</u>epeat if you want the video clip to play repeatedly.
4. Select <u>C</u>ontrol Bar On Playback if you want the Media Player controls to be available while a video clip is playing inside another document.
5. Select <u>B</u>order Around Object if you want a border around the video while it is playing.
6. Select <u>P</u>lay In Client Document if you want the video to play in the document instead of as a separate window.
7. Select <u>D</u>ither Picture To VGA Colors if the color of your video looks distorted.

TROUBLESHOOTING

When I attempt to play an AVI file, I see a message like, `Video not available, cannot find 'vids:cvid' decompressor.` This is an indication that the codec needed to play this movie is not installed. Open the Control Panel and double-click the Add/Remove Programs icon. Then, in the Windows Setup page, click Multimedia, and then click Details. Select the Video Compression check box and choose OK. Close the Add/Remove Programs page to install the codecs.

If you want to play a movie compressed with specialized hardware or a third party codec, you'll have to install the appropriate hardware or contact the manufacturer for a specialized decompressor.

When I attempt to play an AVI file, I see a message like, `MMSYSTEM266: The device could not be loaded. Verify the driver is installed correctly.` You need to reinstall several Multimedia files that have been lost or corrupted. Unfortunately, the Add/Remove Programs tool won't capture them if you simply re-install the Multimedia components. Instead, you need to run the Windows 95 Setup from within Windows 95 by selecting Run from the Start menu and typing **Setup**. When prompted, choose to copy all the Windows files again.

Customizing Windows 95

CHAPTER 13

Customizing with Property Sheets

by Ron Person and Bob Voss

The more you use Windows, the more you'll appreciate its customization options.

There are a number of simple things you can do to make working in Windows easier. For example, you can customize your taskbar to appear only when you want it to, in order to give your applications more room on-screen. You also can position the taskbar in locations other than at the bottom of the screen. If you frequently use the same applications, you can add them to the Start menu so they're easy to find.

If you work with different types of Windows software and have a more up-to-date video adapter and monitor, you will want to take advantage of Windows' capability to switch between different display resolutions. This can be useful when you're running different types of applications or when you're switching a mobile computer between mobile and desktop operation. ■

Why should you customize the taskbar?

In this chapter, you'll find ways to resize and move the taskbar as well as ways to modify the taskbar options.

Why you would modify the Start menu

Ways to add and remove programs in the Start menu and clearing the documents list are explained here.

Why should you need to customize the Send To menu?

You learn why and how to add items to the Send To menu and to create submenus.

Why you should customize the shortcut menu

You can find out how to register a new file type, edit an existing file type, remove a file type, and more in this section.

Why would you change the colors on your screen?

In this chapter, you learn to change the desktop and background colors and color schemes of Windows, and change wallpaper and background patterns.

Why would you adjust Plus! Visual Settings?

This chapter shows you how to change icon size and spacing.

Customizing the Taskbar

In Chapter 3, "Windows Navigation Basics," you learned how to use the taskbar to navigate between your open applications. The taskbar is one of the most useful new features in Windows 95; it's a tool you'll use constantly throughout the day. When you first start Windows 95, the taskbar is located at the bottom of the screen and remains visible all the time—even when you maximize an application. In this section, you learn how you can customize the taskbar to give it the look and feel that best suits your needs and preferences.

Resizing the Taskbar

You can change the size of the taskbar to accommodate a large number of buttons or to make it easier to read the full description written on a button. To resize the taskbar, follow these steps:

1. Point to the edge of the taskbar. The pointer becomes a double-pointing arrow.

2. Hold down the left mouse button and drag to the size you want.

The taskbar resizes in full button widths. If the taskbar is horizontal against the top or bottom of the screen, you can change its height. If the taskbar is positioned vertically against a side, you can change its width.

Moving the Taskbar

The taskbar can be positioned horizontally along the top or bottom (default) of the desktop or vertically along the side of the desktop (see fig. 13.1). To reposition the taskbar, point to a position on the taskbar where no button appears, hold down the left mouse button, and drag to the edge of the screen where you want to position the taskbar. A shaded line indicates the new position of the taskbar. Release the mouse button to place the taskbar.

When the taskbar is positioned at the side of the desktop, it can be so wide that you don't have enough space to work. If so, you can drag the edge of the taskbar to give it a new width. When the taskbar is against a side, you can change its width in pixel increments, not just in full button widths.

Using the Taskbar Menu

As in other Windows screen areas, you can click the right mouse button in a gray area of the taskbar to display a shortcut menu (see fig. 13.2). Use the taskbar menu to rearrange windows on the desktop, to reduce applications to buttons, and to change the properties of the taskbar.

FIG. 13.1
Reposition the taskbar for
your convenience.

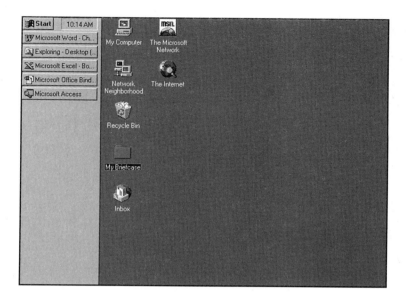

FIG. 13.2
Right-click in the gray area of
the taskbar to display the
shortcut menu.

The following table describes each of the commands on the taskbar menu.

Command	Description
Cascade	Displays windows one over the other from left to right, top to bottom.
Tile Horizontally	Displays windows top to bottom without overlapping.
Tile Vertically	Displays windows left to right without overlapping.
Minimize All Windows	Reduces all open windows to buttons on the taskbar.
Properties	Displays the Taskbar Properties sheet, where you can change the Start menu or taskbar options.

▶ **See** "Customizing the Start Menu," **p. 369**

Changing the Taskbar Options

You can hide or display the taskbar using the Taskbar Properties sheet. Figure 13.3 shows
the commands available from the Taskbar Options tab. You also can turn the clock area of
the taskbar on and off.

Part

IV

Ch

13

To change taskbar properties, follow these steps:

1. Point to a position on the taskbar where no button appears, either below or between buttons, and right-click. Choose Properties.

   or

   Open the Start menu and choose Settings, Taskbar.

2. Click the Taskbar Options tab.

3. Select or deselect a check box to turn an item on or off. The options are explained in the following table.

4. Click OK.

Option	Description
Always on Top	The taskbar displays over all open windows.
Auto Hide	Hides the taskbar to make more space available on your desktop and in application windows. To see the taskbar, move your mouse pointer to the bottom of the screen (or where the taskbar is if you moved it) and the taskbar reappears. When you move the pointer away, the taskbar disappears again.
Show Small Icons in Start Menu	Displays the Start menu with small icons and without the Windows banner. This enables you to see more of what's on-screen while in the Start menu.
Show Clock	Hides or displays the clock in one corner of the taskbar.

FIG. 13.3

Right-click in the gray area of the taskbar and choose Properties when you want to change how your taskbar operates.

When you select the Auto Hide option, the taskbar is reduced to a gray line at the edge of the screen. When you move the mouse pointer over this line, the taskbar reappears. You can modify the width of this line by right-clicking the desktop and choosing Properties. Select the Appearance tab, and select Active Windows Border from the Item list. Modify the value in the Size text box to the desired width and choose OK. Note that this affects the border width of your application windows as well.

Customizing the Start Menu

You can customize the contents of the Start menu. You can add a list of applications you use frequently, and then launch those applications directly from the Start menu. By adding programs to the Start menu, you avoid having to display additional menus.

 To quickly add a program to the highest level of the Start menu, drag the program's file from Explorer or the My Computer window and drop it on the Start button.

Adding and Removing Programs in the Start Menu

To add a program to the Start menu, follow these steps.

1. Right-click on a gray area between buttons on the taskbar. Choose Properties.

   or

   Open the Start menu and choose Settings, Taskbar.

2. Click the Start Menu Programs tab (see fig. 13.4).

FIG. 13.4
The Start Menu Programs tab enables you to add programs to the Start menu.

Part
IV

Ch
13

3. Click <u>A</u>dd to display the Create Shortcut dialog box shown in figure 13.5.

FIG. 13.5
In the Create Shortcut dialog box, type or select the file of the program you want to add to the Start menu.

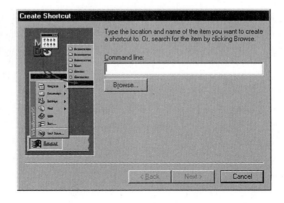

4. Click B<u>r</u>owse to display the Browse dialog box. This dialog box looks very similar to an Open File dialog box.

5. Find and click the file for the program or document you want to add to the Start menu. Choose <u>O</u>pen after you select the file.

TIP Adding a document's file to the Start menu enables you to open the document in its related application, assuming the document type is registered. See "Customizing the Shortcut (Right-Click) Menu," later in this chapter.

You can limit the displayed files to program files by selecting Programs from the Files of <u>T</u>ype list at the bottom of the dialog box. For example, if you want to start Excel, open the Office95 folder, open the Excel folder, and then click EXCEL.EXE. Most program files use an EXE extension.

6. Click Next to display the Select Program Folder dialog box (see fig. 13.6).

FIG. 13.6
You can position your document or application anywhere on the Start menu.

7. Select the folder that corresponds to the location on the Start menu where you want the program to appear. Choose Next.

   For example, if you want the program you selected to appear at the top of the Start menu, select the Start Menu folder. If you want the program to appear as an item on the Programs menu, then you select the Programs folder.

8. Type the name or words you want to appear on the Start menu in the Select a Name for the Shortcut text box. Choose Finish.

T I P You can make it easy to launch the applications you added to the top of the Start menu by using the keyboard. Right-click the Start button and choose Open. Rename each application item, adding a number to the beginning of the name. To launch an application from the Start menu, press Ctrl+Esc to open the Start menu and then type the number for the application you want to start.

To remove a program from the Start menu, you follow a similar process:

1. Display the Taskbar Properties sheet as described earlier in this chapter.

2. Click the Start Menu Programs tab.

3. Click Remove to display the Remove Shortcuts/Folders dialog box shown in figure 13.7.

FIG. 13.7
You can easily remove any item from the Start menu using the Remove Shortcuts/Folders dialog box.

Part
IV
Ch
13

4. Select the shortcut or folder you want to remove from the Start menu.

5. Click Remove to remove the file or folder.

6. Remove additional items or choose Close. Choose OK when you return to the Taskbar Properties sheet.

▶ **See** "Starting from Shortcuts," **p. 39**

▶ **See** "Opening Programs and Documents from Explorer or My Computer," **p. 78**

Clearing the Documents List in the Start Menu

The Start menu contains a Documents item that shows a list of recently used documents. At times, this list can become too long, or you might want to clear the list so documents are easier to find. To clear documents from the Documents menu, follow these steps:

1. Display the Taskbar Properties sheet.

2. Click the Start Menu Programs tab.

3. Click Clear in the Documents Menu area.

4. Choose OK.

Adding the Control Panel, Dial Up Network, and Printers Menus to the Start Menu

You can directly access all the items in the Control Panel by adding a special Control Panel folder to the Start Menu folder. To create this folder, follow these steps:

1. Right-click the Start button and choose Open. The Start Menu window appears.

2. Right-click in a blank area of the Start Menu window and choose New, Folder.

3. Name the folder Control Panel.

Now, when you click the Start button, you see Control Panel at the top of the Start menu. When you select Control Panel, a cascading menu of all the Control Panel items opens.

N O T E   It might seem simpler to create a folder named Control Panel in the Start Menu folder, select all the items in the Control Panel window, and then drag-and-drop them into the new folder to create shortcuts. This works just fine, but the words Shortcut to will appear in front of each item. The previous method results in a cleaner-looking menu. ∎

You can create menus on the Start Menu for two other items using this method.

For the Dial Up Network folder, create a folder in the Start Menu folder with the following name:

Dial Up Net.{992CFFA0-F557-101A-88EC-00DD010CCC48}

For the Printers folder, create a folder in the Start Menu folder with the following name:

Printers.{2227A280-3AEA-1069-A2DE-08002B30309D}

Customizing the Send To Menu

The Send To menu is a very useful tool for using the mouse to move, open, print, fax, and perform many other actions with files and folders. The Send To command is instantly available by right-clicking a file or folder in the Explorer, in a folder window, or on the desktop.

Adding Items to the Send To Menu

When you first start Windows 95, there are a few standard items that appear in the Send To menu, such as your floppy disk drive and My Briefcase (if you installed the Briefcase). However, you can add many other items to the Send To folder, including folders, printers, zip drives, applications, and so on.

To add items to the Send To menu, follow these steps:

1. Open the Send To folder, which is in the Windows folder.
2. Open the folder containing the item you want to add to the Send To menu.
3. Drag-and-drop the item into the Send To folder using the right mouse button.

   You also can drag items from the desktop into the Send To folder.
4. Click Create Shortcut(s) Here.
5. Edit the file name to remove the words Shortcut to.
6. Repeat steps 2 through 5 for any other items you want to add to the Send To menu.

Some suggestions for items you can add to the Send To menu are:

- Folders, for moving files to commonly used folders.
- External drives, such as a zip drive.
- Printers.
- Applications for opening a file (WordPad, for example).

 TIP If you have more than one printer, add each one to the Send To menu. That way, you can choose what printer to use to print a file. Or, if you set up different configurations for the same printer (such as high and low resolution modes), include both of them in the Send To menu.

Figure 13.8 shows a Send To menu with several items that have been added.

Part
IV

Ch
13

FIG. 13.8
You can add many items to
the Send To menu to speed
up processing your files.

 N O T E   When you send a file to a folder on the same disk, the file is moved. If you send the
file to a different disk, it is copied. Be careful not to move EXE files using the Send To
menu. ■

T I P   Add the Recycle Bin to the Send To menu to quickly delete a file or selection of files. One benefit
of using the Send To menu to send files to the Recycle Bin is that you don't have to see the
Confirm File Delete message box.

You can even add Send To to the Send To menu. Create a shortcut to the SendTo folder in the
SendTo folder. Now, when you want to add an item to the Send To menu, right-click the item and
choose Send To, SendTo.

Creating Submenus in the Send To Menu

If you routinely use the Send To menu to move files from folder to folder, you might want
to create submenus of folders on the Send To menu. This will keep the main Send To
menu from becoming cluttered with a long list of folders. Using this technique, you can
categorize your folders, making it easier to find the folder you want to send a file to. For
example, you might create a folder named Book Chapters in the Send To folder that contains shortcuts to the folders you create for each chapter.

To create submenus on the Send To menu, follow these steps:

1. Create a new folder in the Send To folder and assign a name indicating what
   category of folders it will contain.

   Using the previous example, you would name the folder Book Chapters.

2. Open the new folder and create shortcuts to the destination folders that you want to appear in the submenu.

In this example, you would create shortcuts for each of the chapter folders.

You might want to edit the names of the folders to remove the words Shortcut to.

Now, when you open the Send To menu and select the parent folder (Book Chapters), a submenu appears with a list of folders from which you can select to move your files (refer to fig. 13.8).

You can use this same procedure to create submenus for other items. If you have several printers, for example, you could create a Printers folder in the Send To folder and create shortcuts to each of the printers inside this folder.

Customizing the Shortcut (Right-Click) Menu

You can add or modify the commands on the shortcut menu that opens when you right-click a file in the Explorer, in a folder window, or on the desktop. You can do this by speci-fying the application(s) that will act on this type of file. For each application, you can specify different actions the application will take on, such as opening, printing, or running a macro with the file. Applications that have macro languages or startup switches can use those macros or startup switches to control what happens when you start the application using the shortcut menu command.

There are many actions that can occur with a file type. When you double-click a file, the action that has been designated as the default action is executed. Usually, the default ac-tion is opening the file, but you can change the default to another action. In this section, you learn how to register a new file type (when the file type is not already registered) and you learn how to customize the actions associated with a file type.

Registering a New File Type

Registering a file type is analogous to associating a file in Windows 3.1, although you now do a lot more than simply tell Windows with what application to open a file. You can asso-ciate multiple applications with one file type and specify several actions that can occur with a file type; for example, you can tell Windows to print the document or open a new document of the same type.

To register a new file type, follow these steps:

1. In Explorer, choose View, Options.

Part

IV

Ch

13

2. Click the File Types tab of the Options dialog box (see fig. 13.9).

FIG. 13.9

Register and modify file types on the File Types page of the Options dialog box.

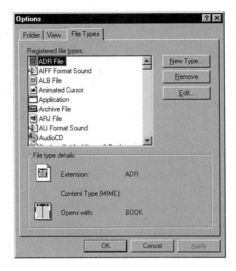

3. Choose New Type. The Add New File Type dialog box appears (see fig. 13.10).

FIG. 13.10

Enter the information for a new file type in the Add New File Type dialog box.

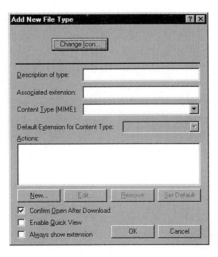

4. Enter a description of the file type in the Description of Type text box.

    This description appears in the Registered File Types list on the File Types page of the Options dialog box. For example, if you want to be able to double-click mainframe text files that use commas to separate data and have that file load into Excel, you might use a description similar to Comma Separated Values (CSV).

5. Enter the file extension to be associated with this file type in the Associated Extension text box. This is the three-letter file extension associated with DOS-based files. For example, a comma-separated values file uses the extension CSV.

6. Choose New to add a new action to the file type in the New Action dialog box.

   The action is actually a custom command that appears on the shortcut menu when you right-click the file.

7. Type an action—for example, **Open CSV in Excel**—in the Actions text box.

   What you type appears as an item on the shortcut menu for this file type. You can type anything, but commands usually start with a verb. If you want the command to have an accelerator key, precede that letter with an ampersand (&).

8. Select the application to be used to perform the action in the Application Used to Perform Action text box.

   You could enter the path and directory to the EXCEL.EXE file—for example, **C:\Office95\Excel\EXCEL.EXE**. You also can choose Browse to find and select the application to use.

   Figure 13.11 shows the completed New Action dialog box.

FIG. 13.11

Designate a shortcut menu action and the program used to perform that action in the New Action dialog box.

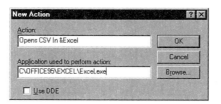

9. While the New Action dialog box is still displayed, select the Use DDE check box if the program uses DDE (dynamic data exchange).

   If you select the Use DDE check box, the dialog box expands (see fig. 13.12), displaying the DDE statements used to communicate with the DDE application. If you know how to write DDE statements, you can customize the action performed with the associated application.

10. Click OK.

11. If you have more than one action listed in the Actions box, select the one you want to be the default action and choose the Set Default button.

   The default action is the one that is performed when you double-click a file of this type in Explorer or My Computer.

Part
IV

Ch
13

FIG. 13.12
You can enter your own DDE
statements to customize the
action associated with a
registered file type.

12. Select the Enable Quick View check box if the file type supports Quick View.
    Quick View allows you to view a file without opening it.

13. Select Always Show Extension if you want the MS-DOS file extension for this file
    type to always be displayed in Explorer and My Computer, even when you have
    selected the Hide MS-DOS File Extensions option on the View page of the Options
    dialog box.

14. Choose Close twice.

    ▶ **See** "Previewing a Document with Quick View," **p. 112**

Adding a Shortcut Menu Action for Unknown File Types

You might want a command to appear in the shortcut menu for any unrecognized file type
on which you right-click. You can use Regedit to modify the Registry to add a custom
command to the shortcut menu for unknown file types. You can accomplish this using the
following steps:

1. Use Notepad or WordPad to create a text file named UNKTYPE.REG. The file should contain
   the following lines:

   ```
   REGEDIT4
   [HKEY_CLASSES_ROOT\Unknown]
   "EditFlags"=hex:02,00,00,00
   ```

   The new type added is Unknown.

2. Save UNKTYPE.REG in any folder.

3. Find and select UNKTYPE.REG in the Explorer and right-click it.

4. Choose Merge from the shortcut menu.

Now, when you open the File Types tab in the Options dialog box, a new file type appears in the Registered File Types list: Unknown. You can use the procedures you learned in the preceding sections to assign new actions to this file type.

Editing an Existing File Type

At times, you might want to change existing file-type options. For example, say you want to change the action that opens BMP files in Paint so they will open in a different image editor. You would edit the BMP open action to include the path and file name for that image editor instead of Paint.

You also can add new commands to the shortcut menu for a registered file type. For example, you might want the option of opening BMP files with either Paint or another image editor. Instead of editing the open action already in place, you would add a new open command associated with the other image editor. You also can change the description, icon, and other aspects.

To edit an existing file type, follow these steps:

1. In Explorer, choose View, Options.
2. Click the File Types tab to display the File Types page of the Options dialog box (refer to fig. 13.9).
3. Select the file type you want to edit in the Registered File Types list.
4. Click Edit.
5. Edit the characteristics for the file type using the same procedures outlined earlier for creating a new file type in the section "Registering a New File Type."

   To edit an action, you must first select that action from the list. Actions for a file type depend on parameters or arguments understood by that file type. Some applications can accept macro names as actions, others accept "switches," and still others accept arguments left over from DOS commands. To learn more about the actions, check the technical reference manual for the application you are starting.

   To add a new action for a file type already registered, click New in the Edit File Type dialog box and follow the procedures outlined earlier for creating a new file type. This is how you customize the shortcut menu for a file type to include new commands for acting on that file type. For example, **Open with CorelDRAW!**.
6. Click OK.

7. Repeat steps 3 through 6 for any other file types you want to edit.

8. Click Close.

 TIP You are not limited to one occurrence for a particular action in a shortcut menu. For example, you can have two Open commands in the shortcut menu for a registered file type, each of which uses a different application to open files of that type. The example for opening BMP files with either Paint or CorelDRAW! is such a case. When you name the action in the New Action dialog box, give the command a name that allows you to distinguish it from the other commands in the menu.

Removing a File Type

If you no longer want a document to start a specific application, you can remove its file type description.

To remove a file type description, follow these steps:

1. In Explorer, choose View, Options.

2. Click the File Types tab to display the File Types page of the Options dialog box (refer to fig. 13.9).

3. Select the file type you want to remove in the Registered File Types list.

4. Click Remove.

5. Click OK.

Changing the Icon for a File Type or Other Object

You can change the icon used to designate a file type, drive, folder, and other objects on your computer. To change the icon used for a particular file type or object, follow these steps:

1. In Explorer, choose View, Options.

2. Click the File Types tab to display the File Types page of the Options dialog box (refer to fig. 13.9).

3. Select the file type or other object whose icon you want to change in the Registered File Types list.

4. Choose Edit.

5. Click Change Icon to display the Change Icon dialog box shown in figure 13.13.

FIG. 13.13
Use the Change Icon dialog box to select a new icon for a file type or other type of object.

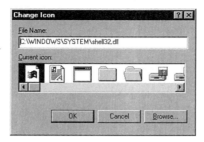

6. Select a new icon from the Current Icon scrolling list.

   The name of the file containing the icons currently shown is listed in the File Name text box. You can use Browse to search for a new file containing different icons. All Windows programs come with their own icons, and you can obtain collections of icons from bulletin boards, the Internet, and other sources. Programs are even available that allow you to create your own icons.

7. Click OK three times.

Adding an Open New Window Command to the Folder Shortcut Menu

When you are browsing through folders, you probably use a single window so you don't have a multitude of folder windows on your desktop. Sometimes, however, it is handy to be able to quickly open a second window: for example, when you want to move files from one folder to another. You can add a command to the shortcut menu that appears when you right-click a folder by editing the Registry. To add a command for opening a new window, follow these steps.

1. Open the Start menu, choose Run, and type **regedit** in the Open text box.
2. Expand the HKEY_CLASSES_ROOT branch and locate the Directory entry.
3. Expand the Directory entry and right-click the shell entry.
4. Choose New, Key and type **opennew**.
5. Double-click the Default entry for the new key in the right pane and type **Open New &Window**.
6. Right-click the opennew entry and add another key. Name it command.
7. Double-click the Default entry for this key and type **explorer %1**.
8. Exit Regedit.

Now, when you right-click any folder, the Open <u>N</u>ew Window command appears in the shortcut menu.

▶ **See** "Alternatives to Editing the Registry," **p. 425**

Customizing the Desktop Colors and Background

Changing colors is just one way you can customize the windows you see on-screen. You also can change the pattern used in the desktop background, add a graphical wallpaper as a background, change the border width of windows, and more.

Wallpaper options you select for the desktop background can include graphics that come with Windows—including some wild and colorful ones—and designs you create or modify with Windows Paint. The graphic images you use as wallpaper are nothing more than computer drawings saved in a bitmap (BMP) format. You also can use the Windows Paint program to create your own bitmap drawings to use as screen backgrounds.

You can put wallpaper over just the center portion of the desktop, or you can tile the desktop with wallpaper. When tiling, the wallpaper reproduces itself to fill the screen.

▶ **See** "Saving Paint Files," **p. 548**

Changing Windows Colors

After working in the drab and dreary DOS or mainframe computer world, one of the first changes many people want to make is to add color to their Windows screens. You can pick colors for window titles, backgrounds, bars—in fact all parts of the window. Predesigned color schemes range from the brilliant to the cool and dark. You also can design and save your own color schemes and blend your own colors.

Using Existing Color Schemes   Windows comes with a list of predefined color schemes. Each color scheme maps a different color and text to a different part of the screen.

You can select from existing schemes, or you can devise your own (described in the next section). To select one of the predefined schemes, follow these steps:

1. Right-click the desktop, choose <u>P</u>roperties, and then select the Appearance tab.

   or

    Open the Start menu and choose <u>S</u>ettings, <u>C</u>ontrol Panel; then open the Display icon and select the Appearance tab.

The Appearance tab of the Display Properties dialog box displays, as shown in figure 13.14.

FIG. 13.14

Select from existing color and text schemes on the Appearance tab to customize Windows appearance.

2. Select the Scheme list and select a predefined color and text scheme from the list. The sample screen at the top of the dialog box illustrates what this color scheme looks like.

3. Choose OK to use the displayed color scheme or return to step 2 for other pre-defined schemes.

Creating Custom Color and Text Schemes   You can change all or some of the colors in a scheme, change the color of the text, and even change the color and width of borders. To create new color schemes while the Appearance tab is open, follow these steps:

1. If you want to use an existing scheme as a base (as opposed to using Windows Standard as a base), select the scheme from the Scheme list.

2. Select from the Item list the screen element you want to modify, or click a screen element in the sample window at the top of the dialog box. You can select elements such as the Menu Bar, Button, Active Border, and so on.

3. Select from the Size, Font, and Color lists how you want to change the selected element. Some options are only available for certain elements.

4. Choose one of these alternatives for the colors you have selected:

   • If you want to color another window element, return to step 2.

Part

IV

Ch

13

- If you want to use these colors now but not save them for the next time you run Windows, choose OK or press Enter.

- If you want to save these colors so you can use them now or return to them at any time, choose Save As. Then type a name in the Save Scheme text box and choose OK.

- If you want to cancel these colors and return to the original scheme, select that scheme from the Scheme list if it was saved, or choose Cancel.

To remove a scheme from the list, select the scheme you want to remove from the Scheme list and click Delete.

Wallpapering Your Desktop with a Graphic

Using a graphic or picture as the Windows desktop is a nice personal touch. For special business situations or for custom applications, you might want to use a color company logo or pictorial theme as the wallpaper.

Windows comes with a collection of graphics for the desktop. You can modify these images or draw new images for the desktop with the Windows Paint program. For high-quality pictorials, use a scanner to create a digitized black-and-white or color image.

Figure 13.15 shows one of the many wallpaper patterns that come with Windows. Figure 13.16 shows a logo used as a backdrop. Many companies scan and then enhance their corporate logo as a BMP file, then use it as the desktop background. Most of the patterns must be tiled to fill the entire screen, which you learn how to do in the following steps.

FIG. 13.15
This is one of the many Windows images you can use to wallpaper your desktop.

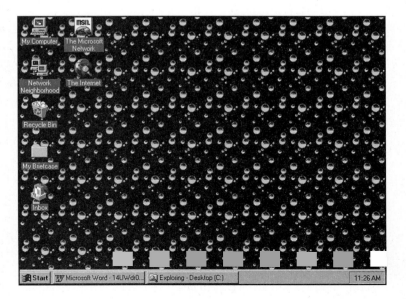

FIG. 13.16
Edit existing wallpaper files
or create your own with
Paint.

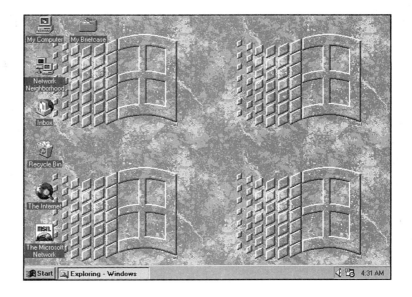

To select wallpaper, follow these steps:

1. Right-click the desktop, choose Properties, and then select the Background tab.

   or

   Open the Start menu and choose Settings, Control Panel; then open the Display icon, and select the Background tab.

   The Background tab of the Display Properties dialog box appears (see fig. 13.17).

FIG. 13.17
Use the Background tab in
Display Properties to select
new wallpapers and
patterns.

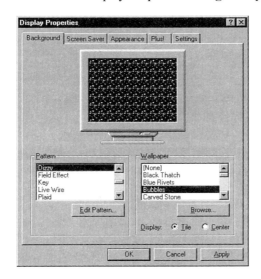

Part
IV

Ch
13

2. Choose a wallpaper from the Wallpaper list box. If the graphic file (with a BMP extension) is located in a folder other than Windows, choose the Browse button to find and select the graphic file.

3. If the graphic is large enough to fill the screen, select Display Center to center the wallpaper in the desktop. If the graphic is small and must be repeated to fill the screen, select Display Tile.

5. Choose OK if you are finished or make other display property changes.

When you choose a wallpaper from the Wallpaper list box, you see a miniature rendition of it in the display shown in the upper part of the Display Properties dialog box. This allows you to preview wallpapers before settling on the one to use.

Remember, however, bitmap images displayed as desktop wallpaper use more memory than a colored or patterned desktop.

Wallpaper is created from files stored in a bitmap format. These files end with the BMP extension and must be stored in the Windows folder. You can edit BMP formats with the Windows Paint program. You also can read and edit files with PCX format in Paint and save them in BMP format to use as a desktop wallpaper.

You can create your own desktop wallpapers in one of three ways:

■ Buy clip art from a software vendor. If the clip art is not in PCX or BMP format, use a graphics-conversion application to convert the image to one of these formats. Use Windows Paint to read PCX format and resave the figure in BMP format. Computer bulletin boards, online services, and the Internet have thousands of BMP graphics files.

■ Scan a black-and-white or color picture using a digital scanner. Save the scanned file as BMP format or convert it to BMP format.

■ Modify an existing desktop wallpaper, or create a new one with Windows Paint or a higher-end graphics program. Save the files with the BMP format.

ON THE WEB

Check out Anonymous FTP: **bongo.cc.utexas.edu** through the path: **/gifstuff/ftpsites**.

You might also look at the Anonymous FTP: **ftp.cica.indiana.edu** through the path: **/pub/pc/ win3/*** for bitmaps for Windows.

Store your new BMP (bitmap) graphics files in the Windows folder so they appear in the Wallpaper Files list box in the Display Properties dialog box.

To remove a wallpaper file from the Wallpaper Files drop-down list, delete or remove its BMP file from the Windows folder. To remove the wallpaper from the desktop, repeat the preceding steps but select None as the type of wallpaper.

Changing the Background Pattern

Wallpapers, while pretty and often amusing, can consume a lot of memory. If you want a simpler background or want to conserve memory, you can use a background pattern. The pattern is a small grid of dots that repeats to fill the screen. In figure 13.18, the Sample area shows how one background pattern appears. Windows comes with predefined patterns you can select; you also can create your own. The color of the pattern is the same as the color selected for Window Text in the Color dialog box.

FIG. 13.18
Background patterns are simpler and conserve memory.

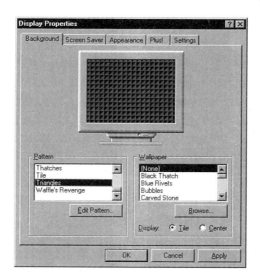

To select a pattern, follow these steps:

1. Right-click the desktop, choose Properties, and then select the Background tab.

   or

    Open the Start menu and choose Settings, Control Panel; then open the Display icon and select the Background tab. The Background tab of the Display Properties dialog box appears.

2. Select a pattern from the Pattern list. Some of the built-in repetitive patterns you can select are 50% Gray, Boxes, Diamonds, Weave, and Scottie.

3. Choose OK to add the pattern to the desktop. Alternatively, use the following procedure to edit the pattern just selected.

Part
IV

Ch
13

You can edit or create new patterns only if you have a mouse. To edit an existing pattern or create a new pattern while the Background tab is displayed, follow these steps:

1. Select a pattern from the Pattern list.

2. Click Edit Pattern to display the Pattern Editor dialog box shown in figure 13.19.

FIG. 13.19

Editing your pattern using an existing pattern as a base can be easier than working from the (None) pattern.

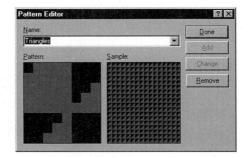

3. Click in the editing grid in the location where you want to reverse a dot in the pattern. Watch the Sample area to see the overall effect.

4. Continue to click in the grid until the pattern is what you want.

5. When you are finished creating or editing, continue with one of the following options:

   - If you want to change an existing pattern, click Change.

   - If you want to add a new pattern, type a new name in the Name list box and choose Add.

6. When you are finished editing, click Done. Choose OK in the Display Properties sheet.

To remove an unwanted pattern from the list, select the pattern and click Remove. Confirm the deletion by choosing Yes. The Remove button is available only after you select a new pattern name.

Working with Desktop Themes

The Microsoft Plus! Desktop Themes provide you with appealing graphics and sounds to decorate your desktop and highlight system events (see fig. 13.20). Each Desktop Theme offers a coordinated set of elements, so you can set the appropriate mood for your computing experience. Plus! provides Desktop Theme combinations for computers displaying in 256 colors and for computers displaying in 16-bit or higher color. If you did not install the high-color Desktop Themes, you can rerun the Plus! Setup at any time to do so. The following are the Desktop Themes provided with Plus!:

256 Color:

Dangerous Creatures

Leonardo da Vinci

Science

The 60's USA

Sports

Windows 95

High Color:

Inside Your Computer

Nature

The Golden Era

Mystery

Travel

FIG. 13.20

Make every workday a safari by choosing the Dangerous Creatures Desktop Theme.

When you choose a Desktop Theme, you can specify whether to replace Windows screen elements you specify using the Control Panel. Desktop Themes provides these desktop elements; you can choose which of these you want to use for your system:

Part
IV

Ch
13

- *Screen Saver.* Displays the Theme screen saver when you leave your computer idle.
- *Sound Events.* Assigns the Theme sounds to system events such as Windows startup and exit.
- *Mouse Pointer.* Applies the Theme pointer styles for different types of pointers, such as the pointer used to select text or the one that appears while Windows is busy performing an operation.

N O T E If you need a high degree of accuracy when pointing with the mouse, the Mouse Pointer option for several Themes might make your pointing more difficult because of the pointer shapes assigned by the Theme. If you have trouble with this, deselect the Mouse Pointer option for the current Theme.

- *Desktop Wallpaper.* Covers the desktop with the decorative background provided by the Theme.
- *Icons.* Assigns custom Theme icons to desktop objects like the My Computer object and Recycle Bin.
- *Icon Size and Spacing.* Makes desktop icons use the icon size and spacing specified by the Theme; remember that larger icons use more computer memory, so if your system is low on memory, don't use this option.
- *Colors.* Applies the Theme colors to windows and other screen elements.
- *Font Names and Styles.* Uses the Theme fonts for screen elements like window titles.
- *Font and Window Sizes.* Uses the Theme font sizes and default window sizes.

As mentioned earlier, the Theme replaces the desktop elements you specify using the Control Panel. You should note, however, that the most recent element you select using either method (Desktop Themes or the Control Panel) becomes active. For example, if you apply a Desktop Theme, but aren't quite satisfied with the screen saver, you can use the Control Panel to choose another screen saver to use.

Selecting and Setting Up a Theme

Plus! Setup! creates an object icon for the Desktop Themes in the Windows 95 Control Panel, which contains other objects for controlling Windows' appearance and operation. Use the following steps to use the Desktop Themes object to select a Theme:

1. Open the Start menu and choose Settings, Control Panel.
2. In the Control Panel window, double-click the Desktop Themes icon (see fig. 13.21).
3. The Desktop Themes dialog box appears, as shown in figure 13.22. Use this dialog box to select and set up a Theme.

FIG. 13.21
Select a Desktop Theme using the Control Panel.

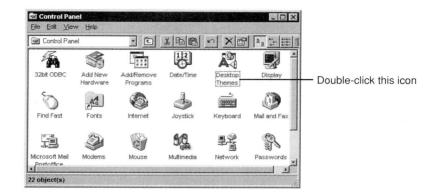

Double-click this icon

FIG. 13.22
Plus! provides numerous options for setting up the Desktop Theme of your choice.

Select a Theme from this drop-down list

Choose which of the Theme settings to use

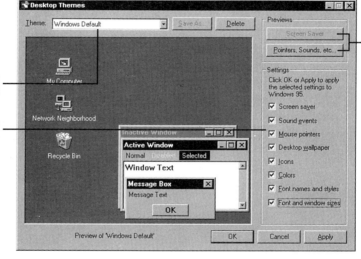

Click one of these buttons to preview a screen saver, sound or other element

Part
IV

Ch
13

Click the down arrow beside the Theme drop-down list to display the available Desktop Themes. Click the name of the Theme you want to use. A dialog box tells you that the Theme files are being imported. When that dialog box closes, the preview area of the Desktop Themes changes to display the appearance of the Theme you selected, as shown in figure 13.23.

4. On the right side of the dialog box, choose the Settings to use for the Theme you selected.

5. (Optional) To preview the selected Theme's screen saver, click Screen Saver in the Previews area. The screen saver appears on-screen. Move the mouse or press a key to conclude the preview.

FIG. 13.23
After you select a Desktop Theme, you see a preview of your Windows desktop.

This is how the Leonardo da Vinci theme looks

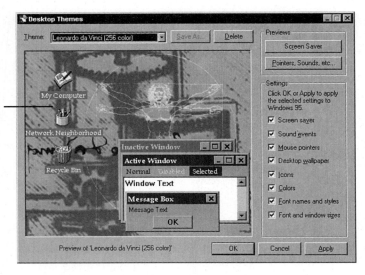

6. (Optional) To preview several of the selected Theme's other elements, click Pointers, Sounds, etc. in the Previews area. A Preview dialog box for the Theme appears; the dialog box has three tabs for Pointers, Sounds, and Visuals. Click the tab you want to view. Each tab offers a list box with the elements for the theme. For the Pointers and Visuals tabs, simply click an element in the list to see a preview in the Preview or Picture area. For the Sounds tab, click an element in the list, then click the right arrow icon near the bottom of the dialog box to hear the sound. Click Close to conclude your preview.

7. After you have selected a theme, chosen settings, and previewed elements to your satisfaction, choose OK to close the Desktop Themes window. The selected Desktop Theme appears on your system.

Saving a Custom Theme

Any Control Panel changes you make after selecting a Theme take precedence over the Theme settings. In fact, you can make desktop setting changes in Control Panel, and save those settings as a custom Theme. To do so, follow these steps:

1. Use Control Panel to change any settings you want, including the wallpaper, screen colors, sounds, and so on.

2. If the Control Panel window isn't open, open the Start menu and choose Settings, Control Panel.

3. In the Control Panel window, double-click the Desktop Themes icon.

TIP To permanently delete a Desktop Theme, select it in the Theme drop-down list, then click Delete. Click Yes in the dialog box that appears to confirm the deletion.

4. Open the Themes drop-down list and choose Current Window settings. The Save As button becomes active.

5. Click Save As. The Save Theme dialog box appears (see fig. 13.24).

FIG. 13.24
Create and save custom desktop themes for interest and variety in your Desktop.

Enter the Theme name here

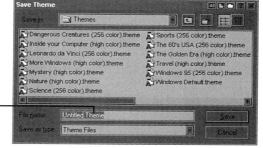

6. (Optional) Choose another folder in which to save the Theme.

7. Enter a unique name for the Theme in the File Name text box.

8. Click Save to save the Theme and return to the Desktop Themes dialog box. The newly saved Theme appears as the Theme selection.

9. Click OK to accept your new Theme and apply it to Windows 95.

Adjusting Plus! Visual Settings

Plus! adds new features to the Display settings available in the Windows 95 Control Panel. These visual settings are designed, primarily, to make your desktop more attractive. Plus! enables you to specify new icons for My Computer, the Network Neighborhood, and the Recycle Bin desktop icons. You can choose to show the contents of a window (rather than just an outline when you drag the window). Choose whether you want to smooth the appearance of large fonts on-screen. You also can choose to show icons with all possible colors or expand the wallpaper (when centered using the Background tab of the Display Properties dialog box from Control Panel) so it stretches to fill the entire screen.

Part
IV

Ch
13

NOTE Most of the Plus! visual settings require more system resources than the normal display settings. In particular, showing window contents while dragging and using all colors in icons consumes more RAM. Consider all your computing requirements before you use up RAM by selecting any of these features. ▪

To work with the Plus! visual settings, open the Start menu and choose Settings, Control Panel. In the Control Panel window, double-click the Display icon. The Display Properties sheet appears. Click the Plus! tab to display its options, as shown in figure 13.25. To assign a new Desktop icon, click the icon you want to change in the Desktop Icons area. Click Change Icon. In the Change Icon dialog box that appears, scroll to display the icon you want, then click OK to accept the change.

FIG. 13.25

Plus! enables you to make additional adjustments to the Windows Display Properties.

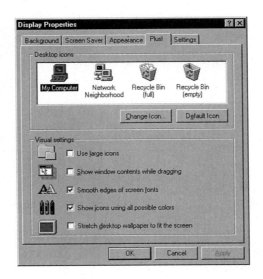

To enable any of the other Plus! display features, select the feature in the Visual settings area of the Plus! page. If you want more information about a particular feature, right-click the feature, then click What's This?. A brief description of the feature appears. Click or press Esc to clear the description. To accept your visual settings and close the Display Properties sheet, click OK. Close the Control Panel window, if you want.

Changing Icon Size and Spacing

You can change the size of the icons and the spacing around icons on the desktop using the Appearance tab of the Display Properties sheet. Click the Item drop-down list. Choose Icon Spacing (Horizontal) to change the text area available for the text below the icons on your desktop. You can enter a number in the Size box from 0 to 150. Using 0 creates a narrow space for the text, so Recycle Bin changes to Re on one line and Bin on one line. Using 150 enables you to use longer names for your icons—43 is the default.

Choose Icon Spacing (Vertical) to adjust the space above and below an icon from 0 to 150 with 43 being the default.

Changing the Name of Desktop Icons

You can change the name of any Desktop icon by clicking the name to select it and then clicking the name again to reveal the Rename text box. Enter the new name and press Enter. Name changes remain until you change them again.

Having Fun with the Screen Saver

Screen savers display a changing pattern on-screen when you haven't typed or moved the mouse for a predetermined amount of time. You can specify the delay before the screen saver activates, and you can set up various attributes—including a password—for most of the screen savers.

To select and set up a screen saver, follow these steps:

1. Right-click the desktop and choose Properties; then select the Screen Saver tab.

   or

    Open the Start menu and choose Settings, Control Panel; then open the Display icon and select the Screen Saver tab.

   The Screen Saver tab of the Display Properties sheet displays (see fig. 13.26).

FIG. 13.26
Customizing your screen saver can display information, attract attention, or warn people away from your computer.

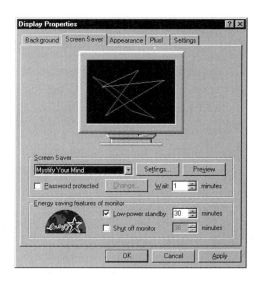

2. Select a screen saver from the Screen Saver list.

3. The miniature display shows you a preview of the screen saver. To see a full screen view, click Preview. Click anywhere on-screen to return to the dialog box from the preview.

4. To customize the appearance and properties of your screen saver, click Settings. The options and settings for each screen saver are different. Figure 13.27 shows the options to customize the Flying Through Space screen saver.

FIG. 13.27

You can customize screen savers so they act differently.

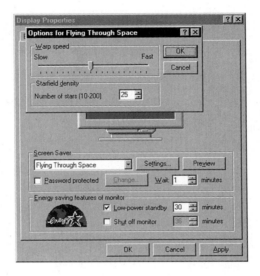

5. In the Wait text box, type or select the number of minutes you want the screen to be idle before the screen saver displays. A range from 5 to 15 minutes is usually a good time.

6. Choose Apply to apply the Display Property changes you have selected so far. You will see the changes take effect, but the Display Properties sheet stays open. Choose OK to accept the changes and close the dialog box.

Protecting Your Computer with a Screen Saver Password

Although each screen saver has unique settings, all except Blank Screen have an area where you can specify password protection. If you don't want uninvited users to use your computer, you can specify a password that is associated with a screen saver, so only those who know the password can clear the screen saver and use your computer.

To protect your computer using a password, follow these steps:

1. Right-click anywhere on the desktop then choose Properties to open the Display Properties sheet.

2. Click the Screen Saver tab.

3. Select a screen saver from the Screen Saver drop-down list and set its options.

4. Select the <u>P</u>assword Protected check box and choose <u>C</u>hange.

5. Type your password in the <u>N</u>ew Password text box, and confirm your password by typing it again in the Con<u>f</u>irm New Password text box.

   Asterisks will appear in the text boxes as you type your password to prevent others from seeing it (see fig. 13.28).

FIG. 13.28

Enter a password for the screen saver in the Change Password dialog box.

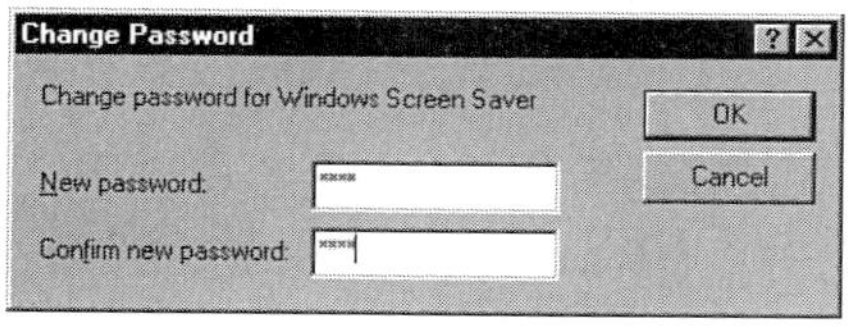

Change Password	? X
Change password for Windows Screen Saver	OK
<u>N</u>ew password: *****	Cancel
Con<u>f</u>irm new password: *****	

6. Choose OK. When the confirmation message appears, choose OK again.

Now, when the screen saver appears and you press a key on the keyboard or move the mouse, a dialog box appears in which you have to type your password to clear the screen saver.

Using Your Display's Energy-Saving Feature

If you leave your computer on continuously, or if you leave your desk for long periods of time while your computer continues to run, you will want to conserve energy by using the energy-saving features that are built into many newer monitors. Although the energy used by one monitor might seem small, when multiplied by the millions of computers in use across the nation it is easy to see that selecting this option one time can save a lot of energy and reduce pollution. When you multiply the cost of running the tens of thousands of monitors in a single large corporation, the dollar savings can be significant.

Monitors that satisfy EPA requirements usually display an "Energy Star" sticker on the monitor or in the manual. Older monitors do not have the energy-saving feature.

If you have a monitor that is an Energy Star but the Energy Saving Features of Monitor options are not available in the Screen Saver tab, you should install the correct display drivers for your monitor. To check which display driver is installed, open the Display Properties sheet, choose the Settings tab, and then choose the Change Display <u>T</u>ype button. From the dialog box that appears, you can install the display driver for your manufacturer and model. After you have the correct driver, select the Monitor is <u>E</u>nergy Star Compliant check box. Selecting this check box does no good if the monitor is not compliant.

To set Windows so it takes advantage of the energy-saving features of Energy Star-compliant monitors, follow these steps:

Part

IV

Ch

13

1. Right-click the desktop and choose Properties.

2. Choose the Settings tab (refer to fig. 13.26).

3. Select the Low-Power Standby check box, and select the number of minutes the computer should be idle before the monitor goes into low-power standby. This mode reduces power requirements but keeps the monitor ready to be instantly used.

4. Select the Shut Off Monitor check box, and select the number of minutes the computer should be idle before the monitor shuts down. This mode completely turns off your monitor.

5. Choose OK.

When you return to your workstation, you can press any key or move the mouse to return to normal monitor use from low-power standby. The Shut Off Monitor mode shuts off the monitor rather than putting it in Standby mode. This saves the most energy. The manual for your monitor describes the best way to turn the monitor on again.

▶ **See** "Understanding the Device Manager," **p. 177**
▶ **See** "Using Power Management," **p. 200**

Changing the Screen Resolution, Font Size, and Color Palette

With Windows 95, you have the ability to change how your application displays even while you work. This can help you if you run applications that operate with different screen resolutions, or use programs that look better in different font sizes. Some applications, such as graphics programs or multimedia, work better when they use 256 colors and higher resolution.

The resolution is the number of dots shown on-screen. The more dots on-screen, the more detail you can work with. However, with a high-resolution screen, icons or fonts that appeared an adequate size on a VGA screen can now appear small.

Changing the resolution while Windows is running enables you to switch between VGA mode (640 × 480 pixels on-screen) to the more detailed and wider view of SVGA mode (1024 × 768 pixels). This can come in handy when you work on different types of tasks. You might, for example, have a laptop computer that displays on its LCD screen in VGA mode. When you work at your desk and have a high-resolution monitor connected to the laptop, you want to work in SVGA mode.

Changing the Screen Resolution

You can change the screen resolution, the number of dots on the screen, if your display is capable of running Super VGA 800 × 600 resolution or better and Super VGA or better is currently set as the monitor type.

You can change or examine your monitor type by following these steps:

1. Open the Display Properties sheet and click the Settings tab.

2. Choose Change Display Type to display the Change Display Type dialog box.

3. Choose the Change button next to the Monitor Type area.

4. Select the resolution you want to use for your monitor from the Select Device dialog box. If you are unsure, choose Standard Monitor Types from the Manufacturers list box and choose a monitor from the Models list box.

5. Choose OK, and then choose Close.

6. When you return to the Display Properties sheet, you can change other display properties. Choose OK.

When you exit the Display Properties sheet, you might need to restart Windows to implement the new monitor type. You will be asked whether you want to restart at that time.

> **CAUTION**
>
> Changing to an incorrect monitor type that cannot be implemented might cause your screen to be unreadable. If that happens, shut off your computer. Restart your computer and watch the screen carefully. When the phrase, "Starting Windows 95" appears, press F8. This displays a text menu that enables you to start Windows in *safe mode.* Safe mode displays Windows on any screen, but many resources will not be available such as networking and CD-ROM. While in safe mode, repeat the steps described in this section and select either a monitor type you are sure of or a resolution that will work from the Standard Monitor Types list.

Part
IV

Ch
13

After your monitor is in Super VGA mode or better, you can change between screen resolutions by dragging the slider in the Desktop area of the Settings tab.

Changing the Number of Colors Available to Your Monitor

Depending on your display adapter and the monitor, you can have the same resolution screen, but with a different palette of colors available. For example, you might have some business applications that use only 16 colors, while most games and multimedia use 256 or more colors.

To change the size of your color palette, click the Color Palette down arrow in the Settings tab, then click the number of colors you need.

Changing Font Sizes

Need glasses to read the screen? You can enlarge (or reduce) the size of the font Windows uses on-screen. All text on-screen will change size. You have to restart Windows, however, to see the change.

You can select from any of the following font size options:

- Small Fonts scales fonts to 100 percent of normal size.
- Large Fonts scales fonts to 125 percent of normal size.
- Custom displays the Custom Font Size dialog box where you can specify your own size.

To change the size of screen fonts, follow these steps:

1. Right-click the desktop and choose Properties. The Display Properties sheet appears.
2. Click the Settings tab. Figure 13.29 shows the Properties sheet.

FIG. 13.29
Change your display's appearance in the Settings tab.

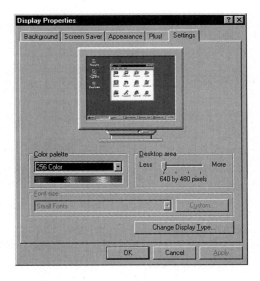

3. Choose Large Fonts or Small Fonts from the Font Size list box.

or

Click Custom to display the Custom Font Size dialog box (see fig. 13.30). Type or select a percentage of normal size in the Scale text box, or drag across the ruler, then release the mouse button to resize. Notice the sample font and its size below the ruler. Choose OK.

FIG. 13.30
You can create your own custom font size.

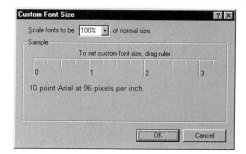

4. Click OK to accept the change and close the Display Properties sheet.

Changing the Sounds Related to Windows Events

Windows 95 has sounds related to different events such as errors, closing programs, shutting down Windows, emptying the Recycle Bin, and so on. You can change the sounds used for each of these events; you can even use your own sound files.

To change the sounds related to an event, follow these steps:

1. Open the Start menu, and choose Settings, Control Panel.

2. Double-click Sounds to display the Sounds Properties sheet shown in figure 13.31.

3. Scroll through the Events list until you see the event sound you want to change, then click that event.

4. Select the WAV file that contains the sound for that event by clicking the Browse button and selecting a WAV file. Click OK.

The Browse dialog box opens in the Windows\Media folder, but you can change to any folder.

FIG. 13.31
You can assign your own sound files to different Windows events.

5. Preview the sound by clicking Go to the right of the Preview icon.

6. Click OK.

N O T E You can create your own collection of WAV files by following the procedures described in Chapter 40, "Working with Audio." You also might want to look on public bulletin boards, online services, and the Internet. They contain thousands of free WAV files. ■

Entire collections of sounds have been grouped already for you as sound schemes. To change all the sounds involved in a sound scheme, select the scheme you want by choosing it from the Schemes list.

If you create your own scheme of sounds/events, you can save it with a name so you can return to it by clicking Save As, entering a name, and clicking OK.

Customizing the Mouse

If you are left-handed, or if you like a fast or slow mouse, you need to know how to modify your mouse's behavior. You can change mouse options in the Mouse Properties sheet, shown in figure 13.32.

To change how your mouse behaves and appears, follow these steps:

1. Open the Start menu and choose Settings, Control Panel; then double-click the Mouse icon. The Mouse Properties sheet appears.

FIG. 13.32
You can change the speed of your mouse and more in the Mouse Properties sheet.

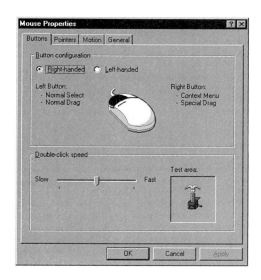

2. Click a tab and make the changes you want.

3. Click Apply to accept the change and to continue making changes, or click OK to accept the change and close the Mouse Properties sheet.

Mouse options are grouped on four tabs—Buttons, Pointer, Motion, and General. The following table describes each tab.

Tab	Description
Button	Select either a Right-Handed mouse or Left-Handed mouse. Set the Double-Click Speed, and then double-click in the Test box to determine whether you set a speed you're comfortable with. When you double-click at the right speed in the Test area, you'll be surprised by what appears.
Pointers	Change the size and shape of the pointer. You can select schemes of pointer shapes so all pointer shapes for different activities take on a new appearance.
Motion	You can set the Pointer Speed to make the mouse move more slowly or quickly across the screen. You can add a Pointer Trail to the mouse to leave a trail of mouse pointers on-screen. This feature is especially useful if you have an LCD screen where the mouse pointer can sometimes get lost. This option cannot be shown for video display drivers that don't support it.

Part
IV

Ch
13

continues

continued

Tab	Description
General	To add a new mouse to your system, click Change and the Select Device dialog box displays. Make your selection from there. You also can add a new mouse with the Add New Hardware Wizard, available from the Control Panel.

 T I P   Double-click a pointer shape while in the Pointers tab to replace one shape in a scheme.

▶ **See** "LCD Screen Mouse Trails," **p. 223**

Customizing the Keyboard

Although changing the keyboard speed doesn't result in a miracle that makes you type faster, it does speed up the rate at which characters are repeated. You also can change the delay before the character repeats.

To change keyboard properties, follow these steps.

 1. Open the Start menu and choose Settings, Control Panel; then double-click Keyboard. The Keyboard Properties sheet appears (see fig. 13.33).

FIG. 13.33
You can change the keyboard repeat and more in the Keyboard Properties sheet.

2. Click a tab and make the changes you want.

3. Click <u>A</u>pply to accept the change and to continue making changes, or click OK to accept the change and close the Keyboard Properties sheet.

Keyboard options are grouped on three tabs: Speed, Language, and General. The following table describes these tabs.

Tab	Description
Speed	Change the keyboard repeat speed. Drag the Slow/Fast pointer to change the Repeat <u>D</u>elay Speed (how long before the first repeat) or the <u>R</u>epeat Rate. Click in the Click Here box to test the results. Drag the Slow/Fast Pointer for Cursor <u>B</u>link Speed to change the speed the cursor blinks.
Language	Use the Language tab to select the language you use. Click A<u>d</u>d to display the Add Language dialog box and select a language from the drop-down list. Click <u>P</u>roperties to select an appropriate keyboard layout. Click <u>R</u>emove to remove a language from the list. Click the up and down arrows to change the order of the languages you have selected. Changing this option enables your applications to accurately sort words that might contain non-English characters, such as accent marks. However, changing the language setting does not change the language used by Windows. You need to purchase a different language version of Windows to accomplish this.
General	To change keyboards, click <u>C</u>hange and the Select Device dialog box appears. Make your selection from there. You also can add a new keyboard with the Add New Hardware Wizard, available from the Control Panel.

Making Windows Accessible for the Hearing, Sight, and Movement Impaired

In an effort to make computers more available to the more than 30 million people who have some form of disability, Microsoft has added Accessibility Properties. You can use these properties to adjust the computer's sound, display, and physical interface.

To make accessibility adjustments, follow these steps:

Part
IV

Ch
13

1. Click the Start button and choose Settings, Control Panel.

2. Double-click the Accessibility Options icon. The Accessibility Properties sheet appears (see fig. 13.34).

3. Make your selections and click OK.

TROUBLESHOOTING

Accessibility Options does not appear in my Control Panel. Reinstall Windows using a custom installation and select Accessibility Options. Appendix A describes how to reinstall options in Windows.

FIG. 13.34
Use the Accessibility Properties sheet to make Windows easier to use for a person with a disability.

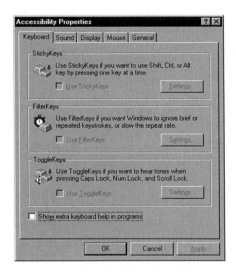

The Accessibility Properties sheet includes the following tabs:

Tab	Description
Keyboard	Make the keyboard more tolerant and patient. Select Use StickyKeys if you need to press multiple keys simultaneously but are able to press keys only one at a time. Select Use FilterKeys to ignore short or repeated keystrokes. Select Use ToggleKeys to make a sound when you press Caps Lock, Num Lock, and Scroll Lock.
Sound	Provide visual warnings and captions for speech and sounds. Select Use SoundSentry to make Windows use a visual warning when a sound alert occurs. Select Use ShowSounds to display captions instead of speech or sounds.

Tab	Description
Display	Select colors and fonts for easy reading. Select Use High Contrast to use color and font combinations that produce greater screen contrast.
Mouse	Control the pointer with the numeric keypad. Select Use MouseKeys to use the numeric keypad and other keys in place of the mouse. The relationship of keys to mouse controls appears in the following table.
General	Turn off accessibility features, give notification, and add an alternative input device. Use Automatic Reset to set Windows so accessibility features remain on at all times, are turned off when Windows restarts, or are turned off after a period of inactivity. Notification tells users when a feature is turned on or off. The SerialKey device enables Windows to receive keyboard or mouse input from alternative input devices through a serial port.

Some of these accessibility features could be difficult for a disabled person to turn on or off through normal Windows procedures. To alleviate this problem, Windows includes special *hotkeys*. Pressing the keys or key combinations for the designated hotkey turns an accessibility feature on or off, or changes its settings. The following table gives the hotkeys for different features.

Feature	Hot Key	Result
High-Contrast Mode	Press left-Alt+left-Shift+Print Screen simultaneously	Alternates the screen through different text/background combinations
StickyKeys	Press the Shift key five consecutive times	Turned on or off
FilterKeys	Hold down right Shift key for eight seconds	Turned on or off
ToggleKeys	Hold down Num Lock key for five seconds	Turned on or off
MouseKeys	Press left-Alt+left-Shift+Num Lock simultaneously	Turned on or off

Part IV

Ch 13

MouseKeys can be very useful for portable or laptop computer users and graphic artists as well as for people unable to use a mouse. Graphic artists will find MouseKeys useful because it enables them to produce finer movements than those done with a mouse.

After MouseKeys is turned on, you can produce the same effects as a mouse by using these keys:

Action	Press this key(s)
Movement	Any number key except 5
Large moves	Hold down Ctrl as you press number keys
Single pixel moves	Hold down Shift as you press number keys
Single-click	5
Double-click	+
Begin drag	Insert
Drop after drag	Delete
Select left mouse button	/
Select right mouse button	-
Select both mouse buttons	*

CAUTION
Use the numeric keypad with MouseKeys, not the numbered keys across the top of the keypad. Make sure the Num Lock key is set so the keypad is in numeric mode rather than cursor mode.

Setting the Date and Time

Use the Date/Time Properties sheet to change the date or time in your system (see fig. 13.35). You also can change the format of the date and time to match another country's standard.

FIG. 13.35
You can change the system date and time in the Date/Time Properties sheet.

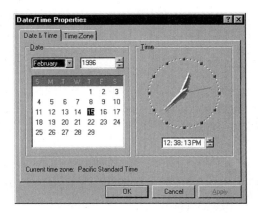

T I P To display the current date, point to the clock on the taskbar and the date will pop up.

To change date and time properties, follow these steps.

1. Double-click the clock on the taskbar.

   or

    Open the Start menu and choose Settings, Control Panel; then double-click Date/Time.

   The Date/Time Properties sheet appears.

2. Click a tab and make the changes you want. See the following table for a description of things you can change.

3. Click Apply to accept the change and to continue making changes, or click OK to accept the change and close the Date/Time Properties sheet.

Date and time options are grouped on two tabs—Date & Time and Time Zone. The following table describes these tabs.

Tab	Description
Date & Time	To change the Date, click the down arrow and select a month, or click the up and down arrows to select a year. Click the day of the month in the calendar.
	To change the time, click the element you want to change in the digital time display. For example, to change hours, click the first two numbers. Click the up and down arrows next to the time display.
Time Zone	Click the down arrow to select a new time zone (see fig. 13.36). Select the Adjust for Daylight Savings Time check box to have the time automatically adjust for daylight savings time.

Part

IV

Ch

13

FIG. 13.36
You can change the time zone to reflect the time in any area of the world.

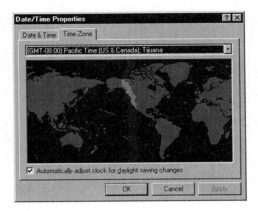

Customizing for Your Country and Language

Windows has the capacity to switch between international character sets, time and date displays, and numeric formats. The international settings you choose in Control Panel affect applications, such as Microsoft Excel, that take advantage of these Windows features.

N O T E Although you can change the language and country formats, doing so does not change the language used in menus or Help information. To obtain versions of Windows and Microsoft applications for countries other than the United States, check with your local Microsoft representative. Check with the corporate offices of other software vendors for international versions of their applications. ■

The Regional Settings Properties sheet provides five tabs (see fig. 13.37). The region you select on the Regional Settings tab automatically affects the settings in the other tabs.

To change Regional Settings properties, follow these steps:

1. Open the Start menu and choose <u>S</u>ettings, <u>C</u>ontrol Panel; then double-click Regional Settings. The Regional Settings Properties sheet appears.

2. Click a tab and make the changes you want.

3. Click <u>A</u>pply to accept the changes and to continue making changes, or click OK to accept the changes and close the Regional Settings Properties screen.

FIG. 13.37
You can change settings,
such as number formats on
the Number tab, to reflect
any region of the world.

The following table describes each tab in the Regional Setting Properties sheet.

Tab	Description
Regional Settings	Click the down arrow and select your geographic region, or click your region on the global map. This selection automatically changes other settings in the dialog box.
Number	To make a change to the format, click the down arrow next to the box you want to change and choose what you want, or click in the box and type what you want.
Currency	To make a change to the format, click the down arrow next to the box you want to change and choose what you want, or click in the box and type what you want. To select some currency symbols, you might have to select a different keyboard first. The No. of Digits After Decimal setting can be overridden by some applications, such as spreadsheet programs.
Time	Change the symbols, separator, and style of the time display. To make a change to the format, click the down arrow next to the box you want to change and choose what you want, or click in the box and type what you want.
Date	To make a change to the format, click the down arrow next to the box you want to change and choose what you want, or click in the box and type what you want.

Changing Custom Settings for Each User

Windows accommodates situations where people share a computer or move between computers. Windows enables you to store your custom settings for colors, accessibility features, and so on with your logon name. When you log on to the computer, Windows resets the computer with your settings.

User profiles are stored with your user logon ID. But you must tell Windows that you want to store user profiles for each different logon ID.

To create or remove a custom user profile for each logon ID, follow these steps:

1. Open the Start menu and choose Settings, Control Panel; then double-click Passwords.

2. Click the User Profiles tab. Figure 13.38 shows the User Profiles tab.

3. Select one of the following:

   - Select All Users of this PC if you want all users to use the same settings. Go to step 5.

   - Select Users Can Customize Their Preferences if you want Windows to use the customization setup during the last use of that logon ID. Go to step 4.

4. If you make the second selection in step 3, you can choose from the following:

   - Select Include Desktop Icons and Network Neighborhood Contents in User Settings if the user profile should remember changes to these items.

   - Select Include Start Menu and Program Groups in User Settings if the user profile should remember changes to these items.

5. Click OK.

FIG. 13.38
You can create user profiles so people sharing the same computer can save their custom settings.

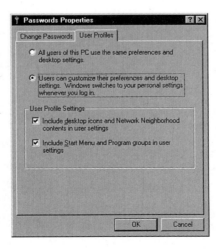

When you are done with a Windows computer shared by multiple users, log off the computer so others can log on and use their custom user profiles. To log off, click the Start button, and choose Sh<u>u</u>t Down, <u>C</u>lose All Programs and Log On as a Different User?. Choose OK.

If you made the selection Users Can Customize Their Preferences, then whenever a person logs on to Windows and customizes settings, those settings are saved with that logon ID. The next time someone logs on with that logon ID, Windows changes to the settings for that ID.

Preventing Others from Using Windows

You might work in an area where you need to keep your computer secure. For example, your work might involve financial, market, or personnel data that is confidential. One way you can help to protect this information is to require a password before Windows will start.

To create or change your Windows password, follow these steps:

1. Open the Passwords Properties sheet as described in the previous section.
2. Click the Change Passwords tab, then click the Change <u>W</u>indows Password button to display the Change Windows Password dialog box.

   If you have network passwords, they will be listed so you can change them to match your Windows password.
3. Type your old password in the <u>O</u>ld Password text box.
4. Type your new password in the <u>N</u>ew Password and Con<u>f</u>irm Password text boxes.
5. Choose OK, then OK again.

Windows provides security for the network environment from the other tabs on the Password Properties sheet.

▶ **See** "Maintaining Workgroup Security," **p. 800**

Part
IV

Ch

13

Reviewing Your Computer's System Information

One of the more gruesome aspects of using DOS or earlier versions of Windows was working with configuration files when you wanted to customize or optimize your computer. People who wanted to install sound cards or network adapters, change memory usage, or specify I/O (Input/Output) or IRQ (interrupt request) settings faced immersion in the arcane world of configuration files. Configuration files gave you no help; yet if you made an error, part of your hardware might not be recognized, your system might run slower, or it might not run at all.

Windows 95 makes specifying configurations easier. Now you can select only allowable options from straightforward dialog boxes, and you can see settings from other hardware devices that might cause conflicts.

Reading Your Registration and Version Number

You can see your registration number, the version number of Windows, and the type of processor on which Windows is running on the General page of the System Properties sheet. To see this page, follow these steps:

1. Open the Start menu and choose Settings, Control Panel to display the Control Panel window.

2. Double-click the System icon.

3. Click the General tab of the System Properties sheet (see fig. 13.39).

FIG. 13.39
View your registration number and Window's version number on the System Properties General page.

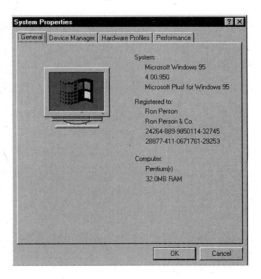

Examine the Hardware on Your Computer

You might need to examine the configuration settings and drivers for hardware connected to your computer. You can use the System Properties sheet to help you troubleshoot hardware. If you need to see a list of IRQ and I/O settings, you need to use the Device Manager.

To display the Device Manager page, follow these steps:

1. Open the Start menu and choose Settings, Control Panel to display the Control Panel window.

2. Double-click the System icon.

3. Click the Device Manager tab of the System Properties sheet (see fig. 13.40).

FIG. 13.40

View the hardware devices and their drivers on the System Properties Device Manager page.

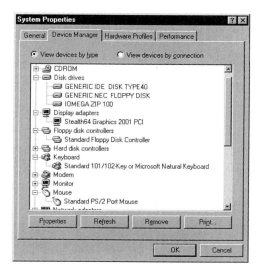

4. To see the drivers installed for a device, click the + sign to the left of the device. To see information about a device or to remove the device, select one of the following buttons:

Button	Action
Properties	Displays a listing of properties appropriate to the device. Select the Computer item to see IRQ and I/O settings.
Refresh	Windows reexamines the installed hardware and attempts to update the list.
Remove	Removes the selected device or driver.
Print	Prints a report of configuration settings.

5. Choose OK.

▶ **See** "Installing Plug and Play Hardware," **p. 158**

▶ **See** "Installing Plug and Play CD-ROM Drives," **p. 319**

Part

IV

Ch

13

Checking IRQ, I/O, DMA, and Memory Settings   Hardware devices each require a unique section of memory (I/O address). Some hardware devices also require an interrupt request (IRQ) or direct memory access (DMA) to operate. If any of these settings conflict with the settings for another device, either or both of the devices might not work.

You can see a list of these settings in your computer by selecting the Computer icon on the Device Manager page of the System Properties sheet and then clicking Properties. Select from the option buttons to display the list of settings you want to see. Figure 13.41 shows the list of IRQ settings.

FIG. 13.41

Use the View Resources page to track down conflicts in IRQ and I/O settings.

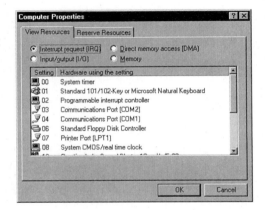

In MS-DOS and in prior versions of Windows, it was difficult to tell the cause of conflicts between hardware devices. In Windows 95, the Device Manager shows you lists of IRQ and I/O settings. You can scan through the lists and see where you accidentally installed two device drivers for the same device or you set two different devices to the same or overlapping IRQ or I/O settings.

If you find you installed two drivers for the same device, you can delete one of them. If you find a conflict because two hardware devices are using the same memory or IRQ settings, you can resolve the conflict easily through the Device Manager. The approach you might take to resolve a conflict is to look through the lists in the Device Manager to find an open IRQ or I/O setting, check the two manuals for the particular devices to determine what other IRQ or I/O settings they will work with, and change the settings for one of the devices so it doesn't conflict.

TROUBLESHOOTING

One of the hardware devices on a computer is not working. Click the Device Manager tab on the System Properties sheet and check for an X through a device. This means the hardware has been disabled. Double-click that device to check its settings. If a device icon has a circled exclamation point, the hardware has a problem. Double-click the icon to inspect the type of problem.

It took a couple of attempts with different driver selections before some of the hardware would work. Now some of the devices on the system work slowly, intermittently, or incorrectly. Check the Device Manager page of the System Properties sheet to see if you have multiple drivers installed for the same hardware device. Delete all the drivers except the driver for your specific manufacturer and model. If there are multiple drivers, but not one specific to your hardware device, keep the generic driver.

The computer works with either a sound card or a network adapter card, but not both. The usual cause of this problem is a conflict between IRQ ports and I/O addresses. Each hardware device must have its own IRQ port and its own I/O address. Sound cards and network adapters are notorious for conflicting with each other over these. To see the IRQ port and I/O address used by each device, display the Device Manager page, select the Computer icon, and choose Properties. On the View Resources page that appears, you can select the Interrupt Request (IRQ) or Input/Output (I/O) option to view a list of settings for each device on your computer. Write down the current settings and watch for conflicts. Then change the settings for devices that conflict with others.

▶ **See** "Installing a Plug and Play Modem," **p. 284**
▶ **See** "Configuring Your Modem," **p. 294**

Creating, Naming, and Copying Hardware Profiles

Part

IV

Ch

13

Hardware profiles are collections of hardware settings; they're useful if you use different collections of hardware on your computer. For example, you might have a laptop computer that uses a VGA LCD monitor on the road, but uses an SVGA large-screen monitor on the desktop.

By saving a collection of hardware settings as a profile, you only need to choose the profile you want rather than manually change hardware settings when you want to run a different combination of hardware.

When you start a Windows 95 computer that has multiple hardware configurations, you have the option of choosing the named hardware profile you want to use. From a text screen in Startup, you see something similar to this:

```
Windows cannot determine what configuration your computer is in.
Select one of the following:

1. Original Configuration
2. Multimedia
3. Desktop
4. None of the above

Enter your choice:
```

Type the number of the profile you want to use and press Enter. Windows 95 then starts with that configuration of hardware, only loading the hardware drivers required.

To make use of the distinct hardware profiles, you must first copy the existing default profile. The default profile is named Original Configuration. After you copy a profile, you can edit the devices included in it and rename it to help you recognize it. To copy or rename a hardware profile, follow these steps:

1. Open the Start menu and choose Settings, Control Panel to display the Control Panel window.

2. Double-click the System icon.

3. Click the Hardware Profile tab of the System Properties sheet (see fig. 13.42).

FIG. 13.42
Keep different combinations of hardware devices stored as a named hardware profile.

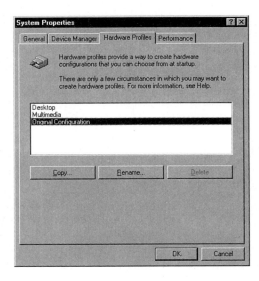

4. Select the hardware profile you want to work with and then click one of the following buttons:

Button	Action
Copy	Displays a Copy Profile dialog box in which you can enter a new name. Copies the hardware configuration from the selected profile to this new profile.
Rename	Changes the name of a profile.
Delete	Deletes a profile.

5. Choose OK.

To create a new profile or change an existing profile, follow these steps:

1. If you want to create a new profile, copy an existing profile as described in the preceding steps. Use a unique, descriptive name for the profile.
2. Click the Device Manager tab on the System Properties sheet.
3. Click the plus sign next to the hardware type you want to change for the configuration; then double-click the specific hardware you want to change. This displays the device's Properties sheet.
4. In the Device Usage area of the Properties sheet, deselect any hardware profile you don't want to use this device with. By default, all of your devices will be used with all of your profiles until you make changes.
5. Choose OK.
6. Repeat steps 3 through 5 until you have configured all the hardware for this profile.
7. Choose OK.

Depending on the changes you made, you might be prompted to restart your computer.

▶ **See** "Using Your Laptop with a Docking System," **p. 192**

Checking Performance Settings

Part
IV
Ch
13

You can check the performance parameters of your computer on the Performance page of the System Properties sheet. To see this page, follow these steps:

1. Open the Start menu and choose Settings, Control Panel to display the Control Panel window.
2. Double-click the System icon.
3. Click the Performance tab of the System Properties sheet (see fig. 13.43).
4. View the performance status parameters on the Performance page, or choose File System, Graphics, or Virtual Memory for advanced performance tuning options.
5. Choose OK.

FIG. 13.43

The System Properties Performance page provides information on your computer's performance parameters.

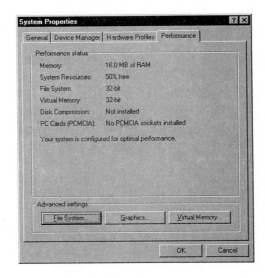

CAUTION

In general, do not change the settings available on the Performance page. Windows 95 usually sets these parameters optimally.

▶ **See** "Improving Performance with Disk Defragmenter," **p. 646**

CHAPTER 14

Introduction to REGEDIT

by Jerry Honeycutt

If you always find yourself tearing apart new technology to learn more about it, you'll undoubtedly want to get knee deep into the Windows 95 Registry Editor (REGEDIT.EXE). The Windows 95 Registry is attracting a lot of attention—as is proven by the number of tips on the Internet about the Registry. Many of the customizations you'll learn about in Chapter 15, "Customizing with REGEDIT," require you to work directly with the Registry.

Even though REGEDIT is very powerful, it is a very simple program. It doesn't have a toolbar, and its menus are fairly straightforward. REGEDIT displays the organization of the Registry on the left side of the window and the actual values on the right side. ■

Back up the Registry before changing it

This chapter shows you how to back up the Registry before changing it with the Registry Editor.

Alternatives to using the Registry Editor

Learn about the Control Panel and other alternatives to using the Registry Editor.

How the Registry is organized

Learning how the Registry is organized will make editing it much easier.

Using the Registry Editor

Learn how to use the Registry Editor to make changes to the Registry and import/export parts of the Registry.

Backing Up the Registry

Because the Registry is the storehouse for all the important configuration information on your computer, you need to treat it with the respect it deserves. *Back it up.* Otherwise, a simple error in your Registry could stop your computer from working properly. If you don't intend to use the Registry Editor, however, you don't need to take any special precautions other than your regular backup.

> **CAUTION**
>
> The "Designed for Windows 95" logo doesn't guarantee that a Windows 95 program won't break your Registry and cause your computer to malfunction. For example, I installed a Windows 95 program that displayed thumbnails of graphics files in Explorer. It broke the Registry because I installed it into a folder that had a space in the name. (Isn't that the point of long file names?) It also prevented The Microsoft Network software from working properly. The best defense against these kinds of problems is to make sure you back up your computer, or at least your Registry, before you install new Windows 95 programs.

Windows 95 backs up your Registry every time you successfully start your computer. Each backup overwrites the previous backup, however, and a successful start doesn't mean that your Registry hasn't been damaged. If you have to restore your Registry after successfully starting Windows 95, you're out of luck. To avoid this problem, you can use backup alternatives, such as backing up the Registry onto tape, copying the Registry files to a safe place, and other techniques discussed in the following sections.

 Start Windows 95 in Safe mode to prevent it from backing up your Registry settings. To start in Safe mode, restart your computer and press F8 when the screen displays the Starting Windows 95 message. Choose Safe Mode Command Property Only from the boot menu.

Copy the Registry Files to a Safe Place

The easiest way to back up the Registry is to copy the files that contain it: SYSTEM.DAT and USER.DAT. Both of these files are in your \Windows folder.

 The SYSTEM.DAT and USER.DAT are hidden system files, so make sure Explorer is set up to show you these type of files. Chose View, Options from Explorer's main menu, select Show All Files, and click OK. While Microsoft does recommend that you back up the Registry from the Safe Mode command prompt, I've successfully backed up and restored my Registry files from Explorer.

Microsoft recommends that you copy these files while in the Safe Mode command prompt. Restart your computer and when the Starting Windows 95 message appears on-screen, press F8. Then, choose Safe Mode Command Prompt Only from the menu. When your computer is started in Safe mode, follow these steps to copy the files:

1. Create a folder in your \Windows folder called Registry so that you now have a path called \Windows\Registry.

2. Change to your \Windows folder, type **attrib -h -s -r system.dat**, and press Enter. Then, type **attrib -h -s -r user.dat**, and press Enter. This makes it possible for you to copy the Registry files.

3. Type **copy system.dat .\Registry**, and press Enter. Then, type **copy user.dat .\Registry**, and press Enter.

4. Type **attrib +h +s +r system.dat**, and press Enter. Then, type **attrib +h +s +r user.dat**, and press Enter. This hides the Registry files again.

 TIP Put the commands shown in steps 3 through 5 in a batch file so that you can quickly back up your Registry.

If you need to restore your Registry, you have to start your computer in Safe mode again. Copy the files from the \Windows\Registry folder back into the \Windows folder, then hide the Registry files, as shown in step 4.

Back Up the Registry onto Tape

Windows 95 comes with a tape backup utility that you can use as part of your regular backup strategy. It's not installed by default, however. You can use the Add/Remove Programs icon in the Control Panel to install it. After it's installed, choose <u>P</u>rograms, Accessories, System Tools, Backup from the Start menu to run it.

Windows 95 Backup doesn't support most of the popular tape drives on the market; for example, it doesn't support Travan TR-3 tape drives, which allow you to back up 3.2G on a single tape. So you'll need to use the Windows 95 backup software provided with your tape drive. If the tape drive you installed didn't come with Windows 95 software, contact the manufacturer for updated software.

A Windows 95 backup program, such as Microsoft Backup or Conner Exec, backs up your Registry when you back up your Windows 95 folder. These backup programs usually export the Registry into a text file, then back up the text file. When you restore files from a tape that contains the Registry, the program usually asks you if you want to restore the Registry. If you choose Yes, the program restores the text file, and imports it back into the Registry.

▶ **See** "Backing Up Your Files," **p. 662**

Part
IV
Ch
14

TROUBLESHOOTING

Can I use my Windows 3.1 or DOS backup software with Windows 95? No. The Windows 3.1 or DOS backup utilities don't back up the Registry correctly. You may not be able to restore your computer in the event that something goes wrong.

I backed up my computer a few weeks ago. Now, I restored an INI file to my \Windows folder and Windows 95 seems to have forgotten a lot of its settings. Windows 95 Backup doesn't ask you if you want to restore the Registry when you restore files from a tape—it just does it. The safest way to restore a file into your \Windows folder is to restore it into a temporary folder, then copy it into your \Windows folder by hand.

Use CfgBack to Back Up the Registry

CfgBack is a configuration backup utility found on the Windows 95 CD-ROM. It lets you make as many as nine different backups of your Registry, and restore any one of them when needed. This utility is located in the \Other\Misc\Cfgback folder. You can copy the files to your hard drive and drag a shortcut to CFGBACK.EXE to your Start menu or desktop.

Don't rely on CfgBack as your only Registry backup, however. CfgBack only runs in Windows 95. It doesn't have a comparable real-mode program. If your computer isn't running properly, you won't be able to use CfgBack to restore your Registry.

> **CAUTION**
> When restoring a backup made by CfgBack, don't attempt to use your computer—not even Explorer. If CfgBack crashes while it's restoring your Registry, you might not be able to restart Windows 95.

Export the Registry into a Text File

You can export the entire contents of the Registry into a REG file. A REG file is a text file that looks very similar to an INI file. You can restore the Registry by running REGEDIT with the /c parameter or by choosing Registry, Import Registry File from REGEDIT's main menu. REGEDIT replaces the current contents of the Registry with the contents of the exported REG file. The section "Useful Command-Line Parameters," later in this chapter shows you how to export the Registry, and how to restore it using the /c parameter. Also, the section "Importing and Exporting Registry Entries," later in this chapter shows you how to import and export the Registry using REGEDIT.

If you can't start Windows 95 because of a corrupted Registry, you can use the real-mode Registry Editor found on your startup disk. This is one of the best reasons I can think of for making a startup disk. If you haven't done so already, do it now. Here's how:

1. Double-click the Add/Remove Programs icon in the Control Panel.
2. Click the Startup Disk tab.
3. Click Create Disk, then follow the instructions.

> **N O T E**   Windows 95 doesn't put CD-ROM or network drivers on your startup disk. If you need access to either of these when you start from your startup disk, copy the drivers to the disk. Then create a CONFIG.SYS and AUTOEXEC.BAT that loads them properly. ▨

Alternatives to Editing the Registry

This section shows you some alternatives to editing the Registry. You'll learn where to change file associations, where to change hardware and system settings, and where to find alternative programs to do some Registry tricks.

Adding and Changing Files Types in Explorer

Windows 95 keeps a list of file type associations just like Windows 3.1. The TXT file type is associated with Notepad, for example, but each file type also can have different types of actions, such as open or print, associated with it. You can even define your own actions for a file type.

You can get to the list of file types through Explorer or a folder view. In either case, choose View, Options from the main menu, and click the File Types tab. Figure 14.1 shows the File Types page.

▶ **See** "Using Windows Explorer," **p. 751**

Changing Your Configuration Through the Control Panel

Most of the truly useful Windows 95 and hardware settings can be changed using the Control Panel icons. You don't need to edit the Registry at all. Table 14.1 shows what settings you can change and which icon to use.

Part
IV

Ch
14

FIG. 14.1
Change file associations and
context menu actions on the
File Types page.

Table 14.1   Control Panel Programs that Change the Registry

Icon	Program	Description
	Accessibility	Visual/Hearing impaired settings
	Add New Hardware	Add new hardware
	Add/Remove Programs	Add or remove programs
	Date/Time	Adjust Date/Time settings
	Display	Most display settings
	Joystick	Joystick settings
	Keyboard	Keyboard settings
	Mail and Fax	Microsoft Exchange settings
	Modems	Modem and TAPI settings
	Mouse	Mouse settings

Icon	Program	Description
	Multimedia	Multimedia settings
	Network	Network hardware and software
	Passwords	Profile and password settings
	Power	Advanced power management
	Printers	Add, change, or remove printers
	Regional Settings	International settings
	Sounds	Assign sounds to events
	System	Hardware/System settings

Using Shareware Applications to Change the Registry

On the CD

Microsoft PowerToys is a freeware product that contains a tool called Tweak UI. Tweak UI lets you set some of the most popular Registry entries, such as an entry that controls window animation. Previously, you had to actually change the Registry. Figure 14.2 shows the Tweak UI's General page. You learn more about using Tweak UI in Chapter 15, "Customizing with REGEDIT." The Win95 shortcut is on the companion CD.

ON THE WEB

http://www.microsoft.com/windows/software/powertoy.htm

Setting Options in Application Programs

Just about all Windows 95 programs save their settings in the Registry. In Word, for example, you change most of your settings by choosing Tools, Options from the main menu (see fig. 14.3). Most other Windows 95 programs have similar methods for changing settings. You don't need to change them in the Registry.

FIG. 14.2
Tweak UI is a safe alternative to making changes to the Registry.

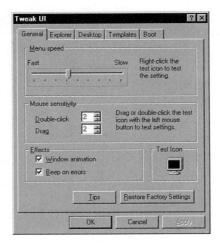

FIG. 14.3
Change a program's options through the menu, not the Registry.

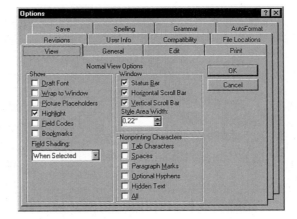

Letting Hardware Detection Maintain Your Configuration

There's really no good reason for changing your hardware settings in the Registry. You can change all of these settings using the Device Manager and the Add New Hardware Wizard. You can change settings for configurable devices using the Device Manager. If you want to change the drive that's assigned to your CD-ROM, for example, you can change it in the Device Manager, as shown in figure 14.4.

The Add New Hardware Wizard adds the necessary entries to the Registry for any new devices you install. In most cases, you won't have to change your CONFIG.SYS, and you'll never have to add entries to the Registry for any hardware you install.

▶ **See** "Adding or Changing Hardware Drivers," **p. 332**

FIG. 14.4
Configure your devices using the Device Manager, not the Registry.

Updating the Registry with REG and INF Files

When you find a description of a great Registry hack you'd like to try, look for a REG file that contains all the changes. These are text files that look similar to INI files. These files are created by exporting a portion of the Registry. You can merge the changes contained in the REG file by double-clicking the file. The entries in the REG are merged with your Registry, replacing any entries by the same name, or adding any new entries.

You'll also find INF files that contain the information Windows 95 needs to make changes to your Registry. Microsoft PowerToys comes with an EXPLORE.INF file, for example, that adds an entry to a folder's context menu. This entry lets you open Explorer with the current folder at the root of the view.

Understanding How the Registry is Organized

The Registry represents the evolution of Windows 3.1's registration database into the central repository for all configuration information in Windows 95 and your computer. It's much more complicated than INI files ever were, but also adds significantly more power and flexibility.

In this section, you learn about how the Registry is organized through such topics as:

- What Windows 95 stashes in the Registry
- How INI files and the registration database evolved into the Windows 95 Registry
- How the Registry is organized and what types of values you'll find in each part

Part
IV

Ch
14

What Goes in the Registry?

Windows 95 and Windows 95 programs store virtually all your settings, both hardware and software, in the Registry. Here are some of the types of information you'll find in the Registry:

- Windows 95 stores information about your computer's hardware in the Registry. This includes hardware detected by the Add New Hardware Wizard and any Plug-and-Play devices.

- Windows 95 stores your desktop configuration in the Registry. Chapter 15, "Customizing with REGEDIT," teaches you how to use these Registry entries to personalize your desktop.

- Windows 95 loads 32-bit protected-mode device drivers from the Registry instead of from your CONFIG.SYS. You no longer need to load a bunch of drivers in your CONFIG.SYS.

- Individual programs that you run on your computer store their settings in the Registry. While 16-bit programs still use the classic INI file, newer Windows 95 programs use the Registry.

How INI Files Compare to the Registry

Editing your configuration using the Registry Editor is definitely an improvement over editing INI files with a text editor. Most notably, it's easier to find the configuration entries you want using REGEDIT, because almost all the entries are stored in one place. Contrast this to finding a configuration entry in 20, 30, or even 100 different INI files. You can hardly do it, unless you have some prior knowledge of the entry you're looking for. Table 14.2 compares various aspects of editing an INI file to editing the Registry using REGEDIT.

Table 14.2   Editing INI Files Versus the Registry

Editing an INI file	Editing the Registry
Items in many INI files	Most items in the Registry
Edit with text editor	Edit with REGEDIT
Text editor uses Flat view	REGEDIT uses Outline view
Two levels of hierarchy	Unlimited levels of hierarchy
Easy to repair	Difficult to repair
Easy to make serious errors	Easy to make serious errors

Editing an INI file	Editing the Registry
Text entries only	Text and binary entries
No remote editing	Remote editing
Changes not always immediate	Changes not always immediate
Entries sometimes unreadable	Entries make more sense
INI files limited to 64K	Registry files unlimited

How the Registry is Organized

As I alluded to earlier, Windows 95 keeps track of two types of configuration information: system and user. The system database contains information about the hardware and software that is installed on your computer. The user database keeps track of each user's preferences, such as desktop settings and program settings. These roughly correspond to two different Registry files named SYSTEM.DAT and USER.DAT. You'll find both of these files in your Windows 95 folder. You'll also find backup copies of your Registry files called SYSTEM.DAO and USER.DAO. Each time Windows 95 successfully starts, it copies your current Registry to the backup files.

Each entry in the Registry is called a *key*, and the Registry organizes keys hierarchically. Your computer is at the top level, a handful of *root keys* at the next level, and each root key has any number of *subkeys* under it. You can think of it like a major corporation, with a CEO at the top level, a handful of vice presidents at the next level, and then a number of managers and workers reporting to each vice president on the next level.

Windows 95 stores the actual configuration data in *value entries*. Every key in the Registry, no matter in which level of the hierarchy you find it, can have one or more of these value entries. Each value entry has a name and data associated with it. The data can be a string, a DWORD (32-bit value), or binary data. Figure 14.5 shows you the relationship between value entries and keys.

When you look at the Registry through the Registry Editor, you see six or more root keys. There are actually only two: HKEY_Local_Machine and HKEY_Users. The other root keys are aliases that refer to branches within either of these two root keys. That is, they are a bit like shortcuts: if you change a value in one of the aliases, that value is actually changed in either HKEY_Local_Machine or HKEY_Users. Table 14.3 gives you an overview of the root keys you commonly find in the Registry.

Part

IV

Ch

14

FIG. 14.5

The Registry Editor displays keys in the left pane and the value entries for the selected key in the right pane.

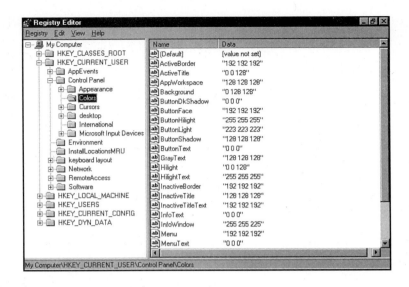

Table 14.3   Root Keys in the Registry Editor

Root Key	Description
HKEY_Local_Machine	Contains configuration data that is specific to the computer, such as installed hardware and program settings. The information in this key applies to all the users who log onto the computer.
HKEY_Classes_Root	An alias for a branch in HKEY_Local_Machine that contains program settings for OLE, drag-and-drop, shortcuts, and file associations.
HKEY_Current_Config	An alias for HKEY_Local_Machine\Config that contains the current configuration data for the computer.
HKEY_Dyn_Data	An alias for a branch in HKEY_Local_Machine that contains dynamic information such as the status of Plug-and-Play devices and performance data.
HKEY_Users	Contains configuration data for all the users who log onto the computer. This includes information that applies to all users and information specific to each user. You'll find a subkey for each user.
HKEY_Current_User	An alias for the branch in HKEY_Users that belongs to the current user.

The sections that follow describe each root key in more detail.

HKEY_Local_Machine   Windows 95 stores the configuration data for your computer in HKEY_Local_Machine. The information in this root key and any of its aliases applies to the computer itself, not to each user who logs onto it. Here are some examples of the information contained in HKEY_Local_Machine:

- Individual program settings, such as paths, that apply to every person who uses the computer.

- Device driver configuration, such as the drive letter assignment of your CD-ROM or your modem's configuration.

- Hardware configuration, such as information about all the hardware (Plug and Play and legacy) installed on your computer.

- Windows 95 configuration, such as your desktop preferences, installation paths, and more.

HKEY_Local_Machine has several subkeys, as described in table 14.4. Some of these subkeys are also aliased by other root keys.

Table 14.4   Subkeys in HKEY_Local_Machine

Subkey	Description
Config	Contains configuration data for alternate hardware configurations as defined using hardware profiles. If you have a docked and an undocked configuration for your notebook computer, both configurations are stored here.
Enum	Contains the device information you'll find in the Device Manager. For each device in your computer, you'll find information such as the type of device, hardware manufacturer, device driver, and configuration.
Hardware	Contains information for the Windows 95 HyperTerminal.
Network	Contains information about the user and the network when a user logs onto a network.
Security	Contains information about network security.
Software	Contains information about the software installed on the computer, including file associations and program settings.
System	Contains information that controls what device drivers Windows 95 loads at startup and how to configure each of the drivers. This subkey also controls many aspects of how Windows 95 works. It is one of the most interesting branches in the Registry.

Part
IV

Ch
14

HKEY_Classes_Root   HKEY_Classes_Root is an alias for the HKEY_Local_Machine\ Software\Classes branch. So why do you need an alias? Windows 3.1 programs used HKEY_Classes_Root in the Registry database, so it's in the Registry to maintain compatibility with those programs.

The HKEY_Classes_Root branch contains:

■ File associations that associate specific classes with different file extensions. The MID file extension is associated with the "midfile" class, for example.

■ Class definitions that describe all the actions associated with a file class. You'll also find information about the icon associated with a class, any shell extensions installed for the class, and the class's OLE information. For example, the "midfile" class contains information about its associated icon, OLE configuration, actions, and shell extensions.

HKEY_Current_Config   HKEY_Current_Config is an alias for the currently used hardware configuration found in HKEY_Local_Machine\Config. You won't have multiple configurations unless you're using hardware profiles.

HKEY_Dyn_Data   Some of the information that Windows 95 stores in the Registry needs to be updated quickly. Thus, Windows 95 keeps part of the Registry in memory instead of on the hard drive. It stores performance data in memory, for example, because it needs quick access to this information. You'll find this type of information in HKEY_Dyn_Data. Table 14.5 shows the two subkeys under it.

Table 14.5   Subkeys in HKEY_Dyn_Data

Subkey	Description
Config Manager	Contains the *hardware tree*, which is a record of all the hardware in the current configuration indicated by HKEY_Current_Config. You'll find status information and any problem codes for each device in the current profile. The HardwareKey value entry contains the subkey relative to HKEY_Local_Machine\Enum for each device, too.
PerfStats	Contains performance information about the network and other components in your system. You can easily view this information using System Monitor.

HKEY_Users   HKEY_Users contains the Default subkey and an additional subkey for each user who has logged onto the computer. If the computer isn't configured for multiple user profiles, you won't see additional subkeys for each user—only the Default subkey. If the computer is configured for multiple users, you'll see additional subkeys for each user.

Each subkey, including .Default, contains preferences that are specific to that user. You'll find information that's updated from the Control Panel, Dial-up Networking, and individual program settings stored here. For example, each user who logs onto your computer can have his own settings for Word. Table 14.6 describes some of the typical subkeys in HKEY_Users.

Table 14.6 Subkeys in HKEY_Users

Subkey	Description
AppEvents	Contains the path to the sound file that Windows 95 plays when a specific event occurs.
Control Panel	Contains the settings defined in the Control Panel that used to be stored in WIN.INI and CONTROL.INI.
Keyboard Layouts	Contains an entry that identifies the current keyboard layout as set in the Control Panel.
Network	Contains subkeys that describe current and recent network connections.
Software	Contains individual program settings for each user. This information used to be found in WIN.INI and private INI files.

HKEY_Current_User   HKEY_Current_User is an alias for the current user in HKEY_Users. If the computer isn't configured to allow each user to maintain his own configuration in the Control Panel's Password Properties, HKEY_Current_User always points to the Default subkey.

Using the Registry Editor

Microsoft's philosophy about the Registry Editor is that if you never had it, you'll never miss it. They don't install it in your Start menu when you install Windows 95. Probably just as well, too. They want to prevent inexperienced users from accidentally breaking their computer system by tampering with the Registry. By reading this chapter, you'll learn how to do it safely.

The Registry Editor is not on your Start menu, but it is in your Windows folder. The file name is REGEDIT.EXE. Choose Programs, Run from the Start menu, type **REGEDIT.EXE**, and then click OK to produce the Registry Editor window.

 Drag REGEDIT.EXE from your Windows folder to your Start menu.

 If you're using a computer in a networked environment, your system administrator may have disabled it. You'll have to plead your case to the system administrator for access to the Registry Editor. Note that the system administrator can also prevent REGEDIT.EXE from being installed on your computer if you're installing Windows 95 from the network.

The Registry Editor Window

The Registry Editor shows two panes in its window (see fig. 14.6)

- The left pane shows the organization of the Registry. The first entry is My Computer. It contains several keys that the Registry Editor represents as folders. Each key can contain subkeys, and so on. Click a plus sign to open a folder, or click a minus sign to close a folder.

- The right pane shows the values entries for a particular key in the Registry. Each key can contain several values entries that have both a value name and its value data.

FIG. 14.6
The left pane of Registry Editor works similarly to the left pane of Explorer.

Key
Subkey
Value entry

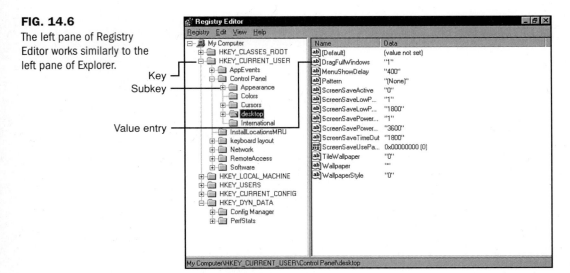

Notice that each value entry in the Registry Editor is preceded by an icon. The icon indicates what type of data that value entry stores within the Registry. These icons are described in table 14.7.

Table 14.7   Types of Data in the Registry

Type	Description
ab	Values represented as strings that you can read.
011 110	Binary values that the Registry Editor displays as hexadecimal text.

Working with Keys and Value Entries

Before you learn how to edit the Registry, remember the advice you read in the section "Alternatives to Editing the Registry," earlier in this chapter. If you can find a safer alternative to editing the Registry directly, use it. You can change many entries using the Control Panel, for example.

If you're absolutely sure that the only way to do what you want is to edit the Registry, follow the instructions in this section for searching for, adding, changing, and deleting keys and values entries.

Searching for Keys and Value Entries

When you search the Registry, the Registry Editor looks for both keys and value entries that match the text you give it. Choose Edit, Find; the Registry Editor displays the dialog box shown in figure 14.7.

FIG. 14.7
Deselect Keys, Values, or Data if you don't want the Registry Editor to search those corresponding parts of the Registry.

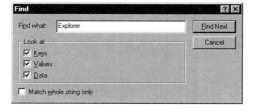

TIP Start your search from the top of the Registry to make sure the Registry Editor looks at all of the entries.

Click Find Next, and the Registry Editor searches for a match. This can sometimes take quite a while—up to a few minutes on slower machines. After the Registry Editor has found a match, it opens the folder that contains the match and highlights the matching key or value. If the result isn't exactly what you had in mind, press F3 to repeat the search. When the Registry Editor reaches the bottom of the Registry, it displays a dialog box telling you it has finished searching.

Editing a Key

You'll change value entries more than you'll add or delete them. You may want to change something on your desktop or you might not like how long it takes a menu to pop up after it's selected. Either way, you can change Windows 95's behavior by changing values in the Registry.

Part
IV

Ch
14

N O T E   Changes that you make to the Registry may not be reflected immediately in Windows 95 or the programs that are running when you make the changes. To ensure that the changes are in place, close the Registry Editor and restart Windows 95.

To restart Windows 95 quickly, choose S<u>h</u>ut Down from the Start menu. Then, select <u>R</u>estart the Computer in the Shut Down Windows dialog box and hold down the Shift key while you click <u>Y</u>es. Windows 95 restarts without rebooting your computer.   ■

Remember that each value entry can be a string, DWORD, or binary data. Double-click a value entry to open the Edit dialog box. This dialog box looks different depending on the type of data stored in the value. Figures 14.8, 14.9, and 14.10 show you what each dialog box looks like. After you've made your changes, click OK.

FIG. 14.8
The Edit String dialog box shows you the original data before you start editing.

FIG. 14.9
Choose <u>D</u>ecimal if your hexadecimal math is a bit rusty.

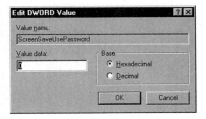

FIG. 14.10
You can use the Windows 95 calculator (in Scientific mode) to convert decimal values to hexadecimal values for use with this dialog box.

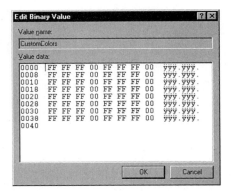

Creating a New Key or Value Entry

Creating a new key or value entry is generally harmless, but your efforts are wasted unless you know for sure that either Windows 95 or another program will use your new key. So when will you need to add a key to the Registry? Well, you might find an interesting customization in Chapter 15, "Customizing with REGEDIT," that involves adding a key or value entry. Also, a support person may ask you to add a key or value entry to fix a problem you're having. Here's how to create a new key or a new value entry:

- *New key.* Select an existing key under which you want your new subkey to appear. Choose <u>E</u>dit, <u>N</u>ew, <u>K</u>ey; type the name of your key; and press Enter.

- *New value entry.* Select an existing key under which you want your new value entry to appear. Choose <u>E</u>dit, New, and choose either <u>S</u>tring Value, <u>B</u>inary Value, or <u>D</u>WORD Value. Type the name of your new value entry, and press Enter. You can edit your key as described in "Editing a Key" earlier in this chapter.

Deleting a Key or Value Entry

Be very careful about deleting keys from your Registry. If you don't know for sure what will happen, don't do it. In some cases, you may made need to delete a key or value entry to customize Windows 95. To turn off those silly arrows that Windows 95 uses for a shortcut's icon, you have to delete two value entries (see Chapter 15, "Customizing with REGEDIT"). Highlight the key or value entry you want to delete, and press Delete. The Registry Editor asks you to confirm that you want to delete it; click OK if you're sure.

Importing and Exporting Registry Entries

There are two ways you can work with the Registry. You can work with it in its current form: SYSTEM.DAT and USER.DAT. Or, you can also export it to a text file and edit it with your favorite text editor, such as WordPad (the file is too big for Notepad). If you export your Registry to a text file, you can use your text editor's search and replace features to make massive changes to it. Be careful doing this, however, because an accidental typo can inadvertently change a value you didn't mean to change. And you might not discover any problems until much later.

You're not limited to exporting your entire Registry to a text file. You can export a specific key and all of its subkeys and value entries (branch). That way you can work with a smaller subset of your Registry, and then import it back into the Registry when you're done.

Part

IV

Ch

14

T I P If you're exporting the Registry as a backup, make sure you export the entire Registry.

Here's how to export your entire Registry or just a specific branch:

1. Select the key that represents the branch you want to export in the left pane of the window. (If you're exporting the entire Registry, you can skip this step.)

2. Choose <u>R</u>egistry, <u>E</u>xport Registry File. The Registry Editor displays the dialog box shown in figure 14.11.

FIG. 14.11

If you don't type a file extension, the Registry Editor uses the default file extension (REG).

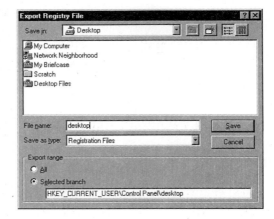

3. If you're exporting the entire Registry, make sure <u>A</u>ll is selected. Otherwise, choose S<u>e</u>lected Branch . The key you selected in step 1 is filled in for you.

4. Type the name of the file into which you want to export the Registry in File <u>N</u>ame, and click <u>S</u>ave.

 The resulting file looks very much like a classic INI file. Figure 14.12 shows what exported Registry entries look like in a text file.

The file is split into sections, with each Registry key being one section. The name of the key is given between two brackets, and it is the full path of that key in the Registry file. Each value entry for a key is listed in the appropriate section. The value entry's name is quoted. The value entry's data looks different depending on its type, as shown in table 14.8.

FIG. 14.12
A Registry export file looks
similar to an INI file.

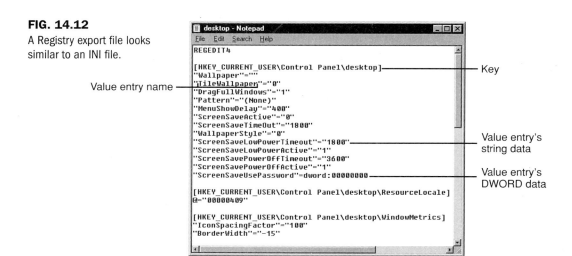

Value entry name

Key

Value entry's
string data

Value entry's
DWORD data

Table 14.8   Formats for String, DWORD, and HEX Data

Type	Example
String	*This is a string value*
DWORD	DWORD:00000001
HEX	HEX:FF 00 FF 00 FF 00 FF 00 FF 00 FF 00

After you've made changes to your exported file, you may want to import it back into the Registry—particularly if you've chosen to edit the Registry as a text file as described earlier in this section. Double-click an exported Registry file, and Windows 95 updates your Registry.

CAUTION

Don't accidentally double-click a REG file. Windows 95 automatically merges it with the Registry because merge is the default action for that file type.

Useful Command-Line Parameters

Part
IV

Ch
14

The Registry Editor has a few command-line parameters. To use the command-line parameters, choose <u>R</u>un from the Start menu, type **regedit** followed by any of the parameters you want to use, and press Enter. Table 14.10 describes what each of these parameters do. If you don't specify the /e or /c parameters, the Registry Editor looks for one or more file names on the command line. It imports each file into the existing Registry—updating entries that already exist, and adding any new entries.

Table 14.10   Command-Line Parameters for REGEDIT.EXE

Command Line	Description
/L:SYSTEM	Specifies location of SYSTEM.DAT.
/R:USER	Specifies location of USER.DAT.
/e FILENAME.REG [*key*]	Exports Registry to given file. If a key is given, exports entire branch under the key.
/c FILENAME.REG	Replaces entire contents of the Registry with the contents of this file.

CHAPTER 15

Customizing with REGEDIT

by Jerry Honeycutt

Windows 95 offers many more ways to customize your desktop than Windows 3.1. You can add actions to context menus and put shortcuts and folders on your desktop to make things more accessible. You can even tell Windows 95 to use a BMP file's image as the file's icon. Many of these customizations are possible because of the Registry.

Most of the customizations discussed in this chapter involve editing the Registry directly. In some cases, however, you learn about tools that edit the Registry for you. And for every customization you learn about in this chapter, you may discover five more of your own. After you've tried out the customizations in this chapter, you should be ready to start experimenting with your own customizations. ◼

Understand what's the worst that can happen

You'll learn about the consequences of changing the Registry using the Registry Editor.

Learn how Windows 95 uses the Registry

You need to understand a few basic concepts before customizing Windows 95 using the Registry.

Customize Windows 95 using the Registry Editor

Changes—called "Registry Hacks"—you can make to the Registry to customize Windows 95.

Learn how to use Tweak UI to customize Windows 95

Tweak UI is a free program from Microsoft that helps you safely customize Windows 95 using the Registry.

The Consequences of Editing the Registry by Hand

Changing the Registry by hand is risky business. If you want to customize Windows 95's behavior, however, and a utility isn't available, you may have little choice but to use the Registry Editor to change the Registry. Note that if you have backed up the Registry, no mistake is unrecoverable.

> **CAUTION**
>
> Backup the Registry before using the Registry Editor to do the customizations described in this chapter.

Here are some examples of some of the most common mistakes:

- The Registry Editor doesn't validate your changes—period. The Editor doesn't warn you if you enter a bad value in a value entry, so you only discover your error when your system fails to function properly. If you accidentally change a file association to an incorrect path, for example, you have no indication of any problem until you discover that you can't open that particular file type and are unable to do so.

- Some of the entries in the Registry have siblings; if you change those entries, you must change the related entries as well. When you edit manually, there's a good chance that you will miss related entries that alternative methods of editing the Registry will catch and change for you.

- The Registry Editor doesn't have an undo feature, and you can't exit the Editor without saving your changes, as you can with Notepad. Once you've made the change, it's a done deal, so be very careful.

 Before changing a value entry in the Registry, record its current value so that you can replace it if you make a mistake.

▶ **See** "Backing Up the Registry," **p. 422**

What You Need To Know about HKEY_CLASSES_ROOT

One of the Registry's primary duties is to keep track of what documents belong to what programs. One way it does this is with file associations. The Registry associates a DOC file extension with Word, for example, and a TXT file extension with Notepad. When you double-click a registered file type, Windows 95 launches the associated application, which then loads the file.

Windows 95 keeps additional information for each file type in the Registry. For example, the Registry contains information about the icon that you see when viewing a file type in Explorer. It also contains information about a file type's context menu entries; edit, open, and print commands; and whether the file type has Quick View support.

ON THE WEB

You can learn about the Registry's organization on the Internet, too. *PC Magazine* has a three-part description of the Registry on the Web that you can read by pointing your Web browser at:

www.zdnet.com/~pcmag/issues/1418/pcm00083.htm

www.zdnet.com/~pcmag/issues/1419/pcm00116.htm

www.zdnet.com/~pcmag/issues/1422/pcm00140.htm

The key (see Chapter 14, "Introduction to REGEDIT," if you don't know what a key is) HKEY_Classes_Root is where you'll find file associations and information describing how OLE should handle various file types. There are three parts to HKEY_Classes_Root:

- *File-extension subkeys* associate extensions with file types
- *Class-definition subkeys* associate file types with programs
- *CLSID subkeys* provide further information about OLE objects and documents

N O T E HKEY_Classes_Root is an alias for HKEY_Local_Machine\Software\Classes. In other words, both Registry keys point to the same data. HKEY_Classes_Root is provided for compatibility with Windows 3.1 applications. ■

▶ **See** "How the Registry Is Organized," **p. 431**

File-Extension Subkeys

The first part of HKEY_Classes_Root is a set of subkeys named after registered file extensions. These subkeys all begin with a dot (period), so the Registry Editor's alphabetical sorting places them conveniently at the top of HKEY_Classes_Root. Most of the file-extension subkeys specify the file type associated with that extension. These file types are defined in greater detail in the class-definition section of HKEY_Classes_Root.

Some extension subkeys have no corresponding class definition. In these cases, the file-extension subkey contains additional information that tells Windows what to do when opening or printing a file.

Other subkeys, like the .TXT subkey in figure 15.1, have matching class definitions, but the file-extension subkey contains additional data that, in most cases, tells Windows how to create a new text file.

FIG. 15.1

File-extension subkeys tell you which class definition is associated with each registered extension. Here, the short name "txtfile" indicates a text document.

For example, when you right-click your desktop or a folder and choose New, then choose Text Document from the resulting menu, Windows checks the .\ShellNew subkey to see whether there's a special command it should use in creating a new file of that type. Most ShellNew subkeys that need a special command don't contain any specific instructions. To see an example of one that does, look at the .LNK\ShellNew subkey to see the command used when creating a new Windows shortcut (.LNK file).

TIP The very first subkey in HKEY_Classes_Root is * (asterisk). It tells Windows how to handle the default items on the context menu and properties dialog box for *all* file types.

Using Explorer to Create File Associations

To create a new file-extension association using Explorer, double-click a file with an extension that's not yet associated with any application. Windows will give you an Open With dialog box. To create a new association, type a description for the new file type, select the program you want to use to open the file, and select the Always Use This Program To Open This File check box. Click OK to create the association and launch the program.

If an extension is already assigned to another application and you want to change it, select a file with that extension and hold down the Shift key while you right-click it. Choose Open With from the context menu and create the new association as described in the previous paragraph.

TIP If you can't successfully change an association, it's probably due to a corrupted Registry entry. Try deleting the old association first, then create a new one from scratch. The easiest way to delete a single file-extension association is to use REGEDIT to remove that extension's subkey from the Registry.

Class-Definition Subkeys

The short names in the file-extension subkeys usually correspond to subkeys in the class-definition section of HKEY_Classes_Root. These class-definition subkeys determine:

- The properties of registered file types, including the icon used
- Whether QuickView is enabled for that file type
- The path and file name of the associated application
- What commands to pass to that application in order to open or print a document

Each subkey is named after a registered file type's short name ("txtfile" in fig. 15.2), and contains the full name for that file type ("Text Document" in the illustration), as well as instructions to Windows on how to handle that type of file.

FIG. 15.2

Class-definition subkeys in HKEY_Classes_Root contain information about registered file types.

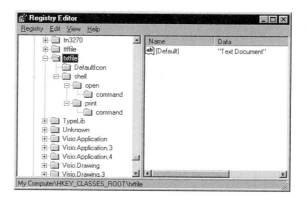

Some file extensions, as mentioned earlier, don't have a corresponding file type. These extensions contain OLE and DDE information under their file-extension subkey.

N O T E A single file type may include more than one associated file extension. For example, the file type "Microsoft Word Document," which is created when you install Word for Windows, includes DOT template files as well as DOC documents. Both DOT and DOC have file-extension entries in the Registry, each of which points to the file-type entry for Word documents. Also, when you use the Open With dialog box to associate a new file extension with an existing file type, it adds to the list of extensions registered to that file type. ■

Here's some of the information found in class-definition subkeys:

- The first value in the class-definition subkey, called Default, contains the full name of the file type. This is the name that appears in the Type column of an Explorer window.

- A CLSID subkey contains the class identifier CLSID for that file type, if one exists. This class identifier corresponds to an entry in HKEY_Classes_Root\CLSID (see "CLSID Entries" later in this chapter).

- The DefaultIcon subkey contains a value that indicates the file and icon number to use for documents of that type. For example, C:\Windows\System\Shell32.DLL,0 tells Windows to use the first icon stored in Shell32.DLL, C:\Windows\System\Shell32.DLL,1 points to the second icon, and so forth.

- A Protocol subkey contains OLE 2.0 information that tells Windows how to handle embedded objects of that type. For example, in the subkey PBrush\Protocol\StdFileEditing (for the file type Paintbrush Picture) the subkey "server" tells Windows which application to use (pbrush.exe) for editing embedded Paintbrush Picture objects, while the "verb" subkey tells Windows what OLE commands that application supports (such as Edit).

- A QuickView subkey tells Windows whether it can use QuickView to display files of that type.

- The Shell subkey includes command lines for opening and printing associated files. For example, the subkey Txtfile\Shell\Print\Command contains a value with the data "C:\Windows\Notepad.Exe /p %1"—the complete command line for opening and printing a text file in Notepad. The /p switch tells Notepad to print, and the %1 is a variable that contains the name of the file you selected.

TIP You can choose a new default action; set the default value entry for the Shell subkey to the name of the action of your choice (the default action is what happens when you double-click that file type).

You can easily change, delete, or add file types using Windows 95's Explorer. Chapter 16, "Installing, Running, and Uninstalling Windows Applications," teaches you how to use Explorer's file type dialog box.

When you follow the instructions in Chapter 16, you're creating a new file type and a new file-extension association at the same time—so you can't use an extension that's already been associated. If you do, Windows will tell you that the extension is already in use and will give you the short name of the file type using that extension.

TROUBLESHOOTING

I've found a file type that has several extensions registered to it, and I want to change just one of them. I can use the Open With dialog box to remove an entire file type, but I can't use it to delete a single file-extension association. How do I get rid of that extension association and assign it to another file type? Open REGEDIT and locate that extension in the file-extension section of HKEY_Classes_Root. Then delete the offending file-extension subkey. The extension is now unassociated.

Alternately, open Explorer and select a file with the extension you want to change. Hold down the Shift key while you right-click the file, and choose Open With. Make sure there's a check mark in the Always Use This Program To Open This Type of File check box. Then click OK to assign the new association and launch the application.

CLSID Entries

The most daunting section of HKEY_Classes_Root is contained in an innocuous-looking subkey called CLSID, buried among the class-definition subkeys. Every type of Windows OLE object has a unique class identifier, or CLSID, recorded in this section. The CLSIDs help Windows to organize various OLE objects, including DLLs, EXE files, Windows functions, and file types. Unfortunately, this section of HKEY_Classes_Root is organized into subkeys named after the CLSIDs, which aren't easily readable by humans.

A CLSID consists of a long string of hexadecimal digits surrounded by curly brackets, and separated by hyphens into a group of eight digits, three groups of four digits, and a group of 12 digits. The CLSID {00000300-0000-0000-C000-000000000046} is represented by the selected subkey that bears the same incomprehensible name. To find a more readable equivalent of a CLSID, you need to select its subkey and note the string contained in the Default value. In this example, the name StdOleLink corresponds to the CLSID selected on the left.

One or more subkeys are found under each CLSID entry. You shouldn't ever need to edit the entries here, unless you move critical DLL or EXE files to new folders. You can, however, use CLSID entries to discover more about the programs used to manage various object types.

Here are a few of the most common subkeys found under CLSID entries:

- *DefaultIcon* specifies the icon used for that CLSID's corresponding objects.
- *InprocHandler* points to an Object Handler, a DLL that works in conjunction with an EXE file to manage objects of the type defined by the CLSID.
- *InprocServer* contains a pointer to the object's In-Process Server, a DLL that handles the type of object defined by that CLSID.
- *InprocServer32* indicates a 32-bit In-Process Server.
- *LocalServer* contains the path and file name of a server application, the EXE file that handles objects of the specified type.
- *ProgID* contains a human-readable identifier for the CLSID, generally the short name for the object type ("txtfile").
- *shellex* contains subkeys that define which DLLs and commands are used to call up the object's context menu or Properties sheet.

TROUBLESHOOTING

I renamed a program's installation folder. How do I get Windows 95 to recognize its new location? If you move an application to a new folder or rename the folder containing it, Windows may not be able to find it the next time you try to open documents or objects associated with that application. If Windows fails to determine the new location of the application, you can use REGEDIT to update the Registry manually. Use the Find function to locate all references to that application—including references in the CLSID section—and make sure every path and file name in the Registry reflects the application's new location.

What Happened to SYSTEM.INI and WIN.INI?

Those two dreaded INI files, SYSTEM.INI and WIN.INI, aren't gone from Windows 95. Microsoft left them behind for compatibility with Windows 3.1 programs that expect to find certain entries in them. Other programs update these files and expect Windows to recognize the updates. Thus, it's not really possible to eliminate them from your system.

Windows 95 moved many of the entries from SYSTEM.INI and WIN.INI to the Registry. Tables 15.1 and 15.2 show the entries that were moved from SYSTEM.INI and WIN.INI into the Windows 95 Registry.

Table 15.1   SYSTEM.INI Entries Moved to the Registry

[386Enh]	[Network]
Network	AuditEnabled
Network3	AuditEvents
SecondNet	AuditLogSize
Transport	AutoLogon
V86ModeLANAs	Comment
	ComputerName
	DirectHost
	EnableSharing
	FileSharing
	LANAs
	LMAnnounce
	LMLogon
	LogonDisconnected
	LogonDomain
	LogonValidated
	Multinet
	PasswordCaching
	PrintSharing
	Reshare
	SlowLanas
	Winnet
	Workgroup

Table 15.2   WIN.INI Entries Moved to the Registry

[Windows]	[WindowsMetrics]
Beep	BorderWidth
BorderWidth	CaptionHeight
CursorBlinkRate	CaptionWidth

continues

Table 15.2   Continued

[Windows]	[WindowsMetrics]
DoubleClickSpeed	MenuHeight
KeyboardDelay	MenuWidth
KeyboardSpeed	MinArrange
MouseThreshold1	MinHorzGap
MouseThreshold2	MinVertGap
MouseSpeed	MinWidth
ScreenSaveActive	ScrollHeight
ScreenSaveTimeOut	ScrollWidth
SwapMouseButtons	SmCaptionHeight SmCaptionWidth

The logical place for these entries is the Registry, because that's where your system's hardware configuration is stored.

Registry Hacks for Customizing Windows 95

Now that you understand a bit more about the Registry, you're ready to customize Windows 95. Armed with the information in the previous section, you can probably figure out the Registry hacks in this section on your own. To get you started, the following sections present some of the most popular Registry hacks.

Each of the following sections describes a single customization. In most cases you'll find step-by-step instructions for performing the customization.

ON THE WEB

Some of the customization in this section can also be found at the Windows 95 Annoyances Web page at

http://www.creativelement.com/win95ann/win95ann2.html

This site also contains hints and tips that don't involve the Registry.

Launching Explorer from My Computer

There are many different ways to get to Explorer. You can launch it from the Start menu or right-click My Computer and choose Explore. You can also double-click My Computer while you hold down the Shift key. You can even launch Explorer just by double-clicking My Computer. Here's how to set it up:

1. Open the Registry Editor and find HKEY_Classes_Root\CLSID\{20D04FE0-3AEA-1069-A2D8-08002B30309D}\shell.

2. Set the default value entry for this key to **explore**.

3. Add the subkey branch \explore\command.

4. Set the default value entry for your new subkey to **explorer.exe**.

5. Close the Registry Editor.

Now when you double-click My Computer, Windows 95 loads Explorer instead of opening the folder view.

> **N O T E** You'll have two entries in My Computer's context menu that say Explore, but this isn't harmful. The first entry is an action that Windows 95 puts in My Computer's context menu—you won't find it in the Registry, and can't get rid of it. The second entry is the one you added in the preceding steps. ▩
>
> ▶ **See** "Class-Definition Subkeys," **p. 447**

Ignoring Changes to Your Desktop

Maybe you like to change your desktop settings as you work, but you don't want those changes to reappear next time you open Windows. If you don't want Windows 95 to remember the arrangement of icons on your desktop, which windows are open, and the position of the taskbar when you close it, follow these steps:

1. Arrange your desktop just the way you want it, and restart your computer.

2. Open the Registry Editor and find HKEY_Current_User\Software\Microsoft\Windows\CurrentVersion\Policies\Explorer.

3. Set the value of NoSaveSettings to **1**. If you don't see a value entry called NoSaveSettings, you'll need to add it.

4. Close the Registry Editor.

Now your desktop will look the same every time you start Windows 95—even if you've messed around with it. Also, if you put Explorer in your Startup group, and forget to close it before you restart Windows 95, you won't have two copies of Explorer running after Windows 95 restarts.

 T I P You can change this entry using PowerToy's Tweak UI as described in "Using Tweak UI," later in this chapter.

Making the Start Menu Snappier

Have you ever noticed the slight delay when you choose a submenu on the Start menu? Many folks think this is annoying. You can eliminate the delay. Here's how:

1. Open the Registry Editor and find HKEY_Current_User\Control Panel\Desktop.

2. Change the value of MenuShowDelay to a smaller number (the default is 400) to make the menus open faster. You can even set this value entry to 0.

3. Close the Registry Editor. This change won't take effect until you restart Windows 95.

 TIP You can change this entry using PowerToy's Tweak UI as described in "Using Tweak UI," later in this chapter.

Adding Actions to the Context Menus

If you have more than one program that accesses the same type of file, you'll want to add an action to that file extension's context menu that allows you to choose between both programs. If you have Word, for example, you can add a new action to the DOC context menu that enables you to open DOC files with WordPad, too. Here's how:

1. Choose View, Options from the Explorer menu, and click the File Types tab. Explorer displays the dialog box shown in figure 15.3.

FIG. 15.3
The File Types page shows all the file types that are registered in your computer. This is where you change file associations in Windows 95.

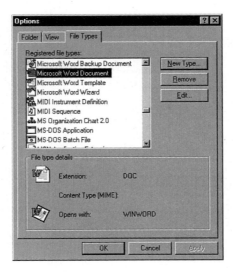

2. Choose the file type to which you want to add an action, then click Edit. In this case, choose Microsoft Word Document, then click Edit. You'll see the Edit File Type dialog box shown in figure 15.4.

FIG. 15.4
Windows 95 adds the actions in the Actions list to this file type's context menu.

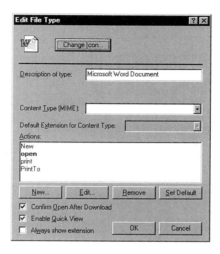

3. Click New, and Windows 95 displays the New Action dialog box. Type the name of the action in the Action text box, and then type the command line used to carry out the action in the Application Used To Perform Action text box. In this case, the name of the action is Open With WordPad and the command line is **"c:\Program Files\Accessories\WordPad.exe" "%1"**.

NOTE The quotes around the %1 in the command line tell Windows 95 to put the file name inside of quotes. It's frequently called a *placeholder*. If you didn't put "%1" in the command line and you selected a long file name with spaces in it, WordPad wouldn't be able to open the file.

4. Click OK to save your changes to the New Action dialog box. Click OK again to save your changes to the Edit File Type dialog box. Click OK again to save your changes to the Options dialog box.

Now you can open DOC files with either Word or WordPad. Double-click a DOC file to open it in Word. Right-click a DOC file and choose Open with WordPad to open it in WordPad.

Changing the Location of System Folders

Have you ever tried to move the \Windows\ShellNew folder to a new location? How about Word's \My Documents folder? You can't, unless you do it through the Registry. Try this:

delete the Recent folder from the \Windows folder. Think it's gone? Nope. Windows 95 will create it again.

Windows 95 keeps a list of shell folders in the Registry. This is how it knows where to find things such as your Start menu, desktop shortcuts, and recent documents. You'll find these shell folders at HKEY_Current_User\Software\Microsoft\Windows\CurrentVersion\Explorer\Shell Folders. Table 15.3 shows you the value entries you'll find by default in Windows 95. Also included are the entries that Microsoft Office adds.

Table 15.3   Default Shell Folders

Value Entry	Default
Desktop	C:\Windows\Desktop
Favorites	C:\Windows\Favorites
Fonts	C:\Windows\Fonts
NetHood	C:\Windows\NetHood
Personal	C:\My Documents
Programs	C:\Windows\Start Menu\Programs
Recent	C:\Windows\Recent
SendTo	C:\Windows\SendTo
Start Menu	C:\Windows\Start Menu
Startup	C:\Windows\Start Menu\Programs\Startup
Templates	C:\Windows\ShellNew

Better Short File Names

If you don't like the tilde (~) that Windows 95 adds to the 8.3 version of long file names, you can show it a better way. If you create a file called A LONG FILE NAME.DOC, its 8.3 file name will be ALONGFIL.DOC instead of ALONGF~1. If you create another file whose first eight characters are the same, however, Windows 95 resorts to using the tilde for that file name. Here's how:

1. Open the Registry Editor, and find HKEY_LocalMachine\System \CurrentControlSet\Control\FileSystem.
2. Add a new binary value entry called NameNumericTail and set its value to **0**.
3. Close the Registry Editor.

Creating Your Own Tips

When you first installed Windows 95, it proudly presented the Welcome dialog box showing you a tip. You probably deselected Show This Welcome Screen Next Time You Start Windows right off the bat.

Why don't you turn it on again and let Windows 95 present tips of your own making? You can add the tips you find in this book, motivational tips from your favorite self-help book, or whatever. Here's how:

1. Open the Registry Editor and find HKEY_Local_Machine\Software\Microsoft \Windows\CurrentVersion\Explorer\Tips. By default, the tips are stored as string value entries with names ranging from 0 to 49. But you can add more.

2. Choose Edit, New, String Value from the main menu, and name the new value entry with the next number available in the key.

3. Double-click the entry, type the text you want to display as the tip, and click OK.

4. Close the Registry Editor.

Adding Sounds for Application Events

In Windows 3.1, you could customize the sounds associated with different application events. You can change the sound associated with an opening menu, for example. In Windows 95, you can also add new events for different programs. Here's how:

1. Open the Registry Editor and find HKEY_Current_User\AppEvents\Schemes\Apps.

2. Create a new subkey with the same name as the program.

3. Create new subkeys under the program's subkey for each event, such as Open and Close.

4. Close the Registry Editor.

5. Double-click the Sounds icon in the Control Panel. Your new application shows up in the list. You can change the sounds associated with each event.

▶ **See** "Changing the Sounds Related to Windows Events," **p. 401**

Changing the Desktop Icons

You're not stuck with the icons Windows 95 uses for My Computer, Recycle Bin, and so on. You can change them all. Here's how:

1. Open the Registry Editor and find HKEY_Classes_Root\CLSID.

2. Look up the icon you want to change in table 15.4. Then find it under Hkey_Classes_Root\CLSID, and open the DefaultIcon subkey underneath it.

Table 15.4 Subkeys for Desktop Icons

Icon Name	Subkey
Briefcase	{85BBD920-42A0-1069-A2E4-08002B30309D}
Control Panel	{21EC2020-3AEA-1069-A2DD-08002B30309D}
Dial-Up Networking	{992CFFA0-F557-101A-88EC-00DD010CCC48}
Inbox	{00020D75-0000-0000-C000-000000000046}
My Computer	{20D04FE0-3AEA-1069-A2D8-08002B30309D}
Network Neighborhood	{208D2C60-3AEA-1069-A2D7-08002B30309D}
Printers	{2227A280-3AEA-1069-A2DE-08002B30309D}
Recycle Bin	{645FF040-5081-101B-9F08-00AA002F954E}
The Internet	{FBF23B42-E3F0-101B-8488-00AA003E56F8}
The Microsoft Network	{00028B00-0000-0000-C000-000000000046}

 T I P Change the name displayed for the icons in table 15.4 by changing its value entry.

3. Change the default value entry to the path of the icon file, and the index of the icon. If you want to use the four icons (0, 1, 2, 3) in SHELL32.DLL, for example, type **C:\Windows\System\Shell32,3**. You can get icons from DLL, EXE, ICO, and other files.

4. Close the Registry Editor.

N O T E Most EXE and DLL files have icons in them. You'll find some DLLs that have a large number of useful icons—such as MOREICONS.DLL, COOL.DLL, PIFMGR.DLL, PROGMAN.DLL, and SHELL32.DLL—in your \Windows or \Windows\System folder. ▩

▶ **See** "CLSID Entries," **p. 449**

Removing Windows 95's Icons from the Desktop

Just because you're using Dial-Up Networking to access the Internet doesn't mean you want the Network Neighborhood icon on your desktop. Likewise, you may care nothing about The Microsoft Network icon on your desktop. You can get rid of any of these icons by following these steps:

1. Open the Registry Editor and find Hkey_Local_Machine\Software\Microsoft \Windows \CurrentVersion\Explorer\Desktop\NameSpace.

2. Delete the subkeys that represent the icons you want to remove from your desktop. Refer to table 15.4 to see what each value represents.

3. Close the Registry Editor.

 T I P Alternatively, you can use Tweak UI's Desktop tab to add or remove icons from your desktop.

Making the Control Panel More Accessible

When you choose <u>S</u>ettings, <u>C</u>ontrol Panel from the Start menu, Windows 95 opens a folder with all the Control Panel icons. But what if you don't want a folder? Wouldn't it be better if you could open a submenu on your Start menu that contains all the Control Panel icons? You can, and here's how:

1. Right-click the Start button, and choose <u>O</u>pen.

2. Create a new folder and rename it **Control Panel.{21EC2020-3AEA-1069-A2DD-08002B30309D}**.

Now when you choose Control Panel from the Start menu, it opens another submenu instead of opening a folder (see fig. 15.5).

FIG. 15.5
Adding the Control Panel to the Start menu in this manner makes the Control Panel icons much more accessible.

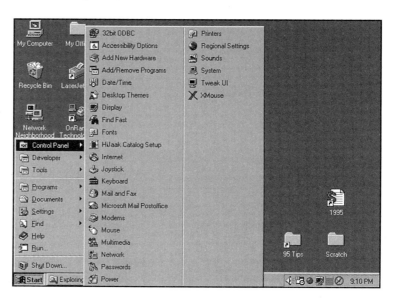

TIP You can also use Tweak UI's Desktop tab to add the Control Panel to the Start menu.

You're not limited to the Control Panel. You can add any of the icons described in table 15.5. Replace the name in step 2 with one of the names from the table.

Table 15.5 Names You Can Add to the Start Menu

Folder name

Briefcase.{85BBD920-42A0-1069-A2E4-08002B30309D}

Control Panel.{21EC2020-3AEA-1069-A2DD-08002B30309D}

Dial-Up Networking.{992CFFA0-F557-101A-88EC-00DD010CCC48}

Inbox.{00020D75-0000-0000-C000-000000000046}

My Computer.{20D04FE0-3AEA-1069-A2D8-08002B30309D}

Network Neighborhood.{208D2C60-3AEA-1069-A2D7-08002B30309D}

Printers.{2227A280-3AEA-1069-A2DE-08002B30309D}

Recycle Bin.{645FF040-5081-101B-9F08-00AA002F954E}

The Internet.{FBF23B42-E3F0-101B-8488-00AA003E56F8}

The Microsoft Network.{00028B00-0000-0000-C000-000000000046}

Killing the Annoying Window Animation

When you minimize or maximize a window, Windows 95 uses animation to show you where it's going. If you have a slow computer, the animation can rob you of that crisp feeling you get when a window pops open or disappears from the screen. Here's how you can turn off the window animation:

1. Open the Registry Editor and find HKEY_Current_User\Control Panel\ Desktop\WindowMetrics.
2. Change the value entry called MinAnimate to **0**.
3. Close the Registry Editor and restart your computer.

 TIP You can also use Tweak UI's General page to change this setting.

Using a Bit Map's Image for Its Icon

If you have a large folder of bit maps, you might have to open a lot of pictures before you find the image you're looking for. Windows 95 enables you to use the bit map's actual image as its icon. Here's how:

1. Open the Registry Editor and find HKEY_Classes_Root\Paint.Picture\DefaultIcon.
2. Change the default value entry to %1.
3. Close the Registry Editor.

 TIP The icons are easier to see if you choose <u>V</u>iew, Large Icons from Explorer's main menu.

It takes a lot longer to display a list of bit maps in an Explorer window this way, because each bit map has to be rendered into an icon. After the first time it's loaded, it'll go much faster because these icons are cached. Figure 15.6 shows what the icons look like in Explorer.

FIG. 15.6

It's sometimes difficult to find bit maps in a crowded folder if you're using their image as their icon.

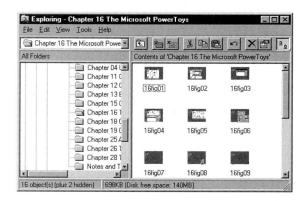

▶ **See** "Using Windows Paint," **p. 537**

Using a Different Icon for Folders

If you don't like the icon that Explorer uses for folders, you can change it. Here's how:

1. Choose <u>V</u>iew, <u>O</u>ptions from Explorer's main menu, and click the File Types tab.
2. Select Folder from the list, and click <u>E</u>dit. Explorer displays the Edit File Type dialog box.
3. Click Change <u>I</u>con, and Explorer displays the Change Icon dialog box.

4. Select an icon from the list, or click <u>B</u>rowse to pick another file to browse for icons. Try MOREICONS.DLL, COOL.DLL, PIFMGR.DLL, PROGMAN.DLL, and SHELL32.DLL as sources for icons. You can also use icons from EXE and ICO files.

5. Click OK to save your changes to the Change Icon dialog box. Click OK again to save your changes to the Edit File Type dialog box. Click OK again to save your changes to the Options dialog box.

Using Tweak UI

You've learned a lot of tips in this chapter. Most of them involve changing settings in the Registry, too. Wouldn't it be great if there was a program that knew about these Registry hacks and would make these changes to the Registry for you? Well, there is. It's called Tweak UI.

ON THE WEB

Tweak UI15 is a Control Panel application that comes with Microsoft PowerToys. PowerToys is a freeware program that you can download from Microsoft's Web site at:

http:\\www.microsoft.com

Installing Tweak UI

Installing Tweak UI is easy. After you've downloaded PowerToys or Tweak UI itself, use these steps:

1. Make a temporary folder, and copy the file you downloaded into the folder.

2. Double-click the self-extracting, compressed file to expand its contents into the temporary folder.

3. Right-click TWEAKUI.INF, and choose <u>I</u>nstall. Windows 95 copies the files it needs from the temporary folder and displays Tweak UI's help file.

4. Delete the temporary folder. Neither PowerToys nor Tweak UI need these files anymore.

Customizing with Tweak UI

You'll find Tweak UI in the Control Panel. From the Start menu, choose <u>S</u>ettings, <u>C</u>ontrol Panel. Then, double-click the Tweak UI application to open it, and you'll see a property sheet with five tabs: General, Explorer, Desktop, Templates, and Boot.

The sections that follow describe the settings on each of these tabs. Click each tab, and change the settings that you want. When you're finished, click OK to save your changes.

General   Click on the General tab, and you'll see the page shown in figure 15.7. This page lets you change settings such as the speed with which Windows 95 displays menus and the sensitivity of the mouse. The options are described in table 15.5.

FIG. 15.7

Double-click, right-click, or drag the test icon to test your settings.

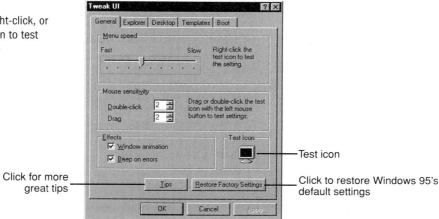

Click for more great tips

Test icon

Click to restore Windows 95's default settings

Table 15.5   General Page Options

Option	Description
Menu Speed	Controls how long Windows 95 waits before popping up a menu after you've clicked on it. Drag the slider to the left to make menus pop up faster or to the right to make menus pop up slower.
Double-click	Determines how many pixels are allowed between two mouse clicks in order for them to be considered a double-click. Make this number larger to increase sensitivity or smaller to decrease sensitivity.
Drag	Determines how many pixels the mouse must move with the button clicked before it's considered a drag. Make this number larger to increase sensitivity or smaller to decrease sensitivity.
Window Animation	Controls whether windows are animated when you minimize, maximize, or restore them. Select this checkbox to turn on animation, or deselect it to turn off animation.
Beep on Errors	Controls whether Windows 95 beeps when an error occurs. Select this checkbox to turn sounds on, or deselect it to turn sounds off.

Explorer   Click on the Explorer tab, and you'll see the page shown in figure 15.8. This page lets you change settings such as the overlay used for shortcuts and whether the words "Shortcut to" are prefixed to new shortcuts. The options are described in table 15.6.

Table 15.6   Explorer Page Options

Option	Description
Shortcut Overlay	Determines the overlay used for shortcuts. The overlay is usually a small arrow that Windows 95 displays in the lower-left corner of the shortcut's icon. Choose either Arrow, Light Arrow, None, or Custom.
Animated "Click Here to Begin"	Controls whether Windows 95 displays "Click here to begin" in the task bar after you log on. Select this checkbox to turn this message on, or deselect it to turn this message off.
Tip of the Day	Controls whether Windows 95 displays the tip of the day when you first log on. Select this checkbox to turn tips on, or deselect it to turn tips off.
Prefix "Shortcut to" on New	Controls whether the words "Shortcut to" are prefixed to new shortcuts. Select this checkbox to turn this message on, or deselect it to turn this message off.
Save Settings on Exit	Controls whether Windows 95 saves the location of any open windows and icons on the desktop when you shutdown. Select this checkbox to let Windows 95 save settings between sessions, or deselect it to keep Windows 95 from saving settings.

CAUTION

On some systems, including mine, setting the shortcut overlay to None causes Windows 95 to behave erratically.

Desktop   Click on the Desktop tab, and you'll see the page shown in figure 15.9. This page lets you add or remove each special desktop icon (My Computer and Network Neighborhood, for example) to or from the desktop. It also lets you create these special icons as files that you can put anywhere on your computer.

To add a special icon to your desktop, click on the box next to the icon in the Special Desktop Icons list until you see a check mark inside of it. To remove a special icon from your desktop, click on the box next to the icon until you don't see a check mark inside of it.

You can also create these special icons as files. Select one of the special icons, and click on Create as File. Choose the folder in which you want to save the file, and click on Save.

FIG. 15.8
Click on Custom to choose
your own icon overlay from a
DLL, EXE, or ICO file.

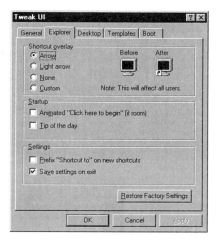

FIG. 15.9
The Printers and Control
Panel icons can't be created
directly on the desktop—you
must create them as files.

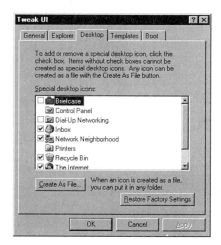

 If you're annoyed that you have to open the Control Panel folder to get access to its applications,
you're in luck. You can put the Control Panel on your Start menu so that all the applications
appear on a sub-menu. Save the Control Panel special desktop icon in the C:\Windows\Start
Menu folder. You'll see the Control Panel menu at the top of the Start menu the next time you
open it.

Templates   Try this: right-click on the desktop, and choose New. You'll see a list of file
types that Windows 95 can create for you. Choose one of the file types such as Text
Document, and Windows 95 creates a new icon on the desktop which is called something
like "New Text Document." Then, double-click the document to open it in Notepad.

You can add your own file types to this list, too. You can even use a template. For example, you might want to create HTM files that have the exact same contents every time. It's easy, here's how:

1. Create a file whose contents you want to use as a template. All new files of this type will have the same contents.

2. Click on the Templates tab, and you'll see the page shown in figure 15.10. This page lets you add your own templates to the list.

FIG. 15.10
You can't delete a template using Tweak UI.

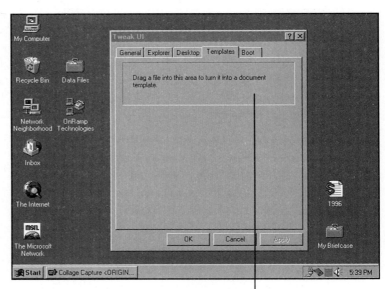

Drop area for new templates

3. Drag the file you created in step 1 to the top part of the Templates page. You can safely delete the original file.

Boot   Click on the Boot tab, and you'll see the page shown in figure 15.11. This page lets you customize how Windows 95 starts. You can disable the animated start up screen, for example. You can also cause Windows 95 to start DOS 7.0 by default, instead of the graphical user interface. Table 15.7 describes the options found on the Boot page.

FIG. 15.11

The boot options are stored in a hidden file called C:\MSDOS.SYS.

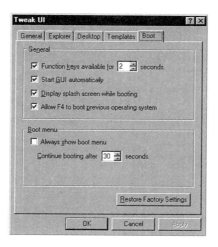

Table 15.7 Boot Page Options

Option	Description
Function Keys Available For # Seconds	Determines how long Windows 95 will wait for you to press one of the function keys before it continues booting.
Start GUI Automatically	Controls whether Windows 95 starts the graphical user interface. Select this checkbox to start the GUI, or deselect it to start DOS 7.0.
Display Splash Screen While Booting	Controls whether Windows 95 displays the animated splash screen while it starts.
Allow F4 to Boot Previous Operating System	Controls whether Windows 95 allows you to start the previous operating system by pressing F4.
Always Show Boot Menu	Determines if Windows 95 will always display the boot menu. Select this checkbox to always display the boot menu, or deselect it to require you to press F8 before displaying it.
Continue Booting After # Seconds	Determines how long Windows 95 will wait for you to choose a boot option if the boot menu is displayed.

Working with Applications

Installing, Running, and Uninstalling Windows Applications

by Michael O'Mara with Bob Voss

Windows applications are bigger, more powerful, and much more complex than DOS-based applications were in the old days. They've become so intertwined with the operating system that it's hard to tell where the dividing line is between Windows and an application. And nearly every Windows application has the potential to interact with any other Windows application on your system.

Not surprisingly, the process of installing and removing applications has grown more complex as well. Fortunately, as application installation grew more complicated, application developers turned to automated setup programs to handle most installation chores. Windows 95 adds new features to further automate adding and removing applications. If you haven't installed Windows 95 yet, see Appendix A, "Installing Windows 95." ∎

Install 16-bit applications in Windows 95

Here is where to look to find out how to install applications that were written for the Windows 3.x environment.

Install Windows 95 applications

This is where you learn how to use Setup to install Windows 95 applications.

Add and remove Windows component applications

Refer to this section to learn how to use the Add/Remove Programs icon in Control Panel to install and uninstall individual components of Windows 95 without having to reinstall Windows 95 from scratch.

Uninstall applications

Look here to find out how to uninstall a Windows application in Windows 95 automatically, using the Add/Remove Programs icon, or manually, if Windows 95 can't do it automatically.

Understanding How Windows Runs Applications

Windows 95 runs applications designed specifically for Windows 95. It also can run most Windows 3.1 applications, DOS-based applications, and applications designed for Windows NT. Windows 95 no longer requires the traditional CONFIG.SYS, AUTOEXEC.BAT, and INI files for configuration information. However, for backward compatibility, Windows 95 uses settings from INI files and maintains its own versions of CONFIG.SYS and AUTOEXEC.BAT to support loading real-mode device drivers.

Although Windows 95 runs various kinds of applications successfully, it provides different kinds of support for each category of application. Windows applications fall into one of two general categories: 32-bit applications (designed for Windows NT and Windows 95) and 16-bit applications (designed for Windows 3.1 and lower versions). This section describes how Windows 95 runs these two types of programs. Chapter 17, "Installing, Running, and Uninstalling DOS Applications," discusses DOS-based applications.

Support for Win32 Applications

Windows 95 offers several significant advantages over Windows 3.1. Some advantages, such as preemptive multitasking and multithreading support, are available only to 32-bit applications.

Support for long file names is one feature of Windows 95's 32-bit operating system that is available to any application designed to make use of it. All Windows 95 applications let you create file names containing as many as 255 characters, allowing you to assign files names such as "First Quarter Sales Results" rather than "1QSALES." Theoretically, program developers can adapt 16-bit applications to use long file names as well. However, don't expect many older Windows applications to add long file name support; the programmers are likely to concentrate on converting the application to full-fledged 32-bit status instead of spending time on minor upgrades.

Most applications benefit from Windows 95's 32-bit architecture, which makes memory addressing more efficient. In addition, Windows 95 runs each 32-bit application in its own memory space. Ordinarily, such details are of interest only to programmers. However, these advantages have a side effect that all users will appreciate. If a 32-bit application hangs or crashes, the problem is isolated, confined to the application's own address space, and thus unlikely to affect other running applications. You can exit the problem application and, without even rebooting, have Windows 95 clean up the affected memory.

▶ **See** "Working with Long File Names," **p. 134**

Advantages of Preemptive Multitasking and Multithreading Despite appearances, single-processor computers can't really perform multiple tasks from several different applications all at the same instant. Generally, PC computers perform only one operation at a time, but do so very fast. But, if the applications are designed to break operations into small tasks, the operating system switches between tasks from several applications so quickly that it seems that all the applications and their processes are running simultaneously.

Programmers designed Windows 3.1 applications to surrender control of the CPU voluntarily at various points of execution, enabling Windows to switch to another task. This is called *cooperative multitasking*. However, some applications were more cooperative than others. If an application was reluctant to share CPU capacity with other applications, Windows 3.1 couldn't do much about it.

Preemptive multitasking enables the Windows 95 operating system to take control away from one running task and pass it to another task, depending on the system's needs. The system doesn't have to wait for an application or process to surrender control of the CPU before another application can take its turn.

With preemptive multitasking, Windows 95 doesn't depend on the foresight of application programmers to ensure that an application performs multitasking successfully. Windows 95 has more power to arbitrate the demands of various running applications.

Multithreading enables an application to create and run separate concurrent *threads* or processes and thus handle different internal operations. Each process gets its own share of Windows 95's multitasking resources. For example, a word processing application might use one thread to handle keyboard input and display it on-screen. At the same time, a separate thread can run in the background to check spelling while another thread prints a document.

Some Windows 3.1 applications implement their own internal multithreading, with varying degrees of success. Windows 95 makes multithreading an integral feature of the operating system, available to all 32-bit applications.

Increased System Resources In Windows 3.1, attempting to launch an application when there was insufficient system resources often resulted in Not Enough Memory errors even though there was ample RAM and disk memory available. In Windows 3.1, things like having lots of installed fonts, running in high resolution, and high color display modes tax system resources. With 32-bit applications, you won't have this problem in Windows 95.

Windows 95 doesn't remove the limitation on system resources completely, but the improvement is dramatic. One way Windows 95 makes more system resources available is to store many data structures in 32-bit memory regions (heaps) instead of in the 16-bit graphical device interface (GDI) and USER heaps used in Windows 3.1 (which are limited to 64K). As a result, the system limits certain types of programming information, such as timers, COM and LPT ports, and data in list boxes and edit controls, are now unlimited. Windows 95 still limits other kinds of programming information, such as for Windows menu handles, items per list box, and installed fonts, but those limits are significantly higher than in Windows 3.1. As a result, you can run more applications, create more windows, use more fonts, and so on—all without running out of system resources. For instance, as I write this I have two very large, resource-hungry applications running, plus a communications program, a personal organizer, Explorer, and CD Player. That's more than enough to exhaust system resources in Windows 3.1 and precipitate a flurry of error messages. But in Windows 95, I still have more than 80 percent of the available system resources free.

Support for Windows 3.1 Applications

Most Windows 3.1 applications run in Windows 95 without modification or special settings. Microsoft claims that 16-bit Windows applications run at least as well in Windows 95 as in Windows 3.1.

Windows 3.1 applications continue to use cooperative multitasking; they cannot use Windows 95's preemptive multitasking and multithreading. However, 16-bit applications benefit from the advantages Windows 95 derives from 32-bit device drivers and 32-bit subsystems, such as the printing subsystem, which uses multitasking at the operating system level.

Windows 3.1 applications running in Windows 95 all run in the same virtual machine and share the same address space—just as they do when running in Windows 3.1. As a result, they don't share the same crash protection as Windows 95 applications. If one 16-bit application hangs or crashes, it's likely to affect other 16-bit applications that are running at the same time. In other words, any application failure that requires rebooting or restarting Windows 3.1 requires you to shut down all the 16-bit applications you're running. However, a failure of a 16-bit application does not affect 32-bit applications, and Windows 95 probably can clean up after an errant 16-bit application without requiring a reboot to recover system resources and clear memory.

▶ **See** "Using Windows 3.1 Applications in Windows 95," **p. 477**

Windows 3.1 and Long File Names

You may wonder what happens to the long file names you assign to files in Windows 95 programs if you open and save these files in 16-bit Window or DOS programs that don't support long file names. Fortunately, Windows 95 uses a technique called *tunneling* to preserve long file names when you open these files in 16-bit programs. Although you won't be able to view the long file names or assign new long file names in these programs, at least you won't lose the existing long file names.

 If you work in an environment that uses both 8.3 and long file names, you will want to understand some of the administrative issues involved in using both. In addition, you may want to modify the Windows Registry to make it easier to work in a mixed name environment. Many users are bothered by truncated long file names that end with a ~1 tail. By modifying the Registry, you can make Windows truncate file names to eight characters. To learn more about long file names and modifying the Registry for truncated names, see "Administering Long File Names" and "Modifying the Registry to Remove Numeric Tails form File Names" in Chapter 4, "Managing Files."

Part
V
Ch
16

When you save a file with a long file name in a 16-bit program, it is saved with the truncated 8.3 version of the name that Windows 95 assigned when you created the long file name. However, Windows 95 is smart enough to recognize that this is happening and to reassign the original long file name to the newly saved file. The technique is called tunneling because the long file name "tunnels" from the old version of the file to the new without being affected by the assigning of an 8.3 file name by the 16-bit program.

There are cases where you need to be able to disable the tunneling feature in Windows 95. If you are using an older backup or disk utility that doesn't preserve long file names, you can run into trouble. The way around this problem is to use a utility called LFNBK.EXE that is included on the Windows 95 CD-ROM. (If you do not have the Windows 95 CD-ROM, you can download the file from one of the support services listed in Appendix C, "Additional Help and Resources.") LFNBK.EXE is used to strip and save all the long file names on your hard disk before you run one of these utilities and then to restore the long file names after you have used the utility. To use LFNBK.EXE, however, you must first disable tunneling. For details on how to disable tunneling and use LFNBK.EXE, see the troubleshooting tip at the end of Chapter 23, "Backing Up and Protecting Your Data."

 Utilities are available that add the capability to use long file names in older programs. Norton Navigator has a feature that enables long file names in many 16-bit Windows programs. Be aware that some Windows programs, such as Excel 5 and Word 6, do not use Windows 95 dialog boxes (such as File Save As and File Open), which are common in applications using the Windows 95 interface. Such applications may not fully benefit from these utilities. In these cases, you may be able to enter a long file name in the File Name text box but not be able to view long file names.

Installing Applications in Windows 95

To install a Windows application, you usually use a setup program or install utility. Installing DOS-based applications is a different matter (and the subject of Chapter 17, "Installing, Running, and Uninstalling DOS Applications"). These setup programs for Windows applications take care of all the details of installing the application. You don't have to concern yourself with creating directories, copying files, and integrating the application into Windows. A manual installation of a major software suite is beyond the capabilities of the average user, and a dreaded chore for even the most advanced user.

▶ **See** "Installing MS-DOS Applications," **p. 518**

What Does Setup Do?

A typical setup or installation program begins by prompting you for some information and then installs the application automatically. The better setup programs provide feedback during installation to keep you informed of what they are doing to your system and the progress of the installation. Depending on the complexity of the application you are installing, the setup program might give you an opportunity to select various options and customize the installation. The program might limit your input to accepting or changing the path where you install the application, selecting whether to install various optional components, or specifying configuration settings for the new application.

After receiving your input, the setup program proceeds to perform some or all of the following steps automatically:

■ Search for an existing copy of the application it's about to install and switch to upgrade mode, if appropriate.

■ Scan your system to determine whether your hard disk has enough room for the necessary files and perhaps check for the existence of special hardware or other system requirements.

■ Create folders and copy files. Often, the setup program must expand files that are stored in a compressed form on the distribution disks.

■ Create a shortcut that you can use to launch the application.

■ Add a folder and/or shortcuts to your Start menu.

■ Update Windows configuration files.

■ Update the Windows Registry.

- Register the application as an OLE server.
- Register the application's file types so Windows can recognize the file name extensions for the application's document and data files.
- Install fonts, support utilities, and so on.
- Configure or personalize the application.

What if There's no Setup Program?

Part

V

Ch

16

A few Windows programs don't include a setup utility to install the application—the developer just didn't supply one. An example could be a small utility program for which installation consists of copying a couple of files to your hard disk and perhaps adding a shortcut to your Start menu to launch the application. You'll find instructions for installing the application in an accompanying manual or README file.

The installation instructions may assume that you're installing the program in Windows 3.1, not Windows 95. (At least that's likely to be the case for awhile after the release of Windows 95.) Fortunately, this isn't a serious problem. Most of the procedures for installing an application in Windows 3.1 work equally well in Windows 95. For instance, although Windows 95 supplies new tools for managing files, the underlying process of creating directories (folders) and copying files is the same in both Windows 95 and Windows 3.1. Also, for backward compatibility, Windows 95 includes full support for WIN.INI and SYSTEM.INI files, so any additions that you're instructed to make to those files should work as expected.

There are two common manual installation procedures that you must adapt for Windows 95. First, if the Windows 3.1 installation instructions require that you create a file association in File Manager, you must substitute the Windows 95 equivalent of registering a file type. Second, instead of creating a program item in Program Manager, you add a program to the Start menu.

▶ **See** "Adding and Removing Programs in the Start Menu," **p. 369**

▶ **See** "Registering File Types Causing Documents to Open Applications," **p. 147**

Using Windows 3.1 Applications in Windows 95

According to Microsoft, Windows 95 features full backward compatibility with 16-bit Windows 3.1 applications, and thus you can install and use your Windows 3.1 applications in Windows 95 without modification. And in fact, with only rare exceptions, Windows 3.1 applications do indeed run successfully in Windows 95.

For a current list of programs with known incompatibility problems with Windows 95 and suggested fixes or workarounds, read the file PROGRAMS.TXT in the Windows folder. You can also search for compatible software programs at the following site on the Internet:

http://www.microsoft.com/windows/queries/search.idc?

If you encounter a compatibility problem with a legacy application—an older application designed for a previous version of DOS or Windows—running in Windows 95, check with the application's developer for a patch or work-around for the problem. In some cases, perhaps the only solution is an upgrade to a Windows 95 version of the application.

 There is an application called MKCOMPAT.EXE, located in the Windows\System folder that helps fix Windows 3.x programs that are not completely compatible with Windows 95. Use the Find command to find MKCOMPAT.EXE, double-click to start, and choose File, Open command to open the EXE file you are having trouble with. Systematically check and uncheck items in the window and try running the program again. You can access additional items by choosing File, Advanced Options.

Using this program is a matter of trial-and-error; there is no Help facility to guide you. Call the software development company that created the Windows 3.x program and ask if they know the MKCOMPAT parameters to make the program run or if they have a Windows 95 compatible version.

Installing Windows 3.1 Applications

The installation instructions for most Windows 3.1 applications direct you to use the Run command to start the setup program and install the application. The instructions might mention that you can find the Run command on the File menu in either Program Manager or File Manager. However, in Windows 95, you find the Run command on the Start menu. The setup program is usually on disk 1 of the installation disks or in the root directory if the program is on a CD-ROM.

NOTE You might prefer a different technique for launching the setup program. Open the My Computer window and double-click the drive icon for the drive that contains the installation disk. Then locate the Setup program's icon and launch the program by double-clicking it.

When you use this technique, you need not type the command in the Run dialog box to start the setup program. This technique also lets you scan the disk for README files before installing the application. ■

CAUTION

Save a copy of your AUTOEXEC.BAT and CONFIG.SYS files before installing any new DOS or Windows 3.x application. After you install a Windows 3.x or DOS application, it is a good idea to check your AUTOEXEC.BAT files to see if any unnecessary programs or configuration lines were added. For example, some applications add a line that loads SHARE.EXE or SMARTDRV.EXE, neither of which are needed in Windows 95. Not only do these programs waste memory, but you may also have problems with your system if they are loaded.

Of course, the setup program for a legacy application is tailored to Windows 3.1 rather than Windows 95. For example, the installation program offers to create Program Manager groups (see fig. 16.1) and update INI files. Fortunately, you can just accept those options when the program offers them. Windows 95 intercepts Program Manager updates and automatically converts them to Start menu shortcuts. Windows 95 also transfers WIN.INI and SYSTEM.INI entries into the Registry.

FIG. 16.1
If you run this setup program in Windows 95, the program is added to the Start menu, which is the equivalent to program groups in Windows 3.x.

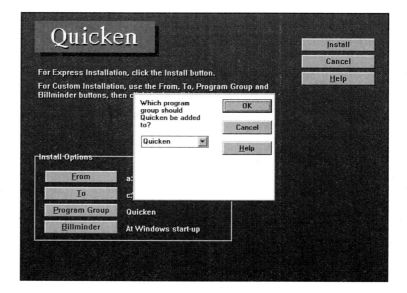

If you install Windows 95 as an upgrade to Windows 3.1, the setup program should take care of such issues. The Windows 95 Setup program automatically transfers information about your existing applications to the Registry when you install Windows 95 into your existing Windows 3.1 directory. As a result, you shouldn't have to reinstall applications.

Setting Up Existing Applications in a Dual-Boot Configuration

If you choose to create a dual-boot system by installing Windows 95 in a folder separate from Windows 3.1, Windows 95 won't know about any Windows 3.1 applications already on your disk. Just adding those applications to your Start menu isn't enough to let you run them successfully in Windows 95.

> **CAUTION**
>
> Before reinstalling a Windows 3.1 application in Windows 95, be sure to note the directory in which the application is currently installed. You must specify *exactly* the same directory when you reinstall the application. Otherwise, you can waste valuable disk space by having two copies of the same application on your system.

In some cases, it may not be necessary to have a separate copy of an application on your hard drive to use it in Windows 95 as well as Windows 3.1. However, most applications expect to find certain initialization and support files in the Windows folder. If you attempt to run the application from Windows 95, it expects to find those files in the Windows 95 folder. But if you installed the program under Windows 3.1, those files are in the Windows 3.1 folder, not in the Windows 95 folder. In some cases, if you copy the Windows 3.1 applications' initialization and support files to the Windows 95 folder, you can run the applications. But usually, you have to reinstall your Windows 3.1 applications in Windows 95 before you can use them. You certainly need to reinstall an application if it uses features such as OLE. However, the application may not run in Windows 3.x when you do this.

The bottom line is that you need to find out for each Windows 3.x application whether it will run in both Windows 3.x and Windows 95 without installing the program twice. You should first try creating a shortcut to the application in Windows 95 and see if the application runs. If not, copy the initialization and support files to the Windows 95 folder and try again. If the application still won't run from Windows 95, reinstall it in Windows 95. Then, if the application doesn't run in Windows 3.x, you have to reinstall from Windows 3.x, using a different directory than the one used when you installed it in Windows 95.

TROUBLESHOOTING

When I try to use the same application under both Windows 3.1 and Windows 95 on a dual-boot system, why does the application keep "forgetting" changes I make in the application's User Preference settings? If you change user settings in an application when running it under Windows 3.1, they may not be there when you run the application under Windows 95—and vice versa. Even though there's only one copy of the application on your hard drive, you may have two sets of the initialization files where User Preference settings are stored: one each in the Windows 3.1 and Windows 95 folders. The application uses the settings from (and stores revised settings in) the initialization files it finds in the default Windows folder for the version of Windows you're running at the time. Unfortunately, there's no way to keep two sets of initialization files in sync automatically.

With some applications, however, you may be able to specify the location of the INI file, in which case you can point to one common INI file (in either the Windows 95 or Windows 3.1 folder). Another possible solution is to move the INI file to the application directory. And a third workaround is to specify the folder containing the INI file as the startup folder for that application.

▶ **See** "Setting Up a Dual-Boot System," **p. 1211**

Running Windows 3.1 Applications

After installing a Windows 3.1 application in Windows 95, you can launch and run the application just like any other Windows application. Windows 95 changes the application's appearance automatically, giving it the new Windows look (see fig. 16.2). The application window's title bar has the new format, complete with the new style of Minimize, Maximize, and Close buttons, and most buttons and other window elements take on the three-dimensional look.

FIG. 16.2
Running a Windows 3.1 application in Windows 95 gives the program an automatic facelift. However, despite the change of appearance, the application performs the same as in Windows 3.1.

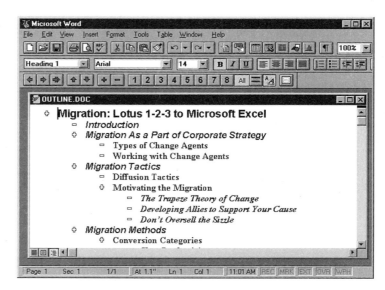

Beneath the superficial appearance changes, the application works the same as it did under Windows 3.1. Windows 16-bit applications continue to use a shared memory space in Windows 95, so they can't preemptively multitask the way the newer 32-bit Windows 95 applications can. The application benefits from some Windows 95 performance improvements such as increased system resources, improved memory management using the Virtual Machine Manager, and some 32-bit Windows subsystems, including the print and communication subsystems. However, to take maximum advantage of the features and capabilities of Windows 95's 32-bit operating system, you must upgrade to a new version of the application. In the meantime, you can continue to use your 16-bit Windows 3.1 applications effectively and efficiently.

▶ **See** "Starting and Quitting Windows," **p. 50**

Installing Windows 95 Applications in Windows 95

To take full advantage of the improvements in performance that Windows 95 offers, you have to upgrade to the Win32-based versions of your applications. By doing this, you will benefit in several ways, as discussed in "Understanding How Windows Runs Applications," later in this chapter.

One new feature of Windows 95 is an optional way to start an application's setup program: a new Install Programs Wizard accessible via the Add/Remove Programs icon in Control Panel. The Add/Remove Programs Properties sheet provides a common starting point for adding and removing Windows applications and Windows system components and accessories.

To run the Install Programs Wizard and use it to install a Windows application, follow these steps:

1. Open the Start menu and choose Settings, Control Panel. This opens the Control Panel window shown in figure 16.3.

2. In the Control Panel window, double-click Add/Remove Programs to open the Add/Remove Programs Properties sheet shown in figure 16.4. By default, the Install/Uninstall tab is active.

3. To start the Install Program Wizard, choose Install.

FIG. 16.3

The Windows 95 Control Panel contains a wizard to make installing applications easier.

Add/Remove Programs Icon

FIG. 16.4

The Add/Remove Programs Properties Properties sheet is the master control for adding and removing applications.

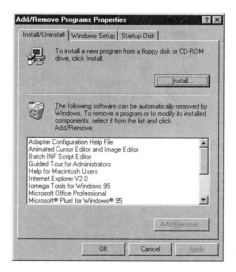

4. When the Install Program From Floppy Disk or CD-ROM dialog box appears (see fig. 16.5), insert the application's distribution disk (the first floppy disk or CD) in the appropriate drive, and click Next.

FIG. 16.5

The Install Program Wizard takes you through each installation step.

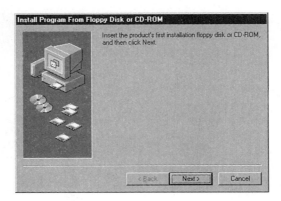

5. The wizard searches the disk's root directory for an installation program (usually named SETUP.EXE or INSTALL.EXE) and displays the command line in the Run Installation Program dialog box (see fig. 16.6).

FIG. 16.6

Usually the wizard finds the application's setup program on the disk.

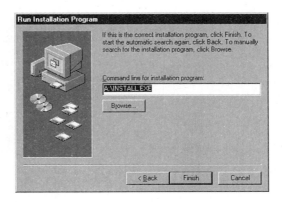

6. If the wizard fails to find the setup program (perhaps because it is in a subdirectory) or you want to run a different setup program (perhaps from a network drive), you can use choose Browse and select a different file in the Browse dialog box (see fig. 16.7). Choose Open to insert the selected file name in the wizard.

7. After the correct command line for the setup program appears in the Run Installation Program dialog box, click Finish to start the setup program and begin the application installation.

FIG. 16.7
If the wizard needs help
locating the setup program,
you can browse for the
correct file.

The application's setup program then installs the application. You'll need to respond to several prompts during the installation process. If the setup program includes a Windows 95-compatible uninstall feature, the wizard notes this and adds the new application to a list of programs that you can remove automatically.

▶ **See** "Removing Windows Applications," **p. 491**

Adding Windows' Component Applications

The Add/Remove Programs icon in Control Panel lets you install and remove Windows components and accessories as well as applications. Therefore, you can reconfigure your copy of Windows 95 without reinstalling it.

Adding and Removing Windows Components

To use the Windows Setup feature to add or remove a Windows component, follow these steps:

1. Open the Start menu and choose Settings, Control Panel.

2. Open the Add/Remove Programs Properties sheet by double-clicking the Add/Remove Programs icon.

3. Click the Windows Setup tab to display a list of Windows components as shown in figure 16.8.

   In the Components list box, a check mark next to an item indicates that the component is already installed on your system. If the check box is gray, the Windows component is composed of more than one subcomponent and some (but not all) subcomponents are currently installed. For instance, in figure 16.8, only some of the subcomponents (accessories such as Calculator, Paint, and WordPad) of the Accessories component are installed. To see what's included in a component, click Details.

Part
V

Ch
16

FIG. 16.8

The Windows Setup page of the Add/Remove Program Properties sheet lets you add and remove parts of Windows.

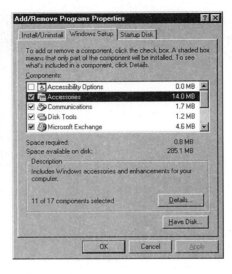

4. Select a component in the Components list box. The Description box in the lower portion of the sheet displays a description of that component and tells you how many of the available subcomponents are selected.

5. If the component you selected consists of more than one subcomponent, click Details to open a dialog box listing the subcomponents. (For example, figure 16.9 shows the Accessories dialog box listing the subcomponents of the main Accessories component.) In some cases, a subcomponent will have additional subcomponents, which you can view by clicking Details again.

FIG. 16.9

The Accessories dialog box lists a component's parts. By choosing Details, you can narrow your selections.

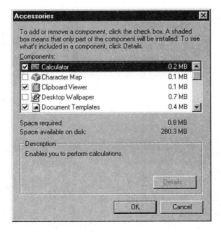

6. Mark components for installation or removal by clicking the check box beside that item in the Components list. Adding a check mark to a blank check box marks that item for installation. Conversely, clearing a checked box instructs Windows to uninstall that component.

7. If you're selecting subcomponents in a dialog box you opened by choosing Details, click OK to close that dialog box and return to the Add/Remove Programs Properties sheet.

8. When the check marks in the Components lists specify the components that you want composing your Windows system, choose Apply in the Add/Remove Programs Properties sheet. You'll need to supply the Windows setup disks or CD when prompted.

Part
V
Ch
16

TROUBLESHOOTING

When I use the Windows Setup feature to add new components, it adds those components, but it also removes other components. Why? If you clear a check box for a component that was checked when you run Windows Setup, this tells Windows to remove the component, rather than to not install it. This can be confusing the next time you run Setup again to add new components. Leave those components that are already installed checked unless you want to uninstall those components.

Installing Unlisted Components

Eventually, you might want to install a Windows component that doesn't appear on the Components list in the Windows Setup page of the Add/Remove Program Properties sheet. For example, you might want to install one of the system-management utilities from the Windows 95 Resource Kit.

To install a Windows component not listed in the Components list box, open the Add/Remove Program Properties sheet, click the Windows Setup tab, and choose the Have Disk button at bottom of the dialog box. This opens the Install From Disk dialog box (see fig. 16.10).

FIG. 16.10
When adding Windows components from a supplemental disk, you must supply the full path to the correct INF file.

In the Copy Manufacturer's Files From field, specify the path to the setup information file (INF) for the Windows component that you want to install. (The setup information file tells Windows Setup what is available to install and how to do it.) You can either type the path and file name or choose Browse and select the file in the Browse dialog box. After specifying the correct path, click OK. Windows opens the Have Disk dialog box (see fig. 16.11), which lists the components available for installation. Check the ones that you want to install, then choose Install. You might have to supply disks and browse for needed files when prompted.

FIG. 16.11

The Have Disk dialog box lists the Windows compo-nents available on the supplemental disk, or at least the components described in the INF file that you selected.

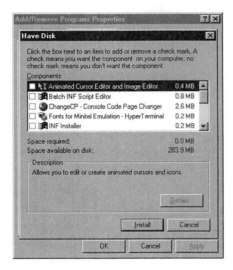

Windows not only installs the component, but also adds the component to the Compo-nents list on the Windows Setup page. Later, you can remove the component just like any other in the list.

Installing components for DOS applications is different from the procedure used with Windows. In most cases, installing many of the major DOS applications requires suspend-ing Windows 95 and switching to the "exclusive" DOS mode. This procedure is described in detail in Chapter 17, "Installing, Running, and Uninstalling DOS Applications."

 A shortcut for suspending Windows 95 and getting to a DOS command prompt is to shut down Windows 95 in the normal way, but when the "It is safe to turn off your computer" screen appears, type **MODE CO80** and press Enter. The DOS command prompt will appear, from which you can run your DOS installation program. Type **WIN** at the command prompt to return to Windows 95.

▶ **See** "Installing MS-DOS Applications," **p. 518**

Running Applications

After you install the application's and Windows' accessories, Windows 95 gives you many options for launching them. The technique that you choose depends on your personal preferences, working style, and what you're doing at the time.

The various methods for launching applications are discussed in more detail in Chapter 3, "Windows Navigation Basics," and Chapter 4, "Managing Files." The following is a summary of the techniques:

Part
V

Ch
16

- Choose the application's shortcut from the Start menu.

 T I P To modify the properties of the shortcut for an application, right-click the shortcut and choose Properties. Select the Shortcut page in the Properties sheet. Here you can specify a folder for the application to start in and a shortcut key for starting or switching to the application from the keyboard. You can also specify whether you want the application to start in a window, maximized or minimized.

- Create and use a shortcut on the desktop.
- Right-click the application's icon in Windows Explorer or the My Computer window, then click Open in the context menu.
- Double-click the application's icon in the My Computer window or Windows Explorer.
- Choose the Run command from the Start menu and then type the path and file name of the application's executable file.
- Choose the Run command from the Start menu, then drag an EXE file from My Computer or Network Neighborhood and drop the file into the Run dialog box.
- Use the Windows 3.1 Program Manager and run the application by double-clicking its program item.

N O T E Windows 95 includes updated versions of both Program Manager and File Manager. The optional 3.1 interface adds applications to the Program Manager during installation. If you opt for the Windows 3.1 interface, you also can add program items to the Program Manager manually.

If you want to start Windows 95 in the Program Manager, you need to install Windows 95 using the Custom option. Choose User Interface in the Computer Settings dialog box and then choose Change. Select Windows 3.1 (Program Manager) and choose OK. If you have already installed Windows 95, add a shortcut to PROGMAN.EXE to the \Windows\Startup folder. PROGMAN.EXE is located in the \Windows folder.

■ Open a document or data file associated with the application. When you open a file, Windows launches the application automatically and then opens the file in that application. There are as many ways to open files as there are ways to launch applications. For instance, you can open files in Explorer by choosing a recently used file from the <u>D</u>ocuments submenu on the Start menu, or by double-clicking a shortcut on your desktop.

■ For a bizarre twist, try this method of launching a Windows application. You can open a MS-DOS window and type the command at the DOS prompt to start the application. You would expect to get an error message saying the program requires Windows to run. But, instead, Windows 95 launches the Windows application for you. You must include the extension for the application's file name, otherwise Start will search for a folder matching the file name and open that folder in Explorer if it finds one. When you exit the Windows application, the DOS window will remain open.

■ Finally, you can be in an MS-DOS window and open a document in a Windows application by typing the following:

> **Start** *pathname\documentname.ext*

If the document has been registered with a Windows application, the application opens and the document loads.

TIP You can set up more than one association for any one file type. By doing this, you will have a choice in the context menu (the right-click menu) of which application you want to use when opening this type of file. You may, for example, want to be able to open an Excel XLS file with either Excel or 1-2-3. By default, when you right-click a file with the XLS extension in My Computer or Explorer and select <u>O</u>pen, the file will be opened in Excel. To add other options to the context menu, see "Editing an Existing File Type" in Chapter 13.

TROUBLESHOOTING

I am unable to specify a working directory in the Properties dialog box for a Windows application. Windows 95 does not allow you to modify the properties of the actual EXE file for Windows applications. You can create a shortcut for the application and then use the Shortcut page in the Properties dialog box for that shortcut to specify a working directory.

TIP You need to use the same media (disk or CD-ROM) that you originally used to install Windows when you install additional components of Windows 95.

▶ **See** "Starting from My Computer or Explorer," **p. 40**
▶ **See** "Compatibility with Windows 3.1 and DOS Programs," **p. 18**

▶ **See** "Starting from Shortcuts," **p. 39**

▶ **See** "Starting from the Start Button," **p. 37**

Removing Windows Applications

Installing a Windows application can be a complicated venture. Windows applications are often tightly integrated with the operating system. Installing such applications not only requires copying the application's files into the application's own directory, but also adds numerous support files to your Windows directory and changes Windows' settings. Fortunately, nearly all applications provide setup programs to automate the installation process.

Removing an application can be similarly complicated. Finding all the support files and settings added or changed during the application's installation can be nearly impossible. Fortunately, many application setup programs now offer an Uninstall option to automate the process when you need to remove the application from your system.

> **CAUTION**
>
> Even uninstall programs can lead to problems. If a program installed a DLL file that is also used by another program, when you uninstall the program, the DLL will be removed and then the remaining program won't run because of the missing file.

Windows 95 takes this welcome trend a step further by adding a facility to remove applications. That facility is in the same Control Panel window that you use to install applications and Windows components.

Removing Applications Automatically

Windows 95's Add/Remove Programs Wizard adds to the capability of individual setup programs by tracking an application's components in the Registry. This lets Windows delete an application's files and settings but still identify and retain any files that another application might share and use.

N O T E Only applications that provide uninstall programs specifically designed to work with Windows 95 appear on the Install/Uninstall page of Add/Remove Programs. ▨

 T I P Use the keywords **uninstall**, **deinstall**, and **remove** to search for uninstall instructions in the online Help for the application you want to remove.

To uninstall an application automatically, start by opening the Control Panel and double-clicking the Add/Remove Programs icon. This opens the Add/Remove Programs Properties sheet—the same sheet used to install the application (see fig. 16.12).

FIG. 16.12
In the Add/Remove Programs Properties sheet, you can remove applications as well as install them.

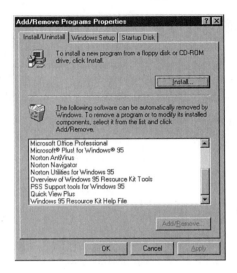

The lower portion of the dialog box lists applications that you can remove. To remove an application, select it from the list and choose <u>R</u>emove. After you confirm that you want to remove the program, Windows runs the selected application's uninstall program.

Removing Applications Manually

If you want to remove an application from your system, just hope that it's one that Windows can remove automatically. Removing an application manually can be difficult, and possibly dangerous. It is very difficult to know if a file you are deleting for one program is also used by another program. If you are not careful, you can end up disabling programs inadvertently and then have to reinstall them.

Removing Files from the Application Directory   Getting rid of the files in an application's own folder is fairly straightforward. In fact, that should probably be the first step in removing an application manually.

Many applications install support files in the Windows directories. It's nearly impossible to tell what application added which files, and to make matters worse, several applications can share the same files. If you ignore the files in the Windows folders when you remove an application, you can leave numerous orphaned files on your system needlessly consuming hard drive space. However, if you make a mistake and delete the wrong file or one that another application also uses, you might render the other application unusable.

If you find support files in your WINDOWS folder that you think are unnecessary, copy them to a separate folder before you remove them. If you don't encounter any problems after a few months, you can delete that folder.

Removing Orphaned DLLs *Dynamic link library files* (*DLLs*) are files associated with one or more applications that contain subroutines used by these applications. When you install a new application, chances are one or more DLLs are placed somewhere on your hard drive. Because there is no easy way to know to which application a particular DLL belongs and where all the DLLs for an application are located, it is difficult to know what DLLs to get rid of when you manually uninstall an application. To make things more complicated, sometimes a DLL is used by more than one application, so if you delete that DLL when you remove one of those applications, you may adversely affect the other applications. This is a major benefit of having an automatic uninstall feature for a Windows application that knows what DLLs to remove when you remove the application.

 Never immediately delete a DLL after manually uninstalling a program. The DLL may be used by other programs that you aren't aware of. A safer practice is to copy the DLL to a disk and delete it from your hard drive. Create a small TXT file with the same name as the DLL telling from which directory the DLL was removed. If any program displays a message saying the DLL you removed is needed, you can copy it back to its original directory.

Here are a few tricks that can help you determine if it is safe to remove a DLL that you suspect is associated with an application you have removed:

- Right-click the DLL in Explorer or My Computer and choose Quick View. Look at the header information for clues indicating which applications use it. If it seems that the only application using the DLL is the one you removed, it is probably safe to delete the DLL.

- Search for references to the DLL in the headers of EXE files, using the Find command. Follow these steps to search through application headers:

  1. Click Start, Find, Files and Folders.
  2. Select the drive you want to search and type ***.DLL;*.EXE** in the Named text box. This tells Find to search for all files with either the DLL or EXE extension.
  3. Check the Include Subfolders option and make sure the Options, Case Sensitive option is not selected.

4. Select the Advanced tab and type the name of the DLL you are checking for in the Containing text box. Do not include the file extension.

5. Choose Find Now. All EXE and DLL files containing the name of the DLL file you specified are listed in the Find dialog box. If no files are found, you can feel reasonably secure about deleting the DLL.

Before you delete any DLL, even if one or both of the methods just described indicates that it is probably safe to do so, it is a good idea to rename the DLL or move it to a floppy disk. If you don't have any trouble running your applications for a period of time, you can get rid of the DLL. Otherwise, restore the any DLLs that appear in error messages when you try to run an application.

 There are several commercial utilities available for helping you uninstall applications, including MicroHelp's UnInstaller 32-bit, Quarterdeck's CleanSweep 95, and Vertisoft's Remove-It for Windows 95. Be sure to get the Windows 95 versions of these programs that are designed to modify the Registry when you uninstall a program. These utilities will also uninstall Windows 3.x programs.

Removing References to Applications in System Files Often an application adds lines to the WIN.INI, SYSTEM.INI, CONFIG.SYS, and AUTOEXEC.BAT files when you install the application. This is mainly true for Windows 3.x applications, because the system information for Windows 95 applications is stored in the Registry. After you have removed an application, search through these files for references to the application. Delete these references to keep your system files from becoming cluttered with unused information.

CAUTION
You should always back up your system files before you edit them, in case you accidentally delete lines that affect how other programs run.

If you get an error message informing you that a particular file is missing after you have removed an application, it may be because there is still a reference to this file in one of the system files. Use Notepad to look through your system files for references to the deleted file. Refer to Chapter 14, "Introduction to REGEDIT," to learn how to search through the REGEDIT file and remove references to files or programs you have deleted.

T I P Click Start, Run, and type **Sysedit** in the Open text box. The System Configuration Editor opens with windows displaying your WIN.INI, SYSTEM.INI, CONFIG.SYS, and AUTOEXEC.BAT files. You can view, edit, and save any of these files using the SYSEDIT.

 Removing Shortcuts and Folders from the Start Menu   After you remove an application's files from your hard drive, you want to get rid of any shortcuts that pointed to the application. To delete a shortcut icon from your desktop, simply drag and drop the shortcut onto the Recycle Bin icon on your desktop.

To remove the application from the Start menu, click the Start button and choose Settings, Taskbar. Then, in the Taskbar Properties sheet, click the Start Menu Programs page. Next, choose Remove to open the Remove Shortcuts/Folders dialog box (see fig. 16.13).

FIG. 16.13

After removing an application, open the Remove Shortcuts/Folders dialog box to remove the application's folder and shortcuts from your Start menu.

The Remove Shortcuts/Folders dialog box, like the Windows Explorer, displays a hierarchical list of folders and files. To expand the display and show a folder's contents, you can click the plus sign beside the folder. Select the folder or shortcut that you want to delete, then choose Remove. To remove other items, repeat the process as necessary. When you finish removing items, click Close.

▶ **See** "Understanding the Most Important Screen Elements in Windows 95," **p. 36**

▶ **See** "Managing Your Files and Folders," **p. 101**

▶ **See** "Emptying the Recycle Bin," **p. 110**

Removing File Associations   After you remove an application, you can remove any associations that might have existed between file extensions and the defunct application. After all, you don't want Windows to try to launch the nonexistent application when you double-click a document file.

To remove the link between a file extension and an application, start by opening the My Computer window. Next, choose View, Options to open the Options dialog box, then click the File Types tab. You then see the screen shown in figure 16.14. Scroll down the Registered File Types list and select the file type that you want to delete, then choose Remove. Windows asks you to confirm your choice. If you answer Yes, Windows abolishes the registration of that file type.

FIG. 16.14

Using the Options dialog box to remove a file type registration is easier and safer than editing the Registry directly.

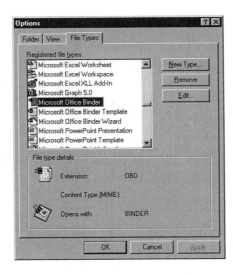

CHAPTER 17

Installing, Running, and Uninstalling DOS Applications

by Dick Cravens

Although Windows 95 is designed from the ground up to shield the user from the often-confusing world of the command line, AUTOEXEC.BAT, CONFIG.SYS, and memory-management practices, it offers surprisingly rich support for those users who still desire or need to work in the MS-DOS environment. If you have a favorite MS-DOS application, utility, or game, there's absolutely no need to give it up or suffer performance loss. In fact, Windows 95 offers greatly enhanced MS-DOS support compared to earlier versions.

None of this comes without a small price: You must learn a few new concepts and controls to master Windows 95 MS-DOS operations. If you're used to adjusting PIF files, you'll be applying some of that knowledge to Windows 95 Properties management, and learning some new tricks as well. The reward is far greater control over MS-DOS application environments under Windows 95 than under previous versions.

If you're currently using another brand of DOS other than Microsoft DOS, have no fear—Windows 95 DOS support is so compatible and configurable, you can

What's new in MS-DOS for Windows 95

Find out about the many improvements in Windows 95 for supporting MS-DOS applications.

How Windows 95 works with MS-DOS applications

Turn here to learn to start, end, and control an MS-DOS session.

Using MS-DOS Mode

Learn how to use MS-DOS mode to work with DOS applications that won't work in the Windows environment.

Installing, configuring, and uninstalling MS-DOS applications

In these sections, you learn how to install a DOS program, then how to alter the default settings using the Properties sheet. You also learn how to remove a DOS program from your computer.

Starting and running MS-DOS programs

Find out how to start your DOS programs from a command prompt and by using the standard Windows 95 methods for starting applications.

easily adjust for any minor variations between DOS versions from other vendors such as IBM's PC-DOS, or Novell/Digital Research DR-DOS. ■

Understanding How Windows 95 Works with MS-DOS Applications

Just as Windows 3.1 improved drastically on version 3.0 support for MS-DOS applications, Windows 95 improves on its predecessor. Applications that simply would not run under earlier versions of the Windows MS-DOS prompt now perform admirably. For applications that still won't run under the new Windows, a special mode helps you run them quickly and easily from within Windows, and then automatically returns you to your Windows session when you're finished.

The following are some of the improvements in Windows 95 for supporting MS-DOS applications:

- Better local reboot support
- Zero conventional memory usage for Protected-mode components
- Consolidated setup for MS-DOS-based applications
- Toolbar support for windowed MS-DOS applications
- Graceful shutdown for windowed MS-DOS sessions
- Long file name support, with full backwards compatibility for "8.3" format file names
- Execution of Windows programs from the MS-DOS session
- The ability to open documents from the command line
- Better control over MS-DOS window fonts
- User-scalable MS-DOS session windows
- Improved Cut, Paste, and Copy commands for integrating MS-DOS and Windows application information
- Universal Naming Convention (UNC) path name support
- Spooling of MS-DOS-based print jobs

Windows 95 makes dealing with MS-DOS/Windows integration quicker and easier than ever, and makes working with MS-DOS applications similar to working on a machine running only MS-DOS. In addition, MS-DOS emulation under Windows 95 gives the user many of the other benefits of Windows 95: the graphical user interface, multitasking, and networking support.

Gone are the confusing variations and limitations of Real, Standard, and Enhanced-mode MS-DOS. Chances are, you'll never have to make an adjustment to Windows MS-DOS support; but if you do, you'll find the controls vastly simplified, well consolidated, and more reliable than ever.

Conventional Memory in Windows 95

An added bonus of the overall design of Windows 95 is the greater conservation of conventional memory (that below the 640K mark). By loading eligible device drivers and TSR (terminate-and-stay-resident) programs in Protected mode, above the first-megabyte mark in memory, Windows frees more working memory for MS-DOS applications than any previous version.

Some MS-DOS applications simply couldn't run under Windows 3.1. By the time mouse, network, SCSI, and other necessary drivers were loaded, there simply wasn't enough RAM below 640K. Windows 95 alleviates this situation by checking each driver specified in your installation against a "safe list" of known drivers, and loading approved ones in extended memory, or substituting equivalent drivers.

For example, if your PC is on a NetWare network, uses a SCSI CD-ROM drive, the SMARTDrive disk cache, DriveSpace disk compression, and an MS-DOS mouse driver, you can save more than 250K in conventional memory using the MS-DOS system in Windows 95.

Part

V

Ch

17

CAUTION

Just as with earlier versions of Windows, don't run anything in a Windows MS-DOS session that alters the File Allocation Table, or other system-critical files. Examples of this type of software are MS-DOS disk defragmenter and unerase or undelete utilities. Windows now comes with many of these utilities, so use the Windows versions instead (don't just boot to MS-DOS to use your older utilities; some of them will corrupt the Windows 95 long file name system).

Starting the MS-DOS Prompt Session

Getting started with MS-DOS under Windows is as simple as selecting a menu item. To begin a session, follow these steps:

1. Open the Start menu and choose Programs. Windows displays a submenu.

2. Choose the MS-DOS Prompt menu item. Windows opens the MS-DOS Prompt window, as shown in figure 17.1.

FIG. 17.1
The MS-DOS Prompt window
awaits your every command.

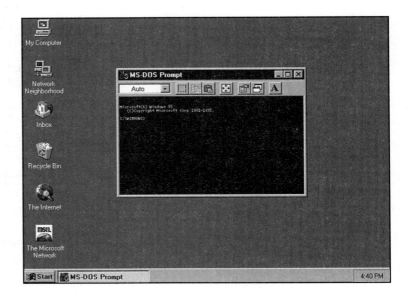

Ending MS-DOS Prompt Sessions

 You can still run DOS batch files, either from the command line, the Run command in the Start menu, or from within Windows, using a shortcut. A nice enhancement in Windows 95 is that you can modify the properties of the BAT file using the Properties sheet. Right-click the shortcut and select the Program tab. Now you can select what mode you want the DOS session to run in (normal window, maximized, or minimized) and assign a shortcut key. You also can specify that the DOS window be closed when the batch file is finished running.

You also can specify a batch file that will be run whenever you start a particular DOS program. Open the Properties sheet for the DOS program, select the Program tab, and type the full path and name for the batch file in the Batch File text box.

Now that you've started an MS-DOS Prompt session, practice closing it before you move on to the finer points of operation. To close the MS-DOS Prompt window, follow these steps:

1. Click in the MS-DOS Prompt window to bring it to the foreground.

2. Find the flashing cursor near the MS-DOS command prompt. At the flashing cursor near the MS-DOS command prompt, type **exit**.

3. Press Enter, and Windows closes the MS-DOS Prompt session window.

TIP Don't leave MS-DOS Prompt sessions open any longer than you need to. Every session takes a big chunk out of available CPU time, slowing down your entire Windows performance in all applications.

N O T E As with most other procedures under Windows, several other ways to close an MS-DOS Prompt session are available. As alternatives, try each of the following:

- Double-click the MS-DOS icon in the top-left corner of the MS-DOS Prompt session window.

- Click the MS-DOS icon; then choose Close from the menu.

- Click the Close icon in the upper-right corner of the MS-DOS Prompt window.

- Right-click anywhere in the MS-DOS Prompt window title bar. Windows displays a menu, from which you can choose Close. ■

Part

V

Ch

17

Ending Sessions with Running Applications

Windows also allows you to close sessions that have applications open; but by default, it warns you if the application is running or has open files.

Besides giving you options for more gracefully ending a session, Windows 95 improves on previous versions by performing better session "cleanup," releasing memory, and deallocating system resources much more consistently.

To close an active session, simply follow the same procedures for closing a session with just an MS-DOS prompt that you used earlier. This time, however, Windows displays the warning dialog box shown in figure 17.2.

FIG. 17.2

Windows warns you if you try to exit an MS-DOS session while an application is active.

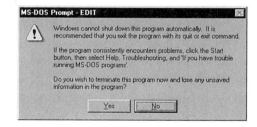

If you choose No, Windows returns you to the MS-DOS Prompt session, and you can exit the program before you close the MS-DOS session.

Otherwise, choose Yes and Windows shuts down the MS-DOS session and terminates the running application. It's not recommended that you close sessions this way, but you can do it in an emergency (for example, if the application is hung and simply won't *let* you exit gracefully).

TROUBLESHOOTING

My MS-DOS application simply won't respond, and none of the close procedures you list are working. What can I do to shut down this bad apple and get back to work? Will I lose all my data in other applications? One great addition to Windows 3.1 was the capability to local reboot, or close crashed applications without closing all of Windows. Windows 95 extends this capability with even greater control over shutting down errant applications.

The method used is the same as under Windows 3.1: use the classic "three-fingered salute," Ctrl+Alt+Del, after which Windows 95 displays the Close Program dialog box, instead of the classic Windows 3.1 "Blue Screen of Impending Doom." Windows 95, however, does a much better job of recovering from application failure, because it gives you a choice of which task to shut down, instead of assuming the one in the foreground is the culprit. After you select the application task to deal with, you have the choice of ending the errant task, shutting down the entire computer, rebooting using Ctrl+Alt+Del again, or canceling.

You learn a way to override the Windows warnings about closing an active MS-DOS Prompt session later in this chapter.

▶ **See** "General Properties," **p. 520**

Controlling the MS-DOS Prompt Session

Now that you know how to get in and out of the car, start the engine, and shut it down, you're ready to get behind the wheel and take her for a spin! Windows 95 offers many great options to dress up the classic MS-DOS session.

Windows 3.x veterans know one of the most basic and useful control tools for MS-DOS sessions: the Alt+Enter key sequence. This great shortcut changes the MS-DOS session from full-screen to windowed and back again, in a flash.

Using DOS Commands

Many of the DOS commands that you are no doubt familiar with from the old days are still available at the DOS prompt. Some of these commands are internal to COMMAND.COM, as they always have been. Dir, Copy, CD, MD, and RD are some examples of these commands. In fact, all the internal DOS commands available in DOS 6.x are still available.

Other DOS commands are external, executable programs and are stored in the \Windows\Command folder (they used to be stored in the \DOS folder). Some examples of the external DOS commands are Attrib, Edit, Find, Mem, and Xcopy. Not all of the external commands that were in MS-DOS 6.x are still with us. Some of the commands you'll notice that are missing are the undelete command, the virus checker, and the DOS backup command. There is now a Windows Backup program for backing up files and the Recycle Bin for recovering deleted files. However, if you delete files from the DOS prompt, they are not sent to the Recycle Bin, so you will have to use a DOS-based recovery utility to retrieve these files. And you will have to purchase a third-party program to check for viruses.

If you want to copy files with long file names from the command prompt be sure to use the XCOPY32.EXE command. You will lose the long file names if you use the XCOPY command.

To get help for a DOS command from the DOS prompt, type the command name followed by **/?**. If the Help text is more than one screenful, type |**more** as well to read the text one screen at a time. For example, **copy /? |more**. The DOS help program included with DOS 6.2 that provided more extensive online help for the DOS commands is not included with Windows 95. However, you can copy this program from MS-DOS 6.2 into your \Winodws\Command folder and run it from a DOS command prompt by typing **Help command.** Be aware of the fact that the program will not include up-to-date information on all the DOS commands that are part of Windows 95.

Even for the diehard Windows user, there are a couple of DOS commands that still come in very handy. If you want to change the attributes of several files at once, the DOS Attrib command is still the quickest way. In Explorer, you can only change the attributes for one file at a time, using the Properties sheet. With the Attrib command, you can use DOS wildcards to change the attributes for many related files at once, or even all the files in a folder. The same holds true for the Ren command, which allows you to use wildcards to rename several related files at once from the DOS prompt, instead of renaming them one-by-one in Explorer.

TIP

Remember how you could type CD.. to move up one directory in the directory hierarchy? Well, now you can type three or more periods to move up two or more levels in the hierarchy with one command.

If you like to use the DOSKEY command-line editing utility when you are working at the command prompt, but only want to load it when you are actually running a DOS prompt window (instead of putting it in your AUTOEXEC.BAT file), open the Properties sheet for the MS-DOS Prompt shortcut, select the Program tab and enter DOSKEY in the Batch File text box on the Program page. Now, whenever you launch an MS-DOS window with this shortcut, DOSKEY is automatically loaded.

Part
V

Ch
17

In fact, you can enter any of the standard DOS commands in the Batch File text box to run them automatically when you double-click the shortcut. For example, you can create a DOS shortcut that runs the XCOPY command to back up a folder and all its subfolders with one double-click:

XCOPY C:\DATA\ D:\ /s

This syntax specifies that the Data folder on drive C and all of its subfolders should be copied to drive D. Put DOS command shortcuts on your desktop for ready access.

TIP If you are working at the DOS command line and you would like to display a folder window showing the contents of the current folder, type **START** followed by a space and a period. Type two periods to open a folder for the parent folder of the current directory.

Another trick when working with the command line is to drag a file or folder onto an MS-DOS window to insert the path and name for the file or folder on the command line. This is handy when you have a long path name and don't want to have to type it on the command line.

Using the MS-DOS Prompt Toolbar

Windows MS-DOS sessions now have a variety of interface controls. The toolbar will be familiar to you if you've been using Explorer. Figure 17.3 shows the MS-DOS Prompt toolbar and its controls.

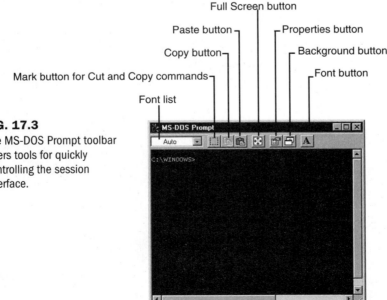

FIG. 17.3
The MS-DOS Prompt toolbar offers tools for quickly controlling the session interface.

T I P To continue running a DOS application in the background when you switch to another application, click the Background button on the Prompt toolbar. If you are downloading a file using a DOS-based communications application, for example, you will want to enable background operation. Normally, you will not want to run the DOS application in the background, so you free up all system resources for the foreground application.

Controlling the MS-DOS Prompt Interface

Although Windows 3.1 offered a choice of fonts for windowed MS-DOS sessions, that choice was limited to bitmapped fonts that restricted the sizing options for the window. It was workable, but it offered nothing like the flexibility available in Windows 95 MS-DOS support.

Windows now offers TrueType scalable fonts in addition to the familiar system fonts, allowing on-the-fly resizing of the entire session window. To try the new font features, open an MS-DOS session and perform the following steps:

1. Click on the toolbar's Font list; then choose TT7 × 14 (the TrueType font for TT7 × 14 resolution). The window should now appear as shown in figure 17.4 (assuming you're using 640 × 480 standard VGA display resolution).

FIG. 17.4
You can use the toolbar to control TrueType fonts in your MS-DOS Prompt session.

2. Grab the window borders in the bottom-right corner and resize the window. Note that the vertical and horizontal window scroll bar controls appear on the window, but the text in the window remains the same, as shown in figure 17.5.

3. Repeat the procedure in the preceding step 1 to select the 4 × 6 font mode. Notice that the text in the window is much smaller, and the window has shrunk to match (see fig. 17.6). Grab the window borders again and try to enlarge the window; note how it is limited to a maximum size.

Part
V

Ch
17

FIG. 17.5

Windows now supports dynamic resizing of the MS-DOS Prompt window. You can access any hidden areas of the session using standard scroll bar controls.

FIG. 17.6

If you choose a font that allows full viewing of the MS-DOS Prompt session, Windows won't let you resize the window larger than the session.

4. Repeat the procedure in the preceding step 1 to select Auto mode. The window does not change.

5. Grab the window borders and pull the window to a larger size. Note how Windows alters the font on the fly. When you change the window size again (try a square, or a vertical rectangle), the font adjusts automatically to the nearest available size.

Using the Windows Clipboard with the MS-DOS Prompt

Windows now offers even easier access to the data in your MS-DOS session, via the toolbar. Copying information from your session into a Windows application is quick and easy. Follow these steps to try it out:

1. Using the mouse, click the Mark tool and select text in your MS-DOS application.

2. Click the Copy tool on the MS-DOS Prompt toolbar. Windows places a copy of the text in the Clipboard.

3. Using the mouse, click your Windows application (for example, NotePad) to make it active. Position the cursor where you want to insert the text; then choose Edit, Paste from the NotePad menu. NotePad displays the text copied from your MS-DOS session window.

TROUBLESHOOTING

I used to be able to use the mouse to highlight text in an MS-DOS session, and then press Enter to copy the text to the Clipboard, but now it doesn't work. This still works under Windows 95; it simply isn't enabled by default. You can use the mouse to select and copy text if the application you're running supports it (for example, EDIT); but the MS-DOS prompt itself won't (for example, you can't mark and copy the results of the `dir` command that MS-DOS writes to your window). If you use the toolbar on your MS-DOS sessions, just click the Mark tool on the toolbar before you select the text. If you've set up your MS-DOS sessions so the toolbar doesn't show, then you can tell Windows 95 to enable the QuickEdit feature.

To enable this feature, simply click the window system icon (the MS-DOS icon in the upper-left corner) and choose Properties; then choose the Misc tab when the Properties sheet appears. Check the QuickEdit box under the Mouse section; then click OK, and you're ready to go.

To copy information from a Windows application to an MS-DOS application, select and copy the information in the Windows application and then choose the Paste tool on the Prompt toolbar. You also can right-click on the MS-DOS window title bar and choose Edit, Paste if you don't have the toolbar displayed. You can use this method to paste information into a DOS application or onto the DOS command line.

Part
V

Ch
17

Using Long File Names

One of the most bothersome limitations of the MS-DOS environment has been the 8.3 file name format. Windows now supports longer file names, and the MS-DOS Prompt offers support for them, too. To see how this works, follow these steps:

1. Using My Computer, create a new folder called Incredibly Long Folder Name on the root of drive C:, as shown in figure 17.7.

2. Using the Start menu, open an MS-DOS Prompt. At the prompt, type **dir c:***. The MS-DOS window displays the folder listing for the root of drive C: (an example is shown in fig. 17.8).

Note the dual display of both the 8.3-format and long-format folder names. Windows and MS-DOS coordinate both naming systems, but not without a price; the 8.3 format name uses the tilde character (~) to show the inevitable truncation. Even under Windows, some long names may be shortened using the ellipsis characters (...) when space is at a premium.

FIG. 17.7
You can use up to 255 characters in a file or folder name.

FIG. 17.8
The MS-DOS Prompt session supports and displays both long and short file and folder (directory) names.

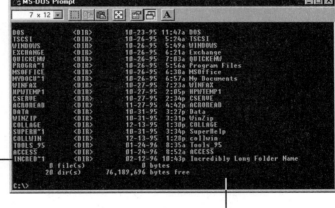

MS-DOS 8.3 format folder (directory) name

Windows 95 format long folder (directory) name

To ensure complete backwards compatibility, Windows still uses file extensions, even though they are not displayed in Explorer or on the Desktop. If you rename a file from the Windows environment, it does not change the hidden file name extension. Windows still uses the extension for file associations with applications and viewers.

N O T E Not all applications support long file names just because Windows does. It's doubtful that any MS-DOS applications will support long file names because most were written prior to this version of Windows. Most 16-bit Windows applications won't support longer file names until their first release after Windows 95, if then (some software companies will probably wait for the first release of their application as a true 32-bit program to include this feature).

Many of the native MS-DOS commands in Windows 95 have been enhanced to provide support for long file names. For example, the `dir` and `copy` commands both support long file names. ■

 TIP   You can use long file names at the DOS command prompt if they don't include spaces. If they do include spaces, enclose the file name in quotes. For example:

CD "MSOFFICE\WINWORD\BUSINESS LETTERS"

▶ **See** "Registering File Types so Documents Open Applications," **p. 147**

Using Universal Naming Convention Path Names

More and more PCs are on *local area networks* (*LANs*). Most shared resources on a LAN are stored on *servers*, or PCs dedicated for a particular network task, such as printing, file storage, or database storage.

Gaining access to other PCs on the network, whether server or workstation, can be a tiresome process of mapping the other machine to a virtual drive letter on your system. The Windows 95 MS-DOS Prompt offers a way around this with *Universal Naming Convention (UNC)* support. This is a fancy way of saying that you can view, copy, or run files on another machine without having to assign it a drive letter on your computer. It also means that if you are running short of logical drive letters, you can get to servers that you use only intermittently with a simple command from the MS-DOS Prompt.

For example, if you want to run an application called SHARED.EXE in the folder Stuff on server FRED1, you can enter the following at the command prompt:

\\fred1\stuff\shared.exe

You also can use this feature with any legal MS-DOS command. For example, to see the contents of the folder Stuff, use the familiar `dir` command as follows:

dir \\fred1\stuff

This yields a standard folder listing of the contents of that area of the server.

Printing from the MS-DOS Prompt

The biggest change in printing support for MS-DOS applications comes in the form of better conflict resolution and print job queuing. Windows now handles printer port contention between MS-DOS and Windows applications by shuttling all MS-DOS print tasks to the same printer management utility used by Windows applications.

▶ **See** "Printing from MS-DOS Applications," **p. 253**

Part
V
Ch
17

Understanding MS-DOS Mode

Even the most perfect host can't entertain someone who really doesn't want to be at the party. Windows has the same problem with some poorly designed MS-DOS applications—some MS-DOS applications demand total control over system resources and access hardware in the most direct way, bypassing "standard" Windows methods.

Windows 95 accommodates a poorly behaved guest to the best of its ability, via *MS-DOS mode.* This mode is the equivalent to the Real mode present in older versions of Windows, with some "real" improvements.

MS-DOS mode works by giving the errant MS-DOS application the entire system for the duration of the session. Windows removes itself from memory, leaving only a small "stub" loader in preparation for its return to power.

▶ **See** "Advanced Program Settings," **p. 520**

To use this mode, the user sets a property in the Advanced Program Settings dialog box. When the MS-DOS application runs, Windows literally shuts down, loads the application, and then returns automatically when the application is finished. This process can be slow and cumbersome, but it's faster and more convenient than exiting Windows manually, using the dual boot option, and reloading Windows.

Knowing When to Use MS-DOS Mode

Before you decide to enable MS-DOS mode for an application, try these other options:

- Confirm that you've optimized the MS-DOS session settings for that application. Check the program's documentation for special memory requirements or other unusual needs. You may be able to adjust Windows' MS-DOS support to make the application work in a standard MS-DOS session.

- Try running the application in full-screen mode, using the Alt+Enter key sequence.

If either of the preceding methods works, you will have a faster, more convenient alternative, allowing you the full benefit of Windows' multitasking and other features, all of which disappear during the MS-DOS mode session.

Setting Up an Application to Run in MS-DOS Mode

Whenever possible, Windows 95 determines that an application needs to run in MS-DOS mode and closes down all other applications and switches to this mode automatically. Unless you specify otherwise, you'll be warned when Windows is about to switch to MS-DOS mode.

In some cases, you may have to manually configure an application to run in MS-DOS mode. If you try to run such an application, you get an error message telling you that you can't run the application in Windows. If this happens, you should manually configure the application to run in MS-DOS mode, using the following steps:

1. If you haven't created a shortcut for the application, create one now. You can only modify the settings of a DOS application using a shortcut.
2. Right-click the shortcut for the application and choose Properties.
3. Select the Program tab and choose Advanced to display the Advanced Program Settings dialog box.
4. Select the Prevent MS-DOS-based Programs from Detecting Windows option.
5. Choose OK.

Double-click the shortcut icon to try running the application. If the application still doesn't run, follow these steps:

1. Open the Advanced Program Settings dialog box again, as in steps 2–3 above.
2. Select the MS-DOS Mode option.
3. Choose OK.

Try running the application again. If it still doesn't run, you have to modify the configuration for the MS-DOS mode, using the following steps:

1. Open the Advanced Program Settings dialog box.
2. Select the Specify a New MS-DOS Configuration option. The dialog box appears as in figure 17.9.

FIG. 17.9

Windows allows you to override the default settings for MS-DOS mode support. You can even run a special CONFIG.SYS and AUTOEXEC.BAT file for each application.

Default settings for MS-DOS sessions

Override settings for MS-DOS mode

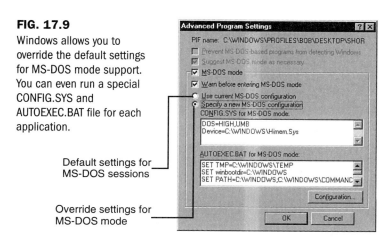

Part

V

Ch

17

Selecting this option allows you to override the default settings for the MS-DOS-mode session.

3. Modify the lines in the CONFIG.SYS for MS-DOS Mode and AUTOEXEC.BAT for MS-DOS Mode windows as needed to allow this application to run.

   The changes you make here only affect this application. In this way, you can customize each application that must run in MS-DOS mode.

4. If necessary, choose the Configuration button and select from the options in the Select MS-DOS Configuration Options dialog box and choose OK.

   Be aware that when you choose from among the options in this dialog box, you remove the entries that already appear in the CONFIG.SYS and AUTOEXEC.BAT text boxes.

CAUTION

Use the Direct Disk Access option with great care. It is possible for an MS-DOS application to destroy long file name support when you select this option.

5. Choose OK twice to close the dialog boxes.

If there are programs or drivers that you want to load for all your MS-DOS mode sessions, edit the file named DOSSTART.BAT that is located in your \Windows folder. For example, if you want to have access to your CD-ROM drive in your MS-DOS sessions, include a line that will enable the CD-ROM. For example:

   MSCDEX.EXE /D:MSCD0001 /M:12

MSCDEX is included with Windows 95 and is located in the \Windows\Command folder. You also need to include a line in your CONFIG.SYS file that loads the CD-ROM real-mode driver. This driver is not loaded into memory when you are running Windows 95.

TROUBLESHOOTING

I set my main MS-DOS Prompt to run in MS-DOS mode, and now whenever I start it, Windows shuts down completely! How can I set it back if I can't get to the properties? You can access the properties of any program or file from the Windows desktop without running the program or opening the file. When Windows restarts after the MS-DOS Mode session, locate the icon for the MS-DOS prompt program (in the Windows\Start Menu\Programs folder) with the Windows Explorer and right-click the icon to get the menu that offers the Properties function.

When the Properties sheet opens, go to the Program page and choose the Advanced button, which opens the Advanced Program Settings dialog box, as shown earlier in figure 17.9. Simply uncheck the MS-DOS Mode box, and choose OK twice to close the Properties sheet and return to the desktop. See "Configuring Your MS-DOS Application" later in this chapter.

▶ **See** "Using the Power of Shortcuts and Desktop Icons," **p. 71**

Using PIF Files

Windows 3.1 offered a straightforward, if awkward, means of controlling the session settings for an MS-DOS application through the use of *Program Information Files (PIF)*. Although PIFs offered a high degree of control over the virtualized MS-DOS environment, the user had to understand the relationship between Windows, MS-DOS, the PIF, the Program Manager icon assigned to the PIF, and the application itself. Advanced training in MS-DOS memory management didn't hurt either. If you add an MS-DOS batch file to the equation, it could be really confusing.

Windows 95 solves this whole mess by using the same mechanism for MS-DOS applications and data that's now used for Windows files: the Properties sheet. With a simple right-click of the mouse, you can directly view and alter the entire gamut of controls for your MS-DOS application. No separate editor, no hunting for the PIF and confirming that it's the correct one. Although Windows 95 still uses PIF files, there's a unified means of viewing the PIF properties for a given application, via the Properties sheet.

One of the more confusing issues under Windows 3.1 was the need to create a PIF file for each MS-DOS application that required custom settings. Windows 95 takes care of that chore automatically—all you need to do is view the properties for your MS-DOS application.

To view an example Properties sheet for an MS-DOS application, follow these steps:

1. Using Explorer, find the Windows folder. Then open the Command folder.
2. Select EDIT.COM in the file list in the right pane of Explorer.
3. Right-click to open the shortcut menu, and choose Properties. Windows displays the Edit Properties sheet, as shown in figure 17.10.

If you're mystified by some of the terms and control types you see here, don't worry. The "Configuring Your MS-DOS Application" section later in this chapter, shows examples of how these controls can help you maximize Windows' performance when you run MS-DOS applications.

FIG. 17.10

The Properties sheet for MS-DOS applications has several tabs unique to the needs of the MS-DOS environment.

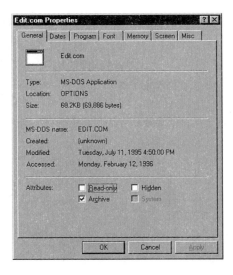

Graphic-Intensive Applications

One great example of the enhanced MS-DOS support available under Windows 95 is the capability to run some applications in graphics mode in a window. Although this doesn't sound like a big trick, remember that earlier versions of Windows don't support this at all; you are forced to run MS-DOS Graphics-mode applications full screen.

Why would you want to take advantage of running MS-DOS applications in a window? For some of the same reasons you like Windows applications: the capability to quickly and easily move back and forth between applications and the capability to easily cut and paste information between programs.

Also, in earlier versions of Windows, moving from a full-screen MS-DOS application in Graphics mode back to Windows involves a time-lag during which the display has to reset for a completely different video mode and resolution; some monitors handle this gracefully, but most don't. Running your MS-DOS program in a window avoids this altogether.

N O T E   Windows 95 contains the capability to self-configure for many popular MS-DOS programs. These configurations are derived from research with the most-used applications and are stored in a file called APPS.INF. When you install an MS-DOS application, Windows checks to see if it's registered in the APPS.INF database; if the application is listed in the APPS.INF file but no PIF file exists, Windows uses the information to create a PIF for future use. ■

Although this new capability is wonderful, be aware that not all MS-DOS applications are supported. Not all applications follow the "official" guidelines for MS-DOS hardware access (some programmers break or bend the rules to gain faster performance, for example writing directly to the video hardware versus using the MS-DOS service calls for video); hence, Windows 95 can't support them in a windowed, virtualized MS-DOS environment. The same application may run perfectly full-screen, because there are fewer layers of virtualization for Windows to provide. Game programs are a great example of this scenario, which constantly attempt to use the system timer, video, and sound resources as directly as possible.

How do you know if your application will run in Graphics mode in a Windows 95 window? The best test is to try it. Follow these steps to test your program:

1. Locate the icon for the MS-DOS graphics program you want to test and double-click it to start the program. Windows starts the program in full-screen mode, unless you've configured it otherwise or the program was installed with a windowed default. If the program opens in a window, press Alt+Enter to return to full-screen mode.

2. If the program supports both Character and Graphics modes, activate the program feature that requires Graphics mode (such as Page or Print Preview).

3. When the screen has reformatted for graphics display, press Alt+Enter to return to windowed display mode. Windows displays the application as shown in the example in figure 17.11.

FIG. 17.11
Windows can display MS-DOS graphics mode for many applications, such as the WordPerfect Print Preview feature.

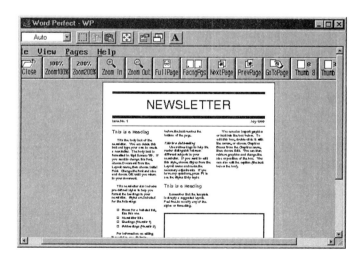

4. If Windows can't support the application in this mode, you see the warning box displayed in figure 17.12.

Part
V

Ch
17

FIG. 17.12

Although Windows now offers improved support for MS-DOS graphics mode, some applications still don't work in a window.

Improved Memory Protection

A bitter lesson learned from running MS-DOS applications under Windows 3.1 was that those applications often inadvertently corrupted the operating system memory areas. MS-DOS programs, not written for a multitasking environment, believe that they have the right to alter the memory for the entire system. This can have catastrophic results in a multitasking environment such as Windows and has been the cause of many a lockup.

Windows 95 offers a much higher level of memory protection for the entire system and specifically for MS-DOS applications. You can specify special protection for conventional system memory by checking the Protected check box on the Memory property page, as shown in figure 17.13.

FIG. 17.13

Windows 95 allows you to protect conventional memory from errant applications via the Protected setting on the Memory property page.

Select to enable MS-DOS session memory protection

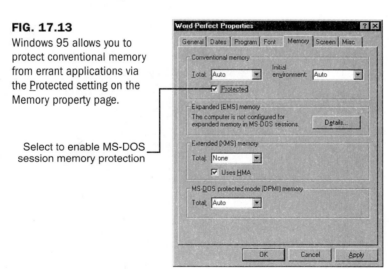

Although it might seem logical to enable this option by default for all MS-DOS applications, enough overhead is involved in tracking this for each session that it's really best to turn it on only for those applications that have proven they require it.

Enhanced Virtual Machine Support

MS-DOS application support requires the presence of a virtual MS-DOS environment, or *virtual machine*. Windows 95 offers many improvements over the virtual-machine model used in previous versions of Windows. Because Windows 95 doesn't require a complete, preexisting Real-mode MS-DOS environment before it runs, you can control almost every aspect of the virtual MS-DOS environment because it is more "truly" virtual. You can even run batch files within the session to customize the environment for your application's needs.

Windows 95 also offers better management of MS-DOS session closings. Under Windows 3.1, not all system memory and resources were released when a virtual machine session ended. This resulted in a slow erosion of performance with the eventual inability to open additional applications, requiring the user to restart Windows.

Part
V

Ch
17

Enhanced Local Reboot Support

Under Windows 3.0, if an application quit working, the user had two options: prayer and prayer. A hung program meant lost data. Windows 3.1 improved on this scenario by allowing *local reboot*, the ability to trap errant application behavior, thus protecting other applications and data. Under Windows 3.1's local reboot, the Ctrl+Alt+Del key sequence didn't restart the machine; it closed the misbehaving application and theoretically left Windows and all other applications fat and happy.

Local reboot had two main problems:

- Users didn't always know which application was hung, so when they used Ctrl+Alt+Del, Windows often closed the wrong one (sometimes offering to shut itself down!).

- Windows 3.1 didn't always respond quickly to the Ctrl+Alt+Del command, and the user "sat" on the keys, resulting in a complete machine reset. (A single Ctrl+Alt+Del would bring up a blue screen warning that a second Ctrl+Alt+Del would reset the system; often this screen was a blue blip as the world came crashing down, and the annual report went to the Great Bit Bucket Beyond.)

Windows 95 improves on this bad scenario by putting a menu between you and data loss. A single Ctrl+Alt+Del displays the Close Program dialog box.

If an application creates a problem or freezes, Windows now indicates that it is "not responding," and you have the choice of ending that task or completing an orderly shutdown of the entire system. Although this doesn't totally insulate your computer from errant applications, it does drastically improve your ability to control otherwise disastrous circumstances.

Installing MS-DOS Applications

Now that you have explored the basic concepts, tools, and techniques behind MS-DOS Prompt session support under Windows 95, look at the steps required to install and configure an MS-DOS application.

You can install any application in the following two ways:

- Locate and run the installation program for the application.
- Create a folder for the application and copy the files to that folder.

N O T E Although Windows can handle complete installations of true Windows applications, it relies on structures and capabilities that are simply not present in most MS-DOS applications. Thus, you need to set up application shortcuts and Start button menu items manually. ■

Using MS-DOS Application Installation Programs

Most professionally written MS-DOS applications have an installation or setup program that handles the details of installation for you. Besides simply creating a storage area for the application and moving the files to it, these installation programs perform the additional operating system configuration chores that may be necessary for successful operation.

N O T E MS-DOS installation programs that are Windows-aware may handle some of the preceding tasks for you, but most won't—you'll have to handle some of the tasks yourself. How do you know what alterations to make? Look for the documentation for the manual program installation instructions in the program folder. Often this is a simple text file, labeled README.TXT or INSTALL.TXT. ■

▶ **See** "Installing Applications in Windows 95," **p. 476**

Installing MS-DOS Applications from the MS-DOS Prompt

While it's just as easy to find and run your MS-DOS application installation program from Explorer or the Start button Run command, you may want to go directly to the MS-DOS Prompt session and install your application directly, or your application may not have a structured installation program. In either case, Windows certainly allows you this level of control.

Using an Installation Program from the MS-DOS Prompt   Running the installation program from an MS-DOS prompt is just like doing it on a machine that's running only MS-DOS. Follow these steps to begin:

1. Open a new MS-DOS session from the Start menu.

2. At the MS-DOS prompt, enter the command to start the installation program (for example, **a:\install.exe**) and press Enter.

3. When the installation program is finished, close the MS-DOS session manually or run the application if you want.

   ▶ **See** "Ending MS-DOS Prompt Sessions," **p. 500**

Installing MS-DOS Programs Manually from the MS-DOS Prompt   Some MS-DOS applications don't have installation programs at all. This is most common with shareware applications or small utility programs.

To install your application manually, follow these simple steps:

1. Open a new MS-DOS session from the Start menu.

2. At the MS-DOS prompt, enter the command to create a folder for your program (for example, **md c:\myprog**) and press Enter.

3. Enter the command to copy the program to the new folder, such as **xcopy a:*.* c:\myprog**. MS-DOS copies the files to the new folder.

N O T E   You may need to alter the preceding routine slightly if your application comes as a compressed archive (such as a ZIP or an ARJ file). Usually all this means is an additional step for decompression once the files are copied. ▨

Configuring Your MS-DOS Application

Before you explore the myriad options for customizing the MS-DOS environment for your application, there's one point that needs to be stressed: The odds are very good that your program will run perfectly without any reconfiguration at all. Microsoft has done a truly admirable job in observing the reality of how people use MS-DOS applications under Windows, and the design of Windows 95 MS-DOS defaults reflects that. Preset configurations for the most popular MS-DOS applications are stored in Windows, awaiting your installation of the program. So before you begin messing around with all the options, be smart and run the program a few times. The old adage truly applies: If it ain't broke, don't fix it. See earlier in this chapter about the APPS.INF file.

Understanding and Configuring MS-DOS Application Properties

You've already been introduced to the Windows Properties sheet and seen how Windows now uses it in place of the PIF Editor. Now you take a closer look at specific property options and how they relate to your application.

▶ **See** "Displaying Properties of Programs, Documents, and Resources," **p. 26**

General Properties The General properties page is primarily informational, with minimal controls other than file attributes (see fig. 17.14).

FIG. 17.14
The General properties page gives you most of the basic information about the file and easy access to control of the file attributes. Context-sensitive help is available at any time by using the "?" tool.

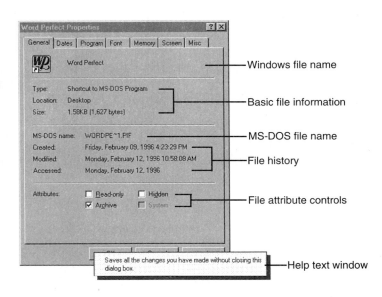

Windows file name

Basic file information

MS-DOS file name

File history

File attribute controls

Help text window

The only real controls exposed in the General properties page are the file attribute settings. These are used mainly to protect documents (by setting the read-only attribute), and you shouldn't alter them unless you have a specific reason.

N O T E A running MS-DOS application displays only six Properties tabs. (The General tab is not shown when the program is in use.) ■

Program Properties The Program properties page gives you control over the basic environment your application starts with (see fig. 17.15).

Advanced Program Settings Clicking the Advanced button in the Program properties page opens the Advanced Program Settings dialog box, shown in figure 17.16.

If you need to run your application in MS-DOS mode, here's where you can enable it. You can even set up custom CONFIG.SYS and AUTOEXEC.BAT values for your session. If you click the Specify A New MS-DOS Configuration radio button, you can edit the special CONFIG.SYS and AUTOEXEC.BAT values right in this dialog box.

If you click the Configuration button, you see the dialog box displayed in figure 17.17.

FIG. 17.15
The Program properties page allows you to alter the variables used to name and start the application.

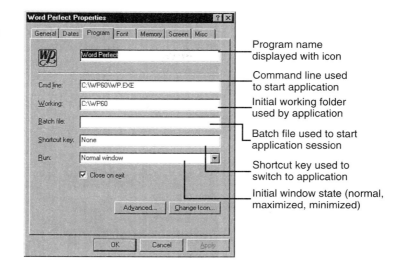

Program name displayed with icon

Command line used to start application

Initial working folder used by application

Batch file used to start application session

Shortcut key used to switch to application

Initial window state (normal, maximized, minimized)

FIG. 17.16
The Advanced Program Settings dialog box enables you to define the precise mode and environment for your MS-DOS session.

Keeps current MS-DOS defaults for Real-mode session

Enables alternate set of defaults for customizing MS-DOS mode

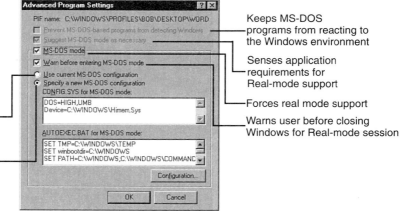

Keeps MS-DOS programs from reacting to the Windows environment

Senses application requirements for Real-mode support

Forces real mode support

Warns user before closing Windows for Real-mode session

FIG. 17.17
The Select MS-DOS Mode Configuration Options dialog box lets you control expanded memory, disk caching, disk access, and command-line editing.

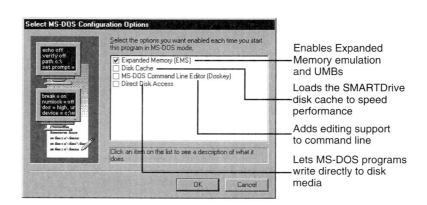

Enables Expanded Memory emulation and UMBs

Loads the SMARTDrive disk cache to speed performance

Adds editing support to command line

Lets MS-DOS programs write directly to disk media

All the settings under the Advanced dialog box should be altered only if your MS-DOS application simply won't run in a standard session with the default settings. For that matter, don't even enable MS-DOS mode unless your application demands it.

▶ **See** "Knowing When to Use MS-DOS Mode," **p. 510**

Changing MS-DOS Application Icons If you click the Change Icon button shown in figure 17.15, the Change Icon dialog box appears (see fig. 17.18).

FIG. 17.18
The Change Icon dialog box lets you customize the icon for your MS-DOS application.

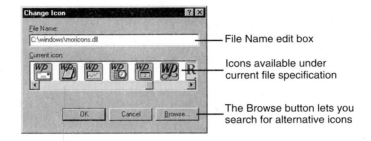

File Name edit box

Icons available under current file specification

The Browse button lets you search for alternative icons

It's likely that your MS-DOS application won't come with any icons. Windows 95 shows you the icons in the file PIFMGR.DLL when you choose Change Icon. You can choose icons from other applications simply by specifying them in this dialog box. Or you may want to look in an icon archive that comes with Windows 3.1, MORICONS.DLL. Microsoft threw in icons for a few of the most popular programs so that you can have a choice. If you didn't upgrade from Windows 3.1, MORICONS.DLL probably won't be on your system.

Font Properties The Font properties page is primarily informational, with minimal controls other than file attributes (see fig. 17.19). It works just like the Font list control on the MS-DOS session toolbar.

TROUBLESHOOTING

When I selected a TrueType font for the display in an MS-DOS window, the font did not change on the screen. If you are running a DOS application in graphics mode, you cannot change the font because DOS graphics applications handle fonts directly. If the application supports text mode, you can switch to text mode (from within the application) and then you will be able to switch screen fonts. The other alternative is to run the application in full-screen mode (press Alt+Enter) and then change the fonts.

▶ **See** "Controlling the MS-DOS Prompt Interface," **p. 505**

Memory Properties The Memory properties page makes simple work of the traditional maze of MS-DOS memory management (see fig. 17.20). With a few mouse clicks, you can configure your application memory precisely as needed.

FIG. 17.19
The Font properties page lets
you choose the font type and
size, and gives you both a
window and font preview.

Select font type
or combination

Window size
relative to desktop

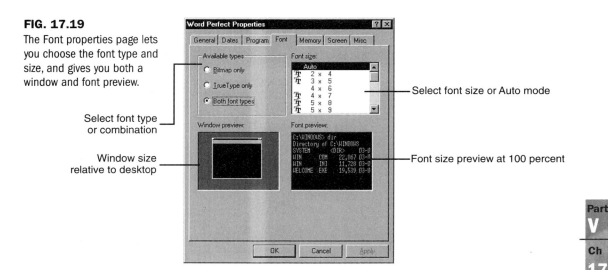

Select font size or Auto mode

Font size preview at 100 percent

FIG. 17.20
The Memory properties page
vastly simplifies this formerly
arcane management issue.

Sets conventional memory
to specific value

Enables protection for
session memory range

Sets XMS emulation value

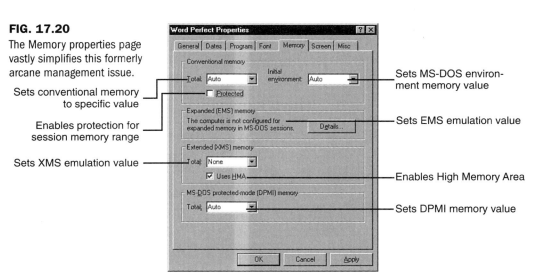

Sets MS-DOS environ-
ment memory value

Sets EMS emulation value

Enables High Memory Area

Sets DPMI memory value

Several dozen books have been written on the subject of MS-DOS memory management.
Let's keep it simple: If your application works without altering these values, *do not change
them.* If your application doesn't work with the default settings, *consult the documentation*
to determine what the appropriate settings are. *Then* you can alter the values in this dialog
box. Proceeding in any other way, unless you have considerable experience with the techniques involved, can severely inhibit the performance of your system.

▶ **See** "Improved Memory Protection," **p. 516**

Screen Properties   The Screen properties page lets you control the appearance of the MS-DOS session (see fig. 17.21).

FIG. 17.21
The Screen properties page gives you control of the size, type, and performance of the MS-DOS interface.

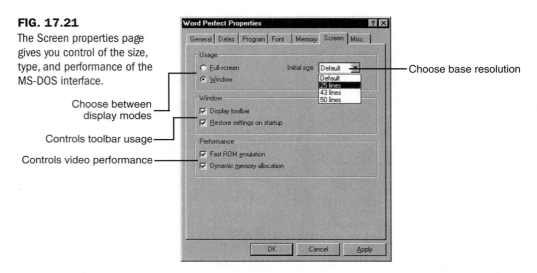

Choose base resolution

Choose between display modes

Controls toolbar usage

Controls video performance

You may find that certain MS-DOS programs (especially those running in Graphics mode) respond poorly to the video emulation used in windowed mode. If so, try defeating the performance defaults by unchecking the Fast ROM Emulation and Dynamic Memory Allocation options. Fast ROM Emulation tells the Windows 95 display driver to mimic the video hardware to help display MS-DOS programs faster. Dynamic Memory Allocation releases display memory to other programs when the MS-DOS session isn't using it. If you experience strange display problems with your MS-DOS programs, try changing these settings.

Miscellaneous Properties   The Misc properties page covers the remaining configuration items that don't fit under the other categories (see fig. 17.22).

■ The *Allow Screen Saver* control lets your default Windows screen saver operate even if your MS-DOS session has the foreground.

■ *Always Suspend* freezes your MS-DOS application when you bring another application (either MS-DOS or Windows) to the foreground. If you have an application that must perform time-sensitive operations (such as a communications program), make sure to disable this option.

■ *Idle Sensitivity* tells your MS-DOS program to yield the system to other applications if it really isn't doing anything important. A word processor, for example, won't have a problem letting go of the system clock when you're not using it. A communications program, however, may need to respond quickly, so you want to set its idle sensitivity to Low.

FIG. 17.22

The Misc properties page controls screen saver, mouse, background operation, program termination, shortcut key, and editing options.

Part

V

Ch

17

- The *Mouse* controls enable *QuickEdit* mode (letting you mark text using just the mouse) and *Exclusive Mode* (the MS-DOS application has control of the mouse cursor when the application is in the foreground, even if you try to move the mouse out of the MS-DOS window).

- The *Warn If Still Active* item in the Termination box tells Windows to notify you before the MS-DOS session is closed. It's really best to leave this enabled, unless you are absolutely certain that the MS-DOS program will never, ever have open data files when you close it.

- The *Fast Pasting* setting simply tells Windows that your MS-DOS program can handle a raw data stream dump from the Windows Clipboard. Some MS-DOS programs clog at full speed, so if you paste to your MS-DOS application and you consistently lose characters, turn this one off.

- *Windows Shortcut Keys* allows you to override the standard quick navigation aids built into the Windows environment, just for your MS-DOS session (some MS-DOS programs think they can get away with using the same keys, and something has to give—Windows!). By default, Windows "owns" these shortcuts, but you can lend them to your MS-DOS application by unchecking them here.

Running Installed MS-DOS Applications

Windows comes set up with a default MS-DOS Prompt configuration designed to run the vast majority of applications. Although your application may have special needs, odds are it will work fine if you start it from within a running MS-DOS Prompt session.

To start your application from an MS-DOS Prompt session, follow these steps:

1. Open a new MS-DOS Prompt session from the Start menu.

2. At the MS-DOS prompt, enter the command to move to the folder of the program you want to start (for example, **cd \wp60**) and press Enter. The MS-DOS prompt now shows the current folder, as shown in figure 17.23.

FIG. 17.23
Once you're in the MS-DOS Prompt session, all the basic MS-DOS commands can be used to start your application.

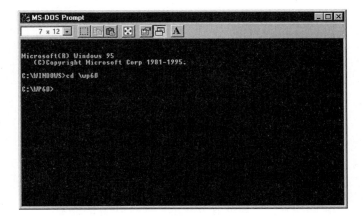

3. At the MS-DOS prompt, enter the command to start your application (for example, **wp**) and press Enter. The MS-DOS Prompt window now displays the application you've started, as shown in figure 17.24.

Although running an application from within the MS-DOS Prompt window works well and seems familiar to the veteran command-line user, it's not really the most convenient method under Windows.

In addition to the default Windows MS-DOS Prompt, Windows 95 offers four other ways to start an application:

- Windows Explorer
- The Start button <u>R</u>un option
- The Start button <u>P</u>rograms menu
- The Application shortcut

FIG. 17.24
Once your application starts, Windows displays it in the MS-DOS Prompt window space. Note that the window title reflects the command name of the program running.

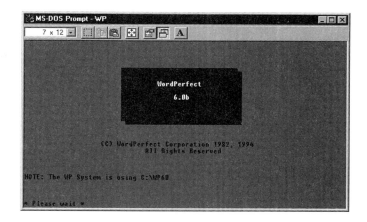

 TIP If you want the opportunity to enter optional (or even required) command-line parameters when you run a DOS application, follow these steps:

1. Right-click the shortcut icon for the application and choose Properties.

2. Select the Program tab and add a question mark to the end of the path in the Cmd Line text box.

3. Choose OK.

Now when you double-click the shortcut, a text box will appear in which you can input the startup parameters for the application.

These startup methods work just like they do for their Windows counterparts.

▶ **See** "Using the Start Menu," **p. 65**, and "Using Windows Explorer to View Files and Folders," **p. 96**

Removing MS-DOS Applications

If you decide to remove your MS-DOS application from your computer, there are two easy ways to do it:

■ Use the MS-DOS Prompt `dir` and `deltree` commands

■ Use Explorer and Recycle Bin

Part
V
Ch
17

> **CAUTION**
>
> Regardless of which technique you use, make sure that you don't have any data stored with the application you're removing. Some applications allow you to store your documents or data files in the same folder as the application code itself. Although this is inherently poor design, it still happens; and if you don't tell the application to save your files to another folder or directory, you may be very sorry after you've deleted the program itself.

Using MS-DOS Commands to Remove an MS-DOS Application

Perhaps the most straightforward way to remove an MS-DOS application is to use the MS-DOS tools themselves. To do this, follow these steps:

1. Open MS-DOS Prompt session from the Start menu.

2. At the MS-DOS prompt, type the command **dir c:*appdir* /p** (where *appdir* is the folder in which your doomed application awaits its final moments). In this example, you'll use **c:\wp60 /p**. The MS-DOS Prompt session displays a folder listing similar to that shown in figure 17.25.

FIG. 17.25

The `dir` command shows the contents of the folder you want to delete. The `/p` switch displays the listing in a page at a time. Simply press any key to continue through the listing.

3. Look for any files that contain your personal data (be sure to check in any subfolders). If necessary, copy or move these files to another location.

4. After you've saved any personal data, delete the application. At the MS-DOS prompt, type **deltree c:*appdir*** (where *appdir* is the folder containing the application to be deleted) and press Enter. MS-DOS displays a message asking you to confirm the deletion. If you're absolutely sure, type **y** and press Enter. MS-DOS deletes the application folder and all subfolders.

▶ **See** "Moving and Copying Files and Folders," **p. 105**

Using Explorer to Remove an MS-DOS Application

An even simpler way to remove an MS-DOS application is to use Explorer and the Recycle Bin. It's really as simple as locating the application folder, checking it for your personal data, and then dragging it to the "trash."

For complete instructions on using Explorer to remove an application, see Chapter 4, "Managing Files."

▶ **See** "Deleting Files and Folders," **p. 107**

Cleaning Up Shortcuts and the Start Menu

Be sure to remove shortcuts to applications after you've removed the application itself. If you don't, Windows will still try to load the application, and ask you to help find it when it can't—a real hassle. If you've placed the shortcut on your Desktop, simply drag it to the Recycle Bin.

If you used the Control Panel Add/Remove Programs feature discussed in Chapter 16 to add the shortcut to the Start menu, just follow the removal steps outlined in that chapter.

ON THE WEB

Check out a shareware utility called Start Clean, written by Firas El-Hasan, which is available at the following Internet site:

http://users.aol.com/felhasan/startcln.htm

This utility scans your system and removes any items in the Start menu folder that are no longer linked to programs.

▶ **See** "Removing Windows Applications," **p. 491**

Part

V

Ch

17

CHAPTER 18

Using Windows 95's Accessories

by Ron Person with Bob Voss

Windows 95 comes with several accessory programs that are useful additions to your usual suite of full-featured applications. WordPad is a word processor that replaces Write, the word processor in earlier versions of Windows. Notepad, a text editor, is still included with Windows 95. Paint is a simple graphics program that will serve the needs of many users for creating, viewing, and editing graphics files. Paint replaces the Paintbrush accessory that came with Windows 3.x. Character Map is a handy accessory that allows you to access the symbol fonts and ANSI characters and insert them into your documents. ■

How to prepare simple word processing documents

You learn to use WordPad for simple, everyday word processing tasks such as creating letters and reports.

How to create and edit bit-mapped images

You learn to use Paint to create and edit pictures that can be inserted into other applications.

How to use special characters in your documents

Here you learn to insert special characters into any Windows document with the Character Map.

Using WordPad

WordPad is a simple but powerful word processor that comes with Windows 95. WordPad offers many of the editing and formatting capabilities—such as cut, copy, and paste—commonly found in more advanced applications, along with the ability to share information with other applications and files using OLE.

WordPad is easy to use. The techniques and features you've learned to use in other word processors—such as how to select commands and how to enter, format, and print text—also work here. Because the margins, a font, and tabs are already set, you can actually begin a new WordPad document as soon as you start the application. WordPad's Help command can assist you if you run up against something new. In this section, you learn a few useful tasks you can accomplish with WordPad.

Starting WordPad

To start WordPad from the desktop, follow these steps:

1. Open the Start menu and choose Programs; then choose Accessories.
2. Choose WordPad. WordPad starts up and displays the WordPad window (see fig. 18.1).

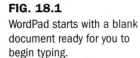

FIG. 18.1
WordPad starts with a blank document ready for you to begin typing.

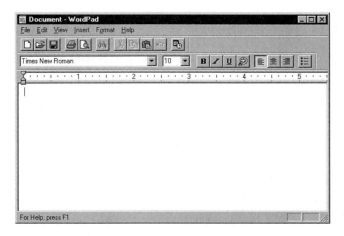

Unlike more robust Windows applications, WordPad does not support MDI (Multiple Document Interface), and therefore can contain only one document at a time. When you open a new blank document you will be asked if you want to save the current document.

TIP Because WordPad is not as resource hungry as "more robust Windows applications," you can open multiple instances of WordPad to edit multiple WordPad documents of different formats, including Word 6.0, ASCII, RTF, and Windows Write.

You can create new documents in any one of three formats in WordPad. When you choose the File, New command, the dialog box shown in figure 18.2 appears. Select one of the following document types:

■ *Word 6 Document.* This format can be opened and edited in Microsoft Word 6.0 or Word for Windows 95 version 7.0. This is handy if you use WordPad on your laptop and Word 6 or Word 7.0 on your desktop.

■ *Rich Text Document.* This format (RTF) is compatible with several word processing programs and includes fonts, tabs, and character formatting. RTF files are also used to create Windows Help files using the Microsoft Help compiler.

■ *Text Document.* This format includes no text formatting and can be used in any word processing program. Use this format for creating DOS batch files.

FIG. 18.2
You can create new documents in any one of three formats.

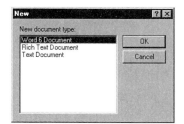

WordPad is an OLE-compliant application, so you can insert objects from other OLE applications into a WordPad document or insert all or part of a WordPad document into an OLE application. You can, for example, insert a graphic created in Windows Paint as an object into a WordPad document and then double-click on the Paint object and edit the graphic in place. The WordPad menus and toolbars are replaced with the Paint menus and toolbars while you edit the object. Use the Insert, Object command or the drag-and-drop method for exchanging information with other OLE applications.

▶ **See** "Benefits of Sharing Data," **p. xxx** (Ch. 19)

WordPad also is MAPI-enabled, which means you can use it with Exchange to send mail and faxes. To mail or fax a document from WordPad, choose the File, Send command.

Part
V

Ch
18

You can drag and drop files and folders from any common File Open dialog box (including WordPad's) into Explorer, onto the desktop, or into any OLE-compliant application such as Word 7.0 for Windows 95. You can, for example, insert a WordPad document into a Word 7 document by dragging it from the File Open dialog box in WordPad and dropping it into the Word document where you want it to be inserted.

TROUBLESHOOTING

When I try to save a file in WordPad with a nondefault extension, WordPad appends the file name with the DOC extension. When you save a file with an extension that is not associated with an application in the Registry, WordPad appends the default DOC extension to the file name. In Notepad, the default extension TXT is appended to the file name. To avoid this, enclose the file name in quotation marks.

I am unable to print multiple or collated copies from WordPad. These features are unavailable in the File Print dialog box. WordPad does not support multiple or collated printing. Unless these features are supported with the printer driver for your printer, you cannot print multiple or collated copies from WordPad.

I selected a block of text in a WordPad document and tried to print just the selection, but the <u>S</u>election option is unavailable in the File Print dialog box. Although this option is shown in the File Print dialog box, the capability to print selected text is not supported in WordPad. To work around this limitation, copy the text to a new WordPad document and print that document.

Using WordPad to Create and Edit System, Batch, and Text Files

WordPad is very useful for creating and editing TXT and system files (files with the extensions BAT, SYS, INI, and so on), especially when the file in question is too large for Notepad. When you open a SYS, INI, BAT, or TXT file in WordPad, edit or view it, and then resave it, it is saved with its original file extension. This feature eliminates any worry about inadvertently saving a system file with the wrong extension, as can happen in a regular word processing program. And, WordPad provides more features (such as the Replace command) for editing your files than does Notepad.

To create a new text file in WordPad, choose <u>F</u>ile, <u>N</u>ew and select Text Document in the New dialog box. When you save the document, it is given the TXT extension automatically. If necessary, change the extension, for example, to BAT for a DOS batch file.

 Create a shortcut for WordPad in the SendTo folder so you can quickly open any file with WordPad from Explorer or a folder window.

▶ **See** "Using the Send To Command for Frequent Operations," **p. 90**

You can change the association for TXT files so that they open in WordPad instead of Notepad when you double-click on them or choose Open in the context menu in Explorer or My Computer. To change the association, follow these steps:

1. Choose Ⅴiew, Ⅺptions in Explorer or My Computer and select the File Types tab.

2. Select Text Document from the Registered File Ⅺypes list.

3. Choose Ⅺdit, select open in the Ⅺctions list of the Edit File Type dialog box and choose Ⅺdit.

4. Choose the Bⅼowse button and locate and select WORDPAD.EXE, which is located in the Program Files\Accessories folder.

5. Choose OK and make sure that .txt is selected in the Default Eⅺtension for Content list.

6. Choose Close twice.

Creating Post-it Notes on Your Desktop

Because WordPad is an OLE 2-compliant application you can drag and drop selected portions of a WordPad document into other OLE applications or onto the desktop. When you drag a selection onto the desktop, you create a scrap; double-click the icon for the scrap, and WordPad opens up and displays the information in the scrap. You can use these scraps as electronic Post-it notes—bits of information you might otherwise lose track of, secured to your desktop.

If you create desktop notes frequently, for example, while on the phone, you can add WordPad to your StartUp folder so that it is immediately available. Or, simply create a shortcut on the desktop to WordPad.

To create a note on your desktop, follow these steps:

1. Open WordPad and create the note.

2. Select the note and drag and drop it on the desktop. The scrap appears as a desktop icon, labeled with the first few words of the note. The data is saved as a file in the desktop folder.

You can rename the scrap. Note that you don't have to save the note in WordPad. Whenever you double-click the scrap icon, the note is opened in WordPad. If you make changes, however, you do need to save the changes—the scrap file isn't saved automatically.

T I P If a Word for Windows file will not open, try opening it in WordPad. If it opens, you may see symbols and characters you do not recognize. Start a new instance of Word for Windows and open a blank document. Base this new document on the same template as the document that would not open. Now return to WordPad and copy the entire document. Switch to the blank document in Word and paste. Reapply paragraph styles as necessary. WordPad seems to be able to open documents that contain file errors that make Word balk.

Using Notepad

Notepad is a miniature text editor. Just as you use a notepad on your desk, you can use Notepad to take notes on-screen while working in other Windows applications. Notepad uses little memory and is useful for editing text that you want to copy to a Windows or DOS application that lacks editing capability.

Notepad retrieves and saves files in text format. This feature makes Notepad a convenient editor for creating and altering text-based files. Because Notepad stores files in text format, almost all word processing applications can retrieve Notepad's files.

Use Notepad to hold text you want to move to another application. Clipboard can hold only one selection at a time, but Notepad can serve as a text scrapbook when you are moving several items as a group.

Starting Notepad

To start Notepad, follow these steps:

1. Open the Start menu and choose Programs; then choose Accessories.
2. Choose Notepad. Notepad starts up and displays a blank document in the Notepad window (see fig. 18.3). You can begin typing.

FIG. 18.3
The initial blank Notepad file is ready for text.

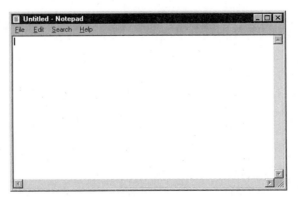

Working with Documents in Notepad

Unlike most word processing applications, Notepad doesn't by default wrap text to the following line. You must choose Edit, Word Wrap to activate this feature.

You can move the insertion point by using either the mouse or the keyboard. You select and edit text in Notepad the same way you select and edit text in WordPad.

Limited formatting is available from the File, Page Setup command. You can change margins and add a header or footer. You cannot format characters or paragraphs in any way, although you can use Tab, the spacebar, and backspace to align text. Tab stops are preset at every eight characters.

With Notepad's Edit commands, you can cut, copy, and move text from one place in a file to another. Text you cut or copy is stored in the Clipboard. When you paste text, this text is copied from the Clipboard to the document at the insertion point.

▶ **See** "Cutting, Copying and Pasting Data," **p. 557**

Creating a Time-Log File with Notepad

By typing a simple entry at the top of a Notepad document, **.LOG**, you can have Notepad enter the current time and date at the end of a document each time you open the file. This feature is convenient for taking phone messages or for calculating the time spent on a project. The text .LOG must be entered on the first line of the document, and must be uppercase. As an alternative, you can choose Edit, Time/Date or press F5 to insert the current time and date at the insertion point.

 TIP Notepad can open binary files, which WordPad cannot. Although most of what you see when you open binary files is unreadable, you can sometimes find helpful information in the header of the binary file. This is a good reason to keep Notepad on your computer, even if WordPad is more suitable for most tasks.

Using Windows Paint

Paint is simple, and easy-to-use, but it may be as powerful a graphics application as you will ever need. With Paint, you can create everything from free-flowing drawings to precise mathematical charts, and you can use your creations in other Windows applications, such as WordPad or Word.

Here are some of the graphic effects you can create with Paint:

- Lines in many widths, shades, and colors
- Brush strokes in a variety of styles, widths, shades, and colors
- Unfilled or filled shapes with shades or colors
- Text in many sizes, styles, and colors
- Special effects such as rotating, tilting, and inverting

Because Paint is a bit-map graphics application, the shapes you create are painted on-screen in one layer. Although you can't layer objects, you can move, flip, and tilt them. You also can change the color of your painting, or erase it completely and paint something new.

Starting Windows Paint

To start Paint, open the Start menu, and choose Programs, Accessories, Paint. Paint starts up and opens a new, empty Paint file (see fig. 18.4).

FIG. 18.4
When you start Paint, a new file opens.

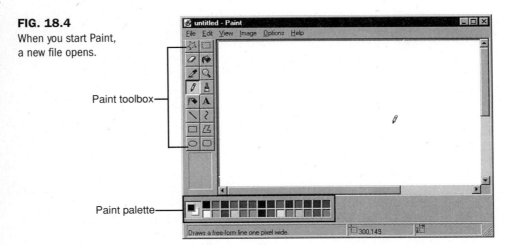

Paint toolbox

Paint palette

To open a previously saved Paint file, choose File, Open. Select the file from the Open dialog box.

T I P Paint can be used to view any PCX or BMP file. If you add Paint to the \Windows\SendTo folder, you can quickly open Paint and view a file from Explorer or My Computer. You can then edit the file in Paint.

Selecting Tools and Colors

To paint, draw, fill, color or shade, write, and edit in Paint, you first must select the appropriate tool and shade or color. Figure 18.5 shows the individual tools in the toolbox located on the left side of the screen.

FIG. 18.5

The Paint toolbox provides the tools you need to create and modify a picture.

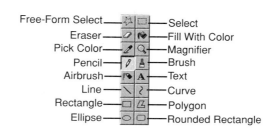

Free-Form Select ——— ——— Select
Eraser ——— ——— Fill With Color
Pick Color ——— ——— Magnifier
Pencil ——— ——— Brush
Airbrush ——— ——— Text
Line ——— ——— Curve
Rectangle ——— ——— Polygon
Ellipse ——— ——— Rounded Rectangle

The palette offers two choices: foreground and background shade or color. At the left end of the palette (see fig. 18.6) is a box overlaying a box. The *top* box is the *foreground* color; the *bottom* box is the *background* color. The color you use depends on which mouse button you use to draw lines, brush strokes, and shapes. The left mouse button draws with the foreground color; the right mouse button draws with the background color. For example, when you draw a shaded box with the left mouse button, the foreground color borders the box and the background color fills the box. If you draw with the right mouse button, the foreground and background colors are reversed. (Drawing is discussed in the next section, "Using the Paint Toolbox.")

FIG. 18.6

Choose foreground and background colors from the Paint palette.

┌Foreground color (left mouse button)

└Background color (right mouse button)

To select a tool or color, position the pointer on the tool or foreground color that you want and click the left mouse button. To select a background color, point to the color you want and click the right mouse button. You must use the left button when selecting a tool; the right mouse button can't be used to select a tool.

Using the Paint Toolbox

The Paint toolbox includes tools for selecting areas, airbrushing, typing text, erasing, filling, brushing, drawing curves or straight lines, and drawing filled or unfilled shapes. Most of the tools operate using a similar process, as described in the following steps.

Part

V

Ch

18

To draw with the tools in the Paint toolbox, follow these steps:

1. Click the tool you want to use.
2. Position the pointer where you want to begin drawing, then press and hold down the mouse button as you draw with the mouse.
3. Release the mouse button to stop drawing.

Three exceptions to this process are

- The Text tool, which you first click to select the text location, and then type the text.
- The Paint Fill tool, which works by pointing and clicking.
- The Curve tool, which works by clicking, dragging, and clicking.

Aligning Drawn Objects   When you want lines or shapes to line up accurately on-screen, refer to the cursor position indicators in the status bar at the bottom of Paint's window. The two numbers that display tell you the position of the insertion point or drawing tool on-screen. The position is given in X, Y coordinates, measured in pixels, from the top left corner of the painting. The left number is the X-coordinate (the position relative to the left edge of the painting); the right number is the Y-coordinate (the position relative to the top of the painting). If the numbers in the Cursor Position window read 42, 100, for example, the cursor is 42 pixels from the left edge of the painting and 100 pixels down from the top of the painting.

Whichever tool you use, Edit, Undo is a useful ally. Use it to undo your most recent action. Undo undoes up to the last three actions. Just continue to select Undo to undo the number of actions you desire.

TROUBLESHOOTING

When I select the Undo command to undo a procedure I am in the middle of completing, the current procedure as well as the previous action are reversed. This is a bug in Paint. If you don't complete an action and you try to undo it, the previous action, as well as the current, incomplete action will be undone. You can reverse the action that was undone by choosing the Edit, Repeat command.

Several tools, including the Selection and Shape tools, use the right mouse button to undo. To cancel the shape you're currently drawing, click the right mouse button *before* you release the left mouse button.

The following sections describe how to use each of the toolbox tools.

 Selecting a Free-Form Area   The Free-Form Select tool enables you to select an area by drawing a free-form boundary. Click the Free-Form Select tool, then select either the Transparent (doesn't include the background) or Opaque (does include the background) tool at the bottom of the toolbox. Draw any shape to enclose an area of the drawing. If you make a mistake while using the Free-Form Select tool, click the left mouse button outside the cutout area to cancel the cutout and try again. Once enclosed, an area can be moved, cut or copied (and then pasted), resized, tilted, flipped, or inverted with the Edit menu commands. If you cut an area, the selected background color shows the color the cleared area will be. With an area selected, press Delete to delete it from the picture.

 Selecting a Rectangular Area   The Select tool enables you to select an area by dragging a rectangular box. Follow the instructions for the Free-Form Select tool to use this tool.

 Erasing Parts of Your Picture   The Eraser tool erases as you drag it over your picture, just like an eraser on a chalkboard. Click the Eraser tool and then select the eraser size from the bottom of the toolbox. Drag across the picture with the left mouse button pressed to erase. The selected background color shows the color the erased area will be. Choose Edit, Undo if you want to restore what you have erased.

 Filling an Area with Color   The Fill With Color tool fills in a shape. Click the Fill With Color tool and select foreground and background colors from the palette. Position the pointed tip of the Fill With Color tool inside the shape that you want to fill. Click the left mouse button to fill with the foreground color, or the right mouse button to fill with the background color.

Part
V

Ch
18

 TIP You can use the Options, Edit Colors command to create a custom color palette from Paint's 48 colors or from colors you define by choosing the Define Custom Colors button in the Edit Colors dialog box.

 TROUBLESHOOTING

I created a custom color palette, but when I try to use the colors in this palette to edit a 256-color bitmap, different colors than those I selected from the palette appear in the picture. This is a known bug in Paint with no current workaround. You have to use the standard color palette to edit 256-color bitmaps.

Picking Up a Color from the Drawing   The Pick Color tool picks up the color on which you click for use in the current tool. To pick up the color of the spot where you click, click the Pick Color tool and then click anywhere in the painting. You can resume using the previous tool or select another tool and paint with the new color.

 Magnifying the View of the Drawing   The Magnifier tool magnifies the view of the drawing. Click the Magnifier tool and then select a magnification value at the bottom of the toolbox (1x, 2x, 6x, or 8x). Position the rectangle over the area you want to enlarge and click the left mouse button. You can work with the individual pixels that make up the painting. You can use any of the tools in the magnified view.

 Drawing a Free-Form Line   The Pencil tool draws a one pixel-wide free-form line in the currently selected color. Draw with the left mouse button pressed to use the foreground color; draw with the right mouse button pressed to draw with the background color.

 Painting with a Brush   The Brush tool provides a selection of brush shapes with which you can paint lines of various widths and shapes. Click the Brush tool button and select from the brush shapes that display at the bottom of the toolbox. Paint with the left mouse button pressed to use the foreground color; paint with the right mouse button pressed to use the background color.

 Painting with an Airbrush   The Airbrush tool paints with a mist of color; the more densely you spray, the heavier your coverage. Click the Airbrush tool and select from the sprayer sizes that display at the bottom of the toolbox. Select a color from the Color palette. The left mouse button sprays with the foreground color; the right mouse button sprays with the background color. Hold the tool in one position longer to spray more densely.

 Adding Text to a Picture   Use the Text tool to add text to your painting. Click the Text tool and, in the area below the toolbox, select Opaque (the background color fills the text box behind the text) or Transparent (the picture appears behind the text). Next, in the picture area, drag to determine the size of the text box. Choose View, Text Toolbar to turn on the display of the Font toolbar (only required the first time you use the Text tool). Select a font, point size, and bold, italic, or underline options. Click in the text box and type. Use the limited set of editing tools, including word-wrap and backspace. Text appears in the foreground color.

 TIP   If your painting will include a lot of text, type the text in Word or WordPad, select and copy it, and then paste it into Paint.

TROUBLESHOOTING

The Text toolbar is not available from the View menu. You must click the Text tool and drag a text area before the Text toolbar is available from the View menu.

An error message appears saying that I need to resize the text box. The text box isn't large enough to hold the text you are pasting into it. Enlarge the box and try again.

I was in the middle of typing text into a Paint picture and I opened Help. The text disappeared and did not reappear when I closed Help. There are a few problems that occur when you open Help in Paint:

- If you open Help when you are using the Text tool, the text disappears.

- If you have selected a portion of a picture with the Select or Free Form Select tools, the selection is lost when you open Help.

- If you are using the Curve or Polygon tools to edit a picture, you will lose what you have created with the tools when you open Help.

One workaround for these problems is to save the picture before you open Help and reopen the saved image after you've closed Help. Or you can click elsewhere in the picture or select another tool to set the element that you were working on before you open Help. Selections made with the selection tools cannot be preserved when you open Help.

 Drawing a Straight Line The Line tool draws a straight line. Click the Line tool and select a line width from the display at the bottom of the toolbox. Drag the mouse to draw a straight line. To cancel the line that you're drawing, click the right mouse button before you release the left mouse button. If you're drawing with the right mouse button, click the left button to cancel the line. To draw a line that is perfectly vertical, horizontal, or at a 45-degree angle, press and hold down the Shift key as you draw.

 Drawing Curves The Curve tool draws a curve. To draw a curve, follow these steps:

1. Click the Curve tool.

2. Select a line width from the display at the bottom of the toolbox.

3. Draw a straight line and release the mouse button.

4. Click the left mouse button and drag away from the line to pull the line into a curve.

5. When you've achieved the shape you want, release the mouse button to complete the line. Repeat the process on the other side of the line to create an *s*-shaped curve.

Drawing Rectangles and Squares   The Rectangle tool draws a rectangle or square with different borders or fill color. Click the Rectangle tool and select Border Only, Border and Fill, or Fill Only from the bottom of the toolbox. To create the size box you want, press and hold down the mouse button and drag to that size. Release the mouse button when you have the size you want. Use the left mouse button to border with the foreground color and fill with the background color; use the right mouse button to border with the background color and fill with the foreground color. The size of the border is determined by the last line size you selected.

T I P   To draw a square, select the Rectangle tool, then press and hold down the Shift key as you draw.

 Drawing Objects with Many Sides (Polygons)   The Polygon tool draws a multisided shape. Each side on the shape is a straight line. To draw a polygon, follow these steps:

1. Click the Polygon tool and select Border Only, Border and Fill, or Fill Only from the bottom of the toolbox.
2. Click and drag to draw the first side of the polygon. As with the Line tool, you can use the Shift key to draw a straight line segment for the polygon.
3. Release the mouse button and click to draw other sides of the polygon.
4. Double-click at the next to last vertex point to finish and close the polygon to its first point.

 Drawing Ellipses and Circles   The Ellipse tool draws an *ellipse* (an oval) or circle. Click the Ellipse tool and select Border Only, Border and Fill, or Fill Only from the bottom of the toolbox. To draw a circle, press and hold down the Shift key as you draw.

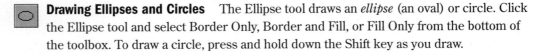 **Drawing Rectangles with Rounded Corners**   Use the Rounded Rectangle tool to draw a rectangle with rounded edges. Click the Rounded Rectangle tool and select Border Only, Border and Fill, or Fill Only from the bottom of the toolbox. Press and hold down the mouse button and drag to create the size rectangle you want. Release the mouse button when you have the size you want.

Editing a Painting

As you edit, be aware that completed objects cannot be edited, only erased or painted over and replaced. You can edit any object while creating it, but not after you complete the object. The method that you use to complete an object depends on the object. To complete a straight line, for example, you *release* the mouse button; to complete text, you *click* the mouse button or select another tool. You can cancel a line or curve before you complete it, for example, by clicking the opposite mouse button; you can change the appearance of text *before* you complete it by making a selection from the Text toolbar.

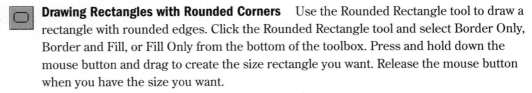

The following paragraphs describe how to use each of the Edit menu commands.

 To undo changes, choose Edit, Undo (or press Ctrl+Z). Choose Edit, Undo again to continue undoing as many as three previous changes.

 Conversely, you can choose Edit, Repeat (or press F4) to redo the last change you made with the Edit, Undo command. Repeat only affects the previous Undo operation, and can't be used to repeat drawing operations.

▶ **See** "Using the Clipboard to Exchange Data," **p. 567**

Using the Clipboard   Use Edit, Cut, or Edit, Copy to remove or copy part of a painting and place it into the Clipboard. Use Edit, Paste to place a copy of the contents of the Clipboard into your painting. Display the area of the painting where you want to paste the contents of the Clipboard and choose Edit, Paste (Ctrl+V). The pasted object appears at the top left of the screen and is enclosed by a dotted line to show that the object is still selected. Drag the selection to the location you want and click outside it.

Removing a Selected Object or Area   Select the area you want to remove. Choose Edit, Clear Selection or press the Delete key and it is deleted from the painting. This option does not place the selected object into the Clipboard.

Copying Part of Your Painting to a File   Use Edit, Copy To to save a portion of your painting in a file. Select the portion of the painting you want to save to a file. Open the Edit menu and choose Copy To. Give the file a name (use the appropriate file extension, such as PCX, for the graphics file you're creating), select a directory or another drive, and click OK.

Pasting a File into Your Painting   Use the Edit, Paste From command to insert a file into your painting. Use the Rectangular Select tool to select the area of the painting into which you want to paste the file. Choose the Edit, Paste From command. Type the file name, select a directory or another drive, and click OK. The file is pasted in the top-left corner of the screen. Drag it to a new location.

Many of the commands described in the preceding sections are also available from a shortcut menu. When you select a portion of your painting with either of the Select tools and click the right mouse button, a context menu appears.

Moving a Selection   You can move an object or area on-screen after you select it. (The object is still selected if you just pasted it.) Paint has several tricks for moving selections.

Part V

Ch 18

To move a selection, follow these steps:

1. Use one of the Select tools to select an object or area of the drawing. Select either Transparent (to leave the background showing) or Opaque (to hide the background). A dashed line encloses the selection.

2. Move the crosshair over the selection. The crosshair becomes an arrow.

3. Press and hold down the left mouse button to drag the selection to its new location. To copy the selection to a new location rather than move it, hold down the Ctrl key as you drag the object to its new location.

4. Release the mouse button to place the selection, then click outside the selection to fix it in its new location.

Getting Different Views of the Painting   You can zoom in to get a closer look at your painting or zoom out to see the whole page. Use either the View, Zoom command or the Magnifier tool.

The larger magnifications of the picture display the *pixels*, or tiny squares of color, that make up your painting. You can paint pixels in the selected foreground color by clicking the dots with the left mouse button, and in the background color by clicking the right mouse button.

To zoom in for a close-up view of your painting, follow these steps:

1. Choose View, Zoom. Select Normal Size (Ctrl+Page Up), Large Size (Ctrl+Page Down), or Custom. If you select Custom, the View Zoom dialog box appears. Select 100%, 200%, 400%, 600%, or 800%.

2. Use the scroll bars to display the part of the painting you want to see.

To zoom back out to regular editing view, choose View, Zoom and select Normal Size. Or, click the Magnifier tool and then click in the picture.

You can choose View, View Bitmap (Ctrl+F) when you are in the regular view to display a reduced picture of the entire page. When you choose View, View Bitmap, all toolboxes, menus, and scroll bars disappear, and your picture expands to fill the window. You can only view in this mode; you cannot edit your painting in Picture mode. Click anywhere in the display to return to normal size.

With an enlarged view of your picture, you can choose to add a grid for more exact drawing. Choose View, Zoom, Show Grid (Ctrl+G). You also can add a thumbnail, which is a small display of the portion of the drawing that has been enlarged. Choose View, Zoom, Show Thumbnail.

You also can switch the Tool Box, Color Box, and Status Bar on or off using the View menu.

Creating Special Effects

Using the Image menu, you can flip, stretch, invert the colors of, shrink, enlarge, or tilt objects you select. You can apply these commands to the entire painting or to selected portions.

 TIP Select the area you want to flip, rotate, stretch, or skew. Place the pointer over it, and click the right mouse button to display a shortcut menu.

Clearing the Painting

The Clear Image command is used to clear the screen of all painting you've done without saving or exiting.

TROUBLESHOOTING

I tried to clear my screen of the current contents, but the Image, Clear Image command is unavailable. The Clear Image command is unavailable if the Text tool is selected. Select any other tool and the command is available.

There's one drawn object in the picture, a circle, that needs to be resized. But there doesn't seem to be a way to change that circle after other objects are drawn. Paint is a bitmap drawing program. When you draw, you change the dots of color on the screen. After you complete the object you are drawing, it becomes part of the screen's pattern, and you can't resize or recolor it. Drawing programs that are object-based enable you to select the individual items that have been drawn and edit them. Items also can be grouped together to act as a single object. There are many standalone object-based drawing programs. Some applications, such as Excel and Word, include object-based drawing tools so you can draw within their documents.

 TIP You can change the appearance of the desktop directly from Paint with File, Set as Wallpaper (Tiled) or Set as Wallpaper (Centered). Select Tiled to repeat the painting over the entire desktop, or Centered to display it once in the center of the desktop.

 TIP To use your painting or part of your painting as wallpaper, follow these steps:

- Display the painting you want to use as wallpaper.
- If you want to use only part of the painting on the desktop, select that part.
- Choose File, Set as Wallpaper (Tiled) to repeat the painting as a pattern over the desktop, or Set as Wallpaper (Centered) to display the painting in the center of the desktop.

Setting Up the Page

Page setup choices affect your printed paintings. You can choose either portrait or landscape paper orientation, change margins, select the size and location of the paper, and select a new printer. To set up your page for printing, choose File, Page Setup, make your selections, and click OK.

▶ **See** "Configuring Your Printer," **p. 232**

Saving Paint Files

When you save a Paint file, Paint assigns the extension BMP to the file name and saves the file in Windows bitmap format.

To save a Paint file, follow these steps:

1. Choose File, Save As.
2. Type a name in the File Name text box and select the directory where you want to save the file from the Directories box.
3. Click the Save As Type box to select one of the following file formats:

Format	File Extension Assigned
Monochrome Bitmap	BMP
16 Color Bitmap	BMP
256 Color Bitmap	BMP
24-bit Bitmap	BMP

4. Choose Save or press Enter.

To resave your file later without changing its name, choose File, Save.

TROUBLESHOOTING

Many graphics files seem to use PCX format, but Paint won't save this format. Paint saves only with the BMP format. You can open PCX files with Paint, but if you want to make any changes and resave the file, you will have to save it as a BMP file. One way you can work around this is to use Microsoft Paintbrush from Windows 3.1 within Windows 95. You can copy the files PBRUSH.EXE, PBRUSH.DLL, PBRUSH.HLP, and PBRUSHX.CDX from the Windows directory in Windows 3.1 into a Windows 95 folder. You can create a new folder within the Programs folder called Paintbrush. With Paintbrush you can open and save PCX files.

You may want to convert your PCX files to BMP format. Microsoft has a graphics converter available, and there are many free converters available through bulletin board services.

Previewing and Printing Paint Files

Paint provides a preview screen where you can see your painting as it will appear in print. Paint gives you great flexibility in printing paintings.

Previewing Your Paintings   When a painting seems complete, you can check its appearance on the page. To preview a painting, choose File, Print Preview. Click the buttons to display the view you want, then click Close to return to the painting, or click Print to display the Print dialog box.

Printing a Painting   You can print all or part of a painting, in draft or final quality, scaled smaller or larger. Before you print, be sure that you have the correct printer selected and set up.

To select and set up a printer and print your document, follow these steps:

1. Choose File, Print. The Print dialog box appears (see fig. 18.7).

FIG. 18.7
Use the Print dialog box
to select a printer.

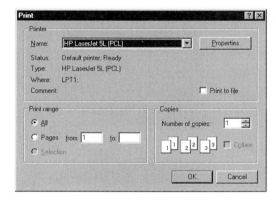

Part
V

Ch
18

2. Select a printer from the Name list.

    After a printer is selected, it remains selected for all documents—you won't have to select a printer again unless you want to change to a different printer.

3. Click the Properties button to make additional choices, such as paper type and graphics quality. Click OK.

4. Select the Print Range All to print all the pages; select Print Range Selection to print only the selected range (including non-text objects), or select the Pages From and To text boxes and type a range of pages to print.

5. Type the number of copies you want to print in the Number of Copies box.

6. Select the Collate check box to collate multiple copies of the document (this option is available if your printer supports collating).

7. Click OK.

▶ **See** "Configuring Your Printer," **p. 232**

 T I P The two screens you see when you shut down Windows are actually BMP files named LOGOW.SYS and LOGOS.SYS. You can customize either of these screens by creating a picture in Paint and giving them one of these two file names. Be sure to rename and save the original files in case you want to revert to them at some point. Both files are located in the Windows folder.

Inserting Symbols with Character Map

The Character Map accessory gives you access to symbol fonts and ANSI characters. *ANSI characters* include the regular character set that you see on the keyboard and more than a hundred other characters, including a copyright symbol, a registered trademark symbol, and many foreign-language characters. One symbol font, Symbol, is included with most Windows applications. Other symbol fonts may be built into the printer. When you set up and indicate the model of the printer, font cartridges, and so on, the printer tells Windows what symbol fonts are available. (Printer fonts appear in Character Map only when they include a matching screen font.)

To start Character Map, open the Start menu and click Programs, then click Accessories. Finally, click Character Map. You are presented with the Character Map window shown in figure 18.8.

FIG. 18.8
Use Character Map to insert any of hundreds of special characters and symbols characters.

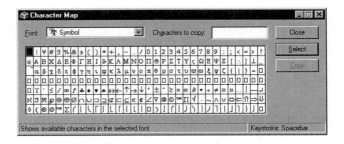

▶ **See** "Creating Shortcuts to Programs or Documents," **p. 72**
▶ **See** "Installing and Deleting Fonts," **p. 274**

The Character Map window includes a drop-down Font list box, from which you can select any of the available fonts on the system. After you select a font, the characters and symbols for this font appear in the Character Map table. Each set of fonts might have different symbols. Some fonts, such as Symbol and Zapf Dingbats, contain nothing but symbols and special characters.

To insert a character in a Windows application from the Character Map, follow these steps:

1. Start the Character Map accessory.
2. Select the font you want to use from the Font list.
3. View an enlarged character by clicking and holding down the mouse button on a character or by moving the selection box over a character by pressing the arrow keys.
4. Double-click the character you want to insert or click the Select button to place the current character in the Characters to Copy text box.
5. Repeat steps 2 through 4 to select as many characters as you want.
6. Click the Copy button to copy the characters you've selected to the Clipboard.
7. Open or switch to the application you want to copy the character(s) to.
8. Place the insertion point where you want to insert the character(s) and open the Edit menu and choose Paste (Ctrl+V).

If the characters don't appear as they did in Character Map, you may need to reselect the characters and change the font to the same font in which the character originally appeared in the Character Map. ●

Part

V

Ch

18

P A R T

VI

Sharing Data Effectively

CHAPTER 19

Simple Ways of Sharing Data Between Applications

by Rob Tidrow with Bob Voss

You can share data from one document or application to another because Windows has *data-exchange* capabilities (also called *data sharing*). These capabilities are as simple as cutting or copying a piece of text from one program to another, and as complex as editing a piece of data in one application that you created in another application. The latter operation, known as *in-place editing*, is a component of OLE, which is discussed in Chapter 20, "Creating Compound Documents with OLE."

Cutting, copying, and pasting are simple operations that make you more efficient in Windows. Although many experienced Windows users are familiar with the data-sharing techniques detailed in this chapter, no discussion of the Windows operating system is complete without mention of them. ∎

How to use the Windows Clipboard and Clipboard Viewer

Learn to transfer information via the Clipboard from one location to another, both within and between applications.

How to use drag and drop to move text, data, and graphics within an application

Here you learn a second method for moving information from one location to another within an application.

How to transfer data with DOS applications

Learn how to transfer information between DOS and Windows applications, and how to copy text from the DOS command line into the Clipboard.

How to transfer data using file converters

Turn here to learn about a third method for transferring information between application.

How to link information between two locations

Learn how to create a link between information located in two documents so that information modified in the source document is automatically updated in the destination document.

Understanding the Data-Sharing Capabilities of Windows 95

Windows 95 supports three types of data exchange: the Clipboard, dynamic data exchange (DDE), and object linking and embedding (OLE). All Windows applications provide some means of sharing data with another application. All applications, for example, have access to the Windows Clipboard, to which you can copy or cut data. Not all Windows applications, however, have DDE or OLE capability.

By sharing data from one source to another, you tap into the strength of a computer in helping automate redundant tasks.

Data-sharing capabilities also enable users to create more powerful, more informative, and more advanced documents. Many applications that adhere to Windows 95 standards let you copy an element from one type of application and use it in another application. You can, for example, create a picture from Paint and use it in a WordPad document, as shown in figure 19.1.

FIG. 19.1
This picture was copied from Paint into WordPad.

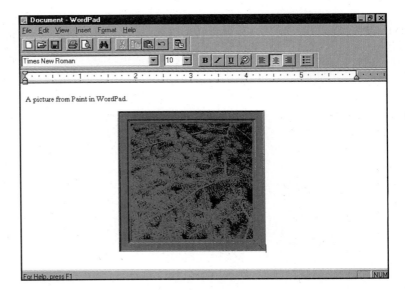

Using the Windows Clipboard

The most basic way to exchange data from one source to another is to use the Windows 95 Clipboard, an area in memory that applications can access to share data. When you use the Clipboard, you *cut* and *copy* data to the Clipboard and then *paste* that data in your document.

Copying places a replica of the material that you selected in the Clipboard. Cutting removes the data from your document and places it in the Clipboard. Pasting places the data from the Clipboard into your document.

N O T E When you paste data from the Clipboard, you don't remove it from the Clipboard. You can paste the data from the Clipboard into your document as many times as you like. The Clipboard retains your cut or copied data until you clear the contents manually, or until you cut or copy something else to the Clipboard. ■

Cutting, Copying, and Pasting Data

Applications that let you access the Clipboard generally use standard menu commands or keyboard shortcuts. In many Windows 95 applications, you can transfer data to and from the Clipboard by choosing commands from the Edit menu.

To cut or copy something from a WordPad document, follow these steps:

1. Select the text in the document that you want to cut or copy, as shown in figure 19.2.

FIG. 19.2
Select the text you want to cut in the source document.

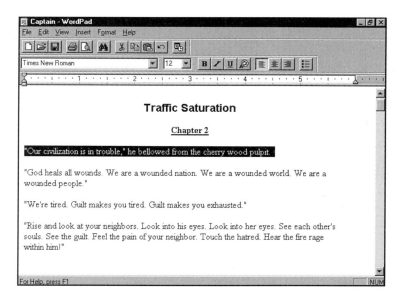

Part
VI

Ch
19

2. Choose Edit, Cut to cut the text to the Clipboard, or choose Edit, Copy to copy the text to the Clipboard.

In many cases, you also can right-click the selection to display a shortcut menu and choose Cut or Copy from the menu.

Now that you have something in the Clipboard, you can paste that element elsewhere in the document, or into another document entirely. To paste, follow these steps:

1. Position your cursor at the place in the document where you want to paste the element (if you're copying to a document in another program, open that program and document, then position the cursor).

2. Choose <u>E</u>dit, <u>P</u>aste to paste the contents of the Clipboard into its new location, Figure 19.3 shows WordPad text pasted into a Paint drawing.

FIG. 19.3
Pasting text from a WordPad document into a Paint drawing.

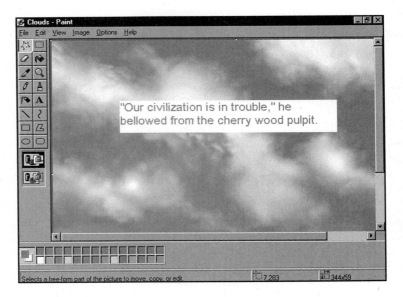

Another standard way to use the Clipboard is to use the buttons in an application's toolbar. Figure 19.4 shows the Cut, Copy, and Paste buttons on the WordPad toolbar.

 Quick View Plus is an add-on product for Windows 95 created by Inso Corporation. Quick View Plus enhances the Quick View feature that comes with Windows 95 in several ways. These include the capabilities to preview many more types of files, and to copy and paste information from a file that you are viewing. This feature allows you to view a file created by an application you don't have on your computer and then to copy and paste information from that file into another document.

For more information on Quick View Plus, contact Inso Corporation at (312) 329-0700. You can download a trialware version of the program from the Internet at the following address:

http://www.inso.com

FIG. 19.4
Cut, Copy, and Paste buttons provided in the WordPad toolbar.

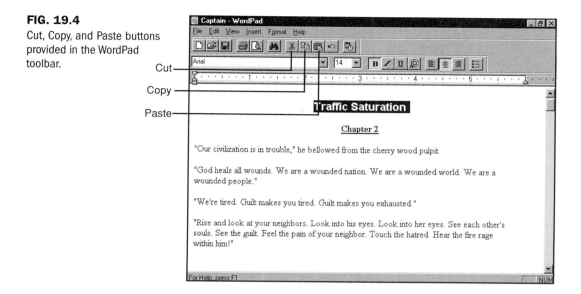

Using Keyboard Shortcuts

Windows 95 supports a common set of keyboard shortcuts that, unless the shortcut has been reassigned, you can use in any application that supports data sharing. Table 19.1 shows these shortcuts.

Part
VI
Ch
19

Table 19.1   Cut, Copy, and Paste Keyboard Shortcuts

Action	Windows 95 Shortcut Keys
Cut	Ctrl+X or Shift+Delete
Copy	Ctrl+C or Ctrl+Insert
Paste	Ctrl+V or Shift+Insert

Copying Information to a Dialog Box

You can use a keyboard shortcut to help you fill in a dialog box. The Letter Wizard dialog box shown in figure 19.5 is requesting your name and address and the recipient's name and address. You can type the information or copy it from somewhere else, if the information is available. For this example, assume that you have the recipient's name and address stored in a Notepad document and that you want to copy and paste that information into the dialog box.

FIG. 19.5

You can cut or copy information to Windows 95 dialog boxes and wizards.

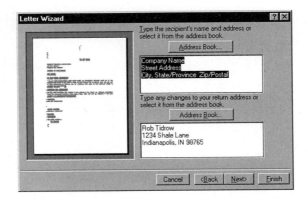

To copy information from the Notepad document to the Word Letter Wizard dialog box, follow these steps:

1. Select the information that you'll replace.

2. Switch to the open Notepad document by clicking the button in the taskbar at the bottom of the screen.

3. In the Notepad window, select the information that you want to copy, as shown in figure 19.6.

FIG. 19.6

Highlight text in the Notepad document to copy to the Clipboard.

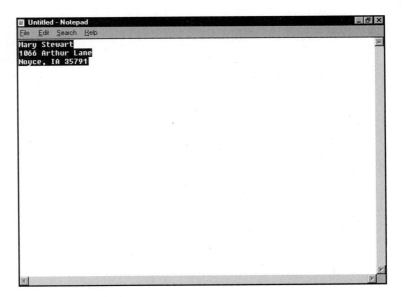

4. To copy the highlighted text, choose Edit, Copy, or press Ctrl+C.

5. Click the Word button on the taskbar to return to the Letter Wizard dialog box in Word. The old entry in the recipient's text box should still be highlighted.

6. Press Ctrl+V to paste the information from the Clipboard to the text box. Figure 19.7 shows the completed text box.

FIG. 19.7
The information from the Clipboard is pasted into the text box.

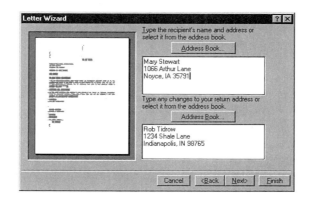

N O T E   You can't use the Edit menu or any button on a toolbar while you're in this dialog box. The only way to copy from the Clipboard is to press Ctrl+V or Shift+Insert. The same holds true when you're trying to cut or copy from a dialog box. Press Ctrl+X to cut or Ctrl+C to copy highlighted text in a text box. ■

Capturing Screens with the Clipboard

Many Windows screen-capturing programs are available, but you also can use the Clipboard to capture the contents of the screen. When the screen image is captured, it's held in the Clipboard in bitmap format.

To capture the entire screen and paste it into a WordPad document, follow these steps:

 TIP   You also can capture the contents of the active window on-screen by pressing Alt+Print Screen or Shift+Print Screen, depending on your keyboard.

1. Press the Print Screen key to capture the entire screen and place it in the Clipboard.

2. Open or switch to WordPad.

3. In a new or existing document, choose Edit, Paste. The screen image, in bitmap format, is pasted into the WordPad document.

   ▶ **See** "Using Windows Paint," **p. 537**

Using the Clipboard Viewer

Windows 95 includes a utility called the *Clipboard Viewer*, which allows you to view and save the contents of the Clipboard. You can start the Clipboard Viewer by choosing Start, Programs, Accessories, Clipboard Viewer. If you recently cut or copied an item to the Clipboard, you see it in the Clipboard Viewer (see fig. 19.8).

> **N O T E** The Clipboard Viewer isn't installed during the typical installation of Windows 95. You need to specify this option during installation, using Custom setup. If Windows 95 is already installed on your computer, start the Add New Programs utility in Control Panel, and install the Clipboard Viewer. ▣
>
> ▶ **See** "Adding and Removing Windows Components," **p. 485**

FIG. 19.8
You can view the contents of the Clipboard using the Clipboard Viewer.

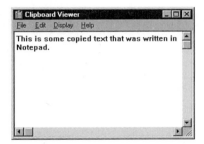

Saving the Contents of the Clipboard Viewer

You can save the information that you cut or copied to the Clipboard to reuse later. You may want to save information if you copy a large amount of data that you can use over and over. To save information that's in the Clipboard Viewer, follow these steps:

1. Choose File, Save As in the Clipboard Viewer. The Save As dialog box appears (see fig. 19.9).

FIG. 19.9
You can save the contents of the Clipboard Viewer.

2. In the File Name text box, type a file name (the Clipboard Viewer automatically uses the extension CLP).

3. Click OK.

If you want to open a saved Clipboard file, follow these steps:

1. Choose File, Open in the Clipboard Viewer. The Open dialog box appears.

2. In the File Name list box, select the file you want to open. If necessary, select the file location in the Folders list box.

N O T E Windows occasionally displays a warning message, asking whether you want to keep the Clipboard's contents. You usually see this message when you've cut or copied a large item (such as an entire spreadsheet or large picture) to the Clipboard. Answer Yes to keep the item in the Clipboard. Answer No to erase that item from the Clipboard to free system memory and resources while you work. ▪

3. Click OK. The Clear Clipboard message appears (see fig. 19.10).

If you already have something in the Clipboard, this message asks whether you want to clear the contents of the Clipboard so that you can open the CLP file that you selected. (Remember that the Clipboard can hold only one cut or copied item at a time.)

FIG. 19.10
The Clear Clipboard message asks whether you want to clear the contents of the Clipboard.

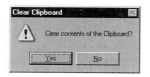

4. If you want to clear the contents and open the selected file, click Yes.

If you don't want to clear the contents of the Clipboard, click No. You return to the Clipboard Viewer.

Viewing Text in the Clipboard Viewer

The Clipboard Viewer lets you view the Clipboard contents in different file formats. The Clipboard stores information in multiple formats so you can transfer information between programs that use different formats.

 The Display menu shows only the formats that are available for the current data in the Clipboard. All other formats are grayed out.

On the Display menu, you have several options for viewing the contents. The most common of these options include:

- *Text.* Displays the contents in unformatted text, using the current Windows system font.

- *Rich Text Format.* Displays the contents in RTF (Rich Text Format). RTF retains any character formatting, such as font and font style.

- *Original Equipment Manufacturer Text.* Displays the contents in the unformatted OEM character set. You usually use this option when you copy text from the Clipboard to DOS applications.

To view the contents in another format, follow these steps:

1. In the Clipboard Viewer, select the Display menu and choose a format. The Clipboard Viewer changes to reflect your choice. In figure 19.13, the content shown in figure 19.11 has changed from text to OEM text.

2. To return to the original format, choose Display, Auto.

FIG. 19.11
Viewing the Clipboard contents with the OEM text option selected.

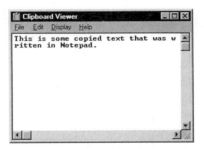

▶ **See** "Reviewing Font Types," **p. 266**

Viewing a Picture in the Clipboard Viewer

The Display menu's Picture option lets you view a picture or formatted text that you cut or copy to the Clipboard. The formatted text shows all the characterizations you add to the text, such as color, fonts, and other formatting. To use the Picture option in the Clipboard Viewer, follow these steps:

 TIP

Use the Picture option to view cut or copied formatted text before you paste it into a document.

1. Cut or copy a picture to the Clipboard, such as from Paint. If you want to view formatted text, open a document in WordPad or similar application and cut or copy formatted text to the Clipboard.

2. Open the Clipboard Viewer.

3. Choose Display, Picture to display the item that you copied or cut to the Clipboard (see fig. 19.12).

FIG. 19.12
Use the Picture option in the Clipboard Viewer to view graphics or formatted text you cut or copy to the Clipboard.

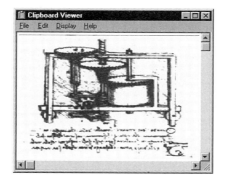

Using Drag and Drop to Move or Copy Information within an Application's Documents

A second method for moving information is to use the mouse to drag and drop selected pieces of information, which can be text, graphics, or data, from one location to another. When you drag and drop information, you are moving or copying it directly from one location to another, without using the Clipboard as a go-between. In this section, you learn how to drag and drop information within an application. In the next chapter, "Creating Compound Documents with OLE," you learn how to drag and drop objects from one application into another.

Part
VI

Ch
19

N O T E   To use drag and drop, you must be working in an application that supports it. Most applications in the Microsoft Office suite, for example, support drag and drop, including Word, Excel, PowerPoint, and Access. Check the manual that comes with your application for information on using drag and drop. ▆

To copy information with drag and drop in WordPad, follow these steps:

1. Open WordPad, and then open a document or create a new document that contains some text.

2. Select the text that you want to move or copy.

3. To move the text, position the mouse pointer over the selected area and drag the text.

To copy the text, hold down the Ctrl key as you drag the text. A plus sign appears next to the mouse pointer.

Up to the point that you release the mouse button to drop the text, you can press or release the Ctrl button to either copy or move the selection.

The mouse pointer changes as you drag, as shown in figure 19.13.

FIG. 19.13
The gray dashed line indicates where the text will be placed.

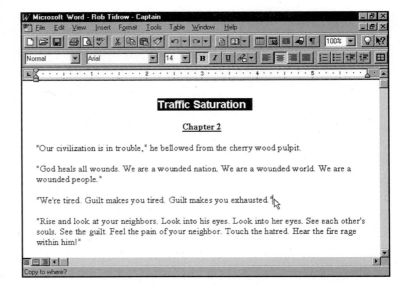

4. Drag the text to the position in the document where you want to place it. The gray vertical bar indicates the position of the new text.

5. Release the mouse button to complete the move or copy procedure.

Some applications, such as Word for Windows, allow you to move or copy text between two documents using drag and drop. To do so, make sure you can see both documents on-screen at the same time, and then drag the item from one document to another following the previous steps.

In Chapter 20, "Creating Compound Documents with OLE," you learn how to use drag and drop to transfer information from one application to another.

TROUBLESHOOTING

When I copy information with drag and drop, the original document loses its information. You used the move feature instead. Make sure that you hold down the Ctrl key throughout the process. Release the mouse button first and then release the Ctrl key. The plus-sign next to the box in the mouse pointer indicates that you are copying the selection.

My copied text appears in the middle of existing text. Don't forget to watch the gray dashed line that's part of the mouse pointer. This line shows exactly where the copied text will be inserted.

I get a black circle with a slash through it when I try to copy. The black circle with the slash indicates that you can't drop the item in the area where the mouse is, such as the title bar or status bar. Make sure that you go all the way into the other document before you release the mouse button.

Although most Windows 95 users use Windows-based applications, millions of copies of DOS applications are used on Windows systems. Applications such as Lotus 1-2-3 for DOS, WordPerfect 5.1 for DOS, and the MS-DOS prompt remain very popular. Windows 95 lets you copy information from a DOS application or from a DOS command prompt to a Windows application.

Windows 95 supports the following ways to transfer information from DOS applications to Windows documents:

- You can transfer text from DOS to Windows, from Windows to DOS, and between DOS applications by means of the Clipboard.
- You can transfer graphics from DOS to Windows applications by means of the Clipboard.
- You can copy text from the MS-DOS command prompt to the Clipboard.

Using the Clipboard to Exchange Data

Some DOS applications use their own Clipboard equivalent, but none provide an area that lets you transfer text and graphics between applications. When you want to transfer text between applications, you usually have to use text converters or file-conversion utilities that transform the text into a format that the application can read. In many cases, you have to convert the text to an ASCII text file; this process strips out your formatting and special character enhancements.

When you want to share data from a DOS application to a Windows application, you use a process known as *mark, copy, and paste*. The Mark, Copy, and Paste commands are located in the control menu of a DOS window. You also can find the Mark button on the MS-DOS Prompt toolbar.

To copy a list of your files at the DOS command prompt to a WordPad document, follow these steps:

1. Open the MS-DOS Prompt into a window (see fig. 19.14). You can change the way your DOS window looks by going into its properties and then changing the font or screen options.

FIG. 19.14

You can copy a directory listing from the DOS window to a Windows document.

2. Click the Mark toolbar button, or choose Edit, Mark from the Control menu. A blinking cursor appears at the top of the DOS window, indicating that you're in marking mode.

3. You now need to mark the area that you want to copy by drawing a box around it with your mouse pointer. To do so, place your mouse pointer where you want to start marking, hold down the left mouse button, and then drag the box around the text that you want to copy. Your screen should look something like the one shown in figure 19.15.

FIG. 19.15

Mark the text that you want to copy.

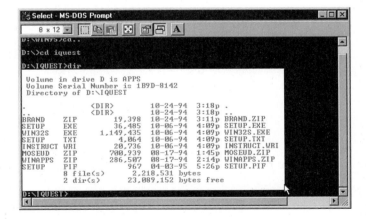

4. When you're satisfied with the selection, release the mouse button.

5. Click the Copy button in the toolbar; choose Edit, Copy from the Control menu; or press Enter to copy the selection to the Clipboard.

6. Switch to WordPad, and place the cursor where you want the text to be placed.

7. Click the Paste toolbar button, or choose Edit, Paste. The text from the DOS window is placed in your WordPad document (see fig. 19.16).

▶ **See** "Understanding and Configuring MS-DOS Application Properties," **p. 519**

FIG. 19.16

You can place a list of your files in a WordPad document by pasting it from the Clipboard.

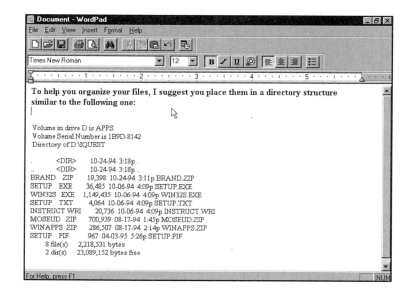

Copying Data from Windows to DOS

You also can copy data from a Windows application to a DOS application by cutting or copying the data to the Clipboard and then pasting the data into the DOS application. When you do this, all the formatting that you placed in the Windows document is lost.

To copy data from Windows to DOS, follow these steps:

1. In your Windows application, such as WordPad, select the text that you want to copy.

2. Choose Edit, Copy, or Edit, Cut.

3. Switch to the DOS application, such as WordPerfect 5.2 for DOS. (Make sure that the application is in a window and not full-screen.)

4. Place the text or mouse cursor where you want to paste the text.

5. Choose Edit, Paste from the Control menu of the DOS application. The text now appears in the document.

Part
VI

Ch
19

Transferring Data by Using File Converters

Rather than cut and paste parts of a document into another document, you sometimes need to import an entire file into a different application. You may, for example, want to import a Windows Write file into WordPad. (Write was distributed with Windows 3.x.) Many software companies distribute Write files with their software to announce updates or changes in the software.

To open files that were created in other programs, many Windows applications include built-in file converters. *File converters* take the file format and transform it to a format that the application can read. During a file conversion, text enhancements, font selections, and other elements usually are preserved. Sometimes, however, these elements are converted to ASCII format.

To convert a Write file to WordPad format, follow these steps:

1. Start WordPad and choose <u>F</u>ile, <u>O</u>pen.

TIP Click the Files of <u>T</u>ype drop-down list to view the types of files you can open in WordPad.

2. Locate a file with the extension WRI and open it. WordPad starts to convert the file. You now can edit the file as a WordPad file.

TIP The type of converters you have installed for an application may depend on the installation options you chose at setup. See the application's documentation for specific converters.

Many other Windows applications include file converters to allow you to read and edit file formats that are created in other applications. Depending on the type of installation you perform, Word for Windows, for example, includes the following set of converters:

- Rich Text Format
- Text File
- Personal Address Book
- Schedule+ Contact List
- Microsoft Excel Worksheets
- Word for DOS 3.x-6.x
- Word for DOS 6.0
- Word for Windows 2.0
- Word 6.0 for Windows/Mac
- Word for Macintosh 4.0-5.1
- Personal Address Book
- WordStar
- WordPerfect 5.x
- WordPerfect 6.x
- WordStar for DOS/Windows
- Works for Windows 3.0
- Works for Windows 4.0
- Write for Windows

TIP Rich text format (RTF) files have become the common language for exchanging files between word processors. You can preserve much of the formatting you apply to a document when you save it as an RTF file. If you don't have the correct converter for exchanging a file from one application to another, try creating an RTF file from the document and importing the document into the receiving application.

Another way to convert files is to save the file in a different format during the Save As process. When you need to import a Word for Windows file into WordPerfect or Word for Macintosh, for example, you can select those formats from the Save As Type drop-down list in the Save As dialog box. This list contains the types of formats in which you can save a Word for Windows document (see fig. 19.17).

FIG. 19.17
Use the Save As Type list options to transfer files to different applications.

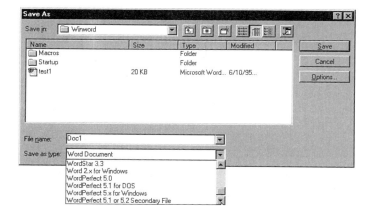

Understanding Data Linking

A more sophisticated way to exchange data in Windows 95 is through the use of linking. Before the arrival of the OLE standard, DDE (dynamic data exchange) was the technology used to link data. Now OLE offers both linking and embedding. OLE allows you to create links from one document or file to another document or file. These links can be between documents that are created in the same application (such as Word) or documents that are created in different applications (such as Word and Excel).

After you establish a link, you can update the information automatically by editing the original source of the information. This procedure lets you use data in various places but update it in only one place. You must set up a *link* between two applications (or two documents) that support OLE. The application that requests data is called the *client* application. The other application, called the *server* application, responds to the client application's request by supplying the requested data.

▶ **See** "Using Embedding To Link Information," **p. 581**

With linked documents, you can work in the client application and make changes in data that's linked to the server application. When you change the data in the client application, Windows 95 automatically changes the data in the server application. The advantage to exchanging data by links is that data is kept up-to-date in the client and server applications.

One possible use of linking is taking data from an Excel worksheet and placing it in a Word document. If you need to change the Excel data, you need to change it only in Excel; the data is updated in Word automatically. In figure 19.18, for example, data for the regional sales of TechTron is shown in an Excel worksheet. Figure 19.19 shows the same numbers in a Word document that can be distributed to the staff in the form of a memorandum.

Suppose that you want to put together a new memo each month to detail sales for the entire year, but you want to create the memo document one time and update the sales data in the Word document automatically. You can do this by using an OLE link. In this example, to change the worksheet data in the Word document, you need to change the data while you're working in Excel.

Windows 95 provides two ways to use linking: interactively and through a macro language. The easiest way to use linking is the interactive method, which is based on the Clipboard copy-and-paste method that you used earlier in this chapter but has some important differences. The macro method, which involves creating a macro in the application's macro language, isn't discussed in this book. See *Special Edition Using Excel Visual Basic for Applications, 2nd ed.,* published by Que, for more information on creating links using a macro language.

FIG. 19.18
Data from an Excel spread-sheet can be linked to a Word document.

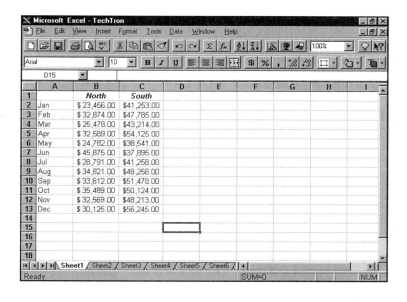

FIG. 19.19
The Word document reflects any changes that you make in the Excel document.

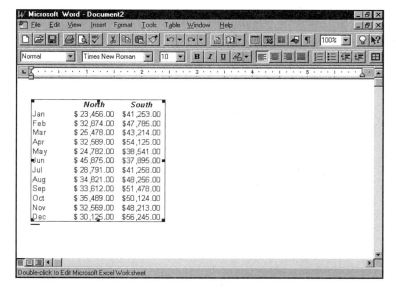

When you establish a link between applications, you use the Edit menu's Copy and Paste Link or Paste Special commands. Suppose that you have an Excel worksheet that you want to link to a Word document. Follow these steps:

1. Open an Excel worksheet. You also can create a new worksheet to link data from.

2. Select some data in the worksheet, as shown in figure 19.20.

Part
VI

Ch
19

FIG. 19.20
Select data in Excel to link to Word.

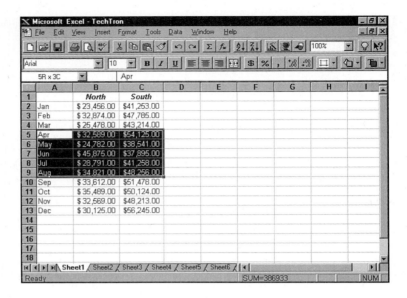

3. Choose <u>E</u>dit, <u>C</u>opy to copy the selected data to the Clipboard.

4. Open Word and then open an existing document or start a new document.

5. Choose <u>E</u>dit, Paste <u>S</u>pecial and the Paste Special dialog box appears.

6. In the Paste Special dialog box, click the Paste <u>L</u>ink option (see fig. 19.21). If you don't click this button, Word inserts the data from Excel as a table without linking.

▶ **See** "Inserting a New Object into Your Document," **p. 585**

FIG. 19.21
Make sure you choose the Paste <u>L</u>ink button to establish a link.

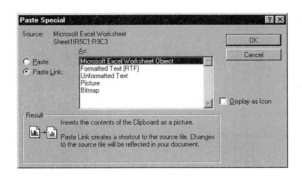

7. Select Formatted Text (RTF) in the <u>A</u>s list box.

If you select Microsoft Excel Worksheet Object, the selected cells will be inserted as an object (using OLE) into the Word document, instead of as a linked table. Sharing information by embedding objects using OLE is covered in Chapter 20, "Creating Compound Documents with OLE."

8. Choose OK. The Excel data is inserted into the Word document as a table (see fig. 19.22).

When changes are made in the data in Excel, those changes are reflected in the Word document.

FIG. 19.22
Excel data is now linked to the Word document.

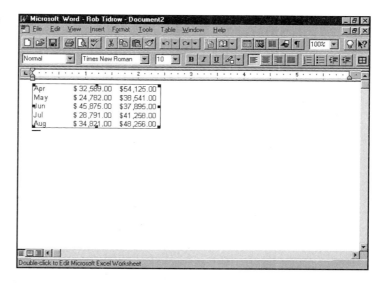

To see changes take place, switch back to the Excel worksheet and then follow these steps:

1. Change some of the data or formatting in the area that you linked to the Word document (see fig. 19.23).

FIG. 19.23
Change some data in the Excel worksheet.

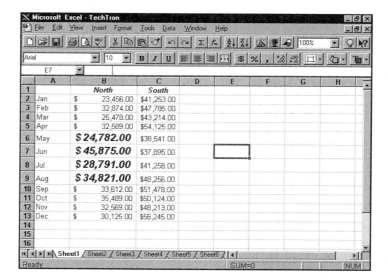

Part
VI

Ch

19

2. Press Enter or click outside the cells that you edited. The data changes in the Word document to reflect your changes.

3. Switch to the Word document to see the updated data (see fig. 19.24).

FIG. 19.24

The Word document is updated to reflect your changes.

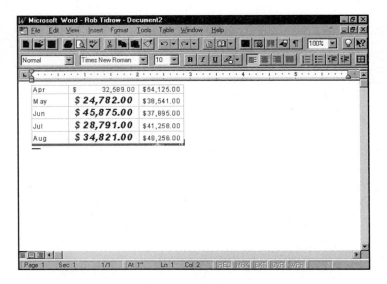

N O T E   If you change the name or path of your client or server documents, you must re-establish your links. You should make a habit of changing or creating file names and directories for your documents before you create a link. Otherwise, your data won't update properly, causing you to work with old data.

CHAPTER 20

Creating Compound Documents with OLE

by Rob Tidrow with Bob Voss

Expanding on the topic of data exchange and information sharing, this chapter introduces you to compound documents and object linking and embedding (OLE). *Compound documents* are documents you create by using multiple types of data. *Object linking and embedding* is a technology invented by Microsoft that allows you to build compound documents. ■

Understand compound documents and objects

Learn about what a compound document is made up of and the terminology used to describe compound documents.

Embed information within documents

Look here to learn the procedures for embedding objects from one application into a document in another application.

Edit OLE objects in a document

Learn how to edit the objects you have embedded in a document.

Create OLE shortcuts on the desktop

Look here to learn how to use OLE technology to create many kinds of shortcuts on your desktop.

Introduction to Compound Documents

As the personal computer industry matures and more powerful operating systems (such as Windows 95) are developed, users are gaining the capability to create documents that include almost any type of data, from almost any source. When you think about the elements that you place within a document—a sound clip, a picture, a spreadsheet—think about them as objects. An *object* is simply a piece of data that has a characteristic (such as sound) and a behavior (it plays a sound when you click it).

Objects are the basic building blocks of Microsoft's programming interface called object linking and embedding, or *OLE* (pronounced "oh-lay"). OLE allows you to build *compound documents*, which are documents that you create in one application but with objects from several different applications.

One technical definition of a compound document is that it's a data file maintained by a container application and that it contains one or more embedded objects. If you break this down, it means that you can, for example, use Word as your container application and have an Excel chart be your embedded object. You might be asking yourself, "What's all the fuss about? I've been doing this using the Clipboard and copy and paste already."

Well, the major difference between OLE (specifically OLE version 2.0) and simple data exchange (via the Clipboard) is that OLE lets you edit your Excel chart (your embedded object) while still in Word for Windows. You can't do that with a simple Clipboard cut-and-paste operation or with linking. With linking, you have to return to the original application (in this case, Excel) to edit or modify the drawing. When you want to edit an OLE object in the compound document (in this case, a Word document), you just double-click the object, and elements common to the Excel interface appear on the Word interface. Figure 20.1 shows an example of this.

The obvious benefit of having the capability to edit an embedded object within a compound document is that you don't have to return to the source application every time you want to change the object. Many times you just need to change the spelling of a word, the position of a graphical element, or one or two entries of data after you place an element in your document. By using OLE 2.0, you double-click the object, wait a few seconds (or minutes, depending on your system) while your application changes, and then make the necessary changes to the object. On the other hand, when you link data, you must open the application that created the data, open the file that contains the data, change the data, and then update the link.

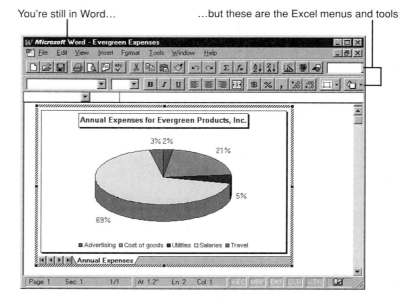

You're still in Word...   ...but these are the Excel menus and tools

FIG. 20.1
While in Word, you can edit
an Excel chart using OLE 2.0
capabilities.

N O T E Microsoft released a Service Pack 1 Update that includes an OLE 32 update. This
update fixes problems that are known to occur with files created by Excel, Word, and
PowerPoint, which use OLE for file storage. What can happen with these applications is that
information from deleted files can end up in current files. Although this information is not visible
within the native application, if you open the file in Notepad, you might be able to see the
information. If this information is of a sensitive nature, this might present a security problem.

You can download the Service Pack 1 Update from The Microsoft Network (**GO WINDOWS**), the
World Wide Web (**http://www.microsoft.com**), or on CompuServe (**GO WINNEWS**). If you
subscribe to Microsoft TechNet, the Service Pack 1 Update was included with the March 1996
CD-ROM. ▨

Part
VI

Ch
20

OLE Terminology

Similar to linking, OLE uses terms for each part of the embedding and linking stages.
Two terms you need to understand are *client* and *server*. The *client* application uses the
services of another application through OLE. The *server* application provides OLE services to a client application.

OLE Technology

Some of the advantages of OLE include:

- *OLE objects can be updated dynamically.* Like links, OLE objects can be updated dynamically when the source data changes.

- *OLE enables applications to specialize.* Rather than have one giant application that tries to be everything for everybody, OLE allows applications to do what they do best. A drawing package, for instance, can focus on drawing; spreadsheets can focus on sorting and analyzing data; word processors can focus on creating documents; and so on.

- *OLE lets users get tasks done.* When users use embedded objects, they can focus on getting their task done rather than on the application necessary to get the job completed.

When you embed an Excel chart in a Word document, for example, Excel is the OLE server and Word is the OLE client. You can think of this relationship the same way you think of a relationship with your attorney. The attorney is the *server* because she provides a service to you (legal help). You're the *client* because you're requesting services from the attorney (better known as the server). The services you obtain from the attorney can then be thought of as *objects*. You can use these objects, but if you need to update them or expand them (gain more knowledge of incorporating your business, for instance), you must go back and request help from your attorney. This is the same way you can update your embedded objects by using OLE. The client requests services from the server to help update the object.

Other OLE terms you need to understand include in-place editing, drag and drop, container object, and OLE Automation. These terms are defined in the following list:

- *In-place editing.* Refers to the capability to modify an embedded object within the client application without leaving the client application.

- *Drag and drop.* Refers to the capability to grab an object, move it across the screen, and place it into a client document. An example of dragging and dropping an object is selecting an Excel chart in Excel, dragging it to Word, and dropping it in a document.

- *Container object.* An object that contains another object or several objects. In the preceding example, the Word document is the container object that holds the Excel object.

- *OLE Automation.* Refers to the capability of a server application to make available (this is known as *expose*) its own objects for use in another application's macro language. This term is used a great deal among advanced users and software developers. One example of this is Visual Basic for Applications (VBA) programming language. VBA Excel version, for example, can use objects in Microsoft Project's VBA environment, enabling developers to create powerful custom applications.

Using Embedding to Link Information

If you're confused by linking and embedding, keep in mind one major difference between the two—where the information is stored. Linked information is stored in the source document. The destination contains only a code that supplies the name of the source application, document, and the portion of the document. Embedded information is stored in the destination document, and the code associated with OLE points to a source application rather than a file.

In some cases, you can't use the source application by itself; you have to use your destination application to start the application. These applications include WordArt, ClipArt, Microsoft Graph, and others. You generally launch the source application by choosing Insert, Object.

Embedding Information in Your Documents

When you embed an object, the information resides in the destination document, but the source application's tools are available for use in editing. You can embed information from a document in one application into a document in another application. You can, for example, embed a table you have created in an Excel worksheet into a document you are creating in Word. You can accomplish this task using the Edit, Copy and Edit, Paste Special commands or by using the mouse to drag and drop the information. The Paste Special command has more flexibility in that it allows you to link or not link the object with its source. When you drag and drop an object, the object is not linked to its source.

Using the Menu to Embed Information To use the menu to embed information from one document into another, follow these steps:

1. Select the information in the source document.
2. Choose Edit, Copy.
3. Switch to the destination and open the document that will contain the object.
4. Choose Edit, Paste Special to display the Paste Special dialog box. The Paste Special dialog box in Word is shown in figure 20.2.
5. Select the object from the As list (see fig. 20.2, Microsoft Excel Worksheet Object).

FIG. 20.2
You can select the type of information you want to paste from the clipboard and whether it is linked to the source in the Paste Special dialog box.

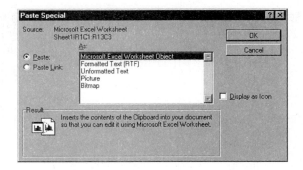

6. Select either the Paste or Paste Link option.

   If you select Paste, the object is embedded but not linked to the source document. When you double-click the object, the menus and toolbars for the source application appear, allowing you to edit in place.

   If you select Paste Link, the object is linked to the source document. When you double-click the object, the original document is opened and the information you linked is selected. You can edit the text in the Word document and the text changes in the Excel worksheet. Even if the worksheet is not opened, if you edit the original text in the linked Word document, the text will be updated in the Excel worksheet the next time you open it.

7. Choose OK.

Using Drag and Drop to Embed Information   OLE 2.0-compliant applications fully support drag and drop operations. This means you can drag an object from a document in one OLE 2.0 application and drop it into a document in another OLE 2.0-compliant application.

To drag and drop information from one application to another, follow these steps:

1. Open both applications and arrange their Windows side-by-side.

2. Select the information in the source document.

3. Drag the selection and drop it at the desired location in the destination document.

 T I P   To copy rather than move the object, hold down the Ctrl key as you drag and drop it into the destination. Otherwise you will move the selected information from the source to the destination. Look for the plus sign next to the mouse pointer when you hold down the Ctrl key. Don't release the Ctrl key until you've released the mouse button.

When you embed information from one application into another using drag and drop, it is not linked to the original data. Changes in the source document will not be reflected in the embedded object. To link an embedded object, use the menu method just described.

 T I P   If the application you want to drop an object in is minimized or hidden by other applications, you can drag the object to the application's button on the taskbar, pause for a few seconds until the application window appears, and then drop the object at the desired location in the destination application.

N O T E   When you drag and drop information from one application to another, it is embedded as an object in the destination document if the data types for the two applications are different. If the data type is the same, the information is inserted in it's native format. When you drag and drop a range of cells from Excel to a Word document, for example, it is inserted as an object. When you drag a text selection from Word to Excel, on the other hand, it is inserted as straight text, since a cell can accept text. To insert a text selection as an object you must use the Edit, Copy and Edit, Paste Special commands. ▨

 T I P   If you accidentally move rather than copy data from one application to another using drag and drop, switch back to the source application and choose Edit, Undo to restore the information in the source document. The object in the destination document will not be affected.

 T I P   If you forget to hold down the Ctrl key as you start the drag-and-drop operation it doesn't matter. As long as you are holding down the Ctrl key when you drop the object, the object will be copied, not moved. You can cancel the drag-and-drop operation by pressing the Esc key.

▶ **See** "Understanding Data Linking," **p. 571**

▶ **See** "Using Drag and Drop to Move or Copy Information within an Application's Documents," **p. 565**

Inserting a File into a Document

You can insert a file into documents by choosing Insert, File, which allows you to insert an entire file as an object. When you use Paste Special to link a file (as you did in Chapter 19), only the text you select before using the Edit, Copy command is part of the target file. If you later go back and insert text before or after the source document selection, the target document doesn't include the entire text. Choosing Insert, File alleviates this problem.

To insert a file into a document, follow these steps:

1. Move to the position in the target document where you want to insert the file.

Part
VI

Ch
20

2. Do one of the following, depending on the application you use:

- In WordPad, choose Insert, Object. Click the Create From File option. The Insert Object dialog box appears (see fig. 20.3).

FIG. 20.3
Enter the file name or use the Browse button to indicate the file you want to embed in a WordPad document.

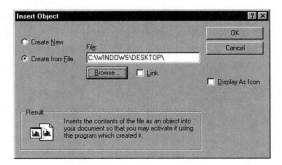

- In Word, choose Insert, File. The Insert File dialog box appears (see fig. 20.4).
- In Excel, choose Insert, Object. The Object dialog box appears. Click the Create From File tab and choose the application and file.

FIG. 20.4
Use Word's Insert, File command to embed a file in a Word document. Here the Preview button was selected to display a thumbnail view of the document.

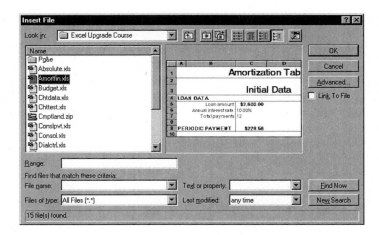

3. Identify the file you want to insert, including the drive and directory, if necessary.
4. Select the Link or Link To File option.
5. Click OK.

To see that the file you inserted is a linked object, click anywhere in the document to show a gray highlight or to show the object's field codes. In Word, you can press Shift+F9 to toggle between viewing the text of the file and the field code for the inserted object.

TIP If you want to insert several word processing documents into a single larger document, bear in mind that each document will retain its original formatting. You will want to give your documents a consistent appearance by formatting them the same. You can use templates and styles to help ensure consistency among documents.

Inserting a New Object into Your Document

If you want to use the features of another application in your compound documents, you can choose Insert, Object and select an application from the provided list. As pointed out at the beginning of this chapter, many applications now support this feature of OLE 2.0, including the standard Microsoft Office applications, the Windows applications (for example, Paint and WordPad), and other Windows applications. Some Windows applications come with small applications that can only be used from within the main application.

As examples of the types of applications that support OLE as a server application or client application, the following list of applications come with Microsoft Office. When you install Office on your system, these applications are installed in a centralized location, usually in a folder called Msapps, which allows many Office applications to access them easily. The WordPad application, which comes with Windows 95, can embed files that have been created in the following list.

Application	Use
Microsoft ClipArt Gallery	Inserts clip art pictures
Microsoft Data Map	Inserts a map showing different levels associated with data
Microsoft Equation	Creates mathematical expressions
Microsoft Graph	Inserts charts from data in a Word table
Microsoft Organization Chart	Creates organization charts
Microsoft Word Picture	Inserts a picture and the tools associated with the Word drawing toolbar
Microsoft WordArt	Creates logos and other special text effects

To use the tools from another application within your document to create a new object, follow these steps:

1. Position the insertion point in the destination document.
2. Choose Insert, Object. The Insert Object dialog box appears (see fig. 20.5).

FIG. 20.5

The Insert Object dialog box lists applications as well as Windows applications.

3. Select the Create New radio button, and then select an application from the Object Type list.

4. If you want to see only an icon for the object, select the Display as Icon check box.

5. When you finish with the Insert Object dialog box, choose OK.

The title bar identifies the application you are viewing. Applications that support OLE 2.0 display the name of the container application. Applications that support OLE 1.0 display the name of the source application.

After you complete these steps, one of two things occurs. A separate window for the application appears with the document active; or you'll remain in your client document window, but the menu bar and toolbar change to reflect the source application (see fig. 20.6).

FIG. 20.6

When you choose Microsoft Excel Worksheet, you get in-place editing. The menu bar and toolbar change to Excel, enabling you to use Excel features such as the AutoSum button.

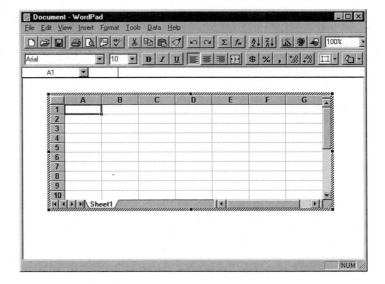

Create the object by using the application's toolbar and menus. When you finish creating the object, you can exit the object in one of two ways:

■ If you launched a separate window for the application, choose File, Exit.

■ If you stayed in your destination document, click outside the object.

Editing an Embedded Object

Regardless of which method you use to embed information into your document, you can edit the embedded object with the tools of the source application. To edit the object, follow these steps:

1. Click the object. Handles appear around the object, and the status bar tells you to double-click the object (see fig. 20.7).

FIG. 20.7

The status bar displays instructions on how to get to the source-application tools.

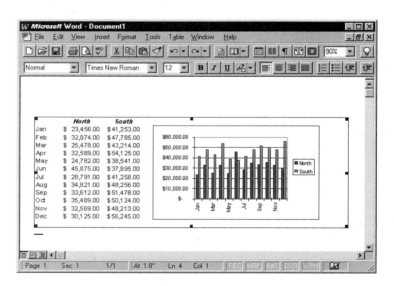

2. Double-click the object. Depending on the source and destination applications, a separate window for the program appears, or the current window's toolbar and menu bar change to those of the source application.

3. Edit the object, using the application's toolbar and menus.

4. When you finish editing the object, exit the object. If you launched a separate window for the application, choose File, Exit. If you stayed in your destination document, click outside the object.

Part
VI

Ch
20

Creating an Example Compound Document

The best way to learn how to use OLE is to actually use it a few times. This section uses Excel and some common Windows 95 applications, such as Paint and Sound Recorder, to show you how to build a compound document. If you don't have Excel, you can use another OLE 2.0-compliant application to simulate this exercise.

Embedding a Paint Object in WordPad

To start your document, open WordPad. WordPad will be the container application where you'll embed server objects. In English, this means you'll use WordPad as your main program and embed a Paint bitmap, an Excel chart, and a sound file into your WordPad document.

1. In WordPad, create some text, such as **Let's embed a Paint object first:**.

2. Switch to Paint and open SANDSTONE.BMP, which is provided with Windows 95.

3. Click the Select tool on the Paint tool box. Mark an area on the drawing that you want to embed in your WordPad document. Choose Edit, Copy.

4. Switch to WordPad and place the cursor where you want to insert the drawing object. Choose Edit, Paste Special. The Paste Special dialog box appears (see fig. 20.8).

FIG. 20.8
You can embed objects using the Paste Special dialog box.

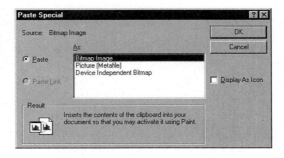

5. In the Paste Special dialog box, make sure that the Paste Link check box isn't marked. You don't want to link this object to your document. Also, select Bitmap Image in the As list box. Click OK.

6. After a few seconds, your WordPad document displays an embedded Paint object. How do you know it's embedded? Click the object, and a thin border surrounds it. This is a frame that WordPad puts around the object. Double-click the object, however, and the entire WordPad interface changes to look like Paint (see fig. 20.9).

FIG. 20.9
Double-clicking the Paint object changes the WordPad interface to show Paint tools and menus.

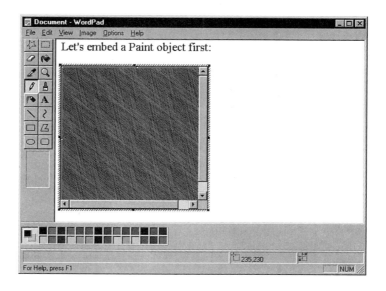

Embedding an Excel Object by Dragging and Dropping

Another way to embed an object into your WordPad compound document is by dragging and dropping it from a server application. To drag a chart from Excel into WordPad, use these steps:

1. Open Excel and create a chart. You don't have to load it down with a lot of data, but do a simple one, as shown in figure 20.10.

FIG. 20.10
You can drag this chart into your WordPad document.

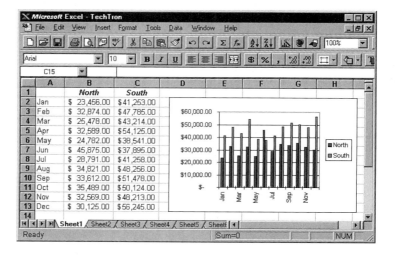

Part
VI

Ch
20

2. Arrange your desktop so that you can see WordPad and Excel at the same time, as shown in figure 20.11.

FIG. 20.11
To drag and drop, you should arrange your desktop to see both applications.

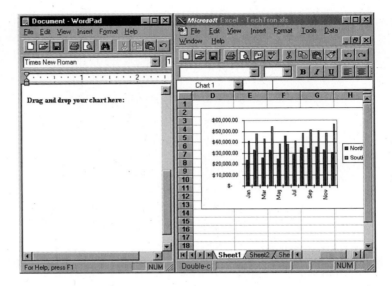

3. Select and drag the chart into the WordPad window. Place the gray box with a plus sign in it at the spot where you want the chart embedded. If you want it in a special place in the document, you should prepare the document for the object before you start the drag-and-drop process.

4. Release the mouse button. The Excel chart now appears in the WordPad document as an embedded object.

Embedding a Sound Clip in WordPad

To add a little flavor to your WordPad compound document, include a sound clip that your readers can click. You need to have a sound card and microphone to create and hear these sounds, but you still can embed the sound clips even if you don't have a sound card installed. To embed a sound clip in your document, follow these steps:

1. In WordPad, choose Insert, Object.

2. In the Insert Object dialog box, select Wave Sound from the Object Type list.

N O T E If you have a specific sound clip that you want to embed, click the Create from File option and select the file you want to embed. If you don't click this option, the default setting is to create a new sound clip. ■

3. Click the Display As Icon check box to embed an icon of the sound clip in your WordPad document. When you use an icon, you reduce the system resources necessary to store the object.

4. Click OK. An icon of the sound object appears in the WordPad document (see fig. 20.12).

5. Double-click the icon to start the Sound Object in Document application (see fig. 20.13). This application allows you to record a new sound clip in your document. After you create a message, you can play it back by double-clicking the sound object in your WordPad document.

FIG. 20.12

The sound object appears as an icon in your document.

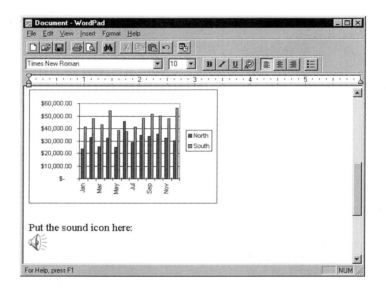

Editing an Embedded Object in Your Compound Document

If your data changes, your taste in art differs now from when it did when you embedded the graphic object, or you want to add something to your sound clip, you can edit each object without leaving WordPad. This section shows you how to edit the Excel chart that you embedded earlier in the section "Embedding an Excel Object by Dragging and Dropping."

To edit the chart, follow these steps:

1. Double-click the Excel chart in your WordPad compound document. The WordPad interface automatically changes to the standard Excel interface (see fig. 20.14).

FIG. 20.13
By double-clicking the sound object icon, you activate the sound recorder application to create a new wave file.

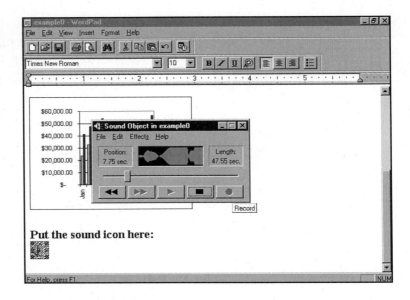

FIG. 20.14
With OLE 2.0, your container application takes on the appearance of the source application.

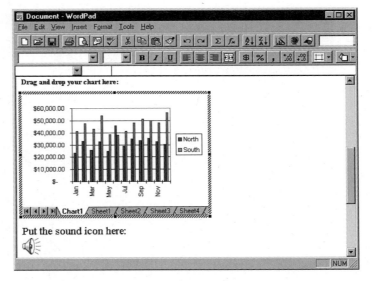

2. Make changes to the chart by using the toolbars and menu options. When you finish, click outside the chart. This returns the WordPad interface to its original state (see fig. 20.15).

FIG. 20.15
WordPad's interface returns to its original state, but the Excel chart has changed.

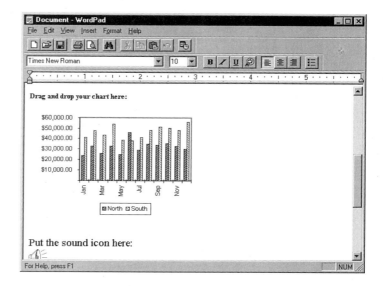

TROUBLESHOOTING

When I double-click a linked or embedded object, a `Cannot edit` error message appears. This means that the source file can't be opened. Make sure that the application needed to edit the file is on your machine. Also make sure that you have enough system memory to run both the container and source applications. Keep in mind that compound documents demand more memory than simple documents.

The margins are 0 (zero) in all my embedded Word objects. Word sets the margins at 0 (zero) inches in a document object to eliminate excessive white space around the object. To change the margins, double-click the Word document object to open it for editing. Choose File, Page Setup; click the Margins tab; then enter new margin settings.

When I double-click an embedded Excel object, Excel doesn't open. You probably have the Ignore Other Applications check box selected, which causes Excel to ignore all requests from other applications. In Excel, choose Tools, Options and then click the General tab. Clear the Ignore Other Applications check box.

Part
VI

Ch
20

Linking Objects to Shortcuts on the Desktop Using OLE

One of the most useful new features in Windows 95 is the ability to create shortcuts to virtually any object, including files, folders, floppy drives, and printers.

In the following sections you learn how to link document objects with icons on your desktop. These shortcuts can expand your ability to share and access the information on your computer.

▶ **See** "Using the Power of Shortcuts and Desktop Icons," **p. 71**

Creating Document Shortcuts

Document shortcuts allow you to quickly navigate to a particular location in a document. You can, for example, create a document shortcut on the desktop to a cell in an Excel worksheet, so that when you double-click the shortcut, Excel is started, the target worksheet opened, and the cell selected. You can create a shortcut to a location or selection in any OLE 2.0-compliant application. You can keep these shortcuts on the desktop, or you place them in a folder on the desktop if you don't want to clutter up your desktop with shortcuts. Using folders to store your document shortcuts also can help you to organize them.

One example of how you can use document shortcuts to save time is if you are working in a document in which you spend a lot of time navigating from one location to another. To ease navigation, you can create document shortcuts to key locations in the document so that you can move to a particular location by simply double-clicking the shortcut for that location. You can collect all the shortcuts for a document in a folder, so that it becomes a computerized table of contents that streamlines navigation.

To create a document shortcut, follow these steps:

1. Make a selection in the document (cells in a worksheet or text in a word processing document).
2. Drag and drop the selection to the desktop using the right mouse button.
3. Choose Create Document Shortcut Here from the menu that appears when you release the mouse button.

When you double-click the shortcut, the document opens at the original selection. You can move the shortcut to a folder that you create on the desktop.

NOTE Not all OLE-compliant applications allow you to create document shortcuts using drag and drop. In these cases, you can create a document shortcut by making a selection, choosing Edit, Copy, right-clicking on the desktop, and choosing Create Shortcut from the menu.

Creating Document Scraps

You also can create document scraps on your desktop. *Scraps* are pieces of information from any OLE document that you store on your desktop or in a folder. At any time, you can drag a scrap into a document in any OLE application to insert it as an embedded object. You can use the scrap as many times as you like in as many different documents as you like.

To create a scrap, follow these steps:

1. Select the information you want to create a scrap from.
2. Drag the selection to the desktop or to a folder.

A scrap consisting of the selected information is created. If you double-click the scrap, the information in the scrap is displayed in the application that created it. You can drag and drop the scrap into any OLE document to embed it as an object in the document.

 TIP Use scraps to create Post-it notes on your desktop. When you want to save a bit of information that you don't want to forget on your desktop, open WordPad (click Start, then choose Programs, Accessories, WordPad), type the note, select the text, and drag it to the desktop. You don't have to save the WordPad file. To read the note, double-click on the scrap. The name of the scrap is taken from the first sentence of the scrap text. You can rename the scrap to give it a more useful name.

Creating Links to Internet and MSN Sites

In Chapter 33, "Getting Connected to the Internet," and Chapter 35, "Using The Microsoft Network," you learn how to create shortcuts on your desktop to sites on the Internet and The Microsoft Network. This is useful if you routinely access certain sites and want to be able to access these sites by double-clicking a shortcut. You also can embed these shortcuts into any OLE document so that you can access these sites from within the document. Imagine distributing a document to your colleagues loaded with shortcuts to useful sites on the Internet. All they have to do is open the document and double-click on the shortcuts.

Part
VI

Ch
20

To embed an Internet or MSN shortcut in a document, drag and drop the shortcut from the desktop into the document. You can then double-click the shortcut to sign on to the Internet or MSN and move to that site. ●

CHAPTER 21

Introduction to Visual Basic for Applications

by Bill Orvis and Ron Person

For years, Microsoft hinted that their long-range strategy included a common application programming language used in all their applications.

Visual Basic for Applications (VBA) offers power users and developers the ability to use the most common Windows programming language, Visual Basic, and apply it to office automation problems. It also enables programmers to more easily control other Microsoft applications. Now that nearly all the major Microsoft applications include VBA, it is significantly easier to create integrated applications. ∎

▬ **Why you should consider using VBA to develop integrated Office applications**

VBA is based on Visual Basic, the world's most widely used language.

▬ **What important concepts form the foundation of VBA?**

You learn about Visual Basic's object model and the objects, properties, methods, statements, and functions that comprise the language.

▬ **How VBA can act on objects in an application—objects such as spreadsheet's cells, database fields, and so on**

Using Excel worksheets as an example, this chapter illustrates how VBA uses properties to change an object's characteristics and uses methods to perform actions related to an object.

If you are familiar with other macro or programming languages, you might want to begin the transition to Visual Basic for Applications immediately. Some of the reasons for using VBA are:

- Learning and supporting synergy increase, because the Microsoft applications share a common application language. While the objects in the language are different, the syntax, concepts, and many programming tools are the same.
- The language is based on Visual Basic, one of the most widely used Windows development languages.
- Applications you write in VBA can be copied into Visual Basic, compiled there, and run as Visual Basic programs that control the application.

Understanding the Importance of Visual Basic for Applications

With the release of the application suite, Office 95 for Windows 95, the VBA language is available in almost all of Microsoft's user-oriented applications. The products in Office 95 Pro that include VBA are:

Microsoft Excel	Includes VBA and can control other VBA applications
Microsoft Access	Includes VBA and can control other VBA applications
Microsoft Project	Includes VBA and can control other VBA applications
Microsoft PowerPoint	Can be controlled by other VBA applications
Microsoft Mail	Can be controlled by other VBA applications
Microsoft SQL Server	Includes VBA and can control other VBA applications

The only major user application that does not include VBA is Microsoft Word. It uses a language with a similar structure: WordBASIC. Although WordBASIC is not a VBA language, it is usually not difficult to integrate Word with other VBA applications.

Understanding the Visual Basic Object Model

The VBA language is based on the Visual Basic programming language with extensions that enable it to control the different types of objects in Excel, Access, Project, and so on.

N O T E Microsoft Excel is used as an example throughout this discussion on VBA. Of the Office 95 suite of applications, the Excel application's object model is the most widely known. ■

VBA can be viewed as having two components—the Visual Basic language constructs and the application object model. The Visual Basic language portion contains statements and functions that are part of the Visual Basic language. *Statements* are commands that produce some action such as controlling the flow of the program. One of Visual Basic's statements is If…Then…Else. This tests whether a condition is true. If that condition is true, Then do some action. If it is not true (Else), do a different action.

Functions are Visual Basic commands that return a result, such as Date, which returns the current date in the computer system.

The application's object models contain objects, properties, and methods that describe the application and its contents. For example, Excel *objects* are items in Excel that can be changed, such as a workbook, worksheet, chart title, range on a worksheet, and so forth. Each object has its own set of *properties* that describe it. These properties are its attributes or characteristics. If you want to set the value of cell A1 to 5, for example, you use a line like

```
Range("A1").Value=5
```

In this example, Value is a property of Range. Other properties of Range are Font, Formula, Height, Hidden, Style, and Left.

Each object also has related *methods*. Methods are actions inherent to an object. To remove the contents of the cell that just had its value changed, for example, you can use

```
Range("A1").Clear
```

where Clear is a method of Range. Other methods you can use on Range are Activate, AutoFill, Borders, CheckSpelling, Copy, Delete, and Sort.

Using Containers to Specify Objects

Objects can be confusing because there can be so many of them in an application. In addition, you might find some code examples confusing because the programmer of Visual Basic has left out some of the objects in a line of code. As a result, the code shows only a property or method and not the object being acted upon.

Think of each object as a container that can hold smaller objects, and those objects in it can contain smaller objects, and so on.

The largest object is the *Application object*. When run in an application such as Excel, the Application object always refers back to the application from which the procedure ran. This helps your Visual Basic program understand which program is being controlled when the Visual Basic procedure is controlling other applications.

Part
VI

Ch
21

One of the objects in an Excel Application is `Workbooks`. `Workbooks` is a *collection*. A collection is a group of objects. In this case, the `Workbooks` object contains a collection of all the open workbooks. You can use a Visual Basic `For Each…Next` statement, for example, to loop through each workbook in the collection `Workbooks`. If you want to refer to a specific workbook, you can use

```
Application.Workbooks("Book3")
```

To refer to a specific worksheet in Book3, you can add

```
Application.Workbooks("Book3").Worksheets("Sheet1")
```

To specify the first row, use

```
Application.Workbooks("Book3").Worksheets("Sheet1").Rows(1)
```

To specify the first cell in the first row, use

```
Application.Workbooks("Book3").Worksheets("Sheet1").Rows(1).Cells(1)
```

Finally, to set the `Formula` property to `"Hi"` in the first cell of the first row, use

```
Application.Workbooks("Book3").Worksheets("Sheet1").Rows(1).Cells(1).
➥Formula="Hi"
```

This gets cumbersome quickly if you have to continually specify this many objects. But you don't. If you are referring to objects in Excel, you don't have to specify `Application` at the beginning of each line. And if the worksheet you are working on is active, you don't need to specify the `Workbooks` and `Worksheets` objects. If the cell in which you want to put information is active, you don't have to specify the row or cell position. You can use a form such as

```
ActiveCell.Formula="Hi"
```

There are many shortcuts to using the object model. You can refer to active objects with the following shortcut object names:

```
ActiveWorkbook
```

```
ActiveSheet
```

```
ActiveWindow
```

```
ActiveCell
```

Another shortcut is to use the object `Selection` to refer to the currently selected object. For example,

```
Selection.Font.Size=24
```

Using *With* to Reduce Code Size

Another way in which you can reduce the amount of Visual Basic code you write is to use the With clause. The With clause enables you to repeat several operations on the same object. If you turn on the Visual Basic recorder when you format selected cells with the Format, Cells command, you see the following code:

```
Sub Formatter()
With Selection
.HorizontalAlignment = xlLeft
.VerticalAlignment = xlBottom
.WrapText = False
.Orientation = xlHorizontal
.AddIndent = False
End With
With Selection.Font
.Name = "Arial"
.FontStyle = "Bold"
.Size = 11
.Strikethrough = False
.Superscript = False
.Subscript = False
.OutlineFont = False
.Shadow = False
.Underline = xlNone
.ColorIndex = xlAutomatic
End With
End Sub
```

In the first With clause, the object (the current selection) has the selection's properties changed by the options in the Alignment page of the Format Cells dialog box. In the second With clause, the Font page of the Format Cells dialog box changes properties. By using the With clause, you do not have to repeat Selection or Selection.Font on each line.

Changing Objects without Selecting Them

As you probably inferred from the object model description, VBA does not require that you select objects to change them or enter data in them. As the example in "Using Containers to Specify Objects" illustrated, however, specifying an object when it is not active can result in long code lines.

Part

VI

Ch

21

Getting and Giving Information Using Parallel Syntax

In some programming languages, retrieving information about an item and putting information into an item require completely different syntax and statements. In Excel 4, for example, this is one of the things that made macros difficult to remember and write. There was no parallel structure between changing an object property and finding the value of a property. Notice in the following example how changing the boldness of a cell uses a different function and syntax than determining whether a cell is already bold. In an Excel 4 macro, you make a cell bold with

```
FORMAT.FONT(,,TRUE)
```

where the third argument in this form of the FONT function is bold. To determine whether a cell is bold, Excel 4 macros use this function

```
GET.CELL(20)
```

where GET.CELL returns True if the active cell is bold and False if the active cell is not.

Because the actual words FORMAT.FONT and GET.CELL are unrelated, it makes the Excel 4 language difficult to remember or learn. You always have to have a function reference manual available to make sure you have the right type number inside GET.CELL.

To do the same thing with Visual Basic is much easier. Both changing a cell to bold and finding out whether it is bold use the same syntax. In this example, the object is the range A1. The property to be changed is Font.Bold. To change cell A1 to bold, you use

```
Sub BoldMaker()
Range("A1").Font.Bold = True
Sub End
```

If you want to determine whether A1 is already bold, you use the same object and properties, just on a different side of the equal sign. In the following code, the variable b stores the True or False result of whether A1 is bold. The code looks like

```
Sub BoldChecker()
b = Range("A1").Font.Bold
MsgBox "Is the cell bold? " & b
Sub End
```

In this example, Font.Bold determines whether the object Range("A1") is bold and returns True or False. If the cell is bold, the MsgBox function displays the message

```
Is the cell bold? True
```

As an aside, the MsgBox function can display only results that are text. The MsgBox normally cannot display the logical values of True or False from b. By joining the text message in quotes with the `True` or `False` result stored in b, the b is coerced into becoming text that `MsgBox` can display.

Referencing Ranges and Cells in Visual Basic

In VBA, you need to reference a cell or range in order to change it.

N O T E VBA objects, like `Range` and `Cells` described here, cannot be used as a line of code by themselves. Use them to specify the object on which to apply the property or method, as in

```
Cells(1,2).Formula="Hello World"
```

or to specify where information is coming from, as in

```
Content = Cells(1,2).Formula note ▪
```

You can refer to the active cell as

```
ActiveCell
```

To refer to a cell or range using a text reference, use one of the following forms:

```
Range("B12")
Range("B12:C35")
Range("MonthReport")
```

The first is the single cell B12 on the active sheet. The second is the range B12:C35 on the active sheet. The `MonthReport` is a named range on the active sheet. None of these objects can be used by themselves; they must be followed by a property or method.

If you need to refer to a cell or range by numeric position or a numeric offset in a row or column, use CELLS as follows:

```
CELLS(1,3)
CELLS(x,y)
```

If you need a specific location on a specific sheet in the active workbook, use the containers that surround the object you want to specify, such as in

```
Worksheets("Sheet6").Rows(3).Cells(2)
```

Other objects that are useful are Rows and Columns. If you need to offset the upper-left corner of a range, use the Offset method. To resize a range, use the Resize method.

Part
VI

Ch
21

N O T E A shortcut to writing cell or range objects on the active worksheet is to use the brackets ([ ]) as an abbreviation. For example,

```
[C14].Value=5
```

puts 5 in cell C14 on the active worksheet. You can even use the shortcut notation

```
[C14]=[B12]*3
```

where the result is that three times the content of B12 on the active worksheet is stored in cell C14 on the active worksheet. ■

Using Variables to Store Information

VBA variables store value, formulas, or references. You also can *type* variables so they store only specific types of data—for example, text or integer numbers. Data typing can reduce troubleshooting problems later because it prevents you from putting the incorrect type of data in a variable.

Another advantage to VBA variables is that they can be *scoped* so they are available only in the Visual Basic procedure containing them, to other procedures in the module, or to other modules globally.

Storing Objects

In VBA, you face the problem of wanting to refer to the same objects over and over throughout your Visual Basic procedure. To store an object for later use, use the Set statement:

```
Set FutureObj=ActiveWorkbook.Sheets("Sheet6").Range("B36")
```

You can use the variable FutureObj later in place of typing the full object specification; for example,

```
FutureObj.Font.Bold=True
```

Creating Dialog Boxes in Visual Basic for Applications

In VBA, you draw dialog boxes on a sheet. Each control on the dialog box, such as edit boxes or lists, can be referred to by a name. In Excel 5, for example, you insert sheets into a workbook and then draw the dialog box directly on the sheet. In Excel 5, you can draw a full gamut of dialog box objects, including spinners and scroll bars (sliders). Other VBA languages have different dialog box capabilities. VBA dialog boxes do not yet have the wide range of capabilities available to dialog boxes created with Visual Basic.

Creating Menus and Toolbars

In VBA, you can create custom menu bars, menus, and menu items, including side or cascading menus. In addition, you can create or modify toolbars. All these customized menus, commands, and toolbar buttons can have your Visual Basic for Application procedures assigned to them.

Getting In-Depth Help Online

One of the best sources of technical information on Visual Basic is the Online Help. To get to the Help index for programming, choose Help, choose the topics command for the application, and then expand the book with a title such as Microsoft Visual Basic Reference.

Each application contains an *object browser*. Object browsers differ between applications but they are designed to show the objects available in an application and what properties and methods can be used with each object. For help on a specific object, property, or method, select an item in the browser, then click the Help button or press F1 to get help specific to the item you selected. When you are looking at an object Help screen, you can choose the `Methods` or `Properties` hypertext link at the top of the Help screen to learn more about related methods or properties. Watch for links that say `Example`. These are links to a segment of sample code that you can copy from the Help file, paste into a module sheet, and run.

Debugging Tools

VBA has more debugging capability than the previous application macros or languages for each application. The debugging tools differ between applications but they follow similar concepts. The following table describes just a few of the debugging tools in Excel 95.

Part
VI

Ch
21

Tool	Description
Breakpoints	Breakpoints are conditions you specify that stop the procedure from running and put the program in break mode. They do this before they run the code containing the breakpoints.
Debugging buttons	The Visual Basic toolbar contains debugging buttons that display when a module (Visual Basic sheet) is active. Using these buttons, you can run one statement or procedure, set breakpoints, set conditional breakpoints, or examine values in variables.
Debug window	The Debug window displays over your application as it runs. It enables you to watch the resulting values and expressions as your procedure runs. You can change values in this window to see how it affects your procedure.

OLE Automation for Interapplication Programming

As mentioned earlier in the chapter, OLE Automation allows developers to use objects from different applications. An Excel program, for example, can create and edit Microsoft Project objects. The following is a list of some of the applications you can use to start OLE Automation:

- Visual Basic
- Access Basic
- Visual Basic for Application, Excel version

Programmers use OLE Automation so they can control and reference objects without worrying about complex and problematic interapplication details during the development cycle. Sophisticated business solutions can be created by using the capabilities of multiple applications with OLE Automation. With more and more applications using OLE 2.0 and exposing objects to programmers, businesses can mix and match the applications on their users' desktops and (hopefully) diversify the vendors who supply the applications. This makes for a much richer computing environment, giving the user more to choose from.

If just one vendor is providing one application to the end user, the end user must devise ways to modify her work to get the desired results. More than likely, these users spend a great deal of time creating workarounds or they don't get the task done, which lowers productivity. With OLE Automation, many customized applications can be created to help businesses get done what they need to get done.

If you're a developer or power user interested in OLE Automation basics, this section briefly describes some of the functions available. By understanding three primary functions in OLE Automation, you can begin developing applications that rely on exposed objects or control objects in other applications.

N O T E For information on OLE Automation, many Que books are available that teach you the fundamentals and expert techniques. A few of these include *Special Edition Using Visual Basic for Applications* and *Special Edition Using Excel for Windows 95*. ▪

The Set function is used to set a variable in the application in which you're programming to reference an object in a different OLE 2.0 application. This reference is commonly referred to as *pointing*. If, for example, you're in Microsoft Project and want to reference the active worksheet in Excel, you would use the following syntax:

```
Set ExampleSheet = MSExcel.ActiveSheet
```

When you reference the properties and methods of the ExampleSheet object in Project, you affect the worksheet in Excel.

The CreateObject function creates the specified object and then returns an object that's linked to the new object. After you get the returned object, you use the Set function to link it to an object variable. To use the CreateObject function, use the syntax CreateObject (*"ApplicationName.ObjectType"*). The following is an example of using the CreateObject function:

```
Set NewObject = CreateObject("Excel.Sheet")
```

In this example, you automatically start Excel, create an object, and create an object variable that can reference the created object. You then use the new object throughout your subroutine.

The last of the primary three OLE Automation functions is GetObject. This function is similar to the CreateObject function, except it accesses its source object from a file. The syntax for GetObject is GetObject(*"completePathname"*). To reference an object that's on your C:\ drive in the OLE folder, for example, use the following syntax:

```
Set ExampleObject = GetObject("C:\OLE\SAMPLE.OBJ
```

Managing Disk Drives and Backups

CHAPTER 22

Working with Disks and Disk Drives

by Ron Person and Bob Voss

Windows 95 comes with several new utilities that allow you to maintain and optimize your floppy disks and hard disks and improve the performance of your system. The 32-bit, protected mode VFAT makes it possible to create disk management utilities that are safe to operate while you are working in Windows and even while you are running another application.

I recommend that you learn to use these utilities so you can get the most performance out of your system and detect and fix problems that could cause you to lose valuable data. ScanDisk and Defragmenter are two utilities you should use on a regular basis to keep your hard disk tuned up. If you want to increase the storage capacity of your hard disk, take a look at DriveSpace, the new disk compression software for Windows 95.

If you have installed Microsoft Plus!, you will want to look at the sections on DriveSpace 3, an enhanced disk compression utility and the System Agent, which is a handy program for scheduling the disk utilities discussed in this chapter to run automatically. ■

Format and partition your disks

Learn how to clean your disks so that they are running at optimum performance.

Improve your performance

With programs like ScanDisk and DriveSpace, you can check for disk damage and increase the effective size of your disks.

Use System Agent for scheduling programs to run automatically

Learn how to run disk-cleaning programs on a routine basis.

Monitor your system's performance

You can increase your computer's performance by conducting regular checks for disk space, disk errors, and viruses. System Monitor helps you keep track of your disk's performance.

The Windows 95 File System

A major architectural change in Windows 95 is the installable file system, which has a new 32-bit, protected-mode Virtual File Allocation Table file system (VFAT) as its primary file system. With the installable file system, Windows 95 can manage multiple file systems, which makes it easy to connect to network computers using different file systems, such as HPFS (OS/2's file system) and NTFS (the Windows NT file system). Note that Windows 95 will not handle HPFS and NTFS on a local hard drive.

VFAT, the primary file system in Windows 95, was actually an optional file system introduced in Windows for Workgroups 3.1. VFAT in Windows 95 has been improved and has many advantages over the original FAT file system used in MS-DOS:

- Faster file accessing and improved multitasking because of the 32-bit, protected-mode data path.
- Improved, dynamic, protected-mode disk caching (VCACHE) for improved performance and stability. Also works with CD-ROMs and network drives.
- No conventional memory used by disk cache driver (VCACHE versus older SmartDrive).
- Cache memory is allocated dynamically, based on available free memory and read/write activity.
- Support for long file names (up to 255 characters).
- Capability to read and write long file names supported by other file systems, such as NTFS and HPFS.
- Support for FAT partitions and short (8.3) file names for backward compatibility.

Formatting Disks

Formatting physically prepares a disk to accept computer data. Formatting checks for and identifies bad areas on the disk's magnetic surface, so that data is not recorded in these areas. Formatting erases any existing data on the disk, so you also can use formatting to clean up a used disk for reuse.

The 32-bit multitasking environment in Windows 95 makes it possible to format floppy disks in the background as you go about your work in other applications. This capability is a real time saver.

Formatting a Floppy Disk

N O T E If you attempt to open an unformatted floppy disk in My Computer or Explorer, you will
be asked if you want to format the disk. The Format dialog box immediately
appears. ▓

To format a floppy disk, follow these steps:

1. Insert the floppy disk to be formatted in the disk drive.

2. Right-click the icon for the drive in a folder window or in the Windows Explorer and
   choose For<u>m</u>at. The Format dialog box appears (see fig. 22.1).

   In a folder window, you also can select the drive icon and choose <u>F</u>ile, For<u>m</u>at.

FIG. 22.1

Set up a formatting
operation in the Format
dialog box.

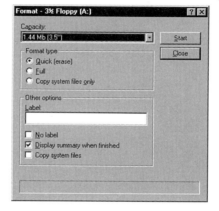

3. Select the size of the floppy disk from the Ca<u>p</u>acity drop-down list.

4. Select the type of format you want from the Format Type options:

<u>Q</u>uick (Erase)	Formats the disk without first scanning it for bad sectors. Speeds up formatting, but you should be sure that the disk is undamaged.
<u>F</u>ull	Checks for bad sectors on the disk before formatting and marks them so that these areas are not used.
Copy System Files <u>O</u>nly	Adds the system files to the disk without formatting it so that the disk can be used to start the computer.

5. If you want to assign a label to the disk, type the label in the <u>L</u>abel text box. Otherwise, select the <u>N</u>o Label option.

6. Select the Display Summary When Finished option if you want to see a screen of information about the disk after it is formatted (see fig. 22.2).

FIG. 22.2
You can get information about a formatted disk in the Format Results message box.

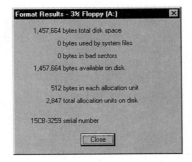

Format Results - 3½ Floppy (A:)

1,457,664 bytes total disk space
0 bytes used by system files
0 bytes in bad sectors
1,457,664 bytes available on disk

512 bytes in each allocation unit
2,847 total allocation units on disk

15C8-3259 serial number

Close

The Format Results message box tells you how much total disk space there is, how many bytes are used by system files and bad sectors, and how many bytes are available.

TIP   If you want to switch to another application while formatting a disk, select the Display Summary option so the Format Results dialog box will notify you when the formatting is completed.

7. If you want to use the disk to start the computer, select the Copy System Files option. Do not use this option unless you need to, because system files use storage space on the disk that can otherwise be used for data.

8. Choose Start. The progress of the formatting operation is displayed at the bottom of the Format dialog box.

TIP   To bypass having to open the Explorer or My Computer, create a shortcut to your floppy disk drive on the desktop. To format a floppy disk, right-click the disk icon and choose Format from the shortcut menu. You also can copy a floppy disk using the Copy Disk command on the shortcut menu.

Formatting Your Hard Disk

Formatting prepares a disk for holding data by setting up a file and directory structure for use by the operating system. Many newer hard drives are already formatted when you purchase them (for example, IDE and EIDE-type drives). However, if you purchase a SCSI drive, or an older ESDI drive, you might have to format the drive. You also might want to format a hard drive that has been used and is cluttered with data or other operating systems, because formatting does more than just erase old data; it magnetically scrubs the disk so files no longer exist.

An essential part of formatting a hard drive for data is *partitioning*. You must create at least one partition on your hard disk, but you can create more than one partition. These additional partitions can be defined as DOS partitions or as non-DOS partitions on which you can install other operating systems. To run Windows 95, you need to create at least one DOS partition, and if you want to start Windows 95 from this disk, you must also define this partition as a primary DOS partition and as the active partition. If you don't use the entire disk for the primary DOS partition, you can create an extended DOS partition from the remaining space and divide this partition into logical drives. Use the FDISK program that comes with DOS and Windows 95 to accomplish all these tasks.

 T I P Re-formatting a hard drive also can help you recover any bad clusters that may have accumulated over the years.

> **CAUTION**
>
> You should format a disk that contains confidential information before giving the computer to someone who should not have access to that data. The erase or delete commands only remove a file's name and location from a disk's table of files. The data still exists on the disk until it is overwritten by another file. Formatting erases the name and location table and magnetically erases the data.

Using FDISK to Partition a New Hard Drive   If you are installing a new hard disk as your primary drive, place the Windows 95 Startup disk in the A: drive and turn on your computer. Windows sees the new drive and asks if you want to allocate all of the unallocated space on your drive. Answer "yes" and it will run FDISK behind the scenes and restart your computer. After the restart, it formats the new partition automatically.

Your other alternative is to boot to DOS Mode by pressing F5 during startup and running FDISK from the DOS Prompt. When you type **FDISK** at the DOS prompt, it puts a menu on the screen. Be sure to check that the drive that you want to partition is the drive that is selected. Option 5 on the menu allows you to select a different drive. After you have confirmed that you have the correct drive selected, choose option 1 from the menu. This option creates a DOS partition on your drive and asks if you want to use the entire drive for your DOS partition. The most common answer is yes. Once the DOS partition is created, your computer will restart and be ready for the formatting of the drive.

As you can see by the two choices of partitioning a hard drive, Windows 95 has made this step much easier.

Using FDISK to Repartition an Existing Drive   You may decide to repartition an existing drive on your computer. One reason for doing this is to create multiple partitions and multiple logical drives to better organize your data and applications. Some users, for example, partition their drive so that they have two logical drives. They then install their applications on one logical drive and store their data on the second logical drive, which they can then back up in its entirety without backing up the applications.

To repartition a drive, you must first delete any existing partitions and then create a new *primary DOS partition*. You must also use FDISK to make the primary DOS partition *active* if you are starting your system from this drive. If you have not opted to use all of your hard disk for the primary DOS partition, you can use FDISK to create an *extended DOS partition,* and you can divide the extended partition into *logical drives*.

> **CAUTION**
>
> When you use FDISK to partition a drive, any existing data on the drive will be destroyed, so be sure to back up the data first.

To delete a partition or logical drive, follow these steps:

1. Back up the files on the drive you want to repartition.
2. Open the Start menu, choose <u>R</u>un, and type **fdisk** in the Run dialog box. Choose OK.

    or

    If you are repartitioning the drive that has Windows 95 on it, use the Startup disk to restart your computer and type **fdisk** at the command prompt.

N O T E   If you don't have a Startup disk, choose the Add/Remove Programs command in Control Panel and select the Startup Disk tab to create a Startup disk. ▪

3. Choose option 3 and follow the menus to delete the desired logical drives and partitions.

To create a primary DOS partition, follow these steps:

1. Choose option 1 in the FDISK opening menu.
2. Choose option 1 in the Create Primary DOS Partition menu.
3. Follow the directions to specify the size for the primary DOS partition or press Enter to use the entire drive for the partition.
4. Return to the opening menu by pressing Esc and make the primary DOS partition active by selecting option 2, if this is the drive from which you start your compute.

To create an extended DOS partition and logical drives, follow these steps:

1. Choose option 2 in the Create DOS Partition or Logical DOS Drive menu.
2. Follow the directions to create the extended partition.
3. Use the same option to divide the extended partition into logical drives, if desired.
4. Press Esc until you exit FDISK.

After you partition a drive, you must use the Format command to format the drive, as described in the following section.

TIP If you have a large hard disk—for example, a 1G drive—you can increase the storage efficiency of your drive by creating two or more logical DOS drives. The minimum number of bytes that a file requires increases as the partition size increases, because the *clusters* DOS uses to allocate disk space are fixed in size and cluster size increases as the partition size increases. For example, the cluster size for partitions in the range from 512M to 1G is 16K versus a cluster size of 32K for 1G to 2G partitions. In this case, a small file 2K in size will use double the space on the larger partitions. Dividing a 1G drive into two smaller logical drives can significantly increase storage efficiency.

To format an uncompressed drive from the MS-DOS prompt, type **Format d:** where d: is the drive letter of the drive you want to format.

TIP If you have installed Microsoft Plus! on your computer, you can increase storage efficiency even more—without repartitioning your hard drive—by using DriveSpace 3, which uses 512-byte sectors instead of clusters as the minimum unit to store files. This is true even if you turn off file compression in DriveSpace 3, which is an option.

▶ **See** "Working with DriveSpace 3 from Microsoft Plus!" **p. 637**

Formatting an Uncompressed Hard Drive from Windows Before you format an uncompressed hard drive, make sure you have backed up or copied any file that may be needed again. Once the formatting process begins, you will be unable to retrieve previous data from the drive.

To format a hard drive, follow these steps:

1. Close all documents and applications that are on the drive you want to format. Close any windows from My Computer that look at that drive. Collapse all folders in Windows Explorer for the hard drive you want to format.
2. Right-click the icon for the drive in either a folder window or in the Windows Explorer and choose Format. The Format dialog box appears (see fig. 22.3).

   In a folder window, you also can select the drive icon and choose File, Format.

FIG. 22.3

You can use the Format dialog box to do a full format, erase files, and copy system files onto a disk.

3. Select the option you want for formatting your disk:

Ca**p**acity	Click the drop-down list arrow to select a different capacity for the drive.

Format type

Quick (erase)	Erases all the files, but does not use ScanDisk to check for bad areas of the disk. The disk must be formatted to use this command. If you think your disk may have bad areas or has shown erratic behavior, be sure to run ScanDisk after the Quick format.
Full	Prepares a disk for use. All files are completely removed. Floppy disks are checked for bad sectors, but hard disks are not. If this is a new hard disk or a disk that has shown erratic behavior, be sure to run ScanDisk after the Full format.
Copy System Files **O**nly	Does not format the disk but it does copy system files to the disk so the floppy or hard disk can be used to start the computer.

Other options

Label	Creates a magnetic label on the disk. This label appears in the title bar of My Computer and Windows Explorer.
No label	Disables the label so the disk will not have a label.

Display Summary When Finished	Displays a report when formatting is complete. The report shows the space available on the disk, the room taken by system files, and the number of bad sectors.
Copy System Files	Copies system files onto the disk after formatting. Select this check box if you need to use this floppy or hard disk to start the computer.

4. Choose OK. A dialog box tells you that all files on the disk will be destroyed. Are you sure you want to format this drive? Choose OK to format or Cancel to stop.

5. If you choose OK, you will see the Format dialog box showing you the progression of the file format (see fig. 22.4).

FIG. 22.4
A progression bar at the bottom of the dialog box shows you the progress of disk formatting.

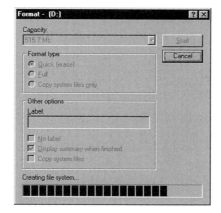

6. When formatting is complete, the Format Results dialog box displays the properties of the formatted drive (see fig. 22.5).

FIG. 22.5
The Format Results dialog box displays a report on disk statistics when formatting is complete.

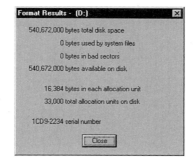

7. Choose Close to close the Format Results dialog box; then choose Close to close the Format dialog box.

If My Computer or Windows Explorer does not display the icon for the hard drive you want to format, then you may need to recheck the drive connections to the drive adapter or partition the hard drive using the FDISK command. You also need to check setup to be sure the proper drive type is selected.

▶ **See** "Using FDISK to Partition a New Hard Drive," **p. 615**

▶ **See** "Using FDISK to Repartition an Existing Drive," **p. 616**

▶ **See** "Using ScanDisk to Check for Disk Damage," **p. 620**

Formatting an Uncompressed Drive from the Windows Startup Disk If you want to reformat the drive that has Windows 95 installed on it, you must use the Windows startup disk:

1. Insert the startup disk in drive A and restart the computer.

2. Type **format** *drive_letter* at the command prompt.

   If you are formatting the boot drive (drive C), type **format C: /s**. The /s parameter will add the system files to the disk.

3. Press Y when the warning message appears.

4. When the formatting is completed, you can add a volume label if you want. Then press Enter to complete the formatting.

5. Remove the startup disk and restart the computer.

Using ScanDisk to Check for Disk Damage

In an ideal world, you would never have to worry about errors occurring on your hard disk or floppy disks. But because this is the real world, Windows 95 comes with a program called ScanDisk, which you can use to check for, diagnose, and repair damage on a hard disk or floppy disk. Part of your routine hard disk maintenance, along with defragmenting your hard disk as described in the previous section, should be to periodically run ScanDisk to keep your hard disk in good repair.

 Run ScanDisk anytime your system is shut down abnormally—for example, when a General Protection Fault (GPF) error or a system crash occurs.

In its standard test, ScanDisk checks the files and folders on a disk for *logical errors*; if you ask it to, ScanDisk also automatically corrects any errors it finds. ScanDisk checks for *cross-linked* files, which occur when two or more files have data stored in the same *cluster* (a storage unit on a disk). The data in the cluster is likely to be correct for only one of the files, and might not be correct for any of them. ScanDisk also checks for *lost file fragments*, which are pieces of data that have become disassociated with their files. Although file fragments can contain useful data, they usually can't be recovered and just take up disk space. You can tell ScanDisk to delete lost file fragments or save them in a file.

You also have the option of having ScanDisk check files for invalid file names and invalid dates and times. When a file has an invalid file name, you might not be able to open it. Invalid dates and times can cause problems when you use a backup program that uses dates and times to determine how current a file is.

You can run a more thorough test, in which ScanDisk checks for both logical errors in files and folders and scans the surface of the disk to check for *physical errors*. Physical errors are areas on your disk that are actually damaged and shouldn't be used for storing data. If ScanDisk finds bad sectors on your hard disk, any data in them can be moved to new sectors, and the bad sectors are marked so data is not stored in them in the future.

Physical Errors

Physical errors can occur if the read head crashes onto the disk. For example, if you jar the computer when the hard disk is being accessed. They also can result from defects or impurities in the magnetic media on the disk platter.

 You can access the Disk Defragmenter and ScanDisk utilities by right-clicking a disk icon in the Explorer or a folder, choosing Properties from the shortcut menu, and clicking the Tools tab.

To check a disk for errors, follow these steps:

1. Open the Start menu and choose Programs, Accessories, System Tools, ScanDisk. The ScanDisk window appears, as shown in figure 22.6.

2. Select the drive you want to check in the Select the Drive(s) You Want To Check for Errors box.

3. To check only for logical errors in the files and folders on the selected disk, make sure the Standard option is selected.

   To check for logical errors and to scan the disk for physical errors, select the Thorough option.

4. Click the Advanced button to change the settings used for checking files and folders for logical errors. The ScanDisk Advanced Options dialog box appears (see fig. 22.7). Use this dialog box to change the options in table 22.1.

FIG. 22.6
Use ScanDisk to check your hard disk for logical and physical errors and repair any damage.

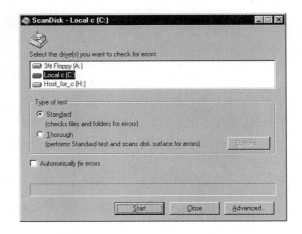

Table 22.1   ScanDisk Advanced Options

Option	Function
Display Summary Options	
Always	A summary with information about your disk and any errors found and corrected is displayed when you run ScanDisk.
Never	A summary is never displayed when you run ScanDisk.
Only If Errors Found	A summary is displayed only if errors are detected.
Log File Options	
Replace Log	Saves the details of a ScanDisk session in a log file named SCANDISK.LOG in the top-level folder on drive C. Replaces any existing file with the same name. Useful if you run ScanDisk automatically during off-hours and want a record of the ScanDisk session.
Append to Log	Saves the details of a ScanDisk session, appending the information to the end of SCANDISK.LOG. Useful if you want to maintain a history of your hard disk's wear-and-tear.
No Log	The results of the ScanDisk operation are not saved to a log file.
Cross-Linked Files Options	
Delete	Deletes cross-linked files when such files are found. Because cross-linked files are usually no good, it frees up hard disk space.
Make Copies	Makes a copy of each cross-linked cluster for each of the cross-linked files. Allows you to check for any salvageable data in the files.

Option	Function
Cross-Linked Files Options	
Ignore	Does not correct cross-linked files in any way. Using a cross-linked file can lead to further file damage and could cause the program using it to crash.
Lost File Fragments Options	
Free	Deletes lost file fragments, freeing up the space they use.
Convert to Files	Converts lost file fragments to files, which you can view to see whether they contain data you need. Files are given names beginning with FILE (for example, FILE0001) and are stored in the top-level folder of the disk.
Check Files For Options	
Invalid File Names	Files are checked for invalid file names. Files with invalid file names sometimes cannot be opened.
Invalid Dates and Times	Files are checked for invalid dates and times, which can result in incorrect sorting and also can cause problems with backup programs.
Check Host Drive First	If the drive you are checking has been compressed using DoubleSpace or DriveSpace, ScanDisk checks the host drive for the compressed drive first. Errors on the host drive often cause errors on the compressed drive, so it is best to check it first.

FIG. 22.7

You can change the settings ScanDisk uses to check files and folders for logical errors in the ScanDisk Advanced Options dialog box.

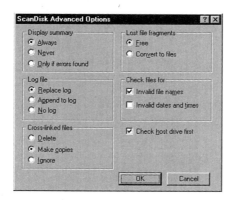

5. If you selected the Thorough option, choose Options to change the settings used to scan the disk for physical errors. The Surface Scan Options dialog box appears (see fig. 22.8). Use this dialog box to change the following options:

Option	Function
System and Data Areas	Scans the entire disk for physical damage.
System Area Only	Scans only the system area of the disk for physical damage. This is the disk area that contains files used to start the computer and holds the operating system.
Data Area Only	Scans only the data area of the disk for physical damage. The data area contains application and data programs. Use this if Windows behaves erratically even if you have reinstalled it.
Do Not Perform Write-Testing	If this option is not selected (the default), ScanDisk reads and writes every sector to verify both read and write functions. If this option is selected, ScanDisk does not write-verify the sectors.
Do Not Repair Bad Sectors in Hidden and System Files	ScanDisk will not move data from bad sectors in hidden and system files. Some programs look for hidden system files at specific locations and will not work if data in these files is moved.

FIG. 22.8

You can change the settings ScanDisk uses to scan the disk for physical errors.

6. Select the Automatically Fix Errors option if you want ScanDisk to automatically fix any errors it finds without first reporting the errors.

    If you don't select this option, ScanDisk informs you when it finds an error, and you can determine how ScanDisk fixes it.

7. Choose Start to begin the test. The progress of the test is displayed at the bottom of the ScanDisk dialog box. You can halt the test by choosing the Cancel button. If you told ScanDisk to scan your disk for physical errors, the test can take several minutes. When the test is complete, a summary report like the one in figure 22.9

might appear, depending on the options you selected in the ScanDisk Advanced Options dialog box. Click Close to close the Results dialog box.

8. Click Close to exit ScanDisk.

FIG. 22.9
The results of a ScanDisk operation can be displayed in the ScanDisk Results dialog box.

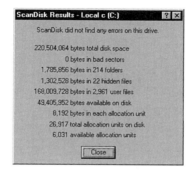

> You can run ScanDisk automatically every time you start your computer to keep your hard disk in top form. To do this, create a shortcut for ScanDisk in the StartUp folder, as follows:
>
> 1. Right-click the Start button and choose Open.
> 2. Open the Programs folder and then the StartUp folder.
> 3. Right-click in a blank area of the StartUp Folder and choose New, Shortcut.
> 4. Type **scandskw.exe** in the Command Line text box and choose Next.
> 5. Type **ScanDisk** in the Select a Name for the Shortcut text box and choose Finish.
>
> You also can use the System Agent to schedule ScanDisk to run automatically. See "Running Disk Performance Utilities with the System Agent," later in this chapter, to learn how to use the System Agent.

You can add any of the following parameters to the command line of the shortcut to control how ScanDisk will run:

/a	Check all local, unremovable hard drives
/n	Runs and exits ScanDisk automatically
/p	Runs ScanDisk in Preview mode, in which errors are reported but not actually fixed.
dblspace.*nnn* or drvspace.*nnn*	Specifies compressed volume file to check, where *nnn* is the file-name extension of the host drive. Use this parameter to check unmounted CVFs. Include the host drive letter, as in c:\drvspace.*nnn*.

TROUBLESHOOTING

When I retrieve a file, the hard disk light comes on a lot. It even sounds like the hard disk is chattering. The more I use the computer the worse this problem gets. ScanDisk didn't show any problems with the disk. The problem is probably not with the physical quality of your hard drive's magnetic surface, which is what ScanDisk checks. The problem is more likely that files on the hard disk are fragmented. Fragmented disks have pieces of files scattered all over the disk. Reading a fragmented file requires a lot more activity for the read head because the clusters that make up the file are not contiguous. This increases the time it takes to load a file and effectively slows down your system. When fragmenting is bad, it gets worse—which is why your computer seems to be slowing down the more you use it. Windows comes with a defragmenting utility that reorganizes your files on the disk so they are contiguous and can be read quickly.

ScanDisk will not check a drive that was compressed using DriveSpace. An error message appears stating that the drive is not properly formatted or a disk utility program has locked it. ScanDisk cannot check a compressed drive if it is unmounted. Open DriveSpace and mount the drive, then run ScanDisk on the drive to check it.

An error message appears when I use ScanDisk to check a drive that was compressed with DriveSpace 3. The message states that the drive was compressed by a program not supported by ScanDisk. When you click OK in the message box, ScanDisk will check the drive. To avoid this error message in the future, replace the DSKMAINT.DLL file by following these steps:

1. Open the Start menu, and choose Programs, MS-DOS Prompt.

2. Type **ren c:j\windows\system\dskmaint.dll dskmaint.xxx** at the command prompt.

3. Insert the Microsoft Plus! CD-ROM (or floppy disk 2) and switch to the drive containing the CD-ROM or floppy disk.

4. Type **extract /l c:\windows\system plus_2.cab dskmaint.dll** at the command prompt and press Enter.

5. Exit the command prompt.

▶ **See** "Improving Performance with Disk Defragmenter," **p. 646**

Compressing a Hard Disk

Windows 95 comes with a new version of DriveSpace, the disk utility used for compressing your hard disks to make room for more files. The Windows 95 DriveSpace is compatible with both DoubleSpace, which was included with MS-DOS 6.0 and 6.2, and

DriveSpace, which was included with MS-DOS 6.22. You can work with compressed drives of either type and the two types of compressed drives can coexist on the same computer.

If you have purchased the optional Microsoft Plus! companion software, you can upgrade to DriveSpace 3, an enhanced disk compression utility that improves on DriveSpace for Windows 95 in several ways. See the later section, "Working with DriveSpace 3 from Microsoft Plus!," to learn how to use DriveSpace 3.

If you already have compressed drives on your computer when you install Windows 95, the DBLSPACE.BIN or DRVSPACE.BIN files on your computer are replaced with new versions of these files that can be unloaded from memory when Windows 95 is started and replaced with a 32-bit driver called DBLSPACX.VXD. This driver is used when you work with compressed drives in Windows 95 and is compatible with the new VFAT file system. The new driver protects the long file names that you can now use with 32-bit Windows 95 applications.

Disk Compression

Despite the name, disk compression doesn't actually compress your hard disk, which is a physical entry, nor does it increase the physical capacity of your disk. What it really does is use software magic to increase the capacity of your hard disk in two ways.

First, disk compression software increases the capacity of your hard disk by reducing the smallest storage unit to 512 bytes, rather than the much larger clusters (8-64K) used in the native DOS environment. This improvement in storage efficiency goes a long way towards reducing the waste of space that occurs when you save a lot of small files.

The second component of disk compression involves the use of a software algorithm that looks for patterns in a data file and codes repeating patterns in a way that takes up less space. Many types of files have lots of repeating information and can be compressed to less than 60 percent of their original size.

 TIP Although DRVSPACE.BIN is the only file you need to work with drives compressed when running Windows 95, you will also find DBLSPACE.BIN in your root directory. DBLSPACE.BIN differs from DRVSPACE.BIN only by name, but you should leave it there. This file is needed if you try to mount older files compressed with DoubleSpace, for example, on a floppy disk you compressed with DoubleSpace.

The Facts about Disk Compression

DriveSpace is an optional program that can be installed when you install Windows 95, or you can install it at a later time. To see if you have DriveSpace available, open the Start menu and choose Programs, Accessories, System Tools. If DriveSpace is not listed in the System Tools menu, you will need to install it. For information on how to install DriveSpace after you have installed Windows, see Appendix A, "Installing Windows 95."

When you run DriveSpace, it creates a compressed drive on your existing hard disk. The compressed drive is actually a file, not a physical hard drive, called a *compressed volume file* (CVF). The CVF is stored on a physical, uncompressed drive, called the *host drive*. The CVF is assigned a drive letter, just like a physical drive, and can be accessed like any other drive. The file that DriveSpace creates on your hard drive is a hidden, read only, system file; thus, is it not acted upon by most normal DOS commands. From the user's point of view, the only difference after running DriveSpace is that the original drive has a lot more free space and there is a new drive, the host drive.

As a rule of thumb, DriveSpace will add 50 to 100 percent more capacity to your disk. The amount of actual compression depends upon the types of files stored on the disk. Some files, like text files or certain graphics files, compress significantly, while other files, like an application's EXE file, may barely change.

You can run DriveSpace in one of two ways. Typically, you use DriveSpace to compress your entire existing drive to free up more storage space. You can run DriveSpace to compress your C drive, for example, which then becomes a compressed volume file on the host drive H. You also can use DriveSpace to compress a specified amount of the free space on your hard drive to create a new, empty compressed drive. The rest of the hard drive is not compressed. If, for example, you have 80M of free space on your C drive, you can use DriveSpace to compress 25M of the free space to create a new drive D with roughly 50M of free space. You then have 55M free on drive C and 50M on drive D for an effective 105M of free space.

The maximum allowable size for a compressed drive using the version of DriveSpace that comes with Windows 95 is 512M. If you have a drive of 420M, for example, you could compress the first 256M to 512M and the remaining 163M to 326M, assuming a compression ratio of 2:1. If you have a drive that already has more than 512M of files on it, you won't be able to compress it using the version of DriveSpace that comes with Windows 95.

To get around this limitation, you can purchase Microsoft Plus!, a companion program for Windows 95 that includes DriveSpace 3, which as an enhanced version of DriveSpace. Among the enhancements is that DriveSpace 3 supports compressed drives up to 2G in size. DriveSpace 3 is discussed in detail later in this chapter in "Working with DriveSpace 3 from Microsoft Plus!"

TROUBLESHOOTING

Large files will not copy onto the compressed drive. The available free space displayed for compressed drives is only an estimate. It is based on the average compression for all files on your disk. If the file you are attempting to save does not compress as much as the average, then it may not fit in the available space.

▶ **See** "Changing the Estimated Compression Ratio for Your Compressed Drive," **p. 634**

Compressing a Drive with Windows 95 DriveSpace

If you are using the DriveSpace program that comes with Windows 95, follow the steps below to compress your drive. If you have installed Microsoft Plus!, see "Working with DriveSpace 3 from Microsoft Plus!," for instructions on how to use DriveSpace 3 to compress your disk.

DriveSpace automatically runs ScanDisk before compressing a drive.

1. Open the Start menu and choose <u>P</u>rograms, Accessories, System Tools, and then choose DriveSpace. The DriveSpace window appears, as shown in figure 22.10.

   A drive that has already been compressed will display the phrase Compressed drive next to it and will have an associated host drive in the list.

FIG. 22.10
Use DriveSpace to create more free space on your hard drive.

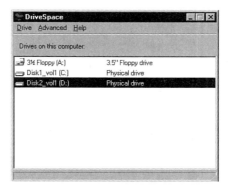

N O T E DriveSpace is optional in installation. If it isn't in the System Tools menu, you need to use Add/Remove Programs, Windows Setup to add it. ■

2. Select the drive you want to compress from the Drives On This Computer list.

> **CAUTION**
>
> If you are using DriveSpace to compress floppy disks, be aware of the compatibility between disks compressed with different versions of Microsoft compression software and the software on the computers used to read the disks. The following table summarizes this information:
>
> | Disk compressed with | Readable on computers with DriveSpace |
> | --- | --- |
> | DriveSpace | for Windows, DriveSpace for MS-DOS, or DoubleSpace for DOS |
> | DoubleSpace for MS-DOS | DoubleSpace for MS-DOS, DriveSpace for Windows |
> | DriveSpace for MS-DOS | DriveSpace for MS-DOS, DriveSpace for Windows |
>
> To use a compressed floppy disk in Windows 95, choose Advance, Options. Select the Automatically Mount Compressed Removable Media option and choose OK.

3. Choose Drive, Compress. The Compress a Drive dialog box appears (see fig. 22.11).

FIG. 22.11
The Compress a Drive dialog box displays information on the size of the selected disk and how much space there will be after running DriveSpace.

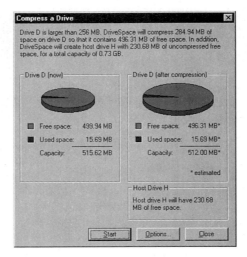

4. Choose Options to change the compression options if you want. The Compression Options dialog box displays (see fig. 22.12). You can change the following three options:

  • To change the drive letter assigned to the host drive, click the down arrow next to the Drive Letter of Host Drive drop-down list and select a new drive letter. You may have to select a new drive letter if you plan on using the default drive letter for another purpose (for example, for a new hard disk).

FIG. 22.12

Change the options used for compressing a drive in the Compression Options dialog box.

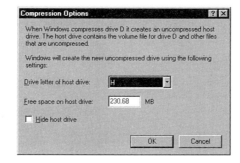

- To change the amount of free space reserved on the host drive, type a new value in the Free Space on Host Drive text box. Windows will calculate the smallest acceptable size for the Host drive and will not allow you to enter a number that is too small.

- If you don't want the host drive to appear in the Windows Explorer, My Computer, or various dialog boxes such as the Open and Save As dialog boxes, select the Hide Host Drive option. You may want to do this if you are creating a system for novices who may accidentally delete important files from the Host drive.

When you finish making changes, choose OK.

5. Choose Start. A confirmation dialog box appears (see fig. 22.13).

FIG. 22.13

Back up your files before you run DriveSpace by choosing the Back Up Files button.

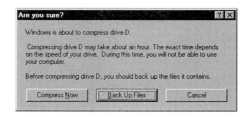

6. If you haven't backed up your files, choose the Back Up Files button to open Backup. See Chapter 23, "Backing Up and Protecting Your Data," for detailed information on how to back up files.

7. Choose Compress Now to start the compression operation. The progress of the compression operation is displayed in the Compress a Drive message box. Choose Close after examining the results.

The DriveSpace program will check your hard disk for errors and defragment it as part of the compression operation.

8. When the compression operation is completed, the Compress a Drive dialog box informs you that the drive has been compressed and displays how much free space is now on the compressed drive (see fig. 22.14).

FIG. 22.14
The results of a drive compression operation are displayed in the Compress a Drive dialog box.

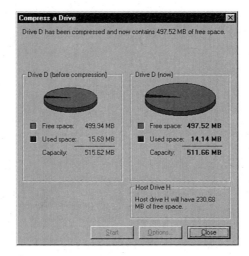

9. A Restart Computer dialog box appears asking you if you want to restart your computer. Choose Yes to restart, No to continue working.

   Do not set up new software, change system settings, or run MS-DOS programs until you restart your computer.

   ▶ **See** "Setting Up Your Floppy or Hard Disk to Read Compressed Files," **p. 643**

Compressing Part of a Disk

You don't have to compress your entire hard disk; you can compress some or all of the free space on your hard disk to create a new compressed drive. To create a new compressed drive from part of a hard disk, follow these steps:

1. Open the DriveSpace window and select the drive with the free space you want to use to create a new compressed drive. You cannot select a compressed drive.

2. Choose Advanced, Create Empty. The Create New Compressed Drive dialog box appears, as shown in figure 22.15.

3. Accept the default name for the new drive or select an alternative name from the Create a New Drive Named drop-down list.

FIG. 22.15

Create a new compressed drive using the free space on your hard disk.

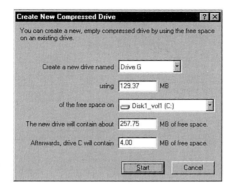

4. Enter the amount of free space (in megabytes) you want to use to create the new drive in the Using text box. The amount displayed in The New Drive Will Contain About...MB of Free Space text box changes to reflect how much free space will be created in the new drive.

5. Select the drive that has the free space you want to use to create the new drive from the Of The Free Space On drop-down list.

6. If you know how much free space you want the new drive to have, enter that number in The New Drive Will Contain About...MB of Free Space text box. If you enter a value here, the amount displayed in the Using text box is automatically adjusted to show how much free space on the selected drive will be used for the new drive.

   The amount of free space that will be left on the uncompressed drive is displayed in the Afterwards, Drive *letter* Will Contain...MB of Free Space text box.

7. Choose Start.

8. When the message box appears informing you that the operation is complete, choose OK.

Adjusting the Size of the Free Space on a Compressed Drive

You can adjust the distribution of free space between a compressed drive and its host. When you increase the free space on the compressed drive, you decrease the free space on the host drive, and vice-versa. To adjust the free space on the compressed and host drives, follow these steps:

1. Open the DriveSpace window and select either the compressed drive or its host from the Drives on This Computer list.

2. Choose Drive, Adjust Free Space; the Adjust Free Space dialog box appears (see fig. 22.16).

FIG. 22.16
Adjust the distribution of free space between a compressed drive and its host in the Adjust Free Space dialog box.

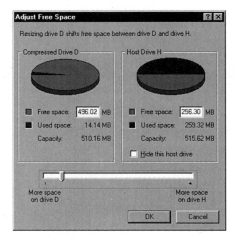

3. Drag the slider to change the distribution of free space between the compressed and host drives. The pie charts will reflect the amount of free space and used space.

4. Choose OK.

   A message box shows you the amount of free space on the compressed and host drives when the operation is complete.

5. A Restart Computer dialog will display asking you if you want to restart your computer. Choose Yes to restart, No to continue working.

   Do not set up new software, change system settings, or run MS-DOS programs until you restart your computer.

TROUBLESHOOTING

There seems to be enough space on the hard disk to store some very large video and sound files, but even after resizing the compressed drive there still isn't enough space. Some files, such as application, video, and music files, may not compress very much. The estimated free space on a compressed drive however, is calculated from the average amount of compression for all files on the drive. As a consequence, files that look like they may fit, may not.

Changing the Estimated Compression Ratio for Your Compressed Drive

DriveSpace contains a command that enables you to change the estimated compression ratio. This ratio does not determine how tightly data is compressed on your hard drive, but Windows 95 uses it to calculate how much free space remains on your hard drive. The remaining free space as calculated by the estimated compression ratio is then used in Windows 95 dialog boxes to give you an estimate of how much drive space remains.

 T I P In general, do not change the compression ratio to more than a two to one (2:1) ratio. Changing the compression ratio to a larger number would not compress files tighter, but it would give you a very misleading idea of how much free space remains.

Windows 95 calculates the estimated compression ratio from an average of the actual file size and the compressed file size for all files on the drive. Every time a file is saved or erased, Windows 95 recalculates the estimated compression ratio and then uses that number to calculate the estimated free space remain. But Windows 95's estimation may not be as accurate as your own.

To understand the problem, you must know that different files compress by different amounts. Files such as text files and some graphics files contain a lot of repetitive information that can be tightly compressed into a small space. Other files, such as an application's EXE files or a video's JPEG or MPEG files, have little room for compression and may not change significantly in size. Windows 95 has no idea what types of files you will be storing on the hard disk, which limits its ability to estimate accurately the compression ratio.

If you have just installed a lot of application files on a compressed drive with few data files, for example, Windows 95 will calculate a low compression ratio. Conversely, if your compressed drive has few application or multimedia files, then the estimated compression ratio will be higher. As long as you continue saving and removing the same type of files, Windows 95 will report a fairly accurate estimated free space. But if you change the type of files you save, the estimated free space will be wrong because the new files compress to a different amount.

> **CAUTION**
> What you see is not necessarily what you get when dealing with compression ratios. Some files, such as EXE application files or JPEG and MPEG video files, compress very little. This means that even though the estimated free space may be 15M, it's doubtful that 12M of JPEG, MPEG, or EXE files would fit because they do not compress as tightly as other files have.

If you will not be adding more application or multimedia files to your compressed drive, but you will be adding a lot more data files, then you may want to increase the estimated compression ratio to get a more accurate reading of free space. Conversely, a drive that has stored word processing files may have much less space available than it appears to have when you begin storing sound, video, and application files on it.

To adjust the compression ratio, follow these steps:

1. Open the DriveSpace window and select the compressed drive whose compression ratio you want to adjust from the Drives on This Computer list.

2. Choose Advanced, Change Ratio; the Compression Ratio dialog box appears (see fig. 22.17).

FIG. 22.17
Adjust the compression ratio of a compressed drive in the Compression Ratio dialog box.

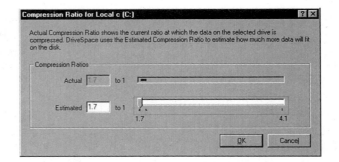

3. Drag the Estimated Compression Ratio slider to adjust the compression ratio.

4. When the message box appears informing you that the operation is complete, choose OK.

Viewing the Properties of a Compressed Drive

You can view the properties of a compressed drive or its host using the Drive Properties command. You can find out the name of the compressed volume file and what drive it is stored on, the amount of free and used space on the drive, and the compression ratio if it is a compressed drive.

To view the properties of a drive, follow these steps:

1. Open the DriveSpace window and select the drive whose properties you want to view from the Drives on This Computer list.

2. Choose Drive, Properties. The Compression Information dialog box appears, as shown in figure 22.18.

3. You can select the Hide Host Drive option to hide the display of this drive when the drive contents display in the Explorer or My Computer window and in some dialog boxes such as Open and Save As. If you select this option, a message box informs you that you will not be able to use the data or free space on the drive. Choose Yes to confirm that you want to hide the drive.

You can use the DriveSpace Properties sheet to show the host drive if you change your mind at a later time.

FIG. 22.18

View the properties of a compressed drive or its host in the Compression Information dialog box.

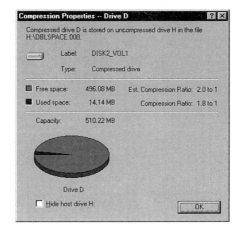

Compression Properties -- Drive D

Compressed drive D is stored on uncompressed drive H in the file H:\DBLSPACE.000.

Label: DISK2_VOL1

Type: Compressed drive

Free space: 496.08 MB   Est. Compression Ratio: 2.0 to 1

Used space: 14.14 MB   Compression Ratio: 1.8 to 1

Capacity: 510.22 MB

Drive D

☐ Hide host drive H: OK

4. Choose OK.

TIP You also can find out how much each file in a CVF is compressed. Open a DOS session and type **dir/c** at the command prompt. The file listing will show the file compression ratio for each file.

Working with DriveSpace 3 from Microsoft Plus!

DriveSpace 3 is the enhanced disk compression utility that comes with the Microsoft Plus! Companion for Windows 95. DriveSpace 3 offers superb disk compression that improves on Windows 95 DriveSpace in the following ways:

- Handles disks up to 2G

- Works with smaller units of data (512-byte sectors versus 32K byte clusters), improving storage efficiency

- Supports two new higher levels of compression (HiPack and UltraPack)

- Has settings for specifying what type of compression to use and when to use it

- Adds a Compression tab to the Properties sheet for floppy and hard disks

Remember that compressed disks can be slow—the greater the compression, the slower your system's performance is likely to be. Also, compressing your system's primary hard disk can take a long time, during which you can't work with your system.

Use the following steps to compress a disk with DriveSpace 3:

1. Open the Start menu and click Programs, Accessories, System Tools. Click DriveSpace (after Plus! installation, the icon beside the DriveSpace will include a 3 to indicate DriveSpace 3). The DriveSpace 3 window appears (see fig. 22.19).

FIG. 22.19
The DriveSpace 3 window displays the available drives on your system.

Click the drive to compress

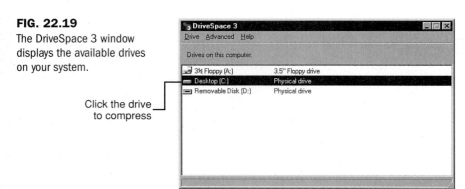

2. Click the drive that you want to compress.

N O T E   If you've previously compressed a hard disk with DoubleSpace or DriveSpace (for Win 95 or for earlier DOS versions), you can select the disk, then choose Drive, Upgrade to convert the disk to DriveSpace 3 format. ▪

3. Choose Advanced, Settings. The Disk Compression Settings dialog box appears (see fig. 22.20).

FIG. 22.20
The compression method you choose affects free disk space and speed.

Leave this check box selected when compressing a floppy disk so Windows will mount it automatically when you insert it in your drive

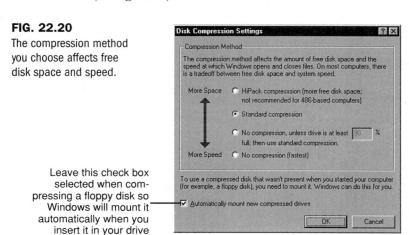

4. Click the option button for the compression method you want to use:

   No Compression

   No Compression, Unless Drive Is at least X% Full only compresses the disk after it's more full than the percentage you specify

   Standard Compression compresses the disk contents by approximately a 1.8:1 ratio

   HiPack Compression compresses the disk contents by up to 2.3:1

N O T E   As always, the compression ratio on your hard drive will depend on the type of files being compressed. ▨

5. Click OK to close the Compression Settings dialog box and accept the specified compression method.

6. Choose <u>D</u>rive, <u>C</u>ompress. The Compress a Drive dialog box appears, informing you of the estimated results of the compression operation—that is, how much free space and used space the disk will have after compression.

7. Click <u>O</u>ptions. The Compression Options dialog box appears. Use it to specify a drive letter and free space for the Host drive where DriveSpace 3 will store compressed information about the drive.

   You should only need to change these first two options if your system is connected to a network that uses drive H for another purpose. If you're compressing a floppy disk you might use on another computer that doesn't have DriveSpace 3, click to select the Use DoubleSpace-Compatible Format check box; note that you do need to select this option for Windows 95 systems without DriveSpace 3 or for systems using DriveSpace from a DOS 6.x version. Click OK to accept the Compression Options you set.

8. Click the <u>S</u>tart button in the Compress a Drive dialog box. The Are You Sure? dialog box appears, asking you to confirm the compression operation.

9. Click the <u>B</u>ack Up Files button to make a backup copy of the files on the disk before you compress it. This is an important safety measure; skipping it isn't recommended.

10. DriveSpace 3 runs the backup utility installed to work with your system. Follow any on-screen instructions to complete the backup process.

11. When the backup is finished, click <u>C</u>ontinue to compress the disk. DriveSpace 3 compresses the disk, then redisplays the Compress a Drive dialog box to report on the compression results.

12. Click <u>C</u>lose to complete compressing the disk.

Part **VII**

Ch **22**

The other commands in DriveSpace 3 work the same way as those in DriveSpace for Windows 95. See the previous sections for information on using these commands.

 TIP When you install DriveSpace 3, a Compression tab is added to the Properties dialog box for the drives on your computer. You can view the properties for any compressed drives on your system and access DriveSpace and the Compression Agent (discussed in the next section) from this tab. To display the Compression tab, right-click on the drive whose properties you want to view and choose Properties. Select the Compression tab in the Properties sheet.

 TROUBLESHOOTING

After compressing a drive using DriveSpace 3, I checked the properties for the drive and found that more space was being used by the files that were already on the disk. The reason it appears that the files are using more disk space after compression is that DriveSpace 3 uses larger clusters (32K) than many hard disks use in order to be able to support very large disk sizes (up to 2G). Because of this, the disk space reported in the Properties dialog box may increase, because small files will seem to take up more disk space than before compression. In fact, DriveSpace 3 allocates physical drive space in 512-byte units, which is much more efficient than the larger clusters that uncompressed drives use. The Properties dialog box determines how much space is being used by files by looking at the cluster level, so it does not give an accurate report.

After reinstalling Windows 95 on a disk compressed with DriveSpace 3, I was unable to create a startup disk that was compatible with DriveSpace 3. The reason for this is that the Windows 95 Setup program overwrites the MSDOS.INF and LAYOUT.INF files, which contained the information needed to create DriveSpace 3-compatible startup disks. To update these files so they contain the necessary information, follow these steps:

1. Open DriveSpace 3 and select an uncompressed drive in the Drives on this computer list box.
2. Choose Advanced, Create Empty.
3. Type **1** in the Using MB text box and choose Start.
4. Choose Yes when prompted to update the current startup disk.
5. Select the newly created compressed drive in the Drives on This Computer list and choose Advanced, Delete.
6. Choose Yes and then OK to confirm deletion of the drive.
7. Exit DriveSpace.

▶ **See** "Backing Up Your Files," **p. 662**

Improving Compression with the Compression Agent

Compression Agent is a new tool that comes with Microsoft Plus! that provides even higher levels of compression and, used in conjunction with DriveSpace 3, allows you to optimize the balance between maximizing disk space and performance. You can specify that particular files and folders are compressed using one of two high compression formats (UltraPack or HiPack), or not at all.

Compression Agent, unlike DriveSpace, doesn't compress files as they are used. Instead, it compresses your files when you run the program. Because it can take a long time to compress your files using the Compression Agent, it is best to run the program when you are not working. You can use the System Agent, discussed in the next section, to schedule the Compression Agent to run after work hours.

To run the Compression Agent, follow these steps:

1. Open the Start menu and click Programs, Accessories, System Tools, and then Compression Agent. The Compression Agent dialog box appears (see fig. 22.21).

FIG. 22.21

The Compression Agent dialog box is used to setup and run Compression Agent.

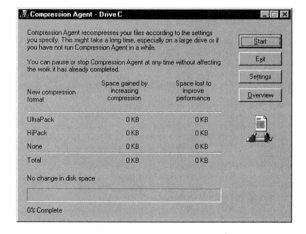

2. Click Start to run Compression Agent using the default settings.

   Compression Agent will recompress the drive file by file, using the best compression method for each file.

3. To change the settings used by Compression Agent, click the Settings button. The Compression Agent Settings dialog box is displayed (see fig. 22.22).

4. Specify which files you want to UltraPack in the first set of options:

   Select the Do Not UltraPack any files option to maximize performance.

Select the UltraPack All Files option to maximize space. Packing and unpacking files using this method is slow, so it is recommended for Pentium systems only.

Select the UltraPack Only Files Not Used Within the Last Days option to specify that only those files that have not been modified in a specified number of days be UltraPacked.

FIG. 22.22

You can specify which compression method should be used on which files in the Compression Agent Settings dialog box.

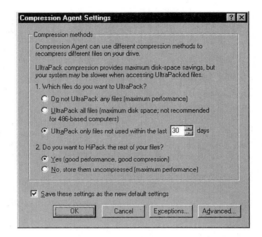

5. Specify whether or not to HiPack the remaining files in the second set of options:

   Select Yes to HiPack the remaining files. This option yields a good balance between performance and space-savings.

   Select No to leave the remaining files uncompressed. Use this option if you want to maximize performance.

6. The Compression Agent can reduce the compression method used for files you have used recently (as specified in step 4). You can override this option when disk space starts to get low by clicking Advanced and specifying a setting in the Advanced Settings dialog box.

   Select the Leave all UltraPacked files in the UltraPack format option if you want files to be UltraPacked even if you have used them recently.

7. If you want to specify different compression settings for particular files or folders, click the Exceptions button and specify which compression method you want to use for which files and folders.

8. Click Start to run the Compression Agent using your settings.

By manipulating the settings used in both DriveSpace 3 and in Compression Agent, you can fine-tune the balance between performance and disk space, depending on your priorities. For example, to maximize performance while still gaining the benefits of disk compression, you can turn off compression in DriveSpace's Disk Compression Settings dialog box and run the Compression Agent at night to compress your files.

After you choose the settings you want in the Compression Agent, use the System Agent as described in "Running Disk Performance Utilities with the System Agent," to run the Compression Agent and recompress the specified disk.

 TIP Even when you tell DriveSpace not to compress files, you save space. This is because DriveSpace 3 uses sectors (512 bytes) instead of clusters (32K in size on a 1G drive) as the minimum storage unit. This significantly improves storage efficiency.

Setting Up Your Floppy or Hard Disk to Read Compressed Files

When you are working with compressed removable storage media (such as floppy disks), you must mount the compressed drive if it wasn't present when the computer was started. Mounting a drive links a drive letter with a compressed volume file (CVF) and enables your computer to access the files on the compressed volume files.

To mount a compressed drive, follow these steps:

1. Open the DriveSpace window and select the drive you want to mount in the Drives on This Computer list.

   For example, if you want to read a floppy disk in drive A and the floppy disk has DriveSpace or DoubleSpace compression, then you would select the A drive.

2. Choose Advanced, Mount.

3. Select the compressed volume file you want to mount.

   After you mount a drive, it shows up in the Drives on This Computer list as a compressed drive.

You can select an option so that newly compressed devices are automatically mounted. Choose Advanced, Settings. Select the Automatically Mount New Compressed Devices option and choose OK. Windows now automatically mounts new compressed devices so that you don't have to mount the compressed device each time you insert it in the computer.

To unmount a compressed drive, follow these steps:

1. Open the DriveSpace window and select the compressed drive you want to unmount from the Drives on this Computer list.

2. Choose Advanced, Unmount.

3. When the message box appears informing you that the operation is complete, choose OK.

TROUBLESHOOTING

DriveSpace is not automatically mounting compressed removable media I am using with my computer. There are two reasons why Windows 95 may not be automatically mounting compressed removable media. The first possibility is that in order for DriveSpace to automatically mount removable media, a compression driver must be loaded in memory. If none of the hard disks on your computer are compressed, you must run DriveSpace to load the driver. To mount the removable media, follow the steps above for mounting a compressed drive. The second possibility is that DriveSpace is opened. Windows 95 will not automatically mount compressed media while DriveSpace is open. Choose Advanced, Mount to mount the compressed drive.

The DISKCOPY command returns an error message when used to make a copy of a floppy disk that has been compressed with DriveSpace. Before you use the DISKCOPY command to copy a floppy disk that has been compressed, you must unmount the compressed volume file, as just described in the previous steps.

Returning a Drive to Normal Compression

DriveSpace also enables you to decompress a drive. Before you decompress a drive, make sure that there will be enough space on the drive to hold the decompressed files.

If there is not enough room, you get an error dialog that tells you how much data you have, how much free space that data requires, and how much data must be deleted or moved elsewhere.

To decompress a drive, follow these steps:

1. Open the Start menu and choose Programs, Accessories, System Tools, DriveSpace. The DriveSpace window appears.
2. Select the drive you want to decompress from the Drives on This Computer list.
3. Choose Drive, Uncompress.
4. Choose Start. A confirmation dialog box appears.

5. If you haven't backed up your files, choose the <u>B</u>ack Up Files button to open Backup. See Chapter 23, "Backing Up and Protecting Your Data," for detailed information on how to back up your files.

6. Choose Uncompress <u>N</u>ow to start the uncompression operation. The progress of the uncompression operation is displayed at the bottom of the Uncompress a Drive dialog box. A message box informs you when the uncompression is completed.

7. Choose OK.

Deleting a Compressed Drive

You can delete a compressed drive, returning it to its original uncompressed state. Deleting a compressed drive is different from decompressing a compressed drive. When you delete a compressed drive, all the data on the drive is destroyed and the drive is decompressed. One situation where you might want to delete a compressed drive is if you are moving the disk to another computer and want to both remove the data and decompress it so it can be used by any MS-DOS computer.

When you delete a compressed drive, Windows 95 deletes the compressed volume file (CVF) that contains all the compressed data and application files. (The contents of the CVF file are what looks like a compressed disk drive.) You could manually delete the DRVSPACE.000 file by changing its system attribute, but it is better to use the Delete command in DriveSpace; this also removes the ACTIVATE= line from the DRVSPACE.INI file for the drive you are deleting.

If you have only one compressed drive on your hard disk, then you will also be asked whether you want to delete the DriveSpace driver, DRVSPACE.BIN. You can delete this driver if you do not have other compressed drives on this drive.

> **CAUTION**
>
> When you delete a compressed drive, you lose all the information stored on that drive, so be sure that you have backed up or moved any files you need on this drive before deleting it.

 TROUBLESHOOTING

An overzealous novice removed the system attribute from the DRVSPACE.000 file and deleted it. Is there a way to recover the data that was on the compressed drive? If the user has not saved files to that disk after deleting DRVSPACE.000, the file may be able to be recovered. Use an undelete utility to restore the deleted DRVSPACE.000 file, then exit Windows and restart. Be sure to restore the system attribute to DRVSPACE.000.

To delete a compressed drive, follow these steps:

1. Open the DriveSpace window and select the compressed drive you want to delete from the Drives on This Computer list.

2. Choose <u>A</u>dvanced, <u>D</u>elete.

3. When the confirmation message box appears, choose Yes.

4. A message box appears asking if you want to delete the DriveSpace driver. Choose <u>Y</u>es if this is the only compressed drive on your computer and you will not be using compressed floppy disks. Choose <u>N</u>o if you have other compressed drives or if you will be using compressed floppy disks.

5. When the message box appears informing you that the operation is complete, choose OK.

6. You will be prompted to restart Windows 95 or continue. Switch to any open applications and save the documents, then choose <u>Y</u>es. If you choose <u>N</u>o, you will not be able to change system settings, install applications, or use MS-DOS until you restart.

If you are in doubt about whether to delete the driver for DriveSpace, remember that it is much easier to reinstall than it is to uninstall the driver. You can remove it now and add it back at any time using the procedure to mount a compressed drive.

▶ **See** "Setting Up Your Floppy or Hard Disk to Read Compressed Files," **p. 643**

Improving Performance with Disk Defragmenter

Information written to a hard disk is not necessarily stored in a *contiguous* (adjacent) block. Rather, fragments of information are more likely spread across the disk wherever the system can find room. The more you use the hard disk, the more fragmented the disk becomes. Obviously, the drive takes more time to hunt for information located in several places than it takes to fetch the same information from a single location. Because of this extra time, disk fragmentation can slow the computer's operation considerably.

The Windows Disk Defragmenter can significantly improve file access time by restructuring files into contiguous blocks and moving free space to the end of the disk.

 TIP   When defragmenting your disk, use the Full Defragmentation option for top performance from your hard drive.

To defragment a disk, follow these steps:

1. Open the Start menu and choose Programs, Accessories, System Tools, Disk Defragmenter. The Select Drive dialog box appears (see fig. 22.23).

FIG. 22.23
Select the drive you want to defragment in the Select Drive dialog box.

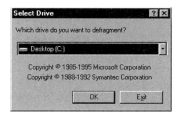

2. Select the drive you want to defragment from the Defragment Which Drive drop-down list and choose OK.

The Disk Defragmenter dialog box appears, as shown in figure 22.24. The percent fragmentation of the selected drive is displayed in the dialog box. You are also informed whether defragmentation will improve performance.

FIG. 22.24
The Disk Defragmenter dialog box tells you how fragmented your drive is and whether defragmenting it will improve its performance.

3. To change the Disk Defragmenter options, choose Advanced. The Advanced Options dialog box appears (see fig. 22.25). Use this dialog box to change the following options:

Option	Function
Full Defragmentation (Both Files and Free Space)	Defragments all the files on the selected disk. This option provides you with the greatest improvement in response time.
Defragment Files Only	Defragments only the files on your hard disk, without consolidating the free space. This takes less time than Full Defragmentation.

continues

continued

Option	Function
Consolidate Free Space Only	Only consolidates the free space on the selected disk without defragmenting the files. This is good for adding new programs and/or a compressed drive.
Check Drive for Errors	Checks the files and folders on the drive for errors before defragmenting. A good idea if you haven't run ScanDisk recently.
This Time Only. Next Time, Use the Defaults Again	Uses the selected options for this defragment operation only.
Save These Options and Use Them Every Time	Saves the selected options and uses them each time you run Disk Defragmenter unless you change them again.

Select the desired options and choose OK. You return to the Disk Defragmenter dialog box.

FIG. 22.25
Change the way Disk Defragmenter works in the Advanced Options dialog box.

4. Choose Start. The progress of the defragmentation operation is displayed in the Defragmenting dialog box (see fig. 22.26).

5. When the defragmentation operation is complete, choose Exit to close the Disk Defragmenter, or choose Select Drive to defragment another drive.

Defragmenting a hard disk can take a long time. Although you can continue working on your computer during the defragmentation operation, you will notice a significant slow-down in your computer's operation. For this reason, it is advisable to run the Disk

Defragmenter during a time when you do not need to use the computer—for example, after you leave work for the day.

FIG. 22.26
Monitor the progress of the defragmentation operation in the Defragmenting dialog box.

You can pause the defragmentation operation if you need to use your computer before defragmentation is completed and you don't want performance slowed down. Choose Pause from the Defragmenting dialog box to pause Disk Defragmenter. To resume defragmentation, choose Pause again. You also can cancel the defragmentation operation by choosing Stop.

Choose Show Details to open a window that displays the details of the defragmentation operation. Choose Legend for an explanation of each of the symbols used in the details window. To close the window, choose Hide Details.

Running Disk Performance Utilities with the System Agent

Microsoft Plus! for Windows 95 provides the System Agent, a program that enables you to schedule when to run the system maintenance utilities discussed in this chapter. The System Agent can run other programs, as well, and notify you when your hard disk is low on space.

By default, the System Agent is enabled after you install Plus!. This means that each time you start Windows 95, the System Agent starts automatically and runs in the background, only becoming active when it needs to start a scheduled program or notify you of low disk space. Even though System Agent is active by default, it isn't fully set up. After you install System Agent, it automatically places Low Disk Space Notification, ScanDisk for Windows (Standard Test), Disk Defragmenter, and ScanDisk for Windows (Thorough Test) programs in the System Agent. You need to manually tell the System Agent which other programs to run, when to run them, and which program features to use.

To schedule programs with the System Agent, use the following steps:

1. Open the Start menu and choose Programs, Accessories, System Tools, System Agent. The System Agent window opens (see fig. 22.27).

FIG. 22.27

The System Agent window lists the currently scheduled programs.

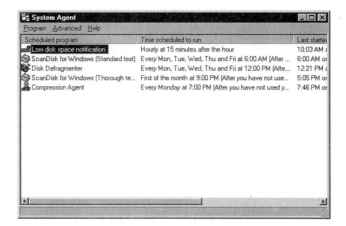

2. Choose Program, Schedule a New Program. The Schedule a New Program dialog box appears (see fig. 22.28).

FIG. 22.28

Use the Schedule a New Program dialog box to select programs for System Agent to run according to the schedule you set.

Choose a program

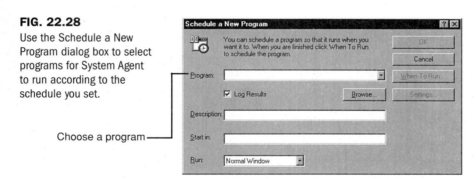

3. Click the drop-down list arrow to open the Program list. Choose a program from the list that appears. You can choose ScanDisk for Windows, Disk Defragmenter, Compression Agent, or Low Disk Space Notification. If you want to run a program other than one of these, click Browse, select the program to run in the Browse dialog box, then click OK. No matter what method you use, the selected program appears as the Program choice.

4. If you want, you can edit the Description for the program and the Start In folder, which specifies the folder containing files the program needs to run.

5. Open the Run drop-down list and specify whether you want the program to run in a Normal Window, Minimized, or Maximized.

T I P Schedule time-consuming programs like Disk Defragmenter for a time you won't normally use your computer. Then, leave your computer on during that time, and System Agent will handle the task for you.

6. To specify the schedule for the program, click the <u>W</u>hen to Run button. The Change Schedule Of... dialog box appears (see fig. 22.29).

FIG. 22.29
Use the Change Schedule dialog box to set up a schedule for the selected program.

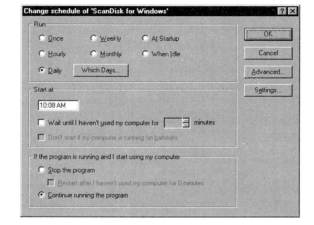

7. Click a Run option, such as <u>W</u>eekly or <u>M</u>onthly. Your choice here affects the options available in the Start At area of the dialog box.

8. Specify the options you want in the Start At area. Although there might be other options depending on your choice in step 7, you always need to enter a starting time. Also, you can specify a number of minutes to tell System Agent to wait if you're using your computer when the scheduled program runtime occurs.

9. Choose whether System Agent should <u>S</u>top the Program or <u>C</u>ontinue Running the Program should you start using your computer when the scheduled program is running. Stopping the program can protect against data loss while running system utilities.

10. Click S<u>e</u>ttings to accept your changed schedule of options and to control which features the selected program uses when the System Agent runs the program. The Scheduled Settings dialog box that appears varies depending on the selected program. For example, figure 22.30 shows the Scheduled Settings dialog box for the Disk Defragmenter program.

11. Specify the settings you want for the selected program, then click OK to close the Scheduled Settings dialog box.

FIG. 22.30

Choose which settings to use for the selected program when System Agent runs it.

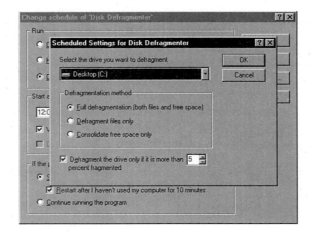

12. Click OK again to finish scheduling the program. System Agent adds the program to the list of scheduled programs.

N O T E Remember that you can schedule the same program to run at different times with different settings. For example, you can schedule a standard ScanDisk check once a week, plus a thorough check once a month. ■

Although you can use the Program menu choices to make changes to the schedule and settings for one of the listed programs, it's faster to simply right-click the program you want to make changes for. A shortcut menu appears, from which you can choose the following:

- ■ Choose Properties to change things like the program startup folder and settings (click the Settings button in the dialog box that appears).

- ■ Use the Change Schedule option to adjust how often System Agent runs the program.

- ■ Choose Run Now to run the program immediately, using the settings you specified.

- ■ Choose the Disable option to prevent the listed program from running at the designated time but leave the program on the list; choose Disable again to reinstate the program's schedule.

- ■ Choose Remove to delete the selected program from the System Agent list; confirm the deletion by clicking Yes at the warning that appears.

The Advanced menu in System Agent offers two commands for controlling System Agent itself. Toggle the Suspend System Agent option off whenever you want to stop all your regularly scheduled programs from running; then toggle this choice back on when you need to. The Stop Using System Agent choice completely stops System Agent operation. After you use this option, System Agent no longer loads when you start Windows, and you have to select System Agent from the System Tools Shortcuts to start using it. To close System Agent after setting it up, choose Program, Exit.

Monitoring Your System

Windows 95 comes with an application called System Monitor, which enables you to monitor the resources on your computer. You can see if you have the System Monitor installed by opening the Start menu, choosing Programs, Accessories, System Tools, and checking for the System Monitor item. If you do not see it on the menu or if it does not start, then you need to rerun Windows 95 and reinstall the System Monitor. To install the System Monitor, follow these steps:

1. Open the Start menu, and choose Settings, Control Panel.
2. Double-click Add/Remove Programs.
3. Select the Windows Setup tab, select Accessories, and choose Details.
4. Select System Monitor in the Components list.
5. Click OK.

You can see information about the 32-bit file system, network clients and servers, and the virtual memory manager, among other things. Most of this information is highly technical in nature and useful only to advanced users. You can display the information in either bar or line charts or as numeric values. To open the System Monitor, open the Start menu and choose Programs, Accessories, System Tools, System Monitor. The System Monitor window appears, as shown in figure 22.31.

FIG. 22.31
Use the System Monitor to monitor the resources on your computer.

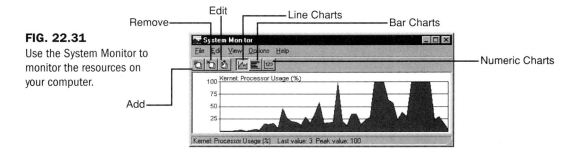

To monitor an item in System Monitor, follow these steps:

1. Select the item you want to monitor by choosing Edit, Add Item; alternatively, click the Add button. The Add Item dialog box appears (see fig. 22.32).

FIG. 22.32

Select the items you want to monitor in the Add Item dialog box.

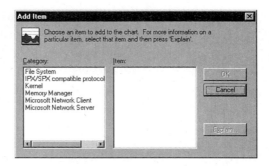

You can obtain information on what an item is by selecting the item and clicking Explain. When you select an item in the right hand box, the Explain button becomes an option.

To select more than one item from the list, select the first item, hold down the Ctrl key, and select additional items. To select several contiguous items in the list, select the first item, hold down the Shift key, and select the last item.

2. Choose OK.

3. Repeat steps 1 and 2 to add additional items to the window.

To remove an item from the window, follow these steps:

1. Choose Edit, Remove Item; alternatively, click the Remove button.

2. Select the item you want to remove and choose OK.

You can edit an item that is being monitored, changing its display color and the scaling used in its chart. To edit an item, follow these steps:

1. Choose Edit, Edit Item, or click the Edit tool, to display the Edit Item dialog box.

2. Select the item you want to edit and choose OK. The Chart Options dialog box appears, as shown in figure 22.33.

FIG. 22.33

Change the display of an item being monitored in the Chart Options dialog box.

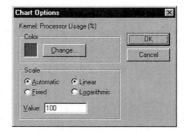

3. Choose Change to change the color of the item.

4. Select Automatic to let System Monitor set the maximum value on the y-axis.

   or

   Select Fixed and type a value in the Value text box to set your own maximum value for the y-axis.

5. Choose OK.

You can display the items being monitored as either a line or bar chart or as a numeric value. To change the display, choose View, Line Charts, Bar Charts, or Numeric Charts; alternatively, click the appropriate button on the toolbar.

 TIP To keep the System Monitor window on top of other windows to facilitate monitoring, choose View, Always on Top. You also can hide the title bar so the System Monitor window is devoted to displaying the chart: choose View, Hide Title Bar. To redisplay the title bar, double-click the chart or press Esc.

You can adjust the frequency at which the chart is updated by choosing Options, Chart and moving the slider to change the update interval. If you are on a network, choose File, Connect to connect to a different computer.

One way to use System Monitor to diagnose problems and bottlenecks on a system is to run System Monitor on a regular basis on a system that is having problems and comparing its performance characteristics to a system that is running well. By monitoring the values for Page Faults in the Memory Manager category, for example, you might find that the values on the low-performance computer are much higher, indicating a shortage of usable RAM. Another useful parameter to look at on a slow system is the Processor Usage (%) in the Kernel category. If the values are consistently high, even when the user isn't doing anything, an open application might be tying up the processor unnecessarily. Identifying the bottlenecks on a system can help you fine-tune a system.

Fine-tuning and Troubleshooting the File System

You can use the File System Properties dialog box to fine-tune the performance of your hard disks and to troubleshoot the file system if you run into applications that do not perform properly with Windows 95. To access the dialog box, open the Start menu, and choose Settings, Control Panel. Double-click the System icon, select the Performance tab, and then choose the File System button to display the dialog box shown in figure 22.34.

FIG 22.34
Use the File System Properties dialog box to fine-tune and troubleshoot your hard disk.

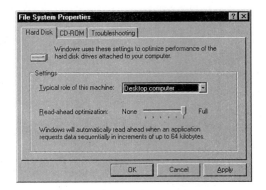

Fine-tuning Your Hard Disk

Windows 95 normally adjusts dynamically to any new hardware configuration and usage to optimize the performance of your hard disk. You can manually adjust two settings on the Hard Disk tab if you have reason to believe this will improve hard disk performance. Table 22.2 describes these settings and how they will affect performance.

Table 22.2 Hard Disk Settings

Setting	Function
Typical role of this machine	Determines amount of RAM used for caching record of most recently accessed folders and files.
• Desktop computer	• 10K of memory used.
• Mobile or docking system	• 5K of memory used.
• Network server	• 40K of memory. This setting will optimize file and folder access but at the expense of slightly more memory usage.
Read-ahead optimization	Determines to what extent Windows 95 will read ahead and cache data, assuming data is being read sequentially. Reduce to conserve RAM or when data is not typically read sequentially.

Troubleshooting the File System

The Troubleshooting tab in the File System Properties dialog box has six settings you can change to help you troubleshoot your file system if you encounter incompatibilities between Windows 95 and an application (see fig. 22.35). Table 22.3 summarizes these settings and how they can be used. You will almost always degrade the performance of your system when you enable one or more of these settings. Typically, they are used to isolate a problem and should not be left on.

FIG. 22.35

Use the Troubleshooting tab in the File System Properties dialog box to isolate file system problems.

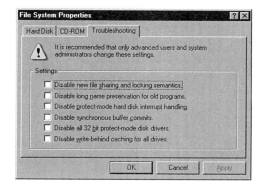

Table 22.3   File System Troubleshooting Settings

Setting	Function
Disable New File Sharing and Locking Semantics	Use with older programs that require SHARE.EXE until program is upgraded. Use with care. Sets Registry setting to SoftCompatMode=0.
Disable Long Name Preservation	Normally, long file names are preserved when files are opened and saved by programs not recognizing long file names. Use with older programs that are incompatible with long file names. Sets Registry setting to PreserveLongNames=0.
Disable Protect-Mode Hard Disk Interrupt Handling	Use if program is having disk-access problems. Allows program to handle Int13h interrupts instead of Windows 32-bit virtual driver. Slows hard disk access. Sets Registry setting to VirtualHDIRQ=1.
Disable Synchronous Buffer Commits	Enabling this option might cause problems with file integrity with some programs. Use only for diagnosing problems with some programs.

continues

Table 22.3 Continued	
Setting	**Function**
Disable All 32-Bit Protect-Mode Disk Drivers	Enable if having problems accessing hard drive. Enables real-mode drivers, which might correct incompatibilities between Windows 95 and some hard drives. Can result in slower hard drive access. Sets Registry setting to ForceRMIO=1.
Disable Write-Behind Caching for All Drives	Turns off write-caching, which slows down writing of data to hard drive, but is safer in situations where you don't want to risk losing data by delaying its writing to disk. Sets Registry setting to DriveWriteBehind=O.

Note: Registry settings listed in table are found in the following key:
Hkey_Local_Machine\System\CurrentControlSet\Control\FileSystem

Configuring Virtual Memory

When RAM is tight, Windows begins to move *pages* of code and data from RAM to the hard disk to make more room in RAM. Windows uses a *least-recently-used* technique to move pages of memory to the disk, selecting first the pages of code and data not recently accessed by a program. If a program requires a piece of data no longer in physical memory, Windows retrieves the information from disk, paging other information from memory to disk to make room. To programs running in Windows, no difference exists between RAM in the system and virtual memory on the disk.

When you install Windows 95, it automatically determines how much hard disk space to use for virtual memory, depending on the amount of free disk space. In most cases, you should let Windows determine the settings used for virtual memory on your computer. Unless you know what you are doing, changing the settings manually can adversely affect the performance of your computer. If you do want to specify your own virtual memory settings, follow these steps:

1. Open the Start menu and choose Settings, Control Panel.
2. Double-click the System icon to display the System Properties dialog box; select the Performance tab.
3. Click the Virtual Memory button to display the Virtual Memory dialog box shown in figure 22.36.

FIG. 22.36

You can let Windows manage your virtual memory settings or specify your own in the Virtual Memory dialog box. Microsoft recommends you let Windows manage virtual memory settings.

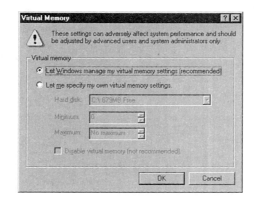

4. Select the Let Me Specify My Own Virtual Memory Settings option.

5. If you want to use a different hard disk for virtual memory than is already specified, select a new disk from the Hard Disk drop-down list. The amount of free space on the hard disk is displayed next to the drive letter.

6. Specify the minimum amount (in megabytes) of hard disk space you want Windows to use for virtual memory in the Minimum text box.

7. Specify the maximum amount of memory (in megabytes) you want Windows to use for virtual memory in the Maximum text box.

8. Choose OK.

The Virtual Memory dialog box contains a Disable Virtual Memory (Not Recommended) check box at the bottom. This turns off all use of virtual memory and is not recommended.

 You can improve the performance of virtual memory in a number of ways:

Locate your swap file on its own partition on your hard disk. This will speed up access, since it is the only file on the disk and it will prevent the swap file from getting fragmented. If you have multiple hard drives, you can partition the second drive (not the boot drive) and locate the swap file in the first partition of that drive. Put the swap file on your fastest drive.

Defragment your hard drive and then create a permanent swap file by specifying the same values for the minimum and maximum values in the steps above. One rule of thumb for how big to make the swap file is to multiply the amount of RAM you have by 1.5. This will increase performance by eliminating the slowdowns caused by the dynamic swap file being resized and by using an unfragmented swap file.

TROUBLESHOOTING

I am receiving "Out of memory" error messages when I try to run multiple programs. When you install Windows 95 on a compressed drive, the Setup program will sometimes locate the swap file on the host drive of the compressed drive. The size of the dynamic swap file may be limited if the host drive has limited free space. You can place the swap file on the compressed drive if you are using Microsoft DoubleSpace or DriveSpace. If you are not using a Microsoft compression program, you must either enlarge the host drive or locate the swap file on another uncompressed drive.

CHAPTER 23

Backing Up and Protecting Your Data

by Ron Person with Bob Voss

Part of any successful file management routine includes creating duplicate copies of data for backup. Virus protection is another critical component of good file management. *Viruses* are computer programs written for the purpose of interrupting or destroying your work.

The backup program that comes with Windows 95 enables you to create backups onto a removable storage device such as a floppy disk, a tape, or a removable hard disk. Windows 95 also includes a virus protection program that can prevent viruses from entering your system and can remove them should they get onto the hard disk. ■

How to back up your files

Look here to learn how to copy one or more files from your hard disk to another disk (usually a floppy disk, a tape drive, or another computer on your network).

How to verify that files are backed up correctly

This chapter explains how to compare files on your backup disks with the original files to ensure their validity.

How to use your backup files

Learn how to restore your backed-up files to any location you choose (including their original locations).

How to protect your system from viruses

This chapter teaches you how to protect your files from viruses and identify a virus that attempts to enter your system.

Backing Up Your Files

The Windows Backup program automatically creates a duplicate image of your hard disk's data on a magnetic tape or spreads an image across multiple floppy disks. During the backup operation, each disk in the set is filled to capacity before the next disk is requested. The collection of all these duplicates files and folders is referred to as the *backup set*.

As hard disks grow in capacity, it becomes more and more laborious to use floppy disks to back up your data. A much more convenient method is to use a tape backup system. You may be able to back up your entire hard drive with one tape. With tape backups, you also avoid the inconvenience of having to sit at your computer swapping floppy disks. In fact, you can initiate the backup when you leave for lunch; when you return, it will be done.

CAUTION

You put the entire concept of having secure data at risk if your backups are not kept in a safe location, physically separate from the original data. For a small company, the physical location for the backup set can be a safe deposit box or the president's house. For a large company, there are services that pick up tapes and store them in disaster-proof vaults. I personally know of two instances in which the backups were lost along with the original system. In one case, a thief stole the backup floppy disks that sat next to the computer. In the other case, the fire that destroyed the legal firm's computers also destroyed their backups, which were in a closet in an adjacent room.

N O T E   Backup does not install as part of a typical or minimum installation. If Backup is not installed and you want it, refer to Chapter 16, "Installing, Running, and Uninstalling Windows Applications," on how to add programs. On the Windows Setup page of the Add/Remove Programs Properties sheet, look for Backup in the Disk Tools items in the Components list. ■

To start the backup program, open the Start menu and click Programs, Accessories, System Tools, Backup. When you first start Backup, you may see a Welcome to Microsoft Backup dialog box that describes the process of making backups. You can select the Don't Show This Again check box if you don't want to see this dialog box again. You also may see a message box that reads Backup has created a Full System Backup file set for you. This means that until you specify otherwise, Backup marks all files and folders to be part of the backup. It's a very good idea to do a Full System Backup at least once a week or once a month, depending on the value of your data and how often program configurations change.

TIP Create a Full System Backup occasionally. It has all the configuration and Registry files necessary to rebuild your system from a disaster.

Once you get past these initial dialog boxes, the Backup dialog box appears, as shown in figure 23.1.

FIG. 23.1

Windows Backup creates duplicate copies of files and folders, compares backups to original files, and restores duplicate files and folders.

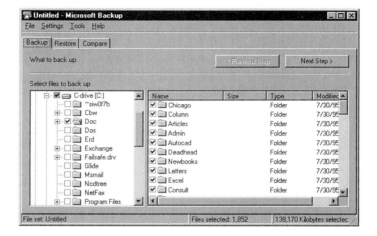

The three basic functions of Backup are divided into tabbed pages in the Backup dialog box:

- *Backup*. Copies one or more files and folders from your hard disk.

- *Restore*. Copies one or more files from your backup set to the hard disk or to another floppy disk.

- *Compare*. Compares the files in a backup set to make sure that they match the source files on the hard disk.

In addition to these major functions, several other operations can be accessed from the pull-down menus:

- The File menu enables you to load and save setup files that define settings to be used when backing up and restoring files. The File menu also enables you to print a list of files contained in a backup set.

- The Settings, File Filtering command enables you to filter the folders or file types you want to include in a backup set (this command is discussed in detail later in this chapter). Using the Settings, Options command, you can set various options for each of the major functions, as well as options that effect the program generally.

■ The Tools menu contains commands for working with tapes.

▶ **See** "Changing Backup Settings and Options," **p. 670**

▶ **See** "Adding Windows' Component Applications," **p. 485**

Understanding Backup

Before you implement a backup strategy, you need to understand the difference between *full* and *incremental* backups, the two types of backups that you can perform with Windows Backup. When you carry out a full backup, all files and folders on the selected drive are backed up. With a full backup set, you can completely restore your system to its original state in the event of a catastrophe. The disadvantages to a full backup are that it can take a lot of time and storage space if you have many files on your hard drive. The first step of your backup strategy, however, should include a full backup.

With an incremental backup, only those files that have changed since the last full or incremental backup (whichever was last), using the same backup set, are backed up. Typically, you start a backup cycle with a full backup and then periodically perform an incremental backup, using a different set of floppy disks or a new tape, for each incremental backup. Each incremental backup set will contain only those files that have changed since the previous backup. If you need to completely restore your hard disk, you need the full backup set and all the incremental backup sets. The advantages of using incremental backups is that it takes much less time and less space than a full backup. The disadvantages are that you must use a new set of disks (or a new tape) each time you perform an incremental backup and restoring your hard disk is more complicated, since you need to use each of the incremental backup sets, in addition to the full backup set, to be sure that you get the most recent version of a file.

> **CAUTION**
>
> To backup all the files you need to completely restore your system, including essential system files used by Windows 95, you need to use the *Full System Backup Set*. This is the only way to safely back up all the files you need to rebuild your system after a catastrophe. Selecting the drive you want to back up in the Select files to Back Up pane *will not* back up important system files needed to fully restore your system.

N O T E You may be used to using *differential backups* in your backup schedule. A differential backup backs up all files that have changed since the last full backup (not just the files that have changed since the last differential backup). Windows 95 does not support differential backups, so you will have to change your backup strategy to one using incremental backups. ■

Creating a full backup is important to preserving your entire system. Full backups take care of merging Registry settings and the file replacements necessary when restoring a Windows system.

An Overview of How to Back Up Your Hard Disk

The Backup program makes it easy to name different sets of backup files so that you don't have to select the files and folders each time. When you aren't using your computer (at lunch time, when you return phone messages, or when you leave work), you can start a backup.

Here is the general procedure for creating a backup:

1. Have enough formatted floppy disks or tapes to store the backup.
2. Start Windows Backup.
3. Select the name of a backup set you previously created. Alternatively, manually select the drives, files, and folders you want to back up.
4. Select the Next Step button, then select the destination to which you want to back up—a tape, a floppy disk drive, or another hard disk.
5. Start the backup.

When Backup is finished, you should store the backup media in a safe location separate from the computers.

 For an extensive list of tape drives compatible with Backup, choose Help, select the Contents tab, and then select the Using Tapes for Backup item.

Windows Backup supports the following tape drives and backup devices:

- Hard disks
- Network drives
- Floppy disks
- QIC 40, 80, 3010, and 3020 tape drives connected to a primary floppy disk controller
- QIC 40, 80, and 3010 tape drives, manufactured by Colorado Memory Systems and connected to a parallel port

 If you own a tape drive manufactured by Colorado Memory Systems that is not supported by Windows 95 Backup, contact Colorado Memory Systems (970-669-8000) for information on a free upgrade to the backup software that came with your backup unit that is compatible with Windows Backup. Or, connect to Colorado's web site at **http://hpcc998.external.hp.com/cms/index.htm**

Part
VII

Ch
23

Backup supports compression using the industry standard QIC-113 format. It can read tapes from other backup programs that use the same format with or without compression. Full backups can be restored to a hard disk of another type.

Preparing a Backup Schedule

When you back up important or large amounts of data, it's important to have a backup schedule and a rotation plan for the backup tapes.

Basically, the backup schedule for most businesses should consist of a full system backup followed by incremental backups spread over time. Should your computer ever completely fail, you can rebuild your system using the full backup (restores Windows, the system Registry, all applications, and their data files as they existed on a specific date). You can then use the incremental backups (which store only changed files) to restore the latest versions of any files that changed after the full backup. Do a full system backup once a week and an incremental backup daily.

Some companies create a full system backup every day. At the end of the week, the tapes are taken to an off-site vault and a new set of tapes are started. Multiple sets of backup tapes are used and rotated between the on-site and off-site storage locations.

> **CAUTION**
>
> Never use one set of tapes for all your backups. If you have only one set of tapes, composed of a full backup and incrementals, creating another backup means that you overwrite one of the previous backups. Should the tape fail or the computer fail during backup, you might be left with no backups capable of restoring your system.

Backing Up Files

Running a backup operation consists of selecting the files you want to backup, specifying the destination for the backup files, and starting the backup. The files that you select for backup will be stored in a single backup file with the extension QIC. To perform a backup, follow these steps:

1. Open the Start menu, click Programs, Accessories, System Tools, Backup.
2. Click the check box for the drive containing the files you want to back up in the left pane of the Backup window.

 Whenever you frequently work with the same files and settings, save them as a file set.

In figure 23.1, local drive C is selected. The files and folders on the drive are displayed in the right pane. You can expand and collapse the hierarchical display in the left pane by clicking the plus (+) and minus (–) signs next to the folders.

3. Select the files and folders you want to back up. If you want to back up using a file set you have previously named, choose File, Open File Set and select the file set you want to back up.

   You can select all the files in a folder by clicking the check box next to the folder's name in the left pane of the Backup dialog box.

   To view the files and folders inside a folder, in the left pane, open the folder containing the folders or files you want to view, then in the left pane click the name of the folder whose contents you want to see; its contents are displayed in the right pane. You can then select individual files or folders inside that folder.

   To select the entire drive, click the box next to the drive in the left pane.

   If you select a folder with many files, a File Selection dialog box momentarily appears, notifying you that file selection is in progress; the box displays the number of files and their total size as the selection progresses.

   The total number of files currently selected and their cumulative size appears in the status bar at the bottom of the window.

4. When you have finished selecting the files and folders you want to back up, click Next Step.

5. Select the destination for the backup files (see fig. 23.2).

   If you select a tape drive, the volume name for that tape appears in the Selected Device or Location box. If you select a disk drive, this box shows the drive letter or path, such as A:\.

FIG. 23.2
Select the destination for the files you want to back up.

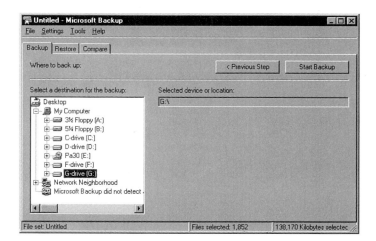

6. Save the file settings for this backup set if you will be doing this backup frequently.

7. Click the Start Backup button.

8. Type a name for the backup set in the Backup Set Label dialog box that appears (see fig. 23.3). This will be the name of the file containing all the files you have selected for backup.

   If you want to prevent unauthorized people from restoring the backup and stealing your data, click Password Protect in the Backup Set Label dialog box and enter a password.

   Give the backup set a meaningful name that will identify the data for you, in case you need to restore or compare it. Names can include spaces, symbols, and numbers. You may want to use a name such as *Accounting, full backup 5/10/95.*

FIG. 23.3

Name the backup set in the Backup Set Label dialog box.

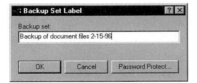

CAUTION

If you forget the password you assign to your backup set, there is no way to use that backup set.

When you have specified a backup label and an optional password, choose OK. The Backup message box appears (see fig. 23.4), showing you the progress of the backup operation. You can cancel the operation by choosing Cancel.

If you are backing up to floppy disks, a message box prompts you when you need to insert the next disk, if necessary.

FIG. 23.4

You can monitor the progress of a backup operation in the Backup message box.

9. When the message box appears informing you that the backup operation is complete, click OK. Click OK again to return to the Backup dialog box.

TROUBLESHOOTING

I tried to back up my hard disk on to my Iomega Zip drive with no success. Is there a way to use Windows Backup with my Zip drive? Windows Backup does not support disk spanning with the Zip drive. In other words, if your backup set requires more than one Zip disk, Backup won't work. You can use the Copy Machine software that comes with your Zip drive to back up an entire disk onto Zip disks.

▶ **See** "Restoring Files," **p. 678**

▶ **See** "Saving File Sets," **p. 672**

Part

VII

Ch

23

Using Backup to Create an Archive The Backup program is a handy way to archive files. Suppose that you want to make room on your hard disk by deleting some files you aren't currently using but want to use at a later date. Use Backup to archive the files to floppy disks or a tape; then delete the files from the hard disk. If you need the files later, use the restore function to put them back on your hard disk.

Using Backup to Copy Files to Another Computer You also can use Backup to transfer folders and files to another computer. The benefit of using Backup for this task is that it takes care of spreading the files across multiple floppy disks when necessary, and it preserves the arrangement of folders, so you can duplicate your folder organization on another computer. If you purchase a laptop, for example, you can use Backup to transfer the information on your desktop computer to the laptop, including the arrangement of your folders.

Scheduling Backups Using System Agent

You can schedule your backups to run automatically when you are not working with your computer using the System Agent that comes with Microsoft Plus! for Windows. The System Agent has a default schedule for running some of the disk utilities that come with Windows 95, so you can schedule additional programs to run at specified times. To schedule Backup to run automatically, follow these steps:

1. Create a backup set following the steps outlined in "Saving File Sets," later in this chapter.

   Before you save the backup set, choose Setting, Drag and Drop and deselect the Confirm Operation Before Beginning and Quit Backup After Operation is Finished options. Choose OK.

2. Exit Backup.

3. Click Start, <u>P</u>rograms, Accessories, System Tools, System Agent.

4. Choose <u>P</u>rogram, Schedule a New <u>P</u>rogram.

5. Type the following in the <u>P</u>rogram text box:

> **"C:\Program Files\Accessories\Backup.exe" C:\Program Files\Accessories***setname.set*

Setname.set is the name of the backup set you created.

6. Choose the <u>W</u>hen to Run button and schedule when you want Backup to run.

7. Exit System Agent.

Be sure to leave your computer running if you have scheduled Backup to run after you leave work. You can create two different schedules, one that does a full backup, perhaps once a week, and another that does daily incremental backups.

Changing Backup Settings and Options

You can change several settings and options that affect your backup operations. To change the settings and options for the backup operation, follow these steps:

1. Open the <u>S</u>ettings menu and choose <u>O</u>ptions.

2. Click the Backup tab to open the dialog box shown in figure 23.5.

FIG. 23.5
Use the Backup page in the Settings—Options dialog box to change the settings and options that affect the way backup operations work.

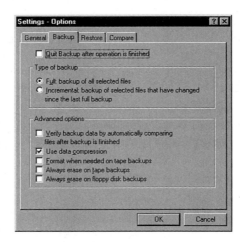

3. Change or select from the following options and then choose OK:

Option	Function
Quit Backup After Operation Is Finished	Closes Backup when the backup operation is completed. Use this option when you use the System Agent to run automatic backups.
Full: Backup of All Selected Files	Backs up all selected files, regardless of whether the file has changed since the last backup. Use this option the first time you run a backup of your hard disk.
Incremental: Backup of Selected Files that Have Changed Since the Last Full Backup	Only backs up selected files that have changed since the last full backup. Use this option between full backups.
Verify Backup Data by Automatically Comparing Files After Backup Is Finished	Compares each file that is backed up with the original file to verify accurate backup.
Use Data Compression	Compresses files as they are backed up to allow more files to be backed up on a tape or floppy disk.
Format When Needed on Tape Backups	Automatically formats an unused tape before backup operation. This only works on tapes that have not already been formatted.
Always Erase on Tape Backups	Erases the tape on backup. When this option is not selected, backups are added to the tape if there is room.
Always Erase on Floppy Disk Backups	Automatically erases floppy disks before they are used in a floppy disk backup operation. When this option is not selected, backups are added to the floppy disk if there is room.

Saving File Sets

If you back up the same set of files regularly, you can save the settings for that file set. Saving backup settings saves you the trouble of reselecting the files and destination each time you want to back up the files.

To save a file set, follow these steps:

1. Open the Backup dialog box and in the Backup page select the files you want to back up, as described earlier in this chapter. Click Next Step.

2. Select the destination for the backup files from the Select a Destination list.

3. Choose File, Save As. The Save As dialog box appears (see fig. 23.6).

FIG. 23.6

Name your file set with a recognizable name for what it contains and when it was created.

4. Type a name for the backup set in the File Name text box.

5. Choose Save.

6. Choose Start Backup if you want to continue the backup operation and create a backup using the file set you just specified.

If you make changes to an existing file set, choose the File, Save command to save the file set with the same name without opening the Save As dialog box.

To open a file set for use in a backup operation, follow these steps:

1. Open the Backup dialog box, then click the Backup tab. Choose File, Open File Set to display the Open dialog box shown in figure 23.7.

2. If you can't see the file set you want to open, open the folder that contains the file set.

3. Select the file set and choose Open.

FIG. 23.7
Open a file set to use in a
backup or restore operation
from the Open dialog box.

Part
VII

Ch
23

The file set is opened, and the files named in this file set are selected in the Backup dialog
box.

TROUBLESHOOTING

**After setting up a backup set and performing the backup, I was unable to save the settings
for the backup set.** You need to save the backup set after you have selected the files to backup
and the destination for the backup but before you start the backup. Once you start the backup by
clicking Start, you will not be able to save the file set.

Filtering Folders and File Types Included in Backup Operations

Backup's file filtering commands enable you to filter out specific folders and types of files
so they are not included in the backup set. These commands can save you a lot of time
when you are creating a file set to be backed up.

You may not want to include all the files on your hard disk in a backup operation. If you
want to back up all but a few folders, you need only specify the folders you *don't* want to
include in the backup set. In most cases, you don't need to include program files in your
daily backups, because you can always reinstall your programs if your system crashes.
You can dramatically reduce the number of disks you use in a backup if you limit the file
set to data files only.

To exclude files of a specific type or date from a backup, follow these steps:

1. Choose Settings, File Filtering. The File Filtering—File Types dialog box appears,
   as shown in figure 23.8.
2. To exclude files modified between two dates, select the Last Modified Date check
   box. Enter From and To dates that *exclude* the files you do not want copied.

FIG. 23.8

You can exclude files of a specific type or files with specific dates.

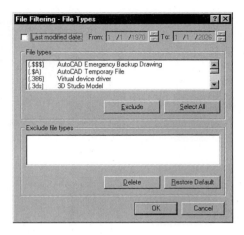

 TIP If you want to exclude all but a few of the file types in the File Types list, click Select All, hold the Ctrl key, and click the types of files you don't want to exclude.

3. To exclude specific file types from the backup operation, select the types of files you want to exclude from the File Types list and click Exclude. Continue to select file types and click the Exclude button until all the file types you want to exclude appear in the Exclude File Types list at the bottom of the dialog box.

To select all of the file types in the list, click Select All.

4. To delete a file type from the list in the Exclude File Types box, select the file type and click Delete.

5. To clear the Exclude File Types box, click Restore Default.

6. When you finish making your selections, choose OK.

Changing the General Settings in Backup

You can change two options in Backup that affect the backup, restore, and compare functions. To change these options, choose Settings, Options. Select the General tab to open the dialog box shown in figure 23.9.

■ Select the Turn on Audible Prompts option if you want to hear beeps from your computer's speaker during backup, compare, and restore operations.

■ Select the Overwrite Old Status Log Files option to replace the old status log with the new one generated by the current backup. The status log records errors and completions of file backups.

FIG. 23.9
Use the General page in the Settings—Options dialog box to change the settings and options that affect the way Backup's operations work.

Backing Up with a Simple Drag and Drop

 Drag and drop is an easy way to back up your files if you have created file sets (as described earlier in this chapter in the section "Saving File Sets"). You can drag a file set and drop it onto the Backup icon or you can double-click a file set name. Either of these actions immediately starts the backup. With the appropriate settings, the entire backup operation can go on in the background and you can continue to use the computer for other tasks.

 Backing up data is so important that if you are an experienced Windows user, you may want to set up other users' computers with drag-and-drop backup so that they can easily protect their data.

To prepare Backup for drag-and-drop operation, follow these steps:

1. Choose Settings, Drag and Drop to open the Drag and Drop dialog box shown in figure 23.10.

FIG. 23.10
Change the Backup settings to make drag-and-drop backup operate in the background while you work.

2. Change or select from the following options and then choose OK:

Option	Function
Run Backup Minimized	After dragging a file set onto the Backup icon, the Backup window minimizes.
Confirm Operation Before Beginning	Displays a message showing which files will be backed up. Asks you to confirm that you want the files backed up.
Quit Backup after Operation Is Finished	Quits Backup after the file set is backed up. Use this option when you use the System Agent to run Backup automatically.

If Backup is operating in the background, you do not see it as a window on-screen. If you need to stop a backup that is in the background, display the title bar and click Backup. A dialog box displays the current backup status and gives you the opportunity to cancel the backup.

N O T E   If you have multiple file sets, but you don't want them all as Shortcuts on your desktop, you can still start them quickly to do a backup. In the Windows Explorer or My Computer window, double-click the name of the file set you want to back up. You are prompted whether you want to make a backup; the backup runs with the settings specified for that file set. ■

Before you can create backups with a drag-and-drop procedure, you must display the Backup program icon. You can open the Program Files\Accessories folder in a window in the Windows Explorer or My Computer. A more convenient method is to create a short-cut to BACKUP.EXE and display it on your desktop.

If you also want a quick way to find and display the SET files that specify your file sets, create a shortcut to the directory containing the SET files. Use the Find command (avail-able on the Start menu) to find all files that end with SET, then create a new folder and drag the SET files into the new folder. Now create a shortcut to this folder and put that shortcut on the desktop (see fig. 23.11). (Creating shortcuts is described in Chapter 3, "Windows Navigation Basics.")

N O T E   Normally, the file sets are stored in the Program Files\Accessories folder. ■

FIG. 23.11
Once drag-and-drop is
enabled, backing up is as
easy as dropping a file-set
icon onto the Backup
shortcut.

To back up a file set, you only need to double-click the shortcut to the folder containing
the file sets. This opens the folder containing the file sets as a Window on your desktop.
Figure 23.11 shows such an open folder. Now drag the file set you want to back up onto
the shortcut to BACKUP.EXE and drop it. You are prompted whether you want to continue with the backup operation. Respond by clicking Yes or No.

▶ **See** "Using Shortcut Icons on the Desktop," **p. 73**

Formatting and Erasing Tapes

If you use tapes to do your backups, Backup includes two tools for working with tapes.
When you purchase a new tape, you must format the tape before you can use it, just as
you format a floppy disk. The Format Tape command formats a tape for you. If you want
to erase the contents on a tape before you use it for a new backup operation, you can use
the Erase Tape command.

To format a tape, follow these steps:

1. Insert the tape in the tape drive.

2. Open the Backup dialog box and choose Tools, Format Tape. If the Format Tape
    command is grayed out, choose the Redetect Tape command, which enables
    Backup to detect the tape.

3. When the Format Tape dialog box appears, type a name for the tape and choose OK.
    You use this name to identify the tape relative to other tapes you use.

    Formatting begins. The progress of the formatting operation is displayed in the
    Format Tape dialog box. Formatting a tape can take a long time; you may want to
    start the formatting operation when you are going to be away from your desk for an
    extended period.

Part
VII

Ch
23

4. When the message box appears telling you the operation is complete, choose OK. Choose OK again to return to the Backup dialog box.

To erase a tape, follow these steps:

1. Insert the tape in the tape drive.

2. Open the Backup dialog box and choose <u>T</u>ools, <u>E</u>rase Tape. If the <u>E</u>rase Tape command is grayed out, choose the <u>R</u>edetect Tape command, which enables Backup to detect the tape.

3. Choose <u>Y</u>es when the confirmation message box appears. The progress of the erase operation is displayed in the Erase dialog box.

4. When the message box appears telling you the operation is complete, choose OK. Choose OK again to return to the Backup dialog box.

Restoring Files

You can restore all the files from a backup set or select specific files or folders to restore. You also can choose where you want to restore the files.

To restore files, follow these steps:

1. Open the Backup dialog box and click the Restore tab (see fig. 23.12).

2. Select the drive containing the backup files from the left panel of the window.

FIG. 23.12
In the Restore page of the Backup dialog box, select the files you want to restore.

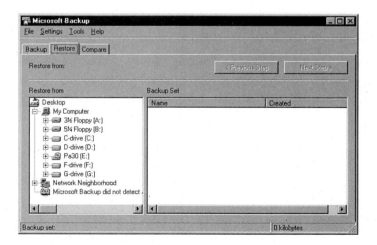

3. Select the backup set containing the files you want to restore from the right pane. If you have more than one backup file on a floppy disk or tape, select the one containing the files you want to restore. A single backup file, with the extension QIC, contains the files you backed up.

4. Click Next Step.

5. Select the folders or files you want to restore as shown in figure 23.13.

Part

VII

Ch

23

FIG. 23.13
You can select all or part of a backup set when you restore.

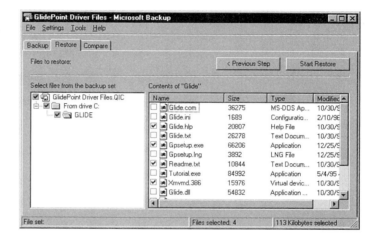

6. Click Start Restore. The Restore message box appears, showing you the progress of the restore operation (see fig. 23.14).

   By default, the files are restored to their original location. You can choose to restore the files to another location by changing one of the restore options.

7. When the Operation Complete message box appears, choose OK.

FIG. 23.14
The Restore message box keeps you informed about how the restore operation is progressing.

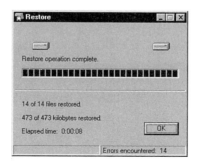

Restoring Files to Other Locations

You can restore files to locations other than their original location (the location from which they were initially backed up). To restore files to an alternate location, follow these steps:

1. Choose Settings, Options.

2. Click the Restore tab.

3. Select the Alternate Location option and choose OK.

4. Perform steps 1 through 6 of the restore procedure described in the preceding section (stop just before you have to click the Start Restore button).

5. Click Start Restore. The Browse for Folder dialog box appears (see fig. 23.15).

FIG. 23.15

Select the location to which you want to restore files from the Browse for Folder dialog box.

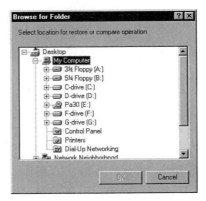

6. Select the location to which you want to restore the files and choose OK.

7. When the Operation Complete message box appears, choose OK.

Changing Restore Settings and Options

You can change several settings and options that affect your restore operations. To change the settings and options for the restore function, follow these steps:

1. Choose Settings, Options.

2. Click the Restore tab to open the dialog box shown in figure 23.16.

FIG. 23.16

Use the Restore page in the
Settings–Options dialog box
to change the settings and
options that affect the way
restore operations work.

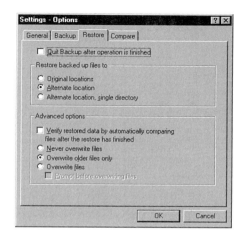

3. Change or select from the following options and then choose OK:

Option	Function
Quit Backup after Operation Is Complete	Closes Backup when the restore operation is completed. Use this option if you use the System Agent to run the restore operation automatically.
Original Locations	Restores files to their original locations.
Alternate Location	Restores files to an alternate location. (See "Restoring Files to an Alternate Location," earlier in this chapter.)
Alternate Location, Single Directory	Restores files to a single directory at an alternate location. Doesn't duplicate original folder structure.
Verify Restored Data by Automatically Comparing Files after the Restore Has Finished	Compares each file to the file on disk or tape after it is restored to check for accuracy of restore.
Never Overwrite Files	Files that are already on the destination location are not overwritten during a restore operation.

| Overwrite Older Files Only | Only files that are older than the files in the backup set are overwritten during a restore operation. |
| Overwrite Files | All files are overwritten during a restore operation. Use the Prompt Before Overwriting Files check box to specify whether you want to be prompted before a file is overwritten. |

TROUBLESHOOTING

I restored my system using Full System Backup.Set but some of my settings, such as the icon arrangement on my desktop and custom colors I had selected, were not properly restored. Some custom settings, including settings for colors, sounds, desktop themes, icon arrangement, and pointers, are saved in the Registry each time you shut down and restart Windows 95. When you do a full system restore, the original custom settings are restored in the Registry, but they are overwritten by the current settings (the default settings) when you restart your computer after the restoration. You must manually restore these custom settings.

A few other settings, namely the desktop pattern, wallpaper, and screen saver will be properly restored only if you restart you computer immediately after you finish the restoration. Otherwise, these settings will automatically be overwritten by the default settings.

I have some files I backed up with an earlier version of Microsoft Backup that I would like to restore on my system which is using Windows 95. Can I do this with Windows 95 Backup? You cannot use Windows 95 Backup to restore files from a backup set created with an earlier version of Backup. To restore these files you need to use either RESTORE.EXE or MSBACKUP.EXE, which are located on your Windows 95 CD-ROM.

Use RESTORE.EXE if your backup set was created with MS-DOS 5.0. RESTORE.EXE is located in the Other\Oldmsdos folder. Copy the program to your hard disk and run it from a command prompt, using the appropriate parameters on the command line. Type **restore /?** for information on the syntax to use with this command. You may receive an error message reading Incorrect DOS version. If this occurs, type **setver restore.exe 6.22** at the command prompt, and press Enter. Restart your computer and try running RESTORE.EXE again.

If your backup set was created with MS-DOS 6.x, use MSBACKUP.EXE, which is located in the Other\Oldmsdos\Msbackup folder. You need to copy all the files in this folder to your hard disk and double-click MSBACKUP.EXE to start it. For information on how to restore files, choose Restore from the Help menu.

Verifying Backup Files

The first time you use a series of disks or a tape for a backup, or any time you want to be absolutely sure of your backup, you should do a comparison. When you compare backups to the original files, you verify that the backup copies are both readable and accurate. To perform a compare, follow these steps:

1. Open the Backup dialog box and click the Compare tab.

2. From the left pane of the dialog box, select the device containing the backup files you want to compare (see fig. 23.17).

FIG. 23.17
Use the Compare function to verify the accuracy of your backup operations.

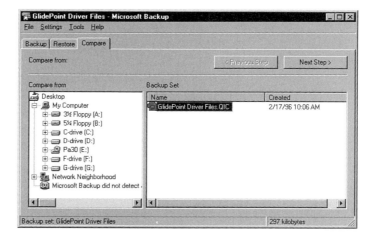

3. From the right pane, select the backup set containing the files you want to compare. Click Next Step.

4. Select the files or folders you want to compare to the original files.

5. Click Start Compare. The Compare message box informs you of the progress of the compare operation.

6. Choose OK when the Operation Complete message box appears; choose OK again to return to the Backup dialog box.

Changing Compare Settings and Options

You can change several settings and options that affect your compare operations. To change the settings and options for the compare function, follow these steps:

1. Choose Settings, Options.

2. Click the Compare tab to open the dialog box shown in figure 23.18.

FIG. 23.18

Use the Compare page in the Settings—Options dialog box to change the settings and options that affect the way compare operations work.

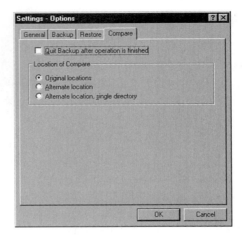

3. Change or select from the following options and then choose OK:

Option	Function
Quit Backup after Operation Is Finished	Closes Backup when the compare operation is completed. Use this option if you use the System Agent to run the compare operation automatically.
Original Locations	Compare files to files at their original locations.
Alternate Location	Compares files to files at an alternate location. (See "Comparing Files to Files at an Alternate Location," earlier in this chapter.)
Alternate Location, Single Directory	Compare files to files in a single directory at an alternate location. Doesn't look for duplicates of the original folder structure.

TROUBLESHOOTING

When I selected specific files to restore from my backup set, a message appeared informing me that my system registry settings were being restored, even though I hadn't selected the system files for restoration. If you use the Full System Backup.Set backup set to restore files, the system registry files are restored automatically, regardless of which files you select for restoration. This backup set is designed to fully restore your system in the event of a disaster. You need to create another backup set that does not include the system files. You can create a backup set for all the files on your hard disk, excluding the system files, by selecting the drive in the Select files to back up pane. You can then do partial restores from this set without restoring the system files.

Windows 95 Backup does not support my backup unit. Is there a way for me to use the DOS backup software that came with my backup unit? You can use the DOS backup software that came with your unit, but you must first go through a procedure to save your long file names, since your DOS software is not compatible with long file names. You need to use a utility called LFNBK.EXE that is on the Windows 95 CD-ROM to backup and restore your long file names. LFNBK.EXE is located in the Admin\Apptools\Lfnbk folder on the CD-ROM. You should copy it to the C:\Windows\Command folder on your hard disk.

To back up your hard disk using DOS backup software, follow these steps:

1. Right-click My Computer, click Properties and select the Performance tab.

2. Choose File System and select the Troubleshooting tab.

3. Select the Disable Long Name Preservation for Old Programs option.

4. Click OK and then Close and then choose Yes when prompted to restart your computer.

5. Open a DOS window from Windows 95 and type the following at the command prompt:

   LFNBK /B d:

   where d is the drive whose long file names you want to back up.

6. Click Start, then Shut Down and restart the computer in MS-DOS mode.

7. Run your DOS backup software, being sure that all Hidden and System files are backed up, if this is optional with your software.

8. Restart your computer and open a DOS window.

9. Type the following at the command prompt:

   LFNBK /R d:

10. Repeat steps 1-4, only deselect the Disable long name preservation for old programs option.

You may need to rearrange your desktop icons. Be sure to save copies of your DOS backup software on your startup disk in case you need to restore your system from scratch. In this case, you can reformat (and if necessary, repartition) your hard disk, using the files that are included on your startup disk (i.e., FORMAT.COM and FDISK.COM). You can then copy the backup software to the hard disk and use it to restore your system.

Protecting Your Files from Viruses

You need to take measures to protect your computer from viruses, a scourge of the modern day computer world. In addition to backing up your system regularly, you should obtain an anti-virus program and make a habit of using it on a regular basis to protect your files against infection, especially if you frequently introduce files onto your hard disk from outside sources.

Part

VII

Ch

23

Understanding How Viruses Damage Your Computer

A *computer virus* is a program designed to do damage to either your computer or your computer's data. Viruses make copies of themselves and spread from one computer to another.

There are only two ways in which viruses can be transmitted between computers:

■ Loading and running infected software

■ Booting up with an infected floppy disk

If you don't do either of these things, your system won't acquire a virus. But because such an insulated approach to computers is virtually impossible, you should consider using an anti-virus program. Used correctly, a good anti-virus program can protect you against the vast majority of known viruses before they damage your computer.

You can simplify the procedure described in the previous Troubleshooting note by using a utility called DOSLFNBK, which can be downloaded from CompuServe. With DOSLFNBK, you don't have to go into the Properties sheet to disable and re-enable long file name preservation. To download DOSLFNBK, type Go MSWIN95 in CompuServe and search for DOSLFN10.ZIP in library 2.

If your system includes a CD-ROM, create simple AUTOEXEC.BAT and CONFIG.SYS files on your startup disk with the commands needed to load the CD-ROM driver at startup. You will also need to copy the driver file onto the disk. Then, if it becomes necessary to reinstall Windows from your Windows 95 CD-ROM, you will be able to access your CD-ROM drive. Your system may have come with a boot disk that includes these files. If so, make a second copy just to be safe, and whenever you create an updated startup disk, copy these files to the new startup disk.

ON THE WEB

For an excellent selection of links to anti-virus software sites, connect to the web at **http://www.primenet.com/~mwest/software.htm.**

Networking with Windows 95

CHAPTER 24

Installing Windows 95 as a Network Client

by Craig Zacker

When you upgrade a network workstation to the Windows 95 operating system, your network client is automatically upgraded as part of the process. Very little user intervention is required during this process, and you usually end up with the same network connectivity that you had before the upgrade.

In this chapter, you learn about the process of manually installing network support to an existing Windows 95 computer. In Windows 95, all network settings are modified using a single interface, as opposed to the multiple text files of other operating systems. In addition, most installations will not require any software other than that which ships as part of the Windows 95 product. After you install and configure a network interface card and the Client for Microsoft Networks, you will be able to share the resources of Windows NT network servers, as well as other peer Windows workstations.

See Chapter 25, "Connecting to a NetWare Network," for a discussion of NetWare clients and connectivity issues. ■

Windows 95's default network client installation

Learn how the Windows 95 installation routine handles an existing network client and automatically upgrades the workstation's network support.

Installing a network interface card

Assuming the physical installation of the card, in this section you learn how to manually install and configure driver support for a network adapter that doesn't conform to the Windows 95 Plug and Play standard.

Installing the Client for Microsoft Networks

Discover how to add networking capability to an existing Windows 95 installation.

Windows 95 networking components

This chapter helps you understand the components of the Windows 95 networking architecture.

Understanding the Default Network Client Installation

When Windows 95 is installed on a networked computer, the network client will, whenever possible, be upgraded to one of the new 32-bit protected-mode clients that ship with the operating system. However, if replacing the existing client will inhibit the workstation's network connectivity, Windows 95 will dynamically modify the client installation. Windows 95 may leave the entire existing client in place, or upgrade only the components that do not hinder network communications.

For example, if Windows 95 detects a client providing mini- or mainframe computer connectivity with a proprietary driver, it will leave that driver in place, because the operating system cannot duplicate these services with its own clients.

The methodical replacement of the network client is a crucial element of the Windows 95 installation process for a number of reasons. Most Windows 95 installations in a business networking environment are performed using source files located on a network drive. This is because installing from CD-ROM or floppy disks to dozens or hundreds of machines would be time-consuming and impractical. When you install an operating system from a network drive, continuous contact with the network must be maintained throughout the entire installation process; otherwise, the installation can be arrested, leaving the workstation without a ready means of accessing the network and completing the process.

Therefore, when the Windows 95 installation program detects an operational network client of any kind, it upgrades the network services if possible, but at the very least, it maintains the same degree of service as when the process began.

Installing the Microsoft Windows Network Client Manually

When networking support is not included as part of the Windows 95 operating system installation, it may be necessary for you to manually install the components needed to achieve network connectivity. This process may include some or all of the following procedures:

- Installing and configuring a network adapter
- Installing and configuring a network client
- Selecting network communications protocols
- Binding protocols to clients and adapters

In the following sections, you learn the basic procedures for accomplishing these tasks. Following that, the various components of the Windows 95 networking architecture will be examined in detail. Once you understand the ways in which the various modules interact, you will be able to configure a Windows 95 workstation to access multiple networks of different types in the most efficient manner possible.

Installing a Network Adapter

A personal computer's network interface consists of two parts: the network adapter device itself, which usually takes the form of an expansion card or NIC (network interface card), and the adapter driver, which allows communication between the hardware and the network client software. Both the hardware and software components must be properly configured for network communication to occur.

Part
VIII

Ch
24

When you install hardware conforming to the Windows 95 Plug and Play (PnP) standard, the operating system performs these configuration tasks for you automatically. However, many networks still purchase and use network interface cards that do not conform to the standard. When you install a non-PnP network adapter, you must configure the hardware and software yourself. Fortunately, even without Plug and Play, Windows 95 makes this configuration process easier than it has ever been before for a PC.

> **N O T E** If you are using a PC Card network adapter, Windows 95 requires that you install a PC Card driver before the driver for the adapter. In many cases, the PC Card driver will provide Plug and Play recognition of the network adapter and its properties, even in computers without a Plug and Play BIOS. ▪

Configuring Network Adapter Hardware

Every network interface card requires access to certain hardware and memory resources of your computer, such as an IRQ, a memory address, an I/O port, or any combination of these. The types of resources required differ for various adapters, but in nearly all cases, you must assign specific resource settings for the exclusive use of the card. The main obstacle to successfully installing a network adapter is locating settings acceptable to the card that are not already being used by the computer's other hardware.

You adjust your network adapter's hardware settings either by physically manipulating jumper blocks or DIP switches on the card itself, or by running a configuration program supplied by the hardware. The program directly addresses the permanent memory on the card and stores your selected settings there.

Unless you are familiar with the IRQ, memory address, and I/O port settings of all the components in your computer, the installation of a network card will be primarily a trial and error process. You insert the card into the computer, load the operating system, and see if there are any conflicts with the other hardware in the computer. If there are, you adjust the settings of the card and try again.

Windows 95 provides tools that can simplify this process, but before you can use them, you must first install driver support for the network adapter. You can do this from the Network icon in the Control Panel, but the easier method is to use the Add New Hardware Wizard.

Using the Add New Hardware Wizard

TIP Before beginning the actual installation process of a new network adapter, it is a good idea to make a note of the adapter's default settings, either by examining the card itself, consulting the card's documentation, or by running the configuration software supplied with it. You may then physically insert the card into the computer (although this also may be done after the driver installation) and start the machine.

The Add New Hardware Wizard takes you through the process of identifying your network interface card to the operating system and installing the appropriate adapter drivers. You may elect to install the adapter hardware before running the wizard (although it is not essential) but it is recommended that you leave the task of resolving any hardware conflicts until afterwards. Once you have installed the adapter driver, you can use the Windows 95 Device Manager to determine what devices are in conflict.

To install support for a network adapter, follow these steps:

1. Select the Add New Hardware icon from the Windows 95 Control Panel.
2. When asked if you want to let Windows 95 attempt to automatically detect your new hardware, select <u>N</u>o.
3. From the list of Hardware Types, choose Network adapters and click the Next button. The Select Device dialog box, shown in figure 24.1, appears.
4. Select the Manufacturer of your network adapter from the scroll box on the left, and select the Model on the right. If your adapter does not appear on the list, or if you have an updated driver that you want to install, click the Have Disk button and specify the location of the files.

FIG. 24.1

The Select Device dialog box lists all of the network adapter drivers that ship with Windows 95.

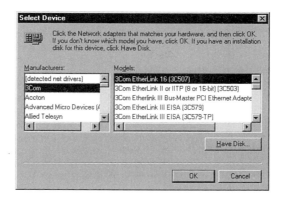

N O T E The drivers supplied with the shipping version of the Windows 95 operating system support a large percentage of the network adapter cards in current use and available on the market today. However, new hardware is continually being released, as are updated drivers. Microsoft has posted a large number of updated hardware drivers on their online services. Updated drivers can also be obtained directly from the hardware manufacturer. While you may encounter cases in which newer drivers are needed to enable certain networking features, you will rarely see the default Windows 95 installation package fail to achieve a network connection using the drivers provided. ▄

ON THE WEB

Microsoft's updated adapter drivers can be found as part of the Windows 95 Driver Library, available on their World Wide Web site at

http://www.microsoft.com/windows/software/drivers/network.html

5. Once you have made a hardware selection, click OK and Windows 95 displays a screen listing the hardware settings that must be specified for the operation of the adapter, as well as the default settings supplied by the driver software. These settings are not necessarily those to which the hardware has been configured. In a non-Plug and Play installation, the operating system is unable to detect the actual settings of the hardware. The values shown are proposed software settings for the driver to be installed.

6. Compare the driver settings displayed by the wizard with the adapter's hardware settings you have previously noted before the installation process began. If these values differ, then you must reconfigure either the hardware or software settings, or both. But first, the driver installation must be completed. Click Next.

7. Windows 95 will now access its installation files and copy the appropriate driver files to the hard drive. You may be prompted to locate your Windows 95 installation source files. Click Yes when you are asked if you want to restart your computer.

TROUBLESHOOTING

After installing a new network interface card, my computer fails to boot properly. It either boots into Safe Mode or fails to boot at all. What's wrong? The network interface card is currently conflicting with the other hardware in your computer. Remove the card, boot the computer, and install support for the card using the Add New Hardware Wizard. (You can do this whether the card is physically installed or not.) Use the Windows 95 Device Manager to find new hardware settings that don't conflict with the rest of the system. Shut down the computer, reinstall the card with the new settings, and reboot.

Using the Windows 95 Device Manager

Unlike older operating systems, Windows 95 can monitor the hardware resources being used by every device in the computer. Windows 95 also includes a Device Manager that displays an inventory of the computer's contents. If you have determined during the adapter driver installation that adjustments to the hardware settings are necessary, you can use the Device Manager to see which hardware devices conflict, and which settings must be altered.

You can access this inventory from the Windows 95 Control Panel by opening the System application and selecting the Device Manager tab. This page displays a collapsible tree, such as that shown in figure 24.2. When you select a device on the tree, click the Properties button and then choose the Resources tab. The hardware resource settings of the device's driver appear.

At the bottom of the Resources sheet, there is a Conflicting Device List. If any of the current settings of your network adapter conflict with another device in the computer, then the setting and the device name are displayed in the Conflicting Device List.

If you attempt to modify a device's configuration to use a resource that has already been allocated, a message box warns you that you must make configuration changes.

FIG. 24.2

The Device Manager screen displays an inventory of the computer's currently installed hardware.

Modifying the Network Adapter Configuration

At this point in the installation of the network adapter, you use the Device Manager to perform two distinct tasks:

- Determine whether the current hardware settings of the adapter are in conflict with other devices

- Modify the resource settings of the network adapter's software device driver

It is important that you distinguish between these two tasks. While you can use the Device Manager to examine the current hardware settings, it cannot modify them. You must do this by using the adapter's configuration program or by adjusting the hardware itself. Use the following procedure to locate proper hardware resource settings and configure the adapter driver to use them.

1. Double-click the System icon in the Control Panel and click the Device Manager tab.

2. In the Device Manager dialog box, select your network adapter by name, and click the Properties button.

3. Click the Resources tab. A display of Resource Settings appears, as shown in figure 24.3.

FIG. 24.3
In the Device Manager, you can modify the Resource Settings.

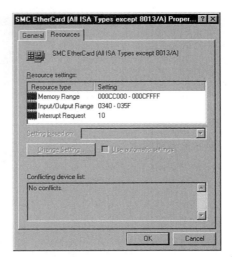

4. Click the first Resource Type in the Resource Settings selector, then click the Change Setting button.

5. Modify the Value in the Edit dialog box to match your adapter's current hardware setting (which you noted before the installation process began). If another installed device appears in the Conflicting Device List window, then that value cannot be used.

6. If necessary, modify the setting again to a Value that displays a No Devices Are Conflicting message in the Conflicting Device List window.

   Notice the new Value that you have selected for later use, and click OK.

7. Repeat steps 4 through 6 for each hardware setting displayed on the Resources page. When you are finished, the Conflicting Device List window on the Resources sheet should indicate that No Conflicts exist.

8. Click OK to close the sheet.

Windows 95 displays a message stating that you should now shut down and power off your computer, and then modify your adapter's hardware settings. You need do this only if you encountered conflicts during the preceding steps. To change the settings, follow the instructions included with your network adapter. You may not have to power down the machine if a software-based setup program is available for the adapter. You do need to reboot the system, however, after any hardware settings are changed.

TROUBLESHOOTING

What do I do if I have tried all of the values for a particular resource setting, and they all result in a conflict? Today's network adapters usually provide a large selection of possible values for their resource settings. Other devices in your computer, however, may offer a different selection. If you cannot locate an unconflicting value for a particular network adapter setting, you will have to modify the configuration of another device in your system to free up a resource for your network adapter. The best way to handle this problem is to remove the network adapter from the computer, and concentrate on reconfiguring another device, using either the Device Manager, a Control Panel application, or a dedicated configuration program to make the changes. Once you are certain that the other device is functioning properly, reinsert the network adapter and modify its resource setting to the newly available value.

I have modified the settings in the Device Manager so that there are no hardware conflicts, but my network adapter still does not function. What's wrong? If you made changes to the adapter driver settings, then you must also configure the hardware itself to use those settings. This can only be done by physically manipulating the hardware, using jumpers or DIP switches, or by using a software-based configuration program.

Part
VIII

Ch
24

> **CAUTION**
>
> The cardinal rule for adapter card installation is that the hardware settings and the software settings must agree in order for communications to take place. A configuration program supplied with an adapter may make it appear as though software settings are being altered, when in fact it is the hardware that is being addressed. Remember, Windows 95 cannot modify the resource settings of non-PnP hardware.

Installing a Network Client

Once you have installed your network adapter, all the other Windows 95 networking components are installed and configured through the Network application in the Windows 95 Control Panel.

You can verify that your adapter has been installed properly by opening the Network application. The name of the adapter should appear in the Configuration page.

> **N O T E** You can modify your network adapter driver's resource settings through the Network application by double-clicking the adapter name and selecting the Resources tab in the adapter's properties sheet. However, while this interface can inform you of the existence of a hardware conflict, it does not specify the name of the conflicting device, as the Device Manager does. ▨

The adapter and its driver are the components that communicate directly with the network. For Windows 95 to access network resources, you must next install a network client, which communicates with the rest of the operating system, and a protocol, which links the client and the adapter.

The next section covers the basic procedure for installing the client and protocol modules that you need to access the resources of a Windows network.

If you understand the basic installation techniques used in the network dialog box and the ways in which the various components interact to form the networking architecture, you can configure a Windows 95 workstation to achieve full connectivity in the most complex multiple network environment.

Installing the Client for Microsoft Networks

The following procedure details the installation of the base Client for Microsoft Networks, and all the other components necessary to gain access to the network and attach to a Windows NT server.

1. Double-click the Network icon in the Control Panel and click Add.

2. In the Select Network Component Type dialog box (see fig. 24.4), double-click Client.

FIG. 24.4
Select the component to be installed from the list.

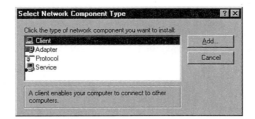

3. Choose Microsoft from the left side of the Select Network Client dialog box (see fig. 24.5) and choose Client for Microsoft Networks from the right side. Click OK. Back at the Network application's Configuration page, the client appears in the component list.

FIG. 24.5
Select the Client for Microsoft Networks to connect to a Windows NT server or a Windows peer-to-peer network.

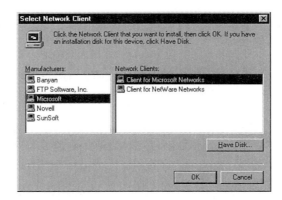

NOTE If you had not already installed an adapter, you would be asked at this time to specify one, or allow Windows 95 to attempt to auto detect one. You can install an adapter directly from the Network application, or see "Using the Add New Hardware Wizard," earlier in this chapter.

4. Click the <u>A</u>dd button again and double-click Protocol in the Select Network Component Type dialog box.

5. Choose Microsoft from the left side of the Select Network Protocol dialog box, and NetBEUI from the right. This is the default protocol for Windows NT and LAN Manager client/server networks, as well as for Windows peer-to-peer networks. Click OK. The Configuration screen of the Network application should list the installed protocol, as shown in figure 24.6.

6. Click OK to complete the component installation process, and click Yes when you are asked if you want to restart the computer.

FIG. 24.6
A Windows 95 Network screen showing all the basic components necessary to attach to a Windows NT client/server network.

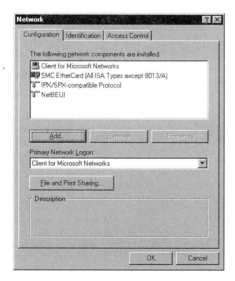

Before clicking the OK button to close the Network application and complete the installation, take note of the items in the next section to ensure that network connectivity is established after you restart your system.

Configuring the Microsoft Client for Network Access

Before your workstation can successfully be logged on to the network, you may have to modify certain client configuration parameters. Check the settings listed in the following sections. Once they are properly configured, click OK to close the Network application and choose Yes when you are asked if you want to restart the computer. Once the operating system is reloaded, if all of the networking components have been installed and configured correctly, Windows 95 should attach to the network and present you with a login dialog box.

> **CAUTION**
>
> When logging on to an existing network, none of the procedures outlined in this chapter, including the installation of the Windows 95 operating system, should be undertaken without first informing the network administrator of your intentions.

The Primary Network Logon   On the Configuration page of the Network application, select Client for Microsoft Networks as the value in the Primary Network Logon display.

The Primary Network Logon selector determines which login dialog box appears each time your computer is restarted. When multiple network clients have been installed, you may select which one is to be the default login using this selector. If you choose the Windows Logon option, then no network login will occur until you attempt to access network resources.

▶ **See** "Logging Into the Network," **p. 744**

The Identification Page   On the Identification page of the Network application, enter a Computer Name and (optionally) a Computer Description. Windows 95 will use the names entered here to identify your computer to the network. Do not confuse the Computer Name with the user name that you use to log in to a network. A single Windows 95 computer can support many users, and a single user can work at many computers.

Also, enter the name of the network workgroup or domain in which your workstation will belong.

Domains versus Workgroups

Microsoft Windows networking recognizes two types of logical machine groupings: domains and workgroups. A domain is a group of machines whose security is administered from a central location—that is, a Windows NT server. All users, groups, and passwords are stored on the server, and administered by the server administrator. If you are logging onto an existing Windows NT network, there is probably a domain to which you will have to be granted access. Domain security information can only be stored on a Windows NT server; you cannot create a domain on a Windows 95 peer-to-peer network.

A *workgroup* is also a collection of Windows machines, any of which may be running Windows 95, Windows NT, or Windows for Workgroups. In a workgroup, each workstation is responsible for maintaining its own security information. The selection of which resources are to be shared and their access passwords are all controlled and stored on each individual workstation itself.

Every Windows computer running a Microsoft network client must declare itself to be a member of a domain or a workgroup, even if the workgroup consists of only one machine. Membership in a workgroup or a domain in no way prevents access to resources in other workgroups or domains.

Domain Logons   If you will be logging into an existing domain on the network, double-click the Client for Microsoft Networks in the Configuration sheet of the Network application, and select the General tab in the Properties sheet. Click to fill the <u>L</u>ogon to Windows NT Domain check box and enter the domain name in the <u>W</u>indows NT Domain field.

During the various procedures covered in this chapter, you have installed three of the four basic network component types used by Windows 95. In the following sections, you will learn about the functions of all four of the following component types, in more general terms:

- Client
- Adapter
- Protocol
- Service

These four entities actually represent groupings of the various network processes that occur behind the scenes in any networking situation. At the very minimum, you must have one client, one adapter and one protocol installed for network communication to take place in Windows 95. The components interact by forming a *stack*, which can be illustrated by arranging them as though they were wooden building blocks, as in figure 24.7.

FIG. 24.7
The basic building blocks of Windows 95 networking stacked to form a communications channel.

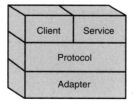

Networking technologies are often illustrated using the OSI Reference Model. The OSI model, as shown in figure 24.8, splits the networking communications processes into seven discrete layers. The Application layer, at the top of the model, represents the user interface at the workstation, and the Physical layer, at the bottom, represents the network medium, usually a cable.

FIG. 24.8
The OSI Reference Model
encompasses the same
procedures as the Windows
95 stack previously
illustrated.

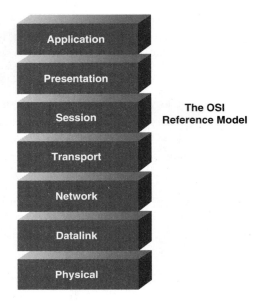

The Windows 95 stack simplifies this model, but represents the same thing, a channel or conduit ranging from the user interface to the network medium, through which data files and network requests are ultimately translated into signals that are then transmitted over the network.

Clients

Although the word is often used in a general sense, to refer to any computer that uses a network to attach to another computer, the term client here refers to a specific networking component. Multiple clients can be installed on a single Windows 95 machine at any one time.

In this sense, the client refers to the network operating system to which the workstation attaches. Windows 95 ships with support for seven clients, two of which have been written by Microsoft, while others use the software developed by the NOS vendor. These clients are:

- Microsoft Client for Microsoft Networks
- Microsoft Client for NetWare Networks
- NetWare (Workstation Shell 3.X [NETX])
- NetWare (Workstation Shell 4.0 and above [VLM])
- Banyan DOS/Windows 3.1

- FTP Software NFS Client (InterDrive 95)
- SunSoft PC-NFS (version 5.0)

Still other clients are available from the manufacturers of network operating systems, and can be installed using the Have Disk button.

The two most commonly installed clients, which Microsoft has created specifically for use with Windows 95, are *the Client for Microsoft Networks* and the *Client for NetWare Networks*. These are both 32-bit protected-mode clients that provide performance levels that are far superior to those of any client previously developed for these network operating systems.

Advantages of a 32-bit protected-mode client

A 32-bit protected-mode client is a great improvement over the traditional 16-bit real-mode clients used for DOS and Windows workstations. 32-bit means that the software can utilize double the communications bandwidth between the computer's memory and its microprocessor. Protected mode means that system memory is addressed linearly by the processor, using a flat memory model. All of the memory required by the client is requested from a common pool, while a real-mode client must address specific individual memory segments of limited size. A flat memory model also eliminates any concern for the use of conventional memory versus extended memory. Thus, the traditional memory management chores associated with the use of real-mode clients (even with Windows 95) are eliminated.

In order to provide backwards compatibility, Microsoft has included support for the standard real-mode clients with Windows 95. These clients use software modules that are loaded from a batch file before Windows loads. You must, however, also perform a client installation using the Control Panel's Network application, so that the client configuration settings stored in the NetWare NET.CFG file are migrated to the Windows 95 Registry.

Support for other clients also is provided with Windows 95, such as those produced by Banyan, FTP Corp., and Sun. Other clients have also become available since the initial Windows 95 release, and still more are currently in development. All clients designed for use with Windows 95 can be installed using the standard Select Network Component Type dialog box in the Network application.

Adapters

As you have seen during the installation procedure, the network adapter is the physical part of the network connection, and is the bottom block upon which the entirety of the networking stack rests. When you install an adapter in Windows 95, you are actually installing the driver through which the adapter hardware will communicate with the operating system. An adapter driver can be installed from the Network application, as well as by using the Add New Hardware Wizard.

When installing a system's first network interface adapter, using the wizard is preferable. When adding a second network adapter, however, the Network application is quite useful. When you install a second adapter into an existing network configuration, it automatically becomes an integrated part of the stack; that is, it is immediately bound with all of the operating protocols. Although it is possible, and sometimes necessary, to install two or more network interface cards into one machine, in most cases a Windows 95 computer's second adapter will be the Dial-Up adapter.

▶ **See** "Installing a Network Adapter," **p. 691**

▶ **See** "Using Novell Real-Mode Clients," **p. 728**

The Dial-Up Adapter Windows 95 treats all types of communications between computers as a form of networking. A telephone line between two modems is just as much a network connection as a cable connecting two network interface cards. The Dial-Up adapter is essentially a driver that allows you to use a modem like any other network interface.

A Windows 95 workstation can access a network by dialing into another modem-equipped Windows 95 or Windows NT machine that has been configured as a remote access server. Likewise, Windows 95 can attach to the Internet using a dial-up PPP (point-to-point protocol) connection that will function just as a LAN Internet connection would (albeit more slowly). Windows 95 can even access shared network drives over the Internet using a Windows NT WINS server that eliminates the need for a modem pool at the host end.

▶ **See** "Using Remote Network Access," **p. 811**

▶ **See** "Sharing Drives over the Internet," **p. 817**

Adapter Configuration Options When you select any installed adapter in the Network application's Configuration page and click the Properties button, a tabbed sheet is displayed that contains the configuration settings that pertain to that adapter. In most cases, the pages discussed in the following sections are displayed:

Driver Type The Driver Type page indicates the standard to which the adapter driver has been written. The choices are:

- Enhanced-mode (32-bit and 16-bit) NDIS driver

- Real-mode (16-bit) NDIS driver

- Real-mode (16-bit) ODI driver

One or more of the choices may be grayed out, indicating that drivers of that type are not available for that adapter.

The Network Device Interface Specification (NDIS) was originally developed by 3Com and Microsoft for use with Microsoft's LAN Manager network operating system. The standard has been revised several times, and is the default adapter driver type used in

Microsoft Windows networking. Windows for Workgroups uses 16-bit real-mode drivers conforming to the NDIS 2.x specification. Windows 95 includes new drivers conforming to version 3.1 of the specification, which provide greatly enhanced performance and resource utilization, due to their 32-bit protected-mode architecture. The new high-performance clients for Microsoft and NetWare networks that ship with Windows 95 both use the 32-bit NDIS driver by default.

> **CAUTION**
>
> Drivers written to conform to the 2.x and 3.1 versions of the NDIS specification can be used with Windows 95; NDIS 3.0 drivers cannot.

The 16-bit real-mode NDIS driver is included in and supported by the Windows 95 operating system, but it is not designed for continued use, as you will realize far better performance with the 32-bit driver. The 16-bit driver is used primarily in cases when a user elects to boot a Windows 95 machine into Safe Mode with Network Support, or in diskless workstation environments, when a PC is booted from a floppy and the real-mode driver is needed to provide access to a shared copy of Windows 95 on the network.

TIP A Windows 95 machine can be booted into Safe mode for troubleshooting purposes by pressing the F8 key during the machine's boot sequence. Selecting *Safe Mode with Network* from the boot menu starts Windows 95 in a minimal mode, bypassing startup files, using a standard VGA video driver, and providing limited real-mode network support.

Just as NDIS is the driver standard for Microsoft networking, so the Open Device Interface, or ODI driver is to NetWare. Although the Microsoft Client for NetWare networks is capable of using the NDIS 3.1 drivers supplied with Windows 95, it also provides real-mode ODI support for when a user elects to install a real-mode network client or when an NDIS 3.1 driver is not available for a particular adapter. Although the situation has now changed, use of the ODI driver was common when Windows 95 was first released, because the 16-bit VLM client was the only way to gain support for NetWare Directory Services.

Bindings Bindings represent the relationships between adapters and protocols. In order for communications to traverse the network stack, an adapter must be bound to at least one protocol that is in turn bound to a client. The Bindings page in the adapter's Properties sheet displays all of the installed protocols and indicates by means of a check box whether they are bound to the adapter. When you remove the check mark from one of the boxes, that protocol is unbound from the adapter. By default, whenever a protocol is installed, it is automatically bound to all of the installed adapters and clients that can use it. Likewise, when a new adapter is installed, it is automatically bound to all existing protocols.

N O T E The Properties sheet for a Protocol also contains a Bindings page, which displays all of the clients to which that protocol is bound. An unbroken link of bindings must exist from adapter to protocol to client for network communications to take place. ▪

Windows 95 provides complete flexibility when it comes to the binding of protocols with adapters, as follows:

- ▪ Multiple protocols can be bound to a single adapter.
- ▪ Multiple adapters can be bound to a single protocol.
- ▪ Separate protocols can be bound to separate adapters.
    - ▶ **See** "Protocols," **p. 707**
    - ▶ **See** "Modifying the Default Installation," **p. 722**

Advanced   The Advanced page is a generic interface for controls and configuration settings that are unique to a particular model of adapter. Depending on the capabilities of the hardware, any number of settings may be located here, for any possible purpose. Each setting in the listing on the left side of the page will display a corresponding selector on the right, from which you can choose possible values.

Resources   The Resources page is where the adapter driver's hardware resource settings are located. The settings appropriate to the adapter are displayed here, along with selectors containing all of the possible value settings for each. When you see an asterisk (*) next to a particular value setting, this indicates that the setting is in conflict with one or more hardware devices in the computer. A pound sign (#) next to a value indicates that the hardware is physically configured to use that setting. Depending on the adapter, Windows 95 may or may not be able to accurately detect the hardware's physical settings.

 T I P Use the Device Manager, located in the System application of the Control Panel, to find out which devices in the computer are using conflicting resource settings.

N O T E Adapters conforming to the Plug and Play standard do not have a Resources page, because Windows 95 handles their configuration automatically. ▪

Protocols

Protocol is, again, a general networking term that has a specific meaning in reference to the Windows 95 stack. A *protocol* is simply a common language used by two network entities to communicate with each other. Protocols vary greatly in nature and use different means to establish communication, just as human languages vary and are composed of different alphabets.

All network communication actually utilizes many different protocols at the same time. Part of the functionality of the OSI reference model shown earlier in this chapter in figure 24.8 is to distinguish between the protocols that are used at different levels of the communications stack. The fundamental, or bottom-most protocol, is the signaling code used by the electrical impulses traveling over the network cable. This is a language understood by the two network adapters at either end of the cable, but it is meaningless to an operating system or a computer application.

One or more unique protocols are used at each level of the OSI model, resulting in a vastly complicated system of communications in which one language is encapsulated within another language, which is in turn packaged within another, and another, and so on. Every language translation process that is performed by the sending computer is also performed in reverse by the receiving computer.

For Windows 95, the technical term protocol refers only to one type of these many languages. It is one that would be located somewhere in the middle of the OSI model, centering around the Network and Transport layers. The purpose of the protocols specified in Windows 95 is to see that a network request or response made by the workstation is properly addressed and arrives intact at its destination.

A protocol selection is usually made according to the network operating system in use, and design decisions made during the creation of the network. In other words, if you were setting up a new network, you could utilize any protocol that is supported by all of the computers and operating systems involved, as long as they were all configured to use the same one. Windows 95 can also use multiple protocols at the same time, either in combination or in parallel.

For example, as shown in figure 24.9, your network adapter could be configured to use both NetBEUI, for connecting to a Windows NT server, and TCP/IP to connect to the Internet. Alternatively, you could use NetBEUI with a network interface card for local network connections, and TCP/IP with the Dial-Up adapter to connect to a dial-up Internet service provider. Both resources would be seamlessly integrated into the Windows 95 interface, but they would actually be separate networking systems, operating in parallel.

FIG. 24.9

Networking protocols can be used in combination or for parallel operations.

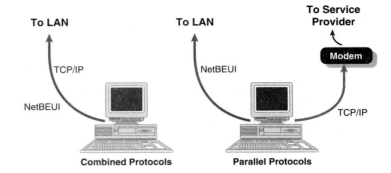

Combined Protocols   Parallel Protocols

NetBEUI The NetBIOS Extended User Interface (NetBEUI) is a protocol that was developed by IBM in the mid-1980s, and which has since become the *lingua franca* of Microsoft Windows networking. The Windows 95 Client for Microsoft Networks uses it by default, allowing communications with other machines running Windows 95, as well as with computers running Windows NT, Windows for Workgroups, and Microsoft LAN Manager.

The NetBEUI support included with Windows 95 is compliant with both protected-mode and real-mode operation, in order to accommodate all of the operating systems listed earlier, and is also compliant with the Plug and Play standard. Thus, if a laptop running Windows 95 is removed from a network docking station, or its PC Card network adapter is removed, the NetBEUI protocol is automatically unloaded, to conserve system resources, and then reloaded when the machine is again connected to the network, all without having to shut down the machine or restart Windows.

NetBEUI and Routability In a client/server networking situation, NetBEUI is often utilized with another protocol. This is because NetBEUI has one outstanding limitation— that it is not routable. Large corporate LANs are composed of multiple segments. Each of these segments is itself a local area network. These segments are combined by routers to form what should strictly be called an internetwork—that is, a network of networks.

Routers and Internetworking

Routers are the devices traditionally used to connect individual segments or networks, thus forming an internetwork. Their job is to let the network traffic through that is destined for the connected segment, and reject all of the traffic that isn't. Thus, if a router connects network A to network B, then only the traffic generated by network A that is destined for a recipient on network B is allowed through the router. All of the rest is blocked, lessening the amount of unnecessary traffic propagated between networks.

Communications using the NetBEUI protocol are incapable of passing through network routers. A Windows 95 workstation running the Client for Microsoft Networks and using only NetBEUI will be able to see only the computers located on the local segment. No communication will be possible with any server or workstation outside that one network.

If you add another protocol, which is routable, to the network configuration, such as the IPX/SPX-compatible protocol or TCP/IP, Windows network communications will be propagated throughout the entire internetwork, and all Windows network computers will be visible and accessible to the workstation.

NetBEUI Configuration Options When you select any installed protocol in the Network application's Configuration page and click the Properties button, a tabbed sheet containing the configuration settings that pertain to that protocol is displayed. The following pages are available:

Bindings The Bindings sheet (see fig. 24.10), present in Properties dialog boxes of all protocols, is similar in format to the Bindings sheet in an adapter's Properties dialog box, except that this page displays the clients to which NetBEUI is bound. As with an adapter, specific bindings can be enabled or disabled through the use of a check box.

FIG. 24.10
The Bindings page indicates which clients are using a particular protocol.

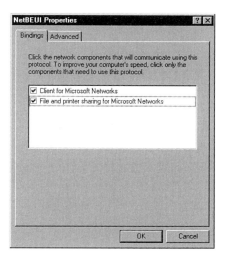

 Windows 95 will not bind a protocol to a client that cannot make use of it (for example, the NetBEUI protocol would never be bound to the Client for NetWare Networks), but the operating system tends to cross-bind all compatible components. Avoid binding protocols to clients (or adapters to protocols) unnecessarily. This practice consumes system resources and does no palpable good.

Part
VIII

Ch
24

Advanced   As with an adapter's Properties sheet, the Advanced page is used for settings specific to this component. NetBEUI's Advanced page contains the following settings:

- *Maximum Sessions.* Indicates the maximum number of remote connections that can be made using the NetBEUI protocol. The default value is 10, and possible values range from 3 to 117. If you intend to access the resources of more than 10 remote server and peer computers at any one time, then increase this value.

- *NCBs (network control blocks).* Indicates the maximum number of NetBIOS commands that can be used. The default value is 12, and possible values range from 7 to 255.

The IPX/SPX-Compatible Protocol

IPX stands for Internetwork Packet Exchange and SPX for Sequenced Packet Exchange. Both of these were created for use as the default protocols for their NetWare network operating system. To this day, IPX is the native protocol for NetWare, and is used on the vast majority of local area networks currently in operation.

IPX/SPX is actually something of a misnomer. IPX/SPX has come to be used as a catchall term for what is actually a collection of protocols used by NetWare for its various communication tasks. IPX is a multi-purpose OSI Network layer protocol NetWare uses as a conveyor for SPX and numerous other higher-level protocols. SPX is a relatively seldom used protocol in NetWare, used for transmission of printer traffic and not very much else.

What Windows 95 refers to as the IPX/SPX-compatible protocol is a collection of protocols designed by Microsoft, specifically for use with Microsoft networking products. They are designed to closely emulate Novell's actual IPX protocol suite, and I have never encountered any compatibility problems with them.

IPX/SPX is required if you are connecting a Windows 95 workstation to a NetWare network. If you will be using Windows 95 to connect only to NetWare servers, then no other protocol is necessary.

N O T E   Although most NetWare networks use IPX/SPX, there is a variant of the network operating system, called NetWare/IP, that uses TCP/IP as its native protocol. However, NetWare/IP is not supported by the Client for NetWare Networks or the Microsoft TCP/IP protocol included with Windows 95. ■

Unlike NetBEUI, IPX/SPX is a routable protocol that you can use with either or both of the 32-bit Microsoft clients for Windows 95. It can also be effectively used with NetBEUI to provide routing services for Windows network traffic.

N O T E Windows 95 also includes Novell's own realization of the IPX protocol suite. It is listed as the Novell IPX ODI Protocol in the Select Network Protocol dialog box of the Network application. Novell's protocol is included for use with the NetWare 16-bit real mode clients, however, and for best performance, should not be used with the 32-bit Microsoft and NetWare clients supplied with Windows 95. ■

IPX/SPX-Compatible Configuration Options   The Properties sheet for the IPX-SPX-compatible protocol contains a Bindings page that is identical to that for the NetBEUI properties sheet (and for every other protocol). There also is a unique NetBIOS page that contains a single check box, indicating whether support for the NetBIOS programming interface should be activated over the IPX/SPX-compatible protocol. Unless you are utilizing client/server applications that require NetBIOS for their communications, leave this box unchecked.

The Advanced page for the IPX/SPX Properties sheet, as shown in figure 24.11, contains a number of parameters that will be familiar to experienced NetWare users.

Part **VIII**

Ch **24**

FIG. 24.11
The Advanced page of the IPX/SPX-compatible protocol properties sheet contains parameter settings specific to the protocol.

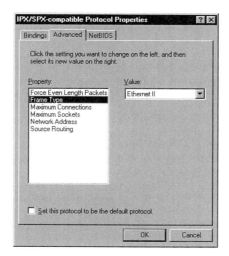

The following are settings that are also found in the NET.CFG file of a DOS/Windows 3.1 NetWare client workstation. Refer to your NetWare documentation for more information as to their use.

■ **Force Even Length Packets**. Possible Values: yes/no/not present—Default: not present—required only for older networks still using monolithic drivers (such as IPX.COM) and frame type 802.3 that cannot handle packets of odd lengths.

- **Frame Type**. Possible Values: auto-detect / 802.2 / 802.3 / Ethernet II / Token Ring / Token Ring SNAP—Default: auto-detect—indicates the frame type that the NetWare operating system is configured to use. NetWare versions 3.12 and later default to 802.2.

- **Maximum Connections**. Possible Values: 1 to 128 / not present—Default: not present (dynamically configured)—indicates the maximum number of IPX connections allowed at one time.

- **Maximum Sockets**. Possible Values: 2 to 255 / not present—Default: not present (dynamically configured)—indicates the maximum number of IPX sockets assigned.

- **Network Address**. Dynamically configured—indicates the IPX network address.

- **Source Routing**. Possible Values: 16, 32, or 64 entries / off—Default: off—used only on Token Ring networks, indicates the number of entries in the cache when source routing is used.

TROUBLESHOOTING

Everything in Windows 95 seems to be configured properly, but I'm having trouble communicating with my NetWare network. What should I do? One of the most common sources of communications problems between Windows 95 and NetWare is the Frame Type auto-detection mechanism. Among the first troubleshooting steps you should take is to change this setting from the default to the specific frame type being used on your NetWare network.

N O T E   *Source routing* is a technique by which a Token Ring workstation queries the network and builds an internal cache of information concerning the location of other workstations. With this information, the source node can determine the route a packet will take to its destination before it is transmitted. ■

N O T E   Several of the settings listed previously have a *Not Present* radio button available, which, when clicked, indicates that the setting is not to be defined at all in the Windows 95 Registry. When this option is selected, there is always a system default for that setting that is observed, despite its absence from the Registry. On more than one occasion, Windows 95 has been known to behave differently when no Registry entry is present for a setting, than when an entry explicitly specifying the default value is present. Obviously, this makes little sense, but keep this fact in mind when troubleshooting obscure problems with Registry settings. Sometimes the complete removal of a setting is preferable to simply reversing it. As always, do not blithely make changes to the Registry unless you are sure of the result, have made a backup copy of the Registry files, and know how to restore it. You may otherwise end up with an unbootable system. ■

TCP/IP

TCP/IP (transmission control protocol/internet protocol) is another convenient term for a set of protocols that cover far more ground than the two mentioned. TCP/IP actually consists of hundreds of different protocols. It was created by the Department of Defense, back when the Internet was known as the ARPAnet, as a common communication language for government computers. It is now the *de facto* standard protocol suite for all UNIX operating systems, as well as for the Internet.

Windows 95 is the first popular desktop operating system to ship with a fully integrated TCP/IP protocol support module that is as simple to use as anyone could possibly ask. It is also compatible with virtually every desktop Internet application available today. Microsoft's TCP/IP is installed like any other protocol, can be used as a general purpose LAN protocol, and can supply internetwork routability to NetBEUI traffic. It can also be used to connect to the Internet, either through a LAN connection, or a dial-up. The Dial-Up adapter driver included with Windows 95 is explicitly made for this purpose.

Part
VIII

Ch
24

TCP/IP Configuration Options   Configuration of the TCP/IP protocol for use on a LAN is more complicated than that of the other protocols we have discussed. There are no default Plug and Play settings. You cannot expect to use the protocol without configuring certain options correctly, because they require unique values for every workstation on the network. In several cases, it will be necessary to ask your network administrator or Internet service provider for the correct settings.

The settings described in this section are intended for the use of TCP/IP over a LAN connection. The configuration procedure is different for a dial-up Internet connection. See Chapter 33, "Getting Connected to the Internet," for more information on this subject.

The TCP/IP Properties sheet (see fig. 24.12) contains the standard Bindings page, as well as an Advanced page that is empty. There are four other pages that you must consider, however, which are cited in the following sections.

IP Address   The IP address is the unique identifying address of your computer. It is composed of four octets of up to three digits each, separated by periods. In some cases, your computer may be assigned a specific IP address by your administrator or service provider. In that case, click the selector that says Select an IP Address, and fill in the address and subnet mask supplied to you.

At other sites, a Windows NT server may be configured to act as a DHCP, or dynamic host configuration protocol server. This is a service that runs on the NT machine that allocates IP addresses to network workstations requesting them, ensuring that no conflicts occur from two workstations using the same address. Such a server can also deliver subnet mask, DNS and WINS information to the workstation.

FIG. 24.12

The TCP/IP Properties sheet contains pages for all essential configuration parameters.

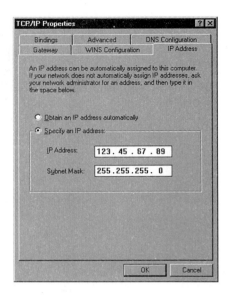

N O T E   If you are using TCP/IP on multiple network adapters, then individual IP addresses, subnet masks, and gateways must be specified for each adapter. ▓

N O T E   If you use dial-up connections to more than one Internet service provider, then individual IP address and DNS settings can be specified for each connection. ▓

Gateway   The gateway is the default IP router on your network. You can specify several gateway addresses. The protocol will proceed to the alternates when the first address is unreachable. This address should be supplied by your network administrator or service provider.

DNS Configuration   A Domain Name Server is a router daemon whose basic function is name resolution. That is, the DNS associates numeric IP addresses, such as 123.45.67.89, with named addresses, such as **www.microsoft.com**. The DNS does this by maintaining static tables of equivalent addresses, and by querying network entities for information to update the table.

Again, the correct DNS address (or addresses) to use should be furnished by your network administrator or service provider. You may enter multiple addresses, so that if an entry is not found on one, the subsequent entries will be checked. You must also enter a host name for your machine, and the domain name for your organization (for example, **microsoft.com**). Use of a DNS is optional, because a DHCP server can be used for the same purpose.

WINS Configuration   WINS, or *Windows Internet Naming Service*, is a realization of an existing published standard, created by Microsoft as a service for their Windows NT Advanced Server product. A WINS server performs essentially the same function as a DNS, except that the WINS server does not require static addresses to maintain its data tables. They can be adjusted dynamically. When using a DHCP server to assign IP addresses, use of a WINS server is almost required, because a DNS server could not keep up with the continual IP address changes.

Configuring the TCP/IP protocol for the use of the WINS server in most cases simply involves entering the addresses of a Primary and Secondary WINS server in the spaces provided in the WINS Configuration page or, alternately, selecting the option that allows a DHCP server to provide the necessary addresses.

▶ **See** "Sharing Drives Over the Internet" **p. 817**

Part
VIII

Ch
24

Services

A *service*, in Windows 95 parlance, is a software module that runs continually, providing a function that is available at all times to the entire system. A service is somewhat akin to a TSR in traditional DOS computing, except that it runs in protected mode and doesn't require the conventional memory that a TSR usually does.

From a networking standpoint, Windows 95 provides services of several different types. They are used as a means of adding extra value to a network client, allowing them capabilities they ordinarily would not have. The installation of a service is as simple as that of any other network component. When you choose a module from the Select Network Service dialog box, it becomes a part of the network configuration, with a Properties sheet that provides any configuration parameters that it needs. Due to the widely divergent functions of different services, the Properties settings may be completely different for each one.

The most commonly used service shipping with Windows 95 is File and Printer Sharing for Microsoft Networks. The network configuration that you installed with the procedures in this chapter will allow your Windows 95 workstation to access the resources of other Windows machines on the network, but in order to be able to share its own local resources with others, you must install this service.

Chapter 28, "Accessing Windows 95 Workstation Resources," looks at this subject in detail.

The Windows 95 operating system also includes a File and Printer Sharing for NetWare Networks service. This service allows a Windows 95 workstation to appear on the network just as though it were a NetWare 3.12 server. Other NetWare users of any sort can log into the machine and access its shared drives as though they were NetWare volumes. You can install this service instead of File and Print Sharing for Microsoft Networks, but both cannot be used at the same time.

One of the most serious omissions from the networking facility of the initial Windows 95 release was the lack of support for NetWare Directory Services. Since that time, Microsoft has remedied this problem by releasing a service that provides the existing Client for NetWare Networks with NDS capabilities. This is a perfect illustration of the way in which services can be used to augment existing software. It was not necessary for the developers to rewrite or for users to reinstall an entirely new client in order to gain additional features.

ON THE WEB

The Service for NetWare Directory Services is available for download from Microsoft's World Wide Web site at **http://www.microsoft.com/windows/software/msnds.htm**.

The other services that ship with the Windows 95 package were all developed by other companies, to provide an interface with their network-based products. Hewlett Packard's JetAdmin services provide extensive network printer control capabilities to Windows 95, and the backup agent services by Cheyenne Software and Arcada Software allow Windows 95 workstations to be backed up to server-based tape drives.

▶ **See** "Using the Microsoft Service for NetWare Directory Services," **p. 734**

▶ **See** "Using the JetAdmin Service," **p. 773**

Other third-party services will no doubt continue to appear on the market, for the service architecture provides an excellent interface to the Windows 95 operating system for the vendors of network-related products. ●

Connecting to a NetWare Network

by Craig Zacker

NetWare is still the most popular network operating system in use today, and Windows 95's ability to function as a NetWare client was a major issue from the very beginning of its development. In attempting to build the ultimate network client, Microsoft knew that it would have to deal with new NetWare client installations, but that the true test would be the workstation upgrade procedure. ■

How to install the Microsoft Client for NetWare Networks to a Windows 95 workstation

You can add NetWare connectivity to the existing configuration with this Windows 95 default.

How the Windows 95 installation program reacts to previously installed NetWare clients

Look here to learn about the many client options for this network operating system.

The various alternative NetWare clients that you may use with Windows 95

Look here for recommendations concerning the alternative clients.

How to connect to a NetWare Directory Services (NDS) database with Windows 95

Look here for detailed information about connecting to an NDS database.

Introducing the Windows 95 Client for NetWare Networks

The arrival of Windows 95 supplied NetWare users with a new client that was immediately heralded as state of the art. With its full 32-bit protected-mode architecture, the Microsoft Client for NetWare Networks uses no conventional memory. Gone are the memory management considerations that have for years plagued the use of DOS terminate-and-stay-resident (TSR) drivers for networking, and in their place is increased performance, simplified configuration and easy installation.

In addition to the key features discussed in following sections, the Windows 95 Client also provides support for login scripts, global drive mappings and command line processing. The one major omission of the initial Windows 95 release was its lack of NDS support, but this has since been addressed.

N O T E   Login script processing, while a major advantage to this client, is not yet completely effective. While there are no problems with the basic commands, such as drive mappings, difficulties have been reported with more complicated scripts, particularly those using IF...THEN loops. It is recommended that you fully test login scripts for successful completion before putting them into regular use. ■

Key Features of the Windows 95 Client

Microsoft's Client for NetWare Networks provides users with several new features not found in any other NetWare client, as well as enhancements of some existing ones. The following sections describe these key features.

Speed   File transfers to and from NetWare drives are noticeably faster under Windows 95. Microsoft claims that its new client is twice as fast on large block transfers as a real-mode client running with Windows 3.1. The client also offers full support for the NetWare Core Protocol Packet Burst protocol as well as Large Internet Packets.

Integrated RAM Caching   Windows 95's protected-mode networking is integrated with its file system. The clients are actually file system drivers, allowing network data to be serviced by Windows 95's 32-bit VCACHE, right along with local files. Files cached in memory do not have to be read and re-read from the network drive during repeated use.

Plug and Play Networking   All of the components of the Client for NetWare Networks are Plug and Play capable, meaning that they can be dynamically unloaded without disturbing running processes or restarting the machine. You can remove a PC Card network adapter from its slot, and all of the networking components associated with it will be unloaded. Replace the card, and all of the components are reloaded, without interruption of other processes.

Network Reconnection   The NetWare client possesses excellent reconnection capabilities. A temporary detachment from the network doesn't disturb other system processes either. Connections, drive mappings, and printer support are resumed when the machine is reattached.

Long File Names   The protected-mode clients allow Windows 95 long file names to be transmitted over the network and stored on NetWare volumes (if they have been appropriately equipped with OS/2 name space).

Installing the Windows 95 Client for NetWare Networks

In Chapter 24, we covered the installation of a new network adapter, the Client for Microsoft Networks, and the NetBEUI protocol. The following procedure will add NetWare connectivity to this equation. Of the components already installed, only the adapter driver is required to attach to a NetWare network. We will be adding an additional client and a second protocol to the configuration. Both clients and protocols will be accessing the same adapter driver, as shown in figure 25.1.

Part
VIII

Ch
25

▶ **See** "Installing a Network Adapter," **p. 691**

FIG. 25.1
Multiple protocols can be bound to a single adapter, each servicing a different client.

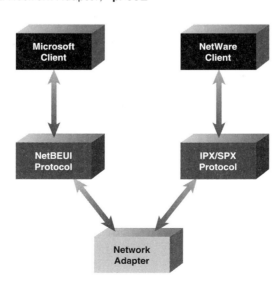

To add NetWare connectivity using the Windows 95 Client for NetWare Networks, use the following procedure:

1. Double-click the Network icon in the Windows 95 Control Panel and choose <u>A</u>dd.

2. In the component list of the Select Network Component Type dialog box, double-click Client.

3. Select Microsoft under the Manufacturers listing and Client for NetWare Networks under the Network Clients listing. Click OK.

4. Select the Client for NetWare Networks, which should now appear in the Configuration page of the Network dialog box (see fig. 25.2), and click <u>P</u>roperties.

FIG. 25.2
Protected-mode clients for Microsoft and NetWare networks can be installed on the same Windows 95 machine.

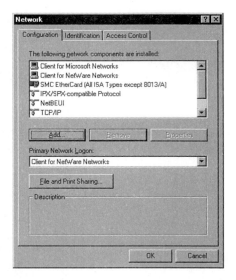

 T I P   The network component listing in the Network dialog box is always sorted by component, in the following order: Clients, Adapters, Protocols, Services.

5. In the Properties sheet, click the General tab, and supply the name of your preferred NetWare server; this will be the server that you always log into first. Your login scripts, if you elect to use them, will reside on this server.

6. Click the check box to <u>E</u>nable Login Script Processing, if you so desire. Click OK.

7. Set the Primary Network <u>L</u>ogon selector on the Configuration page to Client for NetWare Networks, if you want the NetWare login screen to appear first, each time you start Windows 95.

▶ **See** "Logging Into the Network," **p. 744**

T I P NetWare uses the term "login," while Microsoft prefers "logon." The terms are interchangeable.

8. Click OK to close the Network application, and complete the installation. You will be prompted to reboot your system. After you reboot, your computer should be capable of connecting to a NetWare server.

Examining the Installation Process

The preceding installation procedure was a very simple one, but it is worth examining more closely to see what actually occurred.

Step 3 of the process was the selection of the client to be installed. After clicking Add, you may have noticed that not only did the Client for NetWare Networks appear in the Network Configuration screen, but the IPX/SPX-compatible protocol appeared as well. The IPX/SPX protocol is essential for NetWare communications, and Microsoft's client automatically installs the 32-bit version that is supplied with Windows 95. If you remove the IPX/SPX-compatible protocol, the Client for NetWare Networks will be removed as well.

N O T E Novell's own IPX ODI version of the same protocol ships with the operating system as well. It is primarily included for use with Novell's real-mode clients, but it will also function with the Microsoft Client for NetWare Networks in cases where the IPX/SPX-compatible protocol cannot be used. Likewise, the IPX/SPX-compatible protocol can be used with Novell's real-mode clients. ▓

Furthermore, if you select the IPX/SPX-compatible protocol, click the Properties button, and examine its Bindings, you will see that the protocol has been bound to the Client for Microsoft Networks as well. So, what we have at this moment is a network configuration that looks like figure 25.3. Both the NetBEUI and IPX/SPX-compatible protocols are being used by the Client for Microsoft Networks.

For many networks, the binding of the IPX/SPX-compatible protocol to both installed clients is a desirable situation, because the IPX/SPX-compatible protocol can provide internetwork routing services to the Client for Microsoft Networks that NetBEUI cannot. Notice, however, that NetBEUI has not been bound to the Client for NetWare Networks. This is because NetWare can make no profitable use of the protocol, and Windows 95 knows not to bind it.

If you had multiple adapters installed in the Windows 95 system, both protocols would have been automatically bound to both adapters, resulting in an interwoven network configuration in which all adapters are bound to all possible protocols, which in turn are bound to all possible clients.

Part
VIII

Ch
25

FIG. 25.3

Newly installed protocols are automatically bound to all available clients and adapters that can make use of them.

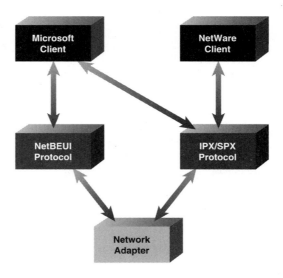

Modifying the Default Installation

In some cases, this cross-binding of clients, protocols, and adapters may be called for, but some of the automatic bindings may be unnecessary. You should remove unnecessary bindings because they consume system resources and slow down network performance.

In the case of our installation, if you are working on a single segment network, or all of the Windows NT machines that you need to access are located on the local network segment, then the binding of the Client for Microsoft Networks to the IPX/SPX-compatible protocol can safely and profitably be removed.

Performing this task is a simple process:

1. Double-click the Network icon in the Control Panel.
2. Select the IPX/SPX-compatible protocol, and choose Properties.
3. Click the Bindings tab, and remove the check mark next to Client for Microsoft Networks (see fig. 25.4).
4. Click OK twice, and the binding will be removed as soon as the system is restarted.

Another situation in which you should remove extraneous bindings is if a Windows 95 machine is using NetBEUI or the IPX/SPX-compatible protocol to connect to a LAN, but is also using a dial-up connection to an Internet service provider. A second adapter, called the Dial-up Adapter, would have to be installed, along with the TCP/IP protocol. In this case, it would be beneficial to remove the bindings of the two LAN protocols from the Dial-up Adapter, as well as that of the LAN adapter to the TCP/IP protocol. You would then have a system in which each adapter was using only the protocols that it needed, conserving system memory and optimizing performance.

FIG. 25.4
Unbinding a protocol from a client is as easy as clearing a check box.

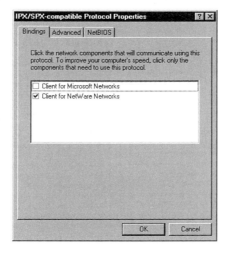

Installing Windows 95 on an Existing NetWare Client

The simplest way to gain network connectivity with Windows 95 is to have a functioning network client present when the operating system is installed.

The Windows 95 setup program scans the machine's configuration files and the DOS memory control blocks (MCBs) for the presence of a Microsoft client, as well as a NetWare shell (NETX.EXE or VLM). The program also looks for other network-related TSRs that are running, all in an attempt to ensure that once Windows 95 has been installed, the workstation retains the same level of network connectivity that it had before the process began.

Always keep in mind that, while Windows 95 examines the contents of startup files like AUTOEXEC.BAT, CONFIG.SYS, and WINSTART.BAT, it bases its installation decisions primarily on the network drivers that it finds in memory at the time of the installation. If, for example, your system is set up to use the NetWare VLM redirector, but you boot the machine from a floppy using NETX.EXE, the installation routine considers this a NETX machine, and behaves accordingly.

T I P In most cases, the recommended method for installing Windows 95 to a network workstation is to start with the machine in its normal working state, before running SETUP.EXE.

In order to maintain the workstation's networking capabilities, Windows 95 modifies its installation routine in accordance with the results of its memory and disk scans. A file called NETDET.INI, located in the Windows directory, contains instructions for the installation program to follow under specific circumstances.

N O T E In networking situations in which you want to upgrade a large number of workstations to Windows 95, you can modify the NETDET.INI file to accommodate the specific needs of the environment. See Chapter 30, "Customizing Windows 95 Networks Installations," for more information on this procedure. ▪

In its default configuration, Windows 95 attempts to install the Microsoft Client for NetWare Networks, using the IPX-SPX-compatible protocol and a 32-bit protected-mode adapter driver. This is the optimum arrangement for Windows 95 running on NetWare. The installation program specifies other components only when they are required to maintain the same level of network connectivity as before the installation began.

This installation process remarks out entries in the AUTOEXEC.BAT and SYSTEM.INI files that are not needed in the new network environment and migrates settings found in configuration files like NET.CFG and PROTOCOL.INI to the Windows 95 Registry. The installation may also move the commands to launch required networking TSRs from the AUTOEXEC.BAT file to WINSTART.BAT. Any configuration settings that conflict with the capabilities of the default client installation may cause other actions to be substituted.

Supporting NetWare Directory Services

In the most common exception to this default installation, an existing real-mode NetWare client is retained because SETUP.EXE detects a workstation running VLMs to connect to a NetWare 4.x NDS tree. At the time of the initial Windows 95 release, no protected-mode client with NDS support was available, and retaining the VLMs was the only alternative. Now that NDS is supported by a Windows 95 service, the default installation will no doubt be modified for the next release.

As you learn later in this chapter, there is now a choice of clients supporting NetWare Directory Services. The installation routine will probably favor Microsoft's implementation, but after comparing the two, you may prefer to use the Novell client.

N O T E Windows 95 is capable of detecting whether a VLM-equipped workstation is logging in to a NetWare Directory Services database. If you are running VLMs to connect to a

NetWare 3.x server, or a NetWare 4.x server in bindery emulation mode, the Microsoft protected-mode client will be installed. ▪

Supporting Other Networking TSRs

Aside from an NDS connection, Windows 95's Setup also attempts to detect any other TSRs that involve network communications. These may include requesters for server-based database engines, network application protocol drivers, or modules providing connectivity to mini- or mainframe computers. When Setup detects such modules, the installation program may take several different actionstops to preserve their functionality:

- TSR load lines may be migrated from AUTOEXEC.BAT to WINSTART.BAT.
- The Client for NetWare Networks may be configured to utilize Novell's IPX ODI protocol, instead of Microsoft's IPX/SPX-compatible protocol.
- A real-mode client may be retained, but the IPX/SPX-compatible protocol is substituted for Novell's IPX ODI protocol.
- A real-mode client may be retained in its entirety.

WINSTART.BAT and Windows 95

WINSTART.BAT is a Windows convention that dates back to version 3.1 and before, but has acquired new significance for Windows 95 users. WINSTART.BAT is simply a batch file that, when located in the Windows directory, automatically executes any commands within it as Windows is loaded. Any TSR programs executed are unloaded from memory when exiting Windows.

When Windows 95 is configured to use any of the Microsoft protected-mode clients, no network connectivity is established until after the processing of the AUTOEXEC.BAT file is completed. Any network-dependent TSRs in that file will, therefore, fail to load. The WINSTART.BAT file, however, is executed after a network connection is established. Migrating these TSR load lines there allows them to initialize properly.

As a result of these measures, a Windows 95 upgrade usually leaves a workstation with the same networking capabilities that it had before the process started.

Using NetWare Client Alternatives

Windows 95's backward compatibility and open architecture provides NetWare users with several alternatives to Microsoft's Client for NetWare Networks. Two of these alternative clients take the form of looking backward: both of Novell's 16-bit real-mode DOS/Windows clients can be used with Windows 95; others look forward, providing even more features than are available with the Windows 95 client. The following sections consider all of these alternatives, outline their capabilities and their drawbacks, and cover their installation processes.

Gateway Services for NetWare

The first alternative method for gaining NetWare connectivity is actually not a client at all, it's a service. And what's more, it doesn't even run on a Windows 95 machine. It's for Windows NT Advanced Server.

Gateway Services for NetWare is a built-in feature of versions 3.5 and higher of the Microsoft network operating system. It allows a Windows NT machine to log into a NetWare server as a single user. As a result, a gateway is created, so that all the Windows network users that are logged into the NT server can access the volumes on the NetWare server, just as though they were normal Windows NT shares.

In this way, a workstation running Windows for Workgroups, Windows NT Workstation or Windows 95 need not have a NetWare client installed at all. With only a Windows client, they can still gain access to NetWare-based file and print services.

Of course, Gateway Services for NetWare is not a practical alternative for prolonged use by a large number of workstations, as it pipes all of the NetWare requests through a single connection. But, for the user who needs only occasional access to NetWare files, or as a temporary measure to facilitate the transition between network operating systems, this can be a very useful tool.

File and Printer Sharing for NetWare Networks

Windows 95 has another unusual method for granting users access to NetWare files, called File and Printer Sharing for NetWare Networks. Just as the File and Printer Sharing service for Microsoft Networks allows the Windows network client to share his or her workstation resources with other users, so File and Printer Sharing for NetWare Networks allows users of Microsoft's Client for NetWare Networks to do the same.

Many people, when first hearing such a description of this feature, give a nod of understanding that gradually changes into a look of puzzlement. How can a NetWare client share drives when NetWare has no resource-naming convention that can be used on workstations?

The answer is to make the NetWare client look like a NetWare server—and this is exactly what this service does. To all NetWare users on the network, a Windows 95 machine running the Client for NetWare Networks along with File and Printer Sharing for NetWare appears to be a NetWare 3.12 file and print server.

Installation of the service creates a subdirectory called Nwsysvol in the machine's Windows directory, which becomes the "server's" SYS: volume. When you share other Windows 95 drives or directories in the normal manner, they become additional volumes on the server.

Only user-level access to this server is allowed, and an actual NetWare server must be used as a "validator." You must select users that are to be allowed access to the shared drives from the actual NetWare server's user list, as shown in figure 25.5. You then grant each user access rights to the shares, according to the standard NetWare model.

FIG. 25.5
Users for the new "server" are selected from a true NetWare server's user list.

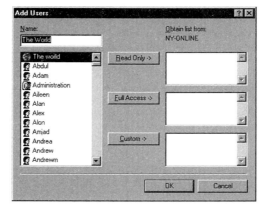

Two options are available, in the service's Properties sheet, for the way in which the new server is to be advertised on the network. *Workgroup advertising* means that the computer will be seen as part of the regular Windows workgroup listing. *SAP Advertising* means that the machine will appear to be a legitimate NetWare server to any other NetWare client workstation, through the SLIST command, or any other utility that lists the NetWare servers on the network. You must use SAP (Service Advertising Protocol) advertising if you want users of the Novell NETX and VLM clients to be able to access the machine.

CAUTION
Use of the SAP advertising feature in the File and Printer Sharing for NetWare service has been known to cause enormous increases in the overall SAP traffic on a network. Be sure to check with your network administrator before enabling this feature.

This service allows up to 250 users to access the Windows 95 machine simultaneously. Theoretically, you can service a huge number of NetWare clients at very little cost by purchasing a 5-user NetWare license, hanging five Windows 95 machines off of that server, and then having up to 1,250 users log into the Windows 95 machines.

I haven't tried this personally, and I wouldn't recommend it but, as an example, it shows how this service adds an extraordinary measure of flexibility to an existing network. On a more practical level, you could grant Windows 3.1 NetWare users remote access to a CD-ROM drive without having to mount it as a volume on a real server, or access to a printer without having to attach it to a NetWare print server and a queue.

Using Novell Real-mode Clients

Although the reasons for doing so are dwindling rapidly, it is possible to use the standard Novell real-mode clients for NetWare on a Windows 95 machine. These clients are the traditional NETX and VLM packages that you have probably been using on DOS and Windows machines for years. Although the use of VLMs with Windows 95 to log into a NetWare Directory Services tree was a common practice during the operating system's beta cycle and immediately after its release, this practice is no longer necessary.

Microsoft's NDS service for the Windows 95 Client for NetWare Networks as well as Novell's Client32 for Windows 95 both provide NDS access while retaining the advantages of a 32-bit protected-mode client. Both of these alternatives will be considered later in this chapter.

While there are other reasons to continue using the Novell real-mode clients, none of them have anything to do with performance. The real-mode clients are slower in every way than their protected-mode counterparts. They are also subject to the same conventional memory utilization problems as they were with Windows 3.1. It may be necessary, even with Windows 95, to implement a full memory management regimen, using the standard tools: EMM386.EXE or a third-party package such as QEMM, to load some of the modules into upper memory.

However, situations such as those mentioned earlier in this chapter, when special TSRs are needed to gain access to critical network services, are still valid cases in which the real-mode clients might be needed, at least until the services in question can be upgraded. These cases are becoming less and less common, though, as many such TSRs are being rewritten as Windows 95 clients and services.

Unlike other 32-bit operating systems, such as Windows NT and OS/2, the marketing effort behind Windows 95 has gathered a much larger pool of users in a shorter span of time. These users represent a significant force exerting pressure on other software developers to upgrade their products to accommodate the new operating system. As more and more networking products are upgraded, there will assuredly be fewer cases in which the real-mode clients will have to be used.

Some sites also have chosen to stick with the older clients out of a misguided desire for system stability. They opine that since NETX and VLMs are "tried and true" technology, they will be inherently more reliable with a brand new operating system than a client that has been written with that operating system specifically in mind. This is not logical thinking, in my opinion. If you going to take the Windows 95 plunge, you may as well jump in with both feet.

Using the NETX Client

When a workstation equipped with the NETX client is upgraded to Windows 95, it is automatically upgraded to the Client for NetWare Networks, unless TSRs are present that are incompatible with the 32-bit protected-mode client. If you wish to continue using NETX with Windows 95 for any other reason, you will have to remove the newly installed client first, in most cases, in order to restore NETX's functionality.

N O T E Even though Windows 95 may disable a workstation's existing networking configuration to install a new one, it will never delete the original files. Reinstalling the original client from the Control Panel locates and reactivates the original files. ■

Part
VIII

Ch
25

Installing the NETX Client

When you install the NETX client in Windows 95, you should have a functional NETX client already installed on the machine, even if it isn't operating. Otherwise, you will be prompted to supply the necessary files during the installation.

> **CAUTION**
>
> The NETX and VLM client files do not ship as part of the Windows 95 package. You are responsible for supplying appropriate versions of all the necessary files. It's strongly recommended that the latest versions be installed on the system before the real-mode client is installed in Windows 95.

To install the NETX client in Windows 95, follow these steps:

1. Double-click the Network icon in the Windows 95 Control Panel.

2. If the Client for NetWare Networks, or any other NetWare client, is currently installed, select it and click the Remove button.

T I P   The NETX client can safely coexist with the protected-mode Client for Microsoft Networks on the same machine. Both can use the same IPX protocol, or two different ones can be installed. However, NETX cannot be used with the real-mode version of the Client for Microsoft Networks. Only one real-mode network client can run on a single machine.

3. In the component list of the Select Network Component Type dialog box, double-click Client.

4. In the Manufacturers list on the left side of the Select Network Client dialog box, select Novell, then on the right side, choose Novell NetWare (Workstation Shell 3.X [NETX]). Click OK.

5. Notice that the NETX client, an adapter labeled Existing ODI Driver, and the Novell IPX ODI protocol have been added to the Network screen (see fig. 25.6). Click OK again to complete the installation. You will then be prompted to restart your system.

FIG. 25.6
Installing the NETX client automatically causes the Existing ODI Driver and the Novell IPXODI Protocol to be installed as well.

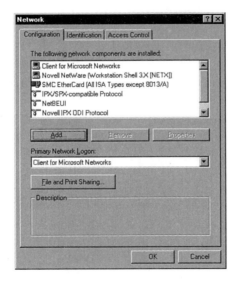

N O T E   While the installation of the NETX client automatically includes the Novell IPX ODI Protocol and a 16-bit real-mode ODI adapter driver, either the Microsoft IPX/SPX-compatible protocol or its protected-mode NDIS 3.1 adapter drivers, or both, can be used instead. ▨

Other NETX Client Issues

You need to consider several other issues when running the NETX client on a Windows 95 machine:

- Windows 95, by default, sets the LASTDRIVE= entry to the letter Z. To use NETX, you must include a line in the CONFIG.SYS file that indicates what the first NetWare drive letter will be. For example, adding LASTDRIVE=E will cause F: to be the first NetWare drive.

- If you will be running a login script that utilizes the %OS_VERSION variable, you must modify the Windows SETVER table by issuing the following command at a DOS prompt:

SETVER NETX.EXE 7.00

TIP SETVER, the MS-DOS version compatibility table, is no longer a separate TSR utility. It is now integrated into Windows 95 and automatically loaded with the operating system.

- Be sure the NETX version of the NETWARE.DRV file is present in the \Windows directory (see the "Windows 95 Clients and NETWARE.DRV" sidebar).

- You will not be able to store Windows 95 long file names on NetWare servers using NETX, or any real-mode client.

Windows 95 Clients and NETWARE.DRV

Whenever you elect to use a NetWare real-mode client with Windows 95, it's crucial that the correct version of the NETWARE.DRV file be installed in the \Windows directory. There are different versions of this file for the NETX and VLM clients, and for Windows 95's own clients. Their approximate sizes are:

NETWARE.DRV	Windows 95	approx. 1.6K
NETWARE.DRV	VLM	approx. 160K
NETWARE.DRV	NETX	approx. 125K

Windows 95 replaces the current NETWARE.DRV with its own version when it updates a real-mode to the protected-mode NetWare client. The old version is renamed, however, as NETWARE.DR~ , so that it can be restored if necessary.

Using the VLM Client

The VLM client, if you are using it to log into a NetWare Directory Services tree, isn't replaced with the protected-mode client by the default Windows 95 installation routine. Its settings are assimilated into the Windows 95 Registry, however, as with the NETX client. Like NETX, it is also loaded into conventional memory, unless you take steps to prevent this occurrence.

In addition, there are other concerns you must be aware of when using the VLM client with Windows 95, as well as issues that you must address when installing the client on an existing Windows 95 machine.

The VLM client offers considerably more functionality than NETX, but some of its features are not compatible with Windows 95. Its primary attribute is its ability to run NetWare NDS utilities like NWADMIN, NETADMIN, and CX, and to log into an NDS tree. To ensure this compatibility, you should use the DOS-based installation routine included with the VLM package to perform a complete client installation (with full Windows support). You should also make sure that you are installing the latest available version of the client software.

Obtaining the Latest Novell Client Software

The latest releases of the Novell NETX and VLM clients are required to run with Windows 95. The most reliable source for Novell upgrade files is the NetWire service on CompuServe. All client software is located in the NetWare Operating System Library forum (**GO NWOSFILES**).

The latest VLM client installation kit is available for download as a six-disk set, with the file names VLMKT1.EXE through VLMKT6.EXE. Note, however, that VLMKT6.EXE contains only the files for the TCP/IP stack. If you won't be running Novell's TCP/IP, you don't need to download this file.

Patch files are also available to update older VLM installations to the current version. As of this writing, the latest releases are VLMUP4.EXE, WINDR3.EXE, and NWDLL2.EXE. Subsequent releases will increment the number in the file name.

Note that the patch files contain upgrades only for the US English version of the clients. Other language code pages are included in the full client installation kit.

NETX users also require NET33X.EXE, which contains the latest version of the workstation shells: NETX.EXE, XMSNETX.EXE and EMSNETX.EXE. The other ODI modules are the same as those used for the VLM client.

You also may require the latest ODI drivers for your adapter, which must be obtained from the manufacturer of the adapter.

All of the Novell release files are self-extracting archives that you should execute in an empty directory. All contain extensive README files that you should read carefully before applying any updates.

Installing the VLM Client

When installing the VLM client onto a Windows 95 machine, use the Novell client installation program for the initial process, rather than the Control Panel. When doing so, you must be sure to retain access to the VLM installation files throughout the process. You should therefore run the installation program either from floppy disks or a CD-ROM, or copy it to a local hard drive, rather than run it from a server drive.

To install the VLM client on a Windows 95 machine, use the following procedure:

1. Double-click the Network icon in the Windows 95 Control Panel and remove all existing network support components. Click OK to close the dialog box.

2. When asked whether to restart the computer, choose <u>N</u>o. Then open the Start menu, select Sh<u>u</u>t Down, choose Restart the Computer in <u>M</u>S-DOS Mode and click <u>Y</u>es.

T I P The computer can also be started in MS-DOS mode by holding down the F8 key during the boot process, and making the appropriate selection from the boot menu.

3. Run the VLM installation program from the DOS prompt in the normal manner. Be sure to include Windows support. If you are asked whether to overwrite the NETWARE.DRV file, select Yes.

4. Restart the computer and again open the Network dialog box. Windows 95 should detect that the VLM client has been installed and add the appropriate settings.

5. Click OK, and restart the computer.

Other VLM Client Issues

You must take note of the following issues when you use the VLM client with Windows 95:

■ Due to a problem in the way that it makes calls to NETWARE.DRV, Windows 95, during its load sequence, attempts to restore any Windows permanent network connections that you have specified before the NetWare login dialog box appears. This situation causes Windows 95 to generate error messages. One workaround is to ignore the errors and use the NWUSER program's Restore Now feature. Alternatively, you can log into the network before loading Windows, to allow the permanent connections to be restored normally.

T I P Placing a LOGIN command in the AUTOEXEC.BAT or STARTNET.BAT file causes the system's boot sequence to pause for user input, allowing you to log into the network before the Windows 95 GUI loads.

■ The VLM client's NWUSER program has an option to allow private drive mappings. These are drive mappings made in a DOS session that exist only in that session. This feature does not function under Windows 95. Be sure to leave the Global Drives and Paths box in the NWUSER program checked at all times. All drive mappings in Windows 95 are global. Changes made to drive mappings within a DOS session are always propagated throughout the whole system.

- As with Windows 3.1, all search drives must be mapped from a DOS prompt or a login script before starting Windows 95. Search drives cannot be mapped from a DOS session within Windows 95.

- As with NETX, Windows 95 long file names cannot be stored on NetWare servers with the VLM client. They will instead be truncated to their DOS 8.3 equivalents. Support for the storage of user profiles on NetWare servers is provided, however.

Using the Microsoft Service for NetWare Directory Services

Microsoft was well aware of the problems created by the lack of NetWare Directory Services (NDS) support in the Client for NetWare Networks at the time of the Windows 95 release. Within two months of that release, Microsoft resolved the problem by providing a Service for NetWare Directory Services.

The networking architecture of Windows 95 contributed to this quick response. NDS support was provided for the existing protected-mode NetWare client through the addition of a Service for NetWare Directory Services. Released as a 371 kilobyte free download, it is a quick and convenient way for users to add full NetWare 4.x compatibility to Windows 95.

The addition of the service provides NDS users with full container, object, and user login script support, the ability to browse for NetWare resources through the NDS hierarchy, and access to all of the NDS-related NetWare utilities.

ON THE WEB

http://www.microsoft.com/windows/software/msnds.htm The Service for NetWare Directory Services is available for download from Microsoft's World Wide Web site.

Installing the Service for NDS

To install NDS support into the Client for NetWare Networks, follow these steps:

1. Download MSNDS.EXE from one of the Microsoft online services.
2. Put the file in a directory by itself and execute MSNDS.EXE to extract the contents of the archive.

3. Double-click the Network icon in the Windows 95 Control Panel.
4. Click Add, double-click Service in the Select Network Component Type dialog box, and click the Have Disk button in the Select Network Service dialog box.

5. Enter the location of the directory containing the MSNDS files into the Install From Disk dialog box, and click OK twice.

6. Select the Service for NetWare Directory Services entry in the Network application's Configuration page and click the Properties button.

7. Enter the name of your preferred NDS tree, and the full context of your workstation. Click OK twice to complete the installation.

> **CAUTION**
>
> When using the NDS Service to connect to a NetWare 4.01 NDS tree, only type full context names can be used. For example, a context of .USER.ORGANIZATION will not be acceptable. .CN=USER.OU=ORGANIZATION must be entered instead.

N O T E The installation of the Service for NetWare Directory Services adds a line to the system's AUTOEXEC.BAT file that runs a batch file called _NWNDS.BAT during the next system reboot. The batch file need only be run once, but this line will remain in the AUTOEXEC.BAT file. You can safely remove it after the installation is complete.

Part VIII

Ch 25

Other Service for NDS Issues

Although the Service for NDS provides users with the ability to access the NetWare Directory, you must address a number of compatibility issues before the service can be a suitable alternative to the VLM client. Some of these issues are easily addressed, some can be avoided by altering usage practices, and others are yet to be corrected. The following sections discuss these issues in detail.

NetWare Library Files Running the NWADMIN directory maintenance utility, as well as many other Windows network utilities, requires the support provided by the following NetWare library files:

- NWCALLS.DLL
- NWNET.DLL
- NWLOCALE.DLL
- NWGDI.DLL
- NWIPXSPX.DLL
- NWPSRV.DLL

These files are part of the NetWare VLM installation kit, and are also available in the NWDLL2.EXE archive, both of which can be downloaded from Novell's NetWire service.

If the VLM client has previously been installed on the workstation, these files should already be available. They must be located in the \Windows\System directory, or in another directory on the computer's path.

Windows 95 does not load these files into memory by default. It is possible that some networking applications may expect these libraries to be available in memory, and will not function properly as a result. To work around this issue, Windows 95's System Policies feature can be used to preload these files. See Chapter 30, "Customizing Windows 95 Network Installations," for more information on using the system policy editor.

> **N O T E**   The NW*.DLL files listed previously are not shipped with Windows 95. They are Novell release files and their use is subject to Novell's licensing restrictions. ■

Other applications may require access to the Unicode tables that are located in the \Public\nls directory on a NetWare 4.x server. Adding this directory to the search path will prevent any "Failed to Find Unicode Tables" errors from occurring.

Adding NDS Printers   When using the Add New Printer Wizard with the Service for NDS to browse for printers, NDS printers will not be visible. Bindery-based printers will appear as they normally do. This discrepancy is due to a problem with the SHELL32.DLL file, which has been remedied by the release of a replacement for this file, available as SHELLUPD.EXE from Microsoft's WWW site at **http://www.microsoft.com/windows/ software/shellupd.htm**.

▶ **See** "Using Network Printers," **p. 766**

Service for NDS and NWUSER   The Microsoft Service for NDS does not support the use of the NWUSER program that is included as part of the VLM client package. Most of the functions performed by NWUSER can be duplicated by other means in Windows 95.

Multiple Login Scripts   When the Client for NetWare Networks and the Service for NDS are used alongside the Client for Microsoft Networks, Windows NT logon scripts will always run before NetWare login scripts, no matter which client is selected in the Primary Network Login dialog box.

Using the Novell Client32 for Windows 95

At about the same time that Microsoft released the Service for NetWare Directory Services, Novell released the first public beta of its Client32 for Windows 95.

Both clients provide Windows 95 users with the basic NDS access that they requested. Novell's client, however, has proven to be a significantly more ambitious project than Microsoft's, and with good reason.

Client32 provides Windows 95 with NDS support, but it goes a great deal further by—for the first time—positioning NetWare Directory Services as a truly beneficial enterprise management platform. Client32's ability to deliver network applications to multiple users in the form of icons on the Windows 95 desktop is the first step toward making the Directory as useful for mid-sized and small networks as it is for giant enterprises.

Installing Client32

Client32 provides a number of options with respect to its installation. Designed for the corporate environment, in which network administrators may be faced with the task of installing the client on hundreds of machines, it offers both automated and customized installation features.

For a network-based installation, Client32 can be added to the Windows 95 source files, and the installation script modified to make Client32 the default instead of Microsoft's NetWare client.

Client32 can also be configured to install itself automatically during a normal NDS login. A user's login script can be used to detect whether the client has already been installed on the workstation, and if it hasn't, perform the installation immediately.

Client32 can also be installed on demand by running a standard Windows 95 SETUP.EXE file from the source directory. All three of these processes can be customized to the administrator's exact preferences, for multiple network installs. By default, they remove all existing NetWare client support from the Windows 95 machine and install the new client in its place. For most single user installations, running the SETUP program (see fig. 25.7) is the recommended installation procedure.

FIG. 25.7
The Novell Client32
SETUP.EXE program
completely automates the
installation process.

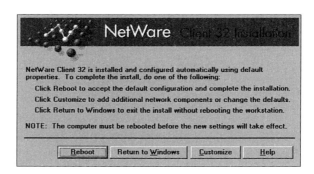

NetWare Client 32 Installation

NetWare Client 32 is installed and configured automatically using default properties. To complete the install, do one of the following:

Click Reboot to accept the default configuration and complete the installation.
Click Customize to add additional network components or change the defaults.
Click Return to Windows to exit the install without rebooting the workstation.

NOTE: The computer must be rebooted before the new settings will take effect.

| Reboot | Return to Windows | Customize | Help |

The package also ships with its own 32-bit ODI drivers that, when compatible with the installed hardware, are recommended for use by Novell. Otherwise, you can use one of the NDIS 3.1 adapter drivers that ship with Windows 95.

Finally, Client32 can be installed using the normal Control Panel procedure, as follows:

1. Download NetWare Client32 from Novell's World Wide Web site, place it in a directory by itself, and execute the file to expand it. (If the files that you downloaded have a ZIP extension, you will need PKWare's PKUNZIP utility to expand them.)

 2. Double-click the Network icon in the Windows 95 Control Panel. Remove any existing NetWare support that has been installed.

N O T E   Client32 is designed to automatically remove any existing NetWare client from Windows 95 before installing itself. However, in some instances it can fail to do so, particularly when the Microsoft Service for NDS is present on the workstation. For large scale client upgrade projects, testing should be conducted on the existing environment, to see if the installation method you choose behaves properly. ◼

3. Click Add, and double-click Client in the Select Network Component Type dialog box.

4. Click Have Disk and set the selector to the drive and directory containing the Client32 installation files.

5. When Client32 for NetWare Networks appears in the Select Network Type dialog box, select it and click OK.

6. After files are copied, the display returns to the Network's Configuration page, where the Novell NetWare Client32 is visible, as well as the IPX 32-bit Protocol for Novell NetWare Client32 (see fig. 25.8). If you wish, and if your hardware is supported, you can manually install one of the 32-bit ODI adapter drivers included with Client32 at this time.

7. Before closing the dialog box, if you will be logging into an NDS tree for the first time, select the client and click the Properties button. Then select the Client32 tab and fill in the names of your preferred server and NDS tree, the context of your user object, and select a letter to be your first NetWare drive letter.

8. Click OK twice to close the dialog box and complete the installation. Restart the computer when you are prompted to do so.

FIG. 25.8
Client32 is integrated into the Windows 95 networking environment, just as a Microsoft client would be.

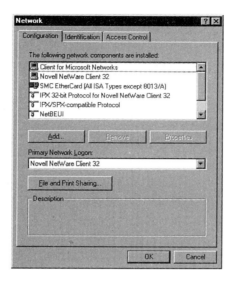

Other Client32 Issues

Once installed, Client32 makes itself your primary login client, and as soon as the machine restarts, you'll see how this client differs from Microsoft's. Additional features abound, from the very first login screen.

Client32 provides support for browsing to a different preferred server or tree, executing a specific login script or user profile, specifying values for login script variables, or just performing a simple bindery login.

The client modifies the My Computer, Network Neighborhood, and Explorer displays to include icons representing NDS trees, as well as other NetWare features not provided by any other client (see fig. 25.9). The network can also be browsed either through the NDS hierarchy or through a server list. Support is even provided for logging into multiple NDS trees simultaneously!

Of course, you can run NWADMIN and all of the other NDS-related NetWare utilities using Client32. All of the necessary library files are included in the package, so even if you have never run a NetWare client on the workstation before, no other downloads are needed.

The benefits of having a NetWare client written by Novell are also obvious. Client32 fully supports the NCP packet burst protocol, large Internet packets, and all of NetWare's packet signature options.

FIG. 25.9
Client32 integrates the NDS tree structure into Explorer.

Most impressively, the package includes a module called APPSNAP. DLL that adds additional schema to the NDS database, that can be used by the NWADMIN utility. Once the module is installed, you can create application objects in the NDS database, just as you would create user, group, or any other NDS objects .

When you assign a user rights to an object representing a network-based application, the icon for the application appears in a window on his desktop when he or she runs the NetWare Application Launcher, a utility that is also included with the client. By placing this launcher in the Windows Startup group on all users' computers, a network administrator can deliver an entire customized suite of applications to as many workstations as needed, simply by assigning rights to users, groups, or containers in NWADMIN.

Choosing an NDS Client

The possibilities suggested by the NetWare Application Launcher are numerous, and most enticing. While it started slowly, NetWare 4 sales are increasing tremendously, and NDS finally seems to be garnering the attention that Novell has always hoped it would, from both users and developers.

With two protected-mode NDS clients available for Windows 95, the only safe bet is that NETX and VLM will finally be retired before long, especially if Novell is successful with its Client32 for Windows 3.1, now in development. Meanwhile, choosing between the two protected-mode Windows 95 NDS clients may not be so easy a task.

For the majority of users, especially those who are better off shielded from the intricacies of NDS and networking in general, the Microsoft Service for NetWare Directory Services is the preferred alternative. It offers excellent performance, all the features that the average user needs, and it merges seamlessly with the existing Windows 95 client installation.

Client32 offers power users a host of very attractive features, but at a price. Navigating through a network server or tree display is markedly slower than with the Microsoft client. Delays of several seconds while scanning network directories are commonplace. When evaluating the client and marveling at its other capabilities, these delays are not as noticeable as when you settle down and try to actually get some work done.

 TIP Client32 ships with files that allow it to be managed by the Windows 95 system Policy Editor. Access to selected features can be restricted in order to customize the interface to suit the users' skill level.

It should be noted that network file transfer performance does not seem to be affected as much as simple directory scanning. Client32 provides its own client-side caching, while the Microsoft clients are able to share the unified Windows 95 system cache (VCACHE). The slower performance of Client32 could also be due to the presence of test code in the 1.14 beta version of the client that was the latest available as of this writing.

Part
VIII

Ch

25

I hope for better performance from future releases of Client32, as this is a client that I would dearly love to use. The concepts introduced in the application launcher could revolutionize the process of network server administration, by moving closer to a true object-oriented environment in which users need only be granted rights to applications. The servers, directories, and files can be allowed to reside invisibly behind the user interface, where they belong. ●

CHAPTER 26

Accessing Client/ Server Network Services

by Craig Zacker

U sers may become expertly proficient with the applications and operating systems that they deal with constantly, but remain largely unaware of the network infrastructure supporting these applications and operating systems. This chapter presents the client/server networking tools and concepts that are part of the Windows 95 operating system, not only as a means to complete your immediate task at hand, but also as a way for you to gain additional insight into how your company network is laid out, and what other resources are available to you.

Chapters 24 and 25 examined the process of selecting and installing the various clients available for Windows 95. In this chapter you learn the process of logging in to Windows NT and NetWare servers, accessing the resources available on the client/server network, and configuring the workstation to provide an integrated and easily accessible interface to both local and network resources. ■

Logging in

How to attach to Windows NT and NetWare servers using the various Windows 95 network clients.

Accessing network drives

Mapping drive letters and browsing network servers.

Accessing network printers

Attaching to server-based printers and monitoring network print queues.

Using Point and Print

Storing drivers on network drives to simplify printer installations in Windows 95.

Logging Into the Network

As stated in Chapter 25, when using either of the Novell real-mode clients (NETX and VLM), the user should always log into the NetWare network from a DOS prompt before the Windows GUI is loaded. In all other cases, however, a network login screen appears when the user loads Windows 95.

The choice of the primary client determines the type of network login screen. When both of the Microsoft protected-mode clients are installed, the Primary Network Logon selector on the Configuration screen of the Control Panel's Network application offers three possible choices:

- Client for Microsoft Networks
- Client for NetWare Networks
- Windows Logon

If you have installed any other protected-mode clients in place of those that ship with Windows 95, such as Novell's Client32, these will appear in the Primary Network Logon selector instead of the Microsoft clients.

When you select one of the network clients, that client's login screen appears first whenever the machine is booted; requiring the entry of a user name and password. The computer name that you have entered in the Identification sheet of the Network application is supplied as the user name, by default, but you can change this to any valid network user name, and the setting is retained for future logins.

When logging into a client/server Microsoft Windows network using the dialog box shown in figure 26.1, Windows 95 uses the Logon Validation option specified in the General page of the Client for Microsoft Networks' Properties sheet to determine whether a domain logon should be performed. You must also specify a domain name on this sheet. The General page also contains an option to choose between a logon sequence that immediately verifies that each network drive is available for use, or one that waits until each individual drive is accessed before verification occurs. The tradeoff is between a brief delay when each drive is accessed, and a cumulative delay during the logon sequence, rarely more than a few seconds.

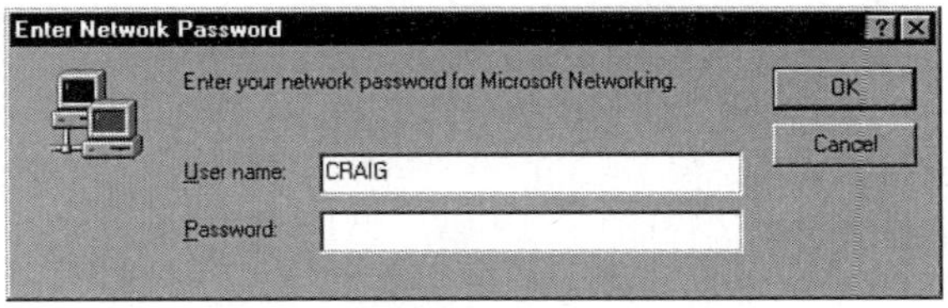

FIG. 26.1
The Microsoft Network logon screen allows access to Windows NT domains as well as peer workgroups.

The Client for NetWare Networks login dialog box allows you to specify a primary NetWare server for the current session, as shown in figure 26.2. In the General page of the Properties sheet for the Client for NetWare Networks, you can opt for the processing of login scripts on NetWare networks by checking a check box. You also can specify a preferred NetWare server, as well as your first network drive letter on this sheet. During the login procedure, you can view the results of the login script processing in a DOS window as it is running, to verify the completion of all scripted tasks.

 T I P When a user has login scripts associated with accounts on both Windows NT and NetWare networks, the Windows NT login script will always run last.

N O T E Windows 95 is incapable of setting environment variables that have been specified in Windows NT logon scripts in the normal manner. As a workaround, a utility called WINSET.EXE is provided in the \Admin\Apptools\Envvars directory of the Windows 95 CD-ROM. You can use this program to set global environment variables from a DOS session command line, a batch file, or a logon script. The syntax of WINSET.EXE is the same as that of the DOS SET command, except that entering the command without any parameters does not display the contents of the environment, as SET does.

FIG. 26.2
The NetWare client login dialog box includes a field for the specification of a preferred login server.

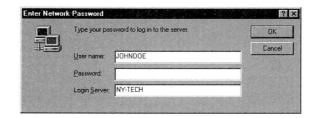

The Primary Network Logon selector controls only which network client logon dialog box is presented first. Access to resources on both Microsoft and NetWare networks is always available, whichever client you select to be the Primary Network Logon. The first time that you log in, Windows 95 presents dialog boxes for both networks, and you must enter a valid user name and password for each. If the user names for both networks are identical, then only the primary network login dialog box will appear in future sessions. The password to this first dialog box will then control access to the file containing the password for the other other network login. This file also contains any other passwords that are cached by the operating system while accessing network resources.

 T I P Password caching can be disabled with the System Policy Editor, forcing the user to log in to each network resource individually. See "Using System Policies" in Chapter 30, "Customizing Windows 95 Network Installations," for more information.

TROUBLESHOOTING

Why doesn't a network login dialog box appear when I start Windows 95, no matter what the setting of the Primary Network Logon selector? If I select Sh̲ut Down from the Start Menu and then choose C̲lose all Programs and log on as a different user, the correct login dialog box appears, after which everything functions normally. To eliminate this problem, open the Windows 95 Registry Editor (REGEDIT.EXE, located in the \Windows directory), and proceed to the following key:

```
HKEY_LOCAL_MACHINE
SOFTWARE
Microsoft
Windows
CurrentVersion
Network
RealModeNet
```

Delete the value *AutoLogon=x*. A value of zero for the AutoLogon parameter causes the failure of the login dialog box to appear, and 1 is the default, but deleting the entire parameter is preferable to just changing the value. Save your changes and restart the computer. The primary login screen should now appear.

Logging in with Microsoft's Service for NetWare Directory Services

The addition of the Service for NetWare Directory Services expands on the functionality of the login dialog box by adding an Advanced button you can click to display the Advanced Login Settings dialog box (see fig. 26.3). In this dialog box, you must select a preferred NDS tree from a selector containing of all the trees on the network, as well as specify the full context for your user object in the NDS database. This information also is visible in the service's Properties sheet. After the user object is validated by Windows 95 as existing in the specified tree, Windows 95 presents the login dialog box containing the user name and password fields. The Advanced Login Setting dialog box also allows you to configure the client for an ordinary NetWare bindery login.

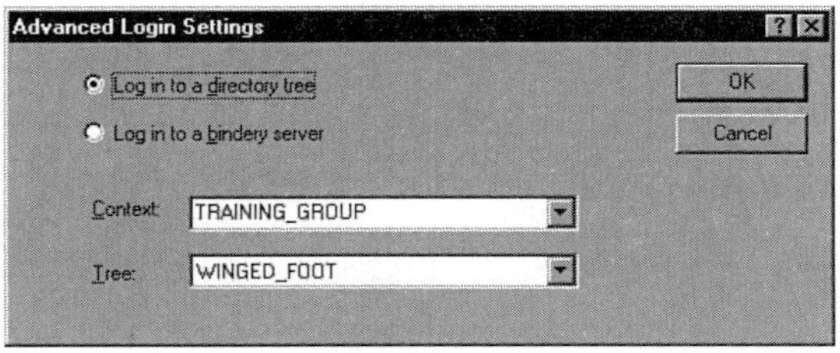

FIG. 26.3

The addition of the Service for NetWare Directory Services allows a selection between bindery and NDS login.

Advanced Login Settings	? X
⦿ Log in to a directory tree	OK
○ Log in to a bindery server	Cancel
Context: TRAINING_GROUP	
Tree: WINGED_FOOT	

◆ **TROUBLESHOOTING**

Why doesn't the login dialog box for the Service for NetWare Directory Services accept my NetWare 4.01 user context? When you specify a context in the Service for NDS login dialog box on a NetWare 4.01 network, only fully distinguished, typeful names can be used. For example, a context of .ORGANIZATION will not be accepted. You must enter .OU=ORGANIZATION instead.

When you choose Windows Logon as the primary logon, the logon dialog box displays the current machine name and prompts for a password. If you don't enter a password, this dialog box will not appear each subsequent time the machine is started. The Windows Logon is designed for use when a network login is not always required, as with a laptop that may only occasionally be connected to a LAN. The appropriate network login will, in this case, only appear when the user first attempts to access a network resource.

Logging In with Novell's Client32

Besides its basic login capabilities (see fig. 26.4), Client32 provides the largest array of login options. Aside from being able to browse the network for a preferred server or NDS tree (see fig. 26.5), you can specify an alternative login script file or user profile (see fig. 26.6), as well as specific values for as many as four login script variables (see fig. 26.7).

FIG. 26.4
The Client32 login tab provides basic login capabilities.

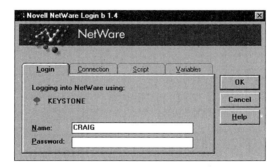

FIG. 26.5
In the Connection tab, you can select login parameters for an NDS or bindery login.

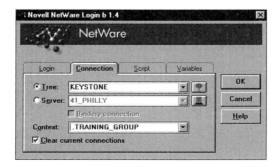

Part
VIII

Ch
26

FIG. 26.6
The Script tab allows you to select specific login and profile script files, and control their appearance on the screen.

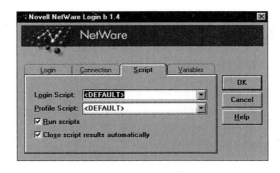

FIG. 26.7
In the Variables tab, you can specify values for up to four variables called by login scripts.

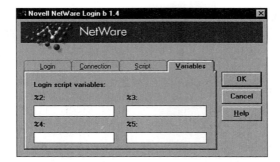

Thus, the working environment can easily accommodate a user or administrator that may log in from different workstations on the network, for different purposes. To troubleshoot specific problems, network support personnel can even script multiple profiles that simulate the working environments of users in different departments.

Controlling Passwords

When logging into more than one network at the start of a Windows 95 session, you do not have to supply a duplicate password for each network, as long as both logins utilize identical user names. Windows 95 automatically stores the secondary password in an encrypted password file called *<USER NAME>*.PWL, located in the workstation's \Windows directory. You can use the Password application in the Windows 95 Control Panel to synchronize differing passwords used by the network logins.

The primary network login password unlocks the password file for use during that Windows 95 session. As work progresses, the operating system automatically caches passwords for NetWare servers, Windows NT machines, and peer workstation resources in this same file. Password-protected applications written to the Master Password API also can store passwords in this file.

All passwords are stored in the file in encrypted form. No unencrypted password is ever sent over the network.

> **CAUTION**
>
> On December 13, 1995, Microsoft released a patch file that significantly enhances the security of Windows 95 PWL files. This was in response to an algorithm posted on the Internet that could be used to crack the existing password files. The fix upgrades the encryption key to 128 bits (from 32), increasing the difficulty of cracking the file by 79228162514264337593543950336 (2^{96}) times. The patch file is called MSPWLUPD.EXE, and is now available as part of the Windows 95 Service Pack 1, on Microsoft's World Wide Web site at **http://www.microsoft.com/windows/software/servpak1/ sphome.htm.**

Most logins to network devices include an option for password caching, such as a checkbox labeled "Save this password in your password list." A network administrator also can use the System Policy Editor to globally disable password caching for specific users or user groups. This action forces users to log into network resources individually, each time they access them.

> **CAUTION**
>
> When you disable password caching and are using share-level access control to network resources, be sure to disable the Quick Logon feature in the Client for Microsoft Networks' Properties dialog box.

Password caching is a useful convenience, but it also can be a dangerous security hole if not used carefully. When system administrators work at a user's machine, for example, they must be careful not to insert their passwords into the user's cache and leave the user with a greater level of access to the system.

If this does occur, one method of repairing the damage is to delete the user's PWL file from the \Windows directory, causing all of his cached passwords to be lost. The user now has to log into each network resource individually until Windows 95 assembles a new cache file.

There is an alternative to this solution, however. On the Windows 95 CD-ROM is a password file editing utility called PWLEDIT.EXE (see fig. 26.8). You can install it by using the Add/Remove Programs application in the Windows 95 Control Panel. Select the Windows Setup tab and use the Have Disk button to get to the \Admin\Apptools\Pwledit directory on the CD-ROM.

Part VIII
Ch 26

FIG. 26.8
Passwords can be safely and
securely removed from a
workstation's cache with the
PWLEDIT utility.

FIG. 26.8
Passwords can be safely and
securely removed from a
workstation's cache with the
PWLEDIT utility.

PWLEDIT is designed to operate only on the PWL files stored on the machine where it is run. It can't be used to open a password file on a network drive, nor can it actually display passwords. PWLEDIT can, however, delete individual passwords from the cache file while leaving the others intact.

▶ **See** "Using System Policies," **p. 862**

Sharing Network Drives

Unquestionably, the first and primary purpose of networking is to enable simultaneous multiple-user access to application and data files stored on hard disk drives. Although networking capabilities continue to expand, disk sharing is still the primary function of most local area networks.

Drive Mappings

Drive mapping, the original network file sharing paradigm, which persists to this day, attempts to package network resources as though they are local devices by mapping server disk locations to workstation drive letters. The DOS conception of the drive letter is thus extended to include not only internal workstation devices, but network drives as well. In this case, the network client functions as a redirector, channeling requests generated by an operating system designed for standalone machines to devices at other locations on the network.

Although drive mapping is still an effective technique, it tends to insulate users from the network rather than integrate them into it. A drive letter provides no indication of where the files are actually located. You must be familiar with the network operating system commands to find this out.

Using the Network Neighborhood

Besides supporting traditional drive mapping methods, Windows 95 also provides another way of accessing network drives for Windows users. The Network Neighborhood window displays all of the servers to which the user is currently attached as icons (see fig. 26.9). Double-clicking a server icon reveals the available NetWare volumes or Windows NT shares as folders.

FIG. 26.9
The Network Neighborhood window displays all of the servers and workstations currently attached to the host machine.

When a user double-clicks the Entire Network icon, all of the servers on the network are displayed, expanding his view even further. A user (with the appropriate permission) can access any shared drive or folder on the network from this interface, simply by double-clicking its icon. If the user is not currently attached to the server containing the share, he is automatically logged in, if a cached password is available, or presented with a login dialog box.

Part
VIII

Ch
26

Using Windows Explorer

Explorer integrates My Computer with the Network Neighborhood to provide a single navigable interface for the more advanced user. Mapped drives coexist with server objects, even when both are referencing the same network machine, and users can manipulate files on both interchangeably by dragging and dropping, as well as with context menus. Many of the same tools are available in Explorer and My Computer.

It is important to understand that local drives as well as network machines all contain folders (or directories) and files within them. You access and manipulate a file on a networked drive just as you do on a local drive. Everyday tasks are just as easy to perform on the network as on a local drive. When the new user becomes accustomed to the network interface, he or she can enjoy the benefits of new network awareness while maintaining previous levels of productivity.

Folders Versus the Tree Display

The Windows 95 default presentation of network files as objects, using the folder paradigm adopted from the Macintosh interface, soon becomes rather unwieldy in a large network environment. When a busy user opens multiple windows to display the contents of different folders, the desktop can rapidly become cluttered, and the folders confusing in their similarity.

Using the Small Icons or List options available in the View menu of either Explorer or the Network Neighborhood can help to make the overall picture of a large network more understandable.

Another factor that may be difficult for the network user to assimilate is the presentation of all files as objects. Network files can, in many cases, have the same file name extensions as local machine files, but actually be used for different purposes. The File Types registered by default in the Windows 95 operating system may therefore not be completely accurate in this respect.

For this reason, especially in a network environment, I personally prefer to view all file types, and to see the entire name of all files, rather than count on the file system to interpret its meaning and produce the appropriate icon and File Type listing. To globally display all file name extensions in all folder or directory displays follow these steps:

1. Choose View, Options in Explorer or Network Neighborhood.

2. Click the View tab, click the Show all Files radio button, and uncheck the Hide MS-DOS File Extensions for file types that are registered box.

3. Click OK.

Understanding Network Naming Schemes

While Windows 95 presents network resources using a graphical, object-oriented display, you can still "get behind" the GUI and use the character-based naming conventions that the operating system uses to address network servers, volumes, directories, and files. One of the drawbacks of the Macintosh file system, on which Windows 95's folders are modeled, is that it is impossible to access files in any way other than through the graphical interface. Microsoft has repeatedly insisted that Windows 95 is based on an entirely new operating system architecture, but in fact it is still a GUI resting on top of a character-based DOS environment. But this arrangement isn't a bad thing. There will always be times when it is preferable to work from a DOS prompt, rather than a GUI display, and a great many users would object, were any attempt made to inhibit this capability.

In a character-based mode in a network environment, you must be able to address objects using a naming convention that incorporates their network location into the object name. Otherwise it would be impossible to have directories of the same name on different machines. When you are working with two network operating systems at the same time, as is so often the case with Windows 95, the workstation operating system must be aware of the different naming conventions used for each NOS.

Using NetWare Object Names

Because NetWare is the older and more common of the two network operating systems most often addressed by Windows 95 workstations, it is essential that Windows 95 understand the syntax by which NetWare files are identified. This syntax is as follows:

```
SERVER/VOLUME:DIRECTORY\FILE
```

Because NetWare is strictly a client/server operating system (that is, one with no peer-to-peer capabilities), only server-based objects have to be addressable. All objects not located on a server can be understood to reside on the local machine, because a NetWare client cannot directly address other workstations. NetWare servers are first broken up into volumes, which are logical divisions that may signify the existence of separate hard drive units. A volume is always followed by a colon (:) in the NetWare syntax, thus preventing it from being confused with a directory. After the colon, the name may include one or more directories and subdirectories, separated by a backslash(\), and then culminate in a file name. In most instances, Windows 95 can process NetWare resources presented in this manner, either in a DOS session or in a Windows dialog box.

Windows 95's ability to understand the NetWare naming convention allows you to use nearly all of the NetWare command line utilities from a DOS prompt. For example, you can map drive letters using the NetWare MAP command in the traditional manner, and the changes you make will immediately be propagated throughout the entire GUI environment.

Part
VIII

Ch
26

> **CAUTION**
>
> The Novell VLM client for NetWare contains a feature through which you can create private drive mappings in a DOS session that do not affect the rest of the Windows environment. When you use the VLM client with Windows 95, this feature is not operational, as all mappings are global. Thus, you should never remove the check mark in the Global Drives and Paths checkbox of the VLM NWUSER program, or serious system instabilities may result.

Using UNC Naming

Windows 95, and all other Microsoft network operating systems, utilize a different syntax for addressing network resources. This is called the *Universal Naming Convention*, or UNC. The syntax for the UNC is as follows:

```
\\SERVER\SHARE\DIRECTORY\FILE
```

Because most Microsoft operating systems offer both client/server and peer-to-peer networking capabilities, you must use naming conventions that are capable of addressing workstation as well as server resources. In actuality, the SERVER name listed in the syntax refers to any machine that is sharing its internal resources over the network, and not just Windows NT servers. A workstation that is configured to share its CD-ROM drive with a neighboring workstation is functioning as a server in that respect, and its machine name is used in place of the SERVER name shown in the preceding example.

SHARE refers to a logical name assigned by a user or administrator to a particular network resource that he is sharing with the rest of the network. All drives, printers, fax modems, and other devices that you can access over a Microsoft network are called *shares*, whether they're located on a server or a workstation. As a result, a share can be an entire drive on a particular machine, a single directory on a drive, a printer, or a fax modem attached to the server.

The name for a share is selected by the person electing to share it. It need not reflect the share's actual location on the server. In other words, in terms of file sharing, you need not give a user any way of knowing on which server drive a share resides, or whether that share represents the entire contents of the drive. As with NetWare volumes, access rights flow downhill on a Microsoft network. When you assign a user rights to a share, you include all of the directories and subdirectories contained beneath it. The directory names are the same as they appear on the server itself, however. You cannot assign them share names unless you configure them separately as additional shares.

 Windows 95 insists (often rather needlessly) on referring to all directories as "folders." The terms can often be used interchangeably, except that a folder also can refer to a SHARE or VOLUME, as well as a directory. All three are represented by the same icon in the Windows 95 visual file windows.

Mapping Network Drives

The most common situation in which you would use NetWare and UNC names is when you are mapping drive letters to network drives. Mapped drives are listed in My Computer and in Explorer as assets of the local machine. For the volumes or shared drives that you access most often, this is still the recommended method for gaining quick access to them, particularly if you sometimes use the DOS prompt to access network directories. You can create drive mappings in several ways with Windows 95.

The most traditional method of mapping drives is through the use of a login script, that is, a text file containing network commands that are executed whenever a user logs in. The login script usually is maintained by the network administrator rather than the individual user, and is a good way of enforcing a particular drive mapping policy on a group of users. Although we want users to understand more about networking and drive access, and perform more configuration tasks themselves, the cost for this knowledge should not be anarchy. Having a dozen bookkeepers each with different sets of drive mappings is sure to cause office work to come to a screeching halt. Users that work together and access the same network resources should use the same drive mappings.

Login scripts are a client/server networking convention and both Windows NT and NetWare support their use. When you log a Windows 95 machine into both networks at the same time, the Windows NT login script will always run last, remapping any drive letters that may also appear in a NetWare script.

Using the Map Network Drive Dialog Box

Within the Windows 95 graphical user interface, the Map Network Drive dialog box (see fig. 26.10) provides a simplified means to map Windows NT, peer workstation, or NetWare drives. The dialog box, which you can access from the Tools menu in Explorer or from the toolbar, contains two fields. The Drive field has a drop-down list with which you select the drive letter that you wish to map. In the Path field, you specify the network resource that you wish to associate with the selected drive letter. The Path field also has a drop-down list, containing all of the network names that you have already entered into this field. To map a drive to a new path, you must manually enter the name of the network resource into the Path field, using either the NetWare naming convention or the UNC. If you are not currently attached to the resource you have specified, and if there is no password information in the cache for that resource, then you will be prompted to log in before the drive mapping is completed. Check the checkbox to order Windows 95 to re-map the drive letter each time the machine is started.

Part
VIII

Ch
26

FIG. 26.10

The Map Network Drive dialog box allows network shares and volumes to be permanently associated with particular drive letters.

TIP While Windows 95, in many cases, can accept either NetWare or UNC names as input, it defaults to UNC. You can always express NetWare resources as UNC names, in the form: \\SERVER\VOLUME\DIRECTORY\FILE.

You also can access the Disconnect Network Drive dialog box from the Tools menu or toolbar of Explorer or Network Neighborhood window. This dialog box displays a listing of the currently mapped drive letters, and performs the opposite function of the Map Network Drive dialog box, allowing you to remove the selected mapping and free up its drive letter.

Mapping Drives from the Command Prompt

Both NetWare and Microsoft networks also provide utilities for mapping drive letters from a DOS prompt. NetWare's is the MAP command, while Windows 95 uses the NET command. When using these utilities, you should be familiar with both of the network naming conventions, because the two are not as interchangeable as they are in the Windows 95 GUI.

The NetWare MAP Command   MAP runs from a Windows 95 DOS prompt in the same way as on a standard DOS computer or in a DOS session under Windows 3.1. When you issue the command MAP from the DOS prompt, all of the NetWare drive mappings and search drives currently active on the workstation are displayed. When you map a new drive letter, the NetWare naming convention must be used to specify a network resource. The syntax is as follows:

```
MAP X:=SERVER/VOLUME:[DIRECTORY]
```

You can map a drive letter to the root of a NetWare volume, or to any directory contained within that volume. Other options of the MAP command allow you to map a subdirectory to a root drive letter, or map the next available drive letter, or create a search drive. See your NetWare documentation for more information on the use of the MAP command.

> **CAUTION**
> When you create drive mappings in a Windows 95 DOS session, they are carried over to the rest of the Windows 95 environment, but newly-created search drives are not. These drive mappings function normally within the confines of that DOS session, but are lost as soon as the session is terminated. Global search drives must be created from a login script, or manually mapped from a DOS prompt before the Windows 95 GUI is loaded.

The Windows 95 NET Command You use the NET.EXE command line utility, with the USE parameter, for mapping drive letters on Microsoft networks. When you issue the NET USE command from any DOS prompt, all of the currently mapped devices on the system are displayed, including peer-to-peer mappings, NetWare drive mappings, and even captured print queues. When you issue the NET VIEW command, all of the shares on the network that are available for mapping are displayed, including NetWare servers.

The syntax for mapping a drive with NET is as follows:

```
NET USE X: \\SERVER\SHARE
```

NET USE also is capable of mapping LPT ports to shared network printers, and contains many other options to control how drive mappings are created. This includes whether passwords are cached, and whether the drive mapping process should be interactive.

While you can use the NET USE command to map a drive letter to any shared network resource, including NetWare drives, it does not support the NetWare naming convention. You would therefore create a drive mapping to a NetWare volume by issuing the following command:

```
NET USE X: \\SERVER\VOLUME
```

Using the Windows 95 NET Command

NET is an extremely powerful command that you can use to perform nearly all the network related tasks that are possible from the Windows 95 GUI. It also has a number of real mode functions that can be used only when you boot Windows 95 to the command prompt; these functions will not operate from a DOS session within the Windows interface. Following is a summary of NET command functions. More detailed information is available by typing the command followed by a /? at a Windows 95 DOS prompt (for example, **NET USE /?**).

NET CONFIG	Displays your current workgroup settings.
NET DIAG	Runs the Microsoft Network Diagnostics program to display diagnostic information about your network.
NET HELP	Provides information about commands and error messages.
NET INIT	Loads protocol and network-adapter drivers without binding them to Protocol Manager.
NET LOGOFF	Breaks the connection between your computer and the shared resources to which it is connected.
NET LOGON	Identifies you as a member of a workgroup.

continues

Part

VIII

Ch

26

continued

NET PASSWORD	Changes your logon password.
NET PRINT	Displays information about print queues and controls print jobs.
NET START	Starts services.
NET STOP	Stops services.
NET TIME	Displays the time on or synchronizes your computer's clock with the clock on a Microsoft Windows for Workgroups, Windows NT, Windows 95, or NetWare time server.
NET USE	Connects to or disconnects from a shared resource or displays information about connections.
NET VER	Displays the type and version number of the workgroup redirector you are using.
NET VIEW	Displays a list of computers that share resources or a list of shared resources on a specific computer.

TROUBLESHOOTING

When using the NET USE command to map drives, why does the utility refuse to read passwords from the cache file, and force me to enter them every time? The patch for the Windows 95 password cache file mentioned earlier in this chapter alters the NET.EXE utility. After the service pack containing the patch is applied, passwords are no longer extracted from the cache when you use NET commands. All passwords must be explicitly specified at all times.

Accessing Network Resources from the DOS Command Prompt

For users who first became acquainted with personal computing through DOS applications, perhaps you remember your first exposure to Windows and how long it took for you to gather up Windows versions of all of the DOS utilities you had collected. During those times when you just couldn't bring yourself to abandon your favorite DOS word processing program or spreadsheet, it was a pleasure to exit from Windows and run that application in native DOS, rather than a DOS session.

Windows 95 is still capable of this, even when network support is required. Bring up the boot menu by pressing F8 as you start your computer, and you can easily boot to a DOS prompt. What you cannot do is boot directly to DOS mode with network support. You can, however, enable Windows 95's real-mode network clients with the NET START command, and map your drives with the NET USE command. Or you could create a batch file to perform all of these steps for you.

> **CAUTION**
>
> NET START can only be issued from the real-mode DOS prompt. It will not function in a Windows 95 virtual machine session. However, NET USE and many other commands can be used in a DOS window in place of their GUI counterparts.

Issue the NET START BASIC command from the DOS prompt to load the real-mode client for Microsoft networking. You then can map drives to any of the Windows shares available on the network, using the following syntax:

```
NET USE D: \\server\share
```

The NET START WORKSTATION command loads Windows 95's real-mode client for NetWare. After you have done this, you can switch to the F: drive (or whatever your first network drive is), and login to your NetWare server, just as you would from any DOS machine. NetWare drives also can be mapped using the NET USE command. UNC naming must be used for the NetWare drive as in *server**volume**directory*.

> **N O T E** Windows 95 cannot use more than one real-mode client at a time, so it is impossible to attach to both Microsoft and NetWare resources simultaneously using this technique. ▨

If you still use WordPerfect for DOS, and need access to your network data files, using the real-mode client from the DOS prompt is the best way to run it under Windows 95. Also, in a troubleshooting situation in which video problems prevent you even from loading the standard VGA driver used by Safe Mode, this technique may help you out. And then of course, there are those network multiplayer DOS games that you've been meaning to check out.

Part
VIII

Ch
26

Browsing Network Drives

As discussed earlier, mapping drive letters is not the only way to access network drives in Windows 95. Using the Network Neighborhood or Explorer, you can easily browse to any server on the network and access it by double-clicking the machine's icon. If a user name and password are stored in the PWL file, then the folders representing the volumes or shares will be displayed immediately. Otherwise, clicking the right mouse button and selecting Attach from the context menu will produce a login dialog box. Detaching can be done the same way. Accessing the Who Am I function on the context menu displays the currently logged user name and the connection number for that server. The Server Information page of the Properties sheet displays the version of the NOS installed on the server, the number of connections in use, and the maximum number of possible connections allowed (see fig. 26.11).

FIG. 26.11
When using the Microsoft Client for NetWare Networks, a server's Properties sheet displays only rudimentary server identification information.

Additional Client Features

The NetWare clients available for Windows 95 provide users with different feature sets. Novell's Client32 provides a larger array of features when accessing NetWare volumes than any of the other clients.

Client32 allows the user to browse for network resources either through a server listing or through the NetWare Directory Services tree.

In addition, Client32 adds extra pages to the Properties sheet for a NetWare directory or file. The NetWare File page shows the additional file attributes maintained by the NetWare file system, such as the last modified date and the object's owner, as well as the user's currently effective rights to that file. As with Microsoft's Client for NetWare Networks, you can modify the file or directory attributes directly from this dialog box. The NetWare Rights page goes even farther, however, by displaying all of the users with trustee rights to the selected object. You can modify these rights, and grant additional trustee rights to any user of that server, as shown in figure 26.12.

Of course, you must have the appropriate NetWare rights yourself before you can alter the rights of other users, but this is yet another way in which Windows 95 brings network properties into the environment of the average network user.

▶ **See** "Using the Novell Client32 for Windows 95," **p. 736**

FIG. 26.12
Novell's Client32 provides the means for manipulation of NetWare trustee rights, directly from the Windows 95 desktop.

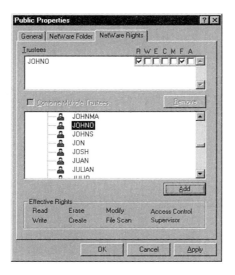

Storing Long File Names on Network Drives

One of the most popular new features of Windows 95 is the ability to give files and directories names with as many as 255 characters. Networking, however, greatly complicates the use of this feature. The primary problem is that the long file names can be lost during several different types of network transactions.

When the Windows NT and Windows 95 file systems use long file names, they also store a standard 8.3 file name with every file. The 8.3 file name is a truncated version of the long file name formed by taking the first six legal characters of the file name and appending a tilde (~) and a numeral, plus the extension. Maintaining the short file name allows the files to remain compatible with any 16-bit applications that they may encounter. A file listing utility, for example, would perform very poorly if many long file names had to be truncated on the fly by the application before they could be displayed.

Unfortunately, any 16-bit application that overwrites or saves changes to the file will use the only name that it understands— the 8.3 version. Because the long file name is not read into memory by the application, it cannot be saved back to the file, and is therefore lost. No notification is provided to the user that the short file name has been used.

You are notified by the Windows 95 file management tools, however, when attempting to copy files with long names to a destination that cannot support them. You are prompted to specify an 8.3 name in place of the truncated version supplied by the system, if desired.

Part
VIII

Ch
26

Windows 95's method for determining 8.3 file names, besides being rather unintuitive, violates the ISO-9660 multiplatform CD-ROM standard through its use of the tilde character. However, by adding a new binary value to the following Registry key, naming it NameNumericTail and assigning it a value of zero (0), the file patterns used by Windows 95 when creating short file names are changed, eliminating the tilde and the numeral except when necessary to avoid the creation of duplicate file names.

See Chapter 15 for more information on using the Registry Editor.

HKEY_LOCAL_MACHINE

System

CurrentControlSet

Control

File System

There are several other circumstances in which long file names can be stripped from Windows 95 files:

- When any 16-bit operating system, such as DOS, Windows 3.1 or Windows for Workgroups, is used to open and save the file.

- When a Windows 95 machine running a real-mode network client is used to open and save the file.

- When the file is stored on a NetWare server volume that has not been properly configured to store long file names.

This last situation is the most common reason that long file names are lost. To store Windows 95 long file names, a NetWare server volume must have OS/2 name space added to its file system. Windows 95's file system was deliberately designed to emulate OS/2 in this respect, so that a new NetWare name space module would not have to be written.

Installing OS/2 Name Space on a NetWare Server

To add support to a NetWare volume for Windows 95 (as well as OS/2) long file names, you need a module called OS2.NAM. From the NetWare server command prompt, or from the STARTUP.NCF file, LOAD this module in the normal manner. You must then issue the command

    ADD OS2 NAME SPACE OS2 TO VOLUME <volume_name>

from the system prompt. The ADD NAME SPACE command need be performed only once (for each volume), while the NAM module must be loaded each time the server is booted. The only way to remove a name space from a volume (without destroying the data) is with the VREPAIR.NLM utility.

There is another issue associated with the use of OS/2 name space on NetWare volumes, however. The original release of NetWare 3.11 contained a problem with its OS/2 name space module, which caused long file names not to be stored on 3.11 volumes. You can obtain a patch that addresses this bug. The patch, called OS2OPNFX.NLM, is located in an archive called 311PTD.EXE, which can be downloaded from the \NWOSFILES forum on Novell's NetWire online service.

Because of this issue, Windows 95 has been configured, by default, not to even attempt to store long file names on NetWare 3.11 servers. To change the default setting, open the Registry Editor and locate the following key:

```
Hkey_Local_Machine
System
Current
ControlSet
Services
VxD
Nwredir
The possible values for this key are as follows:
  • 0-which disables all long file name support on NetWare servers.
  • 1 (default)-which allows long file name support on NetWare servers
    version 3.12 and greater.
  • 2-which allows long file name support on all NetWare servers that
    have OS/2 Name Space.
Change the value to 2, save the changes, and restart the workstation. You
should now be able to store long file names on NetWare 3.11 volumes.
```

Part
VIII

Ch
26

Backing Up Long File Names

Long file names also complicate the process of backing up network workstations. Any network backup package should be able to handle the server-based files, because they are stored just as OS/2 files are. Backing up Windows 95 workstation drives to a server-based tape device is another matter. Not only must the long file names be delivered to the backup software running on the server, but the software must also be able to display the long file names properly so that the user can select files to be restored.

> **CAUTION**
>
> Many people tend to forget that writing to tape is only half of a successful backup operation. The tape is useless unless files can readily and flexibly be restored from it. You should regularly perform test restores from your backup tapes, even if the software indicates that successful backups have been performed.

Using LFNBK.EXE as a Backup Utility   LFNBK.EXE is a command line utility that is included with Windows 95 as a means of maintaining backward compatibility with existing DOS and Windows 3.1 disk utilities. Located in the \Admin\Apptools\Lfnback directory of the Windows 95 CD-ROM, the program can locate files with long file names, strip the long names off into a data file, and restore them at a later time. The idea is that any disk utility that is not Windows 95-aware can be run on a drive that has had its long file names removed.

For the most part, you won't need LFNBK to maintain backward compatibility. Windows 95 ships with its own disk repair and defragmenting utilities, and other companies have released new versions of their disk utility packages, upgraded for use with Windows 95.

You also can use LFNBK as a backup utility, if you are forced to use a backup system that does not support long file names. Use LFNBK.EXE to remove the long file names, perform a system backup with your regular software (including the LFNBK.DAT file, which is the archive containing the long names that have been removed), and then restore the long names again. This leaves you with a complete replica of the system's drives, along with the means to re-create the long file names again, should a restore from the backup tape be necessary.

> **CAUTION**
>
> Be sure to read and follow all of the directions and cautions provided in the LFNBK.TXT file included with the LFNBK.EXE utility. Failure to do so can cause severe problems in Windows 95.

While this type of backup can be done as an interim measure, it is not recommended as a regular backup procedure. The long file names can only be removed and restored for the entire system at one time. As a result, this backup process is useful for a disaster recovery situation, in which the entire contents of a drive have been destroyed, but it won't help you restore individual files. Further, LFNBK works by creating a new 8.3 alias in the

LFNBK.DAT file for each long file name on the drive. This new short file name may not match the existing 8.3 alias that the file already possesses. Thus, the alias on the drive may be changed by the restoration process.

LFNBK also is incapable of saving long file names without removing them from the original files, nor can it restore the original long names to directories that have been changed in any way after the long names were removed.

Backup Software Agents   While an LFNBK backup of your drives is better than no backup at all, you should perform your regular system backups using a software package that is specifically designed for Windows 95 drives. Several software manufacturers have released upgraded versions of backup utilities for use with Windows 95.

Two companies, Cheyenne Software and Arcada Software, have new client agents for their network backup products included with the Windows 95 operating system. These agents are installed as services from the Control Panel's Network application, and allow the server end of these products to contact network clients and back up their drives remotely, even when the user is not logged into the network. The Properties sheets of the client agents (see fig. 26.13) allow you to select specific drives or folders to be backed up, and to designate a password for the backup session, so that the contents of the tapes are protected from intruders.

FIG. 26.13
The ARCserve Agent service is used to back up a Windows 95 workstation to a server-mounted tape drive.

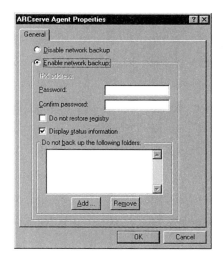

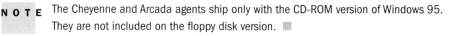

N O T E   The Cheyenne and Arcada agents ship only with the CD-ROM version of Windows 95. They are not included on the floppy disk version. ■

Both of these backup products run on NetWare servers, but there are also Windows NT server-based products with similar abilities. Backups are an essential part of a business computing environment. Even if all of your data is stored on server drives, think of how long it would take you to re-create the customized Windows 95 environment that you've worked so hard to build.

Using Network Printers

Aside from drive sharing and storage capabilities, the other fundamental reason for the widespread adoption of local area networking in the business world is the sharing of printers. As with hard drives, the original method for printer sharing was to redirect the local DOS output to the network, where it was stored in a queue on a print server, until it could be serviced by a printer. The introduction of Windows helped overcome this deception by adding the ability to address network printers directly.

Windows 95 takes this evolution several steps further. Installing support for a network printer is now a far easier process than it ever has been, and with some minor print server configurations, it can be made even easier for every Windows 95 user on the network.

Windows 95 also allows workstations to exert a greater amount of control over network printing than they have been able to in the past, while maintaining the margin of safety important to network administrators. The following section discusses the process of printing to server-based devices located elsewhere on the network.

▶ **See** "Accessing Windows 95 Workstation Resources," **p. 793**

Using the Add New Printer Wizard

Installing a local printer with the Add New Printer Wizard is discussed in Chapter 7, "Controlling Printers." The procedure for installing a network printer is not terribly different. After launching the Add New Printer Wizard, the first question that you are asked is whether you are installing a local or a network printer. When you select Network, you are then asked to furnish the location of the share or queue, as shown in figure 26.14.

It is assumed that the printer you are installing has already been properly configured for network use. This involves the creation of a share on a Windows NT server, or a print queue on a NetWare server. In either case, when you click the Browse button for the Network path or queue name field in the wizard, a Network Neighborhood display appears, in which you can expand servers until you have located the appropriate print queue. The correct path to the share or queue also can be entered directly into the dialog box, but it must be specified using a correct UNC pathname (see the section "Using UNC Naming" earlier in this chapter).

FIG. 26.14

The Add New Printer Wizard simplifies the installation of a network printer.

If the printer cannot be located at the path given, you receive a message to that effect, but you can still proceed with the installation. A network printer may be temporarily invisible to the network for any number of reasons.

The Invisible Printer

One of the basic tenets of network printing is to keep the user working whenever possible. That is why network printing systems are usually designed to function normally, even when the actual printer is not working. Unlike printing to a locally attached device, all network print jobs are *spooled*. Spooling is the process by which a server accepts print jobs from applications and stores them on a disk until the printer can service them. Network users can continue to send jobs to print queues, even when the printer has run out of paper, jammed, or been stolen during the night.

The spooling process has two major effects:

- The actual time that the user's application spends printing is greatly reduced, because a hard drive can accept data at a much greater rate than any printer.

- The user cannot be sure that his job has been successfully printed until he actually walks over to the printer and checks.

The administrative capabilities of Windows 95 can help to make the latter point less of a problem. Printers become more interactive each year, and it is now possible to perform a number of maintenance tasks from a remote network workstation. This eliminates trips to the printer, and avoids a backlog of jobs in the queue.

The second question asked in the Add Printer Wizard dialog box is whether you print from DOS-based programs. While most of the remaining major DOS applications, such as

Part
VIII

Ch
26

WordPerfect and Lotus 1-2-3, are capable of network printing, some Windows users may drop to the DOS prompt to use the small utilities that they have grown accustomed to over the years. These small programs are often not network-aware and print by default to the LPT1 port. What the wizard is asking with this question is whether it should configure the printer driver to capture local printer port output to the network queue.

The wizard then presents a standard Select Hardware dialog box to identify the printer model. Next, the wizard asks you to furnish a name for the printer. You may think it silly to name a locally attached device, but if you're printing on a network, printer naming can be essential.

Part of the advantage of network printing is the ability to access printers all over the network. This has obvious benefits when the printers are of different types. You may need access to a widebed dot-matrix printer for spreadsheets, a laser printer for correspondence and a color printer for presentations. However, even in a company that has 50 identical LaserJets on its network, the ability to send a document to someone in another department simply by printing it to their printer can be a real timesaver. For this reason, it is a good idea to name your various printers descriptively, identifying the printer type and its location.

After its interrogation is complete, the wizard then copies the appropriate printer drivers from the Windows 95 source files (possibly prompting you to insert a floppy or CD-ROM), and creates an additional icon in the Printers window. You may now use this printer just as if it were a local device, dragging and dropping files onto the icon, or selecting it directly from your application.

Using Point and Print

One problem that is often faced by network users is how to know exactly which printer model to select during the installation process, when the printer itself may be some distance away from both their workstation and the file server.

Locating Server-Based Printers

A network printer may have to be associated logically with a network server, but it does not have to be physically attached to it, except through the network medium itself. One of the most popular solutions for network printing today is to install a special network interface card that also functions as a print server into a laser printer.

N O T E   The Hewlett Packard JetDirect card is one of the most popular network interface cards, and Windows 95 includes a service with the operating system that provides an interface to the print server on the card. See "Using the JetAdmin Service," later in this chapter, for more information. ▓

Print jobs can be spooled to a print queue on a server and then systematically fed to a printer located anywhere on the network.

So how do users know which printer to use and what printer driver to install? Point and Print is a Windows 95 mechanism that solves both these problems by associating the appropriate printer model with a print queue, and storing the correct printer drivers on the network, where all users can access them. If you remove from the Add New Printer Wizard the procedures by which the printer is identified and the drivers located, you are left with a ridiculously easy installation process that can be performed by anyone.

In fact, when you have set up network printers for Point and Print, users need only browse the Network Neighborhood for the printer that they want to use and drag it into the Installed Printers window. Users are still asked if they print from DOS applications and whether the selected printer should be the Windows default. After those questions, however, the necessary drivers are automatically downloaded from the server and installed and the printer is ready for use.

Configuring a NetWare Server for Point and Print

Setting up a printer for Point and Print is simply a matter of associating the print queue with the printer's name and a location for its driver files. That information must be stored on the network so that all Windows 95 can have access. For that reason, the user configuring Point and Print must have supervisor rights to the server, at least during the configuration process.

To configure Point and Print, you must know the exact printer model and also have the correct drivers for the printer, if it is not already supported by Windows 95. Once you have this information, use the following procedure to install Point and Print for a NetWare print queue:

1. Open the Network Neighborhood window, and browse until you find the server with the print queue that you want to use.

2. Double-click the server icon to expand it, displaying its volumes and print queues. Choose File, Point and Print Setup.

Part
VIII
Ch
26

   T I P   Point and Print Setup also can be accessed by clicking the printer icon with the right (or secondary) mouse button.

3. Select Driver Path and specify a suitable path to a directory on the server where you will store the printer drivers. All users must have read access to this directory (for NetWare servers, a subdirectory off of SYS:PUBLIC is a good idea). The path must be specified using the UNC syntax, whichever network operating system is being used. For example:

```
\\server\sys\public\hplj
```

4. Click OK, and then select Set Printer Model from the Point and Print Setup menu.

5. Choose the correct printer manufacturer and model from the Select Device dialog box. Click OK. There is no visible change to the icon, but the queue has now been associated with that printer model and looks to the directory furnished for the correct drivers.

6. The final, and perhaps trickiest task is to determine exactly what driver files are needed and copy them to the directory that you have specified. Using Notepad, or any text file viewer, open the MSPRINT.INF file, located in the \Windows\Inf directory. The file is structured much like a Windows 3.1 INI file. As you page through it, you see that each manufacturer from the Select Drive dialog box has its own section, enclosed in brackets (for example,: [HP]). Within each manufacturer section, all of the printer model names are listed on the left. Locate the correct manufacturer section and the line with the model name for your printer. On that line, make note of the information to the right of the equal sign (=). This identifies the appropriate installer section for your printer, found later in the file. Sample entries from the MSPRINT.INF file appear in the code listing that follows:

```
...
;
; The Manufacturer section lists all of the manufacturers that we will
; display in the Dialog box
;
...
[HP]

...
"HP LaserJet 4"                = HPPCL5MS.DRV.BIDI,HP_LaserJet_4
"HP LaserJet 4M"               = HPPCL5MS.DRV.BIDI,HP_LaserJet_4M
"HP LaserJet 4/4M PostScript"  = HP4M_V4.SPD,HP_LaserJet_4/
4M_PostScript
...
;
; Installer Sections
;
; These sections control file installation, and reference all files that
; need to be copied. The section name will be assumed to be the driver
; file, unless there is an explicit DriverFile section listed.
;
...
```

```
[HPPCL.DRV]
CopyFiles=@HPPCL.DRV,FINSTALL,UNI
DataSection=UNI_DATA

[HPPCL5MS.DRV.BIDI]
CopyFiles=@HPPCL5MS.DRV,@PJLMON.DLL,UNI,FINSTALL
DataSection=UNI_DATA
DriverFile=HPPCL5MS.DRV
DataFile=HPPCL5MS.DRV
LanguageMonitor=%PJL_MONITOR%

[HP_COLOR_LASERJET]
CopyFiles=@HPPCL5MS.DRV,@PJLMON.DLL,UNICLR,FINSTALL,COLOR_HP_LASER
DataSection=UNI_DATA
DriverFile=HPPCL5MS.DRV
DataFile=HPPCL5MS.DRV
LanguageMonitor=%PJL_MONITOR%
...
; Copy Sections
;
; Lists of files that are actually copied. These sections are referenced
; from the installer sections, above. Only create a section if it contains
; two or more files (if we only copy a single file, identify it in the
; installer section, using the @filename notation) or if it's a color
; profile (since the DestinationDirs can only handle sections, and not
; individual files).
...
[FINSTALL]
FINSTALL.DLL
FINSTALL.HLP
...
[UNI]
UNIDRV.DLL
UNIDRV.HLP
ICONLIB.DLL
...
```

The CopyFiles line from this section lists the following: @HPPCL5MS.DRV, @PJLMON.DLL,UNI,FINSTALL. The UNI and FINSTALL copy sections each contain additional file names, so that the driver files needed for the HP LaserJet 4 printer are as follows:

HPPCL5MS.DRV

PJLMON.DLL

FINSTALL.DLL

FINSTALL.HLP

UNIDRV.DLL

UNIDRV.HLP

ICONLIB.DLL

Part
VIII

Ch
26

7. Scroll down further in the MSPRINT.INF file until you locate the installer sections, as noted by the remark lines in the listing shown previously. Locate the installer section corresponding to the entry that you noted in step 6.

8. The CopyFiles line in this section indicates the files that should be placed into the Point and Print directory on the server. Names preceded by "@" are exact file names. Make a note of these for use later. The other entries refer to copy sections located farther down in the MSPRINT.INF file.

9. Locate any copy sections listed in the installer section for your printer, and note the file names contained therein. You should now have a list of file names for your printer, taken from the install and copy sections of MSPRINT.INF.

10. Locate the files on your list and copy them to the directory that you specified in step 3. The easiest way to obtain the files from the Windows 95 installation archives is to install the printer using the Add New Printer Wizard. All of the files needed will then be in your \Windows and \Windows\System directories.

T I P Any valid set of printer drivers intended for use with Windows 95 contain a INF file indicating the exact files needed for the installation. The syntax may differ from that shown in the list here, but the file names should be discernible.

Monitoring Network Printers

Aside from simplifying the printer installation process, Windows 95 has also improved the administrative features devoted to network printing. When you double-click a network printer icon in the Printers window, a screen showing the current contents of the network print queue is displayed, as shown in figure 26.15. The source application of each pending job is listed, as well as the network user who generated it, its size, and the time that it was submitted. A user can therefore tell when his job has been completed, or estimate the delay until it is serviced.

FIG. 26.15
The print queue window allows network print jobs to be manipulated directly from within Windows 95.

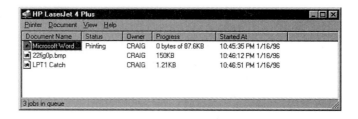

Manipulating Network Print Queues

The print queue interface also allows users to pause or cancel print jobs, on an individual or global basis, assuming that the user has been granted the rights to do so at the print server. On many networks, the typical policy is to allow users to manipulate their own print jobs, but not those of others. You also can modify the service order of the print jobs by dragging and dropping a job to a new position in the queue.

Using the JetAdmin Service

Included in the Windows 95 package is an additional network service that allows improved access to printers using Hewlett Packard JetDirect interface cards. The service installs like any other, through the Network application in the Control Panel. After the installation and a system reboot, an additional Control Panel application is added which, when opened, displays all of the printers on the network using JetDirect cards, as shown in figure 26.16.

FIG. 26.16

The JetAdmin utility allows for more extensive interaction with printers all over the network.

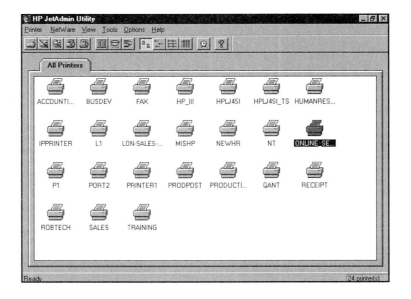

When you select a printer and view its Properties from the File menu, a properties sheet appears providing a tremendous amount of information about the printer, and allowing many of the settings to be modified (see fig. 26.17). When printing from a NetWare print queue, you also can configure the printing rights granted to NetWare users; settings that normally can be changed only by using the NetWare PCONSOLE utility. The service also can automatically install printer drivers to a network server, allowing you to ignore the contents of the MSPRINT.INF file.

Part
VIII

Ch
26

FIG. 26.17
The JetAdmin service brings many of a distant printer's controls to the workstation user's desktop.

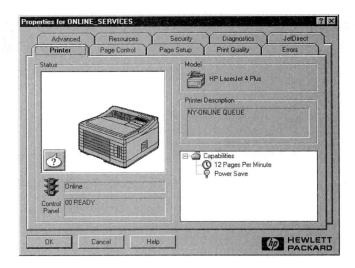

Finally, the ultimate benefit of network printing under Windows 95 is that it differs so little from local printing. Procedures like drag-and-drop printing, as well as virtually all of the other techniques covered in Chapter 7, "Controlling Printers," also can be used on network printers.

Accessing Other Client/Server Services

Networking has, of course, progressed far beyond being merely a means for sharing printers and hard drives. Today's networks provide users with access to all kinds of different resources that would be impractical or impossible to duplicate on every individual computer.

Some of these services are still based on the concept of sharing equipment, such as modem pools and network faxing applications, but the other, more mission-critical, tools are those that share information. From e-mail links, to groupware products such as Lotus Notes, to database engines, and even to the potential services of the future, such as desktop videoconferencing, all of these systems rely on network communications for their basic functionality.

At the practical level, workstation users generally have fewer responsibilities when using these higher-level resources than they have for the more basic services discussed in this chapter. Most of these shared applications operate through Presentation and Application layers, near the top of the OSI reference model (see fig. 26.18). Their functionality is provided through protocols that are transmitted across the network using the lower level protocols, such as IPX/SPX and NetBEUI, as carriers.

FIG. 26.18
Upper layer protocols are
carried as payload within a
frame formed by a lower
level protocol.

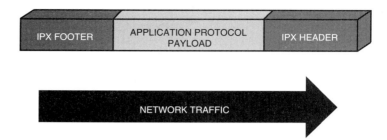

For the most part, this process is automatic. High level protocols such as Windows Sockets and Remote Procedure Calls have been a part of the Windows network standards since long before the release of Windows 95, and their capabilities are fully integrated into the existing network client stack. Users need only install the appropriate client software for the application, and communication with its counterpart at the server end is initiated automatically.

Btrieve

Other services do require some attention from the user, however. A good case in point is the Btrieve client/server database environment. In this system, the databases are maintained at the server by an engine running as a NetWare NLM. In order for a client workstation to contact the databases at the server, a client requester called BREQUEST.EXE must be loaded at the user's workstation.

Brequest initiates the communication between the database engine on the server and the workstation. If no network communication is detected, then the requester cannot load.

Many users place the Brequest command in their AUTOEXEC.BAT files, so that connectivity can be established automatically whenever the machine is booted. Unfortunately, this is not effective under Windows 95 when the workstation is using one of the protected-mode NetWare clients. In these cases, a connection to the network is not established until after the AUTOEXEC.BAT file is read.

For Brequest, as well as certain other network engines, the solution is relatively simple. If you insert the requester load line into the WINSTART.BAT file, access to the databases is allowed, because WINSTART.BAT runs after the IPX connection to the server is established.

Other TSRs

Users of other systems may not be so lucky. Sometimes a terminate-and-stay resident (TSR) program needed to contact a server application is simply incompatible with one or more of the Windows 95 networking modules. These would more typically involve the hardware-sharing applications such as network-faxing or modem-sharing, which redirect local device driver calls to a network server over a middle layer protocol, such as IPX.

In these cases, it is sometimes necessary to retain the real-mode client, protocol, or adapter component (or all three) from an older client software package, such as Novell's NETX or VLM, to maintain compatibility. This can seriously diminish the networking performance of Windows 95, and should be avoided whenever possible. Fortunately, many software developers are rushing to develop Windows 95 compatible clients for their applications, so it should only be a matter of time before more satisfactory solutions are available. ●

CHAPTER 27

Installing Windows 95 Peer-to-Peer Networking

by Craig Zacker

In addition to its client/server capabilities, Windows 95 also is a peer-to-peer network operating system. A peer-to-peer network is one in which every workstation can directly communicate with every other workstation, without the need for an intervening server. You can therefore share a workstation's resources with other users in the same way that a server's resources are shared on a client/server network.

In the Microsoft Windows networking model, the boundaries between the server and the workstation are far less distinct than they are on a Novell NetWare network. All Windows servers are functional clients as well, allowing a user to run an application or access a remote network resource while the machine continues to perform its server duties. Every client workstation also can function as a server, offering access of its resources to other network users. A peer-to-peer network is one in which all of the computers function as both clients and servers. ■

Build a Windows 95 peer-to-peer network

Learn how a Windows 95 peer-to-peer network can operate as part of a client/server network or function on its own.

Create a workgroup

You can organize your network to accommodate almost any need by creating small teams of workers, called workgroups.

Install Windows 95's peer-to-peer networking components

Learn how to install components through the Control Panel by using the Network dialog box.

Add peer-to-peer networking into an existing client/server network

In a client/server network environment, Windows 95 can add the peer-to-peer functionality to an existing infrastructure.

Establish procedures for securing peer network resources against unauthorized access

Learn the difference between user-level and share-level security.

Using the Peer Advantage

A Windows 95 peer-to-peer network can operate as part of a client/server network, or it can function on its own, without the presence of a server. A high-powered client/server NOS like NetWare greatly increases the efficiency of the file and print services for which the local area network was originally designed. It also provides the potential for the evolution to higher level network services such as shared databases and communication applications. However, despite the added power, there is a basic functional drawback to the client/server model.

With the client/server arrangement, when one user needs access to a file on another user's local hard drive, the only solution is to copy the file to a server drive, so that both users can access it from there. There is no direct communication between workstations, as shown in figure 27.1. On a peer-to-peer network, the file can be accessed directly, without bothering its owner. When one user needs to briefly use an application installed on another user's machine, he can simply access the application from the other user's drive.

FIG. 27.1
The client/server model allows a workstation to communicate only with host servers.

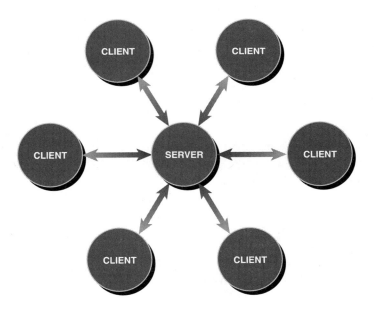

Thus, it is clear that the peer-to-peer networking model does offer something that the client/server model lacks. Instead of every workstation communicating only with a central point—the server—every machine is theoretically capable of communicating with every other machine, as shown in figure 27.2.

FIG. 27.2

Peer-to-peer networking can allow any workstation to access the resources of any other workstation.

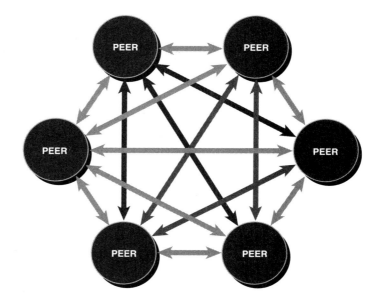

Peer-to-peer networking also allows users to share their workstations' hardware resources more efficiently. With Windows 95, you can allow other network users to access your CD-ROM drive, printer, or fax modem with little effort beyond the normal installation procedure for the device. On a client/server network, configuring any of these devices for network access is a more complicated undertaking, sometimes requiring additional server hardware or software.

Combining client/server with peer-to-peer networking is easy with Windows 95. You can construct a peer-to-peer network for a small business and add servers later, or add peer functionality to your existing client/server network. In either case, Windows 95 simplifies the conversion because all of the necessary client software is integrated into the operating system. You can therefore have a network that grows with the needs of the organization and offers the best features of both the client/server and peer-to-peer networking models.

Part
VIII

Ch
27

Integrating Peer Networking into the Windows Environment

Like Windows for Workgroups and Windows NT before it, Windows 95 incorporates both peer-to-peer and client/server networking functionality into the base operating system package. Windows 95 surpasses its predecessors, however, by automating more of the network configuration process and by providing a user interface in which peer network objects are presented side-by-side with server resources and those of the local machine.

Whichever organizational model you use in your network—client/server, peer-to-peer, or a combination of the two—your users will be working with the same interface. All other computers on the network appear as icons, with their shared resources displayed hierarchically beneath them.

Interestingly, Windows for Workgroups possesses much of the same basic networking capability that Windows 95 now does, that is, the capability to integrate client/server and peer-to-peer functionality into one operating system. The primary and crucial difference between the two is the ease and efficiency by which this is done.

With Windows 95, the process of adding peer-to-peer networking functionality almost never conflicts with the operation of an existing client/server configuration, as it often does in Windows for Workgroups. This allows you to create a business network that takes the fullest advantage of both network types. When every computer is capable of communicating with every other computer, the working environment is completely flexible.

You can create small teams of workers, often called workgroups, that function with a greater amount of autonomy because of the access they are granted to each other's computing resources. You can therefore organize the network to accommodate the needs of the business, rather than organize the business around the constraints of the network.

Creating a New Peer Network with Windows 95

Like Windows for Workgroups and Windows NT before it, you can outfit a group of computers with network interface cards, connect them with cables, and using no software other than Windows 95, have them communicate with each other to great effect. Peer users can share their files, printers, fax modems, and CD-ROM drives without the intervention of a network administrator. You also can provide users with higher-level services, such as e-mail, group scheduling, and remote system administration, just as on a client/server network. Further, the addition of Plug and Play technology eliminates one of the largest stumbling blocks to the do-it-yourself network: selecting, installing, and configuring the hardware.

For a small business or home network of 10 workstations or less, purchase identical thin Ethernet Plug and Play network interface cards, insert one in each machine, connect them with prepackaged 50-ohm coaxial cables, and you have a network. Windows 95 identifies the cards and installs the correct drivers for you, and the basic installation is finished. Configuration and administration of your new network will take a little more effort, but that will be covered in this chapter and those immediately following.

Wiring a Small Network

While Thin Ethernet is not the most recent technology in general use today, it's one of the most inexpensive and the simplest to install (which is why it's also known as *Cheapernet*). The professional standard in office networks is 10BaseT, another Ethernet variety, which uses twisted pair, or telephone type cabling. The complicating factor in a 10BaseT network is the need for a concentrator (or wiring hub), to which every workstation must be connected. This incurs additional expense and installation difficulties. Thin Ethernet cables can simply be strung from one machine to the next, using the T-connectors supplied with the interface cards, and with a terminator plug installed on both ends. This wiring layout is called a *bus topology*. As long you have at least six feet of cable between each pair of machines, and the total bus length does not exceed 186 yards, you virtually can't go wrong. This is, of course, a vast simplification of a very complicated subject, but on this small a network, only the most basic wiring rules are applicable.

Installing Peer-to-Peer Services

Manually installing Windows 95's peer networking capabilities is merely an extension to the network client installation procedure outlined in Chapter 24, "Installing Windows 95 as a Network Client." Windows 95's Client for Microsoft Networks allows a workstation to see and access resources on both client and server machines running the Windows NT, Windows for Workgroups, or Windows 95 operating systems.

▶ **See** "Installing the Client for Microsoft Networks," **p. 698**

All machines with a functioning Windows client are visible to all users on the network, even those that are not configured to share any resources. The only step that remains for a Windows 95 machine with the Client for Microsoft Networks already installed is to add a service into the networking configuration that will allow the computer to share its own resources with other users on the network. This is done through the implementation of a protocol called *SMB* (*server message blocks*) that is common to all of Microsoft's network-capable operating systems. To install the service, follow these steps:

1. Double-click the Network icon from the Windows 95 Control Panel and click <u>A</u>dd.
2. Select Service, click <u>A</u>dd again, highlight Microsoft and then File and Printer Sharing for Microsoft Networks. Click OK.
3. Click <u>F</u>ile and Print Sharing on the Network's Configuration page (see fig. 27.3), and select whether you want to share your drive(s), printer(s), or both. Click OK twice to complete the installation, and restart Windows when you are asked to do so.

FIG. 27.3
The File and Printer Sharing service enables the workstation to share its resources with others.

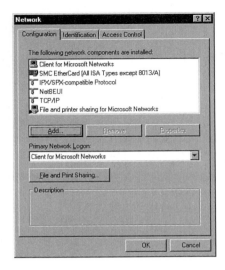

> **CAUTION**
>
> When installing the service, be sure not to choose the File and Print Sharing for NetWare Networks service by mistake. This is a completely different module that performs roughly the same workstation sharing tasks, but in a NetWare environment. It uses NCP, the NetWare Core Protocol, instead of SMBs, and makes a workstation appear to the network just as though it was a NetWare 3.12 server. It cannot run at the same time as the File and Print Sharing for Microsoft Networks service. One must be removed before the other is installed.

Windows Networking and Server Message Blocks

The SMB protocol was developed by Microsoft, Intel, and IBM to provide core networking functions between computers running the Windows network operating systems (Workgroups, NT, and 95), as well as LAN Manager, LAN Manager for UNIX, AT&T StarLAN, IBM LAN Server, 3Com➣, 3+Open➣, 3+Share➣, and DEC PATHWORKS operating systems. Similar in functionality to Novell's NetWare Core Protocol (NCP), SMB provides commands that control four of the most fundamental networking operations: session control, file and print services, and messaging.

Session control is used to establish and break down connections to other machines on the network. File and Print commands initiate communications of the appropriate type for the transmission of data files and print jobs, and messaging commands are used whenever an application sends or receives messages from another workstation.

While the basic Windows 95 Client for Microsoft Networks provides the client-side SMB functionality, the addition of the File and Printer Sharing service adds the capability for the Windows 95 machine to act as a server, by installing the VSERVER.VXD virtual device driver.

Windows 95 machines with both of these components installed are peers in that they possess both client and server functionality in the same machine. This is why you may hear a workstation referred to as a "server," when the discussion involves the sharing of its resources.

Configuration Options

The File and Printer Sharing Service has only two configuration options:

- *Browse Master.* Used to designate whether this workstation should be the Browse Master for the workgroup. A *Browse Master* is a workstation that maintains a list of the other machines in the local workgroup. This arrangement saves time and network traffic by not forcing each machine to search the entire network segment for other machines each time it is browsed. The Windows 95 operating system cooperatively assigns a default Browse Master for each workgroup, but you can use this option to override the assignment. The current workstation can be designated a permanent Browse Master or prevented from ever being assigned Browse Master status.

- *LM Announce.* Used to control whether the workstation's presence should be advertised to LAN Manager 2.x workstations on the network. The default value of this parameter is No, and it only needs to be set to Yes if you have clients running LAN Manager 2.x that will be accessing the resources of your workstation.

These options are accessible from the service's Properties sheet in the Network.

Integrating Windows 95 Peer Services into a Client/Server Network

Part
VIII

Ch
27

In a client/server network environment running Windows NT and/or NetWare servers, Windows 95 can add the peer-to-peer functionality described at the beginning of this chapter to the existing infrastructure, and it can do it far more easily than Windows for Workgroups ever could. What this means is that, in addition to connecting to servers, workstations also can communicate directly with each other.

Thus, Windows 95 users can easily create their own local peer networking groups within the overall structure of the existing client/server network. Nearby users can share hardware conveniently, and users can perform the bulk of the configuration and administration tasks without the constant intervention of corporate MIS personnel.

> **CAUTION**
>
> Always consult with your network administrator before adding peer-to-peer networking to a working environment on any substantial level. You may weaken the performance of the network for other users, and the network administrator may waste a great deal of time trying to track down the cause of the performance degradation.

Users can easily access both client/server and peer networking functions because of Windows 95's improved capability to present and manipulate network entities within a logical, usable interface that fully integrates servers and other workstations into the desktop metaphor. In Chapter 26, you learned how users can access client/server resources, and how the Windows 95 interface can empower network users to achieve a greater level of network understanding than was heretofore the norm. In the rest of this chapter, you see how Windows 95 integrates peer networking entities into the desktop metaphor, how you can organize them into logical groupings, and how to use login and security procedures to grant appropriate access rights to all network users.

Peer Networking and Routability

A large business network is actually more accurately described as an *internetwork*—a network of networks. Individual LANs, or network segments, each containing a limited number of machines, form natural divisions between departments, divisions, or geographical locations within a company. The default transport protocol used in all of the Microsoft networking products is called *NetBEUI*, and unlike NetWare's IPX and TCP/IP, NetBEUI is a non-routable protocol. This means that communication between Windows network machines is limited to those within the local segment, as shown in figure 27.4, unless you take explicit steps to provide routing between networks.

A workstation on LAN A, however, can enter into a peer networking relationship only with the other workstations on the same segment, because the NetBEUI protocol cannot be routed.

▶ **See** "Installing Windows 95 as a Network Client," **p. 689**

In order to route NetBEUI traffic between network segments, you must configure the Client for Microsoft Networks to use a second protocol, in addition to NetBEUI. When you add the Microsoft IPX/SPX-compatible or TCP/IP protocol to the network configuration and bind it to the Client for Microsoft Networks, the new protocol provides the routability that allows users to communicate with workstations on other network segments.

FIG. 27.4

All of the workstations on both LAN A and LAN B can function as clients to the NetWare server, because IPX (the default NetWare protocol) can be routed between network segments.

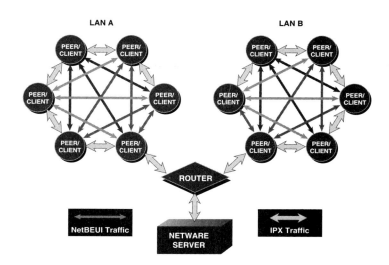

Although perceived by some as a shortcoming, the non-routable nature of NetBEUI can actually be an advantage on large networks where peer and client/server networking are combined. The NetBEUI protocol operates at peak performance on relatively small network segments. Further, using NetBEUI limits the amount of additional network traffic generated when you add peer-to-peer functionality to an existing network.

Peer Networking and Controlling Traffic Levels

The signal traffic on a local area network consists of a great deal more than just the files, print jobs, and other data being sent from one place to another. Networked computers communicate on a great many levels, and countless transactions are being conducted between machines, even when the computers all seem to be idle. Just the practice of a computer making its presence known to the other machines on the network adds traffic.

On a purely client/server NetWare network, for example, each server periodically sends out communications packets to inform all the other servers of its presence. If a large network has 50 servers and 1,000 workstations, the increase in this type of traffic incurred by having all of the workstations advertise their presence would be enormous. This is why it's usually best to keep peer networking traffic limited to the local segment whenever possible. That way, each LAN is subject only to the additional burden generated by its own machines.

In the networking scenario being presented here, it would not be the responsibility of the average Windows 95 user to monitor traffic levels on the network, even if he or she were to function as a peer network administrator. This is a very complex undertaking, requiring special tools and expertise. It's important, however, to be aware of the consequences of your actions. The object here is to remove some of the burden from the professional network administrator, not add to it.

continues

continued

> A network that is already approaching high traffic levels on a regular basis is likely to be pushed into the danger zone by the addition of peer traffic. Users, of course, are not likely to have any knowledge of this and many other factors affecting network performance throughout the enterprise. It's important to always consult your network administrator before implementing any new services that could negatively impact other users.

Creating Workgroups

A single network segment can contain dozens of machines—far more than a normal user would need to access on a regular basis. Microsoft peer networks are therefore broken up into still smaller collections of machines called workgroups, as shown in figure 27.5. A *workgroup* is a number of users whose relationship can be defined by any criteria that is convenient to the organization of the company or the network. Workgroup members may be users performing the same task, members of the same department or project team, or simply a group of people that sit near each other. For whatever reason, these users form a logical grouping based on their need to share the resources of each other's machines.

 When browsing through the Entire Network display of the Network Neighborhood, workgroups are listed at the top level. Expanding a workgroup icon then displays the workstations contained within it. Belonging to a workgroup in no way limits the user's access to resources outside of the group.

The workgroup to which a Windows 95 workstation belongs is defined in the Identification page of the Control Panel's Network dialog box, as shown in figure 27.6. Every Windows machine on a network must have a unique name, and must belong to a logical grouping, either a workgroup or a domain (see the next section for more information on domains). These will later be used as part of a UNC name, to identify the resources on this machine to the rest of the network, when it's time to create and access shares (see Chapter 28, "Accessing Windows 95 Workstation Resources").

A workgroup need not already exist for it to be named in the Identification page. Every machine on the network could create its own workgroup, simply by entering a unique name in this text box. The Computer Description text box has no function other than to further identify this computer to the rest of the network. It could contain the full name of the user, the machine's purpose, or nothing at all, if desired.

FIG. 27.5
A workgroup is a small collection of users within an existing network that have a regular need for access to each other's machines.

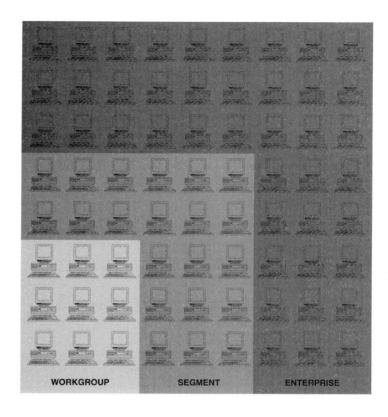

FIG. 27.6
Every networked computer must be identified by name and by a logical grouping.

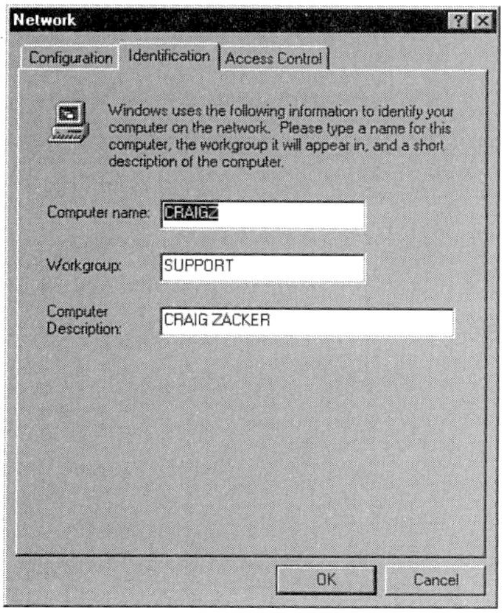

> **CAUTION**
>
> Care should be taken not to assign names to workgroups that duplicate existing server names. This may prevent other users from accessing the server.

When a Windows 95 machine is a part of a workgroup, it is solely responsible for maintaining security over its own resources. As described in the next chapter, shares are created to allow other users access to a machine's drives and printers. These shares are, in a workgroup, individually password-protected by each machine. This is one reason why workgroup computing should be limited to relatively small groups where security is not a major issue.

Using Domains

On a network that uses Windows NT as its network operating system, users are probably already using a domain login to gain access to client/server network resources. A *domain* is a logical grouping of computers that is entirely controlled and administered from a Windows NT server. While share passwords in a workgroup are stored on the individual machines where the shares are located, passwords and all security information for domain users is stored on a server that has been designated as a *domain controller*. In order for one workstation to access a drive on another workstation, both users must have valid accounts on the domain controlling server.

Two screens in the Windows 95 Network dialog box are essential to the use of a domain logon. The Properties sheet for the Client for Microsoft Networks contains a Login Validation section, as shown in figure 27.7. To log on, the user must enable this section and specify a domain name. The Access Control page of the main Network sheet allows the selection of *Share-level* or *User-level* access control to the devices on that workstation. You must specify the domain name here if you intend to use the domain's security information to control access to shared devices.

N O T E User-level access control is not limited to Windows NT domains. A NetWare server also can be specified if the File and Printer Sharing service for NetWare networks has been installed. ■

FIG. 27.7
Logon Validation must be
enabled and a domain name
supplied in order to perform
a Windows NT domain logon.

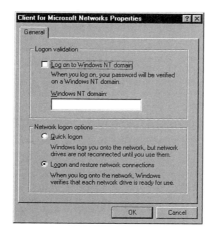

User-Level versus Share-Level Security

When deciding on which type of security validation to use, keep the nature of the resources being protected in mind. Traditional network security policies dictate that sensitive data should always be stored on server drives, for protection against both intrusion and accidental loss.

Adding peer networking as an adjunct to a client/server arrangement is supposed to be a tool of convenience, and user-based security can sometimes defeat that purpose. If you regularly have to disturb a network administrator to have him or her create user accounts on the Windows NT server in order to grant access to workstation devices, then you defeat the purpose of implementing a peer system, in part. You must also consider your network's existing security policies before selecting an access control method.

Share-level security has its drawbacks as well. It is relatively limited in its access rights, allowing only a choice between read-only and full access to a shared drive, while user-level access rights can be more specifically customized. Share-level security also is subject to the whims of each workstation's user. If a member changes passwords, for example, without informing the other workgroup members, problems may result.

Situations like this are not insurmountable. Workgroup members can agree on a set of security policies that may involve, for example, the use of the same passwords for all group resources, or agreements on the sharing of particular resources. Remember, peer-to-peer is not just a technology; it's also a philosophy.

Part
VIII

Ch
27

Building a Workgroup Administrator

Very often the best-run departmental networks are those in which there is a knowledge-able networker among the regular members of the group. Some corporations are moving heavily towards decentralizing a portion of their MIS personnel. Instead of having specialized people concerned with only one aspect of the enterprise network, such as dedicated wide-area technicians and others who deal only with telephony, some companies are hiring (or cross-training) people for more general use and assigning them to specific departments.

This practice has two natural results. First, the corporation develops more well-rounded and generally capable MIS personnel, and second, the administrator becomes a member of the department that he or she is dedicated to servicing. A sense of team spirit develops, that leads the administrator to fight for the rights of co-workers when it comes to allocation of resources and equipment.

Implementing Windows 95 peer networking within a client/server environment will require at least one person who is familiar with the networking capabilities of the operating system, and the administrative tools that are included within it. This workgroup administrator should be responsible for designing and implementing the resource sharing policies observed by the users in the group. The job description is flexible, based on the needs of the users and the services already provided at the corporate level.

The Role of the Workgroup Administrator

The primary function of the workgroup administrator is to make the computing tasks of the less knowledgeable workgroup members easier. This is most often done by limiting their network environment to the resources they actually need to access regularly. One of the ironic qualities of Windows 95 is that it is easily capable of providing the user with an embarrassment of riches. Unlimited access to the contents of 100 different workstations is not going to make an employee's job easier.

A well-functioning workgroup has policies that limit user access to necessary resources. Such policies include the sensible creation of shares on each machine and a well-designed policy for the storage of files as well.

It is a good idea to create similar directory structures on all of the workgroup's computers. This practice gives users a basic familiarity with the layout all of the machines in the workgroup. Synchronizing directories also makes it easier for users to share applications that have been installed on other machines.

The administrator should also designate specific directories for the location of shared data files. The files may be grouped according to application, by project, or using any system convenient to the operation of the department. By collecting them all in the same place on each machine (such as a directory called \SHARED FILES), the administrator can create a documented standard for his workgroup's organization. With such a standard in place, new users can come up to speed quickly, and occasional users of the workgroup's equipment can find themselves in familiar surroundings.

The administrator also works behind the scenes to see that no one computer is carrying too much of the workgroup's weight. One of the primary drawbacks of peer networking is when a computer's background activities as a server detract from its efficiency as a client. If a dozen users are all constantly accessing files on a single computer, the performance level of the machine functioning as the server will suffer. The workgroup administrator must distribute shared hardware and software resources evenly throughout the group, and maintain an even level of traffic for each user, so that all of the group members can remain productive.

Windows 95 provides the administrator with the tools that he needs to perform these organizational tasks. Chapter 28 covers the procedures for creating and accessing peer network shares, and in Chapter 29, you learn how to effectively manage them. ●

Part
VIII

Ch
27

CHAPTER 28

Accessing Windows 95 Workstation Resources

by Craig Zacker

Creating a productive working environment isn't the easiest of tasks. You have to consider the mechanics of sharing workstation resources as well as examining the user policies and limitations of these workstations.

It also is important to balance the load between workstations and to consider the security level you want each workstation to have. With Windows 95, these issues are easily handled. ■

Sharing workstation resources

How to configure your workstation to share its drives, printers, and fax modems with other network users.

Securing shared resources

How to use Windows 95's security measures to prevent unauthorized access to your workstation's shared resources.

Using remote network access

How to access shared network resources from a remote Windows 95 computer using a dial-up connection.

Using the remote access server

How to configure a Windows 95 workstation to function as a remote access server, through which dial-up users can access network resources.

Balancing the load

How to organize a peer workgroup network for convenient and efficient sharing.

Creating Shares

Resources on a Microsoft Windows network are called *shares*. A share can be a hardware device, such as a modem or a printer; it can be a storage device, such as a CD-ROM or optical drive; or a share can be a logical entity on a hard disk drive, such as a volume, a folder, a directory, or a file. The owner of the server or workstation must explicitly designate a particular resource in that machine as shared in order for other users to access it over the network.

N O T E Whenever a computer on a Microsoft Windows network shares any device or resource, that computer is considered to be a server. *Peer-to-peer* means that computers can function as both clients and servers at the same time. ▪

Sharing a Drive

To create a shared drive, make sure that the File and Print Sharing dialog box in the Network dialog box has I Want to be Able to Give others Access to My Files enabled and that you have selected the desired access control method in the Access Control sheet. Then do the following:

1. Open the My Computer window or launch Explorer. Select the local drive or folder you want to share.

N O T E Any storage device attached to the workstation and mounted as a drive letter can be shared with other network users. ▪

2. Choose File, Properties, and click the Sharing tab. Or click the right mouse button and choose Sharing from the context menu.

3. Click Shared As to activate the option fields.

4. Enter a Share Name to identify the device to the network. Any text you enter in the optional Comment field also appears on all share listings.

 When assigning share names, remember these things:

- A share name need not describe the exact location of the share on the server—you can use any descriptive name.

- Appending a dollar sign ($) to the end of the share name prevents the share from being advertised to other machines browsing the network. Remote users gain access by specifying the correct UNC name.

The appearance of the rest of the Sharing page depends upon whether you have chosen to use share-level or user-level access control in the Network dialog box. To complete the drive-sharing process, follow the procedure outlined in the following section that is appropriate for the type of access control you have selected.

▶ **See** "User-level vs. Share-level Security," **p. xxx** (ch 27)

Using Share-Level Access Control

When you configure a workstation to use share-level access control, the Sharing page of the Properties sheet takes on the appearance shown in figure 28.1.

FIG. 28.1
Share-level access enables any user with the correct password to access a shared drive.

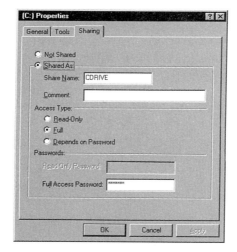

Use the following procedure to grant share-level access:

1. Select an Access Type to denote whether users are granted Read-Only or Full access. The Depends on Password option enables users of both levels to access the share, based on the password entered.

2. Enter password(s) for Read-Only and/or Full Access, depending on your Access Type selection.

3. Click OK. Confirm your password(s). Click OK again to create the share.

 To prevent accidental access, always assign a password for all shares.

Part VIII
Ch
28

Using User-Level Access Control

When you configure a workstation for user-level access, a slightly different Sharing page appears in the Properties sheet (see fig. 28.2).

FIG. 28.2

User-level access requires a Windows NT server for user validation.

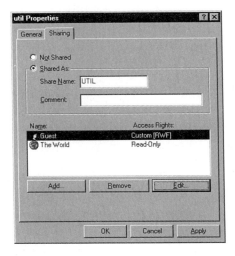

To grant access to shares on workstations configured for user-level access control, use this procedure:

1. Choose <u>A</u>dd and select a user or group from the list presented by the Windows NT validation server (see fig. 28.3).

FIG. 28.3

The list of users and groups presented comes from the Windows NT server specified in the Add Users dialog box.

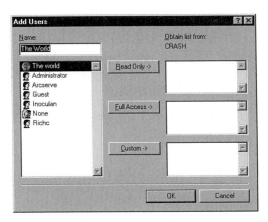

2. Select the level of access for that user—<u>R</u>ead-Only, <u>F</u>ull Access, or <u>C</u>ustom. Selecting <u>C</u>ustom produces the Change Access Rights dialog box, from which you can select for that user any or all of the rights shown in figure 28.4.

FIG. 28.4
You can grant a custom user any combination of these rights.

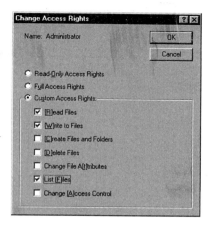

3. Click OK to add the user. Repeat the process for additional users or groups, if necessary. Then click OK to create the share.

After you have shared a drive or a folder, the icon in the local drive displays of the My Computer and Explorer windows changes to include an outstretched hand, as shown in figure 28.5.

FIG. 28.5
An extended hand is added to the icon for a shared local resource.

Shared drive ⎯

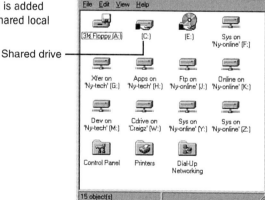

N O T E   When user-level access control is enabled, each user sharing the drive must be added to the access list, either individually or as part of a group. Individual user and group accounts are maintained on a Windows NT machine. This NT machine must be either the primary control server for the domain specified in the Properties sheet of the Client for Microsoft Networks or a Windows NT machine specified by name in the Access Control screen of the Network dialog box.

Part
VIII

Ch
28

continues

continued

Share-level access control enables any network user who furnishes the correct password to access the share. ■

> **CAUTION**
>
> If you switch your workstation's access control method from share-level to user-level (or vice versa) all of your shares will be lost. You must reshare all folders, printers, and fax modems, assigning rights under the new method, before users can access them.

Configuring Access Rights

As with most file systems, the permissions for shared drives in Windows 95 travel downward through the directory structure. When you grant a user full access to the root of your C: drive, you also grant that user rights to every folder and file on that drive. In Microsoft networking parlance, these rights are called *implied rights*. NetWare calls them *inherited rights*. When you use share-level access control, these rights, once granted, cannot be rescinded by any processes, other than disconnecting the user or ceasing to share the drive. You cannot grant or deny rights to individual files in Windows 95, as you can in Windows NT and NetWare. If you share a subdirectory of a previously created share and assign it more limited rights, the network user then has access to two different shares, each with its own permissions. The rights of the original share are unaffected by the creation of the new share.

N O T E As a security precaution, you can share only local drives on a Windows 95 workstation. You cannot "reshare" a network drive to provide access to another user who has insufficient rights to the source of the share. ■

You can effectively overlap shares with different permissions. If you grant read-only access to the root of a drive, and full access to a folder located farther down the tree, you provide the user with both forms of access to that subdirectory, depending on which share the user chooses to access.

 T I P You can tell if a folder is already included as part of another share by looking at the top of the Sharing page of the folder's Properties sheet, where the name of any enclosing share is listed.

Filtering Access Rights

When user-level access control is in effect, you can grant users or groups lesser rights to a subdirectory than they have to the parent. This capability adds an important measure of flexibility to the effective creation of shares on Windows 95 machines.

N O T E Windows 95 uses the term *folders* to refer to what the rest of the PC world calls *directories*. The two terms are, in most instances, interchangeable. ▪

For example, suppose that you are sharing a folder called \Data\IRS and that read-only access has been granted to all users (The World, in Windows NT parlance). If you then create a share of the folder \Data, granting full access to The World, the Change Security dialog box appears and notifies you that folders within the new share have already been granted different security rights (see fig. 28.6).

You are then given several choices:

- ▪ *Apply These Changes to Inside Folders*, causing full access to be granted to the \DATA\IRS folder, in this case.

- ▪ *Do Not Change Any Inside Folders*, retaining the read-only access to \DATA\IRS and granting full access to the rest of \DATA.

- ▪ *Display Each Folder Name Individually*, in which case another dialog box appears, asking if security changes should be applied to the \IRS folder within the \Data share. If you select Yes, then the \IRS folder in both shares will have read-only access. You answer the same question for any other folders within the \Data folder that have been shared.

FIG. 28.6
User-level access control enables you to assign individual access rights to folders within a share.

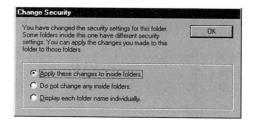

Clearly, the second or third option is preferable in most situations. You can allow users and groups to have full access to \Data and yet limit them to read-only access for \Data\IRS. This arrangement is similar to the Inherited Rights Mask in the NetWare file system.

TIP   Accessing the Sharing page of any shared folder's Properties sheet displays the *effective rights*, that is, the rights currently in force for that folder.

TROUBLESHOOTING

I've created a user-level share and assigned access rights to a particular user, but he is being denied access. What is wrong? Check the status of the user's account on the Windows NT validation server. The user's access will be subject to any restrictions specified on that server.

Maintaining Workgroup Security

The shortcomings of share-level security and the complexities involved in maintaining user-level access are reason enough for many network administrators to reject peer networking as a viable option on a corporate network. Network operating systems like Windows NT and NetWare are more flexible in enabling rights-allocation; you can grant users access to individual files and restrict access to a particular directory branch at any point. On a peer network contained within a client/server network, however, workstation security is less of a concern, because users still have access to server drives where they can store their most highly sensitive files in complete safety.

Even though most workgroups are comprised of users who share a certain degree of trust, you must have sufficient network protection to guard against the inadvertent intrusion, as well as the malicious one. If you organize a workstation's directory structure properly from the outset, you should enable effective sharing.

Connecting to Shared Drives

After you have successfully created a share out of a drive or folder, it immediately appears on the network as a subordinate object to its host machine. The Entire Network display in the Network Neighborhood or Explorer displays the names of all the workstations contained in the workgroup and the names of all the shares on each workstation, as shown in figure 28.7.

Clicking a share for the first time brings up a password validation screen, containing the usual option to save the password to the cache for future access. After access is granted, the folders and files of the share appear on a remote machine no differently than those of a local or a client/server network drive.

FIG. 28.7
Explorer shows all the shares
available on the workgroup.

You also can map a drive letter to a share on a peer workstation. The procedure is exactly the same as the process for mapping to drives on a client/server network. The UNC name specified in the Map Network Drives dialog box, or the NET USE command line, should appear as follows:

\\workstation\share_name

NOTE The NetBEUI protocol, by default, limits a Windows 95 workstation to 10 simultaneous connections to other Windows network machines, including servers. If you work in what is primarily a Microsoft shop, this number may not be sufficient. To increase the limit, open the Network dialog box in the Control Panel. In the Advanced page of the Properties sheet for the NetBEUI protocol, raise the number in the Maximum Sessions setting. You can set this value as high as 117, but set it only as high as you need for normal use. ▦

▶ **See** "Mapping a Network Drive," **p. 152**

Locating Computers

Despite the emphasis of this chapter on peer networking within the workgroup, Windows 95 is in no way limited to accessing the shared resources of nearby machines. You can access any peer workstation on the local network segment, and depending on the protocols being used, possibly any machine on the entire enterprise network as well.

▶ **See** "Peer Networking and Routability," **p. 784**

Part VIII Ch 28

In a large enterprise network environment, the sheer number of available machines may make it difficult to locate a particular server or workstation that you don't access frequently. For this reason, Windows 95 includes in its Find feature the capability to search for networked computers, as well as for files or folders.

To locate a computer on the network, follow these steps:

1. Choose Find from the Start menu, or choose Tools, Find in Explorer or Network Neighborhood. Then choose Computer.

2. Begin entering the UNC name of the machine in the space provided in the Find: Computer dialog box (see fig. 28.8). Entering even a partial name displays all the machines matching your selection.

3. Click the Find Now button to begin the search. The Find utility locates machines of all types: Windows NT servers, Windows NT, 95 or Workgroups workstations, as well as NetWare servers.

4. Use the File, Explore command or double-click a found machine name to view its contents.

FIG. 28.8
The Windows 95 Find utility can locate any machine visible on the network.

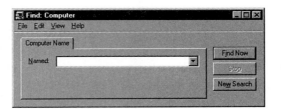

Sharing Workstation Drives

In Chapter 26, "Accessing Client/Server Network Services," you learned about enabling users to access files stored on network server drives. Setting up a workstation drive share is a bit different, though; where a network is a public space, an individual's workstation may seem more like his or her "home."

To make this arrangement work successfully, peer-to-peer networking participants need to follow certain rules of etiquette. Remote users must leave things more or less the way they found them, and the host must keep anything not fit for public display behind closed doors. Establishing specific policies for the workgroup is the best way to ensure that standards are maintained.

Another safeguard is to limit the shared areas of each workstation drive. Allowing a remote user free access to one's entire drive (or house) is asking for trouble, no matter how friendly the relationship between coworkers. Unlimited access also makes finding specific items or files harder for the remote user.

You can choose specific directories or files for shared access on NetWare or Windows NT server drives. On a Windows 95 machine, however, you may need to modify the directory structure to accommodate the need for security. In many cases, if you grant access to a folder, you cannot prohibit access to anything contained within that folder.

Sharing Applications

To create an effective file-sharing arrangement, you must first decide exactly what material on each user's drive needs to be shared. This decision isn't as easy as it used to be. At one time, if you just copied the contents of the \WP51 directory from one computer to another, you had a fully functional copy of WordPerfect. You cannot simply copy a directory with today's Windows applications, which often require INI settings and library files located in several different directories. Even users who have become rather adept at modifying Windows 3.1 INI files may be daunted by the prospect of the Windows 95 Registry.

To effectively share a Windows 95 application, you usually need to perform a network installation to the machine doing the sharing. This way, remote users can install the program themselves from the share, adding the appropriate settings to their own configuration files but leaving the actual executables on the shared drive.

This technique can be an effective means of conserving hard disk space, especially when several people use an application only occasionally. Licensing issues, however, may interfere with this practice. Many applications today protect themselves against users installing multiple copies of a single-user product on a network. In other cases, the terms of the license may deem this practice to be perfectly acceptable, as long as only one person is using the application at a time.

You can effectively share smaller binaries over the network as well. DOS command-line utilities should cause no problems, and many small Windows utilities will function properly from a remote workstation.

N O T E Even the simpler Windows programs, like small utilities used for managing compressed files or viewing graphics, are comprised of several files in addition to the actual executable. Typically, some of the other files are dynamic link libraries (DLLs) that are called while the program is running. Many installation programs copy DLLs to the \Windows\System directory, so they are always available for use. (When a program searches for one of its files, it always checks the \Windows\System directory before running the PATH.)

Storing a copy of any required DLLs in the actual program directory will, in some cases, allow the program to run from another workstation on the network without installing it, as long as the working directory in the remote icon's Properties sheet specifies the program directory on the host machine. Other applications cannot be run this way, because they may require that their OLE objects be entered into the local machine's Registry. ▨

Sharing Data Files

Aside from sharing applications, the other major reason for sharing drives is to access data files. Administrators must take particular care regarding the granting of simultaneous read/write access to such files by multiple users.

Depending on the file type, more than one user may or may not be able to access the file at the same time. Applications usually deal with a second user attempting to open a file in one of three ways:

■ *By denying the user any access at all.* The file locks open, and any attempt to address it by another process generates an error message.

■ *By allowing the user read-only access.* Some applications open a copy of the file, denying write access to the original but enabling the user to save it to another file name, if desired.

■ *By sharing the file between the two users.* Only files specifically designed for sharing should be accessible by multiple users. Usually, this method is possible only with some database file types that lock individual records (divisions within the file) rather than the entire file.

When sharing data files, the administrator needs to be conscious of the way that the associated applications deal with simultaneous accesses. If, for example, a workgroup uses a particular Microsoft Excel spreadsheet file to document and track the progress of a project, then users may need only to refer to the file at some times, and at other times they may need to update it.

Most likely, only one user will have read/write access to the file. Any other users will be in read-only mode, as imposed by the application. However, Microsoft Excel enables a user to explicitly open a file in read-only mode by marking a checkbox in the Open dialog box. In this case, a conscientious workgroup member who requires only read access to the spreadsheet can leave the read/write access available for another person's use.

Successfully enabling the sharing of single-user files represents the essence of well-planned workgroup computing. To construct such a cooperative dynamic, the network administrator must be fully aware of both the system capabilities and the needs of all workgroup members.

Sharing CD-ROMs and Other Removable Drives

Although almost every home computer now sold includes a CD-ROM, this component is not usually standard equipment on the average business machine. One of the outstanding advantages to peer networking is the capability to share a CD-ROM drive among several users without the need to install it on a file server (a complicated process for everyone involved, especially in a NetWare environment).

NetWare and CD-ROM Drives

Loading a CD-ROM onto a NetWare file server requires the use of NLMs devoted to that task. You must allocate memory to support the additional disk space of the CD-ROM, and you must remount the volume every time the disk is changed. These tasks result in increased expense and aggravation for the network administrator.

On the user side of the equation, a NetWare-mounted CD-ROM appears as a new volume on the server. The name of the volume is taken from the volume label of the CD itself, so each disk creates a different volume. Although this technique provides a good way of knowing what disk is currently in the drive, it also forces users to map a new drive letter whenever they access a different CD-ROM.

When a CD-ROM drive is installed on a Windows 95 workstation, sharing the drive is an easy matter. The procedure is the same as that for sharing a local hard drive.

▶ **See** "Creating Shares," **p. 794**

Except in rare cases, you should create a CD-ROM share at the root of the drive. Although you can create a share from a specific directory on a CD-ROM, creating a share at the root enables you to use that same share for any disk loaded in the drive. You need only provide read-only access to a CD-ROM.

N O T E   Even though a CD-ROM is a read-only device, limiting the CD-ROM share to read-only access provides benefits to the user. When a user with full access attempts to save changes to a write-protected drive, an error message is generated, forcing the user to Cancel or Retry the operation. When a user is granted read-only access to the share, issuing a Save command bypasses the error and automatically produces the Save As dialog box. The user can write the changes to another drive if necessary. ▓

Using Networked CD-ROMs

CD-ROMs are rapidly becoming the preferred method of software distribution for users and manufacturers alike. When installing software from a CD-ROM drive accessed over the network, take note of whether the product is being completely installed to the local hard drive, or if it requires later access to the CD-ROM.

Many informational resource CDs, as well as games, install a viewer or other executable to the local drive and access the bulk of their application files from the CD-ROM itself. In these cases, the application sets up pointers to the original location of the drive so it can easily find the drive later. These pointers are nearly always in the form of drive letters.

Therefore, take the following steps to ensure that applications on CD-ROM are installed properly:

- Map a drive to the CD-ROM when installing software that requires access to the disk to run properly. Do not use the Network Neighborhood to browse the drive, unless the software is expressly designed for use with Windows 95.

- Make the drive mapping a permanent one if you want to access the data on the CD repeatedly.

This latter step is necessary because changing the drive letter of the CD-ROM drive may prevent the application from locating its data files. Some applications (like the Windows 95 Setup program) are well-behaved when this obstacle occurs and prompt you to specify the location of the CD when the application cannot find it. Other applications are more belligerent and refuse to run unless you reinstall the application from the new drive letter.

Using Networked Optical Drives

When sharing other types of drives with removable media, follow the same procedure as for a CD-ROM, with the exception of the rights assignment. When you are creating a drive sharing plan, you must consider the access rights to removable drives with read/write capability (such as magneto-optical drives) just like those of any hard disk. Again, though, create the share at the root of the drive so you can change the media without resharing.

 T I P You can share CD-ROM drives mounted on Windows for Workgroups workstations over a Microsoft peer network. To do so, be sure to include the /S switch on the line in the AUTOEXEC.BAT file that loads the Microsoft Windows CD extensions (MSCDEX.EXE).

Networking Tape Drives

Tape drives fall into still another category, because you typically don't mount these devices as drive letters on the local machine. Instead, the devices are directly addressed through software specifically designed for that purpose.

Traditionally, network backup software runs on a server and addresses tape devices directly attached to that server. For a tape drive attached to a workstation, you must instead use a standalone backup software package. However, many workstation backup products can back up network drives as well.

Cheyenne Software and Arcada Software, which also include agent services for their network backup products in Windows 95, have both recently released workstation backup packages for Windows 95. These products can preserve long file names and back up any device (local or network) that is mapped to a drive letter, including Windows NT and NetWare drives. Thus, you can back up an entire workgroup's data to a single tape, not by sharing the tape drive's functionality with the workstations, but by bringing the workstations' data over the network to the tape.

Sharing Workstation Printers

To allow peer network users to access a printer installed on a Windows 95 workstation, you must first install the printer in the normal manner and enable the I Want to be Able to Allow others to Print to My Printer(s) feature in the File and Print Sharing page in the Network dialog box. As with drive sharing, be sure to select the desired access control method in the Access Control page of the Network dialog box.

To create a printer share, use the following procedure:

1. Open the Printers window from the Settings option on the Start menu or through the Control Panel.

2. Highlight the printer you wish to share and choose Sharing from the File menu or from the printer's context menu (see fig. 28.9).

 T I P Notice that the Sharing dialog box is actually one page of the printer's Properties sheet. You can access it via the Sharing tab.

3. Select the Shared As radio button and enter a Share Name. The printer appears with this name to the rest of the network. You also may (optionally) enter further descriptive information for the printer in the Comment field.

4. If you are using share-level access, enter a password to protect access to the printer. For user-level access, select the users or groups who are permitted to use the printer. Click OK to create the share.

Whether your workstation is configured for user-level or share-level access control, a shared printer has only two security options: full access or no access. After you have created the share, an outstretched hand is added to the printer's icon to indicate its status.

▶ **See** "Installing and Deleting Printers," **p. 226**

Part
VIII
Ch

Accessing Shared Printers

Configuring Windows 95 to access a shared workstation printer is no differ printer was installed on a server, except that workstation printers do not s' and Print feature. You can launch the Add New Printer Wizard by any of methods:

FIG. 28.9
Use the Sharing page to assign the printer a networking name and to provide access control.

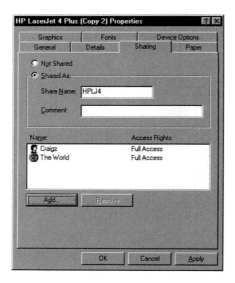

- Open the Printers window and double-click the Add Printer icon.
- Locate the printer share in the Network Neighborhood or Explorer and choose File, Install.
- Drag the shared printer icon from the Network Neighborhood or Explorer window to the Printers window.

- Launch the Add New Hardware icon from the Control Panel and select Printer from the list of devices.

Administering Workstation Print Queues

Windows 95's all-or-nothing printer security limitation affects the administration of print queues on workstations. As with a server-based printer, users can double-click a shared workstation printer's icon and open a window displaying all the pending print jobs in the queue. In Windows 95, all users have equal access to the queue. Any user with permission to access to the printer can reorder the pending jobs, as well as pause or cancel any job in the queue.

However, the queue for a server-based printer is located on that network server, and the rights to manipulate the queue are also controlled by the server. NetWare and Windows NT both have a more extensive array of permissions in regard to accessing print queues. You can limit users' access to only the rights that they require, giving them a distinct advantage in the area of printer management. This should not be a significant problem in a cooperative workgroup, but if the resources of a client/server network coexist with the peer network, you may choose one of several alternatives to workstation-based print queues.

The first alternative is to avoid workstation-based printers entirely and run all printers from the client/server network. A unit equipped with a network adapter such as the HP JetDirect can be located anywhere a network connection exists. HP JetDirect also utilizes a server's print queue, providing additional administrative security and lessening the burden on the workstation that would otherwise be servicing the printer. The additional expense of the network card for the printer is negligible when you consider the average company networking budget.

> **N O T E** You must install the additional RPC (Remote Procedure Call) Print Provider service with the Client for Microsoft Networks to provide Windows 95 with the capability to administer print queues on Windows NT servers. The service is installed through the Network protocol by adding a new service, clicking the Have Disk button, and browsing to the \Admin \Nettools\Rpcpp folder of the Windows 95 CD-ROM.

The other alternative to standard Windows 95 printer sharing is to leave the printer attached to the workstation but utilize a NetWare print queue. ▓

▶ **See** "Using the Microsoft Print Services for NetWare," **p. 842**

▶ **See** "Using Network Printers," **p. 766**

Sharing a Workstation's Fax Modem

Windows 95 incorporates fax services into the operating system using its Microsoft Exchange front end. Users can fax documents directly using the File, Print command of any application or the File, Send command of any application that uses the messaging application programming interface (MAPI). When both sender and recipient are using the Microsoft At Work binary file transfer protocol, you can even edit the faxed documents.

Windows 95 also can share the use of a workstation's fax modem, just as easily as it can share a drive or a printer. The workstation essentially becomes a fax server, enabling multiple network users to submit documents to its queue for sequential servicing by the modem.

> **N O T E** Incoming faxes are held at the workstation where the modem is installed. Windows 95 does not have the capability to automatically route the faxes to their intended recipients. The person designated as the fax server administrator must perform this task manually. ▓

Before configuring a workstation for modem sharing, you must install the modem on the fax server workstation. You also must install Microsoft Exchange and Microsoft Fax on both the fax server and the client workstations.

▶ **See** "Understanding the Windows 95 Communications System," **p. 284**

To configure a workstation modem for network sharing, use the following procedure:

1. Double-click the Mail and Fax icon in the Control Panel. Select Microsoft Fax and click Properties.

 TIP You can access the same sheet from the Microsoft Exchange Inbox window by choosing Tools, Microsoft Fax Tools, Options.

2. Select the Modem tab in the Microsoft Fax Properties sheet and enable the option to Let Other People on the Network Use My Modem To Send Faxes (see fig. 28.10).

FIG. 28.10
You can install and configure modems through the Microsoft Fax Properties sheet.

3. Click Properties, and a sharing sheet appears similar to the sheet box for sharing a drive or a printer.

N O T E When you share a fax modem, a new shared directory is created on the workstation's C: drive. The path to that directory (C:\Netfax, by default) appears in the title box of the Properties sheet. This directory is where queued faxes are stored pending transmission. The seemingly incongruous options for read-only and full access that are provided when you create the modem share are actually referring to the access rights for this directory. You also can control access to network fax services from the directory's own Sharing dialog box. Always assign network users full access rights to the shared directory if they will be using the fax server. ■

4. Click the Shared As radio button and enter a Share Name for the modem. If you are using share-level security, select Full for the access type and enter a password if you want. For user-level security, select users or groups who will have access to the share.

5. Click OK. Verify your passwords, if necessary, and then click OK again to create the share.

Accessing a Shared Fax Modem

After you have completed the preceding steps, any Windows 95 workstation on the network can make use of the shared fax modem. To configure the workstation to utilize the shared modem, use the following procedure:

1. Open the Microsoft Fax Properties sheet as you did in step 1 of the preceding section.

2. Select the Modem tab and click Add.

3. Select Network Fax Modem and click OK.

4. Enter the UNC name for the shared modem in the Connect to Network Fax Server dialog box. Click OK to close each dialog box.

N O T E   The Connect to Network Fax Server dialog box does not contain a browse feature to facilitate the location of the fax modem. Notice the UNC name of the modem before you begin the procedure.

All of the functionality provided by Microsoft Fax is now available to the remote workstation. In fact, performance will be better than using a local modem, because the remote workstation does not have to process the fax transmission in the background. Windows 95 returns all system resources to the user as soon as the printing operation is complete.

Using Remote Network Access

Windows 95 defines the term *networking* more generally than most other operating systems do. The connection of two computers via modems and a telephone line is considered a network interface just as a LAN connection is. Windows 95 integrates these functions into the Network protocol along with the other networking components.

The Windows 95 Dial-up Adapter is a driver like any other adapter driver, except the operating system uses the adapter to direct network traffic to a modem rather than a network

Part

VIII

Ch

28

interface card. A workstation can use this adapter to connect to an Internet service provider, to another Windows 95 workstation, or to a Windows NT remote access server.

This section teaches you how to configure a Windows 95 workstation to be a dial-up server or a client. With this arrangement, a remote machine can dial into a Windows 95 workstation that is connected to the office LAN, and access not only the workstation's resources, but the LAN's resources as well. The remote machine can attach to the network like any workstation with a direct connection and perform any of the normal network functions, albeit more slowly.

> **N O T E**   Do not confuse *remote access* with *remote control*. Some communications products
> enable an offsite computer to dial into a host workstation and commandeer its
> interface by redirecting screen, keyboard, and mouse signals to the modem. When the remote
> user runs a program, all the microprocessing tasks are performed by the host computer. This
> process is remote control.
>
> With Windows 95, the remote machine literally connects to the host as a peer. The host, despite
> functioning as a remote access server, continues to operate as a normal network workstation.
> Both the host and remote users can run different programs, with each machine doing its own
> microprocessing. This procedure is remote access. ■

Before configuring Windows 95 to function as a remote access server (or client), you must install a modem and the Dial-up Networking module from the Windows 95 CD-ROM, as well as the File and Print Sharing for Microsoft Networks service.

▶ **See** "Getting and Installing Internet Explorer," **p. 985**

▶ **See** "Working with Your Modem," **p. 302**

Using the Dial-Up Server

The Windows 95 dial-up server enables a single computer running any one of the following clients to access its internal resources using a modem connection:

- ■ Windows 95
- ■ Windows NT
- ■ Windows for Workgroups
- ■ The Windows 3.1 Remote Access Server (RAS) client
- ■ Any other Point-to-Point Protocol (PPP) client

The server also functions as an IPX/SPX or NetBEUI gateway, enabling these clients to access other network resources that are available to the dial-up server through these protocols.

N O T E Although the Windows 95 dial-up server can route NetBEUI and IPX/SPX traffic to the remote client, it cannot perform this function for TCP/IP. As a result, a remote user cannot access a corporate Internet connection by dialing into a Windows 95 workstation. Such access would require a Windows NT server, which functions as an IP router to its remote access clients. ▓

Configuring the Dial-Up Server

The dial-up server module is available only on the Microsoft Plus! for Windows 95 CD-ROM. You must install the dial-up server during the standard Setup procedure for the package.

After installing the dial-up server, use the following procedure to configure the workstation to be a dial-up server:

1. Open the Dial-up Networking window from the Start, Programs, Accessories menu.
2. Choose Connection, Dial-up Server (see fig. 28.11).

FIG. 28.11
Use the Dial-Up Server dialog box to configure a modem for remote access.

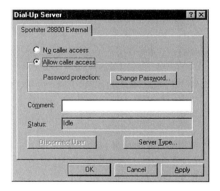

3. Choose the Allow Caller Access radio button.
4. Click the Change Password or Add button, depending on your access control method.
   - For workstations configured for share-level security, click the Change Password button. Enter and verify a password for entry to the server, and click OK twice to close the dialog box.
   - For workstations configured for user-level security, click the Add button to select users or groups who are allowed access to the dial-up server. Click OK to close the dialog box.

When you close the dialog box, the dial-up server is ready to receive calls.

Part
VIII
Ch
28

N O T E The Server Type button in the Dial-up Server dialog box contains settings you should not need to alter for a Windows 95 to Windows 95 connection. The Type of Dial-up Server, when left at its default setting, causes the server to attempt first to initiate a PPP connection, and then drop to a Remote Access Server (RAS) connection, if necessary. The PPP server defaults to the use of software, not hardware, compression. For an RAS connection, the opposite is true. ▪

N O T E The point-to-point protocol (PPP) is a medium-speed Data-link layer protocol used for direct serial communications between two nodes, two routers, or a node and a router. It is most commonly used for Internet communications. ▪

Ensuring Dial-Up Security

Securing a dial-up connection is more important than the workgroup security considerations covered in "Configuring Access Rights," earlier in this chapter. An unprotected phone line is a gateway not only to your workstation, but possibly to your network. Always require a password for any form of dial-up access to any computer.

Windows 95's access control mechanisms, both user-level and share-level, only provide the means to allow or disallow a remote computer's access to the server. Beyond that, the server's resources are protected by the security measures implemented during the creation of the shares. In short, dial-up users are subject to the same share restrictions as any other network users.

When you implement user-level access control for a dial-up server, requiring a correct user name protects the machine against the risk of intrusion by someone outside the company. For this reason, avoid granting access to Guest accounts, or to groups like Everyone or The World when dial-up access is used.

Installing and Configuring a Remote Network Access Client

For the purpose of connecting to another Windows 95 computer, the following instructions assume that the client computer is not already attached to a local area network. Before you configure a Windows 95 machine to be a Remote Network Access (RNA) client, the following components must be installed on the workstation (all the software is available on the Windows 95 CD-ROM):

- A modem
- The Client for Microsoft Networks
- The Dial-up Adapter

■ The NetBEUI protocol (and the IPX/SPX protocol, if your network uses it)

■ The Dial-up Networking module

You must create a new client (and an associated icon) in the Dial-up Networking window for each different computer or service provider you connect to with the Windows 95 machine. Each client maintains its own settings and scripts, if needed, for logging into the host computer. Use the following procedure to create a dial-up client:

1. Double-click the Network icon from the Control Panel and click the Identification tab.

2. Enter the Computer Name and the workgroup of the computer into which you will be dialing.

3. Click the Access Control tab in the Network dialog box and select the type of security the dial-up server uses.

4. Click OK to close the Network dialog box and restart the computer when you are offered this option.

5. After the reboot, open the Dial-up Networking window from the Start, Programs, Accessories menu.

6. Double-click the Make New Connection icon to activate the Make New Connection Wizard, as shown in figure 28.12.

7. Enter an identifying name for the new client you are creating, and be sure that the modem you wish to use on the client machine is specified. You may click the Configure button to alter the settings for the modem, if needed. Click the Next button to proceed to the next screen.

8. Enter the area code, telephone number, and the country code for the computer you will be calling. Click Next to go to the next screen.

9. Click Finish to complete the process and create a new icon in the Dial-up Networking window.

FIG. 28.12
Use the Make New Connection Wizard to configure Windows 95 to dial into a particular host server.

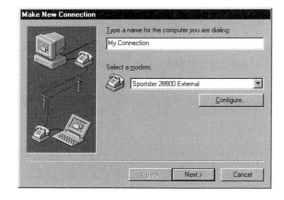

After you have configured the client, double-click the new icon and enter the required password to initiate the call to the host computer. The status of the call attempt appears as you progress through the connection and password-checking sequences. After the computers have successfully established a connection, access to the host computer's resources is available to the remote machine through the normal Windows 95 interface.

The newly created icon in the Dial-up Networking window has a Properties sheet through which you can alter the same modem settings as in step 7 of the preceding steps as well as additional settings provided through an Options page. One setting you may find useful is on the Connection page of this sheet (see fig. 28.13). After you connect to a host, the remote resources are so completely integrated into Windows 95 that you may find yourself forgetting that a dial-up connection is active. Enabling the call disconnect feature under Call Preferences is a good idea so your connection terminates after the specified period of inactivity.

FIG. 28.13

The client's Properties sheet contains a number of settings you may alter to suit that particular client.

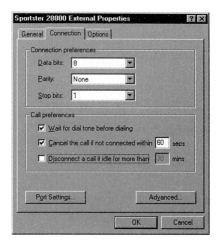

Clicking the Server Type button in the Properties sheet of your new connection icon presents a dialog box that enables you to modify the client for use with a variety of hosts (see fig. 28.14). When you are connecting to a Windows 95 dial-up server, the default settings usually suffice. The sole exception may be the Require Encrypted Password checkbox under Advanced Options. You must set both the client and the server to use password encryption or not to use it.

FIG. 28.14
The Server Types dialog box
enables you to modify the
client for use with various
host computers.

Sharing Drives over the Internet

On a client/server network with Windows NT servers, TCP/IP has become a very popular protocol. Windows NT has features that overcome the protocol's primary administrative drawback—the need to assign unique IP addresses to every machine on the network. NT's *dynamic host configuration protocol* (DHCP) dynamically assigns addresses to network workstations. The *Windows Internet naming service* (WINS) maintains host tables for the rapidly changing network more efficiently than a traditional *domain naming service* (DNS).

WINS also performs routing functions for TCP/IP, and one of the WINS's by-products is its capability to allow Windows NT drives to be shared over the Internet. When you configure a Windows NT server on your network to use the WINS module, and give it an external IP address (that is, an address visible from outside the company's firewall), then you can set up any Windows 95 machine with an Internet connection to contact that server through the WINS.

ON THE WEB

For more information on WINS server try

http://www.winserve.com

Open the TCP/IP Properties sheet in the Network protocol of a remote Windows 95 machine and enable WINS Resolution in the WINS Configuration tab, specifying the correct IP address for your company's WINS server. Once you have done this, you can connect to any Internet service provider using either a dial-up or a direct connection and access shares on the WINS machine.

Unlike a local area network connection to the Windows NT machine, the shared resources are not browsable. In other words, you cannot open the Network Neighborhood window and see your Windows NT machine there. You must know the address of the server and the UNC names of the shares and have appropriate rights to access them. With this information, you can then map a drive or use the Run command on the Start menu to specify the share name and gain access.

This feature could be an enormous convenience for companies that must provide remote network access to distant users. Instead of maintaining a modem pool on the Windows NT machine and having users incur long distance phone charges to dial into the home office, the company can set up the NT server with WINS and have users call a local Internet provider (wherever they happen to be) and gain virtually the same access to that server. Instead of using a high-priced telephone network to establish a remote connection, telecommuters can use the Internet. The possibilities for increasing the flexibility and economy of remote data communications using this technology are unlimited.

Of course, some users may perceive this capability as a gigantic security hole. Some servers may already be accessible from outside the company, without their administrators even knowing it. When administrators are aware of its capabilites, however, WINS can offer users remote network access, with no additional investment in modems and telephone lines.

Balancing the Load

The overall performance of a workstation may degrade significantly if a large number of other users continually access its resources. On a peer network, therefore, the best arrangement is to spread the shared resources of the workgroup evenly among the workstations.

To achieve this balance, you may need to store a shared application on a different computer than its data files, or you may need to distribute files of a similar type among several machines. You also should spread hardware around the workgroup.

Creating a Dedicated Peer Server

There is an alternative approach to the problem of balancing resources within a workgroup. If multiple users rely heavily on Windows 95 to provide fax and print services, then you may want to dedicate a computer to duty as a fax and/or print server.

Windows 95 provides a number of controls that enable the user to adjust the priority allotted to various system activities. You can optimize a machine that is not used as a production workstation to provide peak performance for tasks like printing and faxing, which are usually background processes.

The use of a dedicated machine may seem contradictory on a peer network, and the concept of a *peer server* is something of an oxymoron, but many different factors contribute to the way in which a network is designed. Modest needs call for modest solutions, and Windows 95 has emerged as the much-needed filler of a significant gap between single-user systems and fully realized network systems.

For example, if a limited group of users required fax services, only two ready solutions were available at one time. You could equip each user's workstation with its own modem and its own dedicated telephone line, each of which would remain idle most of the time. You could also invest a significantly greater amount of time, money, and administrative effort on a network server-based faxing system. Now, for the price of a single modem and phone line, users who need fax services can access them using the operating system software they already possess.

Using Workgroup Applications and Utilities

The Windows 95 operating system's peer networking capabilities are by no means limited to hardware sharing. Workgroup members can use Windows 95 to communicate among themselves at many different levels. If you do not already have a corporate e-mail system in place, Microsoft Exchange provides that capability. The \Other folder on the Windows 95 CD-ROM also contains several groupware utilities that have been part of Windows since Windows for Workgroups was first released, but which still may be useful to Windows 95 users.

Chat

Chat enables a Windows 95 user to select another Windows network user from a list and page them for a text-only chat. This feature can be a useful form of intermediate communication, falling somewhere between e-mail and the telephone. Chat is particularly valuable for contacting someone while they are talking on the phone.

Clipbook Viewer

The Clipbook viewer extends the capabilities of the Windows Clipboard, enabling network users to share captured information. Users working with the same data can easily share quotes, excerpts, or boilerplate text between their open applications on different machines. ●

Part
VIII

Ch
28

CHAPTER 29

Windows 95 Network Administration

by Craig Zacker

The Windows 95 operating system includes an assortment of tools and utilities that integrate many day-to-day network administration tasks into the user interface. In support of the scenario presented by the previous chapters, in which the best elements of peer-to-peer and client/server networking are combined into a single workgroup environment, this chapter and the next divide these utilities into two basic groups. This chapter concentrates on tools intended for the workgroup administrator, that will be used on a daily basis. Chapter 30, "Customizing Windows 95 Network Installations," examines the tools that are geared more towards the corporate networking personnel who are responsible for integrating Windows 95 into the enterprise network on a large scale.

Of course, the dividing line between these two administrative positions is sometimes a highly arbitrary one. The decision as to who will perform the day-to-day administration tasks for a workgroup must be based on the skills of the available personnel and the division of responsibilities in the company. However, this chapter presents the material in such a way that the advanced Windows 95 user should be capable of taking on some

Configure a Windows 95 workstation for remote administration

How to install the additional modules and activate the options to monitor and configure a remote Windows 95 workstation over the network.

Monitor the system processes of Windows 95 workstations

How to use the Windows 95 System Monitor to track the activities of a workstation's processing, memory, and networking subsystems.

Monitor the shared resources of a workgroup

How to use the NetWatcher utility to track Windows 95 resources shared on a given workstation.

Edit the Windows 95 Registry from a remote location

How to modify the system configuration of a Windows 95 workstation by directly modifying its Registry from a remote location on the network.

Balance network traffic in a workgroup

How to use the Windows 95 network administration tools to determine if the shared resources of a workgroup are evenly divided among the workstations.

of the tasks that would previously have required the intervention of a professional network administrator. If a serious problem arises, a workgroup administrator may not always be qualified to resolve it, but he may be able to recognize that it exists. Sometimes, in networking, diagnosis is half the battle. ■

Creating a Remote Administration Environment

A remote administration environment is one in which a Windows 95 computer is used to alter the configuration settings and monitor the performance levels of other Windows 95 computers. Much of Windows 95's administrative functionality is based on utilities that can address the local workstation, or that can be directed by the administrator to a remote computer over the network. However, you must first configure each Windows 95 computer that will be addressed in this manner to allow remote administrative access.

Many Windows 95 administrative functions also require the installation of additional software components on one or both of the workstations involved. These components may be executables, network services, or protocols, and most are not part of the default Windows 95 installation.

In nearly all instances, however, a base workstation configuration providing the essential components for administrative communication is also required. Before using any of the tools discussed in this chapter, perform the following prerequisite procedures, unless other instructions are given. See the following sections for details.

- ■ Install the Client for Microsoft Networks, along with the File and Print Sharing for Microsoft Networks Service.
- ■ Configure the workstation for user-level access control.
- ■ Enable the Remote Administration feature.

N O T E The Windows 95 installation routine can be configured to automatically perform all of the preceding actions, whenever the operating system is installed on a workstation. This is done by modifying the script that controls the installation. See "Customizing Windows 95 Installation Routines" in Chapter 30 for more information on this process. ■

Using File and Printer Sharing for Administrative Access

Several of the Windows administrative utilities, when launched, immediately address the workstation on which they are executed. You must then direct them to another machine on the network to apply their functions at the remote location. In many cases, the remote workstation must play a part in advertising its availability on the network or in establishing a communications link for the utility to gain access. This is similar to the way in which shares are advertised to other network users, which helps explain the need for the File and Print Sharing service. Most of the administrative functions involve Windows network processes, requiring the Microsoft network variant of the service. However, there are cases in which the workstation's NetWare connectivity can be addressed, and the File and Print Sharing for NetWare Networks service is useful.

Using User-Level Access Control

Some of the Windows 95 administrative utilities, such as the System Monitor and the NetWatcher, are merely tools of convenience. Either they perform their function more efficiently from a remote location, or they relieve an administrator from having to walk over to each machine and displace its user to make a small modification to his workstation environment.

Other tools, however, are very powerful, and can profoundly affect a remote workstation's performance and/or working environment. A minor typographical error in a Registry entry, for example, can mean the difference between a computer that functions normally and one that doesn't boot at all.

For this reason, security is an important factor, and most of the more powerful administrative utilities will only function when user-level access control is in effect. Administrative access can then be limited to a select few individuals who can be trusted to know what they are doing.

Network Administration and the Fear Factor

Many computer users live in mortal fear of their machines. They are terrified that one day, they may make some small mistake that will cause a national data processing disaster, and bring the government to its knees. It is often difficult to convince people like this that on a well-designed network (where their access is very limited), they should not be able to do any major damage by accident.

Unfortunately, there are an equal number of people who are exactly the opposite in disposition. These are the fearless network heroes, rushing in where angels fear to tread, willing to yank the motherboard or reinstall the network operating system at a moment's notice, despite a distinct lack of knowledge or experience.

Neither of these archetypal figures holds great promise as a workgroup administrator. The fearful do too little, and the fearless too much. There is a definite dividing line between a power user who can provide help to his colleagues and develop a good resource sharing environment for the workgroup, and a person who can be entrusted to impose computing policy on others. A good administrator is an example of moderation—one who is led forward by his enthusiasm, but not blinded by it.

Enabling the Remote Administration Feature

To enable remote administration on a Windows 95 computer, use the following procedure:

1. From the Control Panel, open the Passwords Properties sheet and click the Remote Administration tab (see fig. 29.1).

FIG. 29.1
Select the users who will be granted remote administration access to any Windows 95 workstation with great care.

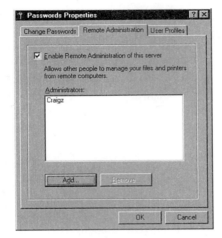

2. Click the Enable Remote Administration of this Server check box.

3. Depending on the type of access control selected for the workstation, either furnish a password for remote administrative access or click the Add button to select users or groups for access (see fig. 29.2).

4. Click OK to close each dialog box, and restart the computer when you are prompted to do so.

FIG. 29.2
User-level access control grants only a single level of access to the selected accounts—Full or None.

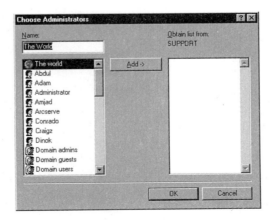

Enabling remote administration on a Windows 95 workstation creates two additional shares that are advertised to the network. They are named ADMIN$ and IPC$. ADMIN$ allows the remote administrator full access to the entire file system of the remote workstation, and IPC$ creates an *interprocess communication* link between the two computers. This link allows the distributed computing needed by some of the administrative tools to take place. Because the ADMIN$ and IPC$ shares both end with a "$," they are not visible to users when they browse the network in the normal manner. They are visible, however, in the Net Watcher application to a user with remote administration privileges.

 T I P When you enable user-level access control on a workstation by using the Network application or a setup script, remote administrative rights are automatically granted to the Domain Administrator group, if a Windows NT domain is the pass-through account validator; the Supervisor account, if a NetWare 3.x server is used; or the Admin account, if a NetWare 4.x server is the validator.

When you enable user-level access control with a system policy file, remote administrative rights are not automatically granted.

▶ **See** "Using System Policies" **p. 862**

Using Windows NT as an Administration Server

If your organization is making a serious commitment to Windows 95, and wishes to use all of its administrative features, the installation of a Windows NT machine may be a worthwhile investment, even in an all-NetWare shop. In addition to maintaining user accounts and providing pass-through user validation, a Windows NT machine also can perform the following valuable administrative functions:

- As a repository for the Windows 95 installation files, the server could be the source from which the operating system is installed to your company's workstations. You can customize Windows 95 setup routines to create workstation environments that contain only the components you select. The installation process also can be completely automatic, requiring no input at all from the user.

- A Windows NT machine also can function as the repository for Windows 95 user profiles and system policies. These are tools you can use to resolve several long-standing administrative problems, such as how to accommodate several users with one computer and single users who work at different computers.

- These functions are all possible in addition to Windows NT usual roles. The machine also could function as a post office for Microsoft Mail, a fax, print, file, or backup server, or any combination of these functions.

It is also not essential for an administrative machine to be running the Windows NT Advanced Server product. An NT workstation will function perfectly well as a pass-through server for user-level access control, as well as for any of the other functions previously listed. It is only if you intend to configure the machine as a high-capacity file server, or to service hundreds of users, that the advanced server product is absolutely necessary.

Remote Windows NT Administration

Whether a dedicated Windows NT machine is set up for workgroup administration purposes or an existing NT machine is used, a Windows 95 user need not have direct physical access to the Windows NT machine to perform the basic administrative functions that user-level access control requires.

Microsoft has released a collection of Windows NT user tools for Windows 95. These are remote access versions of the Windows NT User Manager, Server Manager, and Event Viewer utilities. These tools can give a workgroup administrator the ability to modify Windows NT user accounts and monitor the condition of the server as needed, without giving him access to the secured areas where servers are often kept.

ON THE WEB

The Windows NT User Tools have been released as part of the Service Pack 1 for Windows 95, which is available from Microsoft's World Wide Web site at **http://www.microsoft.com/windows/software/servpak1/sphome.htm**.

Administering Remote Workstations Through the Network Neighborhood

Once you have enabled the remote administration feature on a workstation, one of the easiest ways to access that workstation is through the machine's Properties sheet in the Network Neighborhood. Display the sheet by locating the workstation you wish to administer in Explorer or the Network Neighborhood window. Then select Properties from the workstation's context menu or from the Neighborhood window's File menu, and select the Tools tab to see a screen like that shown in figure 29.3.

The top two buttons launch the Net Watcher and System Monitor utilities, respectively. These are the most frequently used of the Windows 95 administrative tools. When you activate them through this interface, however, you gain an additional measure of convenience over simply running the tools from the Start menu.

FIG. 29.3

The Administrative Tools tab of a workstation's Properties sheet provides quick access to the most commonly used remote administration utilities.

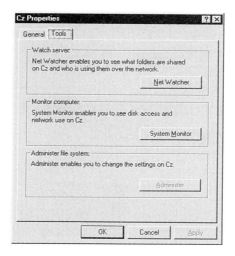

The Administer button opens a window that displays the regular as well as the administrative shares of the selected machine. Through this interface, you can manage the workstation's files with full access, even if the user has not explicitly shared them.

 As stated earlier in this chapter, many of the Windows 95 administrative utilities immediately address themselves to the local machine when you launch them. You must then point them to a remote computer by specifying its name or browsing to it. Activating either the Net Watcher or the System Monitor through a specific computer's Properties sheet omits this extra step. The application launches and immediately attaches to the remote machine.

The following sections cover the procedures for using these two basic utilities and the value that they can provide to the network administrator.

Using the System Monitor

The System Monitor displays the performance levels of selected Windows 95 processes in a graphical format in real time. Real time means that changes in the workstation's performance levels are presented as they happen. Its most beneficial use is in determining the underlying cause of system problems by identifying the process that is acting as a perf‎ mance bottleneck. Once you have identified the problem, steps can be taken to rect‎ and you can then use the System Monitor to measure any improvement resultin‎ changes made to the computer's hardware or software configuration.

While you can use the System Monitor to gauge the processes of the cor‎ it is running, the fact that it presents its data in real time makes it difficult t‎

typical workload for the computer while watching the display. As a result, the program is far more effective when it is run from a machine other than the one with the problem. An administrator can then monitor the processes of the offending workstation while its user continues his normal activities.

Configuring the System Monitor for Remote Administration

The System Monitor is part of the regular Windows 95 installation set. If the program is not already present on your machine, you can install it through the Add/Remove Programs application in the Control Panel by selecting the Windows Setup tab and clicking the appropriate check box in the Accessories section.

In order to use the System Monitor to measure a remote system's processes, however, you must first install the Microsoft Remote Registry service on both machines. This component is installed as a network service, from files located on the Windows 95 CD-ROM.

As with any networking module, you install the Remote Registry service through the Network application in the Control Panel. On the Configuration page, click the Add button, double-click Service, and click Have Disk. Then browse to the \Admin\Nettools\Remotereg folder of the Windows 95 CD-ROM and click OK several times to close all of the dialog boxes. Reboot your computer when you are prompted to do so.

NOTE The System Monitor is simply a program that reads various dynamic data values from the Windows 95 Registry and graphs them. This is why the Remote Registry service is required. This service is also needed for other utilities that can access the Registry on remote machines, such as the Registry Editor and the System Policy Editor. ▓

Running the System Monitor

You can launch the System Monitor from the System Tools group on the Start menu, or through the Administrative Tools page of any remote computer's Properties sheet. When launched for the first time, the program displays a graph like that shown in figure 29.4.

When launched from the Start menu (by choosing Start, Programs, Accessories, System Tools, System Monitor), the System Monitor displays a Line Chart of the local machine's Kernel Processor Usage. This represents the percentage of time that the workstation's microprocessor is busy. To monitor a remote computer, choose File, Connect and type the name of the desired machine in the field provided.

FIG. 29.4
By default, the System Monitor displays the target computer's Kernel Processor Usage.

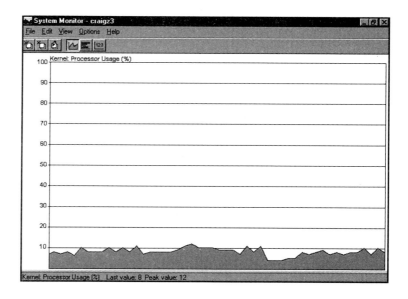

TIP If you create a shortcut to SYSMON.EXE, the System Monitor executable, and include the machine name of another computer on the command line, the System Monitor immediately connects to that machine after loading. You can therefore create an icon for each machine in your workgroup and monitor any activities of any computer at a moment's notice.

Right click the shortcut, select Properties, and then choose the Shortcut page. If you modify the Target field to read

    C:\Windows\SYSMON.EXE JOHND

then the System Monitor, when launched using this shortcut, immediately connects to the machine called JOHND and displays its Kernel Processor Usage.

Customizing the System Monitor Display

Once connected to the desired machine, you can configure the System Monitor to gauge a wide variety of system processes simultaneously. To do this, choose Edit, Add Item, and the dialog box shown in figure 29.5 appears. The category listing on the left side of the display always contains the File System, Kernel, and Memory Manager groups. The other groups are related to network performance, and vary depending on the network components installed.

FIG. 29.5
The System Monitor can be used to gauge a wide variety of workstation processes.

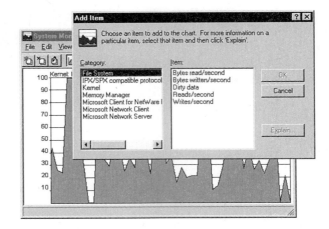

Most of the processes that can be monitored are related to the following basic subsystems:

- Processor utilization
- Memory utilization
- Internal file system performance
- Network traffic

You can select multiple items from a given category and build up a display of as many processes as your monitor can conveniently hold. The processes that you select will be retained when you exit the System Monitor, so you can create a suite of gauges that monitor a wide range of performance parameters (see fig. 29.6). When multiple graphs are displayed, clicking a specific graph provides summary information (such as the parameter's most recent value and its peak value) in the status bar at the bottom of the System Monitor window.

N O T E The Windows 95 Resource Kit contains a complete listing of the parameters that the System Monitor can present, as well as explanations of each parameter and additional ways in which you can use them. ■

CAUTION
The monitoring of some processes, particularly those involving memory and processor utilization, can cause the performance of the workstation to be diminished in those areas. It is not recommended that the System Monitor be left monitoring these processes unnecessarily.

FIG. 29.6
The System Monitor can be
used to track a wide variety
of system parameters at the
same time.

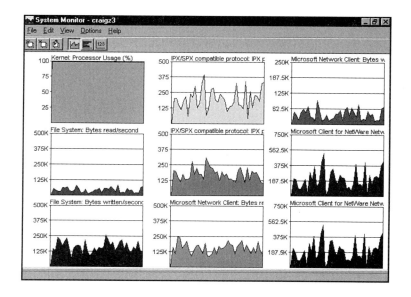

The System Monitor can display its information using three different charts—the line
chart shown in figure 29.6, the bar chart shown in figure 29.7, and a simple numeric chart.
These are selected from the View menu, or from the System Monitor's toolbar. Each chart
type is dynamically updated according to the interval set by choosing Options, Chart from
the menu bar.

FIG. 29.7
System parameters can be
displayed using different
chart types, to save screen
space.

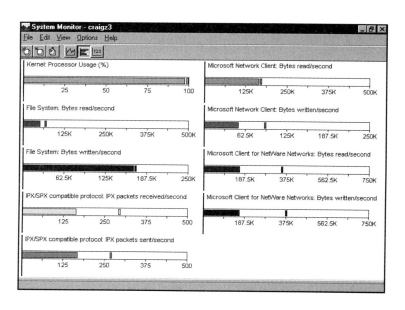

You also can modify the color used to represent each process and the scale used in the graph by choosing Edit, Edit Item, or by clicking the appropriate button on the toolbar.

The different chart types each have advantages, generally trading off the amount of information presented for the amount of screen real estate required. Bar charts and numeric charts can track many more processes on one screen, but they lack the full history displayed by the line chart.

Gauging System Performance

The System Monitor, particularly in its line chart mode, essentially functions as a polygraph for a Windows 95 computer. While a user works at his computer in the usual manner, an administrator can monitor its "vital signs" and see what processes might be negatively affecting system performance.

For example, if you create a display of parameters concerning a workstation's allocated memory, disk cache, and swap file, you should be able to determine whether the workstation has sufficient memory for the user's needs. You could then try installing more memory into the machine, and compare the readings after the upgrade to those before.

This is the basic technique by which the System Monitor is used effectively. Taking an initial reading is called *establishing a baseline* against which future readings can be compared. Readings are then taken after a change is made to the workstation's usage pattern or configuration.

Network traffic monitoring is usually a difficult undertaking, requiring expensive software and no small amount of expertise, but the System Monitor provides you with a basic window into your network's traffic patterns. On a mixed NetWare and Microsoft network, you can easily see which protocols are generating the most traffic. You also can determine whether your workgroup's shared resources are evenly balanced by comparing the Microsoft Network Client traffic for various machines. See "Using the Administrative Tools for Load Balancing," later in this chapter.

NOTE The Windows 95 Installation CD-ROM contains software that is designed to allow Windows 95 traffic to be scrutinized by the Microsoft Network Monitor application that is included with Microsoft's System Management Server product. The software consists of two basic modules—a Network Monitor Agent and a Network Monitor Driver. The agent installs as a network service, and is useless unless you own the Network Monitor application. The Microsoft Network Monitor Driver, however, when installed from the Network application as a protocol, provides the System Monitor with additional graphs that gauge the network traffic generated by Windows 95's NDIS 3.1 protected-mode network adapters. Since only Windows 95 machines use these adapters, this module can help you to quantify the amount of network traffic being produced by Windows 95 workstations in a mixed network environment.

 To install this driver, open the Network application in the Control Panel, click <u>A</u>dd, double-click Protocol, click <u>H</u>ave Disk, and browse to the \Admin\Nettools\Netmon folders of the Windows 95 CD-ROM. ▦

As another example, you may be able to determine that a given workstation is being overtaxed by the users who are sharing its resources. You would do this by comparing readings taken before and after such sharing begins. In cases like these, it is important to be aware of what the user is actually doing while the readings are being taken. As with a polygraph, the monitored readings must be associated with particular events to be of any value.

It is in this area that the System Monitor falls short in its capabilities. Analysis of the monitor's display can only be performed while the workstation activity is actually occurring. The ability to capture the results to a file for later study would be a major improvement to this tool, as would the addition of time stamp markings to the x-axis of the graphs. A time record of the workstation's activities could then be compared to the readings for that moment, resulting in a truly comprehensive analysis.

Using Net Watcher

The Net Watcher utility is used to monitor and control the resource sharing that occurs on a given workstation. With Net Watcher, you can:

- ▦ View the names of the users and computers accessing a given workstation, as well as the shares and files that they currently have open.
- ▦ Disconnect users from the workstation.
- ▦ Close any open file that is being shared.
- ▦ Stop a particular resource from being shared.
- ▦ Create a new shared resource.

Like System Monitor, Net Watcher can be installed as part of the standard Windows 95 setup routine, or from the Accessories group in the Windows Setup page of the Add/Remove Programs application.

Net Watcher monitors a workstation's activity in its role as a server. In other words, the utility is only concerned with the resources that the workstation is making available to other users. Therefore, one of the File and Printer Sharing services must be installed on the workstation to be monitored. Net Watcher will function with either the Microsoft or NetWare version of the File and Print Sharing service, although greater functionality is available for Microsoft network resource servers.

Securing Net Watcher Functions

Net Watcher's capabilities are dependent on the networking configuration on both the host and client computers. The two important factors are:

- The method of access control being used.
- Which File and Printer Sharing service is installed.

When you run Net Watcher on a computer configured for share-level access control, then you can only monitor the shares on other computers using the same share-level access. When you run Net Watcher on a computer configured for user-level access control, then you can monitor the shares on any workstation on the network that is sharing files or printers, including those using share-level access control and those using the File and Printer Sharing for NetWare Networks service.

When you run Net Watcher on a computer running the File and Printer Sharing for NetWare Networks service, then you can only monitor the shares of other machines running the same NetWare service.

When connecting to a remote computer, you must furnish the appropriate password for the type of access control being used on the remote machine. This will be either the Remote Administration password specified in the Passwords application, for share-level access, or the password for a specific user that has been granted administrative access.

Running Net Watcher

When you launch Net Watcher from the Start menu, it displays the resources currently being shared by your workstation. To monitor a remote workstation's shares, you must connect to the other machine using the Select Server item on the Administer menu. Launching Net Watcher from the Properties sheet of a workstation in the Network Neighborhood opens the application and immediately connects it to the remote computer (see fig. 29.8).

As with System Monitor, you also can create a shortcut to NETWATCH.EXE and specify the name of a remote machine on the command line, to establish a remote connection immediately. You must, however, specify the machine using a UNC name, as in NETWATCH.EXE \\WORKSTATION.

FIG. 29.8
Net Watcher displays all of
the shares currently being
advertised by the connected
workstation.

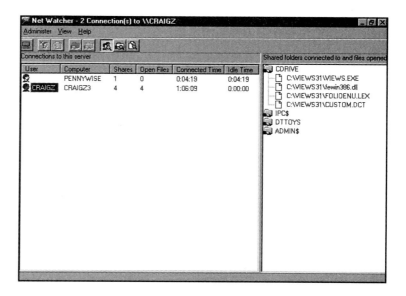

Viewing Shares and Connections with Net Watcher

Once a connection is established to a remote server, you can see all of the users who are currently accessing that server's resources in the left panel of Net Watcher, and the shared folders and files being accessed on the right. This is the View by Connections screen, one of three that can be selected from the View menu, or by using Net Watcher's toolbar. This view provides the most detail regarding the identity and duration of each user connection. From this screen, you also can disconnect any user from the workstation being monitored by simply selecting his name in the User column and clicking Disconnect User on the toolbar or in the Administer menu. After confirming your action, the user's access will be terminated without warning.

Creating and Destroying Shares with Net Watcher

When you select the By Shared Folders view, all of the server's available shares are displayed in the left panel, whether or not they are currently being accessed (see fig. 29.9). The right panel displays the users who are currently connected to each share, as well as the files that they currently have open.

In this view, the Add Shared Folder, Stop Sharing Folder, and Shared Folder Properties items on the Administer menu become available, as do their corresponding buttons on the toolbar. With these tools, you can immediately discontinue the sharing of a resource, or create an additional share, just as though you were seated at the machine being modified.

FIG. 29.9
The Shared Folders view of the Net Watcher window allows new shares to be created and existing ones discontinued.

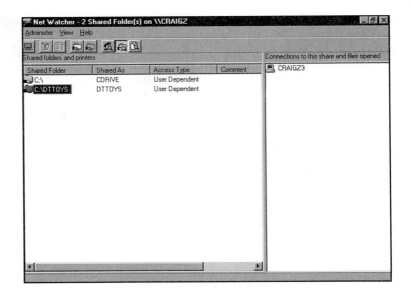

To create a new share with Net Watcher, use the following procedure:

1. With the Net Watcher utility connected to the desired machine, choose View, By Shared Folders.

2. Click the Add Share button on the toolbar, or choose Administer, Add Shared Folder.

3. In the Enter Path dialog box, type the name of the folder that you wish to share, or click the Browse button, which produces a tree display, as shown in figure 29.10.

FIG. 29.10
The Browse for Folder dialog box provides access to both administrative and regular shares.

TIP When entering the path name for the folder to be shared, a UNC name cannot be used. Enter the path as though it were a local resource on the computer, for example: C:\Folder.

If you elect to browse for the path, the tree displayed will contain the computer's existing shares, as well as the administrative shares, such as "c$" (refer to fig. 29.10). Even if the folder desired is contained in one of the existing shares, always use the administrative shares to browse for the path. This is because the existing shares will furnish a UNC path name to the dialog box, which will not be accepted, while the administrative shares will correctly furnish a drive letter and directory name.

4. After you click OK to accept the path name, the standard Sharing dialog box will appear, its form depending on whether the workstation is configured for share-level or user-level access. Complete the normal process of securing the share and click OK. The new share appears in the Net Watcher display.

To discontinue the sharing of a resource, select its name in the Shared Folder column and click Stop Sharing. You also can choose Administer, Stop Sharing Folder. After a dialog box asks you to confirm your decision, the share will be summarily discontinued. All user access to that resource will be immediately cut off.

CAUTION

When you attempt to shut down a Windows 95 workstation while users are attached to its shares, you are pointedly informed of the number of users attached and the dangers that may be involved. Similar warnings appear when using Net Watcher to disconnect a user with the procedure described earlier. However, no such warnings appear when you discontinue a share. If a user has files open on the remote workstation, and you interrupt his access without warning, he may experience a serious system disruption or even a loss of data.

▶ **See** "Configuring Access Rights," **p. 798**

Controlling Open Files with Net Watcher

When you select the by Open Files view of the Net Watcher screen (see fig. 29.11), the left pane of the display contains a listing of all files currently being accessed by all remote users. If you make a selection from the Open File column, you can immediately close that file by clicking Close File on the toolbar or the Administer menu. Again, after confirmation, access to that file by the user will be instantly interrupted.

Depending on the type of file involved, this action may or may not have a serious impact on the user. For example, a small executable may have already been completely read into the remote workstation's memory. Closing the file will probably have no ill effects until the user attempts to terminate or reopen the application. He may be unable to save his changes to a file on the shared drive, but this does not mean that he cannot save the document to a local folder.

FIG. 29.11

Individual shared files can be closed from within Net Watcher.

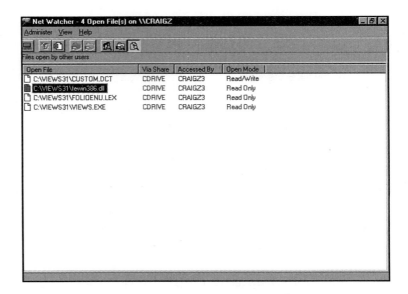

 T I P   If you use Net Watcher to monitor a workstation running the File and Printer Sharing for NetWare Networks service, you cannot close files from a remote location. All other Net Watcher functions operate normally.

Remote Administration with Net Watcher

Clearly, the Net Watcher utility was created primarily for the purpose of monitoring the resource sharing of a Windows 95 network. The program empowers the administrator to immediately terminate any inappropriate access to a shared resource, in several different ways.

However, Net Watcher has other more positive uses as well. The capability to create new shares on a workstation without displacing the user is a boon, especially when not all of the users in the workgroup fully understand the concepts behind resource sharing. Net Watcher allows the administrator to work behind the scenes, insulating the less sophisticated users from the networking infrastructure, and protecting that same infrastructure from the more expert members of the group.

Remote Registry Editing

Having already installed the Windows 95 Remote Registry service for use with the System Monitor, you can now also use the standard Registry Editor program (REGEDIT.EXE) to modify the Windows 95 Registry on remote machines over the network.

From the Registry Editor's Registry menu, select Connect Network Registry and enter the name of the machine to be modified. It appears in the left pane of the editor screen along with the existing entries for your own machine, as shown in figure 29.12. You can then modify the Registry of the remote computer just as if you were sitting at its keyboard.

Many Windows 95 Registry modifications require a system reboot before they have any effect. There is no native mechanism in Windows 95 that can force a reboot of a remote workstation. The administrator must inform the user that changes have been made and that he must reboot at his earliest convenience.

FIG. 29.12

Remote machines appear in the Registry Editor along with the local one.

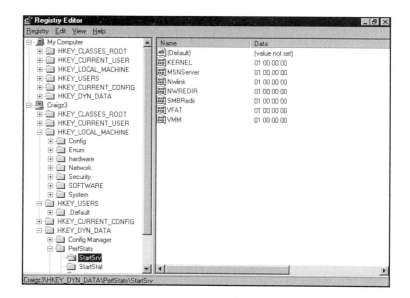

> **CAUTION**
>
> Modifying a remote user's Registry can be just as dangerous as modifying your own. Be sure that an adequate backup exists, and avoid making changes while the user is doing important work.

See Chapter 15, "Customizing with REGEDIT," for more information on modifying the Windows 95 Registry.

Using the Administrative Tools for Load Balancing

It is not simply chance that led the Windows 95 developers to group the System Monitor and Net Watcher utilities with a file management window in the Properties sheet of every remote workstation displayed in the Network Neighborhood. These three tools form the core of the workgroup administrator's arsenal.

As discussed in the last chapter, as well as in this one, balancing shared resources among workgroup computers is one of the tasks that is ideally suited for the workgroup administrator. For the task to be done properly, the person responsible must continually monitor network performance and make regular adjustments. Most corporate network administration departments do not have the manpower to pay close enough attention to individual workstation activities. The workgroup administrator is, by definition, the person most suited to this kind of departmental supervision.

The Net Watcher, System Monitor, and Administer buttons in the Properties sheet provide access to most of the tools you need to balance the distribution of shares around the workgroup. The process of redistributing shares will conform roughly to the following basic steps:

1. Use the System Monitor to determine when a given workstation is too heavily trafficked by other users.
2. Use your administrative file management access to move some of the workgroup's files from the overloaded workstation to another machine.
3. Create a share at the new location using Net Watcher.
4. Modify login scripts or Registry entries to remap users' drive letters to the newly located share.

N O T E A *login script* is a file containing a series of network commands that are executed whenever a user logs into a NetWare or Windows NT network. Login scripts are most commonly used to create uniform drive mappings for users accessing the same network resources. ▓

 T I P The Registry entries containing a Windows 95 workstation's persistent connections (that is, drive mappings) are located at HKEY_CURRENT_USER\Network\Persistent.

By performing a procedure like this, you can detour a certain amount of network traffic to a new locale, without having to leave your own workstation, and without the workgroup's users even being aware of the change. You may have to perform these procedures frequently at first, until you get a feel for the way in which the workgroup's activities affect network traffic patterns. Before long, though, you will get to know your local peer network as you know your own neighborhood.

Dividing Drive Mappings

Another common administrator's technique for balancing network traffic is to place two copies of a particular file or application on two different servers, and then map half of the users to each copy. Windows 95 can complicate this process.

If a user has created a shortcut to a program located on a mapped network drive, Windows 95 seeks out the program's original location, even if the drive mapping has changed. Most of the time, this is a wonderful feature, unless you are trying to balance network traffic. If you create a shortcut to WINWORD.EXE on the G: drive, and the G: drive is mapped to a share on a machine called SERVER1, changing the drive mapping to a share of the same name on SERVER2 will do you no good. The shortcut seeks out SERVER1, changes the drive letter if necessary, and thwarts your attempt to divert traffic to the other server.

There is a command-line utility on the Windows 95 CD-ROM that overcomes this tendency, however. Called SHORTCUT.EXE, it is located in the \Admin\Apptools\Envvars folder. The program needs no installation, and consists of a single executable. You may wish to copy it to your Windows directory, though, so that it is always accessible from the command line.

Windows 95 shortcuts, like nearly every other element of the operating system, are stored as files. A shortcut file is given an extension of LNK, and is located in the folder representing the location of the icon, such as C:\Windows\Desktop. By using the SHORTCUT.EXE utility to modify the LNK file, the shortcut can be converted to a non-tracking or "stupid" shortcut. To do this, use the following syntax in the directory where the shortcut file is located:

SHORTCUT -c -s -n <*filename*>

The <*filename*> variable must be replaced with the name of the actual shortcut file, which appears in its Properties sheet.

To continue the example given here, executing the command

SHORTCUT -c -s -n C:\Windows\Desktop\WINWORD.LNK

will cause the shortcut always to reference the G: drive, no matter what server has been mapped to that drive letter. The shortcut is called non-tracking or stupid because it will no longer search for the executable. If WINWORD.EXE is not present in the directory on the G: drive referenced by the shortcut file, an error message will be generated.

 TIP Shortcuts placed on the desktop or in the Windows 95 Start menu are located in directories called \Windows\Desktop and \Windows\Start Menu, respectively.

If you place a shortcut like this on the desktop or in the Start menu of all of your workgroup's users, you can modify the users' drive mappings between the two servers containing the target file until a balance is achieved, secure in the knowledge that an executable will always be found.

Using the Microsoft Print Services for NetWare

File sharing is not the only source of network traffic problems. In fact, the use of a Windows 95 workstation as a fax or print server can often be far more detrimental to its overall performance than the sharing of its files. The user who is given the workstation with the attached printer may at first feel lucky, but he will soon discover that playing host to a heavily shared device is more trouble than he bargained for.

Aside from the need to service the printer (loading paper, clearing jams, and so on), this is the workstation where all of the pending print jobs are queued, until they can be fed by the operating system to the printer. The burden on the storage subsystem of that computer, as well as the disk space requirements, can make it very difficult for that user to get any other work done.

The best solution is, of course, to detach the printer from that workstation and service it from a client/server operating system like NetWare or Windows NT. A partial solution for a workstation-based printer is available, however. Windows 95 does not only maintain its own print queue, it also provides the capability to service a NetWare print queue, using a workstation-based printer. This practice eliminates the security problem inherent in Windows 95's "all or nothing" printer access, because the queue is administered through the server. Using a NetWare queue also means that the pending print jobs will be stored on the NetWare server's hard drives, rather than the workstation's, as they are waiting to be serviced by the printer. Relocating the queue significantly lessens the burden on the workstation, and reduces the need for temporary hard disk space in the process.

Windows 95's PSERVER capability is provided through an additional service that ships on the installation CD-ROM. Before you use it, however, you should have already installed the workstation printer, as well as the Microsoft Client for NetWare Networks, although the File and Printer Sharing for NetWare Networks service is not needed. Once you have done this, install the Microsoft Print Services for NetWare service from the \Admin\Nettools\Prtagent directory of the CD-ROM, using the Have Disk button in the Control Panel's Network application.

You must also have access to a NetWare print server and print queue that is fully installed and operational, either on a dedicated DOS machine or a NetWare server.

Once the service has been installed and the computer restarted, use the following procedure to configure the printer:

1. Open the Printers window from the Start, Settings menu, or the shortcut in the Control Panel. Select the installed printer that you will use to service the NetWare print queue and open its Properties sheet from the File or context menu.

2. Select the Print Server tab, which the installation of the service has created in the Properties sheet (see fig. 29.13). Enable the Microsoft Print Server for NetWare by clicking the appropriate radio button.

FIG. 29.13
The Print Server tab is added to the Properties sheet of all installed printers by the Microsoft Print Services for NetWare.

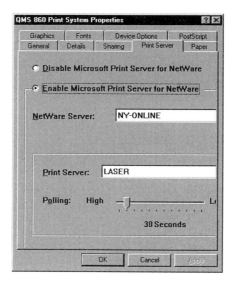

3. The NetWare Server drop-down list contains the names of all of the servers to which the workstation is currently attached. Select the server that is acting as host to the print server.

N O T E If an error message stating Cannot Determine Print Queue Name appears, the NetWare print server is not functioning properly. Consult your NetWare documentation to troubleshoot the print server. ▪

4. Once you have selected a NetWare server, its active print servers appears in the field below the server listing. If there is more than one print server listed, select the one that you intend to use.

5. The Polling selector sets the time interval at which the Windows 95 workstation checks the NetWare queue for the presence of new print jobs. The default value is 30 seconds, with possible values ranging from 15 seconds to 3 minutes. Adjust the value, if desired, depending on the priority allotted to printing on this workstation. Click OK to close the dialog box and complete the configuration.

All NetWare print jobs sent to the selected queue will now be routed to the workstation printer. Double-clicking the printer icon displays the contents of the NetWare queue, instead of a local workstation queue. User permissions for the queue administrative tasks will be controlled by the NetWare server as well, allowing greater flexibility in the assignment of rights to the queue. ●

CHAPTER 30

Customizing Windows 95 Network Installations

by Craig Zacker

The material in preceding chapters focused on enabling advanced users of Windows 95 to take full advantage of the operating system's features. This chapter covers issues related primarily to the corporate network administrator who is responsible for engineering a large scale migration to Windows 95. Using the features discussed in this chapter, administrators can limit users' access to Windows 95's more powerful features.

Access control is an important concern in the corporate world. Not everyone can be a power user, or even wants to be. Many users benefit from a relatively simple and consistent working environment. Such an environment helps users work more efficiently and simplifies the technical support process.

Different organizations take different approaches to workstation standardization; some organizations provide users with a great deal of flexibility in configuring their own computers, and others enforce strict guidelines over all aspects of the interface. Windows 95 can accommodate both of these extremes and any degree in between. Windows 95

- **Customizing the default Windows 95 installation**

  How to alter Windows 95 scripts to adapt the installation process to your users' needs and capabilities.

- **Using Windows 95 user profiles**

  How to resolve the roving user and multiple user problems with Windows 95 user profiles.

- **Using Windows 95 system policies**

  These techniques and features will help everyone to see your work more clearly.

can enable a user to easily take his custom settings with him from machine to machine, or lock everyone into an environment where even wallpaper is a corporate standard. ■

Customizing Windows 95 Installation Routines

When you perform a Windows 95 installation on a single computer, the setup routine offers a choice of installation types; your choice determines what Windows 95 features are installed and the degree of user intervention the system requires during the installation process. Most experienced users select the Custom installation, because it provides the greatest amount of flexibility—allowing the user to select exactly which components to install. This option also requires the most user intervention.

For professional network support personnel, performing individual custom installations on the hundreds of machines they may support is impractical. Windows 95, therefore, includes tools that enable administrators to create customized installation routines and install the operating system source files onto a network drive. You can integrate other software products into the installation routine, so an alternative client or additional utilities are installed to user workstations along with Windows 95.

Customizing the Windows 95 installation has three major advantages:

- You can override normal Windows 95 installation defaults.
- You can specify component selection and configuration with extreme precision.
- You can minimize or even eliminate interaction with the network user during the installation.

As the network administrator, you control the degree of installation customization. For example, you might want to do no more than modify the default network client installation routine. When the Windows 95 installation program detects that a workstation is using NetWare's VLMs to connect to a NetWare Directory Services (NDS) database, it leaves the real-mode client in place. The new protected-mode client is not installed because, at the time of the original Windows 95 release, it had no support for NDS.

Now that Microsoft has released the NDS support service for its protected-mode NetWare client, you might want to have the setup routine install the Microsoft Client for NetWare Networks. You also can add an installation of the NDS service, which was released several months later than the operating system.

These minor modifications are easy to perform because Windows 95 installations are controlled by scripts, which you can easily edit to conform to any requirements. Your task becomes more difficult when you must upgrade a large number of workstations to Windows 95, using a highly customized installation that requires absolutely no user intervention.

You can create an installation routine, for example, that launches automatically one morning when users first log into the network from their Windows 3.1 workstations. As the user watches, the Windows 95 upgrade installation is performed from source files on the network. About 30 minutes later, the system reboots, and the user is immediately using a new operating system. With properly configured system policies, you can even present users with a desktop and a Start menu complete with the applications they need to begin working.

Such elaborate installations inevitably suffer script failures on some workstations. These installation customizations require extensive testing and debugging before the scripts are considered foolproof. The time and convenience gained by the custom installation, however, make the project well worth the effort.

▶ **See** "Using the Microsoft Service for NetWare Directory Services," **p. 734**

Creating a Server-Based Installation

The first step in creating a customized Windows 95 installation is to create a common directory on a server, where all the scripts and source files for the operating system will be located. Use the Windows 95 Server Setup utility (NETSETUP.EXE), located in the \Admin\Nettools\Netsetup folder on the CD-ROM. You don't need to install this utility. Running NETSETUP.EXE from the CD-ROM produces a screen like the one shown in figure 30.1.

FIG. 30.1
Use NETSETUP.EXE to create source file directories and installation scripts on server drives.

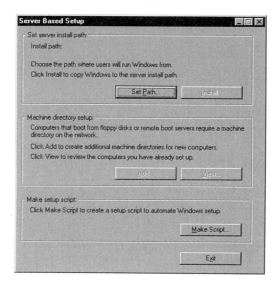

Part

VIII

Ch

30

Creating a Source Directory

To create a source directory from which users can install Windows 95, use the following procedure:

1. Run NETSETUP.EXE and choose Set Path.

2. Enter the UNC path name of the directory where the new source files are to be located. Click OK.

3. Choose Install. Select the option indicating the location where you want to install Windows 95 shared files.

4. Enter the location of the Windows 95 installation media in the Path Install From text box. Click OK to begin the process.

N O T E As with earlier versions of Windows, Windows 95 enables workstations to share operating system files located on a network drive. You even can make provisions for running the operating system on a diskless workstation, a practice that has all but disappeared from modern computing. A strong recommendation is to install individual copies of all operating system files on each workstation, and to select the Local Hard Drive option in step 3 of preceding steps. ■

The source directory created by the Server Setup program differs from the installable files on the Windows 95 CD-ROM or floppy disks. On the original installation media, all of the files are compressed into CAB (for "cabinet") archives. The Server Setup program decompresses these archives into the a set of installation files with which you can add additional software to the default installation routine and use customized scripts.

Using Installation Scripts

A setup, or installation, script is an ASCII file you can modify with any text editor. The default setup script for Windows 95 is called MSBATCH.INF. Although you can run a script of any name from the SETUP.EXE command line, you should retain the INF extension.

You can create installation scripts in three ways—by using a text editor to manually create the script, or by using the graphical user interfaces (GUIs) of the NETSETUP.EXE or BATCH.EXE programs. While the GUI-based programs provide easy point-and-click selection of features, editing the actual script provides you with access to all possible commands and parameters, which the GUI programs do not. However, you need not make a definitive selection between the two methods. You can use NETSETUP or BATCH to create a basic script, and then manually fine-tune it by editing the code directly.

Manually Creating Scripts Creating a script without a GUI is not as difficult a task as you may think. First, Windows 95 includes sample scripts from which you can take code or modify code to meet your needs. These scripts are in the \Admin\Reskit\Samples\ Scripts folder of the installation CD-ROM.

A second source of scripting code is the SETUPLOG.TXT file that is created on the C:\ drive for every Windows 95 installation. Although the setup program creates the file as a record of the installation process, the file does in fact use precisely the same syntax as an installation script. You can therefore perform a single interactive workstation installation, making the selections you require for all your users, and use the log file as the basis of your script.

Obviously, you must remove the code containing machine-specific information, such as the user name and machine name. Any required information not specified in an installation script reverts to the Windows 95 installation default, which may cause the user to receive a prompt for input or a predetermined value to be used. Therefore, your script may end up being very short, supplying only a few selections you want to make on every workstation and leaving everything else to the defaults.

N O T E Many of the administrative modules and/or settings discussed in Chapter 31, "Using the Universal Inbox," are prime candidates for inclusion in setup scripts. If you plan on exercising any administrative control over your workstations, consider some or all of the following modifications:

- Enable remote administration
- Require user-level access control
- Install the Remote Registry service
- Enable user profiles

Remember, whatever selections you don't make globally before the installation, you might end up making individually afterwards.

Creating Installation Scripts with NETSETUP.EXE Windows 95 includes two GUI programs for creating installation scripts. One program is part of the NETSETUP.EXE program, and the other is a separate utility, called BATCH.EXE. Both of these programs are limited to creating new script files; you cannot use the programs to edit existing scripts. Of course, you can manually edit the resulting code in any way you want.

From the main NETSETUP screen, click Make Script. After specifying the name and location of the script to be created, a dialog box like the one in figure 30.2 appears.

FIG. 30.2
The Server Setup program can script a large number of installation variables.

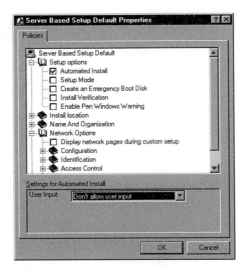

The Server Based Setup Default Properties sheet bears a marked resemblance to the interface used to create system policy files. (See "Using System Policies" later in this chapter.) You select individual options, and the area at the bottom of the sheet changes to enable the entry of required data. As you progress through the list of settings, you supply answers that anticipate the prompts provided by the typical installation routine. Most of the options are self-explanatory and provide drop-down lists or obvious prompts for you to enter data. A few of the entries are quite cryptic, however, and require some explanation—particularly those involved with networking.

For example, when you expand the Network Options/Configuration page, you can specify which clients and protocols to install on your workstations, and you can configure the settings for each (see fig. 30.3). Clicking the Clients to Install option, however, produces an empty text box labeled Clients. The program provides no clue as to how to specify the clients.

The program requires that you create a comma-delimited client list that contains one or more of the following entries:

Module	Client
VREDIR	Indicates the Client for Microsoft Networks
NWREDIR	Indicates the Client for NetWare Networks
VLM	Instructs the program to retain the existing VLM client
NETX	Instructs the program to retain the existing NETX client

FIG. 30.3
The network client selection fields in NETSETUP.EXE are less than intuitive.

Part
VIII
Ch
30

The first client you list in the text box becomes the primary network logon client. In the same manner, you must specify protocols as follows:

Module	Protocol
NWLINK	Indicates the IPX/SPX-compatible protocol
NETBEUI	Indicates the Microsoft NetBEUI protocol
MSTCP	Indicates the Microsoft TCP/IP protocol

Most people need assistance in figuring out how to use these settings. Fortunately, Microsoft provides reference materials for both the NETSETUP and BATCH script-making programs in the Windows 95 Resource Kit (included on the installation CD-ROM in Windows HLP format). The help file also includes a complete listing of the MSBATCH.INF script entries that are made by selecting each configuration item in both programs, as well as the entries you cannot set through the GUIs.

Creating Installation Scripts with BATCH.EXE   Apart from being difficult to use at times, the script-making interface in NETSETUP.EXE is far from complete. The BATCH.EXE utility, located in the same folder on the CD-ROM (\Admin\Nettools\Netsetup), provides a more comprehensive and easy-to-use interface for the selection of script parameters (see fig. 30.4).

N O T E   Neither NETSETUP.EXE nor BATCH.EXE provides an interface that can create all possible setup script parameters. You still must manually script some forms of customization. Consult the Windows 95 Resource Kit for information on the use and syntax of these parameters. ▪

FIG. 30.4
The BATCH.EXE interface allows you to create more complete and detailed installation scripts.

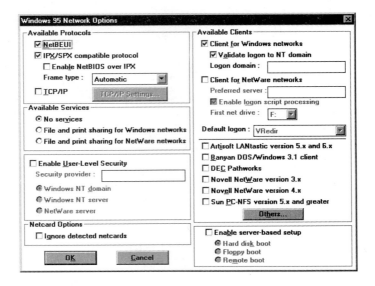

As you can see from the Network Options dialog box shown in figure 30.4, the selection of network clients and protocols is much simpler in the BATCH program than it is in NETSETUP. The selection also is more complete.

BATCH enables you to select individual Windows 95 components for a Custom installation, as shown in figure 30.5.

FIG. 30.5
BATCH.EXE comes far closer to enabling a truly Custom installation to be pre-scripted.

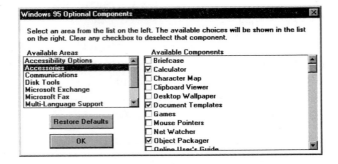

Since the initial release of Windows 95, Microsoft has upgraded the BATCH.EXE program. Version 2.0 is included as part of the Windows 95 Service Pack 1, and consolidates the interface into a tabbed dialog box that takes advantage of the WIN32 Common Controls to provide a familiar look and feel to the user (see fig. 30.6).

BATCH version 2.0 also adds additional parameters to the interface to accommodate some of the other Windows 95 updates released since August 1995. For example, you can now specify NetWare Directory Services login preferences and have them assimilated into the an installation routine, providing that an administrator has installed the Service for NDS into the source file directory. (See "Using INFINST.EXE," later in this chapter.)

FIG. 30.6
Version 2.0 of BATCH.EXE consolidates the interface and updates the script parameter selection.

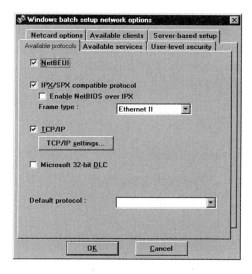

ON THE WEB

http://www.microsoft.com/windows/software/servpak1/sphome.htm   The Windows 95 Service Pack 1 is available for download from Microsoft's WWW server.

TROUBLESHOOTING

I'm trying to create an installation script using BATCH.EXE version 2.0, but it won't run on my Windows 3.1 machine like the old version. What's wrong? The updated version of BATCH.EXE is a 32-bit program. While BATCH version 1 could be run on a Windows 3.1 workstation, version 2.0 runs on Windows 95 and NT only.

Adding Other Software to Installation Scripts and Source Directories

After you have created a script for the basic Windows 95 installation, you can add other software to the setup routine. You can add components on the CD-ROM that are not options in the normal Windows 95 installation program; you can add additional services released by Microsoft, and even the Windows 95 Power Toys installed through your installation script.

Using INFINST.EXE   The INFINST.EXE utility, located in the \Admin\Nettools\Netsetup folder of the Windows 95 CD-ROM, can assimilate any program installed using an INF file into your existing script file and source directory.

When you run the program, you see the dialog box shown in figure 30.7. Choose Set Path and specify the location of your source directory using a fully qualified UNC name. Then choose Install INF and browse to the location of the INF script used to install your additional software. INFINST.EXE parses the program's INF script, copies the appropriate files to your source directory, and assimilates the software installation routine into the existing MSBATCH.INF script.

FIG. 30.7
The INFINST.EXE program enables you to add any INF-installed software to a Windows 95 installation routine.

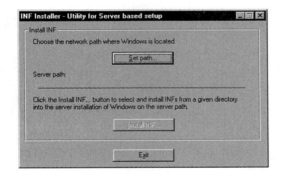

The INFINST.EXE program does more than simply append one script to another. For example, if the additional software you are installing is network-related, then the proper adjustments are made to the [Network] section of MSBATCH.INF.

Using Other Script Files   As part of your custom setup routine, you may want to modify other script files involved in a Windows 95 installation besides MSBATCH.INF.

NETDET.INI   NETDET.INI is the file controlling the actions that Windows 95 takes when it detects different types of network-related drivers during the installation process. NETDET.INI is actually a library of exceptions, because the default action of the setup routine is to remove the workstation's existing network support, migrate its settings from configuration files to the Registry, and install either or both of the new Microsoft protected-mode clients.

If you are using any non-standard networking software on your workstations, examine NETDET.INI and see if the software is listed, and if it is, what action Windows 95 will take.

Each section in the NETDET.INI file is composed of *detection* entries and *event* entries, as shown in this example:

```
;;;;;; NOVELL Directory Services VLM 4.x ;;;;;;;;
[VLM]
detection0=custom_dll
detection_dll=NETOS.DLL
detection_call=NW_IsNDSinUse
full_install0=prevent
```

The first line after the [VLM] section heading indicates the type of detection to use if the event specified on the last line is performed. Detection parameters can require that the specified network software module be located in one or more of the following ways:

Part
VIII

Ch
30

- In an unremarked entry of the CONFIG.SYS file
- In an unremarked entry of the AUTOEXEC.BAT file
- In an unremarked entry of the SYSTEM.INI file
- In the TSR list maintained by DOS in the memory control blocks (MCBs)
- By calling custom detection code in an external DLL

The final method in the preceding list is illustrated in the earlier code example. The first detection entry is checking that the workstation is using the NetWare VLM redirector, and it is checking that the workstation is using the redirector to log into an NDS tree (as opposed to performing a bindery login). This is the condition that is being determined by the NW_IsNDSinUse call in the NETOS.DLL file specified on the subsequent detection entries.

The event called by the satisfaction of the specified detection method can be one of the following:

Event	Action
Prevent	Causes the default protected-mode client not to be loaded.
None	No action is taken.
Remove	Causes the detected module not to be loaded by remarking it out.
Unremove	Causes the detected module to be loaded by unremarking it.
Migrate	Remarks out the module in the AUTOEXEC.BAT file and adds it to the WINSTART.BAT file.
Unmigrate	Reactivates the module in the AUTOEXEC.BAT file and removes it from the WINSTART.BAT file.

In the code shown earlier, the detection of a connection to an NDS database causes the protected-mode Client for NetWare Networks not to be installed.

If you are using your workstations to connect to NDS, then you very likely want to disable this reaction. If you have already scripted the installation of the Microsoft Service for NetWare Directory Services, then you must ensure that the Client for NetWare Networks is installed. In this case, simply removing the entire [VLM] section from NETDET.INI causes the protected-mode client to be installed whenever VLMs are detected, regardless of the existence of an NDS connection.

Other alterations to NETDET.INI are likely to be considerably more complex. In some cases, you can make modifications by emulating the existing entries. In other cases, you need a programmer's familiarity with the modules being detected to script them properly.

WRKGRP.INI   WRKGRP.INI is a text file you can use to provide a selection of workgroups from which a user can choose during a Windows 95 installation. You can specify a domain logon (Windows NT) server and preferred (NetWare) server for each workgroup. You also can control whether the selections you provide are merely suggestions or if the user is required to choose among them.

In its simplest form, a WRKGRP.INI file consists of a [Workgroups] section with multiple entries using the following syntax:

```
group_name=server1,server2,server3...
```

Group_name is the workgroup name, and the servers are replaced with the names of the login servers, in the order they will appear in the drop-down list.

You can add an [Options] section in which the following line specifies whether the user can enter a name not on the workgroup drop-down list:

```
Required=true¦false
```

The following entry performs the same action for the domain logon/preferred server drop-down list:

```
ForceMapping=true¦false
```

N O T E   You can find information on other WRKGRP.INI options in the Windows 95 Resource Kit. ▪

Running Script Files

After you have created your MSBATCH.INF script, running it is a simple matter. Append the full UNC path name to the script file to the Windows 95 SETUP.EXE command, and the script takes over from there:

```
SETUP.EXE \\server\share\msbatch.inf
```

Of course, a script cannot control some aspects of the installation. For example, a workstation that runs out of hard disk space midway through the installation definitely requires manual intervention. Other instances are covered in the Windows 95 Resource Kit.

Part VIII Ch 30

Creating User Profiles

Windows 95 provides the solution to two networking problems that have plagued administrators for years:

- How to enable each user to maintain his or her custom working environment on a shared machine.
- How to enable users to take their custom environments with them as they travel to different machines on the network.

Windows 95 resolves both these problems by providing a simple means for saving the basic workstation settings that comprise the user's working environment. These settings are known as a *user profile*. A user profile consists of a copy of the USER.DAT Registry file and (optionally) copies of the folders containing the contents of the Start menu, the Desktop, the Network Neighborhood, and the Recent Documents list.

Enabling the user profiles feature of the operating system saves these files to a folder. The folder is named for the user logged on to the machine at the end of each session. The profile is then read back into memory the next time that user logs on.

Enabling User Profiles

To turn on the Windows 95 user profiles feature, use the following procedure:

1. Launch the Passwords icon from the Control Panel and click the User Profiles tab (see fig. 30.8).
2. Click the Users Can Customize Their Preferences and Desktop Settings option.
3. If you want, select the check boxes in the User Profile Settings area to enable the inclusion of the Desktop and Start menu settings.
4. Click OK to close the dialog box. Restart the computer.

CAUTION
See the following sections for possible problems that can occur as a result of enabling these options.

FIG. 30.8
Enabling user profiles allows a user to preserve his or her custom settings.

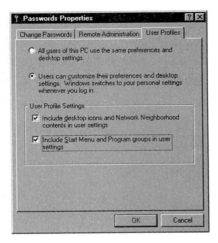

As a result of this procedure, a \Profiles folder is created under the \Windows folder. The \Profiles folder contains subfolders for each user who logs on to the machine. At the end of each Windows 95 session, each user's current settings are copied to his or her folder.

The settings include:

- The USER.DAT Registry file.
- A backup copy of USER.DAT, called USER.DAO.
- Copies of the \Windows\Desktop and \Windows\Nethood directories (if the corresponding check box in the User Profiles dialog box is selected).
- Copies of the \Windows\Recent and \Windows\Start Menu directories (if the corresponding check box in the User Profiles dialog box is selected).

The Windows 95 Registry is stored as two separate files—SYSTEM.DAT and USER.DAT. This arrangement separates the machine settings from the user settings for the purpose of creating user profiles. USER.DAT contains all the settings found in the HKEY_ CURRENT_USER section of the Registry. These settings include all the environment parameters you have configured through the Control Panel, such as color and font selection, wallpaper, screen resolution, the arrangement of icons on the desktop, and so on. USER.DAT also contains settings written to the Registry by specific applications.

TROUBLESHOOTING

My coworker installed a new application on the Windows 95 machine we share, but I can't find it on the Start menu. When I try to run the executable from Explorer, the application won't load. My co-worker says the application works fine. What's wrong? Applications installed while user profiles are in use have their Registry settings, program groups, and Start menu entries added only to the current user's profile. Other users wanting to run the application need to reinstall it (to the same location) to update their own profiles.

With the user profiles capability, several users can share a single Windows 95 workstation, with each user maintaining his or her customized settings. Users with entirely different computing needs can maintain their own Start menu structures, containing only the applications they require. For example, you can use this feature to accommodate part-time workers or shops running multiple shifts.

You do not need to restrict user profiles to specific users. You can create profiles for different positions, allowing the same machine to be instantly configured as an accounting workstation, for example, or a desktop publishing workstation, or a technical support workstation.

Part
VIII
Ch
30

Storing User Profiles on the Network

Now that the user profiles feature has resolved the multiple user problem, how can you address the roving user issue? The answer is simple: store the user profiles on a network drive. In fact, you don't need to take any further action, as long as the following statements are true:

- Each workstation uses a 32-bit protected-mode network client.
- Windows 95 is installed to the same drive and folder (such as C:\Windows) on every workstation where networked profiles will be used.
- Each workstation has enabled support for user profiles.

User profiles are automatically saved to the user's primary login server at the same time they are saved to the local machine. If the user's primary login server is a Windows NT machine, then the profile is saved to the user's designated home directory.

N O T E Windows NT has its own user profiles feature, which is not compatible with the Windows 95 feature. Do not confuse the Windows NT \Profiles folder with the user's home directory, where Windows 95 profiles are stored. ■

If the user's primary login is to a NetWare server, then the profile is saved to the user's Mail folder. Mail is a sub-folder of the SYS:Mail folder, named with the account's eight-character user ID. When you log onto any Windows 95 machine (on which user profiles have been enabled) using that network account, the profile is copied from the network server to the local machine and activated.

N O T E You can determine the NetWare user ID by using the NetWare SYSCON utility. In the User Administration dialog box under the user's account name, the user ID is listed in the Other Information text box. ■

N O T E For the storage of the optional Desktop and Start menu profile information to occur on a NetWare server, the SYS: volume must have the OS/2 name space installed. Long file names and directory names then can be written to the \Mail folder. ■

Accessing and updating your user profile from different workstations can result in Windows 95 finding inconsistent profiles on the local machine and the network. In that situation, Windows 95 always loads the more recently saved profile and updates both the server and the workstation when the session is concluded.

▶ **See** "Storing Long File Names on Network Drives," **p. 761**

Storing User Profiles on Other Networks

You can store user profiles on networks accessed using 16-bit client software, or on peer networks without a Windows NT or NetWare server. Although this method of networking profiles is less convenient, you can do it by following these steps:

1. Create a shared directory of any name on a network drive, to which all users have read-only access (for example, \\Server1\Profiles).

2. Create a text file in that directory, again using any name (for example, PROFILES.INI).

3. In the text file, list all the users who need networked user profiles, along with the location of a home directory for each user, in the following format:

   ```
   [Profiles]

   JohnD=\\SERVER1\USERS\JOHND

   MaryC=\\SERVER1\USERS\MARYC
   ```

   The home directories can be located on any shared network drive, but each user must have full read/write access to his own directory.

4. On each workstation where the networked profiles are going to be used, select the HKEY_LOCAL_MACHINE\NETWORK\LOGON key using the Registry Editor. Add a new String Value called SharedProfileList.

5. Edit the new String and enter the full UNC path to the text file created earlier (for example, \\Server1\Profiles\Profiles.INI). Click OK.

After you perform this procedure, each time a workstation is started, it looks to the PROFILES.INI file for the location of the user's home directory. The machine then treats the profile data as if it were located on a NetWare or Windows NT server. If the user's name is not listed in PROFILES.INI, then the local user profile is used.

▶ **See** "Using the Registry Editor," **p. 435**

Using Shortcuts with User Profiles

If you are creating a profile to use on different machines, be aware of the Windows 95 shortcuts. Consider the following points when creating your desktop configuration, before saving it to a network profile:

- A shortcut placed on the Windows 95 desktop is saved to the network as part of the user profile. Actual files placed on the desktop are saved to the local profile only. These files are not copied to the network.

- A shortcut to a file on a local drive is useless on another machine, unless a file of the same name is located on the other machine. The shortcut searches for the target on the local drive, if necessary.

- If a shortcut to a file on a network drive is launched and Windows 95 cannot find the target, it searches other network drive letters to locate the target and then updates the shortcut.

Disabling the Use of Network User Profiles

You might want to create a profile for use on the network and retain a second profile for use on your own workstation. For example, the network profile can contain shortcuts to applications on the shared drives of your local machine. You need these shortcuts when you log in at another workstation, but not at your local one.

For this or any other reason, you can force a particular Windows 95 machine to always use the local user profile, ignoring even a more recent network copy.

To make a certain Windows 95 machine always use the local user profile, open the Registry Editor and select the HKEY_LOCAL_MACHINE\NETWORK\LOGON key. Create a new DWORD value in this key and call it UseHomeDirectory. Close the Registry Editor and restart the computer.

Enforcing a Mandatory User Profile

Administrators can create a mandatory user profile in a user's directory on a network server. This profile loads when the user logs on to the network. You can use this technique to implement a uniform profile for all users, but it is not the most secure method of enforcing the use of a particular configuration.

When a mandatory user profile is established, users can still modify their settings while they work at the machine. These changes are not saved to the network for later use, however. A user also can disable support for user profiles entirely, forcing the use of the local Registry settings. The administrator can exert a greater degree of control by implementing Windows 95 system policies, which can actually limit users' access to the tools needed to change configuration settings. (See the following section, "Using System Policies.")

To create a mandatory user profile, follow this procedure:

1. Enable user profiles on all machines that will use the mandatory user profile.
2. Create the profile by configuring a workstation to the desired settings and logging it off, causing the settings to write to disk.
3. Rename the newly saved USER.DAT file to USER.MAN.
4. Copy all the user profile folders and files to the home or Mail directories of all the users on the primary network login server.
5. Protect the USER.MAN file from erasure or modification with the appropriate network operating system tools. (Windows 95 never automatically updates a USER.MAN file. This step ensures that the file is not manually overwritten.)

Whenever a user logs on to the network server, Windows 95 reads the user profile from the USER.MAN file, rather than from any USER.DAT file that may exist on the local or network drive. At the end of the session, configuration changes are written to the USER.DAT files in the normal manner, but USER.MAN is not modified.

Using System Policies

When a network administrator must exercise a greater degree of control over the configuration of networked Windows 95 machines, he or she can use the Windows 95 system policies feature.

More comprehensive than user profiles, system policies can alter the values of both computer and user entries in the Windows 95 Registry (that is, both the SYSTEM.DAT and USER.DAT files), and prevent the user from altering them again. With system policies, you can do these things:

- Restrict users' access to specific Control Panel settings.
- Control what menus and applications the user can access.
- Prevent users from accessing specific Windows 95 features (including the MS-DOS prompt).
- Specify network client settings.
- Enforce the use of a preset desktop environment.

In most cases, system policies are not stored on a local machine. Instead, when a user logs on, the workstation automatically downloads the policies from the primary logon server in the form of a file named CONFIG.POL. You can use a single policy file containing multiple user and computer definitions for all users and workstations on a network. You can create different policies in the same file for the default user, for user groups, and for individually named users. In the same way, you can create different policies for different machines on the network, all in that one file.

Preparing a Workstation to Use System Policies

For a workstation to use system policies, it must be configured in the following manner:

- If user settings are included in the policy file, the Windows 95 user profiles feature must be enabled.

- If you are using group policy settings, the Group Policies module must be installed from the \Admin\Apptools\Poledit folder of the Windows 95 CD-ROM. Use the Add/Remove Programs feature in the Control Panel.

Creating a System Policy File

Use the Windows 95 System Policy Editor to create and modify system policy files. This utility is located in the \Admin\Apptools\Poledit folder of the Windows 95 installation CD-ROM. Install the utility from the Windows Setup page of the Add/Remove Programs feature in the Control Panel.

ON THE WEB

http://www.microsoft.com /windows/software/cdextras.htm   For users installing Windows 95 from floppy disks, Microsoft has all of the Windows 95 CD-ROM modules available for free download on their World Wide Web site.

CAUTION

Restrict your users' access to the System Policy Editor and to the policy files themselves. Incorrect changes to a policy file can conceivably lock all network users out of their systems.

Opening a new policy file with the System Policy Editor generates a dialog box similar to the one shown in figure 30.9. The settings found in the Windows 95 Registry's USER.DAT and SYSTEM.DAT files are associated with icons depicting a head and a computer, respectively. Double-click one of the icons, and the program generates a hierarchical display of policy settings, as shown in figure 30.10.

FIG. 30.9

The main dialog box of the System Policy Editor holds icons representing the user and machine types to define.

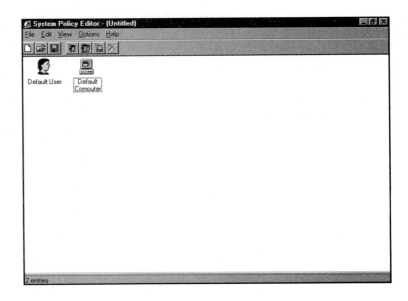

FIG. 30.10

The Default User Properties sheet displays Registry settings in the form of policies.

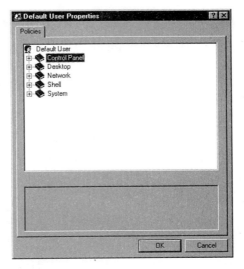

System policies are nothing more than a convenient way of manipulating the Registry entries using plain English rather than cryptic keys and values. Each element in the tree-like display is associated with a particular Registry setting. When a network user logs into his or her server, and a policy file is located in the proper place, the settings the network administrator created in the policy file are downloaded to the local workstation. The changes specified in the policy file are applied to the workstation's Registry, thus modifying the user's environment.

The System Policy Editor uses a template file to determine what Registry entries it can manipulate. The default template included with the Editor is called ADMIN.ADM. This text file is located in the \Windows\Inf folder and can be modified or replaced to include any conceivable Registry setting. A policy file, therefore, can modify Registry entries made by specific applications or third party clients, just as easily as it can modify native Windows 95 settings.

Setting System Policies

When you expand on the tree display of a policy file, entries are displayed in different categories depending on their general purpose. In figure 30.11, policies regarding the Control Panel are separated according to the programs with which they are associated. At the end of each tree "branch" is a policy such as Restrict Display Control Panel. Each policy has a check box where the administrator selects whether to modify the value.

FIG. 30.11
Each system policy can be explicitly enabled, disabled, or left alone.

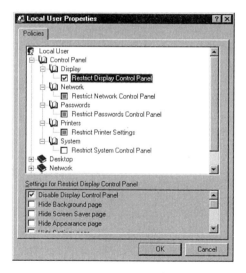

Many of the branch policies, when enabled, display subsettings in the box below the tree display. These subsettings modify various minor aspects of the major setting. The subsettings also enable the administrator to supply specific input that is written to the associated Registry values. In this way, you can configure a workstation to draw a Start menu, Desktop configuration, or even a wallpaper graphic from specific files on the network. The administrator can exert a highly specific degree of control over a user's Windows 95 Registry in this manner.

For example, the policy displayed in figure 30.11 is called Restrict Display Control Panel. Looking in the ADMIN.ADM template file, you find an entry like the following:

```
CATEGORY !!ControlPanel
CATEGORY !!CPL_Display
POLICY !!CPL_Display_Restrict
KEYNAME Software\Microsoft\Windows\CurrentVersion\Policies\System
PART !!CPL_Display_Disable CHECKBOX
VALUENAME NoDispCPL
END PART
```

This entry indicates that this particular policy is associated with a Registry value called SOFTWARE\MICROSOFT\WINDOWS\CURRENTVERSION\POLICIES\SYSTEM. Because this setting is a user setting, the value must be in the HKEY_CURRENT_USER key.

Based on the input of the administrator, a value called NoDispCPL is added to the Registry at this location, removed, or left in its current state. The administrator provides input by manipulating the check boxes located next to each policy.

Each check box in the System Policy Editor has three different states. Knowing which state to use is crucial to creating system policies effectively. The following describes each state:

Selected	Indicates that the associated setting will be added to the workstation Registry (or activated, depending on the type of setting). If the setting does not exist, it is added. If the setting is already added and activated, it is left alone.
Deselected	Indicates that the associated setting will be removed from the workstation Registry (or deactivated). If the setting is currently active, it is deactivated. Otherwise, it is left alone.
Grayed	Indicates a setting that is not controlled by the policy file. The current state of the workstation's Registry is left unchanged.

The administrator's most common error with respect to setting policies is that of mistakenly enforcing a disabled state, when the actual goal is to leave the choice up to the user. Selecting the appropriate state of the check box is a process based on the nature of the Registry entry involved and on the current state of the user's Registry.

For example, in figure 30.11, if the administrator selects the Restrict Display Control Panel policy and then activates the subsetting that hides the screen saver page on all workstations, he or she prevents every user who loads this policy file from modifying the screen saver configuration. (Notice that this setting does not necessarily prevent workstations from using a screen saver; if one is already in use, it only prevents users from changing it).

If the administrator later decides to allow screen saver modifications, he or she would be making a mistake to change the state of the policy and leave the check box grayed. In this situation, a grayed check box forces this Registry entry to remain unchanged. All users who are restricted from using screen savers remain restricted. To relax the ban, the administrator must explicitly remove the Registry value that prevents access to the screen saver configuration page by leaving the check box unselected. After modifying all user's registries, the administrator can dim the check box.

NOTE Removing a policy file from the file server does not undo the changes it has made to the network's workstations. You must explicitly reverse the Registry settings that the policy file modified to restore the machines to their original state. ■

Defining Multiple Policies

The example in the preceding section dealt with user settings located in the Registry in the HKEY_LOCAL_USER key and stored in the USER.DAT file. Many of these settings are the same ones you can set with user profiles. In fact, a Windows 95 workstation must have the user profiles feature enabled for the user settings of a system policy file to take effect.

In addition to user settings, system policies can alter the computer settings located in the HKEY_LOCAL_MACHINE key of the Registry and stored in the SYSTEM.DAT file. These settings are Registry entries that are more machine specific, remaining in effect no matter who logs into the workstation.

A single POL file can contain system policies for as many users and computers as needed (see fig. 30.12). An administrator can therefore assign different system policies to users with varying levels of expertise.

When you create a new policy file, it contains a default user and a default computer. On the Edit menu are commands to add new computers, new users, and new groups. User profile names must match the user account names on the server where the policy file is to be stored—the user's primary logon server. Likewise, take group names from already existing groups on the same server. Computer profiles must match the machine name specified on the Windows 95 workstation's Identification screen in the Network dialog box.

To arrange the order in which group definitions will be loaded, choose Options, Group Priority (see fig. 30.13).

You can use the System Policy Editor to modify a workstation's Registry in real time, using the same interface as that of a POL file. Modifying in real time is a good way for a user to discover the power contained in the Registry without risking a dysfunctional system due to a typographical error. To edit the Registry on the local workstation, choose

File, Open Registry. If you want to edit another workstation's Registry, choose File, Connect and specify the machine's name. The Registry changes you make in this manner don't take effect until the workstation is restarted.

> **CAUTION**
>
> Although using the System Policy Editor to modify the Registry settings eliminates some of the danger inherent in the process, you still can do many things with this tool that can limit or prevent access to your system. Always be careful when modifying your Registry. The System Policy Editor also makes it easy to forget whether you are modifying a policy file or a Registry. Keep an eye on the title bar and be sure you know the target of your modifications.

FIG. 30.12

A policy file can contain user, group, and computer policies for the whole network.

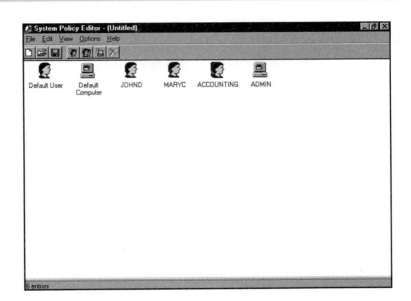

FIG. 30.13

You can prioritize groups to control their load order.

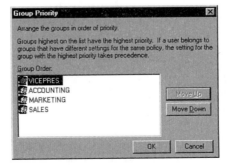

Reading System Policy Files

After you have created all the required profiles, save the file and store it on the proper server, so the workstations can automatically download it. By default, you give a system profile file the name CONFIG.POL and store it in the \Public directory of a NetWare server or in the \Netlogon directory of a Windows NT server.

You can configure workstations to access policy files of different names, stored in different locations, if you want. You perform this task, oddly enough, by using a system policy to enable Windows 95's Remote Update feature, specifying an alternate path and file name where the policies can be located. If you are running workstations using NETX, VLMs, or any other 16-bit network client, you must use this method to apply system policies to them.

When a user logs into his or her home server, Windows 95 reads the policy file and looks for a profile that matches the user's login name. If the operating system finds such a profile, its policies are immediately applied to the workstation. If no specific user profile exists for that login name, Windows 95 begins comparing the available group profiles with the group member lists on the server. Group profiles are always processed in order from the lowest to the highest priority, so the highest-level policies are applied last, taking precedence over all others. If no user or group policies match the login name, then Windows 95 applies the default user policy. The same procedure is then applied to the computer policies found in the file, except no groups are processed.

Developing System Policy

Configuring and implementing system policies is a far easier task for the network administrator than deciding what policies to enforce. A quick examination of the parameters addressable by the System Policy Editor demonstrates that an administrator can wield an enormous amount of power over network users. An administrator can constrain employees into a machine configuration that is absolute, allowing no flexibility in terms of the applications the worker uses, and no variation on the appearance of the desktop.

Many network administrators advocate the use of a standard system configuration for all users, including the software they use. This policy eases the task of providing technical support and ensures that all users' files are compatible. The opposite philosophy, in which users have complete freedom over their systems, results in anarchy and lost production when users' "experiments" malfunction.

Most administrators agree, though, that exercising complete control of the working environment retards the atmosphere of learning and exploration that Windows 95 so deftly creates. Indeed, the entire theory of workgroup networking is based on users who have developed a greater expertise through their experience and experimentation. System policies are ideal for protecting users from the elements of the Windows 95 operating system that they are unqualified to use. Implementing an intelligent array of group policies based on users' perceived capabilities is one way for a network administrator to ensure that workgroup activities do not accidentally affect the performance of other network users.

System policies do not provide the administrator with an impenetrable shield against the inveterate hacker, however. Microsoft recommends its Systems Management Server product for environments in which greater administrative control is required.

ON THE WEB

http://www.microsoft.com/SMSMGMT/default.htm   More information on Microsoft's Systems Management Server product is available from their World Wide Web site.

Using the Internet and Online Services

CHAPTER 31

Using the Universal Inbox

by Gordon Meltzer with Peter Kent and Ken Poore

Microsoft Exchange is a central communications client that organizes the electronic mail and faxes that you receive in one convenient location. Exchange operates not only as your Universal Inbox, but also includes tools that you can use to compose, store, organize, and send messages via e-mail and fax.

In its basic configuration, Exchange coordinates communication among members of your Local Area Network (LAN) workgroup or enterprise and handles communications via The Microsoft Network, yet still finds time to send and receive faxes in several formats. In more advanced configurations, Exchange handles communications with other message services, like CompuServe and Internet mail. ■

Install Microsoft Exchange

Microsoft Exchange is comprised of a core set of programs and utilities for messaging.

Choose and install messaging services

The modular design of Exchange enables it to grow with your needs.

Create and send messages

The primary role of the Universal Inbox is to enable you to create and send e-mail messages.

Work with and organize received messages

Exchange's Personal Folders enable you to sort and manage all your incoming mail messages in organized folders.

Configure your Exchange user profile

The flexibility of Exchange enables you to configure different sets of features collected in user profiles.

Use Exchange remotely from a laptop or other location

Exchange is designed to be used on a networked computer or over a modem that dials into an e-mail system, or both!

Overview of Exchange Features

So that you know how to set up Exchange during the installation process, you should have some detailed information about what Exchange can do. Knowing about Exchange's capabilities will help you to make the right installation and setup choices.

You call on Microsoft Exchange when you want to compose a fax. You visit Exchange again when you want to send a message to a colleague down the hall, to anyone in your enterprise, or possibly anyone connected to the Internet. When one of those folks replies, the message appears in your inbox, no matter where it was sent from. Faxes sent to your fax card head for the Exchange Inbox, too.

Your messages don't have to be just plain text, either. Because Exchange supports Rich Text Format, messages can be delivered in any font on your system, at any size, in any color. The first time you see a mail message that has been passed around your workgroup, and each member has contributed his or her thoughts in a different color, you'll begin to appreciate the power of Exchange.

More important than Rich Text is the ability to work with Object Linking and Embedding (OLE). Your messages can contain OLE documents created in applications that are OLE servers, like Microsoft Word for Windows, Microsoft Excel, or any of the many OLE server applications.

Finally, you can use Exchange to send e-mail via The Microsoft Network, the online service available through Windows 95.

The inclusion of Microsoft Exchange in Windows 95 confirms the notion that e-mail is now a standard feature of personal computing. Exchange's integration with the operating system and applications enables you to easily take full advantage of all the usefulness of e-mail in increasingly complex networked environments.

Clients and Servers

The introduction of this chapter noted that Exchange was a central communications client. The word *client* is so important in Exchange, and in Windows 95 generally, that it needs to be explained along with its complementary counterpart, the *server*.

For the purposes of programs like Exchange, a server is a program, running on a network, that holds information accessible by users on the network. These users employ programs called clients to get at the server-based information.

If the server is a mail or fax server, it provides a place to store mail and fax messages for all the clients (users) on the network. This is the kind of server to which the Exchange client connects.

The Universal Inbox

Discussions of Exchange have commonly referred to it as the "Universal Inbox." The inbox function is a very important part of Exchange, as this section explains.

You'll be using Exchange to communicate, and a large part of communication is finding out what others have to say. You may receive messages by fax or e-mail. In Windows 95, these received messages are directed to Exchange, where they can be conveniently read. Exchange is called a *Universal* Inbox because all messages, both fax and e-mail, no matter where they come from, go to your Exchange inbox.

Windows 95's designers decided that collecting all these messages in one place would be more convenient for users. All of those messages can now be set up to communicate through the Universal Inbox of Exchange, eliminating the need to use different messaging packages to read your e-mail and faxes.

Part
IX
Ch
31

Microsoft Workgroup E-Mail

If you're connected to a Local Area Network (LAN), Exchange is the program you'll use to send and receive e-mail with your workgroup colleagues. Windows 95 contains a Microsoft Mail Postoffice so you can set up an e-mail system on your workgroup network.

Once you have your Postoffice running, Exchange collects all e-mail addressed to you. You can then read, reply to, and forward them, all while using the Exchange program. Other accessory programs, installed on your network, will let Exchange send and receive e-mail over networks wider than your workgroup LAN.

▶ **See** "Installing the Workgroup Postoffice," **p. 910**

Online Service Mail Systems

The Microsoft Network (MSN) is an online service, similar in concept to CompuServe and America Online. Each of these provides e-mail to its members as a service.

Exchange provides a way to dial into MSN and quickly retrieve any e-mail waiting for you. You also can use Exchange to send e-mail to an MSN member.

CompuServe provides an add-in for Exchange to access CompuServe mail in much the same way.

Rich Text Format

Exchange supports Rich Text Format (RTF). This means you can create messages using any font on your system. You also can change the text's size and use different colors.

These text-formatting capabilities let you personalize your messages, and they can be quite useful when messages are routed to various people for comment. Individuals can use different colors, typefaces, and type sizes to help set off each set of comments.

OLE Support

OLE allows you to put part of one document into another. This capability has been used by every major Windows applications publisher. You can highlight a section of a document, copy it into the Windows Clipboard, and paste-link or paste-embed it into another program. The original program might be a spreadsheet, and the target program might be a word processor. It doesn't matter, as long as the source program is an OLE server, and the target program is an OLE client. Most major programs are both.

N O T E   The data you Copy and Paste Link or Paste Embed is called an *OLE object*. Often in Windows 95, OLE objects have an associated icon. You can drag the icon into other programs, or drop it on the Windows desktop. In other cases, the OLE object simply appears in its original format, such as rows from a spreadsheet. ■

Exchange extends your powers to work with OLE objects by allowing you to drop them into mail messages you compose.

Most Windows applications are OLE-enabled. Although Word and Excel were mentioned in the earlier section, "Overview of Exchange Features," any OLE object can be embedded in an Exchange message and sent with that message. More infomation on using OLE can be found in Chapter 20, "Creating Compound Documents with OLE."

Installing and Configuring Exchange

You can install Exchange during your initial Windows 95 installation or afterward. After the first few steps, however, the process is the same. The following sections explain how to install and configure Exchange.

N O T E   Exchange requires a minimum of 6M of memory in your system to run. For good performance, plan on having at least 8M. Exchange also takes 10M of space on your hard drive for required swap files. The Exchange basic program files take 3.7M of disk space. Because Exchange can work with all sorts of different data, you should allow a few megabytes for your incoming messages, too. It's easy to end up with 5M or more of faxes and e-mail. ■

Deciding Whether to Use Exchange

Before you go ahead with loading Exchange, you must first determine whether you really need it. Just because you use e-mail doesn't mean that you will always benefit from using Exchange. Exchange has powerful features and is well integrated into Windows 95; however, Exchange can require some detailed configuration and maintenance, and it does occupy some of your system resources.

To help you make your decision, consider these questions:

- Are you on a network and wish to share e-mail with others in your workgroup?
- Do you have more than one e-mail address on different online services like CompuServe or an Internet service provider?
- Does your current e-mail program poorly manage received messages or have an inadequate address book?
- Do you read e-mail on a laptop computer that is sometimes connected to the network?
- Does more than one person use your computer to read e-mail?
- Do you use The Microsoft Network (MSN)?
- Do you have a fax modem and wish to send and receive faxes?

If you answered Yes to any of these questions, chances are, you'll benefit from using Exchange. Conversely, if you are happy with your current e-mail program and only connect to one online service to send and receive e-mail, then you might want to skip loading Exchange altogether. Of course, the choice is still yours, and you can always load Exchange, try it, and delete it later if you don't seem to get much out of it.

Installing Exchange During Windows Setup

During Windows setup, the Windows 95 Setup Wizard displays the Get Connected dialog box, shown in figure 31.1. In this dialog box, you can choose to install The Microsoft Network online service, Microsoft Mail for use on workgroup networks (LANs), and the Microsoft Fax service.

You can install any or all of these three connectivity components. (You can always add them later, too.) MSN, Microsoft Mail, and Microsoft Fax all require Exchange to work, so when you choose any of them, Exchange is installed for you.

▶ See "Using Custom Setup Mode," p. 1203

Part
IX

Ch
31

FIG. 31.1
The Get Connected dialog
box is the first step to
installing Exchange.

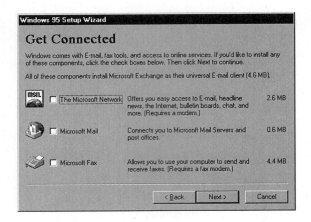

It's also possible to install Exchange without installing any of these items; for instance, if you want to use Exchange for Internet e-mail. To do so, you must choose a Custom installation—you'll then be able to select Exchange from a list of optional components.

Adding Exchange After Windows Is Installed

If you did not install any of the connectivity components during your Windows 95 installation, you can still add Exchange.

 On your Windows desktop is an icon called Inbox. If you right-click the Inbox icon and then choose Properties, Windows confirms that Exchange is not installed (see fig. 31.2).

FIG. 31.2
Windows confirms that
Exchange is not yet installed.

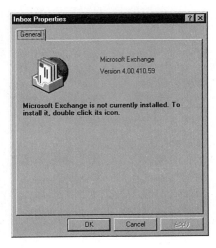

Follow this procedure to install Exchange:

1. Double-click the Inbox icon on your desktop. You'll see a Get Connected dialog box similar to the one shown in figure 31.1, but it's now called the Inbox Setup Wizard.

N O T E If you've installed an Exchange service and now want to install one or more other services, you won't be able to use this procedure. This procedure only works when no Exchange services have been installed. To install Microsoft Fax or The Microsoft Network, open the Start menu and choose Settings, Control Panel: then double-click the Add/Remove Programs icon, click the Windows Setup tab, and select the item from the list of components. To install Microsoft Mail or Internet Mail, right-click the Inbox icon, choose Add, and select the service you want to install. ▓

2. Choose one or more of the three information services you are offered. The services are The Microsoft Network, Microsoft Mail, and Microsoft Fax. (To make this example most useful, what happens when you choose all three will be covered, too.)

3. After selecting the information services you want, choose OK.

4. The Inbox Setup Wizard asks you to insert your Windows 95 CD-ROM or floppy disk. Insert the CD or disk and choose OK. Windows then installs the needed files.

5. The Inbox Setup Wizard asks whether you've used Exchange before. Because you're setting up Exchange for the first time, choose No. Then choose Next. Windows displays the message box shown in figure 31.3.

FIG. 31.3
The Inbox Setup Wizard offers you a choice of services.

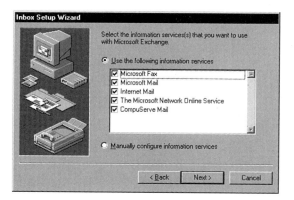

6. The services you selected in step 2 are checked, along with Internet Mail. If you plan to use Exchange for receiving e-mail from an Internet service provider (other than The Microsoft Network), leave this check box checked. If you're not going to use Internet e-mail, deselect this check box.

Part
IX

Ch
31

N O T E   The Microsoft Network has a level of service that provides full Internet access, and it
also allows users at *all* levels to send and receive e-mail across the Internet. However,
the Internet Mail service referred to by the Inbox Setup Wizard is intended for use with other
Internet service providers, not with The Microsoft Network. ■

7. Choose Next to begin configuring your services.

The basic setup of Exchange is done, but the Inbox Setup Wizard continues, setting up
each of the services you have selected. In the next sections, you'll work with the wizard to
configure the individual communications services you just chose to use with Exchange.

TROUBLESHOOTING

**I followed the procedure in the section, "Adding Exchange After Windows Is Installed," but
couldn't get Exchange to install correctly.** The Inbox Setup Wizard may run into problems—it
may even "crash" while setting up your information. For instance, you may get a message telling
you that the wizard was unable to complete something, and telling you to click the Finish button
to end the procedure. If this happens to you, double-click the Inbox icon and the wizard should
start again.

Configuring Microsoft Mail

If you chose to install Microsoft Mail, you see the dialog box shown in figure 31.4. (If you
did not choose to install Microsoft Mail, you can skip this section.)

FIG. 31.4
You need to specify a
Postoffice location to
use Microsoft Mail.

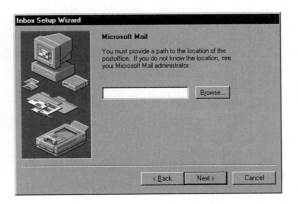

Microsoft Mail requires that one of the computers on the workgroup LAN be set up as a
Postoffice. You may have a network administrator who has already done this. If so, ask the
administrator for the path to the Postoffice. Then put the path to the Postoffice in the text

box shown in figure 31.4 (click the Browse button and search for the path if necessary), and choose Next.

TIP When the administrator creates a Postoffice, a folder called WGPO000 is created. For example, if the administrator creates a folder called Mail and tells the Microsoft Workgroup Postoffice Admin Wizard to place the Postoffice there, the wizard places the WPGO000 folder inside the Mail folder. You must specify where the WPGO000 folder is. In this example, you would enter **C:\MSMAIL\WGPO000**, not C:\MSMAIL.

If you don't have an administrator to set up your Postoffice, turn to the "Installing the Workgroup Postoffice" section later in this chapter. Then return to this section.

You are shown a list of people who have been given access to the Postoffice. Select your name from this list (if it's not on the list, ask the administrator to add it). The Inbox Setup Wizard then asks for your password. Again, ask your administrator what password he used when creating your account, and carefully type that into the text box. Then choose Next.

The Wizard has finished setting up Microsoft Mail, and you are ready to use it on your workgroup LAN.

Configuring Internet Mail

If you chose to install Internet Mail, you see the dialog box shown in figure 31.5. (If you did not choose to install Internet Mail, skip this section.) The first step is to specify your Internet access method.

FIG. 31.5
You need to choose an access method to the Internet for Internet Mail.

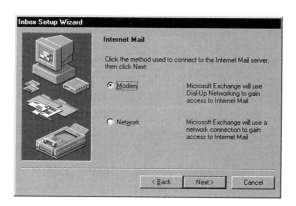

N O T E   In order to use Internet Mail, you must have the TCP/IP protocol installed on your computer. If it isn't, you'll see a message reminding you to install it. To install TCP/IP, open the Start menu and choose Settings, Control Panel; double-click the Network icon and choose Add; select Protocol and choose Add; select Microsoft and TCP/IP, and then choose OK. See Chapter 33, "Getting Connected to the Internet" for more information. ▮

Internet Access Method   The wizard offers Modem and Network options for Internet access. If you connect to the Internet by modem and Dial-Up Networking, follow these steps:

1. Choose Modem, then choose Next.
2. Now select the connection you created in Dial-Up Networking that dials your Internet service provider.

   If you haven't created a connection yet, choose New and create a connection. (Chapter 33, "Getting Connected to the Internet," provides detailed instructions for creating a connection.)

N O T E   If you haven't yet installed the TCP/IP software, the wizard skips step 2; it doesn't ask you which service provider to use. Later you can specify a service provider by choosing Tools, Services on the main Exchange menu, clicking Internet Mail, choosing Properties, and clicking the Connection tab. ▮

3. Choose Next.

If you connect to the Internet via your LAN, choose Network and then choose Next.

Selecting Your Internet Mail Server   Now tell the wizard about your Internet Mail server. You can tell the wizard either the Name of the server where your Internet mail is stored, or you can tell the wizard its IP Address. Figure 31.6 shows an example, with a mail-server name filled in. When you're finished, choose Next.

Internet Mail Transfer Method   You can choose Off-line or Automatic mail transfers:

▮ *Off-line* lets you use Remote Preview to view only incoming mail headers. You selectively decide which messages to download to your inbox, based on the header contents.

▮ *Automatic* instructs Exchange to connect to your Internet Mail server and retrieve all new mail into your inbox automatically. The Automatic option also automatically sends any outbound Internet mail you've created.

Make your choice, and then choose Next.

FIG. 31.6
Enter your Internet Mail server information.

Your Internet E-Mail Address   Next, the Wizard wants you to fill in your e-mail address in the form *user@domain*. Enter this in the text box called <u>E</u>-Mail Address. Also, put your full name in the text box called Your <u>F</u>ull Name. When you're finished, choose Next.

Internet Mailbox Information   The Inbox Setup Wizard needs the <u>M</u>ailbox Name and <u>P</u>assword you use to access your account in your Internet Mail server. Enter them in the text boxes provided and then choose Next.

Internet Mail is now set up and ready to use with Exchange.

Confirming The Microsoft Network Mail System

You cannot set up MSN with the Inbox Setup Wizard. At this point, if you've chosen to install MSN, the Inbox Setup Wizard displays a dialog box confirming that you have chosen to install MSN Mail to work with Exchange (see fig. 31.7).

FIG. 31.7
The wizard confirms that you want to install The Microsoft Network online service mail.

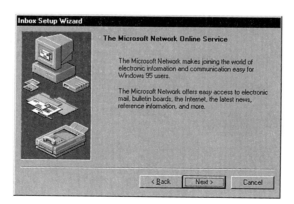

When you choose Next, the wizard confirms that you've chosen to install MSN Mail to work with Exchange. All setup and configuration of MSN is done by the MSN setup program that begins when you double-click the MSN icon on your desktop, or open the Start menu and choose Programs, The Microsoft Network. (Chapter 35, "Using The Microsoft Network," covers MSN installation and setup.)

▶ **See** "Installing and Configuring The Microsoft Network," **p. 1032**

Completing Your Exchange Installation

Now that you've set up the various services you selected, the wizard finishes off the more general Exchange settings. First, it asks you which Personal Address Book it should use.

You probably haven't created a Personal Address Book (assuming that you are installing Exchange for the first time), so simply choose Next.

You see a similar dialog box, this time asking where your Personal Folder file is. This is the file that stores all your messages. Choose Next to accept the file that the wizard is suggesting.

N O T E It is not uncommon for network-based e-mail users (especially if you're using the Microsoft Mail service) to have personal folders exceeding 50M. When backing up your system, be sure to specify the directory in which you've placed your files containing your address book and personal folders (see Chapter 23, "Backing Up and Protecting Your Data"). Also, be sure to exit Exchange before running the backup, otherwise the backup may skip your personal folders file because Exchange has it open. ■

Next, the wizard asks whether you want to run Exchange automatically every time you start Windows. This choice requires some thought; Exchange uses many system resources and can affect performance in low-memory configurations. If you are going to use Exchange only on a dial-up basis, such as with The Microsoft Network or an Internet service provider, choose No.

 T I P If you're connected to a LAN, start Exchange automatically every time you start Windows so that you won't miss any e-mail from workgroup members.

Running Exchange at Windows startup wastes system resources if you don't need to use Exchange's services constantly. If you don't expect much e-mail and use Exchange and its communications services infrequently, select the Do Not Add Inbox to StartUp Group check box.

If your messaging needs require constant connectivity or periodic automatic logon to an online service to check for new mail, choose Add Inbox to the StartUp Group.

To complete the installation, choose Next. The Inbox Setup Wizard displays a final dialog box confirming that Exchange is set up to work with all the communications services you selected (see fig. 31.8).

FIG. 31.8
The Inbox Setup Wizard
confirms that the setup of
services is complete.

Choose Finish. After this long setup and configuration process, you are ready to start using Exchange. (The Exchange window opens automatically immediately after the wizard closes.)

Using the CompuServe Mail Service

The Universal Inbox of Exchange is designed to be a flexible, modular mail system, able to access many different mail services across many different networking and dial-up connections. Earlier in this chapter you were shown how to install the service that allows you to send and receive mail over The Microsoft Network online service. CompuServe has a similar add-in module that allows Exchange to be the inbox for CompuServe mail as well.

Installing the CompuServe Mail Service

You must first add the service to Exchange in order to use it. Follow these steps:

1. The CompuServe mail connector is not included with Exchange, so you first need to obtain the latest version of CompuServe Mail for Exchange from CompuServe. After logging into CompuServe, use **GO CISSOFT** and select CompuServe Mail for Microsoft Exchange (Win 95). Then choose to download the file (CSMAIL.EXE)— it's a free download.

2. CSMAIL.EXE is a self-extracting archive. Once downloaded, copy it into its own directory and run CSMAIL.EXE to extract the setup files. Next, run the extracted SETUP.EXE to start the installation.

3. Follow the instructions provided by the setup program. When the program asks if you would like the service to be installed into your default profile, select Yes. After the service is installed, you are prompted to enter your Name, CompuServe ID, and Password.

Configuring the CompuServe Mail Service

Once installed, you may never need to change how the service is configured. However, if your password changes, or if you would like to set up the service to connect to CompuServe on a scheduled basis, you have to reconfigure it.

Follow these steps to change your CompuServe Mail settings:

1. Open the Start menu and choose Settings, Control Panel.
2. In Control Panel, double-click the Mail and Fax icon.
3. Choose the CompuServe Mail Service and select Properties. You'll see the tabbed sheet shown in figure 31.9. Each tabbed page contains the following configuration settings:

    - *General.* Choose this tab to update your Name, CompuServe ID, or Password.
    - *Connection.* Choose this tab to change the Phone Number to access CompuServe, the modem you use to connect, or the Network type (such as Tymnet or SprintNet). You also can select what type of connection you have to CompuServe. Choose Windows Modem Settings if you're using a modem to connect to CompuServe. Choose Winsock Connection if your computer is directly connected to the Internet. Choose Direct Connection if you have a communications port (for example, COM1) directly wired into CompuServe.
    - *Default Send Options.* Choose Send Using Microsoft Exchange Rich Text Format if you want to preserve all the rich text formatting (fonts, colors, and so on) in your e-mail message. Setting the Release Date holds outgoing messages in your outbox until the date specified; if not set, all mail is sent as soon as possible. The Expiration Date is the date that mail is deleted in your recipient's mailbox.
    - *Advanced.* The Create Event Log option generates a mail message in your inbox each time you connect to CompuServe. The log details how many messages were retrieved and sent, and notifies you if there is a problem connecting. Setting Delete Retrieved messages removes messages from your CompuServe mailbox when Exchange successfully retrieves them. The Change CompuServe Dir option tells the service where your CompuServe access program (for example, WINCIM) resides on your system. Use

Schedule Connect Times to set up when Exchange should automatically connect to CompuServe and retrieve and send mail messages.

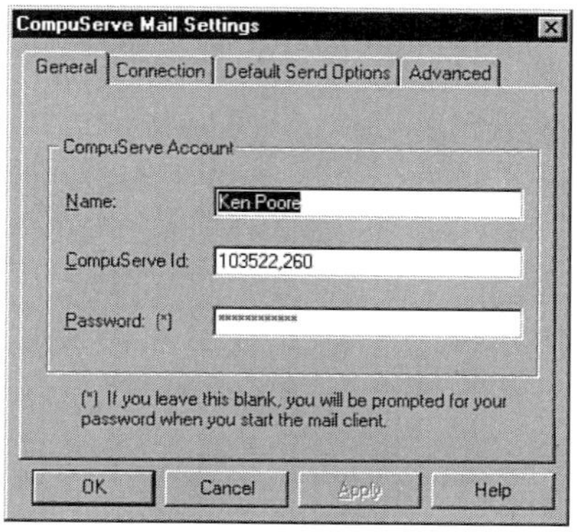

FIG. 31.9

The CompuServe Mail Service is easily configured using the pages on this sheet.

CompuServe Mail Settings

General | Connection | Default Send Options | Advanced

CompuServe Account

Name: Ken Poore

CompuServe Id: 103522,260

Password: [*] ●●●●●●●●●●

[*] If you leave this blank, you will be prompted for your password when you start the mail client.

OK   Cancel   Apply   Help

Creating and Sending Mail Messages

After you configure one or more information services, you can create and send a message with the Exchange client. If Exchange were perfect, it would have a universal composition screen in which you could compose any type of message for any type of recipient and for any delivery method. Because of the differences between fax recipients and e-mail recipients, however, you have to decide whether to compose a mail message or a fax.

This section explains how to create and send a Microsoft Mail e-mail message to members of your workgroup LAN. The next section describes how to compose and send a fax with Microsoft Fax.

Creating a Mail Message

How to send an e-mail message to a member of your workgroup LAN will be explained first. You'll be working with the message form discussed earlier in this chapter. Remember that you'll have all the power of Rich Text Formatting and OLE at your fingertips when you create your e-mail message.

 TIP To quickly e-mail a file from within Explorer, right-click the file name and select Send To, Fax Recipient.

 If the Exchange window is not open, start the Exchange program by double-clicking the Inbox icon on the desktop. Then choose Compose, New Message. If you prefer to use the toolbar, click the New Message button. Exchange opens the New Message window.

Figure 31.10 shows the initial blank composition window, which is Exchange's New Message form, or window. You will see this form frequently while you work in Exchange. Now you can work on your message.

FIG. 31.10

Exchange displays the New Message window in which you compose your message.

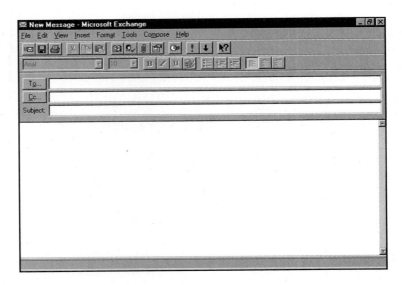

TIP You also can get to the New Message window by pressing Ctrl+N in the main Exchange window.

Choosing a Recipient

When you click To in the New Message window, your Personal Address Book pops up, showing the list of recipients that you have created. Select the names of the people to whom you want to send your message; you can select names for the To box and names for the Cc box.

You may want to send a blind carbon copy, called a Bcc. The blind copy will be sent to any recipients on the Bcc list. The recipients of the original message and any Cc recipients will not know a copy has gone to the Bcc recipient. The New Message form does not show the Bcc text box by default. You can display this text box by choosing View, Bcc Box.

▶ **See** "Working with Your Address Book," **p. 930**

Entering Text

Start with the Subject box and type the subject of the message.

Pressing Tab takes you to the main message-entry space, where you can write what you have to say. Start entering text now.

T I P Enter your text for the message first and format it later.

Formatting Message Text

If you use a word processor, you should see a remarkable similarity between the word processor and the menus and toolbars of the New Message form. The toolbars and menus give you the option of choosing the following formatting options for your message text (the options are listed as they appear on the toolbar, from left to right):

- Font (limited to the fonts on your system)
- Font Size (as small or large as the TrueType font scaler can handle)
- Bold
- Italic
- Underline
- Text Color
- Bullets
- Indents
- Text Alignment (left-align, center, and right-align)

You can combine these options to create messages in Rich Text Format. Whenever you use fonts in varying sizes, colors, and alignments, or other formatting options, you add depth to your communications.

Sending Files and OLE Objects with Exchange

You are not limited to text messages, or even Rich Text Format messages. One of Exchange's most useful capabilities is including files and objects in messages. When you use files and objects in your messages, you can add a lot of extra content to those messages with very little work.

Practically any file on your system can be included in a message. You can send text files, graphics files, and files created by the applications you have. However, if you do send an application file (such as a spreadsheet or database file), be sure that your recipients also have the same applications so they can read what you send them.

N O T E If you want to send a file to a user who retrieves mail from an online service like CompuServe and who may not be using Exchange to read mail, you should not send the file as an OLE object. Send it as a file instead. Few e-mail programs other than Exchange can

continues

continued

interpret an embedded OLE object in an e-mail message. On the other hand, most e-mail programs, including those on nearly all online services, have no difficulty detecting an attached file and can deliver it properly to your recipient. ■

Follow these steps to insert a file (also known as an *attachment*) into an Exchange mail message:

1. After opening up a New Message window by choosing Compose, New Message, choose your recipients and type in the subject of the message. Go to the body of the message and choose Insert, File. A file selection dialog box appears (see fig. 31.11).

FIG. 31.11
Use the Insert File dialog box to insert files into mail messages.

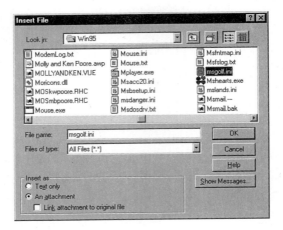

2. Browse through your file system and select the file you want to include inside the message.

3. Use the options in the Insert As section at the bottom of the dialog box to choose how you would like to insert the file into your message:

   - If your message is a straight text file, you can insert the file directly into the mail message, dumping the contents of the file right into the body of your message. Select the Text Only option in the Insert As section at the bottom of the dialog box. Click the OK button to import the text file's content into your mail message.

   - If you are inserting a file containing something other than straight text, you must insert it as an attachment. This preserves the file as a separate item in your mail message. The recipients of the message can save the file to their disk when they read your message, or they can choose to double-click the file icon in the mail message and launch the application associated with the type of file you sent them.

- Related to the previous method of attaching the file and using the mail message as a means to transfer it around, you can choose to just send the recipients a link to the file. This only works, however, if you and all your recipients are on a network that can access the file through Network File sharing. To learn how to send links, continue reading the next section.

Sending File Links with Exchange

Windows 95 introduced a powerful feature called shortcuts, which are simple links to files elsewhere on your system. You can place shortcuts on your desktop, in other directories, or on the Start menu so you can have quick access to what the shortcut points to. You also can send shortcuts in mail messages.

The benefit of doing this is that you are not actually inserting the entire file into your mail message: You are merely inserting a link, or shortcut, to the file. When your recipients receive your mail message and double-click the inserted file link, their application resolves the shortcut to the file on your system, connects to your machine, and accesses the file directly over the network. Sending a link is useful if the file to send is very large or may be accessed by several people simultaneously, like a Microsoft Access database file (MDB file).

Follow these steps to send a file link in a mail message:

1. Verify that the file you want to send is on a shared drive, accessible to all the recipients to whom you want to send the file link.
2. Choose Insert, File from the New Message window's menu. Browse through the file system and locate the file you want to send. Select the file—its name will appear in the File Name field.
3. In front of the file name, type in the UNC name of the network share containing this file. If the file is in a subfolder of the share, be sure to include it in the UNC (see fig. 31.12).
4. In the Insert As box at the bottom of the dialog box, choose to insert the file as An Attachment, Link Attachment To Original File.
5. Choose OK.

    ▶ **See** "Sharing Network Drives," **p. 750**
    ▶ **See** "Using UNC Naming," **p. 754**

FIG. 31.12
Instead of embedding files in messages, you can send links.

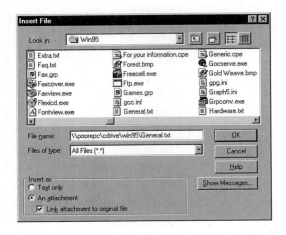

N O T E You can send links to Internet sites in mail messages. In Internet Explorer, choose File, Create Shortcut, when displaying the page you want to mail to someone else. Then in your mail message, choose Edit, Paste to insert the link. ■

If you are only going to send types of files that are common and built into Windows 95, you should send them as embedded OLE objects. This way, the recipient only has to double-click the object and Windows 95 automatically knows how to view it.

You can insert the following types of Windows 95 objects into your messages:

- Audio Recorder
- Bitmap images
- Media clips
- Microsoft Word documents or pictures
- MIDI sequences
- Packages
- Paintbrush pictures
- QuickTime movies
- Video clips
- Wave sounds
- WordPad documents

Each application on your system that is an OLE server can create OLE objects that you can place in your messages, so the preceding list is not exhaustive.

▶ **See** "Creating an Example Compound Document," **p. 588**

Follow these steps to insert an OLE object in an Exchange mail message:

1. In Exchange, choose Insert, Object. The list of available object types appears (see fig. 31.13).

FIG. 31.13
Use the Insert Object dialog box to choose an OLE object type to insert in an Exchange message.

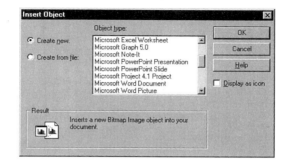

 If you want your OLE option to appear as an icon, select the Display As Icon option while in the Insert Object dialog box. Leave this check box cleared if you want the data—the spreadsheet rows, word processing text, picture, or whatever—displayed rather than the icon. (Some objects—sounds, for instance—can't be displayed, so their icons display automatically.)

2. Select the type of object you want to include in your message, and then choose OK. Select Wave Sound, for example, to insert a sound recording in the message. The application used to create the object starts. In the case of a Sound Wave object, the Sound Recorder application starts.

N O T E Notice that the OLE server application that opens has a special kind of title bar. Instead of saying Sound Recorder, for instance, the title bar would say Sound Object in Mail Message. The OLE server applications also have slightly different menus and options from when they run normally. The File menu in Sound Recorder, for example, has a new option: Exit & Return to Mail Message.

3. Use the application to create the object that you want to mail. In this case, record the audio that you want to send with your mail, and then choose File, Exit & Return to Mail Message. The application disappears, leaving the Wave Sound icon in your message.

If you are inserting a form of data that can be displayed, and if you didn't choose the Display As Icon check box in the Insert Object dialog box, you see the actual data rather than the icon. You can move this data, or the icon, around in your message, and you can give the icon a more useful name than the default name (Bitmap Image).

When recipients get a message containing an icon, they must double-click the icon. This starts the application that created the OLE object. The object is then played or displayed.

N O T E   When you insert objects in Exchange messages, rename the icon, including text such as "Click here to play," to make the icon's intended function obvious to the receiver. To rename the icon, right-click it, choose Rename, and then type the new name in the text box over the old name. Press Enter when you're finished. ■

Embedding an object or file in a message is an example of OLE at work in Exchange.

 T I P   Many applications today have a File, Send command that creates a new e-mail message and automatically embeds the document you're working on in the new e-mail message.

FIG. 31.14
Rich Text Format and Object Linking and Embedding functions are illustrated in this sample Exchange message.

Formatted text ┤

OLE object ──

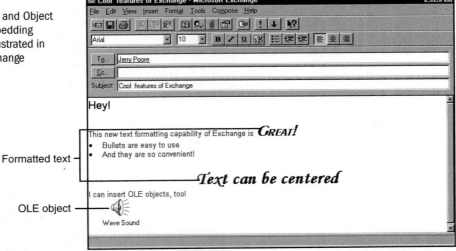

Finishing and Sending Your Mail Message

After you've written your message and added any formatting or OLE objects that you want, there are a few more options you may want to select.

Choose Tools, Options, and then click the Send tab. The following list describes the items on the Send page:

- ■ *Read Receipt and Delivery Receipt.* Requests that a receipt be sent back when the message has been delivered to or read by the recipient.

- *Sensitivity.* Sets sensitivity rankings such as Normal, Personal, Private, and Confidential to your message.

- *Importance Ranking.* Checks whether you want High, Normal, or Low priority for your message. You also can choose the High/Low icons to perform this task.

- *Save a Copy in 'Sent Items' Folder.* Saves a copy of the message in the Sent Items folder.

 Close the Properties box. To send your message, choose File, Send, or click the Send button.

TROUBLESHOOTING

I sent a Microsoft Mail message on my workgroup network, but the message wasn't received.
Make sure that only one Postoffice is installed for your workgroup and that the Postoffice is located in a shared folder that everyone in the workgroup can access.

Using Remote Mail

When you are not connected to a network or your online service and need to read your e-mail, Remote Mail can help you download specific mail messages and optimize your modem connect time. Remote Mail is best used when you expect either a large number of messages to be waiting in your inbox, or you anticipate large messages with attachments that you don't want to download all at once. Remote Mail enables you to connect to your e-mail service, look at the headers of all the mail in your inbox, and pick and choose which mail messages you want to download and read. This section shows how easy Remote Mail is to use.

Setting Up Remote Mail

Most add-in mail services for Exchange support using Remote Mail in addition to the usual way Exchange transfers mail. Some Exchange add-in services require more configuration than others to set up Remote Mail. Some services, like the CompuServe Mail Service for Exchange, require no set up at all—you can use Remote Mail any time without any additional configuration. The Microsoft Mail service, however, has several options important to configuring Remote Mail.

To use Remote Mail with a Microsoft Mail Postoffice, you need to configure the connection and delivery options of Microsoft Mail. However, you must first have a Dial-Up Networking connection established to connect you to the machine where the Postoffice resides.

▶ **See** "Using Dial-Up Networking," **p. 205**

To set up Remote Mail for Microsoft Mail, follow these steps:

1. Open the Start menu and choose Settings, Control Panel.

2. Double-click the Mail and Fax icon.

3. Choose the Microsoft Mail service and click Properties.

4. On the Connection page, select which type of connection you use to access your Microsoft Mail Postoffice:

    • If you're sometimes connected to a LAN and sometimes using a modem to read mail (if you're using a laptop, for instance), choose Automatically Sense LAN or Remote. Exchange figures out how you're connected and uses the right connection type.

    • If you're always on the LAN, select Local Area Network (LAN). You will probably not use Remote Mail if you're always connected to the LAN where your Microsoft Mail Postoffice resides, however, you can still use Remote Mail if you have a slow network connection to the mail server or do not want mail to be automatically delivered to your inbox.

    • If you always use a modem to send and receive mail, choose Remote Using a Modem and Dial-Up Networking.

    • If you do not want to connect via a LAN or a modem, choose Offline. You can compose mail while not connected and reconnect later, if needed.

5. Choose the LAN Configuration page.

6. If you are connected to the LAN and still need to use Remote Mail, choose the Use Remote Mail option. Mail will only be delivered and sent when you use Remote Mail.

7. Choose the Remote Configuration page. These settings are used only when you use a modem to read mail remotely (see fig. 31.15).

8. Choose the Use Remote Mail option. This enables Remote Mail for the Microsoft Mail Service.

9. If you want to keep a local copy of the Postoffice's Address List on your machine so you can select Postoffice mail addresses while not actually connected to the Postoffice, choose the Use Local Copy option. You can later download a copy of the Address Book and store it locally.

10. If you want to connect to your Postoffice automatically during your Exchange session, choose the Remote Session page and choose When This Service Is Started. You can set up scheduled connections to your Postoffice by clicking the Schedule Mail Delivery button. Otherwise, by default, you will only connect to your Postoffice when you choose.

FIG. 31.15

The Remote Configuration Page sets up your Microsoft Mail Service to use Remote Mail.

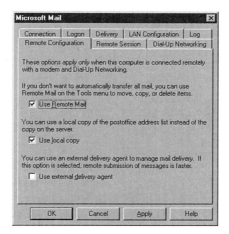

11. If you use Dial-Up Networking to connect to your Postoffice, on the Dial-Up Networking page, select which Dial-Up Networking Connection you use to connect to your Postoffice.

Once configured, Remote Mail is very easy to use. The next section explains how to use Remote Mail after it's configured.

Sending and Receiving Mail Using Remote Mail

Once your mail services are configured to use Remote Mail, the process of connecting to your e-mail service, sending, selecting, and downloading mail is very easy.

Remote Mail has a separate window that is used for viewing the headers of mail messages waiting on the remote e-mail service. When you initially connect to your mail service, you will usually have Remote Mail retrieve the headers of all your new mail, as well as send out what is in your outbox. After completing that and disconnecting, you will review the headers of all your new messages, choosing which ones you would like to download and read. Finally, you reconnect to your mail service and retrieve the messages you've selected. Here are the steps you would typically take to access your mail using Remote Mail:

1. From the Exchange menu, choose Tools, Remote Mail, Microsoft Mail. This displays the dialog box shown in figure 31.16.

2. Click the Update Headers icon or select Tools, Update Headers. The dialog box in figure 31.17 appears.

FIG. 31.16
The Remote Mail window allows you to select which messages you want to receive from your Postoffice.

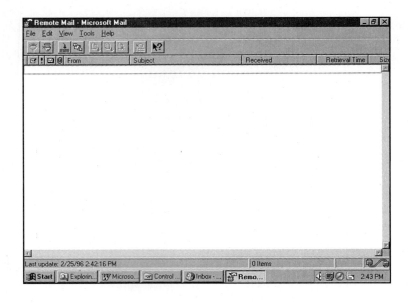

FIG. 31.17
You can do several different tasks when updating the list of message headers.

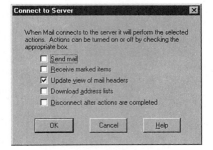

3. While retrieving the waiting message headers, you also can choose the following options:

- Send Mail will take any messages in your outbox addressed to a mail recipient in the Postoffice and send them.

- Receive Marked Items retrieves the messages you've selected from your header list. The first time you enter the Update Headers dialog box you will probably not have chosen to retrieve any messages.

- Download Address Lists should be chosen only when you want to download a local copy of the Postoffice's Address List. This will enable you to select Postoffice mail recipients when you're not connected to the Postoffice. If you think your copy of the address list is out-of-date, you should choose this option. Depending on the number of people in your Postoffice, this could add several minutes to your connection time.

- Choose <u>D</u>isconnect After Actions Are Completed to terminate your modem connection after your headers are downloaded.

4. Click OK to start the transfer. A dialog box with a gauge will keep you informed of what is transpiring during your connection. After a few moments, depending on how many options you've selected, the Remote Mail dialog box will display the headers of the messages waiting in your Postoffice inbox (see fig. 31.18).

FIG. 31.18

The list of waiting messages appears after updating the message headers.

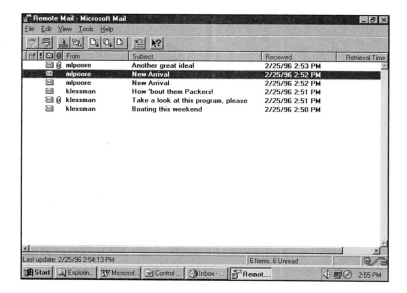

5. Now you can pick and choose which messages you need to retrieve from your Postoffice inbox. When you select which messages to retrieve, you have three options from which to choose (each of these options are also available by right-clicking the message header and choosing it from the pop-up menu):

- Click the Mark to <u>R</u>etrieve button, or choose <u>E</u>dit, Mark to <u>R</u>etrieve, from the menu to retrieve the message and remove it from the Postoffice. The next time you update the message headers, you will not see this message in your Postoffice.

- Click the Mark to Retrieve a Copy, or choose <u>E</u>dit, Mark to Retrieve a <u>C</u>opy, to retrieve a copy of the message, but also keep it in your Postoffice. The message will be marked as read and will not be bolded when you update your headers again.

- Click the Mark to Delete button or choose <u>E</u>dit, Mark to <u>D</u>elete to delete messages without reading them (see fig. 31.19).

FIG. 31.19
You can choose which messages are retrieved from your Postoffice using Remote Mail.

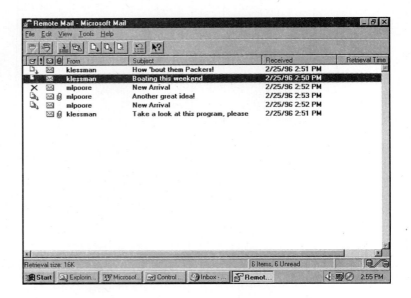

6. Click the Transfer Mail button or choose <u>T</u>ools, <u>T</u>ransfer Mail. A dialog box similar to the Update Headers dialog box seen earlier appears; only this time with the <u>S</u>end Mail, <u>R</u>eceive Marked Items, and Update <u>V</u>iew Of Mail Headers selected by default.

7. Click OK to process your marked items and refresh your view of the waiting message headers. All messages marked for retrieval will be placed in your Exchange Inbox where they can be accessed as usual.

8. If you did not choose to disconnect from the Postoffice automatically and you're finished with Remote Mail for now, you should click the Disconnect button or choose <u>T</u>ools, <u>D</u>isconnect to end your connection with the Postoffice.

9. You can either close the Remote Mail window by selecting <u>F</u>ile, <u>C</u>lose, or select your main Exchange window and continue working with both windows open.

 If you use both a notebook computer and a computer that is connected to your Postoffice over a LAN, choose to Retrieve a Copy of your mail messages. Messages will stay in your Postoffice inbox so you can access them from your LAN-based computer later.

Using Remote Mail with Other Mail Services

The Microsoft Mail service's Remote Mail capabilities are very robust and configurable. Other Exchange services like CompuServe require no special configuration at all. To use Remote Mail to access your CompuServe Mail, from the Exchange menu select <u>T</u>ools,

Remote Mail, CompuServe Mail. The same dialog boxes appear as in Remote Mail for Microsoft Mail explained in the previous section, and they all work the same way.

Viewing Received Mail

To view and work with your received mail, you must have Exchange running. This section explains how you can see your received mail and how to keep the Exchange window organized at the same time.

How Things Are Organized in Exchange

Exchange contains, by default, four Personal folders, each of which holds a different kind of message. The folder names show the function of the folders:

- *Inbox*. This folder is where messages that come in to you are initially stored.

- *Deleted Items*. This folder stores messages that you've deleted from other folders.

- *Outbox*. This folder stores messages you are sending until you actually send them.

- *Sent Items*. This folder stores messages you have sent after they are successfully sent.

> **T I P** It is very useful to be able to see all four Exchange folders on your screen. If you display all four folders, you can tell what kind of message you're seeing.

 To display all four folders described earlier, choose View, Folders on the Exchange menu bar. You also can click the Show/Hide Folder List icon on the Exchange toolbar.

When you choose to display the folder list, your Exchange window divides into two parts. On the left side of the window, you see the list of the four folders. When you highlight a folder on the left side of the Exchange window, the contents of that folder are displayed on the right side of the window.

For example, if you highlight the Inbox folder, you see the contents of your Inbox folder on the right side of the window. The contents of the Inbox folder are your received messages and faxes. If a message in the inbox appears in **boldface**, the message is new and has not yet been read.

The types of messages that you can see in your inbox depend on the Exchange services that you installed. If you installed Microsoft Fax, for example, you can see faxes. If you installed The Microsoft Network, you can see mail from MSN members and from the Internet. If you have Microsoft Mail installed for your workgroup network, you can see workgroup Mail messages. With Internet Mail installed, you can see mail from your own Internet mailbox.

Figure 31.20 shows an Exchange inbox that contains several types of messages. You can manipulate these messages in several ways. You examine how to manipulate and work with those received messages in the next sections.

FIG. 31.20

The Exchange inbox is where all your new messages are placed.

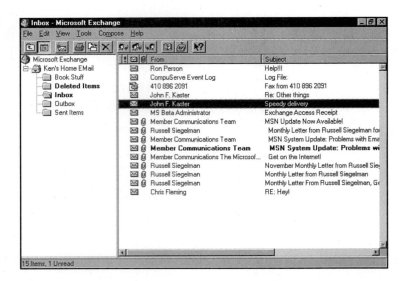

Reading Mail Messages

To read a mail message, double-click the message in your inbox. The standard message form opens, displaying the message. The Subject appears in the message form title bar. Figure 31.21 shows a received mail message.

Editing, Replying to, and Forwarding Messages

The standard message form (refer to fig. 31.10) is an important place where a great deal of messaging action takes place. Notice that the form looks very much like a Windows word processor, complete with formatting toolbar. All the Rich Text tools are available, just as they are when you compose a message. In fact, the standard message form for composing a message is identical to the form for viewing, editing, replying to, and forwarding mail messages.

 TIP As a shortcut to send, reply to, forward, or edit a message without displaying it first, highlight the message in your inbox and then right-click.

FIG. 31.21
Opening a mail message in
your inbox displays the
message.

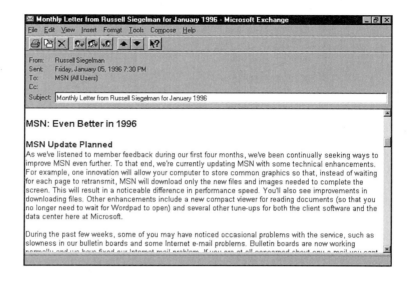

While you're working with a received mail message, you can edit it if you want. Add text, files, or OLE objects, then use the tools in the Compose menu to whisk your reply on its way (see fig. 31.22).

FIG. 31.22
The Compose menu has
Reply and Forward options.

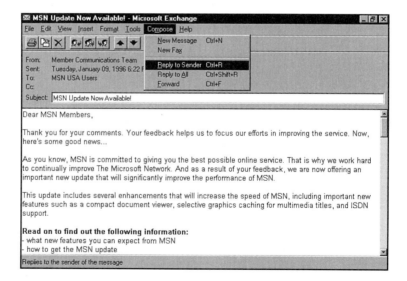

Sorting Messages

Above the messages in any of the Exchange folders are column headings. These headings indicate the following:

■ The importance of the message (according to the sender)

■ The item type

■ Whether files are attached to the message

■ The sender's name

■ The subject

■ The date and time when the message was received

■ The size of the message (in kilobytes)

You can sort the messages in any of the Exchange folders in the following ways:

■ Click the column heading to sort the messages in the folder by the value in that column, in ascending order.

■ Right-click the column heading to change the sort from ascending to descending order.

■ Choose View, Sort in the main Exchange window to access more elaborate sorting functions. Figure 31.23 shows these functions.

FIG. 31.23
You can use these advanced options to sort your messages.

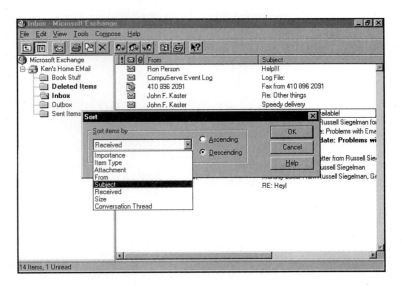

N O T E   The default From, Subject, Received, and Size columns in Exchange are only the tip of the iceberg. You can display many more columns if the column headings are relevant to your work. You'll find loads of column options, many of which are rather obscure. The options available depend on the message services you have installed. What works for one service may not work for another. ■

Deleting Messages

When you finish working with a message in your inbox and you want to delete it, highlight it and press the Delete key. It's removed from the inbox, but it's not really deleted. Rather, it's transferred to the Deleted Items folder.

> **CAUTION**
>
> Deleting a message from the Deleted Items folder completely removes it from your system. It does not place it in the Recycle Bin.

Using the Message Finder

Part IX
Ch
31

Exchange can be used to search through all of your Exchange folders, looking for messages that match certain criteria. You can choose among many options, shown in the following list. You can find items matching

- The name of a sender you specify with the From option.
- A message you sent to a certain recipient with the Sent To option.
- A message sent Directly to you, or Copied (Cc) to you.
- A message with a particular subject, by choosing the Subject option.
- Certain text in the message with the Message Body option.

To use Message Finder, choose Tools, Find in the main Exchange window, then choose the search option you want to use. For example, if you're looking for messages sent to John Jones, enter **John Jones** in the Sent To text box. Exchange displays a list of messages matching the criteria you have chosen.

Working with User Profiles in Exchange

When you installed Exchange, you worked with the Inbox Setup Wizard. You gave the wizard information about yourself, and you installed one or more communications services in Exchange. You also gave the wizard information about the communications services you chose, such as User ID and Mailbox Name.

When you finished installing Exchange, the wizard saved all the information you gave it. The wizard saved your information in something called a *user profile*.

The user profile in Exchange is where all your personal information and the information on all your communications services are stored. The name of the user profile created by the wizard for you is MS Exchange Settings. MS Exchange Settings becomes the default user profile for your computer.

 TIP   You can add as many user profiles as you need by following the steps in the following section.

This default profile is fine for one user. If your computer has more than one user, however, you may want to create a special user profile for everyone who uses your machine.

Suppose that you share a computer with coworkers who work the second shift. If you don't use The Microsoft Network, but your coworkers do, they may want to set up their own user profiles. Then they can configure and personalize Exchange to suit their needs without disturbing the settings that you use during your shift.

Adding Multiple User Profiles in Exchange

To create an additional user profile, follow these steps:

1. Open the Start menu and choose Settings, Control Panel.
2. In Control Panel, double-click the Mail and Fax icon.
3. Choose Show Profiles. You see the list of existing Exchange profiles.
4. Choose Add to create a new user profile. The Inbox Setup Wizard starts to run.
5. Select the communications services that you want to use with the new user profile you're creating (see fig. 31.24). Then choose Next.

FIG. 31.24
Choose the services to use with your new user profile.

6. Type the name for your new user profile in the Profile Name text box (see fig. 31.25). Then choose Next.

FIG. 31.25

In this example, the new user profile is called "Molly's Exchange Settings."

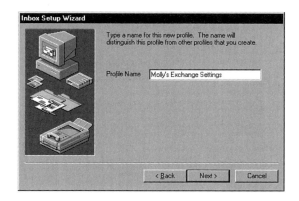

7. You now work with the wizard to set up the communications services you chose in step 5. This works the same way as it did when you first installed Exchange.

▶ **See** "Installing and Configuring Exchange," **p. 876**

When you finish the Inbox Setup Wizard, your new user profile is ready to use. Your screen returns to the Microsoft Exchange Profiles dialog box you saw in step 3. Your new user profile is added to the list of profiles. Figure 31.26 shows Molly's Exchange Settings, along with the default profile, MS Exchange Settings.

FIG. 31.26

Your new user profile has been added to Exchange.

When you have more than one user profile installed, you'll want Exchange to ask you which profile to use each time Exchange starts. Follow these steps to set up Exchange so that it asks which user profile to use:

1. Start Exchange by double-clicking the Inbox icon on your desktop.

2. Choose Tools, Options. The Options dialog box appears.

3. In the When Starting Microsoft Exchange area of the General page, check the Prompt For a Profile To Be Used box (see fig. 31.27).

4. Choose OK.

FIG. 31.27
When you tell Exchange to prompt you for a user profile, you ensure that each user of your computer has the opportunity to pick their own Exchange user profile.

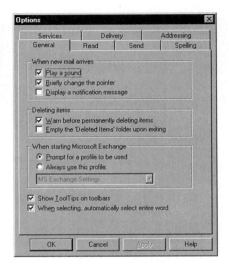

TROUBLESHOOTING

I want to use Microsoft Fax, The Microsoft Network, and Microsoft Mail, but I don't see any references to those services in my Exchange menus. Install the desired services in Exchange. In the Exchange main window, choose Tools, Services, Add, and select the desired service from the list. A wizard guides you in setting up the service, if necessary.

N O T E   If you set up your computer with a different session profile for each user—so the user has to log on when Windows starts—you can ensure that each person's profile starts automatically. Each user should log on to Windows; open Exchange; choose Tools, Options; then click the Always Use This Profile option button and select the appropriate profile. ■

Enabling Mail and Message Security

Normally, when you run Exchange, your mail folders display immediately in the Exchange window. You can see and work with Inbox, Deleted Items, Outbox, and Sent Items as soon as Exchange is running. This means that anyone who starts Exchange on your computer can access all your mail in these four folders.

To make your mail secure, you must set a password for access to your mailbox so that nobody else can open your mailbox and read or work with your messages without your permission. Follow these steps to set up password security for your mail folders:

1. With Exchange running, choose Tools, Options. The Options dialog box appears.
2. Click the Services tab, highlight Personal Folders, and choose Properties.
3. When the Personal Folders Properties sheet appears, choose Change Password. The Microsoft Personal Folders dialog box opens (see fig. 31.28).

FIG. 31.28
Set a password for your mail folders for security.

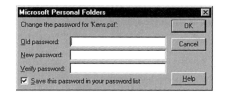

 Don't select the Save This Password in Your Password List option unless you've set up Windows for different users and each user has to log on using a password. If you select this option, you lose password security, because Windows enters the password for you whenever you start Exchange.

4. Enter the password of your choice in the New Password text box. Then repeat the password in the Verify Password text box.
5. Choose OK.

The next time you run Exchange, you have to enter your password to see the contents of your mail folders.

CAUTION
If you forget your mailbox password, you cannot access the contents of your mailbox again. You have to delete your personal folders and set up Exchange again.

If you want to get rid of your mailbox password, follow steps 1 and 2. Then in step 3, type your current password in the Old Password text box. Leave the New Password and Verify Password text boxes blank. This means that you have changed back to having no password security for your mailbox folders. Then choose OK.

Working with the Workgroup Postoffice

Microsoft Mail requires that one of the computers on the workgroup network be set up as a Postoffice. This is usually a job for the network administrator or manager. If this is your function, this section is important for you.

The Postoffice machine is the place where all mail messages are stored for the workgroup. You can choose your machine for Postoffice duties or select a different machine.

The Postoffice must be installed somewhere on the network, in a shared folder that all members of the workgroup can access. Windows 95 comes with the Postoffice and a Wizard that helps you install it.

You have to make the following decisions about your Postoffice:

■ Which machine to install the Postoffice on (choose a machine that has a shared folder that everyone in the workgroup can access)

■ Who will manage and maintain the Postoffice

If you're sure there is no Postoffice installed on your Workgroup LAN, and if you're sure that you are the right person to set it up, the process is simple.

Installing the Workgroup Postoffice

When you are ready to install the Postoffice, follow these steps:

1. Open the Start menu and choose Settings, Control Panel.

2. Double-click the Microsoft Mail Postoffice icon.

3. Select Create a New Workgroup Postoffice, as shown in figure 31.29. Then choose Next.

FIG. 31.29
Use the Microsoft Workgroup Postoffice Admin utility to create a new Workgroup Postoffice.

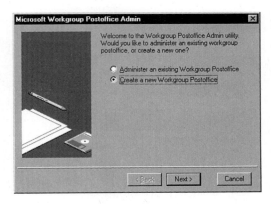

4. Type the full path to the folder you've chosen for the Postoffice in the Postoffice Location text box. Remember, this needs to be a shared folder that everyone on the Workgroup LAN can access. You can click the Browse button to find the folder.

5. Choose Next. The folder you've selected for the Postoffice displays for your approval. Choose Next again.

6. The next dialog box that appears requests administration details. Type your name in the Name text box, your mailbox name in the Mailbox text box, and your mail password in the Password text box (see fig. 31.30). Choose OK.

7. You'll see a message box reminding you to allow other users access to the Postoffice—which can be done from Explorer. Choose OK. You have finished creating your Postoffice.

Part

IX

Ch

31

FIG. 31.30
Enter Postoffice Administrator information in this dialog box.

N O T E The other text boxes shown in figure 31.25 may be filled in as you prefer, but are not required to set up the Postoffice.

CAUTION
Create only one Postoffice on your workgroup network. If you create more than one, the mail system won't work properly.

▶ **See** "Sharing Workstation Drives," **p. 802**

CHAPTER 32

Using Fax, Address Book, and Phone Dialer

by Ken Poore

This chapter covers three topics that are not all directly related, but are all tools you may use every day. ∎

How to create, send, and receive faxes

The first section in this chapter shows how to use Microsoft Fax, a service which you can install into Microsoft Exchange that enables you to send and receive faxes.

How to manage and use all your e-mail and fax addresses

The next section explains the Address Book, an integral part of Microsoft Exchange and Fax that maintains all your fax and e-mail recipient addresses and information, including phone numbers and other personal contact information.

How to set up a speed dialer to dial frequently used numbers

The final section shows how to use the Phone Dialer, a useful accessory which mimics and improves upon a phone speed dialer many of us already use today.

Overview of Microsoft Fax

Microsoft Fax works within Microsoft Exchange's Universal Inbox to provide a convenient place to compose, attach or embed documents, and address a fax. Exchange gives you several ways to create faxes. You can use the Compose New Fax Wizard to send a simple typed message or an attached file. (Yes, you can transfer computer files using Fax, as you'll find out later.) You can use the same New Message window that you use to compose e-mail, or you can create your fax in another application and send or print it to the fax system. Your faxes can include text, pictures, OLE objects, and files. This richness of function is one of the key benefits of using the fax capabilities within Microsoft Exchange.

Installing and Configuring Microsoft Fax

If you chose to install Microsoft Fax while using the Inbox Wizard, you see the dialog box shown in figure 32.1. The wizard asks you to enter information about your telephone number: your area code, the number (if any) that you dial to get an outside line, and whether you are using pulse or tone dialing.

FIG.32.1
The Wizard's Location
Information dialog box.

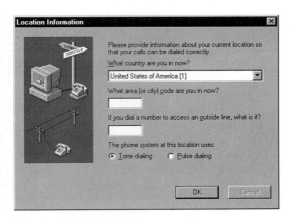

You are then asked whether you want to use a modem or a network-fax service (you can choose only the latter if you have installed network software; if you haven't, the wizard ignores your selection and assumes that you want to use a modem). Select the appropriate option button and choose Next.

The wizard now asks for information about the modem or network-fax service. If you have already installed a modem, you see something like the dialog box in figure 32.2. (If you haven't yet installed a modem, the Install New Modem Wizard starts.)

FIG. 32.2

The Inbox Setup Wizard's Microsoft Fax dialog box lets you specify the kind of device you want to use for sending and receiving faxes.

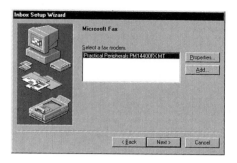

▶ **See** "Configuring Your Modem," **p. 294**

▶ **See** "Installing and Configuring Exchange," **p. 876**

Select which modem you want to use for your fax messages—in the illustration there is only one choice. You can add another fax modem—or a Network Fax Server—by clicking Add. Or modify the selected fax modem's properties by choosing Properties. When you've selected the fax modem (or added a Network Fax Server), choose Next.

 If you want to be prompted to receive a fax when the phone rings, select Properties, Manual Answer mode. You'll still be able to pick the phone and talk, too.

If you select a modem rather than a Network Fax Server, the wizard asks you whether you want Microsoft Fax to answer each incoming call on the phone line the modem is connected to. Choose Yes or No. (If you choose Yes, you may also want to change the Answer After *n* Rings value—you'll probably want the smallest value, 2 rings.) Then choose Next.

The Inbox Setup Wizard now asks for the information that will be used on any fax cover sheets you send along with your outgoing faxes, so people will know who sent them and how to fax back to you.

Enter your name and other information as requested in the dialog box shown in figure 32.3 (you must enter the fax number or you will be unable to continue). Then choose Next.

The Fax service is now installed. If you selected another service to install, the Inbox Setup Wizard now asks for information about that service.

FIG.32.3
Enter the personal information you want included on
your faxes in this dialog box.

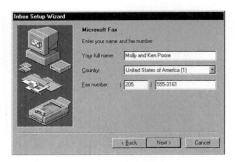

Faxing a Quick Message or a File

You also can send a quick text message, or "fax" a file. This method lets you type a quick
note (you won't be able to format the note) or transmit a file attached to the fax using the
new BFT fax technology. If you want to do more—such as send a nicely formatted fax
message, put pictures inside it, or fax from your word processor—see "Sending a More
Complete Message," later in this chapter. In the main Exchange window, choose Compose, New Fax. The Compose Fax Wizard appears.

 TIP A quick way to fax a file from within Explorer is to right-click the file and select Send To, Fax
Recipient.

▶ **See** "Working with Phone Dialer," **p. 934**

The wizard first verifies the location from which you are sending the message, as shown
in figure 32.4. If you have created other dialing locations and moved your portable computer to one of them, choose I'm Dialing From and specify the new location. (Notice also
that you can click the check box at the bottom of the dialog box to tell the wizard not to
display this next time.) Then choose Next.

FIG. 32.4
The Compose New Fax
Wizard confirms your dialing
location.

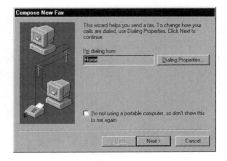

Addressing a Fax

The wizard next prompts you for a recipient and offers to show you your Personal Address Book. If you want to choose a name from the Book, choose Address Book to display the Book (see fig. 32.5). Select a recipient and choose OK.

FIG.32.5
Choose a fax recipient from your Personal Address Book.

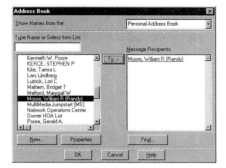

You also can just type the recipient information in the text boxes named To and Fax #, without using the Personal Address Book. Use the Add to List button if you want to send the fax to several different numbers. Select the first and choose Add to List; select the second, and choose Add to List; and so on. Choose Next when you are ready to continue.

▶ **See** "Working with Your Address Book," **p. 930**

▶ **See** "Working with Your Address Book," **p. 930**

Selecting a Cover Page

Next, the wizard asks whether you want to send a cover page with your fax. Windows has the following built-in cover pages:

- Confidential
- For your information
- Generic
- Urgent!

To use a cover page, select the page you want from the displayed list. Click No if you don't want to send a cover page.

 TIP If you don't like any of the predesigned cover pages, use the Cover Page Editor to customize one of them or to create your own. See "Using the Fax Cover Page Editor" later in this chapter.

Options for Fax Transmission

There are a variety of fax options that you can set before you move on. Choose Options to display the Compose New Fax Wizard's Send Options dialog box (see fig. 32.6). Use these options to control when your fax is sent, the format you use to send it, the paper size, and the security applied. In this dialog box, you also can choose the Dialing Location, or a cover page to send with your fax, as you did in the preceding section.

FIG. 32.6

This dialog box lets you specify various fax sending options.

The following sections explain these options and how to use them.

Time to Send You can select a time to send your fax. Your choices are:

- As Soon as Possible

- Discount Rates (nights and weekends)

- Specific Time (which you can choose)

TIP To set up the times for your discount phone rates, from the main Exchange menu, select Tools, Microsoft Fax Tools, Options, and choose the Set button next to the Discount Rates option.

Message Format The Message Format section deals with the new *editable faxes* technology. A traditional fax is a single graphics image. Editable faxes are more like file transfers between computers, with the optional addition of a cover page. In fact, editable faxes are so much like file transfers that the technology behind them is called BFT, for *Binary File Transfer.*

An editable fax can be edited by the recipient in the application that created it or in any application that can open its file type. If you send a document created in Word for Windows (a DOC file), the recipient can open it in Word, WordPad, AmiPro, or WordPerfect, using import filters, if necessary.

Sending editable faxes is very convenient, because the receiver's options are increased. The recipient can view or print the fax as you sent it, or edit the fax first.

You have three choices with the Message Format option:

- *Editable, If Possible.* Editable faxes can be exchanged only between computers using Microsoft Exchange and Microsoft Fax. This is the optimum way to send a fax.

  If the receiver is using a traditional fax machine, using editable format is not possible, so the fax is sent the old-fashioned way, as a graphic. If the recipient has a fax card in a computer but doesn't have Microsoft Exchange installed, the fax is delivered as a graphic. Exchange automatically determines which way to send the fax when it connects to the receiving machine.

N O T E In the near future, other systems may implement *Binary File Transfer* (BFT) in a way that is compatible with the Microsoft system. When that happens, you will be able to exchange editable faxes with those systems, too.

T I P Editable faxes can be exchanged between Microsoft Exchange systems very quickly, because the format used is much more compressed than the format that regular fax machines use.

Part
IX

Ch
32

- *Editable Only.* This option works only for transfers between two Microsoft Exchange systems. If the receiving system is not a Microsoft Exchange system, the fax will not go through.

- *Not Editable.* You use this option when you want all your faxes to be sent as a single graphic image in traditional fax format.

Message Security   Choose the Security button to see the Security options. Security works only with editable faxes. You have two basic choices—None and Password-Protected. If you choose None, your fax can be read immediately upon receipt. Choosing Password-Protected requires the recipient to type the password that you applied to that fax transmission in order to see it.

CAUTION

If you activate password security on a fax that is sent to a non-Microsoft Exchange recipient or fax machine, your fax will not go through.

Paper Size and Orientation, and Image Quality   Choose Paper to access the Paper Size and Orientation options. These options are usable with noneditable faxes. You can choose letter or legal paper. You also can choose Portrait (vertical) or Landscape (horizontal) page orientation.

You also can change the Image Quality in this dialog box. This determines the resolution at which Exchange prepares the fax. As with a laser printer, the higher the resolution, the crisper and cleaner your fax will be when printed.

Pick one of the following three Image Quality options, based on your need for a high-quality fax balanced against the additional time it takes to send the fax at a higher resolution:

- *Best Available.* This setting is recommended; it makes your fax look as good as possible on the receiving end.
- *Fine* (200 dots per inch, or dpi). Fine mode can result in incompatibilities if the receiving side doesn't support it. If it works with your recipient's hardware, it will look as good as possible.
- *Draft* (200×100 dpi). Draft mode looks coarser than Fine or Best Available, but transmits faster.

Cover Page   To send a cover page with your fax, select the Send Cover Page option and choose which type of cover page to send.

When you've finished selecting all the options you want to use, choose Next, and the Compose New Fax Wizard moves on to let you enter the subject of the fax, and, if you wish, a note to put on the cover page.

▶ **See** "Using the Fax Cover Page Editor," **p. 922**

Fax Subject and Note   When you've finished working with all the options described in the preceding sections and you have chosen Next, the Compose New Fax Wizard displays a dialog box where you can enter the subject of the fax and add a note to accompany your fax.

Type the subject in the Subject text box. Optionally, you can type a note in the Note text box to go along with your fax. Click the Start Note on Cover Page check box to start your note on the cover page. If you leave the box unchecked, the note will start on a new page in your fax. Choose Next.

Adding Files to Your Fax

After the Compose New Fax Wizard finishes with the fax subject and note (covered in the preceding section), it offers you a dialog box where you can select files to include with the fax.

To include a file, choose Add File. You can use Explorer to browse and find the file you want to send with your fax.

When you've chosen the file, or files, to send with your fax, the wizard shows the files you've selected in the Files to Send text box. When you've finished selecting files to add to your fax, choose Next.

> **CAUTION**
>
> The files you've chosen can be sent only if the fax is sent in editable format. If you use any other format, Microsoft Fax will not send the fax or cover sheet.
>
> For this reason, choose to add files to your fax only if you are certain that the recipient's system can support editable format, and that both your sending system and the recipient's receiving system are configured for editable faxing. (Configuring your fax in editable format was covered in "Options for Fax Transmission," earlier in this chapter.)

After you have added any files you want to send with your fax, choose Finish, and Microsoft Fax sends your fax.

▶ **See** "Configuring Your Modem," **p. 294**

TROUBLESHOOTING

I'm trying to send a fax, but it won't go through. Do you hear the modem dial the fax? If not, make sure that you have a fax modem selected and that the settings are correct for your modem type. In Exchange, choose Tools, Services, Microsoft Fax, Properties; then click the Modem tab. You should see your fax modem displayed; if not, click Add to configure your modem.

If you can hear the modem dial the phone, but the modem disconnects just after dialing, repeat the preceding procedure. When you see your modem, select it, and then click Properties. Make sure that the modem is set to allow enough time to connect after dialing (60 seconds is a good choice). This parameter often is set to 1 second by Windows for no apparent reason.

Part
IX

Ch
32

Sending a More Complete Message

There are a couple of other ways to send fax messages. First, you may want to use the same window you used to create an e-mail message. The only difference between creating a fax message and an e-mail message is in the way you address it. If you address the message to a Fax "address," the message will be a fax message.

If you don't already have the fax address in your Address Book, you need to add it first. Then use the To button in the New Message window to add this address to the To line of your message.

Choose File, Send Options to modify fax options while working in the New Message window.

The advantage of sending a fax using this method is that you have all the New Message window's tools available. You can write a message, using all the text-editing capabilities. You also can attach files, and insert pictures into your fax.

The other way to fax is directly from an application. For instance, you could fax from your word processor. Many applications have a Send option on the File menu. If an application you want to use *doesn't* have such an option, you can "print" to Microsoft Fax on the FAX print driver.

▶ **See** "Adding Names to Your Address Book," **p. 932**

Using the Fax Cover Page Editor

The Fax Cover Page Editor is a miniature word processor that allows you to work with graphics as well as Rich Text. Use the Fax Cover Page Editor to create your own custom-made cover pages, or to modify one that is supplied with Exchange. You can do the following with Cover pages that you create or edit:

- Insert data from the Personal Address Book into your cover page
- Paste items from the Clipboard into your cover page
- Import text, or graphics (such as a logo) into your cover page

To use the Cover Page Editor, open the Start menu, choose Programs, Accessories, Fax and then click Cover Page Editor. The Cover Page Editor program starts up.

When you first start the Cover Page Editor program, there is no cover page file loaded. From here, you can design a new cover page. If you start designing a new cover page and then decide you want to start over again, choose File, New, or click the New File icon on the toolbar.

 Fax Cover Pages have a file name extension of CPE. The cover pages that come with Exchange are located in the C:\Windows folder.

To edit and customize an existing cover page, choose File, Open on the menu. Then select the cover page you want to work with.

The most useful feature of the Cover Page Editor is the ability to insert information from your Personal Address Book into your cover sheets. You do this by choosing Insert from the menu bar and then choosing from the options on that menu and successive submenus (see fig. 32.7). Information you can insert includes:

- Recipient's or Sender's Name
- Recipient's or Sender's Fax Number
- Recipient's or Sender's Company

FIG.32.7
Insert Address Book information into your fax cover sheet.

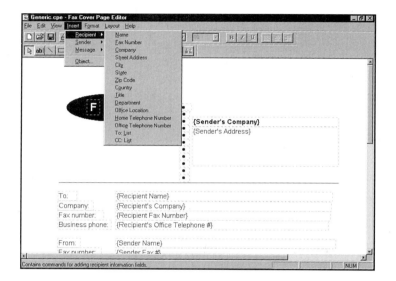

Viewing Received Faxes

The Exchange Inbox can display both e-mail and faxes that you've received (see fig. 32.8). You can see the fax sender's phone number as well as the date and time the fax was received.

When you double-click a normal, noneditable fax, the Fax Viewer opens and displays the fax. When you double-click a received editable fax, or a fax that has attached files, the message window opens. Inside this window, what you see depends on what you received. If you received a fax that the author created in the New Message window, you see exactly what the author saw; the text looks the same, any icons representing attached files look the same, and so on. If, however, you are receiving a fax from another application, (sent using the File, Send option) you see an icon representing the fax. Double-click this icon to open the application associated with that type of file. For instance, if you double-click a DOC file that you've received, the program associated with it opens: Word or WordPad.

FIG. 32.8

The Exchange Inbox shows a received fax.

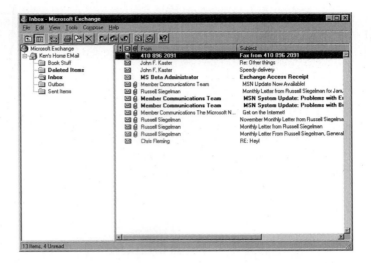

If you receive a fax that the author "printed" to Microsoft Fax on the Fax driver, it comes through as if it were a normal fax from a fax machine; double-clicking the fax in the Inbox opens the Fax Viewer, not the Message window. ■

For instance, figure 32.9 shows a fax received from Notepad. Notice the Notepad icon in the message form to the left of the Notepad window. When the icon was double-clicked, Notepad opened and displayed the fax text. You can edit the text just as though you created the file on your own computer.

TROUBLESHOOTING

Someone is trying to send me a fax, but I'm not receiving it. Make sure that your fax modem is installed. From the Exchange window, choose Tools, Services. Select Microsoft Fax and choose Properties; then click the Modem tab and make sure your modem is shown in the list of Available fax modems. If it is, click the Properties tab and check to see whether the modem is set to answer automatically. If not, select the Answer After check box, and set the number of rings to wait before your fax modem answers calls.

FIG. 32.9
Viewing an editable fax in the application that created the fax.

Notepad icon————

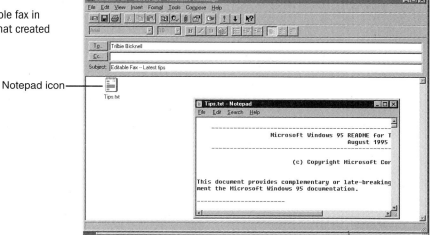

Using Other Fax Options

In addition to the options available when using the Compose New Fax Wizard, there are a few other very useful features that you can enable whenever a fax is sent.

▶ **See** "Options for Fax Transmission," **p. 918**

Using Advanced Fax Security

Security for ensuring that nobody else can view the contents of your faxes is built into Microsoft Fax; by default, however, it is not enabled. To enable the advanced security, select Tools, Microsoft Fax Tools, Advanced Security off the Exchange menu. This type of security is based on key encryption, which is different from the password-based security mentioned earlier. As you would guess, password-based security is based only on a single password; a recipient on the other end must know that password to unlock your fax.

Key encryption is more advanced and more secure, and requires more setup. It works by sending what is called a 'public' version of your key to all the people to whom you will eventually receive encrypted faxes from. They keep this public key on their systems and use it when they only want you to be able to decrypt whatever they're sending. Likewise, you must get their public keys and store them on your system so that you can send them encrypted material that only they can decrypt. Whenever you send them a secure fax, it is encrypted using the public key they've already sent to you. When they receive the encrypted fax, their system uses their own private version of the key to decode the message.

Setting Up Your Encryption Keys   The first steps in using Advanced Fax Security for Microsoft Fax are the creation of your key encryption set, and establishing yourself in the encryption 'system.' For the encryption system to maintain its integrity, the system itself must be protected by your own password; otherwise, anyone else that logs onto your computer might be able to access your encryption system. This is the first line of defense. All of your subsequent key encryption is based on this same password, so you must keep this to yourself or the entire scheme is compromised. Click New Key Set to establish your keys (see fig. 32.10).

FIG. 32.10
Setting up advanced fax security involves the creation of encryption keys.

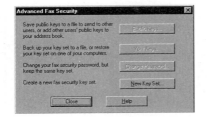

Figure 32.11 displays the dialog box in which you enter your password to build your encryption keys. This same password is used to lock the encryption system. Type in your Password and Confirm it by typing it in again. Checking the Save the Password in Your Password List option saves you from typing in your password each time you receive an encrypted fax, but it also leaves your faxes wide open to anyone who can sit down at your computer and get into your e-mail. If you need the maximum available security, do not select this option. If you keep your password secure, you probably won't have to regenerate your keys in the future. Click OK to return to the Advanced Fax Security dialog box.

FIG. 32.11
You must first establish your password within the key encryption system.

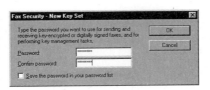

N O T E   Your encryption keys are *not* the same as your password; your keys are made up of an encrypted mixture of your password and your user information. The resulting keys themselves are totally unrecognizable (they're a mish-mash of bits) and virtually unbreakable. ■

Sharing Your Public Keys   To send your public keys to the people who will be sending you encrypted faxes, you must first write your public key to a file so you can later send it via e-mail. Click the Public Keys button on the Advanced Fax Security dialog box, and then click Save (see fig. 32.12).

FIG. 32.12

There are several options to help you manage your Public Keys.

The next dialog box appears, this time asking whose public keys you want to save to the public key file (see fig. 32.13). If you had other public keys available in your address book, they would be listed on the left next to your public key. During the first run through this, only your public key is likely to be available, so click on your name and add it to the To: list, and then click OK.

FIG. 32.13

Selecting your Public Key.

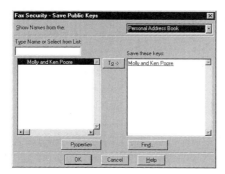

A Save Public Keys dialog box appears (see fig. 32.14), prompting you to write your public key to a file. Choose a folder and click Save.

TIP All public key files end with an AWP extension. It's a good idea to put these files in a folder other than your main Windows folder so you can easily keep track of them.

FIG.32.14

Writing your Public Key to a file.

Now you should send this file in a mail message to those whom you will receive encrypted faxes from (you can send it to them on a floppy, too). Go back to the main Exchange

Window and select Compose, New Message. Select those who will be sending you encrypted faxes, attach the file containing your public keys, and then send it. Be sure to ask them to send you their public keys as well.

When you receive a message from someone containing a public key as a file attachment to an e-mail message, save the attached file. Then, from the Exchange menu, choose Tools, Microsoft Fax Tools, Advanced Security; then select Public Keys from the Managing Public Keys dialog box (refer to fig. 32.12). Click Add and choose the file you just extracted from the e-mail attachment. You see the dialog box shown in figure 32.15.

Choose the names of the users you want to add to your address book's public key list by selecting them from the list and clicking OK.

FIG. 32.15
Adding Public Keys to your system.

Sending a Secure Fax   Now that all your public keys are set up, you can send a key-encrypted secure Fax. Choose Compose, New Message. When the new message dialog box appears, choose File, Send Options, and click the Fax tab. Click the Security button and you can now choose Key-Encrypted Security. If you didn't save your password by using the Save the Password in Your Password List option when you first created your keys, you will have to type in your password next. Close the options dialog boxes and return to composing your fax. Select the recipients, being careful to only choose those recipients for whom you've received a public key. Complete your fax and send it.

Changing Fax Dialing Options

Most fax machines have the ability to continually redial the destination fax if the line is busy—Microsoft Fax does, too. Other options, like making toll calls within your area code and various dialing settings are also available. All these options are available by choosing Tools, Microsoft Fax Tools, Options (see fig. 32.16). The following list describes the options in the Microsoft Fax Properties sheet:

- On the Dialing page, the Toll Prefixes option allows you to select which exchanges in your area code are toll calls requiring the fax to dial 1 and the area code before dialing the number (see fig. 32.17).

FIG. 32.16

Fax dialing options.

FIG. 32.17

Choosing phone exchanges that are toll calls.

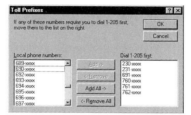

■ Choose <u>D</u>ialing Properties to configure your location and to enter the codes needed to block call waiting and other dialing options.

■ You can change how your modem redials after getting a busy signal by setting the <u>N</u>umber of Retries and the <u>T</u>ime Between Retries.

■ Your user information is inserted into cover pages. If you would like to change your user information, click the User tab and modify it (see fig. 32.18).

▶ **See** "Configuring Your Modem," **p. 294**

FIG. 32.18
Setting up user information for your fax cover pages.

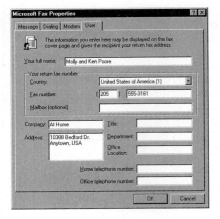

Working with Your Address Book

The Address Book can help you keep track of how to contact your correspondents. You enter names into the Book and specify the type of communications to use (fax, Internet mail, Microsoft LAN Mail, CompuServe Mail, and so on). The Address Book makes sure that your messages are addressed properly.

▶ **See** "Installing and Configuring Exchange," **p. 876**

The entire Address Book in Exchange is built from several different modular, building-block address books. The number of these building-block address books is determined by the communications services you installed when you set up Exchange.

Some of the services you installed come with their own building-block address book modules. For example, if you installed The Microsoft Network online service, a building-block address book for MSN was installed in your Address Book. The MSN Address Book is configured by Microsoft to contain the names and e-mail addresses of all the members of The Microsoft Network.

Microsoft Mail for your workgroup LAN has a building-block address book—built by the network administrator—that is part of your Exchange Address Book. In Exchange, the Microsoft Mail Address Book is called Postoffice Address List.

The final module making up your Address Book is called the Personal Address Book. Here, you can store the names and addresses you use most often. You can transfer names into your Personal Address Book from the other address books.

The Address Book also has options you can use to control how it displays the names you store.

Now, to display and work with the Address Book from the Microsoft Exchange window, choose Tools, Address Book; or press Ctrl+Shift+B.

Setting Display Preferences

By default, names are displayed with the first name followed by the last name (John Jones). If, however, you have a rather long list or know several men called John, you may find viewing the list sorted by last names to be faster.

You can use the Personal Address Book Properties settings to change the order in which first and last names are displayed. To change the order, follow these steps:

1. From the Exchange main window, choose Tools, Address Book. The Address Book opens.

2. Select Personal Address Book from the Show Names From The: drop-down list. The names in your Personal Address Book appear.

3. Choose Tools, Options. The Addressing dialog box appears.

4. In the When Sending Mail list, select Personal Address Book.

5. Click Properties. The Personal Address Book Properties sheet appears.

6. Now you can choose to show names by first name or last name. Click First Name or Last Name on the Personal Address Book page, as shown in figure 32.19.

Part
IX

Ch
32

FIG. 32.19

Use this Properties sheet to select how to display names in the Personal Address Book.

7. You also can give the Personal Address Book a more descriptive name. You, for example, might want to call it Business Contacts. Type the name you want to use for the Personal Address Book in the Name text box.

8. Click the Notes tab and type any information you wish to record about your Personal Address Book in the text box.

Adding Names to Your Address Book

You want to use Exchange as the powerful communications tool it can be. Part of harnessing the power of Exchange is as simple as keeping a well-organized Address Book so that you have all the mail addresses and fax numbers you need conveniently at hand.

1. Open the Address Book by choosing Tools, Address Book. You also can click the Address Book button on the toolbar.

2. In the Show Names From The: drop-down list, select Personal Address Book.

3. Choose File, New Entry. You also can choose the New Entry button on the toolbar. The New Entry dialog box appears (see fig. 32.20).

FIG. 32.20
The power of Exchange is evident in the range of address types to which you can send messages.

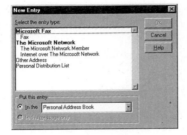

4. Select the type of address you want to add to your Personal Address Book. In this example, we're adding a Microsoft Fax entry to the Book. Then choose OK. The New Fax Properties sheet appears.

5. The Properties sheet that you see in figure 32.21 has text boxes for all the names and numbers required to reach your recipient. Type the pertinent information in each page; then choose OK. The Properties sheet closes, and the new entry appears in your Address Book.

FIG. 32.21
The New Fax Properties sheet is typical of the Properties sheets you fill out when adding entries to your Address Book.

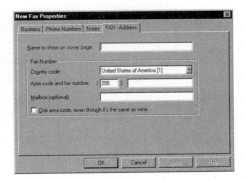

You follow the same steps as those for a Microsoft Fax entry to add different types of addresses, like Microsoft Network addresses or Internet Mail addresses.

The difference between adding the fax address we illustrated and the other possible address types is that after you select the entry type from the New Entry dialog box (step 4 in the previous list), the New Properties sheet that appears is different.

Adding Groups to Your Address Book

To send a message to a group of recipients, create a Personal Distribution List. Once you have a Personal Distribution List, you only have to create a message once, and you can send it to all the members of the list with one click.

Follow these steps to create your Personal Distribution List:

1. Open the Address Book by choosing Tools, Address Book.

2. Choose File, New Entry. The New Entry dialog box appears (refer to fig. 33.20). The New Entry dialog box contains a scrolling list of address types.

3. The last entry in the scrolling list is the Personal Distribution List entry type. Select Personal Distribution List at the bottom of the list.

4. In this example, we're putting our Personal Distribution List in our Personal Address Book. At the bottom of the New Entry dialog box is a setting which says Put This Entry In The. Make sure Personal Address Book shows in the text box. If it doesn't, click the down arrow and scroll to select Personal Address Book.

5. Choose OK. The New Personal Distribution List Properties sheet appears.

6. Name your list. Type the name for your list in the Name text box. In this example, we'll name our Personal Distribution List "Staff Members on Project X."

7. If you want to make some notes about the list, click the Notes tab and type your comments in the text box. You might use this space to document how the group members were chosen. You can enter anything that's useful in this text box.

8. Click the Distribution List tab.

9. Build the Distribution List now. You do this by adding members to the list. Choose Add/Remove Members. A dialog box appears, titled Edit Members of (name of your Distribution List), as shown in figure 32.22.

10. Perhaps one of the people you want to add to the Personal Distribution List is already in another of your building-block address books. If so, choose the proper address book by selecting it from the scrolling list, which is shown in Show Names from the: list. When you choose an address book in Show Names from the:, all the address entries in that address book become visible. In this example, we'll choose to

Part
IX
Ch
32

Show Names from The Microsoft Network. Next, we'll add some addresses from The Microsoft Network online service to our Personal Distribution List.

N O T E You can only use the Microsoft Network address book while online. If you select this address book while offline, the Connect dialog box appears so you can log on. ▇

FIG. 32.22

The Edit Members dialog box has two Microsoft Network member names added to the Personal Distribution List.

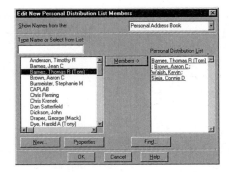

To add other names from existing address books, select Show Names from the:, and select the next address book from the scrolling list. Then repeat the previous step 10.

You also can put people on your Personal Distribution List who are not already in any of your address books. However, you have to put that person into your Personal Address Book first.

Choose New and then follow the steps discussed earlier for adding a name to your Personal Address Book. Once you've made the addition to the book, that name is added to the Personal Distribution List automatically. When you are finished adding members to your Personal Distribution List, choose OK.

Your Personal Distribution List appears in your Personal Address Book, along with any individual addresses you have stored there. By choosing the list as a recipient in a message you create, the message is sent to all members of the Personal Distribution List.

▶ **See** "Adding Names to Your Address Book," **p. 932**

Working with Phone Dialer

The Phone Dialer is a handy accessory built into Windows 95 which acts as a speed dialer, remembering up to eight phone numbers. This may seem a bit redundant if you already have a speed dialer built into your existing phone, but this one is very easy to program and change, plus it can do the more intricate dialing needed to navigate voice-mail systems and make credit card calls. It can even keep a log of your outgoing and incoming calls. The Phone Dialer is accessible from the Start menu, by choosing Programs, Accessories (see fig. 32.23).

FIG. 32.23
Use Phone Dialer to make calls with your modem.

> **N O T E** If you don't see the Phone Dialer on the Accessories menu, open the Start menu and choose Settings, Control Panel; then double-click the Add/Remove Programs icon, click the Windows Setup tab, and select the Communications component. Select Details and be sure the Phone Dialer is selected. Click OK twice to save your changes. ■

Adding Phone Dialer Entries

When first started, your Phone Dialer has no speed dial entries set. Your first task will be to add names and phone numbers to the eight blank dial memories. Click any blank entry and type in the Name and Number to Dial you would like to save (see fig. 32.24).

FIG. 32.24
You can enter a short name for each Phone Dialer entry.

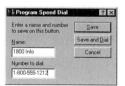

Both the Save and the Save and Dial buttons are now available. You can immediately use your new entry to dial the phone by clicking the Save and Dial button or use the Save button to program your speed dial entry and exit the dialog.

> **TIP** If you have a phone number that contains letters (555-FOOD or 1-800-555-SNOW), just put quotes (") around the letters, like 1-800-555-"SNOW."

Once your number is entered and saved, clicking the speed dial entry immediately starts the phone dialing and opens the dialog box shown in figure 32.25. While waiting for your call to be answered, you can type in a description of the call as you would like it to appear in the phone log.

FIG. 32.25
Enter a log entry while the phone is dialing.

Click <u>H</u>ang Up if you want to abort the call immediately. The Change <u>O</u>ptions button gives you a chance to stop the call and redial with a number you type into the <u>N</u>umber to Redial field (see fig. 32.26). This allows you to specify exactly what you want the modem to dial, ignoring any properties (such as your calling card number) set in the Dialing <u>P</u>roperties sheet. After typing in your number, click the <u>R</u>edial Number button to dial your new entry. If you click the Dialing <u>P</u>roperties button, any changes you made in the <u>N</u>umber to Redial text box are discarded and your original speed dial number appears with your current Dialing <u>P</u>roperties applied to it.

FIG. 32.26
You can make a temporary change to a Phone Dialer number when dialing.

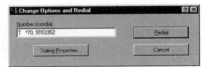

Using Complex Phone Number Sequences

The convenience of voice-mail has had an annoying side effect—all those voice menus prompting you to "Press one to leave a message, Press two to talk with an operator" can drive you crazy and waste a lot of your time. Likewise, credit cards and various long distance carriers have required us to use dozens of numbers and procedures to make connections. A few built-in extras in your modem can handle things like credit card dialing, long-distance service connections, and navigation through many voice-mail hierarchies:

- To wait for the prompts within a voice-mail system, you can use the comma (,) to insert a two second pause within your dialing sequence. Use more than one comma for a longer pause.
- If you need to wait for a secondary dial tone, use the letter W.
- If you need to wait for silence on the line, you can insert an @ sign.

- If you are making a credit card call and need to wait for the tone from your long distance carrier, insert a dollar sign ($) followed by your card number.

- You also can use * and # characters within the phone number to make those voice-mail menu selections.

For example, let's say you want to make a personal long-distance call from your office and charge it to your AT&T calling card. You know that your company's long distance carrier is MCI, so you'll have to access the AT&T network to get the cheapest rates. Here's how to build your Phone Dialer sequence:

1. Type a **9** followed by a **W** to access the outside line and wait for the dial tone.

2. Type the AT&T network access code: **10"ATT"** followed by a zero (**0**) to start the credit card call.

3. Type the phone number you're trying to reach, such as (205)-555-3161

4. To wait for AT&T to give their signal for you to enter your calling card number, type **$**.

5. Type in your credit card number, such as 314-555-2222-4321.

Putting all these pieces of your dialing sequence together, it would read:

- 9W10"ATT"0(205)-555-3161$314-555-222-4321

That would be a definite candidate for saving in the Phone Dialer!

Using the Phone Dialer Log

The Phone Dialer comes with a log in which it will keep a record of your outgoing and incoming calls (see fig. 32.27). Each time you connect a phone call, an entry is placed in this text file. You can cut, copy, and delete from this log using the Edit menu commands, and you can redial an entry in your Log by double-clicking it or by selecting Log, Dial.

FIG. 32.27
Log entries can be used to redial or copy and paste into other documents.

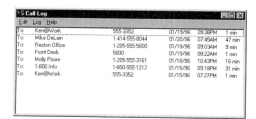

Part
IX

Ch
32

Using the Free Wang Imaging Software to Manage Electronic Documents

There was a time in the early 1980s when people in the computer industry spoke of the paperless office. Instead of paper becoming outmoded, computer's added heavily to the use of paper. However, with the advent of large, cheap hard disks, Fax software, e-mail, and desktop document scanners, it's truly possible for small offices to drastically reduce their use of paper at a nominal cost.

 A new class of hardware, the desktop scanner, has made it possible for individuals to quickly and easily scan and store documents and graphics on their hard disks. The scanners also work well to scan documents or drawings which are then transmitted via Fax software. Most of these $300 scanners come with software to manage documents and reliably convert document images into characters. These scanners are so compact that they sit between your keyboard and monitor, taking up little space. The recognized leader in these units is the PaperPort Vx from Visioneer at 800-787-7007.

Wang has developed imaging software for Microsoft that is designed to run on Windows 95. Wang Image is free software for Windows 95 for people who need to scan, view, annotate, manage, store, and share images that have been created from faxes, scanned documents, or computerized images. Figure 32.38 shows the Wang Image displaying a Fax.

FIG. 32.28
The Imaging software enables you to view, store, and annotate images and faxes.

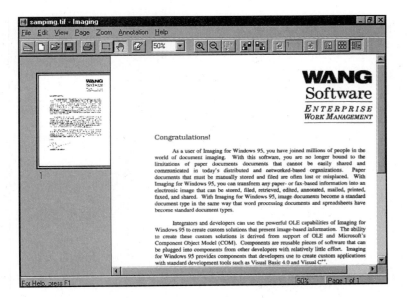

The imaging software works with the Universal Inbox so you can view and store documents from within the Inbox. Faxes or electronic images can be inserted or appended into a multipage document. The documents can be stored as bit-mapped or rasterized images in black and white, grayscale, or color.

You can annotate stored documents with graphics, high-lights, text, and annotations. It even includes pre-defined "rubber stamps" that can be stamped on a document or you can create your own rubber stamps. Documents can be passed on to others as a file. The imaging software is OLE compatible so you can select, then drag documents from the imaging software and drop them into applications such as Word, Exchange, or Lotus Notes. Double-clicking an embedded document image activates the image and switches the applications menus and toolbars to those of the Wang Imaging software.

N O T E The Imaging software is significant for developers and corporations because it will work in conjunction with corporate document imaging systems that Wang will release during the first half of 1996. Developers should examine this free software because it is based on an OLE 2.0 object model and exposes its components for use by other office automation developers. The OLE interface will be released on the Microsoft Developers Network (MSDN) CD-ROM.

If you are an office automation developer, you should check out the software and its developers kit, found in the same setup package, because the Wang Imaging software is OLE capable. Its OLE objects can be used by C++ and Visual Basic developers to incorporate electronic document features in their own software.

Part

IX

Ch

32

File formats read include Microsoft FAX, BMP, DCX, JPG, PCX, and TIF. The software stores documents in an industry standard multi-page TIF 6.0 or Microsoft FAX format. Single bitmap (BMP) files also can be saved.

ON THE WEB

Free copies of the Wang Imaging software developed for Windows 95 are available on the Internet at these sites:

http://www.microsoft.com/windows/software/img_us.htm

http://www.wang.com

Using Microsoft Phone to Manage Telephones

In January, Microsoft announced the release of Microsoft Phone. Microsoft Phone is a new speakerphone and answering machine software designed to work with voice-enabled modems. Hardware vendors will include Microsoft Phone with their voice-enabled modems.

With Microsoft Phone and voice-enabled modems, Windows 95 gives you the following features:

- Speakerphone
- Password protected voice mail boxes
- Fax-on-demand that returns information by fax to callers
- Use a single inbox for voice, e-mail, and Fax
- Read e-mail over the phone using text-to-speech technology
- Give callers a chance to hear announcements
- Call frequently used numbers by speaking a name
- User notification via pager or telephone
- Include caller ID and call forwarding features

Microsoft Phone is only available through hardware vendors who incorporate it with their voice-enabled modems or phone capable computer systems. To learn more about specific features and costs, contact these hardware manufacturers:

Creative Labs Inc.

Diamond Multimedia Systems Inc.

Micron Electronics Inc.

Miro Computer Products

CHAPTER 33

Getting Connected to the Internet

by Francis Moss with Brady P. Merkel

Windows 95 provides a flexible and technically robust means of connecting to the Internet, whether you are connecting from a stand-alone computer or from a network. Windows 95 has built-in support for TCP/IP dial-up access, and it supports 16-bit and 32-bit Windows Internet applications. ■

What is the Internet and how can you benefit from it?

This chapter explains the concept of the Internet, how it came about, and the benefits for business, researchers, and individuals.

What is the means of communication and protocol for the Internet?

TCP/IP is the networking protocol used by many corporate networks as well as the Internet.

How to find a service that can connect you to the Internet and its services.

There are many decisions you need to make before deciding between using The Microsoft Network (Microsoft's Internet connection software and communication package) and using an alternate means of connecting to the Internet through local or national service providers.

How to connect Windows 95 to the Internet.

Wizards in Windows 95 make connecting to the Internet very easy. If you use a non-Microsoft service provider, you will need to know some Internet access information. This chapter explains what you need to complete the wizards dialog boxes.

Understanding the Internet

The Internet is an aggregation of high-speed networks, supported by almost 6,000 federal, state, and local systems, as well as university and commercial networks. It spans worldwide to networks in Canada, South America, Europe, Australia, and Asia, with more than 30,000,000 users. The Internet began with about 200 linked computers; today, there are several million linked computers all over the world. The Internet is growing so fast that no one can say how big it is today, or how large it will grow tomorrow.

The main functions of the Internet are:

- *E-mail (electronic mail)*. You can send a message to anyone, anywhere in the world (as long as they have access to the Internet), almost instantaneously and for less than the cost of a regular letter, or "snailmail."

- The *World Wide Web (the Web,* or *WWW)*. The fastest growing part of the Internet, the Web provides access to files, documents, images, and sounds from thousands of different Web sites using hypertext, which links you to other documents anywhere on the Internet.

- File transfer using *File Transfer Protocol (FTP)*. FTP is an older, but still popular tool for file transfer between computers linked to the Internet. You use FTP to access the hundreds of archives of Windows shareware and freeware software.

- *UseNet newsgroups*. These are "many-to-many" discussion groups on topics ranging from science, current events, music, computers, "alternative" issues, and many others. There are currently more than 10,000 newsgroups, and the list grows daily.

- *Gopher*. Named after the mascot of the University of Minnesota, Gopher allows you to burrow through the Internet to find files. Gopher displays lists of documents and links to other gopher sites.

- *WAIS*. When connected to the Internet, you need a way to search for the information you want. The Wide Area Information Server (WAIS) protocol provides a way to search databases of indexed documents, and return pointers to the documents themselves.

- *Telnet*. Telnet provides an alphanumeric terminal window that allows you to log in to Internet hosts and access character-based programs.

Electronic Mail

The most widely used service the Internet provides is e-mail. With e-mail, you are in almost instantaneous contact with anyone else on the Internet, no matter where they live or work.

How do you send an e-mail message? On the Internet, everyone has a unique e-mail address that looks something like this:

username@anynet.com

Businesses, Internet organizations, and services such as Listserv (a program that keeps track of mailing lists) also have addresses. Your address is composed of your user name (such as *jsmith*) and your provider's domain. When Jane Smith subscribes to The Microsoft Network for her Internet access, she may want to have an e-mail address like this one:

jsmith@msn.com

But, if Joe Smith is already using the "jsmith" login name on MSN, Jane has to pick another one, such as "janesmith" or "jane_s."

The Internet also has *mailing lists*, or e-mail discussion groups, on many topics (such as writing, pets, running a small business, and so on), comprised of members who subscribe to that mailing list. It usually costs nothing to subscribe to most mailing lists.

N O T E To *subscribe* to a mailing list, send an e-mail message to the *listserver* who manages that mailing list. Usually, to subscribe, you send a message with only the word "subscribe" in the message body.

To *send a message* to the members of a mailing list, after you have joined, post a message to the mailing list itself. You respond to messages in the mailing list in the same way you answer an e-mail message from an individual.

▶ **See** "Using the Universal Inbox," **p. 873**

The World Wide Web

The World Wide Web, also called the Web or WWW, is the fastest growing and most exciting part of the Internet. It was developed in 1989 at CERN (which stands for *Centre Européan de Recherche Nuclèaire*, but which most people call the Particle Physics Research Laboratory) at the University of Bern in Switzerland. Although the rest of the Internet is text oriented, the World Wide Web is graphics and sound oriented. Clicking a *hypertext* or *hypermedia link* (a specially encoded text or graphic image) takes you to other documents, called *Web pages*, where you can view images from the Hubble telescope, visit an art museum, watch a video clip of skiers or hear the haunting theme song from the Fox Network's hit show, *The X Files,*—all on your computer.

Unlike other Internet file-retrieval systems, which are hierarchical in nature (you wind your way through descending layers of menus or directories to find what you are looking for), the Web is distributed, offering links to other parts of the same document or other documents, which are not necessarily at the same Web site as the current document. With a *browser*, such as Microsoft's Internet Explorer, you can connect to a location referred to as a Uniform Resource Locator (URL), such as:

http://www.mcp.com

and jump directly to the Web page of Macmillan Publishing USA, as shown in figure 33.1.

FIG. 33.1
The Macmillan Publishing USA page, as viewed from Internet Explorer. Click elements in the graphic to move to the Web pages for those sites.

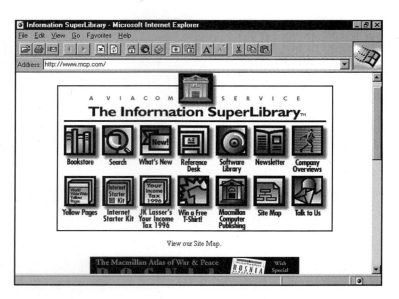

After you install Internet Explorer, you can configure it to view and interact with graphical images on many Web sites, listen to music and voice clips, watch videos, and use hypertext links to jump to other World Wide Web sites around the world.

Web authoring tools, such as Microsoft's Internet Assistant (used with Word for Windows 6.0a or later), allow anyone with an Internet account to create his or her own *Home page* (a kind of display you create that anyone on the Web can see).

▶ **See** "Using Internet Explorer and the World Wide Web," **p. 983**

▶ **See** "Creating Your Own Pages for the World Wide Web," **p. 1013**

▶ **See** "Understanding World Wide Web URLs," **p. 985**

FTP

File Transfer Protocol (FTP) is one of the first functions of the Internet. FTP lets you copy files from the many file repositories, or archives, on the Internet. Computers that permit you to log in to them and download files are called *FTP servers*. You use Internet Explorer to access FTP servers. FTP servers that allow you to log in using the account "anonymous" are called *anonymous-FTP servers*.

There are thousands of anonymous FTP servers all over the globe, each with thousands of files. *Archie servers* index the files available on anonymous FTP sites. Without going to each site and browsing, you can go to an Archie server and search for files by their names. Of course, if the file is about drug use in ancient Egypt, for example, but is named DR3AEG91.TXT, Archie has no clue about what the file contains. After you scan through an index on an Archie server, you can select files from the index you want to download to your computer.

ON THE WEB

Archie Server listing on the YAHOO search engine
http://www.yahoo.com/Computers_and_Internet/Internet/Searching_the_Net/Archie/

UseNet Newsgroups

Newsgroups are another important service on the Internet. Where e-mail is a one-to-one communication, newsgroups are many-to-many discussions, forming global user communities organized by topics. There are over 10,000 newsgroups currently on the Internet, dealing with every imaginable—and unimaginable—topic. You can read messages from a newsgroup to see whether you want to subscribe. Subscribing to newsgroups is free.

Part
IX
Ch
33

ON THE WEB

UseNet Info Center   **http://sunsite.unc.edu/usenet-i/**

UseNet Newsgroup listing on the YAHOO search engine
http://www.yahoo.com/News/Usenet/Newsgroup_Listings/

UseNet Newsgroup Hierarchy with Searchable FAQ Archive
http://www.lib.ox.ac.uk/internet/news/

▶ **See** "Participating in UseNet News," **p. 1005**

Gopher

Gopher servers are computers on the Internet that maintain lists of the files residing on their own as well as other computers. With Internet Explorer you can connect to gopher locations and search files. Gopher allows descriptive comments to be attached to file names. Like the World Wide Web, you can click a file name, and download a file to your computer.

Veronica (Very Easy Rodent-Oriented Netwide Index to Computerized Archives) servers allow you to search menu items on Gopher servers. Veronica servers compile databases of Gopher menus and provide information about the files, in addition to the file names and their locations.

ON THE WEB

Gopher listing on the YAHOO search engine
http://www.yahoo.com/Computers_and_Internet/Internet/Gopher/

Index of Veronica Servers   **gopher://gopher.scs.unr.edu/11/veronica**

WAIS

Let's say that you are looking for as many documents as you can find about drug use in ancient Egypt, but you do not know the names of the files. *WAIS (Wide Area Information Server)* is the most useful search tool for this kind of search. WAIS has an index of keywords contained in all the documents on servers all over the world. Using WAIS, you can type **drugs** and **Egypt** to get information on your topic, even if the file names of the documents containing that information are obscure.

ON THE WEB

WAIS listing on the YAHOO search engine   **http://www.yahoo.com/Computers_and_Internet/Internet/World_Wide_Web/Databases_and_Searching/WAIS/**

Telnet

Telnet allows users to log in to a remote computer and interact with it using a terminal emulation window. Telnet provides a way for participants in *MUD (Multiple User Domain)* games to play one another online.

TIP   Because Telnet uses short keystroke commands to interact with computers, it can be slow and difficult to use. If you have a better way to access a remote site, use that method instead.

Understanding TCP/IP

TCP/IP stands for Transmission Control Protocol/Internet Protocol. TCP/IP is the method used by every computer on the Internet to transfer files. As the name indicates, it is actually two protocols. The first part developed was the Internet Protocol (IP), developed in the days of ARPANET (the Advanced Research Projects NETwork, the original Internet, formed in the 1960s) to send data in *frames* (self-contained units of information, sometimes also referred to as packets) from one computer network to another. The weakness of IP is its inability to deal with poor transmissions. If a frame gets garbled or interrupted, the receiving IP-based machine just removes it from the transmission.

The TCP protocol envelopes the IP. The TCP protocol makes sure every frame is delivered to the receiving network reliably, in the same order it was sent. An error detection system verifies that the frame received is identical to the one sent. Also, TCP ensures that frames have not been garbled during transmission. If a frame arrives that has been garbled, TCP requests the transmitting system to resend the frame.

Every network and every computer on the Internet uses TCP/IP to communicate. Versions of Microsoft Windows after version 3.x have encouraged the development of a Windows TCP/IP standard, called the Windows Sockets Library, or *Winsock*. All manufacturers of Windows-based TCP/IP programs have accepted this standard, which means that, ideally any Windows mail reader you choose will work with the WINSOCK.DLL in your \Windows directory.

But still some problems remain. A version of Winsock bundled with one software manufacturer's application may conflict with another version. Each application may install a version of Winsock in its own directory, causing conflicts with another manufacturer's version, or an Internet provider may customize its version of Winsock, causing conflicts with Internet applications that cannot recognize the new version. Internet jockeys running Windows must periodically comb their hard drives for mismatched Winsocks.

With Windows 95, such conflicts are less of a problem. Microsoft has created two Winsock libraries, one for 16-bit applications and another for 32-bit applications. In addition, a Virtual Device Driver (VxD), called WSOCK.VXD, manages the TCP/IP interface. Most Windows 3.x-based Internet applications work seamlessly with the Windows 95 Winsock. As more Internet software vendors provide Windows 95 versions, Winsock conflicts should disappear.

Part
IX

Ch
33

> **N O T E** Some third-party Internet applications require a WINSOCK.DLL file that conflicts with the Windows 95 version. Known applications that are incompatible with the Windows 95 WINSOCK.DLL are:
>
> - CompuServe NetLauncher version 1.00.66
> - Spry Mosaic In A Box versions 1.0, 1.1, 2.0
> - Network Telesystems TCP Pro Remote

continues

continued

When these applications install, they overwrite the Windows 95 WINSOCK.DLL file. After installing the application, Windows 95 notices the file has changed and renames the file to WINSOCK.OLD. Then Windows 95 copies the WINSOCK.DLL from the \Windows\Sysbckup directory into the Windows directory.

If this happens to you, copy the WINSOCK.OLD from the \Windows directory to the application's directory and rename it WINSOCK.DLL. Then, set the application's working directory to be the application directory, so the correct WINSOCK.DLL is found and used. ■

N O T E By default, Windows 95 installs the 16-bit WINSOCK.DLL in your \Windows folder; it installs a 32-bit version, WSOCK32.DLL, in your \Windows\System folder. If you are using a 32-bit Internet application, Windows 95 knows to use the 32-bit version. ■

Choosing an Internet Service Provider

As the Internet grows, more and more businesses, called *Internet service providers*, are springing up to provide access. Typically, a local provider offers three or more computers, called *servers*, that are linked directly to the Internet. In turn, they provide a dozen or more high-speed (14.4Kbps or 28.8Kbps) modems connected to local telephone lines. In some cities, a service called Integrated Services Digital Network (ISDN) is available, offering speeds up to 128Kbps. Unless you live in a remote part of the world, finding a service provider should not be a problem.

Here are some ways to access the Internet:

- ■ If you attend a college or university, or work at a business of any size, you might already have Internet access. See your supervisor, the computer science department, or an administrator for more information.

- ■ Subscribe to a commercial online service, such as The Microsoft Network, CompuServe, America Online, Prodigy, or Delphi. These services handle the connectivity problems for you; it is just a matter of "pointing and clicking" your way to the Net. Windows 95 is beneficial because of its improved high-speed serial port support.

   The Microsoft Network is especially easy to subscribe to, as Windows 95 comes complete with the MSN tools. Also, The Microsoft Network offers ISDN dial-up connectivity in many cities, providing transfer rates up to 128Kbps. Telephone connections are limited in some areas of the country.

- Sign up with a national Internet provider, such as NETCOM, PSI Pipeline USA, or PSI Instant InterRamp. If you live in a rural area, travel a lot, or want to get many offices online, this may be your best bet. National providers have access phone numbers in major cities and usually offer toll-free numbers for a slightly higher price.

- Sign up with a local Internet provider. This is often the most economical way to get on the Net: many services cost as little as $15 to $25 per month. Every major city in the U.S. and around the world has at least one local provider. Look for advertisements in computer magazines, the newspaper, or your telephone directory.

  This listing offers some useful questions to ask when evaluating Internet service providers. More important, before deciding on an Internet service provider, check with your local Better Business Bureau. Before you enter a long-term relationship with the provider the BBB can confirm that the provider has an ethical business.

Some questions you should ask Internet service providers include the following:

- How long have you been an Internet service provider?

- How are you connected to the Internet? T-1? T-3?

- Do you have plans to upgrade to a higher bandwidth connection?

- Do you offer individual SLIP or PPP accounts?

- How many modems do you have for SLIP and PPP access and how many users will share your connection?

  If so, at what cost? (Setup fee? Flat rate? Hourly rate? Full-time rate? Monthly rate cap?)

- What speed modems do you use for SLIP or PPP access? Do you offer V.42 error control and V.42bis compression?

- Do you offer ISDN dial-up access? At what speeds and cost? Do you support "Bonding" (using both B channels)?

- Does your SLIP provide TCP header compression (also known as CSLIP)?

- Do you use dynamic IP addressing?

- What network services do you provide? E-mail? DNS? UseNet News? Web? FTP?

  If so, do you offer disk space to use these services? Is there a cost associated with these services?

- To which UseNet newsgroups do you provide access? Which newsgroups do you exclude?

- Do you register domain names for IP addresses? At what cost?

Part
IX

Ch
33

■ What are your uptime statistics?

■ Do you offer discounts to students, employees of local businesses, local businesses, or government offices?

■ Do you have a policy as to what constitutes acceptable Internet use?

■ Do you have restrictions on connecting to any part of the Internet?

■ Do you provide a full-time professional support staff?

■ Do you have a 24-hour on-call support line?

■ Do you have online support?

■ What training is available? At what cost?

■ Can you provide a list of references?

Table 33.1 compares what you will spend logging on to the Internet. Although Windows 95, aside from its modem setup and serial port configuration, plays no part in connecting to the commercial services, the service fees are included as a basis for comparison. When you consider your connection rates, you must also factor in that some services provide a limited number of hours (5–10 hours) of free service per month. In addition, consider all the non-financial advantages and disadvantages described in the previous list.

Table 33.1   Sample Monthly Internet Access Fees

	MSN	AOL	CompuServe	Prodigy	IBM Net	Delphi	NETCOM	Local Provider
10 hrs	$19.95	$24.90	$24.70	$29.95	$29.95	$23	$19.95	$25
20 hrs	$19.95	$54	$24.95	$29.95	$29.95	$23	$19.95	$25
30 hrs	$39.95	$83	$44.45	$29.95	$29.95	$41	$19.95	$25
60 hrs	$99.95	$122	$102.95	$118	$89.95	$95	$19.95	$25

It's easy to see, that, for a dedicated 'Net surfer, NETCOM and local providers are the least expensive. But, if you are interested in the additional forums and libraries of the commercial services, and intend to be on the Internet less than 10 or 20 hours a month, you may want to investigate The Microsoft Network, CompuServe, Prodigy or America Online. In fact, setting up an Internet connection through The Microsoft Network is very easy. Windows 95 includes the necessary software for you to subscribe online, and you can be up and running on the Internet in minutes.

▶ **See** "Using The Microsoft Network," **p. 1027**

▶ **See** "Understanding ISDN," **p. 954**

Using The Microsoft Network as Your Internet Service Provider

Windows 95 includes all the necessary software to quickly subscribe to and become a part of The Microsoft Network. Besides the great forums, chat rooms, and e-mail, you can use your MSN account to access the Internet. Also, The Microsoft Network offers ISDN dial-up, with transfer rates up to 128Kbps. Before you go any further, you should subscribe. (See Chapter 35, "Using The Microsoft Network," to find out how.)

After you subscribe, you can change your Microsoft Network connection settings to access the Internet directly. In this case, you use The Microsoft Network as your Internet service provider.

To prepare The Microsoft Network connection settings so MSN can be used as an Internet provider, follow these steps:

1. Double-click The Microsoft Network icon on your desktop.

2. Click the Settings button to change your Microsoft Network connection settings. The Connection Settings dialog box appears as shown in figure 33.2.

FIG. 33.2
Use the Connection Settings dialog box to change the way you access the Microsoft Network.

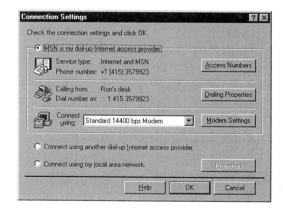

Part
IX

Ch
33

3. Choose the MSN Is My Dial-up Internet Access Provider option.

4. Next, click the Access Numbers button. The Microsoft Network Service Type dialog box appears, as shown in figure 33.3.

FIG. 33.3

Identify the dial-up method and phone numbers you use to access The Microsoft Network.

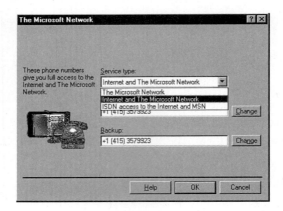

5. In the Service Type list, choose Internet and The Microsoft Network. If you have the necessary equipment, such as an ISDN line and ISDN Terminal Adapter, you can choose the ISDN access to the Internet and MSN option.

6. If the Primary Phone Number text box is blank, click the Change button and select an access number in your local calling area.

   If no local access numbers are listed for your area, the phone list might be out of date. To get the latest phone list, change the Service type to The Microsoft Network and click OK. This reverts to the original phone number. Click OK again to return to the MSN Sign In dialog box. Click Connect to The Microsoft Network.

   When you're online with The Microsoft Network, switch to the MSN Central window that shows Edit, View, and Tools on the menu bar. Choose Tools, Connection Settings. Repeat steps 3 and 4. Click the Change button for the Primary Phone Number, and a message box may indicate that a new phone list is downloading. (This only occurs when your phone list needs updating.) In the ensuing dialog box, select an access number in your local calling area (see fig. 33.4). If no local access numbers are available, you can select a long-distance number. If MSN does not offer a sufficient access number, you may prefer to use a local Internet service provider or different online service instead; see "Choosing an Internet Service Provider," earlier in this chapter.

FIG. 33.4

Choose a local access phone number to avoid long-distance charges.

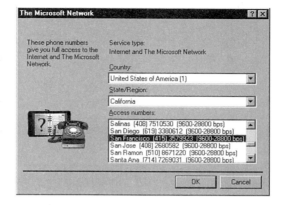

7. Click OK. If you have not installed Dial-Up Networking or the TCP/IP protocol, the Internet Setup Wizard starts (see fig. 33.5). If you have already installed the necessary components, go to step 10.

FIG. 33.5

The Internet Setup Wizard starts if Dial-Up Networking and TCP/IP protocol are not installed.

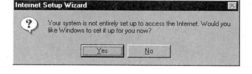

8. The Internet Setup Wizard installs the Dial-Up Networking Adapter and the TCP/IP protocol. A message box appears indicating that you need your Windows 95 installation CD-ROM or floppy disks. Click OK. The Internet Setup Wizard copies files to your hard disk.

9. Restart Windows 95 to finish the installation of the software. MSN asks you to close all applications and DOS sessions. Be sure to save your work, then click OK.

10. Upon restart, you can use The Microsoft Network as your Internet service provider. You have two methods to initiate a connection: double-click The Microsoft Network icon on your desktop, or double-click one of The Microsoft Network icons in your Dial-Up Networking folder (see fig. 33.6). Either way, Microsoft charges you the same rate, based on your connection time.

Part

IX

Ch

33

FIG. 33.6

You can access the Internet using The Microsoft Network connections found in your Dial-Up Networking folder.

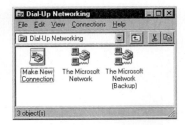

To test your connection, proceed to "Connecting to Your Internet Service Provider," later in this chapter.

▶ **See** "Understanding ISDN," **p. 954**

▶ **See** "Using The Microsoft Network," **p. 1039**

Understanding ISDN

Sometimes ordinary modems just are not fast enough. Corporate or academic users who are accustomed to fast, high-bandwidth connections at work find that, even at 28.8Kbps, file transfers and Web browsing via a modem can be annoyingly slow. If you use the Internet for your daily business, or if you are a dedicated Internet surfer, you might want to take advantage of a new way to get much faster connections: the Integrated Services Digital Network, or ISDN for short.

ISDN offers three channels over a standard two-wire phone circuit. The two *B channels* run at 64Kbps, and the *D channel* carries 16Kbps of data. 64Kbps is the amount of bandwidth required to make a standard analog voice call, so each of the B channels can be used interchangeably for data or voice. You can even talk to ordinary analog phones, modems, and fax machines with your ISDN line. With the right equipment, you can also tie the two B channels together to get 128Kbps of bandwidth. Another feature is that ISDN circuits take about a half-second to complete a call, so dial-on-demand service is pleasingly fast.

N O T E   Some telephone switches only allow you to use 56Kbps of the B channels. Be sure to ask the local phone company if its switches use the full data rate. Even if they do, you will have to use the slower rate if the computers you are calling are served by slow switches. ■

ISDN sounds like a net surfer's dream, but you may never have heard of it. It was originally developed by Bell Communications Research (Bellcore) as a cheap way to move video-on-demand over existing copper cabling, but local phone companies were slow to adopt the technology because they saw little consumer demand for it. The explosion of interest in the Internet has convinced all seven regional Bell companies to offer ISDN to consumers. Most metropolitan areas, and many smaller communities, now offer residential ISDN service for as little as $22 per month (plus the cost of your Internet access).

 TIP To find out if ISDN is available in your area, call the National ISDN Hotline at (800) 992-ISDN. Give it your address and phone number, and it will search your local phone company's database to see if service is available in your area.

ON THE WEB

Frequently Asked Questions about ISDN   **http://www.cis.ohio-state.edu/hypertext/faq/usenet/isdn-faq/faq.html**

ISDN links from the YAHOO Search Engine   **http://www.yahoo.com/Computers_and_Internet/Networking_and_Communications/ISDN/**

Microsoft's home page   **http://www.microsoft.com**

As with most other peripherals, you will have to make some decisions before purchasing your ISDN hardware. The key questions to ask are listed here:

- Do you want a serial, parallel, PCMCIA, or bus *terminal adapter* (or TA, the ISDN equivalent of a modem)?
- Do you want to use analog modems or phones on your ISDN line?

Similar to conventional analog modems, ISDN terminal adapters (TAs) come in internal and external models, with serial, parallel, Ethernet, ISA, EISA, MicroChannel, PCMCIA, and PCI versions available. Which you choose will depend on your existing hardware configuration and your personal preferences. As ISDN becomes more popular, more vendors are getting into the ISDN hardware business. Make sure that whatever TA you buy is compatible with your decision to use analog phone equipment on your ISDN line, and make sure the vendor has Windows 95 drivers available if it is a PCMCIA or bus device.

N O T E Terminal Adapters that use the serial port need to operate as fast as the line speed. You need a fairly fast computer and a 16,550 UART to take full advantage of ISDN speed. You might be better off with a parallel-port, Ethernet, or PCMCIA TA. ■

When your ISDN line installation is complete, you will have a special jack called a *U interface*. Most TAs and other ISDN devices (like ISDN telephones and fax machines) require the *S/T interface*. The U interface requires a terminating device called an *NT-1*, which electrically terminates the ISDN line and converts the U interface into an S/T interface.

Part

IX

Ch

33

Some ISDN TAs include a built-in NT-1; that is a valuable feature, because an NT-1 can cost as much as $200. On the other hand, some "super" NT-1s include not only the NT-1, but standard phone jacks for connecting analog devices and even RS-232 ports which eliminate the need for a separate TA. If you want to combine your two B channels into one 128Kbps virtual channel (known as *bonding*), be sure that your selected TA supports this feature.

Although ISDN lines can communicate with regular analog lines, ISDN TAs cannot communicate with regular modems. This incompatibility can pose problems if you need to dial into a BBS, a commercial service like America Online, or a remote-access server at work that does not support ISDN. One way around this is to select a TA (or "super" NT-1) that has one or two ports for analog devices. You can still use one B channel for data while you use the other for your analog phone, modem, or fax machine.

ISDN telephones are becoming more popular too, because they offer conference calling, advanced caller ID, and other features which either cost more or do not exist on standard phones. Some makers include RS-232 ports or phone jacks to make it easier to use your ISDN telephone with your computer and your analog equipment.

N O T E   ISDN lines do not carry a dial tone. Don't be alarmed when you pick-up your ISDN phone receiver and do not hear a dial tone; just dial the number as you would on an analog phone. █

Using the Internet Setup Wizard from Microsoft Plus!

The Internet Setup Wizard from Microsoft Plus! makes it easy to set up your Internet dial-up connection. If you do not have Microsoft Plus!, you can still set up your Internet connection; refer to "Setting Up Internet Access Manually," later in this chapter.

N O T E   The Internet Setup Wizard simplifies setting up dial-up access to the Internet. If your Windows 95 system is connected to a network with Internet access, see "Connecting to the Internet with a LAN," later in this chapter. █

1. To use the Internet Setup Wizard after you install Plus!, open the Start menu and choose <u>P</u>rograms, Accessories, Internet Tools, and then Internet Setup Wizard. The wizard appears as shown in figure 33.7.

FIG. 33.7

The Internet Setup Wizard guides you through the setup of your Internet connection.

2. Click Next from the Internet Setup Wizard Welcome dialog box to proceed with the setup. The How To Connect dialog box appears, as shown in figure 33.8. Select whether you want to connect to the Internet via a phone line to your modem or through a local area network. Click Next.

FIG. 33.8

The Internet Setup Wizard asks you to specify how you will connect to the Internet—using your phone line or using your local area network.

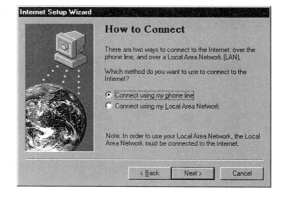

Part

IX

Ch

33

If you have not set up your modem yet, the Internet Setup Wizard will guide you through the process. Simply respond to each wizard dialog box, providing information such as your modem model, maximum speed, and manufacturer. Click Next after you provide each item of information the wizard requests.

3. In the second How To dialog box, specify whether you want to connect via The Microsoft Network or an account you have with an Internet service provider by clicking the appropriate option button. Click Next.

Now your installation process branches depending on whether you are using MSN as an Internet provider or whether you are using a different service provider.

▶ **See** "Configuring Your Modem," **p. 294**

▶ **See** "Using Microsoft Plus!," **p. 1217**

Completing the Internet Installation with MSN

If you elected to use a service provider other than MSN, skip the following procedure. If you selected MSN as the service provider, follow this procedure:

1. If you elect to use The Microsoft Network, you can choose to set up a new Microsoft Network account or connect using an existing Microsoft Network account. Refer to step 5 in "Using The Microsoft Network as Your Internet Service Provider," earlier in this chapter for a description of the dialog boxes you will be asked to complete.

2. After you select telephone numbers for MSN, Windows may request that you restart MSN.

3. Double-click the MSN icon on the desktop to start MSN.

4. Switch to MSN Center. Choose T<u>o</u>ols, <u>F</u>ind and search for **"Internet Center"**. Use quotes around both words so the search is for the phrase rather than separate words.

5. Double-click Internet Center when you find it. This will display a window containing icons for different information about the Internet.

6. Click the icon that updates the Internet Explorer to the latest version. The update installation is automatic, but it takes from 5 to 30 minutes depending on the speed of your modem and computer.

When the update is complete, an Internet icon appears on your desktop. Double-click this icon to start Internet Explorer and access the Internet through MSN.

Completing the Internet Installation with Another Service Provider

If you choose the option to use a service provider other than MSN, follow these steps to continue the Internet installation:

1. The Installing Files dialog box appears, reminding you that you might need your Windows 95 setup CD-ROM or disks. Click Next to continue and copy any needed additional files to your hard disk.

2. The Internet Mail dialog box asks whether you want to use Microsoft Exchange to send and receive mail. Select <u>Y</u>es or <u>N</u>o, then click Next.

3. The Installing Files dialog box tells you that the Setup Wizard will copy any required files from your Windows 95 Setup CD-ROM or disk into the appropriate drive. Click Next.

4. In the Name of Service Provider box, enter a name for this connection (see fig. 33.9). Click Next to continue.

FIG. 33.9
The Internet Setup Wizard asks you to enter the name of your Internet service provider.

5. The Phone Number dialog box appears, as shown in figure 33.10. Enter the Area code, Telephone number, and Country code for the dial-in modems at your Internet service provider. If your provider requires that you perform a login sequence in a terminal window, and does not support PAP or CHAP with PPP, select the Bring Up Terminal Window After Dialing check box. Click Next to continue.

FIG. 33.10
Specify the phone number of your Internet service provider's dial-in modems.

Part
IX

Ch
33

6. The User Name and Password dialog box appears, as shown in figure 33.11. Enter the User name and Password that your Internet service provider gave you. Click Next to continue.

FIG. 33.11
Enter your user name and the password your Internet service provider gave you.

7. The IP Address dialog box appears, as shown in figure 33.12. If your Internet service provider assigns you an IP address at the time of connection, check the option labeled M̲y Internet service provider automatically assigns me one.

   If your Internet service provider gave you a permanent IP address, select the A̲lways Use the Following check box, and enter the I̲P Address and S̲ubnet Mask in the appropriate text boxes. Click Next to continue.

FIG. 33.12
Choose whether to use dynamic IP addressing or specify a permanent one.

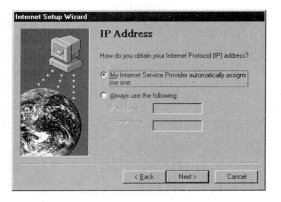

8. The DNS Server Address panel appears, as shown in figure 33.13. Enter the DNS server addresses that your Internet service provider gave you. Click Next to continue.

   DNS servers are used to resolve user friendly host names, such as www.intergraph.com, into the less friendly and difficult to remember IP addresses, like 129.135.1.2. Internet applications use the IP address in the low-level network functions.

FIG. 33.13
Specify your Internet service provider's DNS server addresses. If the first one cannot be contacted the second will be used instead.

9. The Internet Mail panel appears (see fig. 33.14). If your Internet service provider will also act as your e-mail post office, select the Use Internet Mail check box. Doing so will install the necessary software such that you can use Microsoft Exchange to read and send your Internet e-mail. Enter Your Email address and the Internet mail server in the text boxes provided.

   The Internet mail server is also referred to as the Post-Office Protocol (POP) host. Click Next to continue.

FIG. 33.14
Enter your e-mail address and mail server host so that you can read and send Internet e-mail from Microsoft Exchange.

Part
IX
Ch
33

10. A final Setup Wizard dialog box appears, informing you that Setup is complete. Click the Finish button.

11. The Setup Wizard might display a dialog box telling you to restart Windows. If this occurs, complete the setup by clicking Restart Windows.

To test your connection, proceed to "Connecting to Your Internet Service Provider," later in this chapter.

▶ **See** the "Using the Universal Inbox," **p. 873**

Setting Up Internet Access Manually

If you are not using The Microsoft Network, or do not have Microsoft Plus!, you can set up Windows 95 access to your Internet service provider manually.

Windows 95 Dialup Networking supports two kinds of dial-up Internet connections: SLIP (Serial-Line Internet Protocol) and PPP (Point-to-Point Protocol). Both are implementations of the TCP/IP Internet protocol over telephone lines. Unless you access the Net through a LAN and Ethernet cabling, you will probably use telephone lines and SLIP or PPP.

There are both technical and practical differences between the two protocols: technically, SLIP is a *network-layer protocol*; PPP is a *link-level protocol.* Practically, this means that PPP is more fail-safe than SLIP. Windows 95 Dialup Networking is optimized for PPP, which is the protocol to choose if your provider offers a choice.

ON THE WEB

Frequently Asked Questions about PPP   **http://cs.uni-bonn.de/ppp/faq.html**

SLIP versus PPP Performance Comparison
http://www.morningstar.com/MorningStar/slip-ppp-compare.html

If you chose an Internet-only service, you need the following information from your Internet service provider:

- *Connection type.* The kind of connection provided: SLIP or PPP.
- *User name.* Your user name (you can usually choose your own, such as jsmith).
- *Your password.* A password again, you select your own. The most secure passwords have six or more uppercase and lowercase letters, numbers, and punctuation.
- *Provider's phone number.* The provider's local access phone number. Be sure to use a phone number that is both local and has the appropriate modem speeds.
- *Domain and host name.* Your host and domain name are text names that make identification easier.
- *Domain IP.* Your Domain Name Server's IP address (briefly, DNS is the method the Internet uses to associate unique names for each of the servers on the network).
- *Login name.* Authentication technique (some Internet service providers require users to type in their login name and password in a *terminal window*, a command window that opens when you connect to the service. Others have automated authentication methods, called PAP or CHAP, discussed later).

If your Internet service provider gives you a dedicated IP address to use every time you dial in, you may also need the following:

- ■ *IP address for you.* This is your computer's unique address.

- ■ *IP subnet mask.* This is used when your computer communicates to other network devices located at your Internet service provider.

- ■ *Gateway IP address.* The address of your Internet service provider's network router.

Here is an example of the setup requirements for an Internet provider:

IP Address:	127.8.23.61
Subnet Mask:	255.255.255.0
Host Name:	the name of your Internet host
Domain Name:	anynet.com
Dial:	555-0000 (your provider's dial-up networking phone number)
Login:	jsmith
Password:	pAss-WoRd5 (whatever you choose)
Domain Server:	127.8.23.254

Your provider might configure your system for you. It might help you over the phone while you enter the information in the correct Windows 95 Dial-Up Adapter dialog boxes.

▶ **See** "Installing a Plug and Play Modem," **p. 284**

▶ **See** "Using Drivers Provided by Modem Manufacturers," **p. 293**

Installing Dial-Up Networking

The first step when manually setting up Internet access is to install the Dial-Up Networking component. You may have installed Dial-Up Networking when you first set up Windows 95. Here is how you can tell:

1. Double-click My Computer to see whether Dial-Up Networking is installed. If it is, you see a folder named Dial-Up Networking, as shown in figure 33.15.

2. If you have Dial-Up Networking already installed, go to the section titled, "Installing TCP/IP," later in this chapter. If you do not have a Dial-Up Networking folder, install it now. Open the Start menu, choose Settings, Control Panel.

3. Select the Add/Remove Programs option. The Add/Remove Programs Properties sheet appears.

FIG. 33.15
A view of My Computer with Dial-Up Networking installed.

4. Click the Windows Setup tab.

5. Select the Communications option and click the Details button. The dialog box in figure 33.16 appears.

FIG. 33.16
The Communications dialog box, from which you install Dial-Up Networking.

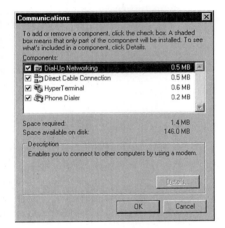

6. Select the Dial-Up Networking option.

7. Click OK in the Communications dialog box; click OK in the Add/Remove Programs Properties sheet to complete the installation.

Installing TCP/IP

Next you have to install the TCP/IP protocol. If you installed the Dial-Up Networking Adapter during the Windows 95 installation, you may have also installed TCP/IP. Here is how you can tell:

1. Open the Start menu and choose Settings, Control Panel. Double-click the Network program icon. If you do not see the TCP/IP protocol listed, install it now.

Click the Add button, select Protocol, and click the Add button. The Select Network Protocol dialog box appears, as shown in figure 33.17. Select Microsoft from the Manufacturers list, select TCP/IP from the Network Protocols list, and click OK.

FIG. 33.17

Select Microsoft from the Manufacturers list and TCP/IP from the Network Protocols list.

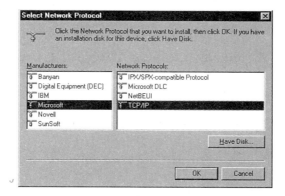

2. Now make sure your dial-up adapter is using (the term is, *is bound to*) the TCP/IP protocol. In the Network dialog box, select the Dial-Up Adapter and then click Properties. Click the Bindings tab, as shown in figure 33.18. Make sure the check box next to the TCP/IP Dial-Up adapter is selected. Click OK to return to the Network dialog box.

FIG. 33.18

The Bindings page in the Dial-Up Adapter Properties sheet, showing TCP/IP bound to the adapter.

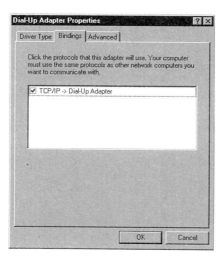

Part
IX

Ch
33

3. Select TCP/IP from the Network list in the Network dialog box and click Properties. Select the IP Address tab and make sure the Obtain An IP Address

Automatically check box is selected. This check box sets your IP address to 0.0.0.0 (this is not visible because the check box is grayed-out), which means your Internet provider will dynamically assign you an IP address when you call in.

N O T E   If your Internet service provider assigns you a permanent IP address, enter that address manually on the IP Address page: in the IP Address box, check the Specify an IP Address option and enter the assigned address in the IP Address field. You must also type the subnet mask address for your provider in the Subnet mask field.

When you connect using PPP, the permanent IP address is used instead of the Internet service provider dynamically assigning one to you. When you connect with SLIP, the permanent IP address shows up in the Specify an IP address box to confirm your IP address for your SLIP connection. ▨

T I P   If the address you are typing has less than three numbers before the period, use the Right Arrow key to jump to the next area between the periods in the field. If you type three numbers before the period, the cursor moves to the next area automatically.

4. In the TCP/IP Properties sheet, click the DNS Configuration tab. Instead of defining the DNS addresses here, you define them as part of the Dial-Up Networking connection in the following section, "Creating a Configuration for Your Internet Service Provider." Select Disable DNS. Click OK to close the TCP/IP Properties sheet.

5. Click OK to close the Network control panel. Exit and restart Windows 95.

Installing SLIP

If you are using a SLIP account, you need to install the SLIP software. Follow these steps to install it:

1. Open the Start menu and choose Settings, Control Panel. Double-click Add/Remove Programs. Select the Windows Setup tab; then select Have Disk.

2. Click Browse. Select the drive and directory where the file RNAPLUS.INF is located. On the Windows 95 CD-ROM, you can find the file in the Admin/Apptools/ Dscript folder. When you have selected the file, click OK.

3. The Have Disk dialog box appears. Select the SLIP and Scripting for Dial-Up Networking check box (see fig. 33.19). Click Install.

FIG. 33.19
To use SLIP, select the SLIP and Scripting for Dial-Up Networking check box.

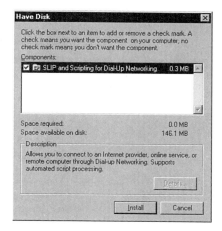

Creating a Configuration for Your Internet Service Provider

In the preceding sections, you configured Windows 95 for TCP/IP connections. Now you need to tell it about the connection you will be making to your Internet service provider. To do this, you create and configure a new connection using the following steps:

1. Open the Dial-Up Networking folder from the My Computer window. If this is the first time you have opened it, a Connection Wizard runs to help you enter all the information necessary for a dial-up connection.

2. Double-click the Make New Connection icon to display the Make New Connection Wizard shown in fig. 33.20. Type the name of your Internet service provider in the Type a Name text box. If you have not already configured Windows 95 for your modem, click Configure to do so now.

Part
IX

Ch
33

FIG. 33.20
Clicking Configure opens the Modem Properties sheet.

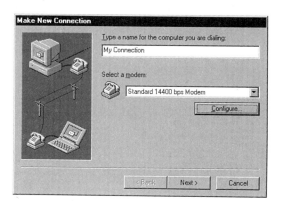

3. If you have configured your modem, continue by clicking Next; then enter the area code and telephone number for your Internet service provider. Select your country code and area code from the drop-down menus. Click Next, and then click Finish to complete the installation. Now you have a new icon in your Dial-Up Networking Box specific to this connection. For easier access, right-drag the icon to your desktop and choose Create Shortcut(s) Here to create a shortcut.

4. If your provider requires you to log on by means of a terminal window, you must enable that function. In the Dial-Up Networking window, right-click the connection icon you just created and choose Properties. In the Connect Using area of the page, click Configure. Now choose the Options tab (see fig. 33.21.) In the Connection Control section, make sure the Bring Up Terminal Window After Dialing check box is selected. Choose OK. This returns you to the first box of the Property sheet.

FIG. 33.21
Check the Bring Up Terminal Window After Dialing option to enable this function.

5. In the Property sheet, click Server Type in the Connect Using section. This displays the Server Types dialog box (see fig. 33.22). Use the Type of Dial-Up Server drop-down menu to select the type of connection, PPP, SLIP, or CSLIP. Your Internet service provider can tell you what type of account you have.

6. In the Advanced Options group, select the Enable Software Compression check box. This improves throughput of your connection, but is only used when both sides of the connection support it.

   Select the Require Encrypted Password check box if you do not want your password to transmit in clear text when you connect. Your Internet service provider must support CHAP for this to work. If it only supports PAP, and you select this option, the connection will fail.

FIG. 33.22

If you are using a PPP connection, your Server Types dialog box should look like this.

The Log On To Network option is not used for Internet access.

N O T E   *PAP* stands for Password Authentication Protocol. *CHAP* stands for Challenge-Handshake Authentication Protocol. Both protocols allow you to log in without typing your user name and password in a terminal window. CHAP provides additional security, as it prevents your password from being transmitted in clear text over the connection. ■

7. From the Allowed Network Protocols group, select the TCP/IP check box. This option provides quicker connect time after dialing the Internet provider. The NetBEUI and IPX/SPX Compatible check boxes are not relevant to connecting to the Internet. Make sure they are unselected.

8. Click the TCP/IP Settings button. The TCP/IP Settings dialog box displays. Figure 33.23 shows a completed TCP/IP Settings dialog box. Any values entered here will override those specified in the Network Control Panel TCP/IP properties sheet.

Part
IX

Ch

33

CAUTION

Be careful when entering server address numbers. Depending on the edit movement keys you use, the zero (0) placeholders might not be replaced by numbers you enter. Make sure inappropriate zeroes do not remain.

Select the Server Assigned IP Address option if your Internet service provider uses dynamic IP addressing. If your Internet service provider gave you a permanent IP address, check the Specify an IP Address option and enter the number in the IP address field.

FIG. 33.23
Use the TCP/IP
Settings dialog box
to define param-
eters only for this
connection.

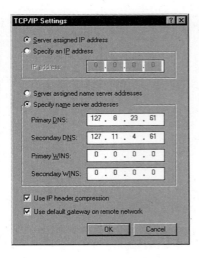

9. When you make a connection to your Internet service provider, addresses for the Domain Name System (DNS) servers can be automatically assigned. If your Internet service provider supports this capability, select the Server Assigned Name Server Addresses option.

    Sometimes, your Internet service provider must give you addresses for its DNS servers. In this case, check the Specify Name Server Addresses option, and enter the addresses into the Primary DNS and Secondary DNS fields. The Windows Internet Naming Service (WINS) addresses do not apply to Internet connections. Leave the Primary WINS and Secondary WINS fields blank.

10. Select the Use IP Header Compression check box. This improves throughput at low modem speeds, but must be supported by your Internet service provider.

11. Select the Use Default Gateway on Remote Network check box. This ensures that all IP traffic is routed through your Dial-Up Internet connection.

12. Click OK. Click OK again. Finally, click OK to close the dialog box for your Dial-Up Connection.

    ▶ **See** "Using the Power of Shortcuts and Desktop Icons," **p. 71**
    ▶ **See** "Configuring Your Modem," **p. 294**

Connecting to Your Internet Service Provider

You are now ready to dial your Internet service provider. Follow these steps:

1. Double-click your New Connection icon (either on the desktop if you have created a shortcut, or in the Dial-Up Networking folder). The Connect To dialog box displays the phone number for your Internet service provider.

2. Enter your user name and password in the Connect To dialog box (see fig. 33.24). If desired, you can check Save Password to avoid having to enter your password each time you dial in.

   If your Internet service provider requires you to log in using a terminal window, you do not have to enter your user name and password here because you enter that information in the terminal window that appears after the modem connects.

FIG. 33.24
Click Connect in the Connect To dialog box to dial your Internet service provider.

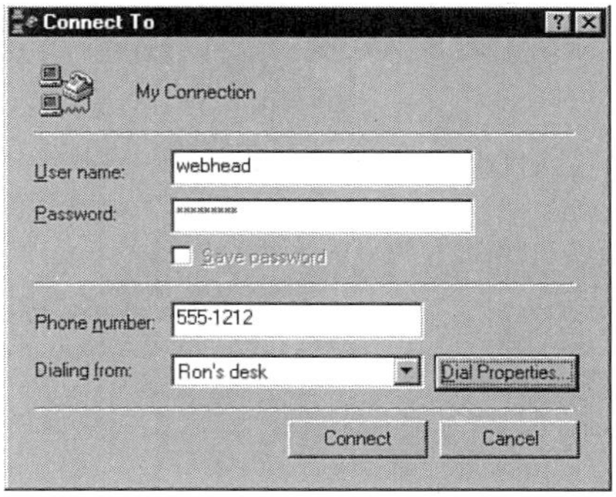

3. Click Connect. The modem dials and connects.

   If your Internet service provider requires you to log in using a terminal window, the Post-Dial Terminal Screen appears, as shown in figure 33.25. Enter your user name and password, and then click Continue or press F7.

Part
IX

Ch
33

CAUTION

If you share files or printers from your system using File and Print Sharing, be aware that Internet users can gain unauthorized access to your shared resources. You can use the Internet Control Panel to perform a security check before your system dials the Internet. See "Using the Internet Control Panel" later in this chapter.

FIG. 33.25
Use the Post-Dial Terminal Screen to enter your user name and password when your Internet service provider does not support PAP or CHAP with PPP.

N O T E Unless you configured Windows 95 not to require a password at the start of each day's session, you will have to retype your password here the first time each day, or after you reboot. ▪

If you are using a SLIP connection, follow these steps to connect:

1. After you enter your user name and password in the terminal window, you should get a message from your provider telling you your IP address for this session. Most providers tell you what your IP address is with a message like `Your IP address is` or `SLIP session from ###.###.###.### to ###.###.###.###`. The second address is usually your IP address. Write down your IP address and click the Continue button.

2. You should see a dialog box like the one in figure 33.26, asking you to confirm your IP address. Type the IP address you just wrote down and click OK. You should be connected in a few seconds.

FIG. 33.26
Use this dialog box to enter your IP address. If you are not sure of the address, ask your Internet provider.

N O T E Most Internet providers can switch your account from SLIP to PPP for no charge. PPP offers better error correction than SLIP. Additionally, PPP accounts may not require you to use the terminal window to log in and do not require you to enter your IP address manually. ▪

TROUBLESHOOTING

I entered all the information in the Property sheet for my connection, and I configured my modem correctly, but I still cannot connect. If you are having problems connecting with your service, make sure that your server type is correct. In the Dial-Up Networking folder, right-click your Connection icon; then select Properties. Click on Server Type. Make sure that the server type in the connection properties is set to PPP, not SLIP or CSLIP. Deselect the Enable Software Compression check box in the Advanced Options section of the page.

If you have a SLIP account, make sure that you have changed the server type to SLIP or CSLIP (PPP is the default). Make sure that you type the correct IP address when prompted during the login process.

When I try to connect to the Internet and The Microsoft Network, I get the error `Cannot` `locate the Microsoft Network Data center, please try again.` **Why?** If you have a static Domain Name Server (DNS) address defined in the Network Control Panel, or a static IP address or gateway associated with your dial-up adapter, you cannot connect to the Internet and The Microsoft Network. This is most likely to occur if you use TCP/IP on a LAN or use Dial-Up Networking to access multiple Internet service providers.

If you use TCP/IP on a LAN, there are three possible solutions.

- Use a different protocol (such as IPX/SPX or NetBEUI) on your LAN. Contact your network administrator for details.

- Use DHCP on your LAN to assign addresses dynamically.

- Change the DNS configuration manually every time you run the Internet and The Microsoft Network. That is, before connecting, delete the static DNS address and restart your computer. After disconnecting, add the static address back and restart so you can see your LAN again.

If you do not use TCP/IP on a LAN, the solution is to remove the addresses from the Network Control Panel. If you use multiple access providers, associate the addresses you remove from the Network Control Panel to the appropriate Dial-Up Networking connection. This procedure ensures that the setup for any access provider does not interfere with the Internet and The Microsoft Network settings. Follow these steps:

1. Open the Start menu and choose Settings, Control Panel. Double-click the Network program icon.
2. If you do not have a network card, select the TCP/IP protocol entry. If you have a network card, select the TCP/IP-> Dial-Up Network Adapter protocol entry.
3. Click the Properties button.
4. Click the DNS configuration tab. Write down any DNS addresses listed. To connect to Internet and The Microsoft Network, you must have the Disable DNS option selected and remove any DNS addresses listed.
5. Click the IP Address tab. Write down any IP address listed. Select the Obtain An IP Address Automatically option.
6. Click the Gateway tab. Select each address listed in the Installed Gateways list and click the Remove button.
7. Click OK until you close all open dialog boxes.

If you use another access provider in addition to the Internet and The Microsoft Network, follow these steps to associate the addresses with the Dial-Up Networking connection:

1. Open the Start menu and choose Programs, Accessories, Dial-Up Networking.
2. Right-click the icon for the Dial-Up connection.

Part

IX

Ch

33

continues

continued

3. Choose Properties.

4. Click the Server Type button.

5. Click the TCP/IP Settings button.

6. Click the Specify an IP Address option, and type the fixed IP address in the IP Address text box.

7. Click the Specify Name Server Addresses option and type the DNS server addresses in the Primary DNS and Secondary DNS text boxes.

8. Click OK until you close all open dialog boxes.

You can find more detailed information in the Microsoft Knowledge base articles Q134288 (Cannot Connect to Internet and MSN with Static DNS) and Q134282 (Cannot Connect to Internet and MSN with Static IP Address). You can access the Microsoft Knowledge base on MSN. From MSN Central, choose Edit, Go to, Other Location, and type **MSKB**. Click OK.

Testing Your Connection

Use Ping (a program that comes with Windows 95) to test if a connection is working. When executed, Ping requests the remote computer you designate to send back a response to let you know you are connected.

To use Ping to test your connection to the Internet, follow these steps:

1. After you are connected to your Internet service provider, open a DOS window.

2. At the DOS prompt, type **ping ftp.microsoft.com**. If the Microsoft server is busy, it may not answer right away. If so, ping your Internet provider's host computer by name. The name may be mail or mach1. Or ping 128.95.1.4, a DNS server. The remote host replies:

```
Pinging ftp.microsoft.com [198.105.232.1] with 32 bytes of data:
Reply from 198.105.232.1: bytes=32 time=180ms TTL=18
Reply from 198.105.232.1: bytes=32 time=185ms TTL=18
Reply from 198.105.232.1: bytes=32 time=176ms TTL=18
Reply from 198.105.232.1: bytes=32 time=181ms TTL=18
```

This tells you that your computer is talking to the server. Unless you have on-going problems connecting, you will only need to use the Ping command once.

N O T E After you make a connection to your Internet service provider, you can use the Winipcfg program to display the TCP/IP configuration of the Dial-Up Adapter. To run Winipcfg, Open the Start menu and choose Run. Type **winipcfg** in the Open text box and click OK. Click More Info to display the detailed information, as shown in figure 33.27. ■

FIG. 33.27

Use Winipcfg to display the TCP/IP parameters of your connection.

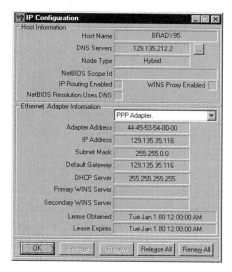

TROUBLESHOOTING

After connecting with my SLIP account, I can ping the server, but still cannot use Winsock applications to connect to a resource. You may have to switch the server type. From My Computer, open the Dial-Up Networking folder. Right-click on your connection to open the Properties sheet. Select Server Type; then try changing the server type in the connection properties from SLIP to CSLIP or CSLIP to SLIP, depending on what it is currently set for.

I can run Internet Explorer, but other network applications will not work. What is wrong? If you have a Winsock application that is not working properly, check to see whether that application requires a specific WINSOCK.DLL file. Some Winsock applications come with their own WINSOCK.DLL, which may not work with Windows 95. First, try renaming the application-provided WINSOCK.DLL to ensure that you are using the WINSOCK.DLL in your Windows directory. If the application does not work with the Windows 95 WINSOCK.DLL, replace it with the application's WINSOCK.DLL file.

Exercise caution, because renaming your Windows 95 WINSOCK.DLL might cause other Winsock applications not to work and is not recommended. Contact the application vendor to see whether it has an updated version that will work with the Windows 95 WINSOCK.DLL.

Everything seems to be configured properly, but I still cannot connect to my Internet service provider. If you are having trouble connecting, open the Networks icon in the Control Panel, select the Dial-Up Adapter, select Properties, select the Advanced tab, and set Record a Log File to Yes. This action writes a file called PPPLOG.TXT to your Windows directory that contains

Part
IX

Ch
33

continues

continued

information recorded during the connecting process. You can use this information when you talk to your provider to find a solution.

I have a PPP connection and sometimes cannot connect to my provider. If you are having problems when connecting with Internet service providers offering PPP accounts, it may help if you turn off IP header compression. To do so, open Control Panel, double-click Network, click Dial-Up Adapter to select it, and click Properties. In the Properties sheet, select the Advanced tab and deselect the Use IP Header Compression option.

Using the Internet Control Panel

Windows 95 includes the Internet Control Panel to provide additional control over your Windows 95 Internet connection. With the Internet Control Panel, you can do the following:

- Set up AutoDial, so Windows 95 automatically dials up your Internet service provider when an application needs access to the Internet.
- Set up Auto Disconnect, so Windows 95 automatically disconnects from the Internet after a specified time of no activity.
- Perform a security check before you connect, to warn you if Internet users may gain access to your File Sharing or Printer Sharing resources.
- Set up and manage your proxy server location, if your organization uses one to control access to the Internet.

Using AutoDial and Auto Disconnect

Use the AutoDial property sheet to configure Windows 95 to automatically dial up your Internet service provider when an application needs access to the Internet. You can also configure Windows 95 to disconnect after a period of inactivity. If your Windows 95 system has access to the Internet through a LAN, do not enable the AutoDial feature.

To configure the AutoDial and Auto Disconnect features, follow these steps:

1. Open the Start menu and choose Settings, Control Panel. Double-click the Internet icon. The AutoDial property sheet appears, as shown in figure 33.28.

FIG. 33.28

Use the Internet Control Panel AutoDial property sheet to automatically dial up your Internet service provider when an application needs access to the Internet.

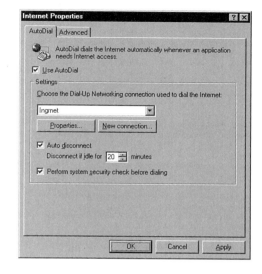

2. Select the Use AutoDial check box. The Settings group should become active.

3. In the Choose the Dial-Up Networking Connection Used To Dial the Internet list, select your Internet service provider. Alternatively, you can create a new entry by clicking the New Connection button. If you create a new connection, refer to step 2 in "Creating a Configuration for Your Internet Service Provider," earlier in this chapter.

   If you want to review or modify the properties of the Dial-Up Networking connection, click the Properties button.

4. If your Internet service provider charges connection time fees, check the Auto Disconnect box to save money when you accidentally leave your system online. In the Disconnect If Idle box, enter the number of minutes of inactivity before the disconnect occurs. Windows warns you one minute before the disconnect occurs, and allows you to remain online if desired.

   If you do not use the Auto Disconnect feature, use the Disconnect button on the Connected to window.

5. To help prevent Internet users from gaining access to your File Sharing and Printer Sharing resources, check the Perform System Security Check Before Dialing box. When you dial your Internet service provider, the system will check for shared folders and printers, and warn you if Internet users can access them.

Part

IX

Ch

33

Using a Proxy Server

A proxy server acts as a gateway between some Internet applications, like Internet Explorer, and the Internet. Normally, proxy servers are set up as a security barrier between your LAN and the Internet. If your Windows 95 system is not on a LAN, you do not have to configure the proxy server settings. Proxy servers perform the following functions:

- Setting up a security barrier between your LAN and the Internet, preventing access of Internet users to information and shared resources on your LAN.

- Auditing and filtering of outgoing requests, to prevent employee access to non-work related sites.

- Caching of Internet information to improve the performance of your Internet connection. The first employee to access a Web page, such as the Wall Street Journal home page, waits the longest because the proxy server fetches the page and stores it in cache. But thereafter, every employee who accesses the same page fetches the page from the proxy server cache instead of over the Internet, and perceived performance is much faster. Algorithms within the proxy server assure that the cache is kept up-to-date and that users always get the correct information.

To configure Windows 95 to use a proxy server, follow these steps:

1. Get your organization's proxy server address and port number from the network administrator.

2. Open the Internet Control Panel, open the Start menu, and choose Settings, Control Panel. Double-click the Internet icon.

3. Select the Advanced tab, as shown in figure 33.29.

FIG. 33.29
Use the Internet Control Panel Advanced page to define your proxy server if your organization uses one.

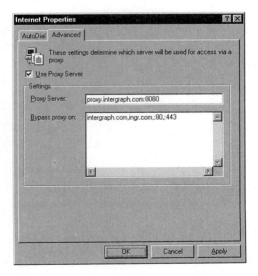

4. Select the Use Proxy Server check box. The Settings group becomes active.

5. In the Proxy Server text box, type in the host name and port number of the proxy server.

6. In the Bypass Proxy On text box, type the names, domains, and port numbers of the hosts which do not use the proxy server. For example, many organizations set up internal webs, which the proxy server offers no added value. Separate your entries with a comma.

Connecting to the Internet with a LAN

If your computer is part of a local area network (LAN), connecting to the Internet with Windows 95 is as easy as connecting a single user. The difference is that instead of getting the information you need from an Internet service provider, you obtain it from your network administrator.

To connect to the Internet with a LAN, follow these steps:

1. Open the Start menu and choose Settings, Control Panel. Double-click the Network icon. If you followed the procedures to install Dial-Up Networking, you will now have both Dial-Up Adapter and TCP/IP installed. Select the TCP/IP protocol and click Properties. If you do not see the TCP/IP protocol in the Network Components list, refer to "Installing TCP/IP," earlier in this chapter.

2. Select the IP Address tab. If your LAN has a Dynamic Host Configuration Protocol (DHCP) Server, click the Obtain an IP Address Automatically button.

3. If your LAN does not have a DHCP server, obtain an IP address from your network administrator. Click the button marked Specify an IP address and fill in the address. Use the arrow key to move between the fields separated by periods. You should also enter the Subnet Mask address at this time.

4. Now click the Gateway tab. This is the address of the connection point between your LAN and the Internet. Enter the address provided by your network administrator.

5. Now select the DNS Configuration tab (see fig. 33.30). Select Enable DNS. Obtain your Host and Domain names from your network administrator and enter them in the spaces provided. If you are part of a smaller organization, you may not have a Domain Name Server of your own, but have a domain name provided by your service provider.

Part
IX
Ch
33

FIG. 33.30
Use the DNS
Configuration page
to identify the DNS
servers on your LAN.

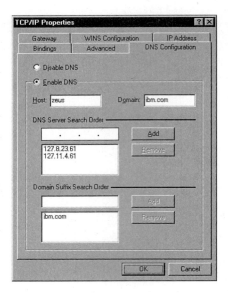

6. In the DNS Server Search Order text box, enter the numeric address of the DNS server your network administrator gives you.

7. If your LAN is running Windows NT, you might have to set up the Windows Internet Naming Service (WINS). Click the WINS Configuration tab and follow your network administrator's instructions.

8. Click OK to close the Network control panel. Exit and restart Windows 95.

TROUBLESHOOTING

I do not run TCP/IP on my LAN and I experience occasional system pauses. How do I fix this? If you are using TCP/IP for your Internet connections and the protocol is bound to both your LAN and dial-up adapter but no DHCP server is present on the LAN, your system may pause for a few seconds every once in a while. The system pauses as it attempts to identify other TCP/IP hosts on your LAN. To avoid this, unbind TCP/IP from your LAN adapter.

Open the Network icon in Control Panel. Select the Network Card; then click Properties. Click the Bindings tab, and deselect the TCP/IP option in the dialog box.

▶ **See** "Installing Windows 95 as a Microsoft Windows Network Client," **p. 689**

Windows 95 Internet Tools

After all the configuration work you went through to get onto the Internet, it may seem that getting connected was the goal. But the real power of the Internet lies not in the connection, but in what you do after you are there. Windows 95 includes the following useful Internet applications.

- *An e-mail program.* Use Microsoft Exchange with the Internet service. For complete details on Microsoft Exchange, see Chapter 31, "Using the Universal Inbox."

- *A World Wide Web browser.* Use Microsoft's Internet Explorer. You may also need programs to view downloaded images, play sound, and watch videos. In some cases, these applications are included with Internet Explorer.

  In addition to navigating Web pages, Internet Explorer supports downloading files using FTP and gopher, as well as the capability to participate with UseNet newsgroups.

- *Telnet* is a Windows-based program used to log on to Internet sites as if your computer were a terminal connected to that computer.

  ▶ **See** "Using Internet Explorer and the World Wide Web," **p. 983**

Part

IX

Ch

33

CHAPTER 34

Using Internet Explorer and the World Wide Web

by Francis Moss with Paul Robichaux and Brady P. Merkel

The World Wide Web, designed by researchers at CERN in Geneva, Switzerland, is a collection of hypertext documents served from computers throughout the world. Web documents, or *pages,* can contain pictures, text, sounds, movies, and links to other documents. Web pages can—and usually do—contain links to documents on other computers. The name "Web" comes from the interlinked nature of the pages.

Internet Explorer is a Web browser. Designed to take advantage of the full range of Windows 95's features, Internet Explorer uses the productive Windows 95 user interface and supports shortcuts and long file names. Figure 34.1 shows Internet Explorer's main window and the default page that ships with the software. Internet Explorer is part of Microsoft's Plus! Pack for Windows 95. If you purchased a new computer with Windows 95 installed, the Internet Explorer might be installed as well. Also, Microsoft offers the Internet Explorer as a free download from its Internet site and The Microsoft Network.

Explore the World Wide Web (WWW)

Use Internet Explorer to access the rich multimedia content on the World Wide Web, the most popular service on the Internet.

Participate in UseNet community forums

Use Internet Explorer to post and read articles that millions of other users can see.

Log in to remote computers on the Internet with Telnet

Connect to distant sites and view alphanumeric information in a Telnet session.

Create your own Web page

Use Microsoft's Internet Assistant to author your own Web pages using the HyperText Markup Language (HTML).

FIG. 34.1

Internet Explorer's main window includes a toolbar for quick access to common functions. This is the introductory Internet Explorer start page.

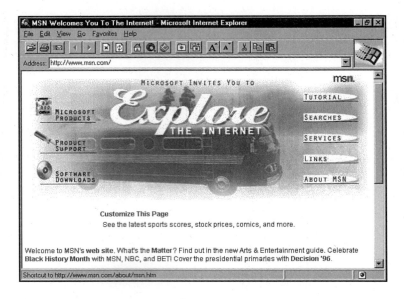

N O T E This book is about Windows 95, so we can only scratch the surface of the Internet. For more coverage of the Internet and related software, check out *Special Edition Using the Internet,* Second Edition; *Special Edition Using the World Wide Web with Mosaic; Using FTP; Using Netscape; Easy World Wide Web with Netscape; Using UseNet Newsgroups; Web Publishing with Word for Windows*; or any of the other Que books about the Internet and its parts. ■

ON THE WEB

Visit the Macmillan Publishing Web page for a complete book list at

http://www.mcp.com

Internet Explorer shares a common look and feel with Microsoft's other applications, and includes Windows 95 features like ToolTips and the common File and Print dialog boxes. It also has many similarities to other Web browsers. If you are already accustomed to another browser, you will find the Internet Explorer both comfortably familiar and excitingly different.

There *is* one difference you need to know about. Microsoft calls hypertext links *shortcuts,* since clicking them takes you to someplace else. To avoid confusion, this chapter refers to hypertext links as "links" or "hyperlinks," and Windows 95 shortcuts as "shortcuts."

The Microsoft Plus! Pack includes the Internet Jumpstart Kit, which contains a World Wide Web browser and an e-mail service for use with the Microsoft Exchange mail client. One feature of the Web browser includes the capability to drag your favorite Internet locations to the desktop to create shortcuts, so you can quickly jump to that Web location. ■

Getting and Installing the Internet Explorer

The Internet Explorer comes as part of the Plus! Pack for Windows 95. (If your computer came preloaded with Windows 95, you may already have the Internet Explorer installed; check your system documentation.) Like many other Windows 95 products, the Plus! Pack is easy to install. Here is what you should do:

1. Insert the first Plus! Pack disk into your floppy or CD-ROM drive.

2. Using the Windows 95 command prompt, Explorer, or a desktop window, run the SETUP.EXE on the floppy or CD-ROM.

3. The Plus! Pack setup installer loads and asks you to choose which modules you want to install. Choose the Internet Explorer option.

Understanding World Wide Web URLs

Uniform Resource Locators (*URLs*) specify the location of resources on the Internet that are part of the World Wide Web (WWW). You use URLs with Internet Explorer to identify where to retrieve information from the Internet. URLs are also used within WWW documents to link to other resources. Figure 34.2 illustrates the makeup of a URL. The first part of a URL defines the Internet protocol used to get the resource. Use a colon to delimit the protocol from the remainder of the URL. The number of supported protocols is growing, and you may find protocols that are not listed below.

Specifier	Protocol
ftp	File Transfer Protocol
http	HyperText Transfer Protocol
https	Another secure HTTP
gopher	Gopher Protocol
telnet	Telnet Terminal Session
news	UseNet News, uses NNTP
mailto	Electronic mail address

Part
IX

Ch
34

ON THE WEB

Information about Internet Protocols on the YAHOO search site
http://www.yahoo.com/Computers_and_Internet/Software/Protocols/

As shown in figure 34.2, the protocol is `http`, which indicates that this resource is retrieved using the HyperText Transfer Protocol. The rest of the URL includes the Internet host name (`www.w3.org`) and the path to the document on the host.

FIG. 34.2
URLs serve as simple
identifiers to resources on
the World Wide Web.

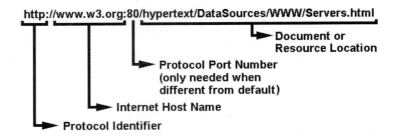

What follows the protocol depends on which protocol is used. Most URLs introduce a server host name by double slashes. If an application protocol is running on a non-standard TCP/IP port (a virtual network location on a host), the TCP/IP port number can follow the server name, delimited by a colon. If no TCP/IP port number is defined, the standard TCP/IP port number for that protocol is used instead.

Paths to specific files, directories, or programs on the server follow the server host name. Finally, arguments or parameters to server programs may be passed at the end of the URL. Consider the following examples of URLs:

- **http://www.intergraph.com/index.html**

  This http: URL identifies a document named index.html on the www.intergraph.com server, using the HyperText Transfer Protocol. Internet Explorer fetches the document and displays it in the window.

- **http://www.intergraph.com/ics/**

  When a directory is specified with no document, an HTTP server usually returns a default file or a listing of the files in the directory, depending on how the HTTP server is configured.

- **https://www.intergraph.com/catalog/order.pl**

  This https: URL identifies a secure HTTP server, which communicates with Internet Explorer in a trusted way. Using these URLs, you prevent Internet hackers from getting the information you submit, such as your credit card number.

- **ftp://ftp.intergraph.com/help/FAQ**

  This ftp: URL identifies a file named FAQ in the help directory on the ftp.intergraph.com anonymous-ftp server. Note that no user name and password are supplied. In this case, the ftp connection is established using the user name anonymous, and your e-mail address as the password.

If required, specify the user name and password before the host name, as in ftp://your-userid@your-password:ftp.intergraph.com/help/FAQ.

■ **gopher://gopher.intergraph.com:70/pub/win32**

Named after the mascot of the University of Minnesota, Gopher allows you to list and find files on the Internet. The gopher: URL requests a listing of the /pub/win32 directory on the gopher.intergraph.com server. The additional :70 after the server name identifies the port number to connect to. Port numbers are optional in URLs, and default to the standard port number for the particular protocol.

■ **news:news.answers**

The news: URL identifies a UseNet newsgroup. In this case, Internet Explorer connects to your Network News Transfer Protocol (NNTP) server, configured in the View Options News Property sheet.

■ **mailto:info@intergraph.com**

The mailto: URL identifies an e-mail address. When you click a mailto: URL, Internet Explorer brings up Microsoft Exchange, which allows you to fill in a subject, return address, and message. The message is sent to the address in the URL.

■ **file:c:\htdocs\default.htm**

To reference local files, as opposed to those on the network, use a file: URL. When you drag and drop a file onto Internet Explorer, the document appears with a file: URL. In general, URLs always use forward slashes, but Internet Explorer allows backslashes as well.

■ **telnet://ausername:apassword@archie.sura.net**

The telnet: URL identifies a host to invoke a terminal session, including the user name and password. When you click a telnet: URL in Internet Explorer, the Telnet application is used to handle the request.

Navigating the World Wide Web

When you start the Internet Explorer, it displays the introductory page shown in figure 36.1 (until you customize it, that is). There are several ways to open a page. The most common way is also the simplest: just click a hyperlink to jump to the page. Hyperlinks are usually shown as underlined and colored text. Another way to jump to any Web document, anywhere, is to use the Open Internet Address dialog box (see fig. 34.3). When you type in a URL address, the Internet Explorer opens the Web document you requested. Select the Open in New Window check box to view the new page in a separate window.

FIG. 34.3

The Open Internet Address dialog box allows you to jump directly to any site on the Internet, or to load Web pages stored on your hard disk.

To go to any page whose URL you know, use the following method:

1. Choose File, Open; or click the Open button on the toolbar.

2. Type in the address or select an address from the pull-down menu.

 TIP
You can open the Start menu and choose Run to display the Run dialog box, then enter a URL in the command line to start Internet Explorer with that resource displayed.

 TIP
To open an HTML document from a drive on your computer, click the Open File button in the dialog box in step 2 or drag the HTML file from the My Computer window or Explorer into the Internet Explorer window.

3. To open a new window for the page you are opening, select the Open in New Window check box. You can easily work with multiple pages just by switching between their windows.

4. Click OK.

There are several other ways to go to Web pages. You can:

- Type an address into the Address Bar menu just below the toolbar.

- Select a previously visited site from the Address Bar pull-down menu.

 TIP
Right-click a picture or background texture in Internet Explorer to save the picture to your disk, copy it to the Clipboard, or set it as your desktop wallpaper. You can also drag images from a Web page to the My Computer window or Explorer to copy them onto your disk, or into Exchange to mail them.

- At any time, you can jump back to your start page (the initial page loaded when you launch the Internet Explorer) by clicking the Home icon or choosing Go, Start Page.

- Jump directly to a Favorite site by opening the Favorites folder and then choosing a site. Click the toolbar icon or choose Favorites, Open, then select the site you want to visit.

■ Use the left-arrow button to go back to a page you have already visited. Once you have gone back to a page, use the right-arrow button to go forward again.

 The Internet Explorer adds pages you have visited to the bottom of the File menu. You can also select File, More History to see a history window of pages you have visited. Windows keeps your history of shortcuts in the Program Files\Plus!\Microsoft Internet\History folder.

Keeping Track of Your Favorite Sites

You probably have some favorite sites that you visit frequently. The Internet Explorer supplies two easy ways to keep track of your favorite sites: the Create Shortcut command and the Favorites list.

Create Shortcut creates a shortcut to the currently displayed page and puts it on your desktop. To create a shortcut, follow these steps:

 Right-click a link to open a new window to the link, create a shortcut to the link, copy a shortcut to the link to the Clipboard, save the linked document to a file, or add the link to your Favorites list.

1. If you are not already there, go to the page for which you want a shortcut.
2. Create the shortcut by choosing File, Create Shortcut.

   When you create a shortcut, you can put it on your desktop, mail it to a friend, or use it anywhere else shortcuts work.
3. You will be asked to confirm that you want to create a shortcut on the desktop. Choose OK to create the shortcut.

Windows keeps your Favorite shortcuts in the Windows\Favorites folder. To add a page to your Favorites list, follow these steps:

1. If you are not already there, go to the page you want to add.

 2. Add the page to your Favorites list by choosing Favorites, Add Favorite, or by clicking the Add to Favorites button.
3. The standard Save File dialog box appears. Choose a location for your entry, then choose OK.

 Drag text from a Web page into any application that accepts text, such as WordPad.

Part
IX

Ch
34

Controlling Page Loading and Display

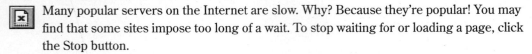

Many popular servers on the Internet are slow. Why? Because they're popular! You may find that some sites impose too long of a wait. To stop waiting for or loading a page, click the Stop button.

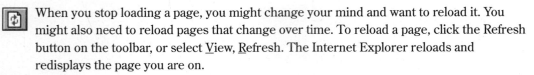

When you stop loading a page, you might change your mind and want to reload it. You might also need to reload pages that change over time. To reload a page, click the Refresh button on the toolbar, or select <u>V</u>iew, <u>R</u>efresh. The Internet Explorer reloads and redisplays the page you are on.

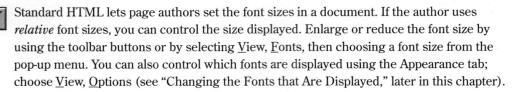

Standard HTML lets page authors set the font sizes in a document. If the author uses *relative* font sizes, you can control the size displayed. Enlarge or reduce the font size by using the toolbar buttons or by selecting <u>V</u>iew, <u>F</u>onts, then choosing a font size from the pop-up menu. You can also control which fonts are displayed using the Appearance tab; choose <u>V</u>iew, <u>O</u>ptions (see "Changing the Fonts that Are Displayed," later in this chapter).

Searching for Information on the World Wide Web

When you are comfortable with the Internet Explorer, you can travel to servers around the world with just a few clicks. There are more than 100,000 Web servers available, with millions of files. Finding what you need can be impossible if you don't know where to start. Internet Explorer makes it easy for you to get started.

To search for Web documents with Internet Explorer, choose <u>G</u>o, S<u>e</u>arch the Internet; or click the Search the Internet button on the toolbar. Internet Explorer displays your search page, where you can type key words and ask for links to related documents. Some Web search sites are faster than others, while others serve to index different sets of documents. To change the search page you use, see "Changing Your Search Page," later in this chapter.

Here are the addresses of some excellent Web search sites that you can use to find what you are looking for:

- **http://www.altavista.digital.com**

  Digital Equipment Corporation sponsors a fast and thorough search engine, which includes timely updates of UseNet News articles. It invites you to search its databases and see if you can find a long-lost friend online!

- **http://www.yahoo.com**

  Yahoo started as a project at Stanford University, but has quickly become such a popular site that it has spun off as a separate server. Yahoo offers a comprehensive list of Web pages, organized into categories like law, entertainment, and business. Yahoo stands for "Yet Another Hierarchically Organized Oracle."

- **http://www.infoseek.com**

  InfoSeek offers a reliable search service that indexes Web pages, articles from computer periodicals, wire-service news articles, and several other sources. Although it is a commercial service, the rates are quite reasonable and it offers free trials.

- **http://www.einet.net**

  EINet, a company that provides electronic commerce consulting and services, operates the Galaxy as a public service. It is organized somewhat like Yahoo, but with a more varied list of topics.

Customizing Internet Explorer

The Internet Explorer lets you control its behavior with the Options dialog box, displayed when you choose <u>V</u>iew, <u>O</u>ptions.

Controlling How Pages Appear

You can control settings used for displaying Web pages with the Appearances page of the Options dialog box. To open this dialog box, choose <u>V</u>iew, <u>O</u>ptions. You can change how hyperlinks are drawn, whether pictures are displayed, the text and background color for pages, and more. Figure 34.4 shows the Options dialog box when the Appearance page is selected.

Part
IX

Ch
34

 Web pictures are usually referred to as *inline graphics* or *inline images*.

Controlling How Graphics are Displayed   You can ask Internet Explorer not to download or display pictures on Web pages. This is helpful when using a modem connection, or when trying to reach a busy server. To turn image loading off or on, choose <u>V</u>iew, <u>O</u>ptions and select the Show Pictures check box until it reflects the setting you want.

FIG. 34.4

The Appearance page gives you control over how Web pages and links appear on your screen.

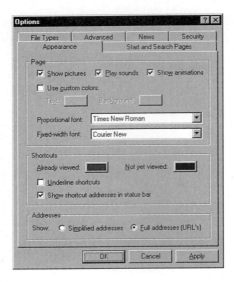

Controlling How Sounds are Played   Internet Explorer can play sounds, such as background music, that accompany Web pages. Using sound can delay page loading, so you may want to turn it off when using a modem connection. Also, if you surf the Web during late hours of the evening, you may want to turn off the sound to allow others in the house to sleep. To turn Web sound off or on, select the Play Sounds check box. A check in the box will make sounds audible; leave the box unchecked to disable sound play.

Controlling How Animations are Displayed   Internet Explorer can display animations in Web pages. Some animation can delay page loading, so you may want to turn it off when using a modem connection. To turn animations off or on, select the Show Animations check box until it reflects the setting you want. Checking the box will show animations. Leave the box unchecked to prevent animations from displaying.

Changing the Text and Background Colors   Internet Explorer lets you control the text and background colors of Web documents. Some Web pages may define their own colors. To set your color preferences, check the Use Custom Colors check box, and select your colors, as follows:

- Click Text to bring up the Color dialog box. Choose a color from the selected palette, or mix a custom color, then choose OK. Internet Explorer uses that color for displaying text on Web pages.

- Click Background to bring up the Color dialog box. Choose a color from the selected palette, or mix a custom color, then choose OK. Internet Explorer uses that color for displaying the background on Web pages.

Changing the Fonts that are Displayed   Internet Explorer lets you control which fonts are used when it displays proportional or fixed-width text. Most Web documents use proportional text, because it is easier to read. Select the proportional font you prefer in the Proportional Font pull-down menu. Fixed-width fonts are sometimes used to align tabular information in a document. Select the fixed-width font you prefer in the Fixed-Width Font pull-down menu.

Some Web authors use different fonts than those you prefer. In that case, the author's fonts will be displayed instead.

 TIP   Serif fonts are easier to read for large amounts of text. The small wings, or *serifs,* on each character help the eye follow the text quickly.

Modifying How Hyperlinks are Displayed   Internet Explorer lets you control how hyperlinks are displayed. Some users prefer their links underlined, while others like them to appear as plain text. You can set your preference using the Underline Shortcuts check box.

Internet Explorer also lets you choose what colors to use when drawing links. To change those colors, choose one of these options:

- Click the Already Viewed button to bring up the Color dialog box. Choose a color from the selected palette, or mix a custom color, then choose OK. Internet Explorer uses that color to indicate links to pages you have already visited.

- Click the Not Yet Viewed button to bring up the Color dialog box. Choose a color from the selected palette, or mix a custom color, then choose OK. Internet Explorer uses that color to indicate links to pages you have not yet seen.

Changing How Addresses are Displayed   Web addresses, or URLs, can be arbitrarily long, and many of them contain confusing query characters or computer-generated indexing markers. If you prefer, you can turn off the display of page addresses, or you can make the Internet Explorer show a shortened, simpler form of the URL for each page.

To control whether the Internet Explorer shows URLs at all, use the Show Shortcut Addresses In Status Bar check box. When unchecked, the Internet Explorer will not show you the URLs. When checked, addresses appear according to the setting of the two radio buttons below it: Simplified Addresses and Full Addresses (URLs). Choose Simplified Addresses if you want to see a shortened, less complex form of page addresses; choose Full Addresses if you want to see the full URL for each link.

A simplified address displays like `Shortcut to HotTopics.htm` at www.microsoft.com. A full address displays like `Shortcut to` http://www.microsoft.com/HotTopics.htm. When you write down an address to use later or share with a friend, use the full address.

Changing Which Page Loads at Startup

 T I P To minimize waiting when first starting the Internet Explorer, specify a page you use often that loads quickly, or run Internet Explorer with the no home command-line argument to prevent loading of the start page. You also can use the Internet Assistant to create your own local start page on your hard drive with links to pages you use often. See "Creating Your Own Pages for the World Wide Web," later in this chapter.

The Start and Search Page tab of the Options dialog box allows you to specify which Web page loads when you launch the Internet Explorer. You can specify a file on your local hard disk, on a shared disk (with a UNC path), or on a Web server.

Here is how to change the start page:

1. Go to the page you want to use as your starting page.

2. Open the Options dialog box (click View, Options) and click the Start and Search Pages tab, as shown in figure 34.5.

3. Select Start Page in the pull-down menu.

4. Click the Use Current button to use the current page, or click Use Default to go back to the previously set start page.

FIG. 34.5
Use the Start and Search Pages tab to set the address of your startup Web page.

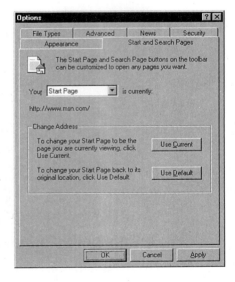

▶ **See** "Using UNC Naming," **p. 754**

Changing Your Search Page

Many Internet sites provide the capability to type in key words and perform a search for documents on the Internet. The Start and Search Pages page of the Options dialog box allows you to specify which Web page loads when you click the search button on the toolbar. You can specify a file on your local hard disk, a shared disk (with a UNC path), or on a Web server.

For a list of excellent Web search sites, refer to "Searching for Information on the World Wide Web," earlier in this chapter.

Follow these steps to change the search page:

1. Go to the page you want to use as your search page.
2. Open the Options dialog box (choose View, Options) and click the Start and Search Pages tab (refer to fig. 34.5).
3. Select Search Page in the pull-down menu.
4. Click the Use Current button to use the current page, or click Use Default to go back to the previously set search page.

Advanced Settings

Internet Explorer allows you to control the size of your History list and how much disk space is used for caching documents. Adjust these parameters to improve performance and conserve disk space. You can also request that Internet Explorer remain your default Internet browser.

Adjust your advanced settings using the Advanced tab in the Options dialog box (choose View, Options), as shown in figure 34.6.

Adjusting the History List Size Internet Explorer saves a shortcut for each Web page you visit, which can take up valuable disk space. To adjust the number of remembered pages in your History list, type a number in the Remember the Last Places Visited text box; or use the up- or down-arrow button to increase or decrease the number. If you want to delete the contents of your current History list, click the Empty button in the History group. To change the folder location for your History files, such as to a different drive, click the Change button in the History group and select a folder in the Browse for Folder dialog box.

Part
IX

Ch
34

FIG. 34.6
Adjust the disk space used
by the Internet Explorer
cache in the Advanced page.

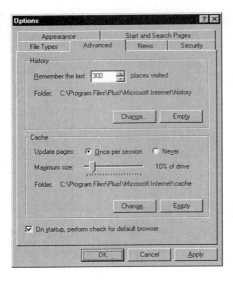

Managing the Cache   Internet Explorer caches Web pages on your hard disk to
increase performance when you return to those pages. Internet Explorer can automatically check for updates to the cached pages when you return to them, or only when
you refresh them. However, be advised, this technique can consume lots of your hard disk
if you are not careful.

To configure Internet Explorer to automatically check for new pages that have been
cached, choose the Once per Session button. Alternatively, if you want to save browsing
time by displaying cached documents and not automatically checking for a new version,
choose the Never button. If you want to make sure you are viewing the latest version of a
Web document, click Refresh on the toolbar; or choose View, Refresh.

To adjust the amount of disk space Internet Explorer uses to cache Web pages, use the
Maximum Size slider. If you are low on disk space; reduce the cache size by moving the
slider to the left. If you want to delete the contents of your current cache folder, click the
Empty button in the Cache group. To change the folder location for your cache, such as to
a different drive, click the Change button in the Cache group and select a folder in the
Browse for Folder dialog box.

TROUBLESHOOTING

**When I navigate to Web sites that update frequently, the documents look the same as when I
last read them. Why?** It is possible you are actually viewing documents that Internet Explorer
found in cache, instead of the latest version available from the Web. To force Internet Explorer to
fetch the latest version of the active document, click the Refresh button.

Always Use Internet Explorer To Browse the Web Sometimes, you may install other Internet browsing software on your system, and that software will register itself as your default browser. If you want to keep Internet Explorer as your Internet browser, check the On Startup, Perform Check for Default Browser check box. When this box is checked and you start Internet Explorer, it will verify that your default browser is Internet Explorer.

Installing Add-Ins and New Document Types

Internet Explorer comes preconfigured to accommodate and use many common file types, including Microsoft Office documents, JPEG and GIF images, WAV and AU sounds, AVI videos, and various other file types. However, you may need to add new file types for documents whose types Microsoft did not anticipate, such as CAD drawings, files compressed on UNIX machines, or MIDI files. You might also want to change the application associated to view a certain file type.

For example, if you want to view Word documents downloaded from the Web, you can associate Word documents with the Word application. If you do not have the Word application, you can use another application that reads Word documents, or use the free Word Viewer available from Microsoft's Web site at **http://www.microsoft.com**. Microsoft also offers Add-Ins for other file types, such as VRML (Virtual Reality Modeling Language). See "Navigating the Web in 3D," later in this chapter.

Figure 34.7 shows an example of adding a file type; in this case, we have added support for ZIP files.

FIG. 34.7
Add new file types through the File Types page in the Options dialog box.

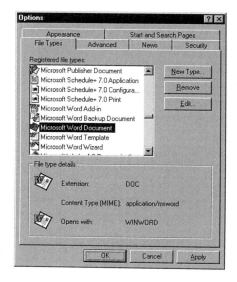

To register a new document type so that the Internet Explorer recognizes it, do this:

1. Open the Options dialog box (click <u>V</u>iew, <u>O</u>ptions) and select the File Types tab. The File Types page appears.

2. Click the <u>N</u>ew Type button.

3. The standard Windows 95 file type dialog box appears. Fill in the fields for the file type you want to add and then choose OK.

  ▶ **See** "Registering File Types Causing Documents to Open Applications," **p. 147**

Working with Internet Security

The Internet is composed of a network of networks. When two computers communicate, data is visible on all the network equipment between them. Internet hackers use this fact to access information that may be considered private. To thwart hackers from accessing private information, such as banking or credit card data, Internet Explorer and many Internet sites employ security software, also known as the Secure HyperText Transfer Protocol and the Secure Sockets Layer. You can use Internet Explorer to view and send private information to these sites, knowing that Internet hackers will not be able to view the information.

 N O T E   Internet Explorer displays the Security Lock button in the status bar when you are connected to a secure Internet site. ▪

You can configure Internet Explorer to warn you when you are about to send information to a site that is not considered secure. Follow these steps to define the level of security you want:

 To view the security certificate information for a Web page, right-click a blank area on the page and select <u>P</u>roperties; then click the Security tab to read the Certificate Information.

1. Open the Options dialog box (click <u>V</u>iew, <u>O</u>ptions) and select the Security tab. The Security page appears, as shown in figure 34.8. If you want to read more about Internet security, click the <u>T</u>ell Me About Internet Security button now.

2. In the Security While Sending group, choose the warning level you prefer. The <u>H</u>igh setting will warn you every time you send information (such as your name and credit card number) to an Internet host that is not secure. Choose the <u>M</u>edium setting to warn you when you send more than one line of information. If you want no warning at all, choose the <u>L</u>ow setting.

FIG. 34.8
Use the Security page to define when security warnings should appear.

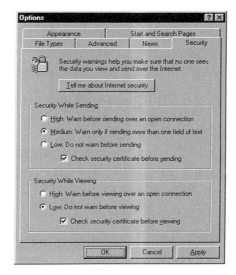

3. Select the Check Security Certificate Before Sending check box to warn you when you are about to send information to an Internet host who claims to be secure, but does not check out.

4. In the Security While Viewing group, choose the warning level you prefer when viewing Web documents. The High setting will warn you when you are about to connect to a secure Internet site, such as your bank. If you want no warning at all, choose the Low setting.

5. Select the Check Security Certificate Before Viewing check box to warn you when you are about to send information to an Internet host who claims to be secure, but whose credentials do not check out.

Navigating the Web in 3-D

Part
IX
Ch
34

One of the World Wide Web's greatest strengths is its rich interactive multimedia content. However, most of that content is presented in a plain, two-dimensional view, using simple text and graphics. The Virtual Reality Modeling Language (VRML) will help to change that fact.

VRML is a sophisticated language that describes 3-D scenes, or *worlds*. VRML worlds are composed of 3-D objects, textures, shadows, light sources, and more. Furthermore, the 3-D objects can have hyperlinks associated with them to allow you to jump to other Internet sites. When viewing VRML worlds, you can interact with the view—rotating, moving, and zooming in and out. All these elements combine to deliver a new experience on the World Wide Web, an experience that allows you to walk through malls, fly around buildings, and glide over cities (see fig. 34.9).

FIG. 34.9
A VRML view of the Microsoft campus in Redmond, Washington.

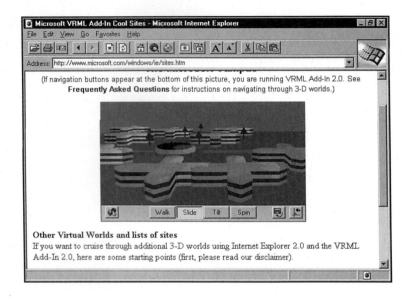

You interact with VRML worlds using an Internet Explorer VRML *Add-In*. The Add-In enables you to interact with VRML worlds that display in the Internet Explorer window, instead of using an external program.

Getting and Installing the VRML Add-In

Before you take the time and effort to install the VRML Add-In, make sure your computer can support it. You must have at least a 486DX 33MHz computer with 8M of memory, 2M of free disk space, and a video card that can support 256 colors or more.

To get and install the Internet Explorer VRML Add-In, follow these steps:

1. Connect to the Internet, if you are not already.

2. Run Internet Explorer and connect to the VRML Add-In site at **http:// www.microsoft.com/windows/ie/vrml.htm**. You can do this all in one step by choosing Start, Run, and typing **www.microsoft.com/windows/ie/vrml.htm** in the Open box. Click OK.

3. Right-click the Download VRML Add-In link. Select Save Target <u>A</u>s and choose a folder in the Save As dialog box. Click <u>S</u>ave. Choose a folder on a drive with at least 2M of free space.

4. Internet Explorer downloads the self-installing executable. The file is about 1.8M and the download will take several minutes when using a modem connection.

5. Once the download of the file has finished, select <u>F</u>ile, E<u>x</u>it from Internet Explorer. When installing the VRML, Add-In may attempt to update files that Internet Explorer keeps open, causing the installation to fail.

   Do not disconnect from the Internet yet. The remainder of the installation will only take a few minutes, and you will need to be online to view your first VRML world.

6. Select Start, <u>R</u>un and type the path to the VRML Add-In self-installing executable. Click the <u>B</u>rowse button if you would rather locate the file by point-and-click. Click OK.

7. A dialog box appears, notifying you that you are installing the VRML Add-In. Click <u>Y</u>es to continue.

8. The installer copies files to a temporary folder on your hard disk, then displays a License Agreement dialog box.

9. Read the license agreement carefully. If you agree with the terms of the license agreement, click the I Agree button.

   If you do not agree with the terms of the license agreement, click the I Disagree button. The installer will close and will not complete the installation of the VRML Add-In.

10. When you click the I Agree button, the installer copies files to your hard disk.

11. A dialog box appears, notifying you that the VRML Add-In installation was successful. Click OK. You are now ready to view and interact with VRML worlds!

Using the VRML Add-In

After you install the VRML Add-In for Internet Explorer, you can begin to experience VRML worlds. Your first VRML stop should be the Microsoft campus (refer to fig. 34.9). To view the Microsoft campus in 3-D and learn how to use the VRML Add-In, follow these steps:

1. Select Start, <u>R</u>un, and type **www.microsoft.com/windows/ie/sites.htm** in the <u>O</u>pen box. Click OK.

Part

IX

Ch

34

2. Internet Explorer starts and loads the Microsoft VRML Add-In Cool Sites page. Depending on your connection speed, it can take a few minutes to download the VRML information. Your VRML Add-In displays a 3D view of the Microsoft campus in the center of the page.

   If you do not see the picture, you may need to enable animations. Select View, Options, and click the Appearance tab. Select the Show Animations check box. Click OK. Alternatively, you can right-click the icon that represents the VRML picture, and select Show Picture.

3. Use your mouse, keyboard, or joystick and the toolbar at the bottom of the picture to pilot your way through the buildings and around the company grounds. If you don't see the toolbar, right-click over the picture and select Show Toolbar.

   Table 34.1 describes the toolbar buttons and how to use them. Table 34.2 shows you how to navigate VRML worlds with your mouse, keyboard, or joystick.

TIP   Double-click an object to automatically walk toward it.

Table 34.1   VRML Add-In Toolbar Functions

Button	Name	Function
	Reset	Return to the starting position and orientation.
	Straighten	Level your orientation with respect to the scene.
Walk	Walk	Move through a scene, as if you were walking forward. You can also double-click an object to automatically walk towards it.
Slide	Slide	Pan the viewpoint horizontally or vertically, as if you move your head.
Tilt	Tilt	Rotate your viewpoint up, down, right, or left, as if you tilt your head.
Spin	Spin	Rotate the scene, as if you stand still and the scene rotates in front of you.
	Menu	Customize your VRML Add-In.

Table 34.2   Navigating VRML Worlds with Your Mouse, Keyboard, or Joystick

Device	Control	Description
Mouse	Walk	Press and hold down the left mouse button. Move the mouse pointer in the direction you want to go.
	Slide	Press and hold down the left mouse button. Move the mouse pointer in the direction you want to slide.
	Tilt	Press and hold down the left mouse button. Move the mouse pointer in the direction you want to tilt.
	Spin	Press and hold down the left mouse button. Move the mouse pointer in the direction you want the VRML world to spin, then release the mouse button.
Keyboard	Walk	Press and hold down the arrow keys.
	Slide	Press and hold down the Shift key while pressing the arrow keys.
	Tilt	Press and hold down the Ctrl key while pressing the arrow keys.
Joystick	Walk	Move the joystick in the direction you want to go.
	Slide	Press and hold down the Shift key while moving the joystick. If your joystick has a Point-Of-View control, you can use it instead of the Shift key.
	Tilt	Press and hold down the Ctrl key while moving the joystick.

 The pointer shape changes to a hand when you point at objects that contain links to other worlds or Web sites. Click the object to go to the link.

4. If you're ready to maneuver other VRML worlds, click the links on the bottom of the HTML page (below the VRML view of the Microsoft campus). Microsoft has provided a jumping-off point to some exciting and wonderful VRML worlds.

Customizing the VRML Add-In

You can customize the VRML Add-In to strike a balance between 3-D realism and improved drawing performance. To customize the VRML Add-In, click the menu button in the toolbar. The pop-up menu appears, as shown in figure 34.10.

 If you don't see the VRML toolbar, right-click the VRML picture and select Show Toolbar. If you still don't see the toolbar, you may need to expand the Internet Explorer window.

FIG. 34.10
Use the VRML Add-In menu to customize your VRML settings.

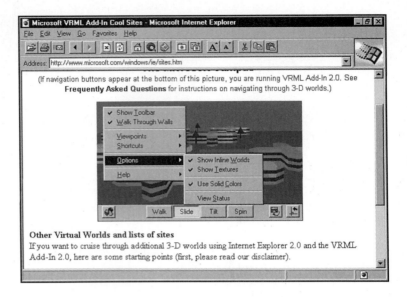

The following list explains the function of each VRML Add-In customization option:

■ If you do not want the toolbar to display, click Show Toolbar until the check mark disappears. You can get back to the toolbar by right-clicking over the VRML picture and checking Show Toolbar again.

■ Check Walk Through Walls to be able to move through the surfaces of objects. When you uncheck Walk Through Walls, VRML Add-In performs collision detection and prevents you from moving through the surfaces of objects.

NOTE Deselecting the Walk Through Walls check box can reduce the drawing performance of VRML worlds because VRML Add-In uses more CPU cycles to detect collisions. Also, some VRML worlds do not support collision detection and will not allow you to move around them unless Walk Through Walls is selected. ■

■ Use the Viewpoints submenu to move to preset views in the VRML world.

■ Use the Shortcuts submenu to jump to URL links from objects in the VRML world.

■ To improve download times and animation performance, uncheck Options, Show Inline Worlds and uncheck Options, Show Textures. However, at the expense of reduced performance, you can increase the realism effect. Check Options, Show Inline Worlds and check Options, Show Textures to display embedded images, VRML worlds, and surface textures inside the current world displayed.

■ To improve animation performance, check Options, Use Solid Colors. However, at the expense of reduced performance, you can increase the realism effect. Uncheck Options, Use Solid Colors to display objects using gradual color shading.

■ Click <u>O</u>ptions, View <u>S</u>tatus to display the VRML Add-In status window with your current view position and orientation. Also, you can see your current animation rate in frames per second.

Participating in UseNet News

One of the most popular services on the Internet, UseNet News serves as user forums on just about every topic imaginable. Topics range from zero-dimensional geometry (alt.0.d), to the wi.* hierarchy, consisting of groups with articles about Wisconsin. Participating in UseNet News is free, excluding your connect-time charges.

UseNet News is arranged into individual groups called *newsgroups*. All of the newsgroups are organized into a hierarchy that orders related topics with a mostly logical naming scheme. Each newsgroup name starts with a three- or four-letter prefix, followed by a newsgroup name. Here are the most common prefixes:

■ *alt.* Alternative topics, everything from alien invasions to xenophobia

■ *biz.* Covers business affairs, commerce, and commercial products

■ *comp.* Computers and computer-related topics

■ *news.* News of interest to the Internet community, such as announcements of new groups

■ *rec.* Recreation, hobbies, and sports

■ *sci.* Scientific

■ *soc.* Social issues

■ *talk.* Discussions and debates

■ *misc.* Everything that won't fit elsewhere

Individual regions, countries, and states have hierarchies too, identified by their postal ID. For example, the **can.general** group is for general discussion about Canada, and **tn.general** is for general discussion about the state of Tennessee. You can find a list of all of the newsgroups in **news.groups**, complete with descriptions.

Group names move from the general to the specific as you read them. For example, the **comp.infosystems.www.announce** and **comp.infosystems.www.servers.unix** groups are both about the World Wide Web. The first has announcements about the Web, and the second is about UNIX Web server software.

Newsgroups are created using a closely watched balloting mechanism, involving impartial people to solicit and count votes by e-mail. Some newsgroups are *moderated,* meaning that when someone posts an article to that group, the article is forwarded to an individual who

Part
IX

Ch
34

approves the article for distribution. Moderated newsgroups usually have high-quality information, at the expense of minor delays for the approval cycle. Conversely, *unmoderated* newsgroups allow anyone to post articles without approval.

The wildest newsgroups are those in the alt hierarchy (alt is an abbreviation for *alternative*), on topics from **alt.0.d** to **alt.zine**, a newsgroup about alternative magazines. All of the alt newsgroups are unmoderated, and anyone is allowed to create a newsgroup in the alt area. This untamed nature causes many organizations to avoid participation in the alt hierarchy. If you do not see the alt hierarchy, contact your Internet service provider or Network Administrator—he or she can explain the policy.

Configuring Internet Explorer for News

You can use Internet Explorer to participate in UseNet News. But first, you must configure Internet Explorer with your news server and preferences. To do that, you need the address or host name of a news server. Internet Explorer connects to the news server to send and receive the UseNet newsgroup articles. If you don't know the address of a news server, consult your Internet service provider or Network Administrator.

Follow these steps to configure Internet Explorer with your News server:

1. In Internet Explorer, open the Options dialog box (click <u>V</u>iew, <u>O</u>ptions) and select the News tab. The News page appears, as shown in figure 34.11.

FIG. 34.11
Use the News page to identify your news server.

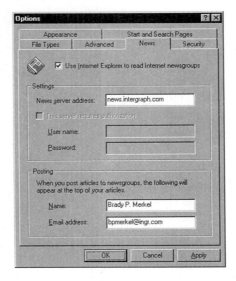

2. Select the Use Internet Explorer to Read Internet Newsgroups check box. If you want to use another program or The Microsoft Network to read UseNet News, do not select this box.

3. In the News Server Address box, type the address or host name of your news server. If the news server also requires an account, select the This Server Requires Authorization check box, and type the User Name and Password into the fields provided. Ask your Internet service provider or Network Administrator for this information if you do not know it.

4. When you *post,* or submit, articles to a newsgroup, Internet Explorer automatically puts your name and e-mail path at the top of the article. This way, other UseNet News users can know that you submitted the article and how to contact you. Type your full name in the Name text box, and type your e-mail address in the Email Address text box.

Listing Newsgroups and Articles

To begin your UseNet News experience, you start with the list of available newsgroups. To download and display the current list of newsgroups from the news server, click the Read Newsgroups icon on the toolbar; or choose Go, Read Newsgroups. With more than 10,000 newsgroups, the download might take a few minutes. Once loaded, Internet Explorer displays the list as if it was a Web page, as shown in figure 34.12.

FIG. 34.12

Click the newsgroup name from the list to show articles in that group.

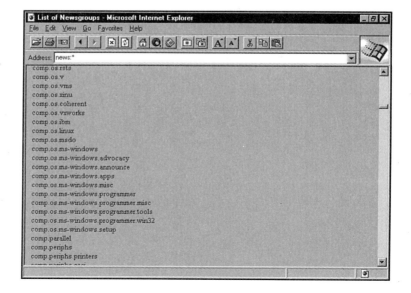

Part

IX

Ch

34

If you are unfamiliar with UseNet News, start with the following newsgroups. They are purposely set up for new users, and can help you understand how to use the UseNet:

- *news.announce.newusers*. Learn about the UseNet.
- *news.newusers.questions*. Ask basic UseNet questions.
- *news.test*. Practice posting your own articles.

Other popular newsgroups include:

- *news.answers*. View the Frequently Asked Question (FAQ) articles of all newsgroups.
- *comp.windows.ms*. For Microsoft Windows information.
- *rec.humor.funny*. A moderated newsgroup with jokes and funny stories.

When you click a newsgroup name, Internet Explorer displays a list of the most recent articles that have been posted there, as shown in figure 34.13. Internet Explorer displays the articles in the order that they arrived at the news server. Sometimes this can be confusing, because you may see a response to an article that has not appeared yet. The reason for this is because UseNet News works in a store-and-forward manner. Articles hop from news server to news server along the Internet, and often arrive out of sequence. For example, if you are in Florida, you will likely see articles posted by users in Georgia well before articles posted by users in California.

FIG. 34.13
Articles appear in the order that your news server receives them.

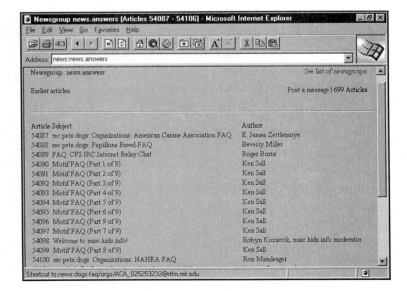

When viewing the list of articles, you also see the name of the newsgroup in the upper-left corner of the page. In the upper-right corner is a link back to the list of newsgroups from whence you came. Also at the top-left and bottom-left of the page is the current count of articles, and a link to a window where you can post a message. To compose and submit a new article, click the Post a Message link. See "Posting Articles," later in this chapter for information on posting articles.

Once you find a newsgroup you wish to visit often, add it to your Favorites list or create a shortcut. Then, when you want to jump directly to the newsgroup without waiting on the list of available newsgroups, just select the link from your Favorites menu or double-click the shortcut.

Reading Articles

To read an article, click its link in the article list. The article appears (see fig. 34.14). Similar to the article listing page, you see the newsgroup name in the upper-left corner, and a link to the newsgroup list in the upper-right. The subject of the article appears in the title bar of the Internet Explorer window.

Newsgroup articles have a format similar to e-mail messages. You can see the article subject, the author's name, his e-mail address, and the date the article was posted. Internet Explorer makes the author's e-mail address a link. Click the link to send e-mail directly to him.

TIP Internet Explorer identifies World Wide Web links and e-mail addresses in UseNet articles. Use the links to jump directly to a Web site, or send e-mail to other users.

To view the previous article in the list, click the Previous Article link. Click the Next Article link to read the next article in the list. Both of these links appear in the upper-left of the page as well as the lower-left corner of the page.

When you read an article and would like to post a *follow-up*, or response, click the Post a Response link, which appears in the upper-right and lower-right corners of the page. See the following section for information on posting articles.

To return to the list of articles, click the See List of Articles link, which appears in the upper-right and lower-right corners of the page.

FIG. 34.14
Click the Next Article link to read the next article in the list.

Next article link ——

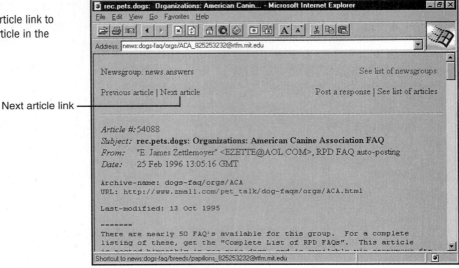

Posting Articles

To post a new article, as shown in figure 34.15, or a response to a previous article, follow these steps:

N O T E It is a good idea to "lurk" (Net-speak for reading articles but not posting any) in a newsgroup for a while. Think of it as being at a party where you don't know anyone. You might prefer to stand around and observe before joining in a conversation. Also, before asking a question in a newsgroup, consult the group's Frequently Asked Question (FAQ) article. Your question may be answered there. ■

FIG. 34.15
Compose your article and then click the Post button to submit it worldwide.

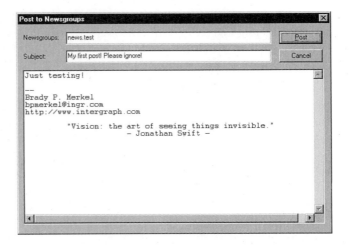

1. Type the name of the target newsgroup in the Newsgroups text box.

    If you want to post your message to multiple newsgroups, also known as *cross-posting,* type the newsgroup names, separated by commas. Be careful when cross-posting articles to newsgroups that don't relate to your article, otherwise you may get *slammed,* or chastised, for wasting bandwidth.

 To practice posting articles, use the news.test newsgroup. Do not expect a reply from other users, though—no one reads that newsgroup regularly. It is used only for practice and testing news software.

2. Enter the subject of your article in the Subject box. For new articles, select a subject that is brief and distinct. UseNet users are more likely to read your article if they notice your subject.

    If you are posting a response to a previous article, keep the subject the same, prefixed with the letters "Re:". Some UseNet users employ news software that orders related articles by subject. If you change the subject, they might miss your article.

3. Type the text of your article in the large scrolling text box. When you respond to a previous article, Internet Explorer automatically copies the article. To avoid wasting bandwidth, remove any of the original text that does not pertain to your response.

4. Check your spelling, then click the Post button to submit your article to the world. In a few minutes, your news server will list your article along with others in the same newsgroup. To see your article, go to the newsgroup you posted to and select the Refresh icon, or select View, Refresh. When your article appears in the list, click it and read it as others would.

A Note About "Netiquette"

In most newsgroups, there are no rules except those enforced by the opinion of group members. However, there are certain community standards for UseNet newsgroups that are generally agreed upon. These standards are referred to as *Netiquette,* short for Network Etiquette:

- Do not *spam.* This refers to the wholesale unsolicited posting of advertisements or self-aggrandizing announcements to many groups. The term "spam" comes from a Monty Python comedy skit that repeats the product name incessantly, in an attempt to make a sale.

- Do not post sexist, racist, or demeaning messages. Doing so will usually bring down the newsgroup's wrath on the poster, whose later postings will be ignored or *flamed.*

Part
IX

Ch
34

To be flamed is to be disparaged in public, and is often accompanied with a barrage of e-mail that will fill your disk drive, or that of your Internet service provider.

■ Avoid excessive cross-talk or chatting between two posters. Keep private discussions in e-mail.

■ Do not post private e-mail that you receive to a newsgroup without permission of the original author.

■ Keep articles short, without overly long quoting of the message to which you are responding. In Net-speak, long, rambling postings are flamed for wasting bandwidth.

Using Telnet

The Internet's Telnet protocol allows you to log in to a remote computer as though you were sitting in front of it. Windows 95 provides a Telnet application you can use to connect to remote systems where you have accounts. In addition to dial-up network access, many Internet service providers allow you to connect to their hosts for access to command-line accounts.

The Windows 95 Telnet client is not flashy, but since Telnet is based on the idea of emulating a plain ASCII terminal, it does not need to be.

Connecting and Disconnecting to Remote Computers

The first step to connecting to remote computers with Windows 95's Telnet is to start the application. To start Telnet, follow these steps:

1. Open the Start menu and choose <u>R</u>un. When the Run dialog box opens, type **telnet**.

2. Choose <u>C</u>onnect, <u>R</u>emote System. The Connect dialog box appears (see fig. 34.16).

FIG. 34.16
Select a host, port, and terminal type from the Connect dialog box. Do not change the port number unless absolutely necessary.

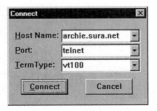

After you are connected, you can use all the remote computer's facilities just as you could if you dialed into that computer via modem, or if you were sitting in front of it.

When you are done, choose Connect, Disconnect to close the connection; if you choose Connect, Exit, Telnet will exit. Unfortunately, you can only connect to one computer at a time.

> **CAUTION**
>
> If you are connected to a remote computer when you choose Connect, Exit, Telnet will exit *without* asking you to confirm.

Keeping a Log of Your Connection

Sometimes it's useful to have a permanent record of a session with a remote computer, such as a financial transaction or an airline reservation. Telnet includes a way for you to capture what appears on your screen and save it in a text file for later review.

To turn on logging, choose Terminal, Start Logging from the Telnet main menu. Telnet prompts you to choose a location and name for your log file. Once you start logging, your communications with the remote system goes into the log file.

To stop logging, choose Terminal, Stop Logging. Telnet closes the log file.

Setting Preferences

Many users like to be able to control the cursor's appearance and behavior in a communications program. Telnet provides a Terminal Preferences dialog box that allows you to adjust the cursor shape, the text font used in Telnet windows, and other aspects of the program's behavior.

To set Telnet's preferences, choose Terminal, Preferences. Set the options the way you want them, then choose OK to save your changes or Cancel to discard them. If you save your changes, Telnet will remember them.

Creating Your Own Pages for the World Wide Web

One of the best things about the Web is that it allows anyone with Internet access to *provide* information, not just consume it. If you have access to a Web server and information to share, the Internet lets you do so in a unique way.

Web pages are written in the HyperText Markup Language (HTML). HTML is made up of *elements*; each element contains a *tag* defining what kind of element it is. Most elements also contain text that defines what the element represents. In figure 34.17, the sample HTML page as displayed by the Internet Explorer is shown at the top; the same page shown as HTML form is shown at the bottom.

FIG. 34.17
Here you see on-screen and HTML versions of a simple page.

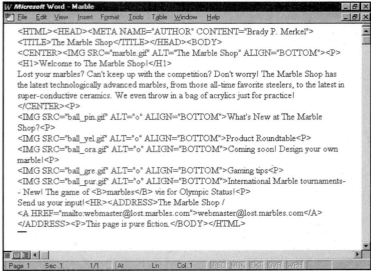

Unlike traditional desktop publishing, the user—not the author—controls how the document is actually displayed. When you create HTML documents, it is important to split the content of your document from its structure and appearance on-screen. The document that looks just right in your 640 × 480 Internet Explorer window may look awful to users of other browsers.

Building Documents with HTML

HTML elements are plain ASCII text, so you can create Web pages with any simple text editor, including WordPad. This section introduces the basic elements of HTML to help familiarize you with the most common elements before we plunge into using Microsoft's Internet Assistant.

> **N O T E** HTML offers many features, including on-screen forms. A complete copy of the HTML specification is available from the World Wide Web Organization (W30)'s Web server at **http://www.w3.org/hypertext/WWW/MarkUp/MarkUp.html**, and the National Center for Supercomputing Applications maintains an excellent HTML tutorial at **http:/www.ncsa.uiuc.edu/ General/Internet/WWW/HTMLPrimer.html**.
>
> For more detailed information on creating Web pages, see Que's *Web Publishing with Word for Windows, Special Edition Using HTML,* and *10 Minute Guide to Internet Assistant.* ▪

> **T I P** Right-click a Web page in Internet Explorer to view the HTML source.

How Documents Are Structured   Like those nesting Russian dolls, elements can contain other elements, and they can be deeply nested. HTML documents usually consist of at least one element: the HTML element, which contains *head* and *body* elements. Each of those elements can, in turn, enclose others.

The head element usually contains a *title* element, and it may also contain comments, author information, copyright notices, or special tags that help indexers and search engines use the contents of the document more effectively.

The body element holds the actual body and content of the document. For typical documents, most of the body element is text, with tags placed at the end of each paragraph. You can also use tags for displaying numbered or bulleted lists, horizontal rules, embedded images, and hyperlinks to other documents.

Tag Basics   All HTML tags are enclosed in angle brackets (<>). Some elements contain two matching tags, with text or hypertext in between. For example, to define a title as part of your document's <head> element, you would put this HTML into your document:

```
<title>A Simple WWW Page</title>
```

The first tag signals the start of the title element, while the same tag, prefixed with a slash (/), tells the browser that it has reached the end of the element. Some tags do not require matching tags, such as <li>, which denotes an item in a list.

The elements most often used in HTML body elements fall into three basic categories: logical styles, physical styles, and content elements.

Using Logical Styles   Logical styles tell the browser how the document is structured. The HTML system of nesting elements gives the browser some information, but authors can use the logical style elements to break text into paragraphs, lists, block quotes, and so on. Like styles in Word, you can use the logical styles in your documents and know that they will be properly displayed by the browser.

Table 34.3 lists some common logical styles you can use to build your document, along with examples for each one.

Table 34.3   Logical Style Elements

Style Tag	What It Does	Sample
<p>	Ends paragraph	This is a very short paragraph. <p>
 	Inserts line break	First line Second line
<Hx>...</Hx>	Section heading	<H1>HTML Is Easy</H1>
...	Emphasis on text	Use this instead of bold text.
...	Stronger emphasis on text	THIS really gets the point across!
<code>...</code>	Displays HTML tags without acting on them	The <code><p></code> tag can be handy.
<quote>...</quote>	Displays a block of quoted text	<quote>No man is an island. </quote>
<pre>...</pre>	Displays text and leaves white space intact	<pre>E x t r a spaces are OK here.</pre>

Using Physical Styles   In ordinary printed documents, **bold**, *italic,* and <u>underlined</u> text all have their special uses. Web pages are the same way; you may want to distinguish the name of a book, a key word, or a foreign-language phrase from your body text. Table 34.4 shows a list of some common physical styles you can use in HTML documents, along with simple examples.

Table 34.4 Physical Style Elements

Style Tag	What It Does	Sample
...	Bold text	Bold text stands out.
<i>...</i>	Italic text	<i>Belle</i> is French for "pretty."
<u>...</u>	Underlined text	<u>Don't</u> confuse underlined text with a hyperlink!
_{...}	Subscript text	Water's chemical formula is H₂O.
^{...}	Superscript text	Writing "x²" is the same as writing "x*x."
<tt>...</tt>	Typewriter text	This tag's <tt>seldom</tt> seen.

Using Content Elements   Many Web documents just contain plain, unadorned text. Content elements enrich your documents by adding embedded graphics, lists, and links to other documents. You can quickly turn a boring, plain-text document into a rich Web page by using content elements.

One of the simplest content elements—and one of the most effective—is the <hr> tag, which inserts a horizontal rule across the page. Use it to separate different sections of material, much as you would add a page break to a Word document to start a new section.

<ul>...</ul> defines a bulleted or "unordered" list, and <ol>...</ol> defines a numbered or "ordered" list. Both use the <li> tag to define list items. The list items are easy to use; if you have ever used Word or PowerPoint to build a list, you already know how to use these. Here are two quick examples:

```
<ul>
<li>First bullet
<li>Second bullet
</ul>

<ol>
<li>Item 1
<li>Item 2
</ol>
```

Many Web pages contain embedded graphics. These graphics must be in GIF or JPEG format, but they can be as large or small as you like. However, be aware that the larger your graphic is, the more time it will take to load it to the local system. Embedding the images in your page is easy with the <img> tag. When a browser sees <img>, it fetches the image and displays it in the body of the document.

Part
IX

Ch
34

The simplest form of <img> lets you specify only the name of the graphics file. This instruction causes the browser to download "picture.gif" from the Web server and display it in the text:

```
<img src="picture.gif">
```

N O T E   If you have an image in PCX or bitmap format, you must convert it to GIF or JPEG before you can use it on the Web. ▩

   Use the alt attribute in <img> tags. Users who are not loading images can see the text tag and decide whether they want the image or not.

You can also add the alt attribute to your <img> tag, which specifies a text string to be displayed instead of the image. Why would you want to do this? Some browsers, like Lynx, cannot display images. Other browsers can display the alt attribute for users who have turned off image loading to boost their connection speed. Adding alt to the previous example, we end up with

```
<img src="picture.gif" alt="A pretty picture">
```

Creating Hyperlinks   Now let's talk about the key element that makes the Web different from plain static documents: hyperlinks. Each link points to an *anchor,* or destination for the link. Most anchors are implied; when you specify a page as the target of the link, it is assumed that you want that entire page to be an anchor.

You can also specify named anchors to let you quickly jump to a particular section of a document. Define anchors with <a name="a-name">...</a>. The "a" stands for "anchor," and the name attribute names the anchor. Anchors can display text labels, but they do not have to. The following anchors work identically, but the first one displays text in the browser and the other does not.

```
<a name="Chapter36">Chapter 36's anchor</a> is the same as <a
name="Chapter36"></a> this one.
```

The basic element for hyperlinks is <a href="URL">...</a>. In this case, the "a" still stands for "anchor," and "href" is a hypertext reference. Let's say you were setting up a Web server containing information about Windows 95. Your start page might link to a page listing new software for Windows 95, like this:

```
New <a href="Software/NewSoftware.htm">software</a> for Windows 95
```

The text in the middle of the link appears as a link on the browser's screen. Notice that the folder "Software" is part of the link. This link points to a file named "NewSoftware.htm" in the directory "Software."

Say you also wanted to include a link to Macmillan Publishing Company's Web page so that people visiting your page could find out about Windows 95 books. Notice that this link contains a full URL instead of the name of a local document.

```
The <a href="http://www.mcp.com">Macmillan Publishing</a> home page has
information on Macmillan's books.<p>
```

Both types of link can include anchors. If the target page contains an anchor with that name, the browser will jump directly to that anchor and display it. For example, you could use a link like:

```
See <a href="http://www.mcp.com/Books/Win95/
UsingWin95.htm#Chapter36">Chapter 36</a>'s outline for more details.<p>
```

to specify a certain position in the link's target document.

N O T E If you would like a tool to check your HTML for correctness, you can use the Weblint tool. Weblint "picks the fluff" off your HTML pages and catches common errors like mismatched tags and bogus attribute names. For more details, see the Weblint page at **http://www.unipress.com/weblint/**. ▓

Using Microsoft's Internet Assistant

If you use Word, you can easily create HTML files with Microsoft's Internet Assistant, a Word add-on that already knows all the rules of HTML previously discussed, and then some!

Internet Assistant gives you an HTML document template with styles representing all the major HTML elements, plus converters to let you turn a Word file into HTML with a simple mouse click.

Getting and Installing Microsoft's Internet Assistant   The Internet Assistant is available at no cost from Microsoft's Web site. There is a version for Microsoft Word 6.0a or later, as well as a 32-bit version for Microsoft Word 95 and Microsoft Word 6 for Windows NT. Use Internet Explorer to get the version you need, open the Start menu, choose <u>R</u>un, and type **http://www.microsoft.com/msword/internet/ia/default.htm**. The files are over 1M and the download will take several minutes when using a modem connection.

Part
IX

Ch

34

CAUTION

You must have Word 95, Word 6 for Windows NT, or Word 6.0a or later to run Internet Assistant. If you have an earlier version of Word 6, you can download the 6.0a patch (WORD60A.EXE) from Microsoft's FTP server.

The Internet Assistant requires the English, French, or German versions of Word 6.0a or later, Word 95, or Word 6 for Windows NT. It *does not* work with older versions, or other languages. After you have downloaded the Internet Assistant, you will probably be in a hurry to install it and start producing HTML files. Fortunately, installation is easy; just download the self-extracting executable and then run it. The executable will install the Internet Assistant on your hard disk.

 Using Microsoft's Internet Assistant as a Browser   After you have installed the Internet Assistant, start Word. You will discover a new button on the Formatting toolbar and a new command on the File menu.

> **N O T E**   Before you can browse the Web with Microsoft's Internet Assistant, you need to have your connection to the Internet running. Either dial up to your Internet service provider to log in to your network connection, or use a LAN connection. ■

To browse the Web, choose File, Browse Web or click the Browse Web button (see fig. 34.18). You will notice that browsing the Web with Internet Assistant isn't as fast as browsing with Internet Explorer. The delays are due to the additional overhead to translate HTML into a format Word can display. Use Internet Explorer for your everyday browsing, and use Internet Assistant's browse mode to review your own Web documents during authoring.

FIG. 34.18
After installing the Internet Assistant, Word has a new button on the Formatting toolbar.

Browse Web button ──┐

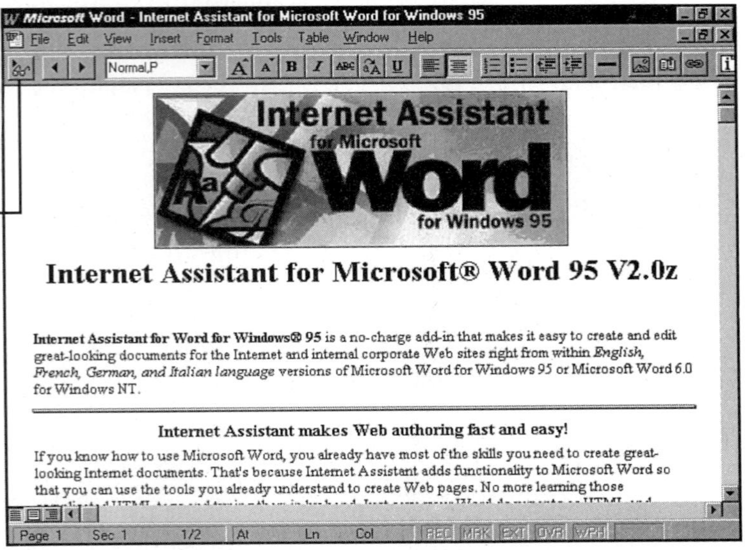

> **Internet Assistant for Microsoft® Word 95 V2.0z**
>
> Internet Assistant for Word for Windows® 95 is a no-charge add-in that makes it easy to create and edit great-looking documents for the Internet and internal corporate Web sites right from within *English, French, German, and Italian language* versions of Microsoft Word for Windows 95 or Microsoft Word 6.0 for Windows NT.
>
> **Internet Assistant makes Web authoring fast and easy!**
>
> If you know how to use Microsoft Word, you already have most of the skills you need to create great-looking Internet documents. That's because Internet Assistant adds functionality to Microsoft Word so that you can use the tools you already understand to create Web pages. No more learning those

After you start the Browse Web mode, the screen changes to look like the screen shown in figure 34.19.

FIG. 34.19
This is Microsoft's Internet Assistant, with the Internet Assistant World Wide Web page on view.

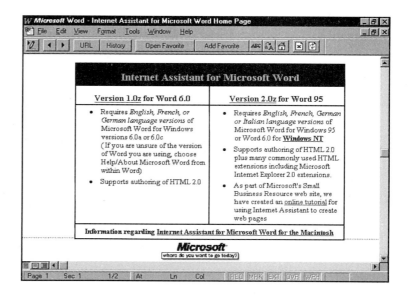

Creating New HTML Documents   When you use Word to create a new HTML document, select the HTML template instead of whatever you normally use. Figure 34.20 shows Word's New dialog box with the HTML template selected.

FIG. 34.20
Select the HTML template to create a new Web page with the Internet Assistant.

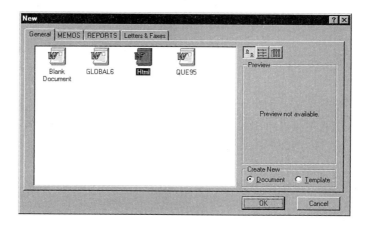

A new document window opens, and you will notice some new icons on the Formatting toolbar along with the familiar ones. These icons allow you to quickly format your document using HTML elements.

Formatting Your HTML Documents   You have probably noticed some new and unusual icons on the Internet Assistant Formatting toolbar. Here's how to use them to format your documents in HTML:

Button	Action
	The Edit and Browse Web buttons toggle Word between HTML Edit mode (the pencil) and Browse Web mode. You can also toggle with the View menu's Web Browse and HTML Edit options.
	Use the Back or Forward button to go backwards or forward among Web pages you have viewed. They do not do anything in normal Word mode.
	These buttons work just like the standard Word Bold, Italic, and Underline buttons. Use them to enhance your text.
	These buttons let you create numbered and bulleted lists, just like in Word or PowerPoint.
	Use this button to insert a horizontal rule into your document.
	Insert pictures (GIF or JPEG only) into your document with this button. You will see a dialog box that allows you to select a picture file and enter an alternative text string for the picture. If you have BMP and PCX files that you want to use on your Web pages, convert your images with a tool like the shareware LView Pro, PaintShop Pro, or Adobe Photoshop.
	Use this icon to set the document's title. Clicking it brings up a dialog box that lets you specify a title to be embedded.

Use the Style pull-down menu (just to the right of the Forward button) to select HTML styles for your documents.

TIP Use Internet Explorer to browse the pages you create with the Internet Assistant—it's faster and uses less memory than Word.

Building Hyperlinks   The Internet Assistant allows you to embed two kinds of links: links to external documents, and links to files and documents on your computer. This is a terrific feature, since you can quickly create links in, and between, several documents at once.

 Insert *bookmarks* with the Add Bookmark button. Bookmarks are HTML anchors; you can embed bookmarks in your Word documents so that you can build hyperlinks to specific pages or items. When you click this icon, the Bookmark dialog box appears, as shown in figure 34.21.

Use these steps to work with bookmarks in your documents:

1. Choose Edit, Bookmark; or click the Bookmark button. The Bookmark dialog box appears.

2. To add a bookmark, type a name for the new bookmark in the Bookmark Name field and click Add.

3. To delete an existing bookmark, select it and click Delete. You will be asked to confirm the deletion.

4. To jump to an existing bookmark, select it and click Go To.

FIG. 34.21

The Bookmark dialog box lets you name specific locations in your document so you can build hyperlinks to them.

 You need to be able to embed hyperlinks in your documents, too. Fortunately, the Internet Assistant has a button for that as well. Clicking the Hyperlink button, or choosing Insert, HyperLink, brings up the Hyperlink dialog box, as shown in figure 34.22.

FIG. 34.22

The Hyperlink dialog box gives you a quick way to build links to Web pages and Word documents on your computer or on other Web servers.

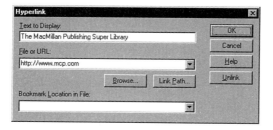

To build hyperlinks, follow these steps:

1. In the Text to Display text box, type the text you want to appear in the link.

2. If you are making a link to a URL somewhere on the Internet, type the URL to which you want to link into the File or URL text box, or pick a previously used URL from the drop-down menu.

3. If you are making a link to a local file, click the Browse button to find the link's target file. Click the Link Path button to verify the URL that will be inserted into the document.

4. If you are linking to a bookmark you have already defined, select the bookmark to which you want to link from the Bookmark Location in File pop-down menu.

5. Click OK to accept your new link, or click Cancel to dismiss the dialog box.

Part
IX
Ch
34

When you no longer want text linked to a document, select the linked text and choose Insert, HyperLink. Click the Unlink button to disassociate the link from the text. Click OK.

TROUBLESHOOTING

When I copy my Web documents to my Web server, the hyperlinks no longer work. How do I fix them? Internet Assistant saves hyperlinks in your Web document as absolute paths unless the hyperlinks point to other documents in the same folder. To correct the broken hyperlinks, open the Web document in Internet Assistant. Select each broken link and click the Hyperlink button. Click the Link Path button and modify the URL to point to the correct location on your Web server.

Saving Your Documents   While you are creating and editing your documents, you will need to save them to disk. You can save your documents—HTML styles and all—as regular Word documents. When you are ready to save the HTML version, see figure 34.23 and follow these steps:

1. Choose File, Save As.
2. When the Save As dialog box appears, type a file name for your HTML file. You can also choose a directory to put it in from the Save In drop-down list.
3. Pull down the Save Files Type combo box and select HyperText Markup Language (HTML) as the file type. Click OK to save the file.

FIG. 34.23
Save your Word documents as HTML with Word's Save As dialog box.

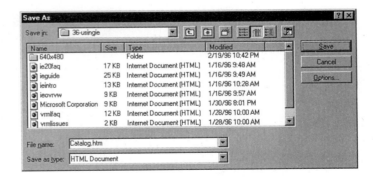

CAUTION
Many Word elements do not have any equivalent in HTML. If you save a Word document as HTML and then reopen it as a Word document, those element types *will be lost.*

For a complete list of Word elements that cannot be translated, use Word's Help facility to view the topic on "What Is Lost When Word Documents Are Converted to HTML."

N O T E   The Internet Assistant works best with relatively small pages. If you have large Word documents, consider breaking them into several smaller documents. Not only will this improve the performance of the Internet Assistant, but also Web surfers who read your pages will appreciate the reduced download time! ▒

Translating Existing Documents to HTML   You may already have a large stock of Word documents that you want to convert into Web pages. Microsoft anticipated this and has made it easy to convert existing documents. Here is what to do:

1. Open the document you want to translate.

2. Add a title using the Title icon on the Formatting toolbar.

3. Add bookmarks as needed by choosing Edit, Bookmark, or clicking the Add Bookmark button.

4. Add links, as desired, by choosing Insert, HyperLink, or by clicking the HyperLink button.

5. Save the new document as an HTML file.

CHAPTER 35

Using The Microsoft Network

by John R. Gordon with Jerry Honeycutt

The *Microsoft Network* (MSN) is Microsoft's powerful online service launched along with the release of Windows 95. Access to MSN is built into Windows 95. If you have Windows 95 installed, you're almost ready to connect to a new world of online information, services, and entertainment.

Microsoft's goal for MSN is to enrich the online experience of its users, by making sure that experience is rewarding. Microsoft wants MSN to be *the* premier online destination. ■

How to install and access MSN

This section explains that all you need to install MSN is an installed modem and a valid credit card.

Send and receive e-mail

The Microsoft Network provides e-mail support for the Internet and other online services.

Navigate MSN and discover its features

MSN has a wide range of databases and services available. In addition to software and troubleshooting information directly from Microsoft, you have access to topics as wide ranging as online encyclopedias, corporate financial data, or gourmet discussion groups.

Find help when you need it

Nearly all the information available to Microsoft's online technical support staff is available to you on MSN. In addition, MSN has free software and driver updates, training courses, and developer information.

What is The Microsoft Network?

One of the great things about MSN is that it's built with Windows 95 as its foundation. You can take advantage of many inherent features of the operating system, such as file naming conventions, folder navigation, using the desktop, and so on. Better still are the features of MSN that set it apart from other online services. Among the best of these features are:

- *Seamless Internet Integration.* MSN lets you quickly set up to browse World Wide Web (WWW) pages all over the Internet. Click a shortcut to automatically launch your WWW browser and find the desired link.

- *VChats (Virtual Chat).* Three-dimensional visual conversation with other MSN subscribers using on-screen images.

- *Shortcuts.* OLE objects that are pointers to MSN and WorldWide Web (WWW) destinations.

- *Guidebooks.* Help you find your way to professionally managed and produced online content tailored to your interests.

- *Download-and-Run (dnr) Files.* Makes viewing files or running online software "point-and-click" simple.

- *Multitasking.* MSN takes full advantage of Windows' multitasking capabilities. If you are downloading a file from a forum, you can chat with colleagues in a chat room and read messages from a bulletin board at the same time.

- *Online Multimedia Titles.* Microsoft Encarta and Microsoft Bookshelf are examples of this emerging online technology.

N O T E What's the difference between MSN the online service and MSN the WWW site?

By definition, MSN was (and still is) an access-controlled online service. Independent Content Providers (mostly non-Microsoft companies that build content and manage individual forums on MSN) and Category Managers (folks employed or contracted by Microsoft to coordinate and organize those forums in various categories) update and maintain the forums and content on the service that can be accessed only after logging in with a Member ID and password.

Although this is still true, Microsoft has broadly redefined MSN as the collection of both online services and a rapidly growing collection of high-quality WWW sites, *together* comprising The Microsoft Network. The next section defines in detail how this relationship works. ■

Web Content + Online Services = The Microsoft Network

MSN actually consists of two services. First is the MSN web site (see fig. 35.1), where the services only cost what your Internet browsing costs. The other is the MSN online service, where services are provided under a subscription fee that includes most forums and areas. Some additional services (called extended services) are fee-based at the time of use.

Access to MSN can be summarized by the three levels shown in table 35.1.

Table 35.1 MSN Access Levels

Level	Content	Price
MSN WWW Sites	General, plus links to other Internet and MSN destinations	Free (normal Internet cost)
MSN Basic	Online forums and services	Standard subscription fee
MSN Extended	Special forums or forum areas, special offers, product purchases, and so on.	Subscription fee plus fee for each extended transaction

FIG. 35.1
Find the MSN Internet
Destination at **http://
www.msn.com** with your
World Wide Web Browser.

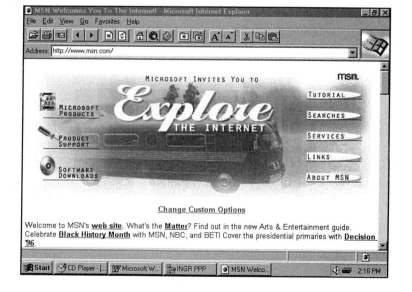

MSN The Internet Destination (www.msn.com)   Microsoft describes the MSN web site as the best place to begin your online experience. Start at **www.msn.com**, and let your imagination chart the course. Access to this web page requires nothing more than a web browser pointed to **http://www.msn.com**, and of course Internet access. If you discover an inviting link on the page that requires access to the MSN online service, you'll be prompted to log in with the standard login screen. You'll find lots of free content at the MSN web site, including Microsoft product information, the latest news, weather (including Maps), sports, Comics, TV Listings, Industry Highlights, great WWW links, and more.

 The **http://www.msn.com** site is highly customizable. Once you get to the page, click Customize Page. You'll notice that you can decide what you see and even hear! Add your favorite links, select your favorite search engine, turn background music on, or change link colors. When you customize to your own time zone, you can even review TV listings and movie schedules in your area. When you have everything set the way you want it, just click the Set Up Page button at the bottom of the screen and every time you visit the MSN home page, you'll see it the way you want to. You can change the options again anytime you want.

MSN the Online Service   Access to the online service (see fig. 35.2) requires that you have installed and configured the MSN client software that is delivered with your Windows 95 installation CD or disks. Also, you must agree to abide by the Member Agreement terms and conditions of membership, and select and agree to pay for a membership plan after you've had awhile (30 days) to get aquainted with the service. When you log in you get:

- *Basic Services.* This includes the vast majority of goods and services that comprise MSN. The monthly fee allows you a specified number of hours per month, and then charges you for additional hours at a flat rate.
- *Fee-for-Service Areas.* These are extensions of the basic services, and have an additional fee associated with them over and above the subscription plan. Examples of extended services are Credit Reports, New Automobile Comparison Reports, Commercial Software purchases, flowers ordered online, and more.

 The latest MSN subscription and pricing information, special membership promotions, or terms and conditions may be obtained by contacting MSN Customer Service in the U.S. and Canada at 1-800-386-5550.

FIG. 35.2
This is MSN Today!, the
online service's home base.

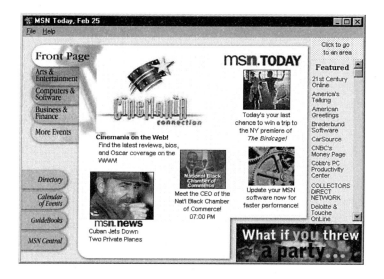

MSN as an Internet Service Provider

One of the greatest assets of MSN is its capability to provide you with Internet access if you don't have an access provider. If you are looking for an all-in-one solution to find your way onto the Internet, MSN can provide the access you need.

This section covers installing and configuring The Microsoft Network client software only. If you intend to use MSN as your Internet Access provider, follow the steps in "Using The Microsoft Network as Your Internet Access Provider" in Chapter 33, "Getting Connected to the Internet."

 You can connect to MSN via the Internet with no connect-time charges. MSN 1.2 supports a new access feature called TPA (Third Party Access), which permits connection to MSN via a third-party Internet access provider (IAP) without connect-time charge. Your normal subscription rates will apply. TPA should work properly on dial-up Internet access providers (IAPs) and most corporate LANs. IAPs must support Point-to-Point Protocol (PPP) with no scripting, and TPA may not work on a LAN connection to the Internet through a proxy server, but most Internet Firewall applications should function properly.

Installing and Configuring The Microsoft Network

In the following sections, you learn what steps to take to install and configure the MSN software. This includes loading the client, updating your local phone numbers, providing personal and payment information, choosing a Member ID and password, and getting out on the system.

> **N O T E**   If you are installing MSN from the original CD or disks, the first time you access MSN you may be required to update immediately to MSN version 1.2. The update provides faster graphics rendering, a better and more compact document viewer, and dramatically improves overall MSN performance.
>
> If given an option, you should always update as soon as possible to the latest MSN software. Don't worry about using up precious connect time for an update. Microsoft generally provides a generous connect time credit for this activity. ■

▶ **See** "Understanding the Windows 95 Communications System," **p. 284**

▶ **See** "Adding and Removing Windows Components," **p. 485**

▶ **See** "Installing and Configuring Exchange," **p. 876**

All you need to set up MSN is a modem (preferably 14.4 Kbps or greater), a phone line, Windows 95 installation media, and a major credit card number to pay for the service. Make sure your modem is installed and working correctly. Also, check to see if Microsoft Exchange is installed. It's required for MSN. If it's not installed, it will be installed and configured as part of the MSN installation process.

Installing the MSN Client

First check to see if you already have MSN installed. If you, your system administrator, or hardware supplier installed Windows 95 for you, it might already be done. Find out by inspecting your Windows 95 desktop. If the MSN icon is there, MSN is installed, but probably needs to be configured, and you can skip ahead to the section entitled "Configuring the MSN Client Software." If you don't see the MSN icon, follow these steps to install MSN:

1. From the Start menu, choose <u>S</u>ettings, <u>C</u>ontrol Panel. The Control Panel window is displayed.

2. Double-click the Add/Remove Programs icon. The Add/Remove Programs Properties sheet appears.

3. Select the Windows Setup tab to see a list of install options.

4. Scroll down until you see The Microsoft Network option and select it.

5. Select OK to start the installation of MSN.

Proceed to the next section.

TROUBLESHOOTING

 I have an MSN icon on my desktop, but when I double-click it, nothing happens. The MSN icon is a Windows 95 Registry Key, not a desktop shortcut to an executable file, like most desktop icons. If it's deleted, or doesn't work, you'll probably need to reinstall the MSN software. If it doesn't do anything, try restarting your system.

Configuring the MSN Client

If you are already an MSN member, and you only need to install the software (say, perhaps on a second computer) but *not* sign up for membership, use the following steps for configuring the MSN client software. You also need to check the dialog box option as shown in the lower-left corner of Fig. 35.3. This skips the membership setup, and goes directly to the client software configuration. You need to know your Member ID and password to make this work properly.

FIG. 35.3
Signing up for MSN
Membership is easy.

To configure MSN, follow these steps:

1. Double-click The Microsoft Network icon on your desktop. The MSN Trial Offer dialog box appears (refer to fig. 35.3).

Part
IX

Ch
35

2. Choose OK. The area code and prefix dialog box appear. Enter your area code and the first three digits of your telephone number.

3. Choose Connect. Your modem dials a toll-free access number that connects to the MSN Data Center. You should see blinking modem lights in your taskbar, indicating modem activity, and a "Starting transfer" message. MSN updates any pricing and service details and updates your system's local phone book of MSN access numbers, then disconnects. No user intervention is required, and the dialog box shows you what it's doing while it's doing it. When it's finished, you'll see the MSN Sign-up dialog box (see fig. 35.4).

FIG. 35.4

Signing up for an MSN membership is a simple three-part process.

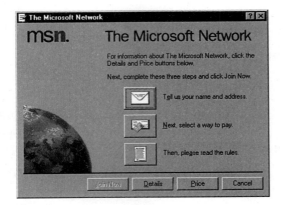

In this three-part dialog box, you provide MSN with your name, address, and credit card information, and you review and accept the MSN Member Agreement. You can optionally review the current pricing and subscription plans, plus any special plans that are being offered by MSN. Each large icon in this dialog box represents a part of the configuration process.

4. Click the envelope (Tell us your name and address) icon and the personal information dialog box appears (see fig. 35.5). Complete all the information on the form and click OK.

5. Click the credit card (Next, select a way to pay) icon. The payment method dialog box appears (see fig. 35.6).

6. Decide on a credit card (currently the only way to pay for MSN). Fill out necessary information in the form and choose OK.

7. Click the Member Agreement (Then, please read the rules) icon and the member agreement dialog box appears (see fig. 35.7). Review the agreement and choose I Agree.

FIG. 35.5
Enter your personal
information here.

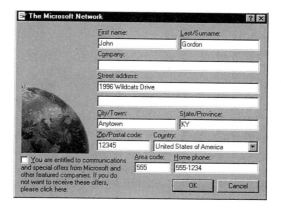

FIG. 35.6
Select a Major Credit Card
and Enter the Number here.

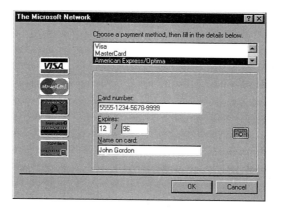

FIG. 35.7
Review the Member
Agreement.

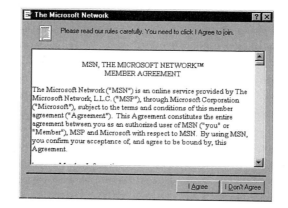

Part
IX

Ch
35

At this time you can examine pricing and/or subscription details by selecting either the Pricing or Details button.

NOTE Notice the small check box in the lower-left corner of the sign-up personal dialog box. The default is unchecked, meaning Microsoft, MSN advertisers, and Content Providers may occasionally send you promotions, solicitations, special offers, and, maybe even junk e-mail, unless you check this box. It's a good idea to leave it unchecked for a while unless it bothers you. You never know what great deal might pop up in your Inbox. ■

Now that you have completed all three parts (as indicated by the giant check marks next to the three icons) the Join Now button is available (see fig. 35.8).

FIG. 35.8
Click the Join Now button to complete the process.

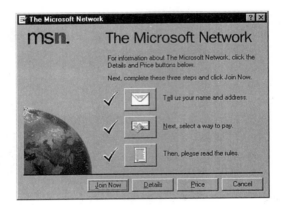

8. Click Join Now. You should see a dialog box similar to figure 35.9, allowing you to verify your connection numbers for MSN.

FIG. 35.9
You can modify your connection settings here.

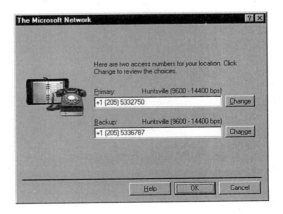

If you don't see this dialog box, but you do see one (similar to fig. 35.10) offering only numbers outside your local calling area, the system has determined that you do not have a local access number for connecting to MSN.

FIG. 35.10
Try to find a local access number for connecting to MSN. If you don't, you may have to pay long-distance charges.

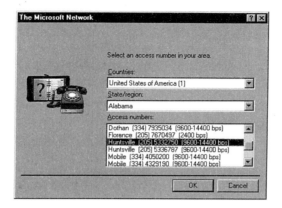

If you need to, select another access number near your location, bearing in mind that long-distance charges will likely apply.

 If you don't see a local access number as described in the steps on this page, don't give up. Microsoft is constantly adding many new access numbers to the local access phonebook. MSN checks frequently to verify that you have current telephone access information. Chances are if there is not a local access number now, there will be in the near future.

 Sometimes it costs less money for an out-of-state phone call than an in-state long-distance call. The connections dialog box (refer to fig. 35.10) doesn't mind what state, city, and phone number you select. Check with your long-distance service provider. It won't beat a local call, but it might keep your bills lower until local access is available in your community.

Setup now connects properly using your own settings and phone numbers, and sends your membership information to the MSN data center. The member ID and password dialog box appear (see fig. 35.11).

N O T E Your Member ID is your unique identifier on MSN. It is used for your MSN login, Chat identifier, and e-mail address. Choose it carefully, preferably before you begin the software configuration. You can't change it later.

Member IDs can be three to 64 characters long, upper- or lowercase, and may include numbers, underscores, and hyphens. No other symbol may be used.

Passwords *can* be changed, and you should consider doing so on a routine basis. Passwords can range in length from 8 to 16 characters, and can only be letters and numbers. Passwords are also not case-sensitive. Guard your password closely. ▨

Part
IX

Ch
35

FIG. 35.11
Select a member ID and
password here.

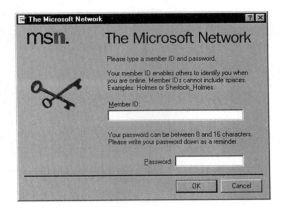

 TIP To change your password, Choose Tools/Password for MSN Central. You'll have to enter your existing password, and then enter your new password twice for verification. Click OK, and the next time you attempt to log in, use your new password.

 TROUBLESHOOTING

I entered my new password, and MSN complained that its length was invalid even though I'm positive it was long enough. MSN tells you that your password length is invalid if your password contains invalid characters, such as spaces or other special characters. Passwords can contain only the characters A through Z, a through Z, 0 through 9, "-", and ".".

9. Enter a Member ID in the appropriate box. If your Member ID is not unique to MSN, you receive a The ID is already in use. Please try a different one. message and you must choose another. Keep trying a different Member ID until your choice is successfully validated by MSN.

CAUTION
Be very careful with your password during the sign-up process. This is the only time that MSN allows your password to appear in the dialog box (see fig. 35.12). Other situations requiring your MSN password will echo asterisks (*) to the screen while you type in your password. Bottom line: Make sure you supply your initial password in a secure environment, with no curious onlookers.

 TIP Member IDs and passwords are *not* case-sensitive, so your member ID could be johnrgordon, JohnRGordon, or JOHNRGORDON and MSN treats them the same.

FIG. 35.12
This is the only time you can
see your password.

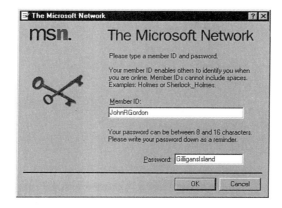

10. Enter a password. If the choice you entered for the password does not meet the
    guidelines, you receive an appropriate error message.

11. Choose OK. You will see the congratulatory dialog box as shown in figure 35.13

FIG. 35.13
Congratulations! You're a
member!

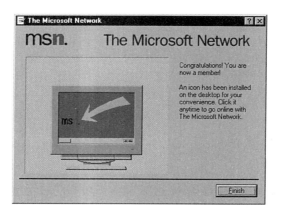

Now you have established your own account on MSN, set up billing, and can log
into the service with your own member ID and password.

12. Click Finish.

Using The Microsoft Network

Now that you have MSN installed, you'll want to log in and learn your way around. The
next few sections introduce you to online features such as MSN Today, MSN Central,
Favorite Places, Categories, Member Assistance, and other services.

Part
IX

Ch
35

Logging In for the First Time

When you log in to MSN for the first time, you see some screens and dialog boxes that only occur the first time. With each subsequent login, you'll just go straight into the service.

To start using MSN, follow these steps:

 1. Double-click the MSN icon on the Windows 95 Desktop. The MSN Sign In dialog box appears (see fig. 35.14).

FIG. 35.14
Enter your name and password here to log into MSN.

TROUBLESHOOTING

When I dial MSN, I get a message saying that the call was canceled or the modem doesn't connect. Your hardware may not support high-speed communications. Change your baud rate to 9600 (or a slower rate) and try again.

---

2. Enter your Member ID and Password. Choose Connect. You can choose Settings to make any changes to your Connection Settings. Your modem dials the access number and connects you to MSN.

    Since this is your first time logging in, you will be greeted by Bill Gates, Chairman and CEO of Microsoft (see fig. 35.15), followed by a screen introducing you to Russ Siegelman, Vice President of MSN at Microsoft.

3. Click the Tell Us About Yourself icon on the introduction to Russ Siegelman screen. This retrieves an optional questionnaire (see figs. 35.16 and 35.17 for an example) that allows Microsoft to gather some demographic data from you.

FIG. 35.15

Enjoy a personal welcome message from the Microsoft chairman, Bill Gates.

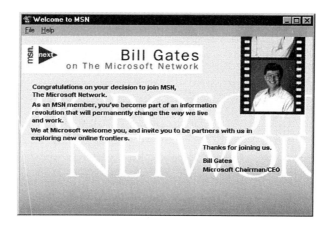

FIG. 35.16

Click Next to respond to the MSN Member Personal Profile Questionnaire.

4. If you decide to participate, complete the forms as desired. Remember, it's optional. You may get some nice promotional information from people with the same interests and background as yourself. Eventually, a screen prompting you to send your member profile appears (see fig. 35.18).

5. If you want to change any of your responses, click Back. When you're satisfied with them, click Send. This completes the Membership Profile registration. Next, The Welcome Committee screen appears (see fig. 35.19), which gives you a chance to meet a cross section of the MSN membership (see fig. 35.20) and learn more about a specific part of the MSN service while doing so.

Part

IX

Ch

35

FIG. 35.17
Here's an example of the questions in the MSN member personal profile questionnaire.

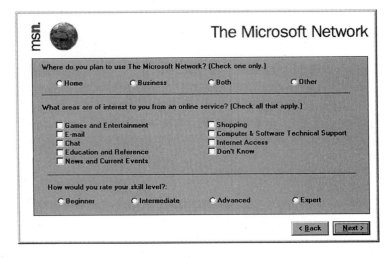

FIG. 35.18
Click the Send button to complete your Membership Profile.

FIG. 35.19
Meet a cross section of MSN members on the Welcome Committee.

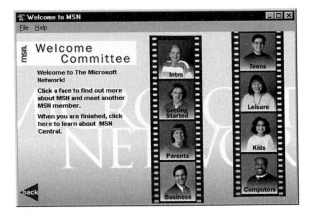

FIG. 37.20
Learn about specific areas of the MSN system from people with similar backgrounds.

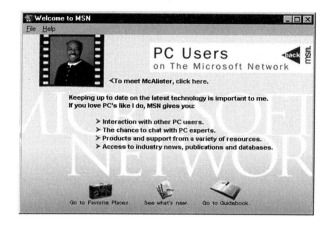

TROUBLESHOOTING

After I complete the questionnaire, I'm prompted to set up my Exchange Inbox. What do I do now? MSN requires Exchange to be installed and will attempt to configure the Inbox for you. See "Installing and Configuring Microsoft Exchange" in Chapter 31 to get your Inbox properly configured.

6. Select a topic on the Welcome Committee screen, or select File, Exit to proceed to MSN Central.

MSN Central

MSN Central is your starting point in MSN. It's the first window you see when you connect to MSN (see fig. 35.21). MSN Central is joined at the beginning of each session by MSN TODAY, and four other main options you can select:

- *E-Mail.* This is the Microsoft Exchange Inbox.
- *Favorite Places.* Empty at first, this folder contains the MSN forums and folders you like to visit most.
- *Member Assistance.* The place to start for any questions you might have.
- *Categories.* Here's where you'll find all the MSN forums.

N O T E If you want to change payment methods (pay with a different credit card), examine your detailed session information (including charges and session times), or review your MSN subscription plan, they can all be accomplished from MSN Central. Choose Tools/ Billing/, and then either Payment Method, Summary of Charges, or Subscriptions. See an example of a detailed account record in figure 35.22. ■

Part
IX

Ch
35

FIG. 35.21
MSN Central is your home base on The Microsoft Network.

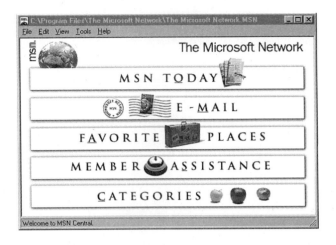

FIG. 35.22
You can review your Summary or Charges anytime.

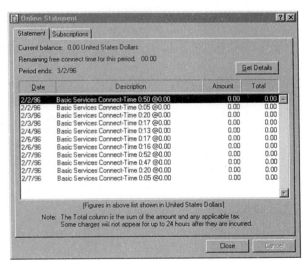

MSN Today

MSN Today keeps you informed about the latest happenings on MSN (see fig. 35.23). It's like the daily newspaper for MSN. Here, you'll find information about upcoming chats; new and exciting forums or additions to the MSN family; or software upgrades.

 Keep up to date by reading MSN Today each day. It's a good reminder of any chats or special events happening on MSN. Plus, its a great place to find lots of information using Guidebooks, the Directory, or the MSN Today screen itself.

MSN displays MSN Today each time you log on. If you don't want it displayed each time you log on, choose <u>V</u>iew, <u>O</u>ptions from the menu, select the General page, and deselect <u>S</u>how MSN Today Title on Startup.

Clicking a graphic or tab in MSN Today opens an MSN title or download-and-run file for you to enjoy or gather more knowledge about a particular topic. Or it might take you directly to the particular forum or area on MSN relating to that topic. For example, clicking the "Computers & Software" tab in MSN Today takes you directly to the "Computers & Software" forum, while clicking on the "Calendar of Events" tab starts a very nice calendar application showing you MSN events happening each day of the upcoming two weeks.

FIG. 35.23
MSN Today has all the latest information about the world of MSN.

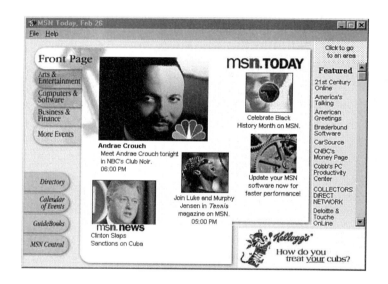

E-Mail

The E-<u>M</u>ail button on MSN Central starts Microsoft Exchange (see fig. 35.24) so you can send and receive e-mail while in MSN. You can send and receive e-mail with other MSN subscribers or Internet users. You can also use Exchange to search for other MSN members with interests similar to yours. See "MSN E-Mail" later in this chapter for more information about using Exchange with MSN.

 Think you might have received an e-mail? You won't need to go look for it on MSN. Each time you log in, the MSN data center will automatically check for e-mail, and you'll be notified if you've received any new e-mail.

▶ **See** "Viewing Received E-Mail," **p. 901**

Part
IX

Ch
35

FIG. 35.24
Check the Microsoft
Exchange Inbox for your
monthly letter from the MSN
team!

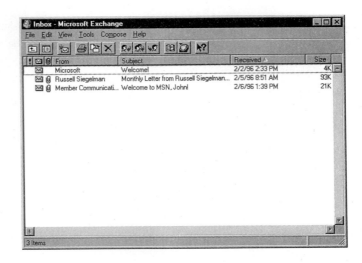

Favorite Places

While you are exploring MSN, you'll come across many forums, BBSs, and other things
you will want to visit again. MSN provides the Favorite Places folder (see fig. 35.25),
which allows you to save a shortcut to a place and then go directly to it without starting
over from the Categories folder. Any document or folder you visit can be stored in Favorite Places.

FIG. 35.25
Favorite Places is one
convenient folder in which
to keep all your most-
frequently visited MSN
Forums.

 Adding a Favorite Place   Most MSN folders allow you to turn the toolbar on by selecting
View, then checking the Toolbar box. This displays the Add to Favorite Places button in
the toolbar. When you find a forum that you want to add to your Favorite Places collection,
simply click the Add to Favorite Places icon on the toolbar. Or choose File, Add to
Favorite Places, and the forum is added to your Favorite Places folder automatically.

Alternatively, you can add an icon to Favorite Places by right-clicking on the icon and
selecting Add to Favorite Places in the context menu.

Going to a Favorite Place After you have saved a place in Favorite Places, you can quickly go there by double-clicking its icon in the Favorite Places folder. To display the Favorite Places folder, click the Go to Favorite Places button in the toolbar.

 Alternatively, right-click the MSN icon in the bottom-right corner of the taskbar and select Go to Favorite Places.

Member Assistance

Member Assistance is the place to go if you need help or have questions about using MSN (see fig. 35.26). Member Assistance is a forum that contains The MSN Member Lobby. This is a useful collection of support features, such as the Reception Desk Member Support, Activities & Promotions, a Member Directory, Suggestion Box, even a Gift Shop, as well as others. Also, the MSN Insider is a weekly update for MSN members from Microsoft. You get great information that is too detailed for *MSN Today.* To go to the Member Lobby, click the Member Assistance picture in MSN Central.

 TIP Consider adding the MSN Member Lobby to your Favorite Places folder. You'll have it handy for quick reference.

FIG. 35.26
Member Assistance is the right place to start when you need help for anything on MSN.

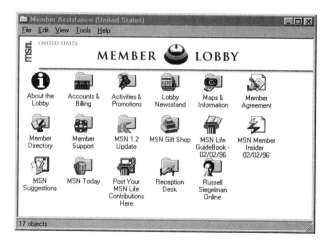

 TIP If you keep receiving an annoying message that MSN wants to disconnect you because you've been idle too long, don't get offended. MSN's trying to watch your pennies for you. By default, if your login session is inactive for 10 minutes, the system will notify you and give you 30 seconds to do something. If you don't hit Cancel, well, goodbye. Here's what you do if you'd like to extend your time-out value. From MSN Central, choose View/Options and then click the General tab on the property sheet. There you'll find a timeout counter that lets you set the inactivity range from 1 to 59 minutes!

Categories

Categories, the last icon in MSN Central, contains most of the actual content on MSN (see fig. 35.27). Here you find forums (organized categorically) from companies and service organizations (known as Independent Content Providers or ICPs) that contain bulletin boards where you can exchange messages with other members. You'll also find chat and V-Chat rooms to participate in live, interactive conversations, file libraries to download files, extended services, such as software products that you can purchase online, and more. Clicking the Categories icon on MSN Central opens the Categories folder. This folder contains icons representing the various categories of forums on MSN. For example, you'll find Arts & Entertainment, Computers & Software, Education & Reference, News & Weather, Science & Technology, and Sports & Recreation to name a few.

Under each category, you'll find subcategories dividing the content into appropriate smaller forums that contain the files, bulletin boards, chat, as well as supporting companies that comprise MSN.

FIG. 35.27

MSN has many categories to choose from. Most of MSN's vast content lies in the Categories section of the service.

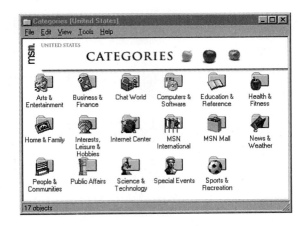

Navigation Tools and Features

You already know about the basic tools in Windows 95, such as folders, shortcuts, Explorer, and many others. MSN is easy to use because it uses these same tools. For example, if you can use Explorer to browse your hard drive, you can easily browse MSN. The following list explains how some of these tools are used:

- *Folders*. These are used to present categories and forums, enabling you to move easily between areas on MSN.

- *Forum*. Although an MSN-specific term, a forum is simply a folder with a collection of related documents and subfolders. For example, a forum on MSN for cat lovers may have a BBS, chat area, and media viewer title explaining the history of cats. It might also contain a subfolder with additional items (BBS, chats, and more) for only long-haired cats, a subcategory of the main topic.

N O T E When you first open a folder, MSN has to download information about it to your computer. This takes time, and it may seem slow. However, MSN caches (saves the information on your computer so it doesn't have to be transmitted again) the folders on your hard drive. Therefore, the next time you open the folder, it will load significantly faster. ▪

- *Explorer*. This tool gives you a bigger view of MSN and enables you to navigate quickly by showing the entire content of MSN in the left pane.
  - ▶ **See** "Using Windows Explorer to View Files and Folders," **p. 96**
  - ▶ **See** "Managing Your Files and Folders," **p. 101**

T I P If it's not obvious what type of folder or document an icon represents, right-click the icon and select Properties to see its type.

- *Property sheets*. These are used to display information about an area on MSN. Choose File, Properties on the forum. Select the Context tab, which displays information such as the Forum Manager, and the forum rating:

  GA-General Audiences

  MA-Mature Audiences

  AO-Adults Only

  NR-Not Rated

CAUTION

Particular areas of MSN (and certainly the Internet) contain content that is intended for individuals age 18 years and above. By default, all new MSN users do not have access rights to these areas. To gain access to these areas, it is necessary to intentionally request what is known as FULL ACCESS rights from MSN (see fig. 35.28). This may be obtained by requesting them via the Full Newsgroups Access e-mail form, found under the Categories/Internet Center/Internet Newsgroups/Full Newsgroup & Adult Access folder.

Alternatively, if you discover any forum on MSN that you want to exlcude your child from exploring, simply contact the forum manager by e-mail (found by File, Properties on the folder) and request that the Member ID that your child uses be restricted from that forum.

FIG. 35.28

In order to obtain full access rights to all MSN areas, you must complete this e-form and return it to MSN.

- *Shortcuts.* Most documents and folders on MSN can be dragged as shortcuts to your desktop, folders, or documents. Double-clicking an MSN shortcut takes you straight to that MSN area.

  ▶ **See** "Using the Power of Shortcuts and Desktop Icons," **p. 71**

  ▶ **See** "Overview of Exchange Features," **p. 874**

As you navigate MSN, you'll find that almost all "objects" or "containers" comprising MSN are of the following types:

- *BBS.* A message area where you can post static messages with other MSN subscribers. BBSs are not live. Some are set up as file distribution areas, which are read-only, where you can download the files attached to messages. BBSs are organized by areas of interest.

- *Chat room.* A place where you can have a live conversation with other MSN members who see your comments immediately. Many conferences by leaders in various industries are held in chat rooms.

 You can convey emotion in a chat room. For example, use the smiley *emoticon*—the emotion icon :-)—to indicate that you're grinning. See your MSN online help for more emoticons.

- *V-Chat.* Virtual Chat is an environment where you participate in a live, 3-D visual chat. You assign yourself the likeness of a virtual on-screen character called an Avatar, and maneuver the Avatar through the three-dimensional V-Chat space on MSN. Avatars are imagery files that convey some visual message such as a frown, smile, wave, and so on, and that can be displayed and easily changed on command via toolbar buttons during a V-Chat. Custom Avatars can be built by anyone having the necessary software, also available online. Links to other shortcuts are possible from within the chat spaces (see fig. 35.29).

FIG. 35.29
An unsuspecting subscriber encounters the author's Avatar in the MSN FishBowl V-Chat.

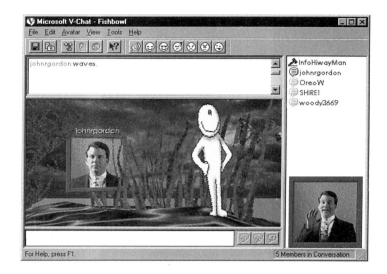

- *MediaView title*. A file that is downloaded to your computer and viewed in the MSN Online Viewer. You view content in the right side of the viewer, and you can select different pages to view in the left side.

- *Internet Studio title*. A multimedia-rich title that can contain sound, moving images, and more.

- *Download-and-run*. A file that is downloaded to your computer and executed. On MSN, this file is typically a Word document. However, it can be any file type registered with Windows, such as a text file or bitmap file.

- *Kiosk*. A download-and-run document that contains important information about the forum. Kiosks typically are used to convey overview materials, welcome messages, and "Read Me First" kinds of information. Quite often the Forum Manager will convey his or her greeting and good information about the forum.

  ▶ **See** "Registering File Types Causing Documents to Open Applications," **p. 147**

MSN E-Mail

In Chapter 31, "Using the Universal Inbox," you learned how to send and receive messages, use the Address Book, use remote mail, and configure your Inbox and Exchange client. When you installed MSN, however, it added additional features to Exchange specifically for MSN. For example, MSN added the capability to search for MSN members in the Address Book or make your personal profile available to other MSN members.

Part
IX

Ch
35

The following sections describe how to use Exchange with MSN. You learn about updating your personal profile, searching for other members, setting options for using Exchange with MSN, and using MSN's Address Book.

▶ **See** "Overview of Exchange Features" **p. 874**

Updating Your Personal Profile   Personal profiles allow other MSN members to see information about you, such as hobbies or profession. Thus, members can search their Address Books to find people with similar interests. Also, personal profiles are useful in chat rooms. If you are chatting with a person in a chat room and want to see more information about that person, such as the company for whom he works, you can right-click his name, and MSN displays his personal profile.

> **N O T E**   Providing all or part of the personal profile is optional. For example, if you don't feel comfortable revealing your company name, age, or gender, simply leave those fields blank. ▓

To make sure that this information is available to other members, you need to fill in your information. To provide your personal profile, follow these steps:

1. Open Exchange by clicking E-MAIL in the MSN Central window.

2. Choose Tools, Address Book or click the Address Book button in the toolbar.

3. Select Microsoft Network from the Show Names From The list. If you are not currently logged on to MSN, Exchange starts MSN, which prompts you to log on. The Address Book displays a list of all the MSN users. This list is updated about every 24 hours.

4. Search for your name by paging down the list. Alternatively, you can start typing your name in the field provided, and MSN displays the entry that matches what you have typed.

5. Right-click your name and choose Properties. The Address Book then displays the property sheet shown in fig. 35.30.

6. Fill in the information in the fields provided on the General, Personal, and Professional pages of the property sheet. Click OK, and MSN updates your profile. However, the updating could take as long as 24 hours.

FIG. 35.30
You should provide useful information in the personal profile so that other users can find you. All the fields in the profile are optional.

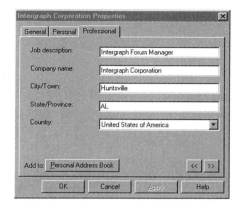

Finding Members in the Address Book   Finding members in the Address Book is a powerful way to find people with similar interests, professions, or even birthdays. To find members in the Address Book, follow these steps:

1. Open the MSN Address Book as described earlier. Click Tools, Find or click the Find button in the toolbar. Exchange displays the property sheet that you used to fill in your own profile.

2. On each page of the property sheet, fill in the information you want to match. Click OK.

3. Exchange redisplays the Address Book with the addresses that match your request. Notice that Exchange sets Show Names From The to Search Results.

4. Select The Microsoft Network in Show Names From The to return to a full list.

TROUBLESHOOTING

After starting a search in the Address Book, Exchange displays this error: The search resulted in too many Address Book entries to display. Your search criteria were not narrow enough. Provide more information in the property sheet to narrow the search.

Setting Properties for The Microsoft Network in Exchange   Chapter 31, "Using the Universal Inbox," describes setting up and configuring the various services used in Exchange, such as Microsoft Fax, Personal Address Book, and Personal Information Store. When you installed MSN, it added an additional service to this list: The Microsoft Network Online Service. This service provides the capability to exchange e-mail with other MSN members.

Part
IX

Ch
35

To set options for the MSN service in Exchange, follow these steps:

1. Choose Tools, Services from the Exchange main menu.

2. Select *The Microsoft Network Online Service* from the list of services. Then click Properties.

3. Set the options on the Transport and Address Book pages of the property sheet. Click OK.

 TIP Remember that your MSN e-mail address is nothing more than your Member ID. That's all you need to send e-mail to other MSN members using Exchange on MSN. If you want to turn your MSN e-mail into an Internet address, however, simply add @msn.com to your Member ID. For example, MSN member jqpublic would be jqpublic@msn.com to the Internet community.

Sending E-Mail on MSN   Composing a message for MSN is the same as for any other message in Exchange. However, you can choose to use MSN addresses when you use the Address Book. To see MSN addresses in the Address Book, select Microsoft Network from the Show Names From The list.

N O T E   When Exchange checks the address for an e-mail message, it automatically looks up the MSN address in the MSN Address Book. For example, if you are addressing an e-mail to "jb_smith" and type only "jb_s" in the address, Exchange completes the address for you. If more than one address matches the characters you typed, Exchange prompts you for the correct address from a list of possible choices. ■

MSN E-Mail with the Internet and Online Services   Sending e-mail to an Internet address is only slightly different from sending e-mail to an MSN address. Instead of typing an MSN address such as JqPublic, you type an Internet address such as jqpublic@msn.com. Receiving e-mail from an Internet user is just as easy. Before an Internet user can send you an e-mail message, the sender needs your Internet ID. Your Internet ID is Member ID@MSN.COM, in which Member ID is your MSN Member ID. See table 35.2 for details.

Table 35.2   Sending E-Mail to Online Destinations

Service	Internet Descriptor	Comment
Standard Internet	emailname@serviceprovider.suffix	Suffix generally .net or .com.
The Microsoft Network	Member ID@MSN.com	Member ID is e-mail name
America Online	ScreenName@AOL.com	Similar to Member ID

Service	Internet Descriptor	Comment
CompuServe	User.ID@CompuServe.com	User IDs are normally separated by a comma, and should be replaced by a period in the Internet Address.
Prodigy	ID@Prodigy.com	Similar to Member ID

TROUBLESHOOTING

I correctly addressed an e-mail message to an Internet user, but when I log on to MSN, it doesn't send the message. Exchange determines which services will be used for Internet addresses by the order of the services in Recipient Addresses are Processed in the Following Order list on the Delivery page of Exchange's Option menu. To use MSN to deliver e-mail to Internet users, choose Tools, Options from the Exchange menu. Then click the Delivery page and move The Microsoft Network Online Service to the top of the list.

Finding What You Want on MSN

There are many ways to find the information you need on MSN. In addition to MSN Find, there is a collection of value-added tools that help: The MSN Directory, Guidebooks, Shortcuts, and GO Words.

Using MSN Find   Finding folders and files on MSN is not much different than finding files on your computer. For example, you may want to find a forum about Windows 95, a chat room about Gourmet Cooking, or any items relating to a particular computer company such as Intergraph Corporation. To find folders and files on MSN, follow these steps:

1. Choose Tools, Find, On The Microsoft Network. MSN displays the Find dialog box.
2. In the Containing field, type the text for which you want to search. Optionally, click Description to include the description of each forum and file in the search.
3. Select the type of service (Name; Topic/Place/People; or forum) in the Of Type list and then click Find Now. MSN performs the search and displays the results.

After MSN displays the search results, you can right-click a file or folder to open it or create a shortcut to it.

Using the MSN Directory   The MSN Directory is a great way to find a forum on MSN (see fig. 35.31). It is actually a very good example of an interactive application, providing detailed information in a concise fashion.

Part
IX

Ch
35

FIG. 35.31

The MSN Directory helps you discover what forums are available. Forums can be searched by category, topic or alphabet.

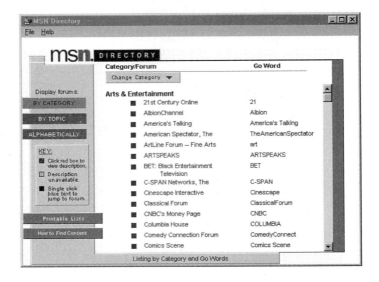

Using Guidebooks Guidebooks (see fig. 35.32) are similar to a helpful magazine online. They are designed and authored to provide detailed information about topics of interest, such as sports, computing, children, and more. Guidebooks contain links and shortcuts to interesting related sites on the Internet and MSN.

FIG. 35.32

Guidebooks are a great way to learn your way around MSN, and find interesting content.

GO Words GO words take you directly to forums on MSN. For example, if you want to move directly to the Woodworking forum, and you know that the "GO" word for the forum is Wood, then from MSN Central, simply choose Edit, Go To, Other Location. A "Go To

Service" dialog box appears. Type in the "GO" word and select OK. Or right-click on the small MSN taskbar icon, and select "Go To" to perform the same operation. This is a great tool if you know your way around. Use the MSN Directory to find popular "GO" words.

Using Shortcuts in MSN   Shortcuts are OLE object pointers that are used extensively in Windows 95, Internet Explorer, and MSN. They are great time-savers, as they can be cut and pasted into any word processing (see fig. 35.33) or spreadsheet document, e-mail message, or OLE-compliant application. They can also be dragged onto the Windows 95 desktop or from any WWW page.

▶ **See** "Using the Power of Shortcuts and Desktop Icon," **p. 71**

FIG. 35.33
MSN Shortcuts are beneficial for helping another individual find a forum, folder, BBS, or other MSN object quickly.

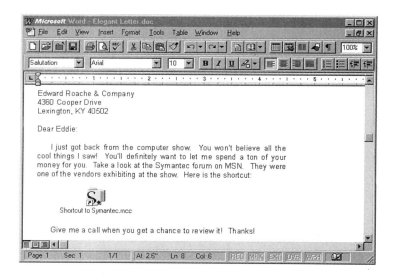

> **N O T E**   You can share your favorite MSN shortcuts with your friends. For example, if you find an interesting BBS on Photography, you can share a shortcut to that BBS with other MSN members so that they can go to the BBS. Create the shortcut on your desktop by dragging an icon from an MSN folder to the desktop. Create and address your e-mail. Then, right-click your shortcut and choose Copy. Right-click in the body of your message and choose Paste. When the recipient opens the e-mail, she can double-click the shortcut to go directly to that item. ■

Many of the MSN programs allow you to save a shortcut to your current location by clicking a toolbar button or selecting a menu option. You can also save a shortcut by dragging an icon from a forum's folder into the open Favorite Places folder.

Part
IX

Ch
35

MSN News   MSN News is the result of a joint venture between Microsoft and NBC. Entitled MSNBC, the service provides online tailored news for MSN subscribers (see fig. 35.34). News is accessed from MSN Today. It is a special application on MSN, which means that it will require some additional files from the MSN Data Center to allow you to view it properly. The first time News is invoked after an MSN installation, you will notice several news reader helper files download before the News application executes. This is a one-time occurrence.

FIG. 35.34
MSN News is comprehensive, current, and easy to navigate.

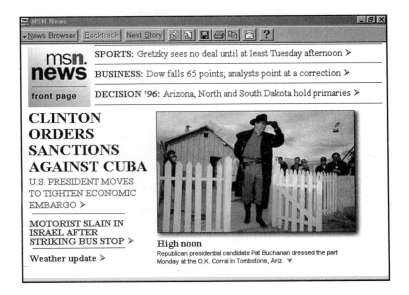

Using MSN Extended (Fee-Based) Services   Most MSN content providers furnish all of their content to MSN subscribers at the standard subscription rates. However, some providers offer extended, value-added products or services such as commercial software, merchandise, or information such as research reports for an additional fee. You are always notified and prompted for your approval of these charges, and the debit amount appears on your MSN billing statement (see fig. 35.35).

FIG. 35.35
Microsoft CarSource's Intellichoice Reports are an example of an MSN Extended, Fee-Based Service.

Getting Help On (and Off) MSN

There are many ways to obtain help for MSN, including the standard Help available in the software, Member Assistance, MSN Customer Support, and several industry-standard support resources.

Online Help

If you encounter problems while using MSN, remember to check the online help support built into the MSN client software. Choose Help/Help Topics from MSN Central, and then choose either the Content, Index, or Find tabs on the help screen. You can skim an introductory overview, find several specific How-to's, and read lots of tips and troubleshooting pointers. You can also search for information using the Help index or search engine.

Get to Know a Forum Manager

Individual forum managers on MSN are very good sources of information about MSN topics, especially regarding subject matter that is their specialty. Check out the Kiosk file in the top level of the forum that you are trying to get help with. You will find a contact, and an e-mail address for the Forum Manager. Drop him or her a line. They are contractually obligated to provide responses to inquiries in a timely fashion.

> **N O T E** Appendix C, "Additional Help and Resources," contains descriptions of other online services, CD-ROMs, and books that can help you with MSN and Windows 95. ▪

Other Sources for Help

You have a wealth of information about MSN available to you on MSN and the Internet. Do some online searching on the following topics, and you'll be amazed at the amount of information that is available to you. Some of these topics are the same databases of tips, troubleshooting, and technical papers used by Microsoft's telephone support professionals when answering questions about Windows 95 and Microsoft applications.

TechNet
Knowledge Base
Windows 95Support
MSN
MSDN

Part
IX

Ch
35

  You can reach MSN Customer Service in the U.S. and Canada at 1-800-386-5550.

CHAPTER 36

Using HyperTerminal

by Jerry Honeycutt with Brady P. Merkel

HyperTerminal is a Windows accessory that enables you to connect your computer to another PC or online service, such as a BBS. Although similar to the Windows 3.1 Terminal program, HyperTerminal is a full-featured communications tool that greatly simplifies getting online. With HyperTerminal, you can connect to a friend's computer, a university, an Internet service provider, or even CompuServe. ■

What HyperTerminal is and how it compares to the other communications tools provided with Windows

Find out what you can and can't do with HyperTerminal.

How to use HyperTerminal for some common tasks such as creating a connection or downloading a file

Look here to learn how to accomplish your everyday communications tasks.

How to configure HyperTerminal and customize your connections

Find out how you can fine-tune your HyperTerminal connections.

Using HyperTerminal

 When you installed Windows, you were given the option to install HyperTerminal as one of your accessories. If you did not install HyperTerminal or you removed it from the Start menu, you can install it at any time by selecting Install/Remove Applications from Control Panel. To run HyperTerminal, click the Start button and choose Programs, Accessories, HyperTerminal.

> **N O T E**   If you have not yet configured your modem, Windows prompts you to set it up the first time you run HyperTerminal.

Figure 36.1 shows the HyperTerminal folder. By default, each connection that you create appears in this folder as an icon.

FIG. 36.1
Double-click Hypertrm to create a new HyperTerminal connection, or double-click another icon to open an existing connection.

▶ **See** "Adding and Removing Windows Components," **p. 485**
▶ **See** "Configuring Your Modem," **p. 294**

What You Can Do with HyperTerminal

HyperTerminal is a communications tool with many uses described in the following list:

- Connect to another computer and exchange files
- Connect to an online service (such as CompuServe) that supports one of HyperTerminal's terminal-emulation modes
- Connect to a school's computer using VT-100 emulation
- Connect to an Internet Service Provider using a shell account, and even access the World Wide Web using Lynx

What You Can't Do with HyperTerminal

Although HyperTerminal is a useful communications tool, it's not the only tool you'll need for your communications activities. The following list describes some things you can't do and refers you to other chapters in this book:

- *Connect to another network.* If you need to connect your computer to another network, use Dial-Up Networking as described in Chapter 28, "Accessing Windows 95 Workstation Resources."

- *Connect to The Microsoft Network.* To connect to The Microsoft Network, use the graphical software provided in Windows 95, as described in Chapter 35, "Using The Microsoft Network."

- *Graphically connect to the Internet.* While many service providers provide Lynx, a character-oriented Web browsing tool, you need a graphical browsing tool to take full advantage of the Web. See Chapter 34, "Using Internet Explorer and the World Wide Web."

You can purchase more powerful communications programs for Windows 95 that have features not found in HyperTerminal. Capabilities you will find in more powerful terminal programs, but not in HyperTerminal, are listed here:

- Support for logon scripts, allowing you to automate your logon to bulletin boards.

- Support for keyboard macros, allowing you to assign repetitive key sequences to function keys.

- Password memory, so you don't have to reenter a password each time you connect.

- Support for more file transfer protocols, such as CompuServe-B, the file transfer protocol used by CompuServe.

- Support for a bulletin board mode and auto-answer. More powerful terminal emulation programs allow remote users to dial-in to your computer, which serves as a bulletin board host.

Creating a New Connection

Before you can connect with HyperTerminal, you need to create a new connection. To do so, follow these steps:

1. Double-click the Hypertrm.exe icon in the HyperTerminal folder. If HyperTerminal is already loaded, choose File, New or click the New button on the toolbar. HyperTerminal prompts you for a new connection description.

2. In the Connection Description dialog box, shown in figure 36.2, type a descriptive name for your new connection, select an icon, and click OK.

FIG. 36.2

Create a new connection and select an icon to help you easily identify it later.

3. HyperTerminal then displays the Phone Number dialog box, as shown in figure 36.3. Type the phone number for your new connection. Verify the country code, area code, and modem choice.

If you are connecting via a direct serial connection, leave the phone number blank, and select the correct port in the Connect Using pop-up menu. You must use a null-modem serial cable between your computer and the host.

FIG. 36.3

Define the phone number of your host in the Phone Number dialog box.

4. Click OK. HyperTerminal opens the Connect dialog box, as shown in figure 36.4.

5. Select your location (usually Default Location) and click Dial if you want to establish your new connection. You can also click Dialing Properties to change the default location, outside line access, and other dialing properties.

Figure 36.5 shows the entire HyperTerminal window with a session in progress. Most of HyperTerminal's features are available on the toolbar. Table 36.1 describes each toolbar button.

FIG. 36.4

After you've set up the connection, just click Dial to get going.

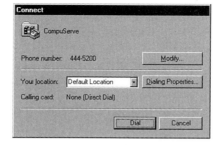

FIG. 36.5

After a connection to the remote computer is established, you interact with it just like a display terminal on the system.

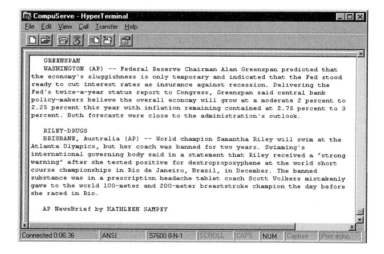

Table 36.1 The HyperTerminal Toolbar

Button	Name	Description
	New	Creates a new connection
	Open	Opens an existing connection
	Connect	Displays the Connect dialog box
	Disconnect	Disconnects the current connection
	Send	Sends a file to the host

continues

Table 36.1 Continued

Button	Name	Description
	Receive	Receives a file from the host
	Properties	Displays the Properties sheet for the connection

To save your new connection, choose File, Save As. HyperTerminal prompts you for a file name. If you want your connections to show up in the HyperTerminal folder, accept the default path. If you quit HyperTerminal without saving your new connection, HyperTerminal prompts you for a file name.

TROUBLESHOOTING

I try to dial a connection, but I get an error that says Another program is using the selected Telephony device. Make sure you don't have any older Windows communications programs running in the background that might be controlling the modem. Although Windows 95 communications tools can share the modem, older Windows communications programs can't.

I connected to the service fine, but all I see on-screen is garbage—usually at the bottom of the screen. Choose File, Properties to display the Properties sheet for your connection, click the Settings tab, and set Emulation to Auto Detect. HyperTerminal automatically determines which terminal emulation your service is using.

 To hang up, choose Call, Disconnect or click the Disconnect button on the toolbar.

▶ **See** "Working with Your Modem," **p. 302**

▶ **See** "Setting Up Direct Cable Connection," **p. 197**

Using an Existing Connection

The next time you want to use the connection you previously created, it appears in the HyperTerminal folder. To establish this connection, double-click the icon in the folder and click Dial.

 To access your connection quicker, make a shortcut to the connection on the desktop or the Start menu.

If HyperTerminal is already running, choose File, Open or click the Open button on the toolbar.

▶ **See** "Shortcuts Add Power," **p. 26**

Capturing Text from the Screen

By capturing text, you can save everything that appears in the HyperTerminal window. You may want to save the information displayed by HyperTerminal for the following reasons:

■ You want to review or use it later.

■ The information is scrolling by so quickly, you can't read it.

You can capture text from the remote computer to a file or to the printer.

 TIP If text is scrolling by faster than you can read it, try pressing Ctrl+S to pause the screen and then press Ctrl+Q to resume.

Capturing Text to a File

To capture text received from the remote computer to a file, follow these steps:

1. Choose Transfer, Capture Text.

2. Type the name for a file in which you want to put the text, or click Browse to select a file. Your screen should look similar to figure 36.6.

FIG. 36.6
Type the name for a file in which to capture text.

3. Click Start. HyperTerminal stores all text it receives from the remote computer in this file.

You can pause text capture by choosing Transfer, Capture Text, Pause and then resume capture by choosing Transfer, Capture Text, Resume. To stop text capture, choose Transfer, Capture Text, Stop. These three options are only available after you have started capturing text to a file. If you stop text capture, you will have to specify a file name again the next time you choose Transfer, Capture Text.

Capturing Text to the Printer

Capturing text to the printer is even easier than capturing to a file. Just choose Transfer, Capture to Printer. All text that HyperTerminal receives will be sent to the default printer. A check mark appears next to Capture to Printer, indicating that the option is turned on. To turn it off, choose it again.

TROUBLESHOOTING

I captured text to a text file, but when I view the file, I can read some of the lines, but the rest of them are garbled. If you are using terminal emulation, such as VT-100, this condition is normal. This emulation uses escape codes, which tell HyperTerminal where to put the cursor or how to format text. Escape codes can't be displayed as normal text. However, they are still captured to the file.

Sharing Text with Other Programs

The cut and paste process is still one of the most useful features in Windows. With a few keystrokes or mouse clicks, you can transfer data from one program to another. HyperTerminal is no exception. To copy data from HyperTerminal using the mouse, select a block of text in the window and choose Edit, Copy or press Ctrl+C.

Pasting is simple, too. After copying data to the Clipboard from another application such as Notepad, choose Edit, Paste to Host or just press Ctrl+V.

CAUTION

In applications such as Notepad, pasting text from the Clipboard puts the text in the document, which is then displayed in the window. When you paste text into HyperTerminal, it actually transmits the text to the remote computer.

▶ **See** "Understanding the Data-Sharing Capabilities of Windows 95," **p. 556**

Exchanging Files with a Remote Computer

You can easily exchange files with another computer using HyperTerminal. For example, you may want to download a program update from the bulletin board of your favorite software vendor. You also can download public domain software from a variety of bulletin board systems (BBSs) around the country.

CAUTION

Before running a program or opening a file downloaded from a remote computer, run it through a virus scan program to make sure that it isn't infected. Otherwise, severe and irreparable damage may occur to your programs and data files if you download a virus.

 ON THE WEB

For information on antivirus software you can purchase, check out these sites on the Internet

http://www.symantec.com/ (Symantec's Norton AntiVirus)

http://www.mcafee.com/ (McAfee's VirusScan for Windows 95)

You also may be asked to upload a data file to a vendor's bulletin board so the vendor can help you fix a problem. HyperTerminal can do it!

Downloading Files

Before you begin downloading a file, you must make sure that you have a connection with a host computer, as described in a previous section "Using an Existing Connection."

To download a file from a host computer, follow these steps:

1. Start the download process on the bulletin board or host computer. Bulletin boards or other host computers vary in how to start a download—follow the instructions given to you online. Make a note of the file transfer protocol you selected on the host. HyperTerminal supports several popular file transfer protocols. Table 36.2 describes each protocol.

Table 36.2   File Transfer Protocols Supported by HyperTerminal

Protocol	Description
Xmodem	Error-correcting protocol supported by virtually every communications program and online service, although it's slower and less reliable than the other protocols.
1K Xmodem	Similar to Xmodem, except that it's faster, transferring files in 1,024-byte blocks as opposed to the slower 128-byte blocks in regular Xmodem.
Ymodem	Offered on many bulletin board systems (another name for 1K Xmodem).
Ymodem-G	Similar to Ymodem, it implements hardware error control and is more reliable than the first three protocols. To use Ymodem-G, your hardware must support hardware error control.

continues

Table 36.2 Continued

Protocol	Description
Zmodem	Preferred by most bulletin board users because it's the fastest protocol of those listed. Zmodem is reliable, too, because it adjusts its block sizes during the download to accommodate bad telephone lines. And if a transfer is aborted midstream, you can resume the file transfer where it left off instead of starting all over. Zmodem's host can initiate the download—you do nothing beyond step 1, and you can download multiple files at one time using Zmodem. The host computer initiates a download for each file you select.
Kermit	Kermit is extremely slow and should not be used if one of the other protocols is available. Kermit is a protocol left over from VAX computers and mainframes.

2. If you selected Zmodem as the protocol, you're done. The host computer initiates the file transfer with HyperTerminal. Otherwise, choose Transfer, Receive File from the menu or click the Receive button. The Receive File dialog box appears.

3. Type a folder name or click Browse to select a folder (see fig. 36.7). Then select a protocol to use for downloading the file. The protocol you use should match the protocol you chose (or the system chose for you) on the host computer.

FIG. 36.7
Tell HyperTerminal where you want to store the file; then click Receive to begin the download.

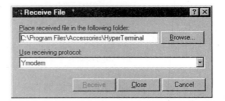

4. Click Receive, type a file name, and click OK. HyperTerminal starts your download. Figure 36.8 shows the dialog box that displays the status of your download. (You may see a different dialog box depending on the file transfer protocol you use.)

Uploading Binary Files

You can upload both binary and text files. Binary files include bitmaps, programs, and word processing documents that contain more than just readable text. For example, a program file contains code and program data that is not readable. On the other hand, text files contain characters that are easily read. This section describes how to upload a binary file.

FIG. 36.8

This dialog box shows the status of your download such as the file name and time elapsed.

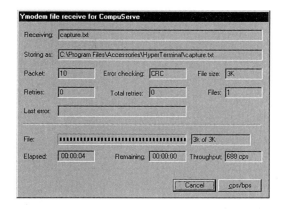

Before you begin uploading a binary file, you must establish the connection to the host computer, as discussed in an earlier section, "Using an Existing Connection." To upload a binary file to a host computer, follow these steps:

1. Initiate the upload on the bulletin board or host computer by following the on-screen instructions. The host displays a message indicating that it is waiting for you to start uploading.

N O T E If you are using Zmodem, you may not need to start the upload on the host computer. Zmodem can initiate the upload on the host for you. To try initiating the upload from your computer, skip step 1. However, if the host computer does not understand how to initiate an upload this way, you will have to start over from step 1. ▓

2. Choose Transfer, Send File or click the Send button on the toolbar. HyperTerminal displays a dialog box similar to the one shown in figure 36.8 in the previous section "Downloading Files."

3. Type a file name or click Browse to select a file.

4. Select a protocol to use for uploading the file. The protocol you use should match the protocol you chose (or the system chose for you) on the host computer.

5. HyperTerminal starts the upload to the host computer. It displays the status of your upload in a dialog box similar to the one shown earlier in figure 36.8.

TROUBLESHOOTING

I'm trying to use Ymodem-G as the transfer protocol, but it does not work. Your modem probably does not support hardware error control. Try using Ymodem instead.

continues

continued

> **I initiated a Ymodem upload from my computer, but the host does not respond.** The host
> computer does not understand how to initiate an upload this way. You need to initiate an upload
> first on the host computer and then on your computer. Alternatively, you may not be at the correct
> prompt on the host computer.
>
> **After reviewing the preceding suggestions, I still cannot download or upload a file.** Make
> sure that you are selecting the exact same file transfer protocol the host computer is using. If you
> continue to have difficulty, contact the system operator of the remote computer.

Uploading Text Files

Before you begin uploading a text file, be sure that you are connected to a host computer, as described in the earlier section, "Using an Existing Connection." To upload a text file to a host computer, follow these steps:

1. Start the upload on the bulletin board or host computer. The host displays a message indicating that it is waiting for you to start the upload.

2. Choose Transfer, Send Text File. HyperTerminal prompts you for a text file name.

> **CAUTION**
>
> Do not try to upload a binary file using the Transfer, Send Text File command. You may think that the
> file transferred OK, but the remote computer will receive a file with garbage in it.

3. Type a file name or click Browse to select a file.

4. Click Open. HyperTerminal starts uploading the text file to the host computer. Note that you do not see a dialog box showing the status of the upload.

Configuring HyperTerminal

HyperTerminal is a flexible communications tool. You can customize all aspects of each of your connections and HyperTerminal automatically saves your settings. For example, you can choose which font a connection uses or which terminal-emulation mode HyperTerminal uses. The next time you use that connection, HyperTerminal uses the settings you previously set. This section shows you how to configure HyperTerminal for each of your connections.

> **TIP**
> When you change configuration items in HyperTerminal, the changes apply only to the connection
> you have loaded. Thus, every connection can be customized differently.

Turning Off the Toolbar and Status Bar

You might want to turn off the toolbar or status bar for a HyperTerminal connection, especially if you don't have enough screen space to display the entire terminal area. To toggle the toolbar, choose View, Toolbar. To toggle the status bar, choose View, Status Bar.

Changing Fonts

You can choose a specific font and style for your HyperTerminal connection. For example, if you want HyperTerminal to display a full screen in a smaller window, choose a smaller font size and resize the window.

> **N O T E** You can't use a small font size to display 132 columns unless you are using VT-100 terminal emulation. HyperTerminal always resizes the display area to 80 columns.

To choose a different font for this HyperTerminal connection, follow these steps:

1. Choose View, Font. HyperTerminal displays the Font dialog box, which is common to most applications.

2. Set the font, style, and size. The Font dialog box shows you a preview of your choice.

3. Click OK. HyperTerminal immediately resizes the display area for 80 columns, using the font you have chosen.

4. Optionally, click the right button in the display area and choose Snap. HyperTerminal resizes the window to fit the display area. This technique is useful if you want to use a smaller font to have a smaller HyperTerminal window.

   ▶ **See** "Understanding Fonts," **p. 262**

Changing a Connection Setup

It's easy to change the properties for a connection after you create it. You can change the connection's icon, name, country code, area code, phone number, and modem in the connection's Properties sheet, as shown in figure 36.9.

To change the properties of your connection, follow these steps:

1. Choose File, Properties or click the Properties button on the toolbar.

2. Click Change Icon, select another icon from the list, and change the connection name.

3. Select a country code.

4. Type the area code and phone number. (If you select the default location when you dial, Windows will not dial the area code if it matches your default area code.)

FIG. 36.9
Change the icon, name, phone number, and modem to use for a connection. Click OK to permanently save your settings.

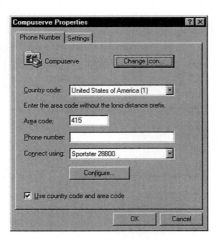

 TIP You can change the HyperTerminal Properties sheet without even running HyperTerminal. Right-click the connection you want to change in the HyperTerminal folder; then choose Properties.

5. Select a modem. Windows displays the modems you currently have installed, or enables you to go directly to a serial port. If you go directly to a serial port, you can bypass the Windows 95 modem configuration, controlling the modem directly. For normal usage, select a configured modem so you can take advantage of centralized modem configuration.

6. Click OK to save your settings.

Configuring the Connection Settings

The Settings page of the Properties sheet enables you to change the terminal properties of HyperTerminal. For example, you can change the terminal-emulation mode. Figure 36.10 shows the Settings page of this sheet. Table 36.3 describes each terminal emulation available in HyperTerminal.

Table 36.3   Terminal Emulation Supported by HyperTerminal

Protocol	Description
ANSI	A popular, generic terminal emulation supported by most UNIX systems that provides full screen emulation
Auto Detect	Automatically determines which terminal emulation the remote computer is using
Minitel	An emulation primarily used in France

Protocol	Description
TTY	Absent of any terminal emulation—simply displays all the characters it receives on the display
Viewdata	An emulation primarily used in the United Kingdom
VT-100	The workhorse of terminal emulations used by many remote systems (such as UNIX)
VT-52	Predecessor to VT-100 that provides full-screen terminal emulation on remote systems that support it

FIG. 36.10
Use the Settings page of the Properties sheet to change the terminal emulation and other useful settings.

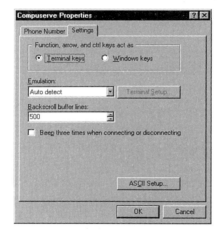

To change the settings for this connection, follow these steps:

1. Choose File, Properties or click the Properties button on the toolbar. Alternatively, right-click a connection document in the HyperTerminal folder and choose Properties.

2. On the Settings page, choose Terminal Keys or Windows Keys. Terminal Keys sends function keys F1 through F12 and arrow keys to the remote computer instead of acting on them in Windows; Windows Keys causes Windows to act on them. For example, if you choose Terminal Keys and press F1, the key would be sent to the host, and the host would respond to it. If you choose Windows Keys and press F1, Windows would display Help.

3. Set Emulation to the terminal emulation you want. HyperTerminal must be using the same terminal emulation the host computer is using.

T I P If you set Emulation to Auto Detect, HyperTerminal automatically determines what emulation the host is using and configures itself appropriately. Use this setting for normal situations.

4. Set the number of lines you want in Backscroll Buffer Lines. In the HyperTerminal main window, the current screen is displayed with a white background. If you press Page Up or use the scroll bar to scroll backwards, you see previously displayed text with a grey background. The default value for Backscroll Buffer Lines is 500 lines, which allows you to review about 20 screens and does not consume a large amount of memory.

5. Turn on Beep Three Times When Connecting or Disconnecting if you want to be notified when you are making or breaking a connection.

6. Optionally, click ASCII Setup and set the options for how text files are sent and received. Figure 36.11 shows the ASCII Setup dialog box, and table 36.4 describes what each option does.

FIG. 36.11
Use the ASCII Setup dialog box to configure how ASCII files will be sent and received. For example, you can choose to send line feeds with line ends.

Table 36.4 ASCII Setup Options

Option	Description
Send Line Ends with Line Feeds	Attaches a line feed to the end of every line that HyperTerminal sends. Enable this option if the remote computer requires it or if you turned on Echo Typed Characters Locally, or if pressing Enter moves you to the beginning of the current line instead of starting a new line.
Echo Typed Characters Locally	Displays each character you type on the keyboard instead of depending on the host to echo each character. Enable this option if you cannot see the characters you type. If you see each character twice (lliikkee tthhiiss), disable this option.

Option	Description
Line Delay	Sets how much time to delay between lines. Increasing the amount of time between lines allows the remote computer time to get ready for the next line. Increase this setting in increments of 100 milliseconds if the remote computer frequently loses portions of each line.
Character Delay	Sets how much time to delay between characters. Increasing the amount of time between characters allows the remote computer time to get ready for the next character. Increase this setting in increments of 5 milliseconds if the remote computer randomly loses characters.
Append Line Feeds to Incoming Line Ends	Attaches a line feed to lines received. Enable this option if the lines you receive from the host computer are displayed one on top of another.
Force Incoming Data to 7-bit ASCII	Changes 8-bit characters to 7-bit. Enable this option if HyperTerminal displays Greek or unrecognizable symbols. This option forces HyperTerminal to stick with readable characters.
Wrap Lines That Exceed Terminal Width	Turns word wrapping on or off. Enable this option if you want lines that are longer than the terminal width to be continued on the following line.

N O T E If you have selected a particular terminal emulation on the Settings page, you can further refine the configuration by selecting Terminal Setup. HyperTerminal displays a different dialog box depending on which emulation you have chosen. The following table shows the options available for each emulation mode:

Emulation	Options
ANSI	Cursor: Block, Underline, or Blink
Minitel	Cursor: Block, Underline, or Blink
TTY	Cursor: Block, Underline, or Blink, Use Destructive Backspace
Viewdata	Hide Cursor, Enter Key Sends #
VT-100	Cursor: Block, Underline, or Blink, Keypad Application Mode, Cursor Keypad, Mode 132-Column Mode Character Set
VT-52	Cursor: Block, Underline, or Blink Alternate Keypad Mode

Configuring Your Modem for HyperTerminal

You probably configured your modem after you installed Windows. However, you can override any of these options in HyperTerminal. For example, if your modem is configured in the Control Panel to connect at 115.2Kbps, you can configure your connection to connect at 2400bps. However, changing your connection does not change your modem's configuration; it is simply overridden by the connection.

Configuring your modem for a particular connection is the same as configuring it in Control Panel.

The first two pages, General and Connection, are the same as those displayed for configuring the modem in Control Panel.

 T I P HyperTerminal automatically detects the configuration of the modem you are calling. Therefore, you don't need to change the data bits, stop bits, or parity settings you might have been familiar with in the past.

The Options page is added to the HyperTerminal modem Properties sheet only when you open it from HyperTerminal. This page enables you to set additional properties for HyperTerminal. To set these options for HyperTerminal, follow these steps:

1. Choose File, Properties or click the Properties button on the toolbar. Alternatively, right-click the appropriate connection icon in the HyperTerminal Connections folder.

2. Click the Configure button and select the Options tab. HyperTerminal displays the page shown in figure 36.12.

FIG. 36.12
You can refine your modem configuration by choosing to display a terminal window before and after dialing, which gives you more control over how the phone is dialed and the connection is made.

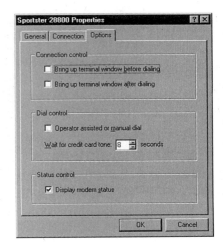

3. Set options as described in table 36.5 and click OK to save.

Table 36.5   Modem Options

Option	Description
Bring Up Terminal Window <u>B</u>efore Dialing	Displays a terminal window, shown in figure 36.13, before HyperTerminal starts dialing, enabling you to enter modem commands directly. (See your modem's manual for a list of commands.)
Bring Up Terminal Window A<u>f</u>ter Dialing	Displays a terminal window after HyperTerminal has dialed the phone number, enabling you to enter modem commands directly.
Operator Assisted or <u>M</u>anual Dial	Enables you to dial the telephone number directly. HyperTerminal prompts you to dial the telephone number.
<u>W</u>ait for Credit Card Tone	Allows you to specify how many seconds HyperTerminal will wait for the credit or dialing card tone.
Display Modem <u>S</u>tatus	Displays the status of the modem. Turning this option off disables the Modem icon in the taskbar.

FIG. 36.13
You can use the terminal window to send commands directly to the modem before and after the phone number is dialed.

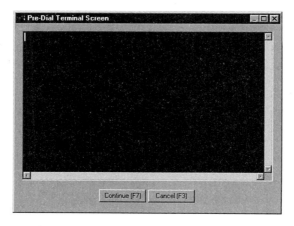

N O T E   HyperTerminal does not have a menu option or toolbar button to answer an incoming
call. However, you can easily answer an incoming call if you have a Hayes-compatible
modem by typing **ATA** and pressing Enter in the HyperTerminal window after the phone rings.
Alternatively, you can place the "A" in your modem's initialization string after the "AT" command
and the modem automatically picks up at the first ring.

▶ **See** "Customizing Your Calling Locations," **p. 302**

▶ **See** "Configuring Your Modem," **p. 294**

▶ **See** "Advanced Settings," **p. 995**

P A R T

X

Exploring Multimedia in Windows 95

CHAPTER 37

Working with Multimedia

by Michael Desmond

Microsoft has touted Windows 95 as a true multimedia operating system, and for good reason. Today, most PCs sold come equipped with a CD-ROM drive and sound board. Not surprisingly, the number of CD-ROM titles sold for these systems has skyrocketed— meaning there's a lot of hardware and software designed to deliver compelling graphics, video, and sound. And with Windows 95, Microsoft has ensured it will be a dominant player in multimedia computing.

There's a lot of interesting material in Windows 95. At the heart of the system is its efficient 32-bit design that lets a PC work on several things at once without sacrificing performance—critical for juggling multimedia tasks. Microsoft also has added a set of multimedia technologies to Windows 95—called DirectX—that provides better game play, improved video and audio performance, and easier connectivity. The operating system offers a variety of controls for adjusting and tweaking multimedia performance as well, including support for dedicated CONFIG.SYS and AUTOEXEC. BAT profiles for DOS games.

What hardware you need to enjoy multimedia with Windows 95

You'll find out how much processing power you need and which peripherals offer the most value.

The new features that give Windows 95 its multimedia edge

A description of the DirectX technologies that enhance multimedia performance under Windows 95.

Autoplay, and tips for using it

A guide to controlling the automatic CD-ROM player in Windows 95.

How to use the Multimedia Properties sheet

The Multimedia Properties sheet lets you control settings for key multimedia drivers and devices.

Customizing the Windows 95 multimedia interface

Add sound and graphics to the Windows 95 interface with these step-by-step tips.

Not that Windows 95 is perfect. For all its improvements over DOS and Windows 3.1, getting to the multimedia features of Windows 95 can be difficult. While useful tools like the Multimedia Properties sheet offer control over a wide range of system settings, the many options make the tools difficult to master. And the DirectX components, which help make Windows 95 a world class multimedia platform, are not even a part of Windows 95. You must add them via an upgrade. ■

▶ **See** "Exploring the Multimedia Properties Sheet," **p. 1092**

Getting the Right Multimedia

The array of peripherals and resources you need to work with multimedia can make choosing the right hardware difficult. To provide guidance in these choices, the Multimedia PC Marketing Group devised a specification called MPC (Multimedia Personal Computer) that mandates specific hardware and software for MPC-labeled machines. The original spec is now several versions old—MPC 3 being the current standard—but its recommendations make a good starting point.

Starting Out with MPC 3

In order for a vendor to market a PC as MPC 3-compliant, it needs to be outfitted with specific hardware. Be warned: the MPC 3 spec represents a lowest common denominator. If you expect to do things like work with rich video files and play demanding games, you'll want to spend some dollars to go beyond the minimum spec.

Table 37.1 provides a profile of the MPC 3 specification, as well as recommendations for adequate multimedia performance. For example, the 75-MHz Pentium mandated by the MPC has already fallen behind the power curve, and is insufficient for playing back high-quality MPEG video. We've also provided two other profiles, one for buyers constrained by a budget, and another for those seeking cutting edge performance.

	Table 37.1 The MPC-3 Specification and Suggested Hardware		
Item	**MPC 3** (about $1,600)	**Mid-range** (about $2,400)	**High-end** (about $3,500)
CPU	Pentium-75	Pentium-100	Pentium 150 or 166
RAM	8M	16M	32M
Hard drive	540M	1.2G	1.6G

Item	MPC 3 (about $1,600)	Mid-range (about $2,400)	High-end (about $3,500)
CD-ROM	4X with 250ms seek, multisession, "Red Book" capable	6X, at least 200ms seek, multisession	6.7X or 8X, at least 150ms seek, multisession
Sound	16-bit digital, multivoice internal synthesizer capable of six simultaneous voice and two percussion tracks	Ditto, but with wave table MIDI hardware	Ditto, but with wave table MIDI, 3-D audio processing
Video	30 frame per second at 352 × 240 pixels, MPEG-1 compliance	64-bit graphics accelerator with 2M of DRAM, on-board video enhancement	64-bit graphics accelerator with 4M of VRAM, on-board video enhancement, 3-D acceleration

Part
X

Ch
37

Understanding Multimedia Hardware

A PC must be well-balanced to handle multimedia demands. A fast processor does little to enhance CD-ROM titles, for example, if your system lacks RAM and has a single-speed CD-ROM drive. For this reason, you need to decide where to spend your money.

Choosing the Right CPU   The CPU is the heart and soul of any multimedia system. While the MPC 3 spec recommends a 75-MHz Pentium, the truth is that anything slower than 100 MHz will not have a lot of staying power as new software demands more and more performance. Even today, any demanding video playback will confound a Pentium-75, particularly complex MPEG video files that are becoming an industry standard. For those playing the hottest flight simulators or working with video compression, 3-D graphics, and image editing, a Pentium running at 150 or 166 MHz is best, though systems based on the 133-MHz Pentium probably give you the most overall value. Of course, there is no reason why you can't buy a system with a CPU from chip makers other than Intel, such as the 100-MHz 6 × 86 from Cyrix—which provides about 100-MHz Pentium performance—and upcoming Pentium-class CPUs from AMD.

Understanding System Memory (RAM)   Aside from the CPU, system RAM is the most important element in multimedia performance. In general, a Windows 95 PC should have no less than 8M of RAM, and 16M or more is recommended for multimedia applications and titles. While some demanding applications like image editing and video capture do better with 32M or more of RAM, most multimedia applications and titles achieve optimal performance in 16M.

N O T E With 16M of RAM, Windows 95 not only avoids the use of slow virtual memory, it enables the use of larger dynamic hard disk and CD-ROM drive caches. The result is faster access from disk and CD-ROM. ▧

System RAM is known as dynamic RAM, or DRAM. Today, many fast Pentium PCs use an enhanced form of DRAM, called Extended Data Out (edo) DRAM. While edo DRAM costs a bit more, it provides about a 10 percent boost in system performance. Today, the fastest Pentium systems all use edo DRAM to get maximum performance. Also, make sure your system has 256K of external cache, which is a layer of fast memory that keeps necessary data close to the CPU for quick access. Smaller caches result in degraded performance, as fast Pentium processors wait for system RAM to deliver data.

N O T E Some vendors are now introducing high-end Pentium PCs that use synchronous DRAM (SDRAM), which is supposed to run more efficiently than current DRAM technologies. The biggest performance boost occurs during large data transfers, common in tasks such as video decompression. ▧

ON THE WEB

For more detail about RAM technology and products, check out the World Wide Web site of Kingston Technology, a maker of RAM and PC upgrade products:

http://www.kingston.com

Choosing a CD-ROM Drive   These days, there is no excuse to go for less than a 4x model, though older 2x drives will suffice for handling most tasks. Still the faster drives sap less CPU resources, and provide greater headroom for coming applications. Most importantly, they can find data on the CD-ROM more quickly, improving overall performance. The best drives operate at 6x and higher drive speeds. If you tend to juggle a lot of CD-ROMs, you might consider a multi-disc CD changer, such as the three-disc model found in some Gateway systems, or the NEC 4 × 4 drive that can accept four discs at once.

Get a quick inventory of multimedia files on your CD-ROM discs by saving a standard search to the Windows 95 desktop. To do this, press F3 in any open folder window, and in the Named: box of the dialog box that appears, type ***.avi *.mpg *.mov *.wav *.mid**. In the Look In drop-down list box, type **D:**; then select File, S<u>a</u>ve Search to save the search as an icon to your desktop.

If you want to make your own CD-ROMs, you might consider a CD-Recorder, also known as a CD-R drive. These drives can write (or *burn*, as it is called) special CD-ROM discs that can be played on any CD-ROM player. Several models now sell for under $1,000, making it possible for small businesses and home publishers to burn their own CD-ROM discs. CD-Rs are excellent for distributing digital video, multimedia presentations, and even archiving important data.

Buying a Sound Board and Speakers   Your sound board must support 16-bit wave audio, and should be equipped for wave table MIDI. Wave table MIDI provides realistic sounding playback of MIDI scores, in contrast to the cheap, synthesized sound provided by FM MIDI sound cards. Most games use extensive MIDI scores for their music tracks, since MIDI files are smaller and require less CPU attention than big wave audio files. The most sophisticated cards, such as Creative Labs' Sound Blaster AWE 32, lets you store custom wave samples as MIDI sounds. This feature allows you to sample sound effects such as a gun shot, and use it in a MIDI score.

Part
X

Ch

37

> **N O T E**   MIDI stands for *musical instrument device interface*, and is an international standard for handling digital scores that play back consistently on synthesizers, PCs, and other devices. ▨

T I P   When buying a sound board, consider going with a major brand such as Creative Labs' Sound Blaster or Advance Gravis UltraSound Pro. You'll find Windows 95 drivers for these brands to be widely available and generally more reliable.

In speakers, look for amplified models, since the small amplifier built into a sound board lacks volume and introduces noise to the original audio signal. Generally, a speaker with about four watts of output is adequate for desktop use, though you'll want 10 watts or more for presentations or group use. Keep in mind that desktop multimedia speakers often can not reproduce low bass sounds. A floor standing subwoofer is the best way to add rich bass to your titles and music. In addition, make sure desktop speakers are shielded, so they don't interfere with the image on your monitor. If you are not sure if the speakers are shielded, ask the vendor about this feature.

Picking a Graphics Board   Your graphics board should come with 2M of graphics RAM to handle the high resolutions and rich colors of multimedia software. Look for 64-bit boards that provide acceleration of full-motion video. These features help Windows 95

PCs achieve full-screen, 30 frame per second video. Also, if you want the fastest performance and the most comfortable viewing, go with a board that uses video RAM (VRAM). This memory is able to produce a more stable, flicker-free image than less-expensive DRAM boards.

> **N O T E** The Diamond Stealth 64 Video 3400XL and the STB Velocity 64 Video are good examples of video-enabled graphics cards. ▦

If you are buying a new system, make sure it has a PCI (Peripheral Component Interconnect) bus, and that the graphics card plugs into a PCI bus slot. PCI provides fast access to the CPU for demanding peripherals such as graphics, video capture, and network cards. PCI also offers a subset of the Plug and Play scheme, helping ease installations.

Input devices If multimedia games are your bag, don't overlook the joystick. While all joysticks enjoy better performance under Windows 95 than they did under DOS, the new generation of digital joysticks provide greater precision, quickness, and features than any analog model can supply. Microsoft's SideWinder Pro 3D joystick is the first digital product on the market.

> **N O T E** Analog joysticks can draw about 15 percent of the CPU's processing power because your system must constantly go to the analog joystick port and check for any changes. Digital joysticks take the load off the system by sending data direct to Windows 95. The result—faster game play. ▦

Understanding DirectX

Windows earned a well-deserved reputation for being slow when handling multimedia tasks. As a result, PC game developers and buyers put up with difficult DOS-based game software, despite the convenience of Windows 3.1's compatibility and interface. Windows 95 changes all that with a set of core technologies—called DirectX—that bring fast graphics, enhanced video, and world-class game play to Windows.

The DirectX technologies address multimedia specifically, turning Windows 95 into an enhanced platform for sound, video, graphics, and game play. To take full advantage of the new capabilities, users need to get Windows 95 drivers for the peripherals they own.

> **N O T E** Future multimedia software will install DirectX components into Windows 95 as needed, in essence doing a field upgrade of your operating system. ▦

To help you understand how Windows 95 handles multimedia, the following sections discuss each of the DirectX technologies and explains what they do and how to take advantage of them. In all cases, advanced hardware can multiply the performance of your system significantly.

The DirectX components are:

- *DirectDraw*. Fast graphics for games and video.
- *DirectVideo*. Video playback enhancements.
- *DirectSound*. Low overhead audio processing.
- *Direct3D*. Industry standard for accelerated 3-D graphics.
- *DirectInput*. Support for digital joysticks, head-mounted displays, and other game devices.
- *DirectPlay*. Built-in, easy-to-use network and modem game play.

TIP At this time, Microsoft provides no easy way to see if your system has DirectX drivers installed. One way you can check is to use Windows 95's Find feature to search for the file names DDRAW.DLL, DSOUND.DLL, and DVIDEO.DLL in the Windows/System subdirectory. You can also search for references to these files in the Windows 95 Registry with the Registry's search function.

▶ **See** "Using the Registry Editor," **p. 435**

DirectDraw: Fast Graphics and Video

For Windows 95 to survive as a game and multimedia platform, it had to get faster graphics. DirectDraw lets everything from flight simulators to video windows enjoy fast screen updates by removing the considerable overhead of Windows' Graphics Device Interface (GDI) engine—a process called *direct frame buffer access*. In addition, DirectDraw-compliant graphics adapters can provide further enhancements. Among the features are *double buffering*, which speeds frame-based screen redraws (common in video and games); and *overlay,* which allows high frame rates even when the video window is partially covered by another window. Most 64-bit graphics cards sold today include hardware for these functions, though you may have to get the DirectDraw drivers for the card separately.

N O T E DirectDraw is actually Microsoft's follow-on to DCI (Display Control Interface), which was developed by Intel for Windows 3.1. Most graphics boards today include DCI drivers for Windows 3.1 operation. ▪

DirectVideo: Accelerated Full-Motion Video

When people think multimedia, they think video. DirectVideo lets inexpensive, video-savvy graphics hardware accelerate key video playback tasks. The result is smooth, full-screen video on properly equipped mid-range Pentium level machines. In addition, if you don't have a dedicated MPEG adapter card installed, you'll need DirectVideo to play high-quality MPEG video. Without the hardware acceleration that DirectVideo enables, even fast systems cannot manage adequate playback of MPEG video clips.

N O T E With DirectVideo, Windows 95 finally catches up to the multimedia functions that DCI pioneered almost a year and a half ago. ■

DirectVideo and DirectDraw work together to let properly-equipped graphics hardware free the system CPU from difficult tasks associated with video decompression and play-back. Most important is *color space conversion*, an operation that accounts for about 30 percent of the CPU's time when playing back compressed video. *Pixel interpolation,* mean-while, allows video clips that were created at lower, space-saving resolutions to be played back at full screen.

DirectSound: Hearing Windows 95

DirectSound helps streamline and enhance the audio handling of Windows 95. It also gives software vendors a standard way to put sophisticated audio into games and titles—relieving the compatibility problems that have been such a problem with DOS-based games. One feature of Windows 95's audio handling is *polymessage MIDI*, which lets the system send multiple MIDI instructions using a single interrupt.

DirectInput: Playing with Windows 95

DirectInput promises to open the door to advanced game interaction. Now, Windows 95 provides a standard interface for game peripherals ranging from joysticks to head-mounted displays, allowing game makers to take advantage of innovative devices like the Forte VR1 headgear, Virtual I/O i-Glasses, and other peripherals. DirectInput also pro-vides a standard interface for digital joysticks, which provides greater precision and better performance.

Direct3D: The Next Generation of Multimedia

Perhaps the most important new multimedia technology to emerge on the PC is 3-D graphics. Windows 95 provides key standards that help bring accelerated, real-time 3-D graphics to games and applications. Called Direct3D, this technology lets software programmers and graphics board makers develop products to a common standard, ensuring that 3-D games and graphics cards can work together. Direct3D enables complex functions like *texture mapping*, which makes object surfaces look realistic; and *polygon draws*, which build 3-D scenes and objects. The promise: Incredible realism when playing games and interactive titles, particularly when a PC is equipped with a 3-D accelerator card.

DirectPlay: Multiplayer Gaming

Still under development, DirectPlay will let games provide multiplayer interaction over modems, LANs, and public network services. It provides a standard, simple to use interface for users, and lets game makers not worry about developing code to handle online game play. DirectPlay also makes possible mixed mode connections, so players can be hooked to a network game via modem, ISDN line, and Ethernet connection; yet all can play each other with no difference in performance. To play together, users will be able to simply log onto an existing game session that another has initiated, whether on a network or via direct modem call.

Autoplay Exposed

Autoplay, one of the most highly touted features of Windows 95 is likely the most simple. When an Autoplay-compliant CD-ROM or an audio CD is put in the CD-ROM drive, Windows 95 recognizes it, and either installs or launches the application (or begins playing the first audio track with audio CDs). The idea is to make playing CD-ROM titles and games as easy as working with cartridge-based game machines such as Nintendo and Sega.

How can you tell if a CD-ROM supports Autoplay? Browse the root directory of the disc, and look for a file called AUTOPLAY.INF. This file tells Windows 95 what the disc is, and how to launch it.

But Autoplay is hardly perfect. For example, most CD-ROM drives take several seconds to spin up and read a newly inserted disc. You have to wait for Windows to either autoplay the disc, or to do nothing. And let's face it, just because you put a disc in the drive doesn't mean you always want it to play *right now*.

 T I P To disable Autoplay when you insert a CD-ROM disc, just hold down the Shift key as you insert the disc into the drive.

You can permanently disable the Autoplay feature by doing the following:

1. From any folder window, click View, Options, and click the File Types tab. In the Registered file types window, scroll down to the AudioCD entry.

2. Click Edit, and select the bold Play item in the Actions box.

3. Turn Autoplay off by clicking the Set Default button. The Play item is no longer bold.

4. Click Close. Now when you insert a CD-ROM or audio CD disc, Windows 95 Autoplay will not be invoked.

Okay, maybe the problem isn't too much Autoplay, but rather, that you can't get enough. Microsoft has posted a number of intriguing utilities, called PowerToys, on its online forums and World Wide Web site.

ON THE WEB

The PowerToys web site is:

http://www.microsoft.com/windows/software/PowerToy.htm

These features enhance the basic functionality of the operating system. One of the PowerToy applications is called Autoplay Extender, and adds buttons for browsing into CD-ROM subdirectories, should no AUTOPLAY.INF file be found.

Exploring the Multimedia Properties Sheet

With all the various components that go into making a multimedia system, it's a good thing that Windows 95 puts many of the critical controls in one easy-to-find place. The Multimedia Properties sheet is a one-stop shop for installing drivers, changing settings, and setting up hardware.

To get to the Multimedia Properties sheet, open the Control Panel, and double-click the Multimedia icon. There, you'll see a tabbed dialog box that lets you run the multimedia gamut. Among the things in the Multimedia Properties sheet:

- *Audio*. Changes the volume level on a multimedia device.
- *Video*. Varies the size of the standard window in which a video clip is displayed, and offers detailed information on the selected clip.
- *MIDI*. Sets up a new MIDI instrument.

■ *CD Music.* Adjusts the volume of an installed CD player.

■ *Advanced.* Configures multimedia properties associated with specific attached devices.

 T I P Put the Multimedia Properties sheet in easy reach by placing it into your Start menu. From the Control Panel, drag the Multimedia icon onto the Start button and let go. When you click the Start button, you'll see the Multimedia item on your Start menu.

Part
X

Ch
37

Exploring the Audio Page

Here you can adjust the volume of multimedia devices, as well as set defaults for device usage and audio recording quality.

1. Click the Audio tab (see fig. 37.1).

2. Adjust the volume for Playback or Recording by dragging the respective Volume slider. Drag the slider to the right for more volume, and to the left for less.

3. Select the device you want used for playback or recording if it is not the default in the Preferred device list.

4. Check the Show Volume Control on the Taskbar item if you want the volume control displayed on the Windows 95 desktop.

5. Select an option from the Preferred Quality list to adjust the quality of the recording (for example, CD Quality).

6. If you want to customize the recording quality, click the Customize button in the Recording area. The Customize dialog box appears (see fig. 37.2).

FIG. 37.1
You can adjust the default volume and other settings of multimedia devices using the Audio page on the Multimedia Properties sheet.

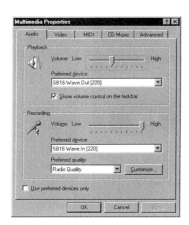

FIG. 37.2
Adjust the default quality of recorded sound using the Customize option.

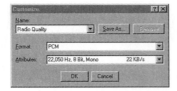

With this option, you can select the sound quality, format, and attributes, and then save the customized format as a special file by clicking the Save As button.

Exploring the Video Page

Here you can adjust the size of the standard window in which a video clip is displayed. After the Multimedia Properties sheet appears, follow these steps:

 TIP To achieve the smoothest video playback, select the Original Size option from the Window drop-down list.

1. Open the Video page, shown in figure 37.3. In the Show Video In area, choose Window to customize the display the window, or choose Full Screen to use the entire screen.
2. If you chose Window, select the window size you want from the drop-down list that appears when you click the down arrow.
3. Click OK to make the changes take effect.

N O T E The Full screen setting plays video in a special graphics mode that deactivates the rest of the Windows desktop. You won't see any video controls during playback, and you have to press Esc or click the screen to stop the video and reassert the Windows interface.

FIG. 37.3
Adjust the default size of video clip windows using the Video page of the Multimedia Properties sheet.

MIDI

You can use the MIDI page of the Multimedia Properties sheet to set up a new MIDI instrument connected to your PC. Before you open the sheet, make sure you've connected the MIDI instrument hardware to a MIDI port on your installed sound card.

N O T E MIDI peripherals, such as keyboards, connect to your PC via the MIDI/joystick port on the back of your sound card.

1. Open the MIDI page (see fig. 37.4).
2. Click the Add New Instrument button near the bottom of the page.
3. Follow the instructions on-screen to install the MIDI device, and then click the Single Instrument button.
4. The device you just installed will be displayed in the list window in the center of the MIDI page. Select the device and click OK.

FIG. 37.4

You can set up a MIDI instrument using the MIDI page in the Multimedia Properties sheet.

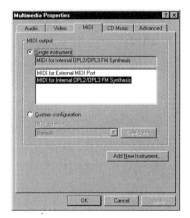

CD Music

T I P If you have multiple CD-ROM drives installed, you can set separate default volume levels for each drive.

You can adjust the default volume of the CD player's headphone output by using the CD Music page on the Multimedia Properties sheet.

After you display the Multimedia Properties sheet, follow these steps.

1. Open the CD Music page (see fig. 37.5).

2. To increase the volume, drag the slider to the right. To decrease the volume, drag the slider to the left.

3. Click OK after you have selected the correct volume level.

> **N O T E** This setting only affects sound coming out of the CD-ROM player's headphone jack or pass through line—common for audio CDs—not WAV or MIDI audio playing off of CD-ROM titles. ▨

FIG. 37.5

You can change the volume level for a specific CD-ROM drive using the CD Music page on the Multimedia Properties sheet.

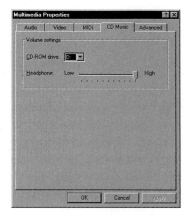

If you have more than one CD player installed, you can switch between CD players using the same Multimedia page:

1. Select the CD drive you want to use from the CD-ROM drive list.

2. Click OK.

Advanced Page

Clicking the Advanced tab of the Multimedia Properties sheet displays multimedia properties associated with different devices attached to your PC (see fig. 37.6). The Advanced page offers you access and control over the various video and audio compression schemes installed in your computer. It also provides a means of quickly taking stock of your system's multimedia playback capabilities.

FIG. 37.6

To display multimedia properties related to different devices, click the Advanced tab.

To configure the multimedia device of your choice, follow these steps:

1. Click the plus sign next to the type of multimedia device you are interested in. A sublist of associated devices appears.

2. Select the device you want to configure.

3. Click the Properties button at the bottom of the window.

4. Make the necessary changes on the Properties sheet and click OK. The Properties sheet is different for each type of device.

T I P You can change the default names for audio-specific devices listed under the Advanced page of the Multimedia Properties sheet. Click the plus (+) sign next to the device type you wish to customize, then right-click the device, and click Friendly Name from the context menu. Click Yes when prompted to change the name, and then type the new name of the device directly into the text box.

The Advanced sheet can be helpful for troubleshooting multimedia conflicts. For example, some systems may have multiple versions of the same codec installed on their system, a situation that can degrade or disable video playback. To remove a duplicate version of the Cinepak video compression/decompression driver (called a codec), do the following:

1. In the Advanced page, click the plus (+) sign next to the Video Compression Codecs item.

2. Select Cinepak (TM) and click the Properties button.

3. In the Cinepak (TM) Properties sheet, click the Settings button to view specific version information about the codec.

4. Return to the Cinepak (TM) Properties sheet, and click the Remove button.

5. Click Yes in the Remove Confirmation dialog box, and Windows 95 uninstalls the driver.

> **CAUTION**
>
> Removing drivers using the Multimedia Properties sheet can be dangerous. These items are removed from the hard disk and will not be available to your system unless you reinstall the software as the original medium. Some video files associated with the removed codec may not play back.

Customizing Windows 95's Multimedia Interface

Windows 95 is probably the first operating system that can talk, sing, and generally flash its way around. Click a button, and get a sound. Graphics come up at boot up, and application windows animate when they are opened and closed.

Get busy giving your system its own trademark style, whether it's playing classic movie lines at shut down, or putting your family photo on screen at boot up in lieu of those mildly-annoying Microsoft clouds. These tips will help you put the fun into your daily grind.

Sound Off: Playing with Audio

You probably know the sounds of Windows 95 all too well. That not-quite-winsome bell sound you get at boot up, and the familiar, if unloved, jangle of CHORD.WAV when you do something wrong. Windows 95 knows to play these sounds because they are associated with a scheme. Windows comes with a default scheme, and the Microsoft Plus! pack offers a variety of theme schemes that will drive you buggy with random whizzes and chirps at every mouse click (see fig. 37.7).

FIG. 37.7
Roll your own Windows sound
schemes from the Sound
Properties sheet.

But you can do better. To set your own audio scheme, double-click the Audio icon in the
Control Panel. You see the Sound Properties sheet, which controls all the interface noises
for your multimedia PC. To associate a sound with a Windows action—like when you
minimize a window—do the following:

1. In the Events scroll window, select the Minimize item.

2. In the Sound area, click the Name drop-down list box and select from the sound in
   the list.

 Can't find the sound you want on the list? Click the Browse button to find a WAV file anywhere on
your hard disk. Just don't go to your CD-ROM! Windows needs those systems sounds to be there
all the time.

3. Test a sound selected in the Name drop-down list box by clicking the Play icon to
   the right of the Preview window.

4. Now save your change to a custom sound scheme by clicking Save As, and entering
   a name in the Save this Sound Scheme As text entry box (see fig. 37.8).

FIG. 37.8
Save custom schemes, or
change existing ones, by
typing in the name in the
Save Scheme As dialog box.

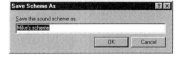

Registry Secret   While scrolling around the Events window of the Sounds Properties sheet, you may have noticed that the top-most Windows item is not the only entry beneath which indented events are displayed. The Windows Explorer entry, for example, includes an indented event entry for Empty Recycle Bin. And you may have noticed other entries installed by programs such as Delrina's CyberJack.

Did you know you can create new application entries, and assign sounds to specific events? To do this, you have to do a little Registry diving; but the results give you a great deal of power over the Windows 95 interface. For example, you can make your system play a WAV file whenever Media Player is opened or closed.

▶ **See** "Using the Registry Editor," **p. 435**

To add a new Media Player application item to the Sounds Properties' Events box, do the following:

1. From the Run command dialog box, launch REGEDIT.EXE.

2. Clicking the plus (+) sign next to each item, move down the directory tree to HKEY_CURRENT_USER/AppEvents/Schemes/Apps (see fig. 37.9).

3. Right-click Apps, and select New, then Key, from the fly-out context menu.

4. Enter **MPlayer** into the new key's text box.

5. Now right-click MPlayer, and select New and then Key from the fly-out context menu.

FIG. 37.9

With a little Registry diving, you can add new applications to Windows 95's sound schemes.

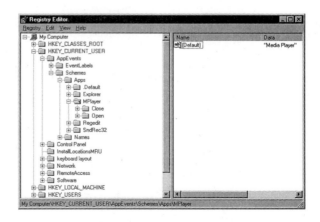

6. Type **Open** in the new key's text box.

7. Repeat step 5, and then type **Close** in the second new key's text box.

8. Close the Registry.

9. Now go back to the Sounds Properties sheet and scroll down the Events scroll window. You'll see a new entry called MPlayer, along with events called Close program and Open program, to which you can assign sounds.

Messing with the Sacred Cow—Changing Logo Graphics

When you finish fine-tuning Windows' audio settings, you can move on to graphics. During start up, Windows 95 displays a cloud-spotted splash screen. When you shut down your system, you see two screens, one warning you not to shut off the system yet, and the other confirming that your system can be shut down.

The files used to display these screens are stored in the Windows directory, and are called LOGO.SYS, LOGOW.SYS, and LOGOS.SYS. Don't be fooled by the SYS extensions, these are actually standard 256-color Windows bitmap files that are cloaked as hidden system files. To put your own images in their place—say, a family photo or special message—you need to save 320×200 pixel BMP files as LOGO.SYS, LOGOW.SYS, and LOGOS.SYS. Here's what you do:

N O T E Messing around with basic system files can cause problems booting up the system. Be sure to make back ups of the original image files to a floppy disk before making any changes. Some images may also not come out well at the resolution and colors required by Windows 95. ▓

1. Save the original images by copying LOGO.SYS, LOGOW.SYS, and LOGOS.SYS to a separate directory.

2. Create or open a 640×480 pixel image in Microsoft Paint (or another image editing program that can output to 256-color BMP format).

3. To match Windows' splash screen format, select Image, Stretch/Skew. In the dialog box, enter the value **50** in the Horizontal item found in the Stretch section, and press Enter.

4. Now adjust the vertical aspect ratio. Select Image, Stretch/Skew, and in the Stretch area enter **104** in the Vertical: box. Press Enter, and then select Image, Stretch/Skew again. Now enter **80** in the same Vertical box and press Enter.

5. Now save this 320 × 200 pixel image to 256-color BMP format, naming it LOGO.SYS, LOGOW.SYS, or LOGO.SYS.

6. Repeat the above steps for each splash screen file. Now, when you start or exit Windows, you'll see your custom images. ●

CHAPTER 38

Working with Graphics

by Michael Desmond

To enjoy the full potential of Windows 95's exciting new multimedia features, you have to know how to deal with graphics. Everything from home accounting software to CD-ROM titles to fast-action shoot-em-ups rely on fast, full-color graphics. In fact, graphics performance is vital to the quality of multimedia applications.

Fortunately, Windows 95 provides a vast improvement over the graphics tools of its predecessor. Gone is Windows 3.1's unhelpful System icon and its drop-down list of seemingly random driver choices. In its place is the Display Properties sheet and the Settings page, which provide logical tools to change resolutions, colors, and graphics drivers.

But there's more here than meets the eye. Windows 95 brings a variety of new graphics talents—not the least of which is the DirectDraw and Direct3D technologies—that enhance multimedia performance and game play. But you'll need the proper hardware and software to take advantage of these talents. Furthermore, there are a variety of tips and tricks that can help you squeeze more performance and greater convenience out of Windows 95. ■

Optimizing the Windows 95 display

This section shows you how to control colors, resolutions, and other key display settings of the Windows desktop.

Understanding Microsoft's DirectDraw technology

This graphics-boosting technology delivers fast game play and enhanced multimedia graphics to Windows 95 software.

Introducing 3-D graphics under Windows 95

Learn about Microsoft's big plans for interactive 3-D graphics, and what you need to take advantage of it.

Working with Windows 95's Graphics Tools

Windows 3.1 helped introduce multimedia applications by allowing colorful, high-resolution graphics on the PC. In addition, for the past two years virtually all PCs have shipped with accelerated graphics, which means the graphics board handles common Windows display tasks directly on the card. The result was quick display of scrolling text, color bitmaps, and other tasks that can otherwise overwhelm an unaccelerated PC.

Unfortunately, most people couldn't figure out how to take full advantage of these features. The ability to display multiple resolutions and color depths in Windows 3.1, for example, was hopelessly buried in the Windows Setup icon. And often users would be running their PC without the benefit of graphics acceleration, because they did not know the wrong driver software was installed. Thankfully, Windows 95 changes all that, with the Settings page of the Display Properties sheet (see fig. 38.1).

N O T E Windows 3.1's difficult interface and limited features prompted graphics card vendors to provide utilities that let users work with graphics settings. Now ATI, Diamond, Matrox, and other vendors provide utilities for Windows 95 that enhance and extend the features available to users. ▓

FIG. 38.1
The Display Properties Setting page provides a single, convenient place to change the resolution, color depth, and driver settings of Windows 95.

From the Display Properties sheet, you can customize your graphics displays to meet the demands of your applications. For example, a simple slider bar lets you explore the range of resolutions provided by your graphics card—and unlike Windows 3.1, you don't have to restart Windows after making the change. This sheet also lets you change the number of colors displayed and to change the driver for your graphics card—you'll need to restart your system for these changes to take effect.

N O T E The Windows 95 software that comes with some graphics cards may add a tabbed page or other element to the Display Properties sheet, where features specific to that card can be accessed. ▪

To bring up the graphics settings, right-click anywhere on the Windows desktop, click Properties on the context menu, and then click the Settings tab of the Display Properties sheet. You'll see items to change color depth and pixel resolutions, as well as driver settings.

T I P Make sure you get the most out of your graphics card by maximizing the acceleration settings. Double-click the System icon under Control Panel, click the Performance tab, and then click the Graphics button (see fig. 38.2). Drag the Hardware Acceleration slider bar all the way to the right, and click OK.

Part
X

Ch
38

FIG. 38.2
The Performance tab of the System Properties sheet includes settings for graphics acceleration.

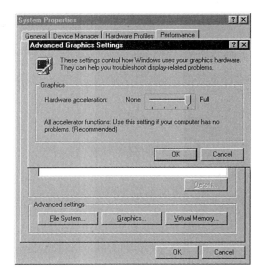

Changing the Screen Resolutions

Windows 95 makes it easy to change the number of pixels your graphics card displays on-screen, with a simple slider bar mechanism found in the Settings page of the Display Properties sheet. Increasing the resolution of the display allows you to view a much greater area of a document or program on-screen, reducing the time spent scrolling and searching for items off the screen. In fact, many multimedia applications require specific resolutions in order to run, so being able to change the pixel density of the display is important.

Windows 95 supports a variety of resolutions, depending on the amount of RAM on your graphics card. The following is a list of some of the settings you may find, and the size of monitor they are appropriate for:

- 640 × 480 pixels—best for text display on 14-inch monitors
- 800 × 600 pixels—best for text and graphics on 15-inch monitors
- 1024 × 764 pixels—best for text, graphics, and multimedia on 17-inch monitors
- 1280 × 1024 pixels—best for design work and graphics on 19- to 21-inch monitors
- 1600 × 1200 pixels—best for design work and document imaging on 21-inch and larger monitors

N O T E While you can run most multimedia software using a graphics card with 1M of RAM, you'll be able to support more colors and pixels—and even enjoy enhanced performance—with a 2M card. ▨

To change resolutions, go to the Settings tab of the Display Properties sheet, and do the following:

1. Click the Desktop Area slider bar, dragging it to the left to decrease screen resolution, and to the right to increase the resolution.

N O T E When you move the Desktop Area slider bar, the image of the Windows 95 desktop in the monitor screen on the Display Properties Settings page changes. This gives you an idea what the new setting looks like. ▨

2. Once you've set the desired resolution, click either the OK or Apply button at the bottom of the sheet.
3. Windows 95 displays a preview of the new graphics setting. If the resulting image is acceptable, click the OK button; if you wish to return to your original setting, click Cancel (see fig. 38.3).

FIG. 38.3
Once you've changed your graphics settings, Windows 95 gives you a chance to back out gracefully.

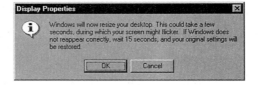

 If the image displayed in the preview mode is so garbled that you cannot make out the button to return to the original display, do not panic. Windows 95 waits 15 seconds for the user to accept or reject the new resolution setting, after which, it defaults back to the original setting.

Changing the Color Depth

Windows 95 also provides a standard way to change the number of colors displayed on the screen—a setting known as *color depth*. A drop-down list called Color Palette lets you choose from the available color settings. While most graphics cards can display as many as 16.7 million colors, by default Windows 95 provides four main options:

- *16 Colors*—rarely used
- *256 Colors*—best for productivity apps
- *High Color (16 bit)*—best for most multimedia apps
- *True Color (32 bit)*—best for detailed image editing and high-quality video

As you can see, Windows 95 refers to number of bits when talking about color depth. This refers to the number of bits of color information that is stored for each pixel on the display. For example, a 256 color display uses 8 bits per pixel of color information ($2^8 = 256$), while a High Color display uses 16 bits per pixel to display 65,536 colors ($2^{16} = 65,536$). As a result, you'll often see color settings referred to as 8-bit, 16-bit, and 24-bit graphics.

Windows 95 doesn't have a built-in setting for 24-bit color; instead it jumps straight to 32 bits. Unfortunately, if you have a 2M graphics card, using the 32-bit color setting limits you to a low pixel resolution of 640×480 pixels. The reason: So much graphic memory is used to store data for each pixel that there is no room to display a larger number of pixels.

▶ **See** "How Much is Enough: Graphic RAM," **p. 1109**

But no multimedia application or video file really needs true, 32-bit color, since the 16,777,216 colors in 24-bit color pixels already exceeds the visual acuity of the human eye. You should call your graphics card vendor or log onto one of their online forums to download a custom driver that will put a 24-bit color option in the Color Palette drop-down list.

 T I P While most multimedia programs need at least 256 colors to run, you'll want to set Windows 95 to High Color (16 bit) to get acceptable visual quality from video and graphics.

To change the color depth, go to the Settings tab of the Display Properties sheet, and do the following:

1. Click the Color palette drop-down list, and select the desired setting.
2. Click either the OK or Apply button at the bottom of the sheet.
3. Windows 95 displays a preview of the new graphics setting. If the resulting image is acceptable, click OK; or click Cancel to retain the original setting.

Part
X
Ch
38

4. If you click OK, Windows 95 informs you that the system needs to restart for the new settings to take effect. Click OK to restart your system under the new color depth.

TIP Once again, Microsoft's PowerToys freeware can help you out. The QuickRes utility lets you change resolutions *and* color depths on the fly, without restarting Windows. It also puts a graphics setting pop-up menu in the taskbar next to the Volume control, so you can switch settings without going to the Display Properties sheet. PowerToys is available online from Microsoft's forums and Web site.

ON THE WEB

http://www.microsoft.com/windows/software/PowerToy.htm PowerToys web site

> **CAUTION**
>
> Increasing the number of colors displayed significantly increases the work load on your system, particularly on the graphics card and CPU. If you have a slower 486 system or a PC without fast, local bus graphics, avoid using High Color and True Color settings.

Changing Refresh Rates

If you spend long hours working in front of PCs, you may have noticed that some displays seem to flicker more than others. That is not your imagination. Your graphics hardware actually sends an updated image to the monitor about 70 times a second. The frequency of screen updates, called *refresh rate*, determines how stable the image appears to the human eye. In general, your graphics board and display need to provide a refresh rate of 70 Hz, or 70 times per second, in order to avoid the perception of excessive flicker.

NOTE Low refresh rates can cause headaches and eyestrain, particularly during prolonged periods of work in front of a display. Generally, a refresh rate of 80 Hz and higher will provide comfortable viewing even on larger displays over long periods of time. ■

Unfortunately, Windows 95—like Windows 3.1—fails to provide tools for setting refresh rates. In general, Windows 95 sets your screen to industry-standard refresh rates of about 72 Hz, provided your graphics board and monitor are up to the task. While this setting is acceptable for most users with 15-inch monitors, those with sensitive eyes or with larger, brightly lit displays, may perceive excessive flicker.

To change the refresh rate, you'll need to contact your graphics card maker and request software that lets you adjust the settings. Some cards may even have Windows 95 driver software that puts refresh rate controls right into the Display Properties sheet.

Those with newer monitors and graphics boards may enjoy the benefits of a new Plug and Play standard, called Display Device Control or DDC. DDC automatically sets your hardware to the highest available refresh rate at any given resolution and color depth. However, both your monitor and graphics hardware must be DDC-aware in order to provide this service. When buying a monitor or graphics board, look for products that comply with the DDC-lab specification.

 If you can't eliminate the flicker on your display, go to the Appearance page of the Display Properties sheet and set the Windows background color to a neutral color, like gray (see fig. 38.4). This helps reduce perceived screen flicker.

FIG. 38.4
You can reduce eyestrain by setting the Windows color properties to a neutral color such as gray.

How Much is Enough: Graphic RAM

More than any other component, graphics RAM can limit the capability of your multimedia PC, particularly when it comes to displaying high-resolution, full-color video, graphics, and animation. Most PCs come with either one or two megabytes of RAM on their graphics card. We strongly recommend you get a 2M card, for two reasons:

- 64-bit graphics cards enjoy faster performance with 2M of RAM than with 1M.
- Your card can display more pixels and colors at the same time.

So how much memory do you need? To get 24-bit color, which is to say, 16.7 million colors, at 640×480 resolution, you need about 0.9M of memory. At 800×600 resolution, you need about 1.4M to get true-color 24-bit capability. Because graphics card memory comes configured by the megabyte, you'll end up needing either a 1M or 2M graphics frame buffer on your card.

Table 38.1 shows you how much memory you need to handle specific resolutions and color depths. Use this table to determine what you need for your multimedia apps.

Table 38.1 Graphics RAM table

	8-bit	16-bit	24-bit	32-bit
640×480	.3	.6	.9	1.2
800×600	.5	.9	1.4	1.8
1024×768	.8	1.5	2.3	3
1280×1024	1.3	2.5	3.8	5

Changing Graphics and Monitor Drivers

Like any multimedia hardware device, graphics boards and monitors must use a driver in order to talk to Windows. In Windows 3.1, changing graphics card drivers was a difficult and unintuitive task. Windows 95 eases this operation greatly, putting access to driver installation right in the Settings page of the Display Properties sheet.

To change your graphics board drivers, do the following:

1. Open the Display Properties sheet and click the Settings tab.
2. Click the Change Display Type button. The Change Display Type dialog box appears (see fig. 38.5).
3. To change the graphics board driver, click the Change button in the Adapter Type area. To change the monitor display driver, click the Change button in the Monitor Type area.
4. To select from compatible device drivers detected by Windows 95, click the Show Compatible Devices radio button in the Select Device screen (see fig. 38.6).
5. To manually select from Windows 95's installed list of drivers, click the Show All Devices radio button, and select the appropriate items from the Manufacturers scroll box and the Models scroll box.
6. If you wish to install drivers from an external source, say a floppy disk or CD-ROM, click the Have Disk button.

FIG. 38.5
To change the currently installed graphics board or monitor drivers, click the Change button in the appropriate area.

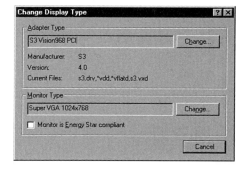

FIG. 38.6
Windows 95 comes with an exhaustive list of drivers for graphics boards and monitors. Choose from it by clicking the Show All Devices radio button.

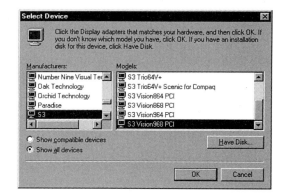

CAUTION
Be careful when setting your monitor drivers. If you tell Windows that an older, low-resolution monitor is some hot-shot 21-inch model, you could damage your hardware. Windows 95 may try to send signals beyond your monitor's range, potentially harming the unit.

Taking Advantage of DirectDraw

Microsoft spent a lot of time, effort, and money developing a way to make Windows 95 faster than its predecessor. At the core of that effort is graphics performance, which is critical to multimedia software and games. Microsoft developed a set of standard graphics shortcuts—called DirectDraw—to enable smooth video playback, fast screen updates, and satisfying game play.

DirectDraw is essentially the sequel to Intel's Display Control Interface (DCI). DCI debuted on Windows 3.1, but was replaced in Windows 95 with Microsoft's own homegrown technology. DirectDraw is the most important technology behind Microsoft's effort to make Windows 95 a premiere platform for games, and comprises several talents that let properly-equipped graphics adapters handle key tasks for the host CPU.

How DirectDraw Works

Actually, DirectDraw may not be on your system—yet. When Microsoft shipped Windows 95 in August 1995, DirectDraw was still under construction. So Microsoft designed it as a technology that can be added to Windows 95. Most users will install DirectDraw into their systems when they install Windows 95 games that use DirectDraw and the other DirectX technologies. Once DirectDraw and the appropriate graphics drivers are installed on your system, you'll see better performance from DirectDraw-compliant Windows 95 software.

▶ **See** "Installing and Enabling DirectDraw," **p. 1113**

DirectDraw does several things to streamline the slow performance of Windows' Graphics Device Interface (GDI). Most importantly, DirectDraw provides a feature called *direct frame buffer access.* (A frame buffer is the physical memory located on a graphics card.) This lets multimedia software send graphics commands straight to your graphics hardware—without a lot of translation among various layers of Windows software. The result is a significant performance boost, particularly in frame-based graphics such as video, animation, and game play (see fig. 38.7).

FIG. 38.7
Id Software's Doom95 is an example of a DirectDraw-compliant Windows 95 game.

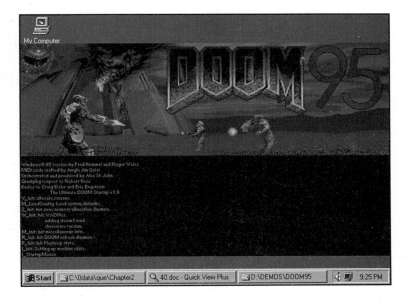

Doom for Windows 95, Microsoft Fury3, and The Hive are all examples of games using DirectDraw to speed graphics performance. Even video playback benefits because DirectDraw reduces the time it takes to put each frame of video into the graphics boards' memory. All boards with a DirectDraw driver, regardless of their hardware, should be able to provide efficient direct frame buffer access. DirectDraw also enables quicker block transfers, critical for applications like video and games, which move large chunks of data from memory to screen.

Installing and Enabling DirectDraw

Windows 95 does not ship with DirectDraw built in, so you need to upgrade it by one of several different methods. Microsoft has worked with makers of Windows 95 games to have DirectDraw, DirectSound, and DirectInput installed into the operating system at the same time the game itself is installed (see fig. 38.8). For those with existing systems, this is the most likely method of upgrade. The procedure is somewhat similar to the way that some titles install Video for Windows or QuickTime onto systems, with the installation routine checking the Windows 95 Registry for the existence of DirectDraw. If the routine fails to find DirectDraw—or finds an older version—it will install the DLLs into your Windows/System subdirectory and update your Registry.

Part

X

Ch

38

FIG. 38.8
During installation, Trimark Interactive's The Hive game tells you that it will install DirectDraw into your system.

TIP To see if DirectDraw is installed on your system, go into your Windows/System directory and look for a file called DDRAW.DLL.

But this performance boosting tool is of little use if your graphics card lacks the software to take advantage of it. For this reason, you need to upgrade your graphics card's driver software with a version that includes DirectDraw capability. Generally, you can use the Install/Remove New Hardware icon to setup new drivers.

T I P Call your graphics board vendor or check its online forums or web page to get a copy of the latest DirectDraw-enabled drivers software.

Double-click the file DXSETUP.EXE in the Directx subdirectory of the The Hive CD-ROM, and you'll see what version of DirectDraw and other DirectX items are installed into your Registry (see fig. 38.9).

FIG. 38.9
The DirectX Setup window displays the files installed into your Registry.

Enter the New Age: Windows 95 and 3-D Graphics

If you thought video and audio were the end-all of multimedia, you're selling yourself short. A series of rapid advances in both hardware and software have enabled the introduction of a whole new media to the multimedia stable—realtime 3-D graphics—and the result will be a profound change in computing. Unlike video, which is linear by nature and consumes tons of disk space, 3-D graphics allows complete freedom of movement and virtually endless creative possibilities. World building and exploration, rapid-fire shoot-em-ups, and mind-bending interfaces are but a few of the possibilities.

In fact, if you've played any flight simulator game such a Falcon Gold or EF2000, you've already got an idea of what 3-D graphics look like. The problem is that even the fastest Pentium PC gets bogged down in the ridiculous amount of math that it takes to put all those 3-D objects in the right place. Worse, these games must skimp on visual detail, realistic lighting, and other effects in order to provide smooth action. Figure 38.10 displays the tools in place to improve these graphics.

Part
X

Ch
38

FIG. 38.10

Applications like CorelDREAM 3D will improve vastly once Windows 95's 3-D tools are in place.

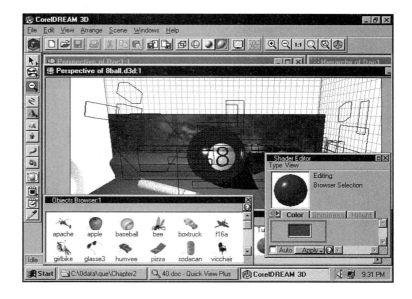

Windows 95 is helping to bring smooth, rich, detailed 3-D graphics and game play to the PC. Microsoft has developed a series of 3-D standards that will enable games and applications to work with a wide range of 3-D accelerating graphics hardware.

How 3-D Graphics Works

Yes, 3-D graphics hold a lot of promise, but the technology is radically different from the handling of the traditional 2-D graphics used to display your Windows desktop and icons. Instead of just giving a color value to a pixel and drawing it up on screen, Windows must literally build 3-D scenes brick by brick. Worse, your system has to paint those bricks, provide the lighting, and even account for atmospheric effects like fog, mist, or smoke.

Think of it as a paper maché model. When a Windows 95 game wants to put a 3-D scene onto your screen, it first builds a framework using thousands of little triangles or polygons. The software determines where each polygon goes and where it meets with its neighbor polygons. Next the software applies color or texture to the polygon surfaces, in effect laying the newspaper on top of the paper mache frame. In this process, referred to as *texture mapping*, the software will actually drape a pattern drawn from a small bitmapped graphic—say, an image of green grass—over the appropriate polygons in the scene. The result is striking visual realism.

After the structure is built, the software provides lighting. Here, your system figures things like how much light reflects off various surfaces, how much the light color affects the color of the surfaces, and so on. Effective lighting can provide dramatic effect—as anyone who has played Myst can attest—but the process of working with multiple lights of varying intensities, types, and color will bog down any system. Finally, your system has to determine what this built world will look like from the current user's perspective. That means juggling polygons to determine which ones go in front.

This detailed approach yields tremendous realism, but overtaxes even powerful systems. While there are specialized graphics cards that can handle polygon building, texture mapping, and other processes in hardware, none have been available to the mass market.

That's where Microsoft's Direct3D technology comes in. Direct3D is a layer in Windows 95 that will let a wide range of 3-D hardware and software work together. Better yet, Direct3D acts as a kind of 3-D diplomat, letting 3-D graphics hardware accelerate functions it's built for—say, texture mapping and polygon draws—and handing off to the CPU those tasks which need to be done manually. So if you upgrade your early-model 3-D card down the road for a deluxe model that features all the bells and whistles, Windows 95 will recognize the improvements, and automatically take advantage of it.

How to Get Interesting 3-D Graphics on Your PC

Microsoft is still working hard on the Direct3D components and other 3-D technologies, but hopes to deliver the tools necessary to make Windows 95 based 3-D games and hardware a reality by Christmas of 1996. When that time comes, getting Direct3D on your system will be a simple matter of installing the required software, probably as part of a game installation or graphics driver routine. The 3-D upgrade should, in effect, work just like it did with DirectDraw and other DirectX technologies.

In the meantime, you can enjoy accelerated 3-D graphics and game play, but it will be through any one of a number of proprietary systems. For example, Caligari's popular trueSpace 3-D authoring package uses Intel's 3-D handling technology called 3DR. Used in conjunction with a 3-D capable graphics card, such as the Matrox Millennium, that includes 3DR drivers, you are able to get accelerated 3-D now. But most games won't work with the Matrox card—in fact, Matrox includes a CD-ROM with several custom games with the Millennium board—so it's hard to justify the expense of dedicated hardware.

There are a number of 3-D software interfaces now on the market. The following list includes those you may find with current cards from companies like Diamond Multimedia, Matrox Graphics, and Creative Labs.

- Microsoft Direct3D
- Intel 3DR
- Argonaut BRender
- Creative Labs Creative Graphics Library (CGL)

Other popular 3-D boards include the Diamond Edge 3D and the Creative Labs 3D Blaster. The Edge board, for instance, is a dedicated Windows 95 card, and like the Millennium, comes with bundled games designed specifically for its hardware.

If you are excited about 3-D graphics and want to take advantage of the Direct3D technology when it arrives, buy for the future. You'll want a Pentium PC, 16M of RAM, and a PCI bus to plug a fast, 3-D aware card into. Then just hunker down and wait. By all accounts, this Christmas should see a rush of 3-D games and hardware. ●

Part

X

Ch

38

CHAPTER 39

Working with Video and Animation

by Michael Desmond

It's hard to overstate the importance of digital video in multimedia computing. PC-based video is cropping up everywhere, whether it's to deliver dramatic effect in CD-ROM titles and games, or provide informative tutorials for tax and finance software. But despite rapid advances in PC hardware, desktop video demands compromises in quality and system performance.

Windows 95 builds on two key technologies that emerged over the past year: Intel's Display Control Interface (DCI) that lets properly-equipped graphics boards enhance video playback, and MPEG video (for Motion Picture Expert Group), a high-quality, low-bandwidth video compression scheme that has emerged as a standard.

PC video has improved significantly, but a variety of challenges still face video quality. This chapter will help you get the most out of Windows 95 video, with tips and tricks for enhancing display and understanding playback. ∎

Working with the video tools in Windows 95

A discussion of video compression/decompression drivers in Windows, including MPEG video.

Understanding video file formats

A description of the video-boosting DirectVideo technology, and how to take advantage of it.

Understanding DirectVideo Acceleration

A discussion of video capture, and the hardware and software it requires.

How to capture video

Learn about breaking technologies like MPEG-2, Intel's Indeo Video Interactive, Apple's QuickDraw VR, and Microsoft's SurroundVideo.

Working with the Video Tools in Windows 95

Windows 95 has certainly given a boost to digital video. The 32-bit architecture of Windows 95 helps streamline video playback and eliminate pesky resource problems. Better yet, Windows 95 puts video capability directly into the operating system, which means that virtually anyone who has Windows 95 will be able to work with AVI files.

At the core of Windows-based video is the Media Control Interface, or MCI. MCI is an architecture that gives programs a standard, script-based interface to Windows multimedia resources, such as the Media Player, video playback windows, and audio controls. In addition, MCI enables programmatic control of video and audio, so development tools like Visual Basic, or even application macro scripts, can invoke and control video playback and editing. MCI is also at the core of object linking and embedding (OLE) video clips, where video clips are played within OLE-aware documents such as spreadsheets.

Beyond MCI and the familiar Media Player interface, users will notice that the device and video compression drivers needed to work with video are all pre-installed in Windows 95. As a result, you can distribute AVI video files to virtually any Windows 95 user, and be assured the file can be played back.

Windows 95 puts a wealth of video-centric tools into the hands of PC users. To help you get up to speed, here is a rundown of their operation.

The Video Properties Sheet

The Properties sheet for AVI files displays valuable data that can help you optimize video playback. Right-click any AVI file in an Explorer or Browser window, and select Properties from the context menu. You'll see a tabbed sheet that opens to the General page. Here, you're able to browse all the usual file information, like file name, size, and creation date.

Click the Details tab. Here you'll see the length of the video clip, the audio compression and fidelity, as well as the compression scheme, resolution, color depth, and frame rates of the clip (see fig. 39.1). It even provides the data rate, in KB/Sec (kilobytes per second), so you can tell if your CD-ROM drive is up to the task of playing the clip.

You also can preview the AVI file from the Properties sheet. Click the Preview tab, and you'll see the opening frame of the video (see fig. 39.2). To view the video, click the play button; or drag the slider control to move through the clip.

FIG. 39.1
The Details page reveals information such as data rates, color depth, and resolution.

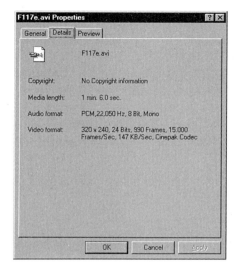

FIG. 39.2
The Preview page lets you sample AVI files.

Using the Windows 95 Media Player

The Media Player is the multimedia headquarters for Windows 95, and closely resembles the application found in Windows 3.1. One key exception: this Media Player is a native Windows 95, 32-bit application, with all the advantages and benefits that implies.

Media Player supports a wide variety of formats, such as Video for Windows video (AVI), sound (WAV), MIDI (MID), animation (FLC and FLI), and CD audio. It also accepts driver updates that let it support a variety of other formats, including QuickTime for Windows (MOV), MPEG video files, and other media types.

To play videos with Media Player, double-click an AVI file in an Explorer or Browser window. Media Player loads the AVI file and immediately starts playing it. You can open an AVI file from Media Player, by following these steps:

1. Choose Device, then click the Video for Windows option.

N O T E   The numbered hot key for selections beneath the Device menu vary depending on what multimedia drivers are loaded onto your system. ■

2. Select an AVI file in the Open dialog box, then click Open.
3. Click the play button in Media Player (see fig. 39.3).

FIG. 39.3

The Windows 95 Media Player uses simple, VCR-like controls.

When a video is playing, the play button changes to a pause button. You can stop the video by clicking the stop button or pause the video by clicking the pause button. To fast forward or rewind the video, click the double-arrow buttons. You also can advance to the beginning and end of a clip or section of video by clicking the Previous Mark and Next Mark controls. Finally, the Scroll Forward and Scroll Backward buttons just to the right of the slider bar allow you to do single-frame playback, great for finding a specific frame of video.

Sizing Video Windows   Media Player gives you the option of playing back a video clip at various sizes. While you can stretch a video window by grabbing it by the edge, doing so may distort the original image.

Most AVI clips measure either 320×240 or 160×120 pixels, an aspect ratio of 4:3. To change the video window size while preserving the aspect ratio, go to Media Player's properties sheet by choosing Device, Properties.

Click the Windows drop-down list box to see the available selection of window sizes for video playback (see fig. 39.4). You can select from Double Original Size, 1/16 of Screen Size, 1/4 of Screen Size, 1/2 of Screen Size, and Maximized. The monitor image in the Video Properties sheet will show an approximation of what the resized video will look like, complete with blocky pixelation.

FIG. 39.4
Expand and shrink video
windows from the Video
Properties sheet.

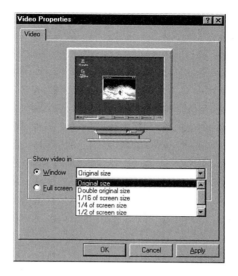

TIP Unless you have video enhancing hardware and drivers for Windows 95, you will usually get best results by playing videos at Original Size. Stretching or shrinking video forces the CPU to do additional processing, causing lost frames.

TIP If you want the best full screen video, click the Full Screen radio button, and not the Maximized setting on the drop-down list. Windows 95 can streamline video playback when it does not have to manage graphical user interface (GUI).

Working with Scale Settings   When Media Player plays a video clip, it uses a frame- or time-based scale to measure progress. This scheme lets you find specific points in the video, so you can easily edit, play, or copy selected parts of video files. For example, a frame-based scale lets you perform frame-accurate video editing and tracking. To have Media Player display the scale by frames, choose Scale, Frames. To have the scale expressed in minutes and seconds, choose Scale, Time. The display beneath the video progress slider bar will change to reflect the new setting. You can even do this while a clip is playing.

Setting Playback Options   Media Player lets you customize the look and function of a video window during playback. For instance, you can set a video to play back continually, starting again at the beginning after it is completed. Choose Edit, Options (or press Ctrl+O) to see the Options dialog box (see fig. 39.5). When checked, the controls in this dialog box allow you to do the following:

Part
X

Ch
39

FIG. 39.5

Media Player's Options dialog box lets you control the look and behavior of video clips.

- *Auto Rewind* queues the video clip back to the beginning after the clip is finished playing.
- *Auto Repeat* forces the clip to play in a loop until the user stops playback.
- *Control Bar On Playback* puts start/stop and slider bar controls on video files embedded into other applications using Windows' (OLE) technology.
- *Caption* lets you change the text that appears in the control bar on OLE embedded video clips.
- *Border Around Object* draws a border around an embedded video while it plays.
- *Play in Client Document* lets the embedded video run inside the OLE application document, without invoking a separate video window.
- *Dither Picture to VGA Colors* if the color in a video clip looks distorted.

Control the Volume   If a clip is too loud for your tastes, you can adjust the volume by choosing Device, Volume Control. The Windows 95 Volume Control dialog box appears, with slider controls to handle the volume, balance, and mute settings for all the various audio inputs and outputs.

 You also can adjust volume by clicking the speaker icon located in the taskbar, invoking a slider control that adjusts volume.

▶ **See** "Understanding the Audio Properties Box,"**p. 1140**

Media Player Secrets   There are a lot of features in Media Player that you won't find in the interface or the Help file. Some of these features can help you understand and take advantage of video on your multimedia PC.

For example, pressing Ctrl+F5 when the Media Player application is open invokes the Send MCI String Command dialog box. From here, you can enter a variety of powerful text commands to play, adjust, or get information on video files.

Here's a quick list of Media Player secrets:

■ *Count frames.* Media Player tracks how many frames drop during playback. To see how many frames dropped after a clip has played, press Ctrl+F5 to invoke the Send MCI String Command dialog box (see fig. 39.6). Type **status frames skipped** in the Command box, and click Send. You'll see how many frames were dropped during video playback.

FIG. 39.6
Use the status frames skipped MCI call to see how many frames were dropped during playback.

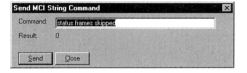

■ *More MCI command tricks.* You can type other commands in the Command box that appear after pressing Ctrl+F5. For example, to pause a video, press Ctrl+F5, and type **pause**. You also can type **stop**, **play**, and **close** in the MCI String Command dialog box.

■ *Drag-and-drop video.* Media Player won't look at your CD-ROM drive for video by default, forcing lots of pointing and clicking. Take a shortcut by dragging the icon of an AVI file in a Browser or Explorer window onto the Media Player application. You'll see the telltale mouse cursor with a plus sign. Release the button, and the file will open and begin playing right away in the background.

Part
X

Ch
39

■ *Compact video playback.* With a video window open, double-click the Media Player application title bar. You'll get a consolidated video window (without a separate Media Player window) that includes start/stop and pause buttons and a slider bar (see fig. 39.7).

FIG. 39.7
The consolidated video window saves screen space.

■ *Change video size.* This tip is particularly useful when using the compact playback window. Expand a video window to full screen by pressing Ctrl+4, and return to original size by pressing Ctrl+1. Ctrl+2 doubles the window size, and Ctrl+3 quadruples it.

Understanding Video File Formats and Compression

Digital video puts excessive strain on the most powerful PCs. Video files consist of a long string of color images, which are played one after the other in rapid succession to create the illusion of fluid motion. For digital video, 30 frames per second is considered full-motion, though many video clips are recorded at 15 or 24 frames per second to ease play-back. And don't forget the work that goes into synchronizing the audio that goes with each video image.

To enable digital video, there obviously needed to be standard file formats and compression technologies. But standards could not overcome the challenge of managing so much data. For that, technologies had to be created that took the pressure off the PC's CPU. In 1992, Video for Windows 1.0 helped establish some key standards. More recently, the PC platform has embraced the elements needed to enhance video.

Understanding Video File Formats

To handle this flood of data, there needed to be video file formats that gave the PC a place to start. Today, there are a variety of video formats. Among those you are most likely to encounter are: Video for Windows (AVI), QuickTime for Windows (MOV), MPEG (MPG), and Motion JPEG (MJG). These video formats are described in the following section.

Audio Visual Interleave—AVI   This is the standard video file format for Windows. AVI is the most common Windows video file format, and can be played back on virtually any PC running Windows 3.11 or later.

As the name suggests, the audio data and video data are meshed together in the file, allowing systems to synchronize sound and images. Ironically, video playback is slaved to the audio track, ensuring that you will always hear all of the audio, even if your system drops video frames. While you can still make sense of a video that drops even a majority of its frames, the loss of audio data makes it impossible to understand what's being presented. For this reason, even when frames are lost, the soundtrack goes on uninterrupted—except in extreme cases.

AVI video files can be compressed using a variety of schemes, including Intel's Indeo, Radius' Cinepak, and Microsoft's Video1. While each of these will produce a video with distinctive characteristics, the AVI format itself is unchanged. You can play the video, provided that you have the proper decompression driver (Windows 95 ships with all of these).

Apple's QuickTime Video for Windows—MOV   Apple made a splash in the video world with its QuickTime technology, which multimedia developers snatched up for use in their titles. When Apple developed QuickTime for Windows, it immediately became a force on the PC, since so many multimedia titles used QuickTime as their video format. While Windows 95 does not ship with QuickTime drivers, a large percentage of multimedia titles use QuickTime video, so they will install the drivers during setup.

Like AVI files, QuickTime MOV files can be compressed using a variety of compression schemes, though Radius' Cinepak is most popular. The QuickTime drivers include tools for handling decompression; so as long as you have QuickTime installed, you should be able to play back MOV files (see fig. 39.8).

FIG. 39.8
Select the Advanced tab of the Multimedia Properties sheet to see if QuickTime for Windows is installed.

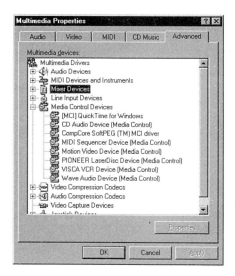

Part
X

Ch
39

N O T E   To see if your system is QuickTime-ready, click the Multimedia icon in the Control Panel; then click the Advanced tab, and click the plus sign next to Media Control Devices. You should see an entry called (MCI) QuickTime for Windows. If you don't, you will need to install QuickTime before MOV files can be played. ▦

The Next Big Thing in Video—MPEG   Unlike Video for Windows and QuickTime for Windows, MPEG is both a file format and a codec scheme. MPEG videos are crunched down to a very small size using the MPEG compression scheme, which does all sorts of mathematics and interframe comparisons. The result is video of much higher visual quality than other schemes, yet using a tiny 150 kilobits per second (kb/sec) of data—low enough to run off a single-speed CD-ROM drive. But MPEG is very complex, and high-end PCs have only recently reached the level where they can play back MPEG video without expensive add-in cards.

> **N O T E**   As with QuickTime, you can check the Advanced page of the Multimedia Properties
> sheet for MPEG drivers. Click the plus sign next to Media Control Devices, and look for
> an entry that refers to MPEG. ▨

To get MPEG playback capability, you need one of several MPEG software players. Xing, Mediamatics, and CompCore all sell MPEG player software. In addition, many graphics boards come with MPEG player software as part of their bundle. Those with Pentium-75 or slower machines should buy a dedicated MPEG add-in board to get acceptable MPEG performance. Number Nine's FastMPEG and Elsa, Inc.'s ElsaMotion are examples of PCI-based MPEG decoders that pipe decompressed MPEG video to the monitor.

Understanding Video Compression Schemes (codecs)

The only way digital video can be played on a PC is to reduce the amount of data required to store and move it. Video compression/decompression algorithms, referred to as *codecs*, do just that, reducing streams of full-color images into compact code. Your system's CPU must decode the compressed video before it can be displayed to screen, a time-consuming task that often results in dropped frames.

> **N O T E**   Don't confuse video codecs with video file formats. A file format like AVI or MOV can
> often be compressed using a number of codecs. For example, AVI files can be
> compressed using Indeo, Cinepak, Video1, and TrueMotion codecs, just to name a few. ▨

Unlike file compression utilities like PKZip or Stacker, video compression schemes actually throw out a good deal of image data to achieve compact file sizes. For this reason, video codecs are referred to as "lossy," while file compressors are referred to as "lossless."

> **N O T E**   While lossless compression schemes like PKZip will achieve compression ratios of
> about 2:1, lossy video compression schemes can shrink files sizes by 100 times or
> more, for ratios of 100:1. ▨

Video codecs save a great deal of space by discarding redundant data. For example, MPEG only saves changes that occur between video frames, instead of storing all the data in every single frame. In addition, codecs can discard color, brightness, and other visual data, because much of the detail is not actually visible to the human eye. However, most software codecs, such as Indeo and Cinepak, must throw out a great deal of visual information to achieve data rates of about 300 kbps. The result is grainy video and visual artifacts such as banding and color distortion.

Before your system can decompress a video file, you need to have a driver installed that lets the system know how to do it. To see if you have drivers installed to handle, say, Cinepak video, go back to the Multimedia Properties sheet from Control Panel's Multimedia icon. Click the Advanced tab, and then click the plus (+) sign next to Video Compression Codecs. You'll see a list of installed codecs (see fig. 39.9).

FIG. 39.9
Windows 95 comes standard with seven codecs, though you can install more.

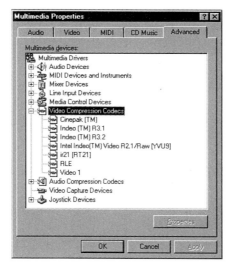

Among the most common video codecs are:

- Indeo
- Cinepak
- Video1
- RLE
- TrueMotion
- MPEG
- Motion JPEG

Intel Indeo 3.2   Intel's Indeo codec was among the first on the PC, and is among the most prevalent. Indeo 3.2 is included with Windows 95, making it a universal playback compression scheme. To play an Indeo-compressed AVI file, you need to open the file from Media Player. Media Player automatically detects the codec used to compress the file, and invokes the Indeo driver to decode it. Indeo is generally favored for video clips that contain less motion and activity, such as interviews and speeches.

Radius Cinepak 8.02   Cinepak was developed by Radius, and is also bundled with Windows 95. The Cinepak codec is popular with title vendors, because it is able to compress high-action sequences without too much loss of visual quality and CPU effort. However, the latest release of Indeo (3.2) has largely closed the performance gap. Cinepak-compressed files can be found in both Video for Windows and QuickTime for Windows files.

Microsoft Video1   Microsoft Video1 was included in the first Video for Windows release in 1992, but lacks the sophistication to handle rich, full-color video. While the Video1 codec works well for animation and other simple video compression tasks, it is limited to 8-bit color and lacks interframe compression.

MPEG   MPEG doesn't ship with Windows 95—at least, it doesn't yet. Microsoft plans to include support for this high-quality, low-bandwidth video codec in a future version of the Windows 95 operating system, perhaps by the summer of 1996. Users can get MPEG playback now by purchasing a separate playback utility, from companies like Xing, CompCore, and Mediamatics. Microsoft, for instance, is licensing Mediamatics MPEG player for use in Windows 95.

 TIP   Many graphics boards come bundled with MPEG playback software. Check your board's software for MPEG video drivers.

The secret to MPEG is its complex interframe compression, where only changes between frames are stored in the MPEG video file. The problem is that this scheme requires a lot of processing horsepower, which is why it takes a Pentium-90 PC (or better) to handle MPEG adequately in software. Older systems can play back MPEG video using an add-in card, such as the RealMagic Rave or Number Nine MPEG-Plus, to handle the decompression.

The Editor's Choice—Motion JPEG   Motion JPEG, like MPEG, is both a file format and a codec. Actually, Motion JPEG is an outgrowth of the JPEG (Joint Photographers Expert Group) file format, which is a popular still image compression scheme for files posted on the Internet. Motion JPEG's main appeal is to video artists and editors, because every frame is compressed individually. By contrast, MPEG compression stores only the changes that occur between frames of video—so if you want to go back and edit a frame, it's likely that some visual data will be missing.

Video capture boards such as the Reveal VideoStudio Pro and miroVideo DC-20 capture to Motion JPEG format. Files compressed to Motion JPEG format often look better than QuickTime or Video for Windows clips, but require more CPU and greater data bandwidth. But the files can be recompressed to AVI or MOV, though video quality will likely degrade.

The Future of Codecs—MPEG-2   New codecs are constantly being developed and updated to meet the needs of digital video. MPEG-1, for example, has a big brother by the name of MPEG-2, which is a broadcast-quality compression scheme used with DSS services such as DirecTV. MPEG-2 excels where MPEG-1 breaks down—for instance, in the display of high-action sequences where the efficiencies of interframe compression are lost. But MPEG-2 requires 10 times the bandwidth of MPEG-1—as much as 1.5Mbps— which means current CD-ROM drives are unable to keep up. In addition, MPEG-2's large file sizes mean that CD-ROM discs could only hold scant minutes of MPEG-2 video. For this reason, MPEG-2 is likely to remain a consumer video codec until PC users adopt super density compact discs with several gigabytes of storage capacity.

The Future of Codecs—Indeo Video Interactive   Perhaps more relevant is Intel's Indeo Video Interactive, also known as Indeo 4.0. This intriguing codec breaks with the past by adopting a wavelet-based compression scheme that reduces access times and visual artifacts. Intel has claimed—and some independent CD-ROM title developers have confirmed—that Indeo 4.0 can challenge MPEG video for visual quality. However, like MPEG, Indeo 4.0 really needs a Pentium CPU to handle the complex decompression; and it's unclear if Indeo 4.0 can really match MPEG quality at the low 150kbps data rate that MPEG maintains.

Indeo 4.0 provides powerful streaming and branching technologies, enabling video to be used in interactive games. For example, multiple video streams can be played on a single display—providing, say, a simultaneous rear view video while the player looks forward. The format also enables much faster access, so video can be employed in fast-action games without annoying delays. These features could turn Indeo 4.0 into *the* codec for Windows 95.

Finally, Indeo 4.0 includes powerful chromakey and overlay support. For example, Indeo 4.0 videos do not have to be constrained to a video window. Instead, video images can float on the Windows desktop and interact with other Windows elements. These features provide exciting new opportunities for hobbyists and publishers alike.

Part
X

Ch
39

Windows Video Primer: DirectVideo, and Other Nifty Things in Windows 95

To lessen the load, video files are compressed down to smaller sizes to conserve disc space, ease bus traffic, and enable higher frame rates. In fact, without compression, video playback would be impossible on even the most powerful PCs. But compression has its own costs, since the CPU must take time to decode the encoded video stream.

There's more to playing digital video than simply decompression. The CPU also must handle a variety of other tasks to turn an encoded pile of bits into a smooth train of images that make video:

- *Decompression.* The encoded video file is reassembled by the CPU, using the appropriate driver, such as an Indeo, Cinepak, or MPEG decoder. Some compression/decompression schemes require a great deal of computing power, but yield better looking images at lower data rates.

- *Color space conversion.* To save disc space, the color data in video files is usually saved using a compact format called YUV, which is optimized to the sensitivities of the human eye. This YUV color data must be converted to the standard RGB (Red, Green, Blue) format recognized by graphics cards and monitors. Color space conversion can take up to 30 percent of the CPU processing time during video playback.

N O T E   YUV stands for luminence, hue, and saturation, and is a method for composing color video signals that was originally applied to television broadcasting. The main advantage of YUV color is that it is much more compact than the RGB format used by computers. ■

- *Image scaling.* This step occurs when the user changes the size of the video window from its original size. Often, 320 × 240 pixel videos are displayed at full screen to ease viewing. However, the CPU must calculate and create all the new pixels that appear in the image, further straining the system. In addition, the image that results appears blocky and pixelated, since the CPU simply replicates pixels to fill in the larger window.

Improved Video Performance

The big problem with video is that it's, well, big. Real big. A modest video saved at 320 × 240 pixels and 15 frames per second would push 3M per second of data through your system if played uncompressed. Even with compression, video floods your system with data, taxing your CD-ROM drive, clogging the system bus, and pushing your processor to the limit. When these demands outstrip your PC, Windows has no choice but to drop frames to keep up.

A number of recent performance enhancements make it possible for Windows 95 to playback 320 × 240 video files at 30 frames per second. Even better, these videos can be stretched up to 640 × 480 pixels and beyond, and still enjoy smooth motion, provided you have the right drivers and multimedia hardware installed. Among the enhancements are:

- *DirectDraw.* DirectDraw allows accelerated access to the memory on your graphics card, key for pushing 30 frames of video each second. In essence, DirectDraw is a graphics shortcut that lets video software talk directly to your graphics hardware, eliminating Windows' slow graphics engine. DirectDraw also provides pixel scaling and color space conversion features.

■ *DirectVideo.* The second half of Microsoft's video improvement plan, DirectVideo opens the door to hardware accelerated video under Windows 95. DirectVideo lets inexpensive graphics hardware take over key video playback tasks from the CPU, by providing an interface into DirectDraw.

N O T E Like other DirectX components, DirectDraw and DirectVideo both ship separately from the Windows 95 operating system. Most users will get DirectDraw and DirectVideo when they install software that uses DirectX technology, such as games or titles. ■

■ *CDFS.* The CD File System improves throughput from the CD-ROM by providing an optimized, 32-bit, protected-mode file system. The result is improved performance of CD-ROM drives in Windows 95, which reduces dropped frames. CDFS also takes some of the burden off the system CPU, allowing it more time to decompress video files (see fig. 39.10).

FIG. 39.10
Windows 95 may not recognize your CD-ROM drive, and use slower compatibility-mode drivers. Check the Performance page of the System Properties sheet to see if your CD-ROM drive is not fully optimized.

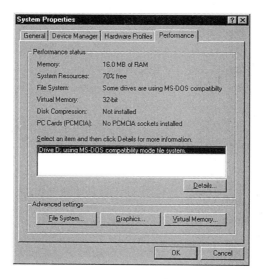

■ *Multitasking.* Windows 95's preemptive multitasking minimizes pauses and delays during video playback; these breaks in the continuity can ruin the viewing experience. Video can continue to play even while other processes, such as display of separate graphics, run in the background.

Enhanced CD-ROM and file management benefit all aspects of your computer's performance, but DirectDraw and DirectVideo are aimed squarely at improving multimedia and video. The good news is that you don't need to throw out your existing graphics hardware to play games and software using Direct X technologies. However, you will enjoy much better video playback if your graphics card includes the proper drivers and video-intelligent hardware.

DirectVideo works by first checking the graphics card and finding out what video-accelerating features, if any, are supported in the hardware. Windows then knows to send key tasks like color space conversion and pixel scaling straight to the graphics card, if it is properly configured. If the card lacks enhanced video support, all the video handling tasks are sent straight to the system CPU.

N O T E   The newest graphics hardware does little good without the proper drivers. Otherwise, Windows 95 will send all the video tasks straight to the system CPU, even if you have a video-accelerating card. In fact, Windows 95 can fail to install the specific driver you need. Check the installed driver from the Display Properties sheet by clicking the Change Display Type button. ▦

Older boards, such as those based on graphics chips such as S3's Vision864 and Vision964, lack video enhancing hardware; you won't see much improvement in video performance even with DirectVideo installed. However, most mid-range graphics boards sold over the last two years are video savvy. Look for boards based on S3's Vision868, Vision-968, and Trio64 graphics chips. Matrox's Millennium board, which uses the company's own MGA chip, also provides video acceleration features.

Of course, you'll need DirectDraw and DirectVideo drivers to let Windows 95 know that the multimedia features are there. Contact your graphics card vendor and make sure you have the latest DirectVideo-enabled drivers.

CAUTION
If you only have 16-bit drivers for multimedia graphics boards such as the Jazz Jakarta or miroVideo 20TD, Windows 95 will probably be unable to provide the full functionality that these boards had under Windows 3.1. Contact the board's vendor to get 32-bit drivers.

New Developments in Windows 95 Video

Windows 95 delivers many improvements to desktop video playback, but there is more to come. Microsoft has announced a limited road map of features, functions, and new video types that should enhance the quality of CD-ROM games and titles. This section gives you a sneak peek at what to expect next.

Among the key technologies promised by Microsoft are:

- Surround Video
- WinToon
- Active Movie

Surround Video   Microsoft's Surround Video, a scheme similar to Apple's QuickTime VR, lets developers build 360-degree photo-realistic scenes. Users will be able to interact with on-screen objects, images, and videos as they traverse immersive scenes.

Surround Video scenes consist of a series of photographs stitched together into a 360-degree panorama, allowing users to turn and view an entire scene. Games can use Surround Video to put photo-realistic backgrounds behind interactive elements. But Surround Video is even better suited for creating virtual tours built from actual photos.

For users, Surround Video is something that comes as part of the games and other software they purchase.

WinToon   Another content creation tool is Wintoon. Aimed at high-quality animation playback, WinToon lets developers create full-screen, high frame rate animations. Best of all, it lets animators work in the familiar cel format, so they don't have to adapt their techniques for publishing to CD-ROM. WinToon playback support within Windows 95 means that software developers can count on WinToon being available for their products.

Active Movie   Just recently announced, Active Movie is a multimedia development technology in Windows 95 that will let developers create interactive content. Details are sketchy at this point, but the technology should allow developers to enable user interaction with video streams. In addition, Active Movie will enable mixed video, animation, and 3-D graphics playback, for a true multimedia experience in games and titles.

Part
X

Ch
39

Creating Digital Video in Windows 95

Perhaps more than anywhere else, Windows 95 improved the lot of those who wish to create multimedia content, particularly digital video clips. In fact, Windows 95 is able to deliver video capture performance on a par with that of Windows NT 3.51, a true workstation-level operating system.

Windows 95 also improves the editing of captured video. Whether it's splicing digital video, adding special effects, or compressing clips to a new format, Windows 95's efficient architecture improves the editing experience.

Capturing Video   Capturing video is probably one of the most difficult tasks you can ask of a desktop PC. The process strains virtually every component of your computer—from the capture card that's hooked to the analog video device, to the system bus that must carry data to the CPU, to the CPU that must process video in real-time.

T I P   To get the best video capture results, scan and defragment your hard drive before the capture session using Windows 95's built-in disk tools found by choosing Start, Programs, Accessories, System Tools (see fig. 39.11). This will improve data throughput, since the drive head won't have to jump around to find free space on the disk.

FIG. 39.11
Pave a smooth road for your captured video files by using Windows 95's defragment utility.

Windows 95's preemptive multitasking and 32-bit memory addressing are a welcome improvement. Gone is the frantic hop-scotch of 16-bit memory addressing, which builds transactional overhead into every process. Meanwhile, preemptive multitasking lets direct memory access (DMA) peripherals like capture cards send a steady flow of data, without being rudely interrupted by unrelated system events.

Capturing video is not cheap. Or easy. Here's what you'll need:

- *A video capture board*, such as the $999 miroVideo DC20 or the $450 Reveal Video Artist. Those capturing to MPEG format might consider the $5000 Sigma Designs RealMagic Producer or even the $8000 Optibase MPEG Encoder, which is aimed at professionals. If you have a PCI-based system—and you'll be much better off if you have one—make sure the capture board is designed for the PCI bus. You'll get much better video capture data rates and enjoy smoother installations.

- *A big and fast SCSI hard disk.* Get at least 1.6G of data capacity or more, and look for disk access times of 10 milliseconds or below. A fast PCI connection is also vital. Seriously consider a so-called A/V drive, which boosts data rates by foregoing data integrity features such as thermal recalibration of the disk. You can go with a less expensive drive using EIDE (enhanced integrated device electronics) logic.

- *Lots of RAM.* You'll need at least 16M to even consider playing around with video capture. Video professionals often use 64M or even 128M of RAM to ensure that data flows smoothly, and doesn't get hung up by having Windows go to slow virtual memory. Also make sure your system has a 256K cache, to maintain quick flow of data to the processor.

- *A fast processor.* A 90 MHz or faster Pentium CPU is needed for adequate results.

- *An analog video source*, such as a TV, VCR, camcorder, or laser disc player. The analog source must have an output that feeds directly to the capture card, via a connector such as an S-Video or Composite output.

To capture incoming video, you'll need video capture software. Virtually all video capture cards feature a capture utility, though programs such as Adobe Premiere feature capture utilities as well.

T I P When possible, you should use the capture utility that came with the video capture card. Vendors often optimize their hardware to work with their own capture utility, so you may get better results than if you use the generic capture feature in Adobe Premiere, for example.

Windows 95 also provides a way to control specific analog components. In the Multimedia Properties sheet's Advanced page, you'll see a list of entries under the Media Control Devices item. Two of these, the VISCA VCR Device (Media Control) and the PIONEER LaserDisc Device (Media Control) entries, are drivers that let you control attached components from your PC.

Windows 95 is set up to control only a few prosumer-oriented analog components. The VISCA driver, for example, lets you work with Sony video editing equipment connected to your PC over a COM port (see fig. 39.12).

Part
X

Ch
39

FIG. 39.12
The VISCA VCR Device Properties sheet gives you remote control of some prosumer-level video editing equipment from Sony.

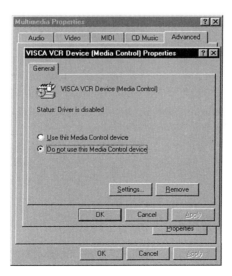

CHAPTER 40

Working with Audio

by Michael Desmond

Just as digital video has improved over the last three years, PC audio has come a long way. The original Sound Blaster board delivered audio quality about on par with that of a dashboard AM radio. Today, sound boards have evolved to handle CD-quality sound, reproduce realistic MIDI scores, and even create compelling 3-D audio for games and titles. Most importantly, the majority of PCs sold now include installed sound boards.

In the past, intractable audio conflicts and difficult installations made PC-based audio difficult to manage. Windows 95 has improved the situation, providing a set of standard interfaces and applications that make working with audio easier than before. In addition, Windows 95 reduces the amount of CPU processing needed to play back audio, which enhances game play. ■

Working with audio tools in Windows 95

Learn how to handle digital sounds to get the most out of your PC.

Understanding the Windows audio architecture and DirectSound

See how Windows 95 makes audio controls a snap to access and use.

Understanding 3-D audio

Learn about the latest development in audio hardware and software. While virtually any application can make use of 3-D audio, game and title software developers are most aggressive about adopting it.

N O T E Your sound card's drivers determine the advanced features that you can access from Windows 95. For example, some drivers provide controls for bass/treble adjustments, while others only support the most basic volume settings. ■

Using Audio Tools in Windows 95

Handling digital sounds can be a difficult task, and understanding how audio works is vital to making the most of your PC. For example, uncompressed Windows wave audio files (WAV) can consume up to 10M of hard disk space per minute, as well as clog your PC's performance.

PC-based audio comes in two forms, wave audio and MIDI. *Wave audio*, or *WAV* files, are essentially digital recordings of the sounds you hear. When you record your voice on the PC, for example, you are creating a wave audio file that is a digital representation of your analog voice.

MIDI files (or *musical instrument device interface*), on the other hand, use a series of commands to tell your PC's sound hardware what notes and instruments to play. Similar to a music roll on a player piano, MIDI scores tell your PC which notes to play. This makes for smaller files, but you are limited by the library of instruments available to your hardware and software.

Windows 95 provides a number of tools to help you play, edit, and create audio files. This section will help you master those capabilities.

Understanding the Audio Properties Box

Windows 95 gives you information on any file when you right-click the file and select Properties from the shortcut menu. The Properties sheet for WAV and MIDI files displays key information on the size, length, and format of the file. The General page features the usual file size and type information. If you click the Details tab, you'll see its audio fidelity and how the WAV file was compressed (see fig. 40.1). If you want to hear a WAV or MIDI clip, click the Preview tab, and then click the play button. The clip will play without opening Media Player (see fig. 40.2).

For more on how to use Media Player, see Chapter 37, "Working with Multimedia."

FIG. 40.1

The Details page of the Properties sheet shows you the audio fidelity of a WAV clip, as well as its length in seconds.

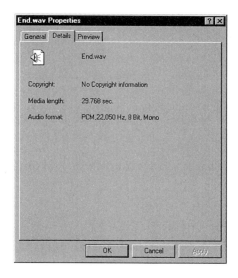

FIG. 40.2

You can even play WAV and MIDI files from the Properties sheet's Preview page.

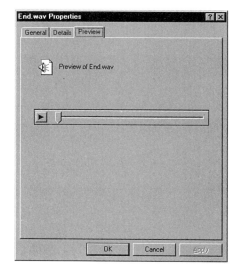

Part

X

Ch

40

Using the Windows 95 Media Player with Audio

The 32-bit Media Player in Windows 95 plays WAV and MIDI audio files. Media Player can accept drivers for additional audio formats, which are added to the list of options available under the Device menu item.

You can open a WAV or MIDI file using Media Player in a couple of ways. The easiest method is to double-click a file that has a WAV or MID extension. Windows 95 automatically associates these file types with Media Player, so Media Player launches and the selected file immediately begins playing.

You also can open a WAV or MID file from within Media Player. To do so, follow these steps:

1. Click the Device menu.
2. Click the option for either Sound or MIDI Sequencer.

N O T E The numbered hotkey for the displayed media types vary according to what drivers are installed in your system. ▨

3. In the Open dialog box, select a WAV or MID file and click Open.
4. Click the play button in Media Player.

The Media Player controls are identical to those used to play and control AVI video files, with a few exceptions. The Options dialog box (choose Edit, Options) contains an item called Dither Picture to VGA Colors, which is disabled for audio playback because it optimizes video playback with 16 colors. Also, the Scales menu is limited to Time because there are no frames in digital audio.

▶ **See Chapter 39**, "Using the Windows 95 Media Player," **p. 1121**

When an audio file is playing, the play button changes to a pause button. You can stop the video by clicking the stop button or pause the video by clicking the pause button. To fast forward or rewind the video, click the appropriate double-arrow button. You can also advance to the beginning and end of a clip or section of video by clicking the Previous Mark and Next Mark controls. Finally, the Scroll Forward and Scroll Backward buttons just to the right of the slider bar allow you to do single-frame playback—great for finding a specific frame of video.

For WAV file playback, the Media Player lets you set memory buffer settings. To access this control, choose Device, Properties (see fig. 40.3).

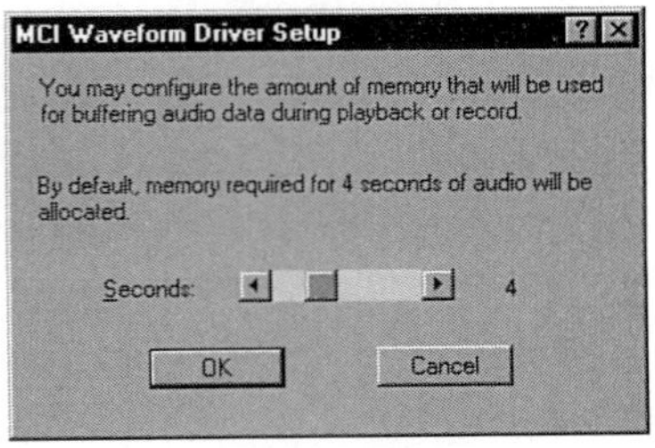

FIG. 40.3

Avoid choppy audio playback by increasing the memory buffer in the MCI Waveform Driver Setup dialog box.

MCI Waveform Driver Setup

You may configure the amount of memory that will be used for buffering audio data during playback or record.

By default, memory required for 4 seconds of audio will be allocated.

Seconds: ◀ ▢ ▶ 4

OK   Cancel

> **TIP** If you are experiencing choppy audio playback, try increasing the size of Windows' audio buffer. Choose <u>D</u>evice, <u>P</u>roperties, and move the scroll bar to the right.

Placing an Audio Clip in a Document

Windows 95 OLE capability enables OLE-compliant applications to feature WAV and MIDI audio clips. From Media Player, you can copy a clip or section of a clip, and paste it directly into an Excel spreadsheet, Word for Windows document, or Lotus Freelance presentation.

To take part of a MIDI clip and place it in a Word document, follow these steps:

1. With a MIDI file loaded into Media Player, move the slider bar to the point of the clip you want to begin with, and click the Start Selection button.

2. Move the slider bar to the end point, and click the End Selection button.

3. Click <u>E</u>dit, <u>C</u>opy Object.

4. Move to the Word document, right-click where you want the audio clip icon to appear, and select Paste from the context menu.

5. Right-click the MIDI clip icon, and select Play Media Clip from the context menu.

> **N O T E** Some applications display somewhat different menu options when you right-click an embedded OLE audio clip. For example, OLE clips embedded in WordPad show an option for <u>M</u>edia Clip Object when right-clicked.

6. If you want to edit the embedded clip, right-click the icon and select Edit Media Clip from the context menu (see fig. 40.4).

Part
X

Ch
40

FIG. 40.4
Click Edit Media Clip from the audio icon context menu, and Word transforms into an audio editing environment.

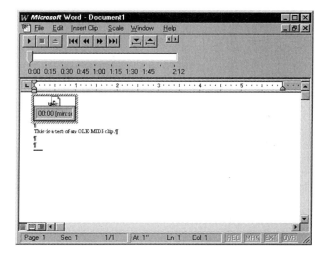

Working with the Taskbar Audio Tool

Windows 95 makes audio controls a snap to access and use. Many audio controls can be accessed from the speaker icon on the right side of the taskbar. You can perform the following actions with the speaker icon:

- Double-click the speaker icon to launch the Windows 95 Volume Control box.
- Click the speaker icon to invoke a mini-volume control next to the speaker icon (see fig. 40.5).

FIG. 40.5
Clicking the speaker icon
brings up the volume mini-
control.

- Right-click the speaker icon to invoke a shortcut menu that can launch the Volume Control box or the Audio Properties sheet.

 TIP If you don't see a speaker icon on your taskbar, open the Multimedia Properties sheet in the Control Panel. On the Audio page, check the Show Volume Control box on the taskbar. Click OK to exit the sheet, and the icon will appear in the taskbar.

Using the Volume Control

To make system-wide adjustments to audio levels, balance, and other settings, the Volume Control dialog box is a powerful tool (see fig. 40.6). You can launch this dialog box by double-clicking the speaker icon on the right side of the taskbar.

 TIP You can change the volume output for all audio devices using the mini-volume control. Single-click the speaker icon, and click and drag the slider item. The volume of all devices will change as you move the slider.

To adjust volume settings, simply drag the slider bar up or down for the item you want to affect. Moving the Wave Volume slider bar down will cause WAV files to play less loudly, but will not affect the playing volume of MIDI files and audio CDs. However, moving the Volume Control Volume slider bar will cause all audio device volume levels to change.

FIG. 40.6

The Volume Control dialog box lets you adjust the individual volume and balance settings for wave, MIDI, and CD audio playback, as well as other settings.

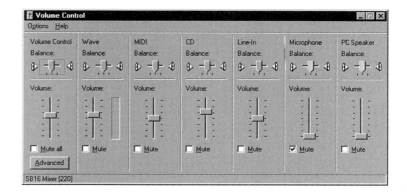

You also can adjust the balance of individual or all audio devices, by moving the appropriate Balance slider bars left or right. In addition, some drivers let you mute one or more devices by clicking the Mute check box at the bottom of each item. A Mute All check box will silence all audio devices.

To add or delete audio devices shown on the Volume Control dialog box, click Options, Properties. In the Properties box, you can select devices associated with playback, recording, and other functions. In the scrolling box at the bottom of the dialog box, you can then select individual devices for inclusion in the Volume Control dialog box.

Some users will also see an Advanced button in the bottom-left corner of the dialog box, provided their sound card drivers offer further capabilities. Clicking this button brings up controls for adjusting bass and treble output, for example (see fig. 40.7). In some cases, Advanced controls may be available, but the button must be set properly to be visible in the dialog box. If the button is not visible, you may be able to click Options, Advanced Controls to make the button available.

Part

X

Ch

40

FIG. 40.7

With some sound boards, you can adjust bass and treble output by clicking the Advanced button in the Volume Control dialog box.

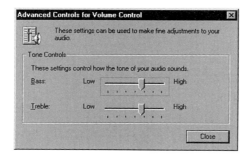

Using the Sound Recorder

Windows 95 includes an application for recording and editing audio files. While Sound Recorder is modest compared to full-featured editing software such as Blue Ribbon SoundWorks' Software Audio Workshop, it provides a good introduction to audio recording and editing concepts. Sound Recorder, shown in figure 40.8, lets you record sound files to your hard drive, which can be included in multimedia presentations or documents via object linking and embedding (OLE). You can find Sound Recorder in the Start menu under Programs, Accessories, Multimedia.

▶ **See** "Placing an Audio Clip in a Document," **p. 1143**

FIG. 40.8

Sound Recorder lets you record and edit sounds for playback.

The menu bar lists the menus that are discussed briefly here. Position represents the current position in the audio file, while Length tells you the complete length of the file in seconds. The visual wave display offers a visual representation of the audio file, and the progress bar indicates how far along in the file you are. Finally, the Control buttons control such operations as fast forward and rewind, just like a regular tape recorder.

The File menu contains a number of familiar and self-explanatory options, in addition to two not-so-common ones. Revert enables you to undo a deleted section of a sound file, and Properties enables you to change the properties of the file and change the quality of the recording (see fig. 40.9).

N O T E The Revert command works only if you have *not* saved the sound file you partially deleted. ■

The Edit menu offers a variety of options, some of which may sound familiar but actually accomplish tasks not normally associated with those commands:

- Copy copies a sound to the Windows Clipboard for insertion elsewhere.
- Paste Insert inserts a sound file into the open sound file.
- Paste Mix mixes two sound files together. The open file and the pasted clips are mixed and played at the same time.

FIG. 40.9

The Properties option on the File menu enables you to change the quality of the recording by changing the format.

- Insert File enables you to insert a file into the open file at the point where you position the slider.

- Mix with File enables you to mix another file with the file playing at the point where you position the slider.

- Delete Before Current Position deletes everything before a specified point, once you have moved the slider to the point in the sound file where you want to cut.

- Delete After Current Position deletes everything after a specified point, once you have moved the slider to the point in the sound file where you want to cut.

- Audio Properties opens the Audio Properties sheet, where you can change various properties for both recording and playback, such as volume.

Part
X

Ch
40

The Effects menu offers options that allow for effects to be added to the sound file:

- Increase Volume (by 25 percent) increases the volume of a sound file.

- Decrease Volume decreases the volume of a sound file.

- Increase Speed (by 100 percent) increases the speed of playback of a sound file.

- Decrease Speed decreases the speed of a sound file.

- Add Echo adds an echo effect to a sound file.

- Reverse plays a sound file in reverse.

T I P If a sound file is compressed, you cannot change the speed of playback or add an echo to the file.

Playing Audio CDs

Windows 95 can play your audio CDs from your system's CD-ROM drive while you are working on another application. The CD Player application offers many of the controls found in stand-alone CD players, and it looks and operates much the same way (see fig. 40.10). In addition, CD Player lets you edit your play list that corresponds to the audio CD being played, so that you can play the tracks in the order you specify.

To launch CD Player, open the Start menu and choose Programs, Accessories, Multimedia, CD Player.

FIG. 40.10

The CD Player allows you to play audio CDs and edit play lists just like a regular high-end CD player.

CD Player includes a number of advanced functions that you access from the menu bar, such as Random Order, Continuous Play, and the capability to edit your play list.

The main CD Player screen offers four menus: Disc, View, Options, and Help. The Disc menu offers two options:

■ Edit Play List enables you to edit your personal play list (see fig. 40.11).

A *play list* is a list of tracks from an audio CD that you want to play. With CD Player, you can specify the tracks you want played from a CD and the order in which they should run.

The left window shows the desired Play List, and the right window lists all Available Tracks on the audio CD. To remove a track from the Play List, highlight it and click Remove. To add a track to the Play List from the Available Tracks list, highlight it and click Add.

FIG. 40.11

You can customize each CD's play list by choosing the Edit Play List option from the Disc menu.

■ Exit closes the CD Player window and turns off the audio CD at the same time.

The View menu offers three sets of options. The first set of options enables you to customize the general CD Player screen:

■ Toolbar enables you to display or remove the toolbar. There are seven icons on the toolbar:

- Edit Play List enables you to edit your play list.

- Track Time Elapsed tracks the time since the start of the track.

- Track Time Remaining lets you know how much time is remaining on the track.

- Disc Time Remaining shows how much time is left on the audio CD currently playing.

- Random Track Order plays the tracks in random order.

- Continuous Play starts the CD over again after the last track has played.

- Intro Play plays the beginning 10 seconds of each track before moving to the next one.

■ Disc/Track Info enables you to display or remove the CD disc and track information at the bottom of the general CD Player screen.

■ Status Bar enables you to display or remove the status bar at the bottom of the windows.

Part
X

Ch
40

The second set of options in the <u>V</u>iew menu enable you to change the time displayed in the time indicator window:

- Track Time <u>E</u>lapsed shows how much time has elapsed on the current track.
- Track Time <u>R</u>emaining shows how much time is left on the current track.
- Dis<u>c</u> Time Remaining shows how much time is left on the current CD.

The third set on the <u>V</u>iew menu has a single option:

- Volume Control enables you to set the control levels for volume, wave, MIDI, and other devices.

The <u>O</u>ptions menu offers four options:

- <u>R</u>andom Order enables you to play tracks from different CDs in random order, which can be useful if you have more than one CD drive.
- <u>C</u>ontinuous Play enables you to repeat the track.
- <u>I</u>ntro Play plays the first 10 seconds of each track and then moves to the next track.
- <u>P</u>references enables you to set preferences for your CD Player (see fig. 40.12).

FIG. 40.12
Preferences enables you to set general preferences for CD Player, such as the length of the introduction for each track in seconds for when you choose <u>I</u>ntro Play from the <u>O</u>ptions menu.

Finally, the <u>H</u>elp menu provides help concerning CD Player, and a memory status dialog box under the <u>A</u>bout CD Player item.

 You can enjoy enhanced audio CD capabilities with the FlexiCD application that is part of Microsoft's PowerToys shareware add-ons for Windows 95. Download PowerToys from Microsoft's Web site at **http://www.microsoft.com/windows/software/powertoy.htm**.

Understanding DirectSound and Windows' New Audio Features

In addition to the variety of audio controls and applications, Windows 95 includes core features for improving the quality and flexibility of audio in applications and games. While

Plug and Play helps reduce hardware conflicts, the DirectSound technology and other innovations make Windows 95 a better platform for handling digital audio than its predecessor.

DirectSound, alongside other DIRECT X technologies, is a key component of Microsoft's game strategy. DirectSound enables low overhead audio transactions under Windows 95, so system performance does not slow down while digital audio and MIDI scores are played. According to Microsoft, DirectSound gives applications direct access to audio buffers, and enables easy digital mixing and 3-D positional audio. The result is fast, reliable, consistent implementation of sound in Windows 95 applications and games.

Perhaps more importantly, DirectSound provides a compelling standard interface for software and hardware to work with the Windows 95 operating system. For sound board makers, this scheme eliminates the need for Sound Blaster compatibility. Cards providing Sound Blaster compatibility in software often suffer from compatibility problems.

Does DirectSound mean that Sound Blaster compatibility is irrelevant? Not hardly. DOS-based games like Wing Commander and Doom will continue to look for specific audio hardware, and the most-supported hardware remains Creative Labs' Sound Blaster line. In addition, Windows 95 provides strong driver support for Sound Blaster boards within the operating system, because these boards make up a large percentage of the installed base.

Beyond DirectSound, Windows 95 introduces support for *polymessage MIDI*. This technology is a streamlined MIDI handling scheme that lets Windows 95 send multiple MIDI instruction at one time, within a single interrupt. This scheme reduces processor overhead and allows closer integration of MIDI playback with graphics updates, game play, and other multimedia applications.

Part
X

Ch
40

N O T E   Your sound board must provide support for polymessage MIDI in order for you to enjoy the reduced overhead it puts on systems. ■

▶ **See** "Understanding DirectX," **p. 1088**
▶ **See** "Understanding MIDI Files," **p. 1155**

Understanding WAV Files

Digital audio comes in two forms: waveform audio (WAV files) and MIDI. *WAV files* are digital representations of analog sound, much the way a graphics bitmap is a representation of a real-world image. In fact, Windows WAV files are similar to the digital audio stored on audio CDs.

When your system records a WAV file, the incoming signal is converted to a series of bits that represent the curve of the original analog signal. The quality of a digital audio file—and also its size—is related to its resolution and frequency. For example, CD-quality audio has a resolution of 16 bits and frequency of 44.1KHz, while the audio found in most AVI video clips is about 8 bits and 22KHz.

To understand what goes into a wave file, you need to know its components.

- *Sampling rate.* The number of times each second that the system takes a snapshot of the analog audio signal. Sampling rate is measured in kilohertz (KHz), which represents thousands of samples each second. Audio CDs store sound at 44.1KHz.
- *Bit depth.* The number of bits that are dedicated to each sample. 16-bit audio, which is the same used by audio CDs, puts two bytes of data to each sample.
- *Stereo/mono.* Stereo means you are storing two channels of sound, which can vary to provide spatial quality to the audio playback. Mono playback uses a single channel.

The audio format determines the digital quality of the sound, but sound hardware is important, too. Interference inside the PC and the quality of audio components affect sound output. Many sound boards have inferior frequency response, which means they do not accurately reproduce sounds at the high and low range of human hearing. Most boards also produce poor *signal-to-noise ratios*—a measure of how much noise is in the output—with performance that falls below that of CD players.

For best results, look for a board that provides superior audio outputs. The Multisound Monterey sound card from Turtle Beach has consistently produced the best results among mainstream sound boards. Other good choices are the Creative Labs' Sound Blaster 32-AWE and the Ensoniq SoundScape 32.

Audio hardware aside, why don't all clips use 16-bit, 44.1KHz audio? Table 40.1 shows just how large a minute of uncompressed digital audio can get.

Table 40.1 Size of One Minute of Uncompressed Stereo Wave Audio

Frequency	8-bit	16-bit
11KHz	1.2M	2.6M
22KHz	2.6M	5.2M
44.1KHz	5.2M	10.4M

To conserve disk space, you can reduce the number of bits dedicated to modeling the curve of analog audio. For example, by capturing to mono format instead of stereo, you cut the size of the file in half, because only one channel of information is being stored. After that, you can reduce the number of times each second that you sample the incoming analog signal. By going from 44.1KHz (or 44,100 samples per second) to 22.05KHz (22,050 samples), you can cut the file size by half again. Dropping to 11.025KHz provides further economies. Finally, you can lower the number of bits dedicated to each audio sample. Dropping from 16-bit to 8-bit resolution again shaves the file size in half.

Unfortunately, the less information you store, the less realistic the audio playback. Losing the stereo data can render audio playback flat, and leave it without spatial cues such as when instruments or sounds come from one speaker or another. Dropping the bit depth can add audible hiss to sound files, and lessens the precision of reproduction. Lowering the frequency means that the audio is being sampled less often, so the card is unable to smoothly re-create changes in sound.

Another way to conserve space is through compression. Like video files, audio compression techniques reduce file size by coding redundant information in compact format and even by throwing out some aural information. Windows includes several compression schemes:

- *Microsoft IMA ADPCM.* Best general-purpose scheme.
- *Microsoft ADPCM.* General purpose codec.
- *Microsoft GSM 6.10 Audio.* General purpose codec.
- *Microsoft CCITT G.711 A-Law and u-Law.* Standard scheme for video conferencing.
- *DSP Group TrueSpeech.* Dedicated to handling speech.
- *Microsoft PCM Converter.* General purpose codec.

The codecs in the Multimedia Properties sheet are ordered by priority (see fig. 40.13). Windows 95 uses this prioritization to determine which codec to use to compress audio files. You can change the priority of each codec, as well as other characteristics, by selecting the appropriate codec and clicking the Properties button (see fig. 40.14). You also can specify when to use the compression scheme (see fig. 40.15).

FIG. 40.13

The Advanced page of the Multimedia Properties sheet shows the installed audio compression drivers.

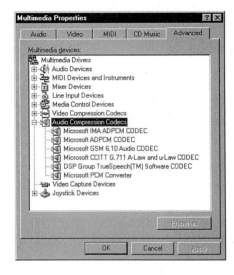

FIG. 40.14

Double-click an audio codec item, and you can change the codec's priority and enable or disable it. Clicking the Settings button lets you specify when to use the compression scheme.

FIG. 40.15

You can specify the maximum real-time conversion rate of the compression scheme.

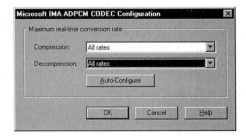

If you install an audio codec that you want to use for all your compression needs, change its priority. Double-click the codec item in the Multimedia Properties sheet's Advanced page, and then use the Change Priority From drop-down list to make this your top-priority codec.

Understanding MIDI Files

The other half of the Windows audio scheme is MIDI. MIDI is actually a standard from the music industry, developed for synthesizers and other professional audio equipment. Unlike WAV files, which are a digital representation of analog sound, MIDI files are composed of simple instructions that tell a MIDI device what to do. A MIDI file consists of instructions that tell your sound card what notes to play, with which instruments, and at what volume.

Of course, in order for these instructions to work, your sound board must be able to understand MIDI instructions. More importantly, all sound boards and MIDI audio equipment must work with the same set of instructions, so that when a MIDI file calls for instrument number 98, the same instrument is played on all hardware. Instrument identifications are standardized under the General MIDI standard, which comprises 128 MIDI instruments.

 Make sure your sound card supports the General MIDI standard. General MIDI consists of 128 instruments, and defines their identification for all audio equipment. Some boards can have more than 128 instrument sounds, but they must comply with General MIDI to work reliably with MIDI files.

Part **X**

Ch **40**

Today, most PCs can handle MIDI scores using FM synthesis. *FM synthesis* is an innovative scheme in which two or more signals are mixed to emulate the sound of actual instruments. Unfortunately, FM synthesis generally fails to produce realistic sounds, particularly with complex, orchestral scores that include numerous instruments.

N O T E Creative Labs' Sound Blaster Pro and Sound Blaster 16 are examples of boards that support FM synthesis MIDI.

For top-quality MIDI playback, you need a board that supports wavetable MIDI. Wavetable MIDI cards use dedicated memory to store samples of actual instrument sounds on the card. When a MIDI score tries to play a C note on a trumpet, the board plays an actual sample of that instrument. In addition, the board may transform the sample to reflect the specific note, and other characteristics that the MIDI score call for.

T I P Not all MIDI samples are equal. The quality of MIDI sounds stored in a sound board can depend on how much memory is used to store the samples. For example, cards that use 1/2 megabyte of ROM to store samples generally cannot store as much sample data as those with 2M. Other factors can also make a difference, such as the algorithms used to transform the base samples, and the compression schemes used to compact them.

The difference in quality is significant. FM synthesis often sounds fake and tinny, like a cheap synthesizer. Wavetable MIDI, on the other hand, can produce the full richness of real instruments, including orchestral scores that feature 20 or more simultaneous instruments.

To get best results, your sound hardware should provide at least 16-voice polyphony. *Polyphony* refers to the capability to play more than one sound at once. For example, many MIDI scores play a veritable desktop orchestra, requiring 20 or even 32 MIDI voices to play at the same time.

N O T E Creative Labs' Sound Blaster AWE 32 and Sound Blaster 32 are two examples of sound cards that provide wavetable MIDI playback. ∎

Some higher-end boards feature customizable wavetable MIDI, which enables you to store samples that *you* record. For example, the Sound Blaster AWE 32 lets you load custom sounds from your hard drive into RAM installed onto the sound board. These custom sounds can then be played back as part of a MIDI score, so you can introduce strange instruments or neat effects like screeching tires or gun shots into your scores.

You will also find some products that feature software-based wavetable MIDI, in which your system's CPU is used to handle the processing of sampled MIDI sounds. This allows less expensive PCs to produce rich, wavetable MIDI playback under Windows—but at a price. Processing wavetable MIDI sounds can consume a good deal of CPU time, impairing performance. If you want wavetable MIDI for demanding games or video presentations, you should use a sound board that offers wavetable processing in hardware. Otherwise, you may be able to save a buck with a software-based wavetable MIDI scheme.

CAUTION
If you want wavetable MIDI playback for your demanding DOS-based games, be warned. Software wavetable MIDI schemes do not operate in Windows 95's DOS mode (though they will work for programs operating in a DOS box). That means that the most demanding flight simulators and other DOS games still need compatible hardware MIDI.

Understanding 3-D Audio

The latest development in audio hardware and software is the introduction of 3-D audio. Like 3-D graphics, 3-D audio is supposed to create the illusion of immersive reality on the desktop. While virtually any application can make use of 3-D audio, game and title software developers are most aggressive about adopting it.

There are several varieties of 3-D audio on the market today. Among the most popular are

- Spatializer
- SRS
- QSound

SRS and Spatializer are similar schemes, in that they add 3-D effects to the sound after the sound has been processed. This allows external modules to be hooked to your sound card to introduce 3-D enhancements as the sound is output.

With Spatializer, software makers can encode 3-D information into their audio streams, so a fighter jet can sound like it is moving from left to right during game play. SRS, meanwhile, relies on the spatial information available within a recording, and brings it out during playback. A recording of a car racing past you would sound very realistic, provided the person who recorded the sound used a pair of microphones to get a stereoscopic audio image of the sound. Because stereo music recordings are captured using two microphones, SRS sound can bring out the positional information during playback.

 TIP Some speakers and sound boards now feature SRS or Spatializer 3-D circuitry. Labtec sells speakers with built-in Spatializer 3-D audio. You can also add Spatializer or SRS 3-D audio modules that plug in between your speakers and sound board, including Labtec's Spatializer LCS-9210 and NuReality's Vivid Pro-ex.

Part **X**

Ch **40**

NOTE The SRS 3-D audio scheme actually comes from the home entertainment market, where it has been built into RCA televisions and some home audio equipment. ▪

QSound is a processor-driven scheme, where spatial data is imposed on the sound before playback. QSound lets you take a sound and make it seem like it is moving around you, with the PC's processor figuring out how to balance the speaker output to achieve the desired effect.

QSound relies on the assumption that the user will be in a certain position with respect to his or her speakers, which limits its usefulness beyond the desktop.

 T I P To get the best results from 3-D audio, position your speakers about six inches from either side of the monitor.

CHAPTER 41

Playing with Windows 95: The Games

by Michael Desmond

Until the release of Windows 95, virtually all PC-based game software ran under DOS, despite poor compatibility and a hard-to-use interface. The reason, quite simply, was performance. Game software ranging from shoot-em-ups like Doom and Terminal Velocity to adventures like Myst require all the resources they can get. But Windows 3.1 was designed for spreadsheets, e-mail, and word processors, where compatibility and a standard interface are more important than split-second performance. Even graphics accelerator boards, which speed up scrolling text and drop-down menus, cannot boost the unpredictable, free-form graphics of most games.

In designing Windows 95, Microsoft sought to create a premiere gaming platform, even as it attempted to replace and improve upon the "corporate" functions of Windows 3.1 (see fig. 41.1). Even more challenging, Windows 95 had to maintain strong compatibility with the wide universe of DOS games, so users wouldn't face the unacceptable choice of throwing out all their favorite game titles.

Microsoft's Game SDK and what it brings to Windows 95 games

Learn about the set of libraries, tools, and resources available in this kit.

Calibrating Joysticks in Windows 95

Visit this one-stop shop for joystick management.

Tips and strategies for dealing with DOS games

Learn how to handle the transition to the new tools that Windows 95 gives you for working with DOS applications.

FIG. 41.1

Windows 95 lets you multitask work and play.

Windows 95 has delivered on these goals with mixed success. The sections that follow will help you understand how Windows 95 works with games, and how you can get the most from the coming generation of Windows 95-based game software. It will also give you insights in to how to deal with DOS games. ■

Understanding Game SDK

To turn Windows 95 into a legitimate game platform, Microsoft developed Game SDK (software development kit), which is a set of libraries, tools, and resources to let software companies create native Windows 95 games that rival DOS performance. Game SDK consists of three DirectX technologies—DirectDraw, DirectInput, and DirectPlay—which bring powerful capabilities to the Windows 95 operating system. In addition, Game SDK includes sample game code, key utilities, and other tools to help developers begin making games.

N O T E   Game SDK did not get to developers until November 1995—a full three months after Windows 95 hit the streets. For this reason, native Windows 95 games have been slow to ship, as vendors waited on the tools required to build optimized software. But Game SDK and DirectX technologies are receiving a warm welcome from major publishers like Lucas Arts and TriMark. For users, that means that Windows 95 will probably emerge as a popular game platform. ■

The DirectX technologies built into Game SDK help Windows 95 enjoy DOS-like performance, while preserving hardware compatibility. Generally, Windows 95 puts a co-joining layer between hardware (like sound and graphics boards) and software (like games and titles). This layer, called a hardware abstraction layer (or HAL), provides a single, stable development target for the people who write drivers and applications. The trick to Games SDK and DirectX, then, is to remove the cumbersome overhead of Windows 95 while keeping a thin layer that ensures compatibility.

To get the most out of the coming generation of Windows 95 games, you'll need to outfit your system with the proper hardware and driver software. Actually, Windows 95's gaming technologies will boost game performance regardless of the hardware you have installed, but you won't be getting the full benefit. To turn your PC into the ultimate Windows 95 game machine, you'll need the proper hardware.

The sections that follow help you understand the components of Game SDK—DirectDraw, DirectInput, and DirectPlay—and how to use them.

▶ **See** "Taking Advantage of DirectDraw," **p. 1111**

▶ **See** "Understanding DirectSound and Windows' New Audio Features," **p. 1150**

DirectDraw: The Key to DOS-like Graphics Performance

Graphics performance is at the core of computer gaming, and Windows 95's DirectDraw aims to deliver graphics speed in line with DOS based systems. Features like direct frame-buffer access and double-buffering deliver important advantages to demanding game software. However, if you don't have the proper driver software already installed, you'll need to get DirectDraw drivers from your board vendor.

 As a rule, popular graphics boards from larger vendors—such as the Diamond Stealth, STB Powergraph, and Matrox Millennium lines—are more likely than older and less-known boards to have DirectDraw and other Windows 95 updates available.

Even if the graphics board in your system is from a small, local vendor, you still may have a decent shot at getting full-function DirectDraw drivers for your graphics board. That's because many boards use the same graphics chip. S3, for example, is the leading maker of chips for Windows graphics accelerators, and the company provides base-level drivers for its hardware. So even if the company who made your board went out of business, you might be able to get updated drivers from the people who made the chip on your board (see fig. 41.2).

Part

X

Ch

41

Among the popular graphics chips are:

- S3 Vision868/968
- S3 Vision864/964
- S3 Trio64V+
- Cirrus Logic GD5434
- Cirrus Logic GD5428/5426
- ATI Mach64
- Matrox MGA 64

TROUBLESHOOTING

I don't know which chip is on my graphics board. Go to the Display Properties sheet by right-clicking your desktop. Click the Change Display Type button, then click the Change button in the Adapter Type area. You should see a driver entry that identifies your graphics chip.

FIG. 41.2
While it's best if Windows 95 recognizes your specific board model, the driver for the specific graphics chip should give you most of the features you need.

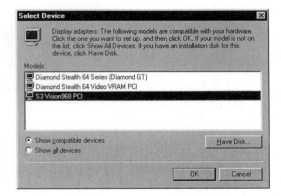

What else should you look for in a gaming graphics card? Most important is fast graphics memory, specifically video RAM (VRAM) or some other graphics RAM equivalent. Because games push vast amounts of graphics data, the memory on the graphics card can be a key performance bottleneck.

 Make sure your graphics board is a 64-bit product. 64 bits refers to the data width of the graphics chip, and is a key factor in fast graphics updates. Older 32-bit boards will not be able to keep up with demanding games and other multimedia applications.

Dynamic RAM (DRAM) and Extended Data Our (EDO) DRAM, which are used for system memory and on budget-minded graphics boards, cannot provide the fast graphics performance and high refresh rates required for fast-action games. As a result, games like Wing Commander and EF2000 run at lower frame rates, and suffer distracting delays that can mean the difference between sweet victory and ignominious defeat.

You should also have at least 2M of memory on the board. While most games run at resolutions and color depths that will fit in a single megabyte of RAM, the second megabyte buys you improved performance for games. Why? Because the memory chips on graphics boards have a limited number of ports for moving data in and out. With 1M of RAM, there are not enough ports to your graphics chip to enable true 64-bit transactions—so data must move 32 bits at a time, which is a lot like closing two lanes on a four lane highway.

> **N O T E** Even though most games run at 320 × 240 pixel resolution and 8-bit color, you should consider going with 2M of RAM on 64-bit graphics boards. You'll see better performance, particularly with fast-action games. ▪

> ▶ **See** "How DirectDraw Works," **p. 1112**

DirectInput: Control Freaks Rejoice

One frequently overlooked aspect of game play (particularly among PC users) is the input device. Whether you're flying the latest flight simulation, or racing on the open road in a virtual Corvette ZR-1, one thing is certain: You won't go far trying to do it from the cursor keys on your PC keyboard. But even if you sprang for a joystick for DOS games, you still had to struggle with tricky calibration and spotty support for the controls on your joystick (see fig. 41.3).

FIG. 41.3
With Windows 95 games, you don't have to settle for a clumsy, separate joystick program; you can access Windows 95's joystick controls in the middle of game play.

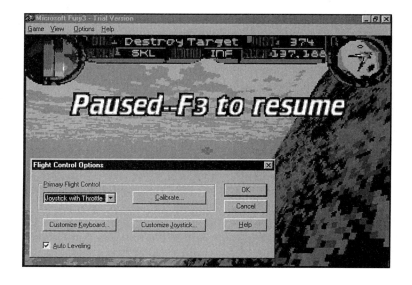

Game SDK addresses game interaction with DirectInput, a technology that provides a standard, digital interface to a wide universe of input devices. DirectInput does several important things for Windows 95 games:

- It places a standard layer between hardware devices and game software, so games can support a wide variety of Windows 95-compliant peripherals.
- It allows multiple input devices, including multiple joysticks, to connect to a single PC for head-to-head gaming.
- It provides support for digital joysticks and other devices.
- It provides a standard Windows interface for calibration and management of joysticks and other peripherals.

DirectInput the Enabling Diplomat   Perhaps the most exciting prospect is the universal device interface that DirectInput puts into the Windows 95 operating system. Today, most games recognize two, or maybe three, popular joystick models, providing partial or full support for the push buttons, top hat buttons, and throttle controls built into the device. If you don't have one of the supported models, and your joystick can't emulate the features of one of those models, you end up with dumbed-down support. That means you get support for stick action and usually two buttons.

And if support is that slim for joysticks, imagine what it's like for new, exotic devices like head-mounted displays and 3-D mice. Windows 95 DirectInput builds in universal support by putting a standard interface that both game software and game hardware talk to. A game maker, for example, writes code so that it can accept direction from DirectInput. The game itself doesn't have to know whose joystick or HMD is calling the shots, since DirectInput passes along the data using known standards regardless of the hardware. Of course, the hardware company will have to write a Windows 95 driver for their device so it can speak to DirectInput. But once that is done, virtually all Windows 95 games should be able to work with the hardware.

Of course, writing driver software is no easy task, so some hardware will enjoy an early lead in Windows 95 support. It's no surprise, for example, that Microsoft's Sidewinder joystick is the first digital, Windows 95-compliant joystick on the market. As usual, you should contact your device vendor about driver updates to let the hardware work with DirectInput.

Digital Performance   The good news about DirectInput is that you can use your existing analog joystick to play Windows 95 games. The bad news is that you won't be getting the most out of them. That's because DirectInput enables a new class of digital joysticks which enjoy greater precision, quicker response, and better system performance than current models.

TIP Analog joysticks require constant attention from the CPU, grabbing up to 15 percent of your system's processing capacity.

One very good reason for getting a digital joystick is the drag that analog models put on your system CPU. With analog joysticks, your system must constantly poll the joystick port in order to get updates, a task that holds up vital processing needs. Digital joysticks, however, simply send their updates directly to the processor, freeing up the CPU and boosting game performance.

Finally, digital joysticks are able to support functions unheard of in analog models, including yaw controls and software-programmable buttons. Digital models also don't require problematical calibration routines—their digital architecture eliminates the loss of centering that occurs with analog models.

Not surprisingly, Microsoft released the first digital joystick, the Sidewinder Pro 3D. Other major vendors, such as Advance Gravis, plan to develop digital joysticks as well. However, to take advantage of these products, your PC must have a digital interface. You can upgrade your system with a digital joystick interface by purchasing an add-in card.

The benefit of DirectInput goes beyond joysticks, addressing the lack of support for specialized game devices. DirectInput solves this by offering a standard interface that lets games take advantage of all DirectInput-compliant hardware. For example, with Microsoft's Fury3, you could use a digital joystick to enjoy precise response, while a DirectInput-compliant head-mounted display lets you really immerse yourself in the game.

> **CAUTION**
> Head-mounted displays have been known to cause disorientation and nausea, as well as neck injury.

Head-mounted displays are not the only peripherals: Steering columns, throttle controls, foot pedals, and other such exotica can enjoy widespread support via DirectInput drivers. DirectInput also offers support for up to TK simultaneous joysticks or other devices. Advance Gravis GrIP module, for example, provides a splitter box that lets you hook two joysticks to a single PC for head-to-head game play.

Part
X
Ch
41

DirectPlay: Bringing Windows 95 Games Together

Ever since the first NetTrek game beeped and flickered across old VAX and PDP-11 midframe machines over 10 years ago, computer gamers have yearned for multiplayer competition. Today, games like Doom, Descent, and Command & Conquer enjoy enormous popularity among users competing over local area networks (LANs). Meanwhile, modem-based play over the Internet and dedicated services like DWANGO and Imagination Network are gaining popularity.

Unfortunately, making remote games work together can be harder than staying alive in a Deathmatch Doom session. Microsoft's answer to the problem is DirectPlay, the final piece of the Windows 95 Game SDK. DirectPlay is an API that makes it easy for multiple systems to play Windows 95 games together. More than anything, DirectPlay lets game vendors concentrate on making games, not communications interfaces.

DirectPlay provides several services to enable easy, effective game play over multiple systems. For example, DirectPlay:

- Provides a standard, universal communication interface between game software and communication hardware and drivers.
- Provides a method for PCs communicating over different infrastructures to play together without degradation of performance.
- Provides users with a standard interface for initiating and managing remote game communications.

Man in the Middle   As with all the other DirectX APIs, DirectPlay's most important contribution is its role as a standard, universal interface. Game vendors, network game service providers, and makers of network cards, modems, and ISDN peripherals can all aim their development at a single standard. In this way, game vendors need only write code to send and receive data with the DirectPlay interface. Hardware and service providers, meanwhile, write code for their drivers to the other side of the DirectPlay API, handing off all the arbitration to DirectPlay.

DirectPlay allows a wide range of inter-computer communications for gaming. Among them:

- Parallel port and null modem connections
- Analog modem
- Digital ISDN phone lines
- Local area networks (LAN)
- Wide area networks and Internet

DirectPlay works because it is part of your operating system. So if you have a modem or network card already working, DirectPlay immediately knows how to manage the hardware. You don't, for example, have to tell your game software what COM port and address your modem is using in order to fire up remote game play. Instead, you tell the game you want to play remotely, and DirectPlay will be able to access the appropriate system resources automatically.

As with other DirectX APIs, however, you will need the appropriate driver software to let your hardware speak to DirectPlay. A network adapter, for instance, needs a native Windows 95 driver that lets it access DirectPlay's functionality and talk to the interface. While drivers for some popular hardware come with the Windows 95 disc, you can get the latest version by contacting the hardware vendor dirrectly.

 T I P In general, Microsoft bundles baseline drivers that may lack customized tweaks and features. You should always contact the hardware vendor directly to see if enhanced drivers are available.

One if by Land, Two if by Sea   DirectPlay has the further advantage of allowing gamers to play over a variety of communication modes. So one player can be hooked into a group via an analog phone line using a 28.8-kbps modem, while others are connected to each other over a LAN. Most importantly, DirectPlay enables this mixed-mode game play while providing a similar game experience for all participants. That means the player on a 28.8-kbps modem is getting the same level of play as the person on a 10 megabit per second (mbps) LAN adapter.

For example, let's say you have a group of four playing a heated game of Deathmatch Doom over a local area network at a small marketing firm (after hours, of course). But the reigning Deathmatch champ, Tim, is on the road in Topeka, Kansas. He can hook into the game by launching his local copy of Doom and calling into the system on the network that acts as the game server. Tim will see the name of the current Deathmatch game on his system, and can jump in. DirectPlay handles incoming and outgoing data on Tim's computer, sending it in packeted bits that the PC at the office can recognize.

N O T E   DirectPlay is a work in progress, and Microsoft has yet to complete development on many features. For this reason, details on DirectPlay's specific functions remain sketchy. ■

DirectPlay works over modems and LANs alike because most head-to-head games only send positional information. The heavy work of creating graphical scenes happens locally on each player's machine. However, modems and LANs can delay even the small amounts of data that get sent over the wire, which can affect game play.

Part
X

Ch
41

Working with 3-D Games and Graphics

The final piece in the graphics gaming puzzle is 3-D. While the 3-D pieces to Windows 95 are not yet in-place, board vendors are already working hard to build the hardware to take advantage of it when 3-D graphics arrive. The Matrox Millennium was the first general-purpose graphics board with 3-D acceleration, but new products from Diamond Multimedia, Number Nine Visual Technologies, and others are coming. Many of these products will use S3's ViRGE chip, which provides 2-D graphics, video playback, and 3-D acceleration in boards costing about $300 on the street.

Look for boards based on the following graphics chips for 3-D acceleration:

- S3 ViRGE and ViRGE VX
- 3D Labs Permedia
- NVideo NV1
- SGS Thompson STS2000
- Rendition Verite

The bad news is that all the talk about 3-D graphics is probably premature. Today, 3-D graphics boards provide truly astounding enhancements to game play, enabling realistic, real-time interaction with six degrees of freedom. But until Microsoft's Direct3D standard reaches the market (or some other standard gains ascendancy), any software that works with a 3-D board must be designed specifically for its hardware (see fig. 41.4). That means a narrow selection of 3-D titles for 3-D boards. Case in point: 3-D boards such as the Matrox Millennium, Diamond Edge 3D, and Creative Labs 3D Blaster all ship with their own cast of 3-D titles.

▶ **See** "Enter the New Age: Windows 95 and 3-D Graphics," **p. 1114**

FIG. 41.4
Until 3-D acceleration and support becomes standard, games must employ tricks like mist effects to let 3-D work on standard systems.

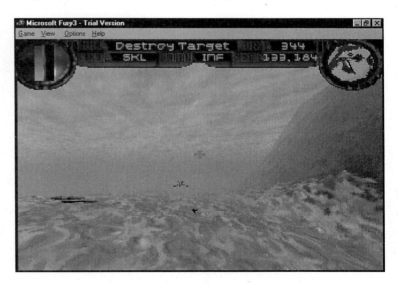

Calibrating Joysticks in Windows 95

Windows 95 provides a standard interface for joystick, setup, calibration, and testing. While DOS games will require you to use the often-clumsy setup routines that come with their software, Windows 95 games rely on this one-stop shop for joystick management. You can find these tools in the Joystick Properties sheet, launched from the Control Panel.

FIG. 41.5
Look familiar? The Joystick Properties sheet is the same one invoked by Windows 95 games like Fury3 for their joystick setup.

The Joystick properties sheet allows you to:

- Select among joystick configurations
- Customize and select controls available on the joystick
- Calibrate the joystick for precise game play
- Test the joystick to confirm button functions, throttle controls, and calibration accuracy

To calibrate a joystick, click the <u>C</u>alibrate button in the Joystick Properties sheet . Then follow the step-by-step instructions (see fig. 41.6).

FIG. 41.6
Use the Joystick Calibration dialog box to get precise performance out of your joystick, and to avoid annoying—and often fatal—drift in your controls.

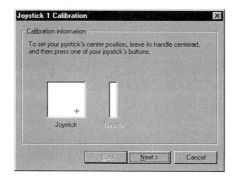

Part
X
Ch
41

The Test function is an excellent way to explore the specific behavior of your joystick *before* you find yourself in the heat of battle. Use the Test dialog box to see which buttons correspond to 1, 2, 3, and 4 on your joystick, as well as where the throttle control (if any) is located (see fig. 41.7).

FIG. 41.7
The Joystick Test dialog box lets you make sure your calibration took, and confirm which buttons do what.

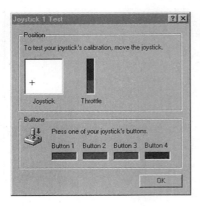

Setting Up DOS Games

Windows 95 fixes a lot of things, both for games and general multimedia applications. But, old habits die hard, and DOS games will surely remain around for years to come. After all, many companies have huge investments of time, money, and intellect in their finely-honed DOS-based games, and moving these to Windows 95 is no trivial task.

That means DOS games running under Windows 95 will continue to have the usual problems. Conventional memory limits, hardware incompatibilities, and multi-boot configurations are just a few of the enduring joys that await those who use Windows 95 to play DOS-based games. Unfortunately, Windows 95 changes a lot of the old rules, forcing even the most adept DOS gamer to learn new tricks.

N O T E Windows 95 doesn't leave you all alone to deal with DOS software. The operating system comes with a file called APPS.INF, which is a configuration database of all sorts of DOS applications and games. This file tells Windows 95 what settings to use for a DOS program whenever it runs (see fig. 41.8). ■

This section helps you deal with the transition, guiding you through the new tools that Windows 95 gives you for working with DOS applications. With Windows 95, you run into three classes of games:

- ■ Native Windows 95 and Windows 3.x games
- ■ DOS games that run in a Windows 95 DOS box
- ■ DOS games that run only in a Windows 95 DOS session
  - ▶ **See** "Installing, Running, and Uninstalling DOS Applications," **p. 497**

FIG. 41.8
Wondering if Windows 95 knows how to handle your DOS game? Use QuickView or other file viewers to look for a listing of the program in the APPS.INF file.

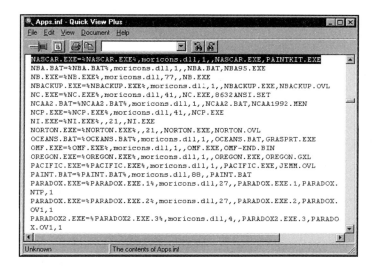

```
NASCAR.EXE=%NASCAR.EXE%,moricons.dll,1,,NASCAR.EXE,PAINTKIT.EXE
NBA.BAT=%NBA.BAT%,moricons.dll,1,,NBA.BAT,NBA95.EXE
NB.EXE=%NB.EXE%,moricons.dll,77,,NB.EXE
NBACKUP.EXE=%NBACKUP.EXE%,moricons.dll,1,,NBACKUP.EXE,NBACKUP.OVL
NC.EXE=%NC.EXE%,moricons.dll,41,,NC.EXE,8632ANSI.SET
NCAA2.BAT=%NCAA2.BAT%,moricons.dll,1,,NCAA2.BAT,NCAA1992.MEN
NCP.EXE=%NCP.EXE%,moricons.dll,41,,NCP.EXE
NI.EXE=%NI.EXE%,,21,,NI.EXE
NORTON.EXE=%NORTON.EXE%,,21,,NORTON.EXE,NORTON.OVL
OCEANS.BAT=%OCEANS.BAT%,moricons.dll,1,,OCEANS.BAT,GRASPRT.EXE
OMF.EXE=%OMF.EXE%,moricons.dll,1,,OMF.EXE,OMF-END.BIN
OREGON.EXE=%OREGON.EXE%,moricons.dll,1,,OREGON.EXE,OREGON.GXL
PACIFIC.EXE=%PACIFIC.EXE%,moricons.dll,1,,PACIFIC.EXE,JEMM.OVL
PAINT.BAT=%PAINT.BAT%,moricons.dll,88,,PAINT.BAT
PARADOX.EXE=%PARADOX.EXE.1%,moricons.dll,27,,PARADOX.EXE.1,PARADOX.
NTP,1
PARADOX.EXE=%PARADOX.EXE.2%,moricons.dll,27,,PARADOX.EXE.2,PARADOX.
OV1,1
PARADOX2.EXE=%PARADOX2.EXE.3%,moricons.dll,4,,PARADOX2.EXE.3,PARADO
X.OV1,1
```

Native Windows 95 and Windows 3.1 Games

Generally, Windows-native games, whether they are designed for Windows 95 or Windows 3.1, will give you few problems. That's because these programs are designed to work under the memory and device management structure of Windows. However, 16-bit Windows 3.x games will not be able to take full advantage of DirectX capabilities, since the software is not designed to recognize interfaces to DirectInput and DirectPlay.

Note that Windows 3.x games bring all the limitations of 16-bit software. For example, if you multitask a 16-bit Windows game with your 32-bit Windows 95 applications, the preemptive multitasking capability of the Windows 95 operating system will be lost. The reason: In order to ensure integrity of 16-bit and 32-bit software operating at the same time, Windows 95 limits itself to processing one operation at a time.

▶ **See** "Installing, Running, and Uninstalling DOS Applications," **p. 497**

Working with DOS Games

Of course, DOS games don't play by the usual Windows rules. Many games run under Windows 95 in a DOS box, allowing you to switch between the DOS game and your Windows 95 desktop and applications. However, the most demanding games will require you to start your system in DOS mode. For these programs, you are limited to running the DOS game—in order to get back to the Windows 95 desktop, you'll have to quit the game and restart your system.

Part
X

Ch
41

DOS Games That Run in a DOS box   DOS games that run in a DOS box fall into two categories:

- Games that can run in a box on the Windows desktop
- Games that can run only in a full-screen DOS box

Actually, very few games will run in a box on the Windows 95 desktop. That's because games usually load a graphics interface that can't run side-by-side with that of the Windows interface. The exception is text-based games such as old dungeon adventure programs.

 TIP   Even if a game will run on the Windows 95 desktop in a DOS box, you get better performance by going to a full-screen DOS box.

Much more common are games that run in a DOS session such as SimCity, Tetris, and Doom but require the entire screen to work. While these games do take up the entire screen, you are able to multitask applications by running other programs in the background.

 TIP   To switch from a running full-screen DOS game to your Windows desktop, press Alt+Tab.

DOS Games That Require DOS-mode   Not all games will run side-by-side with Windows 95, however. Fans of flight simulations and other graphically-intense games probably know this already. For these games, you need to shut down Windows and restart the machine in DOS-mode, a special configuration that does not load the entire Windows 95 operating system.

In DOS mode, Windows 95 foregoes all the fancy protected-mode drivers and memory management schemes to closely emulate a 16-bit DOS machine. For example, instead of loading the 32-bit CDFS driver for your CD-ROM drive, a system running in DOS-mode will load MSCDEX.EXE and the appropriate 16-bit CD-ROM driver software. Under DOS-mode operation, your system reads from the AUTOEXEC.BAT and CONFIG.SYS files in your hard disk's root directory, just as the old MS-DOS operating system did.

While this scheme works well for maintaining compatibility with old DOS applications, it invites all the problems and headaches of life under DOS. In fact, for DOS-mode games, you'll notice little change under Windows 95.

Tips for DOS Games

To help you deal with DOS games, we provide a guide to configuring and managing Windows 95 for game players. If you want more detailed information on dealing with

DOS configurations and how they work, see Chapter 17, "Installing, Running, and Uninstalling DOS Applications."

The File Properties Sheet   To get a recalcitrant DOS game to work under Windows 95, follow these steps:

1. Right-click the icon used to launch the program under Windows 95, and click the Properties item in the context menu (see fig. 41.9).

FIG. 41.9
If you run DOS games, you should become very familiar with the File Properties sheet. It holds the key to making your DOS software run under Windows 95.

2. Click the Program tab, and then click the Advanced button at the bottom of the sheet (see fig. 41.10).

FIG. 41.10
The Avanced Program Settings dialog box lets you fine-tune a specific DOS start-up configuration for your games.

Part
X

Ch
41

3. Check the MS-DOS mode area check box to have the system restart in DOS mode whenever the program is launched.

4. If you still have problems running the application, click the Specify a New MS-DOS Configuration radio button.

5. Edit the lines in the CONFIG.SYS for MS-DOS mode and the AUTOEXEC.BAT for MS-DOS mode scroll boxes to reflect the start-up configuration you need. To free up conventional memory, you can remove unnecessary drivers by typing **REM** in the front of the lines you want to omit.

6. If you still cannot get the game to launch, click the Configuration button to go to the Select MS-DOS Configuration Options page (see fig. 41.11).

FIG. 41.11

The Select MS-DOS Configuration Options page lets you fine-tune DOS memory management, file handling, and other options.

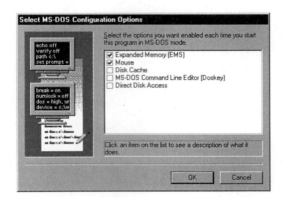

7. Click the check boxes in figure 41.11 to enable or disable Expanded Memory (EMS), Mouse, Disk Cache, MS-DOS Command Line Editor (DOSKEY), and Direct Disk Access.

Booting Straight to DOS   Rebooting in DOS mode is useful for making demanding games run. However, those who frequently play DOS-mode games will waste a lot of time restarting their system. That's because they must wait for Windows 95 to assemble itself and build the desktop, only to restart the system without Windows 95 around.

You can save a lot of time by booting straight to a standard MS-DOS session. Here's how:

1. Restart the system.

2. When you see the text message Starting Windows 95..., press the F8 key.

3. At the list of start-up options, press the 6 key in response to the menu item "6, Command line only."

4. Using the DOS command line, go to the appropriate directory and launch the game.

N O T E In order for this tip to work, your game must use the default MS-DOS configuration, as defined in the AUTOEXEC.BAT and CONFIG.SYS files in the root directory of your hard drive. ▨

T I P Access the list of start-up options at every boot up by editing the file MSDOS.SYS in the root directory. First, open the Properties sheet for MSDOS.SYS and deactivate the Read Only and Hidden check boxes. Now, open the file in a text editor such as Notepad, and add the line `BootMenu = 1` near the top of the file. Save the file, and restart your system.

Appendixes

Installing Windows 95

by Dick Cravens with Bob Voss

Microsoft has completely rewritten Setup for Windows 95, adding significant capabilities and stability to the program. This appendix explains the basics of installing Windows 95 for the first time. ■

How to set up Windows 95

Learn the Windows 95 system requirements.

What's new in the Windows 95 setup

Look here to find the improvements in the Windows 95 Setup.

How Windows 95 Setup works

Learn about the four basic phases involved in Setup.

Advanced installation techniques

Find out about the different Windows installations.

How to configure for dual-boot operation

Learn how this allows you to return to your previous operating system as needed or desired.

How to remove Windows 95

Look here to learn how to reverse the setup.

Understanding Windows 95 Setup Requirements

Before you begin to install Windows 95, be sure that your system meets the minimum system requirements. To run Windows 95, you need a system that includes the following:

- An 80386 or later processor (25MHz or faster) minimum (use at least a 486/33 for serious multitasking)
- A Microsoft- or Logitech-compatible mouse (if you have another type of mouse, be sure to have the drivers for it handy when you begin installation)
- A high-density (1.44M) 3.5-inch floppy drive or CD-ROM drive
- 4M of RAM (8M recommended, 16M preferred)
- VGA graphics video display (Super VGA recommended)
- Microsoft Windows 3.0 or later (including Windows for Workgroups) if you're installing the upgrade version of Windows 95 (the full, non-upgrade version of Windows 95 doesn't require a previous installation of Windows)
- 417K free conventional memory
- 25M to 40M of free hard drive storage space (depending on your upgrade path and installation options) partitioned with the FAT file system
- Up to 14M of additional free hard drive storage space for the Windows 95 swap file (depending on the amount of RAM installed on your system)

Microsoft designed the retail version of Windows 95 as an upgrade-only product, which means you must have a previous version of MS-DOS (version 3.2 or higher), Windows 3.x, or Windows for Workgroups to install Windows 95.

N O T E   While Windows 95 will install on a 386 computer with 4M of RAM, you won't be able to do a lot with it. To experience the full performance potential of Windows 95, you really need at least 8M of memory.

Processor speed is certainly important, but if you have an older 386 system, you may be better off adding additional RAM, or upgrading to a faster hard drive or video system before you splurge on a 486 or Pentium. Processors are usually bottlenecked by one or more of these subsystems. Lack of RAM causes Windows to swap portions of its own code, mostly application code, to the hard drive. Quick drive access is thus critical to Windows performance, but the fastest hard drive appears slow if your display takes seconds to paint.

On the other hand, if you're looking at adding significant amounts of memory, plus replacing *both* your drive and video subsystems, it may pay to check out a completely new computer, with the faster CPU. Check with your hardware vendor and review your options.

N O T E   You may run into trouble installing Windows 95 if you have an older BIOS. If your BIOS is older than January 1994, you should consider replacing it. Contact the BIOS manufacturer to verify compatibility with Windows 95. This is especially true of laptop computers that have a BIOS with power management controls, as these often conflict with Windows 95. ■

N O T E   Windows 95 works with these major drive compression utilities:

- Microsoft DriveSpace and DoubleSpace
- Stacker versions 3.x and 4.x
- Addstor SuperStor

Other compression software may work fine, but it's best to check with the vendor to confirm this prior to installation.

Also, be aware that disk compression may affect the estimate of free drive space available for installation. If you're using compression, be cautious about trusting space estimates. Compression yield depends on many factors, including data types, so allow extra space if you're installing on a compressed drive.

For the best results with drive compression in Windows 95, use the new DriveSpace 3 software that comes with the Microsoft Plus! pack. ■

Improvements in Windows Setup

Microsoft has worked hard to strengthen the Setup program for Windows 95. Among the major improvements:

- New modular architecture for greater customization and flexibility
- Vastly improved hardware detection and configuration accuracy
- Smart recovery modes for problem installations
- Automatic verification of installed components, with correction and replacement of corrupted files or components
- Completely graphical-based installation
- Support for automated installation
- Integrated network installation

Windows 95 is a complete operating system for the PC. As such, it is responsible for installing and integrating the disk operating system, the graphical user interface, and all network support. In addition, it provides support for an incredible number of peripheral devices including monitors, video systems, sound cards, scanners, removable drive media, and modems. While Windows 95 Setup is not perfect, you will be impressed by the simplicity and thoroughness of the new installation approach, the burdens it lifts from the average user, and the backward-compatibility it provides for older peripheral systems and legacy applications.

Preparing for Windows 95 Setup

While Windows 95 Setup does an amazing job configuring most systems, there are some useful tips and tricks for preparing your machine for installation that will save you time and trouble. Before you begin your installation, be sure to do the following:

- Confirm your system meets the minimum Windows 95 hardware and software requirements
- Confirm the boot drive sequence for your system
- Confirm you have a working boot floppy disk for your current operating system configuration
- Back up your critical data and system configuration files (a complete system backup is preferred)
- Confirm that your current Windows installation is in the best possible working order
- Defragment your hard drive(s)
- Know the location of all required drivers for any peripherals (including network interface cards)
- Know all user names and passwords you'll need to log in to your network
- Disable all memory-resident programs (loaded in AUTOEXEC.BAT and CONFIG.SYS files)
- Disable antivirus programs, screen savers, diskscan utilities, and any similar programs
- Disable third-party memory managers, replacing them with HIMEM.SYS and EMM386.EXE
- Remove any substitute shells or shell extensions, such as Norton Desktop for Windows
- Prune your program groups in Program Manager

You should follow most of these procedures for any major change in your computing system.

N O T E While it's usually wise to make backup copies of the installation disks for a new program before you begin, you can forget about it with Windows 95. Microsoft uses a proprietary disk format for Windows 95 floppies that neither MS-DOS nor Windows 3.x can duplicate. Take care of your original disks! ▨

The first step is to confirm that your system meets the minimum hardware requirements. Part of this process is to check the README and SETUP.TXT files that come on the installation disks or check the CD-ROM for notes about hardware-related issues that may need to be considered when you install Windows.

ON THE WEB

You can search the Microsoft Windows Knowledge Base for information that may pertain to your hardware. The Knowledge Base is found on the Microsoft TechNet CD-ROM, on CompuServe by typing **GO Microsoft**, or on the Internet at **http://www.microsoft.com**.

You can download a "Comprehensive Guide to Troubleshooting Setup in Windows 95" at **http://www.microsoft.com/TechNet/ps/win95/setup.htm**.

A precaution is to have a confirmed boot backup plan for your system. This comes in two parts: having a boot floppy disk and configuring your system to use it. A good boot disk is not just a bootable floppy but one that configures your system as closely as possible to the current boot session configurations you normally use via your hard drive. This means you should copy your AUTOEXEC.BAT and CONFIG.SYS files onto the boot disk, and include all the device drivers you need to access the hardware devices in your computer, such as the CD-ROM. It's worth the time it takes to create this "boot backup." The few minutes to do this can save you hours of hair-pulling later.

A great boot disk is worthless if your system can't read it. Most systems are configured to search the drives during startup to find a bootable disk, but some are configured to look only at a specific drive, to save time at startup, or for security reasons. If in doubt about your system, *test it*. If you create a boot disk and the system won't read it from a cold start, check the system CMOS settings and correct the boot sequence (see your computer's manual regarding access to the CMOS setup). The ideal is for the system to search drive A and then continue to the next floppy (if present) before looking for startup information on drive C. While you can configure a system for a reverse of this order (C, then A), some systems will fail by looking at C and then staring off into digital space. Check your system to make sure it's set to search A first, before you learn the hard way.

While having a system backup is obvious to experienced users, the new and the brave may blithely exist without such safety nets. If you don't have a backup plan or system, get one before you invest hours of valuable time configuring your system, and before you lose hours of work due to a power failure or drive crash. This is especially true when installing a new operating system, which involves changes to the configuration of almost every component of your computer, including the storage media systems. Much effort has gone into making today's operating systems and hardware as reliable as is affordably possible, but *nothing* can prevent *all* accidents.

If your Windows 3.x system is working, Windows 95 can use those previous settings to confirm your peripheral configurations. If those settings are incorrect, Windows 95 has no real choice but to try them and fail. Even if your current installation and peripherals are working perfectly, be sure to have your device driver floppy disks handy in case Windows 95 Setup needs to refer to them during installation (especially if you're setting up a dual-boot system).

Defragmenting your hard drive prior to installation ensures that Windows 95 will find enough contiguous drive space to create the swap files it needs for virtual memory support. Defragmentation also makes your system run faster (especially during file copy sessions) because the drive system doesn't have to search frantically for free drive clusters.

 TIP   When you run Setup, it automatically uses DOS ScanDisk to check your hard disk. If you have already checked your disk using another utility, you can bypass this check by adding the /iq and /is switches to the SETUP command. These switches tell Setup to skip the check for cross-linked files and the DOS ScanDisk check.

Another worthwhile precaution is to disable all memory-resident programs (TSRs), antivirus programs, screen savers, utilities that scan your disk automatically checking for errors, and any other programs of this nature that might interfere with the setup procedure. Also, if you have a laptop that is set to automatically go into suspend mode after a period of inactivity, disable this feature.

Also disable any third-party memory managers and replace them with HIMEM.SYS and EMM386.EXE. You may run into problems after you install Windows 95 if you don't do this.

If you have installed a substitute shell for Program Manager, such as Norton Desktop for Windows, you should remove it. Edit the SHELL= line in the [boot] section of SYSTEM.INI to read SHELL=PROGMAN.EXE.

Although there is no harm in leaving the program groups you have set up in Program Manager as they are, because they are all placed in the Programs submenu of the Start menu, your Programs menu is much easier to read and use if you consolidate your program groups into about ten groups. Put all your file and disk management programs into a group called System Maintenance, for example. After you have installed Windows 95, you can easily reorganize the Start Menu submenus to suit your needs.

Backing Up Your Critical Files

A complete system backup is part of the preparation for any system change. If you don't have the facility for a full backup, then consider backing up your critical operating system data as a minimum preparation. These are the recommended files to back up:

- CONFIG.SYS and AUTOEXEC.BAT (located in the root directory of your boot drive, usually C)
- Any files listed in CONFIG.SYS and AUTOEXEC.BAT
- Any network configuration files (include any login scripts) such as CFG, INI, or DAT files in your network driver or root directory
- Your complete DOS directory
- Any initialization (INI) files for Windows applications
- Any Program Information Files (PIF) for MS-DOS applications
- Registry data files (DAT) in your Windows directory
- Password files (PWL) in your Windows directory

 T I P You can search by using the recursion function of the MS-DOS `dir` command (for example, dir c:*.ini /s searches your entire C drive for initialization files).

While most INI and PIF files reside in the Windows directory, some applications store them in their own directory.

Or you can skip the search step and copy all the desired files using the recursion switch for the `xcopy` command. For example, the `xcopy c:\*.pif /s a:` command copies all PIF files on drive C to your A drive, complete with a directory structure if you need to re-create it later.

If you routinely use a backup utility, you may want to simply rely on your last backup prior to installation, or make a new one for just the files types mentioned here. Consult your backup software documentation for more information on how to accomplish this.

Part
XI

App
A

How Windows 95 Setup Works

Before you begin to install Windows 95, it's probably a good idea to know what to expect and when to expect it. Windows 95 Setup has four basic phases:

- Detection
- Question and answer
- File copy
- Startup

Phase One: Setup Detection—Software, then Hardware

Windows 95 Setup starts by detecting what environment it was started from. If you opt to install from within a running Windows 3.1x installation, Setup skips a few steps and gets straight to the business of analyzing your hardware. If you don't have Windows installed, or choose to start from the MS-DOS prompt, Setup first copies and executes a "mini-window" that runs the remainder of the Setup program and then moves on to hardware detection.

Setup checks your system for the following:

- An extended memory manager and cache program. If neither is found, HIMEM.SYS or SMARTDRV.EXE is loaded.
- Installed hardware devices
- Connected peripherals
- IRQs, I/O, and DMA addresses available
- IRQs, I/O, and DMA addresses in use

Don't be surprised if the hardware detection phase takes a few minutes. Windows 95 Setup uses a variety of techniques to perform this hardware query. Most PCs respond well to this procedure, which results in the creation of a hardware tree in the Registry. Older PCs may represent a problem if the devices are not industry-standard for IRQs or I/O addresses; newer machines with Plug and Play technology report their configurations more quickly, fully, and accurately.

When the hardware detection phase finishes, Setup displays a dialog box offering you an opportunity to review the detected equipment and settings for accuracy. If they are correct, you can proceed to the next phase. If there's a problem, you can deal with it directly or tell Windows to ignore it for the time being.

Phase Two: Providing Additional Information

After Setup has the basic information regarding your hardware, it knows most of what it needs to know to install Windows on your system. However, there's still a few details to complete, and you also can exercise options regarding exactly which Windows components you want to install. Setup guides you through this process with a few clear dialog boxes. These options are discussed in more detail later in this chapter.

Phase Three: Copy Chores

Unlike Windows 3.1, Windows 95 Setup asks most questions up front and lets you relax during the actual installation process. After you tell it what you want, it completes the chores by itself, asking only for disk changes. (If you are installing from a CD-ROM drive, you don't even have to worry about that!)

When all Windows 95 files are copied, Setup upgrades the existing version of MS-DOS on your boot drive with the Windows 95 operating system.

Phase Four: Home Stretch—System Startup

When it has replaced the MS-DOS operating system, Setup then restarts your system and finishes the final cleanup chores required for installation. When this is finished, you're ready to roll with Windows 95.

Using Windows 95 Setup

This section begins by showing you two primary ways to install Windows 95:

- Installing from a working Windows 3.1x system
- Installing from an MS-DOS-only system (or Windows 3.0, Windows NT, and OS/2)

How do you know which way to install Windows 95? If at all possible, run Setup from within a working installation of Windows 3.1x or later (this includes all versions of Windows for Workgroups). Started this way, Setup can use your existing Windows installation for information on how best to configure your system.

If Windows is not on your computer, Setup installs a "mini-window" to run from. If you're running Windows NT, you need to return your system to MS-DOS (via NT's dual-boot option) before starting Windows 95 Setup. The same is true if you're running OS/2 or Windows 3.0.

If your computer system is completely new and has no operating system installed, be sure you have the non-upgrade version of Windows 95. Otherwise, you'll be up the creek, because the standard upgrade version requires a previous version of Windows or DOS, or at least installation disk one of one of these operating systems, to operate.

The question of when to install a dual-boot system is inherently problematic. There are many variables involved, but you can boil it down to a simple question: Am I truly prepared to kiss my current Windows installation good-bye? If you're installing Windows 95 for the first time, you may want to keep your previous installation intact until you've proven Windows 95 is compatible with all of your applications and peripherals. If you do opt for the "dual-Windows" approach, be prepared for some serious impact on your disk space reserves, and be prepared to mentally juggle when you switch from version to version. No matter which approach you choose, *make a backup before you begin.*

▶ **See** "Setting Up a Dual-Boot System," **p. 1212**

Installing Windows 95 from Windows 3.x

You can run Windows 95 Setup from any installation of Windows 3.1 or later. If you don't have at least version 3.1, then skip to "Installing Windows from MS-DOS," later in this chapter.

Starting Windows 95 Setup is just like running any other Windows Setup program. If you haven't already, start your current version of Windows. Once it's running, you have a couple of choices of how to start Setup: from the Program Manager or File Manager.

Before you go further, make sure you have the installation disk set or CD-ROM in the appropriate drive. These examples assume you are using floppies in drive A. If you have a CD-ROM drive, simply substitute the appropriate drive letter for A.

Starting Setup from Program Manager   To start Setup from Program Manager, choose File, Run from the main Program Manager menu. Windows displays the Run dialog box (see fig. A.1). Type **a:setup** and click OK to begin the installation process.

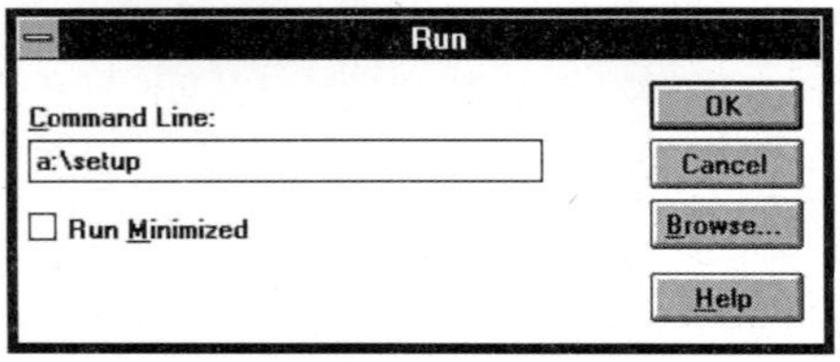

FIG. A.1
Specify the appropriate drive letter, and type **setup**.

There are several switches you can use to control how Setup will run. Enter these switches after the setup command in the Run dialog box. These switches are useful if you know you can safely bypass certain Setup procedures and save some time. The following table describes these switches. Note that two of the switches can only be used when running Setup from MS-DOS (see "Installing Windows 95 from MS-DOS").

Table A.1   Setup Switches

Switch	Function
/C	Doesn't load SmartDrv (when running Setup from MS-DOS)
/T:*\<path\>*	Specifies the directory to be used for the temporary files created during setup. You must create the directory first. The directory is deleted after Setup is finished.
/I	Bypasses hardware detection
/ID	Bypasses disk space check
/IM	Bypasses convention memory check
/IN	Bypasses Network Setup module
/IQ	Bypasses cross-linked file check
/IS	Bypasses hard disk check (using DOS ScanDisk)
\<batch filename\>(no /)	Specifies a batch file containing Setup options (when running Setup from MS-DOS)
/?	Help

If you're not sure what drive your Windows 95 Setup disk is in, don't despair. You can choose Browse to find it. Windows displays the Browse dialog box to help you (see fig. A.2).

FIG. A.2

You can search for the Setup disk using the Browse dialog box.

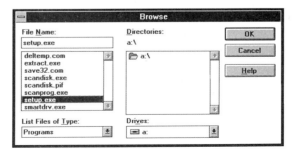

When you select SETUP.EXE, Windows loads and runs the Windows 95 Setup program. After a few seconds, Setup displays the welcome screen shown in figure A.3.

FIG. A.3
You're on your way when you see the big blue screen.

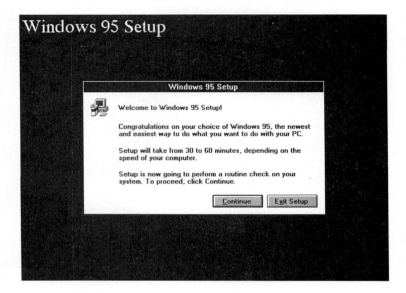

Starting Setup from File Manager   Start File Manager from the Program Manager Main program group by double-clicking the File Manager icon. When the File Manager window appears, click on the icon for the appropriate drive where you've loaded your Windows 95 installation disk or CD-ROM. File Manager then displays the contents of the drive as shown in figure A.4.

FIG. A.4
You can start Windows 95 Setup from File Manager.

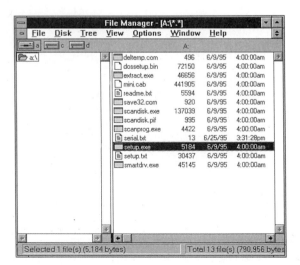

To start Setup, double-click SETUP.EXE. Windows loads the program, and Setup displays the welcome screen.

Getting Down to Business with Setup To continue Windows 95 Setup, click <u>C</u>ontinue. Setup displays the message box shown in figure A.5.

FIG. A.5
Setup keeps you posted during its investigations.

Setup performs a brief check of your hardware, current operating system, and current running programs before proceeding. It then displays the End-User License Agreement. Read it and click <u>Y</u>es to continue.

TROUBLESHOOTING

When I run Setup it hangs during the system check. The first thing to do is check your hard disk for viruses. Viruses are a common cause for Setup hanging during the routine check performed by ScanDisk. After you check for viruses, run ScanDisk from the DOS prompt and then run Setup again. If Setup still hangs, run it again with the /IS switch to bypass the routine check.

When the Setup loader finishes creating the Setup Wizard, Windows may display the dialog box seen in figure A.6. If you have any open programs, it "strongly" suggests you close them before proceeding. This is especially wise if you have any unsaved documents in other applications.

FIG. A.6
While Windows 95 Setup is well-behaved, it's always better to be safe than sorry.

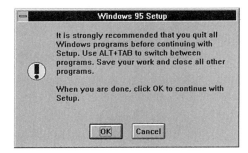

Take the time to use Alt+Tab to close any other open applications or documents. (You won't be able to close Program Manager without exiting Windows.) When you finish, use Alt+Tab to return to Windows 95 Setup, and click OK to proceed. Setup then displays the main Windows 95 Setup Wizard dialog box (see fig. A.7).

FIG. A.7
The Windows 95 Setup Wizard leads you through the entire process of installing Windows 95 on your computer.

Setup begins the first major phase requiring user interaction by collecting information about your system and how you'll use it. Click Next to proceed. Windows displays the Choose Directory dialog box (see fig. A.8).

FIG. A.8
Most users choose to install Windows 95 as an upgrade to their existing Windows 3.x installation (usually in C:\WINDOWS). Choose Next to confirm this option.

If you want to install Windows 95 over your current Windows installation, click Next to proceed. If you want to install to another directory, choose Other Directory and Next; then refer to "Setting Up a Dual-Boot System" later in this chapter.

The next option is a great idea. Windows 95 Setup presents the dialog box shown in figure A.9 and asks you if you want to save your Windows 3.1 and DOS system files. Saving these files takes only about 6–9M of disk space and it's highly recommended that you do this. Saving these files allows you to uninstall Windows 95 (as described later in this appendix) if you ever need to revert to your Windows 3.1 setup. Notice this is *not* a full backup of your system or applications. This just saves files needed to start DOS, Windows, and Windows configuration files. Choose to save these files and then click Next to continue.

FIG. A.9
Save your old Windows 3.1 and DOS system files now and save yourself some grief if you ever need to uninstall Windows 95.

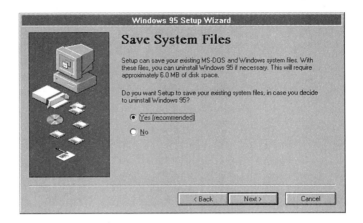

T I P If, after using Windows 95 for a while, you decide that you don't need to keep the Windows 3.x and DOS system files any longer, you can uninstall these files and free up 6–9M of hard disk space. To remove the uninstall files, follow these steps:

1. Open Add/Remove Programs from the Control Panel.

2. Select Old Windows 3.x/MS-DOS System Files in the software list in the Install/Uninstall tab.

3. Choose the Add/Remove button.

Be aware that when you remove these files you can no longer use the Uninstall feature to remove Windows 95.

Setup next checks your system for available installed components and disk space. You don't need to take any action for Setup to move to the next stage. As soon as Setup determines your available drive space, it asks you to confirm what type of installation you need (see fig. A.10).

FIG. A.10
You can choose from Typical, Portable, Compact, or Custom installation profiles.

Your choice here depends on how you use your computer and how you use Windows. With the Typical installation option, you need only provide some user and computer information, and tell Setup whether you want an emergency startup disk (highly recommended).

The Custom option allows you to select exactly which components will be installed. You can, for example, choose not to install Windows accessories you know you won't be using, and select components that are not installed when you choose the Typical installation. If you want to install Microsoft Exchange (the MAPI mail service), Microsoft Fax, The Microsoft Network, the Network Administration Tools, or the Online User's Guide, you must use the Custom installation.

You will want to use the Custom installation if Setup is having trouble detecting your hardware. You can then manually select what hardware Setup should automatically detect and set the configurations for any hardware that is causing problems. When you use the Custom installation, you can make these selections in the Hardware Detection dialog box.

The Custom installation option allows the experienced user near-total control over Windows installation. If you are the master of your computing domain, this selection lets you specify network settings, device configurations, and most other variables in your Windows 95 setup. For more information on the Custom option see "Using Custom Setup Mode" later in this chapter.

N O T E   When you use the Typical option, you can't be sure what is being installed. Not all of the Windows accessories and games are installed, for example. Using the Custom option gives you the opportunity to review exactly what is being installed, so in most cases it is worth the extra few moments it takes to go this route, no matter what kind of system you are installing Windows 95 on. ■

The Portable setup option is best for laptop or mobile computer users. Setup installs the Windows Briefcase tools for file synchronization and transfer.

The Compact setup option is for systems where you must absolutely minimize the Windows "footprint." This option is for those with frugal drive budgets. Windows is completely installed, but all extraneous accessories are not (disk compression and maintenance tools are the only accessories installed).

T I P   To find out the differences between the types of installation, look in the Resource Kit, which is located in the \Admin\Reskit\Helpfile folder on the CD-ROM version of Windows 95. Double-click on WIN95RK.HLP and type **typical** in the text box of the Index tab. Click Display and you get a summary of the different types of installations.

▶ **See** "Using Custom Setup Mode," **p. 1203**

The Typical Windows 95 Setup Process

For now, let's look at a typical setup, as that is what most Windows 95 users will need. To continue the installation, click Next or Press Enter to confirm the default selection (Typical). Windows displays the User Information dialog box (see fig. A.11).

FIG. A.11
Providing your name helps Windows properly identify you in later application installations and helps Windows identify your system on the Windows Network.

Fill in the appropriate information for your installation, and click Next or press Enter. The next stage in Setup is further analysis of your peripheral hardware. Setup displays the Analyzing Your Computer dialog box as shown in figure A.12. Be sure to check any items you want Windows to sense, or it will skip them!

FIG. A.12
Depending on what hardware is installed on your system, Windows displays several options in this dialog box. Confirm or deny your peripheral stance, and Setup does the rest.

Click Next or press Enter and Setup then checks your entire system to profile your peripherals (display adapter, sound cards, CD-ROM drives, and so on). When Setup finishes this investigation, the Windows Components dialog box appears (see fig. A.13).

N O T E If you don't check an item, Setup won't try to detect that class of device. If you do
have a network adapter or multimedia card, and you want Setup to find it, you much
check these options. ■

FIG. A.13
In the Typical setup mode,
Setup allows you to alter
the Windows component
defaults.

If you're setting Windows up on a single-user, non-networked machine, odds are the
default settings are just fine for you. Click Next or press Enter, and Setup displays
the Startup Disk dialog box (see fig. A.14).

FIG. A.14
Create a Startup Disk now
and avoid regrets later.

Click Next or press Enter to tell Setup to create a startup disk. Setup won't prompt you to
do it immediately, so you have a few minutes to find a blank floppy disk. The Startup Disk
contains all the files your computer needs to run if the system files on your hard drive
become corrupt.

TIP You may want to add some files to your Startup disk to help you recover from a system crash. If you have a CD-ROM, you should include the driver file for the CD-ROM and AUTOEXEC.BAT and CONFIG.SYS files with the commands for loading the driver. If you have other devices that are necessary to run in MS-DOS mode, then make copies of these drivers and their lines from the CONFIG.SYS or AUTOEXEC.BAT files. This will save you time if you have to reinstall Windows 95 from the DOS prompt using your Windows 95 CD-ROM.

Click Next or press Enter, and Setup proceeds to the next major section of Windows 95 installation.

The Big Copy Job Having completed its inquiries, Setup can now begin moving the Windows 95 program(s) to your hard drive. Setup displays the Start Copying Files dialog box.

Click Next or press Enter, and Setup continues. The next displayed screen is the familiar Windows 95 Setup background, with a "gas gauge" at the bottom to indicate copy progress (see fig. A.15). If you are installing from CD-ROM, you won't have to do much at this point. If you are installing from floppy disks, be prepared to swap disks as prompted. Windows Setup will prompt you to insert a disk to create the Startup Disk if you selected this option (see fig. A.16).

FIG. A.15
Windows 95 Setup prompts you for installation disks as needed.

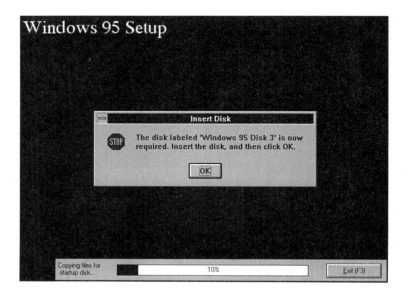

Right in the middle of installation may seem like a strange time to create a boot disk, but this also is a good way to get you to do it.

FIG. A.16

Now's the time to invest in some computing insurance by creating your Windows 95 Startup Disk.

 TROUBLESHOOTING

My system froze up while the Startup disk was being made. You have two options to work around this problem:

Remove the `device=symevnt.386` line in the [386enh] section of your SYSTEM.INI file and run Setup again.

or

Run Setup again and bypass making a Startup disk during setup. After Windows 95 is installed, create a startup disk using the Startup Disk tab in the Add/Remove Programs Properties sheet.

When the gas gauge shows full, your Startup Disk is done, and Setup returns you to the installation.

Completing the Setup Process

After Setup has copied all Windows 95 files to your hard drive, the Finishing Setup dialog box appears, as shown in figure A.17.

FIG. A.17

Setup needs to restart your system to complete the installation process.

Up to this point, Setup has operated as a 16-bit Windows 3.1 application. When you choose Finish and your system reboots, you'll actually be entering the world of Windows 95 computing for the first time.

Restarting Setup, Starting Windows 95

During the Copy phase of Setup, all primary Windows 95 files were created on your hard drive, and many other components of the operating system were initialized as well. When you restarted Windows 95 Setup, MS-DOS was replaced with the new Windows 95 Real Mode kernel, and your hard drive's boot sector was updated to run only the new operating system.

When Setup resumes, it continues the Windows 95 installation by updating remaining configuration files and asking you a few more questions regarding your system peripherals. Most of these tasks are done by a system called the Run-Once Module, which fires up the appropriate system wizards to help you complete your installation.

The process begins with a quick scan of the system hardware. After this quick scan, Setup runs several short routines that can only be performed from within Windows 95 (setting up Control Panels for all appropriate devices, setting up program icons in the Start menu, initializing Windows Help, and confirming the local time zone) as shown in figure A.18.

FIG. A.18
After Windows 95 is running, it can complete Windows 95-specific setup tasks.

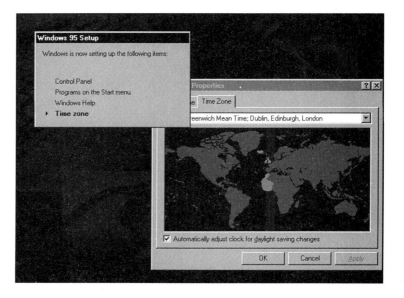

A nice touch is the Time Zone dialog box. Click on the map near your part of the planet, and Windows 95 adjusts the system clock accordingly, even down to daylight savings time (if you've already adjusted your system clock, you may want to uncheck the DST option).

When the Run-Once tasks are complete, Setup is complete, and you're in the world of Windows 95 at last (see fig. A.19).

FIG. A.19
The Welcome to Windows 95 dialog box gives you the basic tips for navigation and registration.

 TROUBLESHOOTING

When Setup attempts to reboot and start up Windows 95, my system hangs. Reboot your system with a bootup disk and comment out any lines in your SYSTEM.INI file that reference an old swapfile. This may do the trick.

Installing Windows 95 from MS-DOS

If you don't have an installation of Windows version 3.1 or later, or are using Windows NT or OS/2, you need to start Windows 95 Setup from the venerable MS-DOS prompt.

Starting Windows 95 Setup from MS-DOS is just like running any other MS-DOS program. If you're using a plain MS-DOS machine, you need version MS-DOS 3.2 or later. To begin, boot the machine just as for any other computing session. If you're using another operating system, you need to use the dual-boot feature or boot from a floppy disk to attain MS-DOS operation.

This example assumes you are using floppy disks in drive A. If you have a CD-ROM drive, substitute the appropriate drive letter for A in the following examples.

The first step in starting Windows 95 Setup from the MS-DOS prompt is to type **a:setup** and press Enter.

There are several command-line switches you can use with the `setup` command to customize how Setup will run. These switches are described in Table A.1 earlier in this appendix.

MS-DOS then runs the Windows 95 Setup program, which starts by running the Windows 95 version of ScanDisk. The first thing you see on-screen is a message saying `Please wait while Setup initializes. Setup is now going to perform a routine check on your system. To continue, press ENTER. To quit Setup, press ESC.` Press Enter to continue. Setup then starts ScanDisk (as shown in fig. A.20), which runs automatically to check out your drives. Follow the prompts to deal with any drive anomalies.

FIG. A.20
Setup needs to check out your disk before it begins. When ScanDisk finishes, exit back to MS-DOS, where Setup continues.

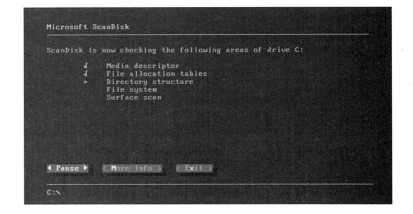

Setup copies a small version of Windows 3.1 to your system so the graphical portions of Setup can run. After that is complete, Setup displays the Welcome screen shown in figure A.21.

FIG. A.21
From this point on, Setup is the same whether you started from MS-DOS or the latest version of Windows.

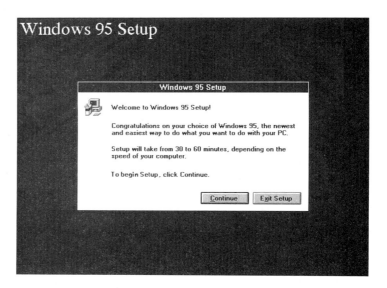

The remaining Setup procedures are nearly identical to those listed earlier in this chapter for installing from Windows 3.1. If you're installing Windows 95 as your first version of Windows, you have to install all of your Windows applications after Windows 95 Setup is complete. If you installed from MS-DOS but didn't install over your existing Windows subdirectory, you'll have to do the same.

▶ **See** "Installing Windows 95 from Windows 3.x," **p. 1188**

Doing a Clean Install

A disadvantage to installing Windows 95 on a system with Windows 3.x is that you inevitably end up with bits and pieces of Windows 3.x left on your hard disk. It is very difficult—if not impossible—to remove all the traces of Windows 3.x. A solution to this problem is to do a clean install by repartitioning and reformatting your hard disk and then installing Windows 95 from scratch. Although this process takes you much longer than installing from Windows 3.x, you have the satisfaction of starting with a very clean system. In some cases, users have reported that the performance of Windows 95 improved significantly when they did a clean install.

To clean install Windows 95, follow these steps:

1. Create a boot disk for your system and copy FDISK.EXE and FORMAT.COM from the \DOS subdirectory onto the disk.

   If you have a CD-ROM on your system and you will be installing Windows 95 from a CD-ROM, be sure to copy the drivers for the CD-ROM on the disk, as well as AUTOEXEC.BAT and CONFIG.SYS files for loading the drivers at startup.

2. Carefully back up all of your data files, configuration (INI) and DAT files for your applications, and so on.

3. Reboot your computer using the boot disk.

4. Repartition your hard disk using FDISK.

   Now is the time to partition your hard disk into two or more logical drives if you want to use separate drives for your data and applications or you want to improve the storage efficiency of a large hard drive by reducing the cluster size. See "Using FDISK to Repartition an Existing Drive," in Chapter 22 for details on how to use FDISK to repartition a drive.

CAUTION

Repartitioning your hard drive destroys all the information on it. Make sure you have a reliable backup of all your important data.

5. Reformat the drive using FORMAT.COM.

6. Reinstall MS-DOS.

   You must use MS-DOS version 3.2 or higher (or an equivalent OEM version). If you use version 3.2, make sure it supports partitions greater than 32M.

7. Reboot your computer and run Setup from the DOS prompt.

8. Reinstall all of your applications and restore your data files from your backups.

N O T E   If you are installing the final version of Windows 95 on a system that had beta versions of Windows 95, Microsoft recommends that you perform a clean install to remove any traces of the earlier versions.

Advanced Installation Techniques

As simple as Windows 95 Setup can be, there are still situations that demand special considerations to meet special needs. There are as many different Windows installations as there are Windows users, and Windows 95 Setup is flexible enough to meet most needs.

Using Custom Setup Mode

Microsoft's Windows 95 development team has done an admirable job of establishing compatibility with a variety of peripheral components, but no one can perfectly predict all of the equipment variables in the churning world of the PC hardware market.

Installing Windows 95 for special setups is straightforward if you have the appropriate information ready before you begin. The Custom setup option allows you to specify application settings, network configuration options, device configurations, and gives you more control over the installation of Windows 95 components.

> **CAUTION**
>
> The Custom installation mode puts a lot of power in your hands. If you don't have the specific experience in network or device configuration, you're better off leaving this to Windows 95 Setup auto-detection, or your MIS department.

Before you begin, know the exact name and model number of the card or device you're installing, and have any special device driver files handy (the original floppy disk is fine, if you don't know where the drivers are on your hard drive). Find out the logical memory address defaults for the component, if applicable (see the peripheral documentation).

 T I P To obtain useful information about your system that can help you during the installation of Windows 95, exit Windows 3.x and type **MSD** at the command prompt. Choose File, Print Report, select Report All *, and choose OK. The information on the printout may assist you in answering questions presented during Windows 95 setup.

To use Windows 95 Setup in Custom mode, proceed with installation as described earlier in this chapter up to the point of selecting the Setup Options dialog box (shown in figure A.22).

FIG. A.22
Select the Custom option to gain more control over your system configuration.

At this point, select the Custom option and click Next. Don't expect Setup to change drastically from this point on; you see a few more dialog boxes, where Setup asks you the appropriate questions regarding additional options. The next screen you see is the User Information dialog box. When you complete this dialog box, Setup displays the Analyzing Your Computer dialog box shown in figure A.23.

FIG. A.23
If you know you're going to need to alter your device configurations, you can select the option easily in this dialog box.

Customizing Hardware Support   If you know you have nonstandard or unsupported devices in your installation, select the N<u>o</u>, I Want to Modify the Hardware List radio button. Then click Next to proceed. Setup displays the screen shown in figure A.24.

FIG. A.24
Select the device type in the left window and the specific device name in the right. Changing the item on the left changes the list on the right.

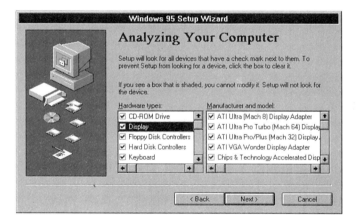

This is where you need the information about your system mentioned earlier. If you *know* that you have an unusual peripheral, look for it here. Setup guides you through installing any special drivers for the device at the appropriate time.

If your device doesn't appear in the lists here, it means one of two things: either Windows 95 has native 32-bit support for the device or no support for it. If Setup didn't detect your device earlier in the installation, you need to tell it to install it now. Or, if it was detected, and the Windows installation didn't work, you can tell Windows to skip it this round.

You can manually install the device later using the Add New Hardware control panel. When you've selected all the device types you want configured, click Next. After completing its analysis of your selected equipment, Setup displays the Select Components dialog box, shown in figure A.25.

FIG. A.25
Select the Windows 95 components you want Setup to install. Setup provides additional information about each option when you click Details.

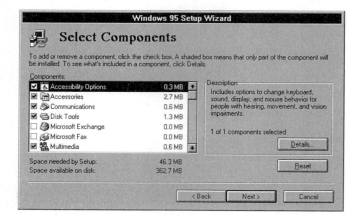

When you've selected all of the Windows 95 components you want installed, click Next. The remainder of the installation depends on what hardware and software component options you've selected. Setup attempts to locate your devices and prompts you when it needs additional information such as device driver files. The next section looks at the basic steps to install network support under Windows 95.

N O T E If Setup fails to correctly detect your hardware device, you can try several things to correct the problem:

- Reinstall the drivers for the hardware, using the original drivers that came with the hardware.

- If there seem to be conflicts between hardware devices, remove all of the devices (for example, sound cards, modems, CD-ROMS) and then use the Add New Hardware Wizard in the Control Panel to reinstall them one-by-one. This will help you isolate the problem.

- You can use the generic video drivers that come with Windows 95 if your monitor does not appear in the monitor list. You can also try to use the driver for a closely related monitor. This may optimize the features for your monitor better than the generic drivers. ▪

TROUBLESHOOTING

Setup has repeatedly crashed on my system. When I checked the DETLOG.TXT file, it seems that it always gets hung up when it checks for one particular device. How can I get around this problem? In most cases, Setup uses the information it gathers while detecting devices to bypass any device that caused it to crash when you restart Setup. However, if it seems a device on your system is repeatedly causing problems, you can turn off the detection module for that device so Setup won't crash trying to detect it. To turn off a device module, follow these steps:

1. When Setup gets to the Setup Options screen, choose Custom.

2. When the Analyzing Your Computer screen is displayed, select No, I Want to Modify the Hardware List.

3. Disable detection for the type of hardware and the specific device by checking the appropriate items in Hardware Detection dialog box.

4. Continue with the setup.

Installing Windows 95 Network Features   If you've selected network support, Setup next displays the Network Configuration dialog box. You can install network support for multiple adapters and protocols from this one Setup screen.

N O T E   See Part VIII, "Networking with Windows 95," for additional information on configuring network support in Windows 95. ▧

To begin configuring your network options, click Add. Setup displays the Select Network Component Type dialog box (see fig. A.26).

FIG. A.26
Click on the network component type you want to install.

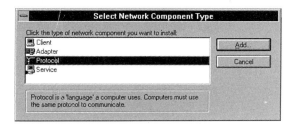

When you select the component type you want to install, Setup displays another selection dialog box for that component classification. For example, if you select Protocol and then click Add, Setup displays the Select Network Protocols dialog box shown in figure A.27.

FIG. A.27
Select the protocol manufacturer in the left list and then
the specific protocol type in
the right list.

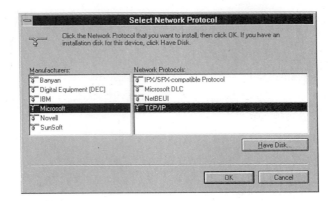

When you've selected the appropriate protocols network adapter, you can either click OK
(to let Setup determine if Windows 95 has native drivers for these types) or click Have
Disk to install your own drivers.

Setup may make assumptions about other network support components based on the
adapter type you select. For example, selecting the Intel EtherExpress 16 or 16TP results
in Setup selecting clients and protocols for both Netware and The Microsoft Network
types, as shown in figure A.28.

FIG. A.28
Setup may make additional
choices based on your
hardware selection. You can
override this by using the
Remove button, but be sure
you don't need the compo-
nent before you proceed.

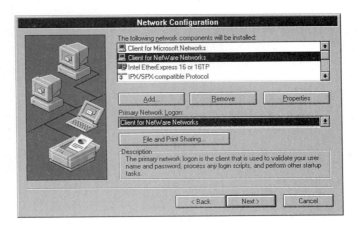

Using Smart Recovery

If Setup fails during your installation, it has the capability to recover gracefully. Two files
are created during the setup process that help Setup to learn from any errors that occur
during installation. DETLOG.TXT records all the devices that Setup looks for during installation and whether they were found. If Setup fails while it is attempting to detect a

device, a file named DETCRASH.LOG is created so that when you restart Setup, the problem device will be bypassed.

A second file, SETUPLOG.TXT records additional information about the progress of the Setup process. Using the information in these files, Setup Safe Recovery is able to automatically skip problem configuration items to allow the installation to finish, and then allows you to go back to the problem and correct it.

If Setup fails during installation, you need to power off your system and then restart it. Pressing Ctrl+Alt+Del (warm boot) is not sufficient to completely reset your system. When you restart your computer, do not delete any files on your hard disk. Restart Setup and choose the Smart Recovery option. If Setup fails again, repeat this process. Each time you repeat the process, Setup moves further along in the installation process, because it doesn't trip on the same problem twice. In most cases, you can eventually complete the installation. You can then look in the two files discussed previously (DETLOG.TXT and SETUPLOG.TXT) to find out where Setup stumbled and fix the problems.

Safe Recovery also can be used in repairing damaged installations. If you run Setup after a complete Windows 95 installation, it first asks whether you want to confirm or repair your installation, or whether you want to completely reinstall Windows 95 (see fig. A.29).

FIG. A.29
You also can use Safe Recovery after a complete installation to repair damage.

 TROUBLESHOOTING

I seem to have tried everything to get Windows 95 to install on my system, but with no success. What else can I try? One more trick worth trying is to clean boot your system and run Setup again.

continues

continued

To clean boot a system that doesn't have any disk-compression or disk-partitioning software or any other third-party software needed to boot your system, follow these steps:

1. Rename CONFIG.SYS to **CONFIG.XXX** and AUTOEXEC.BAT to **AUTOEXEC.XXX**.

2. Reboot your system and run Setup.

If you have third-party software on your system that is needed to boot up, use one of the two following methods to restart your system and rerun Setup. In each method you must create or edit a CONFIG.SYS or AUTOEXEC.BAT as shown, then restart your computer, and then rerun Setup.

If you are installing Windows 95 from MS-DOS, create the following CONFIG.SYS and AUTOEXEC.BAT files, restart your computer, then rerun Setup:

CONFIG.SYS

```
FILES=45
BUFFERS=20
<Third-party disk partitioner>
<Third-party disk compression driver>
<Other required third-party driver>
SHELL=C:\<dir>\COMMAND.COM  /E:1024 /P
```

AUTOEXEC.BAT

```
PROMPT $P$G
PATH=C:\DOS;C:\
```

If you are installing Windows 95 from Windows 3.x, create the following CONFIG.SYS and AUTOEXEC.BAT files, restart your computer, then rerun Setup:

CONFIG.SYS:

```
FILES=45
BUFFERS=20
DEVICE=C:\<dir>\HIMEM.SYS
<Third-party disk partitioner>
<Third-party disk compression driver>
<Other third-party drivers>
STACKS=9,256
SHELL=C:\<dir>\COMMAND.COM  /E:1024 /P
```

AUTOEXEC.BAT

```
PROMPT $P$G
PATH=C:\WINDOWS;C:\DOS;C:\
SET TEMP=C:\<dir>
```

If you are installing from Windows 3.x, you should be sure all other Windows applications are closed and you should use the Enhanced icon in the Control Panel to turn off 32-bit file access if you are using Windows for Workgroups.

Using Safe Detection

Windows 95 Setup looks for system components in a variety of ways. Setup can detect communication ports, display adapters, processor types, drive controllers, sound cards, and network adapters. Setup also looks for system hardware resources such as IRQs, DMA channels, and I/O addresses to avoid conflicts between devices. Setup can detect both the newer Plug and Play devices and older "legacy" peripherals.

Safe Detection works on four classes of devices:

- Sound cards
- Network adapters
- SCSI controllers
- CD-ROM controllers

One problem with auto-detection routines is failure during the detection process itself. Plug and Play devices identify or announce themselves to the system, but older adapters require interactive tests to locate them and confirm operation. While most devices respond well to this, some don't. In addition, if there's any duplication of IRQ, DMA, or I/O addresses between devices, your system can lock up tighter than a drum during installation.

Windows 95 Setup can recover from such failures. Setup keeps track of the process of testing devices during installation and knows at what point a device failed. When you restart it, Setup knows not to touch that subsystem again until corrections have been applied, such as loading 16-bit device drivers, if the 32-bit native Windows 95 drivers have failed.

ON THE WEB

Search the Microsoft Knowledge Base for articles related to specific hardware issues if you are still having problems with setting up Windows 95 using the steps outlined in this section. You can find the Knowledge Base at the following Internet address: **http://www.microsoft.com/kb/**.

Setting Up a Dual-Boot System

A very popular installation option for new Windows 95 users is the *dual-boot setup*. Installing Windows 95 this way allows you to return to your previous operating system as needed or desired.

There are several ways to accomplish a dual-boot installation and several motivations for doing so. The following sections explain the techniques and options available to you under Windows 95.

Setting Up a Dual-Boot System During Installation

The simplest technique for establishing dual-boot is to simply select a new directory for Windows 95 when installing for the first time (see fig. A.30). You still have to configure Windows 95 for many of the applications in your previous Windows installation.

FIG. A.30
Specify a new directory for Windows 95, and Setup takes care of basic dual-boot details.

Setup preserves your current MS-DOS and Windows 3.1x settings if you follow this route, but it can't transfer settings for your current Windows applications to the new Windows 95 installation (see fig. A.31). In addition, Windows 95 disables, redirects, or outright deletes certain files from your DOS directory, so you may want to restore the complete DOS directory from the backup you made before installation.

FIG. A.31
Setup warns you of the additional work dual-boot operation installation may cause.

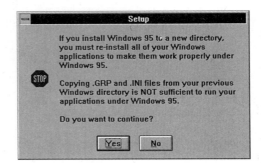

If you're prepared to reinstall your Windows applications after Windows 95 Setup is completed, this is a clean, simple way to proceed. After you install Windows 95 this way, you can return to your previous MS-DOS installation (and from there to your previous Windows installation) with a single F4 keystroke during system startup.

Setting Up a Dual-Boot System After Installation

If you've already installed Windows 95 over your existing Windows 3.1x directory, you can easily set your system up for dual-booting back to MS-DOS. However, because your previous Windows installation was stomped, you can't return to it. In addition, you may notice that some of your favorite MS-DOS commands such as XCOPY are now dust, even when you dual-boot back to MS-DOS (Windows 95 disables some MS-DOS commands, so you'll need to restore your DOS directory from that backup you made prior to installation).

To set your system up for dual-boot to your previous version of MS-DOS, follow these steps:

1. Locate your boot floppy disk for your previous version of MS-DOS (version 5.0 or later). Make a copy of it.

2. On the copy of your boot disk, change the attributes of the IO.SYS, MSDOS.SYS, and COMMAND.COM files to allow you to rename them. (The attrib -h -r -s filename.ext command works for each file.)

3. Rename the IO.SYS, MSDOS.SYS, and COMMAND.COM files on your boot floppy to **IO.DOS**, **MSDOS.DOS**, and **COMMAND.DOS**, respectively.

4. Reset the attributes of the IO.DOS, MSDOS.DOS, and COMMAND.DOS files to protect them. (Use the attrib +r filename.ext command for each file.)

5. Rename the AUTOEXEC.BAT and CONFIG.SYS files on your MS-DOS boot disk to **AUTOEXEC.DOS** and **CONFIG.DOS**, respectively. You may want to set these files to read-only also. (Use the attrib +r filename.ext command for each file.)

6. Copy IO.DOS, MSDOS.DOS, COMMAND.DOS, AUTOEXEC.DOS, and CONFIG.DOS to the boot directory of the Windows 95 drive.

You can now return to your previous MS-DOS installation with a single F4 keystroke during system startup. You also can use the F8 key during startup (when "Starting Windows 95" appears on-screen) and then select item 7, "Previous version of MS-DOS." Bear in mind that you may need to restore certain MS-DOS files that Windows 95 has removed from your DOS directory. (You can use that DOS directory backup you made prior to Windows 95 installation.)

Removing Windows 95

If you decide you want to return to your previous Windows 3. x installation, want to clean up your system before you trade or sell it, or you simply don't want to use Windows 95, you can remove all traces of Windows 95. To use the uninstall feature to uninstall Windows 95, you had to use the (highly recommended) option to save your old Windows 3.12 and DOS system files during Windows setup.

If you were using drive compression with Windows 95, you need to uncompress your hard drive before uninstalling Windows 95. If you have more files than will fit on your uncompressed drive, you will need to delete files before proceeding.

If you have installed any programs since installing Windows 95, they probably will have to be reconfigured to work with Windows 3.1, or you may have to uninstall them from Windows 95 and reinstall them in Windows 3.1. Of course, any applications written to work with Windows 95 (like Office 95) will not run in Windows 3.1.

Once you are ready to uninstall, open the Start menu and choose Settings, Control Panel. Double-click the Add/Remove Programs icon. Click the Install/Uninstall tab. This shows the Properties sheet shown in figure A.32.

FIG. A.32

The Install/Uninstall Programs page of the Add/ Remove Programs Properties sheet includes an option to uninstall Windows 95.

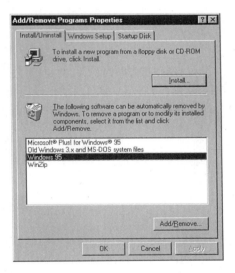

Select Windows 95 and the click Add/Remove. This opens the warning dialog box shown in figure A.33.

Your system should now boot straight to your previous version of MS-DOS. You may need to set up a new Windows 3.1 swap file as your old swap file (if you were using a permanent swap file) no longer exists.

FIG. A.33
If you are sure you want to uninstall Windows 95, click Yes. The uninstaller removes Windows 95 and restores your old DOS and Windows system files.

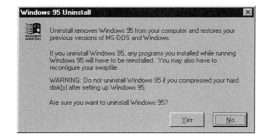

 TROUBLESHOOTING

When I start my system after uninstalling Windows 95, I get an error message saying I have a corrupt swapfile. What should I do? This is normal after uninstalling Windows 95. Choose OK in the Delete dialog box that appears. Next, open Control Panel, open the Enhanced application, and choose the Virtual Memory button. Set the swap file size to none. Reboot the computer and use the Enhanced application to set up a new permanent swap file.

Using Microsoft Plus!

by Rob Tidrow

The Microsoft Plus! Companion for Windows 95 is an add-on software package (you must buy it separately from Windows 95) of utilities and desktop enhancements left out of Windows 95. Plus! provides Desktop Themes to let you customize wallpaper settings, mouse pointers, and sound events. It provides new visual settings to improve the appearance of large fonts, desktop wallpaper, and windows you're dragging. A 3D pinball game is also included.

In addition, Plus! provides a few handy utilities, including System Agent, ScanDisk 3, the Internet Explorer, and Dial-Up Networking Server. System Agent enables you to schedule applications to automatically start at predefined times. ScanDisk 3 is an enhanced version of the ScanDisk compression technology that comes with Windows 95. If you want to connect to the Internet quickly, you can use the Internet Explorer World Wide Web browser that is included with Plus! Finally, the Dial-Up Networking Server is used with Windows 95's Dial-Up feature to let other users dial in to your computer. ■

Install Plus! on your computer

Learn how to install Plus! using the Plus! Setup Program. Also learn the proper system requirements needed to run Plus!

Customize your desktop with Plus! Desktop Themes

You can select themes to customize your desktop while installing Plus! or by using the Desktop Themes icon in Control Panel after installation.

Uninstalling Plus!

See how to use the Windows 95 Add/Remove Programs feature to remove some or all or the Microsoft Plus! companion.

Installing Plus!

After you install Windows 95 on your system, you can install the Microsoft Plus! companion separately. Plus! is available in both the 3.5 inch floppy disk and CD-ROM formats. Before you start the Plus! Setup program, make sure you have the required system resources. Because of the enhanced features of Plus!, your computer must meet higher system requirements than the basic Windows 95 requirements. These requirements are as follows:

- At least an 80486 processor (a Pentium processor is recommended).
- CD-ROM drive or floppy drive and mouse (or similar pointing device).
- Windows 95 operating system installed.
- 50M of hard disk space for a complete installation.
- 8M or more of RAM (12 to 16M recommended).
- Monitor and video card that displays 256 colors or more. Some of the Desktop Themes require a 16-bit display (16 million colors or more).
- Modem/fax modem to use the Internet and dial-up networking features.
- Sound card and speakers are recommended, but is required to hear the 3D pinball sounds and music.
- Windows 95 installation disks or CD-ROM.

Like the Windows 95 Setup program, the Plus! Setup program enables you to install the complete Plus! package using the Typical installation option. Alternatively, use the Custom installation option to install selected components.

Starting the Plus! Setup Program

You can use the Typical Setup option to install all components of Microsoft Plus!. Typical Setup requires up to 16M of hard disk space. If your system is low on hard disk space, or if you don't want to install all of Plus!'s features, perform a Custom Setup. Both of these options are covered in the following procedures.

1. For the CD-ROM version, insert the Plus! CD-ROM in the CD-ROM drive on your system. For the floppy disk version, insert Disk 1 in the appropriate drive on your system.

2. If the Windows 95 AutoRun feature is activated, the Microsoft Plus! for Windows 95 screen appears. Click on the Install Plus! icon. Skip to step 6.

3. If AutoRun is not activated (and for all floppy disk installs), start the Add/Remove Programs option in Control Panel and click the Install/Uninstall tab.

4. Click Install and click Next on the Install From Floppy Disk or CD-ROM Wizard.

5. Windows automatically searches your floppy and CD-ROM drives for setup programs. When it finds the Plus! setup program, click Finish.

   The Microsoft Plus! for Windows 95 Setup screen appears.

6. Click Continue. The Name and Organization Information dialog box appears, as shown in figure B.1.

Part

XI

App

B

FIG. B.1

Enter your name and business name. Your business name is optional.

7. In the Name and Organization Information dialog box, enter your Name and Organization. Click OK. When the confirmation dialog box displays, click OK to confirm your entries.

8. In the next dialog box, enter the 10-digit CD-key number from your Plus! package in the dialog box that appears. Click OK.

9. The Microsoft Plus! for Windows 95 Setup dialog box appears, which shows you the Plus! product ID number. You should write down this number and store it with your Plus! CD or floppy disks. Click OK to confirm the Product ID number and continue Setup.

10. Next, Setup searches your system and displays a dialog box listing the folder Setup creates to store the Plus! files (see fig. B.2). At the dialog box asking whether Windows 95 should create the destination folder, click Yes to continue. Whether you accepted the folder recommended by Setup or specified another one, click OK to accept the Install folder.

FIG. B.2
The Plus! Setup program tells you which folder the Plus! files will be installed in.

 If you want to install Plus! in a different folder, click the Change Folder button. In the Change Folder dialog box, specify the drive and folder to use by selecting them from the list or typing a path in the Path text box. Click OK.

---

11. You now need to specify which type of installation to perform (see fig. B.3). Select Typical or Custom.

N O T E When you select the Custom installation option, you can customize how a particular component installs. To do so, click the component name in the Options list, then click the Change Option button. In the dialog box that appears, click to deselect features you don't want to install in the Options list, then click OK to return to the Custom screen. Repeat this step for each of the components you want to customize.

When you've finished specifying which of the components to install in the Custom screen, click the Continue button. After you click Continue, the Setup process progresses the same as for a Typical Setup. ■

FIG. B.3

If you want to install the default Plus! components, select Typical. To choose the components that Setup installs, select Custom.

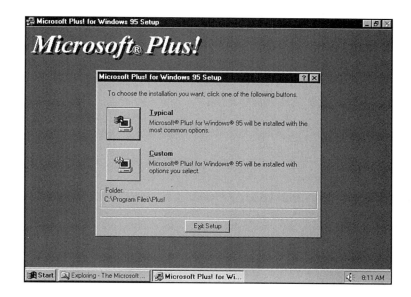

12. If you selected to install the System Agent, Windows prompts you to choose whether to run system maintenance tasks (such as ScanDisk) at night or during your business day. Click Yes to run these utilities at night, but you must keep your computer on at night. Click No to run these utilities during the day, but during times when you normally don't use your PC, such as during the lunch hour.

13. Setup checks your system's video installation. If your display runs in 256 colors, Setup displays the Video Resolution Check dialog box. This dialog box asks whether you want to install the high-color Desktop Themes, even if your monitor currently displays only 256 colors. If your display is capable of displaying more colors (operating in 16-bit color or higher) and you have ample hard disk space, click Yes. Otherwise, click No.

    Setup checks your system for necessary disk space, then begins copying files to your computer. Setup displays a message that it's updating your system.

N O T E After the preceding step, Plus! Setup displays the initial screen for the Internet Setup Wizard, if you selected to install this option earlier. If you don't want to set up the connection now, click Cancel. The Internet Setup Wizard asks you to confirm that you want to exit the Internet Setup Wizard. Click Yes to do so. You can return to it later. If you do want to set up your Internet connection, click Next. ▨

14. The Set up a Desktop Theme dialog box appears. Click OK to continue.

    The Desktop Themes dialog box appears, enabling you to select your first Desktop Theme (see fig. B.4). You can select a theme now, or use the Desktop Themes icon in Control Panel after installation to set up a theme. For now, click OK to continue.

FIG. B.4

You can select a Desktop Theme at this point, or choose one after you have Plus! installed.

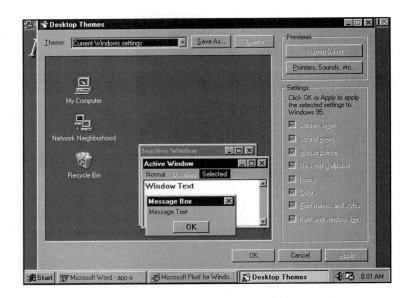

TIP   Click the Add/Remove Programs icon in Control Panel to remove Plus! items from your computer.

---

15. Setup displays a dialog box telling you that it needs to restart Windows to complete the setup. Click the Restart Windows button. Your computer and Windows 95 restart. When Windows 95 restarts, you should see the word Plus! on the Windows 95 startup screen to indicate that you've successfully installed Microsoft Plus!.

You now can start using the features of Plus!.

▶ **See** "Wallpapering Your Desktop with a Graphic," **p. 384**

Uninstalling Plus!

You can use the Windows 95 Add/Remove Programs feature to remove some or all of the Microsoft Plus! companion. To uninstall Plus!:

1. Open the Start menu and choose Settings, Control Panel. The Control Panel Window opens.

T I P Use this process to install parts of Plus! you didn't initially install during the Plus! Setup.

2. Double-click the Add/Remove Programs icon. The Add/Remove Program Properties sheet appears (see fig. B.5).

FIG. B.5

Use the Add/Remove
Programs feature to uninstall
part or all of Plus!.

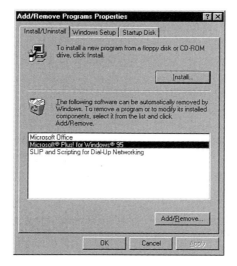

3. In the Install/Uninstall page, a list shows the programs that can be added or removed from your system. Double-click Microsoft Plus! for Windows 95 in the list.

   The Microsoft Plus! for Windows 95 Setup installation maintenance screen appears.

4. To uninstall all of Plus!, click the Remove All button. Or, to choose individual components to remove, click the Add/Remove button to display the Maintenance Install screen (see fig. B.6). In the Options list, click to clear the check mark beside each Plus! component to remove from your system, then click Continue.

5. A dialog box appears asking you to confirm the removal of the selected item(s). Click Yes to continue the uninstall process. Setup removes the Plus! files from your system.

6. A dialog box displays telling you that it needs to restart Windows. To complete the uninstalling Plus!, click the Restart Windows button. Your computer and Windows 95 restart.

FIG. B.6

You can remove a Plus!
component by clearing its
check box.

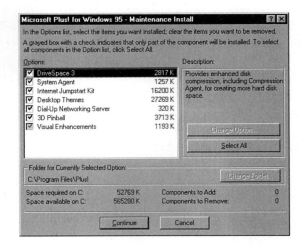

Additional Help and Resources

by Ron Person

■ **Finding the right type of help**

This appendix lists additional resources that offer help and support for Windows 95.

■ **Using online help**

This appendix includes a listing of Internet addresses that offer Windows 95 information.

Although this is one of the most comprehensive books written on Windows 95, there are many additional resources you can turn to for answers to user and technical questions. I have attempted to make this a comprehensive list of resources that includes all major sources. Over time, these sources will change—books are revised and online services change their directories. To stay in contact with online services, use the Find feature found in most services to search for topics on Windows 95. To stay current with new books, call Macmillan Computer Publishing at the number listed later in this appendix. ■

Getting Telephone and Fax Support for Windows 95 and Microsoft Products

Microsoft has a wide array of telephone support systems for Windows 95. There are also numerous third-party companies dedicated to supporting individuals and corporations who use Windows 95.

If Windows 95 or other applications came preinstalled on your computer, your technical support for the preinstalled software will probably be through the hardware vendor who supplied your equipment.

Microsoft Telephone and Fax Support

For customer service and product upgrade information, call (800) 426-9400.

At the time this book was published, Microsoft used three methods of supporting Windows 95 with live support personnel. These numbers and support levels are:

Description	Type	Telephone
Support for 90 days from your first support call.	Free. Initial 90-day support.	(206) 635-7000
$35 charge to a credit card until the specific problem is resolved. Make sure you keep the charge code ID and incident ID assigned by Microsoft.	$35 per incident charged to a credit card.	(800) 936-5700
$35 charge to a telephone number until the specific problem is resolved. Incident ID is assigned by Microsoft.	$35 per incident charged to telephone.	(900) 555-2000

This support is available Monday through Friday, 6:00 am to 6:00 pm, Pacific time, excluding holidays.

You also can receive help on Windows 95 by receiving a fax, which lists the most frequently asked questions and their answers. To get answers from FastTips call (800) 936-4200.

Telephone Support from Non-Microsoft Vendors

Microsoft encourages a stable of service providers who can give you or your company help on Windows 95. These service providers are:

Name	Description	Support Options	Telephone
Keane, Inc.	TeleSolve Help Desk Center; offers a wide range of support around the clock, seven days a week.	One time call costs $30. Five support calls cost $120.	(800)77WIN95 (800) 77WIN95
Softmart	Exton Technology Group; home and corporate support services. Open 24 hours,seven days a week.Credit card	Wide range of services. $30 per incident $1.99 per minute, billed to your telephone number.	(800) 328-1319 (800) 337-6908 (900) 555-8300
Stream International	Backup for in-house support or staff. Using over 2,000 specialists for 1,200 products.	Windows 95 education and training. Windows 95 migration and implementation.	(800) 274-4707 (800) 507-0363
Unisys Corporation	Support for home users and businesses.	$35 per incident $1.95 per minute $150 per five incidents includes DOS, Windows 3.1, and Windows for Workgroups.	(800) 863-0436 (900) 555-5454 (800) 757-8324

Part XI
App C

Online Technical Support

You can also find support online, through The Microsoft Network, World Wide Web, and other computer bulletin board forums.

The Microsoft Network

The Microsoft Network (MSN) is available to users of Windows 95 who have a modem installed. After you sign on to the MSN, you have access to forums, libraries of software, and technical support forums.

To start The Microsoft Network, double-click the MSN icon on the desktop. After you are connected, the MSN Today Front Page appears. From the Front Page, you can select the Computers & Software tab to see featured and new topics related to computers and software.

Switch to MSN Central, the main control panel for the MSN, by clicking the MSN Central tab or by pressing Alt+Tab until a window with the title The Microsoft Network appears. Its large buttons contain categories such as MSN Today, E-Mail, and Favorite Places.

From MSN Central, you can find the same high value resources and help you find on the Web or CompuServe. To find a topic in MSN, use the topical search facility by following these steps:

1. Click Tools, Find, on The Microsoft Network to open the Find dialog box.
2. Type a keyword that describes what you are searching for in the Containing text box.
3. Select the Name, Topic, or Description check box to specify where to search.
4. Select the area where you want the search to take place in the Of Type list.
5. Click OK.

Locations that contain the keyword you entered will appear in the bottom of the Find dialog box.

Other areas of this appendix describe resources that are also available in The Microsoft Network. To find those resources in The Microsoft Network, you might want to search for keywords such as:

Knowledge Base
TechNet
Windows
Windows 95
Windows Support
Windows Software

TIP   Learn how to combine searches with And and Or by selecting the Containing text box in the Find dialog box and pressing F1.

Microsoft Download Service

Microsoft maintains a software library containing sample programs, device drivers, patches, software updates, and programming aids. You have free access to the software in this library. Use Hyperterminal, which comes with Windows 95 and other PC communication software, to connect, search, and download files. Connect to Microsoft Download Service at:

(206) 936-6735

World Wide Web

The World Wide Web is a huge, constantly changing collection of data. Because of this, you can waste considerable time searching for specific information on the Web. Your most productive searches for information will be through sites sponsored by Microsoft, PC Magazine, and vendors. Some valuable URLs are:

Part
XI

App
C

Name	Description	URL
Microsoft	Main Microsoft Web page	**http:// www.microsoft.com/**
Microsoft	Table of contents for Windows	**http:// www.microsoft.com/ Windows/**
	Windows page and Windows 95 topics and software	**http:// www.microsoft.com/ windows/**
Microsoft Knowledge Base	Searchable database of white papers, technical notes, troubleshooting, tips, bugs, and workarounds	**http:// www.microsoft.com/ kb/**
Microsoft technical support	Table of contents for technical support issues, frequently asked questions, migration and planning issues, and white papers	**http:// www.microsoft.com/ windows/ techsup.htm**
Microsoft software updates	Table of contents to a library of free software and tools; files on the CD-ROM but not on disk; free Service Pack upgrades; and drivers	**http:// www.microsoft.com/ windows/ software.htm**
Microsoft TechNet	Troubleshooting database, drivers, upgrades; all the information from the TechNet CD-ROM	**http:// www.microsoft.com/ technet.htm**

▶ **See** "Understanding the Internet," **p. 942**

▶ **See** "Navigating the World Wide Web," **p. 987**

Computer Bulletin Board Forums

Computer bulletin boards are computer services that enable you to retrieve information over the telephone line. Some bulletin boards contain a wealth of information about Windows and Windows applications. One of the largest public bulletin boards is CompuServe.

CompuServe contains *forums* in which Windows and Windows applications are discussed. You can submit questions electronically to Microsoft operators, who will answer questions usually within a day. CompuServe also contains libraries of sample files and new printer and device drivers. The Knowledgebase available in Microsoft's region of CompuServe has much of the same troubleshooting information that Microsoft's telephone support representatives use. You can search through the Knowledgebase by using key words. The Microsoft region of CompuServe is divided into many areas, such as Windows users, Windows software developers, Microsoft, Excel, Microsoft languages, and sections for each of the major Microsoft and non-Microsoft applications that run under Windows.

After you become a CompuServe member, you can access the Microsoft user forums, library files, and Knowledgebase. (You must join CompuServe and get a passcode before you can use the bulletin board.) When you join CompuServe, make sure you get a copy of WinCIM, the Windows CompuServe Information Manager. It enables you to avoid typing many commands, and thus makes using CompuServe significantly easier.

Some of the Windows 95 services available on CompuServe are:

Name	Description	Access with:
Windows Support	CompuServe's table of contents for Windows support, shareware, and so on	GO WIN95
Microsoft Connection	Entry service for Microsoft services	GO MICROSOFT
Microsoft TechNet	Technical database (see the section "Technical Support on Microsoft CD-ROM")	GO TECHNET
Microsoft Knowledge-Base	Searchable database of troubleshooting tips, technical papers, and so on	GO MSKB
Microsoft Software Libraries	Free libraries of tools, software, patches, and drivers	GO MSL
Microsoft Windows Service Pack 1 upgrade	Free upgrades to Windows 95	GO WINNEWS

Name	Description	Access with:
Windows 95 Setup	Specific setup questions for Windows 95	GO SETUP95
Windows Users Group Network	Collections of useful software and information gathered by WUGNet	GO WINUSER

For information on joining CompuServe, contact a retail software store for a CompuServe starter kit or contact CompuServe at the following address:

CompuServe
5000 Arlington Centre Blvd.
P.O. Box 20212
Columbus, OH 43220
(800) 848-8990

Technical Support on Microsoft CD-ROM

One of the most valuable resources of technical knowledge on Windows and Windows applications is TechNet. TechNet is a compilation of troubleshooting procedures, technical papers, product descriptions, product announcements, drivers, and so on. It is available on a monthly CD-ROM for a fee or available over the World Wide Web for free. If you are a company with many Windows users or a consultant using Microsoft products, you must learn how to use TechNet.

ON THE WEB

You can connect to TechNet for free on the Web at

http://www.microsoft.com/technet

If you support only a few people or do not have to frequently download files, then the free TechNet on the Web might work well for you. TechNet on the Web is updated weekly. The Web version does not contain all technical documents as does the CD-ROM version.

Although TechNet is available for free on the Web, there are many times when you might want it on CD-ROM. If you frequently need files or need large files from TechNet, then the CD-ROM is much more convenient than slogging through the Web. TechNet on CD-ROM has a much more flexible and faster search engine so you can quickly browse for related topics; for example, you can quickly find an answer while a client is on the phone. With the advent of CD-ROM drives built-in to portables, the TechNet CD is an indispensable tool for the traveling Windows consultant.

The TechNet CD subscription for a single user is $299 per year for 12 issues of two CDs. Each month you receive the TechNet CD and the Supplemental Drivers and Patches CD. A single-server license for unlimited users is $699.

To subscribe to TechNet, contact them at:

Microsoft TechNet
One Microsoft Way
Redmond, WA 98052-6399
Fax: (206) 936-7329, Attn: TechNet
Voice: (800) 344-2121
Internet: **technet@microsoft.com**
CompuServe: **GO TECHNET**

The Microsoft Windows 95 Resource Kit

Microsoft split the user documentation for Windows 95 in two parts. The first part contains the User's Guide, help files, tutorial, and so on. This part is aimed at the average Windows 95 user and covers the Windows 95 user interface and features.

The Windows 95 Resource Kit comprises the *rest* of the Windows 95 user documentation. This kit provides more depth and detail about topics that (in Microsoft's estimation) the average user isn't likely to need. You can find information about customized setup and installation, network configuration, and so on. The Windows 95 Resource Kit is a manual, help files, and supplementary software utilities aimed at network administrators and others who must support other Windows 95 users.

It's important to understand that the Windows 95 Resource Kit is *not* a programmer's reference or software development kit—that's another area entirely. The Windows 95 Resource Kit is still part of the user-level documentation; it's just aimed at a higher-level user than the rest of the Windows 95 documentation.

The Microsoft Windows 95 Resource Kit is a book-software combination. The book and software come on the Windows 95 CD-ROM from which you might have installed Windows 95. You can also download the book and software from online services or purchase it as a bound book from larger book stores.

If you have the full CD-ROM version of Windows 95, you already have a copy of the Windows 95 Resource Kit. The Resource Kit chapters appear in the Windows 95 Resource Kit Help file, WIN95RK.HLP, which is located in the /Admin/Reskit/Helpfile folder. Double-click this file to open its help window. You can search and print in the file as you would any Help file.

You can also find a number of useful user and network utilities on the Windows 95 CD-ROM. Look in the /Admin/Apptools and /Admin/Nettools folders to find these utilities. You can find software tools on online bulletin boards. Many of these are listed earlier in the section, "Online Technical Support."

N O T E Microsoft does not include the Windows 95 Resource Kit files when distributing Windows 95 on floppy disks. Also, other suppliers who are licensed to sell Windows 95 with their computer systems might not include the Windows 95 Resource Kit files. ■

Books from Macmillan Computer Publishing

Macmillan Computer Publishing (MCP) is the largest publisher of computer books in the world. Que Corporation is MCP's most successful book imprint. Que is the publisher of *Platinum Edition Using Windows 95,* and of the *Special Edition Using* series of books. Some of the best-selling books in this series are:

- ■ *Special Edition Using Windows 95*
- ■ *Special Edition Using Excel for Windows 95*
- ■ *Special Edition Using Word for Windows 95*

For catalogs or individual or corporate purchases, contact Que and Macmillan Computer Publishing at:

> 201 West 103rd Street
> Indianapolis, IN 46290
> (317) 581-3500
> (800) 428-5331

ON THE WEB
You can also search and browse book descriptions and download software at the Macmillan SuperLibrary site on the World Wide Web. To go there, use the URL

http://www.mcp.com

Online WinNews Newsletter

Microsoft publishes WinNews, an online newsletter. It is available to anyone who can receive e-mail from the Internet (this includes CompuServe and America Online). WinNews includes information about new and free Windows 95 software, operating tips, releases of new hardware drivers, and references to additional information. It is published on the first and third Mondays of every month.

If you want to subscribe to WinNews, follow these steps:

1. Create an Internet e-mail message using the same account in which you want to receive WinNews.

2. Use a blank Subject line.

3. Type only the following as the message body:

   SUBSCRIBE WINNEWS

4. Send this Internet e-mail to:

   enews99@microsoft.nwnet.com

To stop receiving a copy of WinNews, follow the same instructions but use the following text as the only text in the message body:

   UNSUBSCRIBE WINNEWS

Catalog of Windows Products

A catalog of applications, development tools, and hardware for Windows and Windows NT is available from WhiteFox Communications, Inc. by calling:

Voice: (503) 629-5612
Fax: (503) 645-8642

Referrals to Consultants and Training

Microsoft Solution Providers develop and support applications written for the Windows environment with Microsoft products. They are independent consultants who have met the strict qualifying requirements imposed by Microsoft.

Microsoft also certifies training centers. A certified training center has instructors who have passed a competency exam and who use Microsoft-produced training material.

You can find the Microsoft Solution Providers and training centers in your area by calling (800) SOL-PROV. ●

File Listing of the Windows 95 CD

by Rob Tidrow

One of the most overwhelming aspects of Windows 95 is the volume of files it relies on. If you purchase Windows 95 on CD-ROM, you'll find more than 1,600 files that Windows 95 uses. If you're a technician, help desk supporter, or other IS person, you often might not know whether a file is a native Windows 95 file, or whether it was copied from a third-party application. ■

This appendix lists all of the files found on the release version of Windows 95 (CD-ROM version). You can use it as a reference to help you find a file you are searching for, find the correct cabinet file that stores the file, or find the original size of a particular file. (Cabinet files have the extension CAB on the Windows 95 CD-ROM or floppy disks.) Each file listed here includes the following criteria:

- *Date.* Shows the file save date.
- *Size.* Shows the expanded file size after it is installed on your machine.
- *Name.* Lists the expanded name of the file after it is installed on your machine.
- *Location.* Shows you where the file is copied to during Windows 95 Setup.
- *Type.* Lists the extension of the specified file.
- *Location/CD.* Shows the folder in which the specified file is stored on the CD-ROM. If you have Windows 95 on floppy disk, these locations might differ.

N O T E Depending on your specific setup and configuration, some of the listed locations might differ from your actual setup. If you are looking for a specific file or file type, use Windows 95 Find, Files or Folders command (located in Explorer on the Tools menu) and search for a name or file extension. ▩

Date	Size	Name	Location	Type	Location/CD
7/11/95	27,961	VDHCP.386	C:\WINDOWS\SYSTEM	386	\WIN95\CAB_12.CAB
7/11/95	62,614	VIP.386	C:\WINDOWS\SYSTEM	386	\WIN95\CAB_12.CAB
7/11/95	95,969	VNBT.386	C:\WINDOWS\SYSTEM	386	\WIN95\CAB_12.CAB
7/11/95	5,668	VPMTD.386	C:\WINDOWS\SYSTEM	386	\WIN95\CAB_03.CAB
7/11/95	47,377	VTCP.386	C:\WINDOWS\SYSTEM	386	\WIN95\CAB_12.CAB
7/11/95	5,687	VTDI.386	C:\WINDOWS\SYSTEM	386	\WIN95\CAB_12.CAB
7/11/95	98,144	SXCIEXT.DLL	C:\WINDOWS\SYSTEM	3GR	\WIN95\CAB_04.CAB
7/11/95	18,944	IMAADP32.ACM	C:\WINDOWS\SYSTEM	ACM	\WIN95\CAB_08.CAB
7/11/95	17,920	MSADP32.ACM	C:\WINDOWS\SYSTEM	ACM	\WIN95\CAB_08.CAB
7/11/95	10,240	MSG711.ACM	C:\WINDOWS\SYSTEM	ACM	\WIN95\CAB_08.CAB
7/11/95	25,088	MSGSM32.ACM	C:\WINDOWS\SYSTEM	ACM	\WIN95\CAB_08.CAB
7/11/95	8,704	TSSOFT32.ACM	C:\WINDOWS\SYSTEM	ACM	\WIN95\CAB_08.CAB
7/11/95	13,456	WFM0200.ACV	C:\WINDOWS\SYSTEM	ACV	\WIN95\CAB_08.CAB
7/11/95	5,184	WFM0201.ACV	C:\WINDOWS\SYSTEM	ACV	\WIN95\CAB_08.CAB
7/11/95	9,056	WFM0202.ACV	C:\WINDOWS\SYSTEM	ACV	\WIN95\CAB_08.CAB
7/11/95	9,056	WFM0203.ACV	C:\WINDOWS\SYSTEM	ACV	\WIN95\CAB_08.CAB
7/11/95	8,274	APPSTART.ANI	C:\WINDOWS\CURSORS	ANI	\WIN95\CAB_10.CAB
7/11/95	12,144	HOURGLAS.ANI	C:\WINDOWS\CURSORS	ANI	\WIN95\CAB_10.CAB
7/11/95	15,624	GENFAX.APD	C:\WINDOWS\SYSTEM	APD	\WIN95\CAB_05.CAB
7/11/95	410,588	CLOSEWIN.AVI	C:\WINDOWS	AVI	\WIN95\CAB_16.CAB
7/11/95	306,608	DRAGDROP.AVI	C:\WINDOWS	AVI	\WIN95\CAB_16.CAB

Date	Size	Name	Location	Type	Location/CD
7/11/95	872,208	EXPLORER.AVI	C:\WINDOWS	AVI	\WIN95\CAB_16.CAB
7/11/95	488,492	FIND.AVI	C:\WINDOWS	AVI	\WIN95\CAB_16.CAB
7/11/95	754,922	MOVEWIN.AVI	C:\WINDOWS	AVI	\WIN95\CAB_16.CAB
7/11/95	1,011,692	PASTE.AVI	C:\WINDOWS	AVI	\WIN95\CAB_16.CAB
7/11/95	1,510,732	SCROLL.AVI	C:\WINDOWS	AVI	\WIN95\CAB_16.CAB
7/11/95	832,222	SIZEWIN.AVI	C:\WINDOWS	AVI	\WIN95\CAB_16.CAB
7/11/95	425,742	TASKSWCH.AVI	C:\WINDOWS	AVI	\WIN95\CAB_16.CAB
7/11/95	745,920	WHATSON.AVI	C:\WINDOWS	AVI	\WIN95\CAB_16.CAB
7/11/95	576	_PWMOVE.BAT	C:\DOS	BAT	\WIN95\CAB_11.CAB
7/11/95	403	DBLSPACE.BAT	C:\DOS	BAT	\WIN95\PRECOPY2.CAB
7/11/95	339	DEFRAG.BAT	C:\DOS	BAT	\WIN95\PRECOPY2.CAB
7/11/95	329	DRVSPACE.BAT	C:\DOS	BAT	\WIN95\PRECOPY2.CAB
7/11/95	2,456	INSTBE.BAT	C:\PROGRAM FILES\ THE MICROSOFT NETWORK	BAT	\WIN95\CAB_07.CAB
7/11/95	152	SCANDISK.BAT	C:\DOS	BAT	\WIN95\PRECOPY2.CAB
7/11/95	816	SUCHECK.BAT	C:\WINDOWS	BAT	\WIN95\PRECOPY2.CAB
7/11/95	751	SUFAIL.BAT	C:\WINDOWS	BAT	\WIN95\PRECOPY2.CAB
7/11/95	40,742	DCAMAC.BIN	C:\WINDOWS	BIN	\WIN95\CAB_11.CAB
7/11/95	71,287	DRVSPACE.BIN	C:\DOS	BIN	\WIN95\PRECOPY1.CAB
7/11/95	26,880	EAGLECAF.BIN	C:\WINDOWS	BIN	\WIN95\CAB_11.CAB
7/11/95	26,880	EAGLEMAC.BIN	C:\WINDOWS	BIN	\WIN95\CAB_11.CAB
7/11/95	51,350	MDGMPORT.BIN	C:\WINDOWS	BIN	\WIN95\ CAB_11.CAB
7/11/95	4,096	NE3200.BIN	C:\WINDOWS	BIN	\WIN95\CAB_11.CAB
7/11/95	110,720	NETFLX.BIN	C:\WINDOWS	BIN	\WIN95\CAB_11.CAB
7/11/95	3,279	UNICODE.BIN	C:\WINDOWS\SYSTEM	BIN	\WIN95\CAB_13.CAB
7/11/95	407	XLAT850.BIN	C:\WINDOWS\SYSTEM	BIN	\WIN95\CAB_03.CAB
7/11/95	2,754	3DBLOCKS.BMP	C:\WINDOWS	BMP	\WIN95\CAB_02.CAB
7/11/95	590	BAMBOO.BMP	C:\WINDOWS	BMP	\WIN95\CAB_03.CAB
7/11/95	2,118	BUBBLES.BMP	C:\WINDOWS	BMP	\WIN95\CAB_03.CAB
7/11/95	190	CIRCLES.BMP	C:\WINDOWS	BMP	\WIN95\CAB_03.CAB
7/11/95	307,514	CLOUDS.BMP	C:\WINDOWS	BMP	\WIN95\CAB_02.CAB
7/11/95	582	EGYPT.BMP	C:\WINDOWS	BMP	\WIN95\CAB_03.CAB
7/11/95	66,146	FOREST.BMP	C:\WINDOWS	BMP	\WIN95\CAB_03.CAB
7/11/95	32,850	GATOR.BMP	C:\WINDOWS	BMP	\WIN95\CAB_03.CAB
7/11/95	190	HALFTONE.BMP	C:\WINDOWS	BMP	\WIN95\CAB_03.CAB
7/11/95	470	HOUNDS.BMP	C:\WINDOWS	BMP	\WIN95\CAB_03.CAB
7/11/95	36,182	MESH.BMP	C:\WINDOWS	BMP	\WIN95\CAB_03.CAB
7/11/95	578	PSTRIPE.BMP	C:\WINDOWS	BMP	\WIN95\CAB_03.CAB
7/11/95	198	PYRAMID2.BMP	C:\WINDOWS	BMP	\WIN95\CAB_03.CAB
7/11/95	578	REDTILE.BMP	C:\WINDOWS	BMP	\WIN95\CAB_03.CAB

Part
XI

App
D

continues

Date	Size	Name	Location	Type	Location/CD
7/11/95	194	RIVETS2.BMP	C:\WINDOWS	BMP	\WIN95\CAB_03.CAB
7/11/95	32,854	SAND.BMP	C:\WINDOWS	BMP	\WIN95\CAB_03.CAB
7/11/95	38,462	SETUP.BMP	C:\WINDOWS	BMP	\WIN95\CAB_10.CAB
7/11/95	182	THATCH2.BMP	C:\WINDOWS	BMP	\WIN95\CAB_03.CAB
7/11/95	4,678	WEAVE2.BMP	C:\WINDOWS	BMP	\WIN95\CAB_03.CAB
7/11/95	1,189	BACKUP.CNT	C:\WINDOWS\HELP	CNT	\WIN95\CAB_04.CAB
7/11/95	797	MAPIF0.CFG	C:\WINDOWS\SYSTEM	CFG	\WIN95\CAB_06.CAB
7/11/95	799	MAPIF1.CFG	C:\WINDOWS\SYSTEM	CFG	\WIN95\CAB_06.CAB
7/11/95	3,989	MAPIF2.CFG	C:\WINDOWS\SYSTEM	CFG	\WIN95\CAB_06.CAB
7/11/95	795	MAPIF3.CFG	C:\WINDOWS\SYSTEM	CFG	\WIN95\CAB_06.CAB
7/11/95	787	MAPIF4.CFG	C:\WINDOWS\SYSTEM	CFG	\WIN95\CAB_06.CAB
7/11/95	826	MAPIF5.CFG	C:\WINDOWS\SYSTEM	CFG	\WIN95\CAB_06.CAB
7/11/95	1	MIDIMAP.CFG	C:\WINDOWS\SYSTEM	CFG	\WIN95\CAB_08.CAB
7/11/95	9,744	IOSCLASS.DLL	C:\WINDOWS\SYSTEM	DLL	\WIN95\CAB_03.CAB
7/11/95	1,912	AWFAX.CNT	C:\WINDOWS\HELP	CNT	\WIN95\CAB_05.CAB
7/11/95	508	CALC.CNT	C:\WINDOWS\HELP	CNT	\WIN95\CAB_05.CAB
7/11/95	643	CDPLAYER.CNT	C:\WINDOWS\HELP	CNT	\WIN95\CAB_13.CAB
7/11/95	16,384	CHIADI.DLL	C:\WINDOWS\HELP	CNT	\WIN95\CAB_04.CAB
7/11/95	440	CLIPBOOK.CNT	C:\WINDOWS\HELP	CNT	\WIN95\CAB_02.CAB
7/11/95	411	CLIPBRD.CNT	C:\WINDOWS\HELP	CNT	\WIN95\CAB_02.CAB
7/11/95	552	DIALER.CNT	C:\WINDOWS\HELP	CNT	\WIN95\CAB_02.CAB
7/11/95	822	DRVSPACE.CNT	C:\WINDOWS\HELP	CNT	\WIN95\CAB_05.CAB
7/11/95	1,639	EXCHNG.CNT	C:\WINDOWS\HELP	CNT	\WIN95\CAB_06.CAB
7/11/95	653	FAXCOVER.CNT	C:\WINDOWS\HELP	CNT	\WIN95\CAB_05.CAB
7/11/95	204	FAXVIEW.CNT	C:\WINDOWS\HELP	CNT	\WIN95\CAB_05.CAB
7/11/95	342	FILEXFER.CNT	C:\WINDOWS\HELP	CNT	\WIN95\CAB_17.CAB
7/11/95	196	FREECELL.CNT	C:\WINDOWS\HELP	CNT	\WIN95\CAB_05.CAB
7/11/95	3,386	HPJAHLP.CNT	C:\WINDOWS\HELP	CNT	\WIN95\CAB_16.CAB
7/11/95	910	HYPERTRM.CNT	C:\WINDOWS\HELP	CNT	\WIN95\CAB_02.CAB
7/11/95	509	MOUSE.CNT	C:\WINDOWS\HELP	CNT	\WIN95\CAB_05.CAB
7/11/95	1,042	MPLAYER.CNT	C:\WINDOWS\HELP	CNT	\WIN95\CAB_08.CAB
7/11/95	1,221	MSFS.CNT	C:\WINDOWS\HELP	CNT	\WIN95\CAB_06.CAB
7/11/95	206	MSHEARTS.CNT	C:\WINDOWS\HELP	CNT	\WIN95\CAB_05.CAB
7/11/95	13,392	MSN.CNT	C:\WINDOWS\HELP	CNT	\WIN95\CAB_07.CAB
7/11/95	246	MSNPSS.CNT	C:\WINDOWS\HELP	CNT	\WIN95\CAB_07.CAB
7/11/95	1,978	MSPAINT.CNT	C:\WINDOWS\HELP	CNT	\WIN95\CAB_02.CAB
7/11/95	391	NETWATCH.CNT	C:\WINDOWS\HELP	CNT	\WIN95\CAB_13.CAB
7/11/95	571	NOTEPAD.CNT	C:\WINDOWS\HELP	CNT	\WIN95\CAB_05.CAB
7/11/95	940	PACKAGER.CNT	C:\WINDOWS\HELP	CNT	\WIN95\CAB_02.CAB
7/11/95	919	PROGMAN.CNT	C:\WINDOWS\HELP	CNT	\WIN95\CAB_10.CAB
7/11/95	544	REGEDIT.CNT	C:\WINDOWS\HELP	CNT	\WIN95\CAB_06.CAB

Date	Size	Name	Location	Type	Location/CD
7/11/95	392	SNDVOL32.CNT	C:\WINDOWS\HELP	CNT	\WIN95\CAB_08.CAB
7/11/95	157	SOL.CNT	C:\WINDOWS\HELP	CNT	\WIN95\CAB_05.CAB
7/11/95	1,023	SOUNDREC.CNT	C:\WINDOWS\HELP	CNT	\WIN95\CAB_08.CAB
7/11/95	263	SYSMON.CNT	C:\WINDOWS\HELP	CNT	\WIN95\CAB_13.CAB
7/11/95	1,722	W_OVER.CNT	C:\WINDOWS\HELP	CNT	\WIN95\CAB_16.CAB
7/11/95	144	W_TOUR.CNT	C:\WINDOWS\HELP	CNT	\WIN95\CAB_17.CAB
7/11/95	13,743	WINDOWS.CNT	C:\WINDOWS\HELP	CNT	\WIN95\CAB_05.CAB
7/11/95	2,169	WINFILE.CNT	C:\WINDOWS\HELP	CNT	\WIN95\CAB_10.CAB
7/11/95	930	WINHLP32.CNT	C:\WINDOWS\HELP	CNT	\WIN95\CAB_05.CAB
7/11/95	168	WINMINE.CNT	C:\WINDOWS\HELP	CNT	\WIN95\CAB_05.CAB
7/11/95	403	WINPOPUP.CNT	C:\WINDOWS\HELP	CNT	\WIN95\CAB_11.CAB
7/11/95	1,920	WORDPAD.CNT	C:\WINDOWS\HELP	CNT	\WIN95\CAB_03.CAB
7/11/95	5,175	CHOICE.COM	C:\WINDOWS\COMMAND	COM	\WIN95\CAB_08.CAB
7/11/95	92,870	COMMAND.COM	C:\WINDOWS	COM	\WIN95\PRECOPY1.CAB
7/11/95	21,959	DISKCOPY.COM	C:\WINDOWS\COMMAND	COM	\WIN95\CAB_08.CAB
7/11/95	15,431	DOSKEY.COM	C:\WINDOWS\COMMAND	COM	\WIN95\CAB_08.CAB
7/11/95	69,886	EDIT.COM	C:\WINDOWS\COMMAND	COM	\WIN95\CAB_02.CAB
7/11/95	40,135	FORMAT.COM	C:\WINDOWS\COMMAND	COM	\WIN95\CAB_02.CAB
7/11/95	19,927	KEYB.COM	C:\WINDOWS\COMMAND	COM	\WIN95\CAB_08.CAB
7/11/95	29,191	MODE.COM	C:\WINDOWS\COMMAND	COM	\WIN95\CAB_08.CAB
7/11/95	10,471	MORE.COM	C:\WINDOWS\COMMAND	COM	\WIN95\CAB_08.CAB
7/11/95	28	NWRPLTRM.COM	C:\WINDOWS	COM	\WIN95\CAB_17.CAB
7/11/95	13,239	SYS.COM	C:\WINDOWS\COMMAND	COM	\WIN95\CAB_02.CAB
7/11/95	4,357	CONFDENT.CPE	C:\WINDOWS	CPE	\WIN95\CAB_05.CAB
7/11/95	4,473	FYI.CPE	C:\WINDOWS	CPE	\WIN95\CAB_05.CAB
7/11/95	5,935	GENERIC.CPE	C:\WINDOWS	CPE	\WIN95\CAB_05.CAB
7/11/95	4,345	URGENT.CPE	C:\WINDOWS	CPE	\WIN95\CAB_05.CAB
7/11/95	58,870	EGA.CPI	C:\WINDOWS\COMMAND	CPI	\WIN95\CAB_13.CAB
7/11/95	49,754	ISO.CPI	C:\WINDOWS\COMMAND	CPI	\WIN95\CAB_13.CAB
7/11/95	57,344	ACCESS.CPL	C:\WINDOWS\SYSTEM	CPL	\WIN95\CAB_02.CAB
7/11/95	63,488	APPWIZ.CPL	C:\WINDOWS\SYSTEM	CPL	\WIN95\CAB_10.CAB
7/11/95	8,704	DESK.CPL	C:\WINDOWS\SYSTEM	CPL	\WIN95\CAB_03.CAB
7/11/95	48,640	INTL.CPL	C:\WINDOWS\SYSTEM	CPL	\WIN95\CAB_03.CAB
7/11/95	7,680	JETADMIN.CPL	C:\WINDOWS\SYSTEM	CPL	\WIN95\CAB_16.CAB
7/11/95	51,200	JOY.CPL	C:\WINDOWS\SYSTEM	CPL	\WIN95\CAB_08.CAB
7/11/95	67,584	MAIN.CPL	C:\WINDOWS\SYSTEM	CPL	\WIN95\CAB_03.CAB
7/11/95	42,768	MLCFG32.CPL	C:\WINDOWS\SYSTEM	CPL	\WIN95\CAB_06.CAB
7/11/95	193,024	MMSYS.CPL	C:\WINDOWS\SYSTEM	CPL	\WIN95\CAB_08.CAB
7/11/95	52,096	MODEM.CPL	C:\WINDOWS\SYSTEM	CPL	\WIN95\CAB_07.CAB

continues

Date	Size	Name	Location	Type	Location/CD
7/11/95	5,312	NETCPL.CPL	C:\WINDOWS\SYSTEM	CPL	\WIN95\CAB_11.CAB
7/11/95	37,376	PASSWORD.CPL	C:\WINDOWS\SYSTEM	CPL	\WIN95\CAB_11.CAB
7/11/95	221,776	SYSDM.CPL	C:\WINDOWS\SYSTEM	CPL	\WIN95\CAB_03.CAB
7/11/95	33,272	TELEPHON.CPL	C:\WINDOWS\SYSTEM	CPL	\WIN95\CAB_11.CAB
7/11/95	49,152	TIMEDATE.CPL	C:\WINDOWS\SYSTEM	CPL	\WIN95\CAB_03.CAB
7/11/95	32,528	WGPOCPL.CPL	C:\WINDOWS\SYSTEM	CPL	\WIN95\CAB_06.CAB
7/11/95	2,238	WFM0200A.CSP	C:\WINDOWS	CSP	\WIN95\CAB_08.CAB
7/11/95	6,776	WFM0201A.CSP	C:\WINDOWS	CSP	\WIN95\CAB_08.CAB
7/11/95	9,004	WFM0202A.CSP	C:\WINDOWS	CSP	\WIN95\CAB_08.CAB
7/11/95	9,004	WFM0203A.CSP	C:\WINDOWS	CSP	\WIN95\CAB_08.CAB
7/11/95	766	ARROW_1.CUR	C:\WINDOWS\CURSORS	CUR	\WIN95\CAB_17.CAB
7/11/95	766	ARROW_L.CUR	C:\WINDOWS\CURSORS	CUR	\WIN95\CAB_17.CAB
7/11/95	766	ARROW_M.CUR	C:\WINDOWS\CURSORS	CUR	\WIN95\CAB_13.CAB
7/11/95	766	BEAM_1.CUR	C:\WINDOWS\CURSORS	CUR	\WIN95\CAB_13.CAB
7/11/95	766	BEAM_L.CUR	C:\WINDOWS\CURSORS	CUR	\WIN95\CAB_13.CAB
7/11/95	766	BEAM_M.CUR	C:\WINDOWS\CURSORS	CUR	\WIN95\CAB_13.CAB
7/11/95	766	BUSY_1.CUR	C:\WINDOWS\CURSORS	CUR	\WIN95\CAB_13.CAB
7/11/95	766	BUSY_L.CUR	C:\WINDOWS\CURSORS	CUR	\WIN95\CAB_13.CAB
7/11/95	766	BUSY_M.CUR	C:\WINDOWS\CURSORS	CUR	\WIN95\CAB_13.CAB
7/11/95	766	CROSS_1.CUR	C:\WINDOWS\CURSORS	CUR	\WIN95\CAB_13.CAB
7/11/95	766	CROSS_L.CUR	C:\WINDOWS\CURSORS	CUR	\WIN95\CAB_13.CAB
7/11/95	766	CROSS_M.CUR	C:\WINDOWS\CURSORS	CUR	\WIN95\CAB_13.CAB
7/11/95	766	HELP_1.CUR	C:\WINDOWS\CURSORS	CUR	\WIN95\CAB_13.CAB
7/11/95	766	HELP_L.CUR	C:\WINDOWS\CURSORS	CUR	\WIN95\CAB_13.CAB
7/11/95	766	HELP_M.CUR	C:\WINDOWS\CURSORS	CUR	\WIN95\CAB_13.CAB
7/11/95	766	MOVE_1.CUR	C:\WINDOWS\CURSORS	CUR	\WIN95\CAB_13.CAB
7/11/95	766	MOVE_L.CUR	C:\WINDOWS\CURSORS	CUR	\WIN95\CAB_13.CAB
7/11/95	766	MOVE_M.CUR	C:\WINDOWS\CURSORS	CUR	\WIN95\CAB_13.CAB
7/11/95	766	NO_1.CUR	C:\WINDOWS\CURSORS	CUR	\WIN95\CAB_13.CAB
7/11/95	766	NO_L.CUR	C:\WINDOWS\CURSORS	CUR	\WIN95\CAB_13.CAB
7/11/95	766	NO_M.CUR	C:\WINDOWS\CURSORS	CUR	\WIN95\CAB_13.CAB
7/11/95	766	PEN_1.CUR	C:\WINDOWS\CURSORS	CUR	\WIN95\CAB_13.CAB
7/11/95	766	PEN_L.CUR	C:\WINDOWS\CURSORS	CUR	\WIN95\CAB_13.CAB
7/11/95	766	PEN_M.CUR	C:\WINDOWS\CURSORS	CUR	\WIN95\CAB_13.CAB
7/11/95	766	SIZE1_1.CUR	C:\WINDOWS\CURSORS	CUR	\WIN95\CAB_13.CAB
7/11/95	766	SIZE1_L.CUR	C:\WINDOWS\CURSORS	CUR	\WIN95\CAB_13.CAB
7/11/95	766	SIZE1_M.CUR	C:\WINDOWS\CURSORS	CUR	\WIN95\CAB_13.CAB
7/11/95	766	SIZE2_1.CUR	C:\WINDOWS\CURSORS	CUR	\WIN95\CAB_13.CAB
7/11/95	766	SIZE2_L.CUR	C:\WINDOWS\CURSORS	CUR	\WIN95\CAB_13.CAB
7/11/95	766	SIZE2_M.CUR	C:\WINDOWS\CURSORS	CUR	\WIN95\CAB_13.CAB
7/11/95	766	SIZE3_1.CUR	C:\WINDOWS\CURSORS	CUR	\WIN95\CAB_13.CAB

Date	Size	Name	Location	Type	Location/CD
7/11/95	766	SIZE3_L.CUR	C:\WINDOWS\CURSORS	CUR	\WIN95\CAB_13.CAB
7/11/95	766	SIZE3_M.CUR	C:\WINDOWS\CURSORS	CUR	\WIN95\CAB_13.CAB
7/11/95	766	SIZE4_1.CUR	C:\WINDOWS\CURSORS	CUR	\WIN95\CAB_13.CAB
7/11/95	766	SIZE4_L.CUR	C:\WINDOWS\CURSORS	CUR	\WIN95\CAB_13.CAB
7/11/95	766	SIZE4_M.CUR	C:\WINDOWS\CURSORS	CUR	\WIN95\CAB_13.CAB
7/11/95	766	UP_1.CUR	C:\WINDOWS\CURSORS	CUR	\WIN95\CAB_13.CAB
7/11/95	766	UP_L.CUR	C:\WINDOWS\CURSORS	CUR	\WIN95\CAB_13.CAB
7/11/95	766	UP_M.CUR	C:\WINDOWS\CURSORS	CUR	\WIN95\CAB_13.CAB
7/11/95	766	WAIT_1.CUR	C:\WINDOWS\CURSORS	CUR	\WIN95\CAB_13.CAB
7/11/95	766	WAIT_L.CUR	C:\WINDOWS\CURSORS	CUR	\WIN95\CAB_13.CAB
7/11/95	766	WAIT_M.CUR	C:\WINDOWS\CURSORS	CUR	\WIN95\CAB_13.CAB
7/11/95	23,200	ESCP2MS.DRV	C:\WINDOWS\SYSTEM	DRV	\WIN95\CAB_09.CAB
7/11/95	10,098	800950.DAT	C:\PROGRAM FILES\ THE MICROSOFT NETWORK	DAT	\WIN95\CAB_07.CAB
7/11/95	524	850.dat	C:\PROGRAM FILES\ THE MICROSOFT NETWORK	DAT	\WIN95\CAB_05.CAB
7/11/95	13,824	ADVAPI32.DLL	C:\WINDOWS\SYSTEM	DLL	\WIN95\CAB_11.CAB
7/11/95	72,272	AVICAP.DLL	C:\WINDOWS\SYSTEM	DLL	\WIN95\CAB_08.CAB
7/11/95	59,904	AVICAP32.DLL	C:\WINDOWS\SYSTEM	DLL	\WIN95\CAB_08.CAB
7/11/95	88,064	AVIFIL32.DLL	C:\WINDOWS\SYSTEM	DLL	\WIN95\CAB_08.CAB
7/11/95	109,424	AVIFILE.DLL	C:\WINDOWS\SYSTEM	DLL	\WIN95\CAB_08.CAB
7/11/95	41,344	AVWIN.DLL	C:\WINDOWS\SYSTEM	DLL	\WIN95\CAB_13.CAB
7/11/95	10,240	AWBMSC32.DLL	C:\WINDOWS\SYSTEM	DLL	\WIN95\CAB_05.CAB
7/11/95	5,120	AWBTRV32.DLL	C:\WINDOWS\SYSTEM	DLL	\WIN95\CAB_05.CAB
7/11/95	9,216	AWCAPI32.DLL	C:\WINDOWS\SYSTEM	DLL	\WIN95\CAB_05.CAB
7/11/95	22,528	AWCL1_32.DLL	C:\WINDOWS\SYSTEM	DLL	\WIN95\CAB_05.CAB
7/11/95	24,064	AWCL2_32.DLL	C:\WINDOWS\SYSTEM	DLL	\WIN95\CAB_05.CAB
7/11/95	24,576	AWCODC32.DLL	C:\WINDOWS\SYSTEM	DLL	\WIN95\CAB_05.CAB
7/11/95	6,144	AWDCXC32.DLL	C:\WINDOWS\SYSTEM	DLL	\WIN95\CAB_05.CAB
7/11/95	7,248	AWDEVL16.DLL	C:\WINDOWS\SYSTEM	DLL	\WIN95\CAB_05.CAB
7/11/95	6,656	AWDEVL32.DLL	C:\WINDOWS\SYSTEM	DLL	\WIN95\CAB_05.CAB
7/11/95	116,736	AWFAXP32.DLL	C:\WINDOWS\SYSTEM	DLL	\WIN95\CAB_05.CAB
7/11/95	123,392	AWFEXT32.DLL	C:\WINDOWS\SYSTEM	DLL	\WIN95\CAB_05.CAB
7/11/95	15,360	AWFMON32.DLL	C:\WINDOWS\SYSTEM	DLL	\WIN95\CAB_05.CAB
7/11/95	35,840	AWFR32.DLL	C:\WINDOWS\SYSTEM	DLL	\WIN95\CAB_05.CAB
7/11/95	49,152	AWFXAB32.DLL	C:\WINDOWS\SYSTEM	DLL	\WIN95\CAB_05.CAB
7/11/95	116,224	AWFXCG32.DLL	C:\WINDOWS\SYSTEM	DLL	\WIN95\CAB_05.CAB
7/11/95	44,032	AWFXIO32.DLL	C:\WINDOWS\SYSTEM	DLL	\WIN95\CAB_05.CAB
7/11/95	49,152	AWFXRN32.DLL	C:\WINDOWS\SYSTEM	DLL	\WIN95\CAB_05.CAB
7/11/95	27,136	AWKRNL32.DLL	C:\WINDOWS\SYSTEM	DLL	\WIN95\CAB_05.CAB

Part
XI

App
D

continues

Date	Size	Name	Location	Type	Location/CD
7/11/95	34,304	AWLFT332.DLL	C:\WINDOWS\SYSTEM	DLL	\WIN95\CAB_05.CAB
7/11/95	13,312	AWLHUT32.DLL	C:\WINDOWS\SYSTEM	DLL	\WIN95\CAB_05.CAB
7/11/95	32,256	AWLINZ32.DLL	C:\WINDOWS\SYSTEM	DLL	\WIN95\CAB_05.CAB
7/11/95	8,192	AWLZRD32.DLL	C:\WINDOWS\SYSTEM	DLL	\WIN95\CAB_05.CAB
7/11/95	34,304	AWNFAX32.DLL	C:\WINDOWS\SYSTEM	DLL	\WIN95\CAB_05.CAB
7/11/95	20,480	AWPWD32.DLL	C:\WINDOWS\SYSTEM	DLL	\WIN95\CAB_05.CAB
7/11/95	11,264	AWRAMB32.DLL	C:\WINDOWS\SYSTEM	DLL	\WIN95\CAB_05.CAB
7/11/95	8,192	AWRBAE32.DLL	C:\WINDOWS\SYSTEM	DLL	\WIN95\CAB_05.CAB
7/11/95	26,624	AWRESX32.DLL	C:\WINDOWS\SYSTEM	DLL	\WIN95\CAB_05.CAB
7/11/95	6,144	AWRNDR32.DLL	C:\WINDOWS\SYSTEM	DLL	\WIN95\CAB_05.CAB
7/11/95	46,592	AWSCHD32.DLL	C:\WINDOWS\SYSTEM	DLL	\WIN95\CAB_05.CAB
7/11/95	13,824	AWSRVR32.DLL	C:\WINDOWS\SYSTEM	DLL	\WIN95\CAB_05.CAB
7/11/95	33,280	AWT30_32.DLL	C:\WINDOWS\SYSTEM	DLL	\WIN95\CAB_05.CAB
7/11/95	40,448	AWUTIL32.DLL	C:\WINDOWS\SYSTEM	DLL	\WIN95\CAB_05.CAB
7/11/95	11,264	AWVIEW32.DLL	C:\WINDOWS\SYSTEM	DLL	\WIN95\CAB_05.CAB
7/11/95	820,224	BACKUP.EXE	C:\WINDOWS\SYSTEM	DLL	\WIN95\CAB_04.CAB
7/11/95	39,936	BKUPNET.DLL	C:\WINDOWS\SYSTEM	DLL	\WIN95\CAB_17.CAB
7/11/95	40,960	BKUPPROP.DLL	C:\WINDOWS\SYSTEM	DLL	\WIN95\PRECOPY2.CAB
7/11/95	148,528	CARDS.DLL	C:\WINDOWS\SYSTEM	DLL	\WIN95\CAB_05.CAB
7/11/95	29,696	CCAPI.DLL	C:\WINDOWS\SYSTEM	DLL	\WIN95\CAB_07.CAB
7/11/95	13,312	CCEI.DLL	C:\PROGRAM FILES\ THE MICROSOFT NETWORK	DLL	\WIN95\CAB_07.CAB
7/11/95	13,824	CCPSH.DLL	C:\PROGRAM FILES\ THE MICROSOFT NETWORK	DLL	\WIN95\CAB_07.CAB
7/11/95	11,792	CHEYPROP.DLL	C:\WINDOWS\SYSTEM	DLL	\WIN95\PRECOPY2.CAB
7/11/95	15,360	CHIKDI.DLL	C:\WINDOWS\SYSTEM	DLL	\WIN95\CAB_04.CAB
7/11/95	22,016	CHOOSUSR.DLL	C:\WINDOWS\SYSTEM	DLL	\WIN95\CAB_11.CAB
7/11/95	6,304	CMC.DLL	C:\WINDOWS\SYSTEM	DLL	\WIN95\CAB_06.CAB
7/11/95	46,480	COMCTL31.DLL	C:\WINDOWS\SYSTEM	DLL	\WIN95\PRECOPY1.CAB
7/11/95	182,272	COMCTL32.DLL	C:\WINDOWS\SYSTEM	DLL	\WIN95\CAB_10.CAB
7/11/95	92,672	COMDLG32.DLL	C:\WINDOWS\SYSTEM	DLL	\WIN95\CAB_10.CAB
7/11/95	48,112	COMMCTRL.DLL	C:\WINDOWS\SYSTEM	DLL	\WIN95\PRECOPY1.CAB
7/11/95	97,936	COMMDLG.DLL	C:\WINDOWS\SYSTEM	DLL	\WIN95\PRECOPY1.CAB
7/11/95	43,504	COMPLINC.DLL	C:\WINDOWS\SYSTEM	DLL	\WIN95\PRECOPY1.CAB
7/11/95	30,976	COMPOBJ.DLL	C:\WINDOWS\SYSTEM	DLL	\WIN95\CAB_09.CAB
7/11/95	23,552	CONFAPI.DLL	C:\WINDOWS\SYSTEM	DLL	\WIN95\CAB_07.CAB
7/11/95	161,280	CRTDLL.DLL	C:\WINDOWS\SYSTEM	DLL	\WIN95\CAB_03.CAB
7/11/95	17,776	CSPMAN.DLL	C:\WINDOWS\SYSTEM	DLL	\WIN95\CAB_08.CAB
7/11/95	12,800	DATAEDCL.DLL	C:\PROGRAM FILES\ THE MICROSOFT NETWORK	DLL	\WIN95\CAB_07.CAB
7/11/95	6,928	DCIMAN.DLL	C:\WINDOWS\SYSTEM	DLL	\WIN95\CAB_08.CAB
7/11/95	5,632	DCIMAN32.DLL	C:\WINDOWS\SYSTEM	DLL	\WIN95\CAB_08.CAB

Date	Size	Name	Location	Type	Location/CD
7/11/95	32,240	DDEML.DLL	C:\WINDOWS\SYSTEM	DLL	\WIN95\CAB_03.CAB
7/11/95	21,504	DEBMP.DLL	C:\WINDOWS\SYSTEM\ VIEWERS	DLL	\WIN95\CAB_13.CAB
7/11/95	369,664	DECPSMW4.DLL	C:\WINDOWS\SYSTEM	DLL	\WIN95\CAB_16.CAB
7/11/95	241,600	DEFRAG.EXE	C:\WINDOWS	DLL	\WIN95\CAB_04.CAB
7/11/95	8,192	DEHEX.DLL	C:\WINDOWS\SYSTEM\ VIEWERS	DLL	\WIN95\CAB_13.CAB
7/11/95	40,448	DEMET.DLL	C:\WINDOWS\SYSTEM\ VIEWERS	DLL	\WIN95\CAB_13.CAB
7/11/95	83,472	DESKCP16.DLL	C:\WINDOWS\SYSTEM	DLL	\WIN95\CAB_03.CAB
7/11/95	36,352	DESS.DLL	C:\WINDOWS\SYSTEM\ VIEWERS	DLL	\WIN95\CAB_13.CAB
7/11/95	48,128	DEWP.DLL	C:\WINDOWS\SYSTEM\ VIEWERS	DLL	\WIN95\CAB_13.CAB
7/11/95	201,136	DIBENG.DLL	C:\WINDOWS\SYSTEM	DLL	\WIN95\CAB_03.CAB
7/11/95	15,872	DISKCOPY.DLL	C:\WINDOWS\SYSTEM	DLL	\WIN95\CAB_10.CAB
7/11/95	6,992	DISPDIB.DLL	C:\WINDOWS\SYSTEM	DLL	\WIN95\CAB_08.CAB
7/11/95	18,272	DMCOLOR.DLL	C:\WINDOWS\SYSTEM	DLL	\WIN95\CAB_09.CAB
7/11/95	17,408	DOCPROP.DLL	C:\WINDOWS\SYSTEM	DLL	\WIN95\CAB_10.CAB
7/11/95	189,456	DSKMAINT.DLL	C:\WINDOWS\SYSTEM	DLL	\WIN95\PRECOPY2.CAB
7/11/95	94,720	DUNZIPNT.DLL	C:\WINDOWS\SYSTEM	DLL	\WIN95\CAB_07.CAB
7/11/95	6,160	ENABLE3.DLL	C:\WINDOWS\SYSTEM	DLL	\WIN95\CAB_02.CAB
7/11/95	14,336	FAXCODEC.DLL	C:\WINDOWS\SYSTEM	DLL	\WIN95\CAB_05.CAB
7/11/95	5,728	FINDMVI.DLL	C:\WINDOWS\SYSTEM	DLL	\WIN95\CAB_08.CAB
7/11/95	10,752	FINDSTUB.DLL	C:\PROGRAM FILES\ THE MICROSOFT NETWORK	DLL	\WIN95\CAB_07.CAB
7/11/95	188,848	FINSTALL.DLL	C:\WINDOWS\SYSTEM	DLL	\WIN95\CAB_09.CAB
7/11/95	105,984	FONTEXT.DLL	C:\WINDOWS\SYSTEM	DLL	\WIN95\CAB_10.CAB
7/11/95	53,248	FTE.DLL	C:\WINDOWS\SYSTEM	DLL	\WIN95\CAB_17.CAB
7/11/95	66,048	FTMAPI.DLL	C:\WINDOWS\SYSTEM	DLL	\WIN95\CAB_07.CAB
7/11/95	231,936	FTSRCH.DLL	C:\WINDOWS\SYSTEM	DLL	\WIN95\CAB_05.CAB
7/11/95	131,072	GDI32.DLL	C:\WINDOWS\SYSTEM	DLL	\WIN95\CAB_11.CAB
7/11/95	58,368	HOMEBASE.DLL	C:\PROGRAM FILES\ THE MICROSOFT NETWORK	DLL	\WIN95\CAB_07.CAB
7/11/95	21,504	HPALERTS.DLL	C:\WINDOWS\SPOOL	DLL	\WIN95\CAB_16.CAB
7/11/95	45,056	HPARRKUI.DLL	C:\WINDOWS\SPOOL	DLL	\WIN95\CAB_16.CAB
7/11/95	105,984	HPCOLA.DLL	C:\WINDOWS\SPOOL	DLL	\WIN95\CAB_16.CAB
7/11/95	18,496	HPCOLOR.DLL	C:\WINDOWS\SPOOL	DLL	\WIN95\CAB_09.CAB
7/11/95	25,088	HPDMIPX.DLL	C:\WINDOWS\SPOOL	DLL	\WIN95\CAB_16.CAB
7/11/95	5,152	HPJD.DLL	C:\WINDOWS\SPOOL	DLL	\WIN95\CAB_16.CAB
7/11/95	48,640	HPJDCOM.DLL	C:\WINDOWS\SPOOL	DLL	\WIN95\CAB_16.CAB
7/11/95	8,704	HPJDMON.DLL	C:\WINDOWS\SPOOL	DLL	\WIN95\CAB_16.CAB
7/11/95	12,288	HPJDNP.DLL	C:\WINDOWS\SPOOL	DLL	\WIN95\CAB_16.CAB

Part
XI

App
D

continues

Date	Size	Name	Location	Type	Location/CD
7/11/95	48,640	HPJDPP.DLL	C:\WINDOWS\SPOOL	DLL	\WIN95\CAB_16.CAB
7/11/95	116,224	HPJDUI.DLL	C:\WINDOWS\SPOOL	DLL	\WIN95\CAB_16.CAB
7/11/95	23,552	HPJDUND.DLL	C:\WINDOWS\SPOOL	DLL	\WIN95\CAB_16.CAB
7/11/95	15,872	HPNETSRV.DLL	C:\WINDOWS\SPOOL	DLL	\WIN95\CAB_16.CAB
7/11/95	1,431	HPNW416.DLL	C:\WINDOWS\SPOOL	DLL	\WIN95\CAB_16.CAB
7/11/95	18,944	HPNW432.DLL	C:\WINDOWS\SPOOL	DLL	\WIN95\CAB_16.CAB
7/11/95	21,504	HPNWPSRV.DLL	C:\WINDOWS\SPOOL	DLL	\WIN95\CAB_16.CAB
7/11/95	27,648	HPNWSHIM.DLL	C:\WINDOWS\SPOOL	DLL	\WIN95\CAB_16.CAB
7/11/95	18,944	HPPJL.DLL	C:\WINDOWS\SPOOL	DLL	\WIN95\CAB_16.CAB
7/11/95	168,448	HPPJLEXT.DLL	C:\WINDOWS\SPOOL	DLL	\WIN95\CAB_16.CAB
7/11/95	7,680	HPPRARRK.DLL	C:\WINDOWS\SPOOL	DLL	\WIN95\CAB_16.CAB
7/11/95	36,864	HPPRNTR.DLL	C:\WINDOWS\SPOOL	DLL	\WIN95\CAB_16.CAB
7/11/95	7,680	HPPRRUSH.DLL	C:\WINDOWS\SPOOL	DLL	\WIN95\CAB_16.CAB
7/11/95	246,784	HPPRUI.DLL	C:\WINDOWS\SPOOL	DLL	\WIN95\CAB_16.CAB
7/11/95	24,576	HPRUSHUI.DLL	C:\WINDOWS\SPOOL	DLL	\WIN95\CAB_16.CAB
7/11/95	152,064	HPSNMP.DLL	C:\WINDOWS\SPOOL	DLL	\WIN95\CAB_16.CAB
7/11/95	41,472	HPTABS.DLL	C:\WINDOWS\SPOOL	DLL	\WIN95\CAB_16.CAB
7/11/95	5,632	HPTRBIT.DLL	C:\WINDOWS\SPOOL	DLL	\WIN95\CAB_16.CAB
7/11/95	11,264	HPVBIT.DLL	C:\WINDOWS\SPOOL	DLL	\WIN95\CAB_16.CAB
7/11/95	25,216	HPVIOL.DLL	C:\WINDOWS\SPOOL	DLL	\WIN95\CAB_09.CAB
7/11/95	13,280	HPVMON.DLL	C:\WINDOWS\SPOOL	DLL	\WIN95\CAB_09.CAB
7/11/95	21,072	HPVRES.DLL	C:\WINDOWS\SPOOL	DLL	\WIN95\CAB_09.CAB
7/11/95	49,104	HPVUI.DLL	C:\WINDOWS\SPOOL	DLL	\WIN95\CAB_09.CAB
7/11/95	24,576	HPWIZ.DLL	C:\WINDOWS\SPOOL	DLL	\WIN95\CAB_16.CAB
7/11/95	20,480	HTICONS.DLL	C:\PROGRAM FILES\ ACCESSORIES\ HYPERTERMINAL	DLL	\WIN95\CAB_02.CAB
7/11/95	326,144	HYPERTRM.DLL	C:\PROGRAM FILES\ ACCESSORIES\ HYPERTERMINAL	DLL	\WIN95\CAB_02.CAB
7/11/95	77,824	ICCVID.DLL	C:\WINDOWS\SYSTEM	DLL	\WIN95\CAB_08.CAB
7/11/95	140,288	ICM32.DLL	C:\WINDOWS\SYSTEM	DLL	\WIN95\CAB_06.CAB
7/11/95	6,496	ICMP.DLL	C:\WINDOWS\SYSTEM	DLL	\WIN95\CAB_11.CAB
7/11/95	22,016	ICMUI.DLL	C:\WINDOWS\SYSTEM	DLL	\WIN95\CAB_06.CAB
7/11/95	77,712	ICONLIB.DLL	C:\WINDOWS\SYSTEM	DLL	\WIN95\CAB_09.CAB
7/11/95	6,144	IMM32.DLL	C:\WINDOWS\SYSTEM	DLL	\WIN95\CAB_06.CAB
7/11/95	5,120	INDICDLL.DLL	C:\WINDOWS\SYSTEM	DLL	\WIN95\CAB_06.CAB
7/11/95	50,512	INETMIB1.DLL	C:\WINDOWS	DLL	\WIN95\CAB_11.CAB
7/11/95	66,192	INSTL50.DLL	C:\	DLL	\WIN95\CAB_17.CAB
7/11/95	66,192	INSTL51.DLL	C:\	DLL	\WIN95\CAB_17.CAB
7/11/95	193,024	IR32_32.DLL	C:\WINDOWS\SYSTEM	DLL	\WIN95\CAB_08.CAB
7/11/95	411,136	KERNEL32.DLL	C:\WINDOWS\SYSTEM	DLL	\WIN95\CAB_11.CAB

Date	Size	Name	Location	Type	Location/CD
7/11/95	154,880	KOMMCTRL.DLL	C:\WINDOWS\SYSTEM	DLL	\WIN95\PRECOPY1.CAB
7/11/95	13,824	LINKINFO.DLL	C:\WINDOWS\SYSTEM	DLL	\WIN95\CAB_10.CAB
7/11/95	5,632	LZ32.DLL	C:\WINDOWS\SYSTEM	DLL	\WIN95\CAB_11.CAB
7/11/95	9,936	LZEXPAND.DLL	C:\WINDOWS\SYSTEM	DLL	\WIN95\MINI.CAB
7/11/95	23,696	LZEXPAND.DLL	C:\WINDOWS\SYSTEM	DLL	\WIN95\PRECOPY1.CAB
7/11/95	22,096	MAINCP16.DLL	C:\WINDOWS\SYSTEM	DLL	\WIN95\CAB_03.CAB
7/11/95	441,088	MAPI.DLL	C:\WINDOWS\SYSTEM	DLL	\WIN95\CAB_06.CAB
7/11/95	592,896	MAPI32.DLL	C:\WINDOWS\SYSTEM	DLL	\WIN95\CAB_06.CAB
7/11/95	5,440	MAPIU.DLL	C:\WINDOWS\SYSTEM	DLL	\WIN95\CAB_06.CAB
7/11/95	4,384	MAPIU32.DLL	C:\WINDOWS\SYSTEM	DLL	\WIN95\CAB_06.CAB
7/11/95	4,448	MAPIX.DLL	C:\WINDOWS\SYSTEM	DLL	\WIN95\CAB_06.CAB
7/11/95	6,000	MAPIX32.DLL	C:\WINDOWS\SYSTEM	DLL	\WIN95\CAB_06.CAB
7/11/95	5,584	MCIOLE.DLL	C:\WINDOWS\SYSTEM	DLL	\WIN95\CAB_08.CAB
7/11/95	99,840	MCM.DLL	C:\WINDOWS\SYSTEM	DLL	\WIN95\CAB_07.CAB
7/11/95	30,720	MF3216.DLL	C:\WINDOWS\SYSTEM	DLL	\WIN95\CAB_03.CAB
7/11/95	322,832	MFC30.DLL	C:\WINDOWS\SYSTEM	DLL	\WIN95\CAB_02.CAB
7/11/95	133,904	MFCANS32.DLL	C:\WINDOWS\SYSTEM	DLL	\WIN95\CAB_03.CAB
7/11/95	55,808	MFCD30.DLL	C:\WINDOWS\SYSTEM	DLL	\WIN95\CAB_02.CAB
7/11/95	15,872	MFCN30.DLL	C:\WINDOWS\SYSTEM	DLL	\WIN95\CAB_02.CAB
7/11/95	133,392	MFCO30.DLL	C:\WINDOWS\SYSTEM	DLL	\WIN95\CAB_02.CAB
7/11/95	5,632	MFCUIA32.DLL	C:\WINDOWS\SYSTEM	DLL	\WIN95\CAB_09.CAB
7/11/95	4,096	MFCUIW32.DLL	C:\WINDOWS\SYSTEM	DLL	\WIN95\CAB_09.CAB
7/11/95	1,300	MINIKBD.DLL	C:\WINDOWS\SYSTEM	DLL	\WIN95\MINI.CAB
7/11/95	12,048	MLSHEXT.DLL	C:\PROGRAM FILES\ MICROSOFT EXCHANGE	DLL	\WIN95\CAB_06.CAB
7/11/95	13,536	MMCI.DLL	C:\WINDOWS\SYSTEM	DLL	\WIN95\CAB_08.CAB
7/11/95	268,176	MMFMIG32.DLL	C:\WINDOWS\SYSTEM	DLL	\WIN95\CAB_06.CAB
7/11/95	5,152	MMMIXER.DLL	C:\WINDOWS\SYSTEM	DLL	\WIN95\CAB_08.CAB
7/11/95	103,248	MMSYSTEM.DLL	C:\WINDOWS\SYSTEM	DLL	\WIN95\CAB_08.CAB
7/11/95	53,248	MMVDIB12.DLL	C:\PROGRAM FILES\ THE MICROSOFT NETWORK	DLL	\WIN95\CAB_07.CAB
7/11/95	27,504	MODEMUI.DLL	C:\WINDOWS\SYSTEM	DLL	\WIN95\CAB_07.CAB
7/11/95	84,412	MORICONS.DLL	C:\WINDOWS	DLL	\WIN95\CAB_10.CAB
7/11/95	107,520	MOSABP32.DLL	C:\WINDOWS\SYSTEM	DLL	\WIN95\CAB_07.CAB
7/11/95	24,576	MOSAF.DLL	C:\PROGRAM FILES\ THE MICROSOFT NETWORK	DLL	\WIN95\CAB_07.CAB
7/11/95	47,616	MOSCC.DLL	C:\WINDOWS\SYSTEM	DLL	\WIN95\CAB_07.CAB
7/11/95	15,360	MOSCFG32.DLL	C:\WINDOWS\SYSTEM	DLL	\WIN95\CAB_07.CAB
7/11/95	36,864	MOSCL.DLL	C:\WINDOWS\SYSTEM	DLL	\WIN95\CAB_07.CAB
7/11/95	149,504	MOSCOMP.DLL	C:\PROGRAM FILES\ THE MICROSOFT NETWORK	DLL	\WIN95\CAB_07.CAB

Part

XI

App

D

continues

Date	Size	Name	Location	Type	Location/CD
7/11/95	21,504	MOSCUDLL.DLL	C:\WINDOWS\SYSTEM	DLL	\WIN95\CAB_07.CAB
7/11/95	25,600	MOSFIND.DLL	C:\PROGRAM FILES\ THE MICROSOFT NETWORK	DLL	\WIN95\CAB_07.CAB
7/11/95	9,216	MOSMISC.DLL	C:\WINDOWS\SYSTEM	DLL	\WIN95\CAB_07.CAB
7/11/95	26,624	MOSMUTIL.DLL	C:\WINDOWS\SYSTEM	DLL	\WIN95\CAB_07.CAB
7/11/95	56,832	MOSRXP32.DLL	C:\WINDOWS\SYSTEM	DLL	\WIN95\CAB_07.CAB
7/11/95	182,784	MOSSHELL.DLL	C:\PROGRAM FILES\ THE MICROSOFT NETWORK	DLL	\WIN95\CAB_07.CAB
7/11/95	7,680	MOSSTUB.DLL	C:\PROGRAM FILES\ THE MICROSOFT NETWORK	DLL	\WIN95\CAB_07.CAB
7/11/95	87,040	MPCCL.DLL	C:\PROGRAM FILES\ THE MICROSOFT NETWORK	DLL	\WIN95\CAB_07.CAB
7/11/95	40,448	MPR.DLL	C:\WINDOWS\SYSTEM	DLL	\WIN95\CAB_11.CAB
7/11/95	119,296	MPRSERV.DLL	C:\WINDOWS\SYSTEM	DLL	\WIN95\CAB_11.CAB
7/11/95	61,952	MSAB32.DLL	C:\WINDOWS\SYSTEM	DLL	\WIN95\CAB_11.CAB
7/11/95	53,552	MSACM.DLL	C:\WINDOWS\SYSTEM	DLL	\WIN95\CAB_08.CAB
7/11/95	91,648	MSACM32.DLL	C:\WINDOWS\SYSTEM	DLL	\WIN95\CAB_08.CAB
7/11/95	402,944	MSFS32.DLL	C:\WINDOWS\SYSTEM	DLL	\WIN95\CAB_06.CAB
7/11/95	1,264	MSMIXMGR.DLL	C:\WINDOWS\SYSTEM	DLL	\WIN95\CAB_08.CAB
7/11/95	25,600	MSNDUI.DLL	C:\PROGRAM FILES\ THE MICROSOFT NETWORK	DLL	\WIN95\CAB_07.CAB
7/11/95	60,416	MSNET32.DLL	C:\WINDOWS\SYSTEM	DLL	\WIN95\CAB_11.CAB
7/11/95	67,584	MSNP32.DLL	C:\WINDOWS\SYSTEM	DLL	\WIN95\CAB_11.CAB
7/11/95	36,400	MSPCIC.DLL	C:\WINDOWS\SYSTEM	DLL	\WIN95\CAB_09.CAB
7/11/95	32,256	MSPCX32.DLL	C:\PROGRAM FILES\ ACCESSORIES	DLL	\WIN95\CAB_02.CAB
7/11/95	17,920	MSPP32.DLL	C:\WINDOWS\SYSTEM	DLL	\WIN95\CAB_11.CAB
7/11/95	55,872	MSPRINT.DLL	C:\WINDOWS\SYSTEM	DLL	\WIN95\PRECOPY1.CAB
7/11/95	48,128	MSPRINT2.DLL	C:\WINDOWS\SYSTEM	DLL	\WIN95\PRECOPY1.CAB
7/11/95	386,560	MSPST32.DLL	C:\WINDOWS\SYSTEM	DLL	\WIN95\CAB_06.CAB
7/11/95	15,360	MSPWL32.DLL	C:\WINDOWS\SYSTEM	DLL	\WIN95\CAB_11.CAB
7/11/95	11,264	MSRLE32.DLL	C:\WINDOWS\SYSTEM	DLL	\WIN95\CAB_08.CAB
7/11/95	74,752	MSSHRUI.DLL	C:\WINDOWS\SYSTEM	DLL	\WIN95\CAB_11.CAB
7/11/95	26,832	MSTCP.DLL	C:\WINDOWS\SYSTEM	DLL	\WIN95\PRECOPY1.CAB
7/11/95	253,952	MSVCRT20.DLL	C:\WINDOWS\SYSTEM	DLL	\WIN95\CAB_02.CAB
7/11/95	129,536	MSVFW32.DLL	C:\WINDOWS\SYSTEM	DLL	\WIN95\CAB_08.CAB
7/11/95	30,208	MSVIDC32.DLL	C:\WINDOWS\SYSTEM	DLL	\WIN95\CAB_08.CAB
7/11/95	113,664	MSVIDEO.DLL	C:\WINDOWS\SYSTEM	DLL	\WIN95\CAB_08.CAB
7/11/95	147,968	MSVIEWUT.DLL	C:\WINDOWS\SYSTEM\ VIEWERS	DLL	\WIN95\CAB_13.CAB
7/11/95	112,128	MVCL14N.DLL	C:\PROGRAM FILES\ THE MICROSOFT NETWORK	DLL	\WIN95\CAB_07.CAB
7/11/95	51,712	MVPR14N.DLL	C:\PROGRAM FILES\ THE MICROSOFT NETWORK	DLL	\WIN95\CAB_07.CAB

Date	Size	Name	Location	Type	Location/CD
7/11/95	77,312	MVTTL14C.DLL	C:\PROGRAM FILES\ THE MICROSOFT NETWORK	DLL	\WIN95\CAB_07.CAB
7/11/95	10,240	MVUT14N.DLL	C:\PROGRAM FILES\ THE MICROSOFT NETWORK	DLL	\WIN95\CAB_07.CAB
7/11/95	14,032	NDDEAPI.DLL	C:\WINDOWS	DLL	\WIN95\CAB_11.CAB
7/11/95	10,768	NDDENB.DLL	C:\WINDOWS	DLL	\WIN95\CAB_11.CAB
7/11/95	106,960	NETAPI.DLL	C:\WINDOWS\SYSTEM	DLL	\WIN95\PRECOPY1.CAB
7/11/95	4,096	NETAPI32.DLL	C:\WINDOWS\SYSTEM	DLL	\WIN95\CAB_11.CAB
7/11/95	6,656	NETBIOS.DLL	C:\WINDOWS\SYSTEM	DLL	\WIN95\CAB_11.CAB
7/11/95	7,885	NETDET.INI	C:\WINDOWS	DLL	\WIN95\PRECOPY1.CAB
7/11/95	282,832	NETDI.DLL	C:\WINDOWS\SYSTEM	DLL	\WIN95\PRECOPY1.CAB
7/11/95	24,400	NETOS.DLL	C:\WINDOWS\SYSTEM	DLL	\WIN95\PRECOPY1.CAB
7/11/95	5,632	NTDLL.DLL	C:\WINDOWS\SYSTEM	DLL	\WIN95\CAB_03.CAB
7/11/95	6,528	NW16.DLL	C:\WINDOWS\SYSTEM	DLL	\WIN95\CAB_11.CAB
7/11/95	25,600	NWAB32.DLL	C:\WINDOWS\SYSTEM	DLL	\WIN95\CAB_11.CAB
7/11/95	21,504	NWNET32.DLL	C:\WINDOWS\SYSTEM	DLL	\WIN95\CAB_11.CAB
7/11/95	77,312	NWNP32.DLL	C:\WINDOWS\SYSTEM	DLL	\WIN95\CAB_11.CAB
7/11/95	43,008	NWPP32.DLL	C:\WINDOWS\SYSTEM	DLL	\WIN95\CAB_11.CAB
7/11/95	39,744	OLE2.DLL	C:\WINDOWS\SYSTEM	DLL	\WIN95\CAB_09.CAB
7/11/95	57,328	OLE2CONV.DLL	C:\WINDOWS\SYSTEM	DLL	\WIN95\CAB_09.CAB
7/11/95	169,440	OLE2DISP.DLL	C:\WINDOWS\SYSTEM	DLL	\WIN95\CAB_09.CAB
7/11/95	153,040	OLE2NLS.DLL	C:\WINDOWS\SYSTEM	DLL	\WIN95\CAB_09.CAB
7/11/95	557,664	OLE32.DLL	C:\WINDOWS\SYSTEM	DLL	\WIN95\CAB_09.CAB
7/11/95	232,720	OLEAUT32.DLL	C:\WINDOWS\SYSTEM	DLL	\WIN95\CAB_09.CAB
7/11/95	82,944	OLECLI.DLL	C:\WINDOWS\SYSTEM	DLL	\WIN95\CAB_09.CAB
7/11/95	12,288	OLECLI32.DLL	C:\WINDOWS\SYSTEM	DLL	\WIN95\CAB_09.CAB
7/11/95	40,576	OLECNV32.DLL	C:\WINDOWS\SYSTEM	DLL	\WIN95\CAB_09.CAB
7/11/95	112,640	OLEDLG.DLL	C:\WINDOWS\SYSTEM	DLL	\WIN95\CAB_09.CAB
7/11/95	24,064	OLESVR.DLL	C:\WINDOWS\SYSTEM	DLL	\WIN95\CAB_09.CAB
7/11/95	6,144	OLESVR32.DLL	C:\WINDOWS\SYSTEM	DLL	\WIN95\CAB_09.CAB
7/11/95	79,424	OLETHK32.DLL	C:\WINDOWS\SYSTEM	DLL	\WIN95\CAB_09.CAB
7/11/95	20,480	PANMAP.DLL	C:\WINDOWS\SYSTEM	DLL	\WIN95\CAB_10.CAB
7/11/95	82,816	PIFMGR.DLL	C:\WINDOWS\SYSTEM	DLL	\WIN95\CAB_03.CAB
7/11/95	12,288	PJLMON.DLL	C:\WINDOWS\SYSTEM	DLL	\WIN95\CAB_09.CAB
7/11/95	48,880	PKPD.DLL	C:\WINDOWS\SYSTEM	DLL	\WIN95\CAB_03.CAB
7/11/95	11,776	PKPD32.DLL	C:\WINDOWS\SYSTEM	DLL	\WIN95\CAB_03.CAB
7/11/95	26,608	PMSPL.DLL	C:\WINDOWS\SYSTEM	DLL	\WIN95\CAB_11.CAB
7/11/95	55,152	POINTER.DLL	C:\WINDOWS	DLL	\WIN95\CAB_08.CAB
7/11/95	12,800	POWERCFG.DLL	C:\WINDOWS\SYSTEM	DLL	\WIN95\CAB_03.CAB
7/11/95	72,192	PRODINV.DLL	C:\WINDOWS\SYSTEM	DLL	\WIN95\CAB_07.CAB

Part
XI

App
D

continues

Date	Size	Name	Location	Type	Location/CD
7/11/95	28,672	PSMON.DLL	C:\WINDOWS\SYSTEM	DLL	\WIN\CAB_09.CAB
7/11/95	1,632	RASAPI16.DLL	C:\WINDOWS\SYSTEM	DLL	\WIN95\CAB_10.CAB
7/11/95	147,456	RASAPI32.DLL	C:\WINDOWS\SYSTEM	DLL	\WIN95\CAB_10.CAB
7/11/95	178,176	RICHED32.DLL	C:\WINDOWS\SYSTEM	DLL	\WIN95\CAB_04.CAB
7/11/95	11,776	RNANP.DLL	C:\WINDOWS\SYSTEM	DLL	\WIN95\CAB_10.CAB
7/11/95	5,408	RNASETUP.DLL	C:\WINDOWS\SYSTEM	DLL	\WIN95\PRECOPY1.CAB
7/11/95	5,120	RNATHUNK.DLL	C:\WINDOWS\SYSTEM	DLL	\WIN95\CAB_10.CAB
7/11/95	54,272	RNAUI.DLL	C:\WINDOWS\SYSTEM	DLL	\WIN95\CAB_10.CAB
7/11/95	31,232	RNDSRV32.DLL	C:\WINDOWS\SYSTEM	DLL	\WIN95\CAB_05.CAB
7/11/95	8,192	RPCLTC1.DLL	C:\WINDOWS\SYSTEM	DLL	\WIN95\CAB_11.CAB
7/11/95	7,584	RPCLTC3.DLL	C:\WINDOWS\SYSTEM	DLL	\WIN95\CAB_11.CAB
7/11/95	9,200	RPCLTC5.DLL	C:\WINDOWS\SYSTEM	DLL	\WIN95\CAB_11.CAB
7/11/95	8,128	RPCLTC6.DLL	C:\WINDOWS\SYSTEM	DLL	\WIN95\CAB_11.CAB
7/11/95	9,168	RPCLTS3.DLL	C:\WINDOWS\SYSTEM	DLL	\WIN95\CAB_11.CAB
7/11/95	10,736	RPCLTS5.DLL	C:\WINDOWS\SYSTEM	DLL	\WIN95\CAB_11.CAB
7/11/95	9,696	RPCLTS6.DLL	C:\WINDOWS\SYSTEM	DLL	\WIN95\CAB_11.CAB
7/11/95	30,832	RPCNS4.DLL	C:\WINDOWS\SYSTEM	DLL	\WIN95\CAB_11.CAB
7/11/95	202,240	RPCRT4.DLL	C:\WINDOWS\SYSTEM	DLL	\WIN95\CAB_11.CAB
7/11/95	23,040	RPLIMAGE.DLL	C:\WINDOWS\SYSTEM	DLL	\WIN95\PRECOPY2.CAB
7/11/95	1,312	RSRC16.DLL	C:\WINDOWS\SYSTEM	DLL	\WIN95\CAB_02.CAB
7/11/95	4,608	RSRC32.DLL	C:\WINDOWS\SYSTEM	DLL	\WIN95\CAB_02.CAB
7/11/95	29,184	SACLIENT.DLL	C:\PROGRAM FILES\ THE MICROSOFT NETWORK	DLL	\WIN95\CAB_07.CAB
7/11/95	9,216	SAPNSP.DLL	C:\WINDOWS\SYSTEM	DLL	\WIN95\CAB_11.CAB
7/11/95	32,256	SCCVIEW.DLL	C:\WINDOWS\SYSTEM\ VIEWERS	DLL	\WIN95\CAB_13.CAB
7/11/95	25,088	SECUR32.DLL	C:\WINDOWS\SYSTEM	DLL	\WIN95\CAB_11.CAB
7/11/95	15,360	SECURCL.DLL	C:\PROGRAM FILES\ THE MICROSOFT NETWORK	DLL	\WIN95\CAB_07.CAB
7/11/95	12,032	SERIALUI.DLL	C:\WINDOWS\SYSTEM	DLL	\WIN95\CAB_03.CAB
7/11/95	6,240	SETUP4.DLL	C:\WINDOWS\SYSTEM	DLL	\WIN95\CAB_10.CAB
7/11/95	355,136	SETUPX.DLL	C:\WINDOWS\SYSTEM	DLL	\WIN95\PRECOPY1.CAB
7/11/95	41,600	SHELL.DLL	C:\WINDOWS\SYSTEM	DLL	\WIN95\PRECOPY1.CAB
7/11/95	817,664	SHELL32.DLL	C:\WINDOWS\SYSTEM	DLL	\WIN95\CAB_10.CAB
7/11/95	24,576	SHSCRAP.DLL	C:\WINDOWS\SYSTEM	DLL	\WIN95\CAB_10.CAB
7/11/95	16,512	SLENH.DLL	C:\WINDOWS\SYSTEM	DLL	\WIN95\CAB_07.CAB
7/11/95	91,136	SPOOLSS.DLL	C:\WINDOWS\SYSTEM	DLL	\WIN95\CAB_09.CAB
7/11/95	7,168	STEM0409.DLL	C:\WINDOWS\SYSTEM	DLL	\WIN95\CAB_05.CAB
7/11/95	4,208	STORAGE.DLL	C:\WINDOWS\SYSTEM	DLL	\WIN95\CAB_09.CAB
7/11/95	9,936	SUEXPAND.DLL	C:\WINDOWS\SYSTEM	DLL	\WIN95\PRECOPY1.CAB
7/11/95	11,264	SVCPROP.DLL	C:\WINDOWS\SYSTEM	DLL	\WIN95\CAB_07.CAB
7/11/95	13,312	SVRAPI.DLL	C:\WINDOWS\SYSTEM	DLL	\WIN95\CAB_11.CAB

Date	Size	Name	Location	Type	Location/CD
7/11/95	55,296	SYNCENG.DLL	C:\WINDOWS\SYSTEM	DLL	\WIN95\CAB_05.CAB
7/11/95	151,040	SYNCUI.DLL	C:\WINDOWS\SYSTEM	DLL	\WIN95\CAB_05.CAB
7/11/95	12,880	SYSCLASS.DLL	C:\WINDOWS\SYSTEM	DLL	\WIN95\CAB_09.CAB
7/11/95	318,304	SYSDETMG.DLL	C:\WINDOWS\SYSTEM	DLL	\WIN95\PRECOPY1.CAB
7/11/95	16,432	SYSTHUNK.DLL	C:\WINDOWS\SYSTEM	DLL	\WIN95\CAB_03.CAB
7/11/95	161,712	TAPI.DLL	C:\WINDOWS\SYSTEM	DLL	\WIN95\CAB_11.CAB
7/11/95	11,776	TAPI32.DLL	C:\WINDOWS\SYSTEM	DLL	\WIN95\CAB_11.CAB
7/11/95	20,616	TAPIADDR.DLL	C:\WINDOWS\SYSTEM	DLL	\WIN95\CAB_11.CAB
7/11/95	12,112	TOOLHELP.DLL	C:\WINDOWS\SYSTEM	DLL	\WIN95\CAB_03.CAB
7/11/95	967,104	TOURANI.DLL	C:\WINDOWS\SYSTEM	DLL	\WIN95\CAB_17.CAB
7/11/95	9,568	TOURSTR.DLL	C:\WINDOWS\SYSTEM	DLL	\WIN95\CAB_17.CAB
7/11/95	638,528	TOURUTIL.DLL	C:\WINDOWS\SYSTEM	DLL	\WIN95\CAB_17.CAB
7/11/95	17,408	TREEEDCL.DLL	C:\PROGRAM FILES\ THE MICROSOFT NETWORK	DLL	\WIN95\CAB_07.CAB
7/11/95	16,384	TREENVCL.DLL	C:\WINDOWS\SYSTEM	DLL	\WIN95\CAB_07.CAB
7/11/95	17,408	TSD32.DLL	C:\WINDOWS\SYSTEM	DLL	\WIN95\CAB_08.CAB
7/11/95	177,856	TYPELIB.DLL	C:\WINDOWS\SYSTEM	DLL	\WIN95\CAB_09.CAB
7/11/95	1,952	UMDM16.DLL	C:\WINDOWS\SYSTEM	DLL	\WIN95\CAB_03.CAB
7/11/95	6,144	UMDM32.DLL	C:\WINDOWS\SYSTEM	DLL	\WIN95\CAB_03.CAB
7/11/95	197,024	UNIDRV.DLL	C:\WINDOWS\SYSTEM	DLL	\WIN95\CAB_09.CAB
7/11/95	44,544	USER32.DLL	C:\WINDOWS\SYSTEM	DLL	\WIN95\CAB_11.CAB
7/11/95	398,416	VBRUN300.DLL	C:\WINDOWS\SYSTEM	DLL	\WIN95\CAB_17.CAB
7/11/95	4,096	VDMDBG.DLL	C:\WINDOWS\SYSTEM	DLL	\WIN95\CAB_03.CAB
7/11/95	9,008	VER.DLL	C:\WINDOWS\SYSTEM	DLL	\WIN95\MINI.CAB
7/11/95	9,008	VER.DLL	C:\WINDOWS\SYSTEM	DLL	\WIN95\PRECOPY2.CAB
7/11/95	6,656	VERSION.DLL	C:\WINDOWS\SYSTEM	DLL	\WIN95\CAB_10.CAB
7/11/95	14,768	VERX.DLL	C:\WINDOWS\SYSTEM	DLL	\WIN95\PRECOPY2.CAB
7/11/95	42,496	VLB32.DLL	C:\WINDOWS\SYSTEM	DLL	\WIN95\CAB_06.CAB
7/11/95	48,640	VSAMI.DLL	C:\WINDOWS\SYSTEM\ VIEWERS	DLL	\WIN95\CAB_13.CAB
7/11/95	17,920	VSASC8.DLL	C:\WINDOWS\SYSTEM\ VIEWERS	DLL	\WIN95\CAB_13.CAB
7/11/95	24,064	VSBMP.DLL	C:\WINDOWS\SYSTEM\ VIEWERS	DLL	\WIN95\CAB_13.CAB
7/11/95	29,184	VSDRW.DLL	C:\WINDOWS\SYSTEM\ VIEWERS	DLL	\WIN95\CAB_13.CAB
7/11/95	38,400	VSEXE2.DLL	C:\WINDOWS\SYSTEM\ VIEWERS	DLL	\WIN95\CAB_13.CAB
7/11/95	64,512	VSFLW.DLL	C:\WINDOWS\SYSTEM\ VIEWERS	DLL	\WIN95\CAB_13.CAB
7/11/95	25,088	VSMP.DLL	C:\WINDOWS\SYSTEM\ VIEWERS	DLL	\WIN95\CAB_13.CAB
7/11/95	33,792	VSMSW.DLL	C:\WINDOWS\SYSTEM\ VIEWERS	DLL	\WIN95\CAB_13.CAB

Part
XI

App
D

continues

Date	Size	Name	Location	Type	Location/CD
7/11/95	37,376	VSPP.DLL	C:\WINDOWS\SYSTEM\VIEWERS	DLL	\WIN95\CAB_13.CAB
7/11/95	86,016	VSQPW2.DLL	C:\WINDOWS\SYSTEM\VIEWERS	DLL	\WIN95\CAB_17.CAB
7/11/95	34,816	VSRTF.DLL	C:\WINDOWS\SYSTEM\VIEWERS	DLL	\WIN95\CAB_13.CAB
7/11/95	43,520	VSW6.DLL	C:\WINDOWS\SYSTEM\VIEWERS	DLL	\WIN95\CAB_13.CAB
7/11/95	78,848	VSWK4.DLL	C:\WINDOWS\SYSTEM\VIEWERS	DLL	\WIN95\CAB_13.CAB
7/11/95	35,328	VSWKS.DLL	C:\WINDOWS\SYSTEM\VIEWERS	DLL	\WIN95\CAB_13.CAB
7/11/95	28,160	VSWMF.DLL	C:\WINDOWS\SYSTEM\VIEWERS	DLL	\WIN95\CAB_13.CAB
7/11/95	64,512	VSWORD.DLL	C:\WINDOWS\SYSTEM\VIEWERS	DLL	\WIN95\CAB_13.CAB
7/11/95	28,672	VSWORK.DLL	C:\WINDOWS\SYSTEM\VIEWERS	DLL	\WIN95\CAB_13.CAB
7/11/95	43,008	VSWP5.DLL	C:\WINDOWS\SYSTEM\VIEWERS	DLL	\WIN95\CAB_13.CAB
7/11/95	51,712	VSWP6.DLL	C:\WINDOWS\SYSTEM\VIEWERS	DLL	\WIN95\CAB_13.CAB
7/11/95	27,136	VSWPF.DLL	C:\WINDOWS\SYSTEM\VIEWERS	DLL	\WIN95\CAB_13.CAB
7/11/95	81,408	VSXL5.DLL	C:\WINDOWS\SYSTEM\VIEWERS	DLL	\WIN95\CAB_13.CAB
7/11/95	81,168	WGPOADMN.DLL	C:\WINDOWS\SYSTEM	DLL	\WIN95\CAB_06.CAB
7/11/95	3,888	WHLP16T.DLL	C:\WINDOWS\SYSTEM	DLL	\WIN95\CAB_05.CAB
7/11/95	10,240	WHLP32T.DLL	C:\WINDOWS\SYSTEM	DLL	\WIN95\CAB_05.CAB
7/11/95	3,200	WIN32S16.DLL	C:\WINDOWS\SYSTEM	DLL	\WIN95\CAB_03.CAB
7/11/95	11,904	WIN87EM.DLL	C:\WINDOWS\SYSTEM	DLL	\WIN95\CAB_03.CAB
7/11/95	12,800	WIN87EM.DLL	C:\WINDOWS\SYSTEM	DLL	\WIN95\MINI.CAB
7/11/95	342,640	WIN95BB.DLL	C:\WINDOWS\SYSTEM	DLL	\WIN95\PRECOPY2.CAB
7/11/95	3,536	WINASPI.DLL	C:\WINDOWS\SYSTEM	DLL	\WIN95\CAB_03.CAB
7/11/95	49,152	WINMM.DLL	C:\WINDOWS\SYSTEM	DLL	\WIN95\CAB_08.CAB
7/11/95	2,000	WINNET16.DLL	C:\WINDOWS\SYSTEM	DLL	\WIN95\CAB_11.CAB
7/11/95	42,080	WINSOCK.DLL	C:\WINDOWS	DLL	\WIN95\CAB_11.CAB
7/11/95	211,456	WMSFR32.DLL	C:\WINDOWS\SYSTEM	DLL	\WIN95\CAB_06.CAB
7/11/95	877,568	WMSUI32.DLL	C:\WINDOWS\SYSTEM	DLL	\WIN95\CAB_06.CAB
7/11/95	16,384	WNASPI32.DLL	C:\WINDOWS\SYSTEM	DLL	\WIN95\CAB_03.CAB
7/11/95	13,824	WNPP32.DLL	C:\WINDOWS\SYSTEM	DLL	\WIN95\CAB_11.CAB
7/11/95	4,096	WOW32.DLL	C:\WINDOWS\SYSTEM	DLL	\WIN95\CAB_11.CAB
7/11/95	462,848	WPS_UPDT.DLL	C:\WINDOWS\SYSTEM	DLL	\WIN95\CAB_10.CAB
7/11/95	8,672	WPSAPD.DLL	C:\WINDOWS\SYSTEM	DLL	\WIN95\CAB_05.CAB
7/11/95	13,312	WPSMON.DLL	C:\WINDOWS\SYSTEM	DLL	\WIN95\CAB_10.CAB
7/11/95	8,080	WPSMON16.DLL	C:\WINDOWS\SYSTEM	DLL	\WIN95\CAB_10.CAB

Date	Size	Name	Location	Type	Location/CD
7/11/95	16,896	WPSUNIRE.DLL	C:\WINDOWS\SYSTEM	DLL	\WIN95\CAB_05.CAB
7/11/95	66,560	WSOCK32.DLL	C:\WINDOWS\SYSTEM	DLL	\WIN95\CAB_11.CAB
7/11/95	4,608	WINWORD.DOC	C:\WINDOWS	DOC	\WIN95\CAB_10.CAB
7/11/95	1,769	WINWORD2.DOC	C:\WINDOWS	DOC	\WIN95\CAB_10.CAB
7/11/95	11,105	AM2100.DOS	C:\WINDOWS\COMMAND	DOS	\WIN95\CAB_11.CAB
7/11/95	16,955	CPQNDIS.DOS	C:\WINDOWS\COMMAND	DOS	\WIN95\CAB_11.CAB
7/11/95	46,573	DC21X4.DOS	C:\WINDOWS\COMMAND	DOS	\WIN95\CAB_11.CAB
7/11/95	15,593	DEPCA.DOS	C:\WINDOWS\COMMAND	DOS	\WIN95\CAB_11.CAB
7/11/95	35,647	DNCRWL02.DOS	C:\WINDOWS\COMMAND	DOS	\WIN95\CAB_11.CAB
7/11/95	22,192	E100.DOS	C:\WINDOWS\COMMAND	DOS	\WIN95\CAB_11.CAB
7/11/95	16,332	E20ND.DOS	C:\WINDOWS\COMMAND	DOS	\WIN95\CAB_11.CAB
7/11/95	8,832	E21ND.DOS	C:\WINDOWS\COMMAND	DOS	\WIN95\CAB_11.CAB
7/11/95	10,512	E22ND.DOS	C:\WINDOWS\COMMAND	DOS	\WIN95\CAB_11.CAB
7/11/95	16,002	E30ND.DOS	C:\WINDOWS\COMMAND	DOS	\WIN95\CAB_11.CAB
7/11/95	8,031	E31ND.DOS	C:\WINDOWS\COMMAND	DOS	\WIN95\CAB_11.CAB
7/11/95	17,430	EL59X.DOS	C:\WINDOWS\COMMAND	DOS	\WIN95\CAB_11.CAB
7/11/95	9,792	ELNK16.DOS	C:\WINDOWS\COMMAND	DOS	\WIN95\CAB_11.CAB
7/11/95	15,519	ELNK3.DOS	C:\WINDOWS\COMMAND	DOS	\WIN95\CAB_11.CAB
7/11/95	11,322	ELNKII.DOS	C:\WINDOWS\COMMAND	DOS	\WIN95\CAB_11.CAB
7/11/95	9,542	ELNKMC.DOS	C:\WINDOWS\COMMAND	DOS	\WIN95\CAB_11.CAB
7/11/95	17,116	ELNKPL.DOS	C:\WINDOWS\COMMAND	DOS	\WIN95\CAB_11.CAB
7/11/95	19,230	EPNDIS.DOS	C:\WINDOWS\COMMAND	DOS	\WIN95\CAB_11.CAB
7/11/95	16,995	EPRO.DOS	C:\WINDOWS\COMMAND	DOS	\WIN95\CAB_11.CAB
7/11/95	14,544	ES3210.DOS	C:\WINDOWS\COMMAND	DOS	\WIN95\CAB_11.CAB
7/11/95	11,299	EVX16.DOS	C:\WINDOWS\COMMAND	DOS	\WIN95\CAB_11.CAB
7/11/95	9,509	EWRK3.DOS	C:\WINDOWS\COMMAND	DOS	\WIN95\CAB_08.CAB
7/11/95	10,478	EXP16.DOS	C:\WINDOWS\COMMAND	DOS	\WIN95\CAB_11.CAB
7/11/95	14,299	HPFEND.DOS	C:\WINDOWS\COMMAND	DOS	\WIN95\CAB_11.CAB
7/11/95	15,470	HPLAN.DOS	C:\WINDOWS\COMMAND	DOS	\WIN95\CAB_11.CAB
7/11/95	11,744	HPLANB.DOS	C:\WINDOWS\COMMAND	DOS	\WIN95\CAB_11.CAB
7/11/95	17,936	HPLANE.DOS	C:\WINDOWS\COMMAND	DOS	\WIN95\CAB_11.CAB
7/11/95	12,640	HPLANP.DOS	C:\WINDOWS\COMMAND	DOS	\WIN95\CAB_11.CAB
7/11/95	10,279	I82593.DOS	C:\WINDOWS\COMMAND	DOS	\WIN95\CAB_11.CAB
7/11/95	10,112	IBMTOK.DOS	C:\WINDOWS\COMMAND	DOS	\WIN95\CAB_11.CAB
7/11/95	59,448	IRMATR.DOS	C:\WINDOWS\COMMAND	DOS	\WIN95\CAB_11.CAB
7/11/95	42,802	NCC16.DOS	C:\WINDOWS\COMMAND	DOS	\WIN95\CAB_11.CAB
7/11/95	34,880	NDIS39XR.DOS	C:\WINDOWS\COMMAND	DOS	\WIN95\CAB_11.CAB
7/11/95	35,160	NDIS89XR.DOS	C:\WINDOWS\COMMAND	DOS	\WIN95\CAB_11.CAB
7/11/95	38,251	NDIS99XR.DOS	C:\WINDOWS\COMMAND	DOS	\WIN95\CAB_11.CAB

Part

XI

App

D

continues

Date	Size	Name	Location	Type	Location/CD
7/11/95	14,020	NE1000.DOS	C:\WINDOWS	DOS	\WIN95\CAB_11.CAB
7/11/95	13,964	NE2000.DOS	C:\WINDOWS	DOS	\WIN95\CAB_11.CAB
7/11/95	33,582	NE3200.DOS	C:\WINDOWS	DOS	\WIN95\CAB_11.CAB
7/11/95	78,996	NETFLX.DOS	C:\WINDOWS\COMMAND	DOS	\WIN95\CAB_11.CAB
7/11/95	10,472	NI5210.DOS	C:\WINDOWS\COMMAND	DOS	\WIN95\CAB_11.CAB
7/11/95	11,070	NI6510.DOS	C:\WINDOWS\COMMAND	DOS	\WIN95\CAB_11.CAB
7/11/95	55,710	OLITOK16.DOS	C:\WINDOWS\COMMAND	DOS	\WIN95\CAB_11.CAB
7/11/95	50,400	PCNTND.DOS	C:\WINDOWS\COMMAND	DOS	\WIN95\CAB_11.CAB
7/11/95	30,721	PE2NDIS.DOS	C:\WINDOWS\COMMAND	DOS	\WIN95\CAB_11.CAB
7/11/95	22,266	PENDIS.DOS	C:\WINDOWS\COMMAND	DOS	\WIN95\CAB_11.CAB
7/11/95	29,090	PRO4.DOS	C:\WINDOWS\COMMAND	DOS	\WIN95\CAB_11.CAB
7/11/95	33,770	PRO4AT.DOS	C:\WINDOWS\COMMAND	DOS	\WIN95\CAB_11.CAB
7/11/95	22,810	PROTMAN.DOS	C:\WINDOWS	DOS	\WIN95\CAB_12.CAB
7/11/95	13,578	SLAN.DOS	C:\WINDOWS\COMMAND	DOS	\WIN95\CAB_11.CAB
7/11/95	88,809	SMARTND.DOS	C:\WINDOWS\COMMAND	DOS	\WIN95\CAB_11.CAB
7/11/95	20,327	SMC_ARC.DOS	C:\WINDOWS\COMMAND	DOS	\WIN95\CAB_11.CAB
7/11/95	12,271	SMC3000.DOS	C:\WINDOWS\COMMAND	DOS	\WIN95\CAB_11.CAB
7/11/95	35,584	SMC8000.DOS	C:\WINDOWS\COMMAND	DOS	\WIN95\CAB_11.CAB
7/11/95	62,496	SMC8100.DOS	C:\WINDOWS\COMMAND	DOS	\WIN95\CAB_11.CAB
7/11/95	31,232	SMC8232.DOS	C:\WINDOWS\COMMAND	DOS	\WIN95\CAB_12.CAB
7/11/95	17,184	SMC9000.DOS	C:\WINDOWS\COMMAND	DOS	\WIN95\CAB_12.CAB
7/11/95	41,946	STRN.DOS	C:\WINDOWS\COMMAND	DOS	\WIN95\CAB_12.CAB
7/11/95	37,939	T20ND.DOS	C:\WINDOWS\COMMAND	DOS	\WIN95\CAB_12.CAB
7/11/95	45,388	T30ND.DOS	C:\WINDOWS\COMMAND	DOS	\WIN95\CAB_12.CAB
7/11/95	19,972	TCCARC.DOS	C:\WINDOWS\COMMAND	DOS	\WIN95\CAB_12.CAB
7/11/95	24,954	TCCTOK.DOS	C:\WINDOWS\COMMAND	DOS	\WIN95\CAB_12.CAB
7/11/95	12,426	TLNK.DOS	C:\WINDOWS\COMMAND	DOS	\WIN95\CAB_12.CAB
7/11/95	10,896	TLNK3.DOS	C:\WINDOWS\COMMAND	DOS	\WIN95\CAB_12.CAB
7/11/95	24,930	UBNEI.DOS	C:\WINDOWS\COMMAND	DOS	\WIN95\CAB_12.CAB
7/11/95	20,257	UBNEPS.DOS	C:\WINDOWS\COMMAND	DOS	\WIN95\CAB_12.CAB
7/11/95	94,768	ATIM32.DRV	C:\WINDOWS\SYSTEM	DRV	\WIN95\CAB_04.CAB
7/11/95	66,336	ATIM64.DRV	C:\WINDOWS\SYSTEM	DRV	\WIN95\CAB_04.CAB
7/11/95	128,800	ATIM8.DRV	C:\WINDOWS\SYSTEM	DRV	\WIN95\CAB_04.CAB
7/11/95	24,336	AVCAPT.DRV	C:\WINDOWS\SYSTEM	DRV	\WIN95\CAB_13.CAB
7/11/95	42,080	AZT16C.DRV	C:\WINDOWS\SYSTEM	DRV	\WIN95\CAB_08.CAB
7/11/95	43,664	AZT16W.DRV	C:\WINDOWS\SYSTEM	DRV	\WIN95\CAB_08.CAB
7/11/95	9,962	BIGMEM.DRV	C:\WINDOWS\SYSTEM\IOSUBSYS	DRV	\WIN95\CAB_03.CAB
7/11/95	13,648	BRHJ770.DRV	C:\WINDOWS\SYSTEM	DRV	\WIN95\CAB_10.CAB
7/11/95	16,464	BROTHER9.DRV	C:\WINDOWS\SYSTEM	DRV	\WIN95\CAB_10.CAB
7/11/95	32,528	BROTHR24.DRV	C:\WINDOWS\SYSTEM	DRV	\WIN95\CAB_10.CAB

Date	Size	Name	Location	Type	Location/CD
7/11/95	29,104	CANON330.DRV	C:\WINDOWS\SYSTEM	DRV	\WIN95\CAB_10.CAB
7/11/95	10,000	CANON800.DRV	C:\WINDOWS\SYSTEM	DRV	\WIN95\CAB_10.CAB
7/11/95	80,864	CANONLBP.DRV	C:\WINDOWS\SYSTEM	DRV	\WIN95\CAB_10.CAB
7/11/95	25,328	CHIPS.DRV	C:\WINDOWS\SYSTEM	DRV	\WIN95\CAB_04.CAB
7/11/95	57,632	CIRRUS.DRV	C:\WINDOWS\SYSTEM	DRV	\WIN95\CAB_04.CAB
7/11/95	35,344	CIRRUSMM.DRV	C:\WINDOWS\SYSTEM	DRV	\WIN95\CAB_04.CAB
7/11/95	40,544	CIT24US.DRV	C:\WINDOWS\SYSTEM	DRV	\WIN95\CAB_10.CAB
7/11/95	29,184	CIT9US.DRV	C:\WINDOWS\SYSTEM	DRV	\WIN95\CAB_10.CAB
7/11/95	5,360	CITOH.DRV	C:\WINDOWS\SYSTEM	DRV	\WIN95\CAB_10.CAB
7/11/95	5,856	COMM.DRV	C:\WINDOWS\SYSTEM	DRV	\WIN95\CAB_03.CAB
7/11/95	9,280	COMM.DRV	C:\WINDOWS\SYSTEM	DRV	\WIN95\MINI.CAB
7/11/95	82,080	COMPAQ.DRV	C:\WINDOWS\SYSTEM	DRV	\WIN95\CAB_04.CAB
7/11/95	12,048	DEC24PIN.DRV	C:\WINDOWS\SYSTEM	DRV	\WIN95\CAB_10.CAB
7/11/95	14,192	DEC3200.DRV	C:\WINDOWS\SYSTEM	DRV	\WIN95\CAB_10.CAB
7/11/95	181,840	DESKJETC.DRV	C:\WINDOWS\SYSTEM	DRV	\WIN95\CAB_09.CAB
7/11/95	5,136	DICONIX.DRV	C:\WINDOWS\SYSTEM	DRV	\WIN95\CAB_10.CAB
7/11/95	25,168	EPSON24.DRV	C:\WINDOWS\SYSTEM	DRV	\WIN95\CAB_09.CAB
7/11/95	31,776	EPSON9.DRV	C:\WINDOWS\SYSTEM	DRV	\WIN95\CAB_10.CAB
7/11/95	43,936	ES1488.DRV	C:\WINDOWS\SYSTEM	DRV	\WIN95\CAB_08.CAB
7/11/95	50,128	ES1688.DRV	C:\WINDOWS\SYSTEM	DRV	\WIN95\CAB_08.CAB
7/11/95	36,976	ES488.DRV	C:\WINDOWS\SYSTEM	DRV	\WIN95\CAB_08.CAB
7/11/95	47,008	ES688.DRV	C:\WINDOWS\SYSTEM	DRV	\WIN95\CAB_08.CAB
7/11/95	17,920	ESSFM.DRV	C:\WINDOWS\SYSTEM	DRV	\WIN95\CAB_08.CAB
7/11/95	9,904	ESSMPORT.DRV	C:\WINDOWS\SYSTEM	DRV	\WIN95\CAB_08.CAB
7/11/95	8,240	ESSMPU.DRV	C:\WINDOWS\SYSTEM	DRV	\WIN95\CAB_08.CAB
7/11/95	15,152	EXPRSS24.DRV	C:\WINDOWS\SYSTEM	DRV	\WIN95\CAB_10.CAB
7/11/95	16,752	FRAMEBUF.DRV	C:\WINDOWS\SYSTEM	DRV	\WIN95\CAB_04.CAB
7/11/95	32,176	FUJI24.DRV	C:\WINDOWS\SYSTEM	DRV	\WIN95\CAB_10.CAB
7/11/95	12,224	FUJI9.DRV	C:\WINDOWS\SYSTEM	DRV	\WIN95\CAB_10.CAB
7/11/95	90,560	HPDSKJET.DRV	C:\WINDOWS\SYSTEM	DRV	\WIN95\CAB_09.CAB
7/11/95	202,992	HPPCL.DRV	C:\WINDOWS\SYSTEM	DRV	\WIN95\CAB_09.CAB
7/11/95	525,856	HPPCL5MS.DRV	C:\WINDOWS\SYSTEM	DRV	\WIN95\CAB_09.CAB
7/11/95	66,976	HPPLOT.DRV	C:\WINDOWS\SYSTEM	DRV	\WIN95\CAB_10.CAB
7/11/95	15,024	IBM238X.DRV	C:\WINDOWS\SYSTEM	DRV	\WIN95\CAB_10.CAB
7/11/95	30,560	IBM239X.DRV	C:\WINDOWS\SYSTEM	DRV	\WIN95\CAB_10.CAB
7/11/95	19,216	IBM5204.DRV	C:\WINDOWS\SYSTEM	DRV	\WIN95\CAB_10.CAB
7/11/95	25,920	IBMPPDSL.DRV	C:\WINDOWS\SYSTEM	DRV	\WIN95\CAB_10.CAB
7/11/95	73,440	JP350.DRV	C:\WINDOWS\SYSTEM	DRV	\WIN95\CAB_10.CAB
7/11/95	12,688	KEYBOARD.DRV	C:\WINDOWS\SYSTEM	DRV	\WIN95\CAB_06.CAB

Part
XI

App
D

continues

Date	Size	Name	Location	Type	Location/CD
7/11/95	7,568	KEYBOARD.DRV	C:\WINDOWS\SYSTEM	DRV	\WIN95\MINI.CAB
7/11/95	30,608	KYOCERA.DRV	C:\WINDOWS\SYSTEM	DRV	\WIN95\CAB_10.CAB
7/11/95	7,984	LMOUSE.DRV	C:\WINDOWS\SYSTEM	DRV	\WIN95\CAB_08.CAB
7/11/95	12,928	LMOUSE31.DRV	C:\WINDOWS\SYSTEM	DRV	\WIN95\MINI.CAB
7/11/95	34,160	MANTAL24.DRV	C:\WINDOWS\SYSTEM	DRV	\WIN95\CAB_10.CAB
7/11/95	22,992	MANTAL9.DRV	C:\WINDOWS\SYSTEM	DRV	\WIN95\CAB_10.CAB
7/11/95	67,520	MCIAVI.DRV	C:\WINDOWS\SYSTEM	DRV	\WIN95\CAB_08.CAB
7/11/95	12,800	MCICDA.DRV	C:\WINDOWS\SYSTEM	DRV	\WIN95\CAB_08.CAB
7/11/95	13,712	MCIPIONR.DRV	C:\WINDOWS\SYSTEM	DRV	\WIN95\CAB_13.CAB
7/11/95	18,672	MCISEQ.DRV	C:\WINDOWS\SYSTEM	DRV	\WIN95\CAB_08.CAB
7/11/95	95,776	MCIVISCA.DRV	C:\WINDOWS\SYSTEM	DRV	\WIN95\CAB_13.CAB
7/11/95	22,016	MCIWAVE.DRV	C:\WINDOWS\SYSTEM	DRV	\WIN95\CAB_08.CAB
7/11/95	110,528	MGA.DRV	C:\WINDOWS\SYSTEM	DRV	\WIN95\CAB_04.CAB
7/11/95	16,976	MIDIMAP.DRV	C:\WINDOWS\SYSTEM	DRV	\WIN95\CAB_08.CAB
7/11/95	3,104	MMSOUND.DRV	C:\WINDOWS\SYSTEM	DRV	\WIN95\CAB_03.CAB
7/11/95	7,712	MOUSE.DRV	C:\WINDOWS\SYSTEM	DRV	\WIN95\CAB_08.CAB
7/11/95	21,872	MSACM.DRV	C:\WINDOWS\SYSTEM	DRV	\WIN95\CAB_08.CAB
7/11/95	7,744	MSJSTICK.DRV	C:\WINDOWS\SYSTEM	DRV	\WIN95\CAB_08.CAB
7/11/95	10,672	MSMOUS31.DRV	C:\WINDOWS\SYSTEM	DRV	\WIN95\MINI.CAB
7/11/95	8,704	MSMPU401.DRV	C:\WINDOWS\SYSTEM	DRV	\WIN95\CAB_08.CAB
7/11/95	7,072	MSNET.DRV	C:\WINDOWS\SYSTEM	DRV	\WIN95\CAB_12.CAB
7/11/95	17,952	MSOPL.DRV	C:\WINDOWS\SYSTEM	DRV	\WIN95\CAB_08.CAB
7/11/95	40,848	MSSBLST.DRV	C:\WINDOWS\SYSTEM	DRV	\WIN95\CAB_08.CAB
7/11/95	39,728	MSSNDSYS.DRV	C:\WINDOWS\SYSTEM	DRV	\WIN95\CAB_08.CAB
7/11/95	8,304	MTLITE.DRV	C:\WINDOWS\SYSTEM	DRV	\WIN95\CAB_10.CAB
7/11/95	12,640	MVI401.DRV	C:\WINDOWS\SYSTEM	DRV	\WIN95\CAB_08.CAB
7/11/95	38,432	MVI514MX.DRV	C:\WINDOWS\SYSTEM	DRV	\WIN95\CAB_08.CAB
7/11/95	41,232	MVIFM.DRV	C:\WINDOWS\SYSTEM	DRV	\WIN95\CAB_08.CAB
7/11/95	19,760	MVIWAVE.DRV	C:\WINDOWS\SYSTEM	DRV	\WIN95\CAB_08.CAB
7/11/95	59,568	MVMIXER.DRV	C:\WINDOWS\SYSTEM	DRV	\WIN95\CAB_08.CAB
7/11/95	26,128	MVPROAUD.DRV	C:\WINDOWS\SYSTEM	DRV	\WIN95\CAB_08.CAB
7/11/95	23,424	NEC24PIN.DRV	C:\WINDOWS\SYSTEM	DRV	\WIN95\CAB_10.CAB
7/11/95	416	NOMOUSE.DRV	C:\WINDOWS\SYSTEM	DRV	\WIN95\MINI.CAB
7/11/95	40,848	OKI24.DRV	C:\WINDOWS\SYSTEM	DRV	\WIN95\CAB_10.CAB
7/11/95	18,336	OKI9.DRV	C:\WINDOWS\SYSTEM	DRV	\WIN95\CAB_10.CAB
7/11/95	48,720	OKI9IBM.DRV	C:\WINDOWS\SYSTEM	DRV	\WIN95\CAB_10.CAB
7/11/95	24,176	OLIDM24.DRV	C:\WINDOWS\SYSTEM	DRV	\WIN95\CAB_10.CAB
7/11/95	33,232	OLIDM9.DRV	C:\WINDOWS\SYSTEM	DRV	\WIN95\CAB_10.CAB
7/11/95	19,040	P351SX2.DRV	C:\WINDOWS\SYSTEM	DRV	\WIN95\CAB_10.CAB
7/11/95	53,200	PA3DMXD.DRV	C:\WINDOWS\SYSTEM	DRV	\WIN95\CAB_08.CAB

Date	Size	Name	Location	Type	Location/CD
7/11/95	7,664	PAINTJET.DRV	C:\WINDOWS\SYSTEM	DRV	\WIN95\CAB_10.CAB
7/11/95	31,312	PANSON24.DRV	C:\WINDOWS\SYSTEM	DRV	\WIN95\CAB_10.CAB
7/11/95	28,000	PANSON9.DRV	C:\WINDOWS\SYSTEM	DRV	\WIN95\CAB_10.CAB
7/11/95	1,920	POWER.DRV	C:\WINDOWS\SYSTEM	DRV	\WIN95\CAB_07.CAB
7/11/95	12,192	PROPRINT.DRV	C:\WINDOWS\SYSTEM	DRV	\WIN95\CAB_10.CAB
7/11/95	11,120	PROPRN24.DRV	C:\WINDOWS\SYSTEM	DRV	\WIN95\CAB_10.CAB
7/11/95	13,856	PS1.DRV	C:\WINDOWS\SYSTEM	DRV	\WIN95\CAB_10.CAB
7/11/95	393,200	PSCRIPT.DRV	C:\WINDOWS\SYSTEM	DRV	\WIN95\CAB_09.CAB
7/11/95	5,776	QUIETJET.DRV	C:\WINDOWS\SYSTEM	DRV	\WIN95\CAB_10.CAB
7/11/95	17,648	QWIII.DRV	C:\WINDOWS\SYSTEM	DRV	\WIN95\CAB_10.CAB
7/11/95	57,632	S3.DRV	C:\WINDOWS\SYSTEM	DRV	\WIN95\CAB_04.CAB
7/11/95	46,000	SB16SND.DRV	C:\WINDOWS\SYSTEM	DRV	\WIN95\CAB_08.CAB
7/11/95	23,216	SBAWE32.DRV	C:\WINDOWS\SYSTEM	DRV	\WIN95\CAB_08.CAB
7/11/95	4,128	SBFM.DRV	C:\WINDOWS\SYSTEM	DRV	\WIN95\CAB_08.CAB
7/11/95	31,376	SEIKO24E.DRV	C:\WINDOWS\SYSTEM	DRV	\WIN95\CAB_10.CAB
7/11/95	18,736	SEIKOSH9.DRV	C:\WINDOWS\SYSTEM	DRV	\WIN95\CAB_10.CAB
7/11/95	3,440	SOUND.DRV	C:\WINDOWS\SYSTEM	DRV	\WIN95\MINI.CAB
7/11/95	63,088	STAR24E.DRV	C:\WINDOWS\SYSTEM	DRV	\WIN95\CAB_10.CAB
7/11/95	38,160	STAR9E.DRV	C:\WINDOWS\SYSTEM	DRV	\WIN95\CAB_10.CAB
7/11/95	52,320	SUPERVGA.DRV	C:\WINDOWS\SYSTEM	DRV	\WIN95\CAB_04.CAB
7/11/95	2,288	SYSTEM.DRV	C:\WINDOWS\SYSTEM	DRV	\WIN95\CAB_03.CAB
7/11/95	2,304	SYSTEM.DRV	C:\WINDOWS\SYSTEM	DRV	\WIN95\MINI.CAB
7/11/95	6,752	THINKJET.DRV	C:\WINDOWS\SYSTEM	DRV	\WIN95\CAB_10.CAB
7/11/95	5,056	TI850.DRV	C:\WINDOWS\SYSTEM	DRV	\WIN95\CAB_10.CAB
7/11/95	10,880	TOSHIBA.DRV	C:\WINDOWS\SYSTEM	DRV	\WIN95\CAB_10.CAB
7/11/95	28,864	TSENG.DRV	C:\WINDOWS\SYSTEM	DRV	\WIN95\CAB_04.CAB
7/11/95	31,152	TTY.DRV	C:\WINDOWS\SYSTEM	DRV	\WIN95\CAB_10.CAB
7/11/95	52,064	VGA.DRV	C:\WINDOWS\SYSTEM	DRV	\WIN95\CAB_04.CAB
7/11/95	73,200	VGA.DRV	C:\WINDOWS\SYSTEM	DRV	\WIN95\MINI.CAB
7/11/95	21,680	WD.DRV	C:\WINDOWS\SYSTEM	DRV	\WIN95\CAB_04.CAB
7/11/95	3,552	WINSPL16.DRV	C:\WINDOWS\SYSTEM	DRV	\WIN95\CAB_09.CAB
7/11/95	18,944	WINSPOOL.DRV	C:\WINDOWS\SYSTEM	DRV	\WIN95\CAB_09.CAB
7/11/95	145,456	WPSUNI.DRV	C:\WINDOWS\SYSTEM	DRV	\WIN95\CAB_05.CAB
7/11/95	12,864	XGA.DRV	C:\WINDOWS\SYSTEM	DRV	\WIN95\CAB_04.CAB
7/11/95	24,734	PRORAPM.DWN	C:\WINDOWS\SYSTEM	DWN	\WIN95\CAB_12.CAB
7/11/95	5,378	RCV0000.EFX	C:\WINDOWS\SYSTEM	EFX	\WIN95\CAB_05.CAB
7/11/95	293	ENVOY.EVY	C:\WINDOWS\SHELLNEW	EVY	\WIN95\CAB_10.CAB
7/11/95	24,576	ACCSTAT.EXE	C:\WINDOWS	EXE	\WIN95\CAB_02.CAB
7/11/95	14,336	ADDREG.EXE	C:\WINDOWS\SYSTEM	EXE	\WIN95\CAB_09.CAB

Part
XI

App
D

continues

Date	Size	Name	Location	Type	Location/CD
7/11/95	168,448	ARCSRV32.EXE	C:\WINDOWS\SYSTEM	EXE	\WIN95\CAB_17.CAB
7/11/95	19,536	ARP.EXE	C:\WINDOWS	EXE	\WIN95\CAB_12.CAB
7/11/95	15,252	ATTRIB.EXE	C:\WINDOWS\COMMAND	EXE	\WIN95\CAB_02.CAB
7/11/95	9,728	AWADPR32.EXE	C:\WINDOWS\SYSTEM	EXE	\WIN95\CAB_05.CAB
7/11/95	74,240	AWFXEX32.EXE	C:\WINDOWS\SYSTEM	EXE	\WIN95\CAB_05.CAB
7/11/95	35,328	AWSNTO32.EXE	C:\WINDOWS\SYSTEM	EXE	\WIN95\CAB_05.CAB
7/11/95	23,834	BACKUP.CFG	C:\PROGRAM FILES\ ACCESSORIES	EXE	\WIN95\CAB_04.CAB
7/11/95	33,018	BACKUP.HLP	C:\WINDOWS\HELP	EXE	\WIN95\CAB_04.CAB
7/11/95	61,952	BKUPAGNT.EXE	C:\WINDOWS	EXE	\WIN95\CAB_17.CAB
7/11/95	59,392	CALC.EXE	C:\WINDOWS	EXE	\WIN95\CAB_02.CAB
7/11/95	27,296	CARDDRV.EXE	C:\WINDOWS	EXE	\WIN95\CAB_09.CAB
7/11/95	22,016	CCDIALER.EXE	C:\PROGRAM FILES\ THE MICROSOFT NETWORK	EXE	\WIN95\CAB_07.CAB
7/11/95	88,064	CDPLAYER.EXE	C:\WINDOWS	EXE	\WIN95\CAB_13.CAB
7/11/95	14,752	CHARMAP.EXE	C:\WINDOWS	EXE	\WIN95\CAB_13.CAB
7/11/95	27,248	CHKDSK.EXE	C:\WINDOWS\COMMAND	EXE	\WIN95\CAB_02.CAB
7/11/95	57,664	CLIPBOOK.EXE	C:\WINDOWS	EXE	\WIN95\CAB_02.CAB
7/11/95	17,376	CLIPBRD.EXE	C:\WINDOWS	EXE	\WIN95\CAB_02.CAB
7/11/95	16,608	CLIPSRV.EXE	C:\WINDOWS	EXE	\WIN95\CAB_02.CAB
7/11/95	14,596	CONAGENT.EXE	C:\WINDOWS\SYSTEM	EXE	\WIN95\CAB_03.CAB
7/11/95	2,112	CONTROL.EXE	C:\WINDOWS	EXE	\WIN95\CAB_10.CAB
7/11/95	7,954	CPQAE05.EXE	C:\WINDOWS\SYSTEM	EXE	\WIN95\CAB_09.CAB
7/11/95	7,288	CPQAE06.EXE	C:\WINDOWS\SYSTEM	EXE	\WIN95\CAB_09.CAB
7/11/95	20,522	DEBUG.EXE	C:\WINDOWS\COMMAND	EXE	\WIN95\CAB_02.CAB
7/11/95	19,019	DELTREE.EXE	C:\WINDOWS\COMMAND	EXE	\WIN95\CAB_08.CAB
7/11/95	63,240	DIALER.EXE	C:\WINDOWS	EXE	\WIN95\CAB_02.CAB
7/11/95	60,416	DIRECTCC.EXE	C:\WINDOWS	EXE	\WIN95\CAB_10.CAB
7/11/95	3,584	DNR.EXE	C:\PROGRAM FILES\ THE MICROSOFT NETWORK	EXE	\WIN95\CAB_07.CAB
7/11/95	336,736	DRVSPACE.EXE	C:\WINDOWS	EXE	\WIN95\CAB_08.CAB
7/11/95	125,495	EMM386.EXE	C:\WINDOWS	EXE	\WIN95\CAB_08.CAB
7/11/95	20,240	EXCHNG32.EXE	C:\PROGRAM FILES\ MICROSOFT EXCHANGE	EXE	\WIN95\CAB_06.CAB
7/11/95	204,288	EXPLORER.EXE	C:\WINDOWS	EXE	\WIN95\CAB_10.CAB
7/11/95	33,280	EXPOSTRT.EXE	C:\WINDOWS	EXE	\WIN95\CAB_16.CAB
7/11/95	191,488	FAXCOVER.EXE	C:\WINDOWS	EXE	\WIN95\CAB_05.CAB
7/11/95	166,912	FAXVIEW.EXE	C:\WINDOWS	EXE	\WIN95\CAB_05.CAB
7/11/95	20,494	FC.EXE	C:\WINDOWS\COMMAND	EXE	\WIN95\CAB_08.CAB
7/11/95	59,128	FDISK.EXE	C:\WINDOWS\COMMAND	EXE	\WIN95\CAB_02.CAB
7/11/95	48,128	FILEXFER.EXE	C:\WINDOWS	EXE	\WIN95\CAB_17.CAB
7/11/95	6,658	FIND.EXE	C:\WINDOWS\COMMAND	EXE	\WIN95\CAB_08.CAB

Date	Size	Name	Location	Type	Location/CD
7/11/95	6,656	FONTREG.EXE	C:\WINDOWS\SYSTEM	EXE	\WIN95\CAB_11.CAB
7/11/95	36,352	FONTVIEW.EXE	C:\WINDOWS	EXE	\WIN95\CAB_11.CAB
7/11/95	28,560	FREECELL.EXE	C:\WINDOWS	EXE	\WIN95\CAB_05.CAB
7/11/95	46,592	FTMCL.EXE	C:\PROGRAM FILES\ THE MICROSOFT NETWORK	EXE	\WIN95\CAB_07.CAB
7/11/95	37,520	FTP.EXE	C:\WINDOWS	EXE	\WIN95\CAB_12.CAB
7/11/95	312,208	GDI.EXE	C:\WINDOWS\SYSTEM	EXE	\WIN95\CAB_03.CAB
7/11/95	149,456	GDI.EXE	C:\WINDOWS\SYSTEM	EXE	\WIN95\MINI.CAB
7/11/95	33,280	GRPCONV.EXE	C:\WINDOWS	EXE	\WIN95\CAB_11.CAB
7/11/95	110,080	GUIDE.EXE	C:\PROGRAM FILES\ THE MICROSOFT NETWORK	EXE	\WIN95\CAB_07.CAB
7/11/95	30,720	HPPROPTY.EXE	C:\WINDOWS\SYSTEM	EXE	\WIN95\CAB_16.CAB
7/11/95	6,144	HYPERTRM.EXE	C:\PROGRAM FILES\ ACCESSORIS\HYPERTERMINAL	EXE	\WIN95\CAB_02.CAB
7/11/95	12,800	INTERNAT.EXE	C:\WINDOWS\SYSTEM	EXE	\WIN95\CAB_06.CAB
7/11/95	693,760	JETADMIN.EXE	C:\WINDOWS\SYSTEM	EXE	\WIN95\CAB_16.CAB
7/11/95	124,416	KRNL386.EXE	C:\WINDOWS\SYSTEM	EXE	\WIN95\CAB_03.CAB
7/11/95	75,490	KRNL386.EXE	C:\WINDOWS\SYSTEM	EXE	\WIN95\MINI.CAB
7/11/95	9,260	LABEL.EXE	C:\WINDOWS\COMMAND	EXE	\WIN95\CAB_08.CAB
7/11/95	32,768	LIGHTS.EXE	C:\WINDOWS\SYSTEM	EXE	\WIN95\CAB_10.CAB
7/11/95	4,785	LMSCRIPT.EXE	C:\WINDOWS\SYSTEM	EXE	\WIN95\CAB_12.CAB
7/11/95	12,135	LOGIN.EXE	C:\WINDOWS\	EXE	\WIN95\CAB_12.CAB
7/11/95	7,488	MAPISP32.EXE	C:\WINDOWS\SYSTEM	EXE	\WIN95\CAB_07.CAB
7/11/95	24,272	MAPISRVR.EXE	C:\WINDOWS\SYSTEM	EXE	\WIN95\CAB_07.CAB
7/11/95	32,082	MEM.EXE	C:\WINDOWS\COMMAND	EXE	\WIN95\CAB_08.CAB
7/11/95	33,792	MKCOMPAT.EXE	C:\WINDOWS\SYSTEM	EXE	\WIN95\CAB_03.CAB
7/11/95	6,367	ML3XEC16.EXE	C:\WINDOWS\SYSTEM	EXE	\WIN95\CAB_07.CAB
7/11/95	24,336	MLSET32.EXE	C:\PROGRAM FILES\ MICROSOFT EXCHANGE	EXE	\WIN95\CAB_07.CAB
7/11/95	69,632	MOSCP.EXE	C:\PROGRAM FILES\ THE MICROSOFT NETWORK	EXE	\WIN95\CAB_07.CAB
7/11/95	55,296	MOSVIEW.EXE	C:\PROGRAM FILES\ THE MICROSOFT NETWORK	EXE	\WIN95\CAB_07.CAB
7/11/95	27,235	MOVE.EXE	C:\WINDOWS\COMMAND	EXE	\WIN95\CAB_09.CAB
7/11/95	147,968	MPLAYER.EXE	C:\WINDOWS	EXE	\WIN95\CAB_08.CAB
7/11/95	12,800	MPREXE.EXE	C:\WINDOWS\SYSTEM	EXE	\WIN95\CAB_12.CAB
7/11/95	25,473	MSCDEX.EXE	C:\WINDOWS\COMMAND	EXE	\WIN95\CAB_04.CAB
7/11/95	31,284	MSDLC.EXE	C:\WINDOWS\COMMAND	EXE	\WIN95\CAB_12.CAB
7/11/95	10,192	MSGSRV32.EXE	C:\WINDOWS\SYSTEM	EXE	\WIN95\CAB_09.CAB
7/11/95	122,240	MSHEARTS.EXE	C:\WINDOWS	EXE	\WIN95\CAB_05.CAB
7/11/95	17,408	MSNEXCH.EXE	C:\WINDOWS\SYSTEM	EXE	\WIN95\CAB_07.CAB
7/11/95	52,224	MSNFIND.EXE	C:\PROGRAM FILES\ THE MICROSOFT NETWORK	EXE	\WIN95\CAB_07.CAB

Part
XI

App
D

continues

Date	Size	Name	Location	Type	Location/CD
7/11/95	311,808	MSPAINT.EXE	C:\PROGRAM FILES\ ACCESSORIES	EXE	\WIN95\CAB_02.CAB
7/11/95	33,371	NBTSTAT.EXE	C:\WINDOWS	EXE	\WIN95\CAB_12.CAB
7/11/95	375,962	NET.EXE	C:\WINDOWS	EXE	\WIN95\CAB_12.CAB
7/11/95	54,992	NETDDE.EXE	C:\WINDOWS	EXE	\WIN95\CAB_12.CAB
7/11/95	23,776	NETSTAT.EXE	C:\WINDOWS	EXE	\WIN95\CAB_12.CAB
7/11/95	63,488	NETWATCH.EXE	C:\WINDOWS	EXE	\WIN95\CAB_17.CAB
7/11/95	6,940	NLSFUNC.EXE	C:\WINDOWS\COMMAND	EXE	\WIN95\CAB_09.CAB
7/11/95	34,304	NOTEPAD.EXE	C:\WINDOWS	EXE	\WIN95\CAB_02.CAB
7/11/95	13,824	NWLSCON.EXE	C:\WINDOWS\SYSTEM	EXE	\WIN95\CAB_12.CAB
7/11/95	71,680	NWLSPROC.EXE	C:\WINDOWS\SYSTEM	EXE	\WIN95\CAB_12.CAB
7/11/95	4,197	ODIHLP.EXE	C:\WINDOWS\HELP	EXE	\WIN95\CAB_12.CAB
7/11/95	74,240	ONLSTMT.EXE	C:\PROGRAM FILES\ THE MICROSOFT NETWORK	EXE	\WIN95\CAB_07.CAB
7/11/95	65,024	PACKAGER.EXE	C:\WINDOWS	EXE	\WIN95\CAB_02.CAB
7/11/95	4,608	PBRUSH.EXE	C:\WINDOWS	EXE	\WIN95\CAB_02.CAB
7/11/95	23,299	PCSA.EXE	C:\WINDOWS	EXE	\WIN95\CAB_17.CAB
7/11/95	23,506	PE3NDIS.EXE	C:\WINDOWS	EXE	\WIN95\CAB_12.CAB
7/11/95	12,128	PING.EXE	C:\WINDOWS	EXE	\WIN95\CAB_12.CAB
7/11/95	37,344	POINTER.EXE	C:\WINDOWS	EXE	\WIN95\CAB_08.CAB
7/11/95	113,456	PROGMAN.EXE	C:\WINDOWS	EXE	\WIN95\CAB_11.CAB
7/11/95	14,952	PROTMAN.EXE	C:\WINDOWS	EXE	\WIN95\CAB_12.CAB
7/11/95	20,992	QUIKVIEW.EXE	C:\WINDOWS	EXE	\WIN95\CAB_13.CAB
7/11/95	13,312	REDIR32.EXE	C:\WINDOWS\SYSTEM	EXE	\WIN95\CAB_03.CAB
7/11/95	120,320	REGEDIT.EXE	C:\WINDOWS	EXE	\WIN95\CAB_02.CAB
7/11/95	176,640	REGWIZ.EXE	C:\WINDOWS\SYSTEM	EXE	\WIN95\CAB_07.CAB
7/11/95	25,600	RNAAPP.EXE	C:\WINDOWS\SYSTEM	EXE	\WIN95\CAB_10.CAB
7/11/95	23,696	ROUTE.EXE	C:\WINDOWS	EXE	\WIN95\CAB_12.CAB
7/11/95	81,644	RPCSS.EXE	C:\WINDOWS\SYSTEM	EXE	\WIN95\CAB_12.CAB
7/11/95	15,360	RSRCMTR.EXE	C:\WINDOWS	EXE	\WIN95\CAB_02.CAB
7/11/95	4,912	RUNDLL.EXE	C:\WINDOWS	EXE	\WIN95\CAB_11.CAB
7/11/95	8,192	RUNDLL32.EXE	C:\WINDOWS	EXE	\WIN95\CAB_11.CAB
7/11/95	11,264	RUNONCE.EXE	C:\WINDOWS\SYSTEM	EXE	\WIN95\CAB_10.CAB
7/11/95	4,608	SCANDSKW.EXE	C:\WINDOWS\SYSTEM	EXE	\WIN95\CAB_09.CAB
7/11/95	264,384	SCANPST.EXE	C:\PROGRAM FILES\ MICROSOFT EXCHANGE	EXE	\WIN95\CAB_07.CAB
7/11/95	240,322	SELECT.EXE	C:\WINDOWS	EXE	\WIN95\CAB_17.CAB
7/11/95	57,209	SETMDIR.EXE	C:\WINDOWS\COMMAND	EXE	\WIN95\CAB_17.CAB
7/11/95	18,939	SETVER.EXE	C:\WINDOWS\COMMAND	EXE	\WIN95\CAB_09.CAB
7/11/95	108,544	SF4029.EXE	C:\WINDOWS\COMMAND	EXE	\WIN95\CAB_10.CAB
7/11/95	10,304	SHARE.EXE	C:\WINDOWS\COMMAND	EXE	\WIN95\CAB_09.CAB

Date	Size	Name	Location	Type	Location/CD
7/11/95	202,752	SIGNUP.EXE	C:\PROGRAM FILES\ THE MICROSOFT NETWORK	EXE	\WIN95\CAB_07.CAB
7/11/95	6,122	SNAPSHOT.EXE	C:\WINDOWS	EXE	\WIN95\CAB_17.CAB
7/11/95	105,472	SNDREC32.EXE	C:\WINDOWS	EXE	\WIN95\CAB_08.CAB
7/11/95	54,784	SNDVOL32.EXE	C:\WINDOWS	EXE	\WIN95\CAB_08.CAB
7/11/95	171,392	SOL.EXE	C:\WINDOWS	EXE	\WIN95\CAB_05.CAB
7/11/95	25,802	SORT.EXE	C:\WINDOWS\COMMAND	EXE	\WIN95\CAB_03.CAB
7/11/95	20,992	SPOOL32.EXE	C:\WINDOWS\SYSTEM	EXE	\WIN95\CAB_09.CAB
7/11/95	9,216	START.EXE	C:\WINDOWS\COMMAND	EXE	\WIN95\CAB_09.CAB
7/11/95	17,904	SUBST.EXE	C:\WINDOWS\COMMAND	EXE	\WIN95\CAB_09.CAB
7/11/95	352,608	SUWIN.EXE	C:\WINDOWS\SYSTEM	EXE	\WIN95\PRECOPY2.CAB
7/11/95	19,488	SYSEDIT.EXE	C:\WINDOWS\SYSTEM	EXE	\WIN95\CAB_02.CAB
7/11/95	65,024	SYSMON.EXE	C:\WINDOWS	EXE	\WIN95\CAB_17.CAB
7/11/95	26,112	SYSTRAY.EXE	C:\WINDOWS\SYSTEM	EXE	\WIN95\CAB_07.CAB
7/11/95	1,784	TAPIEXE.EXE	C:\WINDOWS\SYSTEM	EXE	\WIN95\CAB_11.CAB
7/11/95	7,632	TAPIINI.EXE	C:\WINDOWS	EXE	\WIN95\CAB_11.CAB
7/11/95	28,672	TASKMAN.EXE	C:\WINDOWS	EXE	\WIN95\CAB_11.CAB
7/11/95	66,672	TELNET.EXE	C:\WINDOWS	EXE	\WIN95\CAB_12.CAB
7/11/95	53,248	TEXTCHAT.EXE	C:\PROGRAM FILES\ THE MICROSOFT NETWORK	EXE	\WIN95\CAB_07.CAB
7/11/95	339,456	TOUR.EXE	C:\WINDOWS	EXE	\WIN95\CAB_17.CAB
7/11/95	9,056	TRACERT.EXE	C:\WINDOWS	EXE	\WIN95\CAB_12.CAB
7/11/95	76,496	UNINSTAL.EXE	C:\WINDOWS	EXE	\WIN95\CAB_02.CAB
7/11/95	462,112	USER.EXE	C:\WINDOWS\SYSTEM	EXE	\WIN95\CAB_03.CAB
7/11/95	264,016	USER.EXE	C:\WINDOWS\SYSTEM	EXE	\WIN95\MINI.CAB
7/11/95	10,240	VVEXE32.EXE	C:\WINDOWS\SYSTEM	EXE	\WIN95\CAB_17.CAB
7/11/95	16,384	WELCOME.EXE	C:\WINDOWS	EXE	\WIN95\CAB_11.CAB
7/11/95	155,408	WINFILE.EXE	C:\WINDOWS	EXE	\WIN95\CAB_11.CAB
7/11/95	2,416	WINHELP.EXE	C:\WINDOWS	EXE	\WIN95\CAB_05.CAB
7/11/95	306,688	WINHLP32.EXE	C:\WINDOWS	EXE	\WIN95\CAB_05.CAB
7/11/95	40,801	WININIT.EXE	C:\WINDOWS	EXE	\WIN95\CAB_10.CAB
7/11/95	38,912	WINIPCFG.EXE	C:\WINDOWS	EXE	\WIN95\CAB_12.CAB
7/11/95	24,176	WINMINE.EXE	C:\WINDOWS	EXE	\WIN95\CAB_05.CAB
7/11/95	27,600	WINPOPUP.EXE	C:\WINDOWS	EXE	\WIN95\CAB_12.CAB
7/11/95	3,632	WINVER.EXE	C:\WINDOWS	EXE	\WIN95\CAB_10.CAB
7/11/95	183,296	WORDPAD.EXE	C:\PROGRAM FILES\ ACCESSORIES	EXE	\WIN95\CAB_03.CAB
7/11/95	5,120	WRITE.EXE	C:\WINDOWS	EXE	\WIN95\CAB_02.CAB
7/11/95	6,960	WSASRV.EXE	C:\WINDOWS\SYSTEM	EXE	\WIN95\CAB_12.CAB
7/11/95	3,878	XCOPY.EXE	C:\WINDOWS\COMMAND	EXE	\WIN95\CAB_09.CAB

Part
XI

App
D

continues

Date	Size	Name	Location	Type	Location/CD
7/11/95	40,960	XCOPY32.EXE	C:\WINDOWS\COMMAND	EXE	\WIN95\CAB_09.CAB
7/11/95	26,624	PCXIMP32.FLT	C:\PROGRAM FILES\ ACCESSORIES	FLT	\WIN95\CAB_02.CAB
7/11/95	10,992	8514FIX.FON	C:\WINDOWS\SYSTEM	FON	\WIN95\CAB_05.CAB
7/11/95	12,288	8514OEM.FON	C:\WINDOWS\SYSTEM	FON	\WIN95\CAB_05.CAB
7/11/95	9,600	8514SYS.FON	C:\WINDOWS\SYSTEM	FON	\WIN95\CAB_05.CAB
7/11/95	44,320	APP850.FON	C:\WINDOWS\SYSTEM	FON	\WIN95\CAB_05.CAB
7/11/95	23,424	COURE.FON	C:\WINDOWS\SYSTEM	FON	\WIN95\CAB_05.CAB
7/11/95	31,744	COURF.FON	C:\WINDOWS\SYSTEM	FON	\WIN95\CAB_05.CAB
7/11/95	44,304	DOSAPP.FON	C:\WINDOWS\SYSTEM	FON	\WIN95\CAB_05.CAB
7/11/95	7,968	MODERN.FON	C:\WINDOWS\SYSTEM	FON	\WIN95\CAB_05.CAB
7/11/95	57,952	SERIFE.FON	C:\WINDOWS\SYSTEM	FON	\WIN95\CAB_05.CAB
7/11/95	57,936	SERIFE.FON	C:\WINDOWS\SYSTEM	FON	\WIN95\MINI.CAB
7/11/95	81,744	SERIFF.FON	C:\WINDOWS\SYSTEM	FON	\WIN95\CAB_05.CAB
7/11/95	24,352	SMALLE.FON	C:\WINDOWS\SYSTEM	FON	\WIN95\CAB_05.CAB
7/11/95	19,632	SMALLF.FON	C:\WINDOWS\SYSTEM	FON	\WIN95\CAB_05.CAB
7/11/95	64,544	SSERIFE.FON	C:\WINDOWS\SYSTEM	FON	\WIN95\CAB_05.CAB
7/11/95	64,544	SSERIFE.FON	C:\WINDOWS\SYSTEM	FON	\WIN95\MINI.CAB
7/11/95	89,680	SSERIFF.FON	C:\WINDOWS\SYSTEM	FON	\WIN95\CAB_05.CAB
7/11/95	56,336	SYMBOLE.FON	C:\WINDOWS\SYSTEM	FON	\WIN95\CAB_05.CAB
7/11/95	80,928	SYMBOLF.FON	C:\WINDOWS\SYSTEM	FON	\WIN95\CAB_05.CAB
7/11/95	5,232	VGA850.FON	C:\WINDOWS\SYSTEM	FON	\WIN95\CAB_03.CAB
7/11/95	5,360	VGAFIX.FON	C:\WINDOWS\SYSTEM	FON	\WIN95\CAB_05.CAB
7/11/95	5,360	VGAFIX.FON	C:\WINDOWS\SYSTEM	FON	\WIN95\MINI.CAB
7/11/95	5,168	VGAOEM.FON	C:\WINDOWS\SYSTEM	FON	\WIN95\CAB_05.CAB
7/11/95	5,168	VGAOEM.FON	C:\WINDOWS\SYSTEM	FON	\WIN95\MINI.CAB
7/11/95	7,296	VGASYS.FON	C:\WINDOWS\SYSTEM	FON	\WIN95\CAB_05.CAB
7/11/95	7,280	VGASYS.FON	C:\WINDOWS\SYSTEM	FON	\WIN95\MINI.CAB
7/11/95	47,506	31USERS.HLP	C:\WINDOWS\HELP	HLP	\WIN95\CAB_06.CAB
7/11/95	34,923	ACCESS.HLP	C:\WINDOWS\HELP	HLP	\WIN95\CAB_02.CAB
7/11/95	58,872	APPS.HLP	C:\WINDOWS\HELP	HLP	\WIN95\CAB_05.CAB
7/11/95	8,651	AUDIOCDC.HLP	C:\WINDOWS\HELP	HLP	\WIN95\CAB_05.CAB
7/11/95	58,931	AWFAX.HLP	C:\WINDOWS\HELP	HLP	\WIN95\CAB_05.CAB
7/11/95	8,679	AWPRT.HLP	C:\WINDOWS\HELP	HLP	\WIN95\CAB_05.CAB
7/11/95	31,886	CALC.HLP	C:\WINDOWS\HELP	HLP	\WIN95\CAB_05.CAB
7/11/95	20,579	CDPLAYER.HLP	C:\WINDOWS\HELP	HLP	\WIN95\CAB_13.CAB
7/11/95	20,029	CLIPBOOK.HLP	C:\WINDOWS\HELP	HLP	\WIN95\CAB_02.CAB
7/11/95	13,015	CLIPBRD.HLP	C:\WINDOWS\HELP	HLP	\WIN95\CAB_02.CAB
7/11/95	22,233	COMMON.HLP	C:\WINDOWS\HELP	HLP	\WIN95\CAB_05.CAB
7/11/95	235,199	DECPSMW4.HLP	C:\WINDOWS\HELP	HLP	\WIN95\CAB_16.CAB
7/11/95	19,193	DIALER.HLP	C:\WINDOWS\HELP	HLP	\WIN95\CAB_02.CAB

Date	Size	Name	Location	Type	Location/CD
7/11/95	23,816	DRVSPACE.HLP	C:\WINDOWS\HELP	HLP	\WIN95\CAB_05.CAB
7/11/95	10,790	EDIT.HLP	C:\WINDOWS\COMMAND	HLP	\WIN95\CAB_05.CAB
7/11/95	100,371	EXCHNG.HLP	C:\WINDOWS\HELP	HLP	\WIN95\CAB_06.CAB
7/11/95	9,079	EXPO.HLP	C:\WINDOWS\HELP	HLP	\WIN95\CAB_17.CAB
7/11/95	15,185	FAXCOVER.HLP	C:\WINDOWS\HELP	HLP	\WIN95\CAB_05.CAB
7/11/95	12,186	FAXVIEW.HLP	C:\WINDOWS\HELP	HLP	\WIN95\CAB_05.CAB
7/11/95	14,007	FILEXFER.HLP	C:\WINDOWS\HELP	HLP	\WIN95\CAB_17.CAB
7/11/95	21,491	FINSTALL.HLP	C:\WINDOWS\SYSTEM	HLP	\WIN95\CAB_09.CAB
7/11/95	11,618	FREECELL.HLP	C:\WINDOWS\HELP	HLP	\WIN95\CAB_05.CAB
7/11/95	57,660	HPJDUND.HLP	C:\WINDOWS\HELP	HLP	\WIN95\CAB_16.CAB
7/11/95	10,119	HPPLOT.HLP	C:\WINDOWS\HELP	HLP	\WIN95\CAB_10.CAB
7/11/95	26,913	HPPRARRK.HLP	C:\WINDOWS\HELP	HLP	\WIN95\CAB_16.CAB
7/11/95	81,937	HPPRNTR.HLP	C:\WINDOWS\HELP	HLP	\WIN95\CAB_16.CAB
7/11/95	17,166	HPVDJC.HLP	C:\WINDOWS\HELP	HLP	\WIN95\CAB_10.CAB
7/11/95	21,473	HYPERTRM.HLP	C:\WINDOWS\HELP	HLP	\WIN95\CAB_02.CAB
7/11/95	285,953	JETADMIN.HLP	C:\WINDOWS\HELP	HLP	\WIN95\CAB_16.CAB
7/11/95	26,905	LICENSE.HLP	C:\WINDOWS\HELP	HLP	\WIN95\CAB_03.CAB
7/11/95	13,101	MFCUIX.HLP	C:\WINDOWS\HELP	HLP	\WIN95\CAB_05.CAB
7/11/95	9,584	MMDRV.HLP	C:\WINDOWS\HELP	HLP	\WIN95\CAB_08.CAB
7/11/95	16,577	MOUSE.HLP	C:\WINDOWS\HELP	HLP	\WIN95\CAB_05.CAB
7/11/95	26,940	MPLAYER.HLP	C:\WINDOWS\HELP	HLP	\WIN95\CAB_08.CAB
7/11/95	34,832	MSFS.HLP	C:\WINDOWS\HELP	HLP	\WIN95\CAB_06.CAB
7/11/95	11,661	MSHEARTS.HLP	C:\WINDOWS\HELP	HLP	\WIN95\CAB_05.CAB
7/11/95	17,780	MSN.HLP	C:\WINDOWS\HELP	HLP	\WIN95\CAB_07.CAB
7/11/95	52,454	MSNBBS.HLP	C:\WINDOWS\HELP	HLP	\WIN95\CAB_07.CAB
7/11/95	28,695	MSNCHAT.HLP	C:\WINDOWS\HELP	HLP	\WIN95\CAB_07.CAB
7/11/95	107,361	MSNFULL.HLP	C:\WINDOWS\HELP	HLP	\WIN95\CAB_06.CAB
7/11/95	32,773	MSNINT.HLP	C:\WINDOWS\HELP	HLP	\WIN95\CAB_06.CAB
7/11/95	48,932	MSNMAIL.HLP	C:\WINDOWS\HELP	HLP	\WIN95\CAB_07.CAB
7/11/95	34,974	MSNPSS.HLP	C:\WINDOWS\HELP	HLP	\WIN95\CAB_07.CAB
7/11/95	43,620	MSPAINT.HLP	C:\WINDOWS\HELP	HLP	\WIN95\CAB_02.CAB
7/11/95	164,352	MSWD6_32.WPC	C:\WINDOWS\HELP	HLP	\WIN95\CAB_03.CAB
7/11/95	12,339	NETWATCH.HLP	C:\WINDOWS\HELP	HLP	\WIN95\CAB_13.CAB
7/11/95	88,385	NETWORK.HLP	C:\WINDOWS\HELP	HLP	\WIN95\CAB_05.CAB
7/11/95	11,708	NOTEPAD.HLP	C:\WINDOWS\HELP	HLP	\WIN95\CAB_05.CAB
7/11/95	255,760	OVERVIEW.HLP	C:\WINDOWS\HELP	HLP	\WIN95\CAB_16.CAB
7/11/95	23,529	PACKAGER.HLP	C:\WINDOWS\HELP	HLP	\WIN95\CAB_02.CAB
7/11/95	24,466	PROGMAN.HLP	C:\WINDOWS\HELP	HLP	\WIN95\CAB_11.CAB
7/11/95	20,439	PSCRIPT.HLP	C:\WINDOWS\HELP	HLP	\WIN95\CAB_09.CAB

Part
XI

App
D

continues

Date	Size	Name	Location	Type	Location/CD
7/11/95	57,437	QIC117.VXD	C:\WINDOWS\HELP	HLP	\WIN95\CAB_04.CAB
7/11/95	18,338	REGEDIT.HLP	C:\WINDOWS\HELP	HLP	\WIN95\CAB_06.CAB
7/11/95	14,135	SCANPST.HLP	C:\WINDOWS\HELP	HLP	\WIN95\CAB_07.CAB
7/11/95	22,948	SERVER.HLP	C:\WINDOWS\HELP	HLP	\WIN95\CAB_05.CAB
7/11/95	11,120	SNDVOL32.HLP	C:\WINDOWS\HELP	HLP	\WIN95\CAB_08.CAB
7/11/95	10,145	SOL.HLP	C:\WINDOWS\HELP	HLP	\WIN95\CAB_05.CAB
7/11/95	24,895	SOUNDREC.HLP	C:\WINDOWS\HELP	HLP	\WIN95\CAB_08.CAB
7/11/95	10,558	SYSMON.HLP	C:\WINDOWS\HELP	HLP	\WIN95\CAB_13.CAB
7/11/95	7,315	TELEPHON.HLP	C:\WINDOWS\HELP	HLP	\WIN95\CAB_11.CAB
7/11/95	24,099	TELNET.HLP	C:\WINDOWS\HELP	HLP	\WIN95\CAB_12.CAB
7/11/95	11,606	TTY.HLP	C:\WINDOWS\SYSTEM	HLP	\WIN95\CAB_05.CAB
7/11/95	15,343	UNIDRV.HLP	C:\WINDOWS\SYSTEM	HLP	\WIN95\CAB_09.CAB
7/11/95	519,340	WINDOWS.HLP	C:\WINDOWS\HELP	HLP	\WIN95\CAB_05.CAB
7/11/95	43,833	WINFILE.HLP	C:\WINDOWS\HELP	HLP	\WIN95\CAB_11.CAB
7/11/95	27,507	WINHLP32.HLP	C:\WINDOWS\HELP	HLP	\WIN95\CAB_06.CAB
7/11/95	9,133	WINMINE.HLP	C:\WINDOWS\HELP	HLP	\WIN95\CAB_05.CAB
7/11/95	11,591	WINPOPUP.HLP	C:\WINDOWS\HELP	HLP	\WIN95\CAB_12.CAB
7/11/95	28,422	WORDPAD.HLP	C:\WINDOWS\HELP	HLP	\WIN95\CAB_03.CAB
7/11/95	13,623	HPVCM.HPM	C:\WINDOWS\SYSTEM	HPM	\WIN95\CAB_10.CAB
7/11/95	829	AT&TMA~1.HT	C:\PROGRAM FILES\ ACCESSORIS\HYPERTERMINAL	HT	\WIN95\CAB_02.CAB
7/11/95	829	COMPUS~1.HT	C:\PROGRAM FILES\ ACCESSORIS\HYPERTERMINAL	HT	\WIN95\CAB_02.CAB
7/11/95	829	MCIMAI~1.HT	C:\PROGRAM FILES\ ACCESSORIS\HYPERTERMINAL	HT	\WIN95\CAB_02.CAB
7/11/95	12,504	BJC600.ICM	C:\WINDOWS\SYSTEM\COLOR	ICM	\WIN95\CAB_10.CAB
7/11/95	12,684	BJC800.ICM	C:\WINDOWS\SYSTEM\COLOR	ICM	\WIN95\CAB_10.CAB
7/11/95	12,628	EPSONSTY.ICM	C:\WINDOWS\SYSTEM\COLOR	ICM	\WIN95\CAB_10.CAB
7/11/95	12,716	HP1200C.ICM	C:\WINDOWS\SYSTEM\COLOR	ICM	\WIN95\CAB_06.CAB
7/11/95	24,600	HP1200PS.ICM	C:\WINDOWS\SYSTEM\COLOR	ICM	\WIN95\CAB_06.CAB
7/11/95	12,176	HPCLRLSR.ICM	C:\WINDOWS\SYSTEM\COLOR	ICM	\WIN95\CAB_10.CAB
7/11/95	12,956	HPDESK.ICM	C:\WINDOWS\SYSTEM\COLOR	ICM	\WIN95\CAB_10.CAB
7/11/95	6,514	HPSJTW.ICM	C:\WINDOWS\SYSTEM\COLOR	ICM	\WIN95\CAB_06.CAB
7/11/95	12,700	HPXL300.ICM	C:\WINDOWS\SYSTEM\COLOR	ICM	\WIN95\CAB_10.CAB
7/11/95	24,596	HPXL30PS.ICM	C:\WINDOWS\SYSTEM\COLOR	ICM	\WIN95\CAB_10.CAB
7/11/95	24,416	KODAKCE.ICM	C:\WINDOWS\SYSTEM\COLOR	ICM	\WIN95\CAB_06.CAB
7/11/95	59,564	MNB22G15.ICM	C:\WINDOWS\SYSTEM\COLOR	ICM	\WIN95\CAB_06.CAB
7/11/95	59,564	MNB22G18.ICM	C:\WINDOWS\SYSTEM\COLOR	ICM	\WIN95\CAB_06.CAB
7/11/95	59,564	MNB22G21.ICM	C:\WINDOWS\SYSTEM\COLOR	ICM	\WIN95\CAB_06.CAB
7/11/95	59,964	MNEBUG15.ICM	C:\WINDOWS\SYSTEM\COLOR	ICM	\WIN95\CAB_06.CAB
7/11/95	59,964	MNEBUG18.ICM	C:\WINDOWS\SYSTEM\COLOR	ICM	\WIN95\CAB_06.CAB
7/11/95	59,964	MNEBUG21.ICM	C:\WINDOWS\SYSTEM\COLOR	ICM	\WIN95\CAB_06.CAB

Date	Size	Name	Location	Type	Location/CD
7/11/95	59,980	MNP22G15.ICM	C:\WINDOWS\SYSTEM\COLOR	ICM	\WIN95\CAB_06.CAB
7/11/95	59,980	MNP22G18.ICM	C:\WINDOWS\SYSTEM\COLOR	ICM	\WIN95\CAB_06.CAB
7/11/95	59,980	MNP22G21.ICM	C:\WINDOWS\SYSTEM\COLOR	ICM	\WIN95\CAB_06.CAB
7/11/95	24,348	PS4079.ICM	C:\WINDOWS\SYSTEM\COLOR	ICM	\WIN95\CAB_06.CAB
7/11/95	24,716	QMS10030.ICM	C:\WINDOWS\SYSTEM\COLOR	ICM	\WIN95\CAB_10.CAB
7/11/95	24,844	TPHA200I.ICM	C:\WINDOWS\SYSTEM\COLOR	ICM	\WIN95\CAB_06.CAB
7/11/95	24,804	TPHAIII.ICM	C:\WINDOWS\SYSTEM\COLOR	ICM	\WIN95\CAB_06.CAB
7/11/95	766	MAPIF0L.ICO	C:\WINDOWS\SYSTEM	ICO	\WIN95\CAB_06.CAB
7/11/95	766	MAPIF0S.ICO	C:\WINDOWS\SYSTEM	ICO	\WIN95\CAB_06.CAB
7/11/95	766	MAPIF1L.ICO	C:\WINDOWS\SYSTEM	ICO	\WIN95\CAB_06.CAB
7/11/95	766	MAPIF1S.ICO	C:\WINDOWS\SYSTEM	ICO	\WIN95\CAB_06.CAB
7/11/95	766	MAPIF2L.ICO	C:\WINDOWS\SYSTEM	ICO	\WIN95\CAB_06.CAB
7/11/95	766	MAPIF2S.ICO	C:\WINDOWS\SYSTEM	ICO	\WIN95\CAB_06.CAB
7/11/95	766	MAPIF3L.ICO	C:\WINDOWS\SYSTEM	ICO	\WIN95\CAB_06.CAB
7/11/95	766	MAPIF3S.ICO	C:\WINDOWS\SYSTEM	ICO	\WIN95\CAB_06.CAB
7/11/95	766	MAPIF4L.ICO	C:\WINDOWS\SYSTEM	ICO	\WIN95\CAB_06.CAB
7/11/95	766	MAPIF4S.ICO	C:\WINDOWS\SYSTEM	ICO	\WIN95\CAB_06.CAB
7/11/95	766	MAPIF5L.ICO	C:\WINDOWS\SYSTEM	ICO	\WIN95\CAB_06.CAB
7/11/95	766	MAPIF5S.ICO	C:\WINDOWS\SYSTEM	ICO	\WIN95\CAB_06.CAB
7/11/95	654	GENERAL.IDF	C:\WINDOWS\CONFIG	IDF	\WIN95\CAB_08.CAB
7/11/95	4,788	ADAPTER.INF	C:\WINDOWS\INF	INF	\WIN95\PRECOPY2.CAB
7/11/95	2,578	APM.INF	C:\WINDOWS\INF	INF	\WIN95\PRECOPY2.CAB
7/11/95	22,326	APPLETPP.INF	C:\WINDOWS\INF	INF	\WIN95\PRECOPY2.CAB
7/11/95	45,231	APPLETS.INF	C:\WINDOWS\INF	INF	\WIN95\PRECOPY2.CAB
7/11/95	62,339	APPS.INF	C:\WINDOWS\INF	INF	\WIN95\CAB_06.CAB
7/11/95	19,824	AWFAX.INF	C:\WINDOWS\INF	INF	\WIN95\PRECOPY2.CAB
7/11/95	2,191	AWUPD.INF	C:\WINDOWS\INF	INF	\WIN95\PRECOPY2.CAB
7/11/95	2,893	BKUPAGNT.INF	C:\WINDOWS\INF	INF	\WIN95\PRECOPY2.CAB
7/11/95	35,608	CEMMF.INF	C:\WINDOWS\INF	INF	\WIN95\PRECOPY2.CAB
7/11/95	1,657	CHEYENNE.INF	C:\WINDOWS\INF	INF	\WIN95\PRECOPY2.CAB
7/11/95	2,213	CLIP.INF	C:\WINDOWS\INF	INF	\WIN95\CAB_10.CAB
7/11/95	2,497	CONTROL.INF	C:\WINDOWS\SYSTEM	INF	\WIN95\CAB_11.CAB
7/11/95	33,338	COPY.INF	C:\WINDOWS\INF	INF	\WIN95\PRECOPY2.CAB
7/11/95	2,436	DECPSMW4.INF	C:\WINDOWS\INF	INF	\WIN95\PRECOPY2.CAB
7/11/95	36,793	DEL.INF	C:\WINDOWS\INF	INF	\WIN95\PRECOPY2.CAB
7/11/95	765	DISKDRV.INF	C:\WINDOWS\INF	INF	\WIN95\PRECOPY2.CAB
7/11/95	1,121	DRVSPACE.INF	C:\WINDOWS\INF	INF	\WIN95\CAB_09.CAB
7/11/95	2,971	ENABLE.INF	C:\WINDOWS\INF	INF	\WIN95\PRECOPY2.CAB
7/11/95	24,626	FONTS.INF	C:\WINDOWS\INF	INF	\WIN95\PRECOPY2.CAB

Part
XI

App
D

continues

Date	Size	Name	Location	Type	Location/CD
7/11/95	5,297	HPNETPRN.INF	C:\WINDOWS\INF	INF	\WIN95\PRECOPY2.CAB
7/11/95	2,049	ICM.INF	C:\WINDOWS\INF	INF	\WIN95\PRECOPY2.CAB
7/11/95	2,830	JOYSTICK.INF	C:\WINDOWS\INF	INF	\WIN95\PRECOPY2.CAB
7/11/95	6,953	KEYBOARD.INF	C:\WINDOWS\INF	INF	\WIN95\PRECOPY2.CAB
7/11/95	51,173	LAYOUT.INF	C:\WINDOWS\INF	INF	\WIN95\PRECOPY2.CAB
7/11/95	12,922	LICENSE.TXT	C:\WINDOWS\INF	INF	\WIN95\PRECOPY2.CAB
7/11/95	40,671	LOCALE.INF	C:\WINDOWS\INF	INF	\WIN95\PRECOPY2.CAB
7/11/95	30,827	MACHINE.INF	C:\WINDOWS\INF	INF	\WIN95\PRECOPY2.CAB
7/11/95	4,993	MAPISVC.INF	C:\WINDOWS\INF	INF	\WIN95\CAB_07.CAB
7/11/95	12,865	MDMATI.INF	C:\WINDOWS\INF	INF	\WIN95\CAB_07.CAB
7/11/95	29,686	MDMATT.INF	C:\WINDOWS\INF	INF	\WIN95\CAB_07.CAB
7/11/95	35,436	MDMAUS.INF	C:\WINDOWS\INF	INF	\WIN95\CAB_07.CAB
7/11/95	23,455	MDMBOCA.INF	C:\WINDOWS\INF	INF	\WIN95\CAB_07.CAB
7/11/95	25,304	MDMCOMMU.INF	C:\WINDOWS\INF	INF	\WIN95\CAB_07.CAB
7/11/95	33,941	MDMCPI.INF	C:\WINDOWS\INF	INF	\WIN95\CAB_07.CAB
7/11/95	40,135	MDMCPQ.INF	C:\WINDOWS\INF	INF	\WIN95\CAB_07.CAB
7/11/95	37,416	MDMDSI.INF	C:\WINDOWS\INF	INF	\WIN95\CAB_07.CAB
7/11/95	37,676	MDMEXP.INF	C:\WINDOWS\INF	INF	\WIN95\CAB_07.CAB
7/11/95	23,617	MDMGATEW.INF	C:\WINDOWS\INF	INF	\WIN95\CAB_07.CAB
7/11/95	33,192	MDMGEN.INF	C:\WINDOWS\INF	INF	\WIN95\CAB_07.CAB
7/11/95	47,472	MDMGVC.INF	C:\WINDOWS\INF	INF	\WIN95\CAB_07.CAB
7/11/95	42,229	MDMHAYES.INF	C:\WINDOWS\INF	INF	\WIN95\CAB_07.CAB
7/11/95	28,232	MDMINFOT.INF	C:\WINDOWS\INF	INF	\WIN95\CAB_07.CAB
7/11/95	17,067	MDMINTEL.INF	C:\WINDOWS\INF	INF	\WIN95\CAB_07.CAB
7/11/95	26,967	MDMINTPC.INF	C:\WINDOWS\INF	INF	\WIN95\CAB_07.CAB
7/11/95	23,124	MDMMCOM.INF	C:\WINDOWS\INF	INF	\WIN95\CAB_07.CAB
7/11/95	4,576	MDMMETRI.INF	C:\WINDOWS\INF	INF	\WIN95\CAB_07.CAB
7/11/95	30,549	MDMMHRTZ.INF	C:\WINDOWS\INF	INF	\WIN95\CAB_07.CAB
7/11/95	36,008	MDMMOTO.INF	C:\WINDOWS\INF	INF	\WIN95\CAB_07.CAB
7/11/95	22,953	MDMMTS.INF	C:\WINDOWS\INF	INF	\WIN95\CAB_07.CAB
7/11/95	2,972	MDMNOKIA.INF	C:\WINDOWS\INF	INF	\WIN95\CAB_07.CAB
7/11/95	12,342	MDMNOVA.INF	C:\WINDOWS\INF	INF	\WIN95\CAB_07.CAB
7/11/95	9,964	MDMOSI.INF	C:\WINDOWS\INF	INF	\WIN95\CAB_07.CAB
7/11/95	26,351	MDMPACE.INF	C:\WINDOWS\INF	INF	\WIN95\CAB_07.CAB
7/11/95	33,251	MDMPNB.INF	C:\WINDOWS\INF	INF	\WIN95\CAB_07.CAB
7/11/95	25,055	MDMPP.INF	C:\WINDOWS\INF	INF	\WIN95\CAB_07.CAB
7/11/95	25,804	MDMRACAL.INF	C:\WINDOWS\INF	INF	\WIN95\CAB_08.CAB
7/11/95	62,394	MDMROCK.INF	C:\WINDOWS\INF	INF	\WIN95\CAB_08.CAB
7/11/95	50,109	MDMROCK2.INF	C:\WINDOWS\INF	INF	\WIN95\CAB_08.CAB
7/11/95	9,208	MDMSIER.INF	C:\WINDOWS\INF	INF	\WIN95\CAB_08.CAB

Date	Size	Name	Location	Type	Location/CD
7/11/95	23,370	MDMSONIX.INF	C:\WINDOWS\INF	INF	\WIN95\CAB_08.CAB
7/11/95	11,458	MDMSPEC.INF	C:\WINDOWS\INF	INF	\WIN95\CAB_08.CAB
7/11/95	15,275	MDMSUPRA.INF	C:\WINDOWS\INF	INF	\WIN95\CAB_08.CAB
7/11/95	5,864	MDMTDK.INF	C:\WINDOWS\INF	INF	\WIN95\CAB_08.CAB
7/11/95	31,377	MDMTELBT.INF	C:\WINDOWS\INF	INF	\WIN95\CAB_08.CAB
7/11/95	5,861	MDMTI.INF	C:\WINDOWS\INF	INF	\WIN95\CAB_08.CAB
7/11/95	45,577	MDMTOSH.INF	C:\WINDOWS\INF	INF	\WIN95\CAB_08.CAB
7/11/95	50,070	MDMUSRCR.INF	C:\WINDOWS\INF	INF	\WIN95\CAB_08.CAB
7/11/95	44,991	MDMUSRSP.INF	C:\WINDOWS\INF	INF	\WIN95\CAB_08.CAB
7/11/95	50,051	MDMUSRWP.INF	C:\WINDOWS\INF	INF	\WIN95\CAB_08.CAB
7/11/95	33,304	MDMVV.INF	C:\WINDOWS\INF	INF	\WIN95\CAB_17.CAB
7/11/95	16,156	MDMZOOM.INF	C:\WINDOWS\INF	INF	\WIN95\CAB_08.CAB
7/11/95	23,916	MDMZYP.INF	C:\WINDOWS\INF	INF	\WIN95\CAB_08.CAB
7/11/95	9,166	MDMZYXEL.INF	C:\WINDOWS\INF	INF	\WIN95\CAB_08.CAB
7/11/95	7,887	MF.INF	C:\WINDOWS\INF	INF	\WIN95\PRECOPY2.CAB
7/11/95	7,288	MFOSI.INF	C:\WINDOWS\INF	INF	\WIN95\PRECOPY2.CAB
7/11/95	5,315	MIDI.INF	C:\WINDOWS\INF	INF	\WIN95\PRECOPY2.CAB
7/11/95	37,061	MMOPT.INF	C:\WINDOWS\INF	INF	\WIN95\PRECOPY2.CAB
7/11/95	1,773	MODEMS.INF	C:\WINDOWS\INF	INF	\WIN95\PRECOPY2.CAB
7/11/95	37,649	MONITOR.INF	C:\WINDOWS\INF	INF	\WIN95\PRECOPY2.CAB
7/11/95	55,766	MONITOR2.INF	C:\WINDOWS\INF	INF	\WIN95\PRECOPY2.CAB
7/11/95	56,254	MONITOR3.INF	C:\WINDOWS\INF	INF	\WIN95\PRECOPY2.CAB
7/11/95	42,030	MONITOR4.INF	C:\WINDOWS\INF	INF	\WIN95\PRECOPY2.CAB
7/11/95	46,923	MOS.INF	C:\WINDOWS\INF	INF	\WIN95\PRECOPY2.CAB
7/11/95	47,846	MOTOWN.INF	C:\WINDOWS\INF	INF	\WIN95\PRECOPY2.CAB
7/11/95	58,621	MSBASE.INF	C:\WINDOWS\INF	INF	\WIN95\PRECOPY2.CAB
7/11/95	951	MSCDROM.INF	C:\WINDOWS\INF	INF	\WIN95\PRECOPY2.CAB
7/11/95	21,472	MSDET.INF	C:\WINDOWS\INF	INF	\WIN95\PRECOPY2.CAB
7/11/95	40,877	MSDISP.INF	C:\WINDOWS\INF	INF	\WIN95\PRECOPY2.CAB
7/11/95	10,998	MSDOS.INF	C:\WINDOWS\INF	INF	\WIN95\PRECOPY2.CAB
7/11/95	3,657	MSFDC.INF	C:\WINDOWS\INF	INF	\WIN95\PRECOPY2.CAB
7/11/95	12,267	MSHDC.INF	C:\WINDOWS\INF	INF	\WIN95\PRECOPY2.CAB
7/11/95	36,068	MSMAIL.INF	C:\WINDOWS\INF	INF	\WIN95\PRECOPY2.CAB
7/11/95	13,322	MSMOUSE.INF	C:\WINDOWS\INF	INF	\WIN95\PRECOPY2.CAB
7/11/95	9,510	MSPORTS.INF	C:\WINDOWS\INF	INF	\WIN95\PRECOPY2.CAB
7/11/95	46,309	MSPRINT.INF	C:\WINDOWS\INF	INF	\WIN95\PRECOPY2.CAB
7/11/95	37,350	MSPRINT2.INF	C:\WINDOWS\INF	INF	\WIN95\PRECOPY2.CAB
7/11/95	1,891	MTD.INF	C:\WINDOWS\INF	INF	\WIN95\PRECOPY2.CAB
7/11/95	11,024	MULLANG.INF	C:\WINDOWS\INF	INF	\WIN95\CAB_13.CAB

Part

XI

App

D

continues

Date	Size	Name	Location	Type	Location/CD
7/11/95	25,665	MULTILNG.INF	C:\WINDOWS\INF	INF	\WIN95\PRECOPY2.CAB
7/11/95	21,393	NET.INF	C:\WINDOWS\INF	INF	\WIN95\PRECOPY2.CAB
7/11/95	31,895	NET3COM.INF	C:\WINDOWS\INF	INF	\WIN95\PRECOPY2.CAB
7/11/95	19,762	NETAMD.INF	C:\WINDOWS\INF	INF	\WIN95\PRECOPY2.CAB
7/11/95	153	NETAUXT.INF	C:\WINDOWS\INF	INF	\WIN95\PRECOPY2.CAB
7/11/95	4,152	NETBW.INF	C:\WINDOWS\INF	INF	\WIN95\PRECOPY2.CAB
7/11/95	25,234	NETCABLE.INF	C:\WINDOWS\INF	INF	\WIN95\PRECOPY2.CAB
7/11/95	30,838	NETCD.INF	C:\WINDOWS\INF	INF	\WIN95\PRECOPY2.CAB
7/11/95	2,810	NETCEM.INF	C:\WINDOWS\INF	INF	\WIN95\PRECOPY2.CAB
7/11/95	16,390	NETCLI.INF	C:\WINDOWS\INF	INF	\WIN95\PRECOPY2.CAB
7/11/95	28,011	NETCLI3.INF	C:\WINDOWS\INF	INF	\WIN95\PRECOPY2.CAB
7/11/95	6,816	NETCPQ.INF	C:\WINDOWS\INF	INF	\WIN95\PRECOPY2.CAB
7/11/95	16,782	NETDCA.INF	C:\WINDOWS\INF	INF	\WIN95\PRECOPY2.CAB
7/11/95	20,208	NETDEC.INF	C:\WINDOWS\INF	INF	\WIN95\PRECOPY2.CAB
7/11/95	10,275	NETDEF.INF	C:\WINDOWS\INF	INF	\WIN95\PRECOPY2.CAB
7/11/95	12,788	NETDLC.INF	C:\WINDOWS\INF	INF	\WIN95\PRECOPY2.CAB
7/11/95	22,103	NETEE16.INF	C:\WINDOWS\INF	INF	\WIN95\PRECOPY2.CAB
7/11/95	2,634	NETEVX.INF	C:\WINDOWS\INF	INF	\WIN95\PRECOPY2.CAB
7/11/95	7,168	NETFLEX.INF	C:\WINDOWS\INF	INF	\WIN95\PRECOPY2.CAB
7/11/95	4,125	NETFTP.INF	C:\WINDOWS\INF	INF	\WIN95\PRECOPY2.CAB
7/11/95	4,039	NETGEN.INF	C:\WINDOWS\INF	INF	\WIN95\PRECOPY2.CAB
7/11/95	10,111	NETHP.INF	C:\WINDOWS\INF	INF	\WIN95\PRECOPY2.CAB
7/11/95	17,817	NETIBM.INF	C:\WINDOWS\INF	INF	\WIN95\PRECOPY2.CAB
7/11/95	19,419	NETIBMCC.INF	C:\WINDOWS\INF	INF	\WIN95\PRECOPY2.CAB
7/11/95	25,842	NETMADGE.INF	C:\WINDOWS\INF	INF	\WIN95\PRECOPY2.CAB
7/11/95	16,525	NETNCR.INF	C:\WINDOWS\INF	INF	\WIN95\PRECOPY2.CAB
7/11/95	3,808	NETNICE.INF	C:\WINDOWS\INF	INF	\WIN95\PRECOPY2.CAB
7/11/95	22,774	NETNOVEL.INF	C:\WINDOWS\INF	INF	\WIN95\PRECOPY2.CAB
7/11/95	21,733	NETOLI.INF	C:\WINDOWS\INF	INF	\WIN95\PRECOPY2.CAB
7/11/95	3,811	NETOSI.INF	C:\WINDOWS\INF	INF	\WIN95\PRECOPY2.CAB
7/11/95	11,080	NETPCI.INF	C:\WINDOWS\INF	INF	\WIN95\PRECOPY2.CAB
7/11/95	2,883	NETPPP.INF	C:\WINDOWS\INF	INF	\WIN95\PRECOPY2.CAB
7/11/95	12,890	NETPROT.INF	C:\WINDOWS\INF	INF	\WIN95\PRECOPY2.CAB
7/11/95	8,055	NETRACAL.INF	C:\WINDOWS\INF	INF	\WIN95\PRECOPY2.CAB
7/11/95	12,223	NETSERVR.INF	C:\WINDOWS\INF	INF	\WIN95\PRECOPY2.CAB
7/11/95	7,524	NETSILC.INF	C:\WINDOWS\INF	INF	\WIN95\PRECOPY2.CAB
7/11/95	36,024	NETSMC.INF	C:\WINDOWS\INF	INF	\WIN95\PRECOPY2.CAB
7/11/95	2,593	NETSMC32.INF	C:\WINDOWS\INF	INF	\WIN95\PRECOPY2.CAB
7/11/95	4,543	NETSMCTR.INF	C:\WINDOWS\INF	INF	\WIN95\PRECOPY2.CAB
7/11/95	8,345	NETSNIP.INF	C:\WINDOWS\INF	INF	\WIN95\PRECOPY2.CAB

Date	Size	Name	Location	Type	Location/CD
7/11/95	3,155	NETSOCK.INF	C:\WINDOWS\INF	INF	\WIN95\PRECOPY2.CAB
7/11/95	16,149	NETTCC.INF	C:\WINDOWS\INF	INF	\WIN95\PRECOPY2.CAB
7/11/95	4,828	NETTDKP.INF	C:\WINDOWS\INF	INF	\WIN95\PRECOPY2.CAB
7/11/95	37,248	NETTRANS.INF	C:\WINDOWS\INF	INF	\WIN95\PRECOPY2.CAB
7/11/95	1,980	NETTULIP.INF	C:\WINDOWS\INF	INF	\WIN95\PRECOPY2.CAB
7/11/95	13,101	NETUB.INF	C:\WINDOWS\INF	INF	\WIN95\PRECOPY2.CAB
7/11/95	24,805	NETXIR.INF	C:\WINDOWS\INF	INF	\WIN95\PRECOPY2.CAB
7/11/95	3,831	NETZNOTE.INF	C:\WINDOWS\INF	INF	\WIN95\PRECOPY2.CAB
7/11/95	2,572	NODRIVER.INF	C:\WINDOWS\INF	INF	\WIN95\PRECOPY2.CAB
7/11/95	25,550	OLE2.INF	C:\WINDOWS\INF	INF	\WIN95\PRECOPY2.CAB
7/11/95	10,079	PCMCIA.INF	C:\WINDOWS\INF	INF	\WIN95\PRECOPY2.CAB
7/11/95	2,538	PRECOPY.INF	C:\WINDOWS\INF	INF	\WIN95\PRECOPY2.CAB
7/11/95	20,851	PRTUPD.INF	C:\WINDOWS\INF	INF	\WIN95\PRECOPY2.CAB
7/11/95	7,703	REN.INF	C:\WINDOWS\INF	INF	\WIN95\PRECOPY2.CAB
7/11/95	10,611	RNA.INF	C:\WINDOWS\INF	INF	\WIN95\PRECOPY2.CAB
7/11/95	35,741	SCSI.INF	C:\WINDOWS\INF	INF	\WIN95\PRECOPY2.CAB
7/11/95	55,858	SETUPC.INF	C:\WINDOWS\INF	INF	\WIN95\PRECOPY2.CAB
7/11/95	4,242	SETUPP.INF	C:\WINDOWS\INF	INF	\WIN95\PRECOPY2.CAB
7/11/95	48,580	SHELL.INF	C:\WINDOWS\INF	INF	\WIN95\PRECOPY2.CAB
7/11/95	46,936	SHELL2.INF	C:\WINDOWS\INF	INF	\WIN95\PRECOPY2.CAB
7/11/95	7,272	SHELL3.INF	C:\WINDOWS\INF	INF	\WIN95\PRECOPY2.CAB
7/11/95	1,046	TAPI.INF	C:\WINDOWS\INF	INF	\WIN95\PRECOPY2.CAB
7/11/95	46,060	TIMEZONE.INF	C:\WINDOWS\INF	INF	\WIN95\PRECOPY2.CAB
7/11/95	462	UNKNOWN.INF	C:\WINDOWS\INF	INF	\WIN95\PRECOPY2.CAB
7/11/95	2,158	VIDCAP.INF	C:\WINDOWS\INF	INF	\WIN95\PRECOPY2.CAB
7/11/95	62,619	WAVE.INF	C:\WINDOWS\INF	INF	\WIN95\PRECOPY2.CAB
7/11/95	1,932	WINPOPUP.INF	C:\WINDOWS\INF	INF	\WIN95\CAB_12.CAB
7/11/95	56,062	WINVER.INF	C:\WINDOWS	INF	\WIN95\PRECOPY2.CAB
7/11/95	10,491	WORDPAD.INF	C:\WINDOWS\INF	INF	\WIN95\PRECOPY2.CAB
7/11/95	8,622	AVWIN.INI	C:\WINDOWS	INI	\WIN95\CAB_13.CAB
7/11/95	52,899	CPQMODE.INI	C:\WINDOWS	INI	\WIN95\CAB_04.CAB
7/11/95	41,810	CPQMON.INI	C:\WINDOWS	INI	\WIN95\CAB_04.CAB
7/11/95	67	DESKTOP.INI	C:\WINDOWS	INI	\WIN95\CAB_03.CAB
7/11/95	10,398	IOS.INI	C:\WINDOWS	INI	\WIN95\CAB_03.CAB
7/11/95	328	PSCRIPT.INI	C:\WINDOWS	INI	\WIN95\CAB_09.CAB
7/11/95	7,270	SCANDISK.INI	C:\WINDOWS\COMMAND	INI	\WIN95\CAB_02.CAB
7/11/95	358	SYSTEM.INI	C:\WINDOWS	INI	\WIN95\MINI.CAB
7/11/95	165	WIN.INI	C:\WINDOWS	INI	\WIN95\MINI.CAB
7/11/95	611	KBDBE.KBD	C:\WINDOWS\SYSTEM	KBD	\WIN95\CAB_06.CAB

Part
XI

App
D

continues

Date	Size	Name	Location	Type	Location/CD
7/11/95	403	KBDBLL.KBD	C:\WINDOWS\SYSTEM	KBD	\WIN95\CAB_13.CAB
7/11/95	403	KBDBLR.KBD	C:\WINDOWS\SYSTEM	KBD	\WIN95\CAB_13.CAB
7/11/95	613	KBDBR.KBD	C:\WINDOWS\SYSTEM	KBD	\WIN95\CAB_06.CAB
7/11/95	403	KBDBUL.KBD	C:\WINDOWS\SYSTEM	KBD	\WIN95\CAB_13.CAB
7/11/95	621	KBDCA.KBD	C:\WINDOWS\SYSTEM	KBD	\WIN95\CAB_06.CAB
7/11/95	804	KBDCZ.KBD	C:\WINDOWS\SYSTEM	KBD	\WIN95\CAB_13.CAB
7/11/95	796	KBDCZ1.KBD	C:\WINDOWS\SYSTEM	KBD	\WIN95\CAB_13.CAB
7/11/95	603	KBDDA.KBD	C:\WINDOWS\SYSTEM	KBD	\WIN95\CAB_06.CAB
7/11/95	398	KBDDV.KBD	C:\WINDOWS\SYSTEM	KBD	\WIN95\CAB_06.CAB
7/11/95	693	KBDFC.KBD	C:\WINDOWS\SYSTEM	KBD	\WIN95\CAB_06.CAB
7/11/95	610	KBDFI.KBD	C:\WINDOWS\SYSTEM	KBD	\WIN95\CAB_06.CAB
7/11/95	574	KBDFR.KBD	C:\WINDOWS\SYSTEM	KBD	\WIN95\CAB_06.CAB
7/11/95	520	KBDGK.KBD	C:\WINDOWS\SYSTEM	KBD	\WIN95\CAB_13.CAB
7/11/95	499	KBDGK220.KBD	C:\WINDOWS\SYSTEM	KBD	\WIN95\CAB_13.CAB
7/11/95	495	KBDGK319.KBD	C:\WINDOWS\SYSTEM	KBD	\WIN95\CAB_13.CAB
7/11/95	539	KBDGL220.KBD	C:\WINDOWS\SYSTEM	KBD	\WIN95\CAB_13.CAB
7/11/95	569	KBDGL319.KBD	C:\WINDOWS\SYSTEM	KBD	\WIN95\CAB_13.CAB
7/11/95	547	KBDGR.KBD	C:\WINDOWS\SYSTEM	KBD	\WIN95\CAB_06.CAB
7/11/95	547	KBDGR1.KBD	C:\WINDOWS\SYSTEM	KBD	\WIN95\CAB_06.CAB
7/11/95	786	KBDHU.KBD	C:\WINDOWS\SYSTEM	KBD	\WIN95\CAB_13.CAB
7/11/95	501	KBDHU1.KBD	C:\WINDOWS\SYSTEM	KBD	\WIN95\CAB_13.CAB
7/11/95	670	KBDIC.KBD	C:\WINDOWS\SYSTEM	KBD	\WIN95\CAB_06.CAB
7/11/95	509	KBDIR.KBD	C:\WINDOWS\SYSTEM	KBD	\WIN95\CAB_06.CAB
7/11/95	424	KBDIT.KBD	C:\WINDOWS\SYSTEM	KBD	\WIN95\CAB_06.CAB
7/11/95	518	KBDIT1.KBD	C:\WINDOWS\SYSTEM	KBD	\WIN95\CAB_06.CAB
7/11/95	575	KBDLA.KBD	C:\WINDOWS\SYSTEM	KBD	\WIN95\CAB_06.CAB
7/11/95	635	KBDNE.KBD	C:\WINDOWS\SYSTEM	KBD	\WIN95\CAB_06.CAB
7/11/95	610	KBDNO.KBD	C:\WINDOWS\SYSTEM	KBD	\WIN95\CAB_06.CAB
7/11/95	774	KBDPL.KBD	C:\WINDOWS\SYSTEM	KBD	\WIN95\CAB_13.CAB
7/11/95	528	KBDPL1.KBD	C:\WINDOWS\SYSTEM	KBD	\WIN95\CAB_13.CAB
7/11/95	593	KBDPO.KBD	C:\WINDOWS\SYSTEM	KBD	\WIN95\CAB_06.CAB
7/11/95	473	KBDRU.KBD	C:\WINDOWS\SYSTEM	KBD	\WIN95\CAB_13.CAB
7/11/95	403	KBDRU1.KBD	C:\WINDOWS\SYSTEM	KBD	\WIN95\CAB_13.CAB
7/11/95	615	KBDSF.KBD	C:\WINDOWS\SYSTEM	KBD	\WIN95\CAB_06.CAB
7/11/95	727	KBDSG.KBD	C:\WINDOWS\SYSTEM	KBD	\WIN95\CAB_06.CAB
7/11/95	592	KBDSP.KBD	C:\WINDOWS\SYSTEM	KBD	\WIN95\CAB_06.CAB
7/11/95	781	KBDSV.KBD	C:\WINDOWS\SYSTEM	KBD	\WIN95\CAB_13.CAB
7/11/95	610	KBDSW.KBD	C:\WINDOWS\SYSTEM	KBD	\WIN95\CAB_06.CAB
7/11/95	430	KBDUK.KBD	C:\WINDOWS\SYSTEM	KBD	\WIN95\CAB_06.CAB
7/11/95	398	KBDUS.KBD	C:\WINDOWS\SYSTEM	KBD	\WIN95\CAB_06.CAB

Date	Size	Name	Location	Type	Location/CD
7/11/95	794	KBDUSX.KBD	C:\WINDOWS\SYSTEM	KBD	\WIN95\CAB_06.CAB
7/11/95	95,719	FONTS.MFM	C:\WINDOWS\SYSTEM	MFM	\WIN95\CAB_10.CAB
7/11/95	20,861	CANYON.MID	C:\WINDOWS\MEDIA	MID	\WIN95\CAB_13.CAB
7/11/95	23,165	PASSPORT.MID	C:\WINDOWS\MEDIA	MID	\WIN95\CAB_13.CAB
7/11/95	4,313	REDIRECT.MOD	C:\WINDOWS\SYSTEM	MOD	\WIN95\CAB_04.CAB
7/11/95	8,592	AHA154X.MPD	C:\WINDOWS\SYSTEM\IOSUBSYS	MPD	\WIN95\CAB_04.CAB
7/11/95	5,040	AHA174X.MPD	C:\WINDOWS\SYSTEM\IOSUBSYS	MPD	\WIN95\CAB_05.CAB
7/11/95	23,824	AIC78XX.MPD	C:\WINDOWS\SYSTEM\IOSUBSYS	MPD	\WIN95\CAB_05.CAB
7/11/95	13,600	ALWAYS.MPD	C:\WINDOWS\SYSTEM\IOSUBSYS	MPD	\WIN95\CAB_05.CAB
7/11/95	13,264	AMSINT.MPD	C:\WINDOWS\SYSTEM\IOSUBSYS	MPD	\WIN95\CAB_05.CAB
7/11/95	34,848	ARROW.MPD	C:\WINDOWS\SYSTEM\IOSUBSYS	MPD	\WIN95\CAB_03.CAB
7/11/95	8,144	BUSLOGIC.MPD	C:\WINDOWS\SYSTEM\IOSUBSYS	MPD	\WIN95\CAB_05.CAB
7/11/95	12,000	DPTSCSI.MPD	C:\WINDOWS\SYSTEM\IOSUBSYS	MPD	\WIN95\CAB_05.CAB
7/11/95	10,736	FD16_700.MPD	C:\WINDOWS\SYSTEM\IOSUBSYS	MPD	\WIN95\CAB_05.CAB
7/11/95	8,352	FD8XX.MPD	C:\WINDOWS\SYSTEM\IOSUBSYS	MPD	\WIN95\CAB_05.CAB
7/11/95	53,264	MKECR5XX.MPD	C:\WINDOWS\SYSTEM\IOSUBSYS	MPD	\WIN95\CAB_05.CAB
7/11/95	21,968	MTMMINIP.MPD	C:\WINDOWS\SYSTEM\IOSUBSYS	MPD	\WIN95\CAB_05.CAB
7/11/95	11,120	NCR53C9X.MPD	C:\WINDOWS\SYSTEM\IOSUBSYS	MPD	\WIN95\CAB_05.CAB
7/11/95	9,920	NCRC700.MPD	C:\WINDOWS\SYSTEM\IOSUBSYS	MPD	\WIN95\CAB_05.CAB
7/11/95	10,352	NCRC710.MPD	C:\WINDOWS\SYSTEM\IOSUBSYS	MPD	\WIN95\CAB_05.CAB
7/11/95	10,848	NCRC810.MPD	C:\WINDOWS\SYSTEM\IOSUBSYS	MPD	\WIN95\CAB_05.CAB
7/11/95	25,056	NCRSDMS.MPD	C:\WINDOWS\SYSTEM\IOSUBSYS	MPD	\WIN95\CAB_05.CAB
7/11/95	4,304	PC2X.MPD	C:\WINDOWS\SYSTEM\IOSUBSYS	MPD	\WIN95\CAB_05.CAB
7/11/95	31,632	SLCD32.MPD	C:\WINDOWS\SYSTEM\IOSUBSYS	MPD	\WIN95\CAB_05.CAB
7/11/95	16,960	SPARROW.MPD	C:\WINDOWS\SYSTEM\IOSUBSYS	MPD	\WIN95\CAB_05.CAB
7/11/95	18,944	SPARROWX.MPD	C:\WINDOWS\SYSTEM\IOSUBSYS	MPD	\WIN95\CAB_05.CAB
7/11/95	5,280	SPOCK.MPD	C:\WINDOWS\SYSTEM\IOSUBSYS	MPD	\WIN95\CAB_05.CAB

Part
XI
App
D

continues

Date	Size	Name	Location	Type	Location/CD
7/11/95	11,104	T160.MPD	C:\WINDOWS\SYSTEM\IOSUBSYS	MPD	\WIN95\CAB_05.CAB
7/11/95	11,584	T348.MPD	C:\WINDOWS\SYSTEM\IOSUBSYS	MPD	\WIN95\CAB_05.CAB
7/11/95	13,984	T358.MPD	C:\WINDOWS\SYSTEM\IOSUBSYS	MPD	\WIN95\CAB_05.CAB
7/11/95	12,048	TMV1.MPD	C:\WINDOWS\SYSTEM\IOSUBSYS	MPD	\WIN95\CAB_05.CAB
7/11/95	4,912	ULTRA124.MPD	C:\WINDOWS\SYSTEM\IOSUBSYS	MPD	\WIN95\CAB_05.CAB
7/11/95	4,624	ULTRA14F.MPD	C:\WINDOWS\SYSTEM\IOSUBSYS	MPD	\WIN95\CAB_05.CAB
7/11/95	4,256	ULTRA24F.MPD	C:\WINDOWS\SYSTEM\IOSUBSYS	MPD	\WIN95\CAB_05.CAB
7/11/95	4,448	WD7000EX.MPD	C:\WINDOWS\SYSTEM\IOSUBSYS	MPD	\WIN95\CAB_05.CAB
7/11/95	1,632	NETWARE.MS	C:\WINDOWS\SYSTEM	MS	\WIN95\CAB_12.CAB
7/11/95	109,229	NET.MSG	C:\WINDOWS	MSG	\WIN95\CAB_12.CAB
7/11/95	73,275	NETH.MSG	C:\WINDOWS	MSG	\WIN95\CAB_12.CAB
7/11/95	4	THEMIC~1.MSN	C:\PROGRAM FILES\THE MICROSOFT NETWORK	MSN	\WIN95\CAB_07.CAB
7/11/95	214,528	BBSNAV.NAV	C:\PROGRAM FILES\THE MICROSOFT NETWORK	NAV	\WIN95\CAB_07.CAB
7/11/95	31,744	DSNAV.NAV	C:\PROGRAM FILES\THE MICROSOFT NETWORK	NAV	\WIN95\CAB_07.CAB
7/11/95	40,960	GUIDENAV.NAV	C:\PROGRAM FILES\THE MICROSOFT NETWORK	NAV	\WIN95\CAB_07.CAB
7/11/95	36,864	DSNED.NED	C:\PROGRAM FILES\THE MICROSOFT NETWORK	NED	\WIN95\CAB_07.CAB
7/11/95	88,544	COMMDLG.NEW	C:\WINDOWS	NEW	\WIN95\CAB_11.CAB
7/11/95	14,757	DLLNDIS.NEW	C:\WINDOWS	NEW	\WIN95\CAB_17.CAB
7/11/95	16,588	DLLNDIST.NEW	C:\WINDOWS	NEW	\WIN95\CAB_17.CAB
7/11/95	116,144	SHELL.NEW	C:\WINDOWS	NEW	\WIN95\CAB_11.CAB
7/11/95	5,329	SRM.NEW	C:\WINDOWS	NEW	\WIN95\CAB_17.CAB
7/11/95	12,144	VER.NEW	C:\WINDOWS	NEW	\WIN95\CAB_10.CAB
7/11/95	61,680	WINOA386.NEW	C:\WINDOWS	NEW	\WIN95\CAB_03.CAB
7/11/95	9,124	CP_1250.NLS	C:\WINDOWS\SYSTEM	NLS	\WIN95\CAB_13.CAB
7/11/95	6,868	CP_1251.NLS	C:\WINDOWS\SYSTEM	NLS	\WIN95\CAB_13.CAB
7/11/95	9,194	CP_1252.NLS	C:\WINDOWS\SYSTEM	NLS	\WIN95\CAB_09.CAB
7/11/95	6,856	CP_1253.NLS	C:\WINDOWS\SYSTEM	NLS	\WIN95\CAB_13.CAB
7/11/95	9,522	CP_437.NLS	C:\WINDOWS\SYSTEM	NLS	\WIN95\CAB_09.CAB
7/11/95	6,600	CP_737.NLS	C:\WINDOWS\SYSTEM	NLS	\WIN95\CAB_13.CAB
7/11/95	9,826	CP_850.NLS	C:\WINDOWS\SYSTEM	NLS	\WIN95\CAB_09.CAB
7/11/95	9,618	CP_852.NLS	C:\WINDOWS\SYSTEM	NLS	\WIN95\CAB_13.CAB
7/11/95	7,316	CP_866.NLS	C:\WINDOWS\SYSTEM	NLS	\WIN95\CAB_13.CAB
7/11/95	7,240	CP_869.NLS	C:\WINDOWS\SYSTEM	NLS	\WIN95\CAB_13.CAB

Date	Size	Name	Location	Type	Location/CD
7/11/95	127,912	LOCALE.NLS	C:\WINDOWS\SYSTEM	NLS	\WIN95\CAB_09.CAB
7/11/95	34,676	UNICODE.NLS	C:\WINDOWS\SYSTEM	NLS	\WIN95\CAB_09.CAB
7/11/95	7,188	MVIFM.PAT	C:\WINDOWS\SYSTEM	PAT	\WIN95\CAB_08.CAB
7/11/95	41,369	PHONE.PBK	C:\PROGRAM FILES\ THE MICROSOFT NETWORK	PBK	\WIN95\CAB_07.CAB
7/11/95	851	STATE.PBK	C:\PROGRAM FILES\ THE MICROSOFT NETWORK	PBK	\WIN95\CAB_07.CAB
7/11/95	23,758	ESDI_506.PDR	C:\WINDOWS\SYSTEM\ IOSUBSYS	PDR	\WIN95\CAB_05.CAB
7/11/95	18,998	HSFLOP.PDR	C:\WINDOWS\SYSTEM\ IOSUBSYS	PDR	\WIN95\CAB_05.CAB
7/11/95	13,229	RMM.PDR	C:\WINDOWS\SYSTEM\ IOSUBSYS	PDR	\WIN95\CAB_05.CAB
7/11/95	23,133	SCSIPORT.PDR	C:\WINDOWS\SYSTEM\ IOSUBSYS	PDR	\WIN95\CAB_05.CAB
7/11/95	545	DOSPRMPT.PIF	C:\WINDOWS	PIF	\WIN95\CAB_03.CAB
7/11/95	995	LMSCRIPT.PIF	C:\WINDOWS	PIF	\WIN95\CAB_12.CAB
7/11/95	12,288	POWERPNT.PPT	C:\WINDOWS	PPT	\WIN95\CAB_11.CAB
7/11/95	12,701	FREELANC.PRE	C:\WINDOWS	PRE	\WIN95\CAB_11.CAB
7/11/95	11,971	MAPIRPC.REG	C:\WINDOWS\SYSTEM	REG	\WIN95\CAB_07.CAB
7/11/95	144,902	BACHSB~1.RMI	C:\WINDOWS\MEDIA	RMI	\WIN95\CAB_13.CAB
7/11/95	92,466	BEETHO~2.RMI	C:\WINDOWS\MEDIA	RMI	\WIN95\CAB_13.CAB
7/11/95	27,940	CLAIRE~1.RMI	C:\WINDOWS\MEDIA	RMI	\WIN95\CAB_14.CAB
7/11/95	20,906	DANCEO~2.RMI	C:\WINDOWS\MEDIA	RMI	\WIN95\CAB_14.CAB
7/11/95	21,312	FURELI~1.RMI	C:\WINDOWS\MEDIA	RMI	\WIN95\CAB_14.CAB
7/11/95	38,444	HALLOF~2.RMI	C:\WINDOWS\MEDIA	RMI	\WIN95\CAB_14.CAB
7/11/95	18,130	MOZART~2.RMI	C:\WINDOWS\MEDIA	RMI	\WIN95\CAB_14.CAB
7/11/95	4,570	AMIPRO.SAM	C:\WINDOWS	SAM	\WIN95\CAB_11.CAB
7/11/95	728	HOSTS.SAM	C:\WINDOWS	SAM	\WIN95\CAB_12.CAB
7/11/95	3,691	LMHOSTS.SAM	C:\WINDOWS	SAM	\WIN95\CAB_12.CAB
7/11/95	34,832	SYNTHGM.SBK	C:\WINDOWS\SYSTEM	SBK	\WIN95\CAB_08.CAB
7/11/95	15,872	BEZIER.SCR	C:\WINDOWS\SYSTEM	SCR	\WIN95\CAB_11.CAB
7/11/95	9,728	SCRNSAVE.SCR	C:\WINDOWS\SYSTEM	SCR	\WIN95\CAB_11.CAB
7/11/95	14,336	SSFLYWIN.SCR	C:\WINDOWS\SYSTEM	SCR	\WIN95\CAB_11.CAB
7/11/95	18,944	SSMARQUE.SCR	C:\WINDOWS\SYSTEM	SCR	\WIN95\CAB_11.CAB
7/11/95	20,992	SSMYST.SCR	C:\WINDOWS\SYSTEM	SCR	\WIN95\CAB_11.CAB
7/11/95	15,872	SSSTARS.SCR	C:\WINDOWS\SYSTEM	SCR	\WIN95\CAB_11.CAB
7/11/95	461	PRESENTA.SHW	C:\WINDOWS\SHELLNEW	SHW	\WIN95\CAB_11.CAB
7/11/95	7,098	A_PNT518.SPD	C:\WINDOWS\SPOOL	SPD	\WIN95\CAB_10.CAB
7/11/95	22,106	APLW8101.SPD	C:\WINDOWS\SPOOL	SPD	\WIN95\CAB_10.CAB
7/11/95	19,120	APLWIIF1.SPD	C:\WINDOWS\SPOOL	SPD	\WIN95\CAB_10.CAB
7/11/95	15,266	APLWIIG1.SPD	C:\WINDOWS\SPOOL	SPD	\WIN95\CAB_10.CAB

continues

Part
XI

App
D

Date	Size	Name	Location	Type	Location/CD
7/11/95	8,913	APLWNTR1.SPD	C:\WINDOWS\SPOOL	SPD	\WIN95\CAB_10.CAB
7/11/95	13,016	APLWSEL.SPD	C:\WINDOWS\SPOOL	SPD	\WIN95\CAB_10.CAB
7/11/95	5,681	APPLE230.SPD	C:\WINDOWS\SPOOL	SPD	\WIN95\CAB_10.CAB
7/11/95	6,046	APPLE380.SPD	C:\WINDOWS\SPOOL	SPD	\WIN95\CAB_10.CAB
7/11/95	15,105	APTOLLD1.SPD	C:\WINDOWS\SPOOL	SPD	\WIN95\CAB_10.CAB
7/11/95	14,580	APTOLLW1.SPD	C:\WINDOWS\SPOOL	SPD	\WIN95\CAB_10.CAB
7/11/95	4,436	AST__470.SPD	C:\WINDOWS\SPOOL	SPD	\WIN95\CAB_10.CAB
7/11/95	16,062	CP_PS241.SPD	C:\WINDOWS\SPOOL	SPD	\WIN95\CAB_10.CAB
7/11/95	16,432	CPPER241.SPD	C:\WINDOWS\SPOOL	SPD	\WIN95\CAB_10.CAB
7/11/95	17,878	CPPMQ151.SPD	C:\WINDOWS\SPOOL	SPD	\WIN95\CAB_10.CAB
7/11/95	19,463	CPPMQ201.SPD	C:\WINDOWS\SPOOL	SPD	\WIN95\CAB_10.CAB
7/11/95	5,794	CPPRO518.SPD	C:\WINDOWS\SPOOL	SPD	\WIN95\CAB_10.CAB
7/11/95	9,343	CPPSNB10.SPD	C:\WINDOWS\SPOOL	SPD	\WIN95\CAB_10.CAB
7/11/95	8,806	CPPSX241.SPD	C:\WINDOWS\SPOOL	SPD	\WIN95\CAB_10.CAB
7/11/95	94	D17_MS.SPD	C:\WINDOWS\SPOOL	SPD	\WIN95\CAB_16.CAB
7/11/95	99	D1712_MS.SPD	C:\WINDOWS\SPOOL	SPD	\WIN95\CAB_16.CAB
7/11/95	98	D176_MS.SPD	C:\WINDOWS\SPOOL	SPD	\WIN95\CAB_16.CAB
7/11/95	99	D20_MS.SPD	C:\WINDOWS\SPOOL	SPD	\WIN95\CAB_16.CAB
7/11/95	89	D2150_MS.SPD	C:\WINDOWS\SPOOL	SPD	\WIN95\CAB_10.CAB
7/11/95	89	D2250_MS.SPD	C:\WINDOWS\SPOOL	SPD	\WIN95\CAB_10.CAB
7/11/95	94	D32_MS.SPD	C:\WINDOWS\SPOOL	SPD	\WIN95\CAB_16.CAB
7/11/95	94	D40_MS.SPD	C:\WINDOWS\SPOOL	SPD	\WIN95\CAB_16.CAB
7/11/95	93	D5100_MS.SPD	C:\WINDOWS\SPOOL	SPD	\WIN95\CAB_16.CAB
7/11/95	5,593	DATAP462.SPD	C:\WINDOWS\SPOOL	SPD	\WIN95\CAB_10.CAB
7/11/95	9,476	DC1152_1.SPD	C:\WINDOWS\SPOOL	SPD	\WIN95\CAB_10.CAB
7/11/95	11,025	DC1152F1.SPD	C:\WINDOWS\SPOOL	SPD	\WIN95\CAB_10.CAB
7/11/95	9,072	DC2150P1.SPD	C:\WINDOWS\SPOOL	SPD	\WIN95\CAB_10.CAB
7/11/95	13,611	DC2250P1.SPD	C:\WINDOWS\SPOOL	SPD	\WIN95\CAB_10.CAB
7/11/95	29,406	DC5100_1.SPD	C:\WINDOWS\SPOOL	SPD	\WIN95\CAB_10.CAB
7/11/95	4,545	DCCOLOR1.SPD	C:\WINDOWS\SPOOL	SPD	\WIN95\CAB_10.CAB
7/11/95	9,656	DCD11501.SPD	C:\WINDOWS\SPOOL	SPD	\WIN95\CAB_10.CAB
7/11/95	9,552	DCLF02_1.SPD	C:\WINDOWS\SPOOL	SPD	\WIN95\CAB_10.CAB
7/11/95	10,914	DCLF02F1.SPD	C:\WINDOWS\SPOOL	SPD	\WIN95\CAB_10.CAB
7/11/95	3,851	DCLN03R1.SPD	C:\WINDOWS\SPOOL	SPD	\WIN95\CAB_10.CAB
7/11/95	10,167	DCLPS171.SPD	C:\WINDOWS\SPOOL	SPD	\WIN95\CAB_10.CAB
7/11/95	10,876	DCLPS321.SPD	C:\WINDOWS\SPOOL	SPD	\WIN95\CAB_10.CAB
7/11/95	6,908	DCLPS401.SPD	C:\WINDOWS\SPOOL	SPD	\WIN95\CAB_10.CAB
7/11/95	18,566	DCPS1721.SPD	C:\WINDOWS\SPOOL	SPD	\WIN95\CAB_10.CAB
7/11/95	18,213	DCPS1761.SPD	C:\WINDOWS\SPOOL	SPD	\WIN95\CAB_10.CAB
7/11/95	7,935	DCTPS201.SPD	C:\WINDOWS\SPOOL	SPD	\WIN95\CAB_10.CAB

Date	Size	Name	Location	Type	Location/CD
7/11/95	11,669	DEC3250.SPD	C:\WINDOWS\SPOOL	SPD	\WIN95\CAB_10.CAB
7/11/95	7,376	EPL75523.SPD	C:\WINDOWS\SPOOL	SPD	\WIN95\CAB_10.CAB
7/11/95	5,476	F71RX503.SPD	C:\WINDOWS\SPOOL	SPD	\WIN95\CAB_10.CAB
7/11/95	9,435	HP_3D522.SPD	C:\WINDOWS\SPOOL	SPD	\WIN95\CAB_10.CAB
7/11/95	7,743	HP_3P522.SPD	C:\WINDOWS\SPOOL	SPD	\WIN95\CAB_10.CAB
7/11/95	12,334	HP1200C1.SPD	C:\WINDOWS\SPOOL	SPD	\WIN95\CAB_10.CAB
7/11/95	9,365	HP3SI523.SPD	C:\WINDOWS\SPOOL	SPD	\WIN95\CAB_10.CAB
7/11/95	14,273	HP4M_V4.SPD	C:\WINDOWS\SPOOL	SPD	\WIN95\CAB_10.CAB
7/11/95	12,236	HP4ML_V4.SPD	C:\WINDOWS\SPOOL	SPD	\WIN95\CAB_10.CAB
7/11/95	12,605	HP4MP_V4.SPD	C:\WINDOWS\SPOOL	SPD	\WIN95\CAB_10.CAB
7/11/95	18,906	HP4MV_V4.SPD	C:\WINDOWS\SPOOL	SPD	\WIN95\CAB_10.CAB
7/11/95	12,996	HP4PLUS4.SPD	C:\WINDOWS\SPOOL	SPD	\WIN95\CAB_10.CAB
7/11/95	14,880	HP4SI_V4.SPD	C:\WINDOWS\SPOOL	SPD	\WIN95\CAB_10.CAB
7/11/95	8,617	HPIID522.SPD	C:\WINDOWS\SPOOL	SPD	\WIN95\CAB_10.CAB
7/11/95	7,581	HPIII522.SPD	C:\WINDOWS\SPOOL	SPD	\WIN95\CAB_10.CAB
7/11/95	7,288	HPIIP522.SPD	C:\WINDOWS\SPOOL	SPD	\WIN95\CAB_10.CAB
7/11/95	9,632	HPLJ_31.SPD	C:\WINDOWS\SPOOL	SPD	\WIN95\CAB_10.CAB
7/11/95	14,102	HPLJ_3D1.SPD	C:\WINDOWS\SPOOL	SPD	\WIN95\CAB_10.CAB
7/11/95	11,136	HPLJ_3P1.SPD	C:\WINDOWS\SPOOL	SPD	\WIN95\CAB_10.CAB
7/11/95	14,100	HPLJP_V4.SPD	C:\WINDOWS\SPOOL	SPD	\WIN95\CAB_10.CAB
7/11/95	14,442	HPPJXL31.SPD	C:\WINDOWS\SPOOL	SPD	\WIN95\CAB_10.CAB
7/11/95	9,076	IB401917.SPD	C:\WINDOWS\SPOOL	SPD	\WIN95\CAB_10.CAB
7/11/95	10,431	IB401939.SPD	C:\WINDOWS\SPOOL	SPD	\WIN95\CAB_10.CAB
7/11/95	10,784	IB402917.SPD	C:\WINDOWS\SPOOL	SPD	\WIN95\CAB_10.CAB
7/11/95	12,152	IB402939.SPD	C:\WINDOWS\SPOOL	SPD	\WIN95\CAB_10.CAB
7/11/95	12,116	IBM20470.SPD	C:\WINDOWS\SPOOL	SPD	\WIN95\CAB_10.CAB
7/11/95	5,825	IBM30505.SPD	C:\WINDOWS\SPOOL	SPD	\WIN95\CAB_10.CAB
7/11/95	4,586	IBM31514.SPD	C:\WINDOWS\SPOOL	SPD	\WIN95\CAB_10.CAB
7/11/95	12,095	IBM4039.SPD	C:\WINDOWS\SPOOL	SPD	\WIN95\CAB_10.CAB
7/11/95	15,322	IBM4039P.SPD	C:\WINDOWS\SPOOL	SPD	\WIN95\CAB_10.CAB
7/11/95	6,451	IBM4079.SPD	C:\WINDOWS\SPOOL	SPD	\WIN95\CAB_10.CAB
7/11/95	5,725	KDCOLOR1.SPD	C:\WINDOWS\SPOOL	SPD	\WIN95\CAB_10.CAB
7/11/95	5,825	L100_425.SPD	C:\WINDOWS\SPOOL	SPD	\WIN95\CAB_10.CAB
7/11/95	7,838	L200_471.SPD	C:\WINDOWS\SPOOL	SPD	\WIN95\CAB_10.CAB
7/11/95	7,845	L300_471.SPD	C:\WINDOWS\SPOOL	SPD	\WIN95\CAB_10.CAB
7/11/95	7,843	L500_493.SPD	C:\WINDOWS\SPOOL	SPD	\WIN95\CAB_10.CAB
7/11/95	13,705	LH330__1.SPD	C:\WINDOWS\SPOOL	SPD	\WIN95\CAB_10.CAB
7/11/95	13,953	LH530__1.SPD	C:\WINDOWS\SPOOL	SPD	\WIN95\CAB_10.CAB
7/11/95	12,216	LH630__1.SPD	C:\WINDOWS\SPOOL	SPD	\WIN95\CAB_10.CAB

continues

Date	Size	Name	Location	Type	Location/CD
7/11/95	6,427	LWNT_470.SPD	C:\WINDOWS\SPOOL	SPD	\WIN95\CAB_10.CAB
7/11/95	6,379	LWNTX470.SPD	C:\WINDOWS\SPOOL	SPD	\WIN95\CAB_10.CAB
7/11/95	3,853	MT_TI101.SPD	C:\WINDOWS\SPOOL	SPD	\WIN95\CAB_10.CAB
7/11/95	5,925	N2090522.SPD	C:\WINDOWS\SPOOL	SPD	\WIN95\CAB_10.CAB
7/11/95	5,227	N2290520.SPD	C:\WINDOWS\SPOOL	SPD	\WIN95\CAB_10.CAB
7/11/95	5,472	N890_470.SPD	C:\WINDOWS\SPOOL	SPD	\WIN95\CAB_10.CAB
7/11/95	5,483	N890X505.SPD	C:\WINDOWS\SPOOL	SPD	\WIN95\CAB_10.CAB
7/11/95	3,403	NCCPS401.SPD	C:\WINDOWS\SPOOL	SPD	\WIN95\CAB_10.CAB
7/11/95	4,658	NCCPS801.SPD	C:\WINDOWS\SPOOL	SPD	\WIN95\CAB_10.CAB
7/11/95	4,563	NCOL_519.SPD	C:\WINDOWS\SPOOL	SPD	\WIN95\CAB_10.CAB
7/11/95	6,713	NCS29901.SPD	C:\WINDOWS\SPOOL	SPD	\WIN95\CAB_10.CAB
7/11/95	8,307	NCSW_951.SPD	C:\WINDOWS\SPOOL	SPD	\WIN95\CAB_10.CAB
7/11/95	4,264	O5241503.SPD	C:\WINDOWS\SPOOL	SPD	\WIN95\CAB_10.CAB
7/11/95	5,136	O5242503.SPD	C:\WINDOWS\SPOOL	SPD	\WIN95\CAB_10.CAB
7/11/95	5,830	OKI830US.SPD	C:\WINDOWS\SPOOL	SPD	\WIN95\CAB_10.CAB
7/11/95	6,899	OKI840US.SPD	C:\WINDOWS\SPOOL	SPD	\WIN95\CAB_10.CAB
7/11/95	7,028	OKI850US.SPD	C:\WINDOWS\SPOOL	SPD	\WIN95\CAB_10.CAB
7/11/95	10,570	OKOL8701.SPD	C:\WINDOWS\SPOOL	SPD	\WIN95\CAB_10.CAB
7/11/95	5,551	OL830525.SPD	C:\WINDOWS\SPOOL	SPD	\WIN95\CAB_10.CAB
7/11/95	6,641	OL840518.SPD	C:\WINDOWS\SPOOL	SPD	\WIN95\CAB_10.CAB
7/11/95	6,651	OL850525.SPD	C:\WINDOWS\SPOOL	SPD	\WIN95\CAB_10.CAB
7/11/95	6,481	P4455514.SPD	C:\WINDOWS\SPOOL	SPD	\WIN95\CAB_10.CAB
7/11/95	4,128	PAP54001.SPD	C:\WINDOWS\SPOOL	SPD	\WIN95\CAB_10.CAB
7/11/95	7,607	PAP54101.SPD	C:\WINDOWS\SPOOL	SPD	\WIN95\CAB_10.CAB
7/11/95	3,458	PHIIPX.SPD	C:\WINDOWS\SPOOL	SPD	\WIN95\CAB_10.CAB
7/11/95	79	Q2200_MS.SPD	C:\WINDOWS\SPOOL	SPD	\WIN95\CAB_10.CAB
7/11/95	79	Q2210_MS.SPD	C:\WINDOWS\SPOOL	SPD	\WIN95\CAB_10.CAB
7/11/95	7,328	Q2220523.SPD	C:\WINDOWS\SPOOL	SPD	\WIN95\CAB_10.CAB
7/11/95	78	Q800_MS.SPD	C:\WINDOWS\SPOOL	SPD	\WIN95\CAB_10.CAB
7/11/95	78	Q810_MS.SPD	C:\WINDOWS\SPOOL	SPD	\WIN95\CAB_10.CAB
7/11/95	84	Q810T_MS.SPD	C:\WINDOWS\SPOOL	SPD	\WIN95\CAB_10.CAB
7/11/95	78	Q820_MS.SPD	C:\WINDOWS\SPOOL	SPD	\WIN95\CAB_10.CAB
7/11/95	5,699	Q820T517.SPD	C:\WINDOWS\SPOOL	SPD	\WIN95\CAB_10.CAB
7/11/95	11,333	Q860PLS2.SPD	C:\WINDOWS\SPOOL	SPD	\WIN95\CAB_10.CAB
7/11/95	10,440	QCS1000.SPD	C:\WINDOWS\SPOOL	SPD	\WIN95\CAB_10.CAB
7/11/95	4,763	QCS10503.SPD	C:\WINDOWS\SPOOL	SPD	\WIN95\CAB_10.CAB
7/11/95	4,786	QCS30503.SPD	C:\WINDOWS\SPOOL	SPD	\WIN95\CAB_10.CAB
7/11/95	8,236	QM1700_1.SPD	C:\WINDOWS\SPOOL	SPD	\WIN95\CAB_10.CAB
7/11/95	8,620	QM2000_1.SPD	C:\WINDOWS\SPOOL	SPD	\WIN95\CAB_10.CAB
7/11/95	8,006	QM825MR1.SPD	C:\WINDOWS\SPOOL	SPD	\WIN95\CAB_10.CAB

Date	Size	Name	Location	Type	Location/CD
7/11/95	7,238	QMPS4101.SPD	C:\WINDOWS\SPOOL	SPD	\WIN95\CAB_10.CAB
7/11/95	9,083	QMS1725.SPD	C:\WINDOWS\SPOOL	SPD	\WIN95\CAB_10.CAB
7/11/95	9,873	QMS3225.SPD	C:\WINDOWS\SPOOL	SPD	\WIN95\CAB_10.CAB
7/11/95	8,507	QMS420.SPD	C:\WINDOWS\SPOOL	SPD	\WIN95\CAB_10.CAB
7/11/95	10,650	QMS45252.SPD	C:\WINDOWS\SPOOL	SPD	\WIN95\CAB_10.CAB
7/11/95	7,717	QMS860.SPD	C:\WINDOWS\SPOOL	SPD	\WIN95\CAB_10.CAB
7/11/95	5,395	QMS8P461.SPD	C:\WINDOWS\SPOOL	SPD	\WIN95\CAB_10.CAB
7/11/95	7,933	QMSCS210.SPD	C:\WINDOWS\SPOOL	SPD	\WIN95\CAB_10.CAB
7/11/95	8,673	QMSCS230.SPD	C:\WINDOWS\SPOOL	SPD	\WIN95\CAB_10.CAB
7/11/95	33,024	SKPSFA_1.SPD	C:\WINDOWS\SPOOL	SPD	\WIN95\CAB_10.CAB
7/11/95	4,779	STLS04SS.SPD	C:\WINDOWS\SPOOL	SPD	\WIN95\CAB_10.CAB
7/11/95	4,832	STLS08LP.SPD	C:\WINDOWS\SPOOL	SPD	\WIN95\CAB_10.CAB
7/11/95	4,938	STLS5TTU.SPD	C:\WINDOWS\SPOOL	SPD	\WIN95\CAB_10.CAB
7/11/95	7,063	TIM17521.SPD	C:\WINDOWS\SPOOL	SPD	\WIN95\CAB_10.CAB
7/11/95	8,179	TIM35521.SPD	C:\WINDOWS\SPOOL	SPD	\WIN95\CAB_10.CAB
7/11/95	17,135	TIMLP232.SPD	C:\WINDOWS\SPOOL	SPD	\WIN95\CAB_10.CAB
7/11/95	17,049	TK200172.SPD	C:\WINDOWS\SPOOL	SPD	\WIN95\CAB_10.CAB
7/11/95	9,742	TK220171.SPD	C:\WINDOWS\SPOOL	SPD	\WIN95\CAB_10.CAB
7/11/95	18,748	TKP200I2.SPD	C:\WINDOWS\SPOOL	SPD	\WIN95\CAB_10.CAB
7/11/95	11,782	TKP220I1.SPD	C:\WINDOWS\SPOOL	SPD	\WIN95\CAB_10.CAB
7/11/95	18,614	TKP2SDX1.SPD	C:\WINDOWS\SPOOL	SPD	\WIN95\CAB_10.CAB
7/11/95	21,941	TKP300I1.SPD	C:\WINDOWS\SPOOL	SPD	\WIN95\CAB_10.CAB
7/11/95	10,995	TKPH4801.SPD	C:\WINDOWS\SPOOL	SPD	\WIN95\CAB_10.CAB
7/11/95	19,639	TKPHZR22.SPD	C:\WINDOWS\SPOOL	SPD	\WIN95\CAB_10.CAB
7/11/95	27,202	TKPHZR32.SPD	C:\WINDOWS\SPOOL	SPD	\WIN95\CAB_10.CAB
7/11/95	2,185	TRIUMPH1.SPD	C:\WINDOWS\SPOOL	SPD	\WIN95\CAB_10.CAB
7/11/95	3,260	TRIUMPH2.SPD	C:\WINDOWS\SPOOL	SPD	\WIN95\CAB_10.CAB
7/11/95	4,900	U9415470.SPD	C:\WINDOWS\SPOOL	SPD	\WIN95\CAB_10.CAB
7/11/95	1,969	VT600480.SPD	C:\WINDOWS\SPOOL	SPD	\WIN95\CAB_10.CAB
7/11/95	9,719	ANSI.SYS	C:\WINDOWS\COMMAND	SYS	\WIN95\CAB_09.CAB
7/11/95	1,105	ASPI2HLP.SYS	C:\WINDOWS	SYS	\WIN95\CAB_03.CAB
7/11/95	24,626	CMD640X.SYS	C:\WINDOWS	SYS	\WIN95\CAB_03.CAB
7/11/95	20,901	CMD640X2.SYS	C:\WINDOWS	SYS	\WIN95\CAB_03.CAB
7/11/95	27,094	COUNTRY.SYS	C:\WINDOWS\COMMAND	SYS	\WIN95\CAB_09.CAB
7/11/95	13,390	CSMAPPER.SYS	C:\WINDOWS\COMMAND	SYS	\WIN95\CAB_09.CAB
7/11/95	2,100	DBLBUFF.SYS	C:\WINDOWS	SYS	\WIN95\CAB_09.CAB
7/11/95	35,328	DC21X4.SYS	C:\WINDOWS	SYS	\WIN95\CAB_12.CAB
7/11/95	17,175	DISPLAY.SYS	C:\WINDOWS\COMMAND	SYS	\WIN95\CAB_09.CAB
7/11/95	15,831	DRVSPACE.SYS	C:\WINDOWS\COMMAND	SYS	\WIN95\PRECOPY1.CAB

Part

XI

App

D

continues

Date	Size	Name	Location	Type	Location/CD
7/11/95	39,424	E100.SYS	C:\WINDOWS	SYS	\WIN95\CAB_12.CAB
7/11/95	14,256	E20N3.SYS	C:\WINDOWS	SYS	\WIN95\CAB_12.CAB
7/11/95	15,328	E21N3.SYS	C:\WINDOWS	SYS	\WIN95\CAB_12.CAB
7/11/95	31,744	E22N3.SYS	C:\WINDOWS	SYS	\WIN95\CAB_12.CAB
7/11/95	16,896	EE16.SYS	C:\WINDOWS	SYS	\WIN95\CAB_12.CAB
7/11/95	24,064	EWRK3.SYS	C:\WINDOWS	SYS	\WIN95\CAB_08.CAB
7/11/95	32,935	HIMEM.SYS	C:\WINDOWS	SYS	\WIN95\CAB_03.CAB
7/11/95	3,708	IFSHLP.SYS	C:\WINDOWS	SYS	\WIN95\CAB_12.CAB
7/11/95	34,566	KEYBOARD.SYS	C:\WINDOWS\COMMAND	SYS	\WIN95\CAB_09.CAB
7/11/95	31,942	KEYBRD2.SYS	C:\WINDOWS\COMMAND	SYS	\WIN95\CAB_09.CAB
7/11/95	129,078	LOGOS.SYS	C:\WINDOWS	SYS	\WIN95\CAB_11.CAB
7/11/95	129,078	LOGOW.SYS	C:\WINDOWS	SYS	\WIN95\CAB_11.CAB
7/11/95	41,616	MDGMPORT.SYS	C:\WINDOWS	SYS	\WIN95\CAB_12.CAB
7/11/95	6,140	NDISHLP.SYS	C:\WINDOWS	SYS	\WIN95\CAB_13.CAB
7/11/95	18,432	NE1000.SYS	C:\WINDOWS\SYSTEM	SYS	\WIN95\CAB_12.CAB
7/11/95	18,256	NE2000.SYS	C:\WINDOWS\SYSTEM	SYS	\WIN95\CAB_12.CAB
7/11/95	19,152	NE3200.SYS	C:\WINDOWS\SYSTEM	SYS	\WIN95\CAB_12.CAB
7/11/95	30,992	NETFLX.SYS	C:\WINDOWS\SYSTEM	SYS	\WIN95\CAB_12.CAB
7/11/95	85,504	OCTK16.SYS	C:\WINDOWS	SYS	\WIN95\CAB_12.CAB
7/11/95	12,663	RAMDRIVE.SYS	C:\WINDOWS	SYS	\WIN95\CAB_09.CAB
7/11/95	1,536	RPLBOOT.SYS	C:\WINDOWS	SYS	\WIN95\CAB_17.CAB
7/11/95	129,078	SULOGO.SYS	C:\WINDOWS	SYS	\WIN95\CAB_10.CAB
7/11/95	24,224	TDKCD02.SYS	C:\WINDOWS	SYS	\WIN95\CAB_12.CAB
7/11/95	223,148	WINBOOT.SYS	C:\WINDOWS	SYS	\WIN95\PRECOPY1.CAB
7/11/95	5,532	STDOLE.TLB	C:\WINDOWS\SYSTEM	TLB	\WIN95\CAB_09.CAB
7/11/95	7,168	STDOLE32.TLB	C:\WINDOWS\SYSTEM	TLB	\WIN95\CAB_09.CAB
7/11/95	4,136	MAPIWM.TPL	C:\PROGRAM FILES\ MICROSOFT EXCHANGE	TPL	\WIN95\CAB_07.CAB
7/11/95	1,168	MMTASK.TSK	C:\WINDOWS\SYSTEM	TSK	\WIN95\CAB_08.CAB
7/11/95	28,896	UNIMDM.TSP	C:\WINDOWS\SYSTEM	TSP	\WIN95\CAB_03.CAB
7/11/95	65,412	ARIAL.TTF	C:\WINDOWS\SYSTEM	TTF	\WIN95\CAB_04.CAB
7/11/95	66,952	ARIALBD.TTF	C:\WINDOWS\SYSTEM	TTF	\WIN95\CAB_04.CAB
7/11/95	73,984	ARIALBI.TTF	C:\WINDOWS\SYSTEM	TTF	\WIN95\CAB_04.CAB
7/11/95	62,968	ARIALI.TTF	C:\WINDOWS\SYSTEM	TTF	\WIN95\CAB_04.CAB
7/11/95	98,872	COUR.TTF	C:\WINDOWS\SYSTEM	TTF	\WIN95\CAB_04.CAB
7/11/95	84,360	COURBD.TTF	C:\WINDOWS\SYSTEM	TTF	\WIN95\CAB_04.CAB
7/11/95	85,152	COURBI.TTF	C:\WINDOWS\SYSTEM	TTF	\WIN95\CAB_04.CAB
7/11/95	82,092	COURI.TTF	C:\WINDOWS\SYSTEM	TTF	\WIN95\CAB_04.CAB
7/11/95	138,332	LARIAL.TTF	C:\WINDOWS\SYSTEM	TTF	\WIN95\CAB_13.CAB
7/11/95	139,284	LARIALBD.TTF	C:\WINDOWS\SYSTEM	TTF	\WIN95\CAB_13.CAB

Date	Size	Name	Location	Type	Location/CD
7/11/95	159,720	LARIALBI.TTF	C:\WINDOWS\SYSTEM	TTF	\WIN95\CAB_13.CAB
7/11/95	139,172	LARIALI.TTF	C:\WINDOWS\SYSTEM	TTF	\WIN95\CAB_13.CAB
7/11/95	168,792	LCOUR.TTF	C:\WINDOWS\SYSTEM	TTF	\WIN95\CAB_13.CAB
7/11/95	174,376	LCOURBD.TTF	C:\WINDOWS\SYSTEM	TTF	\WIN95\CAB_13.CAB
7/11/95	179,848	LCOURBI.TTF	C:\WINDOWS\SYSTEM	TTF	\WIN95\CAB_13.CAB
7/11/95	187,948	LCOURI.TTF	C:\WINDOWS\SYSTEM	TTF	\WIN95\CAB_13.CAB
7/11/95	184,328	LTIMES.TTF	C:\WINDOWS\SYSTEM	TTF	\WIN95\CAB_13.CAB
7/11/95	177,800	LTIMESBD.TTF	C:\WINDOWS\SYSTEM	TTF	\WIN95\CAB_13.CAB
7/11/95	166,456	LTIMESBI.TTF	C:\WINDOWS\SYSTEM	TTF	\WIN95\CAB_13.CAB
7/11/95	176,736	LTIMESI.TTF	C:\WINDOWS\SYSTEM	TTF	\WIN95\CAB_13.CAB
7/11/95	17,412	MARLETT.TTF	C:\WINDOWS\SYSTEM	TTF	\WIN95\CAB_05.CAB
7/11/95	60,096	SYMBOL.TTF	C:\WINDOWS\SYSTEM	TTF	\WIN95\CAB_05.CAB
7/11/95	85,240	TIMES.TTF	C:\WINDOWS\SYSTEM	TTF	\WIN95\CAB_04.CAB
7/11/95	83,228	TIMESBD.TTF	C:\WINDOWS\SYSTEM	TTF	\WIN95\CAB_04.CAB
7/11/95	77,080	TIMESBI.TTF	C:\WINDOWS\SYSTEM	TTF	\WIN95\CAB_04.CAB
7/11/95	79,672	TIMESI.TTF	C:\WINDOWS\SYSTEM	TTF	\WIN95\CAB_04.CAB
7/11/95	71,196	WINGDING.TTF	C:\WINDOWS\SYSTEM	TTF	\WIN95\CAB_04.CAB
7/11/95	17,752	CONFIG.TXT	C:\WINDOWS	TXT	\WIN95\CAB_03.CAB
7/11/95	15,954	DISPLAY.TXT	C:\WINDOWS	TXT	\WIN95\CAB_03.CAB
7/11/95	7,072	EXCHANGE.TXT	C:\WINDOWS	TXT	\WIN95\CAB_03.CAB
7/11/95	2,685	EXTRA.TXT	C:\WINDOWS	TXT	\WIN95\CAB_03.CAB
7/11/95	40,378	FAQ.TXT	C:\WINDOWS	TXT	\WIN95\CAB_03.CAB
7/11/95	17,965	GENERAL.TXT	C:\WINDOWS	TXT	\WIN95\CAB_03.CAB
7/11/95	21,548	HARDWARE.TXT	C:\WINDOWS	TXT	\WIN95\CAB_03.CAB
7/11/95	3,277	INTERNET.TXT	C:\WINDOWS	TXT	\WIN95\CAB_03.CAB
7/11/95	5,532	MOUSE.TXT	C:\WINDOWS	TXT	\WIN95\CAB_03.CAB
7/11/95	42,205	MSDOSDRV.TXT	C:\WINDOWS	TXT	\WIN95\CAB_03.CAB
7/11/95	4,111	MSN.TXT	C:\PROGRAM FILES\ THE MICROSOFT NETWORK	TXT	\WIN95\CAB_03.CAB
7/11/95	4	MSNVER.TXT	C:\PROGRAM FILES\ THE MICROSOFT NETWORK	TXT	\WIN95\CAB_07.CAB
7/11/95	18,538	NETWORK.TXT	C:\WINDOWS	TXT	\WIN95\CAB_03.CAB
7/11/95	16,199	PRINTERS.TXT	C:\WINDOWS	TXT	\WIN95\CAB_03.CAB
7/11/95	35,070	PROGRAMS.TXT	C:\WINDOWS	TXT	\WIN95\CAB_03.CAB
7/11/95	24,482	SUPPORT.TXT	C:\WINDOWS	TXT	\WIN95\CAB_03.CAB
7/11/95	2,640	TESTPS.TXT	C:\WINDOWS	TXT	\WIN95\CAB_09.CAB
7/11/95	28,617	TIPS.TXT	C:\WINDOWS	TXT	\WIN95\CAB_03.CAB
7/11/95	1,056	WINNEWS.TXT	C:\WINDOWS	TXT	\WIN95\CAB_06.CAB
7/11/95	64,432	THREED.VBX	C:\WINDOWS\SYSTEM	VBX	\WIN95\CAB_17.CAB
7/11/95	25,402	AFVXD.VXD	C:\WINDOWS\SYSTEM	VXD	\WIN95\CAB_12.CAB

Part

XI

App

D

continues

Date	Size	Name	Location	Type	Location/CD
7/11/95	22,631	AM1500T.VXD	C:\WINDOWS\SYSTEM	VXD	\WIN95\CAB_12.CAB
7/11/95	29,404	APIX.VXD	C:\WINDOWS\SYSTEM	VXD	\WIN95\CAB_03.CAB
7/11/95	25,737	ATI.VXD	C:\WINDOWS\SYSTEM	VXD	\WIN95\CAB_04.CAB
7/11/95	11,860	AVVXP500.VXD	C:\WINDOWS\SYSTEM	VXD	\WIN95\CAB_14.CAB
7/11/95	24,214	AZT16.VXD	C:\WINDOWS\SYSTEM	VXD	\WIN95\CAB_08.CAB
7/11/95	32,841	BIOS.VXD	C:\WINDOWS\SYSTEM	VXD	\WIN95\CAB_09.CAB
7/11/95	18,077	BIOSXLAT.VXD	C:\WINDOWS\SYSTEM	VXD	\WIN95\CAB_03.CAB
7/11/95	58,620	CDFS.VXD	C:\WINDOWS\SYSTEM\IOSUBSYS	VXD	\WIN95\CAB_03.CAB
7/11/95	13,883	CDTSD.VXD	C:\WINDOWS\SYSTEM\IOSUBSYS	VXD	\WIN95\CAB_03.CAB
7/11/95	14,962	CDVSD.VXD	C:\WINDOWS\SYSTEM\IOSUBSYS	VXD	\WIN95\CAB_03.CAB
7/11/95	38,352	CE2NDIS3.VXD	C:\WINDOWS\SYSTEM	VXD	\WIN95\CAB_08.CAB
7/11/95	22,617	CENDIS.VXD	C:\WINDOWS\SYSTEM	VXD	\WIN95\CAB_12.CAB
7/11/95	18,590	CHIPS.VXD	C:\WINDOWS\SYSTEM	VXD	\WIN95\CAB_04.CAB
7/11/95	16,950	CIRRUS.VXD	C:\WINDOWS\SYSTEM	VXD	\WIN95\CAB_04.CAB
7/11/95	22,109	CM2NDIS3.VXD	C:\WINDOWS\SYSTEM	VXD	\WIN95\CAB_08.CAB
7/11/95	10,401	COMBUFF.VXD	C:\WINDOWS\SYSTEM	VXD	\WIN95\CAB_03.CAB
7/11/95	17,913	COMPAQ.VXD	C:\WINDOWS\SYSTEM	VXD	\WIN95\CAB_04.CAB
7/11/95	85,613	CONFIGMG.VXD	C:\WINDOWS\SYSTEM\IOSUBSYS	VXD	\WIN95\CAB_09.CAB
7/11/95	31,837	CPQNDIS3.VXD	C:\WINDOWS\SYSTEM	VXD	\WIN95\CAB_12.CAB
7/11/95	50,775	CTNDW.VXD	C:\WINDOWS\SYSTEM	VXD	\WIN95\CAB_08.CAB
7/11/95	18,639	DBKVSSD.VXD	C:\WINDOWS\SYSTEM	VXD	\WIN95\CAB_09.CAB
7/11/95	15,062	DECCORE.VXD	C:\WINDOWS\SYSTEM	VXD	\WIN95\CAB_17.CAB
7/11/95	27,213	DECLAN.VXD	C:\WINDOWS\SYSTEM	VXD	\WIN95\CAB_12.CAB
7/11/95	36,587	DECLICL.VXD	C:\WINDOWS\SYSTEM	VXD	\WIN95\CAB_17.CAB
7/11/95	16,478	DISKTSD.VXD	C:\WINDOWS\SYSTEM\IOSUBSYS	VXD	\WIN95\CAB_03.CAB
7/11/95	10,094	DISKVSD.VXD	C:\WINDOWS\SYSTEM\IOSUBSYS	VXD	\WIN95\CAB_03.CAB
7/11/95	106,862	DOSMGR.VXD	C:\WINDOWS\SYSTEM	VXD	\WIN95\CAB_03.CAB
7/11/95	13,912	DOSNET.VXD	C:\WINDOWS\SYSTEM	VXD	\WIN95\CAB_03.CAB
7/11/95	54,207	DRVSPACX.VXD	C:\WINDOWS\SYSTEM	VXD	\WIN95\CAB_09.CAB
7/11/95	26,982	DYNAPAGE.VXD	C:\WINDOWS\SYSTEM	VXD	\WIN95\CAB_03.CAB
7/11/95	31,636	E30N3.VXD	C:\WINDOWS\SYSTEM	VXD	\WIN95\CAB_12.CAB
7/11/95	31,636	E31N3.VXD	C:\WINDOWS\SYSTEM	VXD	\WIN95\CAB_12.CAB
7/11/95	17,993	EBIOS.VXD	C:\WINDOWS\SYSTEM	VXD	\WIN95\CAB_03.CAB
7/11/95	23,129	EE16.VXD	C:\WINDOWS\SYSTEM	VXD	\WIN95\CAB_12.CAB
7/11/95	13,669	EISA.VXD	C:\WINDOWS\SYSTEM	VXD	\WIN95\CAB_09.CAB
7/11/95	48,710	EL59X.VXD	C:\WINDOWS\SYSTEM	VXD	\WIN95\CAB_12.CAB
7/11/95	29,379	ELNK16.VXD	C:\WINDOWS\SYSTEM	VXD	\WIN95\CAB_12.CAB

Date	Size	Name	Location	Type	Location/CD
7/11/95	30,773	ELNK3.VXD	C:\WINDOWS\SYSTEM	VXD	\WIN95\CAB_12.CAB
7/11/95	31,325	ELNKII.VXD	C:\WINDOWS\SYSTEM	VXD	\WIN95\CAB_12.CAB
7/11/95	28,787	ELNKMC.VXD	C:\WINDOWS\SYSTEM	VXD	\WIN95\CAB_12.CAB
7/11/95	29,785	ELPC3.VXD	C:\WINDOWS\SYSTEM	VXD	\WIN95\CAB_12.CAB
7/11/95	43,197	ENABLE.VXD	C:\WINDOWS\SYSTEM\ VMM31	VXD	\WIN95\CAB_02.CAB
7/11/95	25,154	ENABLE2.VXD	C:\WINDOWS\SYSTEM\ VMM32	VXD	\WIN95\CAB_02.CAB
7/11/95	21,629	ENABLE4.VXD	C:\WINDOWS\SYSTEM	VXD	\WIN95\CAB_02.CAB
7/11/95	25,152	EPRO.VXD	C:\WINDOWS\SYSTEM	VXD	\WIN95\CAB_12.CAB
7/11/95	18,072	ES1488.VXD	C:\WINDOWS\SYSTEM	VXD	\WIN95\CAB_08.CAB
7/11/95	22,168	ES1688.VXD	C:\WINDOWS\SYSTEM	VXD	\WIN95\CAB_08.CAB
7/11/95	18,071	ES488.VXD	C:\WINDOWS\SYSTEM	VXD	\WIN95\CAB_08.CAB
7/11/95	19,607	ES688.VXD	C:\WINDOWS\SYSTEM	VXD	\WIN95\CAB_08.CAB
7/11/95	23,025	FILESEC.VXD	C:\WINDOWS\SYSTEM	VXD	\WIN95\CAB_12.CAB
7/11/95	3,706	FLS1MTD.VXD	C:\WINDOWS\SYSTEM	VXD	\WIN95\CAB_09.CAB
7/11/95	3,810	FLS2MTD.VXD	C:\WINDOWS\SYSTEM	VXD	\WIN95\CAB_09.CAB
7/11/95	35,629	HPEISA.VXD	C:\WINDOWS\SYSTEM	VXD	\WIN95\CAB_12.CAB
7/11/95	39,494	HPFEND.VXD	C:\WINDOWS\SYSTEM	VXD	\WIN95\CAB_12.CAB
7/11/95	43,588	HPISA.VXD	C:\WINDOWS\SYSTEM	VXD	\WIN95\CAB_12.CAB
7/11/95	43,588	HPMCA.VXD	C:\WINDOWS\SYSTEM	VXD	\WIN95\CAB_12.CAB
7/11/95	39,250	IBMTOK.VXD	C:\WINDOWS\SYSTEM	VXD	\WIN95\CAB_12.CAB
7/11/95	35,086	IBMTOK4.VXD	C:\WINDOWS\SYSTEM	VXD	\WIN95\CAB_12.CAB
7/11/95	165,029	IFSMGR.VXD	C:\WINDOWS\SYSTEM	VXD	\WIN95\CAB_03.CAB
7/11/95	9,934	INT13.VXD	C:\WINDOWS\SYSTEM	VXD	\WIN95\CAB_03.CAB
7/11/95	68,289	IOS.VXD	C:\WINDOWS\SYSTEM	VXD	\WIN95\CAB_03.CAB
7/11/95	41,075	IRMATRAC.VXD	C:\WINDOWS\SYSTEM	VXD	\WIN95\CAB_12.CAB
7/11/95	18,817	ISAPNP.VXD	C:\WINDOWS\SYSTEM	VXD	\WIN95\CAB_09.CAB
7/11/95	69,231	LMOUSE.VXD	C:\WINDOWS\SYSTEM	VXD	\WIN95\CAB_08.CAB
7/11/95	11,637	LOGGER.VXD	C:\WINDOWS\SYSTEM	VXD	\WIN95\CAB_10.CAB
7/11/95	35,479	LPT.VXD	C:\WINDOWS\SYSTEM	VXD	\WIN95\CAB_03.CAB
7/11/95	17,179	LPTENUM.VXD	C:\WINDOWS\SYSTEM	VXD	\WIN95\CAB_09.CAB
7/11/95	9,818	MGA.VXD	C:\WINDOWS\SYSTEM	VXD	\WIN95\CAB_04.CAB
7/11/95	11,844	MMDEVLDR.VXD	C:\WINDOWS\SYSTEM	VXD	\WIN95\CAB_08.CAB
7/11/95	46,746	MRCI2.VXD	C:\WINDOWS\SYSTEM	VXD	\WIN95\CAB_09.CAB
7/11/95	15,804	MSMOUSE.VXD	C:\WINDOWS\SYSTEM	VXD	\WIN95\CAB_08.CAB
7/11/95	12,972	MSMPU401.VXD	C:\WINDOWS\SYSTEM	VXD	\WIN95\CAB_08.CAB
7/11/95	23,897	MSODISUP.VXD	C:\WINDOWS\SYSTEM	VXD	\WIN95\CAB_12.CAB
7/11/95	13,462	MSOPL.VXD	C:\WINDOWS\SYSTEM	VXD	\WIN95\CAB_08.CAB
7/11/95	17,562	MSSBLST.VXD	C:\WINDOWS\SYSTEM	VXD	\WIN95\CAB_08.CAB

Part

XI

App

D

continues

Date	Size	Name	Location	Type	Location/CD
7/11/95	28,400	MSSNDSYS.VXD	C:\WINDOWS\SYSTEM	VXD	\WIN95\CAB_08.CAB
7/11/95	21,657	MSSP.VXD	C:\WINDOWS\SYSTEM	VXD	\WIN95\CAB_12.CAB
7/11/95	8,898	MVPAS.VXD	C:\WINDOWS\SYSTEM	VXD	\WIN95\CAB_08.CAB
7/11/95	99,084	NDIS.VXD	C:\WINDOWS\SYSTEM	VXD	\WIN95\CAB_12.CAB
7/11/95	23,744	NDIS2SUP.VXD	C:\WINDOWS\SYSTEM	VXD	\WIN95\CAB_12.CAB
7/11/95	9,929	NECATAPI.VXD	C:\WINDOWS\SYSTEM	VXD	\WIN95\CAB_03.CAB
7/11/95	45,756	NETBEUI.VXD	C:\WINDOWS\SYSTEM	VXD	\WIN95\CAB_12.CAB
7/11/95	22,609	NICE.VXD	C:\WINDOWS\SYSTEM	VXD	\WIN95\CAB_12.CAB
7/11/95	23,606	NSCL.VXD	C:\WINDOWS\SYSTEM	VXD	\WIN95\CAB_12.CAB
7/11/95	51,001	NWLINK.VXD	C:\WINDOWS\SYSTEM	VXD	\WIN95\CAB_12.CAB
7/11/95	46,653	NWNBLINK.VXD	C:\WINDOWS\SYSTEM	VXD	\WIN95\CAB_12.CAB
7/11/95	123,963	NWREDIR.VXD	C:\WINDOWS\SYSTEM	VXD	\WIN95\CAB_12.CAB
7/11/95	130,636	NWSERVER.VXD	C:\WINDOWS\SYSTEM	VXD	\WIN95\CAB_12.CAB
7/11/95	14,438	NWSP.VXD	C:\WINDOWS\SYSTEM	VXD	\WIN95\CAB_12.CAB
7/11/95	14,476	OAK.VXD	C:\WINDOWS\SYSTEM	VXD	\WIN95\CAB_04.CAB
7/11/95	72,655	OCTK32.VXD	C:\WINDOWS\SYSTEM	VXD	\WIN95\CAB_12.CAB
7/11/95	39,827	OTCETH.VXD	C:\WINDOWS\SYSTEM	VXD	\WIN95\CAB_12.CAB
7/11/95	13,905	PAGESWAP.VXD	C:\WINDOWS\SYSTEM	VXD	\WIN95\CAB_03.CAB
7/11/95	23,105	PARALINK.VXD	C:\WINDOWS\SYSTEM	VXD	\WIN95\CAB_10.CAB
7/11/95	9,801	PARITY.VXD	C:\WINDOWS\SYSTEM	VXD	\WIN95\CAB_03.CAB
7/11/95	77,661	PCCARD.VXD	C:\WINDOWS\SYSTEM	VXD	\WIN95\CAB_09.CAB
7/11/95	24,535	PCI.VXD	C:\WINDOWS\SYSTEM	VXD	\WIN95\CAB_09.CAB
7/11/95	35,461	PCNTN3.VXD	C:\WINDOWS\SYSTEM	VXD	\WIN95\CAB_12.CAB
7/11/95	30,811	PE3NDIS.VXD	C:\WINDOWS\SYSTEM	VXD	\WIN95\CAB_12.CAB
7/11/95	22,583	PERF.VXD	C:\WINDOWS\SYSTEM	VXD	\WIN95\CAB_12.CAB
7/11/95	18,458	PPM.VXD	C:\WINDOWS\SYSTEM	VXD	\WIN95\CAB_08.CAB
7/11/95	135,264	PPPMAC.VXD	C:\WINDOWS\SYSTEM	VXD	\WIN95\CAB_10.CAB
7/11/95	38,995	PROTEON.VXD	C:\WINDOWS\SYSTEM	VXD	\WIN95\CAB_12.CAB
7/11/95	9,787	QEMMFIX.VXD	C:\WINDOWS\SYSTEM\ VMM32	VXD	\WIN95\CAB_03.CAB
7/11/95	22,127	REBOOT.VXD	C:\WINDOWS\SYSTEM	VXD	\WIN95\CAB_03.CAB
7/11/95	17,087	S3.VXD	C:\WINDOWS\SYSTEM	VXD	\WIN95\CAB_04.CAB
7/11/95	54,363	SB16.VXD	C:\WINDOWS\SYSTEM	VXD	\WIN95\CAB_08.CAB
7/11/95	40,014	SBAWE.VXD	C:\WINDOWS\SYSTEM	VXD	\WIN95\CAB_08.CAB
7/11/95	19,189	SCSI1HLP.VXD	C:\WINDOWS\SYSTEM\ IOSUBSYS	VXD	\WIN95\CAB_05.CAB
7/11/95	19,899	SERENUM.VXD	C:\WINDOWS\SYSTEM	VXD	\WIN95\CAB_03.CAB
7/11/95	18,572	SERIAL.VXD	C:\WINDOWS\SYSTEM	VXD	\WIN95\CAB_03.CAB
7/11/95	31,838	SETP3.VXD	C:\WINDOWS\SYSTEM	VXD	\WIN95\CAB_12.CAB
7/11/95	78,964	SHELL.VXD	C:\WINDOWS\SYSTEM\ IOSUBSYS	VXD	\WIN95\CAB_11.CAB
7/11/95	36,959	SMC8000W.VXD	C:\WINDOWS\SYSTEM	VXD	\WIN95\CAB_12.CAB

Date	Size	Name	Location	Type	Location/CD
7/11/95	28,765	SMC80PC.VXD	C:\WINDOWS\SYSTEM	VXD	\WIN95\CAB_12.CAB
7/11/95	71,773	SMC8100W.VXD	C:\WINDOWS\SYSTEM	VXD	\WIN95\CAB_12.CAB
7/11/95	28,767	SMC8232W.VXD	C:\WINDOWS\SYSTEM	VXD	\WIN95\CAB_12.CAB
7/11/95	29,433	SMC9000.VXD	C:\WINDOWS\SYSTEM	VXD	\WIN95\CAB_12.CAB
7/11/95	13,884	SNAPSHOT.VXD	C:\WINDOWS\SYSTEM	VXD	\WIN95\CAB_17.CAB
7/11/95	27,217	SNIP.VXD	C:\WINDOWS\SYSTEM	VXD	\WIN95\CAB_12.CAB
7/11/95	27,217	SOCKET.VXD	C:\WINDOWS\SYSTEM	VXD	\WIN95\CAB_12.CAB
7/11/95	9,806	SOCKETSV.VXD	C:\WINDOWS\SYSTEM	VXD	\WIN95\CAB_09.CAB
7/11/95	9,908	SPAP.VXD	C:\WINDOWS\SYSTEM	VXD	\WIN95\CAB_10.CAB
7/11/95	17,996	SPENDIS.VXD	C:\WINDOWS\SYSTEM	VXD	\WIN95\CAB_12.CAB
7/11/95	2,596	SPLITTER.VXD	C:\WINDOWS\SYSTEM	VXD	\WIN95\CAB_07.CAB
7/11/95	27,196	SPOOLER.VXD	C:\WINDOWS\SYSTEM	VXD	\WIN95\CAB_09.CAB
7/11/95	3,202	SRAMMTD.VXD	C:\WINDOWS\SYSTEM	VXD	\WIN95\CAB_09.CAB
7/11/95	63,935	T20N3.VXD	C:\WINDOWS\SYSTEM	VXD	\WIN95\CAB_12.CAB
7/11/95	64,027	T30N3.VXD	C:\WINDOWS\SYSTEM	VXD	\WIN95\CAB_12.CAB
7/11/95	37,616	TCTOKCH.VXD	C:\WINDOWS\SYSTEM	VXD	\WIN95\CAB_12.CAB
7/11/95	52,627	TLNK3.VXD	C:\WINDOWS\SYSTEM	VXD	\WIN95\CAB_12.CAB
7/11/95	14,531	TSENG.VXD	C:\WINDOWS\SYSTEM	VXD	\WIN95\CAB_04.CAB
7/11/95	31,311	UBNEI.VXD	C:\WINDOWS\SYSTEM	VXD	\WIN95\CAB_12.CAB
7/11/95	41,598	UNIMODEM.VXD	C:\WINDOWS\SYSTEM	VXD	\WIN95\CAB_03.CAB
7/11/95	95,387	V86MMGR.VXD	C:\WINDOWS\SYSTEM	VXD	\WIN95\CAB_03.CAB
7/11/95	19,566	VCACHE.VXD	C:\WINDOWS\SYSTEM	VXD	\WIN95\CAB_03.CAB
7/11/95	23,939	VCD.VXD	C:\WINDOWS\SYSTEM	VXD	\WIN95\CAB_03.CAB
7/11/95	22,408	VCDFSD.VXD	C:\WINDOWS\SYSTEM	VXD	\WIN95\CAB_03.CAB
7/11/95	32,638	VCOMM.VXD	C:\WINDOWS\SYSTEM	VXD	\WIN95\CAB_03.CAB
7/11/95	53,438	VCOND.VXD	C:\WINDOWS\SYSTEM	VXD	\WIN95\CAB_04.CAB
7/11/95	73,592	VDD.VXD	C:\WINDOWS\SYSTEM	VXD	\WIN95\CAB_04.CAB
7/11/95	9,768	VDEF.VXD	C:\WINDOWS\SYSTEM	VXD	\WIN95\CAB_03.CAB
7/11/95	41,844	VDMAD.VXD	C:\WINDOWS\SYSTEM	VXD	\WIN95\CAB_03.CAB
7/11/95	57,917	VFAT.VXD	C:\WINDOWS\SYSTEM	VXD	\WIN95\CAB_03.CAB
7/11/95	16,831	VFBACKUP.VXD	C:\WINDOWS\SYSTEM	VXD	\WIN95\CAB_03.CAB
7/11/95	5,857	VFD.VXD	C:\WINDOWS\SYSTEM	VXD	\WIN95\CAB_03.CAB
7/11/95	7,723	VFLATD.VXD	C:\WINDOWS\SYSTEM	VXD	\WIN95\CAB_04.CAB
7/11/95	14,624	VGAFULL.3GR	C:\WINDOWS\SYSTEM	VXD	\WIN95\CAB_04.CAB
7/11/95	42,749	VGATEWAY.VXD	C:\WINDOWS\SYSTEM	VXD	\WIN95\CAB_07.CAB
7/11/95	14,938	VIDEO7.VXD	C:\WINDOWS\SYSTEM	VXD	\WIN95\CAB_04.CAB
7/11/95	20,590	VJOYD.VXD	C:\WINDOWS\SYSTEM	VXD	\WIN95\CAB_08.CAB
7/11/95	45,371	VKD.VXD	C:\WINDOWS\SYSTEM	VXD	\WIN95\CAB_03.CAB
7/11/95	13,973	VMCPD.VXD	C:\WINDOWS\SYSTEM	VXD	\WIN95\CAB_03.CAB

Part

XI

App

D

continues

Date	Size	Name	Location	Type	Location/CD
7/11/95	9,815	VMD.VXD	C:\WINDOWS\SYSTEM	VXD	\WIN95\CAB_08.CAB
7/11/95	411,132	VMM32.VXD	C:\WINDOWS\SYSTEM	VXD	\WIN95\CAB_03.CAB
7/11/95	32,815	VMOUSE.VXD	C:\WINDOWS\SYSTEM	VXD	\WIN95\CAB_08.CAB
7/11/95	30,931	VMPOLL.VXD	C:\WINDOWS\SYSTEM	VXD	\WIN95\CAB_03.CAB
7/11/95	16,030	VMVID.VXD	C:\WINDOWS\SYSTEM	VXD	\WIN95\CAB_08.CAB
7/11/95	27,221	VNETBIOS.VXD	C:\WINDOWS\SYSTEM	VXD	\WIN95\CAB_12.CAB
7/11/95	19,129	VNETSUP.VXD	C:\WINDOWS\SYSTEM	VXD	\WIN95\CAB_12.CAB
7/11/95	18,494	VOLTRACK.VXD	C:\WINDOWS\SYSTEM\ IOSUBSYS	VXD	\WIN95\CAB_03.CAB
7/11/95	21,094	VPASD.VXD	C:\WINDOWS\SYSTEM	VXD	\WIN95\CAB_08.CAB
7/11/95	22,618	VPD.VXD	C:\WINDOWS\SYSTEM	VXD	\WIN95\CAB_03.CAB
7/11/95	46,543	VPICD.VXD	C:\WINDOWS\SYSTEM	VXD	\WIN95\CAB_03.CAB
7/11/95	19,669	VPOWERD.VXD	C:\WINDOWS\SYSTEM	VXD	\WIN95\CAB_07.CAB
7/11/95	140,343	VREDIR.VXD	C:\WINDOWS\SYSTEM	VXD	\WIN95\CAB_12.CAB
7/11/95	5,721	VSD.VXD	C:\WINDOWS\SYSTEM	VXD	\WIN95\CAB_03.CAB
7/11/95	108,264	VSERVER.VXD	C:\WINDOWS\SYSTEM	VXD	\WIN95\CAB_12.CAB
7/11/95	14,926	VSHARE.VXD	C:\WINDOWS\SYSTEM	VXD	\WIN95\CAB_05.CAB
7/11/95	31,684	VTD.VXD	C:\WINDOWS\SYSTEM	VXD	\WIN95\CAB_03.CAB
7/11/95	18,546	VTDAPI.VXD	C:\WINDOWS\SYSTEM	VXD	\WIN95\CAB_03.CAB
7/11/95	54,497	VWIN32.VXD	C:\WINDOWS\SYSTEM	VXD	\WIN95\CAB_04.CAB
7/11/95	35,112	VXDLDR.VXD	C:\WINDOWS\SYSTEM	VXD	\WIN95\CAB_03.CAB
7/11/95	18,328	WD.VXD	C:\WINDOWS\SYSTEM	VXD	\WIN95\CAB_04.CAB
7/11/95	5,816	WSHTCP.VXD	C:\WINDOWS\SYSTEM	VXD	\WIN95\CAB_12.CAB
7/11/95	14,521	WSIPX.VXD	C:\WINDOWS\SYSTEM	VXD	\WIN95\CAB_12.CAB
7/11/95	15,522	WSOCK.VXD	C:\WINDOWS\SYSTEM	VXD	\WIN95\CAB_12.CAB
7/11/95	92,244	WSVV.VXD	C:\WINDOWS\SYSTEM	VXD	\WIN95\CAB_17.CAB
7/11/95	20,151	XGA.VXD	C:\WINDOWS\SYSTEM	VXD	\WIN95\CAB_04.CAB
7/11/95	135,876	MSSOUND.WAV	C:\WINDOWS\MEDIA	WAV	\WIN95\CAB_08.CAB
7/11/95	15,932	CHIMES.WAV	C:\WINDOWS\MEDIA	WAV	\WIN95\CAB_14.CAB
7/11/95	24,994	CHORD.WAV	C:\WINDOWS\MEDIA	WAV	\WIN95\CAB_14.CAB
7/11/95	11,586	DING.WAV	C:\WINDOWS\MEDIA	WAV	\WIN95\CAB_14.CAB
7/11/95	336,938	JUNGLE~1.WAV	C:\WINDOWS\MEDIA	WAV	\WIN95\CAB_14.CAB
7/11/95	142,888	JUNGLE~2.WAV	C:\WINDOWS\MEDIA	WAV	\WIN95\CAB_14.CAB
7/11/95	145,450	JUNGLE~3.WAV	C:\WINDOWS\MEDIA	WAV	\WIN95\CAB_14.CAB
7/11/95	184,872	JUNGLE~4.WAV	C:\WINDOWS\MEDIA	WAV	\WIN95\CAB_14.CAB
7/11/95	89,126	JUNGLEAS.WAV	C:\WINDOWS\MEDIA	WAV	\WIN95\CAB_14.CAB
7/11/95	143,914	JUNGLECL.WAV	C:\WINDOWS\MEDIA	WAV	\WIN95\CAB_14.CAB
7/11/95	175,146	JUNGLECR.WAV	C:\WINDOWS\MEDIA	WAV	\WIN95\CAB_14.CAB
7/11/95	140,330	JUNGLEDE.WAV	C:\WINDOWS\MEDIA	WAV	\WIN95\CAB_14.CAB
7/11/95	166,954	JUNGLEER.WAV	C:\WINDOWS\MEDIA	WAV	\WIN95\CAB_14.CAB
7/11/95	147,754	JUNGLEEX.WAV	C:\WINDOWS\MEDIA	WAV	\WIN95\CAB_14.CAB

Date	Size	Name	Location	Type	Location/CD
7/11/95	169,010	JUNGLEMA.WAV	C:\WINDOWS\MEDIA	WAV	\WIN95\CAB_14.CAB
7/11/95	74,026	JUNGLEME.WAV	C:\WINDOWS\MEDIA	WAV	\WIN95\CAB_14.CAB
7/11/95	169,010	JUNGLEMI.WAV	C:\WINDOWS\MEDIA	WAV	\WIN95\CAB_14.CAB
7/11/95	129,578	JUNGLEOP.WAV	C:\WINDOWS\MEDIA	WAV	\WIN95\CAB_14.CAB
7/11/95	145,446	JUNGLEQU.WAV	C:\WINDOWS\MEDIA	WAV	\WIN95\CAB_14.CAB
7/11/95	159,782	JUNGLERE.WAV	C:\WINDOWS\MEDIA	WAV	\WIN95\CAB_14.CAB
7/11/95	474,238	JUNGLEWI.WAV	C:\WINDOWS\MEDIA	WAV	\WIN95\CAB_14.CAB
7/11/95	21,816	MUSICA~1.WAV	C:\WINDOWS\MEDIA	WAV	\WIN95\CAB_15.CAB
7/11/95	8,288	MUSICA~2.WAV	C:\WINDOWS\MEDIA	WAV	\WIN95\CAB_15.CAB
7/11/95	12,490	MUSICA~3.WAV	C:\WINDOWS\MEDIA	WAV	\WIN95\CAB_15.CAB
7/11/95	12,054	MUSICA~4.WAV	C:\WINDOWS\MEDIA	WAV	\WIN95\CAB_15.CAB
7/11/95	28,338	MUSICAAS.WAV	C:\WINDOWS\MEDIA	WAV	\WIN95\CAB_15.CAB
7/11/95	45,816	MUSICACL.WAV	C:\WINDOWS\MEDIA	WAV	\WIN95\CAB_15.CAB
7/11/95	10,272	MUSICACR.WAV	C:\WINDOWS\MEDIA	WAV	\WIN95\CAB_15.CAB
7/11/95	6,262	MUSICADE.WAV	C:\WINDOWS\MEDIA	WAV	\WIN95\CAB_15.CAB
7/11/95	20,344	MUSICAER.WAV	C:\WINDOWS\MEDIA	WAV	\WIN95\CAB_15.CAB
7/11/95	9,584	MUSICAEX.WAV	C:\WINDOWS\MEDIA	WAV	\WIN95\CAB_15.CAB
7/11/95	8,608	MUSICAMA.WAV	C:\WINDOWS\MEDIA	WAV	\WIN95\CAB_15.CAB
7/11/95	8,186	MUSICAME.WAV	C:\WINDOWS\MEDIA	WAV	\WIN95\CAB_15.CAB
7/11/95	7,800	MUSICAMI.WAV	C:\WINDOWS\MEDIA	WAV	\WIN95\CAB_15.CAB
7/11/95	43,096	MUSICAOP.WAV	C:\WINDOWS\MEDIA	WAV	\WIN95\CAB_15.CAB
7/11/95	11,932	MUSICAQU.WAV	C:\WINDOWS\MEDIA	WAV	\WIN95\CAB_15.CAB
7/11/95	20,596	MUSICARE.WAV	C:\WINDOWS\MEDIA	WAV	\WIN95\CAB_15.CAB
7/11/95	49,026	MUSICAWI.WAV	C:\WINDOWS\MEDIA	WAV	\WIN95\CAB_15.CAB
7/11/95	249,570	ROBOTZ~1.WAV	C:\WINDOWS\MEDIA	WAV	\WIN95\CAB_15.CAB
7/11/95	71,868	ROBOTZ~2.WAV	C:\WINDOWS\MEDIA	WAV	\WIN95\CAB_15.CAB
7/11/95	49,578	ROBOTZ~3.WAV	C:\WINDOWS\MEDIA	WAV	\WIN95\CAB_15.CAB
7/11/95	109,688	ROBOTZ~4.WAV	C:\WINDOWS\MEDIA	WAV	\WIN95\CAB_15.CAB
7/11/95	70,426	ROBOTZAS.WAV	C:\WINDOWS\MEDIA	WAV	\WIN95\CAB_15.CAB
7/11/95	94,818	ROBOTZCL.WAV	C:\WINDOWS\MEDIA	WAV	\WIN95\CAB_15.CAB
7/11/95	54,150	ROBOTZCR.WAV	C:\WINDOWS\MEDIA	WAV	\WIN95\CAB_15.CAB
7/11/95	44,546	ROBOTZDE.WAV	C:\WINDOWS\MEDIA	WAV	\WIN95\CAB_15.CAB
7/11/95	49,284	ROBOTZER.WAV	C:\WINDOWS\MEDIA	WAV	\WIN95\CAB_15.CAB
7/11/95	30,194	ROBOTZEX.WAV	C:\WINDOWS\MEDIA	WAV	\WIN95\CAB_15.CAB
7/11/95	74,722	ROBOTZMA.WAV	C:\WINDOWS\MEDIA	WAV	\WIN95\CAB_15.CAB
7/11/95	13,920	ROBOTZME.WAV	C:\WINDOWS\MEDIA	WAV	\WIN95\CAB_15.CAB
7/11/95	150,442	ROBOTZMI.WAV	C:\WINDOWS\MEDIA	WAV	\WIN95\CAB_15.CAB
7/11/95	81,390	ROBOTZOP.WAV	C:\WINDOWS\MEDIA	WAV	\WIN95\CAB_15.CAB
7/11/95	79,002	ROBOTZQU.WAV	C:\WINDOWS\MEDIA	WAV	\WIN95\CAB_15.CAB

Part
XI
App
D

continues

Date	Size	Name	Location	Type	Location/CD
7/11/95	119,134	ROBOTZRE.WAV	C:\WINDOWS\MEDIA	WAV	\WIN95\CAB_15.CAB
7/11/95	275,950	ROBOTZWI.WAV	C:\WINDOWS\MEDIA	WAV	\WIN95\CAB_15.CAB
7/11/95	27,516	TADA.WAV	C:\WINDOWS\MEDIA	WAV	\WIN95\CAB_15.CAB
7/11/95	86,798	UTOPIA~1.WAV	C:\WINDOWS\MEDIA	WAV	\WIN95\CAB_15.CAB
7/11/95	2,692	UTOPIA~2.WAV	C:\WINDOWS\MEDIA	WAV	\WIN95\CAB_15.CAB
7/11/95	5,120	UTOPIA-3.WAV	C:\WINDOWS\MEDIA	WAV	\WIN95\CAB_15.CAB
7/11/95	15,372	UTOPIA~4.WAV	C:\WINDOWS\MEDIA	WAV	\WIN95\CAB_15.CAB
7/11/95	95,708	UTOPIAAS.WAV	C:\WINDOWS\MEDIA	WAV	\WIN95\CAB_15.CAB
7/11/95	4,616	UTOPIACL.WAV	C:\WINDOWS\MEDIA	WAV	\WIN95\CAB_15.CAB
7/11/95	5,824	UTOPIACR.WAV	C:\WINDOWS\MEDIA	WAV	\WIN95\CAB_15.CAB
7/11/95	9,946	UTOPIADE.WAV	C:\WINDOWS\MEDIA	WAV	\WIN95\CAB_15.CAB
7/11/95	24,596	UTOPIAER.WAV	C:\WINDOWS\MEDIA	WAV	\WIN95\CAB_15.CAB
7/11/95	13,026	UTOPIAEX.WAV	C:\WINDOWS\MEDIA	WAV	\WIN95\CAB_15.CAB
7/11/95	14,922	UTOPIAMA.WAV	C:\WINDOWS\MEDIA	WAV	\WIN95\CAB_16.CAB
7/11/95	3,462	UTOPIAME.WAV	C:\WINDOWS\MEDIA	WAV	\WIN95\CAB_16.CAB
7/11/95	14,990	UTOPIAMI.WAV	C:\WINDOWS\MEDIA	WAV	\WIN95\CAB_16.CAB
7/11/95	10,760	UTOPIAOP.WAV	C:\WINDOWS\MEDIA	WAV	\WIN95\CAB_16.CAB
7/11/95	13,084	UTOPIAQU.WAV	C:\WINDOWS\MEDIA	WAV	\WIN95\CAB_16.CAB
7/11/95	98,330	UTOPIARE.WAV	C:\WINDOWS\MEDIA	WAV	\WIN95\CAB_16.CAB
7/11/95	156,760	UTOPIAWI.WAV	C:\WINDOWS\MEDIA	WAV	\WIN95\CAB_16.CAB
7/11/95	4,017	QUATTRO.WB2	C:\WINDOWS\SHELLNEW	WB2	\WIN95\CAB_11.CAB
7/11/95	2,448	LOTUS.WK4	C:\WINDOWS\SHELLNEW	WK4	\WIN95\CAB_11.CAB
7/11/95	22,679	WIN.CNF	C:\WINDOWS\SYSTEM	WPC	\WIN95\CAB_03.CAB
7/11/95	62,464	WRITE32.WPC	C:\PROGRAM FILES\ ACCESSORIES	WPC	\WIN95\CAB_02.CAB
7/11/95	30	WORDPFCT.WPD	C:\WINDOWS\SHELLNEW	WPD	\WIN95\CAB_11.CAB
7/11/95	2,274	INFORMS.WPF	C:\WINDOWS\SHELLNEW	WPF	\WIN95\CAB_11.CAB
7/11/95	57	WORDPFCT.WPG	C:\WINDOWS\SHELLNEW	WPG	\WIN95\CAB_11.CAB
7/11/95	1,371	WORDPFCT.WPW	C:\WINDOWS\SHELLNEW	WPW	\WIN95\CAB_11.CAB
7/11/95	5,632	EXCEL.XLS	C:\WINDOWS\SHELLNEW	XLS	\WIN95\CAB_11.CAB
7/11/95	1,518	EXCEL4.XLS	C:\WINDOWS\SHELLNEW	XLS	\WIN95\CAB_11.CAB

What's On the CDs

by Kevin Kloss

The following information describes what you will find on the two CDs included with *Platinum Edition Using Windows 95.* ■

Operating system requirements for the CDs

Determine the minimum and recommended requirements you will need to fully utilize these CDs.

The new User Interface (UI) of the Platinum Edition Windows 95 Shareware CD

This section introduces the latest advancements in the User Interface for Que Shareware CDs, and describes their installation.

What's on the Ziff-Davis PC Benchmarks CD-ROM

Ziff-Davis's benchmark utilities, WinBench 97 and Winstone 97, are described here.

Where to go for help

A list of technical support in case everything doesn't go as planned.

System Requirements

You must have Windows 95/NT installed and operating, as well as a CD-ROM drive (even a single speed will do), to install and use the shareware on the Shareware CD. There is, however, a README.EXE program in the root directory of the CD-ROM that allows you to run the CD-ROM shareware catalog (or RomCat for short) from a DOS prompt. Installing the Benchmarking CD from Ziff-Davis requires that your system be fully operational in the Windows 95 or Windows NT 3.51 (or higher) operating system, and have a minimum of 8M RAM for WinBench on Windows 95, 16M for WinBench on Windows NT, 16M for Business Winstone, and 32M for High End Winstone. For more details, see tables E.3 and E.4.

▶ **See** "Understanding Windows 95 Setup Requirements," **p. 1180**

Introducing the *Platinum Edition Using Windows 95* Shareware CD

To bring order to the multitude of shareware available for Windows—while making it easy and convenient to install, run, and uninstall these programs right from the CD—the Que development staff selected Neon Publishing's (an Association of Shareware Professionals member) "RomCat" User Interface. Here are a few of the great things you'll like in this new interface:

- It uses Windows 95's new Autoplay feature—no more hunting the CD for an INSTALL.EXE or SETUP.EXE.

- The interface asks you where you'd like to place the few files it needs to run, and provides an Uninstall on the same screen—no rebooting required!

- Shareware is divided into categories so you don't have to hunt the 150 plus files for an icon editor (see fig. E.1). A search engine also allows a single or multiple category search of the description, file name, or file date.

- The CD includes both ZIP files and unarchived "ready-to-run" versions of each program.

- Selecting a program from a category displays a description of the program's purpose and lets you view the files to be installed. There's also an option to run the program right from the CD, install it, or copy the files to your hard drive.

■ Selected files display the size of the archive, the file date, and the DOS file name, so you can take files right off the CD with Explorer if you prefer.

■ All ZIP's have been CRC (Cyclic Redundancy Check) verified, and unarchived programs have been scanned for viruses.

FIG E.1
You can access a list of files in a category by just clicking it.

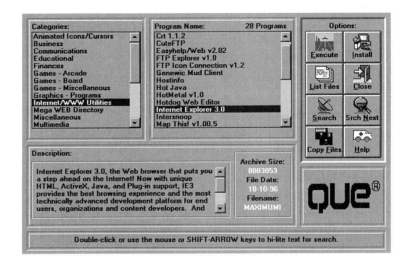

The following is a partial list of the shareware categories you will find on this CD:

Icons/Cursors	Business Software
Communications	Development Tools
Games	Graphics Programs
Internet/Web Utilities	Multimedia
Utilities	Shortcuts to Useful WWW Sites

Part
XI

App
E

Installation

If you have the Auto Insert Notification option selected (default) in your CD-ROM properties, all you have to do is pop the CD into your CD-ROM drive. If you have disabled this feature, follow these steps:

1. Open the Start menu and select Run from the pop-up menu.
2. Type *d:***\autorun** (where *d* is the CD-ROM drive) and press enter.

From here, you simply follow the instructions on-screen.

The Ziff-Davis PC Benchmarks CD-ROM

Anyone familiar with magazines like *PC Magazine*, *PC Week*, *Windows Sources*, or *Computer Shopper*, will be familiar with the Winstone and WinBench benchmark utilities from ZDBOp, the Ziff-Davis Benchmark Operation.

These utilities allow you to

■ Gauge how well your PC compares to systems from other manufacturers

■ Determine if your old video card, for example, is the "weak link" in your system when you are considering an upgrade

■ Confirm that your new system (and/or subsystems) is running at the advertised megahertz and compares well against other brands of similar configuration

■ Determine if that Registry tweak really helped more than hurt

About Winstone 97

The Winstone benchmark runs real applications through a series of scripted activities and times those activities to produce a performance score. Winstone 97 includes two categories of tests: Business Winstone, which runs eight popular applications like Microsoft Word and CorelDRAW, and High-End Winstone, which runs six demanding applications like Photoshop and Visual C++. Some consider Winstone to be a more realistic indicator than WinBench of how a particular machine operates in the test environment. Because Winstone actually loads real applications from the CD to your hard drive, runs a test script, and times its completion, the test process may be time-consuming and may use a lot of space on your hard drive during the test. Extensive documentation and help is available on the CD, as shown in table E.1.

About WinBench 97

WinBench 97 differs from Winstone in that it uses a combination of synthetic, inspection, and playback tests to rate PC subsystems. It doesn't run actual applications like Word or Excel, but simulates their behavior as profiled (or, in the case of the disk, graphics, and CD-ROM playback tests, actually logged) in the ZDBOp Research Center. These tests closely approximate real world applications so you can get a feel for how the applications specifically affect each of your subsystems. Extensive documentation and help is available on the CD, as shown in table E.1.

Table E.1   Additional ZD Benchmark Documentation

This document	Is located in the	And contains:
README.WRI	\ZDBENCH\WS97 or \ZDBENCH\WB97 directory on the CD-ROM.	The license agreement, important notes on the benchmark, and any late-breaking problems as of the benchmark's final release.
Understanding and Using the PC Benchmarks User Interface (UI.DOC)	\ZDBENCH\DOCS\UI directory on the CD-ROM.	Information you need to navigate the PC benchmarks' user interface. Also includes information common to all the benchmarks.
Understanding and Using Winstone 97 Version 1.0 (WS97REF.DOC)	\ZDBENCH\DOCS directory on the CD-ROM.	The Winstone 97-specific reference manual.
Understanding and Using WinBench 97 Version 1.0 (WB97REF.DOC)	\ZDBENCH\DOCS directory on the CD-ROM.	The WinBench 97-specific reference manual.

Table taken from the ZDBUI.DOC file found on the CD.

Installation

Both WinBench and Winstone are on the CD that accompanies this book. This CD uses the Windows Autoplay feature. Simply inserting the disc invokes the installation process and allows you to choose which benchmark to install.

If you have disabled this feature or use a version of Windows NT earlier than 4.0, follow these steps:

1. Open the Start menu and click Run.

2. Type *d:*\install (where *d* is the CD-ROM drive) and press Enter. Then, just follow the on-screen instructions.

> **N O T E**   WinBench requires 6M of free space on the PC's hard disk, an additional 58M, and the size of your RAM (for example, 8M), for temporary files the Disk WinMark 96 suite uses.

The following are the current minimum requirements, taken from the README files.

Winstone 97's minimum hardware and software requirements include:

- Microsoft Windows 95 or later or Windows NT 3.51 (Service Pack 4) or Windows NT 4.0 (build 1381) or later.
- An 80486 (or compatible) or higher processor.
- 16M of RAM to run Business Winstone 97 and 32M of RAM to run High-End Winstone 97.
- About 170M of free disk space for a full install. (To install Business Winstone 97 only requires about 60M of free space. To install High-End Winstone 97 only takes about 110MB of free disk space.) For working space during the tests, the hard drive also needs an additional 54M free disk space to run Business Winstone 97 or 110M free disk space to run High-End Winstone 97.
- A CD-ROM drive if you're planning to run the tests from the CD-ROM.
- For the Photoshop test, the display should have 256 or more colors (this color depth is a Photoshop requirement).
- A VGA resolution (640×480) or higher (a rotated monitor at 480×640 will not work) for the Business Winstone 97 tests; an 800×600 display to run the High-End Winstone 97 tests. (The documentation incorrectly states that a 1024×768 resolution is needed for the High-End tests.)

WinBench 97's minimum hardware and software requirements include:

- Microsoft Windows 95 or later or Windows NT 3.51 (Service Pack 4) or Windows NT 4.0 (build 1381) or later.
- An 80386 (or compatible) or higher processor.
- 8M of RAM, when used with Windows 95; 16 MB of RAM, when used with Windows NT. (WinBench 97 will run in less RAM, but it may produce invalid results due to paging activity.)
- 10M of free disk space for a minimal installation, 73M for a full install.
- 95M plus the size of RAM on the PC as additional free disk space for the Business Disk WinMark 97 tests. About 120M is needed for the High-End Disk WinMark tests.
- A CD-ROM drive if you're planning to run the CD-ROM or video tests.
- A VGA resolution (640×480) or higher graphics adapter.

- A 1024×768 or higher display for the High-End Graphics WinMark tests.
- Small fonts for all Graphics WinMark tests.
- A sound card (for the video tests).
- DirectX 2 or later (available from Microsoft's Web site: **http://www.microsoft.com**) if you want to run the DirectDraw inspection tests.
- ActiveMovie (available from Microsoft's Web site) if you want to run the MPEG Video tests.
- An Indeo 4.1 Video CODEC (available from Intel's Web site: **http://www.intel.com**) if you want to run the Indeo 4.1 Video tests.

Technical Support Numbers

For technical difficulties with the *Platinum Edition Using Windows 95* Shareware CD, contact:

> Neon Publishing Inc.
> 13750 McCormick Drive
> Tampa, FL 33626
> Voice: 813-854-5515
> Fax: 813-854-5516

N O T E For problems with a particular shareware application, please contact the shareware author directly. You can find this information in the README.TXT file included with the program.

For technical or support-related issues regarding the Ziff-Davis PC Benchmarks CD-ROM, go to the ZDBOp Web site at **http://www.zdbop.com** or send e-mail to **zdbopwebmaster@zd.com**.

For issues related to the content or quality of *Platinum Edition Using Windows 95* Shareware CD contact:

> Macmillan Technical Support
> 201 W. 103rd St.
> Indianapolis, IN 46290
> Voice: 317-581-3833
> Internet: **support@mcp.com**
> CompuServe: **GO QUEBOOKS**

Part
XI

App
E

Using the Windows 95 Service Pack

by Michael Desmond

When Microsoft Windows 95 hit store shelves on August 24, 1995, it was still a work in progress. Some promised features had yet to be delivered, while nagging bugs posed a concern for those looking to upgrade from another operating system. In addition, a lack of 32-bit drivers for hardware peripherals meant that many users could not take full advantage of Windows 95's new features.

Enter Windows 95 Service Pack 1. This collection of updates, bug fixes, and device drivers is essentially a slipstream upgrade to the Windows 95 operating system. In this appendix, you learn exactly what is included and why they were necessary. ■

Introducing the Service Pack

An overview of the Service Pack features and how to get and install the software.

New features for Windows 95

A description of the new capabilities that the Service Pack provides and how to take advantage of them.

Bug fixes large and small

A rundown of the various bugs that the Service Pack addresses.

Driver updates

A list of the hardware drivers available as part of the Service Pack.

Introducing the Service Pack

Operating system upgrades can be a tricky business. Installing a new version of an operating system version takes time and effort, and can lead to incompatibilities with existing applications. Microsoft's solution—release occasional updates for its Windows products that address problems and add features and drivers to the original package. The Windows 95 Service Pack consists of a series of files available online from Microsoft's Web site, as well as from other places.

There are actually two versions of the Service Pack, one for individual users and one for information services professionals. Most Windows 95 users will only need the version for individual users; the ISP version adds network specific tools and capabilities to the base set provided in the Individual Users Service Pack.

This section helps you understand if you need the service pack and how to get it.

What is Included in the Service Pack?

While there are two versions of the Service Pack, the vast majority of users will find what they need with the Service Pack for individual users. This Service Pack includes a wide variety of files which address three major areas:

- *Bug fixes*. Addresses problems with OLE, network file management, and passwords.
- *New features*. Adds Microsoft's Internet Explorer as well as infrared communications and other capabilities.
- *Driver updates*. Adds scores of drivers for hardware peripherals.

Who Needs the Service Pack?

Not everyoneneeds the Service Pack. Many systems sold in 1996 come with an updated version of the Windows 95 operating system that includes all the capabilities provided by the Service Pack. In addition, some Microsoft applications, such as the Office suite and its component programs, install many of the Service Pack's features.

One way to tell if you have an updated version of Windows 95 is by checking the version number. To do this, right-click the My Computer icon and select Properties from the context menu. The version number appears on the General page of the Systems Properties sheet (see fig. F.1). If the entry says 4.00.950a or 4.00.950b, your system is already outfitted with the Service Pack updates and you don't need to download the software.

FIG. F.1

Once the system has rebooted, the updates to Windows 95 will take effect.

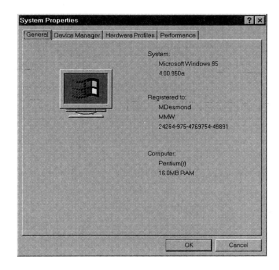

Even if you have the updated Windows 95 version, you may still want some of the Service Pack's features. For example, Microsoft's recently-upgraded Internet Explorer 3.0 Web browser is available from the Service Pack, as are driver updates.

Getting the Service Pack

TheService Pack is a loose collection of files and applications that can be acquired from a variety of sources:

- Download from Microsoft's Web site
- Download from CompuServe information service
- Install from disks ordered from Microsoft

Downloading the Service Pack from Microsoft's Web Site   This is the most popular—and convenient—way to get the Service Pack. To download the various Service Pack elements from Microsoft's Web site, do the following:

1. First, create an empty directory on your hard drive to contain the incoming files.

2. Launch your Web browser and in the address line enter the URL **http:// www.microsoft.com/windows/software/servpak1/sphome.htm**.

3. At the Service Pack Web page, click the Individual Users link near the bottom of the page.

4. Click the link called Windows 95 Service Pack 1 Update to download the 1.2M Service Pack file.

Part

XI

App

F

5. Once you have finished downloading the update file, download the Internet Explorer 3.0 Web browser. Click the link called Microsoft Internet Explorer.

N O T E   At the time the Service Pack was released, it included the Internet Explorer 2.0 Web browser. Microsoft released Internet Explorer 3.0 in May 1996 with a number of important improvements, and the link on the Service Pack Web page now leads you to the download page for Internet Explorer 3.0. If you downloaded the Service Pack some time ago, and are still using Internet Explorer 2.0, you should consider upgrading to the new Web browser. Installing and using Internet Explorer 3.0 is discussed in detail in Appendix G. ■

6. At the page that appears, click the Download Software icon.

7. In the drop-down list box, select IE 3.0 for Windows 95 and click Next. IE 3.0 downloads to the directory you identify.

8. To download driver updates, click Back on your browser until you return to the URL **http://www.microsoft.com/windows/software/servpak1/endusers.htm**. Click the link called Windows 95 Driver File Library, which takes you to the URL **http://www.microsoft.com/windows/software/drivers/drivers.htm**.

9. Click the link that matches the type of driver you wish to download. At the next page, click the link that corresponds to the driver you want, and download it to an empty directory (see fig. F.2).

FIG. F.2
A simple click brings the latest drivers to your hard disk. Be sure to read the instructions that appear on the right side of the page.

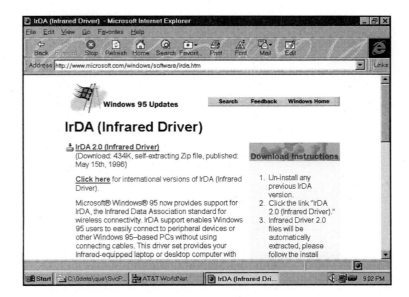

N O T E You can obtain drivers from several other sources. Microsoft's FTP site at **ftp://
ftp.microsoft.com**, SOFTLIB/MSFILES maintains these drivers, or you can also call the
Microsoft Download Service at (206) 936-6735. You can also download drivers from
CompuServe by typing the GO word **MSL**.

Downloading from CompuServe   If you have the CompuServe Information Service, you
can retrieve the Service Pack files from the Microsoft forum. To do this, do the following:

1. Log onto CompuServe.
2. Type **GO MSL** in the Go word dialog box.
3. Double-click the Access the Software Library item.
4. Double-click the File Name item. In the dialog box that appears, type **SETUP.EXE**
   and click OK.
5. Double-click Display Selected Titles.
6. In the dialog box that appears, click Retrieve to begin the download. You can also
   choose to click Retrieve Later to mark the file for download at a later time.

Installing from Disk or CD-ROM   You can also order the Service Pack update directly
from Microsoft. While the disks are free, you will have to pay for shipping and handling.

Installing the Various Service Pack Components

The various components that make up the Service Pack must be installed separately. This
section guides you through the installation for each of the components.

Installing the Service Pack Update Module   With the Service Pack update file called
setup.exe downloaded to an empty directory, installing the software is simple. Do the
following:

1. Close any non-essential applications and, if you use Microsoft Plus!, suspend the
   System Agent by right clicking its icon in the system tray and clicking Suspend
   System Agent.
2. Double-click the setup icon. A dialog box appears, announcing that this will install
   the Update. Click Yes to continue (see fig. F.3).

FIG. F.3
The entire Service Pack
Update is installed from a
single program.

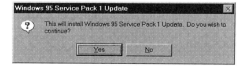

Part

XI

App

F

3. Review the license agreement and click Yes to continue with the installation. A series of dialog boxes tracks updates to your system (see fig. F.4).

FIG. F.4
The OLE32 file update is among the most critical in the Service Pack.

4. When the setup program has finished, you are prompted to restart your computer.

5. After your computer has restarted, deselect the Suspend System Agent menu item by right-clicking the Microsoft Plus! System Agent.

 TIP   To see if the Update installed successfully, click the My Computer icon with the right mouse button. The General page of the Systems Properties sheet will report that Windows is version 4.00.950a.

CAUTION

If you cancel the setup program, your computer may erroneously report a successful installation anyway. The update is not properly installed; you must run the program again to ensure correct configuration.

 TIP   You can remove the Service Pack update using the Windows 95 uninstall utility. From the Control Panel, double-click the Add/Remove Programs icon, and select Windows 95 Service Pack 1 from the list. Click the Add/Remove button to begin uninstalling the Service Pack update (see fig. F.5).

FIG. F.5
Windows 95 gives you a chance to back out before you uninstall the Service Pack. Be sure to keep your original Windows 95 CD-ROM or floppy disks on hand.

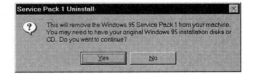

Installing Drivers from the Driver Library The Service Pack comes with nearly 100 drivers, though most users will probably need only two or three at most. To install a new driver, do the following:

> **CAUTION**
>
> Do not attempt to install or use Windows 95 drivers under Windows 3.1. They may be unstable, and some will not work at all.

1. Go to the empty directory containing the file you downloaded and double-click the assist file to extract the installation files.

2. Right-click the My Computer icon on the Windows 95 desktop and select Properties from the context menu.

3. Select the Device Manager tab and double-click the type of hardware you are modifying. Then select the device you wish to update (see fig. F.6).

FIG. F.6
Using the Device Manager, we are about to change the driver controlling a Diamond Stealth 64 Video VRAM graphics card.

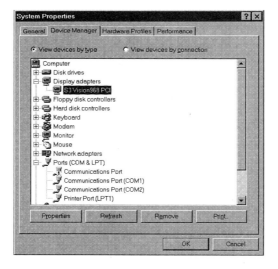

4. Select the Driver tab and click the Change Driver button (see fig. F.7).

5. Click the Have Disk button and navigate to the directory in which you placed the new driver.

6. When the installation is done, you must restart Windows.

FIG. F.7
Select the new driver you
downloaded from the
Microsoft Driver Library.

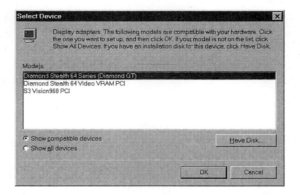

 You should take advantage of new drivers wherever you can. The ones included in the service
pack are faster and more robust than the older drivers they replace. Better yet, you should check
the Web pages of your peripheral vendors for the latest driver updates.

Understanding the Bug Fixes in the Service Pack

At the heart of the Windows 95 Service Pack are a series of updates contained within the
SETUP.EXE file. These updates address bugs in the shipping version of the operating
system, and also enhance some features. The following items are contained within the
SETUP.EXE file:

- *OLE32 Update.* Fixes a serious bug in the file management system. Data deleted in
  the Windows 95 versions of Microsoft Word, Excel, and PowerPoint is not actually
  removed from the document files, and can remain visible to non-Office applications.

- *Microsoft Windows 95 Shell Update.* Fixes a bug that can result in a lost file when a
  file is copied onto itself via two views of the same network resource. Data could also
  be lost when a drive is created with the SUBST command. Also adds the capability
  to access Netware Directory Services printers from the Add Printer wizard.

- *Windows 95 Common Dialog Update for Windows 3.1 Legacy Printer Drivers.* Repairs
  a bug with Windows 95 and Windows 3.1 printer drivers that can cause applications
  to fail.

- *VServer Update.* This update corrects problems with File and Printer Sharing for
  Microsoft Networks in conjunction with Samba's SMBCLIENT.

- *NWServer Update.* Prevents unauthorized access to network data through File and
  Printer Sharing for NetWare Networks when Remote Administration is enabled.

- *Vredir Update.* Fix for Windows 95 and Samba UNIX servers. This update reconciles the valid use of * and / in UNIX file names with the fact that Windows treats those as wildcard characters.

- *Windows 95 Password List Update.* Bolsters Windows security with an enhanced encryption scheme protecting stored passwords.

N O T E Microsoft posted the password encryption update after an algorithm designed to defeat the Windows 95's password scheme was posted on the Internet.

- *Microsoft Plus! Update.* Fixes a small error in floating point calculations caused by the Microsoft Plus! System Agent tool.

- *Printer Port (Lpt.vxd) Update.* This update adds support for Enhanced Communications Parallel (ECP) port and certain printers.

Although the OLE32 update adds no new functionality to Windows 95, it is one of the most important and overdue parts of the service pack. A bug in the way Microsoft Office applications (Word, PowerPoint, and Excel) store data to the hard disk means that much of the text you delete from a given file does not get erased from the document and is actually visible under the right conditions. It isn't apparent to the average user because a document created with Word 7, for instance, will display text properly on any other copy of Word 7. The same document, however, viewed with a different program can reveal the text that was supposed to have been deleted. This can be both an embarrassment and a potential security risk. This update to the OLE32 component of Windows prevents the erroneous display of deleted data from occurring.

More recently, Microsoft released a second OLE32 fix, which you can find at **http://www.microsoft.com/windows/software/oleupd.htm**. This update addresses problems with 16-bit applications that use Microsoft's ODBC database access technology, as well as problems with lost links on files stored on network drives.

Part
XI

App
F

CAUTION

This update only protects documents created or saved after the service pack is installed. Documents created before the fix will continue to be vulnerable to this display of "deleted" data even on a computer with the OLE32 update. To ensure your "deleted" data is secure, load and save the file again after installing this update.

N O T E This problem can affect you even if you are using Word 6, Excel 5, or PowerPoint 4 under Windows 3.1. Microsoft has fixed this behavior with the "C" maintenance update. Check About in the Help menu of these programs to see if you have an affected version.

Exploring the Service Pack's New Features for Windows 95

The Service Pack is more than a bunch of bug fixes. This free software includes a number of drivers and applications that bring exciting new capabilities to the Windows 95 operating system. The major components are:

- Internet Explorer 3.0 Web browser application
- Infrared communication drivers
- ISDN telephone connectivity
- CompuServe Mail for Microsoft Exchange
- Unimodem drivers for modems

This section helps you work with the new capabilities that the Service Pack provides for Windows 95.

Introducing Infrared Communications to Windows 95

The Service Pack adds infrared communications to Windows 95's bag of tricks, adding support for industry standard infrared communications known as IrDA. IrDA, which stands for Infrared Data Association, lets compatible hardware communicate without traditional cables, using infrared (IR) signals to send data across modest distances. Most portable computers now come with IrDa ports, as do some desktop PCs and laser printers. Existing PCs can add infrared capability by plugging an IrDA device into a serial port or expansion slot. The IrDA driver allows Windows 95 to operate infrared communication devices.

▶ **See** "Using Infrared to Communicate with Devices," **p. 210**

ON THE WEB

To learn more about IrDA, visit the home page of the Infrared Data Association, the organization that established the standard. They are located at

http://www.irda.org/

Installing IrDA   To install the IrDA driver, perform the following steps.

1. Before installing the IrDA driver, you must remove any older versions already installed on your computer. If you have one already installed, open the Control Panel and double-click the Add/Remove Programs icon. In the Install/Uninstall page, select the Infrared Support for Windows 95 entry in the scroll down box and click the Add/Remove button. Restart your computer.

N O T E You cannot install the IrDA driver on a computer that is using a "shared" version of
Windows 95 on a network.

2. Go to the Driver Library section of the Service Pack home page, and download the
IrDA (Infrared Driver) file using your Web browser. Save the file in an empty
directory.

3. Extract IrDA by double-clicking the w95ir icon.

4. Double-click the setup icon.

5. The first Wizard page introduces you to the installation process (see fig. F.8). After
clicking Next, the wizard builds a database of the IrDA devices you can choose
from, and presents you with a list. You can select either an internal IrDA device,
such as found in many laptops, or a third-party IrDA device that you've added to
your system (see fig. F.9).

FIG. F.8

The wizard will create
"virtual" ports through
which your IrDA device
will communicate with
the outside world.

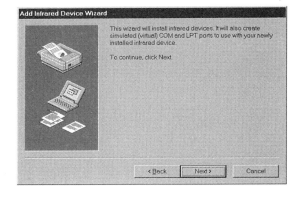

FIG. F.9

Select the appropriate driver.
Unless you purchased a
plug-in IR device, you'll
probably want to select
the Built-in device.

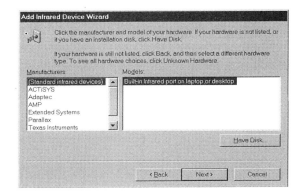

Part

XI

App

F

6. On the next page, select the appropriate COM port. If you don't know which one to
choose, you can go back later and try again.

TROUBLESHOOTING

I've installed the IrDA drivers and the device, but now I can't access my modem or the IrDA port. What's happening? Windows 95 uses the same COM ports used by modems to handle IR devices. Because of this, it's common to experience conflicts between the two peripherals. To check your modem settings, double-click the Modems icon in the Windows 95 Control Panel, and select the Diagnostics tab in the Modems Properties dialog box (see fig. F.10). If both the IR device and modem are using the same COM port, try reassigning the port address for the IR device.

FIG. F.10
Check which COM ports are free for your IR device to use by going to the Modems Properties box in the Windows 95 Control Panel.

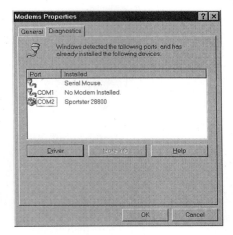

7. Windows must use a simulated LPT and COM port with your IrDA device. You can choose to use the defaults or change them. If you choose to reject the defaults, the next page lets you choose from the available simulated ports (see fig. F.11).

FIG. F.11
This page lets you change the virtual port for the IrDA driver.

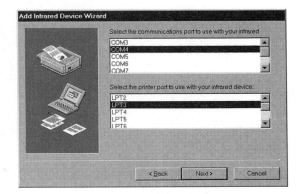

The installation is complete. You can now test your infrared device by starting the Control Panel from the Start menu and double-clicking the new Infrared icon. This launches the Infrared Monitor, a properties sheet with four tabs. It controls the way your IR device interacts with other IR devices.

 T I P A fast way to get to the Infrared Monitor is by clicking the IR icon in the system tray.

There are four tabs on the Infrared Monitor. They are:

- *Status.* This page reports the status of the IrDA link to other IR devices. It indicates what devices are within communications range (about six feet) and how efficiently they are exchanging data.

- *Options.* This page contains important options for controlling your IR device (see fig. F.12). If you move the COM port to which your IrDA device is attached, you need to configure that here. You can also designate how often your computer will poll the device for connection status and whether to limit the IR connection speed, particularly if you encounter problems transferring data at the highest rate.

FIG. F.12
Modify the way your IR device performs on this page. You can disable Plug and Play software from here, for instance, which loads appropriate drivers when an IR device comes within range.

Part
XI

App
F

- *Preferences.* This page lets you disable trouble sounds (such as when connection with a device has been interrupted), turn the system tray icon off, and choose whether to automatically open the Infrared Monitor when a problem occurs.

- *Identification.* This page displays the name of the computer. You need to know this information when connecting two computers together.

Using IrDA   In general, IrDA devices must be more than about six inches away from each other but less than six feet. IrDA can be used to print to an IrDA-capable printer or transfer data between computers with HyperTerminal, Direct Cable Connection, or any other application that supports IrDA.

There are a variety of problems that could cause IrDA to fail to work properly:

- Both devices must be IrDA-compliant. The Apple Newton MessagePad, for instance, has an IR port but isn't currently IrDA-compliant.

- Devices may be too close or too far apart, or aren't pointing toward each other accurately enough. Experiment with the connection by moving the devices around and changing their view angles. Some devices need to be fairly close to initiate communication.

- If one of the devices is battery operated, the batteries may be too weak to operate properly.

- The transmission speed may be too great. If you are having problems, reduce the connection speed to 9600 baud or less on the Options page of the Infrared Monitor.

Getting ISDN

ISDN, or *Integrated Services Digital Network*, is the digital counterpart to standard analog telephone service. In its most basic form, ISDN permits data rates up to 128Kbps, more than four times that of 28.8Kbps modems. While it is more expensive than standard analog phone service, ISDN has become more affordable and is widely available in all but rural locations.

The ISDN portion of the Service Pack requires that you have a lot of things in place in order to provide a benefit. First, you need ISDN lines installed in your home or office. Second, you need an ISDN adapter—simply called an ISDN modem—to work with the digital line. Finally, the services or networks you are calling into must be able to handle fast digital transactions, whether using ISDN or faster connections.

The ISDN Accelerator Pack   The Service Pack gives Windows 95 the capability to work with ISDN peripherals, allowing high-speed access to the Web and remote networks. The ISDN Accelerator Pack is composed of two parts:

- *ISDN Accelerator Pack*. This is the ISDN driver that permits Windows 95 to provide dial-up access to an ISDN line.

- *ISDN Modem driver*. Download the appropriate driver for your ISDN modem, or use the one that the manufacturer provided.

To install the ISDN Accelerator Pack, perform the following steps:

1. Download the ISDN Accelerator Pack file using your Web browser, saving the file to an empty directory.

ON THE WEB

To get the ISDN Accelerator Pack, visit Microsoft's page at

http://www.microsoft.com/software/isdn.htm

2. Double-click the msisdn11.exe icon. Installation is automatic.

3. If necessary, download the appropriate modem driver and install it in accordance with the manufacturer's directions.

ISDN Modem and Software   ISDN modems, like their analog cousins, come in both internal and external varieties. External modems are limited by the serial port's maximum transfer rate, which at 115Kbps is less than the top ISDN rate.

You also need the software to drive the modem and communicate with your service provider. That's where the service pack comes in; The ISDN Accelerator Pack adds ISDN capability to Windows 95. Notice that you must have both Microsoft's ISDN Accelerator Pack (the Windows 95 driver) and software specific to the ISDN modem you own.

N O T E   Drivers for ISDN hardware should be included in the box. Updated versions may be available online, either from Microsoft's Web site, or from the manufacturer's Web site or BBS. ▓

TROUBLESHOOTING

I have an ISDN modem that I use to access the Internet. But I only seem to be getting 64Kbps throughput, even though everything is working properly. The problem may not be your setup. Many Internet Service Providers and other online services provide only 64Kbps ISDN access, which employs only one channel of the ISDN line. Call you service provider and ask specifically if they provide bonded ISDN service, which means that both channels can be tied together for 128Kbps of data throughput.

Part

XI

App

F

CompuServe Mail for Microsoft Exchange

One advantage of Microsoft Exchange is that it can act as a universal inbox, handling e-mail over a wide variety of services. However, the lack of support for third-party mail providers limits its usefulness. The Service Pack addresses this with a driver called

CompuServe Mail for Microsoft Exchange that lets CompuServe members use Exchange to handle e-mail to and from that information service.

The driver can be found from the Driver Library page by clicking the Other link. The software lets you send and receive CompuServe mail directly from Exchange.

To install CompuServe Mail, perform the following steps:

1. Download the CompuServe Mail for Microsoft Exchange file using your Web browser, and save the file to an empty directory.

2. Extract CompuServe Mail by double-clicking the CIS4EXCH.EXE icon.

3. Double-click the setup icon. The program installs necessary files, then asks if you want to make CompuServe Mail a part of your default profile. Click OK.

4. The Inbox Setup Wizard asks for the common directory in which you store CompuServe scripts and the address book. This is the directory that WinCim uses; it is typically C:\Cserve, unless you change WinCim's default installation path (see fig. F.13).

FIG. F.13
Exchange needs to know where you keep your CompuServe files in order to incorporate e-mail from the service. Use the Browse button to specify the top CompuServe directory (not a subdirectory like C:\Cserve\WinCim).

5. As you can see in figure F.14, the next wizard step requires you to input your CompuServe personal data, including local access number and password.

 T I P If you've lost or forgotten your password since the last time you installed WinCim, call CompuServe's customer support center at 1-800-848-8990 for a new password.

6. The next page includes some setup options (see fig. F.15). Create Session Activity generates a log file in the form of a mail message every time you use CompuServe Mail within Exchange. Delete Retrieved Messages removes mail from CompuServe

after it is downloaded into Exchange. Accept Postage Due Messages automatically permits Exchange to get mail that you must pay a fee for, such as when the sender splits charges with you.

FIG. F.14

Enter your CompuServe access information and click Next.

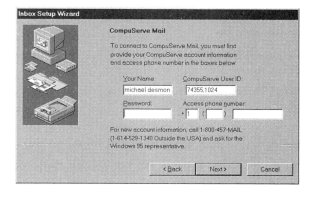

FIG. F.15

You'll probably want to delete messages as they are received and accept all mail, though the Session Log feature can tend to crowd your inbox.

7. If you want Exchange to automatically start when you turn on your computer, select the button for Add inbox to startup group.

Installation is complete. Start Microsoft Exchange, and you'll find CompuServe Mail installed as a service along with Internet Mail, Microsoft Fax, and any other services you might typically use.

Using CompuServe Mail CompuServe Mail is an offline process. This means that there are three steps necessary to send messages:

1. Create your message.
2. Send it to the outbox.

Part

XI

App

F

3. Choose Tools, Deliver Now Using CompuServe Mail. This actually connects you to CompuServe and starts the clock for your connect time charges as your mail is delivered to the recipient.

You can check for new CompuServe mail by selecting Deliver Now Using CompuServe Mail. New messages are created in the same way as other Exchange messages, and your Exchange address book will automatically include the contents of your CompuServe phone book if you specified the correct directory during setup.

Configuring CompuServe Mail   There are a few options for fine-tuning the way CompuServe Mail operates. Select Tools, Services. Find the entry for CompuServe Mail and select the Properties button. The properties sheet has four tabs:

- *General.* This page includes facilities for changing the user ID and password.
- *Connection.* Here you can change the access number, network connection (CompuServe, Tymnet, and so on), and modem settings, if more than one is installed.
- *Default Send Options.* Here you can specify when outgoing messages are sent and when received messages get deleted from the in box. The Split Charges feature divides the cost of message delivery between sender and receiver.
- *Advanced.* The Advanced page offers housekeeping features like event logging for tracking operations, deletion of messages from the CompuServe network after downloading, and automatic acceptance of postage surcharges.

In addition, the Advanced page lets you configure automatic mail retrieval from the Schedule Connect Times button. The following options are available:

- Never (all boxes de-selected). Mail will only be retrieved when you manually select Send Now Using CompuServe Mail from the Tools menu.
- At Startup of Microsoft Exchange.
- At specific intervals, such as every two hours. Select Every and fill in the desired hours and minutes. Exchange must be running for CompuServe Mail to execute this option.
- At a regularly scheduled time. Select Scheduled and fill in the time of day. Again, Exchange must be running at the designated time for your mail to get checked.

N O T E   You can set CompuServe Mail to operate in multiple modes at once. You can, for instance, check your mail at startup and every 90 minutes after that. ■

Remote Mail   Microsoft Exchange's remote mail program is designed for the user who may want to access his mail services via a portable computer while still leaving the messages intact for later retrieval on the desktop system. Remote Mail has these major capabilities:

- Delete mail without reading the message, based on the subject line alone.
- Retrieve the message, deleting it from the mail server just like ordinary mail.
- Download a copy of the message, leaving the original on the server. The message can later be retrieved by Exchange from the desktop PC at home or work.

To use Remote Mail, choose Tools, Remote Mail. You may have several mail service options available depending on your configuration; select CompuServe Mail. A new window appears. If you've never used Remote Mail, it will be empty. This is where Exchange displays information about your messages, like the sender, subject line, and size. From the Tools menu, there are three ways to initiate action in remote mail:

- *Connect.* This option establishes contact with CompuServe, but takes no action on your mail messages.
- *Connect and Update Headers.* Remote mail connects to CompuServe and checks for new messages. If there are any, it displays their subject lines in the Remote Mail window.
- *Connect and Transfer Mail.* Remote mail connects to CompuServe and sends mail waiting in the outbox, if any. If any mail has been marked for action, it acts accordingly.

If you choose to Connect to CompuServe, the last two Tool menu items change to Update Headers and Transfer Mail, respectively.

Once you have chosen to Update Headers, you may then mark your messages for action. The three actions, found in the Edit menu, are:

- *Mark to Retrieve.* This action downloads a message just like Exchange would ordinarily—deleting it from CompuServe.
- *Mark to Retrieve a Copy.* This action retains the original message on CompuServe so you may later download it into Exchange on a different computer.
- *Mark to Delete.* This deletes the message from CompuServe without ever displaying the contents.

Part

XI

App

F

T I P You can mark messages for action with the right mouse button's context menu.

Once you have marked the message headers for action, select Transfer Mail from the Tools menu. Your action will be executed.

You can tell the action-pending status of a message by its symbol at the left side of the window. The first message is set for retrieval. The second will be deleted without downloading from CompuServe and a copy of the last message will be retrieved.

> **CAUTION**
>
> Unlike Exchange, which operates offline from CompuServe, Remote Mail stays online from the first moment you select a Connect option from the Tools menu until you Disconnect or close Remote Mail. Keep this in mind as you use Remote Mail from a potentially expensive telephone connection.

Unimodem V

Unimodem is a general purpose telephony device that monitors the phone line and routes calls to the appropriate application, such as voice mail, fax, and data programs. Unimodem integrates these functions into a single telephony suite. This version of Unimodem supports such features as Caller ID, Call Forwarding, Distinctive Ringing, and voice communication with speakerphones.

To install the Unimodem driver, perform the following steps:

1. Download the Unimodem file using your Web browser, saving the file to an empty directory.
2. Extract Unimodem by double-clicking the UNIMODV.INF icon.
3. Right-click the UNIMODV.INF icon and select Install.
4. There is no wizard for this installation. UNIMOD.INF automatically installs the necessary files and then asks to reboot the computer. Click Yes.
5. After your computer restarts, right-click the My Computer icon, select Properties and click the System tab.
6. Click the Device Manager tab and find your current modem in the list (see fig. F.16). Double-click the modem and click the Remove button.
7. Next, close the Properties sheet and open the Control Panel. Double-click the Modems icon.
8. Figure F.17 shows the Modem Properties sheet. Click Add. The Install New Modem Wizard appears. Find your modem manually or let Windows find it automatically.
9. After Windows locates your modem, the wizard will copy the remaining files to your hard disk.

FIG. F.16
In order to activate Unimodem's new capabilities, you must first remove the driver for the installed modem.

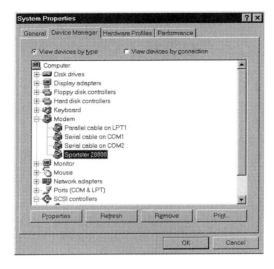

FIG. F.17
Follow the instructions after you click Add to install your modem driver again.

> **TIP** If you have a Plug and Play modem, you simply need to click Refresh after step 6—you don't need to install a modem from the Control Panel.

The Unimodem software has been successfully installed. Unimodem supports a number of advanced features like Distinctive Ringing and Call Forwarding; if your phone line has these features, you can configure your modem to take advantage of them. Select Control Panel from the Start menu and double-click Modems. Click Properties (see fig. F.18). You should have tabs for Distinctive Ring and Forwarding. Enable the appropriate features and configure your modem.

FIG. F.18
Unimodem supports a variety of advanced telephony features. This property sheet allows you to configure settings like Distinctive Ringing and Call Forwarding.

Using the Unimodem Operator

Unimodem comes with its own call manager. To run it, choose Accessories from the Start Menu and select Operator. An icon shaped like a telephone appears in the System Tray.

> **N O T E**   The Unimodem driver currently requires a Windows 95 voice messaging program to be running in order for it to function at all. For that reason, many users cannot take advantage of Operator until it is upgraded or bundled with additional software. ■

Operator will monitor incoming calls and route them to the appropriate application, be it voice, data, or fax. You can configure Operator by double-clicking the System Tray icon. A dialog box appears which lets you suspend the Operator, choose whether to play an introductory telephone greeting, or route the call directly to the applicable application (see fig. F.19). You can also access Operator's Properties sheet. From there, you can:

- Determine the Number of Rings that Operator delays before answering.
- Set Call Routing Priorities. If you select this button, a wizard lets you change the relative order of applications to which Operator sends calls. If a program isn't active when a call comes in, Operator skips it and moves on to the next.
- Initial Greeting. Operator can use any one of several prerecorded messages, or you can record your own. A wizard lets you choose between the prerecorded messages (use Browse to select a greeting you recorded yourself), or, if you select Record a New Greeting, you can make a new one (see fig. F.20).

FIG. F.19
Operator has the features of a consolidated call center, controlled from the system tray.

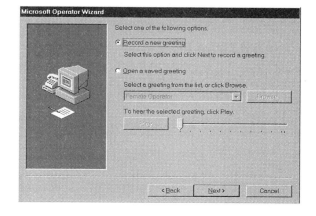

FIG. F.20
Operator comes with two default greetings—a male and female voice—or you can create your own.

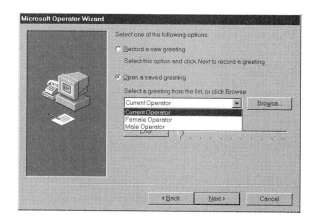

■ Failed Call Message. If the caller selects a program, such as fax, that isn't running, Operator plays a warning message to the caller. This button launches a wizard much like the one for Initial Greeting that allows you to choose the message or create a new one.

Part

XI

App

F

Exploring System Administrator's Tools and Updates

If your goal is to maintain Windows 95 and install the service pack on a network or a group of computers, you can use more assistance than Microsoft provides individuals with the service pack.

An excellent tool that Microsoft provides is the Windows 95 Service Pack 1 Administrator's Guide. This file makes three resources available:

■ *The Windows 95 Support Assistant.* As you can see in figure F.21, this standard Windows 95 help file provides answers to common questions, setup and installation tips, networking solutions, and more.

FIG. F.21

The Support Assistant is a comprehensive database of technical advice and solutions, stored in a common help file.

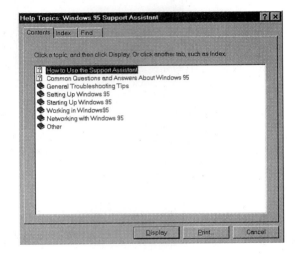

■ *The Windows 95 Application Compatibility List.* This help file provides an alphabetical directory of about 2,500 programs with compatibility notes. It isn't searchable, but you can skip directly to specific letters of the alphabet.

■ *The Windows 95 Hardware Compatibility List.* This help file is a searchable guide to thousands of hardware products. Products are divided into logical categories like Systems, Display, Audio, and Storage. They are further divided into products that bear the Windows 95 logo, and those that do not but are compatible nonetheless.

To install the Guide, perform the following steps:

1. Download the Windows 95 Service Pack 1 Administrator's Guide file using your Web browser, saving the file to an empty directory.

2. Extract the installation files by double-clicking the assist icon.

3. Double-click the setup icon.

4. The installation program allows you to selectively install all three help files or just the ones you want (see fig. F.22).

FIG. F.22
The hardware compatibility list is huge—you probably don't need to install it if you are an individual user.

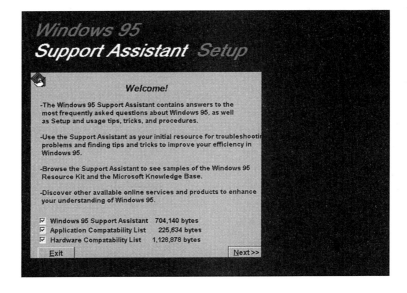

N O T E The Administrator's Guide does not include any new information for the Service Pack; it only discusses the original release of Windows 95. ▨

The ISP Service Pack

The Service Pack for Information System Professionals is available in the form of 14 disks, each one downloaded separately from **http://www.microsoft.com**. If you do not want to retrieve the entire service pack, Microsoft has also made the individual components available elsewhere on the same page. The components are divided into several major categories:

- *Tools.* This set of updates include the Administrator's Guide, installation accessories like the Batch Setup Version 2.0 and INF Generator. The Tools also include the Driver Library.

- *New Components.* This section features Microsoft Explorer, some of the drivers also found in the library, and some enhancements to Network and Connectivity (client support for NetWare Directory Service, an update to Exchange which provides access to Microsoft Mail shared folders, and scripts for automated access to online services).

- *Service Pack Update.* Microsoft includes a folder which updates the distribution point for Windows 95 installations across a network. This program modifies the

Part
XI

App
F

distribution point so future Windows 95 installations automatically incorporate the Service Pack.

■ *Prompted & Silent Update.* These two files allow users who have Windows 95 installed on their own hard disk to update their systems.

Installing the Service Pack to a Network   If you are responsible for maintaining Windows in a network environment, you can ensure each user gets the benefit of the updated Windows 95.

■ *New Windows 95 installations.* Microsoft has included a program which updates Windows 95 network distribution points, ideal for those networks that let users install Windows from a location on the server. Install the SP1NSF.EXE file found in the Folder to update a Windows 95 network distribution point. All subsequent installations from this installation site will yield Windows 95 configurations with the update already installed.

■ *Updating Windows 95 on individual hard disks.* If your users maintain Windows 95 on their own hard disks rather than the server, there are two ways to install the update—the Prompted Update (SETUP.EXE) queries users if they want the update installed and the Silent Update (SP1UPD.EXE) performs the installation without involving the user.

T I P   An easy way to give users access to the service pack update is by attaching a shortcut to the update file in a mail message.

■ *Updating Windows 95 from a server.* If your users run Windows 95 from a common server, you can update that sharepoint in the much same way as if you were updating a distribution point with SP1NSF.EXE.

CAUTION

Advise users not to install the Service Pack Updates by running the files designed for individual hard disks (SETUP.EXE or SP1UPD.EXE). This will cause NET.EXE to be renamed to NETPWL.EXE, and Windows 95 will no longer run.

In addition, you should ensure all network users are logged off before attempting to modify the Windows 95 sharepoint. This ensures that no Windows files will be in use during the update, preventing their modification.

Microsoft Exchange Update   This update provides the capability to access shared folders from Microsoft Mail using Microsoft Exchange. To install this capability, perform the following steps:

1. Download the Microsoft Exchange file using your Web browser, saving the file to an empty directory.

2. Run the installation program by double-clicking the exchupd icon.

3. From the Start Menu, open the <u>C</u>ontrol Panel in <u>S</u>ettings. Open the Mail and Fax icon.

4. If Microsoft Mail is currently installed, select it and click Remove. ·

5. Click Add and select Microsoft Mail (see fig. F.23).

FIG. F.23
You can access Microsoft
Mail from Exchange by
adding that service to
your default profile.

6. The Properties sheet opens automatically. On the Connection page, enter the path to the post office. Also, select the type of connection you use (LAN or Dial-Up).

7. Switch to the Logon tab and enter your Microsoft Mail user name and password.

   The next time you start Microsoft Exchange, Microsoft Mail will be updated to allow access to shared folders.

 Your Microsoft Mail personal data may be different from the user name and password you use with other mail services.

8. Close both the properties sheet and the Add Service dialog box with the OK button.

Scripting and SLIP Support for Dial-Up Networking Tools   This utility adds two important new capabilities to Windows:

■ Dial-up support for SLIP connections

■ The capability to automatically run scripts from a dial-up session to automate log-on and online activities

Using the scripting tool, you can automate the process of entering name and password data, execute activities on an online service (such as retrieving messages) without user intervention, and log-off when done.

Part

XI

App

F

To install the Scripting and SLIP tool, perform the following steps:

1. Download the file using your Web browser, saving the file to an empty directory.
2. Double-click the script icon. Installation is automatic.

Once you have finished installing it, the Dial-Up Scripting Tool can be found in Accessories from the Start Menu. The dialog box displays all of the existing dial-up session on the left, which you can modify using the Properties button.

To use the program, follow these steps:

1. Select the dial-up session to which you want to attach a script from the list on the left.
2. Click Browse. A file requester will display all of the existing scripts (several sample scripts are already included). Choose one (see fig. F.24).

FIG. F.24

Attach an existing script to your dial-up session and Apply to begin using it.

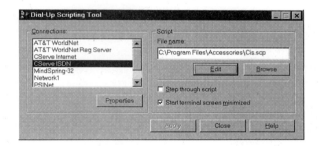

3. Modify an existing script by selecting the Edit button, which lets you work on the selected script in Notepad.
4. If you want to troubleshoot a script as it executes during a dial-up session, check the box for Step through script.

N O T E A guide to the scripting language can be found in your hard disk's Programs/ Accessories directory. It is called SCRIPT.DOC. ▨

Word Viewer for Windows 95 An updated version of the Microsoft Word viewer is included in the Service Pack. This tool displays and prints all versions of Word for Windows and Word for Macintosh on any system, even if no copy of Word is actually installed (see fig. F.25).

This new version of Word Viewer supports hyperlinked text embedded in Word documents. If you load a suitable file, Word Viewer displays the hypertext links much like a Web browser and follows the links to other locations in the document.

FIG. F.25
Word Viewer includes
many of the display options
available in Microsoft Word,
so even users without Word
can view a document the
way it was intended.

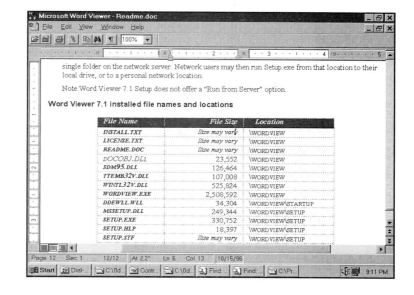

To install the Viewer, perform the following steps:

1. Download the Word Viewer file using your Web browser, saving the file to an empty directory.

2. Double-click the wd95vw71 icon to begin the installation.

3. If you already have a copy of Word Viewer on your computer, the setup program asks permission to overwrite it. Also, if you have a copy of Word on your system, setup asks whether you want Word Viewer or Word to be the default document viewer.

N O T E If your system already has Word installed, you probably don't need the Word Viewer at all—the Quick View utility in Windows 95 provides the capability to view documents without opening Word. The disadvantage of Quick View, however, is that you can neither view embedded OLE objects nor print a document. Both of these capabilities exist in Word Viewer. ■

Update Information Tool

The Update Information Tool is a utility included with both versions of the service pack. It displays information about which components of the service pack update have been installed (see fig. F.26). It is found in the System Tools folder within Accessories using the Start menu.

Part

XI

App

F

FIG. F.26
The Update Information Tool reports on the status of update patches, including whether they are properly installed and logged in the registry.

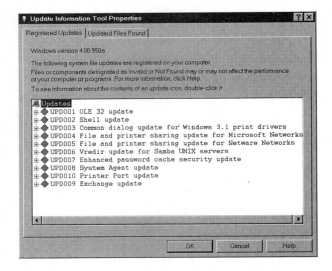

The Registered Updates Tab displays those files which were installed and properly stored in the registry. The Updated Files Found tab provides you the opportunity to search your hard disk for updates which may have been installed without the installation program and hence not properly registered.

> **CAUTION**
>
> Searching for files using the Search Files button on the Updated Files Found page does not update the Registry. To properly configure the Registry, you must re-install the update.

Getting Help

If you need assistance with the service pack, there are a few places you can look for assistance. Some of the best are:

- The Windows 95 Support Assistant provides a wealth of information about Windows 95 installation, support, and troubleshooting. It is available from the following locations:

  http:// www.microsoft.com/windows/software/servpak1/isprof.htm

  ftp://ftp.microsoft.com

  Microsoft Download Service. Dial (206) 936-6735 and download ASSIST.EXE.

  CompuServe. **GO MSL** and search for ASSIST.EXE.

■ The Microsoft Knowledge Base. This database is available both on the Microsoft Network and CompuServe (**GO MSKB**).

■ Microsoft FastTips. 1-800-936-4200.

■ America Online. Keyword **Winnews**.

ON THE WEB

A comprehensive list of Technical Support services is available online from Microsoft at

http://www.microsoft.com/windows/software/servpak1/tech.htm

Using Internet Explorer 3.0

by Ron Person

In the last few years, we have witnessed a shift in information publishing that may have as great a consequence as the invention of the printing press. The printing press did more than just break the medieval church's hold on information, it heralded a new age of thinking that enabled people to question authority and turn to a quest for knowledge. The cause of our new shift in information publishing is the development of the Internet, the World Wide Web, and the visual browsers that make it easy to gather information.

The World Wide Web links together the many resources existing on the Internet. When you use the World Wide Web, you jump among locations (thousands of computer hosts), system applications, and information formats (files and documents). The ease of navigating between documents and the cability to read documents using any computer system has pushed Web technology into corporations. Corporations are rapidly developing their own *intranets*, a proprietary Internet within a company, to publish proprietary information for their employees and business affiliates.

Explore the World Wide Web

Use Internet Explorer 3 to browse the World Wide Web and your corporate intranet.

Work and move seamlessly between Office documents and Web pages

Open and edit Office documents within Internet Explorer 3 even as you browse the Web or your local intranet.

Improve the performance of Internet Explorer 3

Speed up performance with these techniques.

Enhance the capabilities of Internet Explorer 3

Add free components to gain e-mail, newsgroup, streaming audio, video, animation, 3-D worlds, and more.

Microsoft responded to the incredible growth rate of the Internet and the World Wide Web by rapidly developing Internet Explorer 3. From within Internet Explorer 3 you can browse the Internet and work on Word 95, Word 97, Excel 95, and Excel 97 documents. When working on Word or Excel documents the toolbars and menus of Internet Explorer 3 change to match the document type within the browser.

Not surprisingly, Internet Explorer integrates well into Windows 95, allowing you to do things like use Windows 95 shortcuts to access Web sites. Among the technologies included in Internet Explorer 3:

- *HTML 3.0.* Provides full support for the latest version of HTML
- *ActiveX controls.* Applications written in Visual Basic or C++ run within Internet Explorer 3 to add additional features
- *Java.* Applications written in the Java programming language run within Internet Explorer 3 to add additional features
- *Autosearch.* An integrated search tool makes it easy to search the Web

Office and the Internet Explorer will evolve into a single universal viewer and editor, Internet Explorer 4. Internet Explorer 4 will enable you to work with your local drive or Internet files using the same procedures. You will also be able to use Office and other ActiveX applications within Internet Explorer 4 so you won't have to open an application in its own window. ■

ON THE WEB

For the latest information, upgrades, support, and add-ins for Internet Explorer use any Internet browser to go to

> **http://www.microsoft.com/ie/**

For Windows 95 and Microsoft Office tips, training, and add-ins as well as errata for the books *Special Edition Using Windows 95*, *Special Edition Using Word for Windows 95*, and *Special Edition Using Excel for Windows 95*, please point your browser to

> **http://www.ronperson.com/**

Finding and Installing Internet Explorer 3

The Internet Explorer comes on added value CD-ROMs available from Microsoft, pre-installed on Windows computers from many manufacturers, or can be downloaded for free from the Microsoft Web site. If you have The Microsoft Network or Internet Explorer pre-installed on your computer, you will see an icon on your Windows desktop. Double-click this icon to install MSN or the Internet Explorer. The Microsoft Network is

Microsoft's service that connects you to the Internet. There is a monthly subscription fee for its use. Internet access is also available through local Internet Service Providers throughout the United States. You can use the Internet Explorer with any Internet Service Provider.

You also can get the Internet Explorer through added value CD-ROMs, like the ValuPak, available from Microsoft or by accessing Microsoft's Web site (**www.microsoft.com**) with any Web browser and downloading the most current version of Internet Explorer.

When you download the most current version you are given the choices of opening or saving the downloaded file. If you are using an older version of Internet Explorer and you want to immediately upgrade, choose to open the upgrade. This automatically upgrades your computer. If you are using a browser other than Internet Explorer or you want to upgrade at a later time, choose to save the upgrade to a file.

ON THE WEB

Many free Internet Explorer enhancements, Office add-ins, technical support, and hardware drivers are available at the Microsoft Web site. Point your browser to

http://www.microsoft.com/msdownload/

For Windows, Internet Explorer, and Microsoft Office tips and training, point your browser to the author's Web site

http://www.ronperson.com/

To download the latest version of Internet Explorer from the Microsoft Web site, follow these steps:

1. Point your browser to

   http://www.microsoft.com/ie/

2. Click the hyperlink to move to a Web page that will prompt you through downloading and installing.

3. Select the version of Internet Explorer you want installed. Click the Next button to continue with the installation. You will be prompted for the level of installation you want. For Internet Explorer 3 the levels of installation are:

Level of installation	Software included
Minimum	Internet Browser 3
Typical	Internet Browser 3, Internet Mail, and Internet News
Custom	Full installation. This may take as long as 1.45 hours to download on a 14.4 baud modem. You can select which add-ins are installed.

Part

XI

App

G

A full installation includes:

Internet Mail	1.96M
Internet News	1.96M
NetMeeting (Win95)	4.98M
ActiveMovie	2.76M
HTML Layout Control	2.048M

4. When prompted, restart your computer for the Internet Explorer 3 installation to be complete.

5. After restarting your computer, restart Internet Explorer by double-clicking its icon on the desktop or choosing Start, Programs, Internet Explorer.

6. Point your browser to

   http://www.microsoft.com/ie/

7. If prompted, register Internet Explorer 3. If you are not prompted, look on the **www.microsoft.com/ie** Web page for a hyperlink to registration and register your use of Internet Explorer 3. By registering you can be notified of upgrades and free offers.

If you have been using another browser, you may be prompted to make Internet Explorer your registered browser the first time you launch the program. Click Yes at the prompt, and Windows will automatically start Internet Explorer when another application calls a Web browser to display data. There is no penalty for choosing this option; you can register another browser as your default browser later (see fig. G.1).

FIG. G.1
If you don't need to choose among multiple browsers whenever you want to log onto the Web, deselect Always Perform This Check When Starting Up. You won't be bothered with this dialog box again.

T I P   If you have previously installed Internet Explorer 3 you should check the Web site **www.microsoft.com/ie** for the most current version. For example, Internet Explorer 3.01 includes all fixes for Internet Explorer 3 as well as improved handling of Java and Office 97 applications.

ON THE WEB

For troubleshooting tips, known issues, and technical papers on Internet Explorer go to

http://www.microsoft.com/iesupport/

Working and Browsing in Internet Explorer 3

Web sites are posting Office 95 and Office 97 documents on the Web as well as the usual Web pages. Office documents can contain formatting and page layout that isn't possible in HTML documents. Office documents also produce a better quality print than HTML documents. Word 95/97 documents and Excel 95/97 worksheets can be opened, edited, and printed from Web or intranet sites. When you open an Office document within Internet Explorer 3, its menus and toolbars change to include the menu and toolbars for the document's application. (If you do not have Office 95/97 installed you must have the appropriate free Office browser to view and read Office documents. See the section, "Browsing Office Documents without the Application" later in this appendix for more information.)

The advantages to working within Internet Explorer 3 are:

- Accessing files with the same procedures as browsing Web pages.
- Working in a single document container rather than switching between applications.
- Moving forward or backward through the path of opened documents as easily as clicking the Forward and Backward buttons.

The disadvantage to working on Office documents in Internet Explorer 3 is that documents off the hyperlink path are not readily available. In addition, only one document window is open at a time. While you can easily use the Favorites list or History to jump to a previous document, it still must be reopened from disk.

While you are in Internet Explorer 3, you open documents by choosing File, Open to display the Open dialog box. Then click Browse and select the file you want opened. To open Office documents you need to select All Files from the Files of Type list in the Open dialog box.

Part

XI

App

G

CAUTION

When you are working on an Office document from within Internet Explorer 3, don't think you've lost your document or worksheet if you look for Word or Excel on the taskbar and don't see it. Remember that you were working within Internet Explorer 3. Click the Internet Explorer button on the taskbar.

Understanding the Internet Explorer

Internet browsers are simple to use and controls are similar between browsers from different vendors. If you have used another Internet browser, you will quickly understand how to use Internet Explorer. Figure G.2 shows the Internet Explorer page at the Microsoft Web site.

FIG. G.2

It takes only a few buttons to navigate the World Wide Web.

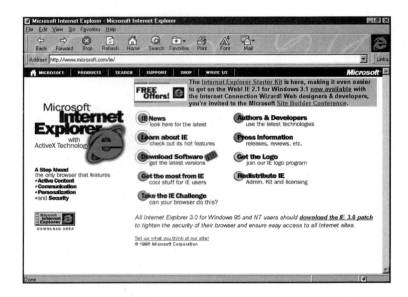

The buttons on the Internet Explorer 3 toolbar are shown in table G.1.

Table G.1 Buttons on the Internet Explorer 3 Toolbar	
Button	**Description**
Back	Displays the previous Web page or document in the history of hyperlink jumps
Forward	Displays the next Web page or document in the history of hyperlink jumps
Stop	Stops the current Web page or document from opening or refreshing
Refresh	Reloads the current Web page or document
Home	Displays the startup page
Search	Displays the search page where you can enter keyword for a search

Button	Description
Favorite	Displays a list of favorite Web pages or documents
Print	Prints the current Web page or document
Font	Cycles the display through a series of predefined font sizes
Address	Entry and edit area for the URL
Address list	Click to display the most recently opened sites
Links	Buttons linked to specific Web pages
Mail	Send or receive e-mail or receive newsgroup files

T I P To display or remove the toolbar, choose View, Toolbar.

To display or remove the Links bar, double-click the word Links.

Move the toolbars or address bar by dragging them by the bar at the left or top edge of each bar.

Starting Internet Explorer 3

You can start Internet Explorer 3 in different ways. You can start it by double-clicking an Internet Explorer icon on your desktop or by clicking Start, Programs, and choosing Internet Explorer. If you have saved a shortcut to a Web page you can double-click the shortcut. You can also double-click HTML files in the Windows Explorer to start Internet Explorer 3.

To go to any page whose URL you know or to any Word or Excel document whose path and file name you know, follow these steps:

1. Choose File, Open.
2. Type in the address or select a previously used page from the list.

   If you do not know the location of a file on your local disk or intranet, choose the Browse button (see fig. G.3).
3. Click OK.

FIG. G.3
The Open dialog box enables you to jump directly to any site on the Internet, or to load Web pages or documents stored on your hard disk or intranet.

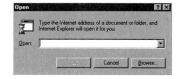

Part

XI

App

G

There are several other ways to go to Web pages. You can:

- Type an address into the Address bar and press Enter.
- Select a previously visited page or Web site from the Address list.

 A quick way to start the Internet Explorer and go directly to the site for an URL is to click Start, Run to display the Run dialog box, then enter an URL in the command line and press Enter.

- At any time, you can jump back to your start page (the initial page loaded when you launch the Internet Explorer) by clicking the Home icon or choosing Go, Start Page.
- Jump directly to a Favorite Web page or document by choosing Favorites, then selecting the site you want to visit. Save the active page as a favorite by choosing Favorites, Add to Favorites.

 Create your own folders in Favorites by clicking Favorites, Add to Favorites. In the Add to Favorites dialog box click Create In, then New and enter the name of the new folder you want underneath Favorites.

◊ "Understanding World Wide Web URLs," **p. 985**

◊ "Navigating the World Wide Web," **p. 987**

Working on Office Documents in Internet Explorer 3

Internet Explorer 3 can open Excel, Word, and PowerPoint applications from Office 95 and Office 97. This means that you can access Office documents stored on the World Wide Web or on your company's intranet and read, edit, and print them from within Internet Explorer.

Figure G.4 shows a Word document on the Internet that has been opened on an HTTP Web site from within Internet Explorer 3. Word's menus and toolbars appear within the Internet Explorer shell so you have access to all of Word's features. Notice that the document opens as a Read-Only file. This means you cannot save it back to the site. You can save it to your local disk or network with a different file name.

N O T E Computers that do not have Word, Excel, or PowerPoint installed can open, read, and print documents from a Web site if they install Microsoft's free viewer software. This software and where to get it are described in the section "Browsing Office Documents without the Application" later in this appendix. ▪

FIG. G.4

Internet Explorer 3 displays Word's menus and toolbars so you can work on Word documents from within Internet Explorer.

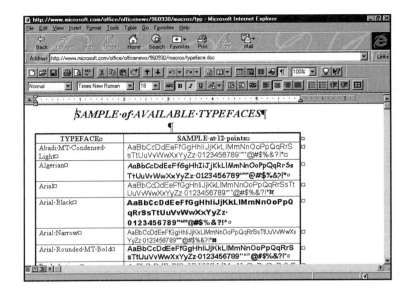

To open a local Word, Excel, or PowerPoint document from within Internet Explorer 3, follow these steps:

1. Choose File, Open to display the Open dialog box.
2. Click Browse to open the Open dialog box.
3. Select All Files from the Files of Type list.
4. Select the file from your local drive or network.
5. Choose Open. Click OK.

Don't be confused if you are working on an Office document in Internet Explorer and the same type of document in its native application. If you press Alt+Tab you will see that the document does not appear in Internet Explorer 3 and the Office application at the same time.

Copying Data and Graphics Out of Web Pages

As you work in Internet Explorer you are bound to come across information you want to save or copy. There are a number of ways you can do this.

You can save the text (but not the graphics) for a Web page to disk by choosing File, Save As File and entering a file name for the HTML file and opening the folder in which you want to save the file. This saves the text document, but does not save the graphics on the page. You can reopen this document in Internet Explorer by double-clicking the file. You can also open it in a word processor because HTML is just a text file.

Part
XI

App

Save a graphic from a Web page by right-clicking the graphic or background in the Internet Explorer. From the shortcut menu, choose Save Picture As and enter a file name and folder. Choose Copy to save the graphic to the clipboard. You also can drag images from a Web page to the My Computer window or a folder in the Explorer. Files saved from a Web page are in GIF or JPEG format.

> **TIP**   Quickly save a graphic from a Web page by dragging it from the Web page and dropping it on your desktop. Be careful that you hold the mouse button down as you drag. An accidental double-click may take you to a hyperlinked location.

The most recent GIF files—Web graphic files—used by Internet Explorer 3 are stored in the WINDOWS\TEMPORARY INTERNET FILES folder.

Using Shortcuts and Favorites   Internet Explorer uses the concept of shortcuts much like Windows does; indeed, one of Explorer's strengths is its nearly seamless integration with Windows. Almost any object in an Explorer window can be turned into a shortcut (see fig. G.5). To turn a hyperlink into a shortcut, for instance, follow these steps:

1. Position the Explorer program so you can see some of the Windows desktop.
2. Click and hold the left mouse button over a link.
3. Drag the link to the desktop and let go of it. A shortcut appears on the desktop.

> **TIP**   To save a shortcut to the current Web page, right-click on the page background and choose Create Shortcut. An alert box will tell you that a shortcut has been placed on your desktop. Double-click this shortcut to open the Web page.

FIG. G.5
You can drag a link to the desktop, or you can right-click a link, as shown here, and use the context menu to copy—and later paste—the link as a shortcut.

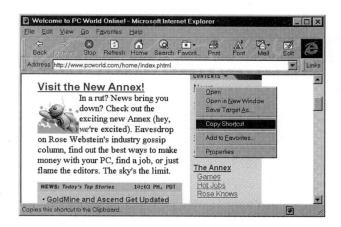

Once you've made a shortcut, you can drag it into a folder, mail it, include it in a Word document, or manage it any other way you would treat a shortcut for an object on your local hard disk.

 TIP You can perform actions like Copy Shortcut in an Explorer window by right-clicking on the desired object (such as a link). A context menu appears with choices like Open and Add to Favorites.

Working with AutoSearch

The sheer quantity of information on the Web can make browsing very difficult. While search engines such as Yahoo!, Lycos, and InfoSeek help sift all the data, they require that you go to a separate page to conduct a search—a time-consuming proposition. Internet Explorer 3 builds Web searching directly into the browser's address line.

To search on the phrase mutual funds, for example, simply type **go mutual funds** in the address line and hit return. The browser sends the search phrase directly to the Yahoo! search engine and returns the results of the query (see fig. G.6).

FIG. G.6
Type **Go valujet** in the URL line, and Internet Explorer 3 returns with the results of a search based on the word valujet.

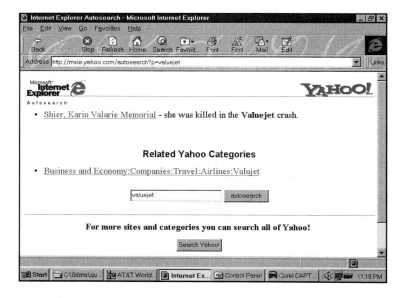

 TIP Want to do heavy-duty searching? Select <u>G</u>o, Search the <u>W</u>eb to jump to Microsoft's all in one search page. Here you can select from among several search engines, as well as click on predefined indexes to find the information you need.

Customizing Web Page and Document Appearance

You can control settings used for displaying Web pages with the Appearances tab of the Options dialog box. To open this dialog box, choose View, Options. On this tab, you can change how hyperlinks are drawn, whether pictures are displayed, the text and background color for pages, and more. Figure G.7 shows the Options dialog box when the General tab is selected.

FIG. G.7
The General page gives you control over how Web pages and links appear on your screen.

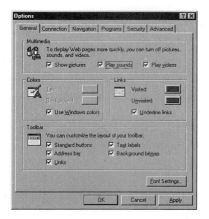

Changing Your Startup Page

The Navigation tab of the Options dialog box allows you to specify which Web page loads when you launch the Internet Explorer. You can specify a file on your local hard disk, on a shared disk (with a UNC path), or on a Web page.

 TIP   Start Internet Explorer quickly and display a start page with the links you want by creating your own start page using the Internet Assistant for Word 5/95 or the Web Page Wizard in Word 97.

To change the start page, follow these steps:

1. Display the page you want as a start page.

2. Choose View, Options and select the Navigation tab, as shown in figure G.8.

3. Choose the Use Current button.

FIG. G.8
Set your start page to any
location you want.

Making URLs Easier to Read

URLs can be arbitrarily long, and many of them contain confusing query characters or computer-generated indexing markers. If you prefer, you can turn off the display of page addresses, or you can make the Internet Explorer show a shortened, simpler form of the URL for each page. To display shorter, more friendly URLs, display the Options dialog box, select the Advanced tab, then select the Show Friendly URLs option. Choose OK.

Selecting Font Appearance

Standard HTML lets Web page authors specify a font size. If the author uses *relative* font sizes, you can control the size displayed. Enlarge or reduce the font size by clicking the Font button on the toolbar. Control which fonts are displayed by choosing View, Options, selecting the General tab, and selecting a font for proportional and fixed-width text.

Changing Hyperlink Text Appearance

Internet Explorer lets you control how hyperlinks are displayed. Some users prefer their links underlined, while others like them to appear as plain text. You can set your preference using the Underline Shortcuts option found on the General tab of the Options dialog box.

Internet Explorer also lets you choose what colors to use when drawing links. To change those colors, choose one of these options from the General tab of the Options dialog box:

■ Click the Visited Links button to bring up the Color dialog box. Choose a color from the selected palette, or mix a custom color, then choose OK. Internet Explorer uses that color to indicate links to pages you have already visited.

Part

XI

App

G

■ Click the Unvisited Links button to bring up the Color dialog box. Choose a color from the selected palette, or mix a custom color, and then choose OK. Internet Explorer uses that color to indicate links to pages you have not yet seen.

Controlling Access to Content with the Content Advisor

Parents and Internet managers in some companies may be interested in limiting the sites accessible by Internet Explorer 3. Internet Explorer 3 has built in the capability to control access to sites who participate in the rating system devised by the Recreational Software Advisory Council.

To set the site ratings that Internet Explorer 3 can access, follow these steps:

1. Click View, Options.
2. Select the Security tab and click Enable Ratings to display the Create Supervisor Password.
3. Enter a password you will remember in the Password box. Reenter it to double-check it in the Confirm Password box, then click OK to display the Content Advisor dialog box shown in figure G.9.

FIG. G.9
Control access to rated sites using the Content Advisor.

4. Select one of the keys in the Category list.
5. Drag the Rating slider to a point on the scale that you deem appropriate. Read the Description box for more details on the level.
6. Repeat from step 4 for another category or click OK.

Not all Web pages have been rated. If you want to prevent viewers from seeing all pages that do not have a rating and therefore might contain some objectionable material, display the Content Advisor dialog box, and select the Users Can See Sites Which Have No Rating option.

Converting Netscape Navigator Bookmarks to Internet Explorer

If you're transitioning from Netscape Navigator to the Internet Explorer, you'll probably want to load your old bookmarks into Explorer. Here is a method for converting those bookmarks into Explorer-style Favorites:

1. Select Open from Explorer's File menu.

2. Click Browse from the Open dialog box, and then click Open in the next dialog box that appears.

3. Enter the location of your Netscape bookmarks, such as C:\Netscape\Program\bookmark.

4. The Explorer window will fill with your Netscape bookmarks, each displayed as a link. Right click each of these and select Add to Favorites from the context menu. You can use the Create New Folder button to categorize your favorites as they are entered.

Improving Internet Explorer 3 Performance

Adjust your advanced settings using the Advanced tab in the Options dialog box (choose View, Options), as shown in figure G.10.

FIG. G.10
Adjust the disk space used by the Internet Explorer cache in the Advanced tab.

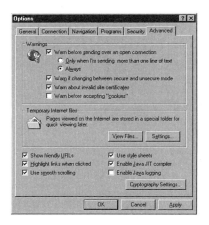

Turn Off Graphics, Video, and Sound for Fast Access

Text transmits over the Internet quicker than graphics. When the Web is slow, you may want to get the text information without the graphics, sound, or video. To turn graphics, sound, or video on or off, choose <u>V</u>iew, <u>O</u>ptions, select the General tab and select or clear the Show <u>P</u>ictures, Play <u>S</u>ounds, or Play <u>V</u>ideos option.

Adjusting the History List Size

Internet Explorer saves a shortcut for each Web page you visit. To adjust the number of remembered pages in your History list, choose the Navigation tab from the Options dialog box, then use the Number of Days to Keep Pages in History spin box to set how many pages are stored.

Managing How Web Pages Store to Disk

Internet Explorer stores Web pages on your hard disk to increase performance when you return to those pages. Internet Explorer can automatically check for updates to the stored pages when you restart the Internet Explorer, return to a page, or only when you refresh them. However, this technique of storing pages on disk, known as caching, can consume lots of your hard disk if you are not careful. To set how Internet Explorer stores and manages Web pages on disk, display the Options dialog box, select the Advanced tab and choose the S<u>e</u>ttings button for Temporary Internet Files. Change the settings as you want for frequency of updates and more or less storage space.

The more frequently you want pages updated the slower your Internet access will be because Internet Explorer is going back to the source more often rather than using files that have been stored on disk. Similarly, if you reduce the amount of storage space for temporary Internet files you will save hard disk space, but Internet Explorer will need to return to the Web site for graphic files or pages that you have recently used.

TROUBLESHOOTING

When I navigate to Web sites that update frequently, the documents look the same as when I last read them. Why?It is possible you are actually viewing documents that Internet Explorer found in its temporary Internet file storage area, instead of the latest version available from the Web. To force Internet Explorer to retrieve the latest version of the active document, click the Refresh button. See the section titled, "Managing How Web Pages are Stored on Disk," to learn about the options that control temporary storage.

Understanding ActiveX and Java

ActiveX controls and Java applications take the Internet Explorer into a new realm. Instead of being just a viewer of Web pages, the capability to run ActiveX controls and Java applications means that the Internet Explorer acts as a shell for applications that download from the Internet and run within the Internet Explorer. Internet Explorer 3 includes the capability to run ActiveX controls and Java applications—there is nothing you need to download or install.

These applications can be as simple as a small data validation program that runs in Internet Explorer before sending data back to the site that hosts the Web page. The applications can also be as complex and robust as applications you are used to running in Windows, such as word processors, spreadsheets, manufacturing controls, and so forth.

Understanding ActiveX

ActiveX controls are a set of programming tools based on Microsoft's Object Linking and Embedding (OLE) architecture. They are modules of code that extend the capabilities of Internet Explorer 3. Users can download ActiveX controls from a Web site to add new browser features (see fig. G.11).

FIG. G.11
ActiveX controls can be simple feature enhancements or robust programs that run over the Internet within Internet Explorer 3.

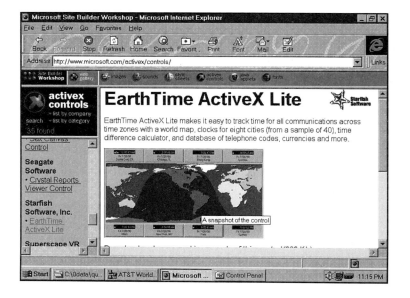

Part
XI

App
G

N O T E   Dozens of useful ActiveX controls, like this handy international time and currency applet from Starfish Software, are available from Microsoft's ActiveX Web page at **http://www.microsoft.com/activex/controls/.** ■

ActiveX controls can simply extend Internet Explorer features, for example, adding new types of animation or checking data entered in a Web page. ActiveX controls can also have the same functionality as normal programs. In fact, many programs written in C++ and Visual Basic 4 can be converted to ActiveX controls so they can be run over the Internet.

One major reason for the success of ActiveX controls is its OLE roots. The enormous Windows developer community can quickly adapt their existing code and expertise to ActiveX, making it a simple matter to create ActiveX controls for IE3. However, ActiveX controls, like IE3 itself, are strictly Windows technologies, so non-Windows systems are unable to take advantage of its capabilities.

Understanding Java

Java is one of the most exciting technologies to emerge on the Internet. Developed by a division of Sun Microsystems, a leading builder of Unix-based workstations, *Java* is a programming language tailored to the needs of the Internet. Developers have flocked to write programs in Java because their code can play on many different types of computers, from a Windows-based PC to a PowerMac to a Unix workstation. For users, Java applications bring life to static Web pages, enabling everything from simple animations to complex interactive applications (see fig. G.12).

FIG. G.12
WallStreetWeb is a Java application that gives you on-the-fly stock information over the Web.

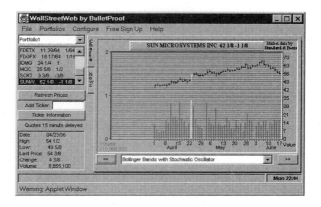

There are a number of reasons why Java has enjoyed such popularity:

- *Platform independence.* Java applications will run on many computers and operating systems without modification.

- *Distributed architecture.* Unlike traditional programs, Java applications don't need to install permanent updates or components in order to run. Applications can run directly within a Web page.

- *Secure design.* Java prohibits access to internal system structures, reducing the possibility that a malicious program will harm the system.

Netscape helped establish Java as an Internet standard when the company included Java support in version 2.0 of the Netscape Navigator browser. The addition of Java support in Internet Explorer is a major enhancement, particularly as Java applications become more prevalent on Web pages.

Internet Explorer 3 includes the Java just-in-time compiler (JIT), a feature that speeds the performance of Java applications. The compiler in Internet Explorer 3 optimizes the code of Java programs just before they run on Windows PCs, taking a little extra time up front but smoothing overall performance.

TROUBLESHOOTING

I can't get some Java applets to run in Internet Explorer 3. I thought they were supposed to work. You may still be using a pre-release, beta version, of the Internet Explorer 3 browser. The pre-release version did not have the full Java functionality built in. If you experience trouble running Java applets, download and install the most current version of Internet Explorer. The previous section, "Finding and Installing Internet Explorer 3," describes how to download and install the current version.

Internet Explorer Add-Ins

At its most basic level, the World Wide Web is an amazing system bringing you information and graphics from thousands of sources around the world. But that basic level of text and graphics has quickly been enhanced with many more ways to communicate over the Web.

Programs to add additional capabilities to the first browsers were first called "helper applications," then "Netscape plug-ins," and now there are "ActiveX controls" and "Java applets." These programs give browsers like Internet Explorer 3 additional capability. By installing free programs to Internet Explorer 3 you can add e-mail, newsgroup downloads, online meetings, sound, video, animation, and 3-D worlds. The number of add-ins continues to expand. Some add-ins are free from Microsoft, others are from third-party vendors who make money from the Web sites that use their enhancements.

Part

XI

App

G

Internet Explorer 3 includes the capability to run ActiveX controls and Java applets. These are *small programs* that add special features and functionality to the Internet browser. Internet Explorer loads the ActiveX control or Java applet when it is needed.

> **CAUTION**
>
> Every one of the Internet Explorer add-ins listed here is worthwhile, but be careful—add-ins can consume a lot of disk space.

Internet Explorer 3 automatically prompts you to install add-ins needed for enhanced Web pages. (Older versions of Internet Explorer and Netscape require that you click a hyperlink and install add-ins before viewing enhanced Web pages.) You do not have to accept the automatic installation and registration of add-ins by Internet Explorer 3, but refusing an installation may mean that you will miss some of the enhanced features on a page.

Microsoft and many other vendors have grouped around a standard to certify add-ins when they download to you. This certification displays like a certificate on your screen to verify that the add-in or file being downloaded is from a specific vendor, such as Microsoft, Adobe, or Macromedia. This doesn't mean the add-in or file does not contain a virus, but it does significantly reduce that likelihood because you know by the certificate which vendor created and packaged the software. For more information on certification, see "Protecting Against Virus" later in this appendix.

Installing Add-Ins and Plug-Ins

If you are upgrading to Internet Explorer 3 from another browser—for example, Netscape—don't be concerned about plug-ins that you used for Netscape enhancements. Internet Explorer detects plug-ins, relocates them, and runs them in Internet Explorer whenever they are required.

When you go to a Web page that requires a Netscape plug-in, Internet Explorer 3 checks to see if there is an ActiveX control at the site that does the equivalent function. If so, you are given the choice of installing either the Netscape plug-in or the ActiveX control. If you select the ActiveX control it will install automatically. If you select the Netscape plug-in, then install it in either the Netscape Navigator plug-in folder or the Internet Explorer plug-in folder. Both of these are found under the Program Files folder.

 URLs for Web sites are dynamic—they change a lot. If you cannot access an add-in through the URLs listed in the following sections, look at the following URL

http://www.microsoft.com/msdownload/

Removing Add-Ins and Plug-Ins

Removing ActiveX controls is fairly easy. Click Start, Settings, Control Panel to display the Control Panel window. Double-click the Add/Remove Programs icon to display the Add/Remove Programs Property window. Select the Install/Uninstall tab, then select from the installed software list the add-in you want removed and click Add/Remove. Choose OK.

Using E-Mail in Internet Explorer 3

E-mail is one of the forces that has made the Internet popular. While removing some of the personal nature of phone calls, e-mail can greatly increase productivity because messages can be retrieved and answered in batches when it fits the respondents schedule. E-mail messages also do away with the pleasantries that can add 20 minutes to 30 seconds worth of information.

Initial releases of Internet Explorer did not have e-mail so people were forced to use an e-mail application independent from the browser. Internet Explorer 3 has a free e-mail add-in from Microsoft that makes sending and receiving e-mail easy.

Microsoft Internet Mail is easy for beginning e-mail users to use, yet contains customization and rule-based filing features useful to advanced users. It works online or offline and creates and displays messages using HTML formatting. You can set Internet Mail to automatically download messages less than a specific size and then read them offline.

Figure G.13 Shows how Internet Mail displays e-mail in a preview window or in a full window. The background window in the figure shows an upper pain that displays message subject and date. The lower pane displays a preview of the selected message. Double-clicking a message in the preview pane opens the message into a full message window, shown in the figure.

FIG. G.13
Internet Mail is a simple e-mail program that works from within Internet Explorer or works on its own.

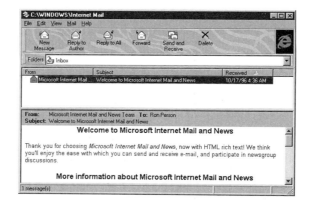

E-mail sent from Internet Mail can include file attachments so you can send application documents or program files. A paper clip icon at the left side of a message in the preview window indicates the message has an attachment. Double-clicking the paper clip opens the attachment if viewer software, such as Word or the Word viewer, is available, or downloads the attachment.

Internet Mail includes an address book that works with nicknames for frequent recipients. It can also do group mailings. It also imports addresses from Microsoft Exchange.

For e-mail users who get a lot of e-mail, Internet Mail includes rule-based message filing. You specify rules by which Internet Mail analyzes e-mail content and it files your mail automatically into folders you've created.

With the volume of e-mail that comes in its easy to lose your hard disk to old mail. To help you preserve your storage Internet Mail includes procedures to compact or delete message folders as well as automatically delete messages older than a specific date.

If you are unsure whether Internet Mail is installed, click Start, Programs, and look for Internet Mail or look on the Internet Explorer toolbar for a Mail icon. If it is not installed or you want to upgrade to a newer version, download a free copy of Internet Mail, by going to:

http://www.microsoft.com/ie/download/

Select Internet Mail & News for Windows 95 and NT 4 from the list. Then click Next. Internet Mail & News will begin downloading.

Setup Internet Mail with the Configuration wizard. This wizard runs the first time you start the program. You will be asked for the name of your Internet server, for example, WWW.MSN.COM, your e-mail address, for example, "*myname@server.com*", and your account name and password to the mail server. Your account name is usually the same name as the name to the left of the @ in your account name. If you have any question about what these are, review the information sent to you by your Internet Service Provider when you started the service or call your Internet Service Provider. Once you complete the installation of Internet Mail & News you will see a Mail button in the Internet Explorer toolbar.

TIP If you are using MSN as your Internet provider, then your account name will be the same as your MSN Member ID and your mail server will be msn.com.

Run Internet Mail as a stand-alone application or with Internet Explorer 3. To run Internet Mail by itself, click Start, Programs, Internet Mail. To run Internet Mail from within Internet Explorer 3, choose Go, Read Mail or click Mail, Read Mail in the toolbar.

For more information on installing Internet Mail or for information on known problems go to:

http://www.microsoft.com/iesupport/

A good place to start is by clicking the button for Frequently Asked Questions (*FAQs*).

◊ **See** "Installing and Configuring Exchange," **p. 876**

Getting the News from Newsgroups

Some people denigrate the Internet and those who use it because they believe computers are taking the personal touch out of human interaction. However, the Internet is bringing together people with common interests that would never have been able to meet. It is creating communities that would never have existed without the Internet and newsgroups.

 T I P Search for newsgroups by using Internet search engines like those described earlier in the section "Searching for Information on the World Wide Web" earlier in this appendix.

Newsgroups are collections of news articles organized by topic and conversations organized by threads. Figure G.14 shows a newsgroup and its articles. Newsgroups include information and conversations on topics that range from classical music, to politics, to finance, to parenting. There are now more than 15,000 newsgroups on nearly every topic imaginable. Newsgroups provide information ranging from hard scientific research to emotional comfort and support for people facing life-threatening illness.

FIG. G.14
Internet News connects you with communities of people with special interests.

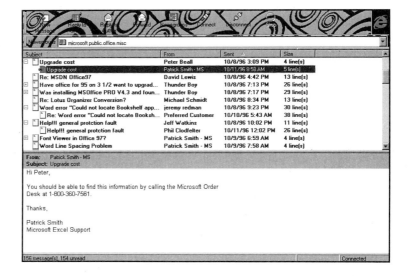

Part
XI

App

G

N O T E   Newsgroups are rather anarchist. The messages they contain are unfiltered so you may find objectionable material from the occasional cretin. Some newsreaders have the capability to filter comments from people on a *Bozo list* or *watch filter*. In its initial release, Microsoft Internet News does not have this capability. This doesn't mean you should shy away from newsgroups—they contain a wealth of information on specialized topics. ■

Internet News is a basic newsreader that includes standard newsreader features. It appears similar to Internet Mail using a preview pane to display contents of selected topics. You can connect to multiple mail servers so you can retrieve different newsgroups coming from different servers. Internet News automatically decodes binary files that can contain images and programs.

You can save storage, download time, and reading time by marking newsgroups, individual messages in newsgroups, or threads for download. You also have the choice of downloading just headers in a newsgroup. From these headers you can select just the topic headers or conversation threads you want to download, again saving you download and reading time.

 T I P   Click Newsgroup in the toolbar of Internet News to download a list of newsgroups available on your news server.

Newsgroup messages are even worse than e-mail for quickly filling you hard disk. To help manage newsgroup infoglut, News can automatically delete newsgroup messages you have read and compress messages when their storage space exceeds a limit you set.

To download a free copy of Internet News, go to:

http://www.microsoft.com/ie/download/ieadd.htm

Select Internet Mail & News for Windows 95 and NT 4 from the list. Then click Next. Internet Mail & News will begin downloading.

The first time you run Internet News, the Configuration wizard will guide you through intalling it. You will be asked for the name of your news server, for example, if MSN is your Internet Provider you news server will be **msnews.microsoft.com**, your e-mail address, for example, "*myname@server.com*", and your account name and password to the mail server. Again, if MSN is your Internet provider your e-mail address will look like, "myname@msn.com." Your account name is usually the same name as the name to the left of the @ in your account name. If you have any questions about what these are, review the information sent to you by your Internet provider when you started the service or call your Internet provider. Once you complete the installation of Internet Mail & News, you see a Mail button in the Internet Explorer toolbar.

Run Internet News as a stand-alone application or with Internet Explorer 3. To run Internet News click Start, Programs, Internet News. To run Internet News from within Internet Explorer 3, choose Go, Read News or click Mail, Read News in the toolbar.

For more information on installing Internet News or for information on known problems go to:

http://www.microsoft.com/iesupport/

Begin your quest for information by clicking the button for Frequently Asked Questions.

Adobe Acrobat for Top Quality Printouts

Web pages have serious limits to their formatting and layout capabilities. When printed they don't have the quality of professionally published materials.

To get around this problem many companies post documents such as forms, product information sheets, or catalogs, in three formats—HTML for viewing online, Word DOC or RTF for editing and printing from Microsoft Word, and Adobe Acrobat.

Anyone having the free Acrobat Reader can view documents on-screen or print and get the same formatting and layout. Users do not have to have a word processor to view or print Acrobat files. In some cases there is the disadvantage that Acrobat documents cannot be edited by readers. Figure G.15 Shows an Adobe Acrobat file being viewed in Acrobat Reader.

FIG. G.15
Adobe Acrobat files produce high-quality images on-screen and in print.

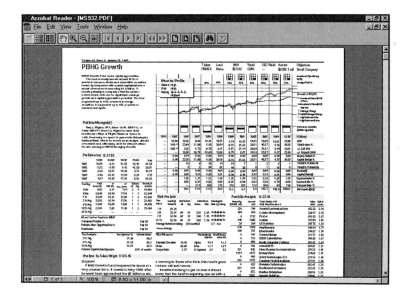

Part

XI

App

G

ON THE WEB

To learn more about Adobe Acrobat or to download the Acrobat Reader go to

http://www.adobe.com/

Loading the HTML Layout Control for Enhanced Pages

The HTML code used to create Web pages does not have the capability to produce the well laid out pages that are possible in good word processors and desktop publishing programs. However, Microsoft is working with the World Wide Web Consortium, the international Internet standards committee, to enhance HTML with additional features.

In preparation for those enhancments, Microsoft has released HTML Layout Controls that add additional graphic and layout capabilities to pages displayed in Internet Explorer 3. Another major improvement added to Internet Explorer 3 that will be copied by other browsers is the addition of Cascading Style Sheets.

Some of the effects possible only with the addition of HTML Layout Control are overlapping graphics, precise positioning of graphics, frame positioning, transparency effects, and some of the onscreen interactive effects we are familiar with in Windows 95 such as ScreenTools that pop-up as the mouse moves over a "hot" region. Figure G.16 shows an HTML page using HTML Layout Controls to enhance its page design. This is a children's game duplicating the venerable Mr. Potato head where vegetables can be dragged onto the eggplant to make a face.

Cascading Style Sheets are a major improvement to the formatting and layout of HTML Web pages. They use a similar concept to Styles in Word and Excel to apply positioning and formatting. Currently they are only implemented in Internet Explorer 3, although Netscape is expected to follow suit in 1997.

ON THE WEB

To upgrade your Internet Explorer 3 to include the display capabilities in HTML Layout Control, visit the Internet Explorer 3.0 HTML Layout Control site at

http://www.microsoft.com/ie/download/ieadd.htm

Online Conferencing with NetMeeting

The technology for social interaction on the Internet has evolved from point-to-point e-mail and file transfer to the typed dialog in chat rooms. Now, with the release of NetMeeting it is possible to have telephone conferencing and collaborative workgroups that share electronic white boards and Windows applications. Figure G.17 shows the NetMeeting window.

FIG. G.16

HTML Layout Controls enable precise control of onscreen items, as well as the capability to drag and drop items as shown in this child's game.

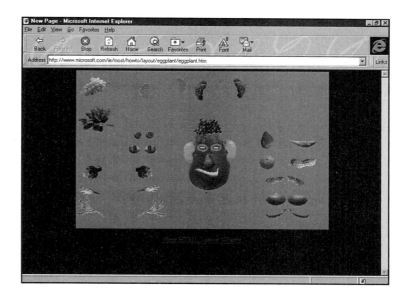

FIG. G.17

NetMeeting makes tele-conferencing and group collaboration feasible and inexpensive.

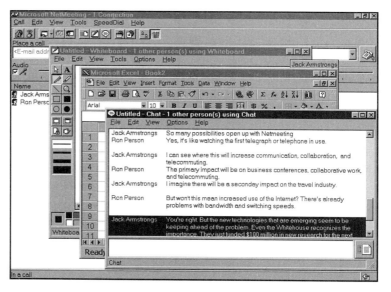

While Internet telephone and collaborative workgroup software for the Internet have been available for about a year, NetMeeting is important because it adheres to international telephone conferencing standards. This means it is compatible with international telephony standards and products from other manufacturers.

Telecommuting and video conferencing have been going on for about 10 years as special cases requiring investment in special equipment. With the advent of NetMeeting, telecommuting becomes widely feasible. Within high-bandwidth corporate intranets, tele-conferencing becomes an affordable option that doesn't require a team of technicians.

NetMeeting can be used in a number of ways. Collaborative work over distance can combine voice, white board, and shared applications. Training becomes cheaper and more flexible because students don't have to travel and classes can be given in hourly doses rather than requiring students to leave work for days. Even relationships between businesses, clients, and associates can change with the possibility of easier communication.

Some of the features available in NetMeeting are:

Feature	Description
Point-to-point audio	High-quality telephone between two individuals anywhere in the world at the low cost of Internet communication.
Multipoint conferencing	Share whiteboard, clipboard, and a Windows application between multiple participants. Any participant can use the host application even when the application is not on their system.
Shared clipboard	Share text and graphics quickly between members of an online conference.
File transfer	Send a file to an individual or all members of a conference as the conference continues.
Shared whiteboard	Share creative and spontaneous ideas on the whiteboard that is accessible to all participants. Write or draw on the multipage board. Drawings are object-oriented so pieces can be rearranged. A pointer and highlighter make presentations easier.
Chat	Use chat for the text-based communication between multiple participants. Or use it to record notes and action items.
User Location Servers	Directory servers hosted by Microsoft, third parties, and within companies that track and connect NetMeeting users.

ON THE WEB

To learn more about NetMeeting go to

http://www.microsoft.com/netmeeting/

To upgrade your Internet Explorer 3 to include NetMeeting, go to

http://www.microsoft.com/msdownload/

or

http://www.microsoft.com/ie/download/ieadd.htm

Playing Sound with RealAudio

Normal Windows sound files can be very large so they take awhile to download before you can play them, but the advent of RealAudio has taken care of that problem. RealAudio is a non-Microsoft add-in that enables Internet Explorer 3 to play streaming audio—sound files that play as they download. The sound quality is acceptable even with a 14.4 modem. With a 28.8 modem you can even download stereo. The developer claims RealAudio can produce CD quality with an ISDN or LAN connection.

RealAudio is free to users. You can order an enhanced version for $29.95 that produces near CD-quality over standard modems, includes hundreds of preset RealAudio sites, and allows you to record your favorite RealAudio sound tracks.

ON THE WEB

To download RealAudio and sample a number of demonstration sites, go to

http://www.realaudio.com/

Playing Video

ActiveMovie is a free Microsoft add-in that plays popular sound and video file formats. The controls are the familiar VCR type controls you've seen in the Windows 95 Media Player accessory. ActiveMovie will play MPEG Audio and Video, AVI files, QuickTime, AU, WAV, MIDI, and AIFF.

To automatically install ActiveMovie go to:

http://www.microsoft.com/msdownload/

select ActiveMovie from the list and click Next.

Adding Animation with ShockWave

Macromedia, famous for their multimedia authoring software, has created ShockWave for the Internet Explorer. ShockWave plays graphics and animation created in Director 5. These multimedia files are compressed and downloaded to Internet Explorer. ShockWave plays streaming audio as the audio is received. Upon receiving the complete animation file ShockWave replays the animation.

Part

XI

App

G

ON THE WEB

To download and install ShockWave go to

http://www.macromedia.com/

Exploring 3-D Worlds with VRML

Technophiles have been entraced by virtual worlds within the *cyberspace* of networked computers every since the release of the mind-breaking science fiction novel "Neuromancer" by William Gibson. In his not-so-distant future world Gibson introduces the idea of working and living within virtual worlds that exist only within computers.

You can participate in some of the first attempts at virtual worlds by adding Virtual Reality Modeling Language (VRML) to Internet Explorer 3. Once you enter a site that has a 3-D world supported by VRML you will be able to move through the world with a mouse, keyboard, or joystick. Some worlds even enable you to take on the *cyberpersona* of an avitar (a visual representation of yourself). Figure G.18 shows one 3-D world. Just remember, what you see is just in its infancy. At current transmission speeds the download of new rooms can be slow and voice and movement may by jerky. But the promise is there and it's definitely worth a visit to some of the sample sites Microsoft has listed.

FIG. G.18
VRML enables you to move
around in a 3-D world.

ON THE WEB

To download the VRML Add-In go to

http://www.microsoft.com/ie/ie3/

Accessibility Features for Internet Explorer 3

Computer users with special access requirements are more and more hindered as the Internet becomes more graphical. For non-Internet programs people who have difficulty seeing computer screens are able to use text-to-speech programs. Web pages present a problem because they are highly graphical and some information and hyperlinks only exist as graphics. They do not have a text conterpart that can be converted to speech. Another problem faces those who have difficulty moving a mouse.

Internet Explorer 3 can reduce some of these impediments. Add-ins can replace mouse movement with keyboard movements. Another add-in displays the Alt text that appears in place of some grahics. This enables text-to-speech readers to read graphics as well as text.

ON THE WEB

To learn more about these add-ins and how custom aids can be built using ActiveX technology look to

http://www.microsoft.com/ie/ie3/access.htm

Browsing Office Documents without the Application

Don't let the absence of an Office application prevent you or others from browsing or viewing Office documents you retrieve from the Web. Microsoft's free Office Viewers are designed to let anyone view or print Word, Excel, and PowerPoint documents.

Viewers are applications that enable you to view or print, but not edit an Office application file. Viewers are associated with a file type just like other Windows applications so you can start the viewer and load a file from disk, or let Internet Explorer 3 automatically load a viewer when you access an Office document on the Web or intranet.

ON THE WEB

The appropriate Web page from which to access viewers for different Microsoft Office applications is

http://www.microsoft.com/msdownload/

CAUTION

Make sure the viewer you download or send to others is the viewer that works with the documents you are distributing.

Protecting against Viruses

Microsoft and others are trying to find ways of slowing the spread of virus over the Internet. One of their techniques is to certify software from major vendors that might be transmitted. Any software that you receive from a reputable vendor will display a certificate stating who the vendor is. This is like the brand image and packaging of products you buy in the store. Software that downloads to the Internet Explorer and has a certification will display the certificate and ask you if you want to install the software. If you recognize the vendor as being reputable you can accept the risk. Software that is not certified prompts you as to whether you want to save the software or open it. If you save this software and then run it to install it, your anti-virus software will have a chance to protect you.

Downloading data from a network, especially the Internet, is a good way to contract a virus. A file with a virus in it cannot only destroy the work you are currently doing, it can destroy all the data on your hard disk and infect others on your network.

There are some things you can do to prevent the spread of virus from the Internet. One form of virus checking checks Word and Excel files for the inconvenient but usually not deadly macro virus. To prevent Word or Excel from transmitting a virus to other Word or Excel documents install the virus protection found on Microsoft's site at

http://www.microsoft.com/msword/

and

http://www.microsoft.com/excel/

ON THE WEB

For product informaton on virus checkers that work when programs execute check with McAfee and Symantec. You can contact them at

http://www.mcafee.com/

http://www.symantec.com/

Administrator's Kit

If you are a corporate computer administrator you will want to get a copy of the Internet Explorer's Administrator's Kit. You can download this kit from

http://www.microsoft.com/ie/ie3/

A wizard in the kit aids you in creating self-installing customized versions of Internet Explorer. You can specify which Internet Explorer add-ins are installed, such as NetMeeting as well as configure user options. ●

Index

S

S-Video cables, 359

safe modes
troubleshooting
problems, 59
Windows 95 startup, 56
minimum networking
functions, 57

sans serif fonts, 263

SAP (Service Advertising
Protocol), NetWare
servers, 727

Save As dialog box, 104

Save Search command
(File menu), 123

Save Theme dialog
box, 393

saving
backup settings, 672
Clipboard Viewer
contents, 562
custom Desktop
Themes, 392
files
Paint program, 548
PCX format, 548
sets, 672
troubleshooting in
WordPad, 534
hardware profiles, 417-419
HTML documents, 1024
search criteria, 123
system files (System
Configuration
Editor), 495

ScanDisk, 611, 620-626
advanced options, 622-623
troubleshooting, 626

ScanDisk Advanced
Options dialog box, 621

ScanDisk error message
(PC Card device
installation), 192

ScanDisk utility, 28

scanners, 938-939

Schedule a New Program
dialog box, 650

Scheduled Settings dialog
box, 651

scheduling backups, 666
System Agent, 669

scraps
document scraps, 595
Post-It notes (WordPad),
535

screens
Clipboard, 561
color depth, 1107-1108
desktop components, 64-65
fonts, switching for DOS
graphics programs, 522
logins for networks, 744
NetWare login, 720
refresh rates, 1108
resolution, 1105-1106
resolutions, 399
savers, 395-398
Desktop Theme, 390
DOS sessions, 524
password protection,
396-397
Windows 95, 36-37

SCRIPT font, 269

scripts
files, running, 856

installing
BATCH.EXE utility, 851
Windows 95
installation, 848-853
login scripts, mapping
network drives, 755
Scripting and SLIP tool,
Service Pack for
Information System
Professionals, 1319-1320

SCSI drives
CD-ROM drives, 321
full-motion video, 358-359

Seagate Barracuda video
hard drives, 358

searching
criteria, saving, 123
drives for networks, 756
files, 119-123
compressed (ZIP),
122-123
pages (Explorer), 995
WWW, 990-991

secure HTTP servers, 986

Secure HyperText Transfer
Protocol, 998

Secure Sockets Layer, 998

security
dial-up servers, 814
Internet, 998-999
passwords, 413
files, 749
user-based and share-level
based peer-to-peer
networks, 789
workgroups (access
rights), 800

Security Lock button
(Internet Explorer), 998

Check out Que® Books
on the World Wide Web
http://www.mcp.com/que

As the biggest software release in computer history, Windows 95 continues to redefine the computer industry. Click here for the latest info on our Windows 95 books

Make computing quick and easy with these products designed exclusively for new and casual users

Examine the latest releases in word processing, spreadsheets, operating systems, and suites

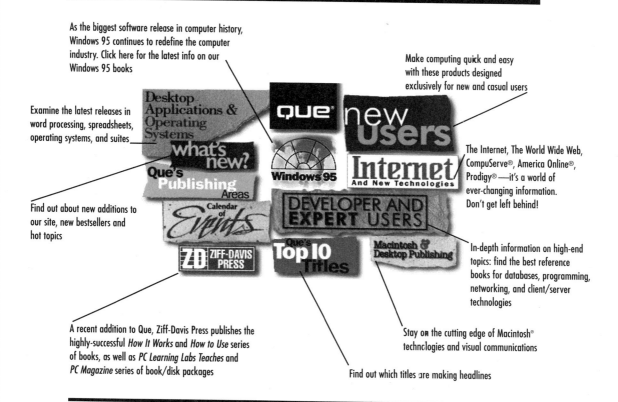

The Internet, The World Wide Web, CompuServe®, America Online®, Prodigy® —it's a world of ever-changing information. Don't get left behind!

Find out about new additions to our site, new bestsellers and hot topics

In-depth information on high-end topics: find the best reference books for databases, programming, networking, and client/server technologies

A recent addition to Que, Ziff-Davis Press publishes the highly-successful *How It Works* and *How to Use* series of books, as well as *PC Learning Labs Teaches* and *PC Magazine* series of book/disk packages

Stay on the cutting edge of Macintosh® technologies and visual communications

Find out which titles are making headlines

With 6 separate publishing groups, Que develops products for many specific market segments and areas of computer technology. Explore our Web Site and you'll find information on best-selling titles, newly published titles, upcoming products, authors, and much more.

- Stay informed on the latest industry trends and products available
- Visit our online bookstore for the *latest information* and editions
- Download software from Que's library of the best shareware and *freeware*

QUE® has the right choice for every computer user

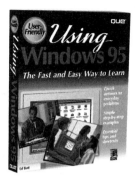

From the new computer user to the advanced programmer, we've got the right computer book for you. Our user-friendly *Using* series offers just the information you need to perform specific tasks quickly and move onto other things. And, for computer users ready to advance to new levels, QUE *Special Edition Using* books, the perfect all-in-one resource—and recognized authority on detailed reference information.

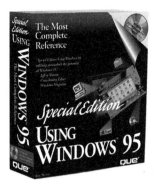

The *Using* series for casual users

Who should use this book?

Everyday users who:

- Work with computers in the office or at home
- Are familiar with computers but not in love with technology
- Just want to "get the job done"
- Don't want to read a lot of material

The user-friendly reference

- The fastest access to the one best way to get things done
- Bite-sized information for quick and easy reference
- Nontechnical approach in plain English
- Real-world analogies to explain new concepts
- Troubleshooting tips to help solve problems
- Visual elements and screen pictures that reinforce topics
- Expert authors who are experienced in training and instruction

Special Edition Using for accomplished users

Who should use this book?

Proficient computer users who:

- Have a more technical understanding of computers
- Are interested in technological trends
- Want in-depth reference information
- Prefer more detailed explanations and examples

The most complete reference

- Thorough explanations of various ways to perform tasks
- In-depth coverage of all topics
- Technical information cross-referenced for easy access
- Professional tips, tricks, and shortcuts for experienced users
- Advanced troubleshooting information with alternative approaches
- Visual elements and screen pictures that reinforce topics
- Technically qualified authors who are experts in their fields
- "Techniques from the Pros" sections with advice from well-known computer professionals

Complete and Return this Card
for a *FREE* Computer Book Catalog

Thank you for purchasing this book! You have purchased a superior computer book written expressly for your needs. To continue to provide the kind of up-to-date, pertinent coverage you've come to expect from us, we need to hear from you. Please take a minute to complete and return this self-addressed, postage-paid form. In return, we'll send you a free catalog of all our computer books on topics ranging from word processing to programming and the internet.

Mrs. ☐   Ms. ☐   Dr. ☐

e (first) ☐☐☐☐☐☐☐☐☐☐☐ (M.I.) ☐   (last) ☐☐☐☐☐☐☐☐☐☐☐☐

ess ☐☐☐☐☐☐☐☐☐☐☐☐☐☐☐☐☐☐☐☐☐☐☐☐☐☐☐☐☐☐

☐☐☐☐☐☐☐☐☐☐☐☐☐☐☐☐☐☐☐☐☐☐☐☐☐☐☐☐☐☐

☐☐☐☐☐☐☐☐☐☐☐☐   State ☐☐   Zip ☐☐☐☐☐☐☐☐☐

e ☐☐☐☐☐☐☐☐☐☐ Fax ☐☐☐☐☐☐☐☐☐☐

any Name ☐☐☐☐☐☐☐☐☐☐☐☐☐☐☐☐☐☐☐☐☐☐☐☐☐☐☐

il address ☐☐☐☐☐☐☐☐☐☐☐☐☐☐☐☐☐☐☐☐☐☐☐☐☐☐☐

ease check at least (3) influencing factors for rchasing this book.

or back cover information on book .... ☐
al approach to the content .... ☐
oleteness of content .... ☐
or's reputation .... ☐
sher's reputation .... ☐
cover design or layout .... ☐
or table of contents of book .... ☐
of book .... ☐
al effects, graphics, illustrations .... ☐
 (Please specify): _____ ☐

w did you first learn about this book?

n Macmillan Computer Publishing catalog .... ☐
mmended by store personnel .... ☐
he book on bookshelf at store .... ☐
mmended by a friend .... ☐
ved advertisement in the mail .... ☐
an advertisement in: _____ ☐
book review in: _____ ☐
 (Please specify): _____ ☐

w many computer books have you rchased in the last six months?

ook only .... ☐   3 to 5 books .... ☐
ks .... ☐   More than 5 .... ☐

4. Where did you purchase this book?

Bookstore .... ☐
Computer Store .... ☐
Consumer Electronics Store .... ☐
Department Store .... ☐
Office Club .... ☐
Warehouse Club .... ☐
Mail Order .... ☐
Direct from Publisher .... ☐
Internet site .... ☐
Other (Please specify): _____ ☐

5. How long have you been using a computer?

☐ Less than 6 months   ☐ 6 months to a year
☐ 1 to 3 years   ☐ More than 3 years

6. What is your level of experience with personal computers and with the subject of this book?

	With PCs	With subject of book
New	☐	☐
Casual	☐	☐
Accomplished	☐	☐
Expert	☐	☐

Source Code ISBN: 0-7897-1052-8

7. Which of the following best describes your job title?

- Administrative Assistant ☐
- Coordinator ☐
- Manager/Supervisor ☐
- Director ☐
- Vice President ☐
- President/CEO/COO ☐
- Lawyer/Doctor/Medical Professional ☐
- Teacher/Educator/Trainer ☐
- Engineer/Technician ☐
- Consultant ☐
- Not employed/Student/Retired ☐
- Other (Please specify): _____ ☐

8. Which of the following best describes the area of the company your job title falls under?

- Accounting ☐
- Engineering ☐
- Manufacturing ☐
- Operations ☐
- Marketing ☐
- Sales ☐
- Other (Please specify): _____ ☐

9. What is your age?

- Under 20 ....
- 21-29 ....
- 30-39 ....
- 40-49 ....
- 50-59 ....
- 60-over ....

10. Are you:

- Male ....
- Female ....

11. Which computer publications do you read regularly? (Please list)

_____
_____
_____
_____
_____
_____
_____
_____
_____
_____
_____

Comments: _____
_____
_____

Fold here and scotch-tape to